University Casebook Series

December, 1980

ACCOUNTING AND THE LAW, Fourth Edition (1978), with Problems Pamphlet (Successor to Dohr, Phillips, Thompson & Warren)

George C. Thompson, Professor, Columbia University Graduate School of Business.
Robert Whitman, Professor of Law, University of Connecticut.
Ellis L. Phillips, Jr., Member of the New York Bar.
William C. Warren, Professor of Law Emeritus, Columbia University.

ACCOUNTING FOR LAWYERS, MATERIALS ON (1980)

David R. Herwitz, Professor of Law, Harvard University.

ADMINISTRATIVE LAW, Seventh Edition (1979), with 1979 Problems Supplement (Supplement edited in association with Paul R. Verkuil, Dean and Professor of Law, Tulane University)

Walter Gellhorn, University Professor Emeritus, Columbia University.
Clark Byse, Professor of Law, Harvard University.
Peter L. Strauss, Professor of Law, Columbia University.

ADMIRALTY, Second Edition (1978), with Statute and Rule Supplement

Jo Desha Lucas, Professor of Law, University of Chicago.

ADVOCACY, see also Lawyering Process

ADVOCACY, INTRODUCTION TO, Third Edition (1981)

Board of Student Advisers, Harvard Law School.

AGENCY, see also Enterprise Organization

AGENCY-ASSOCIATIONS-EMPLOYMENT-PARTNERSHIPS, Second Edition (1977)

Abridgement from Conard, Knauss & Siegel's Enterprise Organization.

ANTITRUST AND REGULATORY ALTERNATIVES (1977), Fifth Edition

Louis B. Schwartz, Professor of Law, University of Pennsylvania.
John J. Flynn, Professor of Law, University of Utah.

ANTITRUST SUPPLEMENT—SELECTED STATUTES AND RELATED MATERIALS (1977)

John J. Flynn, Professor of Law, University of Utah.

BIOGRAPHY OF A LEGAL DISPUTE, THE: An Introduction to American Civil Procedure (1968)

Marc A. Franklin, Professor of Law, Stanford University.

BUSINESS ORGANIZATION, see also Enterprise Organization

BUSINESS PLANNING (1966), with 1980 Supplement

David R. Herwitz, Professor of Law, Harvard University.

BUSINESS TORTS (1972)

Milton Handler, Professor of Law Emeritus, Columbia University.

CIVIL PROCEDURE, see Procedure

CLINIC, see also Lawyering Process

COMMERCIAL AND CONSUMER TRANSACTIONS, Second Edition (1978)

William D. Warren, Dean of the School of Law, University of California, Los Angeles.
William E. Hogan, Professor of Law, Cornell University.
Robert L. Jordan, Professor of Law, University of California, Los Angeles.

COMMERCIAL LAW, CASES & MATERIALS ON, Third Edition (1976)

E. Allan Farnsworth, Professor of Law, Cornell University.
John Honnold, Professor of Law, University of Pennsylvania.

COMMERCIAL PAPER, Second Edition (1976)

E. Allan Farnsworth, Professor of Law, Columbia University.

COMMERCIAL PAPER AND BANK DEPOSITS AND COLLECTIONS (1967), with Statutory Supplement.

William D. Hawkland, Professor of Law, University of Illinois.

COMMERCIAL TRANSACTIONS—Text, Cases and Problems, Fourth Edition (1968)

Robert Braucher, Professor of Law Emeritus, Harvard University, and
The late Arthur E. Sutherland, Jr., Professor of Law, Harvard University.

COMPARATIVE LAW, Fourth Edition (1980)

Rudolf B. Schlesinger, Professor of Law, Hastings College of the Law.

COMPETITIVE PROCESS, LEGAL REGULATION OF THE, Second Edition (1979), with Statutory Supplement

Edmund W. Kitch, Professor of Law, University of Chicago.
Harvey S. Perlman, Professor of Law, University of Virginia.

CONFLICT OF LAWS, Seventh Edition (1978), with 1980 Supplement

Willis L. M. Reese, Professor of Law, Columbia University, and
Maurice Rosenberg, Professor of Law, Columbia University.

CONSTITUTIONAL LAW, Fifth Edition (1977), with 1980 Supplement

Edward L. Barrett, Jr., Professor of Law, University of California, Davis.

CONSTITUTIONAL LAW, Tenth Edition (1980)

Gerald Gunther, Professor of Law, Stanford University.

CONSTITUTIONAL LAW, INDIVIDUAL RIGHTS IN, Third Edition (1981)

Gerald Gunther, Professor of Law, Stanford University.

CONTRACT LAW AND ITS APPLICATION, Second Edition (1977)

Addison Mueller, Professor of Law Emeritus, University of California, Los Angeles.
Arthur I. Rosett, Professor of Law, University of California, Los Angeles.

CONTRACT LAW, STUDIES IN, Second Edition (1977)

Edward J. Murphy, Professor of Law, University of Notre Dame.
Richard E. Speidel, Professor of Law, University of Virginia.

CONTRACTS, Third Edition (1977)

John P. Dawson, Professor of Law Emeritus, Harvard University, and
William Burnett Harvey, Professor of Law and Political Science, Boston University.

CONTRACTS, Third Edition (1980), with Statutory Supplement

E. Allan Farnsworth, Professor of Law, Columbia University.
William F. Young, Professor of Law, Columbia University.

CONTRACTS, Second Edition (1978), with Statutory and Administrative Law Supplement (1978)

Ian R. Macneil, Professor of Law, Cornell University.

COPYRIGHT, Unfair Competition, and Other Topics Bearing on the Protection of Literary, Musical, and Artistic Works, Third Edition (1978)

Benjamin Kaplan, Professor of Law Emeritus, Harvard University, and
Ralph S. Brown, Jr., Professor of Law, Yale University.

CORPORATE FINANCE, Second Edition (1979), with 1980 New Developments Supplement

Victor Brudney, Professor of Law, Harvard University.
Marvin A. Chirelstein, Professor of Law, Yale University.

CORPORATE READJUSTMENTS AND REORGANIZATIONS (1976)

Walter J. Blum, Professor of Law, University of Chicago.
Stanley A. Kaplan, Professor of Law, University of Chicago.

CORPORATION LAW, BASIC, Second Edition (1979), with Documentary Supplement

Detlev F. Vagts, Professor of Law, Harvard University.

CORPORATIONS, see also Enterprise Organization

CORPORATIONS, Fifth Edition—Unabridged (1980)

William L. Cary, Professor of Law, Columbia University.
Melvin Aron Eisenberg, Professor of Law, University of California, Berkeley.

CORPORATIONS, Fifth Edition—Abridged (1980)

William L. Cary, Professor of Law, Columbia University.
Melvin Aron Eisenberg, Professor of Law, University of California, Berkeley.

CORPORATIONS, THE LAW OF: WHAT CORPORATE LAWYERS DO (1976)

Jan G. Deutsch, Professor of Law, Yale University.
Joseph J. Bianco, Professor of Law, Yeshiva University.

CORPORATIONS COURSE GAME PLAN (1975)

David R. Herwitz, Professor of Law, Harvard University.

CREDIT TRANSACTIONS AND CONSUMER PROTECTION (1976)

John Honnold, Professor of Law, University of Pennsylvania.

CREDITORS' RIGHTS, see also Debtor-Creditor Law

UNIVERSITY CASEBOOK SERIES—Continued

CRIMINAL JUSTICE, THE ADMINISTRATION OF, Second Edition (1969)

Francis C. Sullivan, Professor of Law, Louisiana State University.
Paul Hardin III, Professor of Law, Duke University.
John Huston, Professor of Law, University of Washington.
Frank R. Lacy, Professor of Law, University of Oregon.
Daniel E. Murray, Professor of Law, University of Miami.
George W. Pugh, Professor of Law, Louisiana State University.

CRIMINAL JUSTICE ADMINISTRATION AND RELATED PROCESSES, Successor Edition (1976), with 1980 Supplement

Frank W. Miller, Professor of Law, Washington University.
Robert O. Dawson, Professor of Law, University of Texas.
George E. Dix, Professor of Law, University of Texas.
Raymond I. Parnas, Professor of Law, University of California, Davis.

CRIMINAL JUSTICE, LEADING CONSTITUTIONAL CASES ON (1980)

Lloyd L. Weinreb, Professor of Law, Harvard University.

CRIMINAL LAW, Second Edition (1979)

Fred E. Inbau, Professor of Law Emeritus, Northwestern University.
James R. Thompson, Professor of Law Emeritus, Northwestern University.
Andre A. Moenssens, Professor of Law, University of Richmond.

CRIMINAL LAW, Third Edition (1980)

Lloyd L. Weinreb, Professor of Law, Harvard University.

CRIMINAL LAW AND ITS ADMINISTRATION (1940), with 1956 Supplement

Jerome Michael, late Professor of Law, Columbia University, and
Herbert Wechsler, Professor of Law, Columbia University.

CRIMINAL LAW AND PROCEDURE, Fifth Edition (1977)

Rollin M. Perkins, Professor of Law Emeritus, University of California, Hastings College of the Law.
Ronald N. Boyce, Professor of Law, University of Utah.

CRIMINAL PROCEDURE, Second Edition (1980)

Fred E. Inbau, Professor of Law Emeritus, Northwestern University.
James R. Thompson, Professor of Law Emeritus, Northwestern University.
James B. Haddad, Professor of Law, Northwestern University.
James B. Zagel, Chief, Criminal Justice Division, Office of Attorney General of Illinois.
Gary L. Starkman, Assistant U. S. Attorney, Northern District of Illinois.

CRIMINAL PROCEDURE, CONSTITUTIONAL (1977), with 1980 Supplement

James E. Scarboro, Professor of Law, University of Colorado.
James B. White, Professor of Law, University of Chicago.

CRIMINAL PROCESS, Third Edition (1978), with 1979 Supplement

Lloyd L. Weinreb, Professor of Law, Harvard University.

DAMAGES, Second Edition (1952)

Charles T. McCormick, late Professor of Law, University of Texas, and
William F. Fritz, late Professor of Law, University of Texas.

DEBTOR–CREDITOR LAW (1974), with 1978 Case-Statutory Supplement

William D. Warren, Dean of the School of Law, University of California, Los Angeles.
William E. Hogan, Professor of Law, Cornell University.

DECEDENTS' ESTATES (1971)

Max Rheinstein, late Professor of Law Emeritus, University of Chicago.
Mary Ann Glendon, Professor of Law, Boston College.

DECEDENTS' ESTATES AND TRUSTS, Fifth Edition (1977)

John Ritchie, Professor of Law Emeritus, University of Virginia.
Neill H. Alford, Jr., Professor of Law, University of Virginia.
Richard W. Effland, Professor of Law, Arizona State University.

DECEDENTS' ESTATES AND TRUSTS (1968)

Howard R. Williams, Professor of Law, Stanford University.

DOMESTIC RELATIONS, see also Family Law

DOMESTIC RELATIONS, Third Edition (1978) with 1980 Supplement

Walter Wadlington, Professor of Law, University of Virginia.
Monrad G. Paulsen, Dean of the Law School, Yeshiva University.

DYNAMICS OF AMERICAN LAW, THE: Courts, the Legal Process and Freedom of Expression (1968)

Marc A. Franklin, Professor of Law, Stanford University.

ELECTRONIC MASS MEDIA, Second Edition (1979)

William K. Jones, Professor of Law, Columbia University.

ENTERPRISE ORGANIZATION, Second Edition (1977), with 1979 Statutory and Formulary Supplement

Alfred F. Conard, Professor of Law, University of Michigan.
Robert L. Knauss, Dean of the School of Law, Vanderbilt University.
Stanley Siegel, Professor of Law, University of California, Los Angeles.

EQUITY AND EQUITABLE REMEDIES (1975)

Edward D. Re, Adjunct Professor of Law, St. John's University.

EQUITY, RESTITUTION AND DAMAGES, Second Edition (1974)

Robert Childres, late Professor of Law, Northwestern University.
William F. Johnson, Jr., Professor of Law, New York University.

ESTATE PLANNING PROBLEMS (1973), with 1977 Supplement

David Westfall, Professor of Law, Harvard University.

ETHICS, see Legal Profession, and Professional Responsibility

EVIDENCE, Fourth Edition (1981)

David W. Louisell, late Professor of Law, University of California, Berkeley.
John Kaplan, Professor of Law, Stanford University.
Jon R. Waltz, Professor of Law, Northwestern University.

EVIDENCE, Sixth Edition (1973), with 1980 Supplement

John M. Maguire, late Professor of Law Emeritus, Harvard University.
Jack B. Weinstein, Professor of Law, Columbia University.
James H. Chadbourn, Professor of Law, Harvard University.
John H. Mansfield, Professor of Law, Harvard University.

UNIVERSITY CASEBOOK SERIES—Continued

EVIDENCE (1968)

Francis C. Sullivan, Professor of Law, Louisiana State University.
Paul Hardin, III, Professor of Law, Duke University.

FAMILY LAW, see also Domestic Relations

FAMILY LAW (1978), with 1981 Supplement

Judith C. Areen, Professor of Law, Georgetown University.

FAMILY LAW: STATUTORY MATERIALS, Second Edition (1974)

Monrad G. Paulsen, Dean of the Law School, Yeshiva University.
Walter Wadlington, Professor of Law, University of Virginia.

FEDERAL COURTS, Sixth Edition (1976), with 1980 Supplement

Charles T. McCormick, late Professor of Law, University of Texas.
James H. Chadbourn, Professor of Law, Harvard University, and
Charles Alan Wright, Professor of Law, University of Texas.

FEDERAL COURTS AND THE FEDERAL SYSTEM, Hart and Wechsler's Second Edition (1973), with 1981 Supplement

Paul M. Bator, Professor of Law, Harvard University.
Paul J. Mishkin, Professor of Law, University of California, Berkeley.
David L. Shapiro, Professor of Law, Harvard University.
Herbert Wechsler, Professor of Law, Columbia University.

FEDERAL PUBLIC LAND AND RESOURCES LAW (1981)

George C. Coggins, Professor of Law, University of Kansas.
Charles F. Wilkinson, Professor of Law, University of Oregon.

FEDERAL RULES OF CIVIL PROCEDURE, 1980 Edition

FEDERAL TAXATION, see Taxation

FOOD AND DRUG LAW (1980)

Richard A. Merrill, Dean of the School of Law, University of Virginia.
Peter Barton Hutt, Esq.

FUTURE INTERESTS (1958)

Philip Mechem, late Professor of Law Emeritus, University of Pennsylvania.

FUTURE INTERESTS (1970)

Howard R. Williams, Professor of Law, Stanford University.

FUTURE INTERESTS AND ESTATE PLANNING (1961), with 1962 Supplement

W. Barton Leach, late Professor of Law, Harvard University.
James K. Logan, formerly Dean of the Law School, University of Kansas.

GOVERNMENT CONTRACTS, FEDERAL (1975), with 1980 Supplement

John W. Whelan, Professor of Law, Hastings College of the Law.
Robert S. Pasley, Professor of Law Emeritus, Cornell University.

HOUSING—THE ILL-HOUSED (1971)

Peter W. Martin, Professor of Law, Cornell University.

INJUNCTIONS (1972)

Owen M. Fiss, Professor of Law, Yale University.

INSTITUTIONAL INVESTORS, 1978

David L. Ratner, Professor of Law, Cornell University.

INSURANCE (1971)

William F. Young, Professor of Law, Columbia University.

INTERNATIONAL LAW, see also Transnational Legal Problems and United Nations Law

INTERNATIONAL LEGAL SYSTEM (1973), with Documentary Supplement

Noyes E. Leech, Professor of Law, University of Pennsylvania.
Covey T. Oliver, Professor of Law, University of Pennsylvania.
Joseph Modeste Sweeney, Professor of Law, Tulane University.

INTERNATIONAL TRADE AND INVESTMENT, REGULATION OF (1970)

Carl H. Fulda, late Professor of Law, University of Texas.
Warren F. Schwartz, Professor of Law, University of Virginia.

INTERNATIONAL TRANSACTIONS AND RELATIONS (1960)

Milton Katz, Professor of Law, Harvard University, and
Kingman Brewster, Jr., Professor of Law, Harvard University.

INTRODUCTION TO LAW, see also Legal Method, On Law in Courts, and Dynamics of American Law

INTRODUCTION TO THE STUDY OF LAW (1970)

E. Wayne Thode, late Professor of Law, University of Utah.
Leon Lebowitz, Professor of Law, University of Texas.
Lester J. Mazor, Professor of Law, University of Utah.

JUDICIAL CODE and Rules of Procedure in the Federal Courts with Excerpts from the Criminal Code, 1981 Edition

Henry M. Hart, Jr., late Professor of Law, Harvard University.
Herbert Wechsler, Professor of Law, Columbia University.

JURISPRUDENCE (Temporary Edition Hardbound) (1949)

Lon L. Fuller, Professor of Law Emeritus, Harvard University.

JUVENILE COURTS (1967)

Hon. Orman W. Ketcham, Juvenile Court of the District of Columbia.
Monrad G. Paulsen, Dean of the Law School, Yeshiva University.

JUVENILE JUSTICE PROCESS, Second Edition (1976), with 1980 Supplement

Frank W. Miller, Professor of Law, Washington University.
Robert O. Dawson, Professor of Law, University of Texas.
George E. Dix, Professor of Law, University of Texas.
Raymond I. Parnas, Professor of Law, University of California, Davis.

LABOR LAW, Eighth Edition (1977), with Statutory Supplement, and 1979 Case Supplement

Archibald Cox, Professor of Law, Harvard University, and
Derek C. Bok, President, Harvard University.
Robert A. Gorman, Professor of Law, University of Pennsylvania.

LABOR LAW (1968), with Statutory Supplement and 1974 Case Supplement

Clyde W. Summers, Professor of Law, University of Pennsylvania.
Harry H. Wellington, Dean of the Law School, Yale University.

UNIVERSITY CASEBOOK SERIES—Continued

LAND FINANCING, Second Edition (1977)

Norman Penney, Professor of Law, Cornell University.
Richard F. Broude, of the California Bar.

LAW AND MEDICINE (1980)

Walter Wadlington, Professor of Law and Professor of Legal Medicine, University of Virginia.
Jon R. Waltz, Professor of Law, Northwestern University.
Roger B. Dworkin, Professor of Law, Indiana University, and Professor of Biomedical History, University of Washington.

LAW, LANGUAGE AND ETHICS (1972)

William R. Bishin, Professor of Law, University of Southern California.
Christopher D. Stone, Professor of Law, University of Southern California.

LAWYERING PROCESS (1978), with Civil Problem Supplement and Criminal Problem Supplement

Gary Bellow, Professor of Law, Harvard University.
Bea Moulton, Professor of Law, Arizona State University.

LEGAL METHOD

Harry W. Jones, Professor of Law Emeritus, Columbia University.
John M. Kernochan, Professor of Law, Columbia University.
Arthur W. Murphy, Professor of Law, Columbia University.

LEGAL METHODS (1969)

Robert N. Covington, Professor of Law, Vanderbilt University.
E. Blythe Stason, late Professor of Law, Vanderbilt University.
John W. Wade, Professor of Law, Vanderbilt University.
Elliott E. Cheatham, late Professor of Law, Vanderbilt University.
Theodore A. Smedley, Professor of Law, Vanderbilt University.

LEGAL PROFESSION (1970)

Samuel D. Thurman, Dean of the College of Law, University of Utah.
Ellis L. Phillips, Jr., Professor of Law, Columbia University.
Elliott E. Cheatham, late Professor of Law, Vanderbilt University.

LEGISLATION, Third Edition (1973)

Horace E. Read, late Vice President, Dalhousie University.
John W. MacDonald, Professor of Law Emeritus, Cornell Law School.
Jefferson B. Fordham, Professor of Law, University of Utah, and
William J. Pierce, Professor of Law, University of Michigan.

LEGISLATIVE AND ADMINISTRATIVE PROCESSES (1976)

Hans A. Linde, Professor of Law, University of Oregon.
George Bunn, Professor of Law, University of Wisconsin.

LOCAL GOVERNMENT LAW, Revised Edition (1975)

Jefferson B. Fordham, Professor of Law, University of Utah.

MASS MEDIA LAW (1976), with 1979 Supplement

Marc A. Franklin, Professor of Law, Stanford University.

MENTAL HEALTH PROCESS, Second Edition (1976)

Frank W. Miller, Professor of Law, Washington University.
Robert O. Dawson, Professor of Law, University of Texas.
George E. Dix, Professor of Law, University of Texas.
Raymond I. Parnas, Professor of Law, University of California, Davis.

UNIVERSITY CASEBOOK SERIES—Continued

MUNICIPAL CORPORATIONS, see Local Government Law

NEGOTIABLE INSTRUMENTS, see Commercial Paper

NEW YORK PRACTICE, Fourth Edition (1978)

Herbert Peterfreund, Professor of Law, New York University.
Joseph M. McLaughlin, Dean of the Law School, Fordham University.

OIL AND GAS, Fourth Edition (1979)

Howard R. Williams, Professor of Law, Stanford University
Richard C. Maxwell, Professor of Law, University of California, Los Angeles.
Charles J. Meyers, Dean of the Law School, Stanford University.

ON LAW IN COURTS (1965)

Paul J. Mishkin, Professor of Law, University of California, Berkeley.
Clarence Morris, Professor of Law Emeritus, University of Pennsylvania.

OWNERSHIP AND DEVELOPMENT OF LAND (1965)

Jan Krasnowiecki, Professor of Law, University of Pennsylvania.

PARTNERSHIP PLANNING (1970) (Pamphlet)

William L. Cary, Professor of Law, Columbia University.

PERSPECTIVES ON THE LAWYER AS PLANNER (Reprint of Chapters One through Five of Planning by Lawyers) (1978)

Louis M. Brown, Professor of Law, University of Southern California.
Edward A. Dauer, Professor of Law, Yale University.

PLANNING BY LAWYERS, MATERIALS ON A NONADVERSARIAL LEGAL PROCESS (1978)

Louis M. Brown, Professor of Law, University of Southern California.
Edward A. Dauer, Professor of Law, Yale University.

PLEADING AND PROCEDURE, see Procedure, Civil

POLICE FUNCTION (1976) (Pamphlet)

Chapters 1–11 of Miller, Dawson, Dix & Parnas' Criminal Justice Administration, Second Edition.

PREVENTIVE LAW, see also Planning by Lawyers

PROCEDURE—Biography of a Legal Dispute (1968)

Marc A. Franklin, Professor of Law, Stanford University.

PROCEDURE—CIVIL PROCEDURE, Second Edition (1974), with 1979 Supplement

James H. Chadbourn, Professor of Law, Harvard University.
A. Leo Levin, Professor of Law, University of Pennsylvania.
Philip Shuchman, Professor of Law, University of Connecticut.

PROCEDURE—CIVIL PROCEDURE, Fourth Edition (1978), with 1980 Supplement

Richard H. Field, late Professor of Law, Harvard University.
Benjamin Kaplan, Professor of Law Emeritus, Harvard University.
Kevin M. Clermont, Professor of Law, Cornell University.

PROCEDURE—CIVIL PROCEDURE, Third Edition (1976), with 1978 Supplement

Maurice Rosenberg, Professor of Law, Columbia University.
Jack B. Weinstein, Professor, of Law, Columbia University.
Hans Smit, Professor of Law, Columbia University.
Harold L. Korn, Professor of Law, Columbia University.

PROCEDURE—PLEADING AND PROCEDURE: State and Federal, Fourth Edition (1979)

David W. Louisell, late Professor of Law, University of California, Berkeley.
Geoffrey C. Hazard, Jr., Professor of Law, Yale University.

PROCEDURE—FEDERAL RULES OF CIVIL PROCEDURE, 1980 Edition

PROCEDURE PORTFOLIO (1962)

James H. Chadbourn, Professor of Law, Harvard University, and
A. Leo Levin, Professor of Law, University of Pennsylvania.

PRODUCTS LIABILITY (1980)

Marshall S. Shapo, Professor of Law, Northwestern University.

PRODUCTS LIABILITY AND SAFETY (1980), with Statutory Supplement

W. Page Keeton, Professor of Law, University of Texas.
David G. Owen, Professor of Law, University of South Carolina.
John E. Montgomery, Professor of Law, University of South Carolina.

PROFESSIONAL RESPONSIBILITY (1976), with 1979 Problems, Cases and Readings, Supplement, 1980 Statutory (National) Supplement, and 1980 Statutory (California) Supplement

Thomas D. Morgan, Professor of Law, University of Illinois.
Ronald D. Rotunda, Professor of Law, University of Illinois.

PROPERTY, Fourth Edition (1978)

John E. Cribbet, Dean of the Law School, University of Illinois.
Corwin W. Johnson, Professor of Law, University of Texas.

PROPERTY—PERSONAL (1953)

S. Kenneth Skolfield, late Professor of Law Emeritus, Boston University.

PROPERTY—PERSONAL, Third Edition (1954)

Everett Fraser, late Dean of the Law School Emeritus, University of Minnesota.
Third Edition by Charles W. Taintor, late Professor of Law, University of Pittsburgh.

PROPERTY—INTRODUCTION, TO REAL PROPERTY, Third Edition (1954)

Everett Fraser, late Dean of the Law School Emeritus, University of Minnesota.

PROPERTY—REAL PROPERTY AND CONVEYANCING (1954)

Edward E. Bade, late Professor of Law, University of Minnesota.

PROPERTY—FUNDAMENTALS OF MODERN REAL PROPERTY (1974), with 1980 Supplement

Edward H. Rabin, Professor of Law, University of California, Davis.

PROPERTY—PROBLEMS IN REAL PROPERTY (Pamphlet) (1969)

Edward H. Rabin, Professor of Law, University of California, Davis.

PROSECUTION AND ADJUDICATION (1976) (Pamphlet)

Chapters 12–16 of Miller, Dawson, Dix & Parnas' Criminal Justice Administration, Successor Edition.

PUBLIC REGULATION OF DANGEROUS PRODUCTS (paperback) (1980)

Marshall S. Shapo, Professor of Law, Northwestern University.

UNIVERSITY CASEBOOK SERIES—Continued

PUBLIC UTILITY LAW, see Free Enterprise, also Regulated Industries

REAL ESTATE PLANNING (1980), with 1980 Problems, Statutes and New Materials Supplement

Norton L. Steuben, Professor of Law, University of Colorado.

RECEIVERSHIP AND CORPORATE REORGANIZATION, see Creditors' Rights

REGULATED INDUSTRIES, Second Edition, 1976

William K. Jones, Professor of Law, Columbia University.

RESTITUTION, Second Edition (1966)

John W. Wade, Professor of Law, Vanderbilt University.

SALES (1980)

Marion W. Benfield, Jr., Professor of Law, University of Illinois.
William D. Hawkland, Chancellor, Louisiana State University Law Center.

SALES AND SALES FINANCING, Fourth Edition (1976)

John Honnold, Professor of Law, University of Pennsylvania.

SECURITY, Third Edition (1959)

John Hanna, late Professor of Law Emeritus, Columbia University.

SECURITIES REGULATION, Fourth Edition (1977), with 1980 Selected Statutes Supplement and 1980 Cases and Releases Supplement

Richard W. Jennings, Professor of Law, University of California, Berkeley.
Harold Marsh, Jr., Member of the California Bar.

SENTENCING AND THE CORRECTIONAL PROCESS, Second Edition (1976)

Frank W. Miller, Professor of Law, Washington University.
Robert O. Dawson, Professor of Law, University of Texas.
George E. Dix, Professor of Law, University of Texas.
Raymond I. Parnas, Professor of Law, University of California, Davis.

SOCIAL WELFARE AND THE INDIVIDUAL (1971)

Robert J. Levy, Professor of Law, University of Minnesota.
Thomas P. Lewis, Dean of the College of Law, University of Kentucky.
Peter W. Martin, Professor of Law, Cornell University.

TAX, POLICY ANALYSIS OF THE FEDERAL INCOME (1976)

William A. Klein, Professor of Law, University of California, Los Angeles.

TAXATION, FEDERAL INCOME (1976), with 1980 Supplement

Erwin N. Griswold, Dean Emeritus, Harvard Law School.
Michael J. Graetz, Professor of Law, University of Virginia.

TAXATION, FEDERAL INCOME, Second Edition (1977), with 1979 Supplement

James J. Freeland, Professor of Law, University of Florida.
Stephen A. Lind, Professor of Law, University of Florida.
Richard B. Stephens, Professor of Law Emeritus, University of Florida.

TAXATION, FEDERAL INCOME, Volume I, Personal Income Taxation (1972), with 1979 Supplement; Volume II, Taxation of Partnerships and Corporations, Second Edition (1980)

Stanley S. Surrey, Professor of Law, Harvard University.
William C. Warren, Professor of Law Emeritus, Columbia University.
Paul R. McDaniel, Professor of Law, Boston College Law School.
Hugh J. Ault, Professor of Law, Boston College Law School.

TAXATION, FEDERAL WEALTH TRANSFER (1977)

Stanley S. Surrey, Professor of Law, Harvard University.
William C. Warren, Professor of Law Emeritus, Columbia University, and
Paul R. McDaniel, Professor of Law, Boston College Law School.
Harry L. Gutman, Instructor, Harvard Law School and Boston College Law School.

TAXATION OF INDIVIDUALS, PARTNERSHIPS AND CORPORATIONS, PROBLEMS in the (1978)

Norton L. Steuben, Professor of Law, University of Colorado.
William J. Turnier, Professor of Law, University of North Carolina.

TAXES AND FINANCE—STATE AND LOCAL (1974)

Oliver Oldman, Professor of Law, Harvard University.
Ferdinand P. Schoettle, Professor of Law, University of Minnesota.

TORT LAW AND ALTERNATIVES: INJURIES AND REMEDIES, Second Edition (1979)

Marc A. Franklin, Professor of Law, Stanford University.

TORTS, Sixth Edition (1976)

William L. Prosser, late Professor of Law, University of California, Hastings College.
John W. Wade, Professor of Law, Vanderbilt University.
Victor E. Schwartz, Professor of Law, American University.

TORTS, Third Edition (1976)

Harry Shulman, late Dean of the Law School, Yale University.
Fleming James, Jr., Professor of Law Emeritus, Yale University.
Oscar S. Gray, Professor of Law, University of Maryland.

TRADE REGULATION (1975), with 1979 Supplement

Milton Handler, Professor of Law Emeritus, Columbia University.
Harlan M. Blake, Professor of Law, Columbia University.
Robert Pitofsky, Professor of Law, Georgetown University.
Harvey J. Goldschmid, Professor of Law, Columbia University.

TRADE REGULATION, see Antitrust

TRANSNATIONAL LEGAL PROBLEMS, Second Edition (1976), with Documentary Supplement

Henry J. Steiner, Professor of Law, Harvard University.
Detlev F. Vagts, Professor of Law, Harvard University.

TRIAL, see also Lawyering Process

TRIAL ADVOCACY (1968)

A. Leo Levin, Professor of Law, University of Pennsylvania.
Harold Cramer, of the Pennsylvania Bar.
Maurice Rosenberg, Professor of Law, Columbia University, Consultant.

TRUSTS, Fifth Edition (1978)

George G. Bogert, late Professor of Law Emeritus, University of Chicago.
Dallin H. Oaks, President, Brigham Young University.

TRUSTS AND SUCCESSION (Palmer's), Third Edition (1978)

Richard V. Wellman, Professor of Law, University of Georgia.
Lawrence W. Waggoner, Professor of Law, University of Michigan.
Olin L. Browder, Jr., Professor of Law, University of Michigan.

UNIVERSITY CASEBOOK SERIES—Continued

UNFAIR COMPETITION, see Competitive Process and Business Torts

UNITED NATIONS IN ACTION (1968)

Louis B. Sohn, Professor of Law, Harvard University.

UNITED NATIONS LAW, Second Edition (1967), with Documentary Supplement (1968)

Louis B. Sohn, Professor of Law, Harvard University.

WATER RESOURCE MANAGEMENT, Second Edition (1980)

Charles J. Meyers, Dean of the Law School, Stanford University.
A. Dan Tarlock, Professor of Law, Indiana University.

WILLS AND ADMINISTRATION, 5th Edition (1961)

Philip Mechem, late Professor of Law, University of Pennsylvania.
Thomas E. Atkinson, late Professor of Law, New York University.

WORLD LAW, see United Nations Law

University Casebook Series

EDITORIAL BOARD

CASES AND MATERIALS

ON

EVIDENCE

FOURTH EDITION

By

DAVID W. LOUISELL

Late Elizabeth Josselyn Boalt Professor of Law,
University of California, Berkeley

JOHN KAPLAN

Jackson Eli Reynolds Professor of Law,
Stanford University

JON R. WALTZ

Edna B. and Ednyfed H. Williams Professor of Law
and Lecturer in Medical Jurisprudence,
Northwestern University

Mineola, New York
THE FOUNDATION PRESS, INC.
1981

Library of Congress Cataloging In Publication Data

Louisell, David W
  Cases and materials on evidence.

  (University casebook series)
  Includes bibliographical references and index.
  1. Evidence (Law)—United States—Cases. I. Kaplan,
John, joint author. II. Waltz, Jon R., joint author.
III. Title. IV. Series.
KF8934.L6   1981   347.73'6   80-39753

ISBN 0-88277-018-7

Louisell, Kaplan & Waltz Cs. & Mat. on Evid. 4th Ed.
1st Reprint—1981

PREFACE TO THE FOURTH EDITION

We are pleased to present yet another edition of Louisell, Kaplan and Waltz. With the customarily suspicious eye of the legal academic or law student, you may well ask, "Why is this edition different from all other editions?" The answer is that it is newer and, we believe, better.

First of all, we have repaired what was probably the book's greatest inadequacy—the circumstance that, especially for the relatively new teacher, it was somewhat thin in terms of hypotheticals and problem cases. Indeed, candor forces us to admit that "thin" is perhaps the wrong word, and that "emaciated" might do better. On the other hand, we did not want to put in so many hypotheticals that a teacher attempting to plow through the material at anything like the necessary pace would be overwhelmed by the choices, and by the demands from the students to handle this or that problem. As a result, we have added several hypotheticals at the end of each section, the hypotheticals being taken from Judge Bernard Jefferson's remarkable *Benchbook** which, though it relies for its results on California decisions, nonetheless contains the most sophisticated analysis of a large group of evidence problems available in the literature.

Next we have substituted a number of cases for ones that simply did not "teach" well enough. After diligent searching, we have finally found a better case than *Firlotte v. Jesse* to help open the field of relevance. Frankly, despite its use in the First, Second, and Third Editions, we have never really been able to summon up much interest in whether someone had reserved the right to graze animals on a portion of leased land, even if the land *is* now downtown San Francisco. Now we have a case involving a group of Catholic priests who own a rock opera called "Virgin" and are suing a record company for failure to promote it.

In addition to the fact that we have found some more interesting cases to replace those which did not "teach" well, we have also added those which the teacher would probably have had to use as supplementary materials anyway, such as the Supreme Court's latest foray into the spousal incapacity and presumptions in criminal cases. In addition, we have replaced a good number of older cases with recent ones, posing some of the major developing controversies in the interpretation of the Federal Rules of Evidence.

Finally, we have put an end to what had become an annoying feature of our casebook. We have put the California Evidence Code and the Federal Rules of Evidence into an Appendix at the back of the book. We adhere to our firm desire to avoid publishing a Supplement

---

* California Evidence Benchbook, copyright 1975, 1978, Regents of the University of California.

if only on the ground that on any given day a substantial percentage of the students will simply forget to bring it to class.

On the other hand, we have moved to solve a problem which over the past three editions we have found steadily more irritating, the fact that the statutory sections were set out where we then thought each was most appropriately placed—but not necessarily where everyone else would. Now we have used citations to the sections where we had previously placed the sections themselves and have moved the full Codes to the back of the book, so that anyone, including ourselves, can find them quickly.

In short, there are no great break-throughs in this edition but we have continued a process of improvement and modernization. We hope that its users find this new edition even more satisfactory than the past ones.

JOHN KAPLAN
JON R. WALTZ

December, 1980

SUMMARY OF CONTENTS

APPENDICES

*

TABLE OF CONTENTS

TABLE OF CONTENTS

CHAPTER IV. A RETURN TO RELEVANCE

CHAPTER V. IMPEACHMENT AND CROSS EXAMINATION

CHAPTER VI. CONFIDENTIALITY AND CONFIDENTIAL COMMUNICATION

CHAPTER VII. THE PRIVILEGE AGAINST COMPULSORY SELF-INCRIMINATION

TABLE OF CONTENTS

*

TABLE OF CASES

References are to pages.

TABLE OF FEDERAL EVIDENCE RULES

*

TABLE OF CALIFORNIA EVIDENCE
CODE SECTIONS

CASES AND MATERIALS
ON
EVIDENCE

Chapter I

MAKING THE RECORD*

I.

"THE RECORD": WHAT IT MEANS AND HOW IT IS "MADE"

A.

The Meaning and Purpose of the Trial Record

Every experienced trial lawyer realizes as he or she goes into a litigation that his cause may not prevail at the trial level and that his client may wish to appeal to a higher court if, in counsel's opinion, errors occurring at trial contributed significantly to the unhappy outcome. An experienced trial lawyer knows, therefore, that he must be in a position to show a reviewing court precisely what happened during the trial (and perhaps also at any important pre-trial and out-of-court hearings or conferences). It follows that a lawyer must do two things at once—he must operate at two quite different levels—as he goes about the trial of his case. First, he must bend every proper effort to the winning of his client's case at the trial level, which means, essentially, that he must persuade the factfinder—judge or jury—of the rightness of his cause. Second, because counsel can never be absolutely certain of victory at the trial level, he must do everything he can to generate a record of the trial that will serve to convince a reviewing court that justice did not prevail in the court below.

An appellate court can neither speculate about what occurred at trial nor take on faith counsel's uncorroborated description of events in the lower court. A reviewing court can act only on the formal record of the trial that has been officially transmitted to it by the clerk of the trial court.

That record, assembled and bound into one or more volumes after the trial is over, is made up of all the "suit papers," the pleadings in the case (Complaint, Answer, possibly a Reply and perhaps Cross-Complaints, Counterclaims, and Third-Party Complaints and the Answers to them). It will include every other piece of paper that was filed during the course of the litigation: motions, supporting briefs, orders of the trial court, proposed jury instructions, journal entries, everything. The record also contains what in some jurisdictions is called the "Report of Proceedings." This is the ver-

---

*Prepared by Professor Jon R. Waltz.

batim transcript of any on-the-record proceedings in the case. There will be the actual trial transcript—the recordation of all the words that were spoken by the trial's participants (judge, jurors, lawyers, witnesses, and perhaps others)—and there will be transcript from any on-the-record pre-trial or out-of-court hearings and conferences. Attached to the back of the trial transcript, or in the final volumes of a bulky record, will be the exhibits, received and unreceived, that were identified and offered at trial. The record, then, has three basic parts: (1.) the litigation's paperwork, (2.) the verbatim transcript of hearings, conferences, and trial testimony, and (3.) the tangible exhibits that the parties offered into evidence.

B.

How the Record is Made

The active participants in a trial, which means the judge and the lawyers, literally "make" the trial record. They go about it almost as though they were dictating a non-fiction book, or the scenario for a documentary film, to an especially capable secretary. They create the record, in other words, with the assistance of that most important of courtroom functionaries, the court reporter. The reporter has a number of responsibilities during a trial but the most crucial one is the accurate taking down, with high-speed shorthand or by mechanical means such as Stenotype, of everything that is said by the participants. The reporter will take down not only the testimony of the witnesses but the evidentiary objections and arguments of counsel and the comments, rulings, and instructions of the judge. The reporter will ordinarily also be assigned the job of placing identifying markings on tangible exhibits at offering counsel's request and will have the practical responsibility for taking care of the exhibits when they are not in use during the trial.

It thus is no exaggeration to say that during a trial the judge and the lawyers are working with the court reporter in a joint effort that culminates in a complete record of the trial. Competent judges and attorneys are therefore continuously aware of the court reporter and his (or her) importance as the trial process unfolds. This consciousness of the record and of the court reporter's part in the making of it has a discernible effect on the way the judge and counsel go about their work.*

In the first place, it is vital that the court reporter be able to hear and understand everything that is said by the participants in a trial or hearing. It has been said, correctly, that it may even be more important that the reporter hear than the judge, the jurors, and the lawyers, since the reporter can then repeat from his notes any remarks unheard by them.

C.

Conduct of Lawyers that Hampers Court Reporters

Some years ago the National Shorthand Reporters Association catalogued some common practices of trial lawyers that create problems for court reporters. The most frustrating of them are paraphrased below.

1. *"Echoing."* A nervous trial lawyer, or one who is seeking an extra

---

*See Louisell and Pirsig, The Significance of   American Adjudication, 38 Minn.L.Rev. 29
  Verbatim Recording of Proceedings in   (1953).

moment of time in which to frame his next question, sometimes engages in the practice known to court reporters as "echoing." That is, he constantly repeats the witness' response to a question.

Q. What is your name, sir?

A. Clyde Bushmat.

Q. Clyde Bushmat. Where do you reside?

A. At 3730 North Lake Shore Drive in Chicago, Illinois.

Q. 3730 North Lake Shore Drive, Chicago. And how old are you, sir?

A. I'll be forty-two next October 11.

Q. Forty-two in October. What is your present occupation?

Since he must take down everything that is said by the participants in a trial, this unnecessary repetition is distracting to the reporter, wasteful of trial time, and costly to the litigants.

2. *"Overlapping."* It is difficult for a court reporter, no matter how competent, to make an accurate and readable record when more than one person talks at the same time. The reporter may be unable to hear everything that is said or he may be unable to remember all of the overlapping statements long enough to sort out and record them while trying to keep up with the continuing testimony or argument. Counsel, although occasionally forced to prevent a witness from forging ahead with objectionable testimony, generally should avoid interruptions that result in broken sentences and garbled transcripts.

3. *Numbers.* What does a court reporter do when a trial lawyer says "twenty-one-0-two"? Does the lawyer mean 21.02, 2,102.00, or 20,102? Does he mean dollars or something else? He should say, "Twenty-one dollars and two cents" if that is what he means. If he is dealing with a long number, such as the number of an insurance policy, counsel should avoid trying to give the millions, thousands, hundreds, and digits; he is likely to mix up not only himself, the judge, and the jury, but also the court reporter. It is simple enough to say, "Policy Number one-nine-four-seven-nine-six-three." References to dates can also be confusing. Counsel's reference to "October 31" can mean either October the 31st or October, 1931.

4. *Proper Names.* Many proper names have a similar sound. "White, Weit, Whyte, Wight, Wite, Wyatt." Counsel should be particularly careful to enunciate proper names slowly and clearly, in some instances spelling out the name or requesting the witness to do so. Indeed, counsel who is not known to the court reporter would do well to provide the correct spelling of his *own* name at the outset of the trial.

5. *Exhibits.* The Shorthand Reporters Association has observed that trial lawyers are often careless in the way they refer to exhibits. We shall be discussing the correct ways of marking and referring to exhibits. It is enough to mention here that court reporters do not appreciate the lawyer who gets his exhibit properly marked and then fails to make the intended use of the exhibit's number or letter. References to "this photograph" or "that letter" result in an incomprehensible record. Exhibits are marked *for identification.* Counsel's reference should be complete: "I hand you what has been marked Defendant's Exhibit Number 2 for Identification."

6. *Indications and Gestures.*   Unclarified statements such as "About this long," "Approximately that far away," and "He had a jagged scar right here" may be comprehensible enough to those who were present in the trial court to see the witness' physical gestures but they become meaningless on the typed record. Either the witness will have to be asked to give an explicit oral response or, as we shall discuss later, counsel or the court will have to make a clarifying statement for the record.

7. *"Off the Record."*   The practice of lawyers during depositions, pretrial hearings and even occasionally in the midst of trial of directing the court reporter to go "off the record" is often confusing to the reporter. In some instances he may be unclear as to his authority to halt his note-taking, as when neither the trial judge nor opposing counsel has indicated their agreement that recordation can be interrupted; in others he may be uncertain as to precisely when recordation should recommence. If he is unclear of his authority, an experienced court reporter will simply continue to record. And whenever he halts recordation he will protect himself by making a notation in the transcript: "Whereupon discussion off the record was had."

Any confusion about when to resume note-taking can be far more embarrassing to counsel than it is to the reporter where counsel discovers later that an important concession or stipulation did not get on the record or got on it in such a truncated form that it is impossible to determine what it related to. Counsel should give a clear indication when they want to "go back on the record." It is easy to do. A hand signal may be all that is needed, or a statement by counsel such as "Let's go back on now. I want to put our stipulation on the record."

8. *Sidebar Conferences.*   A variation on the off-the-record problem arises when counsel engage in whispered "sidebar" conferences —conferences occurring at the bench. These conferences, usually held in connection with an evidentiary objection, are calculated to be outside the jury's hearing but they may prove to be beyond the court reporter's hearing as well. If anything significant occurs during such a conference, such as a ruling by the judge or a stipulation between the parties, counsel should make certain that the reporter has been able to get it on the record.

9. *Abstruse Terminology.*   In lawsuits that will involve substantial amounts of esoteric terminology, such as patent cases, counsel can contribute to the record's accuracy by supplying the reporter with a glossary of the terms that are likely to come up.

10. *Reading Testimony into the Record.*   In reading deposition testimony or previous trial testimony into the record, counsel should read slowly enough, and enunciate sharply enough, that the court reporter can follow. It helps the reporter if counsel always reads the words "Question" and "Answer" at the appropriate points. Later, counsel should supply to the reporter the deposition or transcript from which he read. This will permit the reporter to check the accuracy of his notes against the written exhibit.

D.

Requesting the Making of a Record

It has already at least been implied that now and then a lawyer's making of the trial record involves little more than remembering to see to it that particular proceedings are "on the record"; that is, that they are being recorded by a court reporter. Many aspects of a litigated matter will not become part of the record unless counsel see to it, first, that there is a court reporter present and, second, that he is recording the proceedings. For example, there usually will not be a reporter present at a pre-trial conference of the sort described in Rule 16 of the Federal Rules of Civil Procedure, or at conferences with the trial judge in his or her chambers, unless counsel requests that one be brought in when needed. Important matters, of both a procedural and an evidentiary nature, are frequently resolved at such sessions and a court reporter should be summoned in order that these stipulations can be put in the record.

In a few jurisdictions the court reporter will not record the examination of prospective jurors—the *voir dire*—or counsel's opening statements to the jury unless specifically instructed by court or counsel to do so. Since error can occur during both of these trial phases (although it rarely does), counsel will request recordation in cases that can support the added expense. (He may also want the opening statements transcribed so that he can refer to them—his own or his adversary's—during his closing argument to the jury.)

Some courts, usually those of less than general jurisdiction (municipal courts, "small claims" courts, traffic courts, and the like), have no official court reporters regularly attached to them. Here the litigants have the obligation to provide and pay for the services of a qualified reporter. Court reporters can be obtained from the same organizations that supply them for the taking of depositions. The Yellow Pages of the Chicago Telephone Directory list 154 individuals and partnerships under the heading, "Reporters —Court and Convention."

E.

Requiring Audible Responses from Witnesses

The principal task of a court reporter, and it is a formidable one, is to take down testimony completely and accurately. The reporter ordinarily cannot take down an answer unless there has been an audible one; it is not the reporter's job to invent words which the witness did not speak. An alert court reporter may have time to insert in the record a bracketed statement of what the witness did—for example, "A: [Witness nodded in the affirmative.]"—but often the pace of the trial leaves no time for this. It is counsel's duty to obtain audible oral answers from witnesses or else, as will be described, he must himself insert an oral statement in the record. When a witness nods or gestures instead of answering audibly, counsel ordinarily should advise him that "The court reporter cannot get your answer unless you say it in words, sir."

F.

Statements for the Record

There are all manner of situations in which counsel or the court find it necessary to make a statement for the record. This means, in effect, that counsel or the trial judge are dictating a statement into the trial record; they, not a witness on the stand, speak and the court reporter takes down what they say as an integral part of the trial record.

Statements for the record are commonly employed to fill in testimonial gaps created by the witness, mentioned above, who provides inaudible responses. Instead of reminding the witness to give audible oral answers, assuming that such an answer was the appropriate mode of response to the question, examining counsel may turn to the court reporter and say, "Let the record show that the witness, in response to the question, nodded his head in the affirmative."

Sometimes witnesses, whether directed to do so or not, will respond to questions with their hands rather than vocally. Counsel inquires, "How long was the blade of the knife?" and the witness, instead of saying "About four inches," indicates the length with the thumb and index finger of one hand. In this situation counsel may make a statement for the record rather than insist on an oral response. "Let the record reflect that in answer to the question the witness, using the thumb and index finger of his right hand, indicated a length of approximately four inches." If opposing counsel objects to the statement, saying it looked more like three inches to him, counsel may have to call for an oral response. If opposing counsel remains silent, the statement for the record stands. If examining counsel inquires of opposing counsel, as out of courtesy he might, whether his statement for the record is satisfactory and gets an affirmative reply, the statement for the record rises to the level of a stipulation between counsel.

Whenever counsel expressly requests a witness to communicate information by means other than oral testimony, a statement for the record will be essential in order to avoid later confusion. Here a typical example involves the drama-conscious prosecutor who asks the witness,

Q. Do you see the man you have described anywhere in the courtroom?

A. I do.

Q. Please come down off the witness stand and place your hand on the shoulder of the man whom you have described as the one who assaulted the little girl. [Witness complies.]

BY THE PROSECUTOR: Let the record show that the witness crossed directly to the accused, Clyde Bushmat, and placed her hand on his right shoulder. [Or he may simply say, 'Let the record show that the witness identified the accused.']

Sometimes a witness will give a response which, although oral and audible, nonetheless calls for a clarifying statement for the record.

Q. How far from the automobile were you when this happened?

A. Oh, about from here to the back wall of the courtroom.

BY EXAMINING COUNSEL: Let the record show that the witness has indicated a distance of approximately fifty feet. Does that meet with your approval, counsel?

BY OPPOSING COUNSEL: Yes, that seems about right.

A statement for the record can be used to place in the trial record pertinent matter that is not in dispute and which would not be expected to come from a witness on the stand; matter which, in a sense, is non-evidentiary. For example, it may from time to time be prudent to make a statement for the record to the effect that described proceedings or events took place while the jury was out, lest it later be suggested that comments, legal arguments, or events such as disruptions by defendants or spectators occurring during the period in question may have prejudiced the jury.

G.

Stipulations

Stipulations by counsel are a near relative of the sort of statements for the record that were discussed in the preceding section. As was suggested there, a statement for the record which opposing counsel affirmatively accepts as accurate rises to the level of a stipulation. An unchallenged statement for the record—one that is not objected to by the opposite side—probably qualifies as an implied stipulation. Stipulations can be extremely important in litigation. They are in the nature of contracts entered into by lawyers acting as special agents of their clients. These agreements between counsel can simplify and expedite trial and fill evidentiary gaps. But they are worse than useless unless they have been carefully made a part of the trial record.

A stipulation is simply a voluntary agreement entered into between counsel for the parties to a litigation respecting some matter that is before the trial court. In the absence of special circumstances that might induce a court to vacate it, a stipulation by counsel binds their principals, the clients. (Courts will usually vacate stipulations that were entered into by mistake, and they will always vacate those that were obtained by fraud or deceit.)

Stipulations can relate either to procedure or to evidence. Typical examples of procedural stipulations can be found in Rule 29 of the Federal Rules of Civil Procedure, which treats of "Stipulations Regarding Discovery Procedure." In order that any such stipulations shall be a discernible part of the record, Rule 29 provides that they must be in writing. (See also FRCP 15, which provides that a party, after the filing of a responsive pleading by the opposing side, can amend his pleading either with the trial court's permission "or by written consent of the adverse party.")

An evidentiary stipulation acts to admit or concede specified facts, relieving a party of the burden of making full-scale proof. Such an evidentiary stipulation constitutes a formal judicial admission—an abandonment of any contention to the contrary—and, unless vacated by the trial court, prevents those who enter into it from offering evidence to dispute it. It is identical in force to an admission contained in a pleading.

Complicated stipulations, like complex hypothetical questions to be posed to an expert witness, are usually written out by counsel and then edited. The final written product can then be filed in the case or read into the record. Simple, single-subject stipulations are stated for the record extemporaneously. Here the only problems involve (a.) remembering to state the stipulation, (b.) making certain that the court reporter is recording it, (c.) making certain that the terms of the stipulation are clear and unambiguous, and (d.) getting on the record opposing counsel's unqualified acquiescence in the stipulation.

Stipulations, whether entered into during a deposition, a pre-trial conference, or in the midst of trial, may evolve in a most informal way.

PLAINTIFF'S COUNSEL [speaking to defense counsel at a pre-trial conference]: George, will you agree to our photographs?

DEFENSE COUNSEL: What have you got, Charlie? I'll be glad to look at them. They're all in living color, I suppose?

PLAINTIFF'S COUNSEL: We're not using photos of the injuries, just some pictures of the accident site, the intersection. And they're black-and-white. We've got a group of four shots, taken about a month after the accident. There haven't been any changes out there and there's nothing staged. Just four shots of the intersection, East, West, North, South. Take a look.

DEFENSE COUNSEL: Well, these are all O.K., I think. Let's put it this way. I'll agree to yours if you'll agree to ours.

PLAINTIFF'S COUNSEL: I've seen yours and they're all right. Now these photos were all used in the depositions we took in this case and each one has an identifying mark put on it by the reporter at those depositions. We can use those numbers for now, and then change them at trial. Can we go on the record for this, Miss Nixon?

THE COURT REPORTER: Yes, I'm ready.

PLAINTIFF'S COUNSEL: Let the record show that it is hereby stipulated by and between the parties to this action, through their counsel, that Plaintiff's Bushmat Deposition Exhibits Numbers 4, 5, 6, and 7 for Identification will be admissible in evidence at the trial of this case, without further foundation or proof, as being true and fair representations of what they purport to show. The same stipulation pertains to Defendant's Bushmat Deposition Exhibits, C, D, E, F, and G for Identification. Is that satisfactory, Charlie?

DEFENSE COUNSEL: Yes, that'll do it.

At trial, counsel will have the court reporter mark the deposition exhibits with new identifying numbers and letters with which the exhibits will be identified from then on. Each lawyer, when offering the exhibits, will inform the court that their admissibility has been stipulated by counsel. Each lawyer will repeat the full stipulation for the record and within the jury's hearing, thus making the record in an orderly and sequential manner. The exhibits will be received by the trial court without further foundation proof, although witnesses may make use of them as adjuncts to their testimony.

Stipulations are often entered into for the first time in the midst of trial. As one lawyer sets about laying the proper foundation for the introduction of a writing, opposing counsel, seeing no reason not to spare his adversary from these laborious preliminaries, may interrupt to say, "We will stipulate that Plaintiff's Exhibit 10 for Identification is what it purports to be." The proposed stipulation, if accepted by offering counsel, serves to authenticate the document. Alert offering counsel will realize, however, that the proposed stipulation goes no further than that; by agreeing only that the writing "is what it purports to be," opposing counsel has reserved the right to assert objections based on evidentiary rules other than those governing authentication. It may go this way:

Q. Handing you what has been marked Plaintiff's Exhibit Number 10 for Identification, Mrs. Stitz, I'll ask you what it is, if you know?

A.   This appears to be a letter dictated by my former employer, Mr. Morton P. Lishniss.

BY OPPOSING COUNSEL: Pardon me, counsel. We will stipulate that your Exhibit 10 is what it purports to be.

BY OFFERING COUNSEL: In that case, your Honor, we now offer in evidence what has been marked Plaintiff's Exhibit 10 for Identification.

BY OPPOSING COUNSEL: Well, now, just a moment. We object to it, your Honor. We agree that it is what it appears to be on its face, a letter from Lishniss to Bushmat dated April 1, 1971, but we don't think it has any relevance to this case. Furthermore, its receipt would violate the hearsay rule.

THE COURT: We'll take a brief recess while I hear argument from both sides on this.

Counsel will ordinarily be required by the trial court to accept any stipulation offered by the opposing side which unequivocally concedes everything that counsel would be entitled to show by making full proof. In such a situation the making of complete proof the laying of every brick in the evidentiary foundation, would be a needless waste of time. On the other hand, offered stipulations do not always supply everything to which counsel is entitled. In that situation he will be free to make a complete record on the matter in question. A common example has to do with the qualifications of an expert witness. Opposing counsel, desiring to keep the jury from hearing all of the witness' impressive credentials, may interrupt the preliminary examination to say, "We'll stipulate that Doctor Faust is a qualified orthopedist, your Honor." But such a stipulation does not give examining counsel everything to which he is entitled in a case that may involve a so-called battle of experts. In order to assign comparative weight to the opinions of opposing experts appearing in the case, the jurors are entitled to hear and assess the qualifications of each of them. And examining counsel is therefore entitled to make full proof of those qualifications, thus:

Q.   Doctor, will you please give the court and jury your full name?

A.   Myron L. Faust.

Q.   Where do you reside?

A.   1000 Astor Place, Chicago, Illinois.

Q.   What is your profession?

A.   Physician and surgeon.

Q.   Are you duly licensed to practice as a physician and surgeon in Illinois?

A.   I am.

Q.   What specialty, if any, have you made in your medical practice?

A.   I specialize in orthopedic surgery.

Q.   We will come back to that, Doctor. How long have you practiced medicine?

A.   Twenty-six years this coming June.

Q.   Of what medical school are you a graduate, Doctor Faust?

A.   The Northwestern Universy Medical School in Chicago.

BY OPPOSING COUNSEL: Excuse me a moment. We're willing to stipulate that Doctor Faust is a qualified orthopedic surgeon and can testify here.

BY EXAMINING COUNSEL: We would prefer to make our proof on this, your Honor. The jury is entitled to hear his training and experience. The jurors have got to decide what weight to give his testimony and they can't very well do that without hearing his qualifications.

THE COURT: It would speed things up if you accepted the stipulation, counsel, but you can't be required to do so. You may proceed to establish the witness' qualifications.

Q.   Very well, your Honor. Doctor Faust what other training or study have you had?

BY OPPOSING COUNSEL: In view of our offer to stipulate, we object to this your Honor.

THE COURT: Overruled.

II.

OFFERING EVIDENCE

Obviously, the making of a trial record consists in large part of offering evidence for the factfinder's consideration. The evidence will be in the form of oral testimony and tangible exhibits. The usual method for offering oral testimony into evidence is by engaging in the direct examination or cross-examination of a witness who has been called to the stand to testify under oath. (Sometimes oral testimony can also be offered by way of a deposition or a transcript of previously recorded testimony.) A tangible exhibit is ordinarily presented through a "sponsoring" witness who can identify or authenticate the item and reveal its relevance to some material issue in the case. After laying the necessary foundation, counsel will say something like "Your Honor, we now offer into evidence what has previously been marked Plaintiff's Exhibit Number 6 for Identification," at which point the trial court will rule on the offer, either receiving or rejecting it.

A.

Direct Examination of Witnesses

Unlike the practice in most European countries, where the witness merely stands up and delivers a long and sometimes rambling narrative concerning what he knows about the case, in Anglo-American law the witnesses relate their stories through the question-and-answer method. We require the witness to give his answers in response to relatively pointed questions so that the opposing counsel, forewarned by the question that the jury may be about to hear inadmissible material, can object in time to prevent receipt of the damaging answer.

In Anglo-American law not only must the parties proceed by question and answer, but they must adhere to certain forms of questions. And the restrictions are far more severe on the side calling the witness to stand. The examination of one's own witness—direct examination as distinguished from cross-examination—is hedged about by a number of rules, the most familiar one being the rule against "leading" questions.

1. *Leading Questions.* A leading question is one that suggests its own answer. A typical leading question is, "You were driving your automobile well under the posted speed limit, isn't that so?" The witness may answer "Yes" but it is the attorney's version of the story that the jury hears. This type of question, at least when it goes to matters at the very heart of the case, is, with some exceptions that we will discuss, objectionable on direct examination. For example, Rule 611(c) of the Federal Rules of Evidence provides that "Leading questions should not be used on the direct examination of a witness except as may be necessary to develop his testimony."

The notion has caught on that any question that can be answered "Yes" or "No" is automatically a leading one. This has led some lawyers to believe that they have only to preface their direct questions with "Did you or did you not ＊ ＊ ＊ ?" or "What is the fact as to whether or not ＊ ＊ ＊?" in order to avoid a successful objection. In fact, a question that is susceptible of a "Yes" or "No" may be essentially non-leading, while the question with the seemingly neutral preface may strongly suggest the desired answer. The point is simply that although questions on direct examination can properly point the witness to a particular subject of inquiry, they should be reasonably balanced and neutral.

"Did you or did you not hear the man say, 'I just killed my wife'?" is a leading question, despite the seemingly neutral alternatives offered in the prefatory "Did you or did you not ＊ ＊ ＊ ?" "And then did you hear the man say anything?" is technically leading but probably is permissible to suggest the desired topic of inquiry: what was *said* rather than what was *done* next. The wholly non-leading approach would be,

Q. What, if anything, happened next?

A. The man blurted out, 'I just killed my wife!'

And everyone knows the all-time favorite non-leading question, "Directing your attention to April 1, 1971, I'll ask you whether anything unusual occurred?"

There are a number of situations in which leading questions are permitted even on direct examination.

(a.) Leading questions are allowed on preliminary matters that do not go to the heart of the case, and they are permitted to provide a transition from one subject of inquiry to another.

Q. And you are employed by the Acme Tool Company, I believe?

A. Yes.

Q. And have been for about ten years?

A. That's true.

＊ ＊ ＊

Q. Now, Mr. Bushmat, turning to the day in question, were you and your family out driving in the country?

A. Yes, we were.

(b.)   Leading questions are permitted with respect to undisputed matters where the question is used as a connective.

Q.   You testified earlier, I believe, that you were driving at about thirty miles an hour, is that right?

A.   Yes.

Q.   Very well, then let me ask you this,   *   *   *

(c.)   An adverse or hostile witness can be asked leading questions. There is very little danger that such a witness would accept a false suggestion contained in a leading question.

(d.)   Leading questions are allowed during direct examination when a witness gives "surprise" answers. Surprise is most commonly demonstrated where the witness' direct testimony is sharply at odds with his deposition testimony or with a previous statement. Of course, examining counsel is not free to call a potentially adverse witness in the blind hope that his testimony will be helpful and then when it proves not to be, commence to lead and impeach him.

(e.)   Leading questions may be allowed in connection with a witness of limited understanding, such as a child, an adult of low mentality, or a foreigner who is experiencing some language difficulty.

(f.)   Leading questions can be put to a witness whose recollection has been exhausted but who apparently possesses additional information of a relevant sort. In other words, it is sometimes proper to refresh a witness' recollection by means of a leading question, thus—

Q.   Can you remember the names of any other people who attended this meeting?

A.   No, I can't. I know there were others but I just can't seem to come up with their names now.

Q.   You have exhausted your recollection of those persons who were present?

A.   I'm afraid so.

Q.   Would it ring any bells if I suggested to you that Mr. Clyde Bushmat also attended that meeting?

A.   You're right! Now I remember. Bushmat was there, too.

Some courts would require that counsel request permission before posing a leading question of this type. Immediately after receiving the response "I'm afraid so," counsel would inquire of the trial court, "Your Honor, may I ask the witness a leading question? His recollection is exhausted and yet he has indicated that he has additional knowledge." Under the circumstances indicated above, this request would undoubtedly be granted.

(g.)   Hypothetical questions of the sort commonly put to expert witnesses are intensely leading, up to a point, but they are permissible as a means of providing a factual basis for the expert's opinion.

Q.   Doctor, I am going to ask you to assume that all of the following facts are true and then I will ask you for your opinion with respect to them. First, please assume that the plaintiff is a woman who on April 1, 1971, was thirty-five years of age. Assume that on that day she *   *   * [Counsel provides additional data, the truth of which is to be assumed by witness.]

Now, assuming all of these facts to be true, do you have an opinion, based on a reasonable degree of medical certainty, as to whether the plaintiff's current condition was caused by the accident that she had on April 1, 1971?

A. I do.

Q. What is that opinion?

2. *Compound and Otherwise Confusing Questions.* In making the testimonial record, counsel should avoid the use of questions that will confuse or mislead the witness. The principal offender is the double or compound question, which may leave everyone in the courtroom baffled. Such questions result in ambiguous or incomplete responses.

Q. State where you were and whether at that time you had a conversation with Clyde Bushmat—was that his first name?—and, if so, what it was.

A. That's right, he said his first name was Clyde, and * * * What was the rest of your question?

BY EXAMINING COUNSEL: Would the court reporter please read the question back?

THE COURT: Maybe it would be better to ask him one question at a time, counsel. Put another question.

Questions should be brief, clear, and cast in reasonably simple terms. The use of negatives in questions is worth avoiding because they generate confusion.

Q. Actually, you don't know whether Bushmat was there, do you?

A. Yes.

THE COURT: Just one moment. Does the witness mean 'Yes, I know,' 'Yes, it is true that I don't know,' or 'Yes, Bushmat was there'?

3. *Questions Assuming Unproved Facts.* The record cannot effectively be made by means of questions that assume the existence of facts that have neither been proved nor conceded. The classic example under this heading is "when did you stop beating your wife?" Nonexistent evidence cannot be supplied by means of "loaded" questions, since counsel is not testifying, and such questions only confuse the witness and the jury.

Expert Witnesses. The direct examination of an expert witness will differ somewhat from that of ordinary witnesses. This is true because of the operation of the so-called opinion rule. Generally speaking, witnesses are required to testify only about facts of which they have direct knowledge and they are not free to unburden themselves of opinions and beliefs about subjects on which any reasonably knowledgeable lay juror could form a conclusion. On the other hand, experts of one sort and another are allowed to express their opinions on relevant matters so long as a proper foundation has been laid.

An expert witness can state an opinion or conclusion if four conditions are satisfied.

1. The validity of the opinion or conclusion depends on special knowledge, skill, or training not ordinarily found in lay jurors;

2. The witness must be qualified as an expert in the pertinent field;

3. He must possess a reasonable degree of certainty (probability) about his opinion or conclusion; and

4. Generally, an expert witness must first describe the data on which his conclusion is based, or he must testify in response to a hypothetical question that sets forth such data. This means that three approaches are open to the expert witness. (a.) He can express an opinion based on facts personally observed, also perhaps taking into account facts communicated to him by another expert—as when a physician bases his opinion in part on the report of an x-ray technician. (b.) The expert who has been present in the courtroom can base his opinion on the evidence if it is not in conflict (the expert will not be permitted to weigh conflicting evidence). (c.) The expert can base an opinion on a hypothetical question embracing undisputed data.

Making the necessary record in connection with an expert witness involves two basic steps. First, he must be "qualified," that is, he must be asked a series of questions that will bring out his qualifications as an expert. Second, the record must show the data on which the witness' opinion is to be based.

Needless to say, the qualifying questions will vary depending on the field of expertise that is involved.

At the conclusion of the direct questions aimed at qualifying a witness as an expert, and before examining counsel gets into substantive questions, opposing counsel is entitled to interrupt and engage in cross-examination as to the witness' expertise. This, somewhat confusingly, is often referred to as a *voir dire* of the witness. At this time the cross-examiner, believing the witness to be unqualified to express an "expert" opinion, makes his record. His cross-questions will be limited strictly to the matter of the witness' qualifications.

The medium of the hypothetical question is employed where the expert witness does not have direct knowledge of the facts, or the evidence, on which an opinion is desired. Careful trial counsel will usually draft the hypothetical question well in advance of its use at trial. In doing this he will usually be assisted by the expert, thus making sure that all the essential facts are included in the question in a sensible sequence. At the beginning of a hypothetical question the witness is called upon to assume as true all of the facts that will be asserted by counsel in the body of the question. The body of the question then sets forth, in hypothetical form, the material facts as to which the expert's opinion is sought. (In the federal practice, it is not necessary to lay out *all* of the underlying facts, however. See Fed.R.Evid. 705: "The expert may testify in terms of opinion or inference and give his reasons therefor without prior disclosure of the underlying facts or data, unless the court requires otherwise.") A hypothetical question's conclusion inquires whether the witness has an opinion, based upon a reasonable degree of certainty, regarding the assumed facts. Thus a hypothetical question may end this way:

Q. Doctor Faust, assuming all of these facts to be true, have you an opinion, based on a reasonable degree of certainty from a surgical point of view, whether the facts assumed in the question and the injury assumed, namely, the dislocation of the vertebrae, and the fracture of the lamina of the fifth cervical vertebra, are sufficient to cause the symptoms and the conditions assumed in my hypothetical question?

    A.   I do have an opinion.

    Q.   What is that opinion, doctor? [At this point any objection to the question will be made and ruled upon.]

For two examples of hypothetical questions, albeit defective ones, the reader is referred to the opinion in Ingram v. McCuiston, reproduced at page ~~1049~~ et seq. in the casebook.

451 *Using an Interpreter.*   When a witness has a serious language barrier—when he speaks no English or very little—the testimonial record will have to be made with the assistance of a qualified interpreter. The interpreter must be shown to be disinterested and will be required to swear or affirm that he "will truly and correctly translate the questions of counsel from English to [German, Spanish, whatever the witness' language may be] and the answers of the witness from [German, Spanish] to English, so help me God." He must translate the questions and the answers verbatim. Counsel will frame his questions just as though he were questioning the witness directly in English. That is, counsel, looking at the witness on the stand and not at the interpreter, will inquire, "What happened next?"; he will not address his question to the interpreter, saying, "Now ask him what happened next."

B.

Cross-Examination of Witnesses

    As was suggested earlier, cross-examination is a much more flexible instrument than direct examination. It is hedged about by far fewer restrictive rules. Relevance is the principal test of a cross-question's propriety; relevance, and whether the cross-questions are ranging too far beyond the contours of opposing counsel's direct examination of the witness.

    The proper purposes of cross-examination are numerous. At its most innocuous, cross-examination may do no more than clarify, supplement, or qualify the direct testimony of a not very damaging witness. However, cross-examination is usually used in a much more aggressive fashion. In an effort to weaken the witness' direct evidence, the cross-examiner's questions may challenge the sources of the witness' knowledge, together with his perception and his memory. The examiner may also try to demonstrate the witness' inability to describe events consistently and accurately. Cross-examination can be employed to extract admissions of fact that undermine the witness' direct testimony. And cross-examination can be used to impeach the witness' veracity, to cast a cloud on his truthfulness.

    On one level a witness' veracity can be put in doubt by inquiries revealing an interest or partisanship, the existence of a bias or prejudice, which might lead him to misrepresent the facts or to twist them. That he is related to or friendly with the opposite party, or hostile to the examining side, can be developed, and any direct or indirect pecuniary interest in the outcome of the lawsuit can be gone into.

    A witness can be impeached, on a somewhat different level, by cross-questions revealing that he has made prior out-of-court statements that are inconsistent with the answers he gave on his in-court direct examination. Occasionally a witness can also be impeached, on yet another level, by evidence of serious criminal convictions or prior "bad acts" tending to cast doubt on his current reliability.

It follows from what has just been said that counsel is free to use leading questions to make his record on cross-examination. (See, e. g., Fed.R. Evid. 611(c): "Ordinarily leading questions should be permitted on cross-examination.") It is virtually impossible to conduct an impeaching cross-examination without asking leading questions. This does not mean, however, that excessively argumentative cross-questions will be countenanced by a trial court. It is one thing to inquire, in altogether leading fashion, "Isn't it a fact that on the night in question you could see only about ten or twelve feet ahead of you?" It is quite another thing, upon being given an unsatisfying response, heatedly to inquire, "Do you really expect the jury to believe that?" The first question is proper on cross-examination, there being scant risk that the opposing party's witness will accept the suggestion built into a leading question and supply the cross-examination party with a favorable but false answer. The second question is improper on either direct or cross-examination; it is unduly argumentative and contributes nothing of value to the trial record.

Questions assuming unproved facts ("loaded" questions), compound and otherwise confusing questions are no more allowable on cross-examination than they are on direct.

C.

Tangible Evidence

Standing in contrast to testimonial evidence is tangible evidence. Tangible evidence may be a writing, a murder weapon, the seized marijuana, a rusted metal container, the scar on a tort plaintiff's face. Putting writings to one side for a moment, because special rules have clustered around them, we can say that there are two basic types of tangible evidence: (1.) real evidence, and (2.) demonstrative evidence. And just as one must qualify oral testimony for admission into evidence by showing, for example, that the witness has personal knowledge of relevant facts, one must also qualify items of tangible evidence for receipt into evidence.

Tangible exhibits should be offered during the direct or re-direct examination of a party's witnesses and not during the cross-examination of the adverse party's witnesses. To put it a different way, *your* exhibits should be offered during *your* direct case, not *his*. It is not reversible error, however, to receive exhibits during cross-examination; the trial court can permit it and the parties can agree to it, expressly or by implication (as when no objection is interposed).

Real Evidence. This is "the real thing"—the actual murder weapon, not a mere example of a weapon of the type said to have been used in the al-alleged crime. Real evidence can be direct evidence, offered to establish facts about the tangible thing itself, such as the extent of plaintiff's disfigurement as a consequence of the observable facial scar. Real evidence can also be circumstantial, as when facts about an object are offered as the basis for an inference that some other fact is true; for example, rust inside a metal container implies the prior presence of moisture in the container.

The procedure for making the record in connection with real evidence is sometimes quite elaborate, depending on the nature of the particular exhibit. (It is usually easier to get a single letter into evidence than a patient's complete medical record, consisting of numerous separate records made by different authors at different times in different places for different reasons.) In general, there are six steps, all of them important:

1. *Marking for Identification.* In order to build a trial record that be understandable and efficient to work with later on, counsel will cause real evidence to be marked for identification, usually by the court reporter. Thereafter, during his examination of witnesses, counsel will refer to the item by its identifying number or letter. Still later, when someone reads the typewritten trial record, he can readily associate the witness' testimony with the marked exhibits that are bound into the record either at the end of testimony or, if the record is a lengthy one, in one or more separate volumes.

With experienced trial counsel the matter of marking exhibits for identification becomes almost automatic: when a trial lawyer picks something with the intention of introducing it in evidence, he will first proceed to the court reporter and ask him to mark it in numerical or alphabetical sequence. Counsel will then subside into silence, since the reporter cannot record counsel's comments or continued questions to a witness while at the same time marking or tagging the exhibit. After the exhibit has been marked, counsel will as a matter of courtesy show the exhibit to the trial judge and opposing counsel unless they have already seen it or, in the case of a writing, diagram, chart, map, or the like, been provided by counsel with copies.

Step No. 1 goes this way, then:

OFFERING COUNSEL [having picked up a letter from the counsel table]: I will ask the court reporter to mark this for identification. If I recall correctly, this would be Plaintiff's 9.

COURT REPORTER [marking the exhibit]: Yes, this will be Plaintiff's 9.

OFFERING COUNSEL: Your Honor, I believe we gave you a Xerox copy of this letter. It is dated April 1, 1971, on the defendant's letterhead.

THE COURT: Yes, I have it.

OFFERING COUNSEL [addressing opposing counsel]: And we supplied you with a copy, too, did we not?

OPPOSING COUNSEL: Yes, we have our copy, although of course we reserve our right to object to it at the appropriate time.

OFFERING COUNSEL: Of course.

2. *Laying the Necessary Foundation.* In the absence of an agreement (stipulation) with opposing counsel that the exhibit is receivable, it will next be necessary to lay the foundation for admission of the item of real evidence. (See, e. g., Fed.R.Evid. 901.) This is usually accomplished through one or more witnesses who "sponsor" the exhibit, identifying authenticating) it and illuminating its relevance to the issues in the case. Basically, this involves testifying that the exhibit is "the genuine article," "the real thing." Examination under Step No. 2 may proceed in this way:

BY OFFERING COUNSEL: Officer, I hand you what has been marked Prosecution Exhibit Number 1 for Identification and ask you if you know what it is?

A.   Yes, I recognize it.

Q.   What is it?

A.   This is the knife that I found next to the victim's body that night.

Q.   And by 'this' you mean Prosecution Exhibit Number 1?

A.   Yes, sir.

Q.   How do you know that Prosecution Exhibit Number 1 is the same knife that you saw that night?

A.   At that time I scratched the date and my initials on the handle of the knife, right here. [Indicating.]

If the witness, unlike the one in the preceding example, is unable to identify the exhibit to the exclusion of all similar objects, the chain of custody, without any hearsay links, must be traced in order to establish that the exhibit is "the real thing." This means that there will be a whole series of witnesses called to the stand, each one accounting for the period during which the exhibit was in his custody. In this manner each link in the chain of custody is forged and it is demonstrated that the exhibit is in fact "the genuine article."

If the condition of the object is significant, the sponsoring witness must be prepared to testify that its condition has not changed in any important way since the pertinent time, thus—

BY OFFERING COUNSEL: Mrs. Stitz, I show you Plaintiff's Exhibit Number 3 for Identification. Do you know what that is?

A.   Yes that's the tin can that I cut my hand on.

Q.   How do you happen to know that?

A.   It's been on a shelf in my kitchen ever since that day, except for the time I brought it to your office to show to you, and I brought it to court today myself.

Q.   Can you tell us whether the condition of Exhibit Number 3 has changed since the day of your accident?

A.   Just that there aren't any green beans in it any more. I cleaned it out.

Q.   Otherwise it looks the same?

A.   Yes, sir. You can still see the jagged metal protrusion that cut my hand. [Indicating.]

Finally, it should be mentioned that the record has not been satisfactorily made where the instrumentality of an alleged crime has not been linked to the crime and to the accused.

3.   *Offering the Exhibit into Evidence.*   The third step involves offering the exhibit into evidence once the proper foundation has been laid. Step No. 3, although sometimes forgotten by inexperienced trial counsel, is a mechanical one:

BY OFFERING COUNSEL: Your Honor, we now offer into evidence, as Plaintiff's Exhibit Number 1, what has previously been marked as Plaintiff's Exhibit Number 1 for Identification.

THE COURT: There being no objection, it will be received.

4. *Securing an Express Ruling on the Record.* In the preceding example the trial court made a prompt and explicit ruling on counsel's offer. Occasionally, however, counsel may find it necessary to request the court to make an unequivocal ruling. The trial court's silence in the face of an offer will not necessarily be taken, on review, as an acceptance of the proferred evidence.

5. *A Precautionary Measure.* Cautious counsel, having obtained a ruling admitting his exhibit into evidence, may foreclose any possible future confusion by requesting the court reporter to scratch out the words "for Identification" in the exhibit-mark, thereby making it doubly clear that the exhibit was received in evidence.

6. *Showing or Reading the Exhibit to the Jury.* Now, for the first time, offering counsel is free to show the exhibit to the jurors or, in the case of written material, read it to them or direct the witness to read it to them. As a matter of courtesy, however, express permission to do so is usually requested of the trial judge.

BY OFFERING COUNSEL: Your Honor, may we now pass the exhibit, Plaintiff's Number 1, to the members of the jury for their examination?

THE COURT: You may.

Counsel will put no new questions to the witness on the stand until the jurors have had an opportunity to inspect the exhibit that has been handed to them.

So-called "testimonial exhibits," such as a deposition that has been placed in evidence, usually must be read into the record (in the fact-finders' hearing, of course) since most jurisdictions will not permit this sort of exhibit to be taken by the jurors to their deliberation room for examination along with the other exhibits in the case. (It is thought that giving the testimonial exhibit to the jurors might unduly highlight an isolated block of testimony.) Counsel can read the exhibit into the record himself or, in the case of a deposition or prior recorded testimony, he can put someone in the witness chair—another lawyer with whom he is associated, even his secretary —to read the deponent's or witness' answers in response to counsel's reading of the questions contained in the deposition or transcript.

Demonstrative Evidence. This is *not* "the real thing." It is tangible material used for explanatory or illustrative purposes only: it is a visual aid, such as an anatomical model, a chart, a diagram, a map, a film, and the like. Evidence that is demonstrative only—that does not qualify as substantive evidence—is not ordinarily offered into evidence in the way real evidence is and it thus does not go to the jury's deliberation room. However, this does not mean that there is no foundational procedure, no record to be made, in connection with demonstrative material.

There are two basic types of demonstrative evidence. First there is "selected" demonstrative evidence, such as handwriting exemplars used as standards of comparison by a handwriting expert. Then there is "prepared" or "reproduced" demonstrative evidence, such as the model or the diagram.

It is in connection with prepared or reproduced demonstrative material that there is the greatest risk of fabrication or distortion. The law seeks to minimize these risks by requiring certain testimonial assurances. These assurances are a part of the foundation, part of the record that must be made, as a precondition to the use of demonstrative materials in the courtroom.

In the first place, it is again true, as it is with real evidence, that conditions shown by the exhibit must not be significantly different from those that existed at the time of the events in question. If conceded changes are irrelevant, they must at least be accounted for, as, for example, in connection with a photograph of the accident site that reveals buildings constructed since the incident in question.

Secondly, there must be testimony that a particular demonstrative exhibit is a "true and fair representation" of what it purports to show. Thus a person familiar with the scene depicted in a photograph (it need not necessarily be the photographer) can lay the foundation for the photograph's use as an item of demonstrative material. In connection with motion picture film, there must be testimony from a knowledgeable witness that it has not been improperly edited by means of splicing and the like.

Writings.   The evidentiary significance of writings frequently depends on their authorship. If the asserted letter of acceptance was dictated and signed by the defendant corporation's president, it will be a crucial item of evidence in a contract case; if it was signed by someone lacking any authority, real or apparent, to do so, it will be of no legal consequence. Accordingly, it often is necessary to make a record on the question of authorship. Is the writing truly what it purports to be on its face, a letter composed and signed by the defendant's president? A writing, in other words, is not receivable in evidence until it has been authenticated. (See e. g., Fed.R.Evid., Arts. IX–X.) Its genuineness must be demonstrated to the trial judge, as a preliminary matter, before the jury can consider it. It cannot be read or shown to the jury until the record has been made and the writing has been formally admitted into evidence by the judge.

A writing can be authenticated in a variety of ways:

1.   By a notice or request to admit genuineness, as under Rule 36 of the Federal Rules of Civil Procedure.

2.   By *direct* evidence that proves the handwriting in question. This can be either the identifying testimony of the writing's author, or the testimony of anyone who observed the writing being made.

3.   By proving the handwriting *circumstantially,* which can be accomplished—

a.   By the identifying testimony of someone who is familiar with the handwriting of the person in question;

b.   By the testimony of a handwriting expert who compares the questioned handwriting with one or more genuine specimens; or

c.   By letting the jurors themselves compare the questioned handwriting with genuine specimens.

4.   By reliance on common law or statutory or rules provisions that render some writings self-authenticating or that set up presump-

tions of authenticity. (A good example is the so-called ancient documents rule.)

The following is a simple example of direct authenticating testimony:

Q. Give your full name to the jury, please.

A. Clyde Bushmat.

Q. Your address?

A. 1313 Euclid Avenue, Cleveland, Ohio.

Q. What is your occupation?

A. I'm a deliveryman for C. D. Pigeon, a jewelry company here in the city.

Q. Do you know Morton P. Lishniss, the defendant in this case?

A. I do.

Q. How do you happen to know him?

A. I have delivered merchandise to him from time to time.

BY EXAMINING COUNSEL [to court reporter]: Please mark this Plaintiff's Exhibit Number 1 for Identification.

Q. Showing you what has just been marked Plaintiff's Exhibit Number 1 for Identification, Mr. Bushmat, I will ask you whether you have ever seen it before?

A. I've seen it before, yes.

Q. When, sir?

A. When I delivered the merchandise that's listed on it.

Q. On the occasion of that delivery did you see Morton P. Lishniss?

A. Sure I did.

Q. Tell us what happened.

A. I delivered the diamond necklace to Mr. Lishniss myself and I requested that he sign the receipt for it.

Q. Did he do so?

A. Yes, sir.

Q. How do you know he did?

A. I saw him do it.

Q. You saw him?

A. Yes I did. He signed it right there while I was watching him.

Q. Whose signature is this on Plaintiff's Exhibit Number 1 for Identification, Mr. Bushmat?

A. That's the signature that Mr. Lishniss made in my presence.

BY EXAMINING COUNSEL: We offer Plaintiff's Exhibit Number 1 for Identification as Plaintiff's Exhibit Number 1, your Honor.

THE COURT: It will be received.

If counsel is offering something other than the original of a writing his making of the record will include an indication of compliance with the "best evidence" rule. The following example begins in mid-stream:

Q.   How many copies of the contract were signed, Mr. McLaren?

A.   Just one.

Q.   Who retained that? Who kept it?

A.   I did.

Q.   Do you have that original agreement that was executed by you and Mr. Bushmat?

A.   No, I don't.

Q.   Do you know where it is?

A.   No, I do not. I can't find it.

Q.   When did you last see it, Mr. McLaren?

A.   The day we signed it.

Q.   What did you do with it?

A.   I put it in one of my desk drawers right after we executed it.

Q.   Have you seen it since then?

A.   No.

Q.   When did you first look for it again?

A.   About ten days ago, but I couldn't find it anywhere.

Q.   Where did you search?

A.   In my desk drawers, on top of the desk, all around my office, at home. Everywhere that I ordinarily keep papers. I looked everywhere.

Q.   Have you tried to find it since then?

A.   Yes. No luck.

Q.   What do you think has happened to the original of the agreement?

A.   Well, it's lost, that's all.

Q.   Did you intentionally lose it or destroy it?

A.   Of course not.

BY EXAMINING COUNSEL: Mark this Plaintiff's Exhibit Number 1 for Identification, if you please.

Q.   Handing you what has been marked Plaintiff's Exhibit Number 1 for Identification, Mr. McLaren, I will inquire whether you have ever seen it before?

A.   Oh, yes.

Q.   Where and when?

A.   In my office. I saw it there at the same time that the original agreement was executed. This is a Xerox copy of the original.

Q.   Can you tell by looking at it whether or not it's a true and correct copy of the original?

A.   Yes.

Q.   Is it, or not?

A. Yes, it is. It was made that day, off the original. The Xerox shows the signatures, everything.

BY EXAMINING COUNSEL: We offer in evidence Plaintiff's Exhibit Number 1 for Identification.

THE COURT: It will be admitted as Plaintiff's Exhibit Number 1.

III.

OBJECTIONS TO EVIDENCE

A.

Party Responsibility for Making Objections

As Professor Charles T. McCormick pointed out long ago, the rules of evidence can be made to work only if a party who contends that opposing counsel's question is improper or that certain evidence should be excluded promptly advises the trial judge, who is the umpire of the litigation, of the contention and the reasons for it. The initiative with respect to evidentiary objections lies with the parties, acting through their counsel, and not with the trial judge. This is simply another example of party responsibility in the adversary trial process. (See, e. g., Fed.R.Evid. 103.)

It is a responsibility gladly assumed by competent trial counsel, who dislike few things more than a trial judge's usurpation of the litigator's obligation to decide which objections, perhaps for purely tactical or strategic reasons, he will forego. Thus it is unusual, although it would not be without precedent, to hear a judge exclude evidence to which counsel has not objected; a competent judge will do this only where the offered evidence is not only incompetent but also irrelevant or potentially prejudicial or where he is preserving the rights of an absent holder of some testimonial privilege. Occasionally, however, one encounters the sort of judge who, possibly because he is himself a frustrated trial lawyer, will interrupt testimony to inquire of one silent side, "Do I hear an objection?" With almost equal frequency one will hear the lawyer for that side respond, "You do not, your Honor." Counsel, for reasons of his own, has made a deliberate decision to dispense with any objection.

B.

Reasons For Foregoing Available Objections

No trial lawyer makes every evidentiary objection that may be open to him. There are a variety of reasons for this. (1.) Trial counsel has no need or wish to complain about every innocuous leading question put by opposing counsel since the use of leading questions as to preliminary matters expedites the examination of witnesses, which is usually advantageous to all concerned and poses no real risk of prejudice. (2.) Counsel may let a questionable objection go by the board because he does not want to run the risk that he will only underscore hurtful testimony. (3.) He may abandon an available objection because he does not want to give the jurors the impression that he is excessively obstructive or that he distrusts them. (4.) Often counsel foregoes objection because the evidence, although arguably inadmissible, actually in some way favors his clients cause. (5.) And sometimes counsel remains silent because the opposing lawyer's offer of objec-tionable evidence "opens the door" for more important evidence that the si-lent lawyer hopes to offer later.

C.

Objections Made for Effect

The truth is that objections that go to nothing more important than the form of the question (e. g., leading) are as often made for jury-effect as they are for any weightier purpose. ("We've been very patient, your Honor, but the jurors might like to have a little more testimony from the witness and a little less from opposing counsel. This is all leading, your Honor, and we have to object to it.") Of course, the use of objections as an excuse to make speeches for the jurors' benefit is ethically questionable, as is their use sole-ly to interrupt a damaging examination or to coach a witness who is under-going effective cross-examination. The making of objections for improper purposes can bring an embarrassing admonition from the bench. It is the practice of an increasing number of trial judges to require that any argumentation in support of an objection be made at the bench, out of the jurors' hearing. Objecting counsel inquires, "May we approach the bench?" If the trial judge is receptive to argument on the objection, he will permit counsel to engage in a whispered sidebar presentation and may even ad-journ to chambers if the arguments are likely to be extensive.

D.

Time for Objecting to Testimony: Waiver

Since the burden of interposing legitimate objections, to "protect the record," is lodged with counsel and not the trial court, the failure to make a timely objection, in proper form, to an offer of evidence will operate to waive any possible basis of complaint about its receipt. "Let him speak now or for-ever hold his peace" is as applicable at trials as it is at weddings.

An objection must be made as soon as the basis for it becomes ap-parent. Counsel is not free to sit back, gambling that the witness will give a harmless or even a favorable answer, and then object when the answer proves to be damaging. The trial court is likely to respond to the belated ob-jection with a terse, "Asked and answered, counsel." Ordinarily examining counsel's question will by its own terms reveal that it calls for inadmissible testimony. Opposing counsel must make an effort to interpose his objection before the witness answers.

Q.   What did your sister tell you about the incident that she had observed?

BY OPPOSING COUNSEL: Just one moment, please. We ob-ject, your Honor. It calls for hearsay and we ask that the witness not be permitted to answer.

THE COURT: The objection is sustained.

If the objection to a question is sustained before any answer is given but the terms of the question disclosed the expected answer, counsel can obtain an instruction to the jury that the question itself is not evidence in the case and should be wholly disregarded.

Q.   Officer, did you issue a traffic ticket to the plaintiff?

PLAINTIFF'S COUNSEL: Now, we object to that question. Irrelevant.

THE COURT: Sustained.

PLAINTIFF'S COUNSEL: We ask that your Honor instruct the jury to disregard the implication contained in defense counsel's question.

THE COURT: Yes, the jurors are instructed to disregard the question completely. It is not evidence in this case and an objection to it has been sustained.

Of course, it is not always feasible neatly to insert one's objection between the question and the answer. For one thing, the witness may respond too quickly. All that opposing counsel can do in this situation is state his objection as soon as he can, adding a two-part request that the witness' answer be stricken and that the trial court instruct the jurors to disregard it. Sometimes an apparently unobjectionable question brings out an inadmissible answer. Here, obviously, counsel, be it examining counsel or opposing counsel, cannot phrase his objection until the infirmity in the witness' response emerges. Perhaps the answer is unresponsive, with the result that examining counsel is entitled to object. He will make what is sometimes referred to as an "after-objection":

Q.   Did you observe the plaintiff enter the crosswalk?

A.   Yes, and he appeared to be looking down at his feet instead of watching where he was going.

BY EXAMINING COUNSEL: Object to everything after the word 'Yes' and ask that it go out, your Honor. We also ask that you instruct the jury to disregard everything except the answer 'Yes' as being unresponsive to the question.

THE COURT: Your objection is sustained, and the jury is so instructed.

It is generally said that only examining counsel is entitled to object to an answer whose only infirmity is its lack of responsiveness. In other words, examining counsel is free to "adopt" an unresponsive but favorable answer, which he does either by expressly saying so or by the simple expedient of foregoing any objection to it. Opposing counsel, not being the author of the question, lacks standing to object to any unresponsive answer unless it is excludable on some evidentiary ground over and beyond unresponsiveness; for example, the witness' answer is not only unresponsive but also violative of the hearsay rule. Here are two examples of correct rulings:

BY PLAINTIFF'S COUNSEL: Did you observe the plaintiff enter the crosswalk?

A.   Yes, and he looked in both directions first.

BY DEFENSE COUNSEL: Object, unresponsive.

BY PLAINTIFF'S COUNSEL: We adopt the entire answer, your Honor.

THE COURT: The objection will be overruled.

The result will be different if the witness' answer is varied somewhat.

BY PLAINTIFF'S COUNSEL: Did you observe the plaintiff enter the crosswalk?

A. No, I didn't, but my sister did and she said that the man looked both ways first.

BY DEFENSE COUNSEL: Object, unresponsive and hearsay, your Honor.

BY PLAINTIFF'S COUNSEL: We adopt the entire answer, your Honor.

THE COURT: The objection is sustained on the ground of hearsay.

Occasionally the inadmissibility of testimony does not emerge clearly until long after it has been received in evidence. This happens where it is revealed only after searching cross-examination that a witness' responses to direct examination were based on hearsay rather than personal knowledge, in which case opposing counsel will move to strike all of the witness' testimony and ask that the jurors be instructed to disregard it. It can also be said to happen in instances of so-called conditional relevance. When one side fails to "tie up" or "connect up" conditionally relevant evidence with other evidence that renders the earlier evidence relevant, a renewed objection to the earlier evidence will be sustained, it will be stricken, and the jury, upon request, will be ordered to disregard it in their deliberations.

E.

Objecting to Exhibits

Objections to an exhibit that constitutes real evidence will normally be made at the time the exhibit is formally offered in evidence. Offering counsel is entitled to accomplish the laying of the necessary evidentiary foundation for receipt of the exhibit. This he will do, as we have seen, through one or more "sponsoring" witnesses who are capable of identifying and otherwise authenticating the exhibit. Objections interjected before offering counsel has had a chance to lay the foundation for the exhibit would ordinarily be premature. Certainly an objection made at the juncture at which an exhibit is marked by the court reporter for identification would be premature in all but the most exceptional of circumstances.

Q. Would you give the court and jury your full name, please?

A. Mrs. Irene Stitz.

Q. And where do you reside, Mrs. Stitz?

A. At 3730 North Lake Shore Drive, in Chicago, Illinois.

Q. What is your present occupation, Mrs. Stitz?

A. I am the Records Librarian at Jefferson Memorial Hospital here in the city.

Q. Would you describe your duties as a records librarian?

A. [Witness details her duties.]

Q. In response to a subpoena which I caused to be issued to you, Mrs. Stitz, have you brought anything with you to court today?

A. I have.

Q. What have you brought?

A. The records of Jefferson Memorial Hospital pertaining to a patient named Clyde Bushmat.

BY OPPOSING COUNSEL: Object, your Honor.

THE COURT: Overruled. Proceed.

Q. Would you hand that folder to me, please? [Witness hands folder to examining counsel.]

BY OFFERING COUNSEL: There appear to be nineteen pages or pieces of paper in the folder that the witness has handed to me. I will ask the court reporter to mark each separate page, front and back. What number have we reached with our exhibits at this point?

BY THE COURT REPORTER: This would be number 8.

BY OFFERING COUNSEL: Then we can begin with 8–A.

[Court reporter marks the group exhibit.]

Q. Mrs. Stitz, handing you what has been marked Plaintiff's Group Exhibit 8–A on the front and 8–B on the back, I'll ask you what it is.

BY OPPOSING COUNSEL: Objection, your Honor.

BY OFFERING COUNSEL: Your Honor, I haven't offered the exhibit yet. I've just barely gotten it marked for identification. May I have an opportunity to lay the proper foundation for its admission? I believe I can do that through this witness. Then I'll offer it and opposing counsel can then interpose any objection he may have.

THE COURT: The objection is overruled. You're jumping the gun, counsel. Wait until the exhibit is offered.

Q. Read the last question back, please.

Of course, an early objection, in advance of the offer, is appropriate if improper use of an exhibit is being made. If, for example, examining counsel displays the exhibit, such as a photograph or diagram, to the jury in advance of its receipt in evidence, or if he asks the sponsoring witness to read a written exhibit to the jury prior to its receipt in evidence, an objection will be sustained.

BY THE COURT REPORTER [reading the last question to the witness]: 'Mrs. Stitz, handing you what has been marked Plaintiff's Group Exhibit 8–A on the front and 8–B on the back, I'll ask you what it is.'

A. It is the admission sheet pertaining to Mr. Clyde Bushmat's admission to Jefferson Memorial Hospital.

Q. Would you just read the first seven lines of that to the jury, please?

BY OPPOSING COUNSEL: Now, I object to any reading of this exhibit, your Honor. He's not doing what he said he would. He hasn't laid an adequate foundation for its admission and he hasn't offered it. It can't be read to the jury yet.

THE COURT: Sustained. Lay your foundation, counsel. Then we'll see whether this exhibit can be read to the jury.

F.

Specificity of Objections

The question naturally comes up, how specific must an objection be? Is it enough simply to stand up and say, "Object, your Honor"? Is something more accomplished where counsel, after the fashion of Perry Mason and other lawyers whose practice is limited to television serials, intones, "Object, your Honor. Irrelevant, incompetent, and immaterial"? Or should a trial lawyer be quite specific: "Object, your Honor. Hearsay"? Or: "Object, the best evidence rule hasn't been satisfied"?

A reading of the countless cases dealing with specificity *versus* generality in the phrasing of objections would lead one to believe that the bare announcement that "I object" is insufficient and that even the somewhat more elaborate "three I's," "Irrelevant, incompetent, and immaterial," which McCormick called a "meaningless ritual," are unavailing except perhaps to preserve the question of relevance. The cases recommend that any objection be accompanied by a reasonably specific statement of the ground(s) for it. (See, e. g., Fed.R.Evid. 103(a) (1)). The idea is that a trial judge cannot be expected to recognize instantly the particular evidentiary rules applicable to the testimony and exhibits being offered in a given case. It may be asked, why should a judge be any less equipped to detect the applicable rules than the lawyers appearing before him? The answer is that the lawyers have had the case for many months, even years, analysing it and preparing it for trial; they have had plenty of time to get a firm grip on the evidentiary questions. Of course, the concept of adversariness is at work here. It is up to the contending lawyers, and not the judge, not only to make objections but to support them with reasons.

In making objections the trial lawyer will have three aims in mind, two of which are directly concerned with the "making" of the record. First counsel is seeking to educate the trial judge on the rule or rules of evidence that authorize the objection and the exclusion of the challenged evidence. Counsel is being an advocate. Second, by being reasonably explicit, counsel is preserving a record for possible appeal in case the judge overrules his objection. Thirdly, and this is nothing more than the reverse of the same coin, he is making a record that will support the trial judge on appeal in the event that he sustains counsel's objection.

An exhaustive catalog of instances in which a specific objection is essential to preserve error would be very lengthy. The following examples are of recurring bases for specific objections, although some of them do not come up with much frequency:

Argumentative question	Foundation for introduction of
Best evidence rule violated	writing inadequate to
Compound question	authenticate
Conclusion of law or fact improperly	Hearsay
called for by the question	Hypothetical question defective
Cross-examination exceeding scope	Impeaching one's own witness
of the direct examination	Instructions of trial court
	incorrect

Dead Man's Act renders witness
  incompetent to testify
Facts not in evidence assumed
  in the question
Foundation for introduction of real
  or demonstrative evidence inadequate (chain of custody, etc.)

Leading question on direct
  examination
Narrative answer called for by
  the question
Parole evidence rule violated
Privileged communication
Unresponsive answer
Witness incompetent

   The rules regarding the required form of objections are heavily weighted in favor of the trial judge. If a generalized objection is made and overruled, appellate courts will not reverse unless a valid basis for the objection is perfectly clear. Obviously, in many situations of a recurring sort it would be a waste of time to require a recitation of reasons for a self-evident objection and the trial court is likely to rule before counsel can do more than say "I object." A common example would be the question that by its terms plainly seeks to elicit hearsay testimony. A simple "I object" should suffice to make the record here.

   Occasionally it is also said that a general objection is enough where receipt of the proferred evidence cannot be justified on any legal basis at all. However, it would be dangerous to gamble on the availability of this argument, which is often grounded on a lawyer's 20–20 hindsight. The rationale behind appellate courts' unwillingness to reverse on the basis of a trial judge's overruling of a general objection is that counsel should not be free to shift to the judge the burden of searching for an applicable exclusionary rule.

   The rules also aid the trial judge when he has sustained a general objection—and here they redound to objecting counsel's benefit, too. On appeal the trial court will be upheld if there was any ground on which the evidence could properly have been excluded. It is assumed that the trial judge had the right reason in mind when he rejected the evidence. To sum up, thn, a trial court will ordinarily be upheld on appeal whether it has sustained or overruled a general objection.

   Where a specific objection ("Object, hearsay") is erroneously overruled, the record thus made will support a reversal if the evidence is prejudicial. If a specific objection is properly sustained, there obviously has been no reversible error. But what if the ground specified by court and counsel is invalid but there existed another and valid but unstated basis for the objection? Again, for common-sense reasons, the rule favors the trial judge and, indirectly, the objecting counsel. It is sometimes said that rejection of the evidence was not prejudicial since there was a good, albeit unmentioned, ground for its exclusion. A more sensible approach is to recognize how futile it would be to reverse the trial court, and remand the case for a new trial, for having rejected the evidence on the wrong ground, only to have the trial court exclude it for the right reason the second time around.

   We have seen that an objector should be explicit about his legal grounds. The precise target at which his objection is aimed should also be made clear. An offer of evidence frequently consists of several statements or parts which make up a whole; for example, an entire deposition, a set of hospital records, or a transcript of previously recorded testimony may be tendered. If only portions of the offer are objectionable, counsel must point them out for the trial judge, who will not himself be required to sift the admissible from the inadmissible. Of course, the real fault may lie with the side offering the evidence as a unit. Where admissibility as a unit is questionable, counsel for the offering party probably should break down the evidence into its component parts, marking and offering those parts separately so that objections can be made and rulings secured in an efficient way. If this is inordinately time-consuming, another approach is for offering counsel to see to it that each page of a voluminous exhibit bears a separate, sequential identifying number so that opposing counsel and the court can make convenient references to any portions objected to, thus:

BY OFFERING COUNSEL: Your Honor, we will ask the court reporter to mark the pages of this group exhibit [a group of medical records, for example] separately. There are twenty-three pages in the group, so they can be marked Plaintiff's Group Exhibit 3–A through 3–X for identification.

THE COURT: We'll just relax for a minute while the reporter marks the exhibits.

BY OPPOSING COUNSEL: Your Honor, we have an objection to 3–B and the reverse side of it, 3–C. That is the history sheet and it contains some inadmissible hearsay.

[Whereupon discussion out of the hearing of the jury is had.]

THE COURT: Certain deletions from exhibits 3–B and 3–C having been made, the objection will be overruled and Plaintiff's Group Exhibit 3–A through 3–X for Identification will be received in evidence as Plaintiff's Group Exhibit 3–A through 3–X.

A general objection is also unavailing where offered evidence is admissible against some parties, although not against all of them, or on a particular issue, although it is not admissible as to some other issue in the case. It is objecting counsel's duty to couple with his objection a request that the evidence be restricted to the particular issue or party. This will be accomplished by means of a brief jury instruction.

BY OPPOSING COUNSEL: On behalf of the defendant Freightco, we object to the witness' testimony concerning what the defendant truck driver, Mr. Bushmat, may have said to plaintiff after the accident. It may be receivable against Bushmat under some exception to the hearsay rule but it certainly isn't binding on us, your Honor. He was not our authorized agent for the making of such statements.

THE COURT: The objection is well taken. The jury is instructed that the testimony they have just heard is received in evidence as against the defendant Bushmat only and is not to be considered by the jury in determining the liability, if any, of the defendant Freightco.

G.

Necessity for Repeating Objections

Where one side, through one or more witnesses, repeatedly offers similar evidence that opposing counsel considers inadmissible, an objection must be interposed each time the evidence is offered unless the trial court permits a single statement of the objection to stand as a "continuing" objection to the entire line of questioning or class of evidence. If opposing counsel's objection to the first of a string of offers of similar evidence is sustained, he will ordinarily find it necessary to object to each subsequent offer. If his initial objection is overruled, however, the trial court may allow a continuing objection in order to conserve time and save opposing counsel from seeming unduly obstructive in the eyes of the jurors.

BY EXAMINING COUNSEL: Had you received any previous complaints about bottles of Dispepsia Cola exploding?

BY OPPOSING COUNSEL: We object, your Honor. Irrelevant and immaterial, since notice is not an issue in this case.

THE COURT: Overruled, counsel. I'm inclined to let it in on the issue of punitive damages.

BY OPPOSING COUNSEL: Can the record show that our objection goes to all similar evidence that plaintiff's counsel may offer? May we have a standing objection, in other words?

THE COURT: You may. The record will show it.

To avoid any possibility of confusion, when additional evidence of the same type is later offered, opposing counsel should point out at least once that his earlier objection is applicable.

The failure to object to an inadmissible item of evidence does not preclude counsel from objecting successfully to subsequent efforts to offer more of the same. Some lawyers, not wishing to object excessively, will wait until it becomes unavoidably apparent that a type of evidence is potentially damaging before objecting to it. The deliberate waiver of objection as to the earlier evidence does not work a waiver as to later offers of similar evidence. For example, the fact that counsel permitted some hearsay to come in on a particular subject matter does not foreclose him from objecting to subsequent offers of hearsay on the same subject.

H.

Necessity for Obtaining a Ruling

The record in connection with an evidentiary objection has not been effectively made where no ruling from the trial judge has been obtained. It is the objector's burden to secure an express ruling on his objection. This is essential to appellate review since a trial judge's silence is not considered tantamount to an overruling of the objection. In the heat of trial the judge may neglect to make an explicit, audible ruling. If the matter is of any importance, objecting counsel can interrupt to forestall the witness from responding to the challenged question and can respectfully request an on-the-record ruling from the trial judge.

Q. What did your friend tell you about the incident?

BY OPPOSING COUNSEL: Object, your Honor, calls for hearsay.

BY EXAMINING COUNSEL: Well, it's perfectly relevant.

BY OPPOSING COUNSEL: It's still hearsay.

BY THE WITNESS: He told me * * *

BY OPPOSING COUNSEL: Just one moment, sir. Your Honor, we would appreciate your instructing the witness not to answer the question until your Honor has ruled. And we would like very much to have a ruling from your Honor on our hearsay objection.

THE COURT: Let me ponder this for a minute. The witness will not answer. Yes, the objection will be sustained. The question clearly calls for a hearsay response.

I.

Exceptions

At one time it was necessary, in many jurisdictions, for counsel to record an express exception to those evidentiary rulings of the trial court that counsel considered erroneous. Today this is rarely required. No longer does one hear the following exchange: "Object, your Honor, irrelevant." "Overruled, counsel." "Please note our exception." Instead, one encounters rules such as FRCP 46: "Formal exception to rulings or orders of the court are unnecessary; but for all purposes for which an exception has heretofore been necessary it is sufficient that a party, at the time the ruling or order of the court is made or sought, makes known to the court the action which he desires the court to take or his objection to the action of the court and his grounds therefor. * * *" Of course, it may subsequently be necessary to set up in a specific and detailed motion for new trial any assignments of error that are based on objections made during trial.

IV.

OFFER OF PROOF

A.

Offer of Evidence as Distinguished from Offer of Proof

In the trial practice the phrase "offer of proof" is something of a term of art. It is a somewhat confusing one because in litigation the word "offer", taken alone, has a common meaning all its own. The two terms need to be distinguished.

The "offer" is the last step, other than possible supportive argumentation, in the introduction of evidence. (We discussed the offering of evidence in section II., above.) The meaning of the word "offer" and of the synonymous phrase "offer of evidence" is perhaps most readily grasped when one thinks in terms of tangible evidence: writings, photographs, murder weapons, and the like. The proponent of a writing, for example, will cause it to be marked for identification and then will do the trial judge and opposing counsel the courtesy of letting them examine the exhibit preliminarily, if they are not already familiar with it as a consequence of pretrial discovery. Counsel will then hand the exhibit to its "sponsoring" witness on the stand and pose questions aimed at authenticating the writing. When this process has been accomplished to the proponent's satisfaction, he will hand the exhibit to the judge and say, Your Honor, we now offer in evidence what has been marked Plaintiff's Exhibit Number 1 for Identification."

As we have seen, one "offers" testimonial evidence, too, although there will be no need to say the word "offer" out loud. Counsel offers oral testimony simply by engaging in the direct examination or cross-examination of a witness on the stand.

The so-called offer of proof is something quite apart from the typical offer of evidence described above and in section II. The offer of proof can come into play before or during an offer of evidence. It can come into play when an objection is made, during the examination of a witness, to the offer either of tangible or testimonial evidence. The offer of proof also comes into play when counsel, with no objection pending and perhaps with no witness as yet on the stand, makes an offer to prove specified matters in order to induce a ruling by the trial court as to the relevance and competence of those matters. We consider first the offer of proof as it is made during the course of examination of a witness on the stand.

B.

Offer of Proof Made During the Examination of a Witness

The necessity for an offer of proof is most commonly encountered during the examination of a witness on the stand. Counsel poses a question to the witness in an effort to elicit testimony; he may value the anticipated testimony for its own sake or because it lays the authenticating or identifying foundation for the introduction of tangible evidence, such as a writing. Opposing counsel, for some stated reason rooted in the rules of evidence, makes a timely objection to counsel's question. Counsel for the introducing party (the "offering" party), either before or after the trial court's ruling on the objection, must make an offer of proof unless he is prepared to concede the merit of his opponent's objection.

The offer of proof has two legitimate purposes: (1.) if properly made, it will permit the trial court to make a fully informed and, hopefully, correct ruling on the objection; (2.) if the ruling is adverse to the introducing party and arguably erroneous, an adequate offer of proof is ordinarily essential to preserve the point for post-trial review.

Harold W. Huff, a Chicago trial lawyer of extensive experience, focused on appellate review when not long ago he described the purpose of an offer of proof:

> * * * sooner or later you can anticipate that you will be placed in a position in which you see your case disintegrating because the man in the black robe will not receive your evidence.
>
> What do you do in that situation? You make a record of what it was that you were not permitted to prove. The record is made, essentially, for the benefit of an appellate court.*

The offer of proof, as Huff indicates, is another aspect of "making the record" or "perfecting the record" for appeal. In the absence of an explicit offer of proof an appellate court often will have no sure way of knowing whether the trial court's evidentiary ruling was correct. Equally important, the reviewing court will have no sure way of knowing whether the loss of the excluded evidence was prejudicial to the introducing party's case; it can hardly weigh the importance of rejected evidence without knowing what that evidence would have been.

*H. Huff, Offers of Proof in Proceedings,   (Ill.Inst. for Cont.Legal Ed.) 4 (1971). Fifth Annual Trial Evidence Seminar

It has occasionally been suggested that the failure to make an offer of proof is excusable where the trial court indicated to counsel in no uncertain terms that an offer would be useless. And a full offer of proof is unnecessary where described evidence has been rejected as a class by the trial court. Here in a very real sense the trial judge has himself made (and rejected) the offer of proof, as when he announces, "I'm not going to allow any evidence of previous reported explosions involving this type of glass container because I don't think any such reports could possibly be relevant to the present case."

It is ordinarily reversible error to refuse counsel an opportunity to make a proper offer of proof. A trial court's refusal to entertain an offer of proof is unjustifiable even where it is based on the court's knowledge of the witness' earlier testimony in the case since the current offer may embrace new matter. So important is counsel's freedom to make his record that it has been stated that any judicial discouraging of offers of proof is improper. However, a trial court need not hear lengthy offers where it is evident that the proposed evidence would not be admissible on any ground.

The necessity of an offer of proof after a sustained objection is generally limited to direct examination, the thought being that while counsel should experience no difficulty describing what his own witness would say in response to a question, he may not be equipped to predict precisely the response of an adverse witness. Certainly it would ordinarily be unfair for a trial court to require an offer of proof during cross-examination. However, enough must be done to show that the sustaining of an objection to a cross-question was error. The cross-question must on its face be proper. Counsel may have to elaborate somewhat to reveal what benefit he expects from his cross-question or line of cross-examination; in other words, it is as incumbent upon counsel during cross-examination as it is during direct examination to make clear the purpose, the materiality, of the anticipated response.

While it may be reasonably accurate to say that no offer of proof —certainly no very explicit or detailed one—is essential during cross-examination, it is also true that counsel is entirely free to make an offer during cross-examination if he can, and, in the absence of effective contradiction, the trial court can rely on it. If counsel has any reason to suspect that the point of his cross-examination is escaping the trial judge (and the sustaining of objections to it is an observable straw in the wind), he will be at pains to give at least some intimation of its purpose.

The required elements of an offer of proof made during the interrogation of a witness can rarely be found in procedural or evidentiary codes. At one time Rule 43(c) of the Federal Rules of Civil Procedure made at least a minimal effort to describe the mechanics of an offer of proof. It read in its entirety as follows:

Rule 43.

EVIDENCE

* * *

(c)   Record of Excluded Evidence. In an action tried by a jury, if an objection to a question propounded to a witness is sustained by the court, the examining attorney may make a specific offer of what he expects to prove by the answer of the witness. The court may require the offer to be made out of the hearing of the jury. The court may add such other or further statement as clearly shows the character of the evidence, the form in which it was offered, the objection made, and the ruling thereon. In actions tried without a jury the same procedure may be followed, except that the court upon request shall take and report the evidence in full, unless it clearly appears that the evidence is not admissible on any ground or that the witness is privileged.

Rules such as FRCP 43(c) are never especially helpful to the practitioner because they are couched in general terms and leave so much to unwritten local practice. In one respect Rule 43(c) may even have been potentially misleading. The rule suggested that a lawyer whose evidence has been excluded "may" make an offer of proof. The word "may" could be read in the sense of "might." As we have said the lawyer *can* make an offer of proof —it would ordinarily be reversible error to refuse him the opportunity to make a proper one—and usually he *must* make one if he is to preserve for review the propriety of the trial court's exclusionary ruling.

FRCP 43(c) has now been superceded by an equally brief Federal Rule of Evidence. Rule 103 of the Federal Rules of Evidence reads in relevant part as follows:

Rule 103.

RULINGS ON EVIDENCE

(a)   Effect of erroneous ruling. Error may not be predicated upon a ruling which admits or excludes evidence unless a substantial right of the party is affected, and

(2)   Offer of proof. In case the ruling is one excluding evidence, the substance of the evidence was made known to the court by offer or was apparent from the context within which questions were asked.

(b)   Record of offer and ruling. The court may add any other or further statement which shows the character of the evidence, the form in which it was offered, the objection made, and the ruling thereon. It may direct the making of an offer in question and answer form.

(c)   Hearing of jury. In jury cases, proceedings shall be conducted, to the extent practicable, so as to prevent inadmissible evidence from being suggested to the jury by any means, such as making statements or offers of proof or asking questions in the hearing of the jury.

Because Rule 103(a) has to do with the preservation for appeal of claimed trial level error in rulings on evidence, subdivision (a) (2) in no way relates to the sort of offer of proof that is sometimes made by counsel prior to any in-court testimony and thus obviously prior to any objection and ruling.

What subdivision (a) (2) does do is require that where the trial court's ruling is one *excluding* evidence, the substance of the evidence must be made known by offer *unless* its substance was evident from the context.

Subdivision (b) of the Rule provides that the trial judge "may" direct that the offer of proof be made in question-and-answer form. This means that questions will be put to the witness by examining counsel and his or her responses will then constitute the offer; otherwise, examining counsel himself simply makes a narrative offer in his own words.

In the Advisory Committee's Preliminary Draft of the Federal Rules of Evidence the question-and-answer method was *required* in non-jury cases, presumably so that a reviewing court would have before it the precise evidentiary basis for possible final disposition of the case in the event of reversal for erroneous exclusion of evidence. This absolute requirement was thought to be an unnecessary intrusion upon judicial discretion and, on revision, it was dropped. It was realized that this requirement would foreclose the sort of offer of proof that is occasionally made with no witness on the stand.

There are three basic ways of making an offer of proof during the course of a witness' oral examination. These three methods can be labelled (1) the tangible offer, (2) the witness offer, and (3) the lawyer offer.

1. *Tangible Offer.*   The tangible offer is easy enough. Any lawyer who knows how to mark, authenticate or identify, and offer into evidence an item of tangible evidence knows, almost *ipso facto,* how to make an offer of proof of the exhibit's contents if his offer of it is successfully objected to by opposing counsel. The proponent of the rejected exhibit need only hand it to the court reporter for inclusion in the trial record. (Or, if the exhibit happens to be a writing, such as a deposition, he might also, out of the jury's hearing, read it into the record at the time of its rejection, thereby ensuring its consideration in context.) Unlike received exhibits, the rejected item will not be handed to the jurors and will not go with them to their deliberation room. It will, however, find its way into the record on appeal, along with all other offered exhibits whether received or rejected. Counsel's only additional task may be to state for the record the evidential purpose of the evidence, if there exists any possibility that its function is unclear. He may also wish to be certain that the record reflects the trial judge's reasons for rejecting the exhibit since the judge may be focusing on a ground for rejection while erroneously disregarding a legitimate basis for admission.

An offer of tangible proof that commingles admissible matter with inadmissible is not a good offer and its rejection *in toto* will not be reversible error. This is not to say that admissible portions of an offer are properly excludable merely because other portions are inadmissible. For example, the competency of a writing in its entirety is not essential to the receipt of unobjectionable parts. It simply means that the inadmissible portions must be omitted from the offer. More than this, it means that the obligation to screen out inadmissible matters belongs to counsel for the offering party; neither the trial court nor the objecting party is obliged to separate the admissible from the inadmissible.

The risk of rejection *in toto* is at its greatest in connection with "omnibus" offers or offers "in bulk." An unsegregated offer of all the hospital records pertaining to the plaintiff in a personal injury action would be a typical example of an omnibus or in bulk offer. Counsel cannot hope to produce error—to provide himself with an ace in the hole, so to speak—by offering, in bulk, a tall stack of pages comprising a patient's entire medical record, which may begin with an admission history, include laboratory and x-ray reports, a report of operation, anesthesia record, progress notes, nurses' notes, and end with a discharge summary. The trial court's rejection of this offer is not improper where counsel has been accorded an opportunity to designate the admissible parts, even though buried in the pile are records which by themselves would be perfectly admissible. Counsel must offer only the admissible portions of his client's medical record or of any other writing or group of writings. Before making his offer he can pull out inadmissible items or mask or cut out inadmissible passages. (In one recent case it was suggested that a piece of paper might be pasted over the inadmissible part of a writing. However, experience teaches that jurors are inclined to peek. A better approach involves masking out the objectionable portion on the original of the exhibit and making a photographic copy for the jury, or using scissors to cut objectionable portions from a photographic copy of the exhibit.)

Counsel must be specific as to what parts of a writing or group of writings are included in his offer of proof. It is not ordinarily enough to make a general representation that all objectionable parts will be deleted. Where an offer of a writing has been rejected, counsel cannot later insist that he offered only its receivable portions unless he in fact designated them explicitly at the trial level. When a writing is offered without such designations it is presumed that the entire exhibit is offered.

When a writing is offered as being impeaching, it is incumbent upon the proponent to isolate those portions thought to be receivable on this ground.

2. *Witness Offer.* The witness offer is an even more simple procedure than the tangible offer. When an objection has been made to a question put to a witness on the stand and an exclusionary ruling is made by the trial judge, examining counsel can make his offer of proof through the witness. He simply proceeds with his examination of the witness, employing the usual question-and-answer method, and the witness' recorded responses, usually taken outside the jurors' hearing, constitute the offer of proof. This is the method adverted to in Rule 103(b) of the Federal Rules of Evidence, discussed above.

As in the case of tangible offers, counsel's only remaining task may be to explain the relevance of the offered testimony more fully than he did at the point of opposing counsel's successful objection to it. Again, offering counsel may want to be sure that the record accurately reflects the judge's reasons for excluding the testimony.

Normally, counsel should state for the record not only the purport (synopsized meaning) but the purpose (relevance, intended function) of the anticipated response. It is sometimes said that a formal offer of proof is unnecessary where counsel's question to a witness clearly calls for admissible evidence. The Illinois Supreme Court has made the broadest generalization on this point:

> It is not necessary that offer of proof be made where the question shows the purpose and materiality of the evidence. It is not necessary that counsel state what the answer would be. If a question is in proper form and clearly admits of an answer relative [*sic.* Relevant?] to the issues, the party by whom the question is propounded is not bound to

state facts proposed to be proved by the answer unless the court requires him to do so.*

This sweeping language seems to disregard the circumstance that a question that quite plainly calls for an admissible answer may be little more than an exercise in optimism in the absence of some discernible assurance that the witness is not only able to answer counsel's question but to answer it favorably to his client's position. In most of the cases suggesting that a formal statement of the expected answer can safely be omitted, the record, in one way or another, showed unmistakably what counsel was after and what he was likely to have gotten had the witness been permitted to answer. Since appellate courts will not invariably presume that an unstated answer would be forthcoming and that it would be both relevant and favorable to the side represented by examining counsel, prudence will ordinarily dictate the making of a reasonably detailed offer of proof following an exclusionary ruling.

If rejection of the offered testimony was based on an exclusionary rule of evidence, such as the hearsay rule or some testimonial privilege, the offer of proof should include any information suggesting the inapplicability of the rule. (A collateral but obviously important possible advantage of a comprehensive and comprehensible offer of proof is that it may cause the trial judge to change his ruling.)

3. *Lawyer Offer.* Where it appears that a question in proper form was posed during the direct examination of a witness on the stand and that, upon objection by opposing counsel, the trial court ruled out the answer, examining counsel's offer of proof may consist of a statement to the court at the time of its ruling, and on the record, showing what the witness' answer would have been. Counsel's statement will include any additional matters essential to demonstrate that the described response would be material and otherwise admissible in evidence. Counsel's statement will also show that the response would benefit his client; that is, that it would be of such a character as could reasonably be expected to affect the finding of the jury in his client's favor.

This so-called lawyer offer will begin this way: the examining counsel poses a question to a witness on the stand, opposing counsel's objection to the question is sustained by the trial judge, and the examining counsel, to make the record for possible appeal, states to the judge, "Your Honor, through this witness we offer to prove [such-and-such]" Of course, there is no magic in the form of words employed in an offer of proof; examining counsel may say, "The witness, were he permitted to answer the last question, would have testified [to such-and-such]."

Ordinarily, the offer of proof should be made immediately after the adverse ruling that cut off the witness' response. Usually it is made out of the jury's presence, as is specifically suggested in Rule 103(c) of the Federal Rules of Evidence, quoted previously. Certainly the time for an offer has arrived when the trial court indicates unequivocally that it will permit no further inquiry along a particular line. At one time it was held in Indiana that the offer must come *after* objection but *before* ruling. In addition to

*Creighton v. Elgin, 387 Ill. 592, 606, 56
N.E.2d 825, 831 (1944).

calling for an impossibly high level of alertness and speed by the offering party's counsel (sometimes there is very little elapsed time between the words "Object" and "Sustained"), this procedure, if adhered to in actual practice, would frequently waste time since, unbeknownst to the offering side, the trial court might be harboring every intention of overruling opposing counsel's objection. In practice, of course, the Indiana trial judge could probably be expected to interrupt counsel long enough to advise that no offer of proof was necessary because he intended to disallow the objection. In any event, the Indiana procedure has never been adopted elsewhere and Indiana itself appears to be in the process of abandoning it.

It has repeatedly been held that a lawyer offer is ineffective where the lawyer's statement of the anticipated answer goes beyond or is unresponsive to the question put to the witness. This rule seems as much an artificial device to avoid reversal as anything else, since counsel presumably could readily have put any number of additional questions to his witness. Furthermore, as will be discussed later, there is no pending question at all in the case of lawyer offers made prior to the calling of a witness to the stand. It is true, of course, that a methodical question and answer approach makes it easier for the opposing counsel to frame specific objections and this may be one reason for the rule. Perhaps this rule simply reflects persistent distrust of the lawyer offer. Although an unethical lawyer could as easily fabricate "anticipated" responsive answers as he could unresponsive ones, the better practice is to proceed by means of questions of limited scope, followed by the statement of an expected answer corresponding to the question.

A possible safeguard against a fabricated lawyer offer lies in the witness' ability—especially upon inquiry by a skeptical trial judge or opposing counsel—to contradict the offer, pointing out that in fact the stated answer would not be his response to the question asked. This, of course, assumes a witness who is sufficiently alert, sufficiently honest, and sufficiently brave to take exception to counsel's narrative.

C.

Offer of Proof Made With No Witness on the Stand

Few commentators on the making of the trial record have considered a special and sometimes difficult type of offer of proof, the type of offer that is made prior to any in-court testimony by a witness and thus obviously prior to any explicit objection and ruling. This is the second principal type of offer. It may be made because offering counsel has a number of witnesses, who are readily available but not presently in court, to establish a line of facts but the trial judge's rulings have strongly suggested that he would exclude their testimony. Such an offer can also be made to induce a ruling with respect to a line of facts. Counsel will make an offer when he is doubtful of the reception that his proposed evidence will receive from the trial judge and wishes to obtain a ruling, and make his record, without first going to the expense and inconvenience of calling and examining the witnesses involved.

This approach permits a trial court, out of the jurors' hearings, to pre-test proposed evidence and avoid possible prejudicing of the jurors. (For those who can recall the incident, this, in effect, was the procedure that was employed by Judge Julius J. Hoffman during the riot conspiracy trial of the

"Chicago 7" in a widely misunderstood episode involving former Attorney General Ramsey Clark, who was not permitted to take the witness stand in open court after the judge concluded, during an out-of-court offer, that all of Clark's proposed testimony was inadmissible.)

An offer of this second type will sound something like this:

BY PLAINTIFF'S COUNSEL: Your Honor, we offer to prove in this case that the defendant had notice, repeated notice, that metal cans containing its product had exploded without warning, causing serious bodily injury. We can call to the stand six eye-witnesses to six separate incidents of this sort, all antedating the incident involving this plaintiff. Those witnesses are readily available on short notice.

COUNSEL FOR DEFENDANT: Well, we would object to that, your Honor. We don't think notice is an element in a strict liability case of this kind. Counsel is just trying to put in some inflammatory evidence.

COUNSEL FOR PLAINTIFF: If nothing else, your Honor, the proposed evidence would be relevant to our prayer for punitive damages.

THE COURT: The offer of proof will be denied. [Or, 'The offer is sustained. You can have until tomorrow morning to get your witnesses here.']

When a trial court rejects an offer of proof of this second type it is taken to have conceded that counsel could have made the described proof if he had been permitted to proceed. The only open question is whether the facts embodied in the offer are properly admissible.

It is the burden of the offering party to include in his offer everything necessary to support the admissibility of the proposed evidence. This must be shown to the trial judge at the time of the making of the offer; if for some reason admissibility cannot be shown until a subsequent time during the trial, the offer, as will be more fully discussed later, should then be renewed. Where the facts supporting admissibility are unclear, no amount of hindsight at the appellate level will put the trial court in error for having rejected the offer.

For instance, an offer must be definite as to the time of events in order that the admissibility of the offer will be apparent. Thus the relevance of prior complaints concerning the condition of a stairway will depend in part on their nearness in point of time to the accident of which the plaintiff complains. Similarly, testimony regarding a post-accident inspection will be rejected where the offer fails to reveal its date.

Often it may also be essential to indicate other facets of relevance, such as similarity of conditions in connection with evidence of prior accidents and the like.

Furthermore, offering counsel may find it necessary to show that the offered evidence would not merely be cumulative to evidence already received in the case.

It will frequently be vital to include foundational elements in an offer of proof. These foundational elements are themselves to be found in the law of evidence. It may, for example, be necessary to state that offered out-of-

court declarations would be admissible because they constituted excited utterances. To cite a much more common example, it may be crucial to include in the offer a clear indication that the witness whose testimony is
being offered is qualified as an expert of some sort. Obviously, there is a serious flaw in an offer "to prove through Clyde Bushmat that cancer can be
induced by trauma"; it will be necessary to include in the offer the fact that
this is *Doctor* Clyde Bushmat, whose training, licensure, and experience
equip him, in to terms of the conventional wisdom respection opinion
evidence, to express a complex medical conclusion.

Much of this is simply one way or another of saying that an offer of
proof must descend into specifics; it is not permissible to couch an offer in
vague generalities. For instance, it is insufficient to announce that evidence
will be adduced "to show bad faith," to show "insolvency," to show that
goods for which a note was given "were not as represented," to show "bias
and prejudice," or to show "surrounding circumstances and conditions." It
is, in other words, not sufficient in an offer of proof to state ultimate facts
that might be more appropriate to a pleading; thus reading the allegations
of a pleading into the record will not result in an effective offer of proof. And
if "ultimate" facts are not good enough it is doubly clear that broad-
gauge conclusions are unavailing in an offer. An offer can be a summari
zation of proposed evidence but it must be cast in terms of evidentiary
facts—what the proposed witnesses said, saw, heard, touched, or smelled;
what the proposed items of tangible evidence reveal.

Needless to say, an offer that is based on nothing more than counsel's
sense of hope and optimism is doomed. Thus the denial of an omnibus or
"in bulk" offer is proper where the offering party, having neglected to employ pre-trial discovery devices to secure and examine the opposing party's
records, bases his offer on nothing more than his unsubstantiated hope that
those records might contain something helpful to his client. An offer of
proof, in other words, must be made in good faith on the basis of evidence
that is known to be available and beneficial.

As an offshoot of the basic premise that the offer must be in good faith,
it is frequently asserted that the offering party must identify the witnesses
who are in a position to testify to the matters described in the offer. From
time to time this requirement has been pushed one long step farther, to demand a showing that the witness is presently in court and ready to testify. It
is even occasionally suggested that a witness must be placed on the stand
and the offer made through him. Any such requirement would effectively
eliminate the second type of offer of proof and restrict counsel to the traditional post-objection witness offer.

It is clear enough, nonetheless, that an offer upon which counsel cannot
possibly make good, because the necessary witnesses are unavailable to
him, is properly rejected. This situation arises most commonly where witnesses, not previously subpoenaed by offering counsel, are shown to be
beyond the trial court's subpoena power at the time of the offer of proof involving them. It is also plain that a trial judge, entertaining doubts about
counsel's ability to make good on his offer, can insist on an offer made
through one or more witnesses called to the stand in an out-of-court session.
However, the weight of authority, which includes a decision of the United
States Supreme Court, is to the effect that a lawyer offer, with no witness on

the stand, is sufficient if an adequate demonstration of good faith is made. In Scotland County v. Hill* the Court said, "[I]f the trial court has doubts about the good faith of an offer of testimony, it can insist on the production of the witness, and upon some attempt to make the proof before it rejects the offer; but if it does reject it ＊ ＊ ＊ and there is nothing else in the record to indicate bad faith, an appellate court must assume that the proof could have been made, and govern itself accordingly."

D.

Renewing Offers of Proof

Occasionally a particular offer of proof must be made more than once or, more precisely, it must be renewed. This happens when an offer, defective when first made, is thereafter perfected. Sometimes an offer will be ruled premature because, for example, some element of its foundation is missing or because it has been made during the wrong stage of the trial. It is vital that counsel renew his offer after having adduced additional evidence by way of essential predicate; otherwise, the trial court is free to treat the earlier offer as having been abandoned.

A renewed offer may be necessary after counsel has put on proof rendering inapplicable some exclusionary rule of evidence, such as the best evidence rule. Where an offer of proof has been rebuffed because it was made during cross-examination of an adverse party's witness rather than in the offering party's own case, counsel usually must renew the offer at the appropriate juncture. Of course, express withdrawal of a question waives any error with respect to the treatment accorded an objection to it. There is, however, no need to make repeated offers of proof where the court has indicated that it will under no circumstances receive the indicated evidence or where the court has sustained an objection to an entire line of questioning. There need be no renewal of an offer where the trial court has not made it clear to counsel that it was excluding evidence only temporarily, as where a witness—usually a medical witness—has been put on the stand out of the regular order.

The need to renew an offer of proof after the taking of additional evidence can be avoided if in the original offer counsel expresses a wllingness to connect up the offered evidence with other testimony that will render the offered evidence material. This is simply another way of saying that an offer of proof must be reasonably complete.

E.

Making Offers of Proof Outside the Jurors' Hearing

The trial court, for a fairly self-evident reason that we will come to shortly, will usually require that counsel present his offer of proof in such a way that although the court, opposing counsel, the witness (if any), and the court reporter can hear it, the jury cannot. (See Fed.R.Evid. 103(c), quoted above.) A court has the right to insist that it be made out of the jury's hearing. Some judicial hints to the contrary notwithstanding, a court is not invariably required to exercise this power, however. Whether an offer of proof

---

*112 U.S. 183, 186 (1884).

shall be presented outside the jury's hearing is a question addressed to the trial judge's discretion.

It would be both disruptive and wasteful of time were a trial court to send the jury out for every offer of proof made during a trial, having in mind that many lawyer offers following objection are one brief sentence in length. Moreover, the content of many offers of proof is quite harmless. If the trial judge believes that an offer is of innocuous material he can properly permit it to be made in the jury's hearing, especially if there is no objection and if he instructs the jurors to disregard the procedure. If opposing counsel disputes the propriety of an offer made in the jury's hearing, he should indicate for the record the jury's presence since this circumstance will not otherwise be apparent unless the trial judge or the court reporter notes it.

Despite what has been said of the trial court's discretion, it is advisable, because of the potential for prejudice, that all but the most neutral and routine offers of proof be presented outside the juror's hearing. The trial judge can send the jury out of the courtroom or he can retire to chambers if the offer is likely to be a lengthy one or if the risk of prejudice would be great were any juror to overhear it; otherwise, the judge can direct that the offer be made at a whispered sidebar conference.

V.

THE INSTRUCTIONS TO THE JURY

A.

Making the Record on Instructions Given and Refused

In almost all jurisdictions, even including those using court-approved "pattern" instructions, the trial judge will either require or at least permit participation by counsel in the preparation of the court's charge to the jury. In some jurisdictions counsel for each side prepares a complete proposed charge; in others counsel prepares only those instructions that apply, at least arguably, to this client's claims or affirmative defenses. Often counsel will have researched and briefed the underlying law and drafted the proposed instructions prior to the commencement of the trial. (Some jurisdictions require that proposed instructions be submitted to the trial judge at the beginning of the trial, although obviously they remain subject to modification as the trial unfolds.)

A conference on the charge is usually conducted in the trial judge's chambers after the parties have rested their cases and before their closing arguments commence. (Counsel prefer to have this conference before rather than after their closing arguments so that they can, with accuracy, make some reference in their arguments to the court's impending instructions.) At this conference the judge, after discussion with counsel, announces what instructions he will give to the jury. It is prudent to have a court reporter present to record the conference although some trial lawyers are content to have the words "Given _____" and "Refused _____" typed at the bottom of each of their requested instructions, the blank lines being for check-marks. Counsel, having submitted his requested instructions separately ("Plaintiff's Requested Instruction No. 1," "Plaintiff's Requested Instruction No. 2," etc.), will place a check-mark after the appropriate term

and deliver his set of requested instructions to the court reporter for inclusion in the record.

B.

Objecting to the Court's Instructions

If counsel has any objections to the jury instructions as given in open
court, over and beyond those recorded during the aforementioned conference, he must make them out of the jury's hearing immediately after the
trial judge has concluded the giving of the charge; otherwise, they are
waived. (Grounds for objection may arise for the first time during the giving
of the charge either because the judge was not explicit in describing some
portion of the instructions during the pre-charge conference or because he
has undertaken extemporaneous amendments to the charge that was agreed
upon in that conference.) A general exception to the instructions is insufficient to preserve error for appellate review. Counsel's objections must be
specific, thus affording the judge an opportunity to correct any errors that
he can be convinced he made. In other words, it is futile to approach the
bench after the charge and say, "We object [or 'except'] to the charge in its
entirety." Counsel must say something like "Your Honor, we object to your
use of the word 'possible,' instead of the word 'probable,' in that portion of
your instructions that dealt with the question of proximate cause."

VI.

VERDICTS

A.

General and Special Verdicts in Civil Cases

A jury's verdict in civil cases is usually a "general" verdict; that is, the
jurors simply find for the plaintiff, stating the amount of damages they have
decided to award to the plaintiff, or they find the defendant not liable. The
jury's foreman enters its findings on printed verdict forms that are supplied
to the jury by the trial court. These forms become a part of the trial record.

Many jurisdictions, including the federal, also provide for "special"
verdicts. With this type of verdict, usually called for only in quite complicated lawsuits, the trial court directs the jury to make a specific written
finding on each fact-issue in the case. The court either submits to the jurors
written questions that are susceptible of categorical (Yes or No) or other
brief answer, or it supplies them with written forms that embody the special
findings that they could make under the pleadings and the evidence. These
questions or special findings are submitted to the court by counsel for the
side requesting them and the record regarding the court's giving or rejection
of them is made in much the same way as it is with requested instructions,
discussed in section V., above.

B.

Demand for Submission of Fact Issues

It is incumbent upon counsel to make a specific demand, on the record,
that the trial court submit particular fact-issues to the jury under the special verdict procedure just described. The federal practice under FRCP 49 is

typical and underscores this point. If in providing the jury with questions or special finding forms the federal court omits any issue of fact, each party is taken to waive its right to jury-trial on that issue unless a specific, on-the-record demand is made before the jurors retire to deliberate. The trial judge can make his own finding as to any fact-issue that he omitted without objection, just as though he were sitting without a jury.

VII.

POLLING THE JURY

In litigation the moment of truth arrives with the reading of the jury's verdict. A buzzer has sounded; the word is that the jury is coming back. Court is reconvened. The jurors file into their places.

THE COURT: Have you reached a verdict?

THE FOREMAN: We have, your Honor.

THE COURT: How do you find the defendant, guilty or not guilty?

THE FOREMAN: Guilty, your Honor.

But perhaps this is not the moment of truth, after all. In many jurisdictions the losing side in either a criminal or a civil case is permitted to have the jurors polled with respect to the announced verdict. Upon request the judge will have his clerk or bailiff inquire of each juror, "Is this your true verdict?" Occasionally this polling process turns up improprieties that occurred during the jury's deliberations and which will require either further deliberations or perhaps even the declaring of a mistrial. (But see Fed.R.Evid. 606(b), restricting jurors to a description of "extraneous prejudicial information" and "outside influence.") The polling of the jury, and any comments made by the jurors during their interrogation, should be on the record.

VIII.

CONCLUSION

We have discussed the most important situations in which trial counsel must "make the record." Consciousness of the record and its significance can have a beneficial influence on a lawyer's effectiveness at the trial level. Awareness of the record induces counsel to make an orderly, logical presentation of evidence and argument. It also tends to inspire clarity of thought and speech. But sometimes counsel's ultimate reward, the real moment of truth, is found in the appellate courts, where the difference between affirmance and reversal may depend on his ability at perfecting the record.

Chapter II

AN INTRODUCTION TO RELEVANCE

HARLOT v. HARLOT

1 Kings 3:16–28 (King James) (c. 650 B.C.).*

Then came there two women, that were harlots, unto the king, and stood before him. And the one woman said, "O my lord, I and this woman dwell in one house; and I was delivered of a child with her in the house. And it came to pass the third day after that I was delivered, that this woman was delivered also: and we were together; there was no stranger with us in the house, save we two in the house. And this woman's child died in the night; because she overlaid it. And she arose at midnight, and took my son from beside me, while thine handmaid slept, and laid it in her bosom, and laid her dead child in my bosom. And when I rose in the morning to give my child suck, behold, it was dead: but when I had considered it in the morning, behold it was not my son, which I did bear." And the other woman said, "Nay; but the living is my son, and the dead is thy son." And this said, "No; but the dead is thy son, and the living is my son." Thus they spoke before the king. Then said the king, "The one saith, 'This is my son that liveth, and thy son is the dead': and the other saith, 'Nay; but thy son is the dead, and my son is the living.' " And the king said, "Bring me a sword." And they brought a sword before the king. And the king said, "Divide the living child in two, and give half to the one, and half to the other." Then spoke the woman whose the living child was unto the king, for her bowels yearned upon her son, and she said, "O my lord, give her the living child, and in no wise slay it." But the other said, "Let it be neither mine nor thine, but divide it." Then the king answered and said, "Give her the living child, and in no wise slay it: she is the mother thereof." And all Israel heard of the judgment which the king had judged; and they feared the king: for they saw that the wisdom of God was in him, to do judgment.

HART AND McNAUGHTON, EVIDENCE AND INFERENCE IN THE LAW

51–56 (1958).**

It will be noticed in the first place that, while the issue to be decided is formally one of fact only, the rule of law is nevertheless functioning importantly. For it is the rule which makes the fact significant. If, for example, a child could not inherit, the question of the claimant's parentage could be left to his biographer or to the genealogists.

The kinds of evidence used by the law in making determinations of adjudicative fact are unlike those used by other disciplines in pursuance of their objectives.

*3 Kings 3:16–28 (Douay).
**The Hayden Colloquium on Scientific Concept and Method edited by Daniel Lerner. Copyright, 1958 by American Academy of Arts & Sciences, copyright, 1959 by The Free Press. Excerpts from material by Henry M. Hart, Jr., and John McNaughton.

The adjudicative facts of interest to the law, being historical facts, will rarely be triable by the experimental methods of the natural sciences. To be sure, ballistics tests in the murder case may prove beyond rational dispute that the bullet which killed the victim came from the defendant's gun. Laboratory tests in the breach-of-warranty case may settle beyond question the quality of the goods. And blood tests in the inheritance controversy may show that it is virtually impossible that the claimant was the child of the deceased. But these instances will be exceptional. For the most part the law must settle disputed questions of adjudicative fact by reliance upon the ambiguous implications of non-fungible "traces"—traces on human brains and on pieces of paper and traces in the form of unique arrangements of physical objects.

Furthermore, the law uses different evidence and uses it in a different way than other disciplines do even when those disciplines are similarly interested in the determination of historical facts. These differences result from the fact that what is involved, when the most distinctive practices of the law in the handling of evidence come into play, is the formal and official settlement of a controversy.

To understand the law's peculiar ways of treating evidence it is necessary to have some appreciation of the role which formal adjudication plays in the total functioning of the legal system.

A contested lawsuit is society's last line of defense in the indispensable effort to secure the peaceful settlement of social conflicts. In the overwhelming majority of instances, the general directions of the law function smoothly with no controversy whatever. When controversies do arise, the overwhelming majority of them are settled informally or, if formally, without a contest, as by plea of guilty in a criminal case. In almost all these situations lawyers are likely to handle evidence in the same common-sense fashion that anybody else would, unless special calculations are called for by a real possibility of formal litigation.

When a question has reached the point of a contested trial, however, its whole context is changed. Victory, and not accommodation, is the objective of the parties. The adversary atmosphere and the delays of litigation naturally repel evidence, especially testimony and things under the control of disinterested persons, so that the litigants have available for use only the partisan and coerced residue after people with ingenuity have made themselves anonymous. That residue is culled by the parties with a view not so much to establishing the whole truth as to winning the case. And the evidence which survives this attrition (and the exclusionary rules of evidence described below) is communicated to the trier of fact in an emotion-charged setting.

In judging the law's handling of its task of fact-finding in this setting, it is necessary always to bear in mind that this is a last-ditch process in which something more is at stake than the truth only of the specific matter in contest. There is at stake also that confidence of the public generally in the impartiality and fairness of public settlement of disputes which is essential if the ditch is to be held and the settlements accepted peaceably.

The law does not require absolute assurance of the perfect correctness of particular decisions. While it is of course important that the court be right in its determinations of fact, it is also important that the court decide the case when the parties ask for the decision and on the basis of the evidence presented by the parties. A decision must be made now, one way or the other. To require certainty or even near-certainty in such a context would be impracticable and undesirable. The law thus compromises.

The compromise is expressed in the formulas used to guide decision of questions of adjudicative fact. In a criminal case, guilt need not be found beyond all doubt; the trier of the fact must be satisfied of the defendant's guilt only "beyond a reasonable doubt." In a civil case, the facts are ordinarily to be found on the basis of "a preponderance of the evidence"; this phrase is generally defined as meaning simply "more likely than not." The formula for determining whether a case should even be submitted to a jury assumes a wide leeway for differing judgments. The question for the trial judge is whether a "reasonable jury" on the evidence submitted could find that the facts have been proved by a preponderance of the evidence. The judge uses a similar formula in determining whether a verdict already rendered by the jury may stand, and so does the reviewing court in deciding whether to upset either the jury's verdict or the trial judge's own finding if the trial judge sat without a jury. * * *

The most conspicuous difference between the law's problems in determining historical facts and those of other disciplines lies in the procedure of decision. Other disciplines rely primarily on the method of inquiry, reflection, and report by trained investigators. In other disciplines the final conclusions as to key facts are drawn by experts, and the conclusions may be changed if they are found later—after further inquiry and reflection—to be wrong. The law, in contrast, depends in most formal proceedings upon presentation by the disputants in public hearing before an impartial tribunal, a tribunal previously uninformed about the matters in dispute. And findings of fact by the tribunal are usually final so far as the law is concerned.

Typical of such formal proceedings is the trial in court. A trial suffers from immobility. It suffers from shortage and inflexibility of time. It is dependent largely upon non-expert sources of information and upon non-expert evaluators of information (the jury). In addition, proof at a trial is rather strictly governed by procedural rules called rules of evidence.

JAMES, RELEVANCY, PROBABILITY AND THE LAW

29 Calif.L.Rev. 689 (1941).

[All footnotes omitted.]

Since scholars first attempted to treat the common law of evidence as a rational system, relevancy has been recognized as a basic concept underlying all further discussion. Thayer gave this recognition its classic form:

"There is a principle—not so much a rule of evidence as a presupposition involved in the very conception of a rational system of evidence, as contrasted with the old formal and mechanical systems —which forbids receiving anything irrelevant, not logically probative."

"The two leading principles should be brought into conspicuous relief, (1) that nothing is to be received which is not logically probative of some matter requiring to be proved; and (2) that everything which is thus probative should come in, unless a clear ground of policy or law excludes it."

* * * Relevancy, as the word itself indicates, is not an inherent characteristic of any item of evidence but exists as a relation between an item of evidence and a proposition sought to be proved. If an item of evidence tends to prove or to disprove any proposition, it is relevant to that proposition. If the proposition itself is one provable in the case at bar, or if it in turn forms a further link in a chain of proof the final proposition of which is provable in the case at bar, then the offered item of evidence has probative value in the case. Whether the immediate or ultimate proposition sought to be proved is provable in the case at bar is determined by the pleadings, by the procedural rules applicable thereto, and by the substantive law governing the case. Whether the offered item of evidence tends to prove the proposition at which it is ultimately aimed depends upon other factors, shortly to be considered. But because relevancy, as used by Thayer and in the Code, means tendency to prove a proposition properly provable in the case, an offered item of evidence may be excluded as "irrelevant" for either of these two quite distinct reasons: because it is not probative of the proposition at which it is directed, or because that proposition is not provable in the case.

* * * Let us analyze a single interesting case, Union Paint & Varnish Co. v. Dean,* an action of assumpsit to recover the purchase price of waterproof roof paint. The defendant relied upon the plaintiff's warranty that the paint would wear for ten years, breach of which he sought to show by proof that another drum of paint of the same brand, which he had purchased six months earlier, not only had failed to prevent leaks but had ruined the shingles to which it had been applied. The drum of paint in issue, purchased just before leaks developed in the first roof painted, had never been opened. Reversing the trial court, the Supreme Court of Rhode Island held that the defendant's offer of proof (apparently almost the only evidence offered in defense) should have been received, saying:

> "If paint of the same brand, sold by the same concern under the same warranty within six months, had proved within that time to be not in conformity with the warranty, in that it was not only not suitable for stopping and preventing leaks but was actually injurious to a roof, a person might well hesitate before using more paint of the same brand when he had no reason to expect the second lot to be any better than the first."

Considered as evidence of the condition of the second drum of paint, proof of the results of use of the first is not very impressive. Waiving any doubts whether the leaks in the first roof were traceable to defects in paint in the first drum, there is no showing whether the defects in the first drum of paint were due to poor ingredients, to a poor formula, or to some error in preparation. If poor ingredients had been used, there is no showing that use of poor ingredients was a policy of, rather than an error of, the plaintiff company. It is easier to believe that one lot of defective paint went out than it is to believe that plaintiff customarily sold, under a ten-year guaranty, water-

*48 R.I. 288, 137 A. 469 (1927) [Ed.].

proof roof paint which would rot out shingles and cause leaks in six months. And the two drums of paint were probably not out of one lot; certainly there was no showing that they were. Proof of the condition of the paint in the first drum was of negligible value in judging the probable character of the paint in the second, unopened drum. It merely showed that plaintiff company sometimes sold bad paint. If the issue was whether the paint in the second drum *was* bad, an issue on which the defendant had the burden, the trial judge's ruling seems sound. At worst, the issue is close enough so that an appellate court should not reverse. Yet there is still a ring of reason to the supreme court's statement that "a person might well hesitate before using more paint of the same brand". He would hesitate to risk ruining a second roof even if he only feared that the second drum of paint might be no better than the first. And if he was reasonable in his hesitation, should the plaintiff be allowed to recover even if it could show at trial that the paint in the second drum was perfectly good? The defendant, reasonably hesitant to use the doubtful paint, by now has probably painted all of his roofs with some other paint and has no further use for the drum which he is tendering back to the vendor. If the customer is to be protected, even against proof that the second drum of paint was in fact satisfactory (as the writer should like to do in such a case), a novel rule of substantive law stands revealed behind a somewhat doubtful ruling on evidence.

But after excluding all cases which turn upon the materiality or immateriality under the pleadings and substantive law of ultimate propositions sought to be proved, there remain many cases in which there is no question of the materiality of the proposition sought to be proved and the probative value of the offered evidence is the real issue. These cases, and these alone, raise the problem of relevancy as a problem in the law of evidence. How should they be handled?

Thayer, after stating the principle which forbids receiving anything not "logically probative", excluded legal criteria from further operation, saying:

"How are we to know what these forbidden things are? Not by any rule of law. The law furnishes no test of relevancy. For this, it tacitly refers to logical and general experience,—assuming that the principles of reasoning are known to its judges and ministers, just as a vast multitude of other things are assumed as already sufficiently known to them." * * *

MORGAN, BASIC PROBLEMS OF EVIDENCE

185–188 (1961).*

* * *

* * * Assume that X has met his death by violence; the proposition to be proved is that Y killed him; the offered item of evidence is a love letter written by Y to X's wife. The series of inferences is about as follows: From Y's letter, (A), to Y's love of X's wife, (B), to Y's desire for the exclusive possession of X's wife, (C), to Y's desire to get rid of X, (D), to Y's plan to get rid of X, (E), to Y's execution of the plan by killing X, (F). The unarticulated premise, (M), conjoined with (A) is, "A man who writes a

*Joint Committee on Continuing Legal Education of The American Law Institute   and The American Bar Association, Philadelphia, 1961.

love letter to a woman is probably in love with her"; that, (N), conjoined with (B) is, "A man who loves a woman probably desires her for himself alone"; that, (O), conjoined with (C) is, "A man who loves a married woman and desired her for himself alone desired to get rid of her husband"; that, (P), conjoined with (D) is, "A man who desires to get rid of the husband of the woman he loves probably plans to do so"; and that, (Q), conjoined with (E) is, "A man who plans to get rid of the husband of the woman he loves is probably the man who killed him." If an arrow represents the drawing of an inference, the series may be represented thus:

A)
+)»»→ B)
M)   +)»»→C)
    N)   +)»»→D)
        O)   +)»»→ E)
            P)   +)»»→F
                Q)

[C1912]

Now it must be obvious that the value of item A as probative of F varies with the degree of probability of the existence of each presumed fact and inversely with the number of inferences between A and F. As A + M cannot possibly equal B but necessarily represent only a fraction of B, and B + N likewise but a fraction of C, and so on through the series it might well be said that the strength of item A as evidence of the existence of F is represented by a fraction which is the product of a series of fractions, each of which represents the portion of certainty of the respective inferences. For in this lawsuit, it must be remembered that the court will begin with the assumption of the nonexistence of A, B, C, D, E and F.

Next, a distinction must be made between the relevance of A as evidence of F on the one hand and its weight on the other. Obviously A standing by itself would not justify the inference F; indeed, it might not justify even D or E. But the proponent of A may offer another item or several other items, each of which will begin a series of inferences leading to F. Thus, suppose that he introduces evidence (1) that two months before X's death Y threatened to kill X; (2) that Y held a pistol pointed toward X, that the pistol fired and X fell over dead; (3) that (a) Y one month before X's death bought a pistol bearing a specified number, (b) that a pistol, Exhibit M, bearing that number was found two weeks after X's death in a near-by abandoned well, (c) that a bullet, Exhibit N, found in X's heart, caused X's death, and (d) that test bullets O and Q fired from Exhibit M bore rifling marks and other surface marks identical with those on Exhibit N. The series of inferences as to the first of these items is from Y's threat to Y's then existing intent, thence to continuance of the intent to the instant of the shooting, thence to the shooting and killing; as to the second item, from the holding of the pistol to the firing of the pistol, thence to the impact of the bullet upon X; as to the third item from the purchase of the pistol to its possession at the time of the shooting, from the identity of the marks on the bullets to the firing of all three from Exhibit M; and from the combination of (a), (b), (c) and (d) to the firing of the bullet N from Exhibit M by Y. Here again the persuasive value of each of these items will depend upon the number of inferences required and the degree of probability of the coexistence of the basic fact of each inference and the fact inferred. But when all the items are considered, the greater the number of items, the stronger will be the foundation for the ultimate inference. Nevertheless, no matter how numerous the items or how short the series of inferences required for each of them, they will never produce certainty. If one witness testified that he saw Y shoot X, the trier may be persuaded that the chances are three out of four that Y did shoot X; but if three others testified to the same effect with equal persuasiveness, the sum of the testimony of all four would not equal three times certainty. On the other hand, no matter how great the number of items established, they will never make the existence of the ultimate fact a question for the trier unless the total would justify reasonable men in concluding that the existence of the ultimate fact is more probable than its nonexistence.

KNAPP v. STATE

Supreme Court of Indiana, 1907.
168 Ind. 153, 79 N.E. 1076.

GILLETT, J. Appellant appeals from a judgment in the above-entitled cause, under, which he stands convicted of murder in the first degree. Error is assigned on the overruling of a motion for new trial.

Appellant, as a witness in his own behalf, offered testimony tending to show a killing in self-defense. He afterwards testified, presumably for the purpose of showing that he had reason to fear the deceased, that before the killing he had heard that the deceased, who was the marshal of Hagerstown, had clubbed and seriously injured an old man in arresting him, and that he died a short time afterwards. On appellant being asked, on cross-examination, who told him this, he answered: "Some people around Hagerstown there. I can't say as to who it was now." The state was permitted, on rebuttal, to prove by a physician, over the objection and exception of the defense, that the old man died of senility and alcoholism, and that there were no bruises or marks on his person. Counsel for appellant contend that it was error to admit this testimony; that the question was as to whether he had, in fact, heard the story, and not as to its truth or falsity. While it is laid down in the books that there must be an open and visible connection between the fact under inquiry and the evidence by which it is sought to be established, yet the connection thus required is in the logical processes only, for to require an actual connection between the two facts would be to exclude all presumptive evidence. Best on Evidence (Morgan's Ed.) § 90. Within settled rules, the competency of testimony depends largely upon its tendency to persuade the judgment. 1 Bentham, Rationale Judicial Ev., 71, et seq.; Chicago, etc., R. Co. v. Pritchard (Ind.Sup.) 79 N.E. 508. As said by Wharton: "Relevancy is that which conduces to the proof of a pertinent hypothesis." 1 Wharton, Ev. § 20. In Stevenson v. Stuart, 11 Pa. 307, it was said: "The competency of a collateral fact to be used as the basis of legitimate argument is not to be determined by the conclusiveness of the inferences it may afford in reference to the litigated fact. It is enough if these may tend in a slight degree to elucidate the inquiry, or to assist, though remotely, to a determination probably founded in truth." See, also, Trull v. True, 33 Me. 367; State v. Burpee, 65 Vt. 1, 25 Atl. 964, 19 L.R.A. 145, 36 Am.St.Rep. 775; Brown v. Clark, 14 Pa. 469; Wells v. Fairbank, 5 Tex. 582; Holmes v. Goldsmith, 147 U.S. 150, 13 Sup.Ct. 288, 37 L.Ed. 118.

We are of opinion that the testimony referred to was competent. While appellant's counsel are correct in their assertion that the question was whether appellant had heard a story to the effect that the deceased had offered serious violence to the old man, yet it does not follow that the testimony complained of did not tend to negative the claim of appellant as to what he had heard. One of the first principles of human nature is the impulse to speak the truth. "This principle," says Dr. Reid, whom Professor Greenleaf quotes at length in his work on Evidence (volume 1, § 7n), "has a powerful operation, even in the greatest liars, for where they lie once they speak truth 100 times." Truth speaking preponderating, it follows that to show that there was no basis in fact for the statement appellant claims to have heard had a tendency to make it less probable that his testimony on this point was true. Indeed, since this court has not, in cases where self-defense is asserted as a justification for homicide, confined the evidence concerning the deceased to character evidence, we do not perceive how, without the possibility of a gross perversion of right, the state could be denied the opportunity to meet in the manner indicated the evidence of the defendant as to what he had heard, where he, cunningly perhaps, denies that he can remember who gave him the information. The fact proved by the state tended to discredit appellant, since it showed that somewhere between the fact and the testimony there was a person who was not a truth speaker, and, appellant being unable to point to his informant, it must at least be said that the testimony complained of had a tendency to render his claim as to what he had heard less probable.

Judgment affirmed.

CONTEMPORARY MISSION, INC. v. FAMOUS MUSIC CORP.

United States Court of Appeals, Second Circuit, 1977.
557 F. 2d 918.

MESKILL, Circuit Judge:

This is an appeal by Famous Music Corporation ("Famous") from a verdict rendered against it in favor of Contemporary Mission, Inc. ("Contemporary"), * * *. Contemporary cross-appeals from a ruling which excluded testimony concerning its prospective damages. * * *

I. *The Facts.*

Contemporary is a nonprofit charitable corporation organized under the laws of the State of Missouri with its principal place of business in Connecticut. It is composed of a small group of Roman Catholic priests who write, produce and publish musical compositions and recordings. In 1972 the group owned all of the rights to a rock opera entitled VIRGIN, which was composed by Father John T. O'Reilly, a vice-president and member of the group. Contemporary first became involved with Famous in 1972 as a result of O'Reilly's efforts to market VIRGIN.

Famous is a Delaware corporation * * * engaged in the business of producing musical recordings for distribution throughout the United States. Famous' president, Tony Martell, is generally regarded in the recording industry as the individual primarily responsible for the successful distribution of the well-known rock operas TOMMY and JESUS CHRIST SUPERSTAR.

The relationship between Famous and Contemporary was considerably more harmonious in 1972 than it is today. At that time, Martell thought he had found, in VIRGIN, another TOMMY or JESUS CHRIST SUPER-STAR, and he was anxious to acquire rights to it. O'Reilly, who was encouraged by Martell's expertise and enthusiasm, had high hopes for the success of his composition. On August 16, 1972, they executed the so-called "VIRGIN Recording Agreement" ("VIRGIN agreement") on behalf of their respective organizations.

The terms of the VIRGIN agreement were relatively simple. Famous agreed to pay a royalty to Contemporary in return for the master tape recording of VIRGIN and the exclusive right to manufacture and sell records made from the master. The agreement also created certain "Additional Obligations of Famous" which included, *inter alia*: the obligation to select and appoint, within the first year of the agreement, at least one person to personally oversee the nationwide promotion of the sale of records, to maintain contact with Contemporary and to submit weekly reports to Contemporary; the obligation to spend, within the first year of the agreement, no less than $50,000 on the promotion of records; and the obligation to release, within the first two years of the agreement, at least four separate single records from VIRGIN.   *   *   *

On May 8, 1973, the parties entered into a distribution contract which dealt with musical compositions other than VIRGIN. This, the so-called "Crunch agreement," granted to Famous the exclusive right to distribute Contemporary's records in the United States. Famous agreed to institute a new record label named "Crunch," and a number of records were to be released under it annually. Contemporary agreed to deliver ten long-playing records and fifteen single records during the first year of the contract. Famous undertook to use its "reasonable efforts" to promote and distribute the records.   *   *   *

   *   *   *   [N]either VIRGIN nor its progeny was ever as successful as the parties had originally hoped, [and]   *   *   *   [C]ontemporary [eventually] brought this action against several defendants   *   *   *   [on the ground that] Famous had failed to adequately promote the VIRGIN and Crunch recordings   *   *   *.

   *   *   *   Famous vigorously contends that the jury's conclusion that it had failed to adequately promote VIRGIN prior to the sale to ABC is at war with the undisputed facts and cannot be permitted to stand.   *   *   *   On the whole [however] we are not persuaded that the jury's verdict should be disturbed.

*   *   *

IV.   *The Cross-Appeal by Contemporary.*

During the trial, Contemporary sought to introduce a statistical analysis, together with expert testimony, in order to prove how successful the most successful of its single recordings, "Fear No Evil," would have become if the VIRGIN agreement had not been breached   *   *   *.   Based upon its projection of the success of that recording, Contemporary hoped to prove what revenues that success would have produced. Judge Owen excluded this evidence on the ground that it was speculative.

* * * This is not a case in which the plaintiff sought to prove hypothetical profits from the sale of a hypothetical record at a hypothetical price in a hypothetical market. * * * [T]he record was real, the price was fixed, the market was buying and the record's success, while modest, was increasing. Even after the promotional efforts ended, the record was withdrawn from the marketplace, it was carried, as a result of its own momemtum, to an additional 10,000 sales and to a rise from approximately number 80 on the "Hot Soul Singles" chart of Billboard magazine to number 61. It cannot be gainsaid that if someone had continued to promote it, and if it had not been withdrawn from the market, it would have sold more records than it actually did. Thus, it is certain that Contemporary suffered some damage in the form of lost royalties. * * *

* * * Because "Fear No Evil" ultimately reached number 61 on the record charts, Contemporary offered a statistical analysis of every song that had reached number 61 during 1974. This analysis showed that 76 percent of the 324 songs that had reached number 61 ultimately reached the top 40; 65 percent reached the top 30; 51 percent reached the top 20; 34 percent reached the top 10; 21 percent reached the top 5; and 10 percent reached number 1. * * *

Famous vigorously maintains, and Judge Owen agreed, that the data was incomplete because it failed to account for such factors as the speed with which the various records rose upward (the most successful records generally rise quickly—passing number 61 in their third or fourth week —"Fear No Evil" had risen relatively slowly—number 61 in ten weeks); the reputations of the various artists performing the recordings (Contemporary had no prior hit records and was relatively unknown); and the size and ability of the company promoting the recordings. We agree that a more accurate prediction of the success of "Fear No Evil" would be likely to result if the statistical analysis accounted for these and other factors. The omission of these factors from Contemporary's study affects only the weight of the evidence, however, and not its admissibility. Evidence need not be conclusive in order to be relevant. Standing alone, the study tended to prove that it was more likely than not that "Fear No Evil" would be among the 51 percent of recordings that reached the top 20. If Famous wished to offer proof that would tend to cast doubt on the accuracy of that prediction, it would be free to do so. In this way, all of the evidence tending to show the probable amount of Contemporary's damages would be placed before the jury. While it is true that the jury would be required to speculate to some degree with respect to whether "Fear No Evil" would be within any particular percentage, such is the nature of estimation. If the amount of damage were certain, no estimation would be required. But the uncertainty exists, and since it is a product of the defendant's wrongful conduct, he will not be heard to complain of the lack of precision.

* * *

* * * [T]he case is remanded to the district court for further proceedings in accordance with this opinion.

[Judge VAN GRAAFEILAND's opinion, concurring in part and dissenting in part, is omitted.]

* * *

FISCH ON NEW YORK EVIDENCE

123–24, 133–38 (1959).*

[Footnotes omitted.]

§ 231. Ability and Opportunity

Proof of physical or mental capacity, or the presence or lack of knowledge, skill, means or opportunity to execute an act is admissible to raise or negative an inference as to its performance by the person charged with its commission. When relevant, however, evidence of financial condition may be introduced, and is frequently used to establish a motive or to show sudden enrichment. It is also commonly received in contested probate proceedings to demonstrate that the testator disregarded the needs, or recognized the good financial condition of those having a claim on his bounty, as these circumstances are indicative of the presence or absence of undue influence, overreaching or testamentary capacity.

A defense of payment or claim of a loan may be negatived by pecuniary inability, and, although financial ability may generally not be introduced to establish the *making* of a loan or the *payment* of a debt, possession by the adversary of sufficient means to have made payment may be proved to rebut evidence of his pecuniary inability to have done so.

On the issue of whether credit was given to A or B, it is improper to receive evidence of financial condition as "(n)o fair inference can be drawn that one person received credit instead of another, because he happened to have the most property. Men are often trusted on account of their good character and strict integrity, and sometimes upon their business capacity, and sometimes upon their future prospects. There are too many circumstances which may exist to cause a credit to be given, to permit the amount of a person's property, to be thrown in the scale upon such a question."

The financial responsibility of the defendant is a factor that may be considered by the jury in awarding exemplary damages as these damages are based on the theory of punishment and deterrence and the sum effective for such purposes depends upon the financial resources of the defendant.

§ 240. Motive

Motive is the inducement by which a person is impelled to act in order to achieve a preconceived goal. Never an essential element of a crime, it is often of probative value in determining whether the accused committed the act charged, since a person who possesses a motive to act or not to act in a certain manner is more likely to do so than one in whom such an impetus is lacking. For this reason lack of motive is also relevant as a circumstance tending towards exoneration of the accused. Evidence of motive is used principally to prove the doing of an act, but even when performance of the act in question by defendant is not disputed, motive may be relevant, and hence admissible, for such other purposes as establishing intent or negativing a defense of accident or mistake.

* * *

The factual situations capable of giving rise to an inference of motive are innumerable and run the entire gamut of human emotions. Because "frequently obscure, often trivial, and never adequate," considerable latitude in proof is allowed, and generally any fact that can possibly tend to establish a motive may be introduced. Proof of the awareness by the defendant of these facts is the only condition of admissibility.

§ 241.   Design, Plan or Scheme

It is to some extent probable that a person will act in accordance with a plan, design or scheme devised by him. Thus, the existence of these factors has probative value in determining whether he did or did not do a particular act. While the variety of acts that may be evidenced by proof of a design, plan or scheme are limitless, such proof most frequently appears in cases involving suicide, the making of a gift or contract, the execution or revocation of a will, or the commission of a criminal act.

Design, plan or scheme may be established by declarations as well as acts, and any act or declaration that according to common sense and experience, would indicate the existence of a design, plan or scheme is admissible. Such circumstances as the possession by the accused of tools or instruments ordinarily used for performing the act in question, other similar acts, prior attempts and threats, whether of a general and specific nature, have been received. However, a defendant, claiming to have killed in self-defense, may introduce the threats of his victim on the theory that they are probative of a plan or design to commit the acts threatened. This inference in turn is used as the basis for concluding that the victim attempted to carry out his plan and was thus the aggressor on the occasion in question. As the circumstances of evidentiary importance is the plan or design to do the act, the fact that the threat was never communicated to the defendant is without legal significance.

The admissibility of threats made by third persons against the victim of a crime, to be used for the purpose of exonerating the accused, has apparently never been adjudicated in this state. While some jurisdictions have refused to admit these statements there appears to be no valid reason for an exclusionary ruling.

§ 242.   Intent

Whenever intent, by which is meant the state of mind that accompanies an act, is a necessary element of the crime charged and the act is one that could have been performed by mistake or accident or with a lawful intent, evidence probative of intent, including proof of emotions that affect the quality or persistence of the intent, may generally be received.

As the defendant is entitled to testify to his lawful intent or lack of guilty knowledge, direct proof of these facts is more readily obtainable than direct evidence of unlawful intent. Consequently, the latter is seldom provable except by circumstantial evidence. Such events as similar offenses, prior attempts to commit the same crime, preparations for the act, threats, quarrels, or other indications of malice or ill-will are often utilized as the basis for inferring unlawful intent. As is true of motive, evidence indicative of intent is not rendered inadmissible because it also tends to prove the commission of another crime.

Intent is often material in civil as well as criminal proceedings, for the legal character of many non-criminal acts is determined by the state of mind with which they were performed. For example, the transfer of property from one person to another is equivocal in that its legal significance can not be determined by the physical act alone. The transfer may have been made in pursuance of an agency, to defraud creditors, for the convenience of the original owner or as a loan or gift. Hence, if it is contended that the transfer was a gift, it becomes necessary to establish a donative intent. This may be accomplished by direct evidence. It may also be established circumstantially by inferring the intent from the declarations of the alleged donor by donee, or from such circumstances as the fact that the alleged donor entirely divested himself of possession and dominion over the property, registered stock on the corporate books in the name of the alleged donee, or owed a moral obligation to the person claiming that a gift was made.

Intent to defraud and fraud in fact are also frequently evidenced circumstantially. Knowledge, or at least the belief, of the person charged that his statement is false, is the usual basis for an inference of intent in fraud actions based upon misrepresentations. Such an inference, however, may be predicated on other circumstances that amount to the same thing, such as the reckless making of the statement, termed "reckless indifference," or from a pretense of exact knowledge. The fact that other acts of the same character have been committed may also give rise to an inference of fraudulent intent.

§ 243. Mental and Physical Condition

An almost endless variety of facts may be admitted to circumstantially establish mental condition. The necessity for this type of proof is most often encountered when the defense of insanity is raised in a criminal case or when probate of a will is opposed on the ground of lack of testamentary capacity.

In determining testamentary capacity, the life, surroundings, relationships and friendships of the testator can properly be considered. Where insanity is relied upon as a defense to a criminal act, the whole previous career of the accused may be relevant to his mental condition at the time of the alleged offense.

The oral and written declarations of the person whose mental condition is in question are admissible as the basis for an inference thereto, and declarations made to him, when introduced to establish that they affected his mind to such an extent as to render him insane, may also be received. Conduct and behavior such as the fact that until his death an individual wisely and prudently supervised a large estate, made an unnatural disposition of his property by disinheriting his expected beneficiaries or suffered from delusions, may be considered in determining mental soundness.

Head injuries, confinement in a mental institution, or the appointment of a committee are also probative of this issue. It may also be proved that other members of the family were afflicted with a hereditary or transmissible disease, provided evidence has been introduced to show that the person in question is similarly afflicted. Consequently, it was held error to exclude hospital records tending to show that an ancestor of the accused suffered from dementia praecox when evidence was introduced in support of the claim of defendant that he too was suffering from this illness, and that it was hereditary. But absent evidence indicating that the person in question is afflicted with the claimed hereditary or transmissible disturbance, its existence may not be inferred solely from the fact that it was present in other members of his family.

That a testator was not intoxicated at the time he executed his will may be shown by the fact that immediately prior thereto he had operated a trolley car and placed it in the car barn without any difficulty.

It is often declared that the circumstances used as the basis for an inference as to mental or physical condition must not be too remote in point of time, but whether the time interval is too long necessarily depends upon the condition to be proved. Thus, if it is sought to prove intoxication, evidence of drinking will not be admitted unless it concerns a period shortly before the event in question. If, on the other hand, mental condition is to be shown, events that occurred in infancy or early childhood may be probative and therefore admissible. Evidence of condition both subsequent as well as prior to the period in question will be received when relevant to establish condition at the time in question.

I JONES, THE LAW OF EVIDENCE

§ 155 (1958).*

[Most footnotes omitted.]

What is Irrelevant.—The following examples of what the courts have held to be irrelevant may serve to illustrate further the theory of relevancy: The reason or motive impelling a party to retain a particular attorney to represent him in the case; a witness' reasons for believing certain facts; a party's personal opinions and prejudices as to matters wholly unrelated to the subject matter of the suit; and, on the issue as to desertion in a divorce suit between persons long married, evidence as to the place where they first lived after marriage.

The success of a discharged employee in similar positions after her discharge is irrelevant to the issue as to the propriety of her discharge from the position in suit for incompetency. And the personal practices of students and faculty members of a state university in another community are irrelevant to the issue as to the propriety of the expulsion from a state normal school of a female student for indulgence in such practices.

The identity of the handwriting of the portion of a writing which contained the defamatory charge with that of other portions of the same writing is irrelevant to the issue as to the truth or falsity of the alleged libel; a rejected bid for public work, which stipulated the damages for delay, is irrelevant to the issue of damages for delay under the accepted bid which contained no such stipulation, and, in an action against a broker for damages for breach of an oral contract, it is irrelevant to show a written contract between the parties relating to an entirely different subject matter.

Likewise, evidence of value or usual price is irrelevant in an action on a contract to pay a fixed sum; proof that a low price was paid for goods is irrelevant to disprove a claim of warranty of quality; and evidence as to the amount of wages paid in a certain employment in towns in another state is

*Copyright 1958 Bancroft-Whitney, San Francisco.

too remote to be relevant to the issue of the proper amount of wages for such work in the place of suit. Other instances of irrelevant evidence are noted below[14] and in the ensuing sections.

See Federal Rules of Evidence 401, 402, 403 at p. 909; California Evidence Code § § 210, 350, 351, 352, at pp. 812, 815.

Hypotheticals

(1) A, a surviving widow, sues X for the wrongful death of B, A's husband. B, a pedestrian, was struck and killed by X's car. X's answer admits liability. A offers evidence that X was driving while intoxicated, and that B was thrown 80 feet by the force of the impact. X objects to this evidence as irrelevant. Is X's objection proper?

(2) P sues D for damages for personal injuries to himself and for the wrongful death of P's wife arising out of D's rear-ending of P's car. P was in his car parked at a curb and his wife was at the car door, starting to get in. P also seeks damages for emotional trauma resulting from his presence at the scene of the accident. P testifies that he did not see his wife after the impact because he was rendered unconscious. D admits liability. P proffers photographs of his wife's body at the accident site to show the condition of her body as a result of the collision, the autopsy report, and testimony of the autopsy surgeon and a friend regarding the reconstruction of the wife's body required to permit an open coffin funeral. D makes an irrelevancy objection to P's proffered evidence. What result?

(3) D is charged with murder of V by kicking him with his boots. D's defense is that he had an argument with V but did not kick him. The prosecutor calls W to testify that D was a member of the X Gang which was known to commit acts of violence and that V belonged to a rival gang. D makes an irrelevancy objection to W's testimony. How should the court rule?

(4) D is charged with the sale of marijuana. The prosecutor introduces evidence that in the company of I, an informer, PO, a police officer, made a purchase of marijuana from D at D's residence. D's defense is entrapment—that PO had the informer plant the marijuana in D's residence. D seeks to introduce evidence that before the alleged sale, D had filed a false arrest suit against the police department growing out of an arrest of D made nine months before the alleged sale. The prosecutor makes an irrelevancy objection to D's proffered evidence. What result?

---

14. Whether or not plaintiff ever paid her bill to defendant private hospital is no justification for her detention in the hospital and is irrelevant in her action for false imprisonment. Gadsden General Hospital v. Hamilton, 212 Ala. 531, 103 So. 553, 40 A.L.R. 294.

Evidence of damages to plaintiff from one libel of him by defendant, which is the subject of one suit between the parties, is irrelevant in another suit between them based upon an entirely different publication. Lehner v. Berlin Pub. Co., 211 Wis. 119, 246 N.W. 579, 86 A.L.R. 1284 and note p. 1297.

That defendant signed the note in suit only as an accommodation maker is irrelevant as against a bona fide holder without notice. Lister v. Donlan, 85 Mont. 571, 281 Pa. 348, 72 A.L.R. 1.

That partners agreed among themselves not to sign a note is irrelevant as against an indorsee without notice on the issue whether one partner did sign the note. Bates v. Forcht, 89 Mo. 121, 1 S.W. 120; Kellogg v. Thompson, 142 Mass. 76, 6 N.E. 860.

The amount of a certain crop grown on a farm in a given year cannot be shown by proof of the average acreage of grass and its yield in other years. Patrick v. Howard, 47 Mich. 40, 10 N.W. 71.

(5)   X is charged with a battery upon A, a police officer, by hitting him with a brick during a demonstration at Y College. The prosecution calls B to testify that several hours before the demonstration he saw several students, including X, enter a room in the Student Union of Y College and that then he heard one student make the statement, "I'm going to sock it to a cop during the demonstration." X makes an irrelevancy objection. Should X's objection be sustained?

(6)   X is charged with the sale of heroin. A, an undercover police officer, testifies that he purchased heroin from X at approximately 8:00 p.m. on January 30, which was six months before X's arrest. X's defense is an alibi. He testifies that on January 30 he and his wife went to the Z Movie Theater and saw the movie "Airport," and that it was raining that night. X's wife corroborates his testimony. X calls the theater manager, who testifies that "Airport" was shown at the Z Movie Theater for seven days, from January 25 to January 31. X then calls B, a meteorologist, to testify that between January 25 and January 31 it rained on January 30 from 6:00 to 10:00 p.m., but not on any other day or night during that period. The prosecution makes an irrelevancy objection to B's testimony. What result?

(7)   D is charged with forgery of a check and of using it to obtain cash from V, a grocer. D offers evidence that he made restitution to V a week after the incident. Should the prosecution's irrelevancy objection to D's proffered evidence be sustained?

IN THE SUPERIOR COURT OF THE STATE OF CALIFORNIA, IN AND FOR THE CITY AND COUNTY OF SAN FRANCISCO.

DEPARTMENT—EXTRA SESSION NO. 3
HONORABLE MILTON D.S_____, Judge

THE PEOPLE OF THE STATE OF CALIFORNIA, Plaintiff, v. JOSEPH T_____ and ERNEST W_____, Defendants	No. 39, 863 A FELONY, to wit: MURDER

REPORTER'S TRANSCRIPT

September 2, 19__

APPEARANCES:

For the PEOPLE:	Hon. EDMUND G. B_____, District Attorney BY:
For Defendant ERNEST W_____: For Defendant JOSEPH T_____:	NORMAN E_____, Assistant District Attorney JOSEPH G_____, Esq. WILLIAM L. F_____, Assistant Public Defender

(On September 10, 19__, Police Officer Charles O_____ was found dead in Dan's Creamery. He had been beaten around the face but the cause of death was a bullet wound through the body.)

People's Exhibit No. 3—A Gun.
No. 17—A bullet.

THE COURT: You may proceed with your closing argument, Mr. E_____.
Mr. E_____: Your Honor, and ladies and gentlemen of the jury:

Page 891 et seq. of transcript:

Now, did this gun, People's Exhibit No. 3, fire the shot that killed Officer O_____?

Now, Tommy F_____ says that it was; this is the gun that Joseph T_____ had with him that night. But we have additional evidence.

We have the testimony of Francis L_____. Francis L_____ says that while sometimes it is possible to tell with scientific exactness that a given bullet was fired from a given gun, because when a bullet is fired through the gun the barrel of the gun leaves on the side of the bullet microscopic markings from the barrel. He said that in this case the barrel is very badly worn. It is worn much more than the barrel of a new gun. So that any bullet which is fired through this gun fits very loosely, and I think that is evidenced too from the killing of Officer O_____. The bullet had no more force than to go through his body; it couldn't even penetrate his outside clothing. And the fact that it wasn't a tight fit leads us to the conclusion there wasn't too much force. Anyway, this gun is too badly worn. In order for him to say with scientific exactitude that this is the gun which fired the bullet which killed Officer Charles O_____, Francis L_____ does say this: He was asked, "What is the caliber of the bullet which killed Officer O_____?" Mr. L_____ says, "It is a .38 caliber." "What is the caliber of this gun?" "This is a .38 caliber gun."—So far exactly the same, except there are a number of different calibers, .22, .25, .30, .32, .38 but they happen to be the same caliber.

Now, he was asked, "What about the rifling? Is it right hand or left hand?"

He says, "The gun had a right hand rifling, right hand lands, and grooves."

"What about the rifling on the bullet?"

"That also was right hand,—was fired by a gun that had right hand lands and grooves."

Then he was asked: "How many lands and grooves?"

Remember, the lands are the high spots inside the barrel and the grooves the low spots.

"How many lands and how many grooves do you find in this gun?"

He says: "There are five lands and five grooves."

Then he was asked: "How many lands and grooves were there in the gun which fired the murder bullet?"

And he said: "There were five lands and five grooves."—Again exactly as this gun.

Then he was asked about whether he found in this gun any misalignment between the revolving cylinder of the gun and the barrel of the gun, and he said: "Yes, the gun is so badly worn that when it is fired the chamber of the cylinder comes to rest not exactly in line, but a little off center, so that when the bullet leaves the chamber of the cylinder, and enters the barrel of the revolver, a portion of the side was shaved off."

Then he was asked: "How about the bullet which killed Officer O_____?"

He says exactly the same thing, that the side of the bullet was shaved off.

Then it is clear to us that the bullet that killed Officer O_____ was fired from a revolver and not from an automatic, an automatic being a gun without the revolving cylinder, one of those black-looking affairs, quite different from this.

We know that that was the case because of the shaving off of the side of the bullet. So the bullet that killed Officer O_____ was fired from a revolver, and this is a revolver.

Now, let's consider the probabilities that are involved in a matter like this. The mathematicians can reduce probabilities to a mathematical formula, I think it is called the law of chance. It is a formula that where you can figure with mathematical precision the probabilities of a given thing happening.

Now, the murder bullet was a .38 caliber, and the gun was a .38 caliber. There are a half dozen different kinds of calibers, starting from .22, .25, .30, .32; there might be a .35. I know there is a .38, .42, .45; that is seven at least.

Let's make it one and five, the chances are one and five that a given gun against a coincidence like this happening that the caliber happens to be exactly the same as the gun, as the gun from which the bullet was fired. Then there is the question of the right and left hand rifling. The chances are one in two that a gun would be right hand or that it would be left hand. So that would be one in two. Then the matter of the five lands and five grooves; Mr. L_____ told us that there were eight lands and eight grooves, there were seven lands and seven grooves, there were six lands and six grooves, there were five, there were four; there are a great many different kinds of numbers of lands and grooves. Let's make it four to one, to make it conservative. It just happens by chance that this bullet happened to have the same number of lands and grooves as the murder revolver. Then there is the fact that the bullet was fired by a revolver with the chamber out of line with the barrel. That is a very unusual thing, but I think it would be safe to say it couldn't happen more than one time in five. I think you will probably agree that it doesn't happen more than one time in fifty, but let's say that one in five would be the probability there. Then the fact that the bullet and the gun happened—the bullet happened to be fired from the revolver, and this gun is a revolver, again one and two, because it might have been an automatic.

Now, Dr. K_____ told us about the law of chance. In the first place, it is one to five; but when you have another one to two probability it becomes one to ten; when you have another one to four probability superimposed on that, it becomes one to forty; when you have another one to five probability on that, it would be—it is one to two hundred, five times forty; when you have another one to two probability it is four hundred. So you have in this case quite a part in the testimony of Tommy F_____, who said "This is the gun we used there that night." And those figures, I think are conservative, one to four hundred, that this is the gun that was used in the killing of Officer Charles O_____ that night.

Those things just don't happen by coincidence. They didn't happen by coincidence; it doesn't happen by coincidence that the bullet was the same caliber as the gun; it doesn't happen that the barrel is out of line with the chambers of the magazine; any one of those things could happen, but it just doesn't happen in the manner that it would have to happen in this case in order that it would be just a coincidence that the bullet happens to fit the gun.

HOUTS, FROM EVIDENCE TO PROOF

132–134 (1956).*

AND IT PROBABLY DIDN'T

My dictionary defines probability as "The state or quality of being probable." Probable is then defined as "1. Having more evidence than the contrary but not proof; likely to be true or to happen, but leaving room for doubt. 2. That which renders something worthy of belief, but falling short of demonstration; as probable evidence."

Unfortunately, it has become the vogue in recent years to bolster sagging cases by applying the law of probability in an attempt to strengthen weak or nonexistent evidence.

I have discussed the matter with several mathematicians and they are unanimous in their opinions that the law of probability has absolutely no application to the forensic field. Its mathematical utility is founded on exact statistical research; and in no field of proof has this research progressed to a point sufficient to warrant the use of precise mathematical equations. I am further advised that the type of research required is not likely to come within the foreseeable future.

It is a relatively simple matter to toss a coin 10,000 times and record the number of times it lands heads and the number tails. It is a totally different matter to compile statistical data on the scale counts of human hair, the lands and grooves of bullets, striations made by crowbars, or the refractive indexes of certain types of plate glass. To achieve statistical accuracy, all possible combinations and variations must be considered—a problem too staggering in magnitude to warrant the expenditures of time and money required to master it.

The proponents of this substitute for proof readily admit that they must assume or assign a probability when they prepare to launch their journeys off into mathematical space. They admit that the assumptions are arbitrary and not founded on research—or if they do claim to have research data, it turns out to be so limited and unreliable that it is actually misleading. They do not realize that to be on sound mathematical ground, the independence or dependence of the numbers or factors used must be firmly established. They then offer to cure this deficiency by meekly pledging conservatism in the assignment.

This may be well and good, except that when you multiply 10 times 10 times 10 for 15 times, the result is far from conservative.

The advocates of the law of probability immediately point to fingerprints and say that this science is founded on probability. I take energetic issue with them. The value of fingerprint evidence rests on our experience in examining millions of sets of prints and in finding no two identical. As a safety factor, twelve points of identity have been established as a minimum standard before two prints are declared exactly alike. If the examiner finds these points, he makes his comparison and declares that he has a match.

He would be scorned by his professional associates if he found only five points of identity to which he assigned a probability of one in twenty and ended up with an assertion that the probabilities are one in 3,200,000 that the two prints are identical—even though only five matching points can be found.

The quickest way to discredit the conclusive probative weight accorded fingerprint evidence is to have some pseudo-expert—and some are now doing it—testify that he has counted the pores in one friction ridge and finds that there are fifteen, to which he assigns a "conservative" probability of one in ten. Thus, on the basis of one friction ridge alone, the probabilities become one in 1,000,000,000,000,000 that the two prints are identical. When it subsequently develops that the two prints were not identical, fingerprint evidence will lose much of its wallop.

A ballistics expert identifies two bullets because their markings are such that he can look at them through a comparison microscope and say that they match positively. He doesn't start counting striations and assigning a probability of one in ten to each line. If he did, he could soon reach an astronomical figure of probability that two bullets were from the same gun —even though his integrity and past experience will permit no such honest conclusion.

The handwriting expert can assume a conservative probability of one in two that the Spencerian characteristics of the questioned writing are the same as those of the known specimen. By the time he has discovered 500 letters in a note, he has a probability of a positive identification of the two writings that would stagger the expert who keeps track of the national debt. Yet, any self-respecting handwriting expert would laugh out loud at this infantile method of establishing handwriting identity.

Two tire impressions are identified because they have a sufficient number of observable, individual characteristics—not because someone reaches into a hat and assigns a probability of one to five to each of fifty or sixty lines and grooves.

I have never seen the law of probability attempted in any case where convincing proof existed. It is only applied where no solid proof exists —where something must be fabricated from nothing before one side can prevail.

As this manuscript is being prepared, Smith Edward Jordan and Robert Otis Pierce await execution in San Quentin for the murder of an Oakland cab driver. The only evidence connecting them with the scene of the crime is the testimony of an expert witness that on the basis of seven matching fiber transfers between the clothing of the victim and the defendants, the probabilities are one in 1,280,000,000 that the defendants contacted the victim and his cab.* This is the same expert who advocated the conservative probability of one in 100 billion in the Trujillo-Woodmansee case.

*Compare People v. Jordan, 45 Cal.2d 697,
290 P.2d 484 (1955).

I have discussed this testimony with a number of leading forensic experts in the United States and they only describe it as "incredible," "unbelievable," and "utterly fantastic."

PEOPLE v. COLLINS

Supreme Court of California, 1968
68 Cal.2d 319, 66 Cal.Rptr. 497, 438 P.2d 33.
[Most footnotes omitted.]

SULLIVAN, Justice. We deal here with the novel question whether evidence of mathematical probability has been properly introduced and used by the prosecution in a criminal case. While we discern no inherent incompatibility between the disciplines of law and mathematics and intend no general disapproval or disparagement of the latter as an auxiliary in the fact-finding processes of the former, we cannot uphold the technique employed in the instant case. As we explain in detail infra, the testimony as to mathematical probability infected the case with fatal error and distorted the jury's traditional role of determining guilt or innocence according to long-settled rules. Mathematics, a veritable sorcerer in our computerized society, while assisting the trier of fact in the search for truth, must not cast a spell over him. We conclude that on the record before us defendant should not have had his guilt determined by the odds and that he is entitled to a new trial. We reverse the judgment.

A jury found defendant Malcolm Ricardo Collins and his wife defendant Janet Louise Collins guilty of second degree robbery (Pen. Code, § § 211, 211a, 1157). Malcolm appeals from the judgment of conviction. Janet has not appealed.[1] * * *

At the seven-day trial the prosecution experienced some difficulty in establishing the identities of the perpetrators of the crime. The victim could not identify Janet and had never seen defendant. The identification by the witness Bass, who observed the girl run out of the alley and get into the automobile, was incomplete as to Janet and may have been weakened as to defendant. There was also evidence, introduced by the defense, that Janet had worn light-colored clothing on the day in question, but both the victim and Bass testified that the girl they observed had worn dark clothing.

In an apparent attempt to bolster the identifications, the prosecutor called an instructor of mathematics at a state college. Through this witness he sought to establish that, assuming the robbery was committed by a Caucasian woman with a blond ponytail who left the scene accompanied by a Negro with a beard and mustache, there was an overwhelming probability that the crime was committed by any couple answering such distinctive characteristics. The witness testified, in substance, to the "product rule," which states that the probability of the joint occurrence of a number of *mutually independent* events is equal to the product of the individual probabilities that each of the events will occur. *Without presenting any statistical evidence whatsoever in support of the probabilities for the factors selected,* the prosecutor then proceeded to have the witness *assume* proba-

---

1. Hereafter, the term "defendant" is intended to apply only to Malcolm, but the term "defendents" to Malcolm and Janet.

bility factors for the various characteristics which he deemed to be shared by the guilty couple and all other couples answering to such distinctive characteristics.[10]

Applying the product rule to his own factors the prosecutor arrived at a probability that there was but one chance in 12 million that any couple possessed the distinctive characteristics of the defendants. Accordingly, under this theory, it was to be inferred that there could be but one chance in 12 million that defendants were innocent and that another equally distinctive couple actually committed the robbery. Expanding on what he had thus purported to suggest as a hypothesis, the prosecutor offered the completely unfounded and improper testimonial assertion that, in his opinion, the factors he had assigned were "conservative estimates" and that, in reality "the chances of anyone else besides these defendants being there, * * * having every similarity, * * * is somewhat like one in a billion."

Objections were timely made to the mathematician's testimony on the grounds that it was immaterial, that it invaded the province of the jury, and that it was based on unfounded assumptions. The objections were "temporarily overruled" and the evidence admitted subject to a motion to strike. When that motion was made at the conclusion of the direct examination, the court denied it, stating that the testimony had been received only for the "purpose of illustrating the mathematical probabilities of various matters, the possibilities for them occurring or re-occurring." * * *

As we shall explain, the prosecution's introduction and use of mathematical probability statistics injected two fundamental prejudicial errors into the case: (1) The testimony itself lacked an adequate foundation both in evidence and in statistical theory; and (2) the testimony and the manner in which the prosecution used it distracted the jury from its proper and requisite function of weighing the evidence on the issue of guilt, encouraged the jurors to rely upon an engaging but logically irrelevant expert

---

10.　Although the prosecutor insisted that the factors he used were only for illustrative purposes—to demonstrate how the probability of the occurrence of mutually independent factors affected the probability that they would occur together—he nevertheless attempted to use factors which he personally related to the distinctive characteristics of defendants. In his argument to the jury he invited the jurors to apply their own factors, and asked defense counsel to suggest what the latter would deem as reasonable. The prosecutor himself proposed the individual probabilities set out in the table below. Although the transcript of the examination of the mathematics instructor and the information volunteered by the prosecutor at that time create some uncertainty as to precisely which of the characteristics the prosecutor assigned to the individual probabilities, he restated in his argument to the jury that they should be as follows:

Characteristic	Individual Probability
A.　Partly yellow automobile	1/10
B.　Man with mustache	1/4
C.　Girl with ponytail	1/10
D.　Girl with blond hair	1/3
E.　Negro man with beard	1/10
F.　Interracial couple in car	1/1000

In his brief on appeal defendant agrees that the foregoing appeared on a table presented in the trial court.

demonstration, foreclosed the possibility of an effective defense by an attorney apparently unschooled in mathematical refinements, and placed the jurors and defense counsel at a disadvantage in sifting relevant fact from inapplicable theory.

We initially consider the defects in the testimony itself. As we have indicated, the specific technique presented through the mathematician's testimony and advanced by the prosecutor to measure the probabilities in question suffered from two basic and pervasive defects—an inadequate evidentiary foundation and an inadequate proof of statistical independence. First, as to the foundation requirement, we find the record devoid of any evidence relating to any of the six individual probability factors used by the prosecutor and ascribed by him to the six characteristics as we have set them out in footnote 10, ante. To put it another way, the prosecution produced no evidence whatsoever showing, or from which it could be in any way inferred, that only one out of every ten cars which might have been at the scene of the robbery was partly yellow, that only one out of every four men who might have been there wore a mustache, that only one out of every ten girls who might have been there wore a ponytail, or that any of the other individual probability factors listed were even roughly accurate.[12]

The bare, inescapable fact is that the prosecution made no attempt to offer any such evidence. Instead, through leading questions having perfunctorily elicited from the witness the response that the latter could not assign a probability factor for the characteristics involved,[13] the prosecutor himself suggested what the various probabilities should be and these became the basis of the witness' testimony (see fn. 10, ante). It is a curious circumstance of this adventure in proof that the prosecutor not only made his own assertions of these factors in the hope that they were "conservative" but also in later argument to the jury invited the jurors to substitute their "estimates" should they wish to do so. We can hardly conceive of a more fatal gap in the prosecution's scheme of proof. A foundation for the admissibility of the witness' testimony was never even attempted to be laid, let alone established. His testimony was neither made to rest on his own testimonial knowledge nor presented by proper hypothetical questions based upon valid data in the record. (State v. Sneed (1966) 76 N.M. 349, 414 P.2d 858.) In the *Sneed* case, the court reversed a conviction based on probabilistic evidence, stating: "We hold that mathematical odds are not admissible as evidence to identify a defendant in a criminal proceeding *so long as the odds are based on estimates, the validity of which have [sic] not been demonstrated.*" (Italics added.) (414 P.2d at p. 862.)

12. We seriously doubt that such evidence could ever be compiled since no statistician could possibly determine after the fact which cars, or which individuals "might" have been present at the scene of the robbery; certainly there is no reason to suppose that the human and automotive populations of San Pedro, California, include all potential culprits—or, conversely, that all members of these populations are proper candidates for inclusion. Thus the sample from which the relevant probabilities would have to be derived is itself undeterminable. (See generally, Yaman, Statistics, An Introductory Analysis (1964), ch. I.)

13. The prosecutor asked the mathematics instructor: "Now, let me see if you can be of some help to us with some independent factors, and you have some paper you may use. Your specialty does not equip you, I suppose, to give us some probability of such things as a yellow car as contrasted with any other kind of car, does it? * * * I appreciate the fact that you can't assign a probability for a car being yellow as contrasted to some other car, can you? A. No, I couldn't."

But, as we have indicated, there was another glaring defect in the prosecution's technique, namely an inadequate proof of the statistical independence of the six factors. No proof was presented that the characteristics selected were mutually independent, even though the witness himself acknowledged that such condition was essential to the proper application of the "product rule" or "multiplication rule." (See Note, supra, Duke L.J. 665, 669–670, fn. 25.)[14] To the extent that the traits or characteristics were not mutually independent (e. g. Negroes with beards and men with mustaches obviously represent overlapping categories[15]), the "product rule" would inevitably yield a wholly erroneous and exaggerated result even if all of the individual components had been determined with precision.

In the instant case, therefore, because of the aforementioned two defects—the inadequate evidentiary foundation and the inadequate proof of statistical independence—the technique employed by the prosecutor could only lead to wild conjecture without demonstrated relevancy to the issues presented. It acquired no redeeming quality from the prosecutor's statement that it was being used "for illustrative purposes" since, as we shall point out, the prosecutor's subsequent utilization of the mathematical testimony was not confined within such limits.

We now turn to the second fundamental error caused by the probability testimony. Quite apart from our foregoing objections to the specific technique employed by the prosecution to estimate the probability in question, we think that the entire enterprise upon which the prosecution embarked, and which was directed to the objective of measuring the likelihood of a random couple possessing the characteristics allegedly distinguishing the robbers, was gravely misguided. At best, it might yield an estimate as to how infrequently bearded Negroes drive yellow cars in the company of blond females with ponytails.

The prosecution's approach, however, could furnish the jury with absolutely no guidance on the crucial issue: *Of the admittedly few such couples, which one, if any, was guilty of committing this robbery?* Probability theory necessarily remains silent on that question, since no mathematical equation can prove beyond a reasonable doubt (1) that the guilty couple *in fact* possessed the characteristics described by the People's witnesses, or even (2) that only *one* couple possessing those distinctive characteristics could be found in the entire Los Angeles area.

---

14.   It is there stated that: "A trait is said to be independent of a second trait when the occurrence or non-occurrence of one does not affect the probability of the occurrence of the other trait. The multiplication rule cannot be used without some degree of error where the traits are not independent." (Citing Huntsberger, Elements of Statistical Inference (1961) 77; Kingston & Kirk, The Use of Statistics in Criminalistics (1964) 55 J. Crim.L., C. & P.S. 516.) (Note, supra, Duke L.J. fn. 25, p. 670.)

15.   Assuming *arguendo* that factors B and E (see fn. 10, ante), were correctly estimated, nevertheless it is still arguable that most Negro men with beards *also* have mustaches (exhibit 3 herein, for instance, shows defendant with both a mustache and a beard, indeed in a hirsute continuum); if so, there is no basis for multiplying ¼ by ⅒ to estimate the proportion of Negroes who wear beards *and* mustaches. Again, the prosecution's technique could *never* be meaningfully applied, since its accurate use would call for information as to the degree of interdependence among the six individual factors. (See Yamane, op. cit. supra.) Such information cannot be compiled, however, since the relevant sample necessarily remains unknown. (See fn. 10, ante.)

As to the first inherent failing we observe that the prosecution's theory of probability rested on the assumption that the witnesses called by the People had conclusively established that the guilty couple possessed the precise characteristics relied upon by the prosecution. But no mathematical formula could ever establish beyond a reasonable doubt that the prosecution's witnesses correctly observed and accurately described the distinctive features which were employed to link defendants to the crime. Conceivably, for example, the guilty couple might have included a light-skinned Negress with bleached hair rather than a Caucasian blond; or the driver of the car might have been wearing a false beard as a disguise; or the prosecution's witnesses might simply have been unreliable.[16]

The foregoing risks of error permeate the prosecution's circumstantial case. Traditionally, the jury weighs such risks in evaluating the credibility and probative value of trial testimony, but the likelihood of human error or of falsification obviously cannot be quantified; that likelihood must therefore be excluded from any effort to assign a *number* to the probability of guilt or innocence. Confronted with an equation which purports to yield a numerical index of probable guilt, few juries could resist the temptation to accord disproportionate weight to that index; only an exceptional juror, and indeed only a defense attorney schooled in mathematics, could successfully keep in mind the fact that the probability computed by the prosecution can represent, *at best,* the likelihood that a random couple would share the characteristics testified to by the People's witnesses—*not necessarily the characteristics of the actually guilty couple.*

As to the second inherent failing in the prosecution's approach, even assuming that the first failing could be discounted, the most a mathematical computation could *ever* yield would be a measure of the probability that a random couple would possess the distinctive features in question. In the present case, for example, the prosecution attempted to compute the probability that a random couple would include a bearded Negro, a blond girl with a ponytail, and a partly yellow car; the prosecution urged that this probability was no more than one in 12 million. Even accepting this conclusion as arithmetically accurate, however, one still could not conclude that the Collinses were probably *the* guilty couple. On the contrary, as we explain in the Appendix, the prosecution's figures actually implied a likelihood of over 40 percent that the Collinses could be "duplicated" by at least *one other couple who might equally have committed the San Pedro robbery.* Urging that the Collinses be convicted on the basis of evidence which logically establishes no more than this seems as indefensible as arguing for the conviction of X on the ground that a witness saw either X or X's twin commit the crime.

Again, few defense attorneys, and certainly few jurors, could be expected to comprehend this basic flaw in the prosecution's analysis. Conceivably even the prosecutor erroneously believed that his equation established a high probability that *no* other bearded Negro in the Los Angeles

16.   In the instant case, for instance, the victim could not state whether the girl had a ponytail, although the victim observed the girl as she ran away. The witness Bass, on the other hand, was sure that the girl whom he saw had a ponytail. The demonstration engaged in by the prosecutor also leaves no room for the possibility, although perhaps a small one, that the girl whom the victim and the witness observed was, in fact, the same girl.

area drove a yellow car accompanied by a ponytailed blond. In any event, although his technique could demonstrate no such thing, he solemnly told the jury that he had supplied mathematical proof of guilt.

Sensing the novelty of that notion, the prosecutor told the jurors that the traditional idea of proof beyond a reasonable doubt represented "the most hackneyed, stereotyped, trite, misunderstood concept in criminal law." He sought to reconcile the jury to the risk that, under his "new math" approach to criminal jurisprudence, "on some rare occasion * * * an innocent person may be convicted." "Without taking that risk," the prosecution continued, "life would be intolerable * * * because * * * there would be immunity for the Collinses, for people who chose not to be employed to go down and push old ladies down and take their money and be immune because how could we ever be sure they are the ones who did it?"

In essence this argument of the prosecutor was calculated to persuade the jury to convict defendants whether or not they were convinced of their guilt to a moral certainty and beyond a reasonable doubt. (Pen.Code, § 1096.) Undoubtedly the jurors were unduly impressed by the mystique of the mathematical demonstration but were unable to assess its relevancy or value. Although we make no appraisal of the proper applications of mathematical techniques in the proof of facts, we have strong feelings that such applications, particularly in a criminal case, must be critically examined in view of the substantial unfairness to the defendant which may result from ill conceived techniques with which the trier of fact is not technically equipped to cope. We feel that the technique employed in the case before us falls into the latter category.

We conclude that the court erred in admitting over defendant's objection the evidence pertaining to the mathematical theory of probability and in denying defendant's motion to strike such evidence. * * *

The judgment is reversed.

Traynor, C.J., and Peters, Tobriner, Mosk and Burke, JJ., concur.

McComb, Justice. I dissent. I would affirm the judgment in its entirety.

APPENDIX

If "Pr" represents the probability that a certain distinctive combination of characteristics, hereinafter designated "C," will occur jointly in a random couple, then the probability that C will *not* occur in a random couple is (1–Pr). Applying the product rule (see fn. 8, ante), the probability that C will occur in *none* of N couples chosen at random is $(1-Pr)^N$, so that the probability of C occurring in *at least one* of N random couples is $[1-(1-Pr)^N]$.

Given a particular couple selected from a random set of N, the probability of C occurring in that couple (i.e., Pr), multiplied by the probability of C occurring in none of the remaining N–1 couples (i.e., $(1-Pr)^{N-1}$), yields the probability that C will occur in the selected couple and in no other. Thus the probability of C occurring in any particular couple, and in that couple alone, is $[(Pr) \times (1-Pr)^{N-1}]$. Since this is true for each of the N couples, the probability that C will occur in precisely *one* of the N couples, without regard to which one, is $[(Pr) \times (1-Pr)^{N-1}]$ added N times, because the probability of the occurrence of one of several *mutually exclusive* events is equal to the *sum* of the individual probabilities. Thus the probability of C occurring in *exactly one* of N random couples (*any* one, but *only* one) is [(N) x (Pr) x $(1-Pr)^{N-1}$].

By subtracting the probability that C will occur in *exactly one* couple from the probability that C will occur in *at least one* couple, one obtains the probability that C will occur in *more than one* couple: [$1-(1-Pr)^N-(N)$ x (Pr) x $(1-Pr)^{N-1}$]. Dividing this difference by the probability that C will occur in at least one couple (i.e., dividing the difference by [$1-(1-Pr)^N$]) then yields *the probability that C will occur more than once in a group of N couples in which C occurs at least once.*

Turning to the case in which C represents the characteristics which distinguish a bearded Negro accompanied by a ponytailed blond in a yellow car, the prosecution sought to establish that the probability of C occurring in a random couple was 1/12,000,000—i.e., that Pr = 1/12,000,000. Treating this conclusion as accurate, it follows that, in a population of N random couples, the probability of C occurring *exactly once* is [(N) x (1/12,000,000) x $(1-1/12,000,000)^{N-1}$]. Subtracting this product from [$1-(1-1/12,000,000)^N$], the probability of C occurring in *at least one* couple, and dividing the resulting difference by [$1-(1-1/12,000,000)^N$], the probability that C will occur in at least one couple, yields the probability that C will occur more than once in a group of N random couples of which at least one couple (namely, the one seen by the witnesses) possesses characteristics C. In other words, the probability of *another* such couple in a population of N is the quotient A/B, where A designates the numerator [$1-(1-1/12,000,000)^N$]−[(N) x 1/12,000,000 x $(1-1/12,000,000)^{N-1}$], and B designates the denominator [$1-(1-1/12,000,000)^N$].

N, which represents the total number of all couples who might conceivably have been at the scene of the San Pedro robbery, is not determinable, a fact which suggests yet another basic difficulty with the use of probability theory in establishing identity. One of the imponderables in determining N may well be the number of N-type couples in which a single person may participate. Such considerations make it evident that N, in the area adjoining the robbery, is in excess of several million; as N assumes values of such magnitude, the quotient A/B computed as above, representing the probability of a second couple as distinctive as the one described by the prosecution's witnesses, soon exceeds 4/10. Indeed, as N approaches 12 million, this probability quotient rises to approximately 41 percent. We note parenthetically that if 1/N = Pr, then as N increases indefinitely, the quotient in question approaches a limit of $(e-2)/(e-1)$, where "e" represents the transcendental number (approximately 2.71828) familiar in mathematics and physics.

Hence, even if we should accept the prosecution's figures without question, we would derive a probability of over 40 percent that the couple observed by the witnesses could be "duplicated" by at least one other equally distinctive interracial couple in the area, including a Negro with a beard and mustache, driving a partly yellow car in the company of a blond with a ponytail. Thus the prosecution's computations, far from establishing beyond a reasonable doubt that the Collinses were the couple described by the prosecution's witnesses, imply a very subsantial likelihood that the area contained *more than one* such couple, and that a couple *other* than the Collinses was the one observed at the scene of the robbery. (See generally: Hoel, Introduction to Mathematical Statistics (3rd ed. 1962); Hodges & Leymann, Basic Concepts of Probability and Statistics (1964); Lindgren & McElrath, Introduction to Probability and Statistics (1959).)

1,000,000,000,000,000,000,000,000,000,000,000 TO 1

Odds Trip Up Pair in New York Race Bet Case*

MINEOLA, L.I.   A Queens woman and a Baldwin, L.I., man have been convicted in an unusual case over disputed claims to a winning parimutuel ticket worth $5,050.

Key elements in the Nassau County Court trial were a Belmont Park racetrack computer printout of more than 350 bets made at a particular betting window on the day in question, and a Hofstra University mathematics professor's testimony that the odds against two different people independently choosing the same combination of nine $2 bets in nine races on the same day were a decillion to one.

The jury trial stemmed from a complaint to racetrack security personnel and later to the Nassau County Police and district attorney's office by a Brooklyn nurse, Rose Grant. She said she had been cheated out of her winning ticket on the track's ninth-race triple bet for May 21, 1974.

The triple is a high-return betting arrangement in which the bettor must pick the first, second and third-place finishers in exact order. At other tracks it is known as the trifecta.

According to Grant's complaint, she went to the track that day but had to leave early. She said she wrote down her picks in each of the nine races on a piece of lavatory paper before leaving. She said she gave the paper and an old, wrinkled $20 bill to a track lavatory matron, Evelyn Jones, with a request that Jones place the $2 bets as listed for her. She said Jones consented.

The next day or so she learned that her triple bet had paid off and was worth $5,050, Grant said. So she went to the track to get her winning ticket from the matron. But she said that Jones told her she had not been able to place the bets after all and that Jones handed her back her paper with the choices and a $20 bill. The bill, Grant said, was a new one and not the one she had had originally. Grant filed a complaint with the track.

Within about a week, Howard R. Graham, a retired restauranteur, tried to cash a winning ticket on that triple. Graham said he had placed his own bet. That ticket was the only winning triple ticket sold at Window 18.

Jones and Graham were indicted in January on charges of second-degree grand larceny and first-degree criminal possession of stolen property.

A computer printout of bets placed at Window 18 on May 21, 1974, showed that the precise series of 27 betting choices noted on Grant's paper had indeed been made that day. Track personnel also testified that the ticket produced by Graham came from Window 18. Assistant Dist. Atty. James Boland produced an expert witness, Hofstra mathematics Professor Sylvia Pines, who said the chances of two strangers deciding on their own to

*Copyright, 1976 by Newsday.

bet the same 27 choices in sequence at the same window the same day were 1,000,000,000,000,000,000,000,000,000,000,000 to 1.

The jury found Jones guilty of grand larceny and Graham guilty of criminal possession.

SMITH v. RAPID TRANSIT, INC.

Supreme Judicial Court of Massachusetts, 1945.
317 Mass. 469, 58 N.E.2d 754.

SPALDING, Justice. The decisive question in this case is whether there was evidence for the jury that the plaintiff was injured by a bus of the defendant that was operated by one of its employees in the course of his employment. If there was, the defendent concedes that the evidence warranted the submission to the jury of the question of the operator's negligence in the management of the bus. The case is here on the plaintiff's exception to the direction of a verdict for the defendant.

These facts could have been found: While the plaintiff at about 1:00 A.M. on February 6, 1941, was driving an automobile on Main Street, Winthrop, in an easterly direction toward Winthrop Highlands, she observed a bus coming toward her which she described as a "great big, long, wide affair." The bus, which was proceeding at about forty miles an hour, "forced her to turn to the right," and her automobile collided with a "parked car." The plaintiff was coming from Dorchester. The department of public utilities had issued a certificate of public convenience or necessity to the defendant for three routes in Winthrop, one of which includes Main Street, and this was in effect in February, 1941. "There was another bus line in operation in Winthrop at that time but not on Main Street." According to the defendant's time-table, buses were scheduled to leave Winthrop Highlands for Maverick Square via Main Street at 12:10 A.M., 12:45 A.M., 1:15 A.M., and 2:15 A.M. The running time for this trip at that time of night was thirty minutes.

The direction of a verdict for the defendant was right. The ownership of the bus was a matter of conjecture. While the defendant had the sole franchise for operating a bus line on Main Street, Winthrop, this did not preclude private or chartered buses from using this street; the bus in question could very well have been one operated by someone other than the defendant. It was said in Sargent v. Massachusetts Accident Co., 307 Mass. 246, at page 250, 29 N.E.2d 825, at page 827, that it is "not enough that mathematically the chances somewhat favor a proposition to be proved; for example, the fact that colored automobiles made in the current year outnumber black ones would not warrant a finding that an undescribed automobile of the current year is colored and not black, nor would the fact that only a minority of men die of cancer warrant a finding that a particular man did not die of cancer." The most that can be said of the evidence in the instant case is that perhaps the mathematical chances somewhat favor the proposition that a bus of the defendant caused the accident. This was not enough. A "proposition is proved by a preponderance of the evidence if it is made to appear more likely or probable in the sense that actual belief in its truth, derived from the evidence, exists in the mind or minds of the tribunal notwithstanding any doubts that may still linger there."

Exceptions overruled.

HART & McNAUGHTON, EVIDENCE AND
INFERENCE IN THE LAW

54–55 (1958).*

It may be suggested parenthetically at this point that, while it is clear that the law satisfies itself with less than certainty, it is not clear that the formulas mentioned above always describe correctly the degree of certainty which the law actually requires. Consider the formula that in a civil case the facts must be determined on a more-likely-than-not basis. In the first place, the probabilities are determined in a most subjective and unscientific way: the trier of fact simply asks itself which of the contesting contradictory propositions according to the trier's limited experience more nearly squares with the evidence. In the second place, the law refuses to honor its own formula when the evidence is coldly "statistical." A court would not, for example hold the government liable to a farmer for injuries inflicted on him by his mule frightened by a "buzzing" jet plane if the only evidence that the pilot was a member of the Air Force (rather than a civilian) was that most of the pilots flying jets that day were Air Force personnel. This would be true even though the farmer could shown that as much as 70 or 80 per cent of the jet pilots in the vicinity that day were of the Air Force.

The court, on the other hand, would certainly allow recovery if the evidence was that 100 per cent of the pilots were Air Force personnel, and would probably allow it if all of them were except a negligible few. Similarly, the court might allow recovery if the farmer, instead of introducing the statistical evidence, testified that he got a fleeting glimpse of the pilot's cap and that it was distinctively Air Force headgear. The court somehow feels more comfortable permitting a finding to be based on such eye-witness testimony even through the probative value of such testimony is itself determined ultimately by home-spun "statistics" in the mind of the trier of fact and even though the eye-witness testimony is probably no more indicative of the truth than is the evidence as to the proportion of Air Force pilots in the air.

Even in the case as originally stated—with the farmer producing solely the statistical evidence—the court might allow recovery if the reason for the farmer's dearth of evidence is the irrelevant fact that the government refused without justification to cooperate in the farmer's search for the offending pilot. And, though according to the more-likely-than-not formula it is irrelevant, the court might be swayed in its demand for evidence by the size of the stakes—a more elaborate presentation would naturally be expected if the farmer was claiming $100,000 in damages than if he was claiming $100.

*The Hayden Colloquium on Scientific Concept and Method edited by Daniel Lerner, Copyright, 1958 by American Academy of Arts & Sciences, Copyright, 1959 by The Free Press. Excerpts from Material by Henry M. Hart, Jr., and John McNaughton.

Chapter III

THE HEARSAY RULE

PART A.   RATIONALE AND MEANING: DEFINITIONS

The general rule excluding hearsay statements did not become firmly fixed in England until the latter part of the 17th Century. Thus Sir Walter Raleigh had his problems with hearsay earlier in that century.

Sir Walter Raleigh's Case (J. G. Phillimore, "History and Principles of the Law of Evidence," 1850, p. 157). (1603. Raleigh was tried for a conspiracy of treason to dethrone Elizabeth and to put Arabella Stuart in her place, by the aid of Spanish money and intrigue. Sir Edward Coke, attorney-general, conducted the prosecution. The principal evidence against him was the assertion of Lord Cobham, a supposed fellow-conspirator, who had betrayed Raleigh in a sworn statement made before trial. Cobham himself was in prison, and was not produced on the trial.)   *   *   *

Raleigh.   "But it is strange to see how you press me still with my Lord Cobham, and yet will not produce him; it is not for gaining of time or prolonging my life that I urge this; he is in the house hard by, and may soon be brought hither; let him be produced, and if he will yet accuse me or avow this confession of his, it shall convict me and ease you of further proof."

Lord Cecil.   "Sir Walter Raleigh presseth often that my Lord Cobham should be brought face to face; if he ask a thing of grace and favour, they must come from him only who can give them; but if he ask a matter of law, then, in order that we, who sit here as commissioners, may be satisfied, I desire to hear the opinions of my Lords, the judges, whether it may be done by law."

The Judges all answered, "that in respect it might be a mean to cover many with treasons, and might be prejudicial to the King, therefore, by the law, it was not sufferable."

Popham, C. J.   "There must not such a gap be opened for the destruction of the King as would be if we should grant this; you plead hard for yourself, but the laws plead as hard for the King. Where no circumstances do concur to make a matter probable, then an accuser may be heard; but so many circumstances agreeing and confirming the accusation in this case, the accuser is not to be produced; for, having first confessed against himself voluntarily, and so charged another person, if we shall now hear him again in person, he may, for favour or fear, retract what formerly he hath said, and the jury may, by that means, be inveigled."   *   *   *

Raleigh.—"I never had intelligence with Cobham since I came to the Tower."

Lord Cecil.—"Sir Walter Raleigh, if my Lord Cobham will now affirm, that you were acquainted with his dealings with Count Aremberg, that you knew of the letter he received, that you were the chief instigator of him, will you then be concluded by it?"

Raleigh.—"Let my Lord Cobham speak before God and the King, and deny God and the King if he speak not truly, and will then say that ever I knew of Arabella's matter, or the money out of Spain, or the Surprising Treason, I will put myself upon it."

Lord Henry Howard.—"But what if my Lord Cobham affirm anything equivalent to this; what then?"

Raleigh.—"My Lord, I put myself upon it."

Attorney-General.—"I shall now produce a witness viva voce:"

He then produced one *Dyer,* a pilot, who, being sworn, said, "Being at Lisbon, there came to me a Portuguese gentleman, who asked me how the King of England did, and whether he was crowned? I answered him, that I hoped our noble king was well, and crowned by this; but the time was not come when I came from the coast of Spain. 'Nay,' said he 'your king shall never be crowned, for Don Cobham and Don Raleigh will cut his throat before he come to be crowned.' And this, in time, was found to be spoken in mid July."

Raleigh.—"This is the saying of some wild Jesuit or beggarly priest; but what proof is it against me?"

Attorney-General.—"It must perforce arise out of some preceding intelligence, and shews that your treason had wings."   *   *   *

Thus on the single evidence of Cobham, never confronted with Raleigh, who retracted his confession, and then (according to the advocates of the Crown) recalled his retraction, did an English jury, to the amazement and horror of the bystanders, and the perpetual disgrace of the English name, find the most illustrious of their fellow subjects guilty of high treason.

UNITED STATES v. BROWN

United States Court of Appeals, Fifth Circuit, 1977.
548 F.2d 1194.

JOHN R. BROWN, Chief Judge:

This case, one of the very few in the recorded annals of the 85 year history of the Fifth Circuit, involves not the trials and tribulations, attempted frauds and other derelictions of taxpayers, which are common grist for our mill. Rather, it involves fraud by a tax preparer, one whose Twentieth Century occupation is now almost indispensable to all save those taxpayers who can use, or risk the use of, a short form with standard deductions. In this Bicentennial foray we see the hazards both to the system and to the protection of rights of the public and the individuals concerned. To be remembered is that it is the fraud or false misstatement of the preparer, not the taxpayer, which counts. Indeed, the tax properly due may be of no, or only secondary, significance.

Defendant-Appellant Amos P. Brown, Sr., a part-time income tax preparer, was convicted by a jury on 12 counts of counseling, procuring and advising the preparation and presentation of fraudulent and false United

States Individual Income Tax Returns for others in violation of 26 U.S.C.A. § 7206(2), Internal Revenue Code. * * * We find that the Trial Judge committed plain error by improperly admitting certain evidence which was highly prejudicial to the defendant. Accordingly, we reverse and remand for a new trial.

* * *

The Peacock's Tale

Among other evidence the Government also introduced the testimony of IRS agent Adrienne Peacock, who testified that between 90% and 95% of about 160 returns prepared by defendant contained overstated itemized deductions.

* * *

Hearsay
* * *

In this case, Peacock's testimony that between 90% and 95% of the returns she audited contained substantially overstated itemized deductions was introduced for the sole purpose of proving, circumstantially, the "willfulness" requirement of § 7206(2). In order to arrive at the conclusion that the deductions in these returns were overstated, Peacock's perusal of the 160 tax returns was not sufficient, since the returns obviously do not show on their face which deductions are overstated. The record shows that Peacock must have gotten her "proof" of the overstatements through conversations with each of the taxpayers audited. Presumably, the proof consisted either of statements by these taxpayers to Peacock that they all gave different information to the defendant tax preparer than defendant put down on their returns, or that they were unable to substantiate their deductions, because they did not have any (or had inadequate) supporting records. The proof might also have consisted of the fact that the IRS had legitimate disagreements with all or some of the deductions claimed. However, a prerequisite to this form of proof would be the initial conversation between Peacock and each taxpayer, so that Peacock could determine the bases for the deductions claimed.

The point to be emphasized, therefore, is that the information obtained by Peacock from the out-of-court statements made by the 160 taxpayers whose returns she audited, was absolutely vital to her ultimate in-court conclusion that between 90% and 95% of the 160 returns she audited contained substantially overstated itemized deductions. Because her testimony had to have been based directly on the out-of-court statements of these taxpayers, defendant had no opportunity to test their ultimate assumptions through cross-examination. He obviously could not cross-examine the taxpayers concerned, because they were not in court. He could not even cross-examine Peacock adequately, because she did not have with her any of the records of conversations she had had with these taxpayers, but was testifying solely from memory, in the most general, amorphous terms. Thus, the jury had no way to examine the trustworthiness of Peacock's testimony, because it could not examine the statements of the declarant taxpayers or others on which Peacock's testimony was directly and substantially founded. Given the rationale of the hearsay rule, a clearer case of hearsay testimony would be difficult to imagine.[20]

* * *

The judgement of conviction against defendant is reversed, and the case remanded for new trial on all counts.

Reversed and remanded.

GEE, Circuit Judge, dissenting:

* * *

Hearsay

The majority's characterization of Agent Peacock's testimony as "hearsay" represents an unprecedented departure from usual hearsay concepts * * * Agent Peacock's statements at trial were (1) that she personally audited all but two or three of the 163 tax returns prepared by appellant and audited by IRS, and (2) that her audit had determined that 90 to 95 percent of those returns contained overstated itemized deductions disallowed under IRS standards. Agent Peacock obviously testified from her own personal knowledge about the results of tax audits she conducted. In her testimony she neither related nor relied upon out-of-court statements by other persons.

It is too plain for argument that Peacock's testimony as to what she knew herself from the returns she individually audited does not fall within Rule 801's hearsay definition. An examination of the record reveals that *all* of Peacock's testimony was based on knowledge she personally acquired while auditing the tax returns prepared by Brown. In fact, the majority points to no *statement* whatever by Agent Peacock which it claims contains hearsay; she mentioned no statements others had made to her during the course of her audit. The majority objects, however, that Agent Peacock's audit necessarily rested on " 'proof' of the overstatements through conversations with each of the taxpayers audited." Since her testimony had to have been based directly on the out-of-court statements of these taxpayers who could not be cross-examined, it is said that "a clearer case of hearsay testimony would be difficult to imagine." I find little difficulty in doing so.

* * *

TRIBE, TRIANGULATING HEARSAY

87 Harvard Law Review 957, 958-61 (1974).*
[Some footnotes omitted.]

I. THE TESTIMONIAL TRIANGLE

The basic hearsay problem is that of forging a reliable chain of inferences, from an act or utterance of a person not subject to contem-

---

20.　Peacock's testimony also inescapably presented by implication the facts leading to her conclusion which she got from other nontestifying declarants, such as the taxpayers concerned. The implication was strong that she satisfied herself from talking to others that what the preparer entered was not what the taxpayer told him. It was an implied assertion that the defen-dant was responsible for the repetitious acts or practices from which the jury could infer the requisite willfulness. It was an assertion, in other words, of the ultimate fact that these faulty returns were due to defendant's acts.

poraneous in-court cross-examination about that act or utterance, to an event that the act or utterance is supposed to reflect. Typically, the first link in the required chain of inferences is the link from the act or utterance to the belief it is thought to express or indicate. It is helpful to think of this link as involving a "trip" into the head of the person responsible for the act or utterance (the declarant) to see what he or she was really thinking when the act occurred. The second link is the one from the declarant's assumed belief to a conclusion about some external event that is supposed to have triggered the belief, or that is linked to the belief in some other way. This link involves a trip out of the head of the declarant, in order to match the declarant's assumed belief with the external reality sought to be demonstrated.

The trier must obviously employ such a chain of inferences whenever a witness testifies in court. But the process has long been regarded as particularly suspect when the act or utterance is not one made in court, under oath, by a person whose demeanor at the time is witnessed by the trier, and under circumstances permitting immediate cross-examination by counsel in order to probe possible inaccuracies in the inferential chain. These inaccuracies are usually attributed to the four testimonial infirmities of ambiguity, insincerity, faulty perception, and erroneous memory. In the absence of special reasons, the perceived untrustworthiness of such an out-of-court act or utterance has lead the Anglo-Saxon legal system to exclude it as hearsay despite its potentially probative value.

There exists a rather simple way of schematizing all of this in terms of an elementary geometric construct that serves to structure its several related elements. The construct might be called the Testimonial Triangle. By making graphic the path of inferences, and by functionally grouping the problems encountered along the path, the triangle makes it easier both to identify when a hearsay problem exists and to structure consideration of the appropriateness of exceptions to the rule that bars hearsay inferences.

The diagram is as follows:

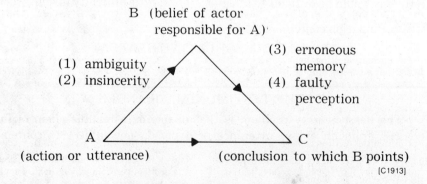

B (belief of actor
responsible for A)

(1) ambiguity
(2) insincerity

(3) erroneous
memory
(4) faulty
perception

A
(action or utterance)

C
(conclusion to which B points)

[C1913]

If we use the diagram to trace the inferential path the trier must follow, we begin at the lower left vertex of the triangle (A), which represents the declarant's (X's) act or assertion. The path first takes us to the upper vertex (B), representing X's belief in what his or her act or assertion suggests, and then takes us to the lower right vertex (C), representing the external reality suggested by X's belief. When "A" is used to prove "C" along the path through "B," a traditional hearsay problem exists and the use of the act or assertion as evidence is disallowed upon proper objection in the absence of some special reason to permit it.

It is of course a simple matter to locate the four testimonial infirmities on the triangle to show where and how they might impede the process of inference. To go from "A" to "B," the declarant's belief, one must remove the obstacles of (1) ambiguity and (2) insincerity. To go from "B" to "C," the external fact, one must further remove the obstacles of (3) erroneous memory and (4) faulty perception.

When it is possible to go directly from "A" to "C" with no detour through "B," there is no hearsay problem unless the validity of the trier's conclusion depends upon an implicit path through "B."[1] Suppose, for example, that the issue in a lawsuit is whether the Government took adequate safety precautions in connection with the nuclear test at Amchitka in 1971. James Schlesinger, then Chairman of the Atomic Energy Commission, "told reporters at Elmendorf Air Force Base outside Anchorage that he was taking his wife * * * and daughters * * * with him [to the site of the Amchitka blast] in response to Alaska Gov. William E. Egan's invitation. Egan strongly disapprove[d] of the test."[2] In these circumstances, the trip from "A," the Chairman's proposed travel with his family to the site of the blast, to "C," the conclusion that the blast was reasonably safe, may appear at first to be purely "circumstantial," but in fact that trip requires a journey into the Chairman's head and out again—a journey through the belief "B" suggested by his willingness to be near the blast with his family. The journey from "A" to "B" involves problems of possible ambiguity and of insincerity in that the Chairman was apparently seeking to dispel fears of danger, so that his act may not bespeak an actual belief in the test's safety. And the journey from "B" to "C" involves problems of memory and perception in that he may not have recalled all the relevant data and may have misperceived such data in the first instance, so that his belief in the test's safety, even if we assume the journey from "A" to "B" safely completed, may not correspond to the facts sought to be demonstrated. On both legs of the triangle, therefore, there are testimonial infirmities that cross-examination contemporaneous with the act "A" could help to expose.

---

1.   An uncompromising behaviorist might insist that no detour through mental states is ever necessary because every trip from an act or utterance "A" to a conclusion "C" is reducible to a circumstantial inference about the statistical frequency with which "C" is present when "A" is present. There are difficulties with accepting the behaviorist perspective as a coherent one. See Chomsky, A Review of B.F. Skinner's Verbal Behavior, 35 Language 26 (1959); Chomsky, The Case Against B.F. Skinner, New York Review of Books, Dec. 30, 1971, at 18. But even if one does adopt such a perspective, it does not follow that the trier's way of using the evidence "A" will in fact mirror that perspective, for the trier is likely to reason about states of mind even if it is in some sense incorrect or unnecessary

to do so. Moreover, the connection between "A" and "C" may well be such that the frequency with which the latter accompanies the former depends upon the actor's testimonial capacities so that, even from a behaviorist perspective, information about a declarant's use of language, tendency to lie, eyesight, and so forth, may increase or decrease the statistical correlation between the utterance and the fact reported.

2.   Boston Globe, Nov. 5, 1971, at 16. The fact pattern of the Amchitka example is remarkably similar to a hypothetical presented by Baron Parke in his opinion in Wright v. Doe dem. Tatham, 7 Ad. & E. 313, 388, 112 Eng. Rep. 488, 516 (K.B. 1837) (experienced ship captain inspecting and setting sail on a ship).

By contrast, when the trier's inference can proceed from "A" directly to "C," the infirmities of hearsay do not arise. For example, the out-of-court statement "I can speak" would be admissible as nonhearsay to prove that the declarant was capable of speech, for it is the fact of his speaking rather than the content of the statement which permits the inference, and that involves no problems of the statement's ambiguity, or of sincerity, memory, or perception.

WHEATON, WHAT IS HEARSAY?

46 Iowa L.Rev. 207, 210–11 (1961).*
[Footnotes omitted.]

I. Definitions

None of the many attempts to define hearsay has produced a generally accepted definition. Scholars have usually been in closer agreement on what constitutes hearsay than have the courts. Dean Ladd has stated that hearsay consists of a statement or assertive conduct which was made or occurred out of court and is offered in court to prove the truth of the facts asserted. Dean McCormick has defined hearsay as testimony in court, or written evidence, of a statement made out of court, such evidence being offered as an assertion to show the truth of matters asserted therein, and which thus rests for its value upon the credibility of the out-of-court asserter. A definition fairly representing the position of Professor Morgan is that hearsay includes the evidence of any conduct of a person, verbal or nonverbal, which he intended to operate as an assertion, if it is used to prove that the assertion is true or that the asserter believes it is true, unless it is subject to cross-examination by the one against whom it is used at the trial at which it is offered. Morgan would also include as hearsay any conduct not intended as an assertion if it is offered to prove both the state of mind of such person and the external event or condition which caused him to have that state of mind. Wigmore has emphasized the importance of the lack of opportunity to cross-examine the declarant as the primary characteristic of hearsay.

While it has been contended that hearsay involves an intention to communicate, Professor Morgan has correctly pointed out that an utterance may be hearsay although there is no intent that it be a communication of thought. For example, when the writer of a letter files it away and the letter is found after the writer's death, the use of the letter to prove the truth of its contents would be an offer of hearsay evidence. Similarly, use of statements overheard from a soliloquy to prove the truth of those statements would involve hearsay.

Judicial definitions of hearsay have been many and varied, perhaps making up in variety for their apparently frequent lack of concision. The lack of consistency may be due to a tendency to define hearsay to meet the requirements of the case before the court. For example, it has been said that hearsay is evidence which derives its value, not solely from the credit to be given the witness upon the stand, but partly from the veracity and competency of some other person. Another court has held that the hearsay rule of exclusion applies only to extra-judicial utterances offered as evidence of

*Copyright 1960–1961 by State University of
Iowa (Iowa Law Review).

the truth of the matter asserted. Further, one court has said that statements are called hearsay because they are not made in court under the sanctity of an oath.

Proposed definitions of hearsay are also found in the Model Code of Evidence and the Uniform Rules of Evidence. Rule 501(1) of the Code states essentially that a hearsay statement includes both conduct found by the judge to have been intended by the person making the statement to operate as an assertion by him, and conduct of which evidence is offered for a purpose requiring an assumption that it was so intended. Rule 501(2) states that a hearsay statement is a statement of which evidence is offered as tending to prove the truth of the matter intended to be asserted or assumed to be so intended except a statement made by a witness in the process of testifying at the present trial or contained in a deposition or other record of testimony taken and recorded pursuant to law for use at the present trial. Rule 62(1) of the Uniform Rules of Evidence says that "statement" includes not only an oral or written expression but also nonverbal conduct of a person intended by him as a substitute for words in expressing the matter stated. Uniform Rule 63 provides that evidence of a statement which is made other than by a witness while testifying at the hearing offered to prove the truth of the matter stated is hearsay evidence.

From these and other definitions, there seems to be agreement that hearsay must be a statement or other communicative conduct offered to prove the truth of the matter asserted. This presupposes a lack of personal knowledge of the truth of the matter asserted on the part of the witness. To qualify as hearsay, the declaration must have been made out of court, at least in the sense that it was not made at the hearing at which it is offered in evidence.

———

See Federal Rules of Evidence 801(b), (c), 802, at pp. 921, 922; California Evidence Code § 1200, at p. 877.

MORGAN, HEARSAY DANGERS AND THE APPLICATION OF THE HEARSAY CONCEPT

62 Harv.L.Rev. 177, 192-93 (1948),* in Selected Writings on
Evidence and Trial, 764, 774-75 (1957).**
[Footnotes omitted.]

Prior Declarations of Witness.—

* * * But there is one situation where the courts are prone to call hearsay what does not in fact involve in any substantial degree any of the hearsay risks. When the Declarant is also a witness, it is difficult to justify classifying as hearsay evidence of his own prior statements. This is especially true where Declarant as a witness is giving as part of his testimony his own prior statement. Although there are numerous dicta accepting Greenleaf's statement that hearsay is "that kind of evidence which does not derive its value solely from the credit to be given to the witness himself, but rests also, in part, on the veracity and competency of some other person," the dictum rarely becomes decision. The courts declare the prior statement

*Copyright, 1948, 1949 By The Harvard Law　　**West Publishing Co., St. Paul, 1957.
　Review Association.

to be hearsay because it was not made under oath, subject to the penalty for perjury or to the test of cross-examination. To which the answer might well be: "The declarant as a witness is now under oath and now purports to remember and narrate accurately. The adversary can now expose every element that may carry a danger of misleading the trier of fact both in the previous statement and in the present testimony, and the trier can judge whether both the previous declaration and the present testimony are reliable in whole or in part." To this Mr. Justice Stone of the Minnesota Supreme Court, speaking of evidence of prior contradictory statements, has framed this reply:

> The chief merit of cross-examination is not that at some future time it gives the party opponent the right to dissect adverse testimony. Its principal virtue is in its immediate application of the testing process. Its strokes fall while the iron is hot. False testimony is apt to harden and become unyielding to the blows of truth in proportion as the witness has opportunity for reconsideration and influence by the suggestions of others, whose interest may be, and often is, to maintain falsehood rather than truth.

He adds "practical reasons" that receipt of such evidence would create temptation and opportunity to manufacture evidence and entrap witnesses, and would require admission of prior consistent statements. Why does falsehood harden any more quickly or unyieldingly than truth? What has become of the idea that truth is eternal and, though crushed to earth, will rise again? Isn't the opportunity for reconsideration and for baneful influence by others even more likely to color the later testimony than the prior statement? Furthermore, it must be remembered that the trier of fact is often permitted to hear these prior statements to impeach or rehabilitate the declarant-witness. In such event, of course, the trier will be told that he must not treat the statement as evidence of the truth of the matter stated. But to what practical effect? Wasn't Judge Swan right in saying, "Practically, men will often believe that if a witness has earlier sworn to the opposite of what he now swears to, he was speaking the truth when he first testified"? Do the judges deceive themselves or do they realize that they are indulging in a pious fraud? * * *

SUBRAMANIAM v. PUBLIC PROSECUTOR

Judicial Committee of the Privy Council, 1956.
100 Solicitor's Journal 566.

This was an appeal, by special leave, by Subramaniam, a rubber tapper, from an order of the Supreme Court of the Federation of Malaya (Court of Appeal at Kuala Lumpur), dated 12th September, 1955, dismissing his appeal against a judgment and order of the High Court of Johore Bahru, whereby he was found guilty on a charge of being in possession of twenty rounds of ammunition without lawful authority, contrary to reg. 4 (1) (*b*) of the Emergency Regulations, 1951, and sentenced to death. It was common ground that on 29th April, 1955, at a place in the Rengam District in the State of Johore, the appellant was found in a wounded condition by certain members of the security forces; that when he was searched there was found around his waist a leather belt with three pouches containing twenty live rounds of ammunition. The defense put forward was that he had been captured by terrorists, that at all material times he was acting under duress, and that at the time of his capture by the security forces he had formed the intention to surrender, with which intention he had come to the place where he was found. He gave evidence describing his capture and sought to give evidence of what the terrorists said to him, but the trial judge ruled that evidence of the conversation with the terrorists was not admissible unless they were called. The judge said that he could find no evidence of duress, and in the result the appellant, as stated, was convicted.

Mr. L. M. D. De Silva, giving the judgment, said that the trial judge was in error in ruling out peremptorily the evidence of conversation between the terrorists and the appellant. Evidence of a statement made to a witness by a person who was not himself called as a witness might or might not be hearsay. It was hearsay and inadmissible when the object of the evidence was to establish the truth of what was contained in the statement. It was not hearsay and was admissible when it was proposed to establish by the evidence, not the truth of the statement, but the fact that it was made. Statements could have been made to the apellant by the terrorists which, whether true or not, if they had been believed by the appellant, might, within the meaning of s. 94 of the Penal Code of the Federated Malay States, reasonably have induced in him an apprehension of instant death if he failed to conform to their wishes. Thus a complete, or substantially complete, version according to the appellant of what was said to him by the terrorists and by him to them had been shut out, and their lordships had to consider whether, in the circumstances of this case, that exclusion of admissible evidence afforded sufficient reason for allowing the appeal. In Muhammad Nawaz v. King-Emperor (1941), L.R. 68 I.A. 126, at p. 128, it was said: "Broadly speaking, the Judicial Committee will only interfere where there has been an infringement of the essential principles of justice. An obvious example would be * * * where [the accused] was not allowed to call relevant witnesses." In the present case the appellant had not been allowed to give relevant and admissible evidence, which was a circumstance very similar in its consequence to not being allowed "to call relevant witnesses." The appellant's version, if believed, could and might have afforded cogent evidence of duress brought to bear on him. He had not been allowed to give relevant and admissible evidence, and it could not be held with any confidence that had the excluded evidence, which went to the very root of the defense of duress, been admitted, the result of the trial would probably have been the same. Their lordships, for those reasons, had humbly advised Her Majesty that the appeal should be allowed.

SAFEWAY STORES, INC. v. COMBS

United States Court of Appeals, Fifth Circuit, 1960.
273 F.2d 295.

Before HUTCHESON, JONES and WISDOM, Circuit Judges.

WISDOM, Circuit Judge. This is a slip-and-fall case.

Mrs. Louella Combs was shopping in a Safeway Store in El Paso, Texas, when she stepped into a puddle of ketchup that had spilled on the floor from a broken bottle. Mr. and Mrs. Combs sued Safeway Stores, Inc., alleging that the defendant was negligent in creating a hazardous condition; in failing to remove the ketchup or in failing to isolate the hazardous condition by placing a barrier around the ketchup; in failing to warn Mrs. Combs of the presence of the ketchup; and in allowing the ketchup to remain on the floor in the immediate vicinity of an eye-catching advertising display that would divert one's attention from the ketchup puddle. Safeway Stores relies upon Mrs. Combs' alleged failure to keep a proper lookout, failure to heed an alleged warning, and on the contention that the hazard, such as it was, was open and obvious.

The case was tried to a jury. The jury rendered a verdict for the plaintiff for $24,500. Judgment was entered upon the verdict. Safeway Stores appealed, citing thirteen specifications of error. We consider two of these specifications of error as meritorious and sufficiently grave to require that the case be reversed and remanded for a new trial.

I.

Safeway contended that Mrs. Combs failed to heed timely warnings. In support of this contention, Kenneth Tunnell, the Safeway Manager, testified that he saw Mrs. Combs walking toward the ketchup and that he called out to her, "Please don't step in that ketchup." At that time he was about ten feet from her. Mrs. Tunnell, the manager's wife, was in the store at the time of the accident. She testified that she saw the broken bottle, left her shopping buggy, and told her husband that there was a broken bottle of ketchup in the frozen-food aisle. He stopped what he was doing, hurried toward the ketchup bottle, picked up the glass, then started toward the back to get a mop. As he came out with a mop she heard him call out. She understood what he said. When she was asked what he had said, plaintiff's
• counsel objected that the question called for hearsay. The trial judge sustained the objection and refused to permit the question to be answered. Had she been permitted to answer—it was stipulated—she would have testified that Tunnell said, "Lady, please don't step in that ketchup".

The hearsay rule is inapplicable to an utterance proved as an operative fact. Tunnell's utterance was a probative verbal act bearing on the critical objective fact whether there was a warning from the defendant, bearing on the plaintiff's state of mind as to notice and knowledge at the danger. The witness testified from her personal knowledge.   *   *   *

Tunnell's warning—if he gave a warning—was a prime element in the defense. The jury was entitled to know if he gave it, and to weigh it with the other evidence. Failure to permit Mrs. Tunnell to testify as to the fact of the warning deprived the defendant of the opportunity of showing whether the plaintiff exercised due care. The trial judge's ruling on this point is sufficient in itself to require the Court to reverse and remand.

[Discussion of the second claimed error is omitted.]

*   *   *

In view of these errors below, we reverse the judgment and remand the case for a new trial.

HANSON v. JOHNSON

Supreme Court of Minnesota, 1924.
161 Minn. 229, 201 N.W. 322.

[Action for conversion. The trial judge, sitting without a jury, gave judgment for plaintiff and the defendants appealed—Ed.]

WILSON, C.J. ＊ ＊ ＊ It is claimed that the court erred in the reception of evidence. Plaintiff owned and leased a farm to one Schrik under a written lease, the terms of which gave plaintiff two-fifths of the corn grown. The tenant gave a mortgage to defendant bank on his share of the crops. The tenant's mortgaged property was sold at auction by the bank with his permission. At this sale a crib of corn containing 393 bushels was sold by the bank to defendant Johnson. If plaintiff owned the corn it was converted by defendants.

1. In an effort to prove that the corn was owned by plaintiff, and that it was a part of his share, he testified over the objection of hearsay and self-serving, that when the tenant was about through husking corn he was on the farm and the tenant pointed out the corn in question (and a double crib of corn) and said:

> "Mr. Hanson, here is your corn for this year, this double crib here and this single crib here is your share for this year's corn; this belongs to you, Mr. Hanson."

A bystander was called, and against the same objection testified to having heard the talk in substantially the same language.

There is no question but that plaintiff owned some corn. It was necessary to identify it. The division made his share definite. This division and identity was made by the acts of tenant in husking the corn and putting it in separate cribs and then his telling Hanson which was his share, and the latter's acquiescence therein. The language of the tenant was the very fact necessary to be proved. The verbal part of the transaction between plaintiff and the tenant was necessary to prove the fact. The words were the verbal acts. They aid in giving legal significance to the conduct of the parties. They accompanied the conduct. There could be no division without words or gestures identifying the respective shares. This was a fact to be shown in the chain of proof of title. It was competent evidence. It was not hearsay nor self-serving. As between plaintiff and the tenant, this evidence would be admissible. It was original evidence. The issues here being between different persons does not change the rule.

＊ ＊ ＊ There is evidence to sustain the findings of the court, and the record is free from error.

Affirmed.

STRAHORN, A RECONSIDERATION OF THE HEARSAY RULE AND ADMISSIONS

85 U.Pa.L.Rev. 484, 490 (1937).＊

Utterances as operative conduct

If the making of the utterance is the ultimate thing sought to be proven in the case, rather than a device for proving that thing, the suspicion of hearsay attaches the least. So it is that the topic of utterances as operative conduct is the one of simplest application under the hearsay rule. No question of possible testimonial or narrative use can arise when the speaking of the words determines the rights being litigated. Thus it is that such typical examples as the making of a promise, the speaking of a slander, the printing of a libel, the speaking of marriage vows are all species of extra-judicial utterances provable despite the hearsay rule because they are the operative conduct of the speaker. For them there is no possible question of the trustworthiness of the utterance.   *   *   *

BRIDGES v. STATE

Supreme Court of Wisconsin, 1945.
247 Wis. 350, 19 N.W.2d 529.

[Defendant was convicted of taking indecent liberties with a child under the age of 16 years. Sharon Schunk, age seven. She was abused by a man in an Army uniform at his house, and the serious question was identification of defendant as that person. This identification in part depended upon whether the house to which Sharon had been taken by her assaulter was the house at 125 East Johnson Street in which defendant concededly resided at the relevant time—Ed.]

FRITZ, Justice. *   *   * This is one of those cases that always gives us great concern. Taking all of her testimony into consideration, it is evident that although the 7 year old complaining witness, Sharon, is apparently somewhat brighter than the average child of her age, her testimony is subject to infirmities that testimony of such children generally is subject to. However, on close analysis and due consideration thereof in connection with many facts established indisputably by other evidence, Sharon's testimony does not appear to be so contradictory as to impair its credibility as a matter of law. The statements made by her to her mother and police officers, prior to their discovery of the location of defendant's room, as to the general appearance of the steps to the porch and the front entrance doors of the house to which she had been taken on February 26, 1945, were fairly accurate for a child of her age and limited schooling and vocabulary, and her first description of the room and articles therein was not too much out of line, although it was not distinctive enough to be of much value either way.

*   *   * Defendant contends the court erred also in admitting testimony by police officers as to matters stated by Sharon in defendant's absence. He claims these statements were hearsay evidence and therefore were not admissible. *   *   * There is testimony by police officers and also Mrs. Schunk as to statements which were made to them by Sharon on February 26 and 27, 1945, and also during the course of their subsequent investigations to ascertain the identity of the man who committed the offense and of the house and room in which it was committed. In those statements she spoke, as hereinbefore stated, of various matters and features which she remembered and which were descriptive of the exterior and surroundings of the house; and of the room and various articles and the location thereof therein. It is true that testimony as to such statements was hearsay and, as such, inadmissible if the purpose for which it was received had been to establish thereby that there were in fact the stated articles in the room, or that they were located as stated, or that the exterior features or surroundings of the house were as Sharon stated. That, however, was not in this case the purpose for which the evidence as to those statements was admitted. It was admissible in so far as the fact that she had made the statements can be deemed to tend to show that at the time those statements were made —which was a month prior to the subsequent discovery of the room and

house at 125 East Johnson Street—she had knowledge as to articles and descriptive features which, as was proven by other evidence, were in fact in or about that room and house. If in relation thereto Sharon made the statements as to which the officers and her mother testified, then those statements, although they were extra judicial utterances, constituted at least circumstantial evidence that she then had such knowledge; and that such state of mind on her part was acquired by reason of her having been in that room and house prior to making the statements.   *   *   *

Hypotheticals

(1)   X is prosecuted for assault with a deadly weapon on A by use of a billiard cue. X's defense is self-defense. In rebuttal the prosecution calls B, who proposes to testify that a week before the fight A told him that X had struck him several times with a baseball bat a month before, because A had said "hello" to X's girl friend at a party. X makes a hearsay objection to B's testimony.

(2)   X is prosecuted for murder of A, his girl friend. A died from a bullet wound received while in X's apartment. X's defense is that he was showing a pistol to A at her request and that he handed her the pistol and it accidentally went off as she was handling it. The prosecution calls B who proposes to testify that a week before A's death, A told him that X had threatened to kill her because she was trying to break up her relationship with X. X objects to B's testimony as hearsay.

(3)   X is prosecuted for the murder of A, his wife. It is undisputed that while A was seated in a chair watching television, X pulled a pistol from his pocket and fired three shots into A, killing her instantly. In order to negate the intent requisite for first degree murder, X testifies to a history of marital difficulties, which he claims impaired his mental condition. In rebuttal, to prove A's state of mind shortly before her death, the prosecution calls B, who proposes to testify that in a telephone conversation with A on the day before her death, A said, "I know X is going to kill me. I wish he would hurry up and get it over with, because he will never let me leave him." X objects to B's proposed testimony on the grounds of hearsay.

WRIGHT v. DOE d. TATHAM

Exchequer Chamber, 1837.
7 Ad. & El. 313.

[This was an action by Tatham as heir at law to recover properties formerly belonging to Marsden, deceased. Wright, formerly a servant of Marsden, claimed as devisee. The issue was whether Marsden was mentally competent to make a will. The trial judge excluded three letters which had been written to Marsden which were offered as evidence that Marsden was sane. One of these letters concerned an important business matter, requesting Marsden to direct his attorney to negotiate for the settlement of a dispute between Marsden and a parish. The other two letters were essentially social. The House of Lords put a question to the judges as to the admissibility of these letters. This litigation was protracted, apparently arousing strong feelings, in England.]

*   *   *   First, then, were all or any of these letters admissible on the issue in the cause as acts done by the writers, assuming, for the sake of argument, that there was no proof of any act done by the testator upon or relating to these letters or any of them,—that is, would such letters or any of them be evidence of the testator's competence at the time of writing them, if sent to the testator's house and not opened or read by him?

Indeed this question is just the same as if the letters had been intercepted before their arrival at his house; for, in so far as the writing and sending the letters by their respective writers were acts done by them towards the testator, those acts would in the two supposed cases be actually complete. It is argued that the letters would be admissible because they are evidence of the *treatment* of the testator *as* a competent person by individuals acquainted with his habits and personal character, not using the word *treatment* in a sense involving any *conduct* of the testator himself; that they are more than mere statements to a third person indicating an opinion of his competence by those persons; they are acts done *towards* the testator by them, which would not have been done if he had been incompetent, and from which, therefore, a legitimate inference may, it is argued, be derived that he was so.

Each of the three letters, no doubt, indicates that in the opinion of the writer the testator was a rational person. He is spoken of in respectful terms in all. Mr. *Ellershaw* describes him as possessing hospitality and benevolent politeness; and Mr. *Marton* addresses him as competent to do business to the limited extent to which his letter calls upon him to act; and there is no question but that, if any one of those writers had been living, his evidence, founded on personal observation, that the testator possessed the qualities which justified the opinion expressed or implied in his letters, would be admissible on this issue. But the point to be determined is, whether *these letters* are admissible as proof that *he did possess these qualities?*

I am of opinion that, according to the established principles of the law of evidence, the letters are all inadmissible for such a purpose. One great principle in this law is, that all facts which are relevant to the issue may be proved; another is, that all such facts as have not been admitted by the party against whom they are offered, or some one under whom he claims, ought to be proved under the sanction of an oath (or its equivalent introduced by statute, a solemn affirmation), either on the trial of the issue or some other issue involving the same question between the same parties or those to whom they are privy.

[T]he question is, whether the contents of these letters are evidence of the *fact to be proved upon this issue,*—that is, the actual existence of the qualities which the testator is, in those letters, by implication, stated to possess: and those letters may be considered in this respect to be on the same footing as if they had contained a direct and positive statement that he was competent. *For this purpose* they are mere hearsay evidence, statements of the writers, not on oath, of the truth of the matter in question, with this addition, that they have acted upon the statements on the faith of their being true, by their sending the letters to the testator. That the so acting cannot give a sufficient sanction for the truth of the statement is perfectly plain; for it is clear that, if the same statements had been made by parol or in writing to a third person, that would have been insufficient; and this is conceded by the learned counsel for the plaintiff in error. Yet in both cases there has been an acting on the belief of the truth, by making the statement, or writing and sending a letter *to* a third person; and what difference can it possibly make that this is an acting of the same nature by writing and sending the letter *to* the testator? It is admitted, and most properly, that you have no right to use in evidence the fact of writing and sending a letter to a third person containing a statement of competence, on the ground that it affords an inference that such an act would not have been done unless the statement was true, or believed to be true, although such an inference no doubt would be raised in the conduct of the ordinary affairs of life, if the statement were made by a man of veracity. But it cannot be raised in a judicial inquiry; and, if such an argument were admissible, it would lead to the indiscriminate admission of hearsay evidence of all manner of facts.

Further, it is clear that an acting to a much greater extent and degree upon such statements to a third person would not make the statements admissible. For example, if a wager to a large amount had been made as to the matter in issue by two third persons, the payment of that wager, however large the sum, would not be admissible to prove the truth of the matter in issue. You would not have had any right to present it to the jury as raising an inference of the truth of the fact, on the ground that otherwise the bet would not have been paid. It is, after all, nothing but the *mere statement* of that fact, with strong evidence of the belief of it by the party making it. Could it make any difference that the wager was between the third person and one of the parties to the suit? Certainly not. The payment by other underwriters on the same policy to the plaintiff could not be given in evidence to prove that the subject insured had been lost. Yet there is an act done, a payment strongly attesting the truth of the statement, which it implies, that there had been a loss. To illustrate this point still further, let us suppose a third person had betted a wager with Mr. *Marsden* that he could not solve some mathematical problem, the solution of which required a high degree of capacity; would payment of that wager to Mr. *Marsden*'s banker be admissible evidence that he possessed that capacity? The answer is certain; it would not. It would be evidence of the fact of competence given by a third party not upon oath.

Let us suppose the parties who wrote these letters to have stated the matter therein contained, that is, their knowledge of his personal qualities and capacity for business, on oath before a magistrate, or in some judicial proceeding to which the plaintiff and defendant were not parties. No one could contend that such statement would be admissible on this issue; and yet there would have been an act done on the faith of the statement being true, and a very solemn one, which would raise in the ordinary conduct of affairs a strong belief in the truth of the statement, if the writers were faith-worthy. The acting in this case is of much less importance, and certainly is not equal to the sanction of an extra-judicial oath.

Many other instances of a similar nature, by way of illustration, were suggested by the learned counsel for the defendant in error, which, on the most cursory consideration, any one would at once declare to be inadmissible in evidence. Others were supposed on the part of the plaintiff in error, which, at first sight, have the appearance of being mere facts, and therefore admissible, though on further consideration they are open to precisely the same objection. Of the first description are the supposed cases of a letter by a third person to any one demanding a debt, which may be said to be a treatment of him *as a debtor,* being offered as proof that the debt was really due; a note, congratulating him on his high state of bodily vigour, being proposed as evidence of his being in good health; both of which are manifestly at first sight objectionable. To the latter class belong the supposed conduct of the family or relations of a testator, taking the same precautions in his absence as if he were a lunatic; his election, in his absence, to some high and responsible office; the conduct of a physician who permitted a will to be executed by a sick testator; the conduct of a deceased captain on a question of seaworthiness, who, after examining every part of the vessel, embarked in it with his family; all these, when deliberately considered, are, with reference to the matter in issue in each case, mere instances of hearsay evidence, mere statements, not on oath, but implied in or vouched by the actual conduct of persons by whose acts the litigant parties are not to be bound.

The conclusion at which I have arrived is, that proof of a particular fact, which is not of itself a matter in issue, but which is relevant only as implying a statement or opinion of a third person on the matter in issue, is inadmissible in all cases where such a statement or opinion not on oath would be of itself inadmissible; and, therefore, in this case the letters which are offered only to prove the competence of the testator, that is the truth of the implied statements therein contained, were properly rejected, as the mere statement or opinion of the writer would certainly have been inadmissible.

* * *

[The letters were held inadmissible in this court and on appeal to the House of Lords, 5 Clark & Finnelly 670.]

COMMONWEALTH v. KNAPP

Supreme Judicial Court of Massachusetts, 1830.
VII American State Trials 395, 515–516.

[John Francis Knapp was tried in 1830 for the murder of one Joseph White. The prosecution, headed by Daniel Webster, claimed that Knapp aided and abetted one Crowninshield, who actually struck the fatal blows. It was therefore crucial to the prosecution to show Crowninshield's guilt —even though Crowninshield himself had committed suicide before the trial. In his closing argument, Daniel Webster discussed the probative value of the suicide on the issue of Crowninshield's guilt—Ed.]

The fatal blow is given! and the victim passes, without a struggle or a motion, from the repose of sleep to the repose of death! It is the assassin's purpose to make sure work, and he yet plies the dagger, though it was obvious that life had been destroyed by the blow of the bludgeon. He even raises the aged arm, that he may not fail in his aim at the heart, and replaces it again over the wounds of the poignard! To finish the picture, he explores the wrist for the pulse! he feels it, and ascertains that it beats no longer! It is accomplished. The deed is done. He retreats, retraces his steps to the window, passes out through it, as he came in, and escapes. He has done the murder—no eye has seen him, no ear has heard him. The secret is his own, and it is safe!

Ah! gentlemen, that was a dreadful mistake. Such a secret can be safe nowhere. The whole creation of God has neither nook nor corner, where the guilty can bestow it, and say it is safe. Not to speak of that eye which glances through all disguises, and beholds everything, as in the splendor of noon, such secrets of guilt are never safe from detection, even by men. True it is, generally speaking, that "murder will out." True it is, that Providence hath so ordained, and doth so govern things, that those who break the great law of heaven, by shedding man's blood, seldom succeed in avoiding discovery. Especially, in a case exciting so much attention as this, discovery must come, and will come, sooner or later. A thousand eyes turn at once to explore every man, every thing, every circumstance, connected with the time and place; a thousand ears catch every whisper; a thousand excited minds intensely dwell on the scene, shedding all their light, and ready to kindle the slightest circumstance into a blaze of discovery. Meantime the guilty soul cannot keep its own secret. It is false to itself; or rather it feels an irresistible impulse of conscience to be true to itself. It labors under its guilty possession, and knows not what to do with it. The human heart was not made for the residence of such an inhabitant. It finds itself preyed on by a torment which it does not acknowledge to God nor man. A vulture is devouring it, and it can ask no sympathy or assistance, either from heaven or earth. The secret which the murderer possesses soon comes to possess him; and, like the evil spirits of which we read, it overcomes him, and leads him whithersoever it will. He feels it beating at his heart, rising to his throat, and demanding disclosure. He thinks the whole world sees it in his face, reads it in his eyes, and almost hears its workings in the very silence of his thoughts. It has become his master. It betrays his discretion, it breaks down his courage, it conquers his prudence. When suspicions, from without, begin to embarrass him, and the net of circumstance to entangle him, the fatal secret struggles with still greater violence to burst forth. It must be confessed, it will be confessed; there is no refuge from confession but suicide, and suicide is confession.

MORTON, THE ROTHSCHILDS*

49-50 (1962).

And there was no news more precious than the outcome of Waterloo. For days the London 'Change[1] had strained its ears. If Napoleon won, English consols[2] were bound to drop. If he lost, the enemy empire would shatter and consols rise.

For thirty hours the fate of Europe hung veiled in cannon smoke. On June 19, 1815, late in the afternoon a Rothschild agent name Rothworth jumped into a boat at Ostend. In his hand he held a Dutch gazette still damp from the printer. By the dawn light of June 20 Nathan Rothschild stood at Folkstone harbor and let his eye fly over the lead paragraphs. A moment later he was on his way to London (beating Wellington's envoy by many hours) to tell the government that Napoleon had been crushed. Then he proceeded to the stock exchange.

Another man in his position would have sunk his worth into consols. But this was Nathan Rothschild. He leaned against "his" pillar. He did not invest. He sold. He dumped consols.

His name was already such that a single substantial move on his part sufficed to bear or bull an issue. Consols fell. Nathan leaned and leaned, and sold and sold. Consols dropped still more. "Rothschild knows," the whisper rippled through the 'Change. "Waterloo is lost."

1. The international currency exchange —Ed.

2. Pounds—Ed.

Nathan kept on selling, his round face motionless and stern, his pudgy fingers depressing the market by tens of thousands of pounds with each sell signal. Consols dived, consols plummented—until, a split second before it was too late, Nathan suddenly bought a giant parcel for a song. Moments afterwards the great news broke, to send consols soaring.

We cannot guess the number of hopes and savings wiped out by this engineered panic. We cannot estimate how many liveried servants, how many Watteaus and Rembrandts, how many thoroughbreds in his descendants' stables, the man by the pillar won that single day.

See Federal Rules of Evidence § 801(a) p. 921; Cal. Evidence Code § 225 p. 812.

UNITED STATES v. RHODES

Trial by General Court Martial, Fort McNair, District of Columbia, 1958.

[During February, 1958, Master Sergeant Roy A. Rhodes, United States Army, was tried by General Court Martial for having conspired with certain named and unnamed persons to violate the espionage laws of the United States by, among things, communicating information concerning the national defense to agents of the Union of Soviet Socialist Republics. Two of the accused's co-conspirators were alleged to be Col. Rudolph Ivanovich Abel and Lt. Col. Reino Hayhanen of the Soviet Secret Police. The evidence showed that in July, 1956, Abel had transmitted to Hayhanen some written information regarding the accused—whose code name was "Quebec"—which Abel had received from Moscow. The information was on "hard" film; Hayhanen had made "soft" film of it and hidden it in a hollowed-out bolt at his home in Peekskill, New York. The bolt and its contents were retrieved by agents of the Federal Bureau of Investigation and a copy of the piece of "soft" film was offered, over objection, and received at Rhodes' trial. The message on the piece of film is reproduced below. Counsel for the accused objected to receipt of this message on grounds of hearsay. On what basis was the exhibit received? Do you agree that it was properly admissible?—Ed.]

PROSECUTION EXHIBIT NO. 7.

QUEBEC, Roy A. Rhodes, born 1917 in Oilton, Oklahoma, U.S., senior sergeant of the War Ministry, former employee of the U.S. Military Attache Staff in our country. He was a chief of the garage of the Embassy.

He was recruited to our service in January 1952 in our country which he left in June 1953; recruited on the basis of compromising materials, but he is tied up to us with his receipts and information he had given in his own hand writing.

He had been trained in code work at the Ministry before he went to work at the Embassy, but as a code worker he was not used by the Embassy.

After he left our country he was to be sent to the school of communications of the Army C-I Service which is at the city of San Luis, California. He was to be trained there as a mechanic of the coding machines.

He fully agreed to continue to cooperate with us in the States or any other country. It was agreed that he was to have written to our Embassy here special letters, but we had received none during the last year.

It has been recently learned that Quebec is living in Red Bank, N. J. where he owns three garages. The garage job is being done by his wife. His own occupation at present is not known.

His father—Mr. W.A. Rhodes resides in the U.S. His brother is also in the States where he works as an engineer at an atomic plant in Camp, Georgia with a brother-in-law of his father.

PEOPLE v. BARNHART

District Court of Appeal of California, 1944.
66 Cal.App.2d 714, 153 P.2d 214.

[Defendant was convicted of keeping a house for the purpose of taking bets on horse races. One of the grounds for the defendant's appeal was that the arresting officers were allowed to testify as to telephone calls received by them on defendant's telephone during the arrest. These calls were received from anonymous callers who stated over the telephone that they wished to place bets—Ed.]

*   *   *

Under the authority of People v. Joffe, 45 Cal.App.2d 233, 235, 113 P.2d 901, and People v. Reifenstuhl, 37 Cal.App.2d 402, 405, 99 P.2d 564, evidence of telephonic conversations between arresting officers and persons calling the establishment are properly admitted as tending to establish the fact that the premises were occupied for the purpose of bookmaking.

*   *   *

For the reasons stated, the judgment is affirmed.

DORAN, J.   I concur in the judgment.—But I know of no rule or principle of law that authorizes or justifies a relaxation of the hearsay rule for expediency. The evidence of the telephone conversations was pure hearsay. Evidence of the fact that a conversation was received would be admissible for the purpose of proving that the telephone was in order and functioning, but for no other purpose; the substance of the conversation is unnecessary for this purpose. The argument in People v. Joffe, supra, namely, that such evidence is admissible because "it tended to establish the fact that the premises were occupied for the purpose of recording wagers on horse races," clearly permits a consideration of hearsay for the purpose of proving the very offense charged. And the same inaccurate reasoning appears in People v. Reifenstuhl, supra, where the court declared, referring to such evidence that "It was not subject to the hearsay rule. The conversation was not admitted for the purpose of proving its own contents but to prove the use to which the telephone was subjected by the public and to demonstrate the reaction of the defendant at the time. The use of the room occupied by defendant was in issue and the nature of the telephonic call was a circumstance to establish the truth. The uses to which a telephone is put reveal more truthfully the character of the establishment that houses the instrument than do the words of description attached to the listing."

It is futile to argue that such evidence is not hearsay. In my judgment the preservation of the hearsay rule is not only important but vital in the administration of justice. To relax the rule just to uphold the conviction of a bookmaker, or for any other purpose, is nothing short of judicial stupidity.

White, J., concurred.

Hearing denied; Carter and Schauer, JJ., dissenting.

McCORMICK, THE BORDERLAND OF HEARSAY

39 Yale L.J. 489, 502–4 (1930).*
[Footnotes omitted.]

[The author, after discussing a number of cases including Wright v. Tatham, supra, concludes:]

Probably the foregoing presents a fair sampling of the cases and comments pro and con on the question. From the data given it seems apparent, first, that Wright v. Tatham expresses the more generally accepted view in holding that conduct, even when not intended as assertive, is hearsay when offered to show the actor's belief and hence the truth of the belief, and second, that this view has, since the leading case, received such slight consideration in subsequent decisions which follow it, and has evoked such contrariety of opinion among the commentators (as well as a sprinkling of contrary decisions) that it is open for re-examination in the light of general policy.

It is only the technique of that general reconsideration that is of any real importance, and the assembling of the foregoing chance driftwood from the decisions is of value only so far as it clears the way for such a reconsideration. These decisions, though casual and inharmonious, serve chiefly to show the situations in real life which call for the application of such theory as we may adopt. And it is just here that the reader may ask, "Why assume that any one solution is likely to work for all the types of cases which seem to occur?" It will have been observed, certainly, that the cases fall into three groups. The first and simplest, for present purposes, are the cases of stark action with no element of communication at all. Such is the ship-captain example, [see p.   ] and most of Parke's other illustrations. But in real life, as the cases show, the element of words enters in. Thus we may distinguish a second group where acts and words explaining them are offered together. Of this type is the evidence of the guest who refuses the hotel-room, objecting that it is too dark, offered to show the undesirability of the room, and the evidence of the rejection of similar goods as defective by other customers, to show breach of warranty. Finally, the third group comprises those cases where the conduct consists of words solely, but words not of *assertion,* but of *action,* such as an offer of a position (to show the *offeree's* skill) or the letters in Wright v. Tatham itself. It seems, however, that to base any difference in results on the mere circumstance that the conduct is verbal or non-verbal would be an undesirable rule of thumb not corresponding to any difference in probable trustworthiness.

If all three types, then, are to be treated alike, what shall that treatment be? The problem is one that will eventually be solved according as the profession adopts one or another general attitude toward the rules of proof.

Possible attitudes might favor the admission of any and all offered items of proof, as seems to be the method in French criminal trials, or might lean toward vesting a large discretion in the trial judge to admit or exclude, guided only by certain general canons and standards, as seems to be the present English tendency, or, on the other hand, the attitude may remain one of adherence to the present system in vogue in the United States, of sharply defined rules prohibiting the admission of many rigidly classified types of evidence.

The advocates of entire exclusion of evidence of conduct to show belief, to show the truth of the fact believed, as being hearsay, hark back to the traditional technique of jury trial administration as it hardened in the eighteenth century. Judges then, to paraphrase a well-worn epigram, were surer about everything than judges today are about anything. That technique consisted of creating large, simple, but definite categories under which offered items of proof could be classified accurately and, above all, quickly. All the contents of each of these classes were either black or white, admissible or inadmissible. The largest of these categories of inadmissible evidence (though its recognition as such was later than we usually supposed) is that of hearsay. The advantages of these clear-cut rules of exclusion are obvious. They enable the lawyer preparing his case to know in advance with fair certainty what he can get in, and what he cannot. If a question as to admissibility does arise, the judge who has no time for subtle discrimination in the heat of trial can make a decision in his stride, as it were. This is splendid, and the only difficulty is that it does not work. The rule excluding all hearsay, clear and simple in its original form, when it was tested by the offer of particular hearsay evidence of a peculiarly indispensable or reliable kind cracked under the strain. To relieve the pressure, exception after exception was recognized until today the rule is riddled with thirteen or more exceptions. The exceptions are in some instances quite as rigidly defined as the rule itself.

To be contrasted with this sort of progress through the mitigation of a rigid rule by numerous rigid exceptions, is the different technique of development of such rules as, for example, those which provide for the order of presenting proof. These have from the outset been merely guides and not limits to the judge's discretion and consequently have never had to be complicated by exceptions. Would it not have been wiser to set up the hearsay rule also in some similar form, as for example: "Hearsay is inadmissible except where the judge in his discretion finds it needed and trustworthy"? The astonishing conservatism of most lawyers and of most judges drawn from their ranks, and their almost religious reverence for these mere procedural rules, will make progress towards such a result slow, but doubtless such a change is on the cards. At all events, newly evolved evidence rules are likely to be of that discretionary type.

Focusing these considerations upon our present problem, we find the orthodox, but not wholly settled or established, view to be that conduct to show belief, to show the fact believed, is invariably to be put in the "hearsay" category and banned as such. The result is that evidence which has the strongest circumstantial guaranties of reliability may be banned. Evidence that a doctor, since deceased, has operated upon a man for appendicitis, would be inadmissible as evidence that the patient actually had that disease. It is true, on the other hand, that very much of such conduct-evidence if admitted would be of trivial value and probably a general inclusionary rule, that all such evidence is admissible wherever the actor's testimony on the stand would be, would be only one degree better than wholesale exclusion. It would seem sensible to conclude that conduct (other than assertions) when offered to show the actor's beliefs and hence the truth of the facts so believed, being merely analogous to and not identical with typical hearsay, ought to be admissible whenever the trial judge in his discretion finds that the action so vouched the belief as to give reasonable assurance of trustworthiness.

MORGAN, BASIC PROBLEMS OF EVIDENCE

248-50 (1961).*
[Footnotes omitted]

C. Where the evidence of declarant's conduct is offered to prove that it truly reflected his then existing state of mind, his sincerity is necessarily involved. Thus where evidence of his abnormal objective conduct is offered as tending to prove his insanity, it has no value if it was feigned. His sincerity is a peculiarly important element where his conduct is a positive assertion and the issue is whether he was suffering an insane delusion that the assertion was true. Thus if a woman asserted "I am the Pope," and the issue is whether she had an insane delusion that she held that high office, her belief in the truth of the statement is determinative. And yet, the courts rarely, if ever, treat such evidence as hearsay, and Wigmore agrees, though Hinton dissented. Speaking generally, where evidence of the declarant's conduct, other than a direct assertion that he has a specified state of mind, is offered as tending to prove his state of mind at the time, and the state of mind at that time or at a later time only is in issue, the evidence is not classed as hearsay. This is difficult to harmonize with the theory of courts and commentators that one of the chief functions of cross-examination is to expose defects in sincerity, and with the accepted justification for most of the recognized exceptions to the hearsay rule on the ground that the circumstances of the utterance furnish a guaranty of sincerity.

BUCK v. STATE

Criminal Court of Appeals of Oklahoma, 1943.
77 Okl.Cr. 17, 138 P.2d 115.

BAREFOOT, Judge. Defendant, G.R. Buck, was charged in the District Court of Okmulgee County with the crime of arson, was tried, convicted and sentenced to serve a term of two years in the State Penitentiary, and has appealed.

The only contention presented in the brief of defendant is that the evidence is insufficient to sustain the judgment and sentence, and that the court erred in refusing to direct a verdict of not guilty.

This case may be said to rest almost wholly upon circumstantial evidence. It presents to this Court for the first time the question of the admissibility in evidence of the trailing of one by bloodhounds. We find that this question has heretofore been presented to the highest appellate courts

*Joint Committee on Continuing Legal Education of The American Law Institute and The American Bar Association, Philadelphia, 1961.

of many states, and that some consideration has been given thereto by text-book writers. However, this Court has never been called upon to consider the question, although the use of bloodhounds at the State Penitentiary has been in vogue for many years.

An investigation of the authorities has been most interesting and profitable. The earliest case in this country is which consideration 385, 39 Am.St.Rep. 17. In that case the death penalty was upheld, and the evidence of tracking by the dog to defendant's home was sustained as competent evidence. Since this case in 1893, many courts have passed upon the question, and by the great weight of authority it has been held that the evidence is admissible under certain rules and conditions, as will be hereinafter stated.

Among the states upholding the rule are Alabama, Florida, Iowa, Kansas, Kentucky, North Carolina, South Carolina, New York, Missouri, Ohio, Texas, Mississippi, Georgia, Tennessee, Arkansas and Louisiana * * * .

The states, some of which recognize that in some cases the evidence might be admissible, yet refuse to follow the rule are Nebraska, Illinois and Indiana, and one case from Iowa.

In the early case of State v. Thomas Hall, 4 Ohio Dec. 147, a history of the bloodhound is given as follows:

"It is a matter of common knowledge, and therefore a matter of which courts will take notice, that the breed of dogs known as blood-hounds is possessed of a high degree of intelligence, and acuteness of scent, and may be trained to follow human tracks with considerable certainty and success, if put upon a recent trail. In Chambers' Encyc., under the title 'Bloodhound,' it is said of this dog, that 'it is remarkable for its exquisite scent and for its great sagacity and perseverance in tracking any object to the pursuit of which it has been trained;' that 'it has been frequently used for the pursuit of felons and deerslayers, and, in America, for the capture of fugitive slaves;' and the writer refers to the use of these dogs in border warfare, and to their importation 'into Jamaica in 1796 to be used in suppressing the Maroon insurrection, but the terror occasioned by their arrival produced the effect without their actual employment.' The Encyc. Britannica (9th Ed.) under the title 'Dog,' bears this testimony to the well known traits of this animal: 'The bloodhound is remarkable for its acuteness of scent, its discrimination in keeping to the particular scent on which it is first laid, and the intelligence and pertinacity with with it pursues its object to a successful issue. These qualities have been taken advantage of not only in the chase, but also in the pursuit of felons and fugitives of every kind. According to Strabo, these dogs were used in an attack upon the Gauls. In the clan feuds of the Scottish Highlands, and in the frequent wars between England and Scotland, they were regularly employed in tracking fugitive warriors, and were thus employed, according to early chroniclers, in pursuit of Wallace and Bruce. The former is said to have put the hound off the scent by killing a suspected follower, on whose corpse the hound stood. For a similar purpose captives were often killed. Bruce is said to have baffled his dogged pursuer as effectually, though less cruelly, by wading some distance down stream, and then ascending a tree by a branch which overhung the water and thus breaking the scent. In the histories of border feuds these dogs constantly appear as employed in the pursuit of enemies, and the renown of the warrier was great, who,

" 'By wily turns and desperate bounds, had baffled Percy's best bloodhounds.'

"In suppressing the Irish rebellion in the time of Queen Elizabeth, the Earl of Essex had, it is said, 800 of these animals accompanying the army. * * *

"Both history, therefore, and natural history testify to the exceptional keenness of scent and capacity for training of this variety of hound. Whatever may be said of the wisdom or humanity of resorting to this means of detecting and securing the apprehension of criminals, there can be no doubt, that, where a well trained dog is set upon a recent track and follows it, in the usual manner of such dogs in following a trail, up to the person or home of the accused, these facts may, on the plain principles governing circumstantial evidence, be shown as tending to connect him with the crime charged. It was so held in the case of Hodge v. State, supra, which is the only case I have found directly in point.

"Of course in such cases full opportunity should be given to inquire into the breeding, training and testing of the dog, and to all the circumstances attending the trailing in the case on trial, and to the manner in which the dog then acted and was handled by the person having it in charge. The weight to be given to the tracking as evidence against the accused will depend largely upon these matters."

Also in the case of Blair v. Commonwealth, 181 Ky. 218, 204 S.W. 67, 68, in which a beautiful tribute is paid to the dog, where it is said:

"If we may credit Sir Walter Scott, such evidence was looked upon with favor as early as the twelfth century. In the Talisman it is related that in the joint crusade of Richard I of England and Phillip II of France, Roswell, the hound, pulled from the saddle Conrade, Marquis of Montserrat, thus mutely accusing him of the theft of the banner of England. Phillip defended the Marquis with the remark:

" 'Surely the word of a knight and a prince should bear him out against the barking of a cur.'

"To which Richard replied:

" 'Royal brother, recollect that the Almighty who gave the dog to be companion of our pleasures and our toils, both invested him with a nature noble and incapable of deceit. He forgets neither friend nor foe; remembers, and with accuracy, both benefit and injury. He hath a share of man's intelligence, but no share of man's falsehood. You may bribe a soldier to slay a man with his sword, or a witness to take life by false accusation; but you cannot make a hound tear his benefactor; he is the friend of man save when man justly incurs his enmity. Dress younder Marquis in what peacock robes you will, disguise his appearance, alter his complexion with drugs and washes, hide himself amidst a hundred men; I will yet pawn my scepter that the hound detects him, and expresses his resentment, as you have this day beheld.'

"The doctrine of the admissibility of bloodhound evidence in criminal prosecutions has been slowly gaining ground during the past 20 years.

* * * "The general rules deductible from these decisions are as follows:

"(1) The bloodhound in question must be shown to have been trained to follow human beings by their tracks and to have been tested as to its accuracy in trailing upon one or more occasions; and,

"(2) The evidence of the acts of bloodhounds in following a trail may be received merely as circumstantial or corroborative evidence against a person towards whom other circumstances point as being guilty of the commission of the crime charged.

"The admission of this class of evidence is therefore hedged about with abundant safeguards in the way of other and human testimony; and as long as these rules are adhered to bloodhound evidence is no more dangerous than any other class of circumstantial evidence.

"In Kentucky it is settled that testimony as to trailing by bloodhounds of one charged with crime may be permitted to go to the jury for what it is worth, as one of the circumstances which may tend to connect the defendant with the crime only after if has been shown by some one having personal knowledge of the facts: (a) That the dog in question is of pure blood and of a stock characterized by acuteness of scent and power of discrimination; (b) is itself possessed of these qualities and has been trained or tested in the tracking of human beings; and (c) that the dog so trained and tested was laid on the trail, whether visible or not, concerning which testimony has been admitted, at the point where the circumstances tend clearly to show that the guilty party had been, or upon a track which such circumstances indicated had been made by him."

* * * The evidence with reference to the history, qualification and experience of the dogs was given by the witness M.I. Stokes. He testified that he was employed by the State of Oklahoma at the State Penitentiary at McAlester. That he had charge of the dogs, about fifteen or twenty in number. That the witness Hubert Wilson was a trusty at the penitentiary who had been appointed to assist him in handling the dogs. That the witness had had fifteen or twenty years' experience in the handling of dogs. That he had been at the State Penitentiary at McAlester in this capacity for about three years, and that the two dogs which he brought to Okmulgee on the 22nd of August, 1938, were "Old Boston," and "Diana." That he selected them as his two best dogs from a pack of fifteen or twenty. "Old Boston" was nine years old and "Diana" a younger dog. He testified at length as to the experience and training which these dogs had received, and especially "Old Boston," and gave individual instances of performances by him in the trailing of human beings. He testifed:

"Q. And they can distinguish between the smells of human beings? A. I will answer that question like this, it has been my experience with bloodhounds, with a trained bloodhound, they have an instinct, we call it, I call it a sense to trail a man better than any other dog would trail anything else, and apparently they have an instinct that will enable them to carry a trail through places that apparently other dogs couldn't carry it at all, and they always know one track from the other. It is impossible for you to cause them to change tracks, they won't do that.

"Q.   You mean, if he is a well trained and experienced blood-hound, if he starts on the track of one human being, he will stay with that particular track?   A.   He will trail no other track than that. It is impossible to get him to change tracks."   *   *   *

"Q.   Does it make a difference whether the trail is fresh or cold? A.   Those two dogs I had there would trail a twenty-four hour track. I have known them to do that. They wouldn't trail as fast as one we call warmer, fresher track, you understand, but those dogs would trail a ten or twelve hour track and move right along with it; but a four or five hour track is nothing at all for them.

"Q.   Would that be considered a comparatively fresh trail?   A. It certainly would.

"Q.   Now then, you used Old Boston as the lead dog, did you? A.   Yes sir. However, we had this Diana there, one of the greatest dogs I ever knew and one of the most accurate dogs.

"Q.   Did you select these two dogs out of a kennel of how many dogs?   A.   We had fifteen or twenty dogs, but on all special occasions I used those two dogs because they were the best I had and the best I ever saw.

"Q.   Let's take, for instance, Old Boston, I understand he has since died, since the trailing of this track up there?   A.   Yes, sir.

"Q.   When did she die?   A.   Boston died, I think, about a month after I left down there.

"Q.   To refresh your memory, was it sometime in March, 1939? A.   Right along then, yes sir.

"Q.   And what age dog was she?   A.   Boston was about nine years of age.

"Q.   Was that dog owned by the state of Oklahoma?   A.   Yes sir. Yes, she was owned by the State.

"Q.   How long were you its keeper or trainer?   A.   Boston individually?

"Q.   Yes.   A.   I only ran Boston about two and a half years. I used him some several years before that when they first got him from Texas. That was before I went to Granite.

"Q.   What age dog was he, if you know, when he was brought to Oklahoma?   A.   He was said to be about three years of age.

"Q.   Have you ever seen him on a man's trail?   A.   Yes, several hundred."

*   *   *

"Q.   Did you ever know Old Boston to lie on any trail?   A.   I never knew him to make a mistake."

* * *

"A. I would have to answer that question like this, that this Master Mind dog of Pennsylvania has greater reputation than Boston. Boston was considered the second dog in the United States at that time."

He then testified to the individual work of these dogs in many cases that came under his personal observation, and where they had successfully tracked human beings, and then testified as to the instant case as above related. On cross examination he was asked:

"Q. There hasn't been any monument or any money or anything appropriated to build a monument to Boston since he died? A. I don't know. There ought to be."

In view of this testimony, we have decided that the tribute to the hound by Richard I of England, as above quoted, shall be a monument or tribute to "Old Boston," and for this reason we perpetuate his name in the law books of this State. Though the State has not erected a monument to his memory, his services will ever be remembered, not only in the instant case but others.

As above stated, the evidence in this case is almost wholly based upon circumstantial evidence, and while we recognize the rule announced in the decisions which have been cited, that a conviction will not be upheld upon the evidence alone of trailing by bloodhounds, yet that evidence being competent as a circumstance, together with the other evidence in the case, where competent proof has been given as to the qualifications, training and experience of the bloodhounds used, as in the instant case, this testimony together with the other evidence in the case presented a question of fact for the jury to pass upon as to the guilt or innocence of the defendant.

There can be no question but that the evidence as to the training and experience of the two dogs, and especially "Old Boston," was such that it entitled the court to submit it to the jury for their consideration, together with the other facts and circumstances and under the law we can not say that the verdict of the jury should be set aside.

We have, therefore, reached the conclusion that the judgment and sentence of the District Court of Okmulgee County should be affirmed.

Jones, P.J., and Doyle, J., concur.

CONVERSATIONS WITH A GORILLA
By Francine Patterson

154 National Geographic 438, 438, 459, 61 (1978).*

KOKO is a 7-year-old "talking" gorilla. She is the focus of my career as a developmental psychologist, and also has become a dear friend.

Through mastery of sign language—the familiar hand speech of the deaf—Koko has made us, her human companions, aware not only that her breed is bright, but also that it shares sensitivities commonly held to be the prerogative of people.

Remembrance of Events and Emotions

A cardinal characteristic of human language is displacement, the ability to refer to events removed in time and place from the act of communication. To learn whether another animal has this ability, we try to find out if the animal uses its sign vocabulary merely to label the events of its world, or if it is framing propositions that re-create a particular event. Does the animal use its symbols to refer to events earlier or later in time?

Koko and I had a revealing conversation about a biting incident. My try at cross-examination—three days after the event—went much as follows:

Me: "What did you do to Penny?"

Koko: "Bite". (Koko, at the time of the incident, called it a scratch.)

Me: "You admit it?"

Koko: "Sorry bite scratch."

(At this point I showed Koko the mark on my hand—it really did look like a scratch.)

Koko: "Wrong bite."

Me: "Why bite?"

Koko: "Because mad."

Me: "Why mad?"

Koko: "Don't know."

The entire conversation concerns a past event and, equally significant, a past emotional state. It is not a discussion one would expect to have with an animal whose memories were dim, unsorted recollections of pain and pleasure. Of striking import to me was that Koko knew she could not remember or express whatever it was that had prompted the bite.

Koko Learns to Lie

Perhaps the most telling, yet elusive, evidence that a creature can displace events is lying. When someone tells a lie, he is using language to distort the listener's perception of reality. He is using symbols to describe something that never happened, or won't happen. Evidence I have been accumulating strongly suggests that Koko expresses a make-believe capacity similar to humans'.

At about the age of 5 Koko discovered the value of the lie to get herself out of a jam. After numerous repeat performances I'm convinced that Koko really is lying in these circumstances and not merely making mistakes. One of her first lies also involved the reconstruction of an earlier happening. My assistant Kate Mann was with Koko, then tipping the scales at 90 pounds, when the gorilla plumped down on the kitchen sink in the trailer and it separated from its frame and dropped out of alignment. Later, when I asked Koko if she broke the sink, she signed, "Kate there bad," pointing to the sink. Koko couldn't know, of course, that I would never accept the idea that Kate would go around breaking sinks.

Some of Koko's lies are startlingly ingenious. Once, while I was busy writing, she snatched up a red crayon and began chewing on it. A moment later I noticed and said, "You're not eating that crayon are you?" Koko signed, "Lip," and began moving the crayon first across her upper, then her lower lip as if applying lipstick.

CITY OF WEBSTER GROVES v. QUICK

St. Louis Court of Appeals, Missouri, 1959.
323 S.W.2d 386

ANDERSON, Judge.   This case arose upon the filing of a complaint against defendant in the City Court of Webster Groves, Missouri, for the violation of a speed ordinance of said city. Defendant was found guilty in said court and thereafter appealed to the Circuit Court of St. Louis County. A trial was had in the Circuit Court resulting in a verdict and judgment finding defendant guilty as charged and assessing as punishment a fine of $10. From this judgment, defendant appealed to the Supreme Court on the theory that because he was convicted on the readings of an electric timer his constitutional rights had been invaded, contrary to Article 1, Sections 10 and 18(a) of the Missouri Constitution, V.A.M.S.; the Fifth Amendment of the Constitution of the United States; and the Sixth Amendment of the Constitution of the United States. The Supreme Court, in an opinion, 319 S.W.2d 543, held that appellant's purported constitutional issues were without substance and colorable only, and transferred said cause to this court.

On March 4, 1957, about 8:00 o'clock a.m., appellant was driving westwardly on Kirkham Boulevard in Webster Groves. As he proceeded westwardly he was driving toward a parked police car which was headed eastward. When appellant reached a point about opposite the police car he was stopped by a police officer and informed he was driving 40 miles per hour in a 30 mile an hour zone. Appellant was advised that an electric timer which was operated by the police showed he was driving at that speed.

The electric timer consists of a control panel which contains a stop watch, a switch and a reset button. In addition, there is a cable, 500 feet long, that plugs into the box. There are two rubber tubes which stretch the width of the street. There are two mercury switches to which the tubes are connected and which are in turn connected to the electric cable, and four weights to anchor the tubes across the street. In the middle of these rubber tubes is a plug to prevent eastbound traffic from having any effect on the unit when the mechanism is set for timing westbound traffic. When laid out for operation the rubber tubes are placed across the street 132 feet apart. The mercury switches to which the tubes are connected are in turn connected to the electric cable which runs from the first tube to the control box on the police car. The first tube is located 500 feet east of the parked police car, and the second tube 368 feet east of said automobile. The police car in the instant case was placed at a point where both tubes could be observed by the occupant of the police car. As the officer sitting in the car observes a car approaching which he wishes to clock he sets the switch on the control panel which opens the first tube. When the tires of the approaching car pass over that tube it activates the mercury switch, which starts a stop watch located in the police car. The switch is then closed to the neutral position, and any automobiles following the car which crossed the first tube have no effect on the unit. Then, as the clocked automobile approaches the second tube, the switch is thrown to the right, which is the control on the second tube, and when the tires of the automobile being clocked run over the second tube it stops the clock. Around the outside of the clock is a calibrated scale laid out in miles which indicates the miles per hour the automobile being observed is traveling. From the point at which the speed of the automobile is indicated on the clock to the police car there is a distance of 368 feet.

A certified steel tape is used to measure the distance between the two tubes to insure that they are laid out exactly 132 feet.

The speed watch device, which had been in use in the city regularly during the two and one-half years before the date of the trial, is checked each day when it is put out by driving a police department vehicle through it at varying speeds. The speedometer reading of the vehicle is checked with the reading of the speed watch. This was done on the day of defendant's arrest. The arresting officer testified he saw no reason why atmospheric disturbances could effect the accurate operation of the machine.

The clock, which is a unit itself, the size of a pocket watch, is checked for accuracy the first week of each month by a watchmaker and jeweler of twelve years' experience. It is the same type of watch used in timing sports, and is tested against the standard of the National Bureau of Standards. The watch is started on a tone put out by the National Bureau of Standards, and is stopped on the tone. The watchmaker checks to see if the watch has the required number of seconds in those tones. The signals of the National Bureau are accurate to one fifty thousandth of a second each twenty-four hours. The watchmaker who testified in this case had never heard of any of the relays of this current or beam being wrong. That is the time used by the Government, and all our ships at sea, and the Air Force, set their watches by it. * * *

The arresting officer, Maurice Paillou, who was sitting in the police car, observed defendant's car approaching from the east. He decided to clock the speed of defendant's car. The officer activated the first tube shortly before defendant crossed it. He saw defendant's car cross the first tube and saw the stop watch start to operate. He then activated the second tube and as defendant crossed the latter the officer observed the stop watch come to a stop. A reading of 40 miles per hour was indicated on the stop watch. The officer then stepped out of the car, flagged down defendant and invited him over to the police car where he showed defendant the reading on the dial and explained to him how the machine worked.

On cross-examination, the police officer testified that there were no other cars on either the eastbound lane or the westbound lane when defendant came through the unit. He could see eastward approximately six to seven hundred feet. He was visually aware of the fact that defendant was traveling at a speed in excess of 30 miles per hour.

Meryle Mikel, a jeweler, testified he checked the watch mechanism during the first week in March, 1957, and found it to be accurate. He also testified he had checked the watch mechanism during the first week of February, 1957, and found it accurate.

Del Reinemer, a Webster Groves Police Sergeant, testified he had taken the stop watch to Mr. Mikel in the first week of February, 1957, the first week of March, 1957, and again in the first week of April, 1957.

Defendant denied he was going over 28 to 30 miles per hour, stating that his recently tested speedometer showed a reading between those figures.

Appellant's first point is that the court erred in permitting Police Officer Paillou to testify as to the readings of the electric timer showing defendant's speed at 40 miles per hour, for the reason that it constituted hearsay evidence.

There is no merit to the point made. The officer himself testified to the reading of the mechanism in question and not to what someone else had told him; thus, the hearsay rule does not apply. The witness when testifying was under oath, and was thoroughly cross-examined, thus satisfying the principal requirements of the hearsay rule. Evidence is called hearsay when its probative force depends, in whole or in part, on the competency and credibility of some person other than the witness by whom it is sought to be produced. It is an extra judicial utterance, including both oral statements and writings. The hearsay rule cannot be applied to what the witness, on the stand and subject to cross-examination, observed, either through his own senses or through the use of scientific instruments. If appellant's contention were sound then results of the use of a measuring device on some object to ascertain its length would be inadmissible; a doctor could not testify to what a fluoroscope revealed concerning the condition of his patient, and, likewise, he would not be permitted to testify as to the results heard through a stethoscope. Many other examples of the absurdity of such a rule could be cited. In such cases, as in the case at bar, the evidence as to the results obtained by the witness is not dependant on the perception, memory, and sincerity of an absent declarant. The circumstantial guarantee of trustworthiness is satisfied by the exerise of the right of cross-examination of the witness on the stand, both as to the results obtained and his testimony as to the reliability and accuracy of the device used. As to the latter, there was sufficient evidence in the case at bar. A police vehicle was operated through the device the morning defendant was arrested, and the device was found to be operating properly. In addition, the stop watch was tested during that week and the first week of the preceding and subsequent months. The witnesses to those facts were produced and were subjected to rigorous cross-examination. We rule there was no error in the court's ruling on the admission of the evidence in question. State of Missouri v. Graham, Mo.App., 322 S.W.2d 188.   *   *   *

[Affirmed]

MORGAN, HEARSAY AND NON-HEARSAY

48 Harv.L.Rev. 1138, 1145-6 (1935).*
[Footnotes omitted.]

*   *   *   The courts constantly and correctly receive as reliable evidence what careful analysis discloses to be hearsay. They sometimes obscure the quesion by a resort to the doctrine of judicial notice. Where a court receives an almanac as evidence of an astronomical fact, it is not taking judicial notice of the fact: it is admitting anonymous hearsay and taking judicial notice of the reliability of the almanac as a source of authentic informa-

tion. Again, nothing is more common than to allow a witness to rely upon a timepiece in stating the time of day when an event happened. If he should testify that he looked at a Western Union clock and noted the time, he would be considered as giving particularly accurate testimony, but would it not be anonymous hearsay upon anonymous hearsay? Certainly the person in charge of the master mechanism which regulated the clock consulted by the witness did not make the astronomical observations in accordance with which that clock was made to indicate the hour and minute of the day. Yet just as certainly an objection upon the ground of hearsay would receive scant attention. Only a little less easy is a demonstration of the hearsay element in the indication of time upon a sundial unless preceded by the testimony of a witness who checked it against his own astronomical observations. Much the same may be said of the automatic weighing machines which in return for a coin furnish a printed assertion of a person's weight, and of non-automatic scales where the position of the marker which produces a balance of the beam announces the weight of the object upon the platform. In each of these cases, the anonymous maker or regulator of the machine intended that the reaction of the machine should operate as an assertion. In each of them he may have fixed the instrument so as to produce a false declaration, as where the faker who gambles upon his pretended ability to guess his victim's weight controls the balance by a hidden mechanism, or a practical joker sets a series of timepieces so as to cause another to miss a appointment. Generally speaking, however, the court regards these mechanisms as sufficiently accurate to justify a trier of fact in relying upon their reactions for most purposes, at least after a preliminary showing of reasonable accuracy. In other words, it takes judical notice of the reliability of these sources of information under ordinary circumstances not withstanding their hearsay character.

Somewhat the same process is used when expert witnesses are permitted to base their opinions upon data as to which they have not the slightest personal knowledge. Though no witness gives first-hand evidence of the truth expressed or implied in these data, the expert is permitted to draw deductions therefrom which the jury may hear and consider.

MORGAN, EVIDENCE EXAM, SUMMER TERM, 1946, HARVARD LAW SCHOOL

Which of the following items is hearsay?

_____ 1. On the issue whether X and D were engaged to be married, D's statement to X, "I promise to marry you on June 1, 1931."

_____ 2. On the issue of the sanity of D, a woman, D's public statement, "I am the Pope."

_____ 3. On the issue of D's adverse possession of Blackacre, D's assertion "I am the owner of this farm."

_____ 4. On the issue of X's provocation for assaulting Y, D's statement to X, her husband, "Y ravished me."

_____ 5. On the issue of D's consciousness after the attack, D's statement, "X shot me, as he often threatened to do."

_____ 6. On the issue of identity of the shooter, D's statement in 5.

_____ 7. On the issue whether X made threats to shoot D, D's statement in 5.

_____ 8. On the issue of X's knowledge of speedily impending death, D's statement to X, "You have only a few minutes to live."

_____ 9. In 8, X's statement, "I realize that I am dying."

_____ 10. On the issue whether a transfer of a chattel from D to X was a sale or gift, D's statement accompanying the transfer, "I am giving you this chattel as a birthday present."

_____ 11. On the issue in 10, D's statement the day following the transfer, "I gave you the chattel as a birthday present."

* * *

_____ 14. On the issue of damages to the family reputation in an action for the seduction of P's daughter, her reputation for chastity.

_____ 15. On the issue of D's ill-feeling toward X, D's statement, "X is a liar and a hypocrite."

_____ 16. On the issue of reasonableness of X's conduct, in the shooting of Y by X, D's statement to X, "Y has threatened to kill you on sight."

_____ 17. On the issue in 16, Y's reputation, known to X, as a violent, quarrelsome man.

_____ 18. Action for malicious prosecution of P by X on the charge of murdering Y. On the issue of probable cause, P's reputation as a gangster, known to X.

_____ 19. In 18, Y's reputation, known to X, as a quiet, peace-loving citizen.

_____ 20. On the issue of the terms of a contract with T negotiated by D, D's statement "I am making this offer to you, as the agent of P."

_____ 21. On the issue whether D was the agent of P, the statement in 20.

_____ 22. As tending to prove that X was suffering from tuberculosis, the fact that D, a physician, ordered X to a tuberculosis sanitarium for six months, concealing from X and X's relatives the character of the hospital.

_____ 23. As tending to prove X's honesty, the mere fact that D, X's employer, promoted him from the position of order clerk to cashier.

_____ 24. As tending to prove D's guilt of the crime of killing X, the fact that D fled under suspicious circumstances immediately after X's murder, in order to draw suspicion upon himself.

_____ 25. As tending to prove X's insanity, the fact that he was confined in an insane asylum.

_____ 26. As tending to prove forgery of a will by X, D's angry statement to X, "Well, I never forged a will, anyway!"

_____ 27. As tending to prove D's guilt of a particular criminal act, the fact that D fled under suspicious circumstances immediately after the criminal act was committed, solely in order to escape.

_____ 28. On the issue whether a transfer of a chattel from D to X was a sale or a gift, D's statement accompanying the transfer, "Here is your birthday gift."

_____ 29. As tending to prove that X was suffering from disease T, the mere fact that D, a physician, treated him for disease T.

_____ 30. On the issue of D's adverse possession of Blackacre, D's statement, "I paid X $5000 for this farm."

_____ 31. To show that X was ill, W offers to testify that X complained of pain in his chest.

_____ 32. In a contest of a will on ground of forgery, to show testator's feelings toward X, the sole legatee, W offers to testify that testator had X arrested for forgery.

_____ 33. In 32, for the same purpose, W offers to testify that testator ordered his superintendent to discharge X from testator's employ.

_____ 34. In 32, for the same purpose, W offers to testify that testator falsely charged X with the crime of bigamy under such circumstances that testator must have known the charge to be false.

_____ 35. Action for $500, the price of an automobile. Plea, payment. On the issue of payment, W offers to testify that he saw defendant hand plaintiff a $500 bill, and say: "This is the payment for that car."

_____ 36. In 35, on the issue of payment, W offers to testify that on the following day plaintiff said to defendant: "I was glad to be able to pay you cash for that car."

_____ 37. Action for conversion of an automobile. To prove value, plaintiff offers a receipt for the purchase price, $5000, signed by the dealer from whom he bought it.

_____ 38. Action for personal injuries by a guest in an automobile against the owner. Defense, contributory negligence and assumption of risk. W offers to testify that an hour before the accident, in the presence of plaintiff, defendant, a mechanic said: "The spindle on that front wheel may break at any moment." If offered to show the spindle defective.

_____ 39. The testimony is 38 offered as tending to show assumption of risk.

_____ 40. As tending to show that D had never repaid a loan, W offers to testify that P hired W to collect the sum from D.

_____ 44. As tending to show that D had a revolver at an affray, W offers to testify that as D passed W's house, W called his wife's attention to a revolver sticking out of D's pocket.

*   *   *

_____ 48. W testified that he saw D do act X, and offers to testify: "I told M within one hour after the event that I had seen D do act X." Offered to show D's conduct.

*   *   *

_____ 50. W testified that he saw D do act X, could not remember the date, but within an hour thereafter reported to M. M offers to testify that at 3:30 p.m. of June 1, 1944, W told M that he had just seen D do act X. M's testimony is offered to fix the time.

_____ 51. To prove that the defendant committed the crime, the prosecution offers a confession made to police officers.

_____ 52. To prove that the defendant committed the crime, the prosecution offers evidence that the defendant remained silent after being arrested for the crime.

_____ 53. To prove that the defendant committed the crime, the prosecution offers into evidence a certified copy of a prior judgement of conviction for the same offense.

_____ 54. To prove that the defendant committed the crime, the prosecution offers a witness to testify that he was present and observed the jury return a verdict of guilty in a prosecution of the defendant for a similar prior offense.

_____ 55. To prove that her husband was insane, a wife offers evidence that he lived in a nest in the top of a tree for the last five years.

_____ 56. In an action for breach of contract, the plaintiff offers into evidence an advertisement conceded to be that of the defendant offering a reward for certain information which the plaintiff claims to have provided.

_____ 57. To prove that the defendant committed a crime, the prosecution offers evidence that the F.B.I. offered a reward for his capture.

_____ 58. In an heirship proceeding, the claimant testifies that the deceased was his father.

_____ 59. To prove paternity, the plaintiff offers evidence that the defendent referred to the child as "my son."

_____ 60. To fix the time of a murder, the prosecution offers a witness who testifies that minutes after he heard the shot, he heard a clock chime three times.

_____ 61. To prove adultery, the husband offers proof that a house guest after a visit had described to one of his cronies a birthmark that the accused wife has on an intimate part of her anatomy. The existence of the mark has previously been testified to by the husband while the wife has testified that only her parents and her husband knew of the mark.

_____ 62. To prove that a couple is married, a witness is offered to testify that he heard the exchange of nuptial vows.

_____ 63. To prove notice of a defect in the defendant's car in a personal injury suit, the plaintiff introduces evidence of the defendant's past attempts to repair his car.

_____ 64. In a common disaster case, in order to establish survivorship, evidence is offered that after the accident one of the victims was heard to cry: "I'm alive."

_____ 65. In a prosecution for the theft of valuable homing pigeons, evidence is offered that when the defendant's pigeon coop was opened, all of the birds flew to the home of the victim.

_____ 66. In a prosecution for sale of pornography, the prosecution offers one hundred letters sent to the defendant's post office box, each of which says, in substance: "Send me some of those dirty books."

_____ 67. Personal injury case. To show pain and suffering, plaintiff calls a nurse who testifies that the plaintiff was screaming when he was brought to the hospital.

_____ 68. In a divorce case, after the husband has testified that his wife was always nagging him at the top of her voice, the wife calls a neighbor to testify that she never heard any nagging.

_____ 69. In a paternity suit, the mother takes the stand and when asked to identify the father of her child, she points to the defendant.

_____ 70. To prove that defendant is the father of her child, the mother offers a letter in evidence from defendant's attorney in which the attorney states that his client has admitted he is the father of the child.

_____ 71. Personal injury litigation. Plaintiff testifies that there was a sign facing the intersection toward the direction that the defendant had come from without stopping and that sign said: "STOP".

_____ 72. To prove that the insured under a life policy is dead, his wife offers a death certificate.

_____ 73. In a plagiarism suit, the plaintiff testifies that he caught the defendant in his apartment copying portions of the plaintiff's typed manuscript in longhand on a sheet of paper.

_____ 74. Murder prosecution. To support a self-defense claim, defendant introduces witnesses who testify that before the killing defendant told them he was afraid of the victim.

_____ 75. To show that defendant was home and thus could have killed his wife the prosecution calls her paramour who testifies that when hubby was gone and the coast was clear, the wife always pulled down a shade on a particular window but when he was home the shade was always open. The prosecution calls a neighbor who testifies that on the night of the murder the shade was open.

PART B. EXCEPTIONS TO THE HEARSAY RULE

---

1. FORMER TESTIMONY

TRAVELERS FIRE INS. CO. v. WRIGHT

Supreme Court of Oklahoma, 1958.
322 P.2d 417, 70 A.L.R.2d 1170.

[Action by J.B. Wright and J.C. Wright to recover under the terms of two fire insurance policies. The defendant insurers defended on the ground that the fire that destroyed plaintiffs' property had been deliberately caused by plaintiff J.B. Wright with the intent to defraud the defendants. Defendants alleged and proved that the plaintiffs were, at all pertinent times, business partners. There was a verdict and a judgment for plaintiffs, from which defendants appealed—Ed.]

JACKSON, Justice. * * * Defendants called Wm. Holland Eppler and Albert Brown as witnesses. Each witne claimed his constitutional privilege against self-incrimination and refused to testify. The claim of each was granted by the trial court. Defendant then offered certified transcripts of testimony given by each witness in the trial of a criminal case wherein one of the plaintiffs herein, J.B. Wright, was charged with the crime of arson in connection with the fire involved in the instant case. Such testimony was to the effect that J.B. Wright, with the aid and assistance of the two named witnesses, actively procured the burning of the property. Each offer was rejected by the trial court. The court reporter who took the evidence in the criminal case testified as to the correctness of his transcript, the nature of the case in which the testimony was taken and the parties involved. In addition to offering the transcript, defendants offered to have the reporter read same in evidence.

In 20 A.M.Jur. § 686, at page 580, it is said that the real basis for the admission of testimony given by a witness at a former trial is to prevent the miscarriage of justice where the circumstances of the case have made it unreasonable and unfair to exclude the same, and where the court perceives no need for the introduction of testimony taken at a former trial of the same issue, such evidence is properly excluded.

There is a difference of opinion upon the right to use in a civil case the testimony given in a criminal case by a witness whose testimony is no longer available. Indeed this court has had difficulty with this question. In Ray v. Henderson, 44 Okl. 174, 144 P. 175, handed down in 1914, without dissent, it was held in the first paragraph of the syllabus as follows:

"The testimony of a witness, since deceased, given at an examining trial before a justice of the peace on the charge of felonious assault, may be used against the defendant, in a civil suit against him, for damages by the person assaulted."

In Concordia Fire Insurance Co. v. Wise, Adm'r, 114 Okl. 254, 246 P. 595, 46 A.L.R. 456, handed down in 1926, with a divided court, 5 to 3, we overruled Ray v. Henderson, supra, and held in the fifth paragraph of the syllabus as follows:

"In an action to recover on a fire insurance policy, the testimony of a witness who had since died, given in the criminal proceedings against the insured for burning the building covered by insurance, is properly excluded."

Since our decisions are binding upon trial courts and litigants, we appreciate the necessity of establishing a rule and following it. However, if we have established the wrong rule, or if our rule is unsound, we should avail ourselves of the first opportunity to correct it lest we perpetuate the wrong. In 142 A.L.R. 673, there appears an Annotation on the question involved herein. At page 701 of the Annotation the author states that he considers it unfortunate that we overruled Ray v. Henderson in the Concordia case.

It is interesting to note that in the Concordia case we followed the rule laid down by the Supreme Court of Illinois (McInturff v. Insurance Co. of North America, 248 Ill. 92, 93 N.E. 369), *believing it to be the majority rule.* However, in 46 A.L.R. (published subsequent to the Concordia decision) there appears an Annotation on page 463, under the subject "Use in civil case of testimony given in criminal case by witness no longer accessible", wherein it is said:

"The weight of authority seems to be to the effect that, on a proper showing of inability to procure the attendance of a witness at the trial of a civil case, his testimony given in a criminal prosecution involving the same transaction is admissible against the person who was defendant therein."

The author lists decisions from five states, Georgia, Iowa, New York, South Dakota, and Wisconsin, as constituting the weight of authority. Three states, Illinois, Pennsylvania, and Oklahoma (citing the Concordia case), are listed as following the minority view.

It is quite often stated that before testimony can be taken from a former trial or proceeding and introduced in a subsequent trial there must be (1) an inability to obtain the testimony of the witness; (2) there must have been an opportunity to cross-examine the witness in the former trial; (3) there must be an identity, or substantial, identity of issues, and (4) parties. These requirements are recognized in the Concordia case. The primary difficulty arises when we attempt to determine if there is an identity of issues. In a Pennsylvania decision, Harger v. Thomas, 1862, 44 Pa. 128, 84 Am.Dec. 422, cited in 46 A.L.R. 463, supra, heavy stress was laid upon the conclusion that a criminal prosecution is not an action, and that the issue in a criminal case is between the government and the prisoner on the question of guilt, and not a question of property. In the Illinois case, McInturff v. Insurance Co. of North America, supra, it was pointed out that the issue in a criminal case is "guilt" and in a civil case the issue is "property." The "issue" as defined by those courts appears to us to be more in the nature of the ultimate issue, or result sought to be obtained by the action or proceeding. In our view it would be more accurate to consider the "issue" as that issue sought to be established by the witness when he testified in the criminal case and weigh it against the issue sought to be proved in the witness in the civil case.

In the case before us, it appears that Eppler and Brown testified in the criminal case to establish the issue of whether J.B. Wright procured the burning of the building. Affirmative proof of this issue was necessary to establish his guilt. In the civil case before us the issue is whether J.B. Wright procured the burning of the building. Affirmative proof of this issue is necessary if defendants herein are to prevail. It may be that there were other issues sought to be proved by other witnesses in the instant case, but the issue sought to be established by Eppler and Brown in both the criminal and civil cases was whether J.B. Wright procured the burning of the building.

From a re-examination of our former decisions, and decisions from other jurisdictions, it becomes apparent that it is impossible to write a rule that will fit all situations. As pointed out in 20 Am.Jur., p. 580, supra, the reason for admitting testimony given at a former trial is to prevent a miscarriage of justice. It naturally follows that testimony from a former trial should not be admitted if to do so would result in a miscarriage of justice.

As a general proposition we think testimony from a criminal case can be introduced in a subsequent civil case where it appears that it is impossible to obtain the testimony of the witness who testified in the criminal case; that there was an opportunity to cross-examine the witness by the party against whom the testimony is sought to be used in the civil case, or by one whose motive and interest in cross-examining was the same; and that there is an identity of issues. As will be hereinafter shown, identity of *all* parties is not an independent requirement in all cases.

As a further safeguard the trial court should give the objecting party an opportunity to point out wherein it would be unjust to admit such testimony. We have examined the transcript of the testimony given by the witnesses Eppler and Brown, in the criminal case and find nothing therein indicating that it would have been unjust to admit the testimony against the plaintiffs in this case.

From our examination of the record herein it appears that the trial court erred in refusing to let the court reporter relate the testimony given by Eppler and Brown in the criminal case. It also follows that the rule is expressed in the fifth paragraph of the syllabus in Concordia Fire Insurance Co. v. Wise, 114 Okl. 254, 246 P. 595, 46 A.L.R. 456, must be, and accordingly is, overruled insofar as in conflict with the views herein expressed.

Is it material that one of the plaintiffs herein, J.C. Wright, was not a party defendant in the criminal case, and apparently did not participate in the alleged burning of the insured property? We think not.

The insurance policies herein, on which recovery is sought, provide that the defendant companies will not be liable for loss by fire caused by neglect of the insured to use all reasonable means to save and preserve the property at and after a loss. In 29 Am.Jur.Insurance § 1028, pp. 777 and 778, it is said:

> "On the other hand, an innocent partner cannot recover on an insurance policy upon partnership property wilfully burned by his copartner, especially where the policy provides that the insured shall use all reasonable means at and after a fire to preserve the property."

This rule of law is supported by cases cited in American Jurisprudence and in an Annotation in 27 A.L.R. beginning at page 948.

Is it important that J.C. Wright did not have an opportunity to cross-examine in the criminal case? J.B. Wright had the same motive and interest in cross-examining the witnesses in the criminal case as would J.C. Wright in the instant case. The issues were the same in both cases. J.B.

Wright had, and has, the same property interest as that of J.C. Wright. In 142 A.L.R. at page 696, the author quotes from 5 Wigmore on Evidence, 3rd ed. § 1368, as follows:

" * * * The principle, then, is that where the interest of the person was calculated to induce equally as thorough a testing by cross-examination, then the present opponent has had adequate protection for the same end. Thus the requirement of identify of parties is after all only an incident or corollary of the requirement as to identity of issue. * * * It ought then, to be sufficient to inquire whether the former testimony was given upon such an issue that the party-opponent in that case had the same interest and motive in his cross-examination that the present opponent has."

The author of the Annotation concludes that the argument and position taken by Wigmore is supported by a considerable number of cases from various jurisdictions and cites the cases in support of that rule. We conclude that J.B. Wright's opportunity to cross-examine the witness in the criminal case on the same issue, and with the same interest and motive that J.C. Wright would have in the instant case, satisfies the rule of substantial identity of issues and parties and opportunity for satisfactory cross-examination.

From the foregoing it is seen that the question of substantial identity of parties is important only with regard to the parties as against whom such testimony is offered; therefore the fact that the state was J.B. Wright's adversary in the first case rather than the insurance companies is immaterial. Such fact has no bearing upon the question of whether there has been an adequate opportunity to thoroughly sift and test such testimony by cross-examination.

In view of our conclusion to remand for new trial, we think it is necessary that we give attention to other questions presented in the briefs which undoubtedly will be presented when the case is retried.

We have herein held that the court reporter should be permitted to relate and testify as to what both witnesses testified to in the criminal trial. This conclusion is upon the assumption that both witnesses, at the subsequent trial of this case, will be subpoenaed and will claim their privilege against self-incrimination, and that their claims will be granted. If so, their testimony is as unavailable as if they were dead. Exleton v. State, 30 Okl.Cr. 224, 235 P. 627.

The judgement is reversed and the cause remanded for a new trial in accordance with the views herein expressed.

Davison, Halley, Johnson, Williams and Carlile, JJ., concur.

Corn, V.C.J., and Blackbird, J., dissent.

JAMES, CIVIL PROCEDURE

575-76, 584-85 (1965).*
[Footnotes omitted.]

D. COLLATERAL ESTOPPEL

§ 11.18.   General

Where an action between two parties terminates in a valid judgment, that judgment may have an effffect in a later action between those parties even where it is brought upon a different claim or cause of action. But, as we have seen, the effect of the judgment in such case is more limited than in the case where both actions are upon the same cause of action. Where the actions are upon different claims the former judgment "operates as an estoppel only as to those matters in issue or points controverted, upon the determination of which the finding or verdict is rendered." It does not preclude inquiry into matters which might have been but actually were not put in issue and determined in the former action. This more limited effect of a judgment is often called "collateral estoppel" and that term will be used here.

Where collateral estoppel is involved between the same parties as those to the original suit the one who claims its benefit (proponent) must show that the very fact or point now in issue was, in the former action, (1) litigated by the parties; (2) determined by the tribunal; and (3) necessarily so determined. Where these conditions are met, collateral estoppel may have a limited effect upon persons who were not parties to the former action. This we shall take up in later sections but the first part of our discussion will assume identity of parties.

§ 11.19. Matter or point must have been litigated

Parties need not and often do not contest every claim to the utmost; they do not always raise every matter or point which might conceivably be relevant to the claim or defense. The reasons why they do not cover a wide range; examples of them given in a famous opinion are " * * * the smallness of the amount or the value of the property in controversy, the difficulty of obtaining the necessary evidence, the expense of litigation, and his own situation at the time." Another reason may be the fear of diverting the tribunal's attention from a good claim or defense by injecting a weak, or confusing, or unpopular issue. Many other considerations may be important in various situations.

If a party omits some matter or point from the first action he is, as we have seen, precluded by a judgment in it from later raising that matter or point either to promote or to defeat the original cause of action. To this extent, then, he is under pressure to litigate the first action to the utmost. The present limitation upon the collateral effect of a judgment represents a decision that the pressure to litigate the first action to the utmost will not be carried so far as to make omissions from the first action fatal * * *

§ 11.23. Introductory

As a rule a person who is entitled to the benefits of the rules of res judicata would also be bound by these rules if the judgment had gone the other way. Where this is so, there may be said to be mutuality with respect to the obligations and rights under a judgment, and (as we shall see) such mutuality has sometimes been erected into a rule or principle requiring it. As we shall also see, however, the requirement of mutuality has been severely attacked and although it has by no means been drained of all vitality it has certainly given ground in the modern scene. The result is that the class of persons who are bound by the res judicata effects of a judgment —including bar, merger, and collateral estoppel—is substantially narrower than the class of those who may take advantage of these effects. The discrepancy is particularly noticeable in the case of collateral estoppel.

———

See Federal Rules of Evidence 804(b)(1), at pp. 926, 927; California Rules of Evidence § § 1290–1292; at pp. 884–885.

Hypotheticals

(1) X is prosecuted for robbery of A, a bartender. At X's preliminary hearing A testified as to the commission of the crime. In addition A stated the address of B Bar where he was then working, and his residence address, but indicated he planned to change his residence address very soon. At X's trial, the prosecutor offers in evidence the preliminary hearing transcript of A's testimony after calling C, a district attorney's investigator, who testifies that he had been unable to locate A; that A no longer worked at B Bar; and that the local phone book and voters' registration list did not contain A's name. On cross-examination by X, C testifies that he did not make inquiry at the Bartenders' Union nor the residence address A gave at the preliminary hearing, because A had said he was planning to move very soon. X makes a hearsay objection to the preliminary hearing transcript testimony of A. What result?

(2) X is prosecuted for robbery of A. The prosecutor offers in evidence the transcript of A's testimony given at the preliminary hearing after calling B, a district attorney's investigator, who testifies that a subpoena had been sent to A's place of employment but was not served because A was in New York; that an hour before testifying, he, B, had made a telephone call to A in New York and A told him that he planned to remain in New York for six months. Should X's hearsay objection to A's transcript testimony be sustained?

(3) A sues X for $1500 property damage to his automobile arising out of a rear-end collision. X takes A's deposition. A moves to New York after his deposition is taken and is living there at the time of trial. A's counsel offers A's deposition testimony in evidence after testifying that a few days before trial, A telephoned and said it was too expensive for him to come back to California and testify. X makes a hearsay objection to A's deposition testimony. What result?

(4) X, a police officer, pursued a suspect felon into a bar. X became involved in a dispute with A, the bar owner, regarding the whereabouts of the suspected felon. X claims that A struck him with a chair. X arrested A on the charge of battery upon a police officer. In the criminal trial of A, A testifies that he didn't touch X and that X struck him with his billy club. B, a bar patron who was present, testifies for A and corroborates A's version of what happened. A was acquitted and then sues X and Y City, X's employer, for damages for battery, false arrest, and imprisonment. At the trial of A's action against X and Y City. A establishes that B's whereabouts are unknown and that he used reasonable diligence to find B to serve him with a subpoena, but to no avail. A then offers in evidence a transcript of B's testimony given in A's criminal trial. X and Y City make a hearsay objection. How should the court rule?

(5) D is charged with possession of narcotics. D is first arrested at his residence for an unrelated offense. At the time of his arrest, X, a female, resided with D. While D is in jail on the unrelated charge, PO, a police officer, secures a search warrant for D's residence and discovers a home-constructed waterbed with hollowed out compartments in the frame in which PO finds the narcotics. D testifies that he had no knowledge of the items in the bedframe compartments, that shortly before his arrest he had observed a pill vial in X's possession similar to the one found in the bedframe compartment, and that he had previously observed X injecting "speed." D offers in evidence in his defense under the former-testimony hearsay exception evidence given by X in another criminal case in a different county. In this prior case

X testified for the prosecution as a witness to the murder of her husband, which took place one week after D's arrest. On cross-examination of X at the former trial, testimony was elicited from her that on the evening of the killing she was under the influence of narcotics, having earlier injected "speed;" that she was a narcotics addict and had possession of narcotics and the necessary paraphernalia for their use. At D's trial it is conceded that X is unavailable as a witness. D contends that X's former testimony is relevant on the question of D's lack of knowledge, possession, and control of the items discovered in the frame of the waterbed. The prosecutor makes a hearsay objection to the proffered former testimony of X. Should the prosecutor's motion be sustained?

2.   DYING DECLARATIONS

CAIRNS, LAW AND THE SOCIAL SCIENCES

173–74 (1935).*
[Footnotes omitted.]

    * * *   A large part of the business of psychology is to ascertain how people generally conduct themselves in certain situations; this is also, but to a much lesser extent, the concern of the law. If, for example, the courts decide that a dying declaration made by an individual, the manner of whose death is being investigated in a criminal proceeding, is admissible because the solemnity of the occasion is likely to impel truthfulness, they are making an assumption more properly describable as psychological then legal. In the establishing of the rule, which is perhaps rooted in a custom which goes back at least to the twelfth century, theological beliefs were perhaps a dominant factor. Psychology may or may not confirm the law's assumption but at least it would be wise for the courts to inquire what it has to offer. * * *

KING JOHN**

Act V, iv, 10–61

SALISBURY

May this be possible? may this be true?

MELUN

Have I not hideous death within my view,
Retaining but a quantity of life,
Which bleeds away, even as a form of wax
Resolveth from his figure 'gainst the fire?
What in the world should make me now deceive,
Since I must lose the use of all deceit?
Why should I then be false, since it is true
That I must die here and live hence by truth?
I say again,   * * *

---

*New York, Harcourt, Brace and Company, 1935.

**The Complete Works of Shakespeare, The Cambridge Edition Text, as edited by W.A. Wright (Rockwell Kent).

SOLES v. STATE

Supreme Court of Florida, 1929.
97 Fla. 61, 119 So. 791.

BROWN, J. Carl Soles was convicted of manslaughter on an indictment charging him with the murder of Clifford Long in May, 1928. The weapon which was alleged to have been used was a 22-caliber rifle.

The judgment is attacked because it is said that the court erred in admitting in evidence the dying declaration of Clifford Long; that it erred in refusing an instruction requested by the defendant upon the subject of dying declaration which embodied the proposition that, if the jury should find from the evidence that the statement admitted as a dying declaration was made "without consciousness on the part of the deceased of impending death," then the jury should not consider it as a dying declaration; and that the evidence was not sufficient to support the verdict.

Arthur Robinson, a witness for the state, was driving the automobile in which the boy, Clifford Long, was sitting when the latter was shot. They had been trying to obtain some whisky for Robinson. While searching for it, or pretending to do so, they were frightened away by what they supposed to be a rifle shot. The two, with one Jesse Jackson, who was also a member of the party, returned to the automobile and drove away. As they proceeded along the road, another shot was fired from a point down the road to their rear, and Clifford Long was wounded in the back of the head. He died as the result of that wound.

About an hour before he died, according to the testimony of his father, who asked who had hurt him, he replied: "Oh Daddy! Carl Soles shot me with a 22 rifle. I have got to die." The statement was made about 20 or 25 minutes after he was shot. The defendant objected to the question propounded to the father of the boy which elicited the above statement from him. The objection was overruled and exception was noted. No motion was made to exclude the answer.

The sister of decreased, a girl about 14 years old, testified to the same fact, and added that about 15 minutes after the decreased was brought to the place where the statement was made the defendant came on the scene driving a truck. No one was with him and he had a "22 rifle." She was permitted to repeat the "conversation," as it was called, which occurred between the boy who had been shot and his father over defendant's objection. The conversation consisted of a question by the father, addressed to no one in particular, as follows: " 'Who has hurt my darling boy?' " and Clifford replied, according to the father: " 'Oh, Daddy! Carl Soles shot me with a 22 rifle. I have got to die.' " According to the girl, the boy replied as follows: " 'Papa, Carl Soles shot me with a 22 rifle and I have got to die.' "

The admission of this evidence constituted the basis of the first and second assignments of error.

It is argued that the statement was inadmissible, not only because the court did not inquire of others present whether the deceased said he had to die, and that one other witness who was present said he did not hear such statement, but that the statement contained no evidence that the declarant made it in the belief that death was impending.

The boy had gone with two negroes in an automobile a short distance from where he lived and was returning when he was shot. After riding a short distance he left the automobile, transferred to a truck, which was about to pass, and was driven to Sammy Long's store, where his father assisted him in getting out of the truck. He soon became unconscious, but before passing into unconsciousness he made the statement.

The defendant's counsel requested the court to give the following instruction to the jury: "The court has admitted in evidence for your consideration an alleged dying declaration of the deceased. In so admitting said dying declaration the Court has only passed upon its admissibility. In order that a statement of the deceased may properly be considered as a dying declaration it must have been made by the deceased with a consciousness of impending death, and if you find from the evidence that such statement by the deceased, if made, was without consciousness on the part of the deceased of impending death you should not further consider it as a dying declaration."

There was no error in admitting the testimony of the two witnesses above referred to.

We are inclined to the opinion that the court below was correct in refusing to give the quoted instruction requested by the defendant, and that the judgment of conviction should be affirmed. While there is some conflict of authority on the question, it appears to us from a careful review of the cases in the notes under section 1451 of Wigmore on Evidence (2d Ed.), that the weight of authority and the trend of our own former decisions is to the effect that such an instruction should not be given. In the text of said section 1451, Dean Wigmore in discussing the question in part says:

Section 1451.   "That the judge is to pass on the preliminary condition necessary to the admissibility of evidence is unquestioned (post Sec. 2550). It follows, as of course, that, since a consciousness of impending death is according to the foregoing principles legally essential to admissibility, the *judge must determine* whether that condition exists before the declaration is admitted.

"After a dying declaration, or any other evidence has been admitted, the *weight* to be given to it is a matter exclusively for the jury. They may believe it or may not believe it; but, so far as they do or do not, their judgment is not controlled by rules of law. Therefore, though they themselves do not suppose the declarant to have been conscious of death, they may still believe the statement; conversely, though they do suppose him to have been thus conscious, they may still not believe the statement to be true. In other words, their canons of ultimate belief are not necessarily the same as the preliminary legal conditions of admissibility, whose purpose is an entirely different one (ante, Sec. 29). It is, therefore, erroneous for the judge, after once admitting the declaration, to instruct the jury that they must reject the declaration, or exclude it from consideration, if the legal requirement as to consciousness of death does not in their opinion exist. No doubt they *may* reject it, on this ground or on any other; but they are not to be expected to follow a definition of law intended for the Judge."

To much the same effect is the treatment of the point by Greenleaf, in vol. 1 (16th Ed.) § 161–b. After laying down the general rule as to the court's determination of the admissibility of the declaration, he adds: "But, after the evidence is admitted, its credibility is entirely within the province of the jury, who of course are at liberty to weigh all the circumstances under which the declaration were made, including those already proved to the judge, and to give the testimony only such credit as upon the whole they may think it deserves."

In the note to section 1451 of Wigmore on Evidence, it is said that a contrary ruling was made in R.V. Woodcock, Leach, Cr.L. (3d Ed.) 563, an English case decided in 1790, but that this was subsequently repudiated in England, and that the principle as stated above does not appear to have since been doubted. He quotes Starkie (1 Stark. 521) as having observed: "It might as well be left to a jury to say whether a witness ought to be sworn, or whether he is not incapacitated by ignorance or infamy or other cause from giving evidence upon oath."

In Holland v. State, 39 Fla. 178, 22 So. 298, this court held that: "The court determines the admissibility, and the jury the credibility, of confessions. It is not error, therefore, for the court to refuse to charge the jury that if they believe from all the evidence that defendant's confession was procured from fear or terror, or hope of reward, they should disregard the confession in making up their verdict." This appears to be the orthodox rule, in regard to confessions. Section 861, Wigmore on Evidence (2d Ed.). The analogy to dying declarations is, in this respect, quite complete. In Roten v. State, 31 Fla. 514, 12 So. 910, it was held that the question of the admissibility of a dying declaration was exclusively one for the court to decide.

Affirmed.

Terrell, C.J., and Whitfield, Strum, and Buford, JJ., concur.

See Federal Rules of Evidence 804(b)(2) at pp. 926, 927; California Evidence Code § 1242 at p. 881.

PRELIMINARY QUESTIONS OF FACT
KAPLAN, OF MABRUS AND ZORGS—AN ESSAY IN HONOR OF DAVID LOUISELL

66 Cal. L.Rev. 987 (1978).*

[Editor's Note: This article has been edited and adapted somewhat for publication in this casebook].

* * *

* * * [A]n infrequently thought about—or at least infrequently written about—area is the distribution of functions between the judge and the jury in determining what are called preliminary questions of fact. In general, we have two rules to cover two different questions that come up in the trial of cases. The first question occurs when the issue is whether a proferred piece of evidence is admissible. Here the elementary rule is that the judge, not the jury, must decide the issue. The second question occurs when

an issue of fact arises and the evidence bearing on it is such that a reasonable person could find either way. There, the equally elementary rule is that the jury, not the judge, is to resolve the question.

In large numbers of cases, we have no trouble telling the two situations a part and the two rules peacefully coexist. Virtually no one would suggest that the jury should determine whether an item of evidence is or is not hearsay, or whether an accountant has or does not have a privilege not to testify against his client. Similarly, most judges would not dream of directing a verdict on the issue of who went through the red light where the usual crowds of drivers, passengers, and bystanders fell to disputing whether the plaintiff or the defendant was the guilty party. It is elementary, however, that we often come across questions that seem to fall within both categories —cases in which the admissibility of a piece of evidence turns on the resolution of a question of fact.

Before examining the conventional wisdom about distinguishing the two rules, let us examine a hypothetical and ask ourselves how a rational legal system—assuming that any legal system which makes use of a two-headed problem solving institution such as a judge and a jury could properly be called rational—should allocate the preliminary factfinding task.

(1) Prosecution of D for the murder of A. W testifies that while A lay in the hospital, two days after suffering a gunshot wound in the stomach, A said, "I saw D shoot me," and, without commenting further on the subject, died shortly thereafter.

Clearly, A's out-of-court declaration is hearsay. Arguably, however, it is within the dying declaration exception to the hearsay rule which provides that in a homicide prosecution a statement of the deceased as to the cause of his death, made on personal knowledge and under a sense of impending death, is admissible to show the truth of the facts asserted.

Let us assume that there is no dispute about A's personal knowledge and that the only real issue as to admissibility is whether the statement was made under a sense of impending death—an issue as to which there is conflicting evidence. One witness testifies that he, a physician, told A, just before A made the statement at issue, that his condition was hopeless and that he would die very shortly. Another witness, a nurse of somewhat dubious credibility because she turns out to have been a girlfriend of D, testifies that, a moment after the statement, the deceased whispered to her that doctors are often wrong and that he felt much better than he had the day before.

Is this question one which the judge should decide on the principle that the court must rule on the admissibility of evidence? Or is it one which the jury should decide (under proper instructions, of course) on the theory that it is the proper trier of the facts?   *   *   *

There are several ways of handling the problem of hypothetical 1. In theory, we could interrupt the trial and empanel a separate jury to listen to the evidence about A's death and decide the sole issue of whether A's statement was made under a sense of impending death. Thus, the question of fact would be decided by a jury, and the judge, bound by this factual finding, could decide the question of admissibility or what was left of it. We would then have two separate questions decided at different times, and our two rules could lie down like the proverbial lion and lamb.[7] If the specially empaneled jury were to decide that A's statement was not made under a sense of impending death, the trial judge would exclude the evidence, and the jury trying the prosecution itself would not hear her testimony. Alternatively, if the specially empaneled jury were to find that A's statement was made under a sense of impending death, would allow the evidence in and the trial jury would then listen to what W had to say.

If questions of preliminary fact were relatively rare, we might seriously consider this course. Such questions, however, are very common and a given trial may raise dozens of them. We have enough difficulty disposing of our litigation with one jury per case. Obviously, it would be that much more time-consuming and expensive to empanel in each case additional juries —or even just one additional jury—to decide all the questions of preliminary fact.

A somewhat less taxing proposal would be to use the trial jury itself to decide each preliminary fact question, but require it to do so before the judge could decide the admissibility of the questioned evidence. Thus, in hypothetical 1, the jurors would first hear all the evidence bearing on the circumstances surrounding A's statement and then, under proper instructions from the judge, retire for their deliberations on this issue. If the jurors were to decide that A's statement was not made under a sense of impending death, they would so inform the judge who would excuse W from the witness stand. If the jurors were to decide the opposite then, on their return, the judge would permit them to hear W's testimony.

Although it is not quite so impractical as the first possibility, this proposal also poses overwhelming problems. First, it would be enormously expensive in terms of time and effort to require many interruptions of the trial while the jury deliberated the numerous preliminary fact questions that arise in the trial of any lawsuit. And this waste of lawyers' and witnesses' time would not be the only problem. We would also have to determine what to do when the jury could not reach unanimous agreement on the preliminary fact issue. Most important, however, we would be unable to cope with the natural inclination of jurors routinely to find the existence of the preliminary facts necessary to the admissibility of evidence so that they could better perform their factfinding duties and satisfy their own curiosities as well.

The next possibility is considerably more administrable than either of the aforementioned, but is itself fatally defective. Why not, one might suggest, simply let the jurors hear both the evidence bearing on the preliminary facts concerning the circumstances surrounding A's statement and W's testimony as to A's statement itself, but instruct them to consider W's testimony as evidence only if they first find that A made his statement under a sense of impending death.

The problem with this course stems from the jury's role being basically quite different from the judge's. A judge's duty is to apply the rules of a legal system which is, one would hope, designed to reach the appropriate fac-

---

7. *Isaiah* 11:6. It has been pointed out, by the way, that in such a situation, the lamb —at best—gets very little sleep.

tual resolution in the largest possible number of cases, giving appropriate weight as well to other societal values. These other values which shape many of our rules of evidence but which are often unrelated to the fact determining role, include privacy, encouragement of certain confidential relations, convenience in administering a complex body of evidence law, and notions of fairness. A jury, on the other hand, focuses on the determination of the facts of one particular case and in doing so frequently is far less interested than a judge in the societal values underlying our rules of evidence or anything else which might get in the way of their determining the facts of the case at hand.

Obviously the jury will not be prepared to enforce the policy of the law to exclude such statements that were not made under a sense of impending death. The jury will be much more interested in whether A had had a grudge against D, whether A wished to shield someone else, and whether his memory and perception of the shooting were good. [T]he jurors might be somewhat interested in the preliminary fact at issue because if A had spoken under a sense of impending death and had been a religious man, that might be an extra guarantee of his sincerity. In most cases, however, they would be much more interested in other facts about the statement. As a result, if anyone is going to enforce the policy of the hearsay exception, it will have to be the judge.

Can we then conclude that in all cases the judge should decide the factual questions which determine the admissibility of evidence and let the jury hear the evidence only if he finds those facts in favor of admissibility? The conventional wisdom is to the contrary, and for good reason. Let us consider another hypothetical:

(2)   Plaintiff, P, injured in an automobile accident, alleges that the defendant, D, was driving at an excessive speed. To help show this, he produces a witness, W, to testify that about a minute before the accident and one mile from the scene he (W) saw D's car travelling at an excessive speed on the road toward the place of impact. D, however, produces evidence that indicates it was another car that W saw, not D's.

Presumably no one would argue that W's testimony is sufficiently relevant to show D's speed if the car W saw was not D's car. Assuming, then, that one mile is close enough to the accident, the relevance of this evidence depends on a question of fact: whether the car observed by W was the defendant's. Is there any reason why this question must be decided by the judge as was the case in the dying declaration hypothetical hypotheticals? Obviously not. The judge can let the jury hear all the evidence on the issue of which car W saw, confident that if the jurors decide that W saw another car and not the defendant's, they will ignore W's testimony as to its speed and decide the case on other evidence.

Similarly, let us examine another hypothetical, illustrating the same point:

(3)   A sues B on a note that purportedly carries B's signature. B's defense is that the note is a forgery, and there is evidence both ways on the question of genuineness. Under the facts of the case, a forged note

would bear no relation to the rights and liabilities of the parties.[8] For this reason, when A attempts to introduce the purported note into evidence, B objects on the ground of relevance.

Here again we have a question to be decided by the jury. If the jurors are at all rational in attempting to perform their job, we would certainly expect them to ignore a forged note in determining the rights and liabilities of A and B.

Even where a preliminary fact question is to be decided by the jury, the judge still retains his function of making sure there is sufficient evidence from which a rational jury could find the preliminary fact. If not, the evidence must be kept from the jury—but not because the judge had decided the preliminary fact question. Rather, the judge would simply be holding that there was, in contemplation of the law, no question to be decided. In our legal system, all jury questions presuppose a situation in which the evidence is sufficient to support a jury finding.

See Federal Rules of Evidence 104 at p. 907; California Evidence Code § § 403, 405 at pp. 817, 818.

Hypotheticals

(1) X is prosecuted for murder in shooting A to death in a barroom brawl. In defense, X calls B and makes an offer of proof that B will testify that he talked with A in the hospital the day before his death, that A had difficulty in breathing, and said: "I don't think I can make it. It was not X's fault. C was going after X with a knife before X drew his gun. C ducked when X fired and that's how I got shot." The prosecutor makes a hearsay objection to B's testimony and offers to prove by Y, a nurse, that five minutes before B talked with A, A told her that he was feeling fine and expected to be able to leave the hospital within a few days. The judge listens to the testimony of B and Y out of the presence of the jury. And believe that both witnesses are telling the truth. Must he then admit A's statement in evidence? Must he then keep it out?

(2) Assume the same facts as given in Illustration (1), except that the judge admits in evidence A's statement to B upon finding that the requirements of the dying declaration exception are satisfied. The prosecutor calls Y, the nurse, to testify before the jury to A's statement made to her. X objects that Y's testimony is inadmissible in view of the court's ruling admitting A's statement to B. What result?

3. SPONTANEOUS AND CONTEMPORANEOUS EXCLAMATIONS

CESTERO v. FERRARA

Supreme Court of New Jersey, 1971.
57 N.J. 497, 273 A.2d 761.

FRANCES, J.   This action arises out of an automobile collision that occurred in Fairfield, N.J. on December 12, 1966, at approximately 10:30 P.M. at a highway intersection where the movement of vehicles was controlled by traffic lights. Plaintiff Julio Cestero, the driver of one car, and members of his family who were passengers in his car sued defendant Jennie Ferrara, the driver of the other car, to recover compensation on account of

---

8. This is not to say that the note would be inadmissible for all purposes. For example, the very fact that A was desperate enough to forge a note might show that he was liable, let us say, on a counterclaim.

property damage, personal injuries and expenses suffered by them in the accident. Defendant Jennie Ferrara counterclaimed against Mr. Cestero seeking a recovery for personal injuries, medical expenses and other losses, including property damage to her car. After trial, the jury brought in a verdict
of $60,000 in favor of defendant Ferrara against the plaintiff Cestero on the
counterclaim and a verdict of no cause of action on the claims of the various
plaintiffs. Following denial of a motion for a new trial, Cestero sought a review in the Appellate Division where the judgments entered on the verdicts
were affirmed. * * * We granted plaintiff Cestero's petition for
certification. * * *

A number of grounds for reversal were raised in the Appellate Division.
They were disposed of adversely to Cestero in the opinion cited above, and
although we agree with the affirmance, we find it advisable to deal somewhat differently with an evidence problem which constituted a major basis
for the appeal.

The liability issue in the case was a relatively simple one. As already
noted, movement of motor vehicles at the intersection in question was controlled by traffic lights. Each driver claimed the light was green as his or her
car entered the intersecting street. It seems obvious from the record that the
verdict would go to the driver in whose favor the jury decided that basic issue.

The testimony of Mrs. Ferrara and Mr. Cestero was diametrically opposed. Each one claimed the favorable green light; each produced a
so-called disinterested witness who agreed with the claim of the party who
produced him. During the trial, the record of Mrs. Ferrara's hospitalization
and treatment following the accident was received in evidence. Plaintiff objected to the portion thereof which set forth as part of the patient's history
her statement as to cause of the accident. The objection claimed that the
statement was self-serving and hearsay, and should be excluded. The trial
court disagreed and admitted the entire record. The criticized portion says:

"Pt. [patient] stopped for red light, started up on green light and got
hit * * *."

Some further reference to the facts is necessary to facilitate discussion
of the problem. As already noted, the accident took place at approximately
10:30 P.M. on December 12, 1966. Mrs. Ferrara was badly hurt and had to
be transported by ambulance to the Mountainside Hospital in Montclair.
She was carried into the emergency room at about 11:00 P.M. She testified
that she did not remember anything after the accident until she was "in the
hospital." Nor could she say how long she was in the hospital before she remembered "anything." In stating the "first thing" she remembered she
said "Well, I opened my eyes, and I looked up and * * * saw a doctor
in front of me." She started to say, "I says to the doctor * * *," but she
was instructed not to tell that. She was in very bad pain when she saw the
doctor.

On admission to the emergency room, it was obvious that Mrs. Ferrara
was severely injured. The nurse's note says "right leg deformed." Apparently, Dr. Robert Greene, an orthopedist, was called immediately and arrived
in a very short time, although the exact time of his appearance was not recorded. The inference is that he was the doctor she saw when she "opened
her eyes." His handwriten notes on the chart record his first observations.

He found a grossly deformed right femur with "severe pain in any motion of the leg." The leg was "tender over the entire shaft" and there was "gross shortening." The patient had a small laceration of the scalp in the right temporal region.

When the doctor recorded the statement about the accident, he noted further that she was complaining of pain in the right thigh, right shoulder and head; also that she believed "she was unconsious, but has no gross loss of memory other than this." After x-rays of the patient's head, shoulder and right hip were taken and a gross neurological examination made, the doctor felt she could withstand the urgently necessary operation on her femur. Accordingly, she was removed to the operating room and the surgery performed. The hospital record notes that she was unable to sign the authorization for the surgery before being taken to the operating room. * * *

Statements and declarations, although self-serving in character, are admissible when they constitute part of the *res gestae*. In the early days of the common law, spontaneous statements, declarations or ejaculations which were made by a person involved in an accident so contemporaneously or concomitantly with the mishap as to explain or characterize it, were treated as part of the event itself and therefore evidential. McCormick, Evidence § 274, p. 585 (1954). But in more recent times the *res gestae* concept has been considerably broadened and the requirement for strict contemporaneity has been modified. Now evidence of declarations made under the immediate influence of the principal transaction or occurrence are admissible. They need not be concomitant or coincident with the exciting stimulus; they may be subsequent providing that in the light of all the circumstances it may be said reasonably that the exciting influence had not lost its sway or had not been dissipated in the interval.

Some discretion must be vested in the trial judge with respect to the propriety of receiving in evidence post-event declarations. It must be remembered that they derive their basic credibility not from the veracity of the witness but rather from their relation to the event out of which they emanate. If the circumstances reveal that there was sufficient time to contrive or devise a self-serving falsehood, admissibility should be denied. It must appear that the statements were unpremeditated emanations of the event and so connected with it as to preclude the idea that they were products of calculated policy. At bottom, the principle rests on the recognized common experience of mankind that:

[U]nder certain external circumstances of physical shock, a stress * * * may be produced which stills the reflective faculties and removes their control, so that the utterance which then occurs is a spontaneous and sincere response to the actual sensations and perceptions already produced by the external shock. Since this utterance is made under the immediate and uncontrolled domination of the senses, and during the brief period when considerations of self-interest could not have been brought fully to bear by reasoned reflection, the utterance may be taken as particularly trustworthy (or, at least as lacking the usual grounds of untrustworthiness), and thus as expressing the real tenor of the speaker's belief as to the facts just observed by him * * * . 6 Wigmore, Evidence § 1747, p. 135 (3d 1940). * * *

Our Rules of Evidence have undertaken to codify this broader *res gestae* principle. Rule 63 (4) provides:

A statement is admissible if it was made (a) while the declarant was perceiving an event or condition which the statement narrates, describes or explains, or (b) while the declarant was under the stress of a nervous excitement caused by such perception, in reasonable proximity to the event, and without opportunity to deliberate or fabricate.

Although the explication might be somewhat more definitive in scope, there is no doubt that it was intended to apply to situations like that now before us.

In the present case we are satisfied that defendant Ferrara's statement about the accident, as it appeared in the hospital record, was properly admitted in evidence. On the basis of her testimony, it was made while she was under the shock and stress of the accident and it was sufficiently proximate in point of time to justify the inference that it was not the product of reasoned reflection. The totality of the circumstances was such that a jury might well find that her terse version of the accident, uttered while she was in shock and severe pain and very soon after her first recollection of the accident, represented an unpremeditated emanation of the event and not the calculated product of a self-serving interest.

It is true that the exact elapsed time between the accident and Mrs. Ferrara's recorded description of it was not stated; nor does it appear how long she had been in the emergency room before she "opened her eyes" and saw the doctor "in front of her." It does not make a significant difference whether she had no memory of the accident in the interval because she was unconscious or because she was in shock until she first became aware of the presence of the doctor. The fact that her utterance about the accident was made very shortly after her return to reality and while she was in severe pain is the important circumstance which satisfies the test of admissibility.

*   *   *

A trial court is not concerned with the ultimate probative force of the utterance. That evaluation must be made by the jury. The legal rule which binds the trial judge respecting admissibility is met when the circumstances reasonably warrant the inference that the statement was made as an uncontrolled response to the shock of the event before reasoned reflection could have stimulated a self-serving response.

An example of application of the principle described appears in Demeter v. Rosenberg,   *   *   *   114 N.J.L. 55, 175 A. 621. There, decedent, a second floor tenant of a tenement house was found by a first floor tenant in an unconscious state at the bottom of the staircase leading from the second to the first floor. The first floor tenant had been awakened from sleep by a thumping noise outside his door. The injured woman was carried into that tenant's apartment where she remained unconscious until her daughter, who had been summoned from her house, arrived about an hour and a half later. On seeing her mother, the daughter screamed "Oh, mama, what happened to you?" The mother who had regained consciousness momentarily said "I missed my step and fell down the stairs." She then lapsed back into unconsciousness and remained in that state until she was taken to the hospital. The former Supreme Court sustained the admission of the utterance

saying there was nothing to indicate that the injured woman had time to reflect and give utterance to a calculated self-serving declaration.   *   *   *

The judgment is affirmed.

HUTCHINS & SLESINGER, SOME OBSERVATIONS ON THE LAW OF EVIDENCE

28 Colum.L.Rev. 432 (1928).*
[Footnotes omitted.]

I. SPONTANEOUS EXCLAMATIONS

Spontaneous utterances, exclamations or declarations are, under certain conditions, admissible in evidence though the party who made them
does not take the stand. According to most courts the occasion must be
startling enough to cause shock, which in turn creates an emotional state.
The utterance must be made under stress of that emotion; it must be "spontaneous and natural; impulsive and instinctive"; it should be immediate, or
"so clearly connected (with the occasion) that the declaration may be said
to be the spontaneous explanation of the real cause." Although in some jurisdictions there is insistence that the declaration be "contemporaneous"
with the act, or "while the act is going on," the progressive view seems to be
that the time interval, beyond which a declaration would no longer be spontaneous, is in the sound discretion of the trial court   *   *   *.

Apparently the type of utterance toward which the courts are most favorably inclined is that which follows a severe shock to the declarant. A
startling invasion of the declarant's repose is assumed to lead to a
trustworthy statement, whether the declarant be a congenital liar, an infant, a murderer, or a minister of the gospel. Whereas an identical blow on
the head might conceivably produce different emotions in a boxer and a
bookkeeper, it is likely that statements made by each would, by many
courts, be admitted in evidence as spontaneous exclamations.

Since the shock is what guarantees the truth of these declarations,
some courts rule that it alone must produce them. Although dying in agony,
if, in response to an inquiry as to the identity of his assailant, the declarant
says that the defendant shot him, the statement must be excluded. As a result of the interpolation of the question, what would otherwise be admissible becomes "not the natural and spontaneous outgrowth of the
murderous assault on him, but a mere narrative of a past transaction, and
hence not a part of the *res gestae.*"

Where no questions have been asked, the courts are willing to concede
that physical shock to the declarant is likely to produce the truth if the utterance comes before time to misrepresent has been afforded him. They are
willing to go a step further and concede that a speaker who has received no
injury, but who is involved in the startling occurrence will, if sufficiently excited, be honest, too. A motorman, a brakeman, or an engineer, although he
escapes unscathed from the wreckage of his train, will not lie about the
cause of the catastrophe until he has regained his equilibrium. But the casual bystander who has no interest in later suits against the railroad, but who
is much affected by the sad spectacle, is by no means so reliable. Some

courts exclude what he has said because he is disinterested. He is not an actor, however much he was moved by the action. The fact that his statement appears to be made without premeditation or design cannot save it. The reason given for admitting an actor's statement is sufficient to exclude his. As the Kentucky court has put it, the admission of the utterances of excited bystanders would open the door to "reckless, thoughtless and ill-considered exclamations," which are precisely the kind, and the only kind that are admitted under the rule as to spontaneous declarations made by injured persons or actors.

Even though most courts do admit the statements of excited bystanders, where there is a stimulus which is not sufficient to produce excitement, they do not ordinarily attribute to it the truth-evoking qualities ascribed to shock. This is so even though there is no conceivable motive to misrepresent, and the person who heard the exclamation is on the stand, subject to cross-examination as to all the circumstances of its making. Thus, if just before an automobile runs down a pedestrian, a witness watching it from a trolley car remarks on its high speed, the statement is inadmissible. If, where the plaintiff's contention is that death was caused by the unnecessary blowing of a whistle which resulted in the frightening of the deceased's horse, he offers a woman's statement, made a block and a half away, that "it was brutish the way they whistled," the evidence cannot come in because the declarant was sitting calmly in her home. The declarant's report that, at the time of the shot, which he heard three-quarters of a mile off, he said someone was trying his pistol, is not admitted as a spontaneous exclamation.

The general theory under which these declarations are admissible has been well stated by Mr. Wigmore. "Under certain external circumstances of physical shock a state of nervous excitement may be produced which stills the reflective faculties and removes their control, so that the utterance which occurs is a spontaneous and sincere response to the actual sensations and perceptions already produced by the external shock." And "since this utterance is made under the immediate and controlled domination of the senses, and during the brief period when considerations of self-interest could not have been fully brought to bear by reasoned reflection, the utterances may be taken to be particularly trustworthy."

This reflective self-interest is a curious doctrine, dating back to a mentalist psychology, and the utilitarian philosophy that made use of it. Man's conduct, according to this theory of behavior, was always personally motivated, his acts being planned by an elaborate calculus of interests, immediate and remote. Since that calculus involved reflection, it clearly followed that by eliminating reflection, self-interested conduct became impossible. The entrance of instinct into psychology shifted the emphasis, without changing the fundamental idea, by putting self-interest on an instinctive basis. The modern tendency is to substitute groups of habits or habit patterns for such general concepts as self-interest. These, if they serve the self, may afterward be called self-interested. That they are not, in fact, due to a force or instinct of self-interest, is shown by their persistence beyond the point of general efficiency. The habit of saving money, for example, is, in certain circumstances, self-interested. But a person having the habit will tend to continue to save even when it is directly against his interest. Reflection plays a part, both in the formation of habits, and in resolving conflicts between them. But once formed, they continue, on their own inertia, creating the illusion of a definite force.

To still, or circumvent this "force," the law relies in part on immediacy. The veracity of a response, according to the courts, varies directly with its speed. The desire to lie requires time and reflection to develop. And the intervention of reflection may be avoided by giving it no time to occur, thus rendering lying difficult, if not impossible.

In order to estimate the time required for reflection, it is necessary to know something of the difficulty of the task reflection is to perform. Ordinarily the choices are very simple ones, involving few alternatives. "John did it!" or "John did not do it!" The gentleman of after-dinner fame who, on being informed that his train had fallen over an embankment while he slept, cried, "Oh, my shoulder" in all probability did not take many moments to respond to the situation. If his general character is pointed to by way of explanation, the answer is simply that it is precisely that sort of character that the courts are guarding against.

A number of laboratory psychological experiments have been performed which throw some light on the problem under consideration. A subject is asked to disobey one of several orders, concealing from the examiner which order he has disobeyed. Or two subjects are sent out of the room, one to perform a series of acts, the other to do nothing, the actor trying to conceal his "crime." To each subject, then, is read a series of words, some of which are directly associated with the crimes in question, with the request that he respond as quickly as possible with the first word that comes to his mind, taking care, however, to avoid giving away his crime. All observers report a delay in reaction time to key words where deception is attempted, although Marston discovered a small group, which he called good liars, whose reaction time to significant words was actually faster than to the rest of the list. It seems, then, that the courts are on the right track in demanding speed as a guarantee of truth, or, at least of the absence of attempted falsehood. The difficulty comes when the speed is considered, not as a general idea, but quantitatively. Here we find that the difference in time between the ordinary reaction and the deception reaction to significant words is so slight, from .83 seconds to 3½ minutes, that it cannot be measured without the aid of instruments. The sound discretion of the trial judge, with the best of intention in these cases, is likely to be fallible.

But it will be remembered that speed is not the only guarantee of truthful response. In order more fully to guard against deceit, a good deal of reliance is placed on shock, and the emotion generated thereby, provided it is severe enough to still the reflective faculties. There is every reason to suppose that such an emotion would render difficult a consciously planned lie. As Mr. Watson inelegantly puts its, emotion is an affair of the guts, beyond control of the intellect, and pretty well running it during its active phase. It halts digestion speeds up heart rate, increases blood pressure, creates general muscular tension throughout the body, pours sugar and adrenin into the blood stream. These bodily changes are certainly discomforting to intellectual activity. They paralyze and distort it all along the line; unfortunately, while they make thinking difficult, they render observation and judgment all but impossible.

One need not be a psychologist to distrust an observation made under emotional stress; everybody accepts such statements with mental reservation. M. Gorphe cites the case of an excited witness to a horrible accident who erroneously declared that the coachman deliberately and vindictively ran down a helpless woman. Fiore tells of an emotionally upset man who testified that hundreds were killed in an accident; that he had seen their heads rolling from their bodies. In reality only one man was killed, and five others injured. Another excited gentleman took a pipe for a pistol. Besides these stories from real life, there are psychological experiments which point to the same conclusion. After a battle in a classroom, prearranged by the experimenter but a surprise to the students, each one was asked to write an account of the incident. The testimony of the most upset students was practically worthless, while those who were only slightly stimulated emotionally scored better than those left cold by the incident. Miss Hyde of Nebraska tells of an unpublished experiment, the results of which differed only in the general inaccuracy of all accounts, regardless of the amount of emotion generated. The conclusion drawn from these, and other similar experiments, is that "emotion may virtually hold connected perception in abeyance so that the subject has only isolated sensations to remember instead of a logically connected unit perception."

That participants, as well as bystanders, have their perceptions clouded by strong emotions will not be doubted. When a carriage containing the inevitable psychologist upset, that worthy gentleman amused himself and his companions by taking depositions while they awaited assistance. He had no known reality to check their stories against, but it was obvious that if any one was right, all the rest were wrong. That even trained observers are fallible is well brought out in an editorial in the *New York World* in which several accounts of newspaper reports of the striking of Kerensky on his recent visit to America are printed. Though the reporters were all experts, and sitting close to the platform, each one told a different story of what must have been a fairly simple event.

The result of these observations is a dilemma. From the point of view of subjective veracity, the speed the courts demand does not necessarily guarantee truth. And from the standpoint of objective accuracy, emotion is little better. If a speedy reaction means nothing without the aid of a stopwatch, an emotional reaction means nothing without eliminating the emotion. What the emotion gains by way of overcoming the desire to lie, it loses by impairing the declarant's power of observation. On the one hand, if reflective self-interest has not had a chance to operate because of emotional stress, then the statement should be excluded because of the probable inaccuracy of observation. On the other, if little emotion is involved, clearly a very short time is sufficient to allow reflected self-interest to assume full sway. On that basis there would seem to be no reason for this hearsay exception. In fact, the emphasis should be all the other way. On psychological grounds, the rule might very well read: Hearsay is inadmissible, especially (not except) if it is by a spontaneous exclamation.

Of course, such a result would be preposterous. The evidence is relevant and should be admitted unless it is so worthless as to mislead the tribunal or waste its time. It would do neither to a tribunal trained to decide the weight to be given to evidence in the light thrown by a knowledge of the background of the declarant, and the circumstances in which an exclamation was made. To this tribunal statements now viewed with suspicion because they are not made under emotional stress, would seem to represent more accurate observation for that very reason. Since an injured person is the one most affected by his injury, his observations would be considered less reliable than those of an uninjured motorman, brakeman, or engineer, and *a fortiori* less than those of a casual, unexcited bystander. And, according to this view, the best evidence of all is a statement made in immediate response to an external stimulus which produces no shock or nervous excitement whatever.

Professor Morgan's insistence on the admissibility of declarations closely connected in time with such a stimulus seems entirely justified. With emotion absent, speed present, and the person who heard the declaration on hand to be cross-examined, we appear to have an ideal exception to the hearsay rule. Statements by passengers before any damage has been done about the roughness of the train ride; observations as to the speed of a train as it is going by; remarks made on hearing a fight in progress some distance away; "why don't the train whistle?", spoken as the declarant saw it approaching the crossing;—all these are exclamations the value of which is indicated by the opportunity to cross-examine the hearer as to the surrounding circumstances, by the speed of the reaction, and the unemotional condition of the speaker.

Thus it appears that the spontaneous declarations regarded with least favor by the courts are more trustworthy than those which most of them admit without question: those where the trial judge rules that the statement was made under the influence of severe physical shock. It is by no means suggested, however, that these last should be excluded simply because other types of evidence assumed to be less reliable turn out, on investigation, to be more reliable. It is suggested, on the contrary, that all these varieties of declarations be admitted. If relevant they should go to the jury; for some are demonstrably more accurate than we have hitherto supposed, and those now admitted are not so inaccurate as to be arbitrarily excluded. To exclude any because they are not the immediate outpourings of an injured person is to insist on requirements shown to be artificial, if not mistaken.

HOUSTON OXYGEN CO., INC. v. DAVIS

Commission of Appeals of Texas, 1942.
139 Tex. 1, 161 S.W.2d 474.

TAYLOR, Commissioner. Pearl Davis, joined by her present husband, Johnie Davis, file this suit against Houston Oxygen Company, Inc., and Oliver O. Stanbury, for damages for injuries sustained by Charles Applebhy, Pearl's minor son, who, according to undisputed testimony, was by a former husband. *   *   *

Defendants contend that the courts below erred in holding inadmissible a statement offered by them, made (according to their testimony) by Mrs. Sally Cooper shortly before the accident occurred. Mrs. Cooper testified that on the date of the accident a Plymouth car headed north on state highway No. 35 (in which the minor and several other colored passengers were riding) passed her about four or five miles from the scene of the accident; that she at the time was driving a car in the same direction on the

highway and that Jack Sanders and M.C. Cooper, her brother-in-law, were
passengers with her. Sanders testified the Plymouth passed them on a curve
of the highway, rough and uneven at that point, travelling "sixty or sixty-five miles" an hour, about four miles from the scene of the accident and
that as it went out of sight it was "bouncing up and down in the back and
zig zagging." When Sanders was asked if anyone in the car made any statement as the Plymouth went by, plaintiffs objected. Defendants' bill of exception discloses that the excluded statement of Mrs. Cooper, made just after the Plymouth passed by, was, as testified to by Sanders for inclusion in
the bill, "they must have been drunk, that we would find them somewhere
on the road wrecked if they kept that rate of speed up." The testimony of
Earnest Cooper as to the speed of the passing car, and what was said by
Mrs. Cooper, was substantially the same as Sanders', except that he (Cooper) said it was ten or fifteen minutes after the Plymouth passed them before
they came to the scene of the collision, and that at the time it passed them
he observed, besides the occupants of the car, a suitcase tied on behind. His
testimony as well as Mrs. Cooper's as to what she said as the car passed by
was substantially the same as that of Sanders.

* * *

We have concluded, though the question is not free from difficulty, that
the statement of Mrs. Cooper was admissible; that the trial court erred in
not admitting the proffered testimony of Cooper and Sanders that Mrs.
Cooper made it, and in not permitting Mrs. Cooper herself to testify she
made the statement; and that the Court of Civil Appeals erred in sustaining
the trial court's ruling holding the statement was hearsay.

It is sufficiently spontaneous to save it from the suspicion of being
manufactured evidence. There was no time for a calculated statement. Mc-
Cormick & Ray in the section cited say: "In one class of cases the requirement of spontaneity is somewhat attenuated. If a person observes some situation or happening which is not at all startling or shocking in its nature,
nor actually producing excitement in the observer, the observer may yet
have occasion to comment on what he sees (or learns from other senses) at
the very time that he is receiving the impression. Such a comment, as to a
situation then before the declarant, does not have the safeguard of impulse,
emotion, or excitement, but there are other safeguards. In the first place,
the report at the moment of the thing then seen, heard, etc., is safe from any
error from defect of memory of the declarant. Secondly, there is little or no
time for calculated misstatement, and thirdly, the statement will usually be
made to another (the witness who reports it) who would have equal opportunities to observe and hence to check a misstatement. Consequently, it
is believed that such comments, strictly limited, to reports of present
sense-impressions, have such exceptional reliability as to warrant their inclusion within the hearsay exception for Spontaneous Declarations."

The statement of Mrs. Cooper is not one the evidential value of which
is purely cumulative, nor is it such as to relegate the determination of its
admissibility to the trial court's discretion. Rather it was one in which the
witness was alluding to an occurrence within her own knowledge in language calculated to make her "meaning clearer to the jury" than would a
mere expression of opinion as to the speed at which the passing car was
moving.

We find neither in the statement nor in the circumstances under which it was made (if it was) any basis upon which to invoke the discretion of the trial court as to its admissibility. It is competent evidence the consideration of which, since it is relevant and not merely cumulative, is determinable as a matter of law under an established rule of evidence. Authorities cited *supra.* The inference to be drawn as to whether the statement was made, and the inferences flowing from it (if made) are solely for the jury, and the trial court erred in excluding the testimony from its consideration.

Defendants contend the making of the statement was too remote in point of time. Had it been made under the stress of emotion, or if the party seeking the benefit of its admission were the one who made it, a different question would be presented. See illustrations referred to in cases noted under the text in McCormick & Ray, sec. 431, pp. 550, 551. It is stated in Vol. 17, Tex.Jur. pp. 623, 624, sec. 262, in discussing the element of time as affecting the admissibility of res gestae statements, that "if they sprang out of the principal transaction (wreck, in the present case), tend to explain it and were voluntary and spontaneous, and made at a time so near it as to preclude the idea of deliberate design, they may be regarded as contemporaneous in point of time and are admissible"; and, further, that "the declarations * * * may either precede the * * * transaction in question, or follow it," citing Gulf, C. & S. F. Ry. Co. v. Compton, 75 Tex. 667, 13 S.W. 667, and other cases in which the point of time preceded the accident. Certainly the statement in the present case (made, if it was, about four miles before the witness reached the scene of the collision) was not so remote in point of time as to be without relevance to its cause. The Court of Civil Appeals erred in affirming the action of the trial court in excluding the testimony. * * *

The judgment of the Court of Civil Appeals affirming that of the trial court is reversed and the case is remanded for another trial.

Opinion adopted by the Supreme Court.

See Federal Rules of Evidence 803 (1) & (2), at p. 922; California Evidence Code § 1240 at p. 881.

Hypotheticals

(1) A, a pedestrian, sues X for damages arising out of being struck by an automobile. X's defense is that he was in the curb lane in his red car and that a blue car passed him in the next lane, struck A, knocking her into the air and onto his red car, and then sped away. A calls B, an ambulance driver, and represents that B will testify that he arrived on the scene ten minutes after the accident, and saw A lying on the ground; that A appeared to be in great pain but not in shock; that B said to A, "Relax now, and take it easy;" and that A then said, "Oh, my God! Help me! That red car hit me while I was in the crosswalk." X makes a hearsay objection.

(2) Assume the same facts as in hypothetical (1). X calls C, a police officer, and represents that C will testify that he arrived at the scene five minutes after the accident occurred; that a number of people were gathered around A; and that he heard someone say, "That lady was hit by a blue car which didn't stop and she was thrown up in the air and landed on the red car," but doesn't know who made the statement. A makes a hearsay objection to C's proposed testimony.

(3) Prosecution of X for the kidnapping of and assault upon Y. Y suffered brain damage, and was hospitalized for seven weeks. W, Y's sister, testified that one week after Y came home from the hospital, W showed her a newspaper article containing a photograph of X. W testified that Y's "immediate reaction was one of great distress", and that Y "pointed to the picture and said very clearly, 'He killed me, he killed me.' " X objects that the statement is hearsay, and that it is not a spontaneous declaration because the startling event was the assault, which occurred eight weeks prior to the statement. What is the proper ruling on X's motion? See United States v. Napier, 518 F.2d 316 (9th Cir. 1975).

(4) Prosecution for the theft of a truck. A state trooper testifies that after receiving a radio report of an abandoned stolen truck, he appealed for information over his citizen's band ("CB") radio. A "CB'er" reported that he saw two men walking away from the point where the truck had been abandoned.

A second "CB'er" informed him that the two men were seen walking five to six miles east of the truck's location. The two men were arrested five miles away from the truck, a few minutes after the first CB statement. Should the first statement have been admitted? See United States v. Cain, 587 F.2d 678 (5th Cir. 1979).

4. ADMISSIONS

REED v. McCORD

Court of Appeals of New York, 1899.
160 N.Y. 330, 54 N.E. 737.

MARTIN, J.   This action was to recover damages for personal injuries to the plaintiff's intestate which occasioned his death, and was based upon the alleged negligence of the defendant.   *   *   *

The only remaining question is whether the statements of the defendant of the circumstances and cause of the accident to the plaintiff's intestate, made while a witness before the coroner, were competent and properly received. The defendant was called and sworn as a witness, and gave evidence as to the accident. Upon the trial of this action the official stenographer for the board of coroners was called and permitted, under the defendant's objection and exception, to testify that upon the hearing before the coroner the defendant gave evidence to the effect that all machines of the make of the one in use when the decedent was killed were alike; that at the time of the injury the dog of the machine was not in position, which caused the accident; and that "the man who had charge of it supposed the dog was in position, and he released his hold on the thing, and it commenced to revolve, and then he got down so as to put his foot on it, and it was going so rapidly that it slipped past." It was admitted that the defendant was not present when the accident occurred, and hence, it is obvious that his statement before the coroner was not based upon his personal knowledge, but upon what he had learned as to the situation and how the accident occurred. The contention of the appellant is that, as his admissions were not based upon his personal knowledge, proof of them should have been excluded, and that his exception to their admission was well taken. The defendant being a party to this action, his admissions against his own interest were evidence in favor of his adversary, if of a fact material to the issue. If he had merely admitted that he heard that the accident occurred in the manner stated, it would have been inadmissible, as then it would only have amounted to an admission that he had heard the statement which he repeated, and not to an admission of the facts included in it. That would have been in no sense an admission of any fact pertinent to the issue, but a mere admission of what he had heard, without adoption or indorsement. Such evidence is clearly inadmissible. Stephens v. Vroman, 16 N.Y. 381. But the admissions proved in this case were not of that character. They were plain admissions of facts and circumstances which attended the intestate's injury. In a civil action the admissions by a party of any fact material to the issue are always competent evidence against him, wherever, whenever, or to whomsoever made. * * * The theory upon which this class of evidence is held to be competent is that it is highly improbable that a party will admit or state anything against himself or against his own interest unless it is true. As the admissions testified to by the stenographer were of facts and circumstances which were material to the issue in this action, they were clearly competent, although not conclusive, evidence of the facts admitted. We find no error in the admission of this evidence, and, as no other questions are raised that we have jurisdiction to review, our conclusion is that the judgment should be affirmed. The judgment should be affirmed, with costs. All concur, except Parker, C.J., not voting, and O'Brien, J., dissenting. Judgment affirmed.

NOTE

The following quotation is from William Shakespeare's Othello, Act III, Sc. iii. The speaker is Iago.

* * * I lay with Cassio lately,
And being troubled with a raging tooth,
I could not sleep.
There are a kind of men so loose of soul,
That in their sleeps will mutter their affairs:
One of this kind is Cassio:
In sleep I heard him say 'Sweet Desdemona,
Let us be wary, let us hide our loves;'
An then, sir, would he gripe and wring my hand,
Cry 'O sweet creature!' and then kiss me hard,
As if he pluk'd up kisses by the roots,
That grew upon my lips: then laid his leg
Over my thigh, and sigh'd and kiss'd, and then
Cried 'Cursed fate that gave thee to the Moor!'

Is this "testimony" of Iago hearsay? Would it on any ground be admissible against Cassio? Or Desdemona? Is it relevant?

UNITED STATES v. HOOSIER

United States Court of Appeals, Sixth Circuit, 1976.
542 F.2d 687.

PER CURIAM.

Appellant seeks to overturn his jury conviction on one count of armed robbery of a federally insured bank. Four witnesses identified him, three of them positively, as the person who robbed the bank in Clarksville, Tennessee.

Another witness, Robert E. Rogers, testified that he had been with the robbery defendant before and after the bank robbery, that before the bank robbery defendant told him that he was going to rob a bank, and that three weeks after the bank robbery, he saw defendant with money and wearing what he thought were diamond rings, and that in the presence of defendant, the defendant's girl friend said concerning defendant's affluence at that point, "That ain't nothing, you should have seen the money we had in the hotel room," and that she spoke of "sacks of money." Although both defendant and his girl friend disputed these facts in their testimony, obviously the resolution of that fact dispute was for the jury, and we must assume the jury resolved it in favor of the government by its verdict of "guilty."

Appellant's sole appellate argument to this court, however, is that the testimony elicited from the fifth witness concerning appellant's girl friend's statement was inadmissible hearsay, and that it was reversible error for the District Judge to fail to grant the objection to its admission.

Relevant to this issue is Rule 801(d)(2)(B) of the Federal Rules of Evidence, which reads in applicable part:

(2) Admission by party-opponent. The statement is offered against a party and is * * * (B) a statement of which he has manifested his adoption or belief in its truth, or * * *

The Advisory Committee's note concerning this rule is as follows:

(B) Under established principles an admission may be made by adopting or acquiescing in the statement of another. While knowledge of contents would ordinarily be essential, this is not inevitably so: "X is a reliable person and knows what he is talking about." See McCormick § 246, p. 527, n. 15. Adoption or acquiescence may be manifested in any appropriate manner. When silence is relied upon, the theory is that the person would, under the circumstances, protest the statement made in his presence, if untrue. The decision in each case calls for an evaluation in terms of probable human behavior. In civil cases, the results have generally been satisfactory. In criminal cases, however, troublesome questions have been raised by decisions holding that failure to deny is an admission: the inference is a fairly weak one, to begin with; silence may be motivated by advice of counsel or realization that "anything you say may be used against you"; unusual opportunity is afforded to manufacture evidence; and encroachment upon the privilege against self-incrimination seems inescapably to be involved. However, recent decisions of the Supreme Court relating to custodial interrogation and the right to counsel appear to resolve these difficulties. Hence the rule contains no special provisions concerning failure to deny in criminal cases.

Fed.R.Evid. (2)(B), Advisory Committee's Notes (1975).

Our analysis of our present problem is made in the context of the Advisory Committee note which is an appropriately guarded one. First, we note that the statement was made in appellant's presence, with only his girl friend and Rogers present. Since appellant had previously trusted Rogers sufficiently to tell him his plan to rob a bank, we see little likelihood that his silence in the face of these statements was due to "advice of counsel" or fear that anything he said might "be used against him." Under the total circumstances, we believe that probable human behavior would have been for appellant promptly to deny his girl friend's statement if it had not been true

—particularly when it was said to a person to whom he had previously related a plan to rob a bank. While we agree with appellant's counsel that more is needed to justify admission of this statement than the mere presence and silence of the appellant, we observe that there was more in this record.

Finding no reversible error, the judgment of conviction is affirmed.

PAWLOWSKI v. ESKOFSKI

Supreme Court of Wisconsin, 1932.
209 Wis. 189, 244 N.W. 611.

FOWLER, J. In the view we take of the case, only two assignments of error need be considered. These are that the court erred (1) in overruling the plea in abatement and (2) in not dismissing the case on the merits for want of evidence to support the verdict. ∗ ∗ ∗

2. To support the judgment findings of the jury (2) that the condition of the tire was such that it was dangerous to inflate it to the degree it was inflated and (4) that defendant knew of the unsafe condition must have support in the evidence. This follows from the rule of this court ∗ ∗ ∗ wherein it was held in effect that the guest assumes the risk of accidents occurring through defective condition of the car unless the host knew, or ought to have known, of that condition and failed to inform the guest of it. That tires are a part of the car within the rule was held in the Waters Case.

It is contended by the appellants that there is no competent evidence of any defective condition of the tire that caused the blowout. All the direct testimony, and there was much of it, for the most part by expert tire dealers and repairmen, was to the effect that the tire appeared in safe condition. The defendant testified that the tire appeared in good condition, and that he had no knowledge or notice that it was not. Even the plaintiff's husband, upon whose testimony alone the finding of unsafety must rest, testified that the tire appeared all right to him, and he had assisted in putting it on shortly before it was inflated. His testimony was to the effect that the tire that blew out was inflated by the defendant at a garage a short time before it blew out; that another man was inflating a tire at the same time; that defendant used the other man's air gauge, and asked the other man what it registered after he had inflated the tire; that the man looked at the gauge, and said that the gauge showed 38 pounds; said that defendant's tires were poor, and that with 38 pounds the tire might go to pieces in a few miles; and that the defendant then stated that he would take a chance on the tire. It is claimed by appellants that this testimony, so far as it goes to the condition of the tire, is hearsay and incompetent to show that condition. That it is hearsay is plain, but respondent claims that it is nevertheless admissible as an admission of the defendant. It was admissible on the point of notice, but its admissibility as an admission depends on whether it falls within the classification of admissions by silence, based on the maxim that "silence gives consent." But " ∗ ∗ ∗ the inference of assent (by silence) may be safely made only when no other explanation is equally consistent with silence; and there is always another such explanation—namely, ignorance or dissent—unless the circumstances are such that a dissent would in ordinary experience have been expressed if the communication had not been correct. This much has always been conceded judicially when the question has been presented." 2 Wigmore, Evidence, § 1071.

The author quoted goes on to say that from the maxim stated a sort of working rule developed that whatever is said in a party's presence is admissible against him because presumably assented to; but that in this broad form it ignores inherent qualifications which the courts recognize and have stated in various situations. The simplest statement of the qualification and perhaps as good as any is that stated in Wiedemann v. Walpole, 2 Q.B. 531, 539, cited by Wigmore: "Silence is not evidence of an admission, unless there are circumstances which render it more reasonably probable that a man would answer the charge made against him than that he would not."

Prolonged discussion of the point would hardly be helpful. We are of the opinion that the statement involved cannot be considered as an admission, for two reasons: The statement of the defendant that he "would take a chance" is as reasonably to be construed as a dissent to the stranger's opinion of the condition of the tire as an assent to it; and there was nothing in the circumstances to render it more reasonably probable that one ordinarily would expressly deny the stranger's statement that the tire was poor than that he would not do so.

The judgment of the circuit court is reversed, with directions to dismiss the complaint.

LA BUY, JURY INSTRUCTIONS IN FEDERAL CRIMINAL CASES

65 (1963).*

Section 6.15   Accusatory Statements

Evidence has been presented that statements accusing the defendant of the crime charged in the indictment were made in his presence, and that such statements were neither denied, nor objected to by him. If the jury finds that defendant actually heard and understood the accusatory statements, and that they were made under such circumstances that defendant would have denied them if they were not true, then the jury should consider whether defendant's silence was an admission of the truth of the statements. However, where defendant is under arrest, his silence in the face of accusatory statements does not in any way constitute an admission of the truth of the statements, nor create any inference of guilt.

THE GOSPEL ACCORDING TO LUKE*

" 'You are the Son of God, then?' they all said, and he replied, 'It is you who say I am.' They said, 'Need we call further witnesses? We have heard it ourselves from his own lips.'

"With that the whole assembly rose, and they brought him before Pilate. They opened the case against him by saying, 'We found this man subverting our nation, opposing the payment of taxes to Caesar, and claiming to/be the Messiah, a king.' Pilate asked him, 'Are you the king of the Jews?' He replied, 'The words are yours.' "

---

*7th Cir. Judicial Conference, West Pub. Co., 1963.   *Luke, 22:70–23:3; The New English Bible, 106–107 (1970).

ADMISSION BY SILENCE—ANOTHER VIEW

"In his funeral oration on Roscoe Conkling, Robert G. Ingersoll said: 'He was maligned, misrepresented and misunderstood, but he would not answer. He was as silent then as he is now—and his silence, better than any form of speech, refuted every charge.' George Bernard Shaw said: 'Silence is the most perfect expression of scorn.' "**

KAPLAN, OF MABRUS AND ZORGS
66 Cal.L.Rev. 987.
1002–03 (1978).

9.   Prosecution of D for rape. Witness, W, wishes to testify that while he sat in a bar with D, the prosecutrix's father, F, entered, pointed at D and said: "You are the man who attacked my daughter," but that D made no reply.

Our black letter law is that when a party is accused of something in circumstances where, had he been innocent of the accusation, he would have denied it, his failure to make any denial is admissible as an admission. The jury must decide the preliminary fact questions so long, of course, as reasonable jurors could differ about them. Thus, whether the party heard the accusation, whether the circumstances were such that if it were untrue he would have been likely to deny it, and whether he did, in fact, deny it, are all issues for the jury.

It would seem, however, that the problem is somewhat more complex than this. Remember that in hypothetical 9, the jury passing on the admission by silence will have to hear not only evidence about the fact of silence and the surrounding circumstances, but it also must hear F's accusation as the necessary predicate for understanding what it is that D allegedly has admitted. Certainly, one can imagine situations where the jurors might decide that D had not heard the accusation or that he had denied it, but that the accusation itself, because of F's reliability, was nonetheless highly probative. In such a situation, they would, of course, ignore the judge's instructions that F's statement should not be considered for the truth of the fact it asserts, but only to show what D did or did not admit.[24]

Are we to conclude that our standard rules as to admission by silence are wrong and that the preliminary questions are to be decided by the judge rather than the jury? Not quite. There are indeed some admissions by silence which are—or at least should be—decided by the jury. Take the case where F's accusation is independently admissible as an exception to the hearsay rule. Let us say it is a spontaneous declaration or, should the jurisdiction's evidence rules permit, a contemporaneous statement. In these cases, the jury would be permitted to consider the hearsay accusation anyway, and hence, the admission by silence would carry no freight of inadmissible hearsay. In such a case, the jury could be trusted to apply the

---

**Commonwealth v. Dravecz, 424 Pa. 582 585 n. 1, 227 A.2d 904, 906 n. 1 (1967).

24.   It can be argued that if the jurors had nothing further to go on than the mere fact of accusation, it would be extremely unlikely that they would rely on its credibility and, hence, the jurors might, in such cases, be permitted to decide the preliminary fact question. This would be quite difficult to determine in many cases, however, since the jury might make many inferences about the credibility of the accuser which were not strictly rational. As a result, the better rule in all such cases where the accusation would be inadmissible would be to have the judge determine the preliminary facts before the jury could hear the evidence.

judge's instructions in its consideration of the significance of D's silence. So too, perhaps, where F has already testified about the facts giving rise to the accusation. Here, though the accusation itself is still hearsay, it is likely in most cases that the jury would not give it any independent weight, over and above F's testimony.

A somewhat more difficult question is presented by the cases where the admission by silence involves a failure to reply, not to an accusation, but to a question. Examine the next hypothetical:

10.   Same as hypothetical 9 except that F asks: "Are you the man who attacked my daughter?"

Although D's failure to reply certainly might be an admission by silence, it is a close case whether the preliminary fact questions should be decided by the judge or the jury. One might argue that since the question is not itself a statement, the jury would not be tempted to rely on the credibility of the questioner. On the other hand, by singling out D to ask, F makes an implied assertion about the existence of some basis for the question. In any event, the question is a difficult one and I am prepared to overlook it here if the reader is as well.

Hypotheticals

(1)   P sues D for damages for personal injuries arising out of an accident in which D was driving and P was a passenger. D testifies that as she was driving on an offramp of the freeway the throttle of her car stuck and she bent over to jiggle it loose; that as she bent over P unzipped the top portion of her dress; that this so surprised and infuriated her that she took her eyes off the road to look at P and the car then smashed into a telephone pole. P testifies that he never touched D at any time and did not unzip her dress. In an evidence-admissibility hearing before trial P makes an offer of proof as to an alleged admission made by D; that P and D had a conversation after P saw the police report for the first time; that the report contained D's statement about her leaning over and P's unzipping the back of her dress; that P made a telephone call to D and told her this was an untrue statement, and that D responded "Well, I did it because I was fearful over my insurance." D objects to P's offer of proof on grounds of hearsay. Should D's objection be sustained?

(2)   A sues B for the price of goods sold to X Enterprises. A claims that B is a partner in X Enterprises. A testifies that, before he sold the goods to X Enterprises, he was at the X Enterprises office and X, the president, introduced him to B with the statement: "Meet my partner in X Enterprises, Mr. B," and that B then shook hands with A and said nothing. B moves to strike A's testimony as hearsay. What result?

MATTHEW v. STATE

Supreme Court of Indiana, 1975.
263 Ind. 672, 337 N.E.2d 821.

ARTERBURN, Justice.

*   *   *

The Appellant stands convicted of reckless homicide while driving under the influence of intoxicating liquor.   *   *   *   The conviction of the Appellant was reversed by the Court of Appeals because of the admission into evidence of certain portions of grand jury testimony by the Appellant.
*   *   *

I.

* * *

* * * The evidence objected to was a portion of Appellant's voluntary statement to the grand jury which had investigated the cause of death at issue, and the testimony of Donna Rogers, a former employee of the Appellant. The record reveals that the Appellant voluntarily went before the grand jury to testify regarding his actions at the time of the accident. He testified that at the time the collision occurred he had just left the Shoreroom cocktail lounge where he had two drinks. He also testified that immediately before that he and his wife had been at the home of his secretary, Donna Rogers, where he had had dinner and had not consumed any alcohol.

After the introduction of this transcript, Donna Rogers took the stand on the behalf of the State and testified that she had supported the Appellant in such testimony before the grand jury, namely that he had dinner at her home on the evening in question. She then testified that in fact this was not true. She further stated that after she had lied to the grand jury she reconsidered the matter and decided she should go back and tell the truth. She stated she had attempted to persuade the Appellant to go back and change his testimony to the truth. He refused and reminded her that she was divorced and had children to support.

* * * Evidence of efforts to manufacture or suppress evidence is competent as a circumstance against a defendant. "Where a person is accused of crime, a guilty consciousness may be inferred from attempted evasion, palpable falsehood, equivocation, or from suppression of facts, and a presumption of guilt is said to arise from the falsification of testimony by accused." 22A C.J.S. Criminal Law § 596, at 375-376 (1961). Where one voluntarily goes before a grand jury to testify in an attempt to cover up by false testimony evidence of guilt, such testimony becomes material as evidence of a consciousness of guilt the same as flight and other such acts.

"No useful purpose would here be served in undertaking to make further classification of the innumerable instances of conduct, both verbal and non-verbal, of a party indicating a consciousness of guilt. The common experience of mankind in dealing with the ordinary affairs of life should offer, it would seem, an indispensable test in making the determination as to whether or not the particular conduct encountered is calculated to raise the inference of a consciousness of guilt." 2 Wigmore on Evidence § 278 at 53 (Supp.1975).

The Appellant voluntarily appeared before the grand jury and deliberately lied. He conspired with his employee in this perjury. When the latter indicated, after the Appellant's first trial, that she had second thoughts and desired to tell the truth, she was reminded that she was divorced and had children to support. The "common experience of mankind" can only conclude that this was a cover-up and raised an inference of a consciousness of guilt. The trial court did not err in admitting this testimony into evidence.

* * *

All Justices concur.

LA BUY, JURY INSTRUCTIONS IN FEDERAL
CRIMINAL CASES

63–64 (1963).*

Section 6.14   Exculpatory Statements

Evidence has been introduced that defendant made certain exculpatory statements outside of the courtroom explaining his actions to
show that he was innocent of the crime charged in the indictment. Evidence
contradicting such statements has also been introduced. If the jury finds
that the exculpatory statements were untrue, and that the defendant made
them voluntarily with knowledge of their falsity, the jury may consider the
statements as circumstantial evidence of defendant's consciousness of guilt.

COKE, THIRD INSTITUTE, 1747

In the county of Warwick there were two brethren, the one having issue
a daughter, and being seized of lands in fee devised the government of his
daughter and his lands, until she came to her age of sixteen years, to his
brother, and died. The uncle brought up his niece very well both at her book
and needle, etc., and she was about eight or nine years of age: her uncle for
some offence correcting her, she was heard to say, Oh good uncle kill me
not. After which time the child after much inquiry, could not be heard of:
whereupon the uncle being suspected of the murder of her, the rather for
that he was her next heir, was upon examination committed to the gaol for
suspicion of murder, and was admonished by the justices of assise to find
out the child, and thereupon bailed him until the next assises. Against
which time, for that he could not find her, and fearing what would fall out
against him, took another child as like unto her both in person and years as
he could find, and apparelled her like unto the true child, and brought her
to the next assises, but upon view and examination, she was found not to be
the true child; and upon these presumptions he was indicted and found
guilty, had judgment, and was hanged. But the truth of the case was, that
the child being beaten over night, the next morning when she should go to
school, ran away into the next county; and being well educated was received
and entertained of a stranger: and when she was sixteen years old, at what
time she should come to her land, she came to demand it, and was directly
proved to be the true child. Which case we have reported for a double
caveat: first to judges, that they in case of life judge not too hastily upon
bare presumption: and secondly, to the innocent and true man, that he never seek to excuse himself by false or undue means, lest thereby he offending
God (the author of truth) overthrow himself, as the uncle did.

Hypotheticals

(1)   P sues D, a physician, for damages for malpractice in failing to diagnose a
lump in her breast as cancerous and thus prevent its spread into other parts of her
body. At the trial, D admits negligence but denies that his negligence was a proximate cause of the spread of the cancer. P offers evidence that D destroyed his original records as to P and produced copies only. D makes an irrelevancy objection,
urging that his admission of negligence rendered any adverse inference from suppression of records irrelevant. What result?

*7th Cir. Judical Conference, West Pub. Co.,
1963.

(2) D, a physician, is charged with the offense of prescribing narcotics to persons not under treatment for a pathology. Various prescriptions written by D are admitted in evidence as exhibits at D's preliminary hearing. D is free on bail. At D's trial, the prosecutor seeks to introduce evidence that during D's preliminary hearing, at D's request, the clerk permitted D to examine the exhibits; that the clerk subsequently discovered that the exhibits comprising the prescriptions were missing; that pieces of the prescriptions were subsequently found floating in a toilet bowl in the men's rest-room in the courthouse. D makes an irrelevancy objection to the prosecutor's proffered evidence, urging that such evidence is too speculative to prove that he took the exhibits. How should the court rule?

(3) D is charged with murder. The prosecutor offers evidence that just prior to his arrest D attempted to flee and conceal his identity. This evidence is offered as corroboration of the testimony of an accomplice, on the theory that such evidence constitutes proof of D's consciousness of guilt. D makes an irrelevancy objection, and offers to prove that the more plausible inference to be drawn from his attempted flight was his belief that a nonsupport warrant for his arrest was outstanding, that he was afraid of being arrested for narcotics hidden in his car, and also that he knew that he had violated his parole. What result?

MAHLANDT v. WILD CANID SURVIVAL & RESEARCH CENTER, INC.

United States Court of Appeals, Eighth Circuit, 1978.
588 F.2d 626.

VAN SICKLE, District Judge.

This is a civil action for damages arising out of an alleged attack by a wolf on a child. The sole issues on appeal are as to the correctness of three rulings which excluded conclusionary statements * * * . Two of them fendant; and the third was in the form of a statement appearing in the records of a board meeting of the corporate defendant.

On March 23, 1973, Daniel Mahlandt, then 3 years, 10 months, and 8 days old, was sent by his mother to a neighbor's home on an adjoining street to get his older brother, Donald. Daniel's mother watched him cross the street, and then turned into the house to get her car keys. Daniel's path took him along a walkway adjacent to the Poos' residence. Next to the walkway was a five foot chain link fence to which Sophie had been chained with a six foot chain. In other words, Sophie was free to move in a half circle having a six foot radius on the side of the fence opposite from Daniel.

Sophie was a bitch wolf, 11 months and 28 days old, who had been born at the St. Louis Zoo, and kept there until she reached 6 months of age, at which time she was given to the Wild Canid Survival and Research Center, Inc. It was the policy of the Zoo to remove wolves from the Children's Zoo after they reached the age of 5 or 6 months. Sophie was supposed to be kept at the Tyson Research Center, but Kenneth Poos, as Director of Education for the Wild Canid Survival and Research Center, Inc., had been keeping her at his home because he was taking Sophie to schools and institutions where he showed films and gave programs with respect to the nature of wolves. Sophie was known as a very gentle wolf who had proved herself to be good natured and stable during her contacts with thousands of children, while she was in the St. Louis Children's Zoo.

* * *

A neighbor who was ill in bed in the second floor of his home heard a child's screams and went to his window, where he saw a boy lying on his back within the enclosure, with a wolf straddling him. The wolf's face was near Daniel's face, but the distance was so great that he could not see what the wolf was doing, and did not see any biting. Within about 15 seconds the neighbor saw Clarke Poos, about seventeen, run around the house, get the wolf off of the boy, and disappear with the child in his arms to the back of the house. Clarke took the boy in and laid him on the kitchen floor.

    * * * An expert in the behavior of wolves stated that when a wolf licks a child's face that it is a sign of care, and not a sign of attack; that a wolf's wail is a sign of compassion, and an effort to get attention, not a sign of attack. * * * The defendant, Mr. Poos, arrived home while Daniel and his mother were in the kitchen. After Daniel was taken in an ambulance, Mr. Poos talked to everyone present, including a neighbor who came in. Within an hour after he arrived home, Mr Poos went to Washington University to inform Owen Sexton, President of Wild Canid Survival and Research Center, Inc., of the incident. Mr. Sexton was not in his office so Mr. Poos left the following note on his door:

> Owen, would you call me at home, 727-5080? Sophie bit a child that came in our back yard. All has been taken care of. I need to convey what happened to you. (Exhibit 11)

Denial of admission of this note is one of the issues on appeal.

    Later that day, Mr. Poos found Mr. Sexton at the Tyson Research Center and told him what had happened. Denial of plaintiff's offer to prove that Mr. Poos told Mr. Sexton, that, "Sophie had bit a child that day," is the second issue on appeal.

    A meeting of the Directors of the Wild Canid Survival and Research Center, Inc., was held on April 4, 1973. Mr. Poos was not present at that meeting. The minutes of that meeting reflect that there was a "great deal of discussion * * * about the legal aspects of the incident of Sophie biting the child." Plaintiff offered an abstract of the minutes containing that reference. Denial of the offer of that abstract is the third issue on appeal.

    Daniel had lacerations of the face, left thigh, left calf, and right thigh, and abrasions and bruises of the abdomen and chest. Mr. Mahlandt was permitted to state that Daniel had indicated that he had gone under the fence. Mr. Mahlandt and Mr. Poos, about a month after the incident, examined the fence to determine what caused Daniel's lacerations. Mr. Mahlandt felt that they did not look like animal bites. The parallel scars on Daniel's thigh appeared to match the configuration of the barbs or tines on the fence. The expert as to the behavior of wolves opined that the lacerations were not wolf bites or wounds caused by wolf claws. * * *

    The jury brought in a verdict for the defense.

    The trial judge's rationale for excluding the note, the statement, and the corporate minutes, was the same in each case. He reasoned that Mr. Poos did not have any personal knowledge of the facts, and accordingly, the first two admissions were based on hearsay; and the third admission contained in the minutes of the board meeting was subject to the same objection of hearsay, and unreliability because of lack of personal knowledge.

The Federal Rules of Evidence became effective in July 1975 (180 days after passage of the Act). Thus, at this time, there is very little case law to rely upon for resolution of the problems of interpretation.

The relevant rule here is: Rule 801(d)(2) [see p.   ].

* * * [T]he statement in the note pinned on the door is not hearsay, and is admissible against Mr. Poos. It was his own statement, and as such was clearly different from the reported statement of another. Example, "I was told that * * *." It was also a statement of which he had manifested his adoption or belief in its truth. And the same observations may be made of the statement made later in the day to Mr. Sexton that, "Sophie had bit a child * * *."

Are these statements admissible against Wild Canid Survival and Research Center, Inc.? They were made by Mr. Poos when he was an agent or servant of the Wild Canid Survival and Research Center, Inc., and they concerned a matter within the scope of his agency, or employment, i.e., his custody of Sophie, and were made during the existence of that relationship.

* * *

* * * This is not an 801(d)(2)(C) situation because Mr. Poos was not authorized or directed to make a statement on the matter by anyone. * * * Weinstein's discussion of Rule 801(d)(2)(D) (Weinstein's Evidence § 801(d)(2)(D)(01), p. 801–137), states that:

Rule 801(d)(2)(D) adopts the approach * * * which, as a general proposition, makes statement made by agents within the scope of their employment admissible * * *. Once agency, and the making of the statement while the relationship continues, are established, the statement is exempt from the hearsay rule so long as it relates to a matter within the scope of the agency.

After reciting a lengthy quotation which justifies the rule as necessary, and suggests that such admissions are trustworthy and reliable, Weinstein, states categorically that although an express requirement of personal knowledge on the part of the declarant of the facts underlying his statement is not written into the rule, it should be. He feels that is mandated by Rules 805 and 403.

Rule 805 recites, in effect, that a statement containing hearsay within hearsay is admissible, if each part of the statement falls within an exception to the hearsay rule. Rule 805, however, deals only with hearsay exceptions. A statement based on the personal knowledge of the declarant of facts underlying his statement is not the repetition of the statement of another, thus not hearsay. It is merely opinion testimony. Rule 805 cannot mandate the implied condition desired by Judge Weinstein.

Rule 403 provides for the exclusion of relevant evidence if its probative value is substantially outweighed by the danger of unfair prejudice, confusion of the issues, or misleading the jury, or by consideration of undue delay, waste of time, or needless presentation of cumulative evidence. Nor does Rule 403 mandate the implied condition desired by Judge Weinstein.

Thus, while both Rule 805 and Rule 403 provide additional bases for excluding otherwise acceptable evidence, neither rule mandates the introduction into Rule 801(d)(2)(D) of an implied requirement that the declarant have personal knowledge of the facts underlying his statement. So we conclude that the two statements made by Mr. Poos were admissible against Wild Canid Survival and Research Center, Inc.

As to the entry in the records of a corporate meeting, the directors as primary officers of the corporation had the authority to include their conclusions in the record of the meeting. So the evidence would fall within 801(d)(2)(C) as to Wild Canid Survival and Research Center, Inc., and be admissible.   *   *   *

But there was no servant, or agency, relationship which justified admitting the evidence of the board minutes as against Mr. Poos.

None of the conditions of 801(d)(2) cover the claim that minutes of a corporate board meeting can be used against a non-attending, non-participating employee of that corporation. The evidence was not admissible as against Mr. Poos.

There is left only the question of whether the trial court's rulings which excluded all three items of evidence are justified under Rule 403. He clearly found that the evidence was not reliable, pointing out that none of the statements were based on the personal knowledge of the declarant.

Again, that problem was faced by the Advisory Committee on Proposed Rules. In its discussion of 801(d)(2) exceptions to the hearsay rule, the Committee said:

> The freedom which admissions have enjoyed from technical demands of searching for an assurance of trustworthiness in some against-interest circumstances, and from the restrictive influences of the opinion rule and the rule requiring first hand knowledge, when taken with the apparently prevalent satisfaction with the results, calls for generous treatment of this avenue to admissibility. 28 U.S.C.A., Volume of Federal Rules of Evidence, Rule 801, p. 527, at p. 530.

So here, remembering that relevant evidence is usually prejudicial to the cause of the side against which it is presented, and that the prejudice which concerns us is unreasonable prejudice; and applying the spirit of Rule 801(d)(2), we hold that Rule 403 does not warrant the exclusion of the evidence of Mr. Poos' statements as against himself or Wild Canid Survival and Research Center, Inc.

*   *   *

The judgment of the District Court is reversed and the matter remanded to the District Court for a new trial consistent with this opinion.

Hypotheticals

(1)   A, a painting subcontractor, sues X, a general contractor, for the balance due on a subcontract with X. A had been paid four progress payments, but X refused to pay the fifth and last progress payment on the ground that A's work was unsatisfactory. B was general superintendent for X and was authorized by X to approve and reject subcontractors' work and to approve progress payments to subcontractors accordingly. When A's painting job for X was 98 percent complete, B wrote a letter of recommendation for A, stating that A had completed the painting job for X to everyone's satisfaction. A offers B's letter in evidence. X objects that the letter is hearsay. What result?

(2) A sues the X market for damages for personal injuries arising out of a slip-and-fall incident. A few minutes after A fell, B, the store manager, arrived and A pointed out a banana peel on the floor. C, a witness to the incident, proposes to testify for A that B then said to A, "Don't worry about this. We will pay your bills. It's the store's fault." X objects that C's testimony is hearsay. Should X's objection be sustained?

MURPHY AUTO PARTS CO. v. BALL

United States Court of Appeals, District of Columbia Circuit, 1957.
249 F.2d 508.
[Most footnotes are omitted.]

BURGER, Circuit Judge. The issue presented by this appeal is whether an alleged out of court utterance of an employee, driving his own car after working hours, stating that he was on an errand for his employer, is admissible to show that he was in fact engaged in his employer's business at the time of a collision with a pedestrian, where the statement is a spontaneous declaration or excited utterance.

The facts are essential to a complete understanding of the precise legal issues presented. Appellee Thomas Ball, a minor, was injured in 1952 when struck by a passenger car owned and driven by James Murphy. James Murphy was employed as a clerk by his stepfather's business concern, appellant here. The injury occurred at 6:30 P.M., one and one-half hour after his regular work day which terminated at 5:00 P.M. Appellee Rita Ball, the mother of the injured child, testified that immediately after the injury and at the scene of the accident, James Murphy "told me that he was sorry, that he hoped my son wasn't seriously hurt, he had to call on a customer and was in a bit of a hurry to get home." James Murphy denied making this or any statement to Mrs. Ball.

It is admitted that James Murphy was employed as a clerk by Murphy Auto Parts Co. on the day of the injury to the minor appellee. It was shown that he received a regular allowance for auto expense but both Murphy and his employer insisted all Murphy's duties were inside clerical work and denied he was authorized to use his personal car for company business. The record shows that at a later date, some months after the accident, James Murphy did make calls on customers using his own car. Thus it is clear that there was a relationship of master and servant, leaving in dispute whether James Murphy was engaged in his employer's business at the precise time appellee's injuries were inflicted. The utterances attributed to James Murphy immediately after the collision tend to show he was at that time on an errand for his employer, and if properly received furnish adequate support for the findings of the jury.

Appellant relies first on the general proposition that the declaration of an agent concerning his authority is inadmissible against his employer and correctly points out that absent the alleged utterance of James Murphy there was not sufficient evidence on which a jury could find that he was acting within the scope of his employment when the accident occurred. Second, appellant urges that under the so-called excited utterance rule such utterances are admissible only and narrowly to explain the exciting occurrence and for no other purpose.

The decided cases dealing with the admissibility of statements of an employee, concerning his authority, are in confusion as to the basis for receiving such evidence. The broadly stated proposition that the authority of an agent cannot be proved "out of the mouth of the agent" is true only if it is considered with its numerous exceptions, which taken together render the general proposition one of relatively little significance. The rationale of excluding such statements seems to rest on the assumed want of reliability; the exceptions to the "rule" tend to rest on finding reliability in the circumstances of the utterance. For example, when made in court under oath, subject to the tests of cross examination and penalties of perjury, those circumstances are regarded as making the statement sufficiently trustworthy to be received. Or, where other independent evidence of authority is present, the assumed want of reliability of the statements is regarded as sufficiently cured by that corroboration. A third category of circumstances regarded as curing the want of reliability or reasonably insuring reliability is the area embraced within the spontaneous declaration, or more aptly called, the excited utterance exception. Here we are still dealing with hearsay but its want of reliability is regarded as satisfied by the circumstances in which the statement is made. The prompt, spontaneous character of the utterance under the impact and stress of the exciting event which "stills the reflective process" provides the circumstances, which, experience shows us, make for reliability.

There has been a general failure to recognize that the rationale of the excited utterance doctrine furnishes a separate and distinct basis for admissibility, not to be confused with the vicarious admissions rule. Under the vicarious admissions rule, a substantive rule of agency, an agent's out of court statements as to his authority (or any other relevant matter) may be received even though hearsay, if other evidence proves he was authorized to speak. There the element of reliability is not a problem since it is the *fact* of the utterance, not its truth which is in issue.

Thus, if the words qualify as a vicarious utterance, i.e., the authorized words of the principal uttered by the agent, it is not necessary that they also qualify as excited utterances. If they qualify as excited utterances there is no rational basis for demanding more, since the want of reliability has been cured by the circumstances, as has been pointed out.

Unfortunately few courts have recognized this and there has been a general tendency to blur the requirements of vicarious utterances and excited utterances. Mecham dispels this confusion, stating:

"Although they thus cannot be regarded as *authorized,* the declarations and admissions of an agent may often be put in evidence upon an entirely different ground, namely, that they constitute [a spontaneous utterance] * * * . The use here * * * does not necessarily depend upon the law of agency at all. It is a rule of evidence, and is just as applicable in a proper case to one who was not an agent at all as to one who was an agent * * * . The theory is that the spontaneous utterances of one who speaks under the excitement of the movement and before he has had time to deliberate—to concoct a self-favoring story—are likely to be true."

Professor Wigmore agrees:

"That there are two distinct and unrelated principles involved must be apparent; and the sooner the Courts insist on keeping them apart, the better * * * ."

We are satisfied, therefore, that when out of court statements qualify as excited utterances, the hearsay rule removes its bar to admissibility. The fact that the utterer is an agent is immaterial so far as admissibility as an excited utterance is concerned.

We turn now to appellant's argument that the part of the alleged utterance of James Murphy tending to show that he was on an errand for his employer did not qualify as an excited utterance, because it did not illuminate the exciting event but rather went to the issue of his authority.

A majority of decided cases and authorities appear to require the presence of three elements in order for an out of court statement to qualify as an excited utterance or spontaneous declaration. These are (a) an exciting event (b) an utterance prompted by the exciting event without time to reflect, i. e., dominated by the nervous excitement of the event, and (c) the utterance must explain or illuminate the exciting event. But a careful analysis of the entire subject demonstrates that the third element, mechanically and narrowly construed, is a spurious element, and that reliability of the utterance is not inflexibly dependent upon the subject matter of the utterance.

The test for receiving the utterance, therefore, should be whether it meets the first two requirements of a spontaneous declaration or excited utterance referred to earlier. This lies essentially with the trial court, and not unlike the evaluation of credibility is one based in part, at least, on observation of the witness, the context of the statement and all surrounding circumstances. It should be kept in mind that as soon as the excited utterance goes beyond description of the exciting event and deals with past facts or with the future it may tend to take on a reflective quality and must be more carefully scrutinized with respect to the second element, that of true spontaneity. In other words, the very fact that the utterance is not descriptive of the exciting event is one of the factors which the trial court must take into account in the evaluation of whether the statement is truly a spontaneous, impulsive expression excited by the event. Most often the excited utterance, as a practical matter, relates to the exciting cause, i. e., description of an accident, an attack, etc., but if the utterance goes beyond a description of the occurrence and still meets the other tests of the excited utterance rule, we think it should be received if it is relevant.[15]

We hold that the alleged out of court statement of James Murphy, uttered at the time of the accident, to the effect that he was on an errand for his employer, and expressly found by the trial court to have been an excited utterance, was properly received in evidence as such.

Affirmed.

UNITED STATES v. MARTORANO

United States Court of Appeals, First Circuit, 1977.
557 F.2d 1, on petition for rehearing, 561 F.2d 406.

COFFIN, Chief Judge.

James Martorano appeals from the judgment of conviction which was entered against him on each count of a four count indictment. Counts one

---

15. See Metropolitan R. Co. v. Collins, 1893, 1 App.D.C. 383, which suggests that the trial court should use its discretion more cautiously when the utterer is an agent, and may have a self-interest in claiming to be within the scope of his employment.

and two charged appellant with conspiring to make, and with making, an extortionate extension of credit in violation of 18 U.S.C. § 892(a). Count three charged conspiracy to use extortionate means to collect an extension of credit in violation of § 894(a).　　*　　*　　*

The charges in this case stem from a loan appellant allegedly made to one Peter Pallotta. The government's evidence, viewed in the light most favorable to it, reflects the following. Pallotta had been running a highly unsuccessful nightclub, and, in late August or early September, 1974, he found himself in need of $2000 to pay some pressing debts. Pallotta's brother took him to see appellant, who agreed to make Pallotta a $2000 loan at five percent interest per week. Told by appellant to return to pick up the money, Pallotta came back the next day and met with appellant and one Matera. Appellant gave Pallotta the money and instructed Matera to go to Pallotta's club each Friday at 7:30 to pick up the weekly payments. No papers were signed, and no collateral was given.

During the next four weeks, Pallotta made the interest payments as follows: once he paid appellant at appellant's club; twice Matera came to Pallotta's club and picked up the money, and once Matera and one Pagano together came to Pallotta's club and received the payment. Sometime in October, Pallotta was forced to close his club for renovations for four weeks, and during this period he did not make any payments. The club reopened on October 30. On that night, appellant and co-defendant Halloran, who was acquitted on all the charges, appeared at Pallotta's club. Because he feared the embarrassment of a beating in his own club, Pallotta left. The next day Pallotta received a telephone call from an unnamed source warning that Pallotta should make himself available to appellant that night. That night Halloran allegedly approached Pallotta in the parking lot outside the club and said that appellant had sent him to get the money. When Pallotta protested that he had no money, Halloran pulled a gun, took Pallotta with him inside the club, and removed some $450 from two separate cash boxes.

Three days later, Pallotta went to see appellant, who asked Pallotta what he was going to do. When Pallotta responded that he had to pay, appellant responded: "Don't be late and see me every week and if you're not going to be here, I want a phone call from you."

Sometime shortly thereafter, Pallotta's club was permanently closed. Because he lacked a source of income and feared physical harm at the hands of several loan sharks, including appellant, Pallotta went into hiding and began living in his car. In late November, 1974, Pallotta contacted the FBI. With Pallotta's consent, the FBI recorded a series of telephone conversations of Pallotta with Halloran, Matera, Pagano, and appellant. In their conversation appellant suggested that Pallotta stop by and see him. When Pallotta expressed his fear of being harmed, appellant replied:

"Don't talk like that on the phone.

*　　*　　*

You can come any time. What do you think I'm gonna do something 'round my own place? Be kind of stupid wouldn't it? Ah, first chance you get drop by and see me."

The conversations between Pallotta and Pagano generally verified the existence of the loan and revealed that Pagano and Matera had supplied half of the money which had been loaned Pallotta.

At the trial Pallota testified as to the reputations of each of the various individuals who allegedly were involved in the transaction. Pallotta testified that appellant was a loan shark and was "100 per cent in getting his collections back   *   *   *   . Nobody missed. If they did, they got hurt." As to Matera and Pagano, Pallotta testified that they had worked together in a loan shark operation for many years and that if any of their borrowers were ever late in repaying a loan, they would hurt the borrower. Pallotta also stated he had known Halloran for a long period of time and that Halloran was "a loan shark, collector and enforcer and a madman" and that he collected for appellant. This reputation testimony was all admitted subject to the limitation that it could be considered only as to Pallotta's state of mind. Finally, Pallotta testified that at the time he accepted the extension of credit he knew he would be physically harmed if he failed to repay on time.

*   *   *

2.   At trial the court permitted the government to introduce the statements Matera and Pagano made during recorded telephone conversations with Pallotta under the co-conspirator exception to the hearsay rule. Appellant objects that there had not been a sufficient prior showing that a conspiracy existed. We find no error.

We recently indicated our view that the new federal rules of evidence, which were in effect at appellant's trial, introduced significant changes in the administration of the co-conspirator exception to the hearsay rule. See United States v. Petrozziello, 548 F.2d 20 (1st Cir. 1977). Without repeating what we said in that case, we read the new rules as committing the question of the admissibility of the statements of an alleged co-conspirator exclusively to the trial judge. The district judge will admit the hearsay declarations if he determines, by a preponderance of the evidence, that a conspiracy existed, that the declarant and the defendant were members of it at the time the statements were made, and that the declarant's statements were made in furtherance of the conspiracy. See Fed.R.Evid. 104(a), 104(b), 801(d)(2)(E). The new rules permit a trial judge to base his determination on hearsay and other inadmissible evidence, including perhaps the very statement seeking admission. Fed.R.Evid. 104(a); see United States v. Petrozziello, supra at 23 n.2.

Here, the trial court made a preliminary determination that there had been a sufficient showing of conspiracy to permit the introduction of the statements of Matera and Pagano, and it followed the pre-federal rules practice of instructing the jury that it could not consider the statements unless it first found that the independent nonhearsay evidence established the existence of a conspiracy beyond a reasonable doubt. Naturally, the only question we must now review is whether the district court erred in making the threshold determination that there had been a sufficient showing that a conspiracy existed to place the statements before the jury. See United States v. Petrozziello, supra at 23. In making this decision, it seems that the district court may have followed the federal rules to the extent of considering evidence other than the independent nonhearsay variety: it allowed the government to argue in favor of the admissibility of some of the statements by referring to the evidence of a conspiracy contained in the statements seeking admission. Although the district court did not make an explicit finding that a conspiracy existed between appellant and the two declarants, appellant requested no such finding and, in view of the fact that *Petrozziello* had yet to be decided, this was not plain error. See id. As we did in *Petrozziello,* we will consider the evidence supporting the existence of the alleged conspiracies. Because, in each instance, we believe the evidence makes the existence of a conspiracy more likely than not, we affirm the district court's evidentiary rulings.

We have already detailed the evidence which was sufficient to permit the jury to find that Matera and Martorano had conspired together, and we believe it preponderates in favor of the existence of the conspiracy. Pagano presents a somewhat closer question. Pallotta testified that he and Matera had been partners in a loan shark operation for years.[9] While this fact alone does not establish that Pagano was a member of the Martorano-Matera conspiracy, there is the additional fact that Pagano and Matera together went to Pallotta's club to collect one of the interest payments. In view of the evidence that the two men were long-time loan shark partners, we think it reasonable to infer that Pagano's presence on this particular occasion was not a coincidence, but rather was because Pagano was taking part in this particular extortionate extension of credit. While this independent, non-hearsay evidence of Pagano's involvement is not terribly compelling, we think the district court could properly take account of a fact which was revealed by the statements seeking admission: that Pagano and Matera had supplied half the money which Martorano gave Pallotta. This additional fact, when considered together with the independent nonhearsay evidence, provides a solid basis for our conclusion that Pagano and appellant were involved in a conspiracy.

We are aware that United States v. Glasser, 315 U.S. 60, 74-75, 62 S.Ct. 457, 86 L.Ed. 680 (1942), rejected the view that the existence of a conspiracy could be proved by the very statement seeking admission. The new rules, however, explicitly contemplate the consideration of such hearsay evidence in making preliminary findings of fact. We believe the new rules must be taken as overruling *Glasser* to the extent that it held that the statement seeking admission cannot be considered at all in making the determination whether a conspiracy exists. *Glasser,* however, still stands as a warning to trial judges that such statements should ordinarily be given little weight. Here, where there is significant independent evidence of the existence of a conspiracy and where the statement seeking admission simply corroborates inferences which can be drawn from the independent evidence, we see no problem with the consideration of that statement.

We also are not persuaded by appellant's further argument that the tapes affirmatively disclose that Pagano had withdrawn from the conspiracy and that his declarations thus did not fall within the ambit of the co-conspirator exception. In the conversations, Pagano expressed his willingness to help arrange further payments to appellant, and we think the district judge reasonably inferred that Pagano was still a member of the conspiracy.

9. Although this evidence was admitted subject to the limitation that it could only be considered as to Pallotta's state of mind, Fed.R. Evid. 104(a) permits the district court to consider such statements for their truth in determining the existence of the preliminary fact of the existence of a conspiracy.

*   *   *

The judgment of conviction is affirmed.

On petition for rehearing.

Having on appellant's petition for rehearing granted leave to file briefs on the issue whether Glasser v. United States, 315 U.S. 60, 62 S.Ct. 457, 86 L.Ed. 680 (1942), has been partially overruled and having now considered the briefs of the parties submitted on this question, we continue to believe that the viability of *Glasser* is in some doubt for the reasons we state below. But our further reflections have persuaded us that we need not face this troublesome issue in this case, for we are satisfied that the tapes of the Pagano-Pallotta conversations were properly admitted under *Glasser.*

Although *Glasser* confines a district court to the "independent" evidence in deciding whether to admit a statement by a co-conspirator, it has never been the case that statements of the declarant were automatically excluded from consideration. The district court has always been permitted to consider statements by the declarant which are not hearsay or which are admissible in their own right under an exception to the hearsay rule. After reconsidering these tapes in light of the government's briefs, we are persuaded that many of Pagano's statements were "verbal acts". These statements, when considered along with the other pieces of independent evidence, provide a solid basis for the conclusion that a conspiracy existed.

The eight Pallotta-Pagano telephone conversations that were admitted into evidence occurred at various times between December 20, 1974 and January 20, 1975. Although many of the statements Pagano made would be most damaging to appellant only if taken as establishing the truth of the matter asserted, e. g., Pagano's assertion that he had supplied appellant with some of the money that had been lent Pallotta or the statements to the effect that Pallotta would be in danger if he went to appellant's nightclub, other statements were significant simply because Pagano had made them. These include: a large number of statements Pagano made indicating his knowledge both of the loan and of Pallotta's delinquent status; see VI Wigmore on Evidence § 1790; and an equally large number of statements which we do not hesitate to characterize as attempts to facilitate and/or to encourage further payments of the loan.[1]

In addition, we note that one of Matera's statements which was admitted into evidence suggests that Pagano was actually in touch with Matera during this period and that Pallotta's situation had been discussed. On January 20, 1975, some twenty minutes after the final call to Pagano, Pallotta telephoned Matera, who answered Pallotta's query with three high-

---

1. All eight calls constituted attempts by Pallotta to find out precisely where he stood with appellant and Matera. Several of the calls consisted of long conversations in which they would talk, sometimes, in Pagano's words, "between the lines" about Pallotta's plight. In virtually each call, Pagano expressed a willingness to get information Pallotta wanted. While Pagano never fully delivered on his promise, in each call he encouraged Pallotta to phone back at some future date when Pagano expected to have the information. While other inferences are of course possible, the simple fact that he was willing to talk to Pallotta at some length about his situation and encourage him to call back suggests that Pagano had an interest in facilitating a normalization of the appellant-Pallotta, creditor-debtor relationship. Pagano also at one time assured Pallotta that one payment must have been received and, in one of the last taped conversations, he offered to help arrange further payments if Pallotta should find himself in a position to make them.

ly suspicious denials of all knowledge concerning the matter and with the statement "[a]nd don't call that other fellow no more." The most natural inference, given the context, is that the "other fellow" was Pagano and that he had been in contact with Matera concerning Pallotta.

The statements we have referred to could properly be considered by the judge in determining the preliminary question whether Pagano and appellant were members of a common venture. The "independent" evidence thus shows the following. First, there is rather overwhelming evidence that appellant and Matera were members of a common illicit venture. Several pieces of evidence tending to link Pagano to that enterprise are that Matera and appellant were co-conspirators; that Matera and Pagano were long time loan shark partners who, inferentially at least, would be involved in each other's ventures; that Pagano accompanied Matera to collect an interest payment from Pallotta; and that Pagano, in late December, 1974, and early January, 1975, was aware of Pallotta's plight, was willing to take steps to find out Pallotta's situation and to facilitate future payments, and had in fact been in touch with Matera and discussed Pallotta's situation. We thus have no difficulty concluding that it preponderates in favor of the existence of a conspiracy between Pagano and appellant. It is true that each of these items is susceptible to an interpretation other than Pagano's participation in the conspiracy. However, when viewed together, each of them gains color from the others and they satisfy us that Pagano and appellant had associated themselves "in a concerted mutual venture".

Having raised the issue of the continued vitality of *Glasser's* requirement that the proof of the existence of the conspiracy be independent of the statement seeking admission, we will briefly outline why we think *Glasser's* survival may be in doubt. Here, the portion of the taped conversation which is relevant to the conspiracy determination is Pagano's statements to the effect that he had put up part of the money appellant loaned Pallotta. Although inadmissible, these statements were highly reliable. * * *

But since the statements were inadmissible, the question here is whether such reliable evidence may be considered by the district court in determining the preliminary fact whether a conspiracy exists. Both the policies and plain terms of Fed.R.Evid. 104(a) seem to indicate that it could be. The rule provides that inadmissible evidence can be considered by the district court in making such determinations, making no distinction between inadmissible evidence generally and the statement seeking admission. And the reason behind the rule—that trial judges, because of their legal experience and training, "will generally be fully cognizant of [the] inherent weakness [of such evidence] * * * and will take such weakness into account in evaluating the preliminary question", Weinstein on Evidence ¶ 104[02](7) at 104-24—is equally applicable to the two kinds of statements. It seems that, once hearsay is placed before the district court, it would be a matter of indifference to the criminal defendant what its source is.

The appellant's argument for the contrary view proceeds from the fact that *Glasser* was premised on the Court's desire to prevent "bootstrapping" of the very hearsay utterance seeking admission to the level of competent evidence. * * * [W]e have to wonder whether a generalized abhorrence of bootstrapping is sufficient justification for barring all use of the trustworthy features of the hearsay statement seeking admission. But under any view of the law we would, as we said in our original opinion, require significant independent evidence of the existence of the conspiracy, deviating from the *Glasser* practice only to the extent of permitting the district court to consider the independent evidence in the light of the color shed upon it by the highly trustworthy and reliable portions of the hearsay utterance seeking admission. This approach would afford the criminal defendants most of the protections provided by the rule of *Glasser,* yet give free play to Rule 104(a)'s policy of recognizing the trial judge's ability to assess the weight to be given otherwise inadmissible evidence.[2]

We emphasize that our opinions in this case should not be understood as deciding anything about the continued viability of *Glasser.* We intend to have done no more than indicate the basis for our doubts. Our decision in this case rests solely upon our view that the "independent" evidence established the existence of a concerted mutual venture.

* * *

KAPLAN, OF MABRUS AND ZORGS

66 Cal.L.Rev. 987, 997–99 (1978).

* * * Let us examine the following hypothetical:

Prosecution of D for aiding and abetting a bank robbery. W testifies that he (W) was in on the plan and that, to bolster his (W's) courage, A, his coconspirator, told him, "You know D is an excellent driver. Well, D told me he'll be waiting outside the bank with the motor going."

Let us temporarily put aside the problem of what to do when the crime charged is conspiracy so that the preliminary question and ultimate issue are the same. Here the crime charged is not conspiracy but bank robbery, and under the California code, as under the common law, the admissibility of W's testimony for the most part turns on whether A, the declarant, and D, the defendant, were members of the conspiracy and whether A's statement was made "in furtherance" of that conspiracy. (Note that W, himself, need not be a member of the conspiracy: the same rule of admissibility would apply if he merely had overheard A's statement to someone else —provided that A's statement was, in fact, in furtherance of the conspiracy and was not simply bragging. W's participation, however, makes it more likely that A's statement was in furtherance of the plan.)

Surely, in principle, the California Statute,* which makes these preliminary fact questions jury questions, is in error. The jury will likely give short shrift to questions such as whether the declarant, A, was himself a member of the conspiracy or whether the statement was made in furtherance of the conspiracy. Rather, the jurors probably will ignore our hearsay rule and decide whether to give the statement weight depending on

2. Although we entertain these doubts about *Glasser's* survival, we note that other courts have assumed that the new federal rules have not affected *Glasser* in the slightest. See United States v. Stanchich, 550 F.2d 1294, 1298–99 n. 4 (2d Cir. 1977); United States v. Trowery, 542 F.2d 623, 626–27 (3d Cir. 1976); United States v. Stroupe, 538 F.2d 1063, 1065, 1066 (4th Cir. 1976); United States v. Savell, 546, F.2d 43, 46–47 (5th Cir. 1977); United States v. Burgard, 551 F.2d 190, 196 (8th Cir. 1977); United States v. Wood, 550 F.2d 435, 442 (9th Cir. 1977). In none of these, however, was the issue specifically considered.

*Cal.Evid. Code § 1223 (West 1966).

whether they think A was knowledgeable and truthful, regardless of whether he was a coconspirator.

Interestingly, in the most common type of case, where the declarant, A, was clearly a conspirator, but the disputed preliminary question is whether the defendant, D, was also a member of the bank robbing conspiracy, the error in the California statute is not so serious. If D's guilt of bank robbery were based on his membership in the conspiracy, and the jury did not believe him to have been a conspirator, it would acquit him. In this case, it would be hard to get upset about whether or not the jury improperly considered A's hearsay statement as to D's guilt.

Of course, it is the other possibility that many find upsetting: that the jurors would believe D to be guilty in part because they considered A's hearsay statement on this issue. This does not mean, however, that the jury would have ignored the policy of the law requiring D's status as a coconspirator as a condition of using A's statement against D. After all, the jury has found that D was a conspirator. The only issue is whether the jury must decide the question as a preliminary fact question—before it decides the same question on the merits of the case. Looked at another way, the issue is whether the jury may consider the hearsay evidence—or more precisely, A's hearsay statement—on the issue of the preliminary fact of D's conspiratorial status. Certainly it is a departure from orthodoxy to do so, but to allow a jury to consider hearsay evidence in making its preliminary fact determination is very different from misallocating our preliminary fact determination so that the jury will consider inadmissible evidence on the merits of the case.

It is in the related exception to the hearsay rule—for authorized admissions—that the California Evidence Code reaches the indefensible result of allowing the preliminary fact to be ignored completely. Section 1222[16] makes the question of authorization a jury question. * * * Here, even more clearly than in the case of the coconspirator exception, a rational jury will pay no attention to the artificial preliminary fact requirement of authorization. Consequently, the question should, of course, be decided by the judge. Nor can one defend the California code's transformation of this issue into a jury question on the ground that the hearsay exception itself is much too narrow. It is true that in the usual case the truck driver's statement as to his own negligence probably should be admissible against his employer even if it is not authorized. By treating the question of authorization as a jury question the California code partially rectifies this arguable error by allowing the jury to hear such statements in a much larger number of cases. On the other hand, if indeed it is the scope of the hearsay exception that is at fault, the proper remedy is to change the exception. When the proponent of the truck driver's statement lacks any evidence of authorization, even the treatment of the question as a jury question will not help produce the "correct" result of admitting the statement. In this case at least, two wrongs do not make a right. Moreover, the California Evidence Code allows the jury to hear what may be unauthorized statements, even in cases in which most of us would regard the lack of authorization as important enough to deny them admissibility, at least so long as we are willing to enforce the hearsay rule.

16.   Cal. Evid. Code § 1222 (West 1966).

The federal rules reach a better result in handling both coconspirator statements and authorized admissions, although the matter is somewhat complicated by the peculiar definition of hearsay in the federal rules which allows both kinds of out-of-court statements into evidence, not as hearsay exceptions, but rather as nonhearsay. In both cases the preliminary issues are not ones merely of relevance, and hence the judge must decide the preliminary fact questions rather than leaving them to the jury.

* * *

LEGO v. TWOMEY

Supreme Court of the United States, 1972.
404 U.S. 553, 92 S.Ct. 619, 30 L.Ed.2d 618.

Mr. Justice WHITE delivered the opinion of the Court.

In 1964, this Court held that a criminal defendant who challenges the voluntariness of a confession made to officials and sought to be used against him at his trial has a due process right to a reliable determination that the confession was in fact voluntarily given and not the outcome of coercion which the Constitution forbids. Jackson v. Denno, 378 U.S. 368, 84 S.Ct. 1774, 12 L.Ed.2d 908 (1964). While our decision made plain that only voluntary confessions may be admitted at the trial of guilt or innocence, we did not then announce, or even suggest, that the factfinder at a coercion hearing need judge voluntariness with reference to an especially severe standard of proof. Nevertheless, since *Jackson,* state and federal courts have addressed themselves to the issue with a considerable variety of opinions.[1] We granted certiorari in this case to resolve the question. * * *

Petitioner Lego was convicted of armed robbery in 1961 after a jury trial in Superior Court, Cook County, Illinois. The court sentenced him to prison for 25 to 50 years. The evidence introduced against Lego at trial included a confession he had made to police after arrest and while in custody at the station house. Prior to trial Lego sought to have the confession suppressed. He did not deny making it but did challenge that he had done so voluntarily. The trial judge conducted a hearing, out of the presence of the jury, at which Lego testified that police had beaten him about the head and neck with a gun butt. His explanation of this treatment was that the local police chief, a neighbor and former classmate of the robbery victim, had sought revenge upon him. Lego introduced into evidence a photograph which had been taken of him at the county jail on the day after his arrest. The photograph showed that petitioner's face had been swollen and had traces of blood on it. Lego admitted that his face had been scratched in a scuffle with the robbery victim but maintained that the encounter did not explain the condition shown in the photograph. The police chief and four of-

---

1. State courts which have considered the question since *Jackson* have adopted a variety of standards, most of them founded upon state law. Many have sanctioned a standard of proof less strict than beyond a reasonable doubt, including proof of voluntariness by a preponderance of the evidence or to the satisfaction of the court or proof of voluntariness in fact. * * * Other States, using state law or not specifying a basis, require proof beyond a reasonable doubt. * * *

Two federal courts have held as an exercise of supervisory power that voluntariness must be proved beyond a reasonable doubt. * * *

ficers also testified. They denied either beating or threatening petitioner and disclaimed knowledge that any other officer had done so. The trial judge resolved this credibility problem in favor of the police and ruled the confession admissible.[2] At trial, Lego testified in his own behalf. Although he did not dispute the truth of the confession directly, he did tell his version of the events which had transpired at the police station. The trial judge instructed the jury as to the prosecution's burden of proving guilt. He did not instruct that the jury was required to find the confession voluntary before it could be used in judging guilt or innocence.[3] On direct appeal the Illinois Supreme Court affirmed the conviction.

Four years later petitioner challenged his conviction by seeking a writ of habeas corpus in the United States District Court for the Northern District of Illinois. He maintained that the trial judge should have found the confession voluntary beyond a reasonable doubt before admitting it into evidence. Although the judge had made no mention of the standard he used, Illinois law provided that a confession challenged as involuntary could be admitted into evidence if, at a hearing outside the presence of the jury, the judge found it voluntary by a preponderance of the evidence. In the alternative petitioner argued that the voluntariness question should also have been submitted to the jury for its separate consideration. After first denying the writ for failure to exhaust state remedies, the District Court granted a rehearing motion, concluded that Lego had no state remedy then available to him and denied relief on the merits. The Court of Appeals for the Seventh Circuit affirmed.

I

Petitioner challenges the judgment of the Court of Appeals on three grounds. The first is that he was not proved guilty beyond a reasonable doubt as required by In re Winship, 397 U.S. 358, 90 S.Ct. 1068, 25 L.Ed.2d 368 (1970), because the confession used against him at his trial had been proved voluntary only by a preponderance of the evidence. Implicit in the claim is an assumption that a voluntariness hearing is designed to enhance the reliability of jury verdicts. To judge whether that is so we must return to Jackson v. Denno, 378 U.S. 368, 84 S.Ct. 1774, 12 L.Ed.2d 908 (1964).

2. In ruling the confession admissible, the judge stated:
    "The petitioner has admitted under oath he had a struggle with the complaining witness over the gun; he was wounded, obtained a facial wound. The Officer testified he was bloody at the time he was arrested.
    "I don't believe the defendant's testimony at all that he was beaten up by the Police. The condition he is in is well explained by the defendant himself."

3. Illinois followed what we described in Jackson as "the orthodox rule, under which the judge himself solely and finally determines the voluntariness of the confession * * *" 378 U.S., at 378, 84 S.Ct. at 1781. While the procedures of all the States could not be neatly classified, we noted that some followed the Massachusetts procedure whereby the judge himself first resolves evidentiary conflicts and determines whether a confession is in fact voluntary. If he is unable so to conclude, the confession may not be admitted into evidence. If judged voluntary and therefore admissible, the jury must also determine the coercion issue and is instructed to ignore a confession it finds involuntary. Id., at 378 n. 8, 84 S.Ct. at 1781. Other States had adopted the New York procedure at issue in Jackson. Our decision in Jackson cast no doubt upon the orthodox and Massachusetts procedures but did call into question the practice of every State which did not clearly follow one of these procedures. A thorough tabulation of what States did in the wake of Jackson appears in 3 J. Wigmore, Evidence 585–593 (Chadbourn rev. 1970).

In New York prior to *Jackson,* juries most often determined the voluntariness of confessions and hence whether confessions could be used in deciding guilt or innocence. Trial judges were required to make an initial determination and could exclude a confession, but only if it could not under any circumstances be deemed voluntary. When voluntariness was fairly debatable, either because a dispute of fact existed or because reasonable men could have drawn differing inferences from undisputed facts, the question whether the confession violated due process was for the jury. This meant the confession was introduced at the trial itself. If evidence challenging its voluntariness were adduced, the jury was instructed first to pass upon voluntariness and, if it found the confession involuntary, ignore it in determining guilt. If, on the other hand, the confession were found to be voluntary, the jury was then free to consider its truth or falsity and give the confession an appropriate weight in judging guilt or innocence.

We concluded that the New York procedure was constitutionally defective because at no point along the way did a criminal defendant receive a clear-cut determination that the confession used against him was in fact voluntary. The trial judge was not entitled to exclude a confession merely because he himself would have found it involuntary, and, while we recognized that the jury was empowered to perform that function, we doubted it could do so reliably. Precisely because confessions of guilt, whether coerced or freely given, may be truthful and potent evidence, we did not believe a jury could be called upon to ignore the probative value of a truthful but coerced confession; it was also likely, we thought, that in judging voluntariness itself the jury would be influenced by the reliability of a confession it considered an accurate account of the facts. "It is now axiomatic," we said,

> "that a defendant in a criminal case is deprived of due process of law if his conviction is founded, in whole or in part, upon an involuntary confession, without regard for the truth or falsity of the confession,   *   *   *

We did not think it necessary, or even appropriate, in *Jackson* to announce that prosecutors would be required to meet a particular burden of proof in *Jackson* hearing held before the trial judge.[9] Indeed, the then-established duty to determine voluntariness had not been framed in terms of a burden of proof, nor has it been since *Jackson* was decided. We could fairly assume then, as we can now, that a judge would admit into evidence only those confessions which he reliably found at least by a preponderance of the evidence, had been made voluntarily.

We noted in *Jackson* that there may be a relationship between the involuntariness of a confession and its unreliability.[12] But our decision was not based in the slightest on the fear that juries might misjudge the accuracy of confessions and arrive at erroneous determinations of guilt or innocence. That case was not aimed at reducing the possibility of convicting innocent men.

9. "Judge" is used here and throughout the opinion to mean a factfinder, whether trial judge or jury, at a voluntariness hearing. The proscription against permitting the jury which passes upon guilt or innocence to judge voluntariness in the same proceeding does not preclude the States from impaneling a separate jury to determine voluntariness.   *   *   *

12. We noted that coerced confessions are forbidden in part because of their "probable unreliability." Jackson v. Denno, 378 U.S., at 385–386, 84 S.Ct., at 1785. How-

Quite the contrary, we feared that the reliability and truthfulness of even coerced confessions could impermissibly influence a jury's judgment as to voluntariness. The use of coerced confessions, whether true or false, is forbidden because the method used to extract them offends constitutional principles. The procedure we established in *Jackson* was designed to safeguard the right of an individual, entirely apart from his guilt or innocence, not to be compelled to condemn himself by his own utterances. Nothing in *Jackson* questioned the province or capacity of juries to assess the truthfulness of confessions. Nothing in that opinion took from the jury any evidence relating to the accuracy or weight of confessions admitted into evidence. A defendant has been as free since *Jackson* as he was before to familiarize a jury with circumstances which attend the taking of his confession, including facts bearing upon its weight and voluntariness. In like measure, of course, juries have been at liberty to disregard confessions which are insufficiently corroborated or otherwise deemed unworthy of belief.

Since the purpose that a voluntariness hearing is designed to serve has nothing whatever to do with improving the reliability of jury verdicts, we cannot accept the charge that judging the admissibility of a confession by a preponderance of the evidence undermines the mandate of In re Winship, 397 U.S. 358, 90 S.Ct. 1068, 25 L.Ed.2d 368 (1970). Our decision in *Winship* was not concerned with standards for determining the admissibility of evidence or with the prosecution's burden of proof at a suppression hearing when evidence is challenged on constitutional grounds. *Winship* went no further than to confirm the fundamental right that protects "the accused against conviction except upon proof beyond a reasonable doubt of every fact necessary to constitute the crime with which he is charged." Id., at 364, 90 S.Ct., at 1072. A high standard of proof is necessary, we said, to ensure against unjust convictions by giving substance to the presumption of innocence. Id., at 363, 90 S.Ct., at 1072. A guilty verdict is not rendered less reliable or less consonant with *Winship* simply because the admissibility of a confession is determined by a less stringent standard. Petitioner does not maintain that either his confession or its voluntariness is an element of the crime with which he was charged. He does not challenge the constitutionality of the standard by which the jury was instructed to decide his guilt or innocence; nor does he question the sufficiency of the evidence which reached the jury to satisfy the proper standard of proof. Petitioner's rights under *Winship* have not been violated.[15]

---

ever, it had been settled when this Court decided *Jackson* that the exclusion of unreliable confessions is not the purpose which a voluntariness hearing is designed to serve. Rogers v. Richmond, 365 U.S. 534, 81 S.Ct. 735, 5 L.Ed.2d 760 (1961). The sole issue in such a hearing is whether a confession was coerced. Whether it be true or false is irrelevant; indeed, such an inquiry is forbidden. The judge may not take into consideration evidence which would indicate that the confession, though compelled, is reliable, even highly so. Id., at 545, 81 S.Ct., at 741. As difficult as such tasks may be to accomplish, the judge is also duty-bound to ignore implications of reliability in facts relevant to coercion and to shut from his mind any internal

evidence of authenticity which a confession itself may bear.

15. Nothing is to be gained from restating the constitutional rule as requiring proof of guilt beyond a reasonable doubt on the basis of constitutionally obtained evidence and then arguing that rights under *Winship* are diluted unless admissibility is governed by a high standard. Transparently, this assumes the question at issue, which is whether a confession is admissible if found voluntary by a preponderance of the evidence. United States v. Schipani, 289 F.Supp. 43 (E.D.N.Y.1968), affirmed, 414 F.2d 1262 (CA2 1969), followed this unsatisfactory course in a Fourth Amendment case but stopped short of basing the decision on the Constitution.

II

Even conceding that *Winship* is inapplicable because the purpose of a voluntariness hearing is not to implement the presumption of innocence, petitioner presses for reversal on the alternative ground that evidence offered against a defendant at a criminal trial and challenged on constitutional grounds must be determined admissible beyond a reasonable doubt in order to give adequate protection to those values which exclusionary rules are designed to serve. Jackson v. Denno, 378 U.S. 368, 84 S.Ct. 1774 (1964), an offspring of Brown v. Mississippi, 297 U.S. 278, 56 S.Ct. 461, 80 L.Ed. 682 (1936), requires judicial rulings on voluntariness prior to admitting confessions. Miranda v. Arizona, 384 U.S. 436, 86 S.Ct. 1602, 16 L.Ed.2d 694 (1966), excludes confessions flowing from custodial interrogations unless adequate warnings were administered and a waiver was obtained. Weeks v. United States, 232 U.S. 383, 34 S.Ct. 341, 58 L.Ed. 652 (1914), and Mapp v. Ohio, 367 U.S. 643, 81 S.Ct. 1684, 6 L.Ed.2d 1081 (1961), make impermissible the introduction of evidence obtained in violation of a defendant's Fourth Amendment rights. In each instance, and without regard to its probative value, evidence is kept from the trier of guilt or innocence for reasons wholly apart from enhancing the reliability of verdicts. These independent values, it is urged, themselves require a stricter standard of proof in judging admissibility.

The argument is straightforward and has appeal. But we are unconvinced that merely emphasizing the importance of the values served by exclusionary rules is itself sufficient demonstration that the Constitution also requires admissibility to be proved beyond reasonable doubt.[16] Evidence obtained in violation of the Fourth Amendment has been excluded from federal criminal trials for many years. Weeks v. United States, supra. The same is true of coerced confessions offered in either federal or state trials. But, from our experience over this period of time no substantial evidence has accumulated that federal rights have suffered from determining admissibility by a preponderance of the evidence. Petitioner offers nothing to suggest that admissibility rulings have been unreliable or otherwise wanting in quality because not based on some higher standard. Without good cause, we are unwilling to expand currently applicable exclusionary rules by erecting additional barriers to placing truthful and probative evidence before state juries and by revising the standards applicable in collateral proceedings. Sound reason for moving further in this direction has not been offered here nor do we discern any at the present time. This is particularly true since the exclusionary rules are very much aimed at deterring lawless conduct by police and prosecution and it is very doubtful that escalating the prosecution's burden of proof in Fourth and Fifth Amendment suppression hearings would be sufficiently productive in this respect to outweigh the public interest in placing probative evidence before juries for the purpose of arriving at truthful decisions about guilt or innocence.

To reiterate what we said in *Jackson:* when a confession challenged as involuntary is sought to be used against a criminal defendant at his trial, he

16. It is no more persuasive to impose the stricter standard of proof as an exercise of supervisory power rather than as a consititutional rule. Cf. Ralph v. Warden, 438 F.2d 786, 793 (CA4 1970), clarifying United States v. Inman, 352 F.2d 954 (CA4 1965); Pea v. United States, 130 U.S.App.D.C. 66, 397 F.2d 627 (1968).

is entitled to a reliable and clear-cut determination that the confession was in fact voluntarily rendered. Thus, the prosecution must prove at least by a preponderance of the evidence that the confession was voluntary. Of course, the States are free, pursuant to their own law, to adopt a higher standard. They may indeed differ as to the appropriate resolution of the values they find at stake.

III.

We also reject petitioner's final contention that, even though the trial judge ruled on his coercion claim, he was entitled to have the jury decide the claim anew. To the extent this argument asserts that the judge's determination was insufficiently reliable, it is no more persuasive than petitioner's other contentions. To the extent the position assumes that a jury is better suited than a judge to determine voluntariness, it questions the basic assumptions of Jackson v. Denno; it also ignores that *Jackson* neither raised any question about the constitutional validity of the so-called orthodox rule for judging the admissibility of confessions nor even suggested that the Constitution requires submission of voluntariness claims to a jury as well as a judge. Finally, Duncan v. Louisiana, 391 U.S. 145, 88 S.Ct. 1444, 20 L.Ed.2d 491 (1968), which made the Sixth Amendment right to trial by jury applicable to the States, did not purport to change the normal rule that the admissibility of evidence is a question for the court rather than the jury. Nor did that decision require that both judge and jury pass upon the admissibility of evidence when constitutional grounds are asserted for excluding it. We are not disposed to impose as a constitutional requirement a procedure we have found wanting merely to afford petitioner a second forum for litigating his claim.

The decision of the Court of Appeals is affirmed.

Affirmed.

The dissenting opinion of Mr. Justice Brennan, with whom Mr. Justice Douglas and Mr. Justice Marshall joined, is omitted. Mr. Justice Powell and Mr. Justice Rehnquist took no part.

5.   DECLARATIONS AGAINST INTEREST

G.M. McKELVEY CO. v. GENERAL CAS. CO. OF AMERICA

Supreme Court of Ohio, 1957.
166 Ohio St. 401, 142 N.E.2d 854, 2 O.O. 2d 345.

MATTHIAS, Judge. The issue raised by this appeal is whether, in a civil action against an insurer by an insured employer upon a policy of fidelity insurance protecting such employer from defalcations by his employees, written and signed confessions by certain employees admitting misappropriations of their employer's funds and stating the amounts of such misappropriations are admissible in evidence to prove both the fact and the amount of the loss.

*   *   *

Early in the history of the law of evidence the courts recognized that, although in most instances hearsay evidence should not be admitted, due to the inability to test the trustworthiness of such evidence, there are condi-tions and circumstances in which hearsay evidence as a matter of necessity must and can be relied upon as being trustworthy.

One of the exceptions to the hearsay rule, which has been found to be based on trustworthiness or a probability of truthfulness and veracity, and which has arisen due to necessity, is a declaration against interest by a third party.

The courts, where confronted with a situation where death, absence from the jurisdiction or insanity makes a witness unavailable, and where such witness is the only source from which his evidence can be obtained, have held that as a matter of necessity a declaration by such witness against his interest should be admitted in evidence. The courts have reasoned that a person does not make statements against his own pecuniary interest un-less they are true and have thus considered such statements trustworthy, even though there is no opportunity to confront the witness or to cross-examine him. 5 Wigmore on Evidence, 204, Section 1421.

Thus, the rule has arisen that a declaration against interest by one not a party or in privity with a party to an action is admissible in evidence, where (1) the person making such declaration is either dead or unavailable as a witness due to sickness, insanity or absence from the jurisdiction, (2) the declarant had peculiar means of knowing the facts which he stated, (3) the declaration was against his pecuniary or proprietary interest and (4) he had no probable motive to falsify the facts stated.

* * *

We realize that element (1) of the rule above is somewhat broader than the dicta spoken by the court in the Stetson case, i. e., "we are clear in the opinion that it could not properly be received while he was a living and com-petent witness," but we are compelled by logic and reason to the conclusion that there may be circumstances other than death which render a witness as unavailable to testify as if he were in fact dead, and that under such circum-stances a declaration, if it meets the other requirements of the rule, loses none of its trustworthiness or probability of truthfulness and veracity. Thus, anything in the dicta of the court in the Stetson case, hereinbefore set out, which is contrary to this conclusion cannot be said to be the law of Ohio on the subject.

At least as applied to written and signed confessions, we are in accord with the rule as stated above, and we will consider the confessions of the employees in the instant case in relation to this rule. First, it is apparent from the record that the employees making them were unavailable as wit-nesses, having been summoned and not found in the jurisdiction by the sheriff. Second, certainly a person who commits an embezzlement has a pe-culiar means of knowing whether he embezzled and how much he took, and, from the record in the instant case, plaintiff's employees are the only per-sons who can accurately indicate both the fact and the amount of the em-bezzlements. Third, it was clearly not to their interest to state such facts, since such declarations render them civilly liable for the amounts of their defalcations. Fourth, there would certainly be no probable motive for plain-tiff's employees to falsify the facts stated unless it would be to minimize the amount of their defalcations, and that question is not raised herein.

* * *

It is our conclusion that, in a civil action by an insured against his fidelity insurer to recover for defalcations by employees of the former, where such employees are unavailable as witnesses, they having been summoned and not found in the jurisdiction by the sheriff, written and signed confessions of such employees are admissible in evidence as declarations against interest as to both the fact and the amount of the loss.

For the reasons herein set out, the judgment of the Court of Appeals is affirmed.

Judgment affirmed.

Weygandt, C.J., and Zimmerman, Stewart, Bell, Taft and Herbert, JJ., concur.

UNITED STATES v. BARRETT

United States Court of Appeals, First Circuit, 1976.
539 F.2d 244.

Before COFFIN, Chief Judge, McENTEE and CAMPBELL, Circuit Judges.

LEVIN H. CAMPBELL, Circuit Judge.

Arthur Barrett appeals from his conviction after a jury trial for crimes arising from the theft and sale of a collection of postage stamps from the Cardinal Spellman Philatelic Museum in Weston, Massachusetts. [Barrett's nickname was "Bucky." Ben Tilley was allegedly a co-conspirator of Barrett's, but died prior to trial. "Buzzy" Adams testified at Barrett's trial as a government witness, in exchange for immunity from prosecution.]

* * *

Barrett * * * argues that the court below erred by refusing to admit the testimony of three defense witnesses. The first was James Melvin. Melvin testified that in February, 1974, he was at a card game on Bowdoin Street, in Dorchester, Massachusetts, with Ben Tilley. When Melvin was asked to recount a conversation which he had there with Tilley, the Government objected. Barrett made an offer of proof that Melvin would testify that Tilley had told Melvin "that he, Tilley, and Buzzy [Adams] were going to have some trouble from the people from California" with respect to the "stamp theft or matter" and that "[Melvin] asked him did he mean Bucky or Buzzy, and then he said, 'No, Bucky [Barrett] wasn't involved. It was Buzzy.' " Barrett argued at the bench that this testimony was admissible under Fed.R.Evid. 804(b)(3) as a declaration against self-interest, apparently on the theory that Tilley's display of inside knowledge of "the people from California," the stamp theft, and the identity of persons "involved", all tended against Tilley's penal interest at the time by advertising his likely complicity. The court excluded the proffered testimony as hearsay on the ground that the relevant part, that Buzzy, not Bucky, was involved, was not against Tilley's interest. The court said, "You are offering it not to prove anything prejudicial to the alleged maker of the statement but to prove that [Buzzy] rather than [Bucky] did it * * * ." Barrett argues on appeal that the entire statement, including the portion exculpating Barrett, should have been admitted.

Rule 804(b)(3) of the new Federal Rules of Evidence provides, with an important qualification, for the admission of a statement by an unavailable declarant that at the time of making tended to subject him to criminal liability. The rule provides in pertinent part,

"(b) *Hearsay exceptions.* The following are not excluded by the hearsay rule if the declarant is unavailable as a witness:

* * *

(3) *Statement against interest.* A statement which was at the time of its making so far contrary to the declarant's pecuniary or proprietary interest, or so far tended to subject him to civil or criminal liability * * * that a reasonable man in his position would not have made the statement unless he believed it to be true. A statement tending to expose the declarant to criminal liability and offered to exculpate the accused is not admissable [sic] unless corroborating circumstances clearly indicate the trustworthiness of the statement."

Rule 804(b)(3) is a departure from the principle laid down in Donnelly v. United States, 228 U.S. 243, 33 S.Ct. 449, 57 L.Ed. 820 (1913), in which the Supreme Court endorsed the exclusion from evidence of a third party's extra-judicial confession to the murder for which the defendant was on trial. In conformity with English precedent, the *Donnelly* court limited the hearsay exception for declarations against interest to declarations against interest of a pecuniary character. Id. at 272-77, 33 S.Ct. 449. Statements subjecting the declarant to criminal liability were held to be outside the exception.

Half a century later, when the present Federal Rules of Evidence were being formulated, *Donnelly* was in disfavor, and provision was made in the various drafts of the new code for the admission of declarations against penal interest. The text underwent several revisions prior to enactment. A provision forbidding prosecutorial use of third party statements or confessions which implicated an accused as well as the declarant was deleted, with the result that subject to sixth amendment and other constraints, a third party's out of court statements against penal interest may now be used against, as well as in favor of, an accused. And, more relevant here, the second sentence of clause (3) was rewritten to require that statements offered to exculpate the accused be corroborated so as to "clearly indicate the trustworthiness of the statement".

As submitted to Congress by the Supreme Court, the Rule required simply that a statement offered to exculpate the accused be corroborated. The Advisory Committee explained this requirement as a way of accommodating the common law's distrust of confessions offered to exculpate an accused:

"The refusal of the common law to concede the adequacy of a penal interest was no doubt indefensible in logic [citing Holmes' *Donnelly* dissent], but one senses in the decisions a distrust of evidence of confessions by third persons offered to exculpate the accused arising from suspicions of fabrication either of the fact of the making of the confession or in its contents, enhanced in either instance by the required unavailability of the declarant. Nevertheless, an increasing amount of decisional law recognizes exposure to punishment for crime as a sufficient stake. The requirement of corroboration is included in the rule in order to effect an accommodation between these competing considerations. When the statement is offered by the accused by way of exculpation, the resulting situation is not adapted to control by rulings as to the weight of the evidence, and hence the provision is cast in terms of a requirement preliminary to admissibility. The requirement of corroboration should be construed in such a manner as to effectuate its purpose of circumventing fabrication." [Citations omitted.]

Notes of Advisory Committee on Proposed Rules, at 28 U.S.C.A. Fed.R.Evid. 804.

The House Judiciary Committee strengthened this corroboration requirement by adding the present language. The Committee noted,

"[The Committee] believed * * * as did the [Supreme] Court [in its earlier version] that statements of this type tending to exculpate the accused are more suspect and so should have their admissibility conditioned upon some further provision insuring trustworthiness. The proposal in the Court Rule to add a requirement of simple corroboration was, however, deemed ineffective to accomplish this purpose since the accused's own testimony might suffice while not necessarily increasing the reliability of the hearsay statement. The Committee settled upon the language 'unless corroborating circumstances clearly indicate the trustworthiness of the statement' as affording a proper standard and degree of discretion. It was contemplated that the result in such cases as Donnelly v. United States, 228 U.S. 243 [33 S.Ct. 449, 57 L.Ed. 820] (1912), where the circumstances plainly indicated reliability, would be changed."

Notes of Committee on the Judiciary, H.R. Rep.No.93–650, Note to Subdivision (b)(3), at 28 U.S.C.A. Fed.R.Evid. 804, U.S.Code Cong. & Admin.News 1974, pp. 7051, 7089.

As finally enacted, Rule 804(b)(3) requires a two-stage analysis: first, do the offered remarks come within the hearsay exception as a "statement against interest"? and second, if they do, is there sufficient corroboration to clearly indicate trustworthiness? Here we believe that the remarks offered were statements against interest within the Rule, and that the district court should have gone on to determine whether there was sufficient corroboration so as to warrant their admission.

Turning to the first stage of analysis, we think that Tilley's alleged remarks sufficiently tended to subject him to criminal liability "that a reasonable man in his position would not have made the statement unless he believed it to be true." * * * A reasonable person would have realized that remarks of the sort attributed to Tilley strongly implied his personal participation in the stamp crimes and hence would tend to subject him to criminal liability. Though by no means conclusive, the statement would be important evidence against Tilley were he himself on trial for the stamp crimes. We cannot say, therefore, that it did not pose the sort of threat to Tilley's interest that the hearsay exception contemplates.

We do not overlook the fact that the proffered remarks came in the course of conversation with acquaintances over cards. In such circumstances, Tilley might not so readily have perceived the disserving character of what was said nor have expected his words to be repeated to the police. But we are unable to say that the contextual circumstances so far impugn the reliability presumed from the remarks' disserving character as to take them outside the first part of the Rule. * * * The factors in question seem better considered under the second part of the Rule in determining whether, overall, there is enough corroboration to "clearly indicate * * * trustworthiness."

Nor do we overlook the fact that exculpating Barrett was not in itself against Tilley's interest, since both could have participated in the crime. Tilley's remarks differ in this respect from the third-party confession in * * * *Donnelly*. In Barrett's trial, the relevance of Tilley's participation is limited to the credence it gives to his views on who else took part. The district court seemed to suggest that in order for exculpatory remarks such as Tilley's to be admissible as against interest, the innocence of the accused must itself be prejudicial to the declarant. On the present facts, we read the first part of Rule 804(b)(3) more broadly, and conclude that so much of Tilley's remarks as exculpated "Bucky" and inculpated "Buzzy" should here be considered as part of the statement against Tilley's interest.

Under the common law exception for declarations against interest, the treatment to be given portions of a declaration collateral to the declarant's interest has been the subject of much debate. A leading commentator, after acknowledging the traditional liberality with which courts have admitted collateral statements, has expressed the opinion that,

> "As long as the courts adhere to the exceptions to the hearsay rule it would be more reasonable to confine the use of statements against interest in all cases to the proof of the fact which is against interest, since the reliability of other parts of the statement is conjectural."

B. Jefferson, Declarations Against Interest: An Exception to the Hearsay Rule, 58 Harv.L.Rev. 1, 62-63 (1944). And more pointedly, in an article criticizing certain conventional exceptions to the hearsay rule, another author has said,

> "Nonetheless, the naming of another as a compatriot will almost never be against the declarant's own interest and thus will contain little assurance of reliability on this ground. * * * The invocation of a name may be gratuitous, may be deliberately false in order to gain advantages for the declarant greater than those that would flow from naming a real participant or no one at all, may be a cover for concealment purposes (another kind of 'advantage'), or may represent an effort to gain some kind of personal revenge." [Footnote omitted.]

D. Davenport, The Confrontation Clause and the Coconspirator Exception in Criminal Prosecutions: A Functional Analysis, 85 Harv.L.Rev. 1378, 1396 (1972).

There are two reasons, however, which make it difficult for us to agree with the district court's view of the statement in issue. First, the Buzzy-Bucky statement, especially in context, is itself arguably disserving to Tilley, since it strengthened the impression that he had an insider's knowledge of the crimes. And second, the case law, while far from settled, has tended to grant at least "[a] certain latitude as to contextual statements, neutral as to interest giving meaning to the declaration against interest * * *", McCormick on Evidence § 279(a), at 676 (2d ed. 1972). While we do not read the federal rule as incorporating the rather broad formulation put forward by Wigmore, who saw the against-interest exception as permitting reception not only of the "specific fact against interest, but also * * * *every fact contained in the same statement"*, Wigmore, supra, § 1465, at 339 (emphasis in original), neither does it appear that Congress intended to constrict the scope of a declaration against interest to the point of excluding "collateral" material that, as here, actually tended to fortify the statement's disserving aspects. See Notes of Advisory Committee, supra; Notes of Committee on the Judiciary, supra. We hold that the Buzzy-Bucky remark was sufficiently integral to the entire statement, and the latter sufficiently against interest, as to come within the first part of Rule 804(b)(3).

It follows that the district court was under an obligation to determine, under the second sentence of the Rule, whether "corroborating circumstances clearly indicate[d] the trustworthiness of the statement", including we would add, the trustworthiness of that part exculpating Barrett. We emphasize that admissibility is conditional upon separate compliance with that standard, which, it is clear from both the statutory language and the legislative history, is not an insignificant hurdle. * * * We would * * * make two observations to guide the district court's judgment, should the question arise upon retrial.

First we would not read the standard of trustworthiness as imposing a standard so strict as to be utterly unrealistic. Even in *Donnelly* * * * the evidence, while strongly corroborated, could have been disbelieved by the jury. On the other hand, there is no question but that Congress meant to preclude reception of exculpatory hearsay statements against penal interest unless accompanied by circumstances solidly indicating trustworthiness. This requirement goes beyond minimal corroboration. * * *

Second, in ruling on trustworthiness courts should be mindful of the possible relationship between constitutional cases * * * and the new federal rule. * * * Rule 804(b)(3) reflects Congress' attempt to strike a fair balance between exclusion of trustworthy evidence, as in * * * *Donnelly,* and indiscriminate admission of less trustworthy evidence which, because of the lack of opportunity for cross-examination and the absence of the declarant, is open to easy fabrication. Clearly the federal rule is no more restrictive than the Constitution permits, and may in some situations be more inclusive. * * *

* * *

Hypotheticals

(1) X is prosecuted for possession of a marijuana cigarette that was found in a jacket in X's car. X's defense is that the jacket belonged to A. X calls A as a witness and A refuses to answer questions about the jacket on the ground of the self-incrimination privilege. X then calls B, who will testify that A told him on the day before X's arrest that he had been riding with X and left his jacket in X's car. The prosecution makes a hearsay objection to B's proposed testimony. How should the court rule?

(2) X is charged with possession of heroin. The heroin was found in X's house while A was present. X establishes that A is in another state at the time of trial. X

calls B, the wife of A, and offers to have her testify that A told her that the heroin found in X's house belonged to A. The prosecution makes a hearsay objection to B's testimony. What result? [Should it matter whether under the laws of the jurisdiction A's statement to his wife was privileged and inadmissible against A?]

(3) A is a guest in a car driven by B, which collides in an intersection with a car driven by X. A, B, and X all receive personal injuries. A sues X for damages, claiming that X ran the red light. X claims that B ran the red light. X offers testimony that B is in Europe. X then calls C and proposes that C will testify that a week after the accident B told him that his accident with X was all B's fault because he blew the red light. Should A's hearsay objection to C's proposed testimony be sustained?

(4) A sues X in a paternity action, claiming that X is the father of a child born to A. X calls B who testifies that he (B) was a friend of C, a married man who now lives in Europe. X proposes to have B testify that C was formerly A's boss and that C told him (B) he (C) was having an affair with A during the time that A's child was conceived. A makes a hearsay objection to B's proposed testimony. What result?

(5) D is charged with murder of V, who was shot to death. The prosecution introduced testimony that D, along with another, was seen beating V prior to the shooting. There was no eyewitness testimony as to whether D did the shooting. Upon D's request, the trial judge conducts an evidence-admissibility hearing out of the presence of the jury. D calls X to testify about whether X did the shooting. X refuses to answer any questions on the ground of self-incrimination. D then calls A, who testifies that he was in the county jail with X and heard X state (1) that he had shot V in the chest and (2) that D was present trying to break up the fight. On cross-examination, A testifies that he also heard X say that X would "take the beef" because he was going to the Youth Authority and couldn't get hurt; that later, at the Youth Authority, he heard X state to a counselor that D had asked him to testify falsely on his behalf and had threatened to get him if he refused. D then offers to have A testify before the jury as to X's statements (1) that X had shot V and (2) that D was trying to break up the fight. The prosecutor makes a hearsay objection and D urges that X's statements would be admissible under the hearsay exception for a declaration against penal interest. The trial judge sustains the prosecutor's hearsay objection. Is this ruling appropriate?

See Federal Rules of Evidence 804(b)(3), at pp. 926, 927; California Evidence Code § 1230, at p. 880.

---

6.   STATE OF MIND

ADKINS v. BRETT

Supreme Court of California, 1920.
184 Cal. 252, 193 P. 251.

OLNEY, J. The action involved in the present appeal is one for damages for the alienation by the defendant of the plaintiff's wife. The cause was tried before a jury, a verdict was returned for the plaintiff, and from the judgment entered upon the verdict the defendant appeals.

The first point made on behalf of the defendant is that the verdict is not supported by the evidence. No question is made but that the evidence supports the conclusion that the husband had lost the affection of his wife, as a result of which she insisted upon a separation, or, if the testimony on behalf of the plaintiff be believed, as it must be taken it was by the jury, that acts of criminal conversation had taken place between the plaintiff's wife and the defendant. The particular in which it is claimed the evidence is insufficient is that, according to counsel's contention, it does not show that the defendant lured and enticed the plaintiff's wife from her husband, was her seducer, so to speak. Passing by the question as to whether or not evidence of adultery by a wife not shown to have theretofore lost her affection for her husband is not sufficient of itself to justify an inference of active seduction on the part of the man involved, it is sufficient for the purposes of this case to say that there was evidence of statements by the defendant to a male companion by the name of Tucker made by the day after a call by the two upon the wife as to what had taken place the night before, which, if true, justified the conclusion that the defendant was the active aggressor against the wife's resistance on the occasion when first they had criminal intercourse. It is only fair to say that the making of the statements was denied by the defendant, as was any guilty relation whatever on his part with the wife, and that the witness Tucker appears in anything but a creditable light. But evidence of the statements by the defendant was competent against him as admissions by him, and we cannot say that the jury was not justified in believing the evidence. It should also be said that there was considerable corroboration. The case is not one of a want of evidence in any particular, but of a flat conflict of evidence in nearly every particular, with gross perjury on one side or the other. Where the truth lay it was for the jury to determine.

The serious questions in the case arise in connection with the admission of evidence of conversations between the plaintiff and his wife, wherein the latter admitted or stated that she had gone automobile riding with the defendant, had dined with him, had received flowers from him, that he was able to give her a good time, and the plaintiff was not, that she intended to continue to accept the defendant's attentions and the plaintiff could do what he pleased about it, and that he was distasteful to her.

One objection to the evidence of these conversations, which may as well be disposed of at the outset as involving the most elementary principles of evidence, is that they were had without the presence of the defendant. The answer to this objection is that it is wholly immaterial whether the defendant was present or not. The competency of evidence of declarations or statements by a person other than the party to the action against whom they are introduced is not affected merely by the latter's presence or absence. If the evidence be not competent if the party against whom it is sought to introduce it was not present when the statements or declarations were made, no more is it competent if he were present. There are apparent exceptions to this, but they are only apparent, and not real, exceptions. One instance is that, when the party to the litigation was present and his conduct in response to the declarations or statements of others or his replies to them are of such character as to amount to admissions by him, his conduct, including his silence or want of action where an inference can fairly be drawn from them, or his replies, may be shown in evidence against him, and as a part of such conduct or replies the statements or declarations of others to which they are a response. But the primary thing which is admitted in evidence in such a case in the party's own conduct or statements, and, unless these are of such a character as to be relevant evidence against him, the declarations or statements of others are not admissible simply because made in his presence. Another instance is where it is sought to charge a party with notice or knowledge, and for that purpose evidence is introduced of a statement made to him notifying or informing him.

The real objection to such evidence as that under consideration is that it is hearsay. The evidence was plainly relevant; that is, it tended to prove matters in issue, and was therefore admissible unless there is some rule of exclusion applicable to it. The only rule of exclusion to which it can be subject is the rule against hearsay. The evidence was, in fact, hearsay, both as to the past matters stated in the conversations and as to the wife's statements of her then feelings toward the plaintiff and the defendant. But the rule is thoroughly well settled that, when the intention, feelings, or other mental state of a certain person at a particular time, including his bodily feelings, is material to the issues under trial, evidence of such person's declarations at the time indicative of his then mental state, even though hearsay, is competent as within an exception to the hearsay rule. In the present case the state of the wife's feelings at the time of these conversations, both toward her husband and toward the defendant, was material, and the conversations were indicative of her feelings, and, this being so, evidence of them, was admissible to show her then state of feelings. This much can hardly be questioned, in view of the settled character of the general rule just stated, its plain applicability to just such cases as the present, and the fact that it has very generally been so applied. See Cripe v. Cripe, 170 Cal. 91, 148 P. 520, and authorities there cited; 13 R.C.L. 1477; 21 Cyc. 1624.

The difficulty in regard to such declarations as those involved here lies in the fact that, while they may be competent upon the point of the wife's feelings, they go very much further. They contain statements as to matters, such as automobile rides, dinners, flowers, and attentions generally by the defendant to the wife, as proof of which the statements are not within any exception to the hearsay rule and are wholly incompetent. The situation is intensified by the fact that those matters are themselves material to the issues, and, if true, very detrimental to the defendant, so that the admission of the evidence involves the placing before the jury of evidence tending to prove matters in issue, for proving which such evidence is not competent, and the proof of which is very prejudicial to the party against whom it is introduced.

Nevertheless, it is clear enough that the evidence, competent for the purpose of showing the state of the wife's feelings, is not rendered incompetent by the fact that it also tends to prove other material matters, to prove which it is not competent. The rule upon this point, which is one of well-nigh everyday application in actual trial, is thus stated by Wigmore (volume 1, p. 42):

"In other words, when an evidentiary fact is offered for one purpose, and becomes admissible by satisfying all the rules applicable to it in that capacity, it is not inadmissible because it does not satisfy the rules applicable to it in some other capacity, and because the jury might improperly consider it in the latter capacity. This doctrine, although involving certain risks, is indispensable as a practical rule."

Cripe v. Cripe, supra, is an illustration of this. A father was sued by the wife of his son for the alienation from her of the son, and at the trial the following question was asked of the father as a witness:

"After the marriage of your son and daughter, and before Dolly [the son's wife] left the ranch at Huasua in August, 1911, did your son ever tell you that Dolly drank to such an extent that he could not control her, or did he ever tell you during that time that she abused him so bad that he could not live with her?"

It is plain that as to the facts that the wife drank to excess and abused her husband, so that he could not live with her, the evidence was hearsay, was not within any exception to the hearsay rule, and was wholly incompetent, and at the same time those facts were material to the case, and, if true, very detrimental to the cause of the wife, so that the introduction of the evidence would be very prejudicial to her as to facts which the evidence was wholly incompetent to prove. Nevertheless the question was held to be proper, and the refusal of the trial court to permit it to be answered reversible error, on the ground that the testimony which it called for was competent to show the state of the son's feelings.

* * * In this situation there is little question but that Cripe v. Cripe should be followed. It is in accord with the great weight of authority and is but the application in this particular class of cases of a general rule of evidence, thoroughly well settled and applied in every kind of case, civil and criminal. One of the most frequent applications of it in civil cases is the admission of declarations by a testator when his mental capacity or his feelings are material. Estate of Arnold, 147 Cal. 583, 594, 82 Pac. 252. A notable instance of its application in a criminal case is Commonwealth v. Trefethen, 157 Mass. 180, 31 N.E. 961, 24 L.R.A. 235, where upon a trial for murder a statement of the decedent, a young unmarried woman, made shortly before her death, that she was five months pregnant, was held admissible for the purpose of showing that she believed this to be her condition, and therefore had a motive for committing suicide. Upon the point that such evidence, admissible to prove one fact, is not rendered inadmissible because tending to prove some other fact, to prove which it is not competent, the court said (page 187 of 157 Mass., page 964 of 31 N.E.):

"The most obvious distinction between speech and conduct is that speech is often not only an indication of the existing state of mind of the speaker, but a statement of a fact external to the mind, and as evidence of that it is clearly hearsay. There is, of course, danger that a jury may not always observe this distinction, but that has not availed to exclude testimony which is admissible for one purpose, and not admissible for another to which there is danger the jury may apply it."

The rule, then, is that the admissibility of such evidence as that under discussion, admissible because competent as to one point, is not destroyed by its incompetency as to other points which it yet logically tends to prove. The danger, however, of the jury misusing such evidence and giving it weight in determining the points as to which it is incompetent is manifest. In such a situation, as Prof. Wigmore puts it immediately following the quotation already made, "the only question can be what the proper means are for avoiding the risk of misusing the evidence." Answering this question, Prof. Wigmore says:

> "It is uniformly conceded that the instruction [to the jury] of the court [that the evidence is competent only as proof of one point and must not be considered as proof of others] suffices for that purpose; and the better opinion is that the opponent of the evidence must ask for that instruction; otherwise he may be supposed to have waived it as unnecessary for his protection."

The general correctness of this statement cannot be doubted. But we doubt if the learned author intended to say more than that the opponent of such evidence is always entitled to such an instruction for his protection, if he asks for it, and that generally it will suffice. But it is not difficult to imagine cases where it would not suffice, and the opponent could justly ask for more. The matter is largely one of discretion on the part of the trial judge. If the point to prove which the evidence is competent can just as well be proven by other evidence, or if it is of but slight weight or importance upon that point, the trial judge might well be justified in excluding it entirely, because of its prejudicial and dangerous character as to other points. A number of the authorities cited by defendant's counsel are distinguishable from the present case upon this ground. This would emphatically be true where there is good reason for believing that the real object for which the evidence is offered is not to prove the point for which it is ostensibly offered and is competent, but is to get before the jury declarations as to other points, to prove which the evidence is incompetent. The same thing would be true as to the introduction of repeated declarations, when once the point for which they are competent has been amply shown. It may also be that the portions of the declaration which there is danger may be misused by the jury are not so interwoven with the balance of the declaration but that they can be disassociated from it without impairing the meaning or effect of the declaration for the purpose for which it is admissible. In such a case evidence of such portions of the declaration may be excluded on proper objection, when offered, if there is opportunity for such objection, or, if there is not, may be stricken out on motion subsequently. The point of the matter is that the opponent of such evidence, so likely to be misused against him, is entitled to such protection against its misuse as can reasonably be given him without impairing the ability of the other party to prove his case, or depriving him of the use of competent evidence reasonably necessary for that purpose.

The question, then, in the present case in connection with the evidence of declarations of the wife reduces itself to a question as to whether the defendant was properly protected from the danger of this evidence being misused by the jury, and considered by them as proof of matters other than that for proving which it was admitted. We think that there can be no doubt but that the defendant was not properly protected in this respect.   *   *   *

[The court holds that the instruction of the trial court was inadequate, and the judgment is reversed.]

———

On the question of limited admissibility. See Federal Rules of Evidence 105, at p. 907; California Evidence Code § 355, p. 816.

GARFORD TRUCKING CORP. v. MANN

United States Court of Appeals, First Circuit, 1947.
163 F.2d 71.
[Most footnotes omitted.]

WOODBURY, Circuit Judge. These are separate appeals from a single judgment entered upon verdicts returned for the plaintiff in an action sounding in tort for negligence brought against both a trucking corporation and one of its drivers. The plaintiff is a resident of New York. The corporate defendant was organized under the laws of New Jersey and the individual defendant was a resident of that State at the time the action was begun. The amount in controversy far exceeds $3,000 exclusive of interest and costs. Federal jurisdiction on the ground of diversity of citizenship and amount in controversy is therefore clear.

Although both defendants have appealed, only the corporate defendant is actively prosecuting. And it does not make the contention that the evidence is insufficient to warrant the reasonable conclusion that it is somewhat more probable then not that its driver's negligent operation of its motor vehicle caused the accident in which the plaintiff was injured. Its contention is that the plaintiff has failed to sustain the burden resting upon him to prove by a balance of the probabilities that at the time of the accident its driver was acting within the scope of his employment. More specifically, its contention is that on the evidence reasonable men could only find that when the accident occurred its driver had deviated from his assigned route on a personal undertaking of his own.

Framingham, Massachusetts, the place where the accident occurred, lies roughly midway between Boston and Worcester on Route 9, a four lane express highway connecting these two cities. Another main highway, but only a two lane one, known as Route 20, also runs from Boston to the vicinity of Worcester. This latter route leaves a more northerly part of the City of Boston than Route 9, passes through Wayland, five or six miles north of Framingham, then trending gradually toward the south, it intersects Route 9 a few miles east of Worcester. Route 20 then swings south of the City of Worcester and continues in a southwesterly direction to connect with routes to New York City and points in New Jersey. Route 126, known in Framingham as Concord Street, runs north and slightly east from Framingham Center (which is south of Route 9), crosses Route 9 at approximately a right angle, and intersects Route 20 in Wayland. Thus Framingham, Wayland, and the point of intersection of Routes 9 and 20 lie at the angles of a rough right triangle; the short leg of which, Framingham to Wayland, is about six miles, the long leg, Framingham to the intersection of Routes 9 and 20 is about 15 miles, and the hypotenuse, Wayland to that intersection of routes, is about 23 miles.

At the time of the accident the individual defendant, Glogowski, was driving one of the corporate defendant's trucks loaded with baled wool on orders to take his load from Framingham Center to his employer's terminal in South River, New Jersey. From the place in Framingham Center where Glogowski picked up his load he drove by what he said was the most direct way he knew to Route 126 and turned north. At or a little beyond the overpass which carries this route over Route 9 he stopped to give a ride to a sailor who said that he was on his way to Saxonville, a small community on

Route 126 between Framingham and Wayland. The accident occurred on this route a half mile to a mile north of the point where it crosses Route 9.

Glogowski testified that the corporate defendant's local manager only gave him general orders to take his load from Framingham to South River. The local manager, however, testified that in addition to such general orders he gave Glogowski specific directions to leave Framingham on Route 9, follow it to the point near Worcester where Route 20 crosses it, and then to take Route 20.

On the evidence summarized above, and it claims that this is all the admissible evidence there is bearing upon Glogowski's choice of route out of Framingham, the corporate defendant contends that reasonable men could not find it more probable than otherwise that Glogowski was acting within the scope of his duties as an employee at the time of the accident. We do not agree.

We pass the question whether the defendant's contention can be sustained on the evidence stated for the reason that there is further competent evidence in the record throwing light upon Glogowski's purpose, intention, or state of mind when he chose to leave Framingham on Route 126 rather than on Route 9. This evidence consists of testimony as to certain remarks made by Glogowski within 10 days after the accident while he was a patient in a hospital, the general tenor of which was that he took Route 126 out of Framingham because it afforded the most direct way to Route 20, and in his opinion he could make better time on that Route, even though it was longer, than he could on Route 9.[2]

When testimony of these remarks of Glogowski was offered, counsel for the defendants objected, and after colloquy the district court admitted the testimony telling the jury, however, that it was to be used only in the action against Glogowski, and that further instructions with respect to this limitation upon the use of the testimony would be given in the charge. Before argument, however, the court below called counsel to the bench and told him that Glogowski's purpose in taking Route 126 was "one of the important facts to determine whether he was within the scope of his authority" and that the jury would be instructed that they might use testimony of Glogowski's remarks generally under the rule "Where the mental condition of a person at a particular time is in issue, his appearance, conduct, acts, and declarations, after as well as before the time in question, have been held admissible in evidence, if sufficiently near in point of time." The jury were later instructed in conformity with this ruling.

We think the district court's final ruling and its instructions to the jury in accordance therewith are correct.

* * * Since we cannot say that Glogowski's detour of some 15 miles in the course of a journey of some 250 miles was so great as to require the conclusion as a matter of law that it amounted to an independent journey as distinguished from a mere deviation from route, the corporate defendant's liability hinges upon the purpose for which Glogowski elected to take the

---

2. There is evidence that Route 9 carries much heavier traffic and is hillier than Route 20.

route which he did. And not only is it established in Massachusetts, as stated by the court below, that an actor's purpose, if that be in issue, can be shown by his reasonably contemporaneous declarations, but it is also established as a general proposition that: "Evidence of statements by an agent introduced in order to show the purpose for which he did an act or to show his knowledge or state of mind is admissible in favor of and against the principal under the rules relating to the introduction of evidence for this purpose. Statements by an agent are not excluded because made by an agent. If his knowledge or condition of mind or purpose is relevant to the cause of action which is being brought, either party may introduce evidence relevant to show this." Am.Law Inst., Restatement of Agency § 289, comment c. See also 6 Wigmore on Evidence, 3d Ed., § 1729.   *   *   *

The judgment of the District Court is affirmed.

MUTUAL LIFE INS. CO. OF NEW YORK v. HILLMON

Supreme Court of the United States, 1892.
145 U.S. 285, 12 S.Ct. 909,36 L.Ed. 706.

[Actions by Sallie E. Hillmon against two insurance companies to recover on policies on the life of her husband, John W. Hillmon. The chief issue was whether a body found at Crooked Creek was that of the insured Hillmon or, as contended by defendants, that of one Walters. To show that the body was that of Walters, defendants offered in evidence letters from Walters to his sister and fiance which expressed his intention to leave Wichita and go with Hillmon to Colorado, where Crooked Creek is located. The trial court rejected these letters. (For an interesting account of the history of this protracted litigation, involving the ouster during the Populist movement of three insurance companies from Kansas, see Wigmore, Problems of Judicial Proof, pp. 856-896 (1913))—Ed.]

Mr. Justice GRAY, after holding for the court that there had been a procedural error, continued:

There is, however, one question of evidence so important, so fully argued at the bar, and so likely to arise upon another tiral, that it is proper to express an opinion upon it.

This question is of the admissibility of the letters written by Walters on the first days of March, 1879, which were offered in evidence by the defendants, and excluded by the court. In order to determine the competency of these letters, it is important to consider the state of the case when they were offered to be read.

The matter chiefly contested at the trial was the death of John W. Hillmon, the insured; and that depended upon the question whether the body found at Crooked Creek on the night of March 18, 1879, was his body, or the body of one Walters.

Much conflicting evidence had been introduced as to the identity of the body. The plaintiff had also introduced evidence that Hillmon and one Brown left Wichita in Kansas on or about March 5, 1879, and travelled together through Southern Kansas in search of a site for a cattle ranch, and that on the night of March 18, while they were in camp at Crooked Creek,

Hillmon was accidentally killed, and that his body was taken thence and buried. The defendants had introduced evidence, without objection, that Walters left his home and his betrothed in Iowa in March, 1878, and was afterwards in Kansas until March, 1879; that during that time he corresponded regularly with his family and his betrothed; that the last letters received from him were one received by his betrothed on March 3 and postmarked at Wichita March 2, and one received by his sister about March 4 or 5, and dated at Wichita a day or two before; and that he had not been heard from since.

The evidence that Walters was at Wichita on or before March 5, and had not been heard from since, together with the evidence to identify as his the body found at Crooked Creek on March 18, tended to show that he went from Wichita to Crooked Creek between those dates. Evidence that just before March 5 he had the intention of leaving Wichita with Hillmon would tend to corroborate the evidence already admitted, and to show that he went from Wichita to Crooked Creek with Hillmon. Letters from him to his family and his betrothed were the natural, if not the only attainable, evidence of his intention.

The position, taken at the bar, that the letters were competent evidence, within the rule stated in Nicholls v. Webb, 8 Wheat. 326, 337, as memoranda made in the ordinary course of business, cannot be maintained, for they were clearly not such.

But upon another ground suggested they should have been admitted. A man's state of mind or feeling can only be manifested to others by countenance, attitude or gesture, or by sounds or words, spoken or written. The nature of the fact to be proved is the same, and evidence of its proper tokens is equally competent to prove it, whether expressed by aspect or conduct, by voice or pen. When the intention to be proved is important only as qualifying an act, its connection with that act must be shown, in order to warrant the admission of declarations of the intention. But whenever the intention is of itself a distinct and material fact in a chain of circumstances, it may be proved by contemporaneous oral or written declarations of the party.

The existence of a particular intention in a certain person at a certain time being a material fact to be proved, evidence that he expressed that intention at that time is as direct evidence of the fact, as his own testimony that he then had that intention would be. After his death there can hardly be any other way of proving it; and while he is still alive, his own memory of his state of mind at a former time is no more likely to be clear and true than a bystander's recollection of what he then said, and is less trustworthy than letters written by him at the very time and under circumstances precluding a suspicion of misrepresentation.

The letters in question were competent, not as narratives of facts communicated to the writer by others, nor yet as proof that he actually went away from Wichita, but as evidence that, shortly before the time when other evidence tended to show that he went away, he had the intention of going, and of going with Hillmon, which made it more probable both that he did go and that he went with Hillmon, than if there had been no proof of such intention. In view of the mass of conflicting testimony introduced upon the question whether it was the body of Walters that was found in Hillmon's camp, this evidence might properly influence the jury in determining that question.

The rule applicable to this case has been thus stated by this court: "Wherever the bodily or mental feelings of an individual are material to be proved, the usual expressions of such feelings are original and competent evidence. Those expressions are the natural reflexes of what it might be impossible to show by other testimony. If there be such other testimony, this may be necessary to set the facts thus developed in their true light, and to give them their proper effect. As independent explanatory or corroborative evidence, it is often indispensable to the due administration of justice. Such declarations are regarded as verbal acts, and are as competent as any other testimony, when relevant to the issue. Their truth or falsity is an inquiry for the jury." Insurance Co. v. Mosley, 8 Wall. 397, 404, 405.

* * *

Even in the probate of wills, which are required by law to be in writing, executed and attested in prescribed forms, yet where the validity of a will is questioned for want of mental capacity or by reason of fraud and undue influence, or where the will is lost and it becomes necessary to prove its contents, written or oral evidence of declarations of the testator before the date of the will has been admitted, in Massachusetts and in England, to show his real intention as to the disposition of his property, although there has been a difference of opinion as to the admissibility, for such purposes, of his subsequent declarations. Shailer v. Bumstead, 99 Mass. 112; Sugden v. St. Leonards, 1 P.D. 154; Woodward v. Goulstone, 11 App.Cas. 469, 478, 484, 486.

In Shailer v. Bumstead, upon the competency of evidence offered to show that a will propounded for probate "was not the act of one possessed of testamentary capacity, or was obtained by such fraud and undue influence as to subvert the real intentions and will of the maker," Mr. Justice Colt said: "The declarations of the testator accompanying the act must always be resorted to as the most satisfactory evidence to sustain or defend the will, whenever the issue is presented. So it is uniformly held that the previous declarations of the testator, offered to prove the mental facts involved, are competent. Intention, purpose, mental peculiarity and condition, are mainly ascertainable through the medium afforded by the power of language. Statements and declarations, when the state of the mind is the fact to be shown, are therefore received as mental acts or conduct." 99 Mass. 120.

In Sugden v. St. Leonards, which arose upon the probate of the lost will of Lord Chancellor St. Leonards, the English Court of Appeal was unanimous in holding oral as well as written declarations made by the testator before the date of the will to be admissible in evidence. Lord Chief Justice Cockburn said: "I entertain no doubt that prior instructions, or a draft authenticated by the testator, or verbal declarations of what he was about to do, though of course not conclusive evidence, are yet legally admissible as secondary evidence of the contents of a lost will." 1 P.D. 226. Sir George Jessel, M.R., said: "It is not strictly evidence of the contents of the instrument, it is simply evidence of the intention of the person who afterwards executes the instrument. It is simply evidence of probability—no doubt of a high degree of probability in some cases, and of a low degree of probability in others. The cogency of the evidence depends very much on the nearness in point of time of the declaration of intention to the period of the execution of the instrument." 1 P.D. 242. Lord Justice Mellish said: "The declarations which are made before the will are not, I apprehend, to be taken as evidence of the contents of the will which is subsequently made—they obviously do not prove it; and wherever it is material to prove the the state of a person's mind, or what was passing in it, and what were his intentions, there you may prove what he said, because that is the only means by which you can find out what his intentions were." 1 P.D. 251.

Upon an indictment of one Hunter for the murder of one Armstrong at Camden, the Court of Errors and Appeals of New Jersey unanimously held that Armstrong's oral declarations to his son at Philadelphia, on the afternoon before the night of the murder, as well as a letter written by him at the same time and place to his wife, each stating that he was going with Hunter to Camden on business, were rightly admitted in evidence. Chief Justice Beasley said: "In the ordinary course of things, it was the usual information that a man about leaving home would communicate, for the convenience of his family, the information of his friends, or the regulation of his business. At the time it was given, such declarations could, in the nature of things, mean harm to no one; he who uttered them was bent on no expedition of mischief or wrong, and the attitude of affairs at the time entirely explodes the idea that such utterances were intended to serve any purpose but that for which they were obviously designed. If it be said that such notice of an intention of leaving home could have been given without introducing in it the name of Mr. Hunter, the obvious answer to the suggestion, I think, is that a reference to the companion who is to accompany the person leaving is as natural a part of the transaction as is any other incident or quality of it. If it is legitimate to show by a man's own declarations that he left his home to be gone a week, or for a certain destination, which seems incontestable, why may it not be proved in the same way that a designated person was to bear him company? At the time the words were uttered or written, they imported no wrongdoing to any one, and the reference to the companion who was to go with him was nothing more, as matters then stood, than an indication of an additional circumstance of his going. If it was in the ordinary train of events for this man to leave word or to state where he was going, it seems to me it was equally so for him to say with whom he was going." Hunter v. State, 11 Vroom (40 N.J. Law) 495, 534, 536, 538.

Upon principle and authority, therefore, we are of opinion that the two letters were competent evidence of the intention of Walters at the time of writing them, which was a material fact bearing upon the question in controversy; and that for the exclusion of these letters, as well as for the undue restriction of the defendants' challenges, the verdicts must be set aside, and a new trial had.

As the verdicts and judgments were several, the writ of error sued out by the defendants jointly was superfluous, and may be dismissed without costs; and upon each of the writs of error sued out by the defendants severally the order will be:

Judgment reversed, and case remanded to the Circuit Court, with directions to set aside the verdict and to order a new trial.

SHEPARD v. UNITED STATES

Supreme Court of the United States, 1933.
290 U.S. 96, 54 S.Ct. 22, 78 L.Ed. 196.

Mr. Justice Cardozo delivered the opinion of the Court.

The petitioner, Charles A. Shepard, a major in the medical corps of the United States army, has been convicted of the murder of his wife, Zenana Shepard, at Fort Riley, Kansas, a United States military reservation. The jury having qualified their verdict by adding thereto the words "without capital punishment" (18 U.S.C. § 567), the defendant was sentenced to imprisonment for life. The judgment of the United States District Court has been affirmed by the Circuit Court of Appeals for the Tenth Circuit, one of the judges of that court dissenting. 62 F.2d 683; 64 F.2d 641. A writ of certiorari brings the case here.

The crime is charged to have been committed by poisoning the victim with bichloride of mercury. The defendant was in love with another woman, and wished to make her his wife. There is circumstantial evidence to sustain a finding by the jury that to win himself his freedom he turned to poison and murder. Even so, guilt was contested and conflicting inferences are possible. The defendant asks us to hold that by the acceptance of incompetent evidence the scales were weighted to his prejudice and in the end to his undoing.

The evidence complained of was offered by the Government in rebuttal when the trial was nearly over. On May 22, 1929, there was a conversation in the absence of the defendant between Mrs. Shepard, then ill in bed, and Clara Brown, her nurse. The patient asked the nurse to go to the closet in the defendant's room and bring a bottle of whisky that would be found upon a shelf. When the bottle was produced, she said that this was the liquor she had taken just before collapsing. She asked whether enough was left to make a test for the presence of poison, insisting that the smell and taste were strange. And then she added the words "Dr. Shepard has poisoned me."

The conversation was proved twice. After the first proof of it, the Government asked to strike it out, being doubtful of its competence, and this request was granted. A little later, however, the offer was renewed, the nurse having then testified to statements by Mrs. Shepard as to the prospect of recovery. "She said she was not going to get well; she was going to die." With the aid of this new evidence, the conversation already summarized was proved a second time. There was a timely challenge of the ruling.

She said, "Dr. Shepard has poisoned me." The admission of this declaration, if erroneous, was more than unsubstantial error * * * [The court held that the statement was not admissible under the dying declaration exception to the hearsay rule, supra.]

2. We pass to the question whether the statements to the nurse, though incompetent as dying declarations, were admissible on other grounds.

The Circuit Court of Appeals determined that they were. Witnesses for the defendant had testified to declarations by Mrs. Shepard which suggested a mind bent upon suicide, or at any rate were thought by the defendant to carry that suggestion. More than once before her illiness she had stated in the hearing of these witnesses that she had no wish to live; and had nothing to live for, and on one occasion she added that she expected some day to make an end to her life. This testimony opened the door, so it is argued, to declarations in rebuttal that she had been poisoned by her husband. They were admissible, in that view, not as evidence of the truth of what was said, but as betokening a state of mind inconsistent with the presence of suicidal intent.

(a) The testimony was neither offered nor received for the strained and narrow purpose now suggested as legitimate. It was offered and received as proof of a dying declaration. What was said by Mrs. Shepard lying ill upon her deathbed was to be weighed as if a like statement had been made upon the stand. The course of the trial makes this an inescapable conclusion. The Government withdrew the testimony when it was unaccompanied by proof that the declarant expected to die. Only when proof of her expectation had been supplied was the offer renewed and the testimony received again. For the reasons already considered, the proof was inadequate to show a consciousness of impending death and the abandonment of hope; but inadequate though it was, there can be no doubt of the purpose that it was understood to serve. There is no disguise of that purpose by counsel for the Government. They concede in all candor that Mrs. Shepard's accusation of her husband, when it was finally let in, was received upon the footing of a dying declaration, and not merely as indicative of the persistence of a will to live. Beyond question the jury considered it for the broader purpose, as the court intended that they should. A different situation would be here if we could fairly say in the light of the whole record that the purpose had been left at large, without identifying token. There would then be room for argument, that demand should have been made for an explanatory ruling. Here the course of the trial put the defendant off his guard. The testimony was received by the trial judge and offered by the Government with the plain understanding that it was to be used for an illegitimate purpose, gravely prejudicial. A trial becomes unfair if testimony thus accepted may be used in an appellate court as though admitted for a different purpose, unavowed and unsuspected. People v. Zackowitz, 254 N.Y. 192, 200; 172 N.E. 466. Such at all events is the result when the purpose in reserve is so obscure and artificial that it would be unlikely to occur to the minds of uninstructed jurors, and even if it did, would be swallowed up and lost in the one that was disclosed.

(b) Aside, however, from this objection, the accusatory declaration must have been rejected as evidence of a state of mind, though the purpose thus to limit it had been brought to light upon the trial. The defendant had tried to show by Mrs. Shepard's declarations to her friends that she had exhibited a weariness of life and a readiness to end it, the testimony giving plausibility to the hypothesis of suicide. Wigmore, § 1726; Commonwealth v. Trefethen, 157 Mass. 180; 31 N.E. 961. By the proof of these declarations evincing an unhappy state of mind the defendant opened the door to the offer by the Government of declarations evincing a different state of mind, declarations consistent with the persistence of a will to live. The defendant would have no grievance if the testimony in rebuttal had been narrowed to that point. What the Government put in evidence, however, was something very different. It did not use the declarations by Mrs. Shepard to prove her present thoughts and feelings, or even her thoughts and feelings in times past. It used the declarations as proof of an act committed by some one else, as evidence that she was dying of poison given by her husband. This fact, if fact it was, the Government was free to prove, but not by hearsay declarations. It will not do to say that the jury might accept the declarations for any light that they cast upon the existence of a vital urge, and reject them to the extent that they charged the death to some one else. (Discrimination so subtle is a feat beyond the compass of ordinary minds.) The reverberating clang of those accusatory words would drown all weaker sounds. It is for ordinary minds, and not for psychoanalysts, that our rules of evidence are framed. They have their source very often in considerations of administrative convenience, of practical expediency, and not in rules of logic. When the risk of confusion is so great as to upset the balance of advantage, the evidence goes out. Thayer, Preliminary Treatise on the Law of Evidence, 266, 516; Wigmore, Evidence, § § 1421, 1422, 1714.

These precepts of caution are a guide to judgment here. There are times when a state of mind, if relevant, may be proved by contemporaneous declarations of feeling or intent. Mutual Life Ins. Co. v. Hillmon, 145 U.S. 285, 295. Thus, in proceedings for the probate of a will, where the issue is undue influence, the declarations of a testator are competent to prove his feelings for his relatives, but are incompetent as evidence of his conduct or of theirs. In suits for the alienation of affections, letters passing between the spouses are admissible in aid of a like purpose. * * * In damage suits for personal injuries, declarations by the patient to bystanders or physicians are evidence of sufferings or symptoms (Wigmore, § § 1718, 1719), but are not received to prove the acts, the external circumstances, through which the injuries came about. * * * Even statements of past sufferings or symptoms are generally excluded, (Wigmore, § 1722 [b]); though an exception is at times allowed when they are made to a physician. * * * So also in suits upon insurance policies, declarations by an insured that he intends to go upon a journey with another, may be evidence of a state of mind lending probability to the conclusion that the purpose was fulfilled. Mutual Life Ins. Co. v. Hillmon, supra. The ruling in that case marks the high water line beyond which courts have been unwilling to go. It has developed a substantial body of criticism and commentary.* Declarations of intention, casting light upon the future, have been sharply distinguished from declarations of memory, pointing backwards to the past. There would be an end, or nearly that, to the rule against hearsay if the distinction were ignored.

The testimony now questioned faced backward and not forward. This at least it did in its most obvious implications. What is even more important, it spoke to a past act, and more than that, to an act by some one not the speaker. Other tendency, if it had any, was a filament too fine to be disentangled by a jury.

The judgment should be reversed and the case remanded to the District Court for further proceedings in accordance with this opinion.

Reversed.

*Maguire, The Hillmon Case, 38 Harvard L.Rev., 709, 721, 727; Seligman, An Exception to the Hearsay Rule, 26 Harvard L.Rev. 146; Chafee, Review of Wigmore's Treatise, 37 Harvard L.Rev., 513, 519.

UNITED STATES v. PHEASTER

United States Court of Appeals, Ninth Circuit, 1976.
544 F.2d 353.

RENFREW, District Judge:

I.   FACTS

This case arises from the disappearance of Larry Adell, the 16-year-old son of Palm Springs multi-millionaire Robert Adell. At approximately 9:30 P.M. on June 1, 1974, Larry Adell left a group of his high school friends in a Palm Springs restaurant known as Sambo's North. He walked into the parking lot of the restaurant with the expressed intention of meeting a man named Angelo who was supposed to deliver a pound of free marijuana. Larry never returned to his friends in the restaurant that evening, and his family never saw him thereafter.

The long, agonizing, and ultimately unsuccessful effort to find Larry began shortly after his disappearance. At about 2:30 A.M. on June 2, 1974, Larry's father was telephoned by a male caller who told him that his son was being held and that further instructions would be left in Larry's car in the parking lot of Sambo's North. Those instructions included a demand for a ransom of $400,000 for the release of Larry. Further instructions regarding the delivery of the ransom were promised within a week. Although the caller had warned Mr. Adell that he would never see Larry again if the police or the F.B.I. were notified, Mr. Adell immediately called the F.B.I., and that agency was actively involved in the investigation of the case from the beginning.

Numerous difficulties were encountered in attempting to deliver the ransom, necessitating a number of communications between the kidnappers and Mr. Adell. The communications from the kidnappers included a mixture of instructions and threats, as well as messages from Larry. Before the kidnappers finally broke off communications on June 30, 1974, Mr. Adell had received a total of ten letters from the kidnappers, nine of which were typed in a "script" style and one of which was handwritten. In addition, Mr. Adell had received two telephone calls from the kidnappers, one of which was tape-recorded by the F.B.I. In these communications, the kidnappers gave instructions for a total of four attempts to deliver the ransom, but it was never delivered for a number of reasons, and Larry was never released.

The instructions for the first delivery, set for June 8th, were nullified by the late delivery of the letter containing them on June 9th. The second delivery failed when, on June 12th, Mr. Adell balked at turning over the money without more adequate assurances that his son would be released. The third delivery on June 23rd was aborted, apparently because of the kidnappers' awareness that the pick-up site was being monitored. A duffel bag containing the ransom money was thrown into the designated spot, but it was never retrieved by the kidnappers. The fourth and final attempt never really began. On June 30th, pursuant to instructions, Mr. Adell went to a designated hotel pay telephone to await further instructions but was never contacted. No further communications were received from the kidnappers, despite Mr. Adell's attempt to renew contact by messages published in the Los Angeles Times.

When it appeared that further efforts to communicate with the kidnappers would be futile, the F.B.I. arrested appellants, who had been under surveillance for some time, in a coordinated operation on July 14, 1974.

* * *

Admissibility of Hearsay Testimony Concerning Statements of Larry Adell

Appellant Inciso argues that the district court erred in admitting hearsay testimony by two teenaged friends of Larry Adell concerning statements made by Larry on June 1, 1974, the day that he disappeared. Timely objections were made to the questions which elicited the testimony on the ground that the questions called for hearsay. In response, the Government attorney stated that the testimony was offered for the limited purpose of showing the "state of mind of Larry". After instructing the jury that it could only consider the testimony for that limited purpose and not for "the truth or falsity of what [Larry] said", the district court allowed the witnesses to answer the questions. Francine Gomes, Larry's date on the evening that he disappeared, testified that when Larry picked her up that evening, he told her that he was going to meet Angelo at Sambo's North at 9:30 P.M. to "pick up a pound of marijuana which Angelo had promised him for free". * * * She also testified that she had been with Larry on another occasion when he met a man named Angelo, and she identified the defendant as that man. Miss Gomes stated that it was approximately 9:15 P.M. when Larry went into the parking lot. Doug Sendejas, one of Larry's friends who was with him at Sambo's North just prior to his disappearance, testified that Larry had made similar statements to him in the afternoon and early evening of June 1st regarding a meeting that evening with Angelo. Mr. Sendejas also testified that when Larry left the table at Sambo's North to go into the parking lot, Larry stated that "he was going to meet Angelo and he'd be right back." * * *

Inciso's contention that the district court erred in admitting the hearsay testimony of Larry's friends is premised on the view that the statements could not properly be used by the jury to conclude that Larry did in fact meet Inciso in the parking lot of Sambo's North at approximately 9:30 P.M. on June 1, 1974. The correctness of that assumption is, in our view, the key to the analysis of this contention of error. The Government argues that Larry's statements were relevant to two issues in the case. First the statements are said to be relevant to an issue created by the defense when Inciso's attorney attempted to show that Larry had not been kidnapped but had disappeared voluntarily as part of a simulated kidnapping designed to extort money from his wealthy father from whom he was allegedly estranged. In his brief on appeal, Inciso concedes the relevance and, presumably, the admissibility of the statements to "show that Larry did not voluntarily disappear." However, Inciso argues that for this limited purpose, there was no need to name the person with whom Larry intended to meet, and that the district court's limiting instruction was insufficient to overcome the prejudice to which he was exposed by the testimony. Second, the Government argues that the statements are relevant and admissible to show that, as intended, Larry did meet Inciso in the parking lot at Sambo's North on the evening of June 1, 1974. If the Government's second theory of admissibility is successful, Inciso's arguments regarding the excision of his name from the statements admitted under the first theory is obviously mooted.

In determining the admissibility of the disputed evidence, we apply the standard of Rule 26 of the Federal Rules of Criminal Procedure which governed at the time of the trial below. Under that standard, the District Court was required to decide issues concerning the "admissibility of evidence" according to the "principles of the common law as they may be interpreted by the courts of the United States in the light of reason and experience."

The Government's position that Larry Adell's statements can be used to prove that the meeting with Inciso did occur raises a difficult and important question concerning the scope of the so-called *"Hillmon* doctrine", a particular species of the "state of mind" exception to the general rule that hearsay evidence is inadmissible. The doctrine takes it name from the famous Supreme Court decision in Mutual Life Ins. Co. v. Hillmon, 145 U.S. 285, 12 S.Ct. 909, 36 L.Ed. 706 (1892). That the *Hillmon* doctrine should create controversy and confusion is not surprising, for it is an extraordinary doctrine. Under the state of mind exception, hearsay evidence is admissible if it bears on the state of mind of the declarant and if that state of mind is an issue in the case. For example, statements by a testator which demonstrate that he had the necessary testamentary intent are admissible to show that intent when it is in issue. The exception embodied in the *Hillmon* doctrine is fundamentally different, because it does not require that the state of mind of the declarant be an actual issue in the case. Instead, under the *Hillmon* doctrine the state of mind of the declarant is used inferentially to prove other matters which are in issue. Stated simply, the doctrine provides that when the performance of a particular act by an individual is an issue in a case, his intention (state of mind) to perform that act may be shown. From that intention, the trier of fact may draw the inference that the person carried out his intention and performed the act. Within this conceptual framework, hearsay evidence of statements by the person which tend to show his intention is deemed admissible under the state of mind exception. Inciso's objection to the doctrine concerns its application in situations in which the declarant has stated his intention to do something *with another person,* and the issue is whether he did so. There can be no doubt, that the theory of the *Hillmon* doctrine is different when the declarant's statement of intention necessarily requires the action of one or more others if it is to be fulfilled.

*   *   *

The *Hillmon* doctrine has been applied by the California Supreme Court in People v. Alcalde, 24 Cal.2d 177, 148 P.2d 627 (1944),   *   *   * In *Alcalde* the defendant was tried and convicted of first degree murder for the brutal slaying of a woman whom he had been seeing socially. One of the issues before the California Supreme Court was the asserted error by the trial court in allowing the introduction of certain hearsay testimony concerning statements made by the victim on the day of her murder. As in the instant case, the testimony was highly incriminating, because the victim reportedly said that she was going out with Frank, the defendant, on the evening she was murdered. On appeal, a majority of the California Supreme Court affirmed the defendant's conviction, holding that *Hillmon* was "the leading case on the admissibility of declarations of intent to do an act as proof that the act thereafter was accomplished." 148 P. 2d at 631.

*   *   *

*   *   * The court found no error in the trial court's admission of the disputed hearsay testimony. "Unquestionably the deceased's statement of her intent and the logical inference to be drawn therefrom, namely, that she was with the defendant that night, were relevant to the issue of the guilt of the defendant." Id. at 632.

*   *   *

In addition to the decisions in *Hillmon* and *Alcalde*, support for the Government's position can be found in the California Evidence Code and the new Federal Rules of Evidence, although in each instance resort must be made to the comments to the relevant provisions.

Section 1250 of the California Evidence Code carves out an exception to the general hearsay rule for statements of a declarant's "then existing mental or physical state". The *Hillmon* doctrine is codified in Section 1250(2) which allows the use of such hearsay evidence when it "is offered to prove or explain acts or conduct of the declarant." The comment to Section 1250(2) states that, "Thus, a statement of the declarant's intent to do certain acts is admissible to prove that he did those acts." Although neither the language of the statute nor that of the comment specifically addresses the particular issue now before us, the comment does cite the *Alcalde* decision and, therefore, indirectly rejects the limitation urged by Inciso.

*   *   * Rule 803 (3) provides an exemption from the hearsay rule for the following evidence:

> "*Then existing mental, emotional, or physical condition.* A statement of the declarant's then existing state of mind, emotion, sensation, or physical condition (such as intent, plan, motive, design, mental feeling, pain, and bodily health), but not including a statement of memory or belief to prove the fact remembered or believed unless it relates to the execution, revocation, identification, or terms of declarant's will."

Although Rule 803(3) is silent regarding the *Hillmon* doctrine, both the Advisory Committee on the Proposed Rules and the House Committee on the Judiciary specifically addressed the doctrine. After noting that Rule 803(3) would not allow the admission of statements of memory, the Advisory Committee stated broadly that

> "The rule of Mutual Life Ins. Co. v. Hillmon [citation omitted] allowing evidence of intention as tending to prove the doing of the act intended, is, of course, left undisturbed." Note to Paragraph (3), 28 U.S.C.A. at 585.

Significantly, the Notes of the House Committee on the Judiciary regarding Rule 803(3) are far more specific and revealing:

> "However, the Committee intends that the Rule be construed to limit the doctrine of Mutual Life Insurance Co. v. Hillmon [citation omitted] so as to render statements of intent by a declarant admissible *only to prove his future conduct, not the future conduct of another person.*" House Report No. 93–650, Note to Paragraph (3), 28 U.S.C.A. at 579 (emphasis added).

Although the matter is certainly not free from doubt, we read the note of the Advisory Committee as presuming that the *Hillmon* doctrine would be incorporated in full force, including necessarily the application in *Hillmon* itself. The language suggests that the Advisory Committee presumed that such a broad interpretation was not the prevailing common law position. The notes of the House Committee on the Judiciary are significantly different. The language used there suggests a legislative intention to cut back on what that body also perceived to be the prevailing common law view, namely, that the *Hillmon* doctrine could be applied to facts such as those now before us.

Although we recognize the force of the objection to the application of the *Hillmon* doctrine in the instant case,[18] we cannot conclude that the district court erred in allowing the testimony concerning Larry Adell's statements to be introduced.

* * *

[Judgment affirmed.]

[Concurring and dissenting opinion omitted.]

18. Criticism of the *Hillmon* doctrine has come from very distinguished quarters, both judicial and academic. However, the position of the judicial critics is definitely the minority position, stated primarily in dicta and dissent.

In his opinion for the Court in Shepard v. United States, 290 U.S. 96, 54 S.Ct. 22, 78 L.Ed.2d 196 (1933), Justice Cardozo indicated in dicta an apparent hostility to the *Hillmon* doctrine. *Shepard* involved hearsay testimony of a dramatically different character from that in the instant case. The Court reviewed the conviction of an army medical officer for the murder of his wife by poison. The asserted error by the trial court was its admission, over defense objection, of certain hearsay testimony by Mrs. Shepard's nurse concerning statements that Mrs. Shepard had made during her final illness. The nurse's testimony was that, after asking whether there was enough whiskey left in the bottle from which she had drunk just prior to her collapse to make a test for poison, Mrs. Shepard stated, "Dr. Shepard has poisoned me." One theory advanced by the Government on appeal was that the testimony was admissible to show that Mrs. Shepard did not have suicidal tendencies and, thus, to refute the defense argument that she took her own life. The Court rejected that theory, holding that the testimony had not been admitted for the limited purpose suggested by the Government and that, even if it had been admitted for that purpose, its relevance was far outweighed by the extreme prejudice it would create for the defendant. In rejecting the Government's theory, the Court refused to "extend the state of mind exception to statements of memory. In his survey of the state of mind exception, Justice Cardozo appeared to suggest the *Hillmon* doctrine is limited to "suits upon insurance policies", id. at 105, 54 S.Ct. 22, although the cases cited by the Court in *Hillmon* refute that suggestion.

The decision in *Shepard* was relied upon by Justice Traynor of the California Supreme Court in his vigorous dissent from the decision reached by the majority in People v. Alcalde, supra, 148 P.2d 627. Justice Traynor argued that the victim's declarations regarding her meeting with Frank could not be used to "induce the belief that the defendant went out with the deceased, took her to the scene of the crime and there murdered her * * * without setting aside the rule against hearsay." Id. at 633. Any other legitimate use of the declaration, in his opinion, was so insignificant that it was outweighed by the enormous prejudice to the defendant in allowing the jury to hear it.

Finally, the exhaustive analysis of a different, but related, hearsay issue by the Court of Appeals for the District of Columbia in United States v. Brown, 160 U.S.App.D.C. 190, 490 F.2d 758 (1974), provides inferential support for the position urged by Inciso. The issue in that case was the admissibility of hearsay testimony concerning a victim's extrajudicial declarations that he was "[f]rightened that he may be killed" by the defendant. Id. at 762. After surveying the relevant cases, the court stated a "synthesis" of the governing principles. One of the cases which was criticized by the court was the decision of the California Supreme Court in People v. Merkouris, 52 Cal.2d 672, 344 P.2d 1 (1959), a case relied upon by the Government in the instant case. The court in *Merkouris* held that hearsay testimony showing the victim's fear of the defendant could properly be admitted to show the probable identity of the killer. The court in *Brown* expressed the following criticism of that holding, a criticism which might also apply to the application of the *Hillmon* doctrine in the instant case:

Hypotheticals

Let us assume that the issue is, "Was the declarant with Angelo that night?" Examine the following hypothetical statements made by the declarant the previous evening:

    a. "Angelo is going to the parking lot at Sambo's North tonight." (Other evidence shows that the declarant went there that night).

    b. "I am going to the parking lot at Sambo's North tonight." (Other evidence shows that Angelo went there that night).

    c. "I am going to meet Angelo at the parking lot at Sambo's North tonight."

    d. "Angelo is coming to my apartment tonight."

    e. "I am going to Angelo's apartment tonight."

    f. "I will not go out with anyone other than Angelo tonight." (Other evidence showing that he went out with someone.)

    g. "I am going to wait at home for Angelo until he picks me up and we will go out." (Other evidence shows that the declarant left his apartment that night).

    h. "I am going out to meet Angelo tonight."

See Federal Rules of Evidence 803(3), at p. 923; California Evidence Code § 1250, p. 881.

McCORMICK, HANDBOOK OF THE LAW OF EVIDENCE

(Hornbook Series), 577–78 (1954).**
[Footnotes omitted.]

    * * * But in one field the courts have not waited for the advance of general hearsay theory. In wills cases the special need for the hearsay use of the testator's declarations to show his previous acts is apparent. The testator is dead and is usually the one who best knew the facts, and is often the only one who had any knowledge of them. The special reliability, though it is arguable that he may often want to deceive his relatives, is strongly supported by his first-hand knowledge and by his lack of selfish interest. Accordingly, by the preponderance of recent decisions, the testator's declarations made after the alleged event are received to show that he has or has not made a will, or a will of a particular purport, or has or has not revoked his will. Some courts reach these results by announcing a special exception to the hearsay rule for retrospective declarations in wills cases. Others look upon the testator's declarations as statements of the mental condition of belief or memory, and hence coming within the present exception for declarations of mental state, and raising the circumstantial inference that the belief must have been prompted by facts. Or again the declarations may be looked on, not as statements, but as conduct evincing a belief circumstantially, and from this the inference as to the previous acts is derived.

"Such an approach violates the fundamental safeguards necessary to the use of such testimony [citation omitted]. Through a circuitous series of inferences, the court reverses the effect of the statement so as to reflect on *defendant's* intent and actions rather than the state of mind of the declarant (victim). This is the very result that it is hoped the limit-ing instruction will prevent." 490 P.2d at 771 (emphasis in original).

For a frequently cited academic critique of the *Hillmon* doctrine, see Maguire, The Hillmon Case—Thirty-Three Years After, 38 Harv.L.Rev. 709 (1925).

As the courts become further accustomed to the hearsay use of retrospective declarations in this important field of wills, it seems likely and desirable that this practice will serve as the core for a wider exception to the hearsay rule. This, by analogy, could take the following shape. The declarations of a person, now unavailable as a witness from death or other cause, as to facts within his knowledge, made under circumstances of apparent sincerity, will be received to evidence these facts.

ZIPPO MFG. CO. v. ROGERS IMPORTS, INC.

United States District Court, S.D. New York, 1963
216 F.Supp. 670

FEINBERG, District Judge. This case involves the attempt of a manufacturer of a popular cigarette lighter to keep others from imitating the lighter's shape and appearance. Plaintiff Zippo Manufacturing Company ("Zippo"), a Pennsylvania corporation, alleges both trademark infringement and unfair competition on the part of defendant Rogers, Inc.[1] ("Rogers"), a New York corporation, by reason of Rogers' sale of pocket lighters closely resembling Zippo's. Plaintiff seeks injunctive relief, an accounting, and damages. * * *

Plaintiff Zippo has been primarily engaged in the manufacture of pocket lighters since 1932, and it has grown spectacularly over the years. Its annual national sales of these lighters grew from about 27,000 units in 1934 to over 3,180,000 in 1958, the year just prior to suit, and well over 4,000,000 in 1961. Today, Zippo produces more units than any other domestic lighter manufacturer. Its pocket lighters are made in two models, the "standard" and the "slim-lighter." The latter accounts for slightly less than twenty-five per cent of the number of pocket lighters sold by Zippo. * * *

After Rogers commenced marketing its allegedly offending lighters in 1957, Zippo began receiving Rogers lighters from consumers who wished to have them repaired through Zippo's free repair policy. At the time of trial, a total of 191 Rogers lighters had been received by Zippo in this manner. Zippo's policy was to return the lighter to the person from whom it was received, together with a form letter stating that the lighter was not a Zippo product, and, therefore, the company would not repair it. * * *

Plaintiff's unfair competition action will be considered first, * * *

* * * plaintiff can obtain relief only if it meets its burden of proving that:

(1) Defendant's lighter copies plaintiff's lighter;

(2) A copied feature has acquired a special significance in the market identifying plaintiff as the source of the lighter, and that purchasers are moved in any degree to buy the lighter because of its source ("secondary meaning");

(3) Such copied feature in defendant's lighter is likely to cause prospective purchasers to regard the lighter as coming from plaintiff;

(4) Such copied feature is nonfunctional. It should be noted, however, that even if the copied feature is functional, plaintiff may

---

1. Defendant was formerly known as Rogers Imports, Inc.

still be entitled to relief if defendant has not taken reasonable steps to set its lighter apart from plaintiff's in the public mind.   *   *   *

Plaintiff has relied heavily on a consumer study to prove the elements of its case. This study was prepared and conducted by the sampling and market research firm of W.R. Simmons & Associates Research, Inc. Mr. Simmons, the head of this firm, and Donald F. Bowdren, the project supervisor, appeared as witnesses; both are qualified experts in the field of consumer surveys. Mr. Bowdren testified that the purpose of the study was to determine whether the physical attributes of the Zippo standard and slim-lighters serve as indicators of the source of the lighters to potential customers and whether the similar physical attributes of the Rogers lighters cause public confusion. The study or project consisted of three separate surveys. In Survey A, the respondents, or interviewees, were shown a Zippo standard lighter which had all the Zippo identification markings removed and were asked, among other things, what brand of lighter they thought it was and why. In Survey B, the same procedure was followed for the Zippo slim-lighter. In Survey C, respondents were shown a Rogers standard lighter that was being sold at the time of the survey, with all of its identifying markings, and they were asked, among other things, what brand of lighter they thought it was and why.

Mr. Simmons' testimony and the project report made clear the principles and procedures by which the surveys were conceived and conducted. Testimony to this effect is important, because it is well settled that the weight to be given a survey, assuming it is admissible, depends on the procedures by which the survey was created and conducted.   *   *   *

There was no overlapping of respondents in the three surveys so that no one respondent would be influenced in one survey by his answers to another survey. The developmental phase of the project involved preparation of questions that could be handled properly by an interviewer, correctly understood by respondents and easily answered by them. This required several drafts of questionnaires and some pretesting. The "universe" to be studied consisted of all smokers aged eighteen years and older residing in the continental United States, which the research project indicated was approximately 115,000,000 ("the smoking population"). All percentage results in the surveys represent projected percentages of the smoking population.

The three separate surveys were conducted across a national probability sample of smokers, with a sample size of approximately 500 for each survey. The samples were chosen on the basis of data obtained from the Bureau of Census by a procedure which started with the selection of fifty-three localities (metropolitan areas and non-metropolitan counties), and proceeded to a selection of 100 clusters within each of these localities—each cluster consisting of about 150-250 dwelling units—and then to approximately 500 respondents within the clusters. The manner of arriving at these clusters and respondents within each cluster was described in detail. The entire procedure was designed to obtain a representative sample of all smoking adults in the country. The procedures used to avoid sampling error and errors arising from other sources, the methods of processing, the instructions for the interviewers, and the approximate tolerance limits for a sample base of 500 were also described. Two of the interviewers testified that they were experienced in interviewing, explained the manner in which the interviews were conducted, and stated that they did not know the purpose of the surveys. All of the original responses to the questions as reported by these interviewers were made available in court.

Plaintiff also called Dr. Robert C. Sorensen as an expert in the field of survey research.[83] Dr. Sorensen stated that the project was conducted objectively and scientifically. Defendant does not deny this generally, but points to specific procedures and questions as being improper and buttresses its arguments with the testimony of its own expert, Professor Charles Winick.

Defendant objects to the admission of the surveys into evidence. It first contends that the surveys are hearsay. The weight of case authority, the consensus of legal writers, and reasoned policy considerations all indicate that the hearsay rule should not bar the admission of properly conducted public surveys. Although courts were at first reluctant to accept survey evidence or to give it weight, the more recent trend is clearly contrary. Surveys are now admitted over the hearsay objection on two technically distinct bases. Some cases hold that surveys are not hearsay at all; other cases hold that surveys are hearsay but are admissible because they are within the recognized exception to the hearsay rule for statements of present state of mind, attitude, or belief. Still other cases admit surveys without stating the ground on which they are admitted.

The cases holding that surveys are not hearsay do so on the basis that the surveys are not offered to prove the truth of what respondents said and, therefore, do not fall within the classic definition of hearsay. This approach has been criticized because, it is said, the answers to questions in a survey designed to prove the existence of a specific idea in the public mind are offered to prove the truth of the matter contained in these answers. Under this argument, when a respondent is asked to identify the brand of an unmarked lighter, the answer of each respondent who thinks the lighter is a Zippo is regarded as if he said, "I believe that this unmarked lighter is a Zippo." Since the matter to be proved in a secondary meaning case is respondent's belief that the lighter shown him is a Zippo lighter, a respondent's answer is hearsay in the classic sense. Others have criticized the non-hearsay characterization, regardless of whether surveys are offered to prove the truth of what respondents said because the answers in a survey depend for their probative value on the sincerity of respondents. One of the purposes of the hearsay rule is to subject to cross-examination statements which depend on the declarant's narrative sincerity. * * * The answer of a respondent that he thinks an unmarked lighter is a Zippo is relevant to the issue of secondary meaning only if, in fact, the respondent really does believe that the unmarked lighter is a Zippo. Under this view, therefore, answers in a survey should be regarded as hearsay.

Regardless of whether the surveys in this case could be admitted under the non-hearsay approach, they are admissible because the answers of respondents are expressions of presently existing state of mind, attitude, or belief. There is a recognized exception to the hearsay rule for such statements, and under it the statements are admissible to prove the truth of the matter contained therein.

---

83.   Tr. pp. 721–22a, 756–57. Dr. Sorensen is the co-author, *inter alia,* of R. C. Sorensen & T. C. Sorensen, The Admissibility and Use of Opinion Research Evidence, 28 N.Y.U.L.Rev. 1213 (1953).

Even if the surveys did not fit within this exception, well reasoned authority justifies their admission under the following approach: the determination that a statement is hearsay does not end the inquiry into admissibility; there must still be a further examination of the need for the statement at trial and the circumstantial guaranty of trustworthiness surrounding the making of the statement. This approach has been used to justify the admissibility of a survey. Necessity in this context requires a comparison of the probative value of the survey with the evidence, if any, which as a practical matter could be used if the survey were excluded. If the survey is more valuable, then necessity exists for the survey, i. e., it is the inability to get "evidence of the same value" which makes the hearsay statement necessary. When, as here, the state of mind of the smoking population (115,000,000 people) is the issue, a scientifically conducted survey is necessary because the practical alternatives do not produce equally probative evidence. With such a survey, the results are probably approximately the same as would be obtained if each of the 115,000,000 people were interviewed. The alternative of having 115,000,000 people testify in court is obviously impractical. The alternatives of having a much smaller section of the public testify (such as eighty witnesses) or using expert witnesses to testify to the state of the public mind are clearly not as valuable because the inferences which can be drawn from such testimony to the public state of mind are not as strong or as direct as the justifiable inferences from a scientific survey.

The second element involved in this approach is the guaranty of trustworthiness supplied by the circumstances under which the out-of-court statements were made. A logical step in this inquiry is to see which of the hearsay dangers are present. With regard to these surveys: there is no danger of faulty memory; the danger of faulty perception is negligible because respondents need only examine two or three cigarette lighters at most; the danger of faulty narration is equally negligible since the answers called for are simple. The only appreciable danger is that the respondent is insincere. But this danger is minimized by the circumstances of this or any public opinion poll in which scientific sampling is employed, because members of the public who are asked questions about things in which they have no interest have no reason to falsify their feelings. While the sampling procedure substantially guarantees trustworthiness insofar as the respondent's sincerity is concerned, other survey techniques substantially insure trustworthiness in other respects. If questions are unfairly worded to suggest answers favorable to the party sponsoring the survey, the element of trustworthiness in the poll would be lacking. The same result would follow if the interviewers asked fair questions in a leading manner. Thus, the methodology of the survey bears directly on trustworthiness, as it does on necessity. Since the two elements of necessity and trustworthiness are satisfied, I would admit these surveys under this approach to the hearsay rule, even apart from the state of mind exception.[104]

104. Irvin v. State, 66 So.2d 288, 291–92 (Fla.1953), cert. denied, 346 U.S. 927, 74 S.Ct. 316, 98 L.Ed. 419 (1954), raises a possible objection not stressed by defendant —"multiple hearsay." The multiple hearsay argument is as follows: when answers made by respondents to interviewers are admissible under a hearsay exception, the interviewers can testify to these answers; but when the interviewers themselves do not testify but instead "tell" these answers to another person in the market research organization who then testifies as to the answers, this testimony is inadmissible hear-

Defendant's next objection to the surveys is that they should not have been conducted in respondents' homes but in stores, the actual places of purchase. While it may be that in general the store is the best place to measure the state of mind at the time of purchase, it would be virtually impossible to obtain a representative national sample if stores were used. An interview at a respondent's home is probative of his state of mind at the time of purchase, although the deviation from the actual purchase situation should be considered in weighing the force of this evidence. Therefore, the surveys are not inadmissible merely because they were conducted in homes.

Defendant also objects to the surveys on the ground that they measured only the popularity of Zippo, as compared with the popularity of Rogers, and that this is not relevant to secondary meaning. However, I find that, by and large, the surveys did, as Dr. Sorensen testified, test brand identification and not brand popularity. They are, therefore, not incompetent because of the small elements of popularity which may have crept in, although that possibility should be considered in the weight to be given their results.

Defendant's next objection is to Survey C. In that survey, 34.7 per cent of respondents thought a Rogers lighter was a Zippo lighter, and plaintiff argues that this is probative of likelihood of confusion between the two lighters. However, respondents were not shown a Rogers display card when they made their mistaken identification. Therefore, defendant contends that the percentage of people who would mistakenly identify a Rogers lighter as a Zippo lighter would be smaller if the Rogers lighter were shown to them on a Rogers display card. This argument is probably correct. This does not mean, however, that the results of Survey C are inadmissible to prove that the appearance of the Rogers lighter is likely to confuse people into thinking that it is a Zippo lighter.

Defendant's argument is implicitly based on two assumptions: (1) that use of the Rogers display card in the interviews would have caused a great number of the respondents who thought the Rogers lighter was a Zippo lighter to give different answers; and (2) that the number left who, even after a display card was shown to them, would still confuse the Rogers lighter with a Zippo lighter would be statistically insignificant. However, these assumptions at best are too speculative to require exclusion of Survey C. Moreover, they are contradicted by other answers in Survey C, which show that about one-half of respondents who mistakenly thought that the Rogers lighter was a Zippo lighter actually saw something stamped on the bottom of the lighter (where the Rogers name was imprinted) and that over one-third of those who thought the Rogers lighter was a Zippo lighter actually saw the Rogers name stamped on the lighter. These results certainly give rise to the inference that if the Rogers display card had been shown to respondents, a significant number of people would have thought the Rogers lighter was a Zippo lighter anyway: although exposed to the display card,

say because the witness is relating what the interviewers told him rather than what respondents in the survey told him. I conclude that this argument should not preclude the admission of a properly conducted survey, possibly because the business entries exception to the hearsay rule covers the transmission of the answers from the interviewers to other people in the organization, at least where the organization involved is in the business of conducting and reporting on surveys, see 52 Mich.L. Rev. 914 (1954), 29 N.Y.U.L.Rev. 751 (1954), or because considerations of necessity and trustworthiness justify an exception for the "second stage" of hearsay as well as for the original answers.

some would not have actually perceived the Rogers name, and others would have seen the Rogers name but would nonetheless think that the lighter was made by Zippo. Therefore, Survey C is not excluded. However, its weight on the issue of likelihood of confusion is less than it would be had a display card been used, and had the same number of respondents nonetheless identified the Rogers lighter as a Zippo lighter. See W. E. Bassett Co. v. H. C. Cook Co., 164 F.Supp. 278, 285 (D.Conn.1958).

Defendant has other objections to admissibility of the surveys, e. g., that a survey is not the best way to prove secondary meaning, but none of these merit further discussion. Surveys A, B, and C were scientifically conducted by a competent and professional research firm, substantially in accordance with the recommendations of Recommended Procedures for the Trial of Protracted Cases, 25 F.R.D. 351, 415–430 (1960). I conclude, therefore, that the surveys are admissible to show secondary meaning for the shape and appearance of the Zippo standard and slim-lighters and likelihood of confusion between these lighters and their Rogers counterparts.

[Judgment was rendered in accordance with the opinion]

Hypotheticals

(1)   A sues X for damages for wrongful death arising out of an automobile accident in which A's husband, B, was killed. A testifies that there was a warm and affectionate relationship between her and B during their five-year marriage which ended with B's death. X calls C, a business associate of B, to testify that about six months before B's death, B said several times that he hated A and that he was very unhappy in his marriage. A makes a hearsay objection to C's testimony. What result?

(2)   Assume the same facts as in Illustration (1). X proposes to have C also testify that on one occasion three months before B's death, B said: "I just can't forget that three months ago I caught A out with another man and that this has changed my love for her into hate." A makes a hearsay objection. What is the appropriate ruling?

(3)   X is prosecuted for murder of A, his wife, X admits that he shot A but his defense is that the shooting was accidental. X calls B, a police officer, to testify that several hours after the shooting he had a conversation with X in which X stated that he was just sick and grief-striken over A's death. The prosecution makes a hearsay objection. Should the objection be sustained?

(4)   X is prosecuted for the murder of A, his girl friend. A was shot to death in X's apartment. X's defense is that A was at his apartment and requested to see his gun collection, that he handed A a pistol, and that while A was examining it she dropped it and it went off, killing her. The prosecution calls B, A's girl friend, to testify that a week before the shooting A told her that she was afraid of X and was deathly afraid of guns. X makes a hearsay objection to B's proposed testimony. How should the court rule?

(5)   Assume the same facts as in Illustration (2). X calls C, a girl friend of A, to testify that two weeks before the shooting, A told her that she was planning to go to Utah the following week and go deerhunting; that upon asking A how were things between her and X, A replied that she was very fond of X and liked to be around him. The prosecution makes a hearsay objection to C's proposed testimony. What result?

(6)   X is prosecuted for the murder of A, his girl friend with whom he was living. X's defense is self-defense—that A was advancing on him with a knife, and that

he then struck her with a beer bottle. The prosecution calls B, a friend of A, to testify that on the day before the killing, A said to her "I am breaking up with X tonight. I might get killed over it but I am going to do it." X makes a hearsay objection to B's proposed testimony. How should the court rule?

7. PHYSICAL CONDITION

Reasons for the Exception. Out-of-court statements concerning then-existing bodily conditions—symptoms, pain, and the like—are thought to have some built-in guarantees of reliability. Often such declarations are truly spontaneous: "Oh, my aching back!" They appear to be especially reliable when made to a treating physician. If the declarant knows that the physician is going to treat him, he is unlikely to give the physician deliberately incorrect information; the joke could prove to be on the patient. Furthermore, the patient is likely to believe that the physician knows a great deal about physical conditions. It is arguable, therefore, that the patient will not supply false data since the physician will only discover its falsity after possibly painful and costly tests. Finally, the physician's expertise is available to corroborate the accuracy of the out-of-court declarant's statements concerning his physical condition.

The hearsay risks are at a minimum here. There is no perception problem since the declarant is relating what he feels at the time. There is no memory problem where the declaration relates to present symptoms. And there is probably no great veracity problem, for the reasons already suggested.

Statements Made to a Nonphysician. Statements concerning present (then-existing) bodily condition are usually received in evidence no matter to whom they were made. They need not have been made to a treating physician; they may have been made to a spouse, to other relatives, to a friend, to a co-worker on the job, to a nurse, or to a hospital roommate. The declaration can relate to symptomology, including the existence of pain. *Past* symptoms are excluded.

Some jurisdictions require that the declarant be unavailable to take the witness stand before this branch of the bodily condition exception can be used.

Statements Made to a Physician. Statements concerning bodily condition may be made to a treating physician or to one whose assignment is only to examine the patient and render a diagnostic opinion.

1. *Statements to a Treating Physician.* Statements of present bodily condition to a treating physician—one who is going to diagnose the patient's problem and prescribe treatment for it—are admissible in evidence to prove the existence of the condition and are generally considered weightier than such statements made to a nontreating physician. Most courts, but not all of them, will exclude declarations about past bodily condition as proof of the existence of that condition. However, all courts will permit receipt of declarations of past symptoms, made to a treating physician, to show the basis for the physician's opinion (diagnosis, prognosis).

Example:

In Ritter v. Coca Cola Co. (Kenosha-Racine) Inc., 128 N.W.2d 439 (S.Ct.Wis.1964), the plaintiff, who had discovered a mouse in her bottle of Coca Cola, consulted a psychiatrist *after* having consulted her lawyer. The psychiatrist treated plaintiff and testified, over objection, that she had sustained psychological injury. The psychiatrist's testimony was ruled admissible.

The Wisconsin Supreme Court said that intrinsic guarantees of trustworthiness apply when treatment was at least part of the reason for consulting a physician. There was enough evidence that the plaintiff had not consulted the psychiatrist solely to secure his expert testimony.

2. *Statements to a Nontreating Physician.* Most courts hold that a nontreating physician's testimony about his patient's narration of present bodily condition is not admissible as proof that the condition actually existed. Such statements can come in only indirectly, where the nontreating physician relied on them in making his diagnosis or prognosis and they help to explain that diagnosis or prognosis.

A minority of courts will permit a nontreating physician—one who has been retained solely to provide an expert opinion and perhaps thereafter to testify in court—to testify only as to objective facts clinically observable to him. The nontreating physician, in other words, cannot testify as to declarations by the patient as to subjective matters, such as pain.

Example a.:

In Gonzales v. Hodson, 420 P.2d 813 (S.Ct.Idaho 1966), a neuropsychiatrist's report was excluded because the consultation had been exclusively for purposes of getting the neuropsychiatrist's testimony for trial.

Example b.:

In Davidson v. Cornell, 30 N.E. 573 (Ct.App.N.Y. 1892), a personal injury case, the plaintiff, just before trial, was examined by a nontreating physician. Plaintiff, mostly in response to questions by the physician, described his physical sensations and abilities—mainly sexual—during the fifteen months between his injury and the physician's examination. The physician's testimony was ruled inadmissible, the New York court saying that declarations of physical condition are receivable only if made to a *treating* physician about *present* conditions.

The new evidence codes make no distinction between statements made to treating physicians and those made to nontreating physicians. Under these codes the jurors are permitted to decide what weight to accord such statements.

Finally, it should be emphasized that involuntary indications of pain, such as groans or grimaces, are not subject to the hearsay rule at all. Anyone who hears them or sees them and then testifies about them is simply giving direct eyewitness or ear-witness testimony.

MEANEY v. UNITED STATES

United States Court of Appeals, Second Circuit, 1940.
112 F.2d 538.

L. HAND, Circuit Judge.

This is an appeal from a judgment entered upon the verdict of a jury, dismissing a petition in an action to recover upon a policy of war risk insur-

ance. The insured was mustered out on December 31, 1918, and the policy lapsed on January 30, 1919; he died of pulmonary tuberculosis on July 6, 1922, and the question was whether he was permanently and totally disabled when the policy lapsed. He had consulted one physician at some time, not definitely fixed, in 1919, and another in December, 1920, who found that he had contracted tuberculosis, and that it was already "moderately advanced". By April of 1921 the disease had so far developed that he had to go to a sanatorium, where he stayed till January, 1922, only six months before his death. The only error we need consider was a ruling, made during the examination of the physician who had first examined him in December, 1920. This witness said that he had taken care of the insured both at that time and after he came back from the sanatorium; and he was allowed to testify as to what he found on his several examinations, but the judge refused to let him say what the insured had told him of the "history of the case".
* * *

The insured's declarations seem to have been offered as a narrative of his past condition; so far as appears they were no part of the basis of the physician's opinion as to his condition; at least they were not offered as such. They were therefore hearsay, and moreover, they did not fall within the generally accepted exception in favor of spontaneous expressions of pain or the like. It is quite true that this exception includes narrative statements as well as mere ejaculations, and that it has been extended to a declaration of present symptoms told by a patient to a physician. The utterances of a patient in the course of his examination, so far as they are spontaneous, may be merely ejaculatory—as when he emits a cry upon palpation—or they may be truly narrative; and it will often be impossible to distinguish rationally between the two; between an inarticulate cry, for example, and a statement such as: "That hurts". The warrant for the admission of both is the same; the lack of opportunity or motive for fabrication upon an unexpected occasion to which the declarant responds immediately, and without reflection. But most of what he tells will not ordinarily be of this kind at all; there may be, and there is in fact, good reason to receive it, but it is a very different reason. A man goes to his physician expecting to recount all that he feels, and often he has with some care searched his consciousness to be sure that he will leave out nothing. If his narrative of present symptoms is to be received as evidence of the facts, as distinguished from mere support for the physician's opinion, these parts of it can only rest upon his motive to disclose the truth because his treatment will in part depend upon what he says. That justification is not necessary in the case of his spontaneous declarations, even when they are narrative; but it is necessary for those we are now considering. * * *

The same reasoning applies with exactly the same force to a narrative of past symptoms. * * * A patient has an equal motive to speak the truth; what he has felt in the past is as apt to be important in his treatment as what he feels at the moment. Thus, in spite of the dicta in Northern Pacific R.R. v. Urlin, supra (158 U.S. 271, 15 S.Ct. 840, 39 L.Ed. 977) and Boston & Albany R.R. v. O'Reilly, supra (158 U.S. 334, 15 S.Ct. 830, 39 L.Ed. 1006) that only declarations of present symptoms are competent, several federal courts have seemed not to take the distinction between declarations of present and past symptoms, provided the patient is consulting the physi-

cian for treatment, and Professor Wigmore appears to assent. Wigmore §
1722. This situation is * * * obviously different from declarations of
facts irrelevant to the declarant's treatment, such as what was the cause of
his injury. It is true that this body of authority is not impressive as such, but
it appears to us that if there is to be any consistency in doctrine, either declarations of all symptoms, present or past, should be competent, or only
those which fall within the exception for spontaneous utterances. Nobody
would choose the second, particularly as the substance of the declarations
can usually be got before the jury as parts of the basis on which the physician's opinion was formed. It it indeed always possible that a patient may
not really consult his physician for treatment; the consultation may be col-
orable. The judge has power to prevent an abuse in such cases, and here as
elsewhere, when the competency of evidence depends upon a question of
fact, his conclusion is final. He must decide before admitting the declarations whether the patient was consulting the physician for treatment and
for that alone. Unless he is so satisfied, he must exclude them, though it is
true that if he admits them, the defendant may still argue that they are untrustworthy. They will be evidence, but in estimating their truth the jury
may have to decide for themselves the very issue on which the judge himself
passed before he admitted them; the competency of evidence is always independent of its weight.

We hold that the insured's "history of the case" as narrated to the physician was competent and that its exclusion was error.

Judgment reversed; new trial ordered.

KENNEDY v. MONROE

Court of Appeals of Washington, Division 2, 1976.
15 Wash. App. 39, 547 P.2d 899.

REED, Judge.

Plaintiff, Jack D. Kennedy, brought this action to recover for personal
injuries allegedly sustained in a rear-end collision on October 5, 1972. Liability was determined in plaintiff's favor by summary judgment and the
case proceeded to trial on the issue of damages only.

The defendants appeal from judgment on a verdict in plaintiff's favor
for $7,775, and the assignments of error present the following issues for our
resolution.

1. May a nontreating physician who has examined a party for the sole
purpose of qualifying as an expert witness at trial relate what that party told him concerning the cause of the injury, subjective symptoms
and course of treatment?

2. If such a history is admissible through the physician, for what
purpose and to what extent may it be considered?

* * *

At trial plaintiff testified concerning the collision, his alleged injuries,
his complaints, suffering and discomfort, and the course of medical treatment he had undergone. * * *

Plaintiff called as his only medical witness one Dr. Bridgeford who had
examined plaintiff for the sole purpose of testifying at trial. Dr. Bridgeford

was allowed, over objection, to relate the entire history given him by the plaintiff as to the facts of the accident, his symptoms of pain, suffering and discomfort, and his course of medical treatment. The doctor further testified that based on the plaintiff's history, he took X-rays and conducted a physical examination, both of which objectively supported the presence of plaintiff's subjective symptoms. Utilizing the history and his findings, it was the doctor's opinion that plaintiff had sustained a subluxation or displacement of a vertebra with attending ligamentous and soft tissue injury resulting in some impairment in his neck movement accompanied by pain and discomfort. Dr. Bridgeford felt that the condition was fixed and plaintiff would continue to experience these symptoms in some degree. The doctor further stated that plaintiff's injuries probably resulted from the collision of October 5, 1972.

* * *

Defendants rely primarily on the case of Petersen v. Department of Labor & Indus., 36 Wash.2d 266, 217 P.2d 607 (1950) and Hinds v. Johnson, 55 Wash.2d 325, 347 P.2d 828 (1959) to support their argument that a nontreating physician is limited to relating objective findings and answering hypothetical questions and is prohibited from testifying concerning subjective symptoms or medical history related to him by a claimant. Because Washington decisions continue to cite *Petersen*'s distinction between the treating and nontreating physician we deem it necessary to commence our discussion by quoting extensively from that decision where the court said at pages 268-270, 217 P.2d at pages 609-610:

> Conclusions as to the health and capacity of a claimant lie in the realm of medical knowledge. * * * We have not been concerned with the credibility of the medical witnesses, since expert and lay witnesses are treated alike as to that. The chief source of our recurring problem, on the question of medical testimony * * * is found in the fact that one rule applies when the medical testimony is given by a doctor who examines a patient for the purpose of treating him, while a different rule applies when the testimony is given by a doctor who examines an individual for the sole purpose of qualifying himself to be a witness as to a person's physical condition. This presents a question of the competence of such evidence in each case, because the element of *hearsay* always inheres in medical conclusions.

> All doctors take the history of their patients, when it is needed to arrive at a correct diagnosis. Their own skilled observations, aided by the best medical equipment, lead only to objective findings. They cannot clinically observe a pain or a functional disorder. Such subjective symptoms must be related to them by the patient, or by someone on his behalf, and are frequently indispensable to a correct diagnosis and course of treatment.

> The doctor receives the statement of these subjective symptoms informally, and they are not given under oath, nor does he attempt to rebut them. The self-interest of the patient is a sufficient guarantee of the trustworthiness of such statements, where the examination is made for the purpose of treatment. Thus, it is the universal rule that, if the doctor who treats a patient later becomes a witness, he may testify as to his medical conclusions, which may be based substantially

on subjective symptoms which are in the realm of hearsay. *This is a recognized exception to the hearsay rule of evidence.*   *   *   *   [Emphasis added.]

The reason for this exception to the rule disappears instantly, when the examination is not made within the doctor-patient relationship for the purpose of treatment, but is made only for the purpose of qualifying the doctor as a witness. Under such circumstances, a claimant may, in describing his symptoms to the doctor, paint a dark picture. He may think his best interest will be served by exaggeration and fabrication of symptoms. Hence, medical conclusions based upon these statements, which were not given under oath or subject to cross-examination, violate the hearsay rule and are not admissible.   *   *   *

  *   *   *   The doctor who examines the party only for the purpose of qualifying as a witness, is limited in his testimony to objective findings and the answering of hypothetical questions.

(Citations omitted.)

In the case of Kresoya v. Department of Labor & Indus., 40 Wash.2d 40, 240 P.2d 257 (1952), our Supreme Court noted that it had held, in a long line of cases, that a physician is not restricted to testimony concerning his objective findings, but may couple those findings with other competent evidence in reaching a medical conclusion. The *Kresoya* court also points out that in Knowles v. Department of Labor & Indus., 28 Wash.2d 970, 184 P.2d 591 (1947) a nontreating doctor was allowed to consider the testimony of lay witnesses together with his own objective findings so as to causally connect an aggravation to the original injury. Using these cases as the springboard, the *Kresoya* court appears to depart from the strict *Petersen* rule regarding the testimony of a physician who saw claimant but once for the purpose of testifying on his behalf, by stating at page 45, 240 P.2d at p. 260:

In order that Dr. Williams might acquire testimonial knowledge of the condition of appellant, it was necessary that he obtain from him some of the history of the case.   *   *   *

  *   *   *   The rule that an expert medical witness may not base his opinion upon subjective symptoms alone is designed to protect *   *   *   against unfounded claims   *   *   *   If such claims could be established by the testimony of a physician who based his opinion entirely upon what the claimant told him, it would open the door to fraudulent claims, as well as those mistakenly made in good faith. A claimant might honestly believe his subsequent condition arose out of his original injury, but this is a medical question and an opinion thereon must be derived from sources other than the claimant's statement. *These protective rules, however, must not be applied to situations where there is a combination of subjective and objective symptoms, which an expert may be able to tie together,*   *   *   *   The physician must of necessity obtain some history from the claimant, and has a right to make proper use of it in connection with objective findings which he as an expert may make by an examination, the making of tests, the use of X-ray pictures and other proper data. [Emphasis added.]

Later decisions cite both *Petersen* and *Kresoya*, but not until Justice Hunter's dissent in Cooper v. Department of Labor & Indus., 54 Wash.2d 428, 342 P.2d 218 (1959) has there been any suggestion that *Kresoya* might have changed the *Petersen* rule. Justice Hunter refers to the *Petersen* rule at page 434, 342 P.2d at page 222 as follows:

> This rules out the consideration of subjective symptoms, even though coupled and related with objective findings. The rule announced by this language in the *Petersen* case, supra, was therefore impliedly overruled in the *Kresoya* case, supra. We should now, for clarification, expressly overrule the *Petersen* case in so far as it is inconsistent with the rule announced in the *Kresoya* case. ＊ ＊ ＊

＊ ＊ ＊

In Hinds v. Johnson, supra, the controversy centered around the testimony of an ophthalmologist who related the claimant's responses during administration of an examination involving the use of a complex lens adjustment instrument. The issue was disposed of when the court held there were sufficient safeguards in the test itself to assure truthful responses, thus qualifying those responses as objective findings rather than subjective complaints. ＊ ＊ ＊

We read the *Hinds* decision as not rejecting the modifications of *Kresoya* because the court was not there faced with an apparent *combination* of both subjective and objective symptoms; having found the patient's responses to be objective it was not necessary to discuss the case in terms of *Kresoya.*

＊ ＊ ＊

From our review of the cases dealing with the point, we see an apparent erosion of the strict rule of *Petersen,* and a growing recognition that in appropriate circumstances and under proper safeguards the admissibility of patient recitals should include those made to a nontreating physician. While the "self-interest" factor used by the *Petersen* court to distinguish between treating and nontreating physicians is valid, the results are not realistic if the rule is strictly applied because it keeps from the jury information which might be helpful and indeed indispensable to their assessment of the doctor's conclusions. Examination of a claimant under oath to reveal any discrepancies within the history given and the use of hypothetical questions to add additional evidentiary facts or point out omissions or embellishments by the claimant in what he told the doctor, are adequate safeguards; the question merely becomes one of the weights to be attached to such testimony and the doctor's conclusions.

We hold, therefore, that an otherwise qualified physician, ＊ ＊ ＊ seen by the plaintiff ＊ ＊ ＊ solely for the purpose of enabling him to testify on plaintiff's behalf, may relate what the plaintiff told him regarding (1) the general nature or cause of the injury insofar as it pertains to treatment and not fault, (2) the plaintiff's past and present subjective complaints and symptoms and (3) the course of medical treatment followed by the plaintiff. The nontreating physician is not limited in his testimony to objective findings and to answering hypothetical questions.

＊ ＊ ＊

By so holding we do not expand upon the limited purpose for which such a narrative of the patient's history is admitted. The historical recitation by the doctor is not admitted as proof of the facts recited, but as proof only that the statements were made and utilized in part by the doctor as a basis for reaching his medical conclusions, *and as such are not hearsay.*

* * *

* * * The statements made by the patient to the doctor, which constitute the basis of his expert opinion, *are not evidence which establishes the fact of the patient's condition.* [Emphasis added.] Smith v. Ernst Hardware Co., supra, at page 79, 377 P.2d at page 261.[4]

* * *

In the instant case, therefore, it was not error to allow Dr. Bridgeford to relate the history given him by Mr. Kennedy as the basis for the doctor's conclusions regarding the nature and extent of the injury and its cause.

* * *

Judgment affirmed.

Petrie, C.J., and Pearson, J., concur.

———

See Federal Rules of Evidence 803(3)–(4) at p. 923.

ADVISORY COMMITTEE'S NOTE TO FEDERAL RULE 803(4)

Even those few jurisdictions which have shied away from generally admitting statements of present condition have allowed them if made to a physician for purposes of diagnosis and treatment in view of the patient's strong motivation to be truthful. The same guarantee of trustworthiness extends to statements of past conditions and medical history, made for purposes of diagnosis or treatment. It also extends to statements as to causation, reasonably pertinent to the same purposes, in accord with the current trend. Statements as to fault would not ordinarily qualify under this latter language. Thus a patient's statement that he was struck by an automobile would qualify but not his statement that the car was driven through a red light. Under the exception the statement need not have been made to a physician. Statements to hospital attendants, ambulance drivers, or even members of the family might be included.

Conventional doctrine has excluded from the hearsay exception, as not within its guarantee of truthfulness, statements to a physician consulted only for the purpose of enabling him to testify. While these statements were not admissible as substantive evidence, the expert was allowed to state the basis of his opinion, including statements of this kind. The distinction thus called for was one most unlikely to be made by juries. The rule accordingly rejects the limitation. This position is consistent with the provision of Rule 703 that the facts on which expert testimony is based need not be admissible in evidence if of a kind ordinarily relied upon by experts in the field.

---

4. A recognition of this distinction will usually lead to a request for a cautionary or limiting instruction to the jury on the effect to be given the recital. * * *

8. PRIOR IDENTIFICATION

PEOPLE v. GARDNER

Supreme Court of Michigan, 1978.
402 Mich. 460, 265 N.W.2d 1.

WILLIAMS, Justice.

INTRODUCTION

This case concerns an attack upon Mr. Anderson, the complaining witness, by three men. The day after the attack Mr. Anderson called the police to inform them that he had seen his attackers. The police then accompanied Mr. Anderson to a poolroom where he pointed out the defendants. At trial Mr. Anderson and a police officer were permitted, over objection, to testify to the circumstances of the poolroom identification. The Court of Appeals found no reversible error. We agree.

* * *

At trial Mr. Anderson identified defendants Gardner and Sanford as two of the men who attacked him. Mr. Anderson testified he had one false eye and his glasses were broken in the struggle. He also testified he had never seen the defendants before that day, but he had seen them in the drug store when he walked into the drug store.

Mr. Anderson also testified on direct examination to having identified the defendants the day after the attack. Mr. Anderson saw the defendants in the same drug store and called the police. By the time the police arrived defendants were in a poolroom. The police joined Mr. Anderson at the poolroom. Mr. Anderson then pointed the defendants out to the police. The relevant portions of that testimony follow:

"*Q. (By Mr. Morgan [Prosecuting Attorney]):* Okay. Now, the next day, Mr. Anderson, February 27, did you have occasion to go back to the drug store?

"*A.* I went back to the drug store.

"*Mr. Ziemba [Defense Counsel]:* Objection. This is entirely irrelevant, Your Honor.

"*The Court:* Overruled.

"*Mr. Ziemba:* Thank you.

"*Q. (By Mr. Morgan):* Would that be in the afternoon some time?

"*A.* Yes. I went back to the drug store, and I saw them come in the drug store.

"*Q.* Who came in the drug store?

"*A.* Those two here.

"*Mr. Ziemba:* May I have a continuing line of this question? [sic].

"*The Court:* Yes.

"*Mr. Ziemba:* Thank you.

"*Q. (By Mr. Morgan):* You saw Mr. Gardner and Mr. Sanford?

"*A.* That's right.

"*Q.*   Did they do anything in the drug store?

"*A.*   They got a pack of cigarettes, I think, and walked out.

"*Q.*   Okay. What did you do next, sir?

"*A.*   I called a policeman.

"*Q.*   Did some police officers come?

"*A.*   That's right.

"*Q.*   What did you do next?

"*A.*   When I called the police, they circled around up and down Owen and Oakland, and then went in the poolroom.

*   *   *

"*Q.*   After the police went into the billiard room, what did you do, sir?

"*A.*   I went in there, too.

"*Q.*   What did you do next?

"*A.*   They was standing around there looking.

"*Q.*   Who do you mean, they?

"*A.*   They was looking, the police, and I pointed him out and him out because them was the ones who robbed me.

"*Q.*   You pointed Mr. Gardner and Mr. Sanford out?

"*A.*   That's right.

"*Q.*   What were they doing in the poolroom?

"*A.*   He was playing pool.

"*Q.*   Mr. Sanford?

"*A.*   Yes, and he was playing checkers.

"*Q.*   Were there any other people in the poolroom?

"*A.*   Yes, about fifteen to sixteen people, something like that.

"*Q.*   Mr. Anderson, did you testify at a prior hearing in this matter?

"*A.*   I [sure] did.

"*Q.*   At that particular time, did you have occasion to identify the defendants?

"*Mr. Ziemba:* I object to this. This is highly objectionable.

"*The Court:* Objection sustained.

"*Mr. Ziemba:* I ask that the answer [sic] be stricken and the jury be instructed to disregard the answer [sic].

"*Mr. Morgan:* Your Honor, may we approach the bench?

"*The Court:* Yes.

(Whereupon a discussion was held off the record.)

"*Q.   (By Mr. Morgan):* Mr. Anderson, is there any doubt in your mind that these are two of the men who attempted to rob you on February 26?

"*A.*   That's right. That's the two right there."

*   *   *

A police officer, over objection, confirmed complainant's testimony concerning the identification made February 27, 1974, in the poolroom. After this testimony the parties rested.

* * *

VI—Prior Identification

Defendants contend it was error "for the trial judge to permit over objection, testimony by the complainant and by a police officer as to the circumstances of defendants' arrests" because it was "irrelevant" and "merely gratuitously bolstered complainant's in-court identification by * * * hearsay." The Court of Appeals stated that after reviewing the issue "discussion is without merit."

We find the question to be whether, over objection, the trial judge should permit testimony concerning an extrajudicial identification by the witness who made the identification and/or by a third party, in this instance a police officer, who witnessed the identification. The problem is whether such testimony is hearsay and if so whether there is an exception which would allow one or both witnesses to testify.

There is a split among the jurisdictions on this question. In Gilbert v. California, 388 U.S. 263, 272–273, fn 3, 87 S.Ct. 1951, 1956, 18 L.Ed.2d 1178 (1967), the United States Supreme Court did not distinguish the two types of testimony and observed:

"There is a split among the States concerning the admissibility of prior extrajudicial identifications, as independent evidence of identity, both by the witness and third parties present at the prior identification. See 71 A.L.R.2d 449. It has been held that the prior identification is hearsay, and, when admitted through the testimony of the identifier, is merely a prior consistent statement. The recent trend, however, is to admit the prior identification under the exception that admits as substantive evidence a prior communication by a witness who is available for cross-examination at trial. See 5 A.L.R.2d Later Case Service 1225–1228."

We agree with the position taken in the Federal Rules of Evidence, which removes the testimony of the identifier from the hearsay category. The Federal Rule of Evidence 801(d)(1)(C) states:

"Rule 801. Definitions

"The following definitions apply under this article:

* * *

"(d) Statements which are not hearsay. A statement is not hearsay if
—

"(1) Prior statement by witness. The declarant testifies at the trial or hearing and is subject to cross-examination concerning the statement, and the statement is * * * (C) one of identification of a person made after perceiving him."

We find that the testimony of the third party limited to the circumstances surrounding the identification is not objectionable as hearsay and is admissible at the discretion of the trial judge subject to such considerations as whether the identification procedures were unfair, biased, or a violation of the accused's constitutional rights.

A. Testimony by the Identifier.

Objections to this type of testimony have usually been based either on its character as hearsay or on the theory that it amounts to impermissible bolstering of the victim's testimony by a prior consistent statement. In my concurring opinion in People v. Poe, 388 Mich. 611, 202 N.W.2d 320 (1972), the importance of such testimony was noted:

> "This case strongly highlights a psychological and legal problem deserving the most serious consideration of the bench and bar. In reading the record and my Brother Adam's [*sic*] opinion, one cannot escape the emphasis on what the witnesses at pretrial identification said and did. Such matters as whether or not an identifying witness did or did not identify the defendant; whether the identifying witness identified another person; whether the identification was 'positive' or 'hesitant'; what the identifying witness said; what the police records of the lineup do or do not show; etc., all are heavily stressed. And no wonder, because punishment or discharge depends on whether the jury finds beyond a reasonable doubt that the witnesses identified the 'right' man.

> *   *   *

> "From this emphasis on what happened and what was said at the pretrial identification procedures it is apparent that both parties thought the jury would be influenced by identifying witness' impressions at the time nearest the crime. This actually is logically and psychologically sound. An important consideration underlining my concurrence in this case is the proposition that, all things being *equal*, identifications made prior to trial are inherently more reliable than those made "in court" ('That's the man.'). Wigmore has characterized in-court identifications as 'violently suggestive.' * * * However, in Gilbert v. California, 388 U.S. 263, 87 S.Ct. 1951, 18 L.Ed.2d 1178 (1967), the United States Supreme Court made testimony as to pretrial identification procedures subject to *per se* exclusion if the defendant was without counsel. *Kirby,* supra [Kirby v. Illinois, 406 U.S. 682, 92 S.Ct. 1877, 32 L.Ed.2d 411], restricted this *per se* exclusion to post-'indictment' situations. This writer believes that the *per se* exclusionary rule should be *eliminated entirely* and an appropriate rule of special qualification of such evidence on the basis of the fairness of the procedures substituted." 388 Mich. 611, 623–625, 202 N.W.2d 320, 326.

The Federal system adopted such a rule by enacting the Federal Rules of Evidence, Rule 801(d)(1)(C), supra.

This Court's most direct pronouncement on the subject was made in conclusory fashion in People v. Londe, 230 Mich. 484, 203 N.W. 93 (1925). There the Court said:

> "It was proper for the witnesses who had seen the men at the time of the robbery to testify that they later identified the defendant as one of them. And it was equally proper for the officer to testify under what circumstances the identification was made. That is as far as the witnesses were allowed to go in giving their testimony. Counsel's objection is without merit. It does not require further discussion." 230 Mich 484, 487, 203 N.W. 93, 94.

Therefore, a literal interpretation of *Londe* would make the testimony concerning the prior identification by the declarant admissible, if the extrajudicial identification was fair. This is consistent with the Federal Rules of Evidence 801(d)(1)(C) and our own proposed Michigan Rule of Evidence 801(d)(1)(C), which is identical to the Federal Rule.

In this case, we are not dealing with the traditional pre-trial line-up, arranged by the police once the suspect is in custody, but a situation where the complaining witness initiated the identification process. Mr. Anderson observed the defendants in a store the day after he was attacked. After observing the defendants, Mr. Anderson called the police and upon their arrival pointed out the defendants, who by then were in a poolroom. There is no suggestion that the identification was unfair, biased or a denial of the defendants' constitutional rights. Surely, so close to the time of the crime this identification had more probative value than one at trial some months later.

* * *

B.   Testimony of Third Party.

Our case law and that of other jurisdictions do not present a clear case for admission of this type of testimony. While most jurisdictions admit the testimony of the identifier as to an extrajudicial identification, most jurisdictions do not admit the testimony of a third party to an extrajudicial identification, except in limited circumstances. The objections to the testimony of the third party are generally the same as those to the testimony of the identifier: its character as hearsay or that it amounts to a bolstering of the identifier's testimony. Where admitted, such testimony has usually been limited to (1) rebuttal of testimony tending to impeach or discredit the testimony of the identifying witness or (2) testimony of the circumstance surrounding the identification.

This Court spoke on the admissibility of such testimony in *Londe,* and allowed the testimony of a police officer as to the circumstances under which the identification was made.

In *Poe,* although the police officer's testimony and handwritten notes concerning the pretrial identification were held inadmissible hearsay, we acknowledged the rule in *Londe* and said:

> "*Londe* restricts the police officer's testimony to 'what took place' and under 'what circumstances the identification was made' and not, as here, the nature or quality of the identification." 388 Mich. 611, 618, 202 N.W.2d 320, 323.

In *Poe,* the facts indicated that the pretrial identification procedures, arranged by the police, were arguably unfair. This Court said:

> "The witnesses were shown a number of police mug shots the night of the holdup and again the next morning. Defendant's photo was in both groups. This would be within standard and proper identification procedures. However, two of the witnesses recalled having been shown photos on the day of the showup and Fannie Evans stated that when she went to the police station for the showup, she was permitted to see defendant before the showup. 'I really didn't look at the others [in the showup] because I saw him [defendant] before I even got there and I recognized him.' When Gary Harbin viewed defendant at a

showup, men used for it, besides the 32-year old defendant, were two teenagers and a 58-year old man." 388 Mich. 611, 616, 202 N.W.2d 320, 322.

This Court concluded that:

"In this case, however, we have identification procedures prior to trial that are at least open to the suspicion of unfairness." 388 Mich. 611, 619, 202 N.W.2d 320, 324.

In this case there is no suspicion that the identification of defendants by the complaining witness was unfair. Mr. Anderson saw the defendants in the drug store. He called the police. When the police arrived, Mr. Anderson pointed out the defendants. This type of identification procedure is one of the fairest available.

* * *

In this case the officer testified to an event he had witnessed, the identification of the defendants by Mr. Anderson, the complaining witness. He was not testifying to the truth of the identification statement but to the fact that it was made and the circumstances surrounding it. Hearsay is defined as a statement, other than one made by the declarant while testifying at the trial or hearing, offered in evidence to prove the truth of the matter asserted.[6] Since the police officer was not testifying to prove that the defendants were the alleged assailants, but only to show that on February 27, 1974 he witnessed an event, the identification of the defendants by Mr. Anderson, his testimony was not hearsay.

* * *

We find the testimony of the complaining witness about calling the police and identifying the defendants to them in a pool hall the day after the crime is not hearsay and was properly admitted under the law expressed in *Londe.* The testimony of the police officer, a third party who witnessed the extrajudicial identification and testified only to the circumstances of the identification procedure, was properly admitted within the discretion of the trial judge.

We affirm.

Moody and Coleman, JJ., concur.

WEINSTEIN'S EVIDENCE

Weinstein-Berger, 1975 (801-3).*

1975 AMENDMENT

Congress amended [Fed.Rule] 801(d) (1)** by adding subparagraph (C) which excludes from the definition of hearsay a statement "of identification of a person made after perceiving him." This subparagraph had been contained in the rules as promulgated by the Supreme Court and as passed by the House of Representatives, but had been struck by the Senate. See *Congressional Changes,* infra. The House had acquiesced in the Senate

*Copyright © 1975 By Matthew Bender & Company Incorporated.

801(d) **Statements which are not hearsay. A statement is not hearsay if—

(1) *Prior statement by witness.* The declarant testifies at the trial or hearing and is subject to cross-examination concerning the statement, and the statement is * * *

version in order to ensure passage of the Rules of Evidence. Statement of Rep. Hungate, Cong.Rec.H. 9653 (daily ed. October 6, 1975). The amendment was signed into law on October 16, 1975 with an effective date of October 31, 1975, P.L. 94-113.

At the Congressional debate on the amendment, it was noted that enactment would return "this section of the hearsay rule to the status it had reached by process of natural judicial evolution," and that this provision had been deleted only because of strenuous objection by Senator Ervin which jeopardized passage of the Rules of Evidence. Cong.Rec. H9654 (daily ed. Oct. 6, 1975).

The Report of the Senate Committee on the Judiciary considering the amendment explained this opposition as stemming from concern "that a conviction could be based upon such unsworn, out-of-court testimony." However, the Report noted that this was a misconception since all constitutional protections were retained and in addition, the requirements of Rule 801(d) (1) that the identifier be available for cross-examination at the trial is continued. The Report reads:

> The purpose of the provision was to make clear, in line with the recent law in the area, that nonsuggestive lineup, photographic and other identifications are not hearsay and therefore are admissible. In the lineup case of Gilbert v. California, 388 U.S. 263, 272 n. 3 (1967), the Supreme Court, noting the split of authority in admitting prior out-of-court identifications, stated, "The recent trend, however, is to admit the prior identification under the exception [to the hearsay rule] that admits as substantive evidence a prior communication by a witness who is available for cross-examination at the trial." And the Federal Courts of Appeals have generally admitted these identifications.

* * *

In the course of processing the Rules of Evidence in the final weeks of the 93d Congress, the provision excluding such statements of identification from the hearsay category was deleted. Although there was no suggestion in the committee report that prior identifications are not probative, concern was there expressed that a conviction could be based upon such unsworn, out-of-court testimony. Upon further reflection, that concern appears misdirected. First, this exception is addressed to the "admissibility" of evidence and not to the "sufficiency" of evidence to prove guilt. Secondly, except for the former testimony exception to the hearsay exclusion, all hearsay exceptions allow into evidence statements which may not have been made under oath. Moreover, under this rule, unlike a significant majority of the hearsay exceptions, the prior identification is admissible only when the person who made it testifies at trial and is subject to cross-examination. This assures that if any discrepancy occurs between the witness' in-court and out-of-court testimony, the opportunity is available to probe, with the witness under oath, the reasons for that discrepancy so that the trier of fact might determine which statement is to be believed.

Upon reflection, then, it appears the rule is desirable. Since these identifications take place reasonably soon after an offense has been committed, the witness' observations are still fresh in his mind. The identification occurs before his recollection has been dimmed by the passage of time. Equally as important, it also takes place before the defendant or some other party has had the opportunity, through bribe or threat, to influence the witness to change his mind.

* * *

See Federal Rules of Evidence 801(d)(1) at p. 922; California Evidence Code § 1238 at p. 880.

Hypotheticals

(1) X is prosecuted for robbery of A. A testifies that he was held up at gunpoint, that the next day he went to the police station and identified the man who robbed him, and that he is sure he picked the right man but can't remember now the person he identified. The prosecution then calls B, a police officer, and represents that B will testify that A came to the station the day after the crime and that, while X was being led through the hall, A yelled: "There goes the man who robbed me" and pointed at X. X makes a hearsay objection to B's proposed testimony. What result?

(2) Assume the same facts as in Illustration (1), except that A has no recollection of making a pretrial identification of X or any other person at the police station. The prosecution then offers B's testimony of A's pretrial identification of X at the police station. X makes a hearsay objection to B's testimony. How should the court rule?

9. PAST RECOLLECTION RECORDED

BAKER v. STATE

Court of Special Appeals of Maryland, April 12, 1977.
35 Md.App. 593, 371, A.2d 699.

MOYLAN, Judge.

This appeal addresses the intriguing question of what latitude a judge should permit counsel when a witness takes the stand and says, "I don't remember." What are the available keys that may unlock the testimonial treasure vaults of the subconscious? What are the brush strokes that may be employed "to retouch the fading daguerreotype of memory?" The subject is that of Present Recollection Revived.[2]

The appellant, Teretha McNeil Baker, was convicted by a Baltimore City jury of both murder in the first degree and robbery. Although she raises two appellate contentions, the only one which we find it necessary to consider is her claim that the trial judge erroneously refused her the opportunity to refresh the present recollection of a police witness by showing him a report written by a fellow officer.

The ultimate source of most of the evidence implicating the appellant was the robbery and murder victim himself, Gaither Martin, a now-dead declarant who spoke to the jury through the hearsay conduit of Officer

---

2. Frequently and alternatively referred to as Present Recollection Refreshed.

Bolton.[3] When Officer Bolton arrived at the crime scene, the victim told him that he had "picked these three ladies up ＊ ＊ ＊ at the New Deal Bar"; that when he took them to their stated destination, a man walked up to the car and pulled him out; that "the other three got out and proceeded to kick him and beat him." It was the assertion made by the victim to the officer that established that his money, wallet and keys had been taken. The critical impasse, for present purposes, occurred when the officer was questioned, on cross-examination, about what happened en route to the hospital. The officer had received a call from Officer Hucke, of the Western District, apparently to the effect that a suspect had been picked up. Before proceeding to the hospital, Officer Bolton took the victim to the place where Officer Hucke was holding the appellant. The appellant, as part of this cross-examination, sought to elicit from the officer the fact that the crime victim confronted the appellant and stated that the appellant was not one of those persons who had attacked and robbed him. To stimulate the present memory of Officer Bolton, appellant's counsel attempted to show him the police report relating to that confrontation and prepared by Officer Hucke.

The record establishes loudly and clearly that appellant's counsel sought to use the report primarily to refresh the recollection of Officer Bolton and that he was consistently and effectively thwarted in that attempt:

"BY MR. HARLAN:

Q. Do you have the report filed by Officer Hucke and Officer Saclolo or Saclolo?

A. Right, I have copies.

Q. Okay.

MR. DOORY: I would object to that, Your Honor.

THE COURT: I will sustain the objection. This is not his report.

BY MR. HARLAN:

Q. Can you look at this report and refresh your recollection as to whether or not you ever had the victim in a confrontation with Mrs. Baker?

MR. DOORY: Objection, Your Honor.

MR. HARLAN: He can refresh—

THE COURT: Well, he can refresh his recollection as to his personal knowledge. That's all right.

A. That is what I am saying, I don't know who it was that we confronted really.

BY MR. HARLAN:

Q. All right. Would you consult your report and maybe it will refresh your recollection.

THE COURT: I think the response is he doesn't know who—

---

3. The exception to the Hearsay Rule urged by the State and utilized by the court to make the out-of-court assertion admissible was the "excited utterance" exception and not the "dying declaration" exception. We are not here considering the admissibility of this hearsay, but are rather assuming it to have been admissible.

MR. HARLAN: He can refresh his recollection if he looks at the report.

THE COURT: He can't refresh his recollection from someone else's report, Mr. Harlan.

MR. HARLAN: I would object, Your Honor. Absolutely he can.

THE COURT: You might object, but—

MR. HARLAN: You are not going to permit the officer to refresh his recollection from the police report?

THE COURT: No. It is not his report.

* * *

MR. HARLAN: Your Honor, I think I am absolutely within my rights to have a police officer read a report which mentions his name in it to see if it refreshes his recollection. If it doesn't refresh his recollection, then fine.

THE COURT: Well, he did that.

MR. HARLAN: You have not afforded him the opportunity to do that yet, Your Honor.

THE COURT: He says he does not know who it was before. So, he can't refresh his recollection if he does not know simply because someone else put some name in there.

MR. HARLAN: He has to read it to see if it refreshes his recollection, Your Honor.

THE COURT: We are reading from a report made by two other officers which is not the personal knowledge of this officer.

MR. HARLAN: I don't want him to read from that report. I want him to read it and see if it refreshes his recollection."

On so critical an issue as possible exculpation from the very lips of the crime victim, appellant was entitled to try to refresh the memory of the key police witness. She was erroneously and prejudicially denied that opportunity. The reason for the error is transparent. Because they both arise from the common seedbed of failed memory and because of their hauntingly parallel verbal rhythms and grammatical structures, there is a beguiling temptation to over analogize Present Recollection Revived and Past Recollection Recorded. It is a temptation, however, that must be resisted. The trial judge in this case erroneously measured the legitimacy of the effort to revive present recollection against the more rigorous standards for the admissibility of a recordation of past memory.

It is, of course, hornbook law that when a party seeks to introduce a record of past recollection, he must establish (1) that the record was made by or adopted by the witness at a time when the witness did have a recollection of the event and (2) that the witness can presently vouch for the fact that when the record was made or adopted by him, he knew that it was accurate. McCormick, Law of Evidence (1st Ed., 1954), describes the criteria, at 15:

"Appropriate safeguarding rules have been developed for this latter kind of memoranda, requiring that they must have been written by the witness or examined and found correct by him, and that they must have been prepared so promptly after the events recorded that these must have been fresh in the mind of the witness when the record was made or examined and verified by him. We have treated such memoranda separately, as an exception to the hearsay rule."

Had the appellant herein sought to offer the police report as a record of past recollection on the part of Officer Bolton, it is elementary that she would have had to show, *inter alia,* that the report had either been prepared by Officer Bolton himself or had been read by him and that he can now say that at that time he knew it was correct. Absent such a showing, the trial judge would have been correct in declining to receive it in evidence.

When dealing with an instance of Past Recollection Recorded, the reason for the rigorous standards of admissibility is quite clear. Those standards exist to test the competence of the report or document in question. Since the piece of paper itself, in effect, speaks to the jury, the piece of paper must pass muster in terms of its evidentiary competence.

Not so with Present Recollection Revived! By marked contrast to Past Recollection Recorded, no such testimonial competence is demanded of a mere stimulus to present recollection, for the stimulus itself is never evidence. Notwithstanding the surface similarity between the two phenomena, the difference between them could not be more basic. *It is the difference between evidence and non-evidence.* Of such mere stimuli or memory-prods, McCormick says, at 18, "[T]he cardinal rule is that they are not evidence, but only aids in the giving of evidence." When we are dealing with an instance of Present Recollection Revived, the only source of evidence is the testimony of the witness himself. The stimulus may have jogged the witness's dormant memory, but the stimulus itself is not received in evidence. Dean McCormick makes it clear that even when the stimulus is a writing, when the witness "speaks from a memory thus revived, his testimony is what he says, not the writing." Id., at 15. McCormick describes the psychological phenomenon in the following terms:

"It is abundantly clear from every-day observation that the latent memory of an experience may be revived by an image seen, or a statement read or heard. It is a part of the group of phenomena which the classical psychologists have called the law of association. The recall of any part of a past experience tends to bring with it the other parts that were in the same field of awareness, and a new experience tends to stimulate the recall of other like experiences." Id., at 14.

The psychological community is in full agreement with the legal community in assessing the mental phenomenon. See Cairn, Law and the Social Sciences 200 (1935):

"In permitting a witness to refresh his recollection by consulting a memorandum, the courts are in accord with present psychological knowledge. A distinction is drawn, in the analysis of the memory process, between *recall,* which is the reproduction of what has been learned, and *recognition,* which is recall with a time-factor added, or an awareness that the recall relates to past experience. It is with recognition that the law is principally concerned in permitting a witness to revive his recollection. The psychological evidence is clear that in thus allowing to be brought to mind what has been forgotten, the law is following sound psychological procedure."

* * *

The catalytic agent or memory stimulator is put aside, once it has worked its psychological magic, and the witness then testifies on the basis of the now-refreshed memory. The opposing party, of course, has the right to inspect the memory aid, be it a writing or otherwise, and even to show it to the jury. This examination, however, is not for the purpose of testing the competence of the memory aid (for competence is immaterial where the thing in question is not evidence) but only to test whether the witness's memory has in truth been refreshed. As McCormick warns, "But the witness must swear that he is genuinely refreshed. * * * And he cannot be allowed to read the writing in the guise of refreshment, as a cloak for getting in evidence an inadmissible document." One of the most thorough reviews of this aspect of evidence law is found in the United States v. Riccardi, 174 F.2d 883 (3rd Cir., 1949), where the court said at 888:

"In the case of present recollection revived, the witness, by hypothesis, relates his present recollection, and under oath and subject to cross-examination asserts that it is true; his capacities for memory and perception may be attacked and tested; his determination to tell the truth investigated and revealed; protestations of lack of memory, which escape criticism and indeed constitute a refuge in the situation of past recollection recorded, merely undermine the probative worth of his testimony."

* * *

When the writing in question is to be utilized simply "to awaken a slumbering recollection of an event" in the mind of the witness, the writing may be a memorandum made by the witness himself, 1) even if it was not made immediately after the event, 2) even if it was not made of firsthand knowledge and 3) even if the witness cannot now vouch for the fact that it was accurate when made. It may be a memorandum made by one other than the witness, even if never before read by the witness or vouched for by him. It may be an Associated Press account. It may be a highly selective version of the incident at the hands of a Hemingway or an Eliot. All that is required is that it ignite the flash of accurate recall—that it accomplish the revival which is sought.

McCormick wrote to just such effect:

"[I]t is probable that most courts today when faced with the clear distinction between the two uses of the memoranda, will adhere to the 'classical' view that any memorandum or other object may be used as a stimulus to present memory, without restriction by rule as to authorship, guaranty of correctness, or time of making."

The Texas dean is in good company, for no less eminent an authority than Lord Ellenborough said in Henry v. Lee, 2 Chitty 124, 125 (1810):

"If upon looking at *any* document he can so far refresh his memory as to recollect a circumstance, it is sufficient; and it makes no difference that the memorandum is not written by himself, for it is not the memorandum that is the evidence but the recollection of the witness."

Not only may the writing to be used as a memory aid fall short of the rigorous standards of competence required of a record of past recollection, the memory aid itself need not even be a writing. What may it be? It may be anything. It may be a line from Kipling or the dolorous refrain of "The Tennessee Waltz"; a whiff of hickory smoke; the running of the fingers across a swatch of corduroy; the sweet carbonation of a chocolate soda; the sight of a faded snapshot in a long-neglected album. All that is required is that it may trigger the Proustian moment.[11] It may be anything which produces the desired testimonial prelude, "It all comes back to me now."

* * *

Although the use of a memorandum of some sort will continue quantitatively to dominate the field of refreshing recollection, we are better able to grasp the process conceptually if we appreciate that the use of a memorandum as a memory aid is not a legal phenomenon unto itself but only an instance of a far broader phenomenon. In a more conventional mode, the process might proceed, "Your Honor, I am about to show the witness a written report, ask him to read it and then inquire if he can now testify from his own memory thus refreshed." In a far less conventional mode, the process could just as well proceed, "Your Honor, I am pleased to present to the court Miss Rosa Ponselle who will now sing 'Celeste Aida' for the witness, for that is what was playing on the night the burglar came through the window." Whether by conventional or unconventional means, precisely the same end is sought. One is looking for the effective elixir to revitalize dimming memory and make it live again in the service of the search for truth.

Even in the more conventional mode, it is quite clear that in this case the appropriate effort of the appellant to jog the arguably dormant memory of the key police witness on a vital issue was unduly and prejudicially restricted.

Judgments reversed; case remanded for a new trial; costs to be paid by mayor and city council of Baltimore.

ADAMS v. THE NEW YORK CENTRAL R. CO.

Court of Common Pleas, Cuyahoga County, Cleveland, Ohio, 1961.
Docket No. 724,072.

[This was an action for the recovery of damages for personal injuries. Defendant's theory was that the injury claimed by plaintiff had in fact never occurred and that plaintiff's quadraplegia stemmed from an injury antedating the claimed injury. One of the few ways in which defendant could hope to establish its theory was by introduction, as past recollection recorded, of a memorandum made by an insurance company employee of an interview with plaintiff. According to the memorandum, plaintiff had mentioned the antecedent injury but had made no reference to any injury of the sort claimed at trial. Following are key portions of the trial transcript showing the efforts of chief defense counsel, James C. Davis, Esq., of the Cleveland Bar, to secure admission of the memorandum—Ed.]

---

11. Marcel Proust, in his monumental epic In Remembrance of Things Past, sat, as a middle-aged man, sipping a cup of lime-flavored tea and eating a madeleine, a small French pastry. Through both media, two long-forgotten tastes from childhood were reawakened. By association, long-forgotten memories from the same period of childhood came welling and surging back. Once those floodgates of recall were opened, seven volumes followed.

DIRECT EXAMINATION

BY MR. DAVIS:

    Q. Will you state your name?

    A. Eugene F. Raith.

    Q. Where do you live?

    A. I live at 20705 Harvard Road, Warrensville Heights, Ohio.

* * *

    Q. What is your business?

    A. Home Office Inspector, employed by the John Hancock Mutual Life Insurance Company.

    Q. How long have you been employed with John Hancock?

    A. 40 years.

    Q. In your capacity with John Hancock, did you in 1957 call on a gentleman named Theodore H. Adams at a time when he was a patient in Highland View Hospital?

    A. I did.

    Q. What was your purpose in calling on Mr. Adams?

    A. To seek any information to be used in evaluation of his disability claim that he had presented to our insurance company as an insured.

    Q. At that time did you interview him?

    A. I did.

    Q. During the interview, or immediately thereafter, did you make a written record of what he told you—of the information you obtained?

    A. Yes, sir.

* * *

    Q. Do you have with you your file on this particular matter?

    A. Yes.

    Q. May I have it? First, the written record which you made, either during your interview or thereafter, was a record in longhand, was it not?

    A. Yes.

    Q. Have you ever testified as a witness before?

    A. No.

    Q. Well, it really is not as painful as it looks.

    A. Thank you. I would change places with you.

* * *

    Q. Now, Mr. Raith, do you at this time have any independent recollection of the subject-matter of the conversation between you and Mr. Adams—that is, what he told you and what you asked him —independent of the notes which you made at that time?

    A. I do not.

Q.   Do you recognize the gentleman at the end of the [counsel] table as the gentleman that you talked to?

A.   I believe so.

Q.   I hand you what has been marked Defendant's Exhibit OO. Now that piece of paper has writing on both sides, does it not?

A.   Yes.

Q.   Tell me, if you will, whether or not the notes that you made of your conversation with Mr. Adams appear on only one side or both sides of that page.

A.   Only on one side.

                    *   *   *

Q.   Now, was the information that is contained on the page that is marked Defendant's Exhibit OO   *   *   *   obtained entirely from the interview with Mr. Adams?

A.   Yes, entirely from Mr. Adams.

Q.   At the time you wrote that Exhibit OO   *   *   *   did it accurately record what he had told you?

A.   Yes.

                    *   *   *

Q.   Was [the interview] recorded in exactly the words which Mr. Adams gave you, or not?

A.   I would be inclined to believe that when I talked to Mr. Adams I made notes rougher than these, and at the conclusion of the interview I made a recap. I say that because of the sequence; it would have been a recap of what I made previously. However, it came from Mr. Adams, no one else.

                    *   *   *

Q.   Are there certain facts recorded on Exhibit OO?

A.   Right.

Q.   When did you record the facts on Exhibit OO with reference to the time of your interview with Mr. Adams?

A.   At the time or shortly thereafter.

Q.   Were the facts obtained from Mr. Adams accurately recorded by you on Exhibit OO?

A.   Yes.

Q.   At the time you made Defendant's Exhibit OO, did you or did you not know it was accurate so far as facts obtained by you from Mr. Adams were concerned?

A.   I did.

Q.   Without telling me what it is, Mr. Raith, is it not a fact that Defendant's Exhibit OO records the fact of an injury which Mr. Adams told you he had received?

A.   Yes.

Q.   Did you record whatever he told you about injuries?

A.   I did.

MR. DAVIS: At this time defendant offers in evidence Defendant's Exhibit OO as evidence of past recollection recorded.

MR. DUDNIK: It is entirely improper.

THE COURT: We will recess until 1:30.

(Thereupon the jury left the Courtroom and the following further proceedings were had in the absence of the jury:)

THE COURT: Proceed, Mr. Davis.

MR. DAVIS: If the Court please, in these circumstances there are two ways in which a witness may properly proceed. First, he may look at a memorandum made at the time and, on the basis of his refreshed recollection, testify. Then he is testifying from his present recollection refreshed. On the other hand, the law is perfectly clear that a witness having no such present refreshed recollection may testify that he made a record of the event at a time in the past and that he knew at the time the record was made that the record was accurate. That record is admissible as past recollection recorded as distinguished from present recollection refreshed. Dean Wigmore says, in Volume 3, Section 734 of the third edition of his work on evidence. * * * [Quotation omitted.]

THE COURT: I will hear from Mr. Dudnik.

MR DUDNIK: My associate, Mr. Nurenberg, will argue the point, your Honor.

MR. NURENBERG: These notes do not fill the bill. Office records might be permitted into evidence, providing certain qualifications are met. The witness stated that even by looking at the exhibit he can't refresh his recollection. * * * The witness said he saw Mr. Adams at Highland View Hospital and, apparently, he has some recollection. * * * The most important thing is that the document [Defendant's Exhibit OO], on its face is not a document at all. It is merely a piece of paper with some pencil jotting; this is not a document. * * * If I talk to you and I go home and jot down with pencil on a piece of paper what you told me, even though they are an accurate recollection * * * I can't come into Court and say they are what you told me, Judge White. I can't come into Court and introduce a pencil note. That is what they are trying to do. That is not past recollection recorded. Past recollection recorded is when a man, in the routine order of business, makes a certain document at or contemporaneous with the subject-matter, not a pencil jotting. * * * That is hearsay in its purest form. Every record is not *ipso facto* a business record.

* * *

MR DAVIS: Your Honor, Mr. Dudnik has given you a case in 156 Northwestern at page 867. That is a case cited by Wigmore. If you will notice, Wigmore does not restrict past recollection recorded to papers that, in the technical sense, constitute business records. The very case cited to you by Mr. Dudnik involved a memorandum taken down by an insurance agent in connection with a policy.

* * *

THE COURT: The Court has examined, necessarily with some haste, the cases cited to it. * * * The fact that the witness has testified that his own recollection is not refreshed [by Defendant's Exhibit OO] persuades the Court that the exhibit is not admissible at this time.

*   *   *

Thereupon the defendant, further to maintain the issues on its part to be maintained, recalled as a witness, EUGENE F. RAITH, who, having been previously duly sworn, was examined and testified further as follows:

BY MR. DAVIS:

Q.   Now, Mr. Raith, I hand you once more Defendant's Exhibit OO, and ask you if you will read it through again. To yourself, not out loud.

Q.   Have you finished?

A.   Yes, sir.

Q.   Having read Exhibit OO, will you tell me whether or not your memory has been refreshed so that you now have a present recollection of your interview with Mr. Adams at Highland View Hospital, and of what he told you on that occasion?

A.   No, it has not.

Q.   It has not what?

A.   It has not been refreshed by reading these notes.

Q.   Then do you or do you not at this time have any present recollection of what Mr. Adams told you at the time you interviewed him at Highland View Hospital?

A.   Other than these notes, I do not.

Q.   Do the notes refresh your recollection so that you now have a recollection, or do they not?

A.   No, they do not refresh my recollection

*   *   *

Q.   Now, at the time you made the writings on Exhibit OO, did you have a clear recollection of what Mr. Adams had told you?

A.   Very clear.

MR. DAVIS: I reoffer Defendant's Exhibit OO, your Honor.

MR. DUDNIK: The same objection.

THE COURT: The objection is sustained.

MR. DAVIS: That is all, Mr. Raith.

NOTE

Do you agree with the rulings of the trial court? Did attorney Davis fail in some significant respect to lay the proper foundation for admission into evidence of the memorandum?

The trial of Adams v. The New York Central R.R. Co. resulted in a verdict for plaintiff in the sum of $300,000. In its motion for a new trial defendant argued that rejection of the proffered memorandum was prejudicial error. Before further proceedings were had, the case was settled for a sum substantially less than the verdict.

———

See Federal Rules of Evidence 803(5) at p. 923; California Evidence Code § 1237 at p. 880.

———

See Federal Rules of Evidence 612 at p. 918; California Evidence Code § 771 at p. 837.

Hypothetical

(1)   X is prosecuted for robbery. The prosecution calls A, who testifies that she saw the getaway car and noticed the license number, and that ten minutes later a police officer came to the scene and she told him exactly what license number she observed, but that she has no recollection now of that number. The prosecution then calls B, a police officer, who testifies that at the robbery scene A told him the license number of the getaway car she had seen and that he wrote correctly on a sheet in his book the number stated by A, and produces the sheet. The prosecutor asks B to read the license number written on the sheet. X makes a hearsay objection to the prosecutor's question. How should the court rule?

10.   BUSINESS AND PUBLIC RECORDS

MARYLAND—DISTRICT OF COLUMBIA—VIRGINIA CRIMINAL PRACTICE INSTITUTE TRIAL MANUAL

2-5, 2-9 (1964).*

2.02   Introducing Business Records**

1.   Your Honor, I would like to have this instrument marked as defense exhibit #1 for identification.

2.   State your name.

3.   Where do you reside, Mr. [witness]?

4.   And what is your occupation?

5.   Where are you employed?

6.   What is the nature of your employer's business?

7.   And what is the nature of your work there?

8.   Were you so employed there on [date in question]?

9.   Now, as the [position title], do you have responsibility of keeping the records concerning [subject matter]?

10.   What is the method utilized for keeping these records?

11.   Is this followed with respect to every [entry] [patient, etc.]?

12.   I show you defendant's exhibit #1 for identification, purporting to be [document title], and ask you whether these are the original records which you have kept in your position?

13.   Were these records in your custody on [date]?

14.   And were they in your custody prior to your bringing them to court this morning?

15.   Where were they kept?

16.   Were the entries made herein made shortly after the transaction they record?

17.   Who provided the information contained therein?

18.   Was it his duty to collect this data and pass it on to you?

---

*Copyright, 1964, by Lerner Law Book Company.   **On the authentication of writings, see Chapter I, Making the Record, supra.

19. And were these entries made in the usual and ordinary course of business?

20. To the best of your knowledge, are they true and correct?

[Then move the admission of defense exhibit #1 for identification into evidence.]

JOHNSON v LUTZ

Court of Appeals of New York, 1930.
253 N.Y. 124, 170 N.E. 517.

HUBBS, J. This action is to recover damages for the wrongful death of the plaintiff's intestate, who was killed when his motorcycle came into collision with the defendants' truck at a street intersection. There was a sharp conflict in the testimony in regard to the circumstances under which the collision took place. A policeman's report of the accident filed by him in the station house was offered in evidence by the defendants under section 374–a of the Civil Practice Act, and was excluded. The sole ground for reversal urged by the appellants is that said report was erroneously excluded. That section reads: "Any writing or record, whether in form of an entry in a book or otherwise, made as a memorandum or record of any act, transaction, occurence or event, shall be admissible in evidence in proof of said act, transaction, occurrence or event, if the trial judge shall find that it was made in the regular course of any business, and that it was the regular course of such business to make such memorandum or record at the time of such act, transaction, occurrence or event, or within a reasonable time thereafter. All other circumstances of the making of such writing or record, including lack of personal knowledge by the entrant or maker, may be shown to affect its weight, but they shall not affect its admissibility. The term business shall include business, profession, occupation and calling of every kind."

Prior to the decision in the well-known case of Vosburgh v. Thayer, 12 Johns. 461, decided in 1815, shopbooks could not be introduced in evidence to prove an account. The decision in that case established that they were admissible where preliminary proof could be made that there were regular dealings between the parties; that the plaintiff kept honest and fair books; that some of the articles charged had been delivered; and that the plaintiff kept no clerk. At that time it might not have been a hardship to require a shopkeeper who sued to recover an account to furnish the preliminary proof required by that decision. Business was transacted in a comparatively small way, with few, if any, clerks. Since the decision in that case, it has remained the substantial basis of all decisions upon the question in this jurisdiction prior to the enactment in 1928 of section 374–a, Civil Practice Act.

Under modern conditions, the limitations upon the right to use books of account, memoranda, or records, made in the regular course of business, often resulted in a denial of justice, and usually in annoyance, expense, and waste of time and energy. A rule of evidence that was practical a century ago had become obsolete. The situation was appreciated, and attention was called to it by the courts and textwriters.

The report of the Legal Research Committee of the Commonwealth Fund, published in 1927, by the Yale University Press, under the title, "The Law of Evidence—Some Proposals for Its Reform," dealt with the question in chapter 5, under the heading, "Proof of Business Transactions to Harmo-

nize with Current Business Practice." That report, based upon extensive research, pointed out the confusion existing in decisions in different jurisdictions. It explained and illustrated the great need of a more practical,
workable, and uniform rule, adapted to modern business conditions and
practices. The chapter is devoted to a discussion of the pressing need of a
rule of evidence which would "give evidential credit to the books upon
which the mercantile and industrial world relies in the conduct of business." At the close of the chapter, the committee proposed a statute to be
enacted in all jurisdictions. In compliance with such proposal, the Legislature enacted section 374–a of the Civil Practice Act in the very words used
by the committee.

It is apparent that the Legislature enacted section 374–a to carry out
the purpose announced in the report of the committee. That purpose was to
secure the enactment of a statute which would afford a more workable rule
of evidence in the proof of business transactions under existing business
conditions.

In view of the history of section 374–a and the purpose for which it was
enacted, it is apparent that it was never intended to apply to a situation like
that in the case at bar. The memorandum in question was not made in the
regular course of any business, profession, occupation, or calling. The policeman who made it was not present at the time of the accident. The memorandum was made from hearsay statements of third persons who happened
to be present at the scene of the accident when he arrived. It does not appear whether they saw the accident and stated to him what they knew, or
stated what some other persons had told them.

The purpose of the Legislature in enacting section 374–a was to permit
a writing or record, made in the regular course of business, to be received in
evidence, without the necessity of calling as witnesses all of the persons who
had any part in making it, provided the record was made as a part of the
duty of the person making it, or on information imparted by persons who
were under a duty to impart such information. The amendment permits the
introduction of shopbooks without the necessity of calling all clerks who
may have sold different items of account. It was not intended to permit the
receipt in evidence of entries based upon voluntary hearsay statements
made by third parties not engaged in the business or under any duty in relation thereto. It was said, in Mayor, etc., of New York City v. Second Ave. R.
Co., 102 N.Y. 572, at page 581, 7 N.E. 905, 909, 55 Am.Rep. 839: "It is a
proper qualification of the rule admitting such evidence that the account
must have been made in the ordinary course of business, and that it should
not be extended so as to admit a mere private memorandum, not made in
pursuance of any duty owing by the person making it, or when made upon
information derived from another who made the communication casually
and voluntarily, and not under the sanction of duty or other obligation."

An important consideration leading to the amendment was the fact
that in the business world credit is given to records made in the course of
business by persons who are engaged in the business upon information given
by others engaged in the same business as part of their duty.

"Such entries are dealt with in that way in the most important undertakings of mercantile and industrial life. They are the ultimate basis of calculation, investment, and general confidence in every business enterprise.

Nor does the practical impossibility of obtaining constantly and permanently the verification of every employee affect the trust that is given to such books. It would seem that expedients which the entire commercial world recognizes as safe could be sanctioned, and not discredited, by courts of justice. When it is a mere question of whether provisional confidence can be placed in a certain class of statements, there cannot profitably and sensibly be one rule for the business world and another for the court-room. The merchant and the manufacturer must not be turned away remediless because the methods in which the entire community places a just confidence are a little difficult to reconcile with technical judicial scruples on the part of the same persons who as attorneys have already employed and relied upon the same methods. In short, courts must here cease to be pedantic and endeavor to be practical." 3 Wigmore on Evidence (1923) § 1530, p. 278.

The Legislature has sought by the amendment to make the courts practical. It would be unfortunate not to give the amendment a construction which will enable it to cure the evil complained of and accomplish the purpose for which it was enacted. In construing it, we should not, however, permit it to be applied in a case for which it was never intended.

The judgment should be affirmed, with costs.

Cardozo, C.J., and Pound, Crane, Lehman, Kellogg, and O'Brien, JJ., concur.

Judgment affirmed.

Hypotheticals

Examine the following hypotheticals involving a suit by A against B arising out of an automobile accident. What should be the result in each case?

The police report contains the following statement:

a. "I was standing at my beat and the red Chevrolet [which we now know to be the defendant's car] went through the red light and struck the green Ford [which other testimony shows as the plaintiff's car]."

b. "I arrived at one thirty [which other evidence indicates was twenty minutes after the accident] and noticed a skid mark, which I measured at 93 feet, leading directly to the rear wheels of the Chevrolet."

c. "I arrived within twenty seconds of the impact and heard a bystander scream, 'Did you see that crazy red car go through the red light?' "

d "I arrived a few minutes after the accident and asked the man in the red Chevrolet what happened. He stated that he had fallen asleep at the wheel and did not rightly know."

e. "I arrived a few minutes after the accident and Officer Jones approached me and said that he had seen the accident and that the red Chevrolet had gone through the red light and hit the green Ford."

f. "I arrived a few minutes after the accident and Officer Jones had told me that he had gotten there just before I did and asked the Chevrolet driver what had happened and that he had said, 'I fell asleep at the wheel and I don't rightly know.' "

g. "I arrived a few minutes after the accident and I asked a bystander what had happened. He said that he had seen it all and the red Chevrolet was going too fast and couldn't stop for the red light and went right through the red light and hit the green Ford."

DEAN JEROME PRINCE, "THE HEARSAY RULE" IN TRIAL EVIDENCE

18-1, 18-8 (Schreiber ed. 1967).*

Johnson v. Lutz has been very severely criticized by commentators on the grounds that the court read into the statute a requirement not expressly to be found in it, a requirement that the informant, or one imparting the information must be under a business duty or obligation to impart the information.

I think that that requirement has much merit.

Business records are trustworthy because they are based upon reports made by persons who are under a routine duty to record it.

The business cannot function if there are reports that are inaccurate and the informant will not long last in the business if his observations or reports are inaccurate.

No such high probability of trustworthiness attaches to reports based upon information supplied by a person unconnected with the business who gives the information voluntarily and casually.

And the Court of Appeals in Cox v. State, 3 N.Y.2d 693, 148 N.E. 2d 879, 171 N.Y.S.2d 818 (1958), reaffirmed the rule announced in Johnson v. Lutz.

2. *The Rule in Kelly v. Wasserman*

The requirement that the informant be under a duty to give information has apparently been disregarded in a recent case. In Kelly v Wasserman, 5 N.Y.2d 425, 158 N.E.2d 241, 185 N.Y.S.2d 538 (1959), the plaintiff conveyed her house to the defendant in exchange for the defendant's oral promise to pay her debts and to allow her to live rent-free in the house.

Later, a dispute arose concerning the terms of the occupancy. The plaintiff said that the oral agreement was that she was to live rent-free in that house for life. The defendant said, "No," the agreement was that she was to live rent-free in that house only so long as the Housing Department did not object to the number of tenants in the house.

The plaintiff was a welfare beneficiary. On the trial the plaintiff offered in evidence an entry in the records of the Welfare Department pertaining to her welfare case. These were entries made by Welfare Department employees in the regular course of their business and were made by persons supervising the plaintiff's welfare case.

The entries offered in evidence were entries to this effect: that in several conversations had between the Welfare Department employees and the defendant, the defendant said that he had agreed to allow the plaintiff to live rent-free for life in that house.

The Court of Appeals held that this entry, or these entries, were admissible under the Statutory Business Records Rule, saying that the entries pertaining to the plaintiff's shelter were germane to the welfare business and the entries were made in the regular course of the business of the Welfare Department.

*Foundation Press, Brooklyn, N.Y.

Now, it is quite plain that the entries were made by the employees of the Welfare Department in the regular course of their business. But, was the defendant a person under a business duty or obligation to impart that information within the contemplation of the rule laid down by Johnson v. Lutz?

The Court of Apeals in Kelly v. Wasserman did not discuss at all, or even mention, the requirement that the informant must be under a business duty or obligation to impart the information.

Regarding Multiple Hearsay, see Federal Rules of Evidence 805 at p. 928; California Evidence Code § 1201, at p. 877.

Hypotheticals

Should a newspaper reporter's notes be admissible as a business record? A newspaper itself? A clipping from the newspaper's back-issue library?

PALMER v. HOFFMAN

Supreme Court of the United States, 1943.
318 U.S. 109, 63 S.Ct. 477, 87 L.Ed. 645.
[Most of the Court's footnotes are omitted.]

Mr. Justice DOUGLAS delivered the opinion of the Court.

This case arose out of a grade crossing accident which occurred in Massachusetts. Diversity of citizenship brought it to the federal District Court in New York. There were several causes of action. The first two were on behalf of respondent individually, one being brought under a Massachusetts statute (Mass.Gen.L. (1932) c. 160, §§ 138, 232), the other at common law. The third and fourth were brought by respondent as administrator of the estate of his wife and alleged the same common law and statutory negligence as the first two counts. On the question of negligence the trial court submitted three issues to the jury—failure to ring a bell, to blow a whistle, to have a light burning in the front of the train. The jury returned a verdict in favor of respondent individually for some $25,000 and in favor of respondent as administrator for $9,000. The District Court entered judgment on the verdict. The Circuit Court of Appeals affirmed, one judge dissenting. 129 F.2d 976. The case is here on a petition for a writ of certiorari which presents three points.

I. The accident occurred on the night of December 25, 1940. On December 27, 1940, the engineer of the train, who died before the trial, made a statement at a freight office of petitioners where he was interviewed by an assistant superintendent of the road and by a representative of the Massachusetts Public Utilities Commission. See Mass.Gen.L. (1932) c. 159, § 29. This statement was offered in evidence by petitioners under the Act of June 20, 1936, 49 Stat. 1561, 28 U.S.C. § 695.[1] They offered to prove (in the lan-

---

1. "In any court of the United States and in any court established by Act of Congress, any writing or record, whether in the form of an entry in a book or otherwise, made as a memorandum or record of any act, transaction, occurrence, or event, shall be admissible as evidence of said act, transaction, occurrence, or event, if it shall appear that it was made in the regular course of any business, and that it was the regular course of such business to make such memorandum or record at the time of such act, transaction, occurrence, or event or within a reasonable time thereafter. All other circumstances of the making of such writing or record, including lack of personal knowledge by the entrant or maker, may be shown to affect its weight, but they shall not affect its admissibility. The term 'business' shall include business, profession, occupation, and calling of every kind."

guage of the Act) that the statement was signed in the regular course of business, it being the regular course of such business to make such a statement. Respondent's objection to its introduction was sustained.

We agree with the majority view below that it was properly excluded.

We may assume that if the statement was made "in the regular course" of business, it would satisfy the other provisions of the Act. But we do not think that it was made "in the regular course" of business within the meaning of the Act. The business of the petitioners is the railroad business. That business like other enterprises entails the keeping of numerous books and records essential to its conduct or useful in its efficient operation. Though such books and records were considered reliable and trustworthy for major decisions in the industrial and business world, their use in litigation was greatly circumscribed or hedged about by the hearsay rule—restrictions which greatly increased the time and cost of making the proof where those who made the records were numerous. It was that problem which started the movement towards adoption of legislation embodying the principles of the present Act. And the legislative history of the Act indicates the same purpose.

The engineer's statement which was held inadmissible in this case falls into quite a different category. It is not a record made for the systematic conduct of the business as a business. An accident report may affect that business in the sense that it affords information on which the management may act. It is not, however, typical of entries made systematically or as a matter of routine to record events or occurrences, to reflect transactions with others, or to provide internal controls. The conduct of a business commonly entails the payment of tort claims incurred by the negligence of its employees. But the fact that a company makes a business out of recording its employees' versions of their accidents does not put those statements in the class of records made "in the regular course" of the business within the meaning of the Act. If it did, then any law office in the land could follow the same course, since business as defined in the Act includes the professions. We would then have a real perversion of a rule designed to facilitate admission of records which experience has shown to be quite trustworthy. Any business by installing a regular system for recording and preserving its version of accidents for which it was potentially liable could qualify those reports under the Act. The result would be that the Act would cover any system of recording events or occurrences provided it was "regular" and though it had little or nothing to do with the management or operation of the business as such. Preparation of cases for trial by virtue of being a "business" or incidental thereto would obtain the benefits of this liberalized version of the early shop book rule. The probability of trustworthiness of records because they were routine reflections of the day to day operations of a business would be forgotten as the basis of the rule. Regularity of preparation would become the test rather than the character of the records and their earmarks of reliability acquired from their source and origin and the nature of their compilation. We cannot so completely empty the words of the Act of their historic meaning. If the Act is to be extended to apply not only to a "regular course" of a business but also to any "regular course" of conduct which may have some relationship to business, Congress not this Court must extend it. Such a major change which opens wide the door to avoidance of cross-examination should not be left to implication. Nor is it any answer to say that Congress has provided in the Act that the various circumstances of the making of the record should affect its weight, not its admissibility. That provision comes into play only in case the other requirements of the Act are met.

In short, it is manifest that in this case those reports are not for the systematic conduct of the enterprise as a railroad business. Unlike payrolls, accounts receivable, accounts payable, bills of lading and the like, these reports are calculated for use essentially in the court, not in the business. Their primary utility is in litigating, not in railroading.

It is, of course, not for us to take these reports out of the Act if Congress has put them in. But there is nothing in the background of the law on which this Act was built or in its legislative history which suggests for a moment that the business of preparing cases for trial should be included. In this connection it should be noted that the Act of May 6, 1910, 36 Stat. 350, 45 U.S.C. § 38, requires officers of common carriers by rail to make under oath monthly reports of railroad accidents to the Interstate Commerce Commission, setting forth the nature and causes of the accidents and the circumstances connected therewith. And the same Act (45 U.S.C. § 40) gives the Commission authority to investigate and to make reports upon such accidents. It is provided, however, that "Neither the report required by section 38 of this title nor any report of the investigation provided for in section 40 of this title nor any part thereof shall be admitted as evidence or used for any purpose in any suit or action for damages growing out of any matter mentioned in said report or investigation." 45 U.S.C. § 41. A similar provision (36 Stat. 916, 54 Stat. 148, 45 U.S.C. § 33) bars the use in litigation of reports concerning accidents resulting from the failure of a locomotive boiler or its appurtenances. 45 U.S.C. §§ 32, 33. That legislation reveals an explicit Congressional policy to rule out reports of accidents which certainly have as great a claim to objectivity as the statement sought to be admitted in the present case. We can hardly suppose that Congress modified or qualified by implication these long standing statutes when it permitted records made "in the regular course" of business to be introduced. Nor can we assume that Congress having expressly prohibited the use of the company's reports on its accidents impliedly altered that policy when it came to reports by its employees to their superiors. The inference is wholly the other way.

The several hundred years of history behind the Act indicate the nature of the reforms which it was designed to effect. It should of course be liberally interpreted so as to do away with the anachronistic rules which gave rise to its need and at which it was aimed. But "regular course" of busienss must find its meaning in the inherent nature of the business in question and in the methods systematically employed for the conduct of the business as a business.

YATES v. BAIR TRANSPORT, INC.

United States District Court, S.D. New York, 1965.
249 F.Supp. 681.
[Footnotes omitted.]

* * * We next proceed to the second class of proffered documents —the reports of various doctors who examined plaintiff.

As appears in the pre-trial order filed herein on March 18, 1964, the plaintiff, who was injured in the course of his employment, made a claim in workmen's compensation for the same injuries arising from the same occurrence as is the subject of this suit. The Liberty Mutual Insurance Company (hereinafter at times referred to as "the Insurance Company"), was the insurance carrier for Charles Noeding Trucking Co. Inc., in connection with that claim and was and is the insurance carrier for defendant Knickerbocker Despatch, Inc.

In accordance with the regular procedure under the Workmen's Compensation Law, and in compliance with Rule 2(b) of the Rules of the Workmen's Compensation Board of the State of New York, reports were submitted by certain physicians to the Insurance Company as well as to the Workmen's Compensation Board. Plaintiff wishes to introduce the reports of Doctors Youmans, Guthrie, Lewis, Fleck and Richman into evidence in lieu of calling them as witnesses, and has requested a pre-trial ruling as to their admissibility.

It appears from ¶ 4C of the Pre-Trial Order herein that all the parties agreed as to the authenticity of the medical reports which are now being proffered. It further appears from the reports themselves, and it can very easily be verified, that Doctors Guthrie and Youmans examined plaintiff on behalf of Liberty Mutual Insurance Company, that Doctor Richman examined plaintiff on behalf of Interboro Mutual Indemnity Insurance Company, and that Doctors Fleck and Lewis were plaintiff's treating physicians. Accordingly, the reports have been sufficiently authenticated.

In ruling on the admissibility of the documents, the reports will be grouped, based on the identity of the party on whose behalf the report was prepared.

In reaching a determination herein, I am assuming, based on the concessions made by defendant Knickerbocker in its memorandum of law (at pg. 3), that Knickerbocker does not seriously contest the fact that the proffered reports of Doctors Youmans and Guthrie were in fact made by them and were made on behalf of Liberty Mutual in the Workmen's Compensation proceeding.

That the report was prepared in the ordinary course of the business of both doctors is indicated by the Court of Appeals decision in White V. Zutell, 263 F.2d 613 (2d Cir. 1959), which involved a medical report made by a specialist who had examined the plaintiff on behalf of the defendant's insurance carrier.

In sustaining the admissibility of the report, the Court stated: "The making of this report was clearly a part of this specialist's 'business'; indeed that is what he was commissioned to do. And it bears its own inherent guaranty of being what it purports to be—a detailed report of what he found medically upon examining the subject. That it might come up in the course of litigation does not affect this guaranty, unless to enhance it; what would be the use of such a report except to aid in fixing legal damage?" Id. at 615.

As stated in McCormick, Evidence § 287 at 604 (1954): "[W]ell reasoned modern decisions have admitted in accident cases the written reports of doctors of their findings from an examination of the injured party when it appears that is the doctor's professional routine or duty to make such report." But, it is argued, all the doctors' reports were prepared specifically for litigation (whether before the Workmen's Compensation Board, or in this suit) and at a time when the motive to misrepresent was present and the reports thus lack the trustworthiness necessary to permit their introduction. Palmer v. Hoffman, 318 U.S. 109, 63 S.Ct. 477, 87 L.Ed. 645 (1943) is cited in support of this argument.

In Palmer v. Hoffman, supra, the Court was concerned with the likely untrustworthiness of materials prepared specifically by a prospective litigant for courtroom use and thus held that the mere fact of regularity of preparation would not in itself be enough to justify the use of the evidence. The Business Records Act was interpreted in Palmer as facilitating the "admission of records which experience has shown to be quite trustworthy." 318 U.S. at 113, 63 S.Ct. at 480.

Accordingly, what must be found in the case at bar is an added element of trustworthiness which will counterbalance the fact that these reports were prepared in clear anticipation of litigation. With respect to the reports of Doctors Guthrie and Youmans, this added element is present.

"In Pekelis v. Transcontinental & W. Air Inc., 187 F.2d 122 (2 Cir.), cert. denied, 341 U.S. 951, 71 S.Ct. 1020, 95 L.Ed. 1374 (1951), we held that the district court was erroneous in refusing to admit the plaintiff's offer of certain accident reports prepared by boards set up by the defendant airline to investigate the crash of one of defendant's airplanes. We interpreted the decision in Palmer v. Hoffman to exclude accident reports only when they were prepared for use in litigation or when there was other indicia of their untrustworthiness. The Pekelis reports, the court pointed out, '* * * were against the interest of the entrant when made, * * * were clearly not part of a story cooked up in advance of litigation in the disguise of business records' and were offered as evidence by the party opposing the one which had had the reports prepared. 187 F.2d at 130.

In Korte v. New York, N. H. & H. R. R., 191 F.2d 86 (2 Cir.), cert. denied, 342 U.S. 868, 72 S.Ct. 108, 96 L.Ed. 652 (1951), another accident case, the district court had admitted certain doctors' reports, offered by the plaintiff, which had been prepared at the request of the defendant railroad. We affirmed the district court. Again, we pointed out that the decision in Palmer v. Hoffman was directed against the admission of hearsay evidence prepared for a litigious or other self-serving purpose. The court in Korte doubted whether the Palmer v. Hoffman rationale extended to reports made by independent doctors. Regardless of this, the Korte court stated that its holding could rest on Pekelis, where it had been held that reports offered by the party adverse to the party for whom the reports were prepared were admissible."

United States v. New York Foreign Trade Zone Operators, 304 F.2d at 798.

Thus the thrust of both opinions supports the admissibility of a doctor's report made in the regular course of business (when litigation was on the horizon) "when offered by one other than the entrant or one for whom the entrant is then working, i. e., the carrier * * *." Rotondi v. McLellan, 194 F.Supp. 415, 417 (E.D.N.Y. 1961).

That other courts have refused to follow Korte and instead have followed Masterson v. Pennsylvania R. Co., 182 F.2d 793, 796-797 (3d Cir. 1950), is not binding on this Court since *Masterson* was sufficiently distinguished, if not disapproved, in *Korte*.

Thus in the case at bar the fact that litigation involving Liberty Mutual was pending when these three reports were made, if anything, enhances the trustworthiness of the documents, since it is the plaintiff, not the defendant, who seeks their introduction (i. e., the party whose interest is adverse to that of the party on whose behalf the reports were made).

Reference must once again be made to White v. Zutell, supra, 263 F.2d 613 (2d Cir. 1959), since it is a case on all fours with the case at bar.

In *White,* the plaintiff was asked whether he had ever been examined by a Doctor Gilshannon, and the defendants conceded that Doctor Gilshannon "a doctor of * * * [their] choosing" (Appellant's Appendix on Appeal at 154a) had examined the plaintiff and made a report to the defendants. The report was turned over to plaintiff, and based on the foregoing foundation, was offered into evidence "as an admission against interest" (id. at 187a) as well as "a document kept by them [the insurance carrier] in the regular course of business * * *." (Ibid.) On the basis of the *Korte* case (id. at 332a) (which decision was also cited by the Court of Appeals), the report was admitted into evidence. In the case at bar, the foundation is, of course, a more solid one. * * *

Accordingly, I am inclined to overrule the objection to the report of Doctors Youmans and Guthrie.

No case, however, has been found or cited wherein a plaintiff was permitted to introduce self-serving reports made by doctors of his own choosing, in anticipation of litigation to shore up his own case. In fact, as noted above, analysis of both *Pekelis* and *Korte* supports the argument that, but for the characteristic of admission against the interest of the maker's principle, they would not have been admitted even though they were technically records kept in the ordinary course of business.

The fact that the record is self-serving is, of course, not determinative if made in the ordinary course of business without a view toward litigation.

As stated in the recent case of Taylor v. Baltimore & Ohio R. R., 344 F.2d 281, 286 (2d Cir. 1965), cert. denied, 382 U.S. 831, 86 S.Ct. 72, 15 L.Ed.2d 75 (10/12/65):

> "The report here was made when, so far as the record shows no one thought Taylor had suffered any serious injury, and it can hardly be assumed that a freight agent would appreciate the witty diversity whereby the difference of a few feet in the place of an employee's injury would result in the imposition of a distinct legal regime."

Thus the situation with respect to the reports of the doctors employed by plaintiff is different than that of defendant's doctors (Doctors Guthrie and Youmans) and warrants a different result, since statements by them would (if statements by defendant's doctors can be deemed admissions) be self-serving with no added degree of trustworthiness. They are thus statements made on behalf of a party by persons more inclined to favor that party's position, and the fact that they were made for the purposes of litigation causes me sufficient concern to refuse to admit them at this time.

The Court, with respect to documents falling under the Business Records Act, has a limited discretion. "The district court's discretion with respect to § 1732 is a discretion in judging whether the document offered 'has an inherent probability of trustworthiness.' Central R. R. v. Jules S. Sottnek Co., 258 F.2d 85, 88 (2 Cir. 1958). It is therefore a necessary premise for its exercise that the document's trustworthiness be in doubt. * * *

Accordingly, where, as here, there is no counterbalancing force to the desire to promote the self-interest of the party on whose behalf the report was made, discretion dictates that the objection at this time be sustained and plaintiff be required to call Doctors Lewis and Fleck. Insofar as Doctor Richman is concerned, his status is not clear with respect to the parties involved in the litigation, and with respect to his report there may not be present this added element of trustworthiness. Therefore, I will place him in the latter group of doctors employed by plaintiff and hold his report at this time inadmissible as well.

The rulings of the Court are as noted above.

So ordered.

WILLIAMS v. ALEXANDER

Court of Appeals of New York, 1955.
309 N.Y. 283, 129 N.E.2d 417.
[Footnotes omitted.]

FULD, Judge. Dessi Williams was struck by defendant's automobile as he was crossing a street in Brooklyn, with the traffic light in his favor. His right leg fractured, he was taken to Kings County Hospital for treatment. At the trial, the testimony of the parties as to the manner in which the accident occurred was sharply discrepant. According to plaintiff, defendant's automobile approached the intersection, at which he was crossing, without diminishing speed and ran into him. Defendant, on the other hand, insisting that he had brought his car to a complete stop at the light, maintained that another vehicle had struck it from the rear and propelled it forward and upon plaintiff.

In the early stages of the trial, plaintiff introduced so much of the Kings County Hospital record as bore upon his injuries and their treatment. Counsel for defendant thereupon offered the balance of the record and it was received in evidence over plaintiff's objection. Specifically challenged by plaintiff as inadmissible hearsay was an entry to the effect that he had stated to a physician at the hospital that "he was crossing the street and an automobile ran into another automobile that was at a standstill, causing this car (standstill) to run into him". Plaintiff denied making any such statement, and the doctor who recorded it was not called as a witness.

Upon this appeal—following a verdict in defendant's favor and an affirmance by a divided Appellate Division—we are called upon to decide whether the statement attributed to plaintiff, relating the manner in which the accident occurred, was properly admitted in evidence as a memorandum or record made "in the regular course of   *   *   *   business". Civil Practice Act, § 374–a.

Section 374–a of the Civil Practice Act permits the introduction in evidence of "Any writing or record   *   *   *   made as a memorandum or record of any act, transaction, occurrence or event," despite its hearsay character, "if the trial judge shall find that it was made in the regular course of any business, and that it was the regular course of such business to make such memorandum or record at the time of such act, transaction, occurrence or event, or within a reasonable time thereafter." The term "business" is broadly defined as including "business, profession, occupation and calling of every kind", and among the records within the section's ambit are those that a hospital keeps in diagnosing and treating the ills of its patients.

The statute, similar to those in effect in most jurisdictions, is designed to harmonize the rules of evidence with modern business practice and give "evidential credit" to the memoranda or other writings upon which reliance is placed in the systematic conduct of business undertakings. See Johnson v. Lutz, 253 N.Y. 124, 127, 170 N.E. 517. It rests upon the probability of trustworthiness which inheres in such records, by virtue of the fact, first, that they are the "routine reflections of the day to day operations of a business", Palmer v. Hoffman, 318 U.S. 109, 114, 63 S.Ct. 477, 480, 87 L.Ed. 645, and, second, that it is the entrant's own obligation, and to his interest, to have them truthful and accurate, made and kept as they are with the knowledge, indeed, for the purpose, that they will be relied upon in the conduct of the enterprise. See Johnson v. Lutz, supra, 253 N.Y. 124, 128, 170 N.E. 517, 518 * * * ; [I]t is this element of trustworthiness, serving in place of the safeguards ordinarily afforded by confrontation and cross-examination, which justifies admission of the writing or record without the necessity of calling all the persons who may have had a hand in preparing it. And it was to assure such accuracy and reliability that the legislature made explicit the condition that the memorandum may be received in evidence—and this is the heart of the provision—only if it was "made in the regular course of [the] business, and * * * it was the regular course of such business to make such memorandum".

As the statute makes plain, and we do not more than paraphrase it, entries in a hospital record may not qualify for admission in evidence unless made in the regular course of the "business" of the hospital, and for the purpose of assisting it in carrying on that "business." The business of a hospital, it is self-evident, is to diagnose and treat its patients' ailments. Consequently, the only memoranda that may be regarded as within the section's compass are those reflecting acts, occurrences or events that relate to diagnosis, prognosis or treatment or are otherwise "helpful to an understanding of the medical or surgical aspects of * * * [the particular patient's] hospitalization."

It follows from this that a memorandum made in a hospital record of acts or occurrences leading to the patient's hospitalization—such as a narration of the accident causing the injury—not germane to diagnosis or treatment, is not admissible under section 374-a, and so it has been almost universally held under the identical or similar statutes of other jurisdictions.

In the words of the Ohio court in Green v. City of Cleveland, supra, 150 Ohio St. 441, 444, 83 N.E.2d 63, 65, typical of those found in the other cases, "it was the business of the hospital to diagnose plaintiff's condition and to treat her for her ailments, not to record a statement describing the cause of the accident in which plaintiff's injuries were sustained."

In some instances, perhaps, the patient's explanation as to how he was hurt may be helpful to an understanding of the medical aspects of his case;

it might, for instance, assist the doctors if they were to know that the injured man had been struck by *an* automobile. However, whether the patient was hit by car A or car B, by car A under its own power or propelled forward by car B, or whether the injuries were caused by the negligence of the defendant or of another, cannot possibly bear on diagnosis or aid in determining treatment. That being so, entries of this sort, purporting to give particulars of the accident, which serve no medical purpose, may not be regarded as having been made in the regular course of the hospital's business. Indeed, in discussing the matter, Wigmore observed that the essential "Guarantee of Trustworthiness" rests upon the fact that "the physicians and nurses * * * themselves rely upon the record" and that the record is designed to be "relied upon in affairs of life and death." 6 Wigmore, op. cit., § 1707, p. 36. Such reasoning, however, will not support the use, or justify the receipt, of a statement detailing the circumstances of the accident where they are immaterial to, and were never intended to be relied upon in, the treatment of the patient. There is no need in that case for the physician to exercise care in obtaining and recording the information or to question the version, whatever it might be, that is given to him. The particulars may be a natural subject of the doctor's curiosity, but neither the inquiry nor the response properly belong in a record designed to reflect the regular course of the hospital's business.

In conclusion, then, that portion of the hospital record containing the statement assertedly made by plaintiff as to the manner in which the accident happened was erroneously admitted, and, since we cannot say that it did not influence the jury in arriving at its verdict for defendant, there must be a new trial.

The judgment of the Appellate Division and that of Trial Term should be reversed and a new trial granted, with costs to abide the event.

Desmond, Judge (dissenting).

I see no error here, and no reason for retrying this simple question of fact.

Plaintiff, for his own convenience, chose to prove his injuries and the hospital treatment he received therefor, by putting a hospital record in evidence and without calling as a witness the physician who made the entries. In so doing, he of course vouched for the accuracy and regularity of that record. Defendant made no objection but in his turn offered in evidence so much of the same hospital record as showed a statement to the hospital physician by plaintiff that the accident had occurred in a manner quite different from that testified to at the trial by plaintiff. Plaintiff objected to any such "history" going into evidence. His alleged ground of objection was stated in the one word: "hearsay". That of course was meaningless in this context. An undoubted exception to the "hearsay" rule makes admissible extra-judicial declarations against interest. Plaintiff's declaration to the hospital physician as to the way the accident happened was directly probative evidence of a main fact in issue. It is, of course, conceivable (but unlikely) that by plaintiff's use of the word "hearsay" he referred to the failure of defendant to call as a witness the physician who had written up the notes. But plaintiff himself had put into evidence the (helpful to him) parts of that identical paper without calling the physician. Surely, plaintiff could not then demand that the other party prove the authenticity of the very record plaintiff had himself presented to the court. Since plaintiff had been allowed to prove by the record alone the diagnosis and treatment of his injuries, it would be absurd to forbid defendant using the same record, written in the same handwriting by the same physician at the same time, to prove an equally relevant, competent and material fact, that is, that plaintiff had stated to the physician that his injuries were caused in the manner asserted by defendant.

It follows from the above that section 374-a of the Civil Practice Act, our statutory rule as to admissibility of records made in the regular course of a business, has little or nothing to do with this case. What we have here is an admission against interest, proved not by the oral testimony of the person to whom it was made but by an authentic document already vouched for to the court by the opposing party himself.

But let us suppose that this is a section 374-a case. "Hospital records concededly are included within the records to which section 374-a of the Civil Practice Act is applicable." People v. Kohlmeyer, 284 N.Y. 366, 369, 370, 31 N.E.2d 490, 492. The physician who made the entries need not be called as a witness. True, as Judge Fuld points out, this court has not yet directly decided whether the section 374-a makes admissible that part of a hospital record which gives the history of the injury. But why should this court not adopt a practical and useful construction, rather than a narrow and unnecessarily restrictive one? And the statute itself seems to furnish the answer: "Any writing or record, whether in the form of an entry in a book or otherwise, made as a memorandum or record of any act, transaction, occurrence or event, shall be admissible in evidence in proof of said act, transaction, occurrence or event, if the trial judge shall find that it was made in the regular course of any business, and that it was the regular course of such business to make such memorandum or record at the time of such act, transaction, occurrence or event, or within a reasonable time thereafter." There is no reason why the "history" part of a hospital record, obtained not from unidentified persons but from the patient himself, should not be used in evidence against the patient. Of course, the writing must have been made in the regular course of the hospital's business and it must have been the regular course of the businesss of the hospital to make such entries. But in this case plaintiff did not object because of any failure to prove those requirements. Indeed, he could not, after himself bringing the record to court, reasonably urge that it was not the regularly made record of this hospital. And he knew, as we all do, that an examining physician, especially in a hospital receiving department, always inquires as to the cause of a trauma. Certainly, in the absence of any suspicious circumstance, it is not up to the courts to decide just how thoroughly a qualified physician may delve into the cause or occasion of the injuries he is diagnosing and treating. Anyhow, all this is by the statute's own words committed to the trial judge's discretion. It is he who is charged with passing on the question of whether the entry was regularly made. Here, no one suggested that it was not so made or called for proof that it was. The trial justice, therefore, had no reason for excluding it, particularly since there was no suggestion that the physician or the hospital had any interest in the case or any possible reason for falsifying these records.

This was a routine trial of a simple issue of fact. Plaintiff said the accident happened one way, defendant said that it happened another way. A hospital book brought to court by plaintiff showed that he himself had described the occurrence in the way that defendant described it. Plaintiff denied that he had made such a statement at the hospital. The jury settled that dispute. It is most unfortunate, especially in these days of congested calendars, that such a case must now be retried.

The judgment should be affirmed, with costs.

Conway, C.J., and Froessel and Van Voorhis, JJ., concur with Fuld, J.

Desmond, J., dissents in an opinion in which Dye and Burke, JJ., concur.

Judgments reversed, etc.

ROBERTS, A PRACTITIONER'S PRIMER ON COMPUTER-GENERATED EVIDENCE

41 U. of Chi.L.Rev. 254, 272-278 (1974).
[Footnotes omitted.]

The courts are just beginning to face the issues raised by computer-generated evidence. No specific evidentiary tools have been developed to deal with this type of evidence, and the courts are trying to deal with the problems of computer-generated evidence through the existing statutory and common law rules of evidence. Several commentators and jurists have maintained that the existing concepts are adequate to deal with the phenomenon of computer-generated evidence. Whether in practice these concepts are sufficiently flexible to accommodate this phenomenon, and whether jurists and practitioners are sufficiently resourceful to deal with the opportunities and challenges of computer-generated evidence, remains to be seen.

A.   Statutory Rules

Computer-generated evidence will inevitably be hearsay, and to be admissible the evidence must therefore be brought within an exception to the hearsay rule. In most cases, the computer-generated evidence will arguably be either business records or generated from business records; as a result, the development of the law has been primarily in the area of the business records exception to the hearsay rule. The Federal Business Records Act represents a significant expansion of the traditional "shop book" rule and can be applied to computer-generated evidence either taken from or representing business records. The general requirements for admissibility under this Act are (1) that the record was made as a record of an act, transaction, occurrence, or event in the regular course of business, and (2) that it must be in the regular course of that business to make the record at the time of the act, transaction, occurrence, or event. The requirements of the Uniform Business Records As Evidence Act, now adopted by a majority of the states, are substantially the same.

In considering the issues raised by computer-generated evidence and the courts' treatment of those issues, it is important to appreciate the flexibility inherent in the relevant rules of evidence. At least in federal courts, there has been a tendency towards liberalization of the rules of evidence in recent years. Rule 803(6) of the Proposed Federal Rules of Evidence, which deals with business records, reflects this trend. Under a stricter set of evidentiary requirements, much computer-generated evidence might be inadmissible or the requirements for its admission might be so burdensome as to destroy its usefulness. There is, however, a danger that computer-generated evidence will be admitted too easily. The computer can package data in a very enticing manner, and, since it might be difficult to look behind that package, there may be a tendency simply to admit the material "for what it is worth." Proper evaluation of computer-generated evidence requires both that a careful evaluation be made of the original source of the evidence and that the proponent make available at least one witness who can answer the questions posed in the analysis outlined above.

B.   The Case Law

* * *

In D & H Auto Parts v. Ford Marketing Corp., Ford offered to show the amount of sales to D & H by introducing monthly sales summaries prepared on Ford's computers from information provided by Ford's parts distributors. The summaries were normally intended for internal use. In support of these documents, Ford offered the testimony of its assistant controller who described the testing of the data. D & H objected to the offer of the sales summaries on the grounds that there was insufficient proof of the accuracy of the printouts and that the testimony offered in support of the evidence was inadequate. The court, citing *DeGeorgia*, ruled that the computer printouts had been properly admitted: "Under the Business Records Act the absence of testimony from other Ford personnel 'may be shown to affect its weight, but such circumstances shall not affect its admissibility.' "

The state courts, acting under the shop book rule and its statutory codifications, have also exhibited a propensity to admit computer-generated material into evidence. A leading case considering the issue of computer-generated evidence is Transport Indemnity Co. v. Seib. To establish the amount of a premium claimed in a civil action, the plaintiff offered a computer-prepared exhibit reporting the defendant's losses and calculating the premium due. The plaintiff offered the testimony of its director of accounting in support of the exhibit; he testified that the computer records were maintained under his control, that the information on losses was fed into and stored in the computer, and that the computer stored and calculated the information in the same manner as plaintiff's previous bookkeeping. The court found that the records and computations were made as a usual and necessary part of the plaintiff's business operation. The Uniform Business Records As Evidence Act had been adopted in that state, and the court refused to construe the statute narrowly:

> No particular mode or form of record is required. The statute was intended to bring the realities of business and professional practice into the courtroom and the statute should not be interpreted narrowly to destroy its obvious usefulness. [Citation omitted].

> The machine here performs the bookkeeping task in the usual course of business. Instead of on paper, the information and calculations are stored on tape and may be retrieved and printed at any time. The taped record furnished a cumulative record based on information flowing into the office of the plaintiff company day by day and fed into the machine in response to a systematic procedure for processing each insured's account.

In King v. State ex rel. Murdock Acceptance Corp., the court, acting without benefit of a statutory business records rule, admitted into evidence computer sheets that purported to reflect the balance due on six conditional sales contracts. The plaintiff's accounting manager testified that the computer sheets were prepared under his supervision in the normal course of business. He traced the flow of data through the EDP system, described verification procedures, and testified that the computer equipment was standard equipment recognized as efficient and accurate. The court stated that the plaintiff's records of customers' accounts would meet the shop book rule if conventional books were used but recognized that the question was whether the printout sheets were inadmissible because they were not the original records. The court, citing *Seib,* decided to admit the printout sheets; the court maintained that it was not departing from the shop book rule but only extending its application to electronic bookkeeping.

The reported cases are not clear about the type of testimony necessary to provide an adequate foundation for the admission of computer-generated data. In *Seib* and *King,* the individual directly responsible for the operation of the EDP system testified and probably could have answered those questions set forth in the analysis outlined above. It could be argued, however, that the party offering the evidence need show only that the computer-generated data was used in the normal course of business or was generated from computer-maintained data used in the normal course of business. Those witnesses who testified in *D & H Auto Parts* and *DeGeorgia* could not have given more than this information; the Hertz employee in *DeGeorgia* apparently could testify only that he relied on the computer printouts in carrying out his duties for the company.

Some cases have raised a question regarding the applicability of the personal knowledge requirement of various evidence rules. A fairly liberal view was adopted in Merrick v. United States Rubber Co. The plaintiff, in support of computer-generated data, offered the testimony of an employee in its credit department who was familiar with the account in question and plaintiff's accounting procedures, but who had no personal knowledge about the operations of the plaintiff's computer system. The court rejected the defendant's contention that this testimony was not an adequate foundation to justify the admission of the computer-generated evidence.

Other courts have applied stricter tests than the *Merrick* court. In Arnold D. Kamen & Co. v. Young, the plaintiff sought to introduce a computer-generated statement of accounts, purchases, and sales. A witness testified that employees transferred information from written order blanks to keypunch cards which were then sent to a tabulating service that ran the cards through a computer and returned the printouts. He further testified that the printout was part of the business records of the company kept for each customer. The defendant argued that the data was not admissible because the plaintiff had not shown that the original data was prepared by someone with personal knowledge of the act or event recorded. The court held that the evidence was inadmissible because "there was no proof that the person who prepared the order blanks or other data had personal knowledge of the data or information allegedly punched into the cards. [The witness] did not attempt to testify that he had knowledge of such information but merely said that the cards were punched by a female employee in the Chicago office based on certain orders not shown on the record."

See Federal Rules of Evidence 803(6)–(7), at p. 923; California Evidence Code § § 1270–1272 at pp. 882–883.

UNITED STATES v. OATES

United States Court of Appeals, Second Circuit, 1977.
560 F.2d 45.

WATERMAN, Circuit Judge:

This is an appeal from a judgment of the United States District Court for the Eastern District of New York convicting appellant, following a six-day jury trial, of possession of heroin with intent to distribute, and of conspiracy to commit that substantive offense.　＊　＊　＊

＊　＊　＊

Appellant　＊　＊　＊　claims that the trial court committed error by admitting into evidence at trial two documentary exhibits purporting to be the official report and accompanying worksheet of the United States Customs Service chemist who analyzed the white powdery substance seized ＊　＊　＊. The documents, the crucial nature of which is beyond cavil, concluded that the powder examined was heroin. Appellant contends, ＊　＊　＊　that under the new Federal Rules of Evidence (hereinafter "FRE") the documents should have been excluded as hearsay　＊　＊　＊.

At trial the government had planned upon calling as one of its final witnesses a Mr. Milton Weinberg, a retired United States Customs Service chemist who allegedly had analyzed the white powder seized from Isaac Daniels. It seems that Mr. Weinberg had been present on the day the trial had been scheduled to commence but he was not able to testify then because of a delay occasioned by the unexpected length of the pretrial suppression hearing. The government claims that by the time Weinberg was rescheduled to testify he had become "unavailable." The Assistant United States Attorney explained the circumstances of this unavailability as follows: "I am told by his wife [he is] very sick. Apparently he has some type of bronchial infection." After a short adjournment the prosecutor added the following comment: "Mr. Weinberg called my office this morning and I was made known about it about 10:30 this morning prior to coming up stairs." Considering these two explanations to be consistent with each other, it appears that Weinberg called the United States Attorney's office to inform them of his unavailability and that subsequently the Assistant United States Attorney attempted to speak to Weinberg personally but was able, for some reason, to speak only to Weinberg's wife who advised that Weinberg had "some type of bronchial infection." There is no indication in the record as to why the Assistant United States Attorney was at that time unable to speak to Weinberg himself, although earlier that day Weinberg had been able to carry on a telephone conversation. Nor is there any other indication in the record that the prosecutor made any further attempts to confirm the fact that Weinberg was ill, and, if so, how ill he might be. No request was made of the district court for a brief continuance for the purpose of determining the nature and expected duration of Weinberg's illness.

＊　＊　＊　[T]he prosecutor had planned to call Weinberg for the purpose of eliciting from him testimony that Weinberg had analyzed the powder seized * * * and found it to be heroin. When Weinberg became "unavailable," the government decided to call another Customs chemist, Shirley Harrington, who, although she did not know Weinberg personally, was able to testify concerning the regular practices and procedures used by Customs Service chemists in analyzing unknown substances. Through Mrs. Harrington the government was successful in introducing Exhibits 13 and 12 which purported to be, respectively, the handwritten worksheet used by the chemist analyzing the substance seized from Daniels and the official typewritten report of the chemical analysis. The report summarizes salient features of the worksheet. Mrs. Harrington claimed to be able to ascertain from the face of the worksheet the various steps taken by Weinberg to determine whether the unknown substance was, as suspected, heroin. When the defense voiced vigorous objection to the attempt to introduce the documents through Mrs. Harrington, the government relied * * * on the modified "business records" exception found in FRE 803(6). [T]he evidence was also claimed to be admissible under FRE 803(8) as a "public record" * * * .

Mrs. Harrington was obviously an experienced chemist, having conducted thousands of tests while working for the Customs Service, including hundreds designed to identify heroin. She was also an experienced witness, having testified "probably a hundred or so" times in the course of her duties with the Customs Service. She had never worked with Weinberg personally and had never observed him perform any chemical tests. She had never received any notes or letters from him, but she identified Weinberg's writing on Exhibit 13 and his signature on Exhibit 12, presumably because she had, in accordance with Customs Service practices, re-analyzed, prior to destruction, substances Weinberg had previously analyzed shortly after the substances were seized.

The defense, in addition to having no opportunity to cross-examine Weinberg, the chemist who had performed the analysis, was also disturbed about two other circumstances surrounding the introduction of Exhibits 12 and 13. In particular, the defense was surprised that Exhibit 12, the official typewritten report, contained Weinberg's signature, for no such signature had appeared on the copy of this exhibit given to the defense beforehand. Moreover, the defense was particularly, and understandably distressed about the absence of Weinberg in view of the fact that the two exhibits differed in one important particular, a particular in which they certainly should have been identical. A notation pertaining to the chain of custody of the powder within the agency appeared on both exhibits, in typewritten form on the official report and in handwriting, presumably Weinberg's on the worksheet. The notation read "Received from and returned to CSO Fromkin." On the typewritten official report, however, this statement had been crossed out, although it still was legible beneath the scribbling. Mrs. Harrington knew nothing about this deletion. There is nothing in the exhibits themselves or in the testimony of any witnesses that would explain why, when and by whom this deletion was made.

* * *

It is eminently clear that the report and worksheet were "written assertions" constituting "statements," FRE 801(a)(1), which were "offered [by the prosecution] in evidence [at trial] to prove the truth of the matters asserted [in them]." FRE 801(c). As such, they were hearsay, and, for our present purposes, under FRE 802 were inadmissible "except as [otherwise] provided by" other provisions of the Federal Rules of Evidence. * * *

* * * On this appeal the government and the appellant are in complete disagreement over the materiality of FRE 803(8) to the issue of whether the chemist's report and worksheet were excludable as hearsay. Although at trial the government placed some reliance on FRE 803(8), the so-called "public records and reports" exception to exclusion, in its brief in this court it completely ignores the provision, apparently abandoning any reliance on it for reasons we shall discuss below. Instead, it urges us to find that the challenged evidence falls easily within the scope of what has traditionally been labeled the "business records exception" to the hearsay exclusionary rule, the codification of which in the Federal Rules of Evidence is found in FRE 803(6). Appellant, on the other hand, vigorously asserts that the issue of whether the chemist's report and worksheet were fatal hearsay can be correctly evaluated only by a careful study of the precise wording of FRE 803(8) and the legislative intent underlying the enactment of that rule.

While the problem presented is not susceptible of any facile solution, we believe that, on balance, appellant's emphasis on the importance of FRE 803(8) is well-founded. It would certainly seem to be the exception which would logically come to mind if a question arose as to the admissibility of reports of the kind we are considering in this case. Moreover, although as a general rule there is no question that hearsay evidence failing to meet the requirements of one exception may nonetheless satisfy the standards of another exception, and there thus might be no need to examine FRE 803(8) at all, we agree with appellant that both the language of Rule 803(8) and the congressional intent, as gleaned from the explicit language of the rule and from independent sources, which impelled that language have impact that extends beyond the immediate confines of exception (8) itself. We therefore regard FRE 803(8) as the proper starting point for our evidentiary analysis.

That the chemist's report and worksheet could not satisfy the requirements of the "public records and reports" exception seems evident merely from examining, on its face, the language of FRE 803(8). That rule insulates from the exclusionary effect of the hearsay rule certain:

> (8) *Public records and reports.*—Records, reports, statements, or data compilations, in any form, of public offices or agencies, setting forth (A) the activities of the office or agency, or (B) matters observed pursuant to duty imposed by law as to which matters there was a duty to report, excluding, however, in criminal cases matters observed by police officers and other law enforcement personnel, or (C) in civil cases and proceedings and against the Government in criminal cases, factual findings resulting from an investigation made pursuant to authority granted by law, unless the sources of information or other circumstances indicate lack of trustworthiness.

While there may be no sharp demarcation between the records covered by exception 8(B) and those referenced in exception 8(C), and indeed there may in some cases be actual overlap, we conclude without hesitation that surely the language of item (C) is applicable to render the chemist's documents inadmissible as evidence in this case, and they might also be within the ambit of the terminology of item (B), a claim appellant argues to us persuasively.

It is manifest from the face of item (C) that "factual findings resulting from an investigation made pursuant to authority granted by law" are not shielded from the exclusionary effect of the hearsay rule by "the public records exception" if the government seeks to have those "factual findings" admitted *against* the accused in a criminal case. It seems indisputable to us that the chemist's official report and worksheet in the case at bar can be characterized as reports of "factual findings resulting from an investigation made pursuant to authority granted by law." The "factual finding" in each instance, the conclusion of the chemist that the substance analyzed was heroin, obviously is the product of an "investigation," * * * supposedly involving on the part of the chemist employment of various techniques of scientific analysis. Furthermore, in view of its reliance on the chemist's report at trial and its representation to the district court that "chemical analys[e]s of unidentified substances are indeed a regularly conducted activity of the Customs laboratory of Customs chemists," the government here is surely in no position to dispute the fact that the analyses regularly performed by United States Customs Service chemists on substances lawfully seized by Customs officers are performed pursuant to authority granted by law.

Though with less confidence, we believe that the chemist's documents might also fail to achieve status as public records under FRE 803(8)(B) because they are records of "matters observed by police officers and other law enforcement personnel." Although in characterizing the chemist's report and worksheet here it is quite accurate to designate those reports as the reports of factual findings made pursuant to an investigation, the reports in this case conceivably could also be susceptible of the characterization that they are "reports * * * setting forth * * * (B) matters observed pursuant to duty imposed by law as to which matters there was a duty to report." If this characterization is justified, the difficult question would be whether the chemists making the observations could be regarded as "other law enforcement personnel." We think this phraseology must be read broadly enough to make its prohibitions against the use of government-generated reports in criminal cases coterminous with the analogous prohibitions contained in FRE 803(8)(C). We would thus construe "other law enforcement personnel" to include, at the least, any officer or employee of a governmental agency which has law enforcement responsibilities. Applying such a standard to the case at bar, we easily conclude that full-time chemists of the United States Customs Service are "law enforcement personnel." The chemist in this case was employed by the Customs Service, a governmental agency which had clearly defined law enforcement authority in the field of illegal narcotics trafficking; the officers who actually seized the suspected contraband were employed by the Customs Service, and the unidentified substance was delivered by them to a laboratory operated by the Customs Service. The unidentified substance was then subjected to analysis by a chemist, one of whose regular functions is to test substances seized from suspected narcotics violators. Chemists at the laboratory are, without question, important participants in the prosecutorial effort. * * * Moreover, the role of the chemist typically does not terminate upon completion of the chemical analysis and submission of the resulting report but participation continues until the chemist has testified as an important prosecution witness at trial. * * * In short, these reports are not "made by persons and for purposes unconnected with a criminal case [but rather they are a direct] result of a test made for the specific purpose of convicting the defendant and conducted by agents of the executive branch, the very department of government which seeks defendant's conviction." It would therefore seem that if the chemist's report and worksheet here can be deemed to set forth "matters observed," the documents would fail to satisfy the requirements of exception FRE 803(8) for the chemist must be included within the category of "other law enforcement personnel."

Our conclusion that the chemist's report and worksheet do not satisfy the standards of FRE 803(8) comports perfectly with what we discern to be clear legislative intent not only to exclude such documents from the scope of FRE 803(8) but from the scope of FRE 803(6) as well.   *   *   *

*   *   *

*   *   * We *   *   * think it manifest that it was the clear intention of Congress to make evaluative and law enforcement reports absolutely inadmissible against defendants in criminal cases. Just as importantly, it must have been the unquestionable belief of Congress that the language of FRE 803(8)(B) and (C) accomplished that very result.

Despite what we perceive to be clear congressional intent that reports not qualifying under FRE 803(8)(B) or (C) should, and would, be inadmissible against defendants in criminal cases, the government completely ignores those provisions *   *   * and argues instead that the chemist's report and worksheet in the case at bar fall clearly within the literal terms of the modified business records exception to the hearsay rule contained in FRE 803(6), entitled *"Records of regularly conducted activity."* (See p. 923).

*   *   *

*   *   * [T]he government's argument that the documents in this case satisfy the requirements of the modified "business records" exception is not altogether unappealing if it is assessed strictly on the basis of the literal language of FRE 803(6) and without reference to either the legislative history or the language of FRE 803(8)(B) and (C). For instance, it is true that, traditionally, a proponent's inability to satisfy the requirements of one hearsay exception does not deny him the opportunity to attempt to meet the standards of another. Secondly, it is clear from the explicit inclusion of the words "opinions" and "diagnoses" in FRE 803(6) that, in one sense anyway, Congress intended to expand, or at least ratify, the view of prior court cases that had expanded the concept of what constitutes a "business record." The Advisory Committee's Notes confirm this. Advisory Committee's Notes, Note to Paragraph (6) of Rule 803, 56 F.R.D. at 309. It is reasonable to assume that a laboratory analysis may well be an "opinion." Thirdly, the testimony of Mrs. Harrington, a "qualified witness," established that it was a regular practice of the Customs laboratory to make written reports of their analyses and that these particular written reports were made in the regular course of the laboratory's activities. However, not nearly as clear is whether under the facts here the "method or circumstances of preparation" might not "indicate lack of trustworthiness." The language contained within the subordinate "unless" clause creates an exception to the general language of FRE 803(6) and, as such, "is *   *   * subject to the rule of strict con-

struction; that is, any doubt will be resolved in favor of the general provision and against the exception, and anyone claiming to be relieved from the statute's operation must establish that he comes within the exception." * * * Here there are some "circumstances of preparation [which tend to] indicate lack of trustworthiness." As already noted, Exhibits 12 and 13 differ from each other in one significant respect in which they should be identical. On both, in handwriting on the worksheet and in typewritten form on the official report, the notation "Received from and returned to CSO Fromkin" appears. Yet, on the report this notation has been crossed out. Nothing indicates who deleted the notation, when it was deleted, or why it was deleted and, as it relates to the issue of chain of custody, it is a matter of some importance. Moreover, before trial defense counsel was given what was purported to be a copy of the official chemist's report. Yet, this document did not contain the signature of the certifying chemist Weinberg. At trial the official report the government offered was signed. Assuming that Weinberg did sign the document the government offered, there is obviously a question as to when this document was signed, it not being unreasonable to assume that it was signed after the government had already given the defense a copy of an originally unsigned report. However, while we are troubled by these concededly unusual circumstances, and it may well be that they raise ample doubts to require exclusion on the face of FRE 803(6) alone, we prefer not to predicate our decision on a finding that the "circumstances of preparation indicate lack of trustworthiness." Instead, we assume for purposes of argument here, that, as sedulously asserted by the government, the chemist's report and worksheet might fall within the literal language of FRE 803(6).

For purposes of our present analysis, we thus consider the situation to be that the chemist's documents might appear to be within the literal language of FRE 803(6) although there is clear congressional intent that such documents be deemed inadmissible against a defendant in a criminal case. This would not be the first time that a court has encountered a situation pitting some literal language of a statute against a legislative intent that flies in the face of that literal language. Our function as an interpretive body is, of course, to construe legislative enactments in such a way that the intent of the legislature is carried out. In recognition of this responsibility numerous courts have either applied, or at least recognized the principle that, despite the existence of literal language that might dictate a contrary result, a court should interpret a statute in such a way as to effectuate clear legislative intent.

* * *

* * * Representative William Hungate, in presenting the report of the Committee of Conference to the House of Representatives, left no doubt that it was the belief of the Committee of Conference that under the new Federal Rules of Evidence the *effect* of FRE 803(8)(B) and (C) was to render law enforcement reports and evaluative reports inadmissible against defendants in criminal cases. It is thus clear that the only way to construe FRE 803(6) so that it is reconcilable with this intended effect is to interpret FRE 803(6) and the other hearsay exceptions in such a way that police and evaluative reports not satisfying the standards of FRE 803(8)(B) and (C) may not qualify for admission under FRE 803(6) or any of the other exceptions to the hearsay rule. * * *

Even if the remarks of Representative Hungate　*　*　*　were not as clear as they are, we could still reach the same conclusion that, in view of the articulated purpose behind the narrow drafting of FRE 803 in general and FRE 803(8) in particular, FRE 803(6) must be read in conjunction with FRE 803(8)(B) and (C). Specifically, the pervasive fear of the draftsmen and of Congress that interference with an accused's right to confrontation would occur was the reason why in criminal cases evaluative reports of government agencies and law enforcement reports were expressly denied the benefit to which they might otherwise be entitled under FRE 803(8). It follows that this explanation of the reason for the special treatment of evaluative and law enforcement reports under FRE 803(8) applies with equal force to the treatment of such reports under *any* of the other exceptions to the hearsay rule. The prosecution's utilization of any hearsay exception to achieve admission of evaluative and law enforcement reports would serve to deprive the accused of the opportunity to confront his accusers as effectively as would reliance on a "public records" exception. Thus, there being no apparent reason why Congress would tolerate the admission of evaluative and law enforcement reports by use of some other exception to the hearsay rule　*　*　*　it simply makes no sense to surmise that Congress ever intended that these records could be admissible against a defendant in a criminal case under *any* of the Federal Rules of Evidence's exceptions to the hearsay rule.　*　*　*

We are not the first court to indulge in a less than literal construction of a hearsay exception so as to effectuate congressional intent. An issue addressed by the D.C. Circuit in United States v. Smith, supra, 521 F.2d at 968-69 n.24, was whether the police reports of FRE 803(8)(B) are admissible *against* the government. While conceding that "[o]n its face, 803(8)(B) appears to [say that they are not, the court was] convinced, however, that 803(8)(B) should be read, in accordance with the obvious intent of Congress and in harmony with 803(8)(C) to authorize the admission of the reports of police officers and other law enforcement personnel at the request of the defendant in a criminal case." 521 F.2d at 968 n.24. The "obvious intent of Congress" in enacting FRE 803(8)(B) was found to be that "use of reports against defendants would be unfair." 521 F.2d at 969 n.24. "Since there [was] no apparent reason to allow defendants to use the reports admitted by 803(8)(C) but not those governed by 803(8)(B) [the court concluded] that a police report　*　*　*　is an exception to the new hearsay rules when introduced at the request of the defense." 521 F.2d at 969 n.24.　*　*　*

*　*　*

*　*　*　Inasmuch as the chemist's documents here can be characterized as governmental reports which set forth matters observed by law enforcement personnel or which set forth factual findings resulting from an authorized investigation, they were incapable of qualifying under any of the exceptions to the hearsay rule specified in FRE 803 and 804. The documents were crucial to the government's case, they were of course, hearsay, and, inasmuch as they were ineligible to qualify for any exception to the hearsay rule, their admission at trial against appellant was prejudicial error.

*　*　*　[W]e reverse the judgment of conviction and remand for a new trial.

UNITED STATES v. GRADY

United States Court of Appeals, Second Circuit, 1976.
544 F.2d 598.

OAKES, Circuit Judge:

The waves of tragedy from the internecine conflict in Northern Ireland have their ripple effects in this country. Appellants here are Frank Grady, a sympathizer with the Catholic minority in Ulster, and John Jankowski, a licensed firearms dealer in Yonkers, New York. Each was convicted of conspiracy to violate the federal firearms law, particularly 18 U.S.C. §§ 922(m) and 923, which together require a licensed firearms dealer to make true entries in a federal firearms record, and of ten substantive counts of making or causing to be made false entries as to ten .30-caliber semiautomatic rifles in Jankowski's record or "logbook"; Grady was also convicted of one count of unlawful exportation without a permit of these same rifles. * * *

* * *

IV. Admission of Irish Police Records.

Much is made in the briefs of the admission into evidence of records of the formidable-sounding Department of Industrial and Forensic Science of the Ministry of Commerce and of the Royal Ulster Constabulary. These were entitled "Material Forwarded for Examination" and "Order for Disposal of Firearms/Ammunition." The ground of objection was that the documents constituted inadmissible hearsay. * * *

For the limited purpose of showing that the specified weapons were found in Northern Ireland on dates subsequent to the May, 1970, purchases, however, we think the records were admissible under the public records exception to the hearsay rule, codified in Fed.R.Evid. 803(8)(B). Rule 803(8)(B) allows admission of records and reports of public offices or agencies setting forth "matters observed pursuant to duty imposed by law as to which matters there was a duty to report," but is subject to an exception for "matters observed by police officers and other law enforcement personnel." In adopting this exception, Congress was concerned about prosecutors attempting to prove their cases in chief simply by putting into evidence police officers' reports of their contemporaneous observations of crime. The reports admitted here were not of this nature; they did not concern observations by the Ulster Constabulary of the appellants' commission of crimes. Rather, they simply related to the routine function of recording serial numbers and receipt of certain weapons found in Northern Ireland. They did not begin to prove the Government's entire case; they were strictly routine records.

* * *

Judgments affirmed.

———

See Federal Rules of Evidence 803(8)–(10) at pp. 923–924. California Evidence Code §§ 1280, 1281, 1284 at pp. 883–884.

Hypotheticals

(1) A sues X Department Store for damages for injuries received in slipping on X's floor. A claims she slipped and fell because the floor was highly waxed and polished and unduly slippery as a result. X offers in evidence a report prepared for X

by B, the store manager. B is no longer in X's employ and could not be found to testify. X's evidence establishes that B's report was prepared the day after the accident, and that X's store manager customarily makes a report after an accident. B's report states that B arrived at the scene a few minutes after A fell and while A was still on the floor, and that B examined the floor and it was not highly waxed or polished but had a dull finish and was not slippery. A objects to the report as hearsay. Should the objection be sustained?

(2)   X is prosecuted for robbery of A. X's defense is an alibi. X testifies that he was in a distant city, having just registered at the B Motel at the time of the robbery. X calls C, a clerk at the B Motel, who identifies a registration card that shows that one X, with defendant's address, registered at the motel at the time of the robbery of A. The registration card does not bear any signature of the guest X on it. C further testifies that motel clerks frequently fill out the registration card from information supplied by the guest and do not require a guest's signature. X offers the registration card in evidence. The prosecution makes a hearsay objection. What result?

(3)   A sues X for fire damage to A's house. A had employed X, a general contractor, to remodel A's kitchen. Just before the work was completed, a fire started in the kitchen and caused the damage. A claims the fire resulted from X's negligence in leaving an open can of highly inflammable cabinet stain too close to the pilot of the water heater. X's defense is that the fire was the result of arson. After laying a proper foundation, X offers in evidence a report by B, a captain in the city fire department. B's report stated that his investigation of the fire included an inspection of the premises and conversations with A's neighbors, and that based upon this investigation, his conclusion was that the fire was of incendiary origin. A objects to the report as hearsay. Is A's objection proper?

(4)   D is charged with murder. D's defense is diminished capacity due to consumption of alcohol and drugs. D's contention is that he killed the victim from being in a rage because of a homosexual advance made by the victim. In his defense, D offers in evidence under the business-records hearsay exception a report concerning the victim made 20 years ago by Dr. A, a psychiatrist. In Dr. A's report was the diagnosis of "alchoholism with sexual psychopathy. This patient is not an outstanding patient for psychiatric treatment." The prosecutor makes a hearsay objection to Dr. A's report. What result?

(5)   P sues D for damages for injuries suffered in an automobile accident. P does not call a doctor to testify but offers into evidence the doctor's report. Foundation is established that the doctor's report is the only record kept by him in the ordinary course of business. The report recites that the doctor examined P on a certain date, had X-rays taken, and diagnosed a fracture of the femur. In a separate paragraph of the doctor's report, a prognosis is stated that, in the doctor's opinion, P will suffer permanent residuals of a limitation of motion. D makes a hearsay objection. How should the court rule?

(6)   A sues X to recover the contract price of goods sold. A and X entered into a written contract for A to sell X 1,000 metric tons of lead fume. The contract price depended on the exact weight and metallic content of the lead fume delivered by A. To prove the weight and metallic content, A testifies that he employed B, a highly respected assayer, to assay a sample of the lead fume; that he later went by B's office and received from a secretary a report on the letterhead of B, purporting to bear B's signature; that he is not, however, familiar with B's signature. A offers in evidence this report, which sets forth the weight and metallic content of a sample of the lead fume allegedly assayed by B. X makes a hearsay objection. What result?

(7)   A sues X for damages for personal injuries and car property damage arising out of an automobile accident. A testifies that he went to Dr. B and C Hospital for treatment, and had his car repaired at D Garage. A offers in evidence bills or in-

voices, which he testifies as having been received from Dr. B, C Hospital, and D Garage. Each bill is stamped with the words "Payment Received." X makes a hearsay objection to the admissibility of the bills. How should the court rule?

(8)   D is charged with robbery of V, a liquor store owner, at his store. V testifies that after the robbery he ran out of the store and obtained D's license number as D drove off. V testifies that the license number of the car was 468 ABC. D's car bore this license number. D calls PO, a police officer, who identifies a police report of the event and establishes the foundation that it was made in the usual course of business and at or near the time of the robbery. A sentence in the report states that 30 minutes after the robbery, the police received a telephone call from A, a neighbor of V, who reported the license number of the robber's car as 416 ABC. D offers the police report in evidence. In response to the prosecutor's hearsay objection, D states that the report is being offered as nonhearsay to establish that a different license number had been reported, but that, if hearsay, the report is admissible under the official-record hearsay exception. Should the prosecutor's objection be sustained?

(9)   Sam D is charged with perjury because he allegedly gave false testimony in the trial of a civil action. The prosecution's contention of the false testimony is that, in the civil action, Sam D identified himself by the name of John D, while his real name was Sam D, and that in qualifying to testify as an expert he said he was a standing consultant in engineering at the U.S. Bureau of Mines. The prosecution offers in evidence a writing stating that C, the signer, was the official custodian of records for the U.S. Bureau of Mines and that C had made a diligent search of the records of the U.S. Bureau of Mines and failed to find any record that any person by the name of Sam D or John D had been an engineering consultant. The writing bears a signature, C, as custodian of records of the U.S. Bureau of Mines, and has stamped thereon a seal purporting to be the seal of the U.S. Bureau of Mines. D makes a hearsay objection to the writing. What result?

11.   MISCELLANEOUS EXCEPTIONS

JUDGMENT OF PREVIOUS CONVICTION

See Federal Rules of Evidence 803(22) at p. 925; California Evidence Code § § 1300–1302 at p. 885.

COMMENT TO CALIF. EVID. CODE § 1300

Analytically, a judgment that is offered to prove the matters determined by the judgment is hearsay evidence. It is in substance a statement of the court that determined the previous action ("a statement that was made other than by a witness while testifying at the hearing") that is offered "to prove the truth of the matter stated." Evidence Code § 1200. Therefore, unless an exception to the hearsay rule is provided, a judgment would be inadmissible if offered in a subsequent action to prove the matters determined.

Of course, a judgment may, as a matter of substantive law, conclusively establish certain facts insofar as a party is concerned. The sections of this article do not purport to deal with the doctrines of res judicata and estoppel by judgment. These sections deal only with the evidentiary use of judgments in those cases where the substantive law does not require that the judgments be given conclusive effect.

Section 1300 provides an exception to the hearsay rule for a final judgment adjudging a person guilty of a crime punishable as a felony. Hence, if a plaintiff sues to recover a reward offered by the defendant for the arrest and conviction of a person who committed a particular crime, Section 1300 permits the plaintiff to use a judgment of conviction as evidence that the person convicted committed the crime. The exception does not, however, apply in criminal actions. Thus, Section 1300 does not permit the judgment to be used in a criminal action as evidence of the identity of the person who committed the crime or as evidence that the crime was committed.

Section 1300 will change the California law. Under existing law, a conviction of a crime is inadmissible as evidence in a subsequent action. The change, however, is desirable, for the evidence involved is peculiarly reliable. The seriousness of the charge assures that the facts will be thoroughly litigated, and the fact that the judgment must be based upon a determination that there was no reasonable doubt concerning the defendant's guilt assures that the question of guilt will be thoroughly considered.

Section 1300 applies to any crime punishable as a felony. The fact that a misdemeanor sentence is imposed does not affect the admissibility of the judgment of a conviction under this section. Cf. Penal Code § 17. The exclusion of judgments based on a plea of nolo contendere from the exception in Section 1300 is a reflection of the policy expressed in Penal Code Section 1016.

COMMENT TO CALIF. EVID. CODE § 1301

If a person entitled to indemnity, or if the obligee under a warranty contract, compiles with certain conditions relating to notice and defense, the indemnitor or warrantor is conclusively bound by any judgment recovered.

Where a judgment against an indemnitee or person protected by a warranty is not made conclusive on the indemnitor or warrantor, Section 1301 permits the judgment to be used as hearsay evidence in an action to recover on the indemnity or warranty. Section 1301 reflects the existing law relating to indemnity agreements. Civil Code § 2778(6). Section 1301 probably restates the law relating to warranties, too, but the law in that regard is not altogether clear.

TREATISES AND OTHER PROFESSIONAL LITERATURE
WALTZ & INBAU, MEDICAL JURISPRUDENCE

85–87 (1971).*
[Some footnotes omitted.]

USE OF MEDICAL TREATISES AS EVIDENCE

Theoretically at least, the problem of securing expertise in support of meritorious malpractice cases could be neatly solved if only plaintiffs were free to offer in evidence relevant medical treatises instead of having to obtain live witnesses. Plaintiff's counsel, after introducing evidence of what the defendant doctor did, could simply introduce a treatise or other item of medical literature that purportedly lays out the proper procedures—the standard of care—to be followed by doctors in the type of case in question. The jury, optimistically, could then consider the contents of the treatise just as it would weigh the statements of expert witnesses actually testifying in court. But for reasons which we shall presently discuss, this alternative is currently available in only a few jurisdictions.

A few states, by either statute or judicial decision, have taken what might at first appear to be a substantial step toward alleviating malpractice plaintiffs' difficulties in producing expert testimony. Alabama, North Carolina, Kansas, Massachusetts, Nevada, Rhode Island and perhaps Connecticut, Maine, and Wisconsin will admit into evidence learned books and articles to be used in establishing the standard of care applicable to the defendant physician. Alabama's rule is judge-made as, apparently, is North Carolina's; Massachusetts, Kansas, Nevada, and Rhode Island have enacted statutes to accomplish the same result. The Massachusetts statute [Mass.Laws Ann., ch. 233, § 79(c) (Supp.1968)] which is typical, reads as follows:

> "A statement of fact or opinion on a subject of science or art contained in a published treatise, periodical, book or pamphlet shall, in the discretion of the court, and if the court finds that it is relevant and that the writer of such statement is recognized in his profession or calling as an expert on the subject, be admissible in actions of contract or tort for malpractice, error or mistake against physicians, surgeons, dentists, optometrists, hospitals, sanitaria, as evidence tending to prove said fact or as opinion evidence; provided, however, that the party intending to offer as evidence any such statement shall, not less than three days before trial of the action, give the adverse party notice of such intention, stating the name of the writer of the statement and the title of the treatise, periodical, book or pamphlet in which it is contained."

Nevada's statute is virtually identical with Massachusetts' except that it is made expressly applicable also to cases involving osteopathic physicians or surgeons, chiropractors, chiropodists and naturopathic physicians.[28]

The primary objection to the treatise approach is that it involves massive doses of hearsay, which is ordinarily an inadmissible brand of evidence in our courts. Hearsay evidence, to put it very simply, is the statement of a witness in court as to what another person has asserted out of court, the out-of-court assertion being offered to establish the truth of its contents. Unless the assertion happens to fall within one of the fairly numerous exceptions to the hearsay rule, it is rejected because of its unreliability. One reason for its rejection is that it was not made under oath. More importantly, it is rejected because secondhand assertions depend for their validity on the perception, training, skill, memory, articulateness, and veracity not of the witness on the stand but of the out-of-court declarant. Since the declarant is not on the witness stand, his possession of these truth-guaranteeing attributes cannot be tested by means of cross-examination. Furthermore, every statement in medical literature is

---

28. Nev.Rev.Stat., § 51.040 (1967). See also Kans.Stat.Ann., § 60–460(cc) (1964); Rhode Island Sess.Laws, H.B. 1833 (1969). The New Jersey Supreme Court recently adopted a code of evidentiary rules. One rule, proposed to the court but not adopted by it, would have permitted the use of medical treatises as substantive evidence under certain circumstances. N.J.S.Ct.R. 63(31) (not adopted). Section 1341 of the Calif.Evid.Code (Supp.1967) provides that medical books cannot be employed to establish the nature of an injury or its probable effect. See also § 721.

more or less a generalization; if the author were available for cross-examination it might develop that the fact situation before the court, although apparently the same as that discussed in the witness's book, was different enough to render the author's statement inapplicable to the immediate case.

There are additional dangers in the use of medical books as evidence. An obvious one is their potential for total confusion when placed in the hands of those who are ill-equipped to comprehend their esoteric language. And there is always the risk that jurors will give greater weight to a dubious treatise or article than to the oral testimony of the defendant's experts merely because the plaintiff's case appears in print between impressive cloth covers.

Only the Massachusetts treatise statute has had comprehensive judicial interpretation but the problems that arise under the Massachusetts law are undoubtedly the same as those encountered in the other states that have a treatise rule. Under the Massachusetts law two preliminary requirements must be met before a treatise or other publication will be admitted in evidence. First, the book, or the designated portion of it, must be relevant to material issues in the litigation. Second, and more significantly, the book must be reliable and authoritative. This second requirement has probably forestalled the publication in Massachusetts and elsewhere of a flood of special-interest medical treatises aimed mainly at the courtroom rather than the operating room.

The most difficult hurdle that plaintiff encounters under a treatise rule is the necessity for qualifying the author as a recognized and reliable authority in his field. In the Massachusetts case of Reddington v. Clayman,[29] medical books were excluded from evidence by the trial judge because he was not satisfied that their authors were recognized experts. If a medical treatise is in fact authoritative, however, plaintiff's counsel can extract this concession from the defendant doctor in a malpractice case by calling him as a witness in the manner previously described in this chapter.

Not surprisingly, it appears that the courts of Massachusetts have looked with disfavor on that state's treatise statute. Lawyers on both sides of the counsel table have agreed that "unsympathetic exercise of the trial judge's discretion has 'emasculated' the Massachusetts malpractice evidentiary statute."[30]

See Federal Rules of Evidence 803(17) & (18) at p. 925; California Evidence Code § § 1340, 1341 at p. 888.

McCORMICK'S HANDBOOK OF THE LAW OF EVIDENCE

745–747 (2d ed. 1972).

Statements and Reputation as to Pedigree and Family History.

One of the oldest exceptions to the hearsay rule encompasses, under certain conditions, statements concerning family history, such as the date and place of births and deaths of members of the family and facts about

---

29. 134 N.E.2d 290 (S.Jud.Ct.Mass. 1956).

30. Kehoe, W.F.: Massachusetts Malprac-

tice Evidentiary Statute—Success or Failure?, 44 Boston Univ.Law Review 10, 26 (1964).

marriage, descent, and relationship. Under the traditional rule, declarations of the person whose family situation is at issue are admissible, as are declarations by other members of the family and even, under a liberal view adopted by some courts, declarations by nonfamily members with a close relationship to the family. These statements are admissible, however, only upon a showing that the declarant is unavailable, that the statement was made before the origin of the controversy giving rise to the litigation in which the statement is offered (i.e., *ante litem motam*) and that there was no apparent motive for the declarant to misrepresent the facts. The firsthand knowledge requirement is not enforced; it is unnecessary to show that the declarant had personal knowledge of the facts of birth, death, kinship, or the like. Special need for this type of evidence is found in the general difficulty of obtaining other evidence of family matters, reflected in the unavailability requirement. Special assurances of reliability are found in the probability that in the absence of any motive for lying, the discussions of relatives (and others intimately related to them) as to family members will be accurate.

The traditional exception goes beyond oral declarations and permits the use of contemporary records of family history, such as entries in a family Bible or on a tombstone,[30] even though the author may not be identifiable. Further, evidence of the traditional reputation in the family as to such facts is admissible, and some courts have extended this to the reputation in the community of matters of family history.

Both the Uniform Rules of Evidence and the Proposed Federal Rules of Evidence adopt liberal positions, abandoning the requirement that declarations have been made *ante litem motam* and providing for the admission of statements of a nonfamily member if the declarant was so intimately associated with the family as to be likely to have accurate information concerning the subject of the statement.

See Federal Rules of Evidence 803(11) & (12), at p. 924, 804 (b)(4) at pp. 926, 927; California Evidence Code § § 1310–1316 at pp. 886–887.

McCORMICK'S HANDBOOK OF THE LAW OF EVIDENCE

747–748 (2d ed. 1972).

Recitals in Ancient Writings and Documents Affecting an Interest in Property.

As discussed in a preceding section, a writing is usually regarded as sufficiently authenticated if the offering party proves that it is at least 30 years old, the trial judge finds that it is unsuspicious in appearance, and the party proves that it was produced from a place of custody natural for such a writing. This "ancient documents" rule, however, traditionally relates only to authentication. American courts have nevertheless sometimes held that if a writing meets these requirements it is admissible to prove the truth of statements made in it. Thus what originated as an exception to general requirements of authentication has become in some jurisdictions also an exception to the hearsay rule.

Is the exception justified? The age requirement probably assures that there will be a special need for dispensing with the hearsay rule, for the same reasons which give rise to the special authentication rule. After passage of such a period of time, witnesses are unlikely to be available or, if available, to recall reliably the events at issue. But it is more doubtful whether there are sufficient assurances of special trustworthiness to justify admissibility. The mere age of the writing it may be contended, offers little assurance of truth; it is unlikely that lying was less common 30 years ago. Advocates of the exception argue, however, that given the special need for the evidence sufficient assurances of reliability exist. First, the dangers of mistransmission are minimized since the rule applies only to written statements. Second, the age requirement virtually assures that the assertion will have been made long before the beginning of the present controversy. Consequently, it is unlikely that the declarant had a motive to falsify, and, in any case, the statements are almost certainly uninfluenced by partisanship. Finally, some additional assurance of reliability is provided by insistence, insofar as practicable, that the usual qualifications for witnesses and out-of-court declarants be met. Thus the writing would be inadmissible if the declarant lacked the opportunity to know firsthand the facts asserted.

Nearly all courts will apply an exception to the hearsay rule when the matter involves ancient deed recitals. Thus deed recitals of the contents and execution of an earlier instrument, of heirship, and of consideration are nearly everywhere received to prove those facts. It is arguable that, especially where possession has been taken under the deed, these cases involve unusual assurances of reliability and the rule should be limited to them. A number of courts, however, have applied the exception to other types of documents. Both Wigmore and the Uniform Rules do not recognize any exception to the hearsay rule for ancient documents as such, but do recognize an exception for recitals in deeds without regard to the age of the deed.[43] The Uniform Rules would extend this to recitals in wills and other documents purporting to transfer land or personal property, but would require that the judge find that the matter stated would be relevant upon an issue as to an interest in the property and that dealings with the property since the statement was made have not been inconsistent with the truth of the statement. The Proposed Federal Rules of Evidence provide a similar exception for statements affecting an interest in property,[44] and also would recognize a specific exception for ancient documents with the common law age requirement reduced from 30 to 20 years.[45]

See Federal Rules of Evidence, 803 (15) and (16) at p. 925; California Evidence Code § 1331 at p. 888.

McNAUGHTON, EVIDENCE EXAM, HARVARD LAW SCHOOL, FIRST SEMESTER, 1960-1961

B. 50 HEARSAY QUESTIONS

Each of the following questions has two parts. (a) Is the item hearsay? Answer "Yes" or "No." And (b), if hearsay, under what exception or exceptions might the item reasonably fall? In the blank following the question, write one of the following three things: (i) "Not applicable" (or "N/A") if

---

43.　5 Wigmore, Evidence §§ 1573–1574; Uniform Rule 63(29).

44.　F.R.Ev. (R.D.1971) 803(15).

45.　F.R.Ev. (R.D.1971) 803(16).

the item is not hearsay; (ii) "None" if the hearsay link falls under no exception; (iii) the appropriate hearsay exception(s) under which the hearsay link might reasonably fall.

SPECIAL INFORMATION: (1) Even if the facts given are insufficient to supply all of the prerequisites of an exception, you should mention the exception if the facts given reasonably suggest and are not inconsistent with it. (2) Treat past recollection recorded, the business entry statute and present sense impression—pg—as separate exceptions to the hearsay rule.

If the item is multiple, or "totem pole," hearsay, indicate in some appropriate way which exceptions (if any) apply to which hearsay link.

Hearsay?
(Yes or No) _____

_____ 76. Prosecution of D for killing V. On the issue of D's fear of V, W1 testifies that he heard W2 say to D, "V has knifed three people in the last year." (Exception(s)_____
_____)

_____ 77. Same as 76 except the issue is whether V or D was the aggressor. (Exception(s)_____
_____)

_____ 78. On the issue whether P and D are bound by a contract, W testifies to D's statement to P, "I accept your offer." (Exception(s)_____
_____)

_____ 79. Action P v. D for injuries sustained when P fell through termite-eaten boards on D's porch. (a) to prove that P was involved in such an accident, P offers the testimony of W: "D said that when he got home from work he heard that P had gone through the porch and that he thought it was too bad." (Exception(s)____
_____)

_____ 80. — (b) to prove that P was involved in such an accident, P offers the testimony of W that N, a neighbor who had been on the porch with P, came rushing across the lawn shouting to D, "P has fallen through your porch." (Exception(s)_____
_____)

_____ 81. — (c) to rebut evidence by D that he had no knowledge of P's alleged accident until 18 months after it was supposed to have occurred, P offers the testimony in 80. (Exception(s)_____
_____)

_____ 82. — (d) to prove that P was involved in such an accident, P offers the transcript of D's testimony in prior litigation between him and his insurance company: "The boards on the porch were so weak that P went right through them." (Exception(s)_____
_____)

_____ 83. Same as 79 except that W is dead and P is offering a transcript of W's testimony, to the indicated effect, given in a prior trial of the same cause. (Exception(s)_____
_____)

_____ 84. As tending to show that D had a revolver in his possession, the state offers the testimony of W that, as D passed W's house,

(Yes or No) ⎯⎯⎯

W called her husband's attention to a revolver sticking out of D's pocket. (Exception(s)⎯⎯⎯⎯⎯⎯⎯⎯⎯⎯⎯⎯⎯⎯⎯⎯⎯⎯⎯⎯⎯⎯⎯⎯⎯⎯⎯)

⎯⎯⎯ 85. On the issue whether plaintiff's decedent (V) was still alive after his car was struck by the first of two cars, W (who was in V's car with V) testifies that, before the second car struck, V said, "My head hurts." (Exception(s)⎯⎯⎯⎯⎯⎯⎯⎯⎯⎯⎯⎯⎯⎯⎯⎯⎯⎯⎯⎯⎯⎯⎯⎯⎯⎯)

⎯⎯⎯ 86. On the issue of the existence of injuries to V's head caused by the first car, the testimony in 85. (Exception(s)⎯⎯⎯⎯⎯⎯⎯⎯⎯⎯⎯⎯⎯⎯⎯⎯⎯⎯⎯⎯⎯)

⎯⎯⎯ 87. On the issue of the sanity of D, a woman, W testifies that D on numerous occasions said publicly, "I am the Pope." (Exception(s)⎯⎯⎯⎯⎯⎯⎯⎯⎯⎯⎯⎯⎯⎯⎯⎯⎯⎯⎯⎯⎯⎯⎯⎯⎯⎯⎯)

⎯⎯⎯ 88. On the issue of D's guilt of the crime of killing V, W testifies that D told him that he (D) fled the scene immediately after V's murder. (Exception(s)⎯⎯⎯⎯⎯⎯⎯⎯⎯⎯⎯⎯⎯⎯⎯⎯⎯⎯⎯⎯⎯⎯⎯⎯)

⎯⎯⎯ 89. On the issue of X's sanity, W testifies that X was confined to an insane asylum. (Exception(s)⎯⎯⎯⎯⎯⎯⎯⎯⎯⎯⎯⎯⎯⎯⎯⎯⎯⎯⎯⎯⎯⎯⎯⎯⎯⎯)

⎯⎯⎯ 90. On the issue whether a transfer of a fountain pen from defendant (D) to plaintiff (P) was a sale or gift, P testifies that D made a statement accompanying the transfer, "I am giving you this pen as a birthday present." (Exception(s)⎯⎯⎯⎯⎯⎯⎯⎯⎯⎯⎯⎯⎯⎯⎯⎯⎯⎯⎯⎯⎯)

⎯⎯⎯ 91. In 90, P testifies instead that D, the day following the transfer, said, "I gave you the pen as a birthday present." (Exception(s)⎯⎯⎯⎯⎯⎯⎯⎯⎯⎯⎯⎯⎯⎯⎯⎯⎯⎯⎯⎯⎯⎯⎯⎯⎯⎯)

⎯⎯⎯ 92. In 90, P testifies instead that D, the day before the transfer, said, "I plan to give you the pen as a birthday present." (Exception(s)⎯⎯⎯⎯⎯⎯⎯⎯⎯⎯⎯⎯⎯⎯⎯⎯⎯⎯⎯⎯⎯⎯⎯⎯⎯⎯)

* * *

⎯⎯⎯ 94. On the issue of plaintiff's (P's) having cancer, N (a nurse) testifies for D that E, a doctor, gave P X-Ray treatments. (Exception(s)⎯⎯⎯⎯⎯⎯⎯⎯⎯⎯⎯⎯⎯⎯⎯⎯⎯⎯⎯⎯⎯⎯⎯⎯⎯⎯)

⎯⎯⎯ 95. In 94, N testifies instead that she heard E tell P that P had cancer. (Exception(s)⎯⎯⎯⎯⎯⎯⎯⎯⎯⎯⎯⎯⎯⎯⎯⎯⎯⎯⎯⎯⎯⎯⎯⎯⎯)

⎯⎯⎯ 96. In 94, instead of using N's testimony, D offers in evidence the hospital record containing a notation made by E to the effect that he had found a malignant tumor in P. (Exception(s)⎯⎯⎯⎯⎯⎯⎯⎯⎯⎯⎯⎯⎯⎯⎯⎯⎯⎯⎯⎯)

⎯⎯⎯ 97. Same as 96 except that the hospital record contains a notation by the hospital receptionist to the effect that P, on entering

(Yes or No) ＿＿＿＿＿

the hospital, said that he had "a cancerous tumor." (Exception(s)＿＿＿＿＿＿＿＿＿＿＿＿＿＿＿＿＿＿＿＿＿＿＿＿＿＿＿＿＿＿
＿＿＿＿＿＿＿＿＿＿＿＿＿＿＿＿＿＿＿＿＿＿＿＿＿＿＿＿＿)

＿＿＿＿＿ 98.　On the issue of X's good eyesight, W testifies that Y, X's commanding officer, assigned X to the position of lookout on the ship. (Exception(s)＿＿＿＿＿＿＿＿＿＿＿＿＿＿＿＿
＿＿＿＿＿＿＿＿＿＿＿＿＿＿＿＿＿＿＿＿＿＿＿＿＿＿＿＿＿)

＿＿＿＿＿ 99.　Action P v. D. On the issue of P's knowledge that D was in the city, D offers X's testimony that Z said to P, "D is in the city." (Exception(s)＿＿＿＿＿＿＿＿＿＿＿＿＿＿＿
＿＿＿＿＿＿＿＿＿＿＿＿＿＿＿＿＿＿＿＿＿＿＿＿＿＿＿＿＿)

＿＿＿＿＿ 100.　The testimony in 99 offered to prove that D was in the city. (Exception(s)＿＿＿＿＿＿＿＿＿＿＿＿＿＿＿＿＿＿＿
＿＿＿＿＿＿＿＿＿＿＿＿＿＿＿＿＿＿＿＿＿＿＿＿＿＿＿＿＿)

＿＿＿＿＿ 101.　Action P v. D. To prove that D was present in the city, D offers W's testimony that P said, "I know that D is in the city." (Exception(s)＿＿＿＿＿＿＿＿＿＿＿＿＿＿＿＿
＿＿＿＿＿＿＿＿＿＿＿＿＿＿＿＿＿＿＿＿＿＿＿＿＿＿＿＿＿)

＿＿＿＿＿ 102.　On the issue of witness W1's hostility toward defendant (D), W2 testifies for D that W1 said to D in an angry tone, while D remained silent, "Well, at least I've never stolen money from my employer like you have!" (Exception(s)＿＿＿＿＿＿＿＿
＿＿＿＿＿＿＿＿＿＿＿＿＿＿＿＿＿＿＿＿＿＿＿＿＿＿＿＿＿)

＿＿＿＿＿ 103.　On the issue of D's stealing money from his employer plaintiff (P) offers the evidence in 102. (Exception(s)＿＿＿＿＿
＿＿＿＿＿＿＿＿＿＿＿＿＿＿＿＿＿＿＿＿＿＿＿＿＿＿＿＿＿)

＿＿＿＿＿ 104.　To prove the license number of the car involved in a hit-run accident, P offers a crumpled slip of paper on which appears the number EE2468 and the testimony of a woman that, though she cannot now recall the number of the car, she did, while the number was fresh in her mind, write the number down on the piece of paper offered in evidence. (Exception(s)＿＿＿＿＿
＿＿＿＿＿＿＿＿＿＿＿＿＿＿＿＿＿＿＿＿＿＿＿＿＿＿＿＿＿)

＿＿＿＿＿ 105.　To prove the license number of the car involved in a hit-run accident, P offers a photograph of a retreating automobile bearing the license plate EE2468 and the testimony of a woman that, though she cannot now remember the number of the car, she did know it at the time and that she took the photograph offered in evidence of the accident car as it left the scene. (Exception(s)＿＿＿＿＿＿＿＿＿＿＿＿＿＿＿＿＿＿＿＿＿
＿＿＿＿＿＿＿＿＿＿＿＿＿＿＿＿＿＿＿＿＿＿＿＿＿＿＿＿＿)

* * *

＿＿＿＿＿ 108.　On the issue of the speed of a locomotive, P introduces the tape printed by an automatic speed-recording device in the train. (Exception(s)＿＿＿＿＿＿＿＿＿＿＿＿＿＿＿＿＿＿＿
＿＿＿＿＿＿＿＿＿＿＿＿＿＿＿＿＿＿＿＿＿＿＿＿＿＿＿＿＿)

＿＿＿＿＿ 109.　On the issue of D's guilt of a crime, P offers a moving picture of D re-enacting the crime. (Exception(s)＿＿＿＿＿＿＿
＿＿＿＿＿＿＿＿＿＿＿＿＿＿＿＿＿＿＿＿＿＿＿＿＿＿＿＿＿)

(Yes or No) _____

_____   110.   On the issue of the voluntariness of D's confession, P offers the moving picture in 109. (Exception(s)_____
_____)

_____   111.   On the issue of D's good faith in discharging X, an employ-ee (W) testifies that the police chief told D that X had been caught burglarizing a store. (Exception(s)_____
_____)

_____   112.   On the issue of D's good faith in discharging X, an employ-ee, D testifies that W told him (D) that the police chief told W that X had been caught burglarizing a store. (Exception(s)_____
_____)

_____   113.   On the issue of D's good faith in discharging X, an employ-ee, W testifies that the police chief told W that he (the police chief) had told D that X had been caught burglarizing a store. (Exception(s)_____
_____)

*   *   *

_____   115.   Action P v. D. W1 testifies for P that D's car was going "over 50 miles an hour." To impeach W1, D offers the testi-mony of W2 that W1 said a day after the accident that D was going "slow." (Exception(s)_____
_____)

_____   116.   The evidence in 115 offered by D to prove that he (D) was going slowly. (Exception(s)_____
_____)

_____   117.   In 115, W2 is a police officer with no present recollection of W1's statement, so D offers the officer's (W2's) accident report, made up the day after the accident, containing the alleged W1 statement. (Exception(s)_____
_____)

_____   118.   To prove that X was ill, W testifies that X, at the time, complained of a pain in his chest. (Exception(s)_____
_____)

_____   119.   Action P v. D for $800, the price of a used automobile. Plea, payment. On the issue of payment, W testifies that he saw D hand P $800 in cash and say, "This is the payment for that car." (Exception(s)_____
_____)

_____   120.   Action P v. D for conversion of a new automobile. To prove value, P offers a receipt for the purchase price, $3000, signed by X, the dealer from whom P bought it. (Exception(s)_____
_____)

_____   121.   Same as 120 except X is D. (Exception(s)_____
_____)

_____   122.   Action for personal injuries by a guest in an automobile against the owner. On the issue of contributory negligence and assumption of risk, W testifies than an hour before the accident, a mechanic said to the owner in the presence of the guest, "The

(Yes or No) _____

spindle on that front wheel may break at any moment." (Exception(s)_____
_____)

_____ 123.   The evidence in 122 offered to show that the spindle was defective. (Exception(s)_____
_____)

_____ 124.   As tending to prove title to Blackacre in defendant (D) by adverse possession under claim of title, D offers the testimony of W that plaintiff (P) said to his sister, "I've been down to the town meeting, and D is telling everyone that he owns Blackacre." (Exception(s)_____
_____)

_____ 125.   Action P v. D. To prove that A was an agent of D's, P offers the testimony of W that A said, "I am an agent of D's." (Exception(s)_____
_____)

SATURDAY REVIEW
June 4, 1966, p. 341 *

"Sure, it's hearsay—but it's great hearsay!"

[C1914]

PART C. THE FUTURE OF HEARSAY

McCORMICK, LAW AND THE FUTURE: EVIDENCE

51 Nw.U.L.Rev. 218 (1956).**
[Footnotes omitted.]

*   *   * The group of rules about hearsay evidence may be liberalized and simplified. A distinctive and cherished ideal of our trial tradition is that evidence in the main should be limited to the statements in court of witnesses who have observed the facts and are produced for cross-examination. But the rational investigation of facts cannot always be so limited. In ordinary life we must base many of our important decisions upon letters, technical books and articles, word of mouth, account books—in short, upon hearsay. So ten to twenty (depending upon minuteness of classification) sharply defined exceptions have been hammered out. But a half-century ago the exceptions had become more or less crystallized and had ceased to grow. Already they were too numerous and too complex to be remembered reliably at the counsel table. They badly need to be consolidated and enlarged. One move in that direction is the Massachusetts hearsay statute which admits the declaration of a deceased person if the judge finds it was made in good faith upon personal knowledge. The English Evidence Act of 1938 admits a written hearsay statement, on personal knowledge, if the writer is unavailable for any reason. The Model Code would admit any hearsay statement, written or oral, based on personal knowledge, if the declarant is unavailable for any cause. Even bolder in conception are those decisions which seem to sanction the practice that when a statement does not fall within an existing exception it still may be admitted if the judge finds that there is a necessity for its use and that it was made under circumstances showing exceptional trustworthiness. These courageous judges have marked the way, and we may eventually see our hearsay canon restated in this fashion: a hearsay statement will be received if the judge finds that the need for and the probative value of the statement render it a fair means of proof under the circumstances. *   *   *

HUFF v. WHITE MOTOR CORP.

United States Court of Appeals, Seventh Circuit, 1979.
609 F.2d 286.

TONE, Circuit Judge.

In the trial of this diversity action for wrongful death, the court excluded a statement of the plaintiff's decedent, made while he was hospitalized for treatment of the injuries from which he later died. We hold that unless the declarant was not mentally competent when he made the statement, it should have been admitted under the so-called residual exception to the hearsay rule established by Rules 803(24) and 804(b)(5) of the Federal Rules of Evidence. *   *   *

* * *

On September 4, 1970 Jessee Huff was driving a truck-tractor manufactured by the defendant White Motor Corporation near Terre Haute, Indiana when it jackknifed on the highway, sideswiped a guardrail, and collided with an overpass support. Aside from the structural damage to the tractor, the fuel tank ruptured and caught fire. The flames engulfed the cab area occupied by Huff. The severe burns he received in the fire caused his death nine days later. Helen L. Huff filed this action seeking damages for wrongful death of her husband based on the theory that the defective design of the fuel system cause the fire [after the collision] that took Huff's life.

At the trial on remand, the jury returned a verdict awarding plaintiff $700,000 in compensatory damages. Defendant appeals from the judgment on the verdict, * * * .

I.

Admissibility of Decedent's Statement

Defendant offered and the trial court excluded the testimony of Melvin Myles, who was the husband of Mrs. Huff's cousin and a friend and neighbor of the Huffs for many years. Myles' testimony, presented out of the presence of the jury, was that when he and one Richard King visited Huff in his hospital room two or three days after the accident, Huff gave the following description of how the accident occurred:

[H]e told us first more or less what happened and this U.S. 41 there has a bad curve there and he told us as he was approaching the curve or starting into it his pant leg was on fire and he was trying to put his pant leg out and lost control and hit the bridge abutment and then the truck was on fire * * * .

The district court excluded this testimony as hearsay, rejecting defendant's argument that Huff's statement was an admission under Rule 801(d)(2) or admissible under the residual exception, Rules 803(24) and 804(b)(5). * * *

Defendant first argues that Huff's statement is admissible as an admission because privity exists between Huff and his widow, who brings this wrongful death action [and hence his admission should be usable against her to show his contributory negligence in allowing his pant leg to catch fire]. * * *

The admissibility of privity-based admissions in the federal courts is now controlled, of course, by the Federal Rules of Evidence. A reading of Article VIII of those rules, the article on hearsay, leads us to conclude that privity-based admissions are to be tested for admissibility under the residual exception provided for in Rules 803(24) and 804(b)(5) rather than under the admissions provision, Rule 801(d)(2). Although neither the rules themselves nor the Advisory Committee Notes refer to privity-based admissions, and Congress added nothing on the subject in its consideration of the rules, the language of Rule 801(d)(2) and the general scheme of the hearsay article support our conclusion. Privity-based admissions are within the definition of hearsay, Rule 801(c), an extra-judicial statement offered "to prove the truth of the matter asserted," and are not among the specifically defined kinds of admissions that despite Rule 801(c) are declared not to be hearsay in Rule 801(d)(2). Nor are they covered by any of the specific exceptions to the hearsay rule listed in Rules 803 and 804. Thus privity-based admissions are not admissible as such, if the rules are to be read literally. Moreover, the very explicitness of Rule 801(d)(2) suggests that the draftsmen did not intend to authorize the courts to add new categories of admissions to those stated in the rule. No standards for judicial improvisation or discretion are provided in Rule 801(d)(2), as they are in Rules 803(24) and 804(b)(5).

The admissibility of Huff's statement depends, therefore, upon the residual exception, which is stated in Rules 803(24) and 804(b)(5):

A statement not specifically covered by any of the foregoing exceptions but having equivalent circumstantial guarantees of trustworthiness, if the court determines that (A) the statement is offered as evidence of a material fact; (B) the statement is more probative on the point for which it is offered than any other evidence which the proponent can procure through reasonable efforts; and (C) the general purposes of these rules and the interests of justice will best be served by admission of the statement into evidence. However, a statement may not be admitted under this exception unless the proponent of it makes known to the adverse party sufficiently in advance of the trial or hearing to provide the adverse party with a fair opportunity to prepare to meet it, his intention to offer the statement and the particulars of it, including the name and address of the declarant.

We recognize at the outset that in applying this exception the district court has a considerable measure of discretion. If, however, we arrive at "a definite and firm conviction that the court below committed a clear error of judgment in the conclusion it reached based upon a weighing of the relevant factors," and that the error was prejudicial, we must reverse. We also recognize that Congress "intended that the residual hearsay exceptions will be used very rarely, and only in exceptional circumstances." Committee on the Judiciary, S.Rep.No.93–1277, Note to Paragraph (24), 28 U.S.C.A. Fed.R. Evid. p. 583 (1975); we think such circumstances are present here.

* * *

Hearsay evidence must fulfill five requirements to be admissible under the residual exception. We apply them to resolve the issue before us.

1. *Trustworthiness*

The circumstantial guarantees of trustworthiness on which the various specific exceptions to the hearsay rule are based are those that existed at the time the statement was made and do not include those that may be added by using hindsight. Evidence admissible under the residual exception must have *"equivalent* circumstantial guarantees of trustworthiness." Rules 803(24) and 804(b)(5) (emphasis added). Therefore, the guarantees to be considered in applying that exception are those that existed when the statement was made. In contrast, the probative value of an admission of a party-opponent, classified as non-hearsay by Rule 801(d)(2), is based on its inconsistency with the position asserted in court, and that probative value does not depend on whether the party knew when making it that it would be against his interest in a later lawsuit. Accordingly, in evaluating the circumstantial guarantees of trustworthiness with respect to Huff's statement, we may not consider its probative value as an admission of one who would be bringing the action if he had survived.

Turning to the circumstances we may properly consider for the present purpose, we note that Huff's statement was an unambiguous and explicit report of the events he had experienced two or three days earlier; it contained neither opinion nor speculation. He was not being interrogated, so there was no reason to give any explanation of how the accident happened unless he wanted to do so. There was no reason for him to invent the story of the pre-existing fire in the cab.   *   *   *

Plaintiff also argues that it is unlikely that Huff made the statement, because Mrs. Huff testified that he was not physically able to carry on a conversation. Even if we were to consider facts bearing on the reliability of Myles' reporting of the incident in determining its admissibility, we would not be persuaded that it should have been excluded for this reason. Mrs. Huff was an interested witness and, moreover, was assisted by her counsel's leading questions in giving the testimony relied on. No reason is suggested why Myles, a friend and relative by marriage, would have manufactured the story. Although the trial judge did not address the residual exception and made no credibility finding, it appears from his remarks that he credited Myles' testimony.

In our view, however, the reliability of the witness' testimony that the hearsay statement was in fact made is not a factor to be considered in deciding its admissibility. We recognize that the Third Circuit [has] said otherwise but, as we have already noted, the circumstantial guarantees of trustworthiness necessary under the residual exception are to be "equivalent" to the guarantees that justify the specific exceptions. Those guarantees relate solely to the trustworthiness of the hearsay statement itself. The specific exceptions to the hearsay rule are not justified by any circumstantial guarantee that the witness who reports the statement will do so accurately and truthfully. That witness can be cross-examined and his credibility thus tested in the same way as that of any other witness. It is the hearsay declarant, not the witness who reports the hearsay, who cannot be cross-examined. Therefore, although we do not think Myles' testimony would fail a reliability test, that test is not to be applied by the court but by the jury, as with any other witness.

For the same reason, the probability that the statement is true, as shown by corroborative evidence, is not, we think, a consideration relevant to its admissibility under the residual exception to the hearsay rule. Because the presence or absence of corroborative evidence is irrelevant in the case of a specific exception, it is irrelevant here, where the guarantees of trustworthiness must be equivalent to those supporting specific exceptions. Accordingly, in reaching our decision we do not rely upon the evidence to which defendant has pointed as corroborating Huff's story of the fire in the cab.

*   *   *

We proceed now to a brief explanation of why we believe the other requirements of the residual exception to the hearsay rule have been met. *   *   *

2. *Materiality*

Rules 803(24) and 804(b)(5) require that the statement be offered as evidence of a material fact, which we take to be a requirement of relevance. Defendant argues that the existence of a fire in the cab before the crash would be relevant to the issue of what caused the fuel to ignite after the crash, plaintiff having pleaded, offered proof, and argued that the location of the battery and battery mechanism as a result of a design error was a likely cause of ignition. Plaintiff responds that there were several possible sources of ignition. Assuming this to be true, the evidence was nevertheless relevant. The "fact that is of consequence" for purposes of the application of Rule 401 is that, as defendant contended, the fuel was ignited by a fire in the cab that was not due to a defect in the vehicle. If proved, that fact would be "of consequence to the determination of the action." The evidence in issue would tend "to make the existence of [that] fact * * * more probable or less probable than it would be without the evidence." Accordingly, the evidence is plainly relevant.

3. *Probative Importance of the Evidence*

To be admissible under the residual exception, the statement must be "more probative on the point for which it is offered than any other evidence * * * [the defendant] can procure through reasonable efforts." Huff's statement satisfies this requirement. The other evidence is expert opinion and [a witness'] circumstantial testimony about what he saw when he arrived at the scene after the crash. Only Huff was in the cab immediately before the crash and knew whether there was a fire in the cab at that time. Unless the hearsay is admitted, there will be no direct evidence on that question. Moreover, the unique probative quality that would lie in Huff's admission if he had survived to bring this action, is not lost when the action is brought by his widow for his wrongful death.

4. *The Interests of Justice*

The hearsay statement is to be admitted only if doing so will best serve the general purposes of the Federal Rules of Evidence and the interests of justice. As we have already said, the circumstantial guarantees of trustworthiness and the probative value of the statement are strong. The need for the only available direct evidence on the issue of whether there was a fire in the cab, which, if it existed, would have been a likely source of ignition of the fuel, is obvious. There is no reason to believe the jury will not be equipped to evaluate the evidence. Admission of the evidence will best serve the interests of justice by increasing the likelihood that the jury will ascertain the truth about the cause of the accident.

5. *Notice*

Finally, the residual hearsay exception requires that the proponent of the hearsay statement notify his opponent of his intent to use the statement sufficiently in advance of the trial to give the opponent a fair opportunity to prepare to meet it. Plaintiff does not argue that defendant failed to comply with this notice provision, and the record reflects that defendant gave sufficient notice to plaintiff and the court.

For reasons that are apparent from our explanation of why we believe the evidence to be admissible under the residual exception if Huff possessed the requisite mental capacity, exclusion of the evidence, if erroneous, was so prejudicial as to require a new trial.

*   *   *

Vacated and remanded   *   *   *   .

UNITED STATES v. WEST

United States Court of Appeals, Fourth Circuit, 1978.
574 F.2d 1131.

HAYNSWORTH, Chief Judge:

Calvin W. West, Floyd Lee Davis and Joseph Lee Dempsey appeal their convictions for distributing heroin and possessing heroin with the intent to distribute it. The most significant question presented is whether the admission of the grand jury testimony of Michael Victor Brown, who was slain prior to trial, was permissible under Rule 804(b)(5) of the Federal Rules of Evidence   *   *   *   . We hold that it was.

The convictions challenged here are the product of an extensive Drug Enforcement Agency (DEA) investigation in which Brown played a vital role. Brown volunteered his assistance to the DEA while he was in jail on a drug charge and under a detainer for parole violation. He agreed to purchase heroin under police surveillance.

Each purchase was similar. Brown would contact West or Davis and arrange to purchase heroin. Twice the DEA monitored Brown's calls to West arranging heroin deals. It also monitored one phone call to Davis. On other occasions it seems that Brown simply notified the DEA that he had arranged a purchase.

Each time that the DEA agents received notice that Brown was about to make a purchase, they made arrangements for extensive surveillance. Before each purchase, DEA agents strip-searched Brown to make sure that he had no drugs, and they concealed a transmitter on him. They then searched his vehicle to be sure that it contained no drugs and gave Brown the money required for the anticipated purchase.

According to the government's evidence, on three occasions, Brown went to West, gave West money, and obtained heroin. Twice Brown went to Davis, gave Davis money and obtained heroin. On another occasion, Brown gave West money then accompanied him to meet Dempsey. West then gave Dempsey money and told Brown that they were to meet Dempsey at Griffin's home. Brown and West went to Griffin's home. Dempsey arrived, went to the open window of Brown's car and then entered Griffin's home and told Brown that everything was all right. Brown then returned to his car to find 30 capsules of heroin.

Each time, law enforcement officials observed Brown's movements and obtained photographs of Brown as he met with West and with Davis. After each transaction Brown returned to the DEA office and surrendered the heroin that he had purchased and any money remaining. Each time the agents searched Brown and his car to be sure that he retained no contraband. Agent Scott then discussed with Brown the events that had taken place and composed a detailed summary of what had occurred, which Brown read, corrected and signed. After one of the purchases Brown himself prepared a statement which Agent Scott revised before Brown read, corrected and signed it. Each time, Scott and Brown listened to the tapes from the body transmitter for audibility and voice identification. By reviewing the tapes with Brown, Scott independently became able to identify the voices of the defendants.

On March 8, 1976, the defendants and others were indicted by a grand jury, apparently without Brown's testimony. On March 16, Brown appeared before a grand jury and testified under oath regarding his knowledge of the drug traffic in Virginia's Tidewater area. The government attorney read the statements that Brown had signed and periodically asked Brown if they were correct.

As a result of his cooperation, Brown was released from jail, the pending drug charge against him was nol prossed, and the detainer for parole violation was lifted. The DEA also gave Brown $855 for his personal use so that he would not arouse suspicion and jeopardize his cover by being without funds immediately after supposedly selling a large amount of heroin.

On March 19 Brown was murdered in a manner suggestive of contract killers. Four bullets were fired into the back of his head while he was driving his car. According to the government, at least four potential government witnesses in this and related narcotics investigations have been murdered after they had agreed to cooperate. But these defendants have not been charged with Brown's murder, and the government did not offer any evidence to show that they were responsible for it.

On April 22, a week before the scheduled trial date, the government notified the defendants, pursuant to Rule 804(b)(5) of the Federal Rules of Evidence, that it intended to introduce Brown's grand jury testimony at trial. It agreed to give defense counsel all of its evidence, including Brown's arrest record, and transcripts of the tapes of Brown's conversations with the defendants.

After a pre-trial hearing, the district court ruled that the grand jury testimony was admissible under Rule 804(b)(5) because, under the circumstances, it was essential and trustworthy. It also gave the defense a week's continuance after it announced that it would admit Brown's grand jury testimony.

During the trial the government introduced the transcript of Brown's grand jury testimony, the photographs, and expert on voice identification and the heroin. It also played the tapes of Brown's conversations with the defendants. Law enforcement agents testified about their observation of Brown's activities and corroborated Brown's highly detailed grand jury testimony. The government sought to introduce transcripts which it had prepared from the tapes from Brown's body transmitter. Although the district judge found that the transcripts were a fair representation of the taped conversations, he permitted the jury to see the transcripts only while they listened to the tapes and instructed the jurors to decide for themselves what the tapes said.

I.

The defendants contend that the district judge erred in concluding that the transcript of Brown's grand jury testimony was admissible under Rule 804(b)(5).

Rule 804(b)(5) provides:

"(b) *Hearsay exceptions.* The following are not excluded by the hearsay rule if the declarant is unavailable as a witness:

* * *

"(5) *Other exceptions.* A statement not specifically covered by any of the foregoing exceptions but having equivalent circumstantial guarantees of trustworthiness, if the court determines that (A) the statement is offered as evidence of a material fact; (B) the statement is more probative on the point for which it is offered than any other evidence which the proponent can procure through reasonable efforts; and (C) the general purposes of these rules and the interests of justice will best be served by admission of the statement into evidence."

The defendants do not contend that the grand jury transcript fails to meet the criteria of clauses (A), (B) and (C). Instead, they focus upon the general requirement that the statement have "equivalent circumstantial guarantees of trustworthiness" as statements the admission of which is authorized by any of the preceding four paragraphs. They find a lack of trustworthiness in Brown's criminal record and their lack of any opportunity to cross-examine him. They point to legislative history indicating that Rule 804(b)(5) applies only where "exceptional circumstances" lend to the extra-judicial statement a degree of trustworthiness equivalent to that of evidence admissible under other § 804(b) exceptions.[1]

There were present very exceptional circumstances providing substantial guarantees of trustworthiness of Brown's grand jury testimony probably exceeding by far the substantial guarantees of trustworthiness of some of the other § 804(b) hearsay exceptions. Before each contact by Brown with West, Davis or Dempsey, the agents took elaborate steps to assure themselves that Brown possessed no drugs or money other than the money supplied by the agents to effect the purchases. Except when he entered a building and became concealed from their view he was under constant surveillance, and photographs were taken when he was with one of the defendants. Moreover, his transmitter was broadcasting his conversations with the defendants, and a tape recorder preserved those conversations. Moreover, immediately after each purchase, he and one of the agents reviewed what Brown had done, said and observed, and a statement of it was prepared and corrected. The immediate transcription and verification of Brown's statements provide an additional guarantee other admissible hearsay statements lack. But the most impressive assurance of trustworthiness comes from the corroboration provided by the observations of the agents, the pictures they took and their recordings of the conversations. Brown had a criminal record, and he was seeking favors to avoid further incarceration,

<hr/>

1. The defendants also rely upon United States v. Fiore, 443 F.2d 112 (2d Cir. 1971) in which it was held that grand jury testimony was inadmissible where the declarant was physically available but refused to take the oath and submit to meaningful cross-examination. *Fiore* is inapposite, for it was decided before the adoption of Rule 804(b)(5). Two cases decided after adoption of the rule have reached opposite re-

sults. *Compare* United States v. Carlson, 547 F.2d 1346 (8 Cir.) (admitting prior grand jury testimony under Rule 804(b)(5)) with United States v. Gonzalez, 559 F.2d 1271 (5th Cir. 1977) (testimony not admissible). Both courts focused for purposes of their analysis of the admissibility of the evidence under the F.R. Evid. on its reliability.

but the circumstances make deception of the agents inconceivable. The agents simply followed, photographed and recorded conversations to such an extent that deception by Brown was substantially impossible. Moreover, his interest in gaining favors to avoid further imprisonment gave him every incentive to be extremely accurate in his reports. He knew what the agents were doing to corroborate and verify his reports, and any attempted deception would only have been calculated to arouse the suspicion of the agents and to lose for Brown their favor.

The substantially contemporaneous sworn written statements by Brown were the basis of Brown's grand jury testimony. The corroborative circumstances and verification procedures lend to his grand jury testimony a degree of trustworthiness probably substantially exceeding that inherent in dying declarations, statements against interest, and statements of personal or family history, all of which are routinely admitted under § 804(b)(2), (3) and (4).

Although Brown's grand jury testimony was not subject to immediate cross-examination, to a large extent what Brown said was corroborated by the observations of the agents. The agents did appear as witnesses and were subject to cross-examination about what they observed, including the possibility of mistake or prevarication by Brown, and their own roles in preparing Brown's statements.　*　*　*

Under all of these circumstances, the absence of an opportunity to cross-examine Brown himself is of considerable less significance than in those cases involving statements against interest, statements of family history, or dying declarations.

Whether the circumstantial guarantees of trustworthiness of Brown's grand jury testimony are equivalent to those which arise from cross or direct examination which underlies the former testimony exception of § 804(b)(1), we need not determine. In this unusual case, those guarantees were probably greater, but the equivalent guarantee of trustworthiness requirement of § 804(b)(5) is met if there is equivalency of any one of the preceding § 804(b) exceptions. Clearly there is such equivalency with the exceptions we find in paragraphs 2, 3, and 4.

The defense lawyers were given every opportunity to attack Brown's credibility, and they fully utilized their opportunities. It may be of passing significance that the jury did not accept all that Brown said, for it acquitted two of the defendants implicated by him. That it convicted West, Davis and Dempsey suggests that it carefully considered the very substantial extent to which the corroborative evidence established their guilt, either directly or through strong demonstration of the trustworthiness of Brown's testimony as to them.

*　*　*

Affirmed.

[Dissenting opinion of Judge Widener omitted.]

———

See Federal Rules of Evidence 803(24) at p. 926, 804(b)(5) at pp. 926, 927.

CIVIL EVIDENCE ACT, ENGLAND, 1968.

2.—(1)   In any civil proceedings a statement made, whether orally or in a document or otherwise, by any person whether called as a witness in those proceeding or not, shall, subject to this section and to rules of court, be admissible as evidence of any fact stated therein of which direct oral evidence by him would be admissible.

(2)   Where in any civil proceedings a party desiring to give a statement in evidence by virtue of this section has called or intends to call as a witness in the proceedings the person by whom the statement was made, the statement—

(a)   shall not be given in evidence by virtue of this section on behalf of that party without the leave of the court; and

(b)   without prejudice to paragraph (a) above, shall not be given in evidence by virtue of this section on behalf of that party before the conclusion of the examination-in-chief of the person by whom it was made, except—

(i)   where before that person is called the court allows evidence of the making of the statement to be given on behalf of that party by some other person; or

(ii)   in so far as the court allows the person by whom the statement was made to narrate it in the course of his examination-in-chief on the ground that to prevent him from doing so would adversely affect the intelligibility of his evidence.

(3)   Where in any civil proceedings a statement which was made otherwise than in a document is admissible by virtue of this section, no evidence other than direct oral evidence by the person who made the statement or any person who heard or otherwise perceived it being made shall be admissible for the purpose of proving it:

Provided that if the statement in question was made by a person while giving oral evidence in some other legal proceedings (whether civil or criminal), it may be proved in any manner authorized by the court.

CALIFORNIA v. GREEN

Supreme Court of the United States, 1970.
399 U.S. 149, 90 S.Ct. 1930, 26 L.Ed.2d 489.
[Some footnotes omitted.]

Mr. Justice WHITE delivered the opinion of the Court.

Section 1235 of the California Evidence Code, effective as of January 1, 1967, provides that "[e]vidence of a statement made by a witness is not made inadmissible by the hearsay rule if the statement is inconsistent with his testimony at the hearing and is offered in compliance with Section 770."[1] In People v. Johnson, 68 Cal.2d 646, 68 Cal.Rptr. 599, 441 P.2d 111 (1968), cert. denied, 393 U.S. 1051, 89 S.Ct. 679, 21 L.Ed.2d 693 (1969), the California Supreme Court held that prior statements of a witness that were not subject to cross-examination when originally made, could not be introduced under this section to prove the charges against a defendant

---

1.   Cal.Evid.Code § 1235 (1966). Section 770 merely requires that the witness be given an opportunity to explain or deny the prior statement at some point in the trial. See Cal.Evid.Code § 770 (1966).

without violating the defendant's right of confrontation guaranteed by the Sixth Amendment and made applicable to the States by the Fourteenth Amendment. In the case now before us the California Supreme Court applied the same ban to a prior statement of a witness made at a preliminary hearing, under oath and subject to full cross-examination by an adequately counseled defendant. We cannot agree with the California court for two reasons, one of which involves rejection of the holding in People v. Johnson.

I

In January 1967, one Melvin Porter, a 16-year-old minor, was arrested for selling marihuana to an undercover police officer. Four days after his arrest, while in the custody of juvenile authorities, Porter named respondent Green as his supplier. As recounted later by one Officer Wade, Porter claimed that Green had called him earlier that month, had asked him to sell some "stuff" or "grass," and had that same afternoon personally delivered a shopping bag containing 29 "baggies" of marihuana. It was from this supply that Porter had made his sale to the undercover officer. A week later, Porter testified at respondent's preliminary hearing. He again named respondent as his supplier, although he now claimed that instead of personally delivering the marihuana, Green had showed him where to pick up the shopping bag, hidden in the bushes at Green's parents' house. Porter's story at the preliminary hearing was subjected to extensive cross-examination by respondent's counsel—the same counsel who represented respondent at his subsequent trial. At the conclusion of the hearing, respondent was charged with furnishing marihuana to a minor in violation of California law.

Respondent's trial took place some two months later before a court sitting without a jury. The State's chief witness was again young Porter. But this time Porter, in the words of the California Supreme Court, proved to be "markedly evasive and uncooperative on the stand." People v. Green, 70 Cal.2d 654, 657, 75 Cal.Rptr. 782, 783, 451 P.2d 422, 423 (1969). He testified that respondent had called him in January 1967, and asked him to sell some unidentified "stuff." He admitted obtaining shortly thereafter 29 plastic "baggies" of marihuana, some of which he sold. But when pressed as to whether respondent had been his supplier, Porter claimed that he was uncertain how he obtained the marihuana, primarily because he was at the time on "acid" (LSD), which he had taken 20 minutes before respondent phoned. Porter claimed that he was unable to remember the events that followed the phone call, and that the drugs he had taken prevented his distinguishing fact from fantasy. See, e.g., App. 7–11, 24–25.

At various points during Porter's direct examination, the prosecutor read excerpts from Porter's preliminary hearing testimony. This evidence was admitted under § 1235 for the truth of the matter contained therein. With his memory "refreshed" by his preliminary hearing testimony, Porter "guessed" that he had indeed obtained the marihuana from the backyard of respondent's parents' home, and had given the money from its sale to respondent. On cross-examination, however, Porter indicated that it was his memory of the preliminary testimony which was "mostly" refreshed, rather than his memory of the events themselves, and he was still unsure of the actual episode.   *   *   *   Later in the trial, Officer Wade testified, relating Porter's earlier statement that respondent had personally delivered the marihuana. This statement was also admitted as substantive evidence.

Porter admitted making the statement, * * * and insisted that he had been telling the truth as he then believed it both to Officer Wade and at the preliminary hearing; but he insisted that he was also telling the truth now in claiming inability to remember the actual events.

Respondent was convicted. The District Court of Appeal reversed, holding that the use of Porter's prior statements for the truth of the matter asserted therein, denied respondent his right of confrontation under the California Supreme Court's recent decision in People v. Johnson, supra. The California Supreme Court affirmed, finding itself "impelled" by recent decisions of this Court to hold § 1235 unconstitutional insofar as it permitted the substantive use of prior inconsistent statements of a witness, even though the statements were subject to cross-examination at a prior hearing. We granted the State's petition for certiorari, 396 U.S. 1001 (1970).

II

The California Supreme Court construed the Confrontation Clause of the Sixth Amendment to require the exclusion of Porter's prior testimony offered in evidence to prove the State's case against Green because, in the court's view, neither the right to cross-examine Porter at the trial concerning his current and prior testimony, nor the opportunity to cross-examine Porter at the preliminary hearing satisfied the commands of the Confrontation Clause. We think the California court was wrong on both counts.

Positing that this case posed an instance of a witness who gave trial testimony inconsistent with his prior, out-of-court statements,[2] the California court, on the authority of its decision in People v. Johnson, supra, held that belated cross-examination before the trial court, "is not an adequate substitute for the right to cross-examination contemporaneous with the original testimony before a different tribunal." People v. Green, supra, 70 Cal.2d, at 659, 75 Cal.Rptr., at 785, 451 P.2d, at 425. We disagree.

Section 1235 of the California Evidence Code represents a considered choice by the California Legislature[3] between two opposing positions concerning the extent to which a witness' prior statements may be introduced at trial without violating hearsay rules of evidence. The orthodox view, adopted in most jurisdictions, has been that the out-of-court statements are inadmissible * * *.

In contrast, the minority view adopted in some jurisdictions and supported by most legal commentators and by recent proposals to codify the law of evidence[6] would permit the substantive use of prior inconsistent

2. See People v. Green, 70 Cal.2d 654, 657 n. 1, 75 Cal.Rptr. 782, 451 P.2d 422, 424 n. 1 (1969).

3. See the comments of the California Law Revision Commission, Cal.Evid.Code § 1235 (1966).

6. Dean Wigmore was the first noted commentator to adopt this position, abandoning his earlier approval, in the first edition of his Treatise, of the orthodox view. See 3 Wigmore § 1018 n. 2. Both the Model Code and the Uniform Rules have since followed the Wigmore position, see Model Code of Evidence Rule 503(b) (1942); Uniform Rule of Evidence 63(1) (1953), as has the recent preliminary draft of the rules of evidence for the lower federal courts, see Committee on Rules of Practice and Procedure of the Judicial Conference of the United States, Preliminary Draft of Proposed Rules of Evidence for the United States District Courts and Magistrates, Rule 8–01(c) (2) (1969). For commentators who have urged views similar to Wigmore's see C. McCormick, Evidence § 39 (1954); Maguire, The Hearsay System: Around and Through the Thicket, 14 Vand.L.Rev. 741, 747 (1961); Morgan, Hearsay Dangers and the Application of the Hearsay Concept, 62 Harv.L.Rev. 177, 192–196 (1948).

statements on the theory that the usual dangers of hearsay are largely non-existent where the witness testifies at trial. "The whole purpose of the Hearsay rule has been already satisfied [because] the witness is present and subject to cross-examination [and] [t]here is ample opportunity to test him as to the basis for his former statement."[7]

Our task in this case is not to decide which of these positions, purely as a matter of the law of evidence, is the sounder. The issue before us is the considerably narrower one of whether a defendant's constitutional right "to be confronted with the witnesses against him" is necessarily inconsistent with a State's decision to change its hearsay rules to reflect the minority view described above. While it may readily be conceded that hearsay rules and the Confrontation Clause are generally designed to protect similar values, it is quite a different thing to suggest that the overlap is complete and that the Confrontation Clause is nothing more or less than a codification of the rules of hearsay and their exceptions as they existed historically at common law. Our decisions have never established such a congruence; indeed, we have more than once found a violation of confrontation values even though the statements in issue were admitted under an arguably recognized hearsay exception. The converse is equally true: merely because evidence is admitted in violation of a long-established hearsay rule does not lead to the automatic conclusion that confrontation rights have been denied.

Given the similarity of the values protected, however, the modification of a State's hearsay rules to create new exceptions for the admission of evidence against a defendant, will often raise questions of compatibility with the defendant's constitutional right to confrontation. Such questions require attention to the reasons for, and the basic scope of the protections offered by the Confrontation Clause.

*   *   *

*   *   * Viewed historically, then, there is good reason to conclude that the Confrontation Clause is not violated by admitting a declarant's out-of-court statements, as long as the declarant is testifying as a witness and subject to full and effective cross-examination.

This conclusion is supported by comparing the purposes of confrontation with the alleged dangers in admitting an out-of-court statement. Confrontation: (1) insures that the witness will give his statements under oath —thus impressing him with the seriousness of the matter and guarding against the lie by the possibility of a penalty for perjury; (2) forces the witness to submit to cross-examination, the "greatest legal engine ever invented for the discovery of truth";[11] (3) permits the jury that is to decide the defendant's fate to observe the demeanor of the witness in making his statement, thus aiding the jury in assessing his credibility.

It is, of course, true that the out-of-court statement may have been made under circumstances subject to none of these protections. But if the declarant is present and testifying at trial, the out-of-court statement for all practical purposes regains most of the lost protections. If the witness admits the prior statement is his, or if there is other evidence to show the statement is his, the danger of faulty reproduction is negligible and the jury can be confident that it has before it two conflicting statements by the same witness. Thus, as far as the oath is concerned, the witness must now affirm,

---

7.   3 Wigmore § 1018.   11.   5 Wigmore § 1367.

deny, or qualify the truth of the prior statement under the penalty of perjury; indeed, the very fact that the prior statement was not given under a similar circumstance may become the witness' explanation for its inaccuracy—an explanation a jury may be expected to understand and take into account in deciding which, if either, of the statements represents the truth.

Second, the inability to cross-examine the witness at the time he made his prior statement cannot easily be shown to be of crucial significance as long as the defendant is assured of full and effective cross-examination at the time of trial. The most successful cross-examination at the time the prior statement was made could hardly hope to accomplish more than has already been accomplished by the fact that the witness is now telling a different, inconsistent story, and—in this case—one that is favorable to the defendant. * * *

The defendant's task in cross-examination is, of course, no longer identical to the task that he would have faced if the witness had not changed his story and hence had to be examined as a "hostile" witness giving evidence for the prosecution. This difference, however, far from lessening, may actually enhance the defendant's ability to attack the prior statement. For the witness, favorable to the defendant, should be more than willing to give the usual suggested explanations for the inaccuracy of his prior statement, such as faulty perception or undue haste in recounting the event. Under such circumstances, the defendant is not likely to be hampered in effectively attacking the prior statement, solely because his attack comes later in time.

Similar reasons lead us to discount as a constitutional matter the fact that the jury at trial is foreclosed from viewing the declarant's demeanor when he first made his out-of-court statement. The witness who now relates a different story about the events in question must necessarily assume a position as to the truth value of his prior statement, thus giving the jury a chance to observe and evaluate his demeanor as he either disavows or qualifies his earlier statement. The jury is alerted by the inconsistency in the stories, and its attention is sharply focused on determining either that one of the stories reflects the truth or that the witness who has apparently lied once, is simply too lacking in credibility to warrant its believing either story. The defendant's confrontation rights are not violated, even though some demeanor evidence that would have been relevant in resolving this credibility issue is forever lost.

It may be true that a jury would be in a better position to evaluate the truth of the prior statement if it could somehow be whisked magically back in time to witness a gruelling cross-examination of the declarant as he first gives his statement. But the question as we see it must not be whether one can somehow imagine the jury in "a better position," but whether subsequent cross-examination at the defendant's trial will still afford the trier of fact a satisfactory basis for evaluating the truth of the prior statement. On that issue, neither evidence nor reason convinces us that contemporaneous cross-examination before the ultimate trier of fact is so much more effective than subsequent examination that it must be made the touchstone of the Confrontation Clause.

Finally, we note that none of our decisions interpreting the Confrontation Clause requires excluding the out-of-court statements of a witness who is available and testifying at trial. The concern of most of our cases has been focused on precisely the opposite situation—situations where statements have been admitted in the absence of the declarant and without any chance to cross-examine him at trial. These situations have arisen through application of a number of traditional "exceptions" to the hearsay rule, which permit the introduction of evidence despite the absence of the declarant usually on the theory that the evidence possesses other indicia of "reliability" and is incapable of being admitted, despite good-faith efforts of the State, in any way that will secure confrontation with the declarant.[14] Such exceptions, dispensing altogether with the literal right to "confrontation" and cross-examination, have been subjected on several occasions to careful scrutiny by this Court. In Pointer v. Texas, 380 U.S. 400, 85 S.Ct. 1065 (1965), for example, the State introduced at defendant's trial the transcript of a crucial witness' testimony from a prior preliminary hearing. The witness himself, one Phillips, had left the jurisdiction and did not appear at trial. "Because the transcript of Phillips' statement offered against petitioner at his trial had not been taken at a time and under circumstances affording petitioner through counsel an adequate opportunity to cross-examine Phillips," 380 U.S., at 407, 85 S.Ct. at 1070, we held that its introduction violated the defendant's confrontation rights. Similarly, in Barber v. Page, 390 U.S. 719, 88 S.Ct. 1318 (1968), the State introduced the preliminary hearing testimony of an absent witness, incarcerated in a federal prison, under an "unavailability" exception to its hearsay rules. We held that that exception would not justify the denial of confrontation where the State had not made a good-faith effort to obtain the presence of the allegedly "unavailable" witness.

We have no occasion in the present case to map out a theory of the Confrontation Clause that would determine the validity of all such hearsay "exceptions" permitting the introduction of an absent declarant's statements. For where the declarant is not absent, but is present to testify and to submit to cross-examination, our cases, if anything, support the conclusion that the admission of his out-of-court statements does not create a confrontation problem. Thus, in Douglas v. Alabama, 380 U.S. 415, 85 S.Ct. 1074, 13 L.Ed.2d 934 (1965), decided on the same day as *Pointer,* we reversed a conviction in which the prosecution read into the record an allege confession of the defendant's supposed accomplice, Loyd, who refused to testify on self-incrimination grounds. The confrontation problem arose precisely because Loyd could not be cross-examined as to his prior statement; had such cross-examination taken place, the opinion strongly suggests that the confrontation problem would have been nonexistent:

> "In the circumstances of this case, petitioner's inability to cross-examine Loyd as to the alleged confession plainly denied him the right of cross-examination secured by the Confrontation Clause. * * * Loyd could not be cross-examined on a statement imputed to but not admitted by him. * * * [S]ince [the State's] evidence tended to show only that Loyd made the confession, cross-examination * * * as to its genuineness could not substitute for cross-examination of Loyd to test the truth of the statement itself. * * *

14. See generally, e. g., 5 Wigmore §§ 1420–1422.

"Hence, effective confrontation of Loyd was possible only if Loyd affirmed the statement as his." 380 U.S., at 419–420.

Again, in Bruton v. United States, 391 U.S. 123, 88 S.Ct. 1620, 20 L.Ed.2d 476 (1968), the Court found a violation of confrontation rights in the admission of a co-defendant's confession, implicating Bruton, where the co-defendant did not take the stand. The Court again emphasized that the error arose because the declarant "does not testify and cannot be tested by cross-examination," 391 U.S., at 136, 88 S.Ct. at 1628, suggesting that no confrontation problem would have existed if Bruton had been able to cross-examine his co-defendant. Indeed, *Bruton's* refusal to regard limiting instructions as capable of curing the error, suggests that there is little difference as far as the Constitution is concerned between permitting prior inconsistent statements to be used only for impeachment purposes, and permitting them to be used for substantive purposes as well.

We find nothing, then, in either the history or the purposes of the Confrontation Clause, or in the prior decisions of this Court, that compels the conclusion reached by the California Supreme Court concerning the validity of California's § 1235. Contrary to the judgment of that court, the Confrontation Clause does not require excluding from evidence the prior statements of a witness who concedes making the statements, and who may be asked to defend or otherwise explain the inconsistency between his prior and his present version of the events in question, thus opening himself to full cross-examination at trial as to both stories.

III

We also think that Porter's preliminary hearing testimony was admissible as far as the Constitution is concerned wholly apart from the question of whether respondent had an effective opportunity for confrontation at the subsequent trial. For Porter's statement at the preliminary hearing had already been given under circumstances closely approximating those that surround the typical trial. Porter was under oath; respondent was represented by counsel—the same counsel in fact who later represented him at the trial; respondent had every opportunity to cross-examine Porter as to his statement; and the proceedings were conducted before a judicial tribunal, equipped to provide a judicial record of the hearings. Under these circumstances, Porter's statement would, we think, have been admissible at trial even in Porter's absence if Porter had been actually unavailable, despite good-faith efforts of the State to produce him. That being the case, we do not think a different result should follow where the witness is actually produced.

This Court long ago held that admitting the prior testimony of an unavailable witness does not violate the Confrontation Clause. Mattox v. United States, 156 U.S. 237, 15 S.Ct. 337, 39 L.Ed. 409 (1895). That case involved testimony given at the defendant's first trial by a witness who had died by the time of the second trial, but we do not find the instant preliminary hearing significantly different from an actual trial to warrant distinguishing the two cases for purposes of the Confrontation Clause. Indeed, we indicated as much in Pointer v. Texas, 380 U.S. 400, 407, 85 S.Ct. 1065, 1069, (1965), where we noted that "[t]he case before us would be quite a different one had Phillips' statement been taken at a full-fledged hearing at which petitioner had been represented by counsel who had been given a complete and adequate opportunity to cross-examine." And in Barber v. Page, 390 U.S. 719, 725–726, 88 S.Ct. 1318, 1322 (1968), although noting that the preliminary hearing is ordinarily a less searching exploration into the merits of a case than a trial, we recognized that "there may be some justification for holding that the opportunity for cross-examination of a witness at a preliminary hearing satisfies the demands of the confrontation clause where the witness is shown to be actually unavailable. * * * " In the present case respondent's counsel does not appear to have been significantly limited in any way in the scope or nature of his cross-examination of the witness Porter at the preliminary hearing. If Porter had died or was otherwise unavailable, the Confrontation Clause would not have been violated by admitting his testimony given at the preliminary hearing—the right of cross-examination then afforded provides substantial compliance with the purposes behind the confrontation requirement, as long as the declarant's inability to give live testimony is in no way the fault of the State.

But nothing in Barber v. Page or in other cases in this Court indicates that a different result must follow where the State produces the declarant and swears him as a witness at the trial. It may be that the rules of evidence applicable in state or federal courts would restrict resort to prior sworn testimony where the declarant is present at the trial. But as a constitutional matter, it is untenable to construe the Confrontation Clause to permit the use of prior testimony to prove the State's case where the declarant never appears, but to bar that testimony where the declarant is present at the trial, exposed to the defendant and the trier of fact, and subject to cross-examination.[16] As in the case where the witness is physically unproducible, the State here has made every effort to introduce its evidence through the live testimony of the witness; it produced Porter at trial, swore him as a witness, and tendered him for cross-examination. Whether Porter then testified in a manner consistent or inconsistent with his preliminary hearing testimony, claimed a loss of memory, claimed his privilege against compulsory self-incrimination, or simply refused to answer, nothing in the Confrontation Clause prohibited the State from also relying on his prior testimony to prove its case against Green.[17]

---

16. The explanation advanced for the contrary conclusion seems to be that where the witness is dead or otherwise unavailable, the State may in good faith assume he would have given the same story at trial, and may introduce the former testimony as reasonably reliable and as prompted by the factor of "necessity." On the contrary, it is argued, where the witness is present to testify but does not relate the same story, "necessity," "reliability," and the assumption that the story would be the same are all destroyed. * * * Surely in terms of protecting the defendant's interests, and the jury's ability to assess the reliability of the evidence it hears, it seems most unlikely that respondent in this case would have been better off, as the dissent seems to suggest, if Porter had died, and his prior testimony were admitted, than he was in the instant case where Porter's conduct on the stand cast substantial doubt on his prior statement. As long as the State has made a good-faith effort to produce the witness, the actual presence or absence of that witness cannot be constitutionally relevant for the purposes of the "unavailability" exception.

17. The hearsay exception itself has generally recognized that a witness is "unavailable" for purposes of the exception where through lapse of memory or a plea of the Fifth Amendment privilege, the State cannot secure his live testimony. See 5 Wigmore §§ 1408, 1409.

IV

There is a narrow question lurking in this case concerning the admissibility of Porter's statements to Officer Wade. In the typical case to which the California court addressed itself, the witness at trial gives a version of the ultimate events different from that given on a prior occasion. In such a case, as our holding in Part II makes clear, we find little reason to distinguish among prior inconsistent statements on the basis of the circumstances under which the prior statements were given. The subsequent opportunity for cross-examination at trial with respect to both present and past versions of the event, is adequate to make equally admissible, as far as the Confrontation Clause is concerned, both the casual, off-hand remark to a stranger, and the carefully recorded testimony at a prior hearing. Here, however, Porter claimed at trial that he could not remember the events that occurred after respondent telephoned him and hence failed to give any current version of the more important events described in his earlier statement.

Whether Porter's apparent lapse of memory so affected Green's right to cross-examine as to make a critical difference in the application of the Confrontation Clause in this case is an issue which is not ripe for decision at this juncture. The state court did not focus on this precise question, which was irrelevant given its broader and erroneous premise that an out-of-court statement of a witness is inadmissible as substantive evidence, whatever the nature of the opportunity to cross-examine at the trial. Nor has either party addressed itself to the question. Its resolution depends much upon the unique facts in this record, and we are reluctant to proceed without the state court's views of what the record actually discloses relevant to this particular issue. * * *

We therefore vacate the judgment of the California Supreme Court and remand the case to that court for futher proceedings not inconsistent with this opinion.

It is so ordered.

Mr. Justice White delivered the opinion of the Court.

Mr. Justice Marshall took no part in the decision of this case.

Mr. Justice Blackmun took no part in the consideration or decision of this case.

[The concurring opinions of Mr. Chief Justice Burger and Mr. Justice Harlan and the dissenting opinion of Mr. Justice Brennan have been omitted.]

GRAHAM, THE RIGHT OF CONFRONTATION AND RULES OF EVIDENCE: SIR WALTER RALEIGH RIDES AGAIN

9 Alaska L.J. 20–23 (1971).*

Despite, or perhaps because of, the Court's desire to preserve the flexibility of the reformers, the opinion in *Green* does little to advance analysis of the confrontation clause. It clearly rejects the reasoning of the California Supreme Court, but beyond that, the opinion is anything but clear.

It is fair to say that the majority opinion could be said to stand for any one of the following propositions:

(1)   Any out-of-court statement may be used by the prosecution in a criminal case if the person who made it is present in court and available for cross-examination.[81]

(2)   Same as (1), but the declarant must take the stand and admit that he did in fact make the out-of-court statement.[82]

(3)   Same as (1), but the declarant must either concede having made the statement *or* it must have been made at a prior judicial hearing or be preserved in some form, such as videotape, that will make it indisputable that the statement was made.[83]

(4)   A prior out-of-court statement may be used aginst a defendant in a criminal case only if the person who made it appears at the trial and tells a story which contradicts the statement and is favorable to the defendant.[84]

(5)   Same as (4) but it is sufficient if his testimony contradicts the statement and is not helpful to the prosecution.[85]

(6)   Same as (4) or (5), but the declarant must also be available for cross-examination at trial by the defendant.[86]

81.   Id. at 158: " * * * there is good reason to conclude that the Confrontation Clause is not violated by admitting a declarant's out-of-court statements, as long as the declarant is testifying as a witness and subject to full and effective cross-examination." Id. at 158: "But if the declarant is present and testifying at trial, the out-of-court statement for all practical purposes regains most of the lost protections." Id. at 161: " * * * none of our decisions interpreting the Confrontation Clause requires excluding the out-of-court statements of a witness who is available and testifying at trial."

82.   Id. at 164: " * * * the Confrontation Clause does not require excluding from evidence the prior statement of a witness who concedes making the statements * * *" The Court also quotes with approval from Douglas v. Alabama, 380 U.S. 415, 420, 85 S.Ct. 1074, 1077, 13 L.Ed.2d 934 (1965): "effective confrontation * * * was possible only if (the witness) affirmed the statement as his." 399 U.S. at 163. In Green the witness admitted making the prior statements, but claimed a present lapse of memory.

83.   Id. at 158: "If the witness admits the prior statement is his, or if there is other evidence to show the statement is his, the danger of faulty reproduction is negligible * * * ." The statement in Green had as noted in the text, been taken at a preliminary hearing and was recorded in a reporter's transcript.

84.   Id. at 159: "The most successful cross-examination at the time the prior statement was made could hardly hope to accomplish more than has already been accomplished by the fact that the witness is now telling a different inconsistent story, and—in this case—one that is favorable to the defendant." Id. at 160: "The defendant's task in cross-examination is, of course, no longer identical to the task that he would have faced if the witness had not changed his story and hence had to be examined as a 'hostile' witness * * * . For the witness, favorable to the defendant, should be more than willing to give the usual suggested explanations for the inaccuracy of his prior statement. * * * "

85.   Although the Supreme Court sometimes claims that the present testimony of the witness was "favorable" to Green, see note 84 supra, nothing in the Court's own description of the testimony suggests that this is more than a relative judgment. It was obviously less damaging than his testimony at the preliminary hearing which inculpated Green, but his present claim that he could not remember the facts is certainly not exculpatory.

86.   Id. at 164: " * * * the Confrontation Clause does not require excluding from evidence the prior statements of a witness who concedes making the statements, and who may be asked to defend or otherwise explain the inconsistency between his prior and his present version of the events in question, thus opening himself to full cross-examination at trial as to both stories."

(7)   Same as (4) or (5), but the declarant must be available for present cross-examination or have been available for cross-examination at a prior hearing.[87]

(8)   Same as (7) but with the added qualifications about the form of the prior statement set forth in (3).[88]

(9)   Same as (8), but the defendant must have actually cross-examined at the prior hearing.[89]

(10)   A prior inconsistent statement of a "turncoat" witness may be used against a defendant in criminal trial without violating the confrontation clause if the witness had previously testified for the prosecution at a trial-type hearing in which the defendant fully cross-examined him *and* the witness appears at trial subject to cross-examination and tells a story that is not as favorable as the prosecutor expected, unless the witness claims a lapse of memory that defeats present efforts to cross-examine him, but this qualification does not apply if his present testimony is wholly favorable to the defendant.[90]

As the reader will have surmised by now, this by no means exhausts the ways in which the holding in *Green* can be read. One can recombine the specific elements mentioned by Mr. Justice White as justifying the use of the statement in a variety of ways to produce results which are numerically impressive. However, the fact that the holding is capable of so many readings would scarcely be a cause for criticism if the opinion were not cast in a rhetoric suggesting that the Court believes it has solved the riddle of the hearsay rule and the confrontation clause.

Mr. Justice White attempts to explain the result in *Green* on three different bases: history, empiricism and the prior decisions of the Court. None of these is entirely satisfactory by itself and each tends to be inconsistent with the others.

According to the majority opinion, history shows that the core value to be protected by the confrontation clause is the "literal right to 'confront' the witness at the time of trial."[91] This motion may find some support in Shakespeare,[92] but it flies in the teeth of all of the Court's recent opinions which have made cross-examination the touchstone of the confrontation

---

87.   The Supreme Court holds in the third part of its opinion that the statements would have been admissible even without respect to the cross-examination at trial because they had been given at a preliminary hearing "under circumstances closely approximating those that surround the typical trial." Id. at 165.

88.   The Court carefully notes that the preliminary hearing testimony was recorded. Id. at 165.

89.   The opinion is unclear on this point. At one place its speaks of the "opportunity" to cross-examine, and at others the Court is at pains to point out that cross-examination was actually conducted without any apparent limitations. Id. at 165, 166.

90.   This fanciful version of the "holding" is a combination of the actual facts of *Green* plus an attempt to explain how the Supreme Court was able to conclude that the case should be remanded to determine whether a statement that the witness had made during a police interrogation could be adequately tested by cross-examination when the defendant now claims a lapse of memory, an inquiry seemingly equally relevant with respect to statements the Court held admissible. Id. at 168–169.

91.   399 U.S. at 157.

92.   "Then call them to our presence; face to face and frowning brow to brow, ourselves will hear the accuser and the accused freely speak." RICHARD II, Act 1, Sc. 1.

clause.[93] Moreover, as the opinion seems to admit by its refusal to recount the historical evidence upon which it relies, history that is very convincing is hard to find.[94]

It is probable that the ambiguity of history is in large measure due to the fact that the Founding Fathers, and the Founding Mothers for that matter, were reacting to a series of abuses of the criminal process which took place over a couple of centuries during which the nature of criminal trials was changing.[95] There is nothing in history to suggest that the drafters of the Sixth Amendment ever considered each of the various rights granted there individually; asking, for example, whether the right of the defendant to call witnesses might not be adequate to prevent the evils of trial by deposition or affidavit.

Even if one could determine with accuracy what our forefathers found objectionable in the trial of Sir Walter Raleigh and which of the various constitutional safeguards were designed to remedy each objection, history would still not tell us what their reaction might have been to subsequent technological and jurisprudential developments. Is the defendant "confronted" with the witness if the testimony is given live but across a continent by closed circuit television? Is a video-tape record of a prior statement under oath subject to the same objections as an affidavit? How, if at all, might the drafters have recast the confrontation clause if they could have foreseen the statute making the defendant a competent witness, the development of the modern police and prosecutorial institutions and the subsequent development of other provisions of the Fourth, Fifth and Sixth Amendments by the Supreme Court?

LILLY, AN INTRODUCTION TO THE LAW OF EVIDENCE

273–278 (1978).

Any assessment of the future role of hearsay evidence, at least in criminal trials, must take account of the Constitution's Sixth Amendment guarantee to an accused of the right "to be confronted with the witnesses against him."[96] Although "the confrontation cases are in disarray and the policies to be served by the constitutional protection are far from clear," certain conclusions may be drawn from the cases.

The confrontation clause never has been read so literally as to preclude generally the use of hearsay evidence in criminal trials. Indeed, the cases are replete with instances of hearsay statements admitted under the recog-

---

93. See, e. g., Barber v. Page, 390 U.S. 719, 88 S.Ct. 1318, 20 L.Ed.2d 255 (1968).

94. The Court says: "The origin and development of the hearsay rules and of the Confrontation Clause have been traced by others and need not be recounted in detail here." 399 U.S. at 156. Upon examination, the sources to which the Court refers turn out to be either discussions of the hearsay rule or statements that the history of the confrontation clause is obscure. Id. at 156 n. 9. The opinion then builds upon this shaky foundation a series of claims about the historical meaning of confrontation.

Mr. Justice Harlan seems more accurate when he says in his concurring opinion: "History seems to give us very little insight into the intended scope of the Sixth Amendment Confrontation Clause." Id. at 174.

95. 380 U.S. 415, 419–420 (1965).

96. This provision applies not only to the federal government but to the states as well. See Pointer v. Texas, 380 U.S. 400 [85 S.Ct. 1065, 13 L.Ed.2d 923] (1965). The clause also can be read as guaranteeing the accused's right to be present at his own trial. See Illinois v. Allen, 397 U.S. 337 [90 S.Ct. 1057, 25 L.Ed.2d 353] (1970).

nized exceptions. It is fairly certain that there is no constitutional prohibition against either the substantive use of a prior extrajudicial declaration of a witness present at trial (at least where it clearly is shown that the prior statements were made) or, in cases of unavailability, against the use of prior testimony in circumstances in which the accused had an earlier opportunity to conduct a fair and full cross-examination.[99] Even admission against the accused of dying declarations apparently is permissible,[1] and most courts have turned aside confrontation clause challenges to such hearsay exceptions as declarations against interest,[2] business entries,[3] and party admissions by coconspirators.[4]

Nonetheless, the confrontation clause places limits, however uncertain, upon the freedom with which the prosecution may deny the accused adequate opportunity to cross-examine witnesses (including, in some circumstances, hearsay declarants) and the right to have adverse statements secured under oath and in the presence of the trier of fact. The Supreme Court apparently has rejected both of the most extreme readings of the confrontation clause. Under one of these constructions, every hearsay declarant would be viewed as a witness against the accused and his presence at trial would be compelled constitutionally, thus blocking substantially all hearsay evidence. Under the opposite reading, the constitutional command would require merely a guarantee that evidence used to convict the accused be presented through trial witnesses. The source of the witness's information, while perhaps raising issues under an exclusionary rule of evidence such as the hearsay rule, would not present a constitutional problem.

In several cases, the Supreme Court has struck down under the confrontation clause evidence of inculpatory statements that the accused could not subject to meaningful cross-examination. Use of a transcript of prior testimony elicited from a witness during the accused's preliminary hearing at which the accused was not represented by counsel[6] was found constitu-

---

99.   California v. Green, 399 U.S. 149 [90 S.Ct. 1930, 26 L.Ed.2d 489] (1970); Mattox v. United States, 156 U.S. 237 [15 S.Ct. 337, 39 L.Ed. 409] (1895). See Barber v. Page, 390 U.S. 719 [88 S.Ct. 1318, 20 L.Ed.2d 255] (1968), which contrary to the language in *Green* indicates that prior testimony at the preliminary hearing may not afford a defendant adequate opportunity to cross-examine because the issue at the preliminary hearing is limited to whether there is probable cause for a trial. See also Government of Virgin Islands v. Aquino, 378 F.2d 540, 549 (3d Cir. 1967).

1.   Mattox v. United States, 156 U.S. 237 [15 S.Ct. 337, 39 L.Ed. 409] (1895), cited with approval in Pointer v. Texas, 380 U.S. 400, 407 [85 S.Ct. 1065, 1069–70, 13 L.Ed.2d 923] (1965).

2.   United States v. White, 553 F.2d 310 (2d Cir.), cert. denied [431 U.S. 972] 97 S.Ct. 2937 [53 L.Ed.2d 1070] (1977).

3.   United States v. Lipscomb, 435 F.2d 795 (5th Cir. 1971). See also Reed v. Beto, 343 F.2d 723 (5th Cir. 1965) (public records); State v. Finkley, 6 Wash.App. 278, 492 P.2d 222 (1972) (hospital's medical records). Contra, State v. Tims, 9 Ohio St.2d 136, 224 N.E.2d 348 (1967) (confrontation clause violated by use of business-hospital record).

4.   Dutton v. Evans, 400 U.S. 74 [91 S.Ct. 210, 27 L.Ed.2d 213] (1970). Further, the confrontation clause does not extend to statements by persons whose declarations are not used to establish guilt at trial, such as witnesses before a grand jury, informers who provide information sufficient for probable cause to search, or probation officers who supply information relevant to sentencing. As one commentator notes, participants in the criminal process whose statements are not considered by a jury in connection with a determination of guilt or innocence are not "witnesses" against the accused as that term is used in the constitution. See Graham, supra note 97, at 125–29.

6.   Pointer v. Texas, 380 U.S. 400 [85 S.Ct. 1065, 13 L.Ed.2d 923] (1965). This case also holds that the confrontation clause is fully applicable to the states through the Fourteenth Amendment.

tionally objectionable. Similarly rejected was improper "evidence" (although not formally admitted) of a prosecutor's use of the confession of the accused's codefendant: after the codefendant-witness invoked the fifth amendment and refused to testify, the prosecutor used the guise of refreshing the witness's recollection to read aloud the codefendant's earlier confession which implicated the accused.[7] In a third case, in which the accused did not take the stand, the use of a codefendant's confession which inculpated the accused was held to violate the latter's right of confrontation;[8] an instruction to the jury that it consider the confession only with regard to the codefendant's guilt was deemed ineffective. The Supreme Court also has indicated that the confrontation clause limits when a witness can be considered "unavailable" for purposes of a hearsay exception. In one case, state authorities who knew that a prosecution witness was in a federal penitentiary in another state made no attempt to secure his presence at trial. The Court held that the state denied the accused's right of confrontation when it used the witness's out-of-state custody as a ground for invoking the exception for prior recorded testimony.[9]

The Court has yet to clarify the reach of the confrontation clause, but reason suggests an analytical framework for future decisions. Like other constitutional provisions, the right of an accused "to be confronted with witnesses against him" should not be inflexible. Confrontation is a relative term to be given a functional meaning. Although the values to be protected by the confrontation clause are not altogether clear. the notion of confronting a witness implies a right to interrogate him effectively under oath and to bring him within the observation of the trier of fact. At a minimum, it guarantees that the accused may effectively confront and cross-examine those who testify against him at trial. Cross-examination may not be limited so as to significantly emasculate its effectiveness.[11] In all probability, the right of confrontation also ensures that an accused will not be convicted on the basis of statements by absent declarants that fall within no recognized exception to the hearsay rule. Thus, prosecutorial use at trial of the ex parte affidavit of an absent declarant to supply significant proof against the accused probably would violate his sixth amendment right to confrontation.

7. Douglas v. Alabama, 380 U.S. 415 [85 S.Ct. 1074, 13 L.Ed.2d 934] (1965). Compare Barber v. Page, 390 U.S. 719 [88 S.Ct. 1318, 20 L.Ed.2d 255] (1968). See supra note 99. In Parker v. Gladden, 385 U.S. 363 [87 S.Ct. 468, 17 L.Ed.2d 420] (1966), the Court found that a bailiff's secret remarks to the jury violated the accused's right to confront witnesses against him.

8. Bruton v. United States, 391 U.S. 123 [88 S.Ct. 1620, 20 L.Ed.2d 476] (1968). But see Nelson v. O'Neil, 402 U.S. 622 [91 S.Ct. 1723, 29 L.Ed.2d 222] (1971) (*Bruton* not controlling where co-defendant takes stand, denies inculpatory admission, and testifies favorably to accused); Harrington v. California, 395 U.S. 250 [89 S.Ct. 1726, 23 L.Ed.2d 284] (1969) (*Bruton* violation can be harmless error; also *Bruton* may not apply when codefendant takes the stand and admits statements).

9. Barber v. Page, 390 U.S. 719 [88 S.Ct. 1318, 20 L.Ed.2d 255] (1968). But see Mancusi v. Stubbs, 408 U.S. 204, 211–13 (1971) (witness who had left country genuinely unavailable therefore defendant could not invoke Barber v. Page). See also California v. Green, 399 U.S. 149, 166–68 [90 S.Ct. 1930, 1939–40, 26 L.Ed.2d 489] (1970) (admission at trial of statement taken from witness at preliminary hearing did not violate confrontation clause where accused had counsel and adequate opportunity to cross-examine at earlier proceeding).

11. Davis v. Alaska, 415 U.S. 308 [94 S.Ct. 1105, 39 L.Ed.2d 347] (1974) (accused must be permitted to show probationary status of juvenile witness against him); Smith v. Illinois, 390 U.S. 129 [88 S.Ct. 748, 19 L.Ed.2d 956] (1968) (accused must be allowed to ask a principal prosecution witness the latter's true name and address).

Beyond these situations, application of the confrontation clause should depend upon whether considerations of trustworthiness and adversarial fairness are satisfied. In ascertaining whether the confrontation of a witness at trial who merely presents documents or who gives testimony which embodies the assertions of absent declarants satisfies the sixth amendment, at least three factors should be determinative: trustworthiness, the ease with which a declarant can be produced, and the importance of the evidence in question. If there is strong reason to distrust the reliability of the evidence, the preference for live testimony should be compelling. If the declarant reasonably can be produced, his courtroom presence should be demanded. In instances where the declarant is deceased or otherwise not available, the question whether the right of confrontation has been violated should depend on the degree of risk that the evidence will produce an erroneous finding. If the statements in question fall within a hearsay exception and thus have the imprimatur of judicial and legislative experience, this fact should weigh heavily in favor of a determination that the right to confrontation has been satisfied.[13] Finally, the significance of an accused's right to confront a witness should bear a direct relation to the significance of the evidence supplied by the witness. When this evidence is comparatively inconsequential, cross-examination of the in-court witness should be sufficient confrontation even though the source of the witness's testimony may be traced to an absent declarant.[14]

The foregoing analysis may fit as comfortably within a due process analysis as it does within the framework of the confrontation clause. Nonetheless, the Supreme Court already has embarked upon a course that accords the confrontation clause content beyond that found in the restrictive interpretation described earlier. A middle ground permitting ample flexibility to accommodate the growth of the hearsay rule seems consonant with the existing cases and highly desirable.

CHAMBERS v. MISSISSIPPI

Supreme Court of the United States, 1973.
410 U.S. 284, 93 S.Ct. 1038, 35 L.Ed. 297.

Mr. Justice POWELL delivered the opinion of the Court.

Petitioner, Leon Chambers, was tried by a jury in a Mississippi trial court and convicted of murdering a policeman. The jury assessed punishment at life imprisonment, and the Mississippi Supreme Court affirmed, one justice dissenting. * * * Subsequently, the petition for certiorari was granted, * * * to consider whether petitioner's trial was con-

---

13. See Hoover v. Beto, 467 F.2d 516, 528–34 (5th Cir. 1972) (confession of principal admissible at accomplice's trial), cert. denied sub nom. Hoover v. Estelle, 409 U.S. 1086 (1972). But see Park v. Huff, 493 F.2d 923 (5th Cir. 1974) (confrontation clause violated by admission of co-conspirator's statements) rev'd en banc 506 F.2d 849, 860 (5th Cir. 1975) (no violation of confrontation clause), cert. denied 423 U.S. 824 [96 S.Ct. 38, 46 L.Ed.2d 40].

14. In Dutton v. Evans, 400 U.S. 74, 87–89 [91 S.Ct. 210, 219–220, 27 L.Ed.2d 213]

(1970) the Supreme Court noted that the hearsay evidence admitted against the accused was not "critical" or "devastating," especially in light of the other inculpatory evidence in the record. Although the significance of evidence which arguably violates the confrontation clause may be an important factor in determining if a constitutional violation has occurred, it would appear that a trial judge, faced with a timely constitutional objection, should reject even insignificant evidence if he thinks that it violates the accused's sixth amendment right.

ducted in accord with principles of due process under the Fourteenth Amendment. We conclude that it was not.

I

The events that led to petitioner's prosecution for murder occurred in the small town of Woodville in southern Mississippi. On Saturday evening, June 14, 1969, two Woodville policemen, James Forman and Aaron "Sonny" Liberty, entered a local bar and pool hall to execute a warrant for the arrest of a youth named C.C. Jackson. Jackson resisted and a hostile crowd of some 50 or 60 persons gathered. The officers' first attempt to handcuff Jackson was frustrated when 20 or 25 men in the crowd intervened and wrestled him free. Forman then radioed for assistance and Liberty removed his riot gun, a 12-gauge sawed-off shotgun, from the car. Three deputy sheriffs arrived shortly thereafter and the officers again attempted to make their arrest. Once more, the officers were attacked by the onlookers and during the commotion five or six pistol shots were fired. Forman was looking in a different direction when the shooting began, but immediately saw that Liberty had been shot several times in the back. Before Liberty died, he turned around and fired both barrels of his riot gun into an alley in the area from which the shots appeared to have come. The first shot was wild and high and scattered the crowd standing at the face of the alley. Liberty appeared, however, to take more deliberate aim before the second shot and hit one of the men in the crowd in the back of the head and neck as he ran down the alley. That man was Leon Chambers.

Officer Forman could not see from his vantage point who shot Liberty or whether Liberty's shots hit anyone. One of the deputy sheriffs testified at trial that he was standing several feet from Liberty and that he saw Chambers shoot him. Another deputy sheriff stated that, although he could not see whether Chambers had a gun in his hand, he did see Chambers "break his arm down" shortly before the shots were fired. The officers who saw Chambers fall testified that they thought he was dead but they made no effort at that time either to examine him or to search for the murder weapon. Instead, they attended to Liberty, who was placed in the police car and taken to a hospital where he was declared dead on arrival. A subsequent autopsy showed that he had been hit with four bullets from a .22-caliber revolver.

Shortly after the shooting, three of Chambers' friends discovered that he was not yet dead. James Williams,[1] Berkley Turner, and Gable McDonald loaded him into a car and transported him to the same hospital. Later that night, when the county sheriff discovered that Chambers was still alive, a guard was placed outside his room. Chambers was subsequently charged with Liberty's murder. He pleaded not guilty and has asserted his innocence throughout.

The story of Leon Chambers is intertwined with the story of another man, Gable McDonald. McDonald, a lifelong resident of Woodville, was in the crowd on the evening of Liberty's death. Sometime shortly after that day, he left his wife in Woodville and moved to Louisiana and found a job at

---

1. James Williams was indicted along with Chambers. The State, however, failed to introduce any evidence at trial implicating Williams in the shooting. At the conclusion of the State's case-in-chief, the trial court granted a directed verdict in his favor.

a sugar mill. In November of that same year, he returned to Woodville when his wife informed him that an acquaintance of his, known as Reverend Stokes, wanted to see him. Stokes owned a gas station in Natchez, Mississippi, several miles north of Woodville, and upon his return McDonald went to see him. After talking to Stokes, McDonald agreed to make a statement to Chambers' attorneys, who maintained offices in Natchez. Two days later, he appeared at the attorneys' offices and gave a sworn confession that he shot Officer Liberty. He also stated that he had already told a friend of his, James Williams, that he shot Liberty. He said that he used his own pistol, a nine-shot .22-caliber revolver, which he had discarded shortly after the shooting. In response to questions from Chambers' attorneys, McDonald affirmed that his confession was voluntary and that no one had compelled him to come to them. Once the confession had been transcribed, signed, and witnessed, McDonald was turned over to the local police authorities and was placed in jail.

One month later, at a preliminary hearing, McDonald repudiated his prior sworn confession. He testified that Stokes had persuaded him to confess that he shot Liberty. He claimed that Stokes had promised that he would not go to jail and that he would share in the proceeds of a lawsuit that Chambers would bring against the town of Woodville. On examination by his own attorney and on cross-examination by the State, McDonald swore that he had not been at the scene when Liberty was shot but had been down the street drinking beer in a cafe with a friend, Berkley Turner. When he and Turner heard the shooting, he testified, they walked up the street and found Chambers lying in the alley. He, Turner, and Williams took Chambers to the hospital. McDonald further testified at the preliminary hearing that he did not know what had happened, that there was no discussion about the shooting either going to or coming back from the hospital, and that it was not until the next day that he learned that Chambers had been felled by a blast from Liberty's riot gun. In addition, McDonald stated that while he once owned a .22-caliber pistol he had lost it many months before the shooting and did not own or possess a weapon at that time. The local justice of the peace accepted McDonald's repudiation and released him from custody. The local authorities undertook no further investigation of his possible involvement.

Chambers' case came on for trial in October of the next year.[2] At trial, he endeavored to develop two grounds of defense. He first attempted to show that he did not shoot Liberty. Only one officer testified that he actually saw Chambers fire the shots. Although three officers saw Liberty shoot Chambers and testified that they assumed he was shooting his attacker, none of them examined Chambers to see whether he was still alive or whether he possessed a gun. Indeed, no weapon was ever recovered from the scene and there was no proof that Chambers had ever owned a .22-caliber pistol. One witness testified that he was standing in the street near where Liberty was shot, that he was looking at Chambers when the shooting began, and that he was sure that Chambers did not fire the shots.

2. Upon Chambers' motion, a change of venue was granted and the trial was held in Amite County, to the east of Woodville. The change of trial setting was in response to petitioner's claim that, because of adverse publicity and the hostile attitude of the police and sheriff's staffs in Woodville, he could not obtain a fair and impartial trial there.

Petitioner's second defense was that Gable McDonald had shot Officer Liberty. He was only partially successful, however, in his efforts to bring before the jury the testimony supporting this defense. Sam Hardin, a life-long friend of McDonald's testified that he saw McDonald shoot Liberty. A second witness, one of Liberty's cousins, testified that he saw McDonald immediately after the shooting with a pistol in his hand. In addition to the testimony of these two witnesses, Chambers endeavored to show the jury that McDonald had repeatedly confessed to the crime. Chambers attempted to prove that McDonald had admitted responsibility for the murder on four separate occasions, once when he gave the sworn statement to Chambers' counsel and three other times prior to that occasion in private conversations with friends.

In large measure, he was thwarted in his attempt to present this portion of his defense by the strict application of certain Mississippi rules of evidence. Chambers asserts in this Court, as he did unsuccessfully in his motion for new trial and on appeal to the State Supreme Court, that the application of these evidentiary rules rendered his trial fundamentally unfair and deprived him of due process of law. It is necessary, therefore, to examine carefully the rulings made during the trial.

II

Chambers filed a pretrial motion requesting the court to order McDonald to appear. Chambers also sought a ruling at that time that, if the State itself chose not to call McDonald, he be allowed to call him as an adverse witness. Attached to the motion were copies of McDonald's sworn confession and of the transcript of his preliminary hearing at which he repudiated that confession. The trial court granted the motion requiring McDonald to appear but reserved ruling on the adverse-witness motion. At trial, after the State failed to put McDonald on the stand, Chambers called McDonald, laid a predicate for the introduction of his sworn out-of-court confession, had it admitted into evidence, and read it to the jury. The State, upon cross-examination, elicited from McDonald the fact that he had repudiated his prior confession. McDonald further testified, as he had at the preliminary hearing, that he did not shoot Liberty, and that he confessed to the crime only on the promise of Reverend Stokes that he would not go to jail and would share in a sizable tort recovery from the town. He also retold his own story of his actions on the evening of the shooting, including his visit to the cafe down the street, his absence from the scene during the critical period, and his subsequent trip to the hospital with Chambers.

At the conclusion of the State's cross-examination, Chambers renewed his motion to examine McDonald as an adverse witness. The trial court denied the motion, stating: "He may be hostile, but he is not adverse in the sense of the word, so your request will be overruled." On appeal, the State Supreme Court upheld the trial court's ruling, finding that "McDonald's testimony was not adverse to appellant" because "[n]owhere did he point the finger at Chambers." 252 So.2d, at 220.

Defeated in his attempt to challenge directly McDonald's renunciation of his prior confession, Chambers sought to introduce the testimony of the three witnesses to whom McDonald had admitted that he shot the officer. The first of these, Sam Hardin, would have testified that, on the night of the shooting, he spent the late evening hours with McDonald at a friend's house after their return from the hospital and that, while driving McDonald home later that night, McDonald stated that he shot Liberty. The State objected to the admission of this testimony on the ground that it was hearsay. The trial court sustained the objection.[4]

Berkley Turner, the friend with whom McDonald said he was drinking beer when the shooting occurred, was then called to testify. In the jury's presence, and without objection, he testified that he had not been in the cafe that Saturday and had not had any beers with McDonald. The jury was then excused. In the absence of the jury, Turner recounted his conversations with McDonald while they were riding with James Williams to take Chambers to the hospital. When asked whether McDonald said anything regarding the shooting of Liberty, Turner testified that McDonald told him that he "shot him." Turner further stated that one week later, when he met McDonald at a friend's house, McDonald reminded him of their prior conversation and urged Turner not to "mess him up." Petitioner argued to the court that, especially where there was other proof in the case that was corroborative of these out-of-court statements, Turner's testimony as to McDonald's self-incriminating remarks should have been admitted as an exception to the hearsay rule. Again, the trial court sustained the State's objection.

The third witness, Albert Carter, was McDonald's neighbor. They had been friends for about 25 years. Although Carter had not been in Woodville on the evening of the shooting, he stated that he learned about it the next morning from McDonald. That same day, he and McDonald walked out to a well near McDonald's house and there McDonald told him that he was the one who shot Officer Liberty. Carter testified that McDonald also told him that he had disposed of the .22-caliber revolver later that night. He further testified that several weeks after the shooting, he accompanied McDonald to Natchez where McDonald purchased another .22 pistol to replace the one he had discarded.[5] The jury was not allowed to hear Carter's testimony. Chambers urged that these statements were admissible, the State objected, and the court sustained the objection.[6] On appeal, the State Supreme Court approved the lower court's exclusion of these witnesses' testimony on hearsay grounds. 252 So.2d, at 220.

In sum, then, this was Chambers' predicament. As a consequence of the combination of Mississippi's "party witness" or "voucher" rule and its hearsay rule, he was unable either to cross-examine McDonald or to present witnesses in his own behalf who would have discredited McDonald's re-

---

4. Hardin's testimony, unlike the testimony of the other two men who stated that McDonald had confessed to them, was actually given in the jury's presence. After the State's objection to Hardin's account of McDonald's statement was sustained, the trial court ordered the jury to disregard it.

5. A gun dealer from Natchez testified that McDonald had made two purchases. The witness' business records indicated that McDonald purchased a nine-shot .22-caliber revolver about a year prior to the

murder. He purchased a different style .22 three weeks after Liberty's death.

6. It is not entirely clear whether the trial court's ruling was premised on the same hearsay rationale underlying the exclusion of the other testimony. In this instance, the State argued that Carter's testimony was an impermissible attempt by petitioner to impeach a witness (McDonald) who was not adverse to him. The trial court did not state why it was excluding the evidence but the State Supreme Court indicated that it was excluded as hearsay. 252 So.2d, at 220.

pudiation and demonstrated his complicity. Chambers had, however, chipped away at the fringes of McDonald's story by introducing admissible testimony from other sources indicating that he had not been seen in the cafe where he said he was when the shooting started, that he had not been having beer with Turner, and that he possessed a .22 pistol at the time of the crime. But all that remained from McDonald's own testimony was a single written confession countered by an arguably acceptable renunciation. Chambers' defense was far less persuasive than it might have been had he been given an opportunity to subject McDonald's statements to cross-examination or had the other confessions been admitted.

III

The right of an accused in a criminal trial to due process is, in essence, the right to a fair opportunity to defend against the State's accusations. The rights to confront and cross-examine witnesses and to call witnesses in one's own behalf have long been recognized as essential to due process. Mr. Justice Black, writing for the Court in In re Oliver, 333 U.S. 257, 273, 68 S.Ct. 499, 507, 92 L.Ed. 682 (1948), identified these rights as among the minimum essentials of a fair trial:

> "A person's right to reasonable notice of a charge against him, and an opportunity to be heard in his defense—a right to his day in court—are basic in our system of jurisprudence; and these rights include, as a minimum, a right to examine the witnesses against him, to offer testimony, and to be represented by counsel."

* * * Both of these elements of a fair trial are implicated in the present case.

A

Chambers was denied an opportunity to subject McDonald's damning repudiation and alibi to cross-examination. He was not allowed to test the witness' recollection, to probe into the details of his alibi, or to "sift" his conscience so that the jury might judge for itself whether McDonald's testimony was worthy of belief. The right of cross-examination is more than a desirable rule of trial procedure. It is implicit in the constitutional right of confrontation, and helps assure the "accuracy of the truth-determining process." It is, indeed, "an essential and fundamental requirement for the kind of fair trial which is this country's constitutional goal." Of course, the right to confront and to cross-examine is not absolute and may, in appropriate cases, bow to accommodate other legitimate interests in the criminal trial process. But its denial or significant diminution calls into question the ultimate " 'integrity of the fact-finding process' " and requires that the competing interest be closely examined.

In this case, petitioner's request to cross-examine McDonald was denied on the basis of a Mississippi common-law rule that a party may not impeach his own witness. The rule rests on the presumption—without regard to the circumstances of the particular case—that a party who calls a witness "vouches for his credibility." Although the historical origins of the "voucher" rule are uncertain, it appears to be a remnant of primitive English trial practice in which "oath-takers" or "compurgators" were called to stand behind a particular party's position in any controversy. Their assertions were strictly partisan and, quite unlike witnesses in criminal trials today, their role bore little relation to the impartial ascertainment of the facts.[7]

Whatever validity the "voucher" rule may have once enjoyed, and apart from whatever usefulness it retains today in the civil trial process, it bears little present relationship to the realities of the criminal process.[8] It might have been logical for the early common law to require a party to vouch for the credibility of witnesses he brought before the jury to affirm his veracity. Having selected them especially for that purpose, the party might reasonably be expected to stand firmly behind their testimony. But in modern criminal trials, defendants are rarely able to select their witnesses: they must take them where they find them. Moreover, as applied in this case, the "voucher" rule's[9] impact was doubly harmful to Chambers' efforts to develop his defense. Not only was he precluded from cross-examining McDonald, but, as the State conceded at oral argument,[10] he was also restricted in the scope of his direct examination by the rule's corollary requirement that the party calling the witness is bound by anything he might say. He was, therefore, effectively prevented from exploring the circumstances of McDonald's three prior oral confessions and from challenging the renunciation of the written confession.

In this Court, Mississippi has not sought to defend the rule or explain its underlying rationale. Nor has it contended that its rule should override the accused's right of confrontation. Instead, it argues that there is no incompatibility between the rule and Chambers' rights because no right of confrontation exists unless the testifying witness is "adverse" to the accused. The State's brief asserts that the "right of confrontation applies to witnesses *'against'* an accused."[11] Relying on the trial court's determination that McDonald was not "adverse," and on the State Supreme Court's holding that McDonald did not "point the finger at Chambers,"[12] the State contends that Chambers' constitutional right was not involved.

The argument that McDonald's testimony was not "adverse" to, or "against," Chambers is not convincing. The State's proof at trial excluded the theory that more than one person participated in the shooting of Liberty. To the extent that McDonald's sworn confession tended to incriminate him, it tended also to exculpate Chambers. And, in the circumstances of this case, McDonald's retraction inculpated Chambers to the same extent that it exculpated McDonald. It can hardly be disputed that McDonald's testimony was in fact seriously adverse to Chambers. The availability of the right to confront and to cross-examine those who give damaging testimony

---

7. 3A J. Wigmore, Evidence § 896, pp. 658–660 (J. Chadbourn ed. 1970); C. McCormick, Evidence § 38, pp. 75–78 (2d ed. 1972).

8. The "voucher" rule has been condemned as archaic, irrational, and potentially destructive of the truth-gathering process. C. McCormick, supra, n. 7; E. Morgan, Basic Problems of Evidence 70–71 (1962); 3A J. Wigmore, supra, n. 7, § 898, p. 661.

9. The "voucher" rule has been rejected altogether by the newly proposed Federal Rules of Evidence, Rule 607, Rules of Evidence for United States Courts and Magistrates (approved Nov. 20, 1972, and transmitted to Congress to become effective July 1, 1973, unless the Congress otherwise determines). [56 F.R.D. 183, 266.]

10. Tr. of Oral Arg. 35–37.

11. Brief for Respondent 9 (emphasis supplied).

12. 252 So.2d, at 220.

against the accused has never been held to depend on whether the witness was initially put on the stand by the accused or by the State. We reject the notion that a right of such substance in the criminal process may be governed by that technicality or by any narrow and unrealistic definition of the word "against." The "voucher" rule, as applied in this case, plainly interfered with Chambers' right to defend against the State's charges.

B

We need not decide, however, whether this error alone would occasion reversal since Chambers' claimed denial of due process rests on the ultimate impact of that error when viewed in conjunction with the trial court's refusal to permit him to call other witnesses. The trial court refused to allow him to introduce the testimony of Hardin, Turner, and Carter. Each would have testified to the statements purportedly made by McDonald, on three separate occasions shortly after the crime, naming himself as the murderer. The State Supreme Court approved the exclusion of this evidence on the ground that it was hearsay.

The hearsay rule, which has long been recognized and respected by virtually every State, is based on experience and grounded in the notion that untrustworthy evidence should not be presented to the triers of fact. Out-of-court statements are traditionally excluded because they lack the conventional indicia of reliability: they are usually not made under oath or other circumstances that impress the speaker with the solemnity of his statements; the declarant's word is not subject to cross-examination; and he is not available in order that his demeanor and credibility may be assessed by the jury. California v. Green, 399 U.S. 149, 158, 90 S.Ct. 1930, 1935, 26 L.Ed.2d 489 (1970). A number of exceptions have developed over the years to allow admission of hearsay statements made under circumstances that tend to assure reliability and thereby compensate for the absence of the oath and opportunity for cross-examination. Among the most prevalent of these exceptions is the one applicable to declarations against interest—an exception founded on the assumption that a person is unlikely to fabricate a statement against his own interest at the time it is made. Mississippi recognizes this exception but applies it only to declarations against pecuniary interest. It recognizes no such exception for declarations, like McDonald's in this case, that are against the penal interest of the declarant.

This materialistic limitation on the declaration-against-interest hearsay exception appears to be accepted by most States in their criminal trial processes, although a number of States have discarded it. Declarations against penal interest have also been excluded in federal courts under the authority of Donnelly v. United States, 228 U.S. 243, 272–273, 33 S.Ct. 449, 459, 57 L.Ed. 820 (1913), although exclusion would not be required under the newly proposed Federal Rules of Evidence.[18] Exclusion, where the limitation prevails, is usually premised on the view that admission would lead to the frequent presentation of perjured testimony to the jury. It is believed that confessions of criminal activity are often motivated by extraneous considerations and, therefore, are not as inherently reliable as statements against pecuniary or proprietary interest. While that rationale has been the

---

18.　Rule 804, supra, n. 9.

subject of considerable scholarly criticism, we need not decide in this case whether, under other circumstances, it might serve some valid state purpose by excluding untrustworthy testimony.

The hearsay statements involved in this case were originally made and subsequently offered at trial under circumstances that provided considerable assurance of their reliability. First, each of McDonald's confessions was made spontaneously to a close acquaintance shortly after the murder had occurred. Second, each one was corroborated by some other evidence in the case—McDonald's sworn confession, the testimony of an eyewitness to the shooting, the testimony that McDonald was seen with a gun immediately after the shooting, and proof of his prior ownership of .22-caliber revolver and subsequent purchase of a new weapon. The sheer number of independent confessions provided additional corroboration for each. Third, whatever may be the parameters of the penal-interest rationale,[20] each confession here was in a very real sense self-incriminatory and unquestionably against interest. McDonald stood to benefit nothing by disclosing his role in the shooting to any of his three friends and he must have been aware of the possibility that disclosure would lead to criminal prosecution. Indeed, after telling Turner of his involvement, he subsequently urged Turner not to "mess him up." Finally, if there was any question about the truthfulness of the extrajudicial statements, McDonald was present in the courtroom and was under oath. He could have been cross-examined by the State, and his demeanor and responses weighed by the jury. See California v. Green, 399 U.S. 149, 90 S.Ct. 1930, 26 L.Ed.2d 489 (1970). The availability of McDonald significantly distinguishes this case from the prior Mississippi precedent, Brown v. State, supra, and from the *Donnelly*-type situation, since in both cases the declarant was unavailable at the time of trial.[21]

Few rights are more fundamental than that of an accused to present witnesses in his own defense. In the exercise of this right, the accused, as is required of the State, must comply with established rules of procedure and

20. The Mississippi case which refused to adopt a hearsay exception for declarations against penal interest concerned an out-of-court declarant who purportedly stated that he had committed the murder with which his brother had been charged. The Mississippi Supreme Court believed that the declarant might have been motivated by a desire to free his brother rather than by any compulsion of guilt. The Court also noted that the declarant had fled, was unavailable for cross-examination, and might well have known at the time he made the statement that he would not suffer for it. Brown v. State, 99 Miss. 719, 55 So. 961 (1911). There is, in the present case, no such basis for doubting McDonald's statements. See Note, 43 Miss. L.J. 122, 127–129 (1972).

21. McDonald's presence also deprives the State's argument for retention of the penal-interest rule of much of its force. In claiming that "[t]o change the rule would work a travesty on justice," the State posited the following hypothetical:

"If the rule were changed, A could be charged with the crime; B could tell C and D that he committed the crime; *B could go into hiding* and at A's trial C and D would testify as to B's admission of guilt; A could be acquitted and B would return to stand trial; B could then provide several witnesses to testify as to his whereabouts at the time of the crime. The testimony of those witnesses along with A's statement that he really committed the crime could result in B's acquittal. A would be barred from further prosecution because of the protection against double jeopardy. No one could be convicted of perjury as A did not testify at his first trial, B did not lie under oath, and C and D were truthful in their testimony." Brief for Respondent 7 n. 3 (emphasis supplied).

Obviously, B's absence at trial is critical to the success of the justice-subverting ploy.

evidence designed to assure both fairness and reliability in the ascertainment of guilt and innocence. Although perhaps no rule of evidence has been more respected or more frequently applied in jury trials than that applicable to the exclusion of hearsay, exceptions tailored to allow the introduction of evidence which in fact is likely to be trustworthy have long existed. The testimony rejected by the trial court here bore persuasive assurances of trustworthiness and thus was well within the basic rationale of the exception for declarations against interest. That testimony also was critical to Chambers' defense. In these circumstances, where constitutional rights directly affecting the ascertainment of guilt are implicated, the hearsay rule may not be applied mechanistically to defeat the ends of justice.

We conclude that the exclusion of this critical evidence, coupled with the State's refusal to permit Chambers to cross-examine McDonald, denied him a trial in accord with traditional and fundamental standards of due process. In reaching this judgment, we establish no new principles of constitutional law. Nor does our holding signal any diminution in the respect traditionally accorded to the States in the establishment and implementation of their own criminal trial rules and procedures. Rather, we hold quite simply that under the facts and circumstances of this case the rulings of the trial court deprived Chambers of a fair trial.

The judgment is reversed and the case is remanded to the Supreme Court of Mississippi for further proceedings not inconsistent with this opinion.

It is so ordered.

[The concurring opinion of Justice White and the dissenting opinion of Justice Rehnquist are omitted.]

NOTE

See the excerpt from Williams, The Proof of Guilt, supra, p.   . Does Chambers v. Mississippi enact the British prosecutor's ethical rule?

WILLIAMS, THE PROOF OF GUILT
209–10 (1955).*
Hearsay as Evidence for the Defense

The books on evidence do not distinguish between the rules of hearsay as applied to the evidence for the Crown and as applied to the evidence for the defense. In fact it has sometimes been ruled with great distinctness that defendants in criminal trials are subject to the same rules of evidence (including the hearsay rule) as the prosecution. Most people would say, however, that there should be a great difference between the position of the defense and that of the prosecution. A miscarriage of justice should not be risked by shutting out any evidence for the defense, even though it may be hearsay. Accordingly, Crown counsel frequently take no objection to defense evidence even when they might technically be able to do so. As Sir Herbert Stephen wrote:

"The counsel for the prosecution ought to make it obvious, and in England he almost always does so, that his object is not to get a con-

*London, Stevens, 1955.

viction, without qualification, but to get a conviction only if justice requires it. He therefore seldom if ever raises any objection to question proposed to be asked in the course of the defense upon any ground except that they are a waste of time, or likely to distract the attention of the jury from the substantial issues of the case."

Chapter IV

A RETURN TO RELEVANCE

PART A.   CHARACTER, HABIT, AND CUSTOM

1.   CHARACTER IN ISSUE

CLEGHORN v. NEW YORK CENTRAL & H. RIVER RY. CO.

Court of Appeals of New York, 1874.
56 N.Y. 44.

CHURCH, Ch. J.   The accident was caused by the carelessness of the switchman, in neglecting to close the switch after the stock train had passed on to the side track, and in giving a false signal to the approaching passenger train, that the track was all right. It was a clear case of negligence; and for the injury to the plaintiff produced thereby the defendant is liable in this action. It is insisted that the court erred in admitting evidence of the intemperate habits of the switchman, and that the case of Warner v. N.Y.C.R.R. Co. (44 N.Y. 465) is a direct authority against it. That was a case of injury at a road crossing. It was proved that the flagman neglected to give the customary signal, and was intoxicated at the time. The Commission of Appeals held it error to show previous habits of intemperance known to the officers of the company, upon the ground that such evidence had no bearing upon the question of negligence at the time. In that view the decision was right. Previous intoxication would not tend to establish an omission to give the signal on the occasion of the accident. In this case it was sought to be proved, not only that Hartman was intoxicated at the time of the accident, but that he was a man of intemperate habits, which were known by the agent of the company, having the power to employ and discharge him and other subordinates, with a view of claiming exemplary damages. For this purpose the evidence was competent.   *   *   *   Judgment reversed. [On other grounds.]

WELLMAN, THE ART OF CROSS-EXAMINATION

199–200 (1962).*

[Suit for libel. The defendant newspaper had published a front page attack upon the plaintiff opera manager which included the sentence:]

"My opinion of you is that you are the sort of man who would steal his mother's bones from the grave and sell them to buy flowers for a harlot."

The plaintiff testified in his own behalf. On cross-examination by Mr. Nicoll it developed that the plaintiff had written the editor who had composed the article an offensive note almost as violent as the one sued upon; that while manager of a trade journal he, himself, had been sued for libel,

*Copyright, 1962 by Collier.

where the verdict was four thousand five hundred dollars against him; and that he was put upon the jail limits for failure to pay the judgment. It also appeared that he had been convicted of assault upon the opposing lawyer, a most respectable member of the bar; that he had been twice bankrupt; that his sister had recovered a judgment against him for money borrowed; and that his wife had been persuaded to help him in his business affairs and had been driven into bankruptcy on his account. During seven of the twenty years of his married life he kept a mistress, and even occupied, with her, on many occasions, a box in his own opera house directly over his wife's box. He also wrote her impassioned letters, and allowed her to use his wife's horses and carriages. The object of the cross-examiner was, of course, to show that the reputation of such a man could not be injured by anything a newspaper might say about him. The jury agreed with counsel that one thousand dollars out of the two hundred and fifty sued for was balm enough for his injured feelings.

In actions for defamation such as the one just described, it is always legitimate to attack the character of the plaintiff, whether or not he becomes a witness in his own behalf. The question in such cases is one of sound tactics rather than of professional ethics. The plaintiff's character is directly material on the issue as to how much he has been damaged by what the defendant has said or written of him.

Hypothetical

P, the widow of H, sues D in a wrongful death action arising out of H's death in 1970. P testifies on the issue of damages that she and H had a happy and affectionate marital relationship. D then proffers evidence that in 1961–63, H left P and lived with a minor female in a meretricious relationship, and that H was convicted in 1967 of the offense of issuing checks without sufficient funds and received a year's jail sentence. P makes an inadmissible-character-evidence objection to D's proffered evidence. D contends that the proffered evidence establishes H's character traits for immorality and dishonesty and that these character traits are relevant to the issue of the pecuniary value of H's companionship to P, his widow. The trial judge overrules P's objection. Is this ruling correct?

2.   CHARACTER AS CIRCUMSTANTIAL EVIDENCE

MICHELSON v. UNITED STATES

Supreme Court of the United States, 1948.
335 U.S. 469, 69 S.Ct. 213, 93 L.Ed. 168.
[Some of the Court's footnotes have been omitted.]

Mr. Justice JACKSON delivered the opinion of the Court.

In 1947 petitioner Michelson was convicted of bribing a federal revenue agent. The Government proved a large payment by accused to the agent for the purpose of influencing his official action. The defendant, as a witness on his own behalf, admitted passing the money but claimed it was done in response to the agent's demands, threats, solicitations, and inducements that amounted to entrapment. It is enough for our purposes to say that determination of the issue turned on whether the jury should believe the agent or the accused.

On direct examination of defendant, his own counsel brought out that, in 1927, he had been convicted of a misdemeanor having to do with trading in counterfeit watch dials. On cross-examination it appeared that in 1930, in executing an application for a license to deal in second-hand jewelry, he answered "No" to the question whether he had theretofore been arrested or summoned for any offense.

Defendant called five witnesses to prove that he enjoyed a good reputation. Two of them testified that their acquaintance with him extended over a period of about thirty years and the others said they had known him at least half that long. A typical examination in chief was as follows:

"Q.   Do you know the defendant Michelson? A. Yes.

"Q.   How long do you know Mr. Michelson? A. About 30 years.

"Q.   Do you know other people who know him? A. Yes.

"Q.   Have you had occasion to discuss his reputation for honesty and truthfulness and for being a law-abiding citizen? A. It is very good.

"Q.   You have talked to others? A. Yes.

"Q.   And what is his reputation? A. Very good."

These are representative of answers by three witnesses; two others replied, in substance, that they never had heard anything against Michelson.

On cross-examination, four of the witnesses were asked, in substance, this question: "Did you ever hear that Mr. Michelson on March 4, 1927, was convicted of a violation of the trademark law in New York City in regard to watches?" This referred to the twenty-year-old conviction about which defendant himself had testified on direct examination. Two of them had heard of it and two had not.

To four of these witnesses the prosecution also addressed the question the allowance of which, over defendant's objection, is claimed to be reversible error:

"Did you ever hear that on October 11th, 1920, the defendant, Solomon Michelson, was arrested for receiving stolen goods?"

None of the witnesses appears to have heard of this.

The trial court asked counsel for the prosecution, out of presence of the jury, "Is it a fact according to the best information in your possession that Michelson was arrested for receiving stolen goods?" Counsel replied that it was, and to support his good faith exhibited a paper record which defendant's counsel did not challenge.

The judge also on three occasions warned the jury, in terms that are not criticized, of the limited purpose for which this evidence was received.[3]

3.   In ruling on the objection when the question was first asked, the Court said: " * * * I instruct the jury that what is happening now is this: the defendant has called character witnesses, and the basis for the evidence given by those character witnesses is the reputation of the defendant in the community, and since the defendant tenders the issue of his reputation the prosecution may ask the witness if she has heard of various incidents in his career. I say to you that regardless of her answer you are not to assume that the incidents asked about actually took place. All that is happening is that this witness' standard of opinion of the reputation of the defendant is being tested. Is that clear?" In overruling the second objection to the question the Court said: "Again I say to the jury there is no proof that Mr. Michelson was arrested for receiving stolen goods in 1920, there isn't any such proof. All this witness has been asked is whether he had heard of that. There is nothing before you on that issue. Now would you base your decision on the case fairly in spite of the fact that that question has been asked? You would? All right."

Defendant-petitioner challenges the right of the prosecution so to cross-examine his character witnesses. The Court of Appeals held that it was permissible. The opinion, however, points out that the practice has been severely criticized and invites us, in one respect, to change the rule.[4] Serious and responsible criticism has been aimed, however, not alone at the detail now questioned by the Court of Appeals but at common-law doctrine on the whole subject of proof of reputation or character.[5] It would not be possible to appraise the usefulness and propriety of this cross-examination without consideration of the unique practice concerning character testimony, of which such cross-examination is a minor part.

Courts that follow the common-law tradition almost unanimously have come to disallow resort by the prosecution to any kind of evidence of a defendant's evil character to establish a probability of his guilt. Not that the law invests the defendant with a presumption of good character, but it simply closes the whole matter of character, disposition and reputation on the

The charge included the following: "In connection with the character evidence in the case I permitted a question whether or not the witness knew that in 1920 this defendant had been arrested for receiving stolen goods. I tried to give you the instruction then that that question was permitted only to test the standards of character evidence that these character witnesses seemed to have. There isn't any proof in the case that could be produced before you legally within the rules of evidence that this defendant was arrested in 1920 for receiving stolen goods, and that fact you are not to hold against him; nor are you to assume what the consequences of that arrest were. You just drive it from your mind so far as he is concerned, and take it into consideration only in weighing the evidence of the character witnesses."

4.   Footnote 8 to that court's opinion reads as follows [165 F.2d 735]:

"Wigmore, Evidence (3d ed. 1940) § 988, after noting that 'such inquiries are almost universally admitted,' not as 'impeachment by extrinsic testimony of particular acts of misconduct,' but as means of testing the character 'witness' grounds of knowledge,' continues with these comments: 'But the serious objection to them is that practically the above distinction —between rumors of such conduct, as affecting reputation, and the fact of it as violating the rule against particular facts —cannot be maintained in the mind of the jury. The rumor of the misconduct, when admitted, goes far, in spite of all theory and of the judge's charge, towards fixing the misconduct as a fact upon the other person, and thus does three improper things,—(1) it violates the fundamental rule of fairness that prohibits the use of such facts, (2) it gets at them by hearsay only, and not by trustworthy testimony, and (3) it leaves the other person no means of defending himself by denial or explanation, such as he would

otherwise have had if the rule had allowed that conduct to be made the subject of an issue. Moreover, these are not occurrences of possibility, but of daily practice. This method of inquiry or cross-examination is frequently resorted to by counsel for the very purpose of injuring by indirection a character which they are forbidden directly to attack in that way; they rely upon the mere putting of the question (not caring that it is answered negatively) to convey their covert insinuation. The value of the inquiry for testing purposes is often so small and the opportunities of its abuse by underhand ways are so great that the practice may amount to little more than a mere subterfuge, and should be strictly supervised by forbidding it to counsel who do not use it in good faith.'

"Because, as Wigmore says, the jury almost surely cannot comprehend the judge's limiting instruction, the writer of this opinion wishes that the United States Supreme Court would tell us to follow what appears to be the Illinois, rule, i.e., that such questions are improper unless they relate to offenses similar to those for which the defendant is on trial. See Aiken v. People, 183 Ill. 215, 55 N.E. 695; cf. People v. Hannon, 381 Ill. 206, 44 N.E.2d 923."

5.   A judge of long trial and appellate experience has uttered a warning which, in the opinion of the writer, we might well have heeded in determining whether to grant certiorari here: " * * * evidence of good character is to be used like any other, once it gets before the jury, and the less they are told about the grounds for its admission, or what they shall do with it, the more likely they are to use it sensibly. The subject seems to gather mist which discussion serves only to thicken, and which we can scarcely hope to dissipate by anything further we can add." L. Hand in Nash v. United States, 2 Cir., 54 F.2d 1006, 1007.

prosecution's case-in-chief. The State may not show defendant's prior trouble with the law, specific criminal acts, or ill name among his neighbors, even though such facts might logically be persuasive that he is by propensity a probable perpetrator of the crime.[8] The inquiry is not rejected because character is irrelevant;[9] on the contrary, it is said to weigh too much with the jury and to so overpersuade them as to prejudge one with a bad general record and deny him a fair opportunity to defend against a particular charge. The overriding policy of excluding such evidence, despite its admitted probative value, is the practical experience that its disallowance tends to prevent confusion of issues, unfair surprise and undue prejudice.

But this line of inquiry firmly denied to the State is opened to the defendant because character is relevant in resolving probabilities of guilt. He may introduce affirmative testimony that the general estimate of his character is so favorable that the jury may infer that he would not be likely to commit the offense charged. This privilege is sometimes valuable to a defendant for this Court has held that such testimony alone, in some circumstances, may be enough to raise a reasonable doubt of guilt and that in the federal courts a jury in a proper case should be so instructed.

When the defendant elects to initiate a character inquiry, another anomalous rule comes into play. Not only is he permitted to call witnesses to testify from hearsay, but indeed such a witness is not allowed to base his testimony on anything but hearsay. What commonly is called "character evidence" is only such when "character" is employed as a synonym for "reputation." The witness may not testify about defendant's specific acts or courses of conduct or his possession of a particular disposition or of benign mental and moral traits; nor can he testify that his own acquaintance, observation, and knowledge of defendant leads to his own independent opinion that defendant possesses a good general or specific character, inconsistent with commission of acts charged. The witness is, however, allowed to summarize what he has heard in the community, although much of it may have been said by persons less qualified to judge than himself. The evidence which the law permits is not as to the personality of defendant but only as to the shadow his daily life has cast in his neighborhood. This has been well described in a different connection as "the slow growth of months and years, the resultant picture of forgotten incidents, passing events, habitual and daily conduct, presumably honest because disinterested, and safer to be trusted because prone to suspect.   *   *   *   It is for that reason that such

---

In opening its cyclopedic review of authorities from many jurisdictions, CORPUS JURIS SECUNDUM summarizes that the rules regulating proof of character "have been criticized as illogical, unscientific, and anomalous, explainable only as archaic survivals of compurgation or of states of legal development when the jury personally knew the facts on which their verdict was based." 32 C.J.S., Evidence, § 433.

8. This would be subject to some qualification, as when a prior crime is an element of the later offense; for example, at a trial for being an habitual criminal. There are also well-established exceptions where evidence as to other transactions or a course of fraudulent conduct is admitted to establish fraudulent intent as an element of the crime charged. [Citations omitted.]

9. As long ago as 1865, Chief Justice Cockburn said, "The truth is, this part of our law is an anomaly. Although, logically speaking, it is quite clear that an antecedent bad character would form quite as reasonable a ground for the presumption and probability of guilt as previous good character lays the foundation of innocence, yet you cannot, on the part of the prosecution, go into evidence as to character." Reg v. Rowton, 10 Cox's Criminal Cases 25, 29–30. And see 1 Wigmore, Evidence (3d ed., 1940) § 55.

general repute is permitted to be proven. It sums up a multitude of trivial details. It compacts into the brief phrase of a verdict the teaching of many incidents and the conduct of years. It is the average intelligence drawing its conclusion." Finch J., in Badger v. Badger, 88 N.Y. 546, 552, 42 Am.Rep. 263.

While courts have recognized logical grounds for criticism of this type of opinion-based-on-hearsay testimony, it is said to be justified by "overwhelming considerations of practical convenience" in avoiding innumberable collateral issues which, if it were attempted to prove character by direct testimony, would complicate and confuse the trial, distract the minds of jurymen and befog the chief issues in the litigation.

Another paradox in this branch of the law of evidence is that the delicate and responsible task of compacting reputation hearsay into the "brief phrase of a verdict" is one of the few instances in which conclusions are accepted from a witness on a subject in which he is not an expert. However, the witness must qualify to give an opinion by showing such acquaintance with the defendant, the community in which he has lived and the circles in which he has moved, as to speak with authority of the terms in which generally he is regarded. To require affirmative knowledge of the reputation may seem inconsistent with the latitude given to the witness to testify when all he can say of the reputation is that he has "heard nothing against defendant." This is permitted upon assumption that, if no ill is reported of one, his reputation must be good.[13] But this answer is accepted only from a witness whose knowledge of defendant's habitat and surroundings is intimate enough so that his failure to hear of any relevant ill repute is an assurance that no ugly rumors were about.

Thus the law extends helpful but illogical options to a defendant. Experience taught a necessity that they be counterweighted with equally illogical conditions to keep the advantage from becoming an unfair and unreasonable one. The price a defendant must pay for attempting to prove his good name is to throw open the entire subject which the law has kept closed for his benefit and to make himself vulnerable where the law otherwise shields him. The prosecution may pursue the inquiry with contradictory witnesses to show that damaging rumors, whether or not well-grounded, were afloat—for it is not the man that he is, but the name that he has which is put in issue. Another hazard is that his own witness is subject to cross-examination as to the contents and extent of the hearsay on which he bases his conclusions, and he may be required to disclose rumors and reports that are current even if they do not affect his own conclusion.[16] It may test the sufficiency of his knowledge by asking what stories were circulating

13. People v. Van Gaasbeck, 189 N.Y. 408, 420, 82 N.E. 718, 22 L.R.A.,N.S., 650, 12 Ann.Cas. 745. The law apparently ignores the existence of such human ciphers as Kipling's Tomlinson, of whom no ill is reported but no good can be recalled. They win seats with the righteous for character evidence purposes, however hard their lot in literature.

16. A classic example in the books is a character witness in a trial for murder. She testified she grew up with defendant, knew his reputation for peace and quiet, and that it was good. On cross-examination she was asked if she had heard that the defendant had shot anybody and, if so, how many. She answered, "Three or four," and gave the names of two but could not recall the names of the others. She still insisted, however, that he was of "good character." The jury seems to have valued her information more highly than her judgment, and on appeal from conviction the cross-examination was held proper. People v. Laudiero, 192 N.Y. 304, 309, 85 N.E. 132.

concerning events, such as one's arrest, about which people normally comment and speculate. Thus, while the law gives defendant the option to show as a fact that his reputation reflects a life and habit incompatible with commission of the offense charged, it subjects his proof to tests of credibility designed to prevent him from profiting by a mere parade of partisans.

To thus digress from evidence as to the offense to hear a contest as to the standing of the accused, at its best opens a tricky line of inquiry as to a shapeless and elusive subject matter. At its worst it opens a veritable Pandora's box of irresponsible gossip, innuendo and smear. In the frontier phase of our law's development, calling friends to vouch for defendant's good character, and its counterpart—calling the rivals and enemies of a witness to impeach him by testifying that his reputation for veracity was so bad that he was unworthy of belief on his oath—were favorite and frequent ways of converting an individual litigation into a community contest and a trial into a spectacle. Growth of urban conditions, where one may never know or hear the name of his next-door neighbor, have tended to limit the use of these techniques and to deprive them of weight with juries. The popularity of both procedures has subsided, but courts of last resort have sought to overcome danger that the true issues will be obscured and confused by investing the trial court with discretion to limit the number of such witnesses and to control cross-examination. Both propriety and abuse of hearsay reputation testimony, on both sides, depend on numerous and subtle considerations, difficult to detect or appraise from a cold record, and therefore rarely and only on clear showing of prejudicial abuse of discretion will Courts of Appeals disturb rulings of trial courts on this subject.[17]

Wide discretion is accompanied by heavy responsibility on trial courts to protect the practice from any misuse. The trial judge was scrupulous to so guard it in the case before us. He took pains to ascertain, out of presence of the jury, that the target of the question was an actual event, which would probably result in some comment among acquaintances if not injury to defendant's reputation. He satisfied himself that counsel was not merely taking a random shot at a reputation imprudently exposed or asking a groundless question to waft an unwarranted innuendo into the jury box.[18]

17. It has been held that the question may not be hypothetical nor assume unproven facts and ask if they would affect the conclusion. And that it may not be so asked as to detail evidence or circumstances of a crime of which defendant was accused. It has been held error to use the question to get before the jury a particular derogatory newspaper article. The proof has been confined to general reputation and that among a limited group such as fellow employees in a particular building held inadmissible.

18. This procedure was recommended by Wigmore. But analysis of his innovation emphasizes the way in which law on this subject has evolved from pragmatic considerations rather than from theoretical consistency. The relevant information that it is permissible to lay before the jury is talk or conversation about the defendant's being arrested. That is admissible whether or not an actual arrest had taken place; it might even be more significant of repute if his neighbors were ready to arrest him in rumor when the authorities were not in fact. But before this relevant and proper inquiry can be made, counsel must demonstrate privately to the court an irrelevant and possibly unprovable fact—the reality of arrest. From this permissible inquiry about reports of arrest, the jury is pretty certain to infer that defendant had in fact been arrested and to draw its own conclusions as to character from that fact. The Wigmore suggestion thus limits legally relevant inquiries to those based on legally irrelevant facts in order that the legally irrelevant conclusion which the jury probably will draw from the relevant questions will not be based on unsupported or untrue innuendo. It illustrates Judge Hand's suggestion that the system may work best when explained least. Yet, despite its theoretical paradoxes and deficiencies, we approve the procedure as calculated in practice to hold the inquiry within decent bounds.

The question permitted by the trial court, however, involves several features that may be worthy of comment. Its form invited hearsay; it asked about an arrest, not a conviction, and for an offense not closely similar to the one on trial; and it concerned an occurrence many years past.

Since the whole inquiry, as we have pointed out, is calculated to ascertain the general talk of people about defendant, rather that the witness' own knowledge of him, the form of inquiry, "Have you heard?" has general approval, and "Do you know?" is not allowed.

A character witness may be cross-examined as to an arrest whether or not it culminated in a conviction, according to the overwhelming weight of authority. This rule is sometimes confused with that which prohibits cross-examination to credibility by asking a witness whether he himself has been arrested.

Arrest without more does not, in law any more than in reason, impeach the integrity or impair the credibility of a witness. It happens to the innocent as well as the guilty. Only a conviction, therefore, may be inquired about to undermine the trustworthiness of a witness.

Arrest without more may nevertheless impair or cloud one's reputation. False arrest may do that. Even to be acquitted may damage one's good name if the community receives the verdict with a wink and chooses to remember defendant as one who ought to have been convicted. A conviction, on the other hand, may be accepted as a misfortune or an injustice, and even enhance the standing of one who mends his ways and lives it down. Reputation is the net balance of so many debits and credits that the law does not attach the finality to a conviction when the issue is reputation, that is given to it when the issue is the credibility of the convict.

The inquiry as to an arrest is permissible also because the prosecution has a right to test the qualifications of the witness to bespeak the community opinion. If one never heard the speculations and rumors in which even one's friends indulge upon his arrest, the jury may doubt whether he is capable of giving any very reliable conclusions as to his reputation.

In this case the crime inquired about was receiving stolen goods; the trial was for bribery. The Court of Appeals thought this dissimilarity of offenses too great to sustain the inquiry in logic, though conceding that it is authorized by preponderance of authority. It asks us to substitute the Illinois rule which allows inquiry about arrest, but only for very closely similar if not identical charges, in place of the rule more generally adhered to in this country and in England.[21] We think the facts of this case show the proposal to be inexpedient.

The good character which the defendant had sought to establish was broader than the crime charged and included the traits of "honesty and truthfulness" and "being a law-abiding citizen." Possession of these characteristics would seem as incompatible with offering a bribe to a revenue agent as with receiving stolen goods. The crimes may be unlike, but both alike proceed from the same defects of character which the witnesses said this defendant was reputed not to exhibit. It is not only by comparison with

---

21. The Supreme Court of Illinois, in considering its own rule which we are urged to adopt, recognized that "the rule adhered to in this State is not consistent with the great weight of authority in this country and in England." People v. Hannon, 381 Ill. 206, 209, 44 N.E.2d 923, 924.

the crime on trial but by comparison with the reputation asserted that a court may judge whether the prior rest should be made subject of inquiry. By this test the inquiry was permissible. It was proper cross-examination because reports of his arrest for receiving stolen goods, if admitted, would tend to weaken the assertion that he was known as an honest and law-abiding citizen. The cross-examination may take in as much ground as the testimony it is designed to verify. To hold otherwise would give defendant the benefit of testimony that he was honest and law-abiding in reputation when such might not be the fact; the refutation was founded on convictions equally persuasive though not for crimes exactly repeated in the present charge.

The inquiry here concerned an arrest twenty-seven years before the trial. Events a generation old are likely to be lived down and dropped from the present thought and talk of the community and to be absent from the knowledge of younger or more recent acquaintances. The court in its discretion may well exclude inquiry about rumors of an event so remote, unless recent misconduct revived them. But two of these witnesses dated their acquaintance with defendant as commencing thirty years before the trial. Defendant, on direct examination, voluntarily called attention to his conviction twenty years before. While the jury might conclude that a matter so old and indecisive as a 1920 arrest would shed little light on the present reputation and hence propensities of the defendant, we cannot say that, in the context of this evidence and in the absence of objection on this specific ground, its admission was an abuse of discretion.

We do not overlook or minimize the consideration that "the jury almost surely cannot comprehend the Judge's limiting instructions," which disturbed the Court of Appeals. The refinements of the evidentiary rules on this subject are such that even lawyers and judges, after study and reflection, often are confused, and surely jurors in the hurried and unfamiliar movement of a trial must find them almost unintelligible. However, limiting instructions on this subject are no more difficult to comprehend or apply than those upon various other subjects; for example, instructions that admissions of a co-defendant are to be limited to the question of his guilt and are not to be considered as evidence against other defendants, and instructions as to other problems in the trial of conspiracy charges. A defendant in such a case is powerless to prevent his cause from being irretrievably obscured and confused; but, in cases such as the one before us, the law foreclosed this whole confounding line of inquiry, unless defendant thought the net advantage from opening it up would be with him. Given this option, we think defendants in general and this defendant in particular have no valid complaint at the latitude which existing law allows to the prosecution to meet by cross-examination an issue voluntarily tendered by the defense.

We end, as we began, with the observation that the law regulating the offering and testing of character testimony may merit many criticisms. England, and some states have overhauled the practice by statute.[22] But

22. Criminal Evidence Act, 61 & 62, Vict. c. 36. See also 51 L.Q.Rev. 443, for discussion of right to cross-examine about prior arrests. For review of English and State legislation, see 1 Wigmore, Evidence (3d ed., 1940) § 194, et seq. The Pennsylvania statute, Act of March 15, 1911, P.L. 20, § 1, discussed by Wigmore has been amended, Act of July 3, 1947, P.L. 1239, § 1, 19 P.S. § 711. The current statute and Pennsylvania practice were considered recently by the Superior Court of that state. Commonwealth v. Hurt, 163 Pa.Super. 232, 60 A.2d 828.

the task of modernizing the longstanding rules on the subject is one of magnitude and difficulty which even those dedicated to law reform do not lightly undertake.[23]

The law of evidence relating to proof of reputation in criminal cases has developed almost entirely at the hands of state courts of last resort, which have such questions frequently before them. This Court, on the other hand, has contributed little to this or to any phase of the law of evidence, for the reason, among others, that it has had extremely rare occasion to decide such issues, as the paucity of citations in this opinion to our own writings attests. It is obvious that a court which can make only infrequent sallies into the field cannot recast the body of case law on this subject in many, many years, even if it were clear what the rules should be.

We concur in the general opinion of courts, textwriters and the profession that much of this law is archaic, paradoxical and full of compromises and compensations by which an irrational advantage to one side is offset by a poorly reasoned, counterprivilege to the other. But somehow it has proved a workable even if clumsy system when moderated by discretionary controls in the hands of a wise and strong trial court. To pull one misshapen stone out of the grotesque structure is more likely simply to upset its present balance between adverse interests than to establish a rational edifice.

The present suggestion is that we adopt for all federal courts a new rule as to cross-examination about prior arrest, adhered to by the courts of only one state and rejected elsewhere.[24] The confusion and error it would engender would seem too heavy a price to pay for an almost imperceptible logical improvement, if any, in a system which is justified, if at all, by accumulated judicial experience rather than abstract logic.[25]

The judgment is

Affirmed.

Mr. Justice Frankfurter, concurring.

Despite the fact that my feelings run in the general direction of the views expressed by MR. JUSTICE RUTLEDGE in his dissent, I join the Court's opinion. I do so because I believe it to be unprofitable, on balance, for appellate courts to formulate rigid rules for the exclusion of evidence in courts of law that outside them would not be regarded as clearly irrelevant in the determination of issues. For well-understood reasons this Court's occasional ventures in formulating such rules hardly encourage confidence in denying to the federal trial courts a power of control over the allowable

23. The American Law Institute, in promulgating its "Model Code of Evidence," includes the comment, "Character, whenever used in these Rules, means disposition not reputation. It denotes what a person is, not what he is reputed to be. No rules are laid down as to proof of reputation, when reputation is a fact to be proved. When reputation is a material matter, it is proved in the same manner as is any other disputed fact." Rule 304. The latter sentence may seem an oversimplification in view of the decisions we have reviewed.

24. See note 21.

25. It must not be overlooked that abuse of cross-examination to test credibility carries its own corrective. Authorities on practice caution the bar of the imprudence as well as the unprofessional nature of attacks on witnesses or defendants which are likely to be resented by the jury. Wellman, Art of Cross Examination (1927) p. 167 et seq.

scope of cross-examination possessed by trial judges in practically all State courts. After all, such uniformity of rule in the conduct of trials is the crystallization of experience even when due allowance is made for the force of imitation. To reject such an impressive body of experience would imply a more dependable wisdom in a matter of this sort than I can claim.

To leave the District Courts of the United States the discretion given to them by this decision presupposes a high standard of professional competence, good sense, fairness and courage on the part of the federal district judges. If the United States District Courts are not manned by judges of such qualities, appellate review, no matter how stringent, can do very little to make up for the lack of them.

[The dissenting opinion of Mr. Justice Rutledge who was joined by Mr. Justice Murphy, though worthy of examination, is not reproduced here.]

CAMUS, THE STRANGER

79–81.*

[The protagonist is awaiting trial before an Algerian Court on a charge of murdering an Arab in a brawl. The defense is self-defense. His lawyer visits him in jail] * * * [H]e said that they'd been making investigations into my private life. They had learned that my mother died recently in a home. Inquiries had been conducted at Marengo and the police informed that I'd shown "great callousness" at my mother's funeral.

"You must understand," the lawyer said, "that I don't relish having to question you about such a matter. But it has much importance, and, unless I find some way of answering the charge of 'callousness,' I shall be handicapped in conducting your defense. And that is where you, and only you, can help me."

He went on to ask if I had felt grief on that "sad occasion." The question struck me as an odd one; I'd have been much embarrassed if I'd had to ask anyone a thing like that.

I answered that, of recent years, I'd rather lost the habit of noting my feelings, and hardly knew what to answer. I could truthfully say I'd been quite fond of Mother—but really that didn't mean much. All normal people, I added as on afterthought, had more or less desired the death of those they loved, at some time or another.

Here the lawyer interrupted me, looking greatly perturbed.

"You must promise me not to say anything of that sort at the trial, or to the examining magistrate."

I promised, to satisfy him, but I explained that my physical condition at any given moment often influenced my feelings. For instance, on the day I attended Mother's funeral, I was fagged out and only half awake. So, really, I hardly took stock of what was happening. Anyhow, I could assure him of one thing: that I'd rather Mother hadn't died.

The lawyer, however, looked displeased. "That's not enough," he said curtly.

After considering for a bit he asked me if he could say that on that day I had kept my feelings under control.

"No," I said. "That wouldn't be true."

He gave me a queer look, as if I slightly revolted him; then informed me, in an almost hostile tone, that in any case the head of the Home and some of the staff would be cited as witnesses.

"And that might do you a very nasty turn," he concluded.

When I suggested that Mother's death had no connection with the charge against me, he merely replied that this remark showed I'd never had any dealings with the law.

A.L.I., MODEL PENAL CODE

Tentative Draft No. 9, art. 207.12.*

(7) Evidence. On the issue whether a place is a house of prostitution the following shall be admissible evidence: its general repute; the repute of the persons who reside in or frequent the place; the frequency, timing, and duration of visits by nonresidents * * * .

MARYLAND—DISTRICT OF COLUMBIA—VIRGINIA CRIMINAL PRACTICE INSTITUTE TRIAL MANUAL

2–7 (1964).*

2.03 *Eliciting Testimony Regarding the Character Trait of Truth and Veracity.*

1. What is your name, please?
2. Where do your reside, Mr. [name]?
3. Where are you employed?
4. How long have you worked there?
5. In what capacity?
6. Do you know the defendant, [name]?
7. How long have you know him?
8. During that period, how often did you see him?
9. What was the nature of your association with him?
10. Did you know other people who knew him?
11. Did you discuss with these people, or hear discussed, the defendant's reputation for truth and veracity?
12. What generally is his reputation for truth and veracity among those people?

THEODORE ROOSEVELT AS CHARACTER WITNESS

10 Journal of the Cleveland Bar Assoc. 36 (Dec. 1938).

[Note—In this installment of the address which was delivered by President Frank J. Hogan, of the American Bar Association, before

*The American Law Institute, Philadelphia, 1959. See Calif. Penal Code § 315.   *Copyright, 1964, by Lerner Law Book Co.

our members at the October meeting, we start with the entrance of the late President Theodore Roosevelt into the courtroom at Washington to testify as a character witness for Charles G. Glover, president of the largest national bank in the capital city.]

As Teddy Roosevelt stepped up into the room it appeared as though he had stepped on a button that would set off the applause, and first the applause started with hand clapping, and then everybody in the courtroom stood up. * * *

When quiet was restored and a few minutes passed and Roosevelt had waved to everybody whether he knew them or not, the Judge ascended the bench and we put Teddy on as the first witness.

Now, all of you, I don't know whether your rule is as strict with respect to reputation witnesses here, but in most states, of course, the witness is allowed to identify himself and then say he knows the defendant, and then he is asked whether the defendant's character or reputation for the trait involved is good or bad, and in some states they tie it down to good, bad or excellent, or very good, or something of that kind. In our jurisdiction we are allowed a little greater latitude, our Court of Appeals having held that one might have a good reputation or a superlatively good reputation, and that also we have a right to show who the character witness is so that the jury can give greater or less weight to the man who thus testifies.

But whether we had those rules of "good" or "bad" or monosyllabic responses would have made no difference to Roosevelt. Rules of evidence might be worshipped by a Wigmore, but if Roosevelt ever heard of them he heard of them only to laugh at them. (Laughter).

He was asked his name, and then many in the audience noticed what the older of this audience must know, that Theodore Roosevelt had a perpetually boy's changing voice—got a great reputation for over-emphasis which he could not help. He had a slight St. Vitus's dance which made him go as though he were going to spit something out, and he could not help it any more than I can help winking one eye every now and then—one of those ties that the psychoanalyst says shows something's wrong up here. When one's voice was changing as a boy, when he was going through that period that makes mother angry when she calls up and says, "Johnny, it's dinner time," and he says, "All right (bass voice). I will be down in a minute (high-pitched voice)," and she says, "Don't both answer at once," and scolds the daughter for joining in—he had almost that kind of a voice, and, as I say, it gave a sort of an added, not practiced, unintentional emphasis to what he had to say.

And when we asked him his name, he said, "Theodore Roosevelt." (Voice breaking from bass to high-pitched). We asked what his profession was, and he said, "Write." (High-pitched voice). We asked where he lived; he said, "Used to be New York." (High-pitched voice). And then without imitating him any more I will tell you he went on that way, getting that up and down. It was fascinating when you realized that the man was intensely interested in what he was saying.

He was asked whether or not he had ever lived in Washington, and he twisted around to the jury, and he said, "May I state what happened without any further question?"

And I said, "Yes, go ahead."

He said, "I came to Washington as Civil Service Commissioner when conditions were very bad. Politics, politics, alone, governed whether—are any of you in the government service? Oh, no. I forgot jurymen can't be in the government service. Well, those of your neighbors would be shoved in and out of office all the time, and we were trying to make something permanent in the tenure of government officials, and we did it. But it was very routine: it wasn't exciting at all; and I was called back to New York—Judge, you will remember this; you are old enough to remember it—called back to New York, and when I got there I became Police Commissioner. Oh, gentlemen of the jury, I know I can't tell you stories about it today, but it was bully fun—it was bully fun. And I was interested in that. It's fine work where the policemen are generally honest policemen, and we made them honest in New York. We did, gentlemen of the jury, and the citizens of New York would be proud of our work. Oh, but I am getting off. I am coming back, Judge. I am coming back.

"Then I came to Washington as Assistant Secretary of the Navy. That got my interest. When this country gets a great big strong navy it won't have any reason to fear anybody, and people won't be going around saying, 'I didn't raise my son to be a soldier.' You won't hear that any more because the navy will take care of it. We need a strong navy.

"I know, Judge, you are just about to tell me, but I am coming now to it. That's when I was in Washington, though." (Laughter). "And at that time I opened—I know you want me, Mr. Hogan, to say this—I opened an account at the Riggs National Bank. You know, I had a deposit at the Riggs National Bank ever since, and I had it because my faith in Mr. Glover was so great, I wouldn't take it out no matter where I lived."

There was still no stopping him. The district attorney had sense enough to know that if you stopped him you would be bowled over in some way.

He said, "Then came the Spanish-American War. That was terrible, but it was interesting, it was fine, and I had a real life for a while. Then I became governor of New York, so I was back there again for quite a while. Then, gentlemen of the jury, they made me Vice-President. It was the most terrible experience, a perfectly terrible experience. I don't think I would have lived through it if I had to take four years, but I had my account here at the Riggs National Bank as Vice-President just as I had it when I was President; and as you know, I was President for about seven and a half years, living here all the time, keeping my account at the Riggs National Bank.

"And by the way, Judge, I knew I had met you somewhere. I appointed you because of your civic righteousness, because of your interest in the poor of this city, on my committee to clean out the slums. That's what I did, and you were one of the best men on the committee I ever had. I know, gentlemen of the jury, you are glad to hear that about your Judge. I knew I recognized him. And you did splendid work." And the Judge, who was just on the soft and kindly side, was agreeing with my man, particularly when he said, "You did that splendid work." He went on for some time. Then he said, "Now, have I covered it?"

And I said, "Well, you have covered the fact that you had an account at the Riggs National Bank."

"And didn't I tell you why I put it there? Because of my confidence in Mr. Glover, because of his integrity, because of the splendid man he was and the fine bank he ran and what a fine credit it had all over the United States."

I said, "Yes, Colonel, you have told us that." Well; we were getting away with it. Now, we weren't doing anything wrong; we were simply presenting a man as nature had made him, and we could no more control him, parenthesis, if we wanted to, and parenthesis, (laughter) than could the judge or the jury, or the district attorney, had he attempted it.

Well, we went a little futher—I won't go into all the details—and finally he was asked, "Do you know the reputation of Mr. Glover for honesty, probity, and integrity and veracity?" Getting them all in, you know.

He said, "Do I know it? Why, everybody in the city of Washington knows it. Of course. Nobody could live here, nobody could at any time have had any dealings that amounted to anything, and not know what his reputation is. It was"—

I said, "Just a moment, Colonel. You know that reputation, do you not? I am speaking now of his reputation in the community among people who knew him as you knew him."

"Well," he said "even everybody knew him, so everybody must have known the reputation as I knew it."

"All right. Now, Colonel, will you tell us what that reputation was?"

He pulled his chair forward almost to the edge of the jury platform, leaned over to the jury—he had very heavy hands, put them down on his knees, and he said "I knew Mr. Glover as a civic minded citizen who did more to make the national capitol the perfectly beautiful, outstanding capitol of the world that it is today than any other man that ever lived in America. I knew Mr. Glover as one who in all philanthropic and charitable enterprises—like the Judge; like you, Judge—would always come forward and respond, whether a neighbor or the President of the United States called him.

"I knew Mr. Glover in his home. We visited. My daughter was out there staying with his daughter. We visited out there. We visited as good old chums, because we have been very friendly, and I knew him as a family man loved by all of his own relatives and reverenced by all of his neighbors, and I knew Mr. Glover as a banker whose credit was so high, whose reputation was so fine, whose word was so good, that nobody ever questioned for a moment the safety of his deposit, whether it be large or small. That is the way I knew Mr. Glover."

And then the district attorney couldn't stand it any longer. He arose with a solemnity that I recall vividly to this day. He said, "If your Honor please, I move to strike out the entire answer of the witness. Colonel Roosevelt has said that he knew Mr. Glover in these various capacities, these various ways. He has not said a word about what his reputation was, and I move"—

The Court said, "I am with you, Mr. District Attorney; I will grant your motion," turned apologetically to Colonel Roosevelt and said, "Colonel, you have testified to your own knowledge of Mr. Glover. The rule is that you can testify only to general reputation, general repute. That's what you can do, and nothing more. So I'll have to strike out your answer. Now, please keep that in mind."

I said, "Go ahead, Colonel. Please give us your answer again, keeping the Judge's admonition in mind."

Again he turned to the Judge, again the thick finger went out. He said, "You are right. I should have known that. Thanks ever so much.

"Gentlemen of the jury, I knew Mr. Glover by general reputation and general repute—I'm right now, Judge, am I not? I am right now." (Laughter). And he went all over the whole thing again, with elaborations.

The district attorney whispered to me, "Oh, hell."

And I said, "I should have known better."

But there was no cross-examination. And then, as though that were not enough, Colonel Roosevelt, whom we had promised to let get the 11:00 o'clock train back to New York if he got through with his testimony as we thought he would, came over, and he was wearing his great big sombrero that all of you who ever saw him or pictures of him would recognize, that he always wore in campaign years, and he grabbed it and swished it in to the ladies. One of my associates was to take him to the train, and he had to pass right in front of the jury on his way out. Getting right in the middle in front of the jury, clenching his hand, using that terrific thick finger, he squatted himself as though for a football rush, and he said, "Judge or no Judge,"— * * * "Goodbye, gentlemen of the jury. I always like to appear before a jury of my fellow citizens, for you are rendering a public service. You are rendering a really great public service, just as much as the Judge there. You are here to do justice. That's why you are here—and I know you are going to do it, I know you are going to do it." (Laughter and applause).

With that he went out leaving the courtroom in a perfect storm of disorder. * * * Of course, may I add, again in parenthesis, that justice was done. (Laughter). * * *

———

Methods of Proving Character (See Federal Rules of Evidence 404 at p. 909).

Advisory Committee's Note 10 Rule 404

The rule deals only with allowable methods of proving character, not with the admissibility of character evidence, which is covered in Rule 404.

Of the three methods of proving character provided by the rule, evidence of specific instances of conduct is the most convincing. At the same time it possesses the greatest capacity to arouse prejudice, to confuse, to surprise, and to consume time. Consequently the rule confines the use of evidence of this kind to cases in which character is, in the strict sense, in issue and hence deserving of a searching inquiry. When character is used circumstantially and hence occupies a lesser status in the case, proof may be only by reputation and opinion. These latter methods are also available when character is in issue. This treatment is, with respect to specific instances of conduct and reputation, conventional contemporary common law doctrine. McCormick § 153.

In recognizing opinion as a means of proving character, the rule departs from usual contemporary practice in favor of that of an earlier day. See 7

Wigmore § 1986, pointing out that the earlier practice permitted opinion and arguing strongly for evidence based on personal knowledge and belief as contrasted with "the secondhand, irresponsible product of multiplied guesses and gossip which we term 'reputation.' " It seems likely that the persistence of reputation evidence is due to its largely being opinion in disguise. Traditionally character has been regarded primarily in moral overtones of good and bad: chaste, peaceable, truthful, honest. Nevertheless, on occasion nonmoral considerations crop up, as in the case of the incompetent driver, and this seems bound to happen increasingly. If character is defined as the kind of person one is, then account must be taken of varying ways of arriving at the estimate. These may range from the opinion of the employer who has found the man honest to the opinion of the psychiatrist based upon examination and testing. No effective dividing line exists between character and mental capacity, and the latter traditionally has been provable by opinion.

According to the great majority of cases, on cross-examination inquiry is allowable as to whether the reputation witness has heard of particular instances of conduct pertinent to the trait in question. Michelson v. United States, 335 U.S. 469, 69 S.Ct. 213, 93 L.Ed. 168 (1948); Annot., 47 A.L.R.2d 1258. The theory is that, since the reputation witness relates what he has heard, the inquiry tends to shed light on the accuracy of his hearing and reporting. Accordingly, the opinion witness would be asked whether he knew, as well as whether he had heard. The fact is, of course, that these distinctions are of slight if any practical significance, and the second sentence of subdivision (a) eliminates them as a factor in formulating questions. This recognition of the propriety of inquiring into specific instances of conduct does not circumscribe inquiry otherwise into the bases of opinion and reputation testimony.

The express allowance of inquiry into specific instances of conduct on cross-examination in subdivision (a) and the express allowance of it as part of a case in chief when character is actually in issue in subdivision (b) contemplate that testimony of specific instances is not generally permissible on the direct examination of an ordinary opinion witness to character. Similarly as to witnesses to the character of witnesses under Rule 608(b). Opinion testimony on direct in these situations ought in general to correspond to reputation testimony as now given, i.e., be confined to the nature and extent of observation and acquaintance upon which the opinion is based. See Rule 701.

STATE v. MIRANDA

Supreme Court of Connecticut, 1978.
176 Conn. 107, 405 A.2d 622.

LONGO, Associate Justice.

A jury found the defendant, Miguel A. Miranda, guilty of the crime of manslaughter in the first degree   *   *   *   . The defendant admitted that he shot the victim, Daniel Germany, and testified that he acted in self-defense when Germany attacked him with a knife. His only claim on appeal is that the trial court erred in excluding from evidence Germany's record of convictions of crimes of violence. We agree.

Germany had a lengthy criminal record. The defendant's offer of proof was limited to two convictions of breach of peace by assault in 1965, a conviction of carrying a dangerous weapon in 1969, and a conviction of assault in the second degree in 1973. Those convictions, of which the defendant was unaware at the time of the shooting in 1975, were offered as evidence of Germany's violent character, as tending to show that Germany was the aggressor in the fatal incident. Thus the evidentiary issue resolves itself into two distinct questions: (1) In a homicide trial where the accused claims self-defense, may the accused introduce evidence of the victim's violent character to establish that the victim was the aggressor, regardless of the accused's lack of prior knowledge of such character or the evidence? (2) If such evidence is generally admissible, is the victim's record of convictions of crimes of violence acceptable proof of character?

I

In a trial for homicide the character of the deceased ordinarily is irrelevant to the accused's guilt or innocence. It is well settled, however, that an accused may introduce evidence of the violent, dangerous or turbulent character of the victim to show that the accused had reason to fear serious harm, after laying a proper foundation by adducing evidence that he acted in self-defense and that he was aware of the victim's violent character. The reason for the rule was explained in State v. Padula, supra: "If the reputation of the deceased be that of a violent, dangerous, or turbulent character, such reputation, if known to the defendant, may be a circumstance contributing to a reasonable belief by the accused that his life is in peril and his consequent state of mind as to the necessity of defending himself and the means justifiably to be taken in so doing."

Logically, evidence of a homicide victim's violent character might be offered by the accused for yet another purpose, to show that the victim was the aggressor in their encounter, irrespective of the accused's knowledge of the victim's character. This view was considered and rejected in State v. Padula, supra, 459, 138 A. 456. We have not had occasion to reconsider the matter since.

The case for admissibility of character evidence on the vital issue of who was the aggressor has been cogently stated by Professor Wigmore. When evidence of the deceased's violent character is offered to show the defendant's state of mind, "it is obvious that the deceased's character, as affecting the defendant's apprehensions, must have become known to him; i.e. proof of the character must indispensably be accompanied by proof of its *communication to the defendant;* else it is irrelevant." 1 Wigmore, Evidence (3d Ed.) § 63, p. 470. But when evidence of the deceased's character is offered to show that he was the aggressor, "this additional element of communication is unnecessary; for the question is what the deceased probably did, not what the defendant probably thought the deceased was going to do. The inquiry is one of objective occurrence, not of subjective belief." 1 Wigmore, loc. cit.

We are no longer persuaded that these forceful arguments are outweighed by the objections raised in State v. Padula, supra, 459, 138 A. 458, that admitting such evidence would unfairly prejudice the prosecution's case and would tempt the jury "to measure the guilt of the accused by the deserts of the victim." When an accused chooses to place the deceased's violent character in issue, the state may enjoy the same right of rebuttal as when the accused places his own nonviolent character in issue. There is always the risk that the jury may be unduly diverted and confused by collateral matters such as character; the sound discretion of the court is relied upon to focus the jury's attention on the material issues in the trial.

In cases which have observed the distinction between using evidence of the deceased's violent character to show the accused's state of mind and using it to show that the deceased was the aggressor, it has generally been held that when competent evidence of character is offered for the latter purpose it is admissible regardless of the extent of the accused's knowledge of such character or of the particular evidence in question. We adopt the majority rule.

II

The next stage of our inquiry is whether it is permissible to prove a homicide victim's violent character and hence the allegation that he was the aggressor by evidence of his prior convictions of crimes of violence. In theory, a trait of character may be proved in three ways: (1) by testimony concerning the individual's reputation in the community as to the trait; (2) by testimony of those who have had an opportunity to form, and have formed, an opinion as to whether the individual possessed the trait; (3) by evidence of specific acts of the individual under similar circumstances, from which the existence of the character trait may be inferred. The first method is universally acceptable in situations where character evidence is permitted. Although the second method is not allowed in a number of states, Connecticut adopted it in Richmond v. Norwich, 96 Conn. 582, 594, 115 A. 11, 16, on the rationale that "[p]ersonal observation and personal knowledge are a more trustworthy reliance than general reputation." Both methods are appropriate to prove the character for violence of a homicide victim.

The third method of proving character, evidence of specific acts, has consistently been disapproved in Connecticut and other jurisdictions except in cases where character is directly in issue. Such evidence of specific instances of conduct is excluded not because it is unconvincing, but because it has the potential to surprise, to arouse prejudice, to multiply the issues and confuse the jury, and to prolong the trial.

These considerations have led many courts to limit proof of a homicide victim's character for violence to reputation testimony and opinion testimony, excluding evidence of prior convictions and other specific acts of violence unknown to the defendant.[1] On the other hand, in similar circumstances a growing number of jurisdictions have recognized an exception to the rule that prior convictions and other specific acts of violence may not be used to prove character.

We are presented in this appeal only with the question of the admissibility of convictions of crimes of violence. We agree with the reasoning of the latter group of decisions that the nature of such evidence and the victim's absence from the trial warrant a narrow exception to the rule that conduct may not be used to prove character. That a homicide victim has a rec-

---

1. There is a marked trend towards admitting evidence of prior convictions and other instances of violent conduct *known* to the defendant as probative of the defendant's state of mind.

ord of violent crime should not come as a surprise to the prosecution. Nor is introduction of the victim's criminal record likely to confuse the jury and waste time, since the fact of the convictions is beyond dispute and inquiry must necessarily be limited to the time the events occurred and the nature of the conduct for which the victim was convicted. Most important, such evidence can be highly relevant in helping the jury to determine whether the victim had a violent disposition and whether the defendant's story of self-defense is truthful.

We hold that in a homicide prosecution where the accused has claimed self-defense, the accused may show that the deceased was the aggressor by proving the deceased's alleged character for violence. The deceased's character may be proved by reputation testimony, by opinion testimony, or by evidence of the deceased's convictions of crimes of violence, irrespective of whether the accused knew of the deceased's violent character or of the particular evidence adduced at the time of the death-dealing encounter. We emphasize that the accused is not permitted to introduce the deceased's entire criminal record into evidence in an effort to disparage his general character; only specific convictions for violent acts are admissible. Nor is the accused authorized to introduce any and all convictions of crimes involving violence, no matter how petty, how remote in time, or how dissimilar in their nature to the facts of the alleged aggression. In each case the probative value of the evidence of certain convictions rests in the sound discretion of the trial court.

In this case, the fatal shooting took place in 1975 and the defendant's offer of proof consisted of two convictions of breach of peace by assault in 1965, a conviction of carrying a dangerous weapon in 1969, and a conviction of assault in the second degree in 1973. Those convictions can perhaps be questioned as being too remote in time or lacking elements of violence, depending on the underlying facts and circumstances. The record indicates, however, that the trial court excluded the convictions not for lack of probative value, but for lack of a showing that the defendant knew of them, which was a correct application of the law stated in State v. Padula, 106 Conn. 454, 459, 138 A. 456. Having concluded that the law should be changed, we cannot say under the circumstances that the court's ruling could not reasonably have affected the jury's rejection of the self-defense claim and was therefore harmless.

There is error, the judgment is set aside and a new trial is ordered.

In this opinion Bogdanski, Speziale and Peters, JJ., concurred.

Loiselle, Associate Justice (dissenting).

I agree with the majority opinion extending the rule of admissibility of evidence of aggression on the part of the victim on the issue of self-defense, but I do not agree that evidence of specific acts are admissible for that purpose.   *   *   *

NOTE

See Federal Rules of Evidence 404, 405, at pp. 909, 910, and 803(21) at p. 925; California Evidence Code § § 110–1104 at pp. 810–873, and § 1324 at p. 888.

Where the defendant introduces evidence attacking the character of the victim does this open the door to the prosecution's similarly attacking the character of the defendant? See Roberson v. State, 91 Okla.Crim. 217, 218 P.2d 414 (1950).

McCORMICK'S HANDBOOK OF THE LAW OF EVIDENCE

447-454 (2d ed. 1972).

Character to Evidence Conduct—(c) Application of Rule of Exclusion to Forbid the Prosecution to Introduce Evidence Initially of Bad Character of Accused: Other Crimes

The disfavor for receiving proof of the character of a person as evidence that on a particular occasion he acted in keeping with his disposition is strongly felt when the state seeks to show that the accused is a bad man and thus more likely to have committed the crime. The long-established rule, accordingly, forbids the prosecution, unless and until the accused gives evidence of his good character, to introduce initially evidence of the bad character of the accused.[31] It is not irrelevant, but in the setting of the jury trial the danger of prejudice outweighs the probative value.

This danger is at its highest when character is shown by other criminal acts, and the rule about the proof of other crimes is but an application of the wider prohibition against the initial introduction by the prosecution of evidence of bad character. The rule is that the prosecution may not introduce evidence of other criminal acts of the accused unless the evidence is substantially relevant for some other purpose than to show a probability that he committed the crime on trial because he is a man of criminal character.[32] There are numerous other purposes for which evidence of other

---

31. United States v. Harris, 331 F.2d 185 (4th Cir. 1964) (reputation); Bedsole v. State, 274 Ala. 603, 150 So.2d 696 (1963) (reputation and prior convictions); State v. McCorvey, 262 Minn. 361, 114 N.W.2d 703 (1962) (reputation); Jones v. LaCrosse, 180 Va. 406, 23 S.E.2d 142 (1942)(character for drunkenness); 1 Wigmore, Evidence §§ 55, 57; Dec.Dig. Crim.Law   376.

32. For a similar formulation see Model Code of Evidence Rule 311: " * * * evidence that a person committed a crime or civil wrong on a specified occasion is inadmissible as tending to prove that he committed a crime or civil wrong on another occasion if, but only if, the evidence is relevant solely as tending to prove his disposition to commit such a crime or civil wrong or to commit crimes or civil wrongs generally.", approved in Swann v. United States, 195 F.2d 689, 690 (4th Cir. 1952) and in State v. Scott, 111 Utah 9, 175 P.2d 1016, 1022 (1947).

See also Uniform Rule 55: "Subject to Rule 47 [see § 188, n. 17] evidence that a person committed a crime or civil wrong on a specified occasion, is inadmissible to prove his disposition to commit crime or civil wrong as the basis for an inference that he committed another crime or civil wrong on another specified occasion but, subject to Rules 45 [see § 185, n. 30] and 48 [see § 189, n. 20], such evidence is admissible when relevant to prove some other material fact including absence of mistake or accident, motive, opportunity, intent, preparation, plan, knowledge or identity." To similar effect is F.R.Ev. (R.D.1971) 404(b).

A frequent form of statement is a general rule that evidence of other crimes is inadmissible except when offered for certain particular named purposes. See, e.g., People v. Molineux, 168 N.Y. 264, 61 N.E. 286, 293, 294 (1901): "The general rule of evidence applicable to criminal trials is that the state cannot prove against a defendant any crime not alleged in the indictment, either as a foundation for a separate punishment, or as aiding the proofs that he is guilty of the crime charged. * * * The exceptions to the rule cannot be stated with categorical precision. Generally speaking, evidence of other crimes is competent to prove the specific crime charged when it tends to establish (1) motive; (2) intent; (3) the absence of mistake or accident; (4) a common scheme or plan embracing the commission of two or more crimes so related to each other that proof of one tends to establish the others; (5) the identity of the person charged with the commission of the crime on trial." In that case, a prosecution for murder by poisoning, the evidence was held not to fit any of these exceptions.

The spirit of the rule condemns not only evidence of other crimes not independently relevant, but also questions which, though negatively answered, carry with them the insinuation that the accused committed the other crimes.

criminal acts may be offered, and when so offered the rule of exclusion is simply inapplicable. Some of these purposes are listed below but warning must be given that the list is not complete, for the range of relevancy outside the ban is almost infinite; and further that the purposes are not mutually exclusive, for a particular line of proof may fall within several of them. Neither are they strictly coordinate. Some are phrased in terms of the immediate inferences sought to be drawn, such as plan or motive, others in terms of the ultimate fact, such as knowledge, intent, or identity which the prosecution seeks to establish.[33] The list follows.

(1) To complete the story of the crime on trial by proving its immediate context of happenings near in time and place.[34] This is often characterized as proving a part of the "same transaction" or the "res gestae."

(2) To prove the existence of a larger continuing plan, scheme, or conspiracy, of which the present crime on trial is a part.[35] This will be relevant as showing motive, and hence the doing of the criminal act, the identity of the actor, and his intention, where any of these is in dispute.

(3) To prove other like crimes by the accused so nearly identical in method as to earmark them as the handiwork of the accused.[36] Here much more is demanded than the mere repeated commission of crimes of the same class, such as repeated burglaries or thefts. The device used must be so unusual and distinctive as to be like a signature.[37]

33. "Motive, intent, absence of mistake, plan and identity are not really all on the same plane. Intent, absence of mistake, and identity are facts in issue—*facta probanda*. Motive, plan, or scheme are *facta probantia*, and may tend to show any *facta probanda*." Stone, op. cit., 51 Harv.L.Rev. 988, 1026n.

34. State v. Villavicencio, 95 Ariz. 199, 388 P.2d 245 (1964) (sales of narcotics to A and B at same time and place; evidence of sale to A admissible in prosecution for the sale to B; "This principle that the complete story of the crime may be shown even though it reveals other crimes has often been termed 'res gestae.' * * * [W]e choose to refer to this as the 'complete story' principle, rather than 'res gestae.' "); State v. Klotter, 274 Minn. 58, 142 N.W.2d 568 (1968) (burglary of sporting goods store; evidence of burglary of home of friend of defendant's family, 5 miles away on same night admissible, where guns from both burglaries found in defendant's possession; "connected closely enough in time, place and manner"); State v. Hendrix, 310 S.W.2d 852 (Mo.1958) (prosecution of convict for damaging penitentiary building by sawing bars on window; evidence of attempted escape of defendant and others, which was the purpose of the sawing, admissible as "circumstantial evidence of guilt").

35. Makin v. Attorney General of New South Wales, [1894] App.C. 57 (Privy Council) (murder of an infant left with defendants for their care, with an inadequate premium; evidence that the bodies of ten other babies were found buried in the gardens of three houses formerly occupied by the accused, properly received, on question whether adoption bona fide and deaths accidental); Leonard v. United States, 324 F.2d 911 (9th Cir. 1963) (defendant obtained Treasury checks payable to others, induced A to forge payees' endorsements, then induced B to obtain false credentials, cash checks and split proceeds with defendant; all admissible to show scheme); State v. Toshishige Yoshimo, 45 Hawaii 206, 364 P.2d 638 (1961) (defendant and others robbed A and obtained from him name and address of B as holder of another sum of money, proceeded to B's house and assaulted and robbed B; evidence of first robbery admissible in prosecution for second); State v. Long, 195 Or. 81, 244 P.2d 1033 (1952) (that defendant after killing owner of truck, for which he is now on trial, in use of truck next day for robbery shot F.B.I. man while leaving scene of robbery properly proved as part of planned course of action); Haley v. State, 84 Tex.Cr. 629, 209 S.W. 675 (1919) (murder: that defendant desiring to continue illicit relations with wife of deceased, formed a plan to kill his own wife and deceased, provable but state's evidence here of his poisoning his wife not sufficiently cogent to be received).

36. R. v. George Joseph Smith (1915), reported in Notable British Trials (1922), and described in Marjoribanks, For the Defense: The Life of Edward Marshall Hall 321 (1937) (the famous "brides of the bath" case; defendant accused of murdering his

(4)   To show a passion or propensity for illicit sexual relations with the particular person concerned in the crime on trial.[38] Other like sexual crimes with other persons do not qualify for this purpose.[39] It has been argued that certain unnatural sex crimes are in themselves so unusual and distinctive that previous such acts by the accused with anyone are strongly probative of like acts upon the occasion involved in the charge,[40] but the danger of prejudice is likewise enhanced here, and most courts have in the past excluded such acts with other persons for this purpose. More recent cases show signs of lowering this particular barrier to admission.[41]

(5)   To show, by similar acts or incidents, that the act on trial was not inadvertent, accidental, unintentional,[42] or without guilty knowledge.[43]

wife, who left her property to him by will, by drowning her in the bathtub: defendant leaves their boarding house on a pretended errand, and then on his return purports to discover his wife drowning in the tub and so reports to the landlady; help proper to show that he had previously married several wives, who left him their property and were discovered by him drowned in the bath); People v. Peete, 28 Cal.2d 306, 169 P.2d 924 (1946) (where defendant had been previously convicted of killing another who was killed by means of a bullet from behind, severing the spinal cord at the neck, and deceased in present prosecution was shot from behind at close range in an attempt to sever the spinal cord, evidence of the prior homicide was admissible as tending to identify defendant as the murderer.); and see Note, 35 Colum.L.Rev. 131 (1935) which at p. 136 examines the distinction between this and purpose (2), above; Whiteman v. State, 119 Ohio St. 285, 164 N.E. 51, 63 A.L.R. 595 (1928) (robbery; evidence of other robberies committed by defendants according to same peculiar plan, as used in the robbery now on trial, that is, by using uniforms, impersonating officers, and stopping cars, thus "earmarking" the crimes as committed by the same persons).

37.   See, e.g., State v. Sauter, 125 Mont. 109, 232 P.2d 731, 732 (1951) (forcible rape by defendant and S in automobile after picking victim up in barroom; held, error to admit evidence of rapes accomplished after similar pickups of other victims; "too common * * * to have much evidentiary value in showing a systematic scheme or plan"; two judges dissenting). A discussion of what is and is not sufficient is in People v. Haston, 69 Cal.2d 233, 70 Cal.Rptr. 419, 444 P.2d 91 (1968).

38.   Woods v. State, 250 Ind. 132, 235 N.E.2d 479 (1968) (rape and incest; other like acts on victim admissible to show "depraved sexual instinct"); State v. Schut, 71 Wash.2d 400, 429 P.2d 126 (1967) (incest; prior acts with victim admissible to show a lustful inclination toward the offended female).

39.   Landon v. State, 77 Okl.Cr. 190, 140 P.2d 242 (1943) (statutory rape on daughter: other offenses with another daughter on other occasions excluded); State v. Pace, 187 Or. 498, 212 P.2d 755 (1949) (statutory rape); State v. Williams, 36 Utah 273, 103 Pa. 250 (1909) (statutory rape). But though not receivable to show propensity the evidence may come in on other theories. Landon v. State, supra ("res gestae"); Comm. v. Ransom, 169 Pa.Super. 306, 82 A.2d 547 (1951), affirmed on lower court's opinion, 369 Pa. 153, 85 A.2d 125 (1952) (charge of robbery and rape; other attempts at forcing intercourse on others during previous two days and up to two hours before offense admitted to show design or intent).

40.   A few decisions have admitted the evidence seemingly on the theory, in part at least, of showing a special propensity. See, e.g., State v. Edwards, 224 N.C. 527, 31 S.E.2d 516 (1944) (incest); State v. Jackson, 82 Ohio App. 318, 81 N.E.2d 546 (1948) (incest). See also Comm. v. Kline, 361 Pa. 434, 65 A.2d 348 (1949) (statutory rape on daughter: State allowed to prove that defendant indecently exposed himself to a neighbor woman, as showing he was an exhibitionist and thus had a moral trait consistent with the crime on trial).

41.   Commentators assert that recently the limitations on proof of other offenses are being reduced in prosecutions for sex crimes, either directly, on the basis of the argument described in the text, or by forcing the evidence into the exceptions relating to design or intention. Examples of cases rejecting evidence of acts on persons other than the present victim: State v. Searle, 125 Mont. 467, 239 P.2d 995 (1952) (sodomy); State v. Start, 65 Or. 178, 132 Pa. 512 (1913).

42.   United States v. Ross, 321 F.2d 61 (2d Cir. 1963), cert. denied 375 U.S. 894 (securities fraud; where defendant claimed he was an unwitting tool of his employer, proper for prosecution to show on cross-examination that he had long drifted among firms engaged in selling worthless securities by similar methods); People v.

(6)   To establish motive.[44] This in turn may serve as evidence of the identity of the doer of the crime on charge, or of deliberateness, malice, or a specific intent constituting an element of the crime.

(7)   To show, by immediate inference, malice, deliberation, ill will or the specific intent required for a particular crime.[45]

Williams, 6 Cal.2d 500, 58 P.2d 917 (1936) (larceny of coin-purse; state's theory and evidence were that defendant posing as customer standing near owner of bag, took purse from bag while owner was shopping; defendant claimed to have picked the purse from the floor, thinking it lost; held, evidence of detectives that they had seen defendant take another purse from another woman's bag in same manner, admissible); State v. Lapage, 57 N.H. 245, 294 (1876) (Cushing, C.J.; "Another class of cases consists of those in which it becomes necessary to show that the act for which the prisoner was indicted was not accidental,—e. g., where the prisoner had shot the same person twice within a short time, or where the same person had fired a rick of grain twice, or where several deaths by poison had taken place in the same family, or where the children of the same mother had mysteriously died. In such cases it might well happen that a man should shoot another accidentally, but that he should do it twice within a short time would be very unlikely. So, it might easily happen that a man using a gun might fire a rick of barley once by accident, but that he should do it several times in succession would be very improbable. So, a person might die of accidental poisoning, but that several persons should so die in the same family at different times would be very unlikely."); 2 Wigmore, Evidence § 302. The similarity of the other acts need not be as great as under purpose (3) in the text above, nor is a connection by common plan as in purpose (2) demanded. The trial judge has a range of discretion in determining whether the probative value justifies admission. Subsequent as well as prior acts have been held admissible for this purpose. However, when the act charged is not equivocal, but the criminal intent is a necessary conclusion from the act, this theory of other acts as showing intent may not be availed of. People v. Lonsdale, 122 Mich. 388, 81 N.W. 277 (1899) (abortion where there was no room for inference of accident or that operation was performed to save life); State v. Barker, 249 S.W. 75, 77 (Mo.1923) (automobile theft); 1 Wharton, Criminal Evidence § 237 (12th ed. 1955).

43.   United States v. Brand, 79 F.2d 605 (2d Cir. 1935), cert. denied 296 U.S. 655 (knowingly transporting stolen car in interstate commerce; evidence of previous sale of a stolen car); People v. Marino, 271 N.Y. 317, 3 N.E.2d 439, 105 A.L.R. 1283 (1936) (similar).

44.   State v. Simborski, 120 Conn. 624, 182 Atl. 221 (1936) (murder of officer who was seeking to arrest defendant; fact that defendant had committed two burglaries a short time before, admissible to show motive and as res gestae); People v. Odum, 27 Ill.2d 237, 188 N.E.2d 720 (1963) (murder; evidence that victim's name had been indorsed as witness on indictment against defendant for another crime, admissible to show motive, although conviction here reversed for other error); Gibbs v. State, 201 Tenn. 491, 300 S.W.2d 890 (1957) (defendant killed A, then killed Mrs. A when she discovered this, then killed A's daughter when she discovered Mrs. A's body; in trial for murder of Mrs. A, evidence as to the other killings admissible to show motive and as "inseparable components of a completed crime;" the killing of A's daughter, however, clearly belongs under (9) infra, as an admission of guilt by conduct, where the prosecution is for the killing of Mrs. A); State v. Simborski, 120 Conn. 624, 182 A. 221 (1936) (murder of an officer who was seeking to arrest defendant; fact that defendant had committed two burglaries a short time previously on the same morning admissible to show motive, and as res gestae); State v. Long, 195 Or. 81, 244 P.2d 1033 (1952) (murder of owner of truck: that defendant a short time afterward used the truck to commit robbery admitted); Comm. v. Heller, 269 Pa. 467, 87 A.2d 287 (1952) (murder of wife: evidence of illicit relations with sister-in-law and attempt to procure her to get divorce admissible); State v. Gaines, 144 Wash. 446, 258 P. 508 (1927) (murder of daughter; evidence of incestuous relations between defendant and deceased and that daughter was threatening to end the relation).

45.   Copeland v. United States, 152 F.2d 769 (D.C.Cir. 1945) (murder in first degree; that defendant after shooting deceased pursued and shot sister of deceased, proper to show first act done, not accidentally or in self-defense but with deliberate intent to kill); Patterson v. United States, 361 F.2d 632 (8th Cir. 1966); Dunson v. State, 202 Ga. 515, 43 S.E.2d 504, 508 (1947) (wife-murder: previous acts of violence to wife, to show malice); Clark v. State, 151 Tex.Cr.R. 383, 208 S.W.2d 637 (1948) (murder, by beating, of five year old stepson: previous whippings, to show malice); State v. Stationak, 1 Wash.App. 558, 463 P.2d 260 (1969).

(8)   To prove identity. This is accepted as one of the ultimate purposes for which evidence of other criminal conduct will be received.[46] It is believed, however, that a need for proving identity is not ordinarily of itself a ticket of admission, but that the evidence will usually follow, as an intermediate channel, some one or more of the other theories here listed. Probably the second (larger plan), the third (distinctive device) and the sixth (motive) are most often resorted to for this purpose.[47]

(9)   Evidence of criminal acts of accused, constituting admissions by conduct, intended to obstruct justice or avoid punishment for the present crime.[48]

(10)   To impeach the accused when he takes the stand as a witness, by proof of his convictions of crime.

Some general observations may be added. In the first place, it is clear that the other crime, when it is found to be independently relevant and admissible, need not be established beyond a reasonable doubt, either as to its commission or as to defendant's connection therewith, but for the jury to be entitled to consider it there must of course be substantial evidence of these facts, and some courts have used the formula that it must be "clear and convincing."[52] And it is believed that before the evidence is admitted at all, this factor of the substantial or unconvincing quality of the proof should be weighed in the balance.

Two considerations, one substantive and the other procedural, affect the ease or difficulty of securing admission of proof of other crimes. The first is that the courts are stricter in applying their standards of relevancy when the ultimate purpose of the state is to prove identity, or the doing by the accused of the criminal act charged than they are when the evidence is offered on the ultimate issue of knowledge, intent or other state of mind.[53] The sec-

46.   People v. McMonigle, 29 Cal.2d 730, 177 P.2d 745 (1947) (murder of girl enticed by accused into his automobile; evidence that a naval T shirt, similar to that worn by murderer, was stolen by accused some weeks before, properly received to show plan to entice, and identity); Hawkins v. State, 199 So.2d 276 (Fla.1967); State v. King, 111 Kan. 140, 206 P. 883, 22 A.L.R. 1006 (1922) (murder; victim, an employee of defendant, disappeared, after which accused was in possession of his effects; ten years later victim's body found burned in defendant's premises; held, finding of other bodies on same premises of persons who had disappeared and whose effects were in defendant's possession, admissible to identify accused as murderer); Helton v. Com., 244 S.W.2d 762 (Ky.1951) (assault committed as member of mob of miners; accused denied being present; "other incidents" on same morning presumably involving accused, admissible to show larger plan, motive and identity); State v. Bock, 229 Minn. 449, 39 N.W.2d 887 (1949) (attempt to pass forged check, by making small purchase and getting cash for balance; evidence of similar subsequent passing of other checks at other stores, under similar plan, admissible in discretion to

identify person who attempted to pass check in question here; but error to exclude evidence of accused that some other person passed these other checks).

47.   See decisions cited under these headings, above and cases in next preceding note.

48.   People v. Gambino, 12 Ill.2d 29, 145 N.E.2d 42 (1957), cert. denied 356 U.S. 904 (escape and attempted escape while awaiting trial); People v. Spaulding, 309 Ill. 292, 141 N.E. 196 (1923) (killing of only eyewitness to crime); State v. Brown, 231 Or. 297, 372 P.2d 779 (1962) (stealing cars to escape); Gibbs v. State, 201 Tenn. 491, 300 S.W.2d 890 (1957), discussed in note 44, supra.

52.   Tucker v. State, 82 Nev. 127, 412 P.2d 970 (1966) ("plain, clear, and convincing"); Wrather v. State, 179 Tenn. 666, 678, 169 S.W.2d 854, 858 (1943). See also State v. Porter, 229 Iowa 282, 294 N.W. 898 (1940) (must be clearly shown).

53.   United States v. Fierson, 419 F.2d 1020 (7th Cir. 1970) (mere formal issue is not sufficient); Jones v. Com., 303 Ky. 666, 198 S.W.2d 969, 970, 971 (1947) ("The applica-

ond is that when the crime charged involves the element of knowledge, intent, or the like, the state will often be permitted to show other crimes in rebuttal, after the issue has been sharpened by the defendant's giving evidence of accident or mistake, more readily than it would as part of its case in chief at a time when the court may be in doubt that any real dispute will appear on the issue.[54]

There is an important consideration in the practice as to the admission of evidence of other crimes which is little discussed in the opinions. This is the question of rule versus discretion. Most of the opinions ignore the problem and proceed on the assumption that the decision turns solely upon the ascertainment and application of a rule. If the situation fits one of the classes wherein the evidence has been recognized as having independent relevancy, then the evidence is received, otherwise not. This mechanical way of handling these questions has the advantage of calling on the judge for a minimum of personal judgment. But problems of lessening the dangers of prejudice without too much sacrifice of relevant evidence can seldom if ever be satisfactorily solved by mechanical rules. And so here there is danger that if the judges, trial and appellate, content themselves with merely determining whether the particular evidence of other crimes does or does not fit in one of the approved classes, they may lose sight of the underlying policy of protecting the accused against unfair prejudice. The policy may evaporate through the interstices of the classification.

Accordingly, some of the wiser opinions (especially recent ones) recognize that the problem is not merely one of pigeonholing, but one of balanc-

tion of the rule of admissibility is more liberal in the matter of establishing guilty knowledge or intent where intent is a material ingredient of the offense charged, for a series of similar offenses tends to show the party knew or intended to do what he was doing on the particular occasion. Where the purpose is to identify the defendant, the circumstances may govern the degree of liberality or strictness. * * * where it is a question of the particular individual committing the particular offense, as it was here, the latitude is much smaller."); and see People v. Molineux, 168 N.Y. 264, 313, 61 N.E. 286, 302 (1901) ("As to identity: Another exception to the general rule is that, when the evidence of an extraneous crime tends to identify the person who committed it as the same person who committed the crime charged in the indictment, it is admissible. There are not many reported cases in which this exception seems to have been affirmatively applied. A far larger number of cases, while distinctly recognizing its existence, have held it inapplicable to the particular facts then before the court.").

54. See, e.g., People v. Knight, 92 Cal.App. 143, 216 P. 96 (1923) (lewd acts with children; defendant testifies that he committed the acts but with no lewd intent; held no error to receive evidence of similar acts with other children: "defendant opened the door"); State v. Gilligan, 92 Conn. 526, 103 A. 649 (1918) (murder by keeper

of old folks' home of one of the inmates: receiving evidence of other poisonings where state's evidence did not suggest possibility of accident, held error, "without prejudice to its possible admission in rebuttal"). The remarks of Lord Sumner in Thompson v. The King, [1918] App.C. 221, 232 are pertinent: "Before an issue can be said to be raised, which would permit the introduction of such evidence so obviously prejudicial to the accused, it must have been raised in substance if not in so many words, and the issue so raised must be one to which the prejudicial evidence is relevant. The mere theory that a plea of not guilty puts everything material in issue is not enough for this purpose. The prosecution cannot credit the accused with fancy defences in order to rebut them at the outset with some damning piece of prejudice."

The issues may be sharpened in advance by the raising of special defenses, such as alibi, insanity, or entrapment. As to entrapment, a contra holding is People v. Benford, 53 Cal.2d 1, 345 P.2d 928 (1959).

Compare the situation where the defendant or his lawyer for him imprudently makes claim to an unblemished character or record. Holding that this opens the door to evidence of other crimes: People v. Westek, 31 Cal.2d 469, 190 P.2d 9, 13, 18 (1948); Molton v. People, 118 Colo. 147, 193 P.2d 271, 272 (1948); but see Keene v. Com., 307 Ky. 308, 210 S.W.2d 926 (1908).

ing,[55] on the one side, the actual need for the other crimes evidence in the light of the issues and the other evidence available to the prosecution,[56] the convincingness of the evidence that the other crimes were committed and that the accused was the actor, and the strength or weakness of the other-crimes evidence in supporting the issue, and on the other, the degree to which the jury will probably be roused by the evidence to overmastering hostility.

Such a balancing calls for a large measure of individual judgment about the relative gravity of imponderables. Accordingly, some opinions stress the element of discretion. It should be recognized, however, that this is not a discretion to depart from the principle that evidence of other crimes, having no substantial relevancy except to ground the inference that accused is a bad man and hence probably committed this crime, must be excluded. The leeway of discretion lies rather in the opposite direction, empowering the judge to exclude the other-crimes evidence, even when it has substantial independent relevancy, if in his judgment its probative value for this purpose is outweighed by the danger that it will stir such passion in the jury as to sweep them beyond a rational consideration of guilt or innocence of the crime on trial.[58] Discretion implies not only leeway but responsibility. A decision clearly wrong on this question of balancing probative value against danger of prejudice will be corrected on appeal as an abuse of discretion.[59]

55.   Quarles v. Com., 245 S.W.2d 947, 948 (Ky.1951) ("* * * evidence of an independent offense is inadmissible even though it may have some tendency to prove the commission of the crime charged, because the probative value of the evidence is greatly outweighed by its prejudicial effect. This is especially so where the evidence is of an isolated, wholly disconnected offense. But the balance of scales is believed to be the other way where there is a close relationship to the offense charge.").

56.   The importance of this is clearly pointed out by Beach, J., in State v. Gilligan, 92 Conn. 526. 103 A. 649, 652, 653 (1918). See also the remarks of Olney, J., in Adkins v. Brett, 184 Cal. 252, 193 P. 251, 254 (1920). In discussing a question of the admission of a declaration, competent for one purpose, incompetent for another, he said: "The matter is largely one of discretion on the part of the trial judge. If the point to prove which the evidence is competent can just as well be proven by other evidence, or if it is of but slight weight or importance upon that point, the trial judge might well be justified in excluding it entirely, because of its prejudicial and dangerous character as to other points."

Another factor mentioned as entitled to consideration is surprise. People v. Kelley, 66 Cal.2d 232, 57 Cal.Rptr. 363, 424 P.2d 947 (1967). The remedy here would seem to be notice, as required in State v. Spreigl, 272 Minn. 488, 139 N.W.2d 167 (1965).

58.   State v. Goebel, 36 Wash.2d 367, 218 P.2d 300, 306 (1950) (Hill, J.: "* * *

this class of evidence, where not essential to the establishment of the state's case, should not be admitted, even though falling within the generally recognized exceptions to the rule of exclusion, when the trial court is convinced that its effect would be to generate heat instead of diffusing light, or, as is said in one of the law review articles above referred to, where the minute peg of relevancy will be entirely obscured by the dirty linen hung upon it. This is a situation where the policy of protecting a defendant from undue prejudice conflicts with the rule of logical relevance, and a proper determination as to which should prevail rests in the sound discretion of the trial court, and not merely on whether the evidence comes within certain categories which constitute exceptions to the rule of exclusion.").

59.   See, e. g., Noor Mohamed v. The King, [1949] App.C. 182, 192, 193 (Privy Council) (murder by poisoning wife; death by poison of previous wife admitted; held, while judge had discretion to balance relevancy against prejudice, here erroneously exercised), critically noted, 12 Mod.L.Rev. 232; State v. Gilligan, 92 Conn. 526, 103 A. 649, 653 (1918) (murder by poisoning: other deaths by poisoning admitted and conviction reversed on this ground; "Courts are not infrequently required in criminal cases to pass upon preliminary questions of fact in order to determine the admissibility of evidence, and no doubt courts are vested with considerable discretionary powers in passing upon such preliminary questions * * * we think it would be an abuse of discretion to permit proof of similar but un-

PEOPLE v. MASSEY

District Court of Appeal of California, 1961.
196 Cal. App.2d 230, 16 Cal.Rptr.402.

KAUFMAN, P. J.   By an information dated August 9, 1960, the appellant, Richard L. Massey, was charged with the burglary (Pen. Code, § 459) of an apartment at 620 Jones Street, San Francisco, on May 2, 1960; and with two prior felony convictions in Iowa. He admitted the prior convictions and entered a plea of not guilty. A jury found him guilty of burglary in the first degree and the court sentenced him for the term prescribed by law, and decreeing that the sentence was to run concurrently with any prior incompleted sentence. On this appeal from the judgment of conviction entered on the verdict and the order denying his motion for a new trial, appellant argues that: *   *   *   the evidence relating to another burglary of which he was acquitted was erroneously admitted   *   *   *

The record reveals the following facts: About 4:30 a.m. on the morning of May 2, 1960, Mrs. Sarah Finley, who lived alone in a one-room apartment, was awakened when she felt "a terrific jerk." She saw a Negro man hovering over her face and screamed. The intruder hurried to the open window, leaped out and ran off. Mrs. Finley took a pill for her heart condition and telephoned for help. The police arrived and discovered that $13 was missing from her purse, as well as a few other small items from the apartment. A large rectangular piece had been cut out of the sheet on Mrs. Finley's bed, probably with the scissors on the nearby table. Later the same day, Mrs. Finley's apartment was dusted for latent fingerprints by an officer from the crime laboratory. A fingerprint was found on the inside of the window in Mrs. Finley's room and a knife outside the window.

Mrs. Finley had lived for several years in the apartment on the first floor of the Gaylord Hotel at 620 Jones Street in San Francisco. Her apartment had only two windows which overlooked the porch and the hotel next door. On the prior evening, May 1, 1960, she retired abut 10 p.m.; as the night was very warm, she opened both windows, locked them with the chain, and covered herself only with a sheet.

The above occurrence remained unsolved for several weeks. About 3 a.m. on the morning of May 26, 1960, Elsie Cox, who lived alone in a two-room apartment at 757 Sutter Street, awoke and in the large mirror facing her bed, saw the reflection of a man entering the living room where she slept. She could see him very clearly as the living-room window extended almost the entire wall and overlooked the brightly lit Trader Vic's parking area next door. The venetian blinds on the window were down but open. She watched the prowler creep around her bed, and noticed that he kept a white cloth over his hand as he flashed a light into the closet and took a leisurely survey. He then turned and lifted up the pillow next to hers and pushed his hand under it. Then he straightened up, proceeded to the end of the bed, and the other side of the room. After he climbed out the kitchen window, she called the police. Later, she discovered that only a dish towel was missing, although several things were awry. Miss Cox's apartment was on the

connected poisonings in a case where the state's evidence had already gone so far toward eliminating accident or mistake as to leave no reasonable doubt, in the absence of rebutting evidence, that the poison, if administered by the accused, must have been knowingly administered."); and cases in next preceding note.

second floor; there were a fire escape and some pipes near the kitchen window. Shortly thereafter, a police officer saw the appellant walking down Post Street near Mason Street, and returned with him to Miss Cox's apartment. Miss Cox positively identified the appellant as the prowler at that time and at the later trial.

On June 9, 1960, while in custody on the Cox matter, the appellant was questioned about the Finley burglary. He denied being at Mrs. Finley's apartment on the morning in question and indicated he did not wish to make any further statements. On July 26, 1960, the preliminary hearing was held in Mrs. Finley's room because of her heart condition. At this time, Mrs. Finley testified that the prowler who was in her room on the morning of May 2 did not look like the appellant but was huskier, fatter and older. At the trial, she testified that the prowler looked very much like the appellant but admitted that she had observed the prowler for only about half a second and that it was so dark that she couldn't tell. She explained that the inconsistency in her identification was due to her nervousness at the preliminary.

The prosecution's expert witness testified that in his opinion, the latent fingerprint found on the window of Mrs. Finley's apartment was appellant's. The appellant took the stand, admitted the two prior felony convictions and being on parole from the Iowa Men's Reformatory for one of them. He testified that on May 1, he had gone to bed around 10 o'clock at the home of his sister and brother-in-law at 184 Hoff Street. The appellant's sister and her husband also testified that the appellant was in his bed on the night of May 1 at their home in the Ingleside district. It was also brought out at the trial that one week earlier, the appellant had been tried and acquitted of the Cox burglary. * * *

Appellant next argues that the evidence relating to the subsequent burglary of Miss Cox's apartment was not admissible because of his acquittal and because of its prejudicial effect. It is well established, however, that an acquittal does not prevent the admissibility of evidence concerning another wrongful act (People v. Huston,* 156 Cal.App.2d 670, 671, 320 P.2d 175; see also People v. Brown, 168 Cal.App.2d 549, 336 P.2d 1 [defendant charged but not yet convicted], and People v. Raleigh, 83 Cal.App.2d 435, 442, 189 P.2d 70 [other charges dismissed at preliminary examination]), as conviction of the offense is not a prerequisite to the introduction of such evidence.

As stated in People v. Brown, supra, at pages 552–553: "The ultimate fact to be proved is the defendant's guilt of the crime with which he is charged and not the other offense. The evidence of the other offense is admissible even though the defendant was not convicted of it, provided such evidence is relevant. Therefore, the rule concerning the admissibility of other offenses expressed in the *Raleigh* case must be limited to those circumstances where the proof is relevant and material to the crime for which the defendant is being tried."

*[In People v. Huston the defendant was charged with three counts of sex offenses with one girl and a fourth count with another girl. He was acquitted on the fourth count and argued on appeal that "The defense could not object to the testimony when given because the witness was the prosecutrix of count IV of the complaint. However, defendant was acquitted of count IV. Thus the admission of the evidence became improper and prejudicial error." The court rejected this argument.]

Appellant here argues that the Cox burglary is not relevant to the Finley burglary; the attorney general argues that the evidence was relevant and admissible as the Cox burglary was committed in the same neighborhood (about 2 blocks from the Gaylord Hotel where Mrs. Finley lived), was committed within the same month in the early hours of the morning, and both involved the use of a white cloth, Miss Cox's dish cloth, and by inference, the piece cut from Mrs. Finley's sheet.

The general rule of the admissibility of other criminal acts is stated in People v. Sanders, 114 Cal. 216, at page 230, 46 P. 153:

"If the evidence of another crime is necessary or pertinent to the proof of the one charged, the law will not thwart justice by excluding that evidence, simply because it involves the commission of another crime. The general tests of the admissibility of evidence in a criminal case are: 1. Is it a part of the *res gestae?* 2. If not, does it tend logically, naturally, and by reasonable inference, to establish any fact material for the people, or to overcome any material matter sought to be proved by the defense? If it does, then it is admissible, whether it embraces the commission of another crime or does not, whether the other crime be similar in kind or not, whether it be part of a single design or not * * * ." We think the evidence of the Cox burglary was pertinent to the issue of intent. * * *

[Affirmed.]

UNITED STATES v. GANO

United States Court of Appeals, Tenth Circuit, 1977.
560 F.2d 990.

William E. DOYLE, Circuit Judge.

This is an appeal from a conviction on three counts of the crime of having carnal knowledge of a female under the age of 16, contrary to 18 U.S.C. § 2032. The questions which are advanced in this effort to obtain a reversal are whether the trial court erred in receiving testimony as to other offenses allegedly committed by the defendant * * * .

The defendant was employed as a social worker at the Veterans Administration Hospital in Topeka, Kansas. His assignment was to counsel members of the families of patients. The patient in this instance was a dentist, who was being treated for psychiatric problems. He had three children, the oldest of whom was 15, the youngest four. The 15-year-old, Cynthia, became acquainted with defendant incident to the defendant counselling her mother and other members of the family.

In September 1974, defendant commenced counselling the mother and sex became the main area of discussion. Soon after this, the family moved to Topeka where the hospital was and the mother began to see defendant two to three times a week. At these sessions sex was the main area which was discussed. This ultimately led to intercourse between the mother and the defendant. Prior to this incident, there was an extensive program of establishing trust, engaging in body massage, plus other actions designed to break down barriers and inhibitions by means of pseudo-treatment methods.

During the several month period in which all of the alleged actions occurred, the 15-year-old daughter, who had been attending school in Missouri, moved to Topeka and immediately defendant's focus was shifted to her. About the same program was followed in his dealings with this young girl. Counselling sessions were had with the 15-year-old about three times a week and sexual topics together with massage were the principal activities. As in dealing with the mother he sought to develop a trusting and uninhibited relationship with her. Finally, on December 17, 1974, he induced her to have sexual relations with him in his Veterans Administration Hospital office. After this he urged her not to tell anyone what had happened because, so he maintained, this would destroy their relationship. However, she refused to return for sessions with him after the December 17 occurrence and eventually did so only as a result of her mother's urging. The mother was also persuaded to surreptitiously give the daughter marijuana in food. This was represented as an attempt to relax the child and to thereby assist the therapy. About this time the child ceased her communication with her mother, and on January 10, 1975, defendant took the girl to a movie after she had had marijuana in her food and then afterwards took her to his office at the Veterans Administration Hospital, where they again had intercourse. Intercourse again occurred at the office on January 15, 1975.

He saw the child frequently thereafter, and in mid-February, there was a weekend trip to Wichita on the pretext that it would be therapeutic. On February 13, 1975, he and the girl traveled to Kansas City, Missouri. There were frequent acts of intercourse during this period of time.

As indicated above, the sole question for our determination is whether it was error to admit testimony pertaining to crimes other than that charged in the indictment. Also received was testimony that defendant had sold marijuana to the mother for her own use and for the purpose of giving it to the child; that this was as a prelude to one of the charged offenses. Further received was evidence that he gave marijuana to the girl. All of this was objected to, and the trial court overruled the objections at the same time cautioning the jury that this evidence was admissible for a limited purpose, that of showing opportunity, preparation, plan, knowledge or absence of mistake or accident in connection with the charged offenses. Following the close of the trial, the judge gave an additional instruction which again limited the evidence received.

The argument of defendant is that the testimony as to other acts, including one act of intercourse with the mother, is not probative and that it does not establish opportunity, preparation, plan, knowledge or absence of mistake or accident. * * * The government maintains that the evidence was admissible because it was relevant to the defense of insanity and because it concerned matters so closely connected to the charged offenses that it is indivisible from the acts which are set forth in the indictment. An alternative position of the government is that the evidence shows a scheme, plan, knowledge, opportunity, etc.

We are of the opinion that the court did not err in receiving this testimony. The part of the evidence which is at first somewhat questionable is that pertaining to the act of sexual intercourse with the mother.[1] This was

---

1. On the question whether evidence of relationship with another person is admissible, it is considered in II Wigmore, 3d Ed., § 398, p. 355. The author states that such evidence of prior sexual acts has been received for the purpose of showing the de-

separated in time from the acts which were perpetrated against the daughter. Also, where the act is against another victim and is separated in time from that which took place with the person described in the indictment, it is at least suspect. However, in this case we see no basis for distinguishing the one act involving the mother from the subsequent ones involving the daughter. In both instances the method employed by defendant was essentially the same. It was under the guise of therapy or treatment. Defendant manipulated both the mother and the daughter and played them one against the other even using marijuana to aid him in carrying out his scheme. Not only do we consider the evidence relevant and material, it appears to us that it would be difficult to divide up the numerous incidents since they were closely interrelated so as to be indispensable to a complete showing.

Rule 404(b) of the Federal Rules of Evidence deals with the present subject. This rule provides:

> Evidence of other crimes, wrongs, or acts is not admissible to prove the character of a person in order to show that he acted in conformity therewith. It may, however, be admissible for other purposes, such as proof of motive, opportunity, intent, preparation, plan, knowledge, identity or absence of mistake or accident.

Thus, the first part of the rule states that evidence of other crimes is inadmissible to prove the character of a person. It in effect provides that it is not permissible to offer other offenses in order to establish that the accused is a person of bad character. This is not different from the general rule which existed prior to the adoption of the rule. Its similarity to the prior law is found in its recognition of the admissibility of other acts which show motive, opportunity, intent, preparation, plan, knowledge, identity, and absence of mistake. In the case at bar the evidence helped to establish the offenses charged by proving motive, preparation, plan and knowledge (or state of mind).

It is no answer that the commission of the act was not disputed in that the defendant relied on insanity. The government is not on that account ex-

---

fendant's propensity for that kind of act. Other cases hold that such acts are remote, irrelevant and inadmissible.

As to the offense of statutory rape, the cases collected by Wigmore show that the admissibility of such evidence depends upon the circumstances of each individual case. Thus, prior sexual acts with the prosecutrix are generally admissible in a statutory rape prosecution. See II Wigmore on Evidence, § 398 n.1, pp. 361–65 and 1975 Supp., pp. 164–66. Generally, such acts with persons other than the named prosecutrix are inadmissible, but there is an exception to this last rule in cases in the Wigmore note where the sexual acts with other children occurred at the same place and on the same day as the charged offense. See State v. Dowell, 47 Idaho 457, 276 P. 39 (1929); State v. Sheets, 127 Iowa 73, 102 N.W. 415 (1905). Close similarity of the charged offense and the previous act enhances the probative value of the evidence so as to overrule the prejudicial effect.

In the instant case, where the daughter is the victim and the mother is the object of another act, the connection is so close as to render the evidence admissible. After all, access was gained to the daughter through the mother. The scheme of false therapy was used to seduce the mother and was repeated with some modifications to overcome the resistance of the daughter. The time period was not so great of itself to cause the evidence to be inadmissible because the defendant was using this time to execute his plan against the daughter.

Cf. Lovely v. United States, 169 F.2d 386 (4th Cir. 1949) (testimony that defendant charged with rape had, fifteen days before charged offense, raped a different woman on the same federal reservation and also in an automobile held to be inadmissible, distinguishable on the fact since there was no connection between the acts or the victims).

cused from proving the elements of its case. If the evidence is relevant, it is admissible even though the defendant promises to finally admit the acts charged.

Moreover, the close relationship of the acts, one with the other, justified their admission.

As to furnishing the marijuana: this was admissible although it tended to show the commission of a somewhat different crime because it was sold to the mother for her own use and as part of the therapy being administered to the daughter. Accordingly, the marijuana was used to lower the resistance of the daughter to defendant's advances, so it cannot be argued that this did not have a bearing on the method employed by defendant to have intercourse with the daughter.

*   *   *

As we have shown above, the sale and the use of marijuana plus the pseudo-treatment efforts were part of the same scheme and looked to the same objective. Also, the fact that these came in as part and parcel of the proof of the offenses charged in the indictment does not render it inadmissible.

In our view then, the trial court did not err in ruling that the evidence was admissible either as proving the offenses charged or as showing the complete picture of the perpetration of a scheme to have relations with the daughter. *   *   *

*   *   *

The judgment is affirmed.

UNITED STATES v. BEECHUM

United States Court of Appeals, Fifth Circuit, 1978.
582 F.2d 898.

TJOFLAT, Circuit Judge:

This case comes before the court en banc for reconsideration of this circuit's doctrine on the admissibility of offenses extrinsic to a defendant's indictment to prove his criminal intent. That doctrine, deriving in part from the case of United States v. Broadway, 477 F.2d 991 (5th Cir. 1973), requires that the essential physical elements of the extrinsic offense include those of the offense charged and that each of these elements be proved by plain, clear, and convincing evidence. We are here called upon to determine the effect of the recently enacted Federal Rules of Evidence on this doctrine, an issue expressly reserved in a number of our cases decided prior to the panel opinion in this case. The panel hearing this case was of the opinion, Judge Gee dissenting, that *Broadway* and its progeny survived intact the enactment of the rules. United States v. Beechum, 555 F.2d 487, 504–08 (5th Cir. 1977). With deference to the panel, we must disagree.

A jury convicted Orange Jell Beechum, a substitute letter carrier for the United States Postal Service, of unlawfully possessing an 1890 silver dollar that he knew to be stolen from the mails, in violation of 18 U.S.C. § 1708 (1976). To establish that Beechum intentionally and unlawfully possessed the silver dollar, the Government introduced into evidence two Sears, Roebuck & Co. credit cards found in Beechum's wallet when he was arrested. Neither card was issued to Beechum, and neither was signed. The

Government also introduced evidence indicating that the cards had been mailed some ten months prior to Beechum's arrest to two different addresses on routes he had serviced. The propriety of the admission of this evidence is the primary issue in this appeal. * * *

* * *

At the time of his arrest, Beechum possessed a silver dollar and two credit cards, none of which belonged to him. The only contested issue concerning the silver dollar was whether Beechum intended to turn it in, as he claimed, or to keep it for himself. Apparently, he had possessed the credit cards for some time, perhaps ten months, prior to his arrest. The obvious question is why would Beechum give up the silver dollar if he kept the credit cards. * * *

* * *

Broadway established two prerequisites to the admissibility of extrinsic offense evidence. First, it required that the physical elements of the extrinsic offense include the essential physical elements of the offense for which the defendant was indicted. Second, the case mandated that each of the physical elements of the extrinsic offense be established by plain, clear, and convincing evidence. The elements of the offense for which Beechum was convicted, violation of 18 U.S.C. § 1708 (1976), include the following: (1) that the defendant possessed the item, (2) that the item was stolen from the mail, (3) that the defendant knew that the item was stolen, and (4) that the defendant specifically intended to possess the item unlawfully. The first three elements were not disputed, except to the extent that a denial of the fourth renders the item not stolen for the purposes of the second and third elements. The physical elements of the crime are the first two. The panel held that the Government's proof as to the credit cards failed to establish the second element, that the cards were stolen from the mail, by the plain, clear, and convincing evidence required by the second prong of the *Broadway* test. For the purposes of the following analysis, we accept this conclusion as valid.

We must overrule *Broadway* because a straightforward application of the Federal Rules of Evidence calls for admission of the cards. The directly applicable rule is Fed.R.Evid. 404(b), which provides as follows:

> *Other crimes, wrongs, or acts.* Evidence of other crimes, wrongs, or acts is not admissible to prove the character of a person in order to show that he acted in conformity therewith. It may, however, be admissible for other purposes, such as proof of motive, opportunity, intent, preparation, plan, knowledge, identity, or absence of mistake or accident.

The rule follows the venerable principle that evidence of extrinsic offenses should not be admitted solely to demonstrate the defendant's bad character. Even though such evidence is relevant, because a man of bad character is more likely to commit a crime than one not, the principle prohibits such evidence because it is inherently prejudicial. Without an issue other than mere character to which the extrinsic offenses are relevant, the probative value of those offenses is deemed insufficient in all cases to outweigh the inherent prejudice. Where, however, the extrinsic offense evidence is relevant to an issue such as intent, it may well be that the evidence has probative force that is not substantially outweighed by its inherent prejudice. If this is so, the evidence may be admissible.

What the rule calls for is essentially a two-step test. First, it must be determined that the extrinsic offense evidence is relevant to an issue other than the defendant's character. Second, the evidence must possess probative value that is not substantially outweighed by its undue prejudice and must meet the other requirements of rule 403. The test for relevancy under the first step is identical to the one we have already encountered. The standards are established by rule 401, which deems evidence relevant when it has "any tendency to make the existence of any fact that is of consequence to the determination of the action more probable or less probable than it would be without the evidence." Where the evidence sought to be introduced is an extrinsic offense, its relevance is a function of its similarity to the offense charged. In this regard, however, similarity means more than that the extrinsic and charged offense have a common characteristic. For the purposes of determining relevancy, "a fact is similar to another only when the common characteristic is the significant one for the purpose of the inquiry at hand." Therefore, similarity, and hence relevancy, is determined by the inquiry or issue to which the extrinsic offense is addressed.

Where the issue addressed is the defendant's intent to commit the offense charged, the relevancy of the extrinsic offense derives from the defendant's indulging himself in the same state of mind in the perpetration of both the extrinsic and charged offenses. The reasoning is that because the defendant had unlawful intent in the extrinsic offense, it is less likely that he had lawful intent in the present offense.[15] Under *Broadway*, that the defendant had unlawful intent in the commission of the extrinsic offense is established by requiring the Government to prove each physical element of that offense by plain, clear, and convincing evidence. And the extrinsic offense is deemed admissible only if its physical elements include those of the offense charged. We think that *Broadway* runs afoul of the Federal Rules of Evidence by imposing on the Government too strict a standard of proof and by requiring too close an identity of elements.

15.   It is crucial to distinguish the use of extrinsic offense evidence to prove issues other than intent. In other contexts different standards apply because the inference to be drawn from the extrinsic offense is not based upon the reasoning applicable here. To illustrate this proposition and to place our discussion in the proper context, we digress briefly and examine the use of extrinsic offense evidence in other settings.

Evidence of extrinsic offenses may be admissible to show motive, which has been defined as "the reason that nudges the will and prods the mind to indulge the criminal intent." Slough & Knightly, Other Vices, Other Crimes, 41 Iowa L.Rev. 325, 328 (1956) (footnote omitted). For example, the prosecution may establish impecuniousness as a motive for robbery by showing that the defendant had been threatened for nonpayment of a debt incurred in a drug transaction. United States v. Johnson, 525 F.2d 999, 1006 (2d Cir. 1975), cert. denied

424 U.S. 920, 96 S.Ct. 1127, 47 L.Ed.2d 327 (1976). The only point of similarity between the charged and extrinsic offenses in this instance is that the same individual committed both. Therefore, overall similarity is not required when the offense is introduced to show motive.

Such evidence is admissible to indicate knowledge. Thus, the Government may prove that the defendant knew that he was passing counterfeit securities by eliciting testimony that the defendant knowingly had purchased counterfeit currency on a prior occasion. Peters v. United States, 376 F.2d 839 (5th Cir. 1967). Again, similarity of the physical elements of the crime need not be established. The extrinsic offense need merely be of such a nature that its commission involved the same knowledge required for the offense charged.

The identity of the defendant may be established by evidence of offenses extrinsic to

Obviously, the line of reasoning that deems an extrinsic offense relevant to the issue of intent is valid only if an offense was in fact committed and the defendant in fact committed it. Therefore, as a predicate to a determination that the extrinsic offense is relevant, the Government must offer proof demonstrating that the defendant committed the offense. If the proof is insufficient, the judge must exclude the evidence because it is irrelevant. The issue we must decide is by what standard the trial court is to determine whether the Government has come forward with sufficient proof.

The standard of proof for ruling upon factual conditions to relevancy is supplied by Fed.R.Evid. 104(b), which states as follows:

> *Relevancy conditioned on fact.* When the relevancy of evidence depends upon the fulfillment of a condition of fact, the court shall admit it upon, or subject to, the introduction of evidence sufficient to support a finding of the fulfillment of the condition.

As the rule provides, the task for the trial judge is to determine whether there is sufficient evidence for the jury to find that the defendant in fact committed the extrinsic offense. * * *

Once it is determined that the extrinsic offense requires the same intent as the charged offense and that the jury could find that the defendant committed the extrinsic offense, the evidence satisfies the first step under rule 404(b). The extrinsic offense is relevant (assuming the jury finds the

---

the indictment. In this instance, the likeness of the offenses is the crucial consideration. The physical similarity must be such that it marks the offenses as the handiwork of the accused. In other words, the evidence must demonstrate a modus operandi. United States v. Goodwin 492 F.2d 1141, 1154 (5th Cir. 1974). Thus, "[a] much greater degree of similarity between the charged crime and the uncharged crime is required when the evidence of the other crime is introduced to prove identity than when it is introduced to prove a state of mind." United States v. Myers, 550 F.2d 1036, 1045 (5th Cir. 1977). As an example, a prior conviction for possession of heroin may not in itself establish that in an unrelated prosecution a defendant possessed heroin with intent to distribute. If, however, that conviction and the charged offense involved white heroin, an extremely rare type in the region, a distinctiveness may be established that is sufficient to allow admission of the prior offense to show identity. United States v. Baldarrama, 566 F.2d 560 (5th Cir. 1978).

Extrinsic offenses may be admitted if part of a common plan, scheme, or design. Although this category encompasses a variety of circumstances, see 2 Weinstein & Berger, Weinstein's Evidence ¶ 404[09] (1976), we shall address only one. If the uncharged offense is "so linked together in point of time and circumstances with the crime charged that one cannot be fully shown without proving the other, the general rule of exclusion does not apply." Slough & Knightly, supra, at 331. Evidence admitted under this test is termed part of the res gestae of the crime charged. E. g., United States v. McDaniel, 574 F.2d 1224, 1227 (5th Cir. 1978). Physical similarity is not a requisite here. Illustrative is the case of United States v. Hughes, 441 F.2d 12 (5th Cir.), cert. denied, 404 U.S. 849, 92 S.Ct. 156, 30 L.Ed.2d 88 (1971). This was an appeal from convictions for printing counterfeit obligations, possessing counterfeit plates and negatives, and possessing counterfeit federal reserve notes. We held that it was not prejudicial error for the trial court to have admitted several sawed-off shotguns found at the premises of the operation. "The record of entry and use of [the premises] for their counterfeiting operation would be grossly incomplete without the account of their guns, intimidations, beatings, and violence. * * * [T]he guns in question were pertinent evidence because they were so closely blended and inextricably bound up with the history of the crime itself as to constitute a part of the plan or system of criminal action involved in this case." Id. at 20.

We have taken this opportunity to digress to point out that the meaning and nature of the "similarity" requirement in extrinsic offense doctrine are not fixed quantities. Each case must be decided in its own context, with the issue to which the offense is directed firmly in mind.

defendant to have committed it) to an issue other than propensity because it lessens the likelihood that the defendant committed the charged offense with innocent intent. * * * It is not necessary that the physical elements of the charged and extrinsic offenses concur for this inference to be drawn and relevancy established. If the elements do match, the extrinsic offense may have greater probative value, but this is not an issue of relevancy. Evidence is relevant once it appears "to alter the probabilities of a consequential fact." Weinstein & Berger, Weinstein's Evidence ¶ 401[06], at 401-18 (1976). The probative value of the evidence is a matter to be weighed against its potential for undue prejudice, and the similarity of the physical elements of the charged and extrinsic offenses figures in at this stage. Therefore, we turn to the second step of the analysis required by rule 404(b), whether the evidence satisfies rule 403.

As we have stated, the central concern of rule 403 is whether the probtive value of the evidence sought to be introduced is "substantially outweighed by the danger of unfair prejudice." * * * In measuring the probative value of the evidence, the judge should consider the overall similarity of the extrinsic and charged offenses. If they are dissimilar except for the common element of intent, the extrinsic offense may have little probative value to counterbalance the inherent prejudice of this type of evidence. Of course, equivalence of the elements of the charged and extrinsic offenses is not required. But the probative value of the extrinsic offense correlates positively with its likeness to the offense charged. Whether the extrinsic offense is sufficiently similar in its physical elements so that its probative value is not substantially outweighed by its undue prejudice is a matter within the sound discretion of the trial judge. * * *

As this case demonstrates, a significant consideration in determining the probative value of extrinsic offense evidence is the posture of the case. If at the commencement of trial it is not certain that the defendant will contest the issue of intent, the judge is in a poor position to weigh the probative value against the prejudice of the evidence because he cannot foresee the nature or extent of either the Government's case or the defendant's response. Whether a mere plea of not guilty justifies the Government in introducing extrinsic offense evidence in its case in chief is an open question in this circuit. * * * cf. United States v. Ring, 513 F.2d 1001 (6th Cir. 1975) (holding extrinsic offense evidence inadmissible in case in chief where innocent intent not pleaded). We need not now answer it. Although the credit cards in this case were introduced by the Government in its case in chief, it was clear before the case went to trial that the crucial issue would be Beechum's intent. In effect all the other elements of the crime for which Beechum was indicted were conceded. * * * Where it is evident that intent will be an issue at trial, we have held the admission of the extrinsic offense as part of the Government's case in chief not to be grounds for reversal. * * *

We shall now apply the precepts we have set forth to the facts of this case. As we have demonstrated above, the credit card evidence is relevant to Beechum's intent with respect to the silver dollar. That Beechum possessed the credit cards with illicit intent diminishes the likelihood that at the same moment he intended to turn in the silver dollar. If there is sufficient evidence to establish that Beechum wrongfully possessed the credit cards, the requirement of the first step under rule 404(b), that the evidence be relevant to an issue other than propensity, is met. This is so even if the evidence were insufficient for a findng that the cards were stolen from the mail. As we have said, relevancy is established once the identity of the significant state of mind is established. The similarity of the physical elements of the extrinsic and charged offenses is a measure of probity.

The standard for determining whether the evidence is sufficient for a finding that Beechum wrongfully possessed the credit cards is provided by rule 104(b): whether the evidence would support such a finding by the jury. We think the evidence in the record clearly supports a finding that Beechum possessed the credit cards with the intent not to relinquish them to their rightful owners. Beechum possessed the credit cards of two different individuals. Neither card had been signed by the person to whom it was issued. When asked about the cards, Beechum answered first that the only cards he had were his own. When confronted with the credit cards, which were obviously not his own, Beechum responded that they had never been used. He refused to respond further because the inspector "had all the answers." The logical inference from this statement is that Beechum was attempting to mitigate his cupability, having been caught red-handed. The undisputed evidence indicated that he could have possessed the cards for some ten months. The jury would have been wholly justified in finding that Beechum possessed these cards with the intent permanently to deprive the owners of them. This is all the rules require the court to determine to establish the relevancy of the extrinsic offense evidence.

We move now to the second step of the rule 404(b) analysis, the application of rule 403. The incremental probity of the extrinsic offense evidence in this case approaches its intrinsic value. Indeed, the posture of this case and the nature of the Government's proof with respect to the intent issue present perhaps the most compelling circumstance for the admission of extrinsic offense evidence. From the very inception of trial, it was clear that the crucial issue in the case would be Beecham's intent in possessing the silver dollar. He took the stand to proclaim that he intended to surrender the coin to his supervisor. The issue of intent was therefore clearly drawn, and the policies of justice that require a defendant to explain evidence that impugns his exculpatory testimony were in full force.

* * *
                              * * *

The overall similarity of the extrinsic and charged offenses in this case generates sufficient probity to meet the rule 403 test that the probative value of evidence not be substantially outweighed by its unfair prejudice. We think this to be true even if it could not be established that the credit cards were stolen from the mail. At the least, there was sufficient evidence for the jury to find that Beechum possessed property belonging to others, with the specific intent to deprive the owners of their rightful possession permanently. That Beechum entertained such intent with respect to the credit cards renders less believable the story that he intended to turn in the coin in this instance. The force of this inference is not appreciably diminished by the failure of the Government to prove that the cards actually were stolen from the mail.

The probity of the credit card evidence in this case is augmented by the lack of temporal remoteness. Although Beechum may have obtained the cards as much as ten months prior to his arrest for the possession of the silver dollar, he kept the cards in his wallet where they would constantly remind him of the wrongfulness of their possession. In effect, Beechum's state of mind with respect to the credit cards continued through his arrest. He maintained contemporaneously the wrongful intent with respect to the cards and the intent as regards the coin. The force of the probity of this circumstance is illustrated by what Beechum would have had to convince the jury in order to avoid it. He would have been forced to argue that his state of mind was schizoid—that he intended at the same time to relinquish the coin but to keep the cards. This situation does not differ significantly from one in which a thief is caught with a bag of loot, is charged with the larceny as to one of the items, but claims that he intended to return that item. Would any reasonable jury believe this story when it is established that he had stolen the rest of the loot?

The remaining considerations under rule 403 do not alter our conclusion as to the admissibility of the extrinsic offense evidence in this case. The extrinsic offense here is not of a heinous nature; it would hardly incite the jury to irrational decision by its force on human emotion. The credit card evidence was no more likely to confuse the issues, mislead the jury, cause undue delay, or waste time than any other type of extrinsic offense evidence. Since the need for the evidence in this case was great, it can hardly be said that the admission of the cards constituted "needless presentation of cumulative evidence."

* * *

Having examined at length the circumstances of this case, we conclude that the credit card evidence meets the requirements of rule 403. Therefore, the conditions imposed by the second step of the analysis under rule 404(b) have been met, and the extrinsic offense evidence in this case was properly admitted at trial.

IV.   *Conclusion*

For the reasons stated above, we AFFIRM Beechum's conviction.

* * *

Affirmed.

Goldberg, Circuit Judge, with whom Godbold, Simpson, Morgan and Roney, Circuit Judges, join, dissenting:

As the lights are being extinguished on Broadway, I feel impelled to light a few candles in requiem.

* * *

At the heart of this dissent is a concern about the proper level of hostility or hospitality to extrinsic offense evidence. But in this dissent I am even more concerned about the practicality and integrity of the analysis this circuit will employ in making these judgments. In this case the majority has obliterated a venerable, well-reasoned body of law for no good reason at all, and has replaced it with a Freudian, difficult to apply subjective test that, outside this and a few other similar cases, will not even accomplish what the majority wants. It is especially ironic that the majority should justify its evisceration of *Broadway* by declaring that the "revolutionary" drafters of Rule 404(b) wanted the old standards cleared from the stage to make room for the free form, uncontrolled balancing-test discretion of the new Theatre of the Absurd. For no sooner were the objective flats and screens of the legitimate *Broadway* stage pulled aside, than the majority brought in the psychological psychedelics of the Theatre of Indulgence. I can only hope that the majority will soon see the error of its ways and return to the Great White Way of *Broadway* with the appreciation and respect that the grand old boulevard deserves.

I would reverse the judgment of the district court and remand the case for a new trial.

WRIGHT v. McKEE

Vermont Supreme Court, 1864.
37 Vt. 161.

ALDIS, J.   The plaintiff delivered to the defendant a package of bank bills and silver—in value $48.86—to carry to Mr. Keith. From the time the defendant took it till he delivered it to Keith it was always in the defendant's possession. He claims to have delivered it to Keith just as he took it. When Keith opened the package there was nothing but waste paper in it. The conclusion seems irresistible that either the defendant stole the money from the package, or that the plaintiff did not put it in. The defendant and plaintiff differ upon one point. The plaintiff says she and the defendant *together* put the money into the package and tied it up with a string; the defendant says that after the money was counted and put into the package and before it was tied up, she took the package, went to another part of the room near a stand, and returned apparently in the act of tying up the package, and when she had tied it up dropped it into a bag in which he carried it to Keith. The defendant's version gives the plaintiff a chance to have slipped the money out of the package unobserved before she handed it to him. The plaintiff's version excludes such supposition and fastens the embezzlement of the money on the defendant.

The material points of the evidence thus resting on the testimony of the two parties and the plaintiff's testimony virtually charging the defendant with the crime of embezzlement—the defendant offered the testimony of witnesses to show that he sustained a good character for honesty and integrity. To this the plaintiff objected upon the ground that the action being trover for the money, the evidence was not admissible. The court excluded the evidence. The question we have here to consider is,—was there error in this ruling?

We are not aware that this point has ever been before this court.

In criminal cases the respondent is permitted to introduce evidence of this kind. In civil cases where the question of character is directly in issue and material as to the amount of damages—as in slander and seduction—it is admitted.

This we think is the extent to which it ought to be admitted in civil suits.

In criminal cases the law allows it to the respondent out of tenderness —to help him if it may in his necessity, as it gives him the benefit of every doubt. And even in criminal cases the law regards it of value only when the other evidence leaves the case in doubt, and general good character may be fairly invoked to rebut suspicious circumstances.

Many considerations concur in rejecting such evidence in civil cases.

Evidence of this character has but a remote bearing as proof to show that wrongful acts have or have not been committed, and the mind resorts to it for aid only when the other evidence is doubtful and nicely balanced. It may then perhaps serve to turn the wavering scales. Very rarely can it be of substantial use in getting at the truth.

It is uncertain in its nature—both because the true character of a large portion of mankind is ascertained with difficulty, and because those who are called to testify are reluctant to disparage their neighbors,—especially if they are wealthy, influential, popular, or even only pleasant and obliging. It is mere matter of opinion, and in matters of opinion men are apt to be greatly influenced by prejudice, partisanship, or other bias, of which they are unconscious; and in cases which are not quite clear they are apt to agree with the one who first speaks to them on the subject, or to form their opinions upon the opinions of others.

The introduction of such evidence in civil causes, wherever character is assailed, would make trials intolerably long and tedious and greatly increase the expense and delay of litigation. It is this kind of evidence that might be easily manufactured—is liable to abuse and if in common use in the courts, as likely to mislead as to guide aright. The authorities are quite unanimous in excluding such testimony. Many of the cases have been referred to by the counsel for the plaintiff.   *   *   *

Judgment affirmed.

JAMES AND DICKINSON, ACCIDENT PRONENESS AND ACCIDENT LAW

63 Harv.L.Rev. 769, 791–94 (1950).*
[Footnotes omitted.]

*   *   *   There is also a question whether evidence of a person's accident proneness is to be admitted to show what he probably did on this occasion. The difficulties spring chiefly from the rule limiting the use of character to show conduct on a specific occasion and the inhibitions against the use of prior specific instances to throw light on what was done in the case at bar.

In civil cases the general rule is that evidence of a party's character is not admissible to show what his conduct was on a particular occasion, but that evidence of his habit or custom of doing or omitting a particular thing may be received for this purpose. The general propensity to be negligent or careful has usually been assimilated to character, and evidence of it excluded, though on no very satisfactory ground. It could scarcely be urged that propensity is totally without probative value, though perhaps its rational probative effect is too slight to warrant the risks of an unduly long excursion into collateral matters and a too facile overpersuasion of uncritical minds. Such reasoning would obviously exclude evidence offered to show that a party was accident-prone for the purpose of proving that he was negligent at the time of the accident. And this would be true however the accident proneness was sought to be evidenced—whether by the opinion of experts, by tests, by a showing of past accidents, or otherwise.

It may be urged with considerable force that the recent studies invite reconsideration of the rule stated in the last paragraph, since they afford a scientific basis for attributing more probative value to accident proneness, when properly shown, than loose conclusions about propensity toward negligence deserve. Moreover, the general rule has not commanded universal acceptance. Some courts, for example, admit evidence of a person's general disposition to be careful in order to show care at the time of the accident, where there are no eyewitnesses to his conduct at that time; and very occasionally courts have admitted this kind of evidence for such a purpose in cases beyond the scope of this exception. Under such rulings, proper evidence of accident proneness should be admitted to show carelessness.

Where it is proper to show accident proneness for this or any other purpose, there is a question of how it may be proven. The results of specific tests of the individual in question should be admissible if introduced through the testimony of a qualified expert who can show that the tests are scientifically approved ones, that they were properly administered in this case, and what the significance of the result is. The last might well be in the form of an expert opinion whether the individual was accident-prone.

As we have seen, a conclusion as to accident proneness may also be based on, or contributed to by, a clinical interview and observation or a past accident record. The former should be admissible in evidence as an admission against a party to the action if a qualified expert will testify as to its meaning. Where, however, the conduct of a nonparty is in issue (as where an employer is sued for his employee's negligence), the subject's narrative as to his case history will run afoul of the hearsay rule if offered through the observer. This difficulty could be obviated by eliciting the narrative, on the stand, from the subject himself and calling the expert simply to interpret it.

The admissibility of past accident records presents more difficulty in view of the traditional reluctance of the law of evidence to receive individual instances for the purpose of showing propensity, character, or the like. Exclusion has been based in part on a supposed lack of strong probative value and on fear of encountering too many collateral issues. The recent studies should reduce the force of both objections. They tend to indicate that accident records have substantial bearing on the actor's conduct at the time of accident. And they show that collateral inquiry into the particular circumstances surrounding the other accidents is largely unnecessary since the crucial fact is the mere repetition itself of involvement in accident.

* * *

LILLY, AN INTRODUCTION TO THE LAWS
OF EVIDENCE

(121–124).*

PROBLEMS OF CIRCUMSTANTIAL PROOF

Evidence of Habit

The line between character and habit is not always easy to discern, but the division can mark the difference between exclusion and admissibility. * * * [E]vidence of habit, used circumstantially to prove particular conduct, generally is admissible. The jurisdictions differ, however, in their degree of receptivity. In some courts, evidence of habit is admissible only if there is no eyewitness to the conduct in question.[64]

Character may be thought of as a trait or disposition which can manifest itself in a variety of activities. Thus viewed, character is more general than habit; the latter is a particular activity, routine, or response that is frequently repeated over a protracted period of time. A person with a character trait for punctuality and orderliness may have a habit of picking up and sorting his mail each day at noon.

The probative value of habit is considered greater than that of character. When evidence of habit is introduced, the desired inference from habit to the conduct in question is grounded upon a series of specific, repetitious actions. The trier is asked to infer that on the occasion in question the actor conformed to habitual practice or procedure. When evidence of character is considered, the desired inference is grounded upon a trait, tendency, or disposition which may be displayed in somewhat varied circumstances. A general tendency to drive carefully could be displayed in a variety of driving activities. Thus, evidence that a person generally exercises care in driving is usually classified as evidence of character and rejected. Conversely, evidence that each workday a person traversed a particular railroad track and always stopped before crossing is generally classified as habit. The character-habit line becomes blurred when the evidence offered is that the actor always stopped at railroad crossings, but surely this is an area where the judge's discretion should be sustained.

The business environment, which is characterized by standardized procedures and routines, offers many opportunities to develop evidence of habit. Frequently, courts refer to habit within a business organization as "custom," but this difference in label does not alter the requirement of a repeated response to a particular circumstance. Some courts have required that the admissibility of evidence of custom be dependent upon corroborating evidence that the custom was followed on the particular occasion in question. This is an inadvisable limitation which loses sight of the rationale of evidence showing a habit or custom: the theory is that a pattern of continuous activity increases the likelihood that the custom was followed on the particular occasion.

The modern approach to the admissibility of habit and custom is expressed in the following provision of the Federal Rules of Evidence:

> Evidence of the habit of a person or of the routine practice of an organization, whether corroborated or not and regardless of the presence of eyewitnesses, is relevant to prove that the conduct of the person or organization on a particular occasion was in conformity with the habit or routine practice.[69]

---

64. McCormick, § 195, at 463. This view is difficult to defend because its premise is the superior reliability of eyewitness testimony—a proposition which is highly dubious. A very good summary of the weaknesses of testimonial proof, which collects many authorities, appears in Maguire et al. at 52. Even if testimonial proof were considered reliable, should evidence of habit be rejected? It seems that this added evidence still should be presented for the trier's evaluation. The case for habit evidence especially is strong when the eyewitness is one of the parties (or identified with one of the parties) and evidence of habit is offered by the adversary.

69. Fed.R.Evid. 406. In a recent criminal case the trial judge was reversed for excluding evidence of business custom. United States v. Callahan, 551 F.2d 733 (6th Cir. 1977).

Note that the Federal Rule expressly rejects of the eyewitness requirement[70] and leaves open the question of what kind of evidence is admissible to prove habit or custom.[71] The usual method of proof is by the testimony of a witness who has observed the habit or custom over a sufficient period to state that it is a routine, repeated practice. Sometimes, however, the proponent must resort to proof of a number of specific instances which, taken together, demonstrate the required regularity. This manner of proof is generally accepted, although dissimilarities between the instances or the apparent lack of a sufficient number to establish a routine may result in the judge's discretionary rejection. The Federal Rule also rejects the requirement, imposed by some courts, that business custom be corroborated as a condition precedent to its admission. Corroboration is viewed correctly as relating to the sufficiency of evidence rather than to its admissibility.[73]

See Federal Rules of Evidence 406 at p. 910; California Evidence Code § 1105 at p. 873.

Hypotheticals

(1) X, a prison inmate, is charged with aggravated assault upon A, a fellow prisoner. The prosecution's case is that X and B, another inmate, assaulted A and stabbed him numerous times. X's defense is that his only part in the fray was to break up a fight between A and B. X calls Y, an inmate who did not witness the fight, to testify that he has known X for one month and that, in his opinion, X is a nonviolent man. The prosecutor makes an inadmissible-character-evidence objection to Y's proposed testimony. What result?

(2) X is charged with first degree murder of A, a police officer. B, a police officer, testifies that he was with A in a police car and that they stopped X, who was driving an automobile in an erratic fashion; that A asked X to step out and X complied; that A then asked X to raise his hands so he could be checked for weapons; that instead, X sprang back, drew a gun from a concealed holster under his shirt and began firing; that A was hit and died the next day; and that B succeeded in disarming X and placed him under arrest. The prosecution offers evidence that (a) X was on parole from a felony sentence in Illinois and his presence in California was in violation of his parole; (b) seven days before the charged offense X committed armed robbery of a market in Denver, Colorado; and (c) the automobile in which X was riding had been stolen from a San Francisco car dealer three days before the charged offense. The prosecutor announces that he is offering the above items of evidence on the issues of motive, intent, and premeditation. X makes an irrelevancy and inadmissible character evidence objection. How should the court rule?

(3) X is charged with grand theft from the person of A. X's defense is an alibi. A testifies that he is 85 years of age; that X approached him on the street, said he was celebrating the birth of a boy, put his arm around A, offered him a cigar and then left; and that immediately thereafter A noticed his wallet from his hip pocket

70. See supra n. 64 and accompanying text.

71. The House Committee on the Judiciary deleted a provision that would have authorized the proof of habit by opinion evidence and evidence of specific instances of conduct. This deletion was made to allow the courts to deal with this issue on a case-by-case basis. The Committee noted that it did not intend to sanction a general authorization for the use of opinion evidence to show habit. H.Rep. 93–650, 93d Cong., 2d Sess. reprinted in 1974 U.S. Code Cong. & Admin. News 7075, 7079. In any event, it would appear that an opinion whether a habit was followed on the occasion in question would not be appropriate unless there was evidence of repetitious conduct.

73. Adv.Comm.Note to Fed.R.Evid.406.

was missing with its contents of $75. The prosecutor calls B and makes an offer of proof that he will testify that he is 84 years of age; that two months after the A incident, he was approached on the street by X who told him he was celebrating the birth of his first boy, offered him a cigar, put his arm around his waist, and asked for some street directions; that X pushed him slightly and then left; that B immediately felt for his wallet in his hip pocket and it was missing; and that he ran after X, saw him get into a car but could not catch him. The prosecutor states that B's testimony is offered on the issue of identity to prove modus operandi and common scheme or plan. X makes an irrelevancy and an inadmissible character-evidence objection. What result?

(4) X is charged with murder of A. X's version of events is that A, who lived in the same apartment building, was visiting X; that an argument developed and A took a karate stance and sprang at X; and that X wrestled A to the floor and stomped his foot in A's stomach. A died from injuries to the abdomen about two weeks later. In rebuttal, the prosecutor offers the following testimony: (1) the testimony of B, a former paramour of X, that about two months before X's fight with A, she and X had a drunken quarrel; that X kicked her in the ribs, causing her to be hospitalized; and that X pleaded guilty to assault and battery; and (2) the testimony of C that he was a longtime acquaintance of X; that a year before X's fight with A, X and several others knocked him, C down without reason; and that X then kicked him in the stomach. The prosecutor states that he is offering the testimony of B and C to establish X's modus operandi to use his feet in a fight. X makes an irrelevancy and an inadmissible character-evidence objection to the proposed testimony of B and C. What result?

(5) A sues X and the Y Bus Company for damages for personal injuries suffered in a collision between a bus driven by X, an employee of the Y Bus Company, and a car driven by A. A claims that X failed to stop at a stop sign. A calls B, who testifies that he has been a regular and daily rider on the bus driven by X during the six-month period preceding the accident, but that he was not on the bus the day of A's accident. A asks B whether, in this six-month period, X habitually failed to come to a stop at the intersection where the accident took place. X and the Y Bus Company make an inadmissible-character and a habit-evidence objection to A's question. Should the objections be sustained?

PART B.   SIMILAR HAPPENINGS

ROBITAILLE v. NETOCO COMMUNITY THEATRES OF NORTH ATTLEBORO

Supreme Judicial Court of Massachusetts, 1940.
305 Mass. 265, 25 N.E.2d 749.

LUMMUS, Justice.   The first action is brought for personal injuries by a woman who will be called the plaintiff. The second is brought by her husband for consequential damages. Each obtained a favorable verdict. There was evidence that while attending the defendant's theatre the plaintiff had occasion to go down stairs; that the carpet on the stairs, which was nearly half an inch thick and fastened by tacks only half an inch long, was loose, because of the pulling out of the tacks, and slipped under her feet, with the result that she fell on her back and was hurt. Witnesses for the defendant testified that the carpet was not loose but was securely fastened. The existence and dangerous nature of the alleged defect constituted, therefore, an important issue.

The judge, over the defendant's exception, admitted evidence that two or three weeks before the plaintiff's injury two girls fell at the same spot. After they fell the tacks fastening the carpet were found to have been pulled out, and the carpet was found to be loose. It was not shown that the looseness existing at that time continued until the time of the plaintiff's injury. On the contrary, the evidence was that it had been repaired in the meantime by fastening the carpet again with tacks. It will be noticed that the evidence admitted was not merely that on an earlier occasion the carpet had become loose under travel, which might have been admissible to show that the tacks used were insufficient to fasten it. The evidence admitted was of a similar fall sustained by other persons because of the loose condition of the carpet at a different time.

The admissibility of evidence of injury to others at other times by reason of the same thing that caused the plaintiff's injury, for the purpose of showing that thing to be dangerous, has often come before this court. Such evidence is open to grave objections. Its persuasive force depends upon similarity in the circumstances of different injuries, of which it is hard to be certain. Substantial identity in the alleged defective condition is only the first essential. The person who was injured at the time to which the offered evidence relates may have been defective in eyesight, feeble, or careless. The fact that he was injured may have little or no bearing upon the danger to a normal traveller. Moreover, though the same defective condition may have been present at both times, the actual causes of the two injuries may have been different. Unless a comparison of the circumstances and causes of the two injuries is made, the injury to another is without significance. But if such a comparison is undertaken, the minds of the jurors must be diverted from the injury on trial into a detailed and possibly protracted inquiry as to injuries received by others at various times. Those injuries have only a collateral and often minor bearing upon the case. As to them the opposing party will often be ill prepared to present evidence. There is danger that a jury may disregard the real differences in the circumstances of the two incidents, and find upon mere superficial similarity that a dangerous condition existed. Similar considerations apply where evidence that other people, confronted at other times with the same alleged danger, suffered no injury, is offered to prove the want of a dangerous condition.

Very likely not all the statements, and perhaps not all the decisions, in reported cases in this Commonwealth, can be reconciled. Usually the failure to show substantial identity of the circumstances of the incident on trial with those of the incidents offered in evidence, or the danger of unfairness, confusion or unreasonable expenditure of time in trying the latter, has led to a justified exclusion of the evidence, in a wise exercise of discretion if not through the application of a positive rule of law. In a few cases the admission of such evidence has been held erroneous, apparently on the theory that it is made inadmissible by such a rule of law.

But where substantial identity in the circumstances appears, and the danger of unfairness, confusion or undue expenditure of time in the trial of collateral issues reasonably seems small to the trial judge, he has generally been left free to admit such evidence in his discretion. [Citations omitted.]

In Bemis v. Temple, 162 Mass. 342, 38 N.E. 970, 26 L.R.A. 254, the exclusion of evidence that other horses were frightened by the same flag was even held erroneous; for where the conduct of animals is concerned evidence of their habitual or occasional conduct is received more freely than in the case of human beings. * * * The recent behavior of machinery in operation may be received to show its condition. * * * The harmless or noxious character of food and other substances may be shown by the effect upon other persons similarly exposed to them. * * *

Where the safety of a device or a method is in issue, evidence has been admitted that it is in common use or that other devices or methods are available. * * *

Where the evidence is of a uniform result in a large number of instances, the objections to the class of evidence under discussion are minimized, and the evidence has been admitted; for example, that no complaint was ever received as to the wholesomeness of many other sandwiches made from the same lot of turkeys * * * or that no explosion ever occurred in a large number of oil refineries using the same process. * * * Evidence that persons intimately associated with a plaintiff remained healthy has been admitted to show that she was not afflicted with a contagious disease. * * *

The evidence admitted in the present case could not have been lawfully admitted, even in the discretion of the judge, without a showing that the condition existing at the time when the two girls fell was substantially the same as that existing when the plaintiff fell. That was not shown. It does not appear that on the earlier occasion the tacks had been pulled out to the same extent, or that the carpet assumed the same form or had the same degree of looseness, as at the later time. The admission of the evidence was erroneous. Other questions argued need not be considered.

Exceptions sustained.

HALLORAN v. VIRGINIA CHEM. INC.

Court of Appeals of New York, 1977.
41 N.Y.2d 386, 393 N.Y.S.2d 341, 361 N.E.2d 991.

BREITEL, Chief Judge.

Defendant Virginia Chemicals appeals in a personal injury products liability action. Plaintiff Frank Halloran, an automobile mechanic, obtained a verdict in his favor, after a jury trial on the issue of liability only, for injuries he sustained while using a can of refrigerant packaged and sold by the chemical company. A divided Appellate Division affirmed, and certified a question of law for review in this court.

* * *

There is one * * * issue meriting extended discussion: whether evidence that the injured mechanic had previously used an immersion heating coil to heat the can of the refrigerant should be admissible to show that on the particular occasion he was negligent and ignored the labeled warnings on the can [which cautioned against using an immersion coil]. Evidently relying on the rubric excluding prior instances of carelessness to create an inference of carelessness on a particular occasion, both the Trial Judge and the Appellate Division, save for two dissenting Justices, agreed that such evidence was not admissible.

There should be a reversal and a new trial. If plaintiff, when necessary to stimulate the flow of the refrigerant, a highly compressed liquified gas, habitually or regularly used an immersion coil to heat the water in which the container was placed, evidence of that habit or regular usage should be admissible to prove he followed such a procedure on the day of the explosion. Evidence of habit or regular usage, if properly defined and therefore circumscribed, involves more than unpatterned occasional conduct, that is, conduct however frequent yet likely to vary from time to time depending upon the surrounding circumstances; it involves a repetitive pattern of conduct and therefore predictable and predictive conduct. On this view, the excluded evidence was offered to show a particular method of executing a task followed by the mechanic, who, on his own testimony, had serviced "hundreds" of air-conditioning units and used "thousands" of cans of the refrigerant. If on remittal the evidence tends to show that the mechanic used an immersion coil a sufficient number of times to warrant a finding of habit, or regular usage, it would be admissible to aid the jury on its inquiry whether he did so on the occasion in question.

On June 1, 1970, the day of the accident, Frank Halloran, a mechanic for 15 years, had been employed by the Hillcrest Service station for over three years. Among his duties was the servicing and charging of automobile air-conditioning units, a job for which he had been specially trained, and for which he used "all [his] own tools." The particular task involved that day was the changing of the air-conditioning compressor on a 1967 Chrysler automobile. Plaintiff testified that he had emptied the system, removed the old compressor, and installed a new one. He then began to charge the unit.

The first two cans of the refrigerant, Freon, flowed into the system without difficulty. By the time he was emptying the third can, however, plaintiff found it necessary to accelerate the flow of the refrigerant. The mechanic described how he filled an empty two-pound coffee tin with warm tap water, used a thermometer to determine that the water temperature was about 90 to 100 degrees, and inserted into the coffee tin the third can of Freon. Having a similar problem with the flow of the fourth can, Halloran again dropped the Freon into the warm water. Noticing that his low pressure gauge showed a rapid increase in the pressure, and aware that "something was wrong", Halloran reached down to remove the can from the water, but was too late. The can exploded before he could touch it.

Neither the thermometer Halloran claimed to have used nor the bottom of the exploded can of Freon was produced at trial. Halloran knew that excessive heating of the can would cause damage, and that the warnings on the can specified 130 degrees as the maximum permissible safe temperature. As discussed earlier, he proved no particular defect in the can, its contents, or in so much of the exploded can which was produced at the trial. Having worked alone that day, Halloran was the only eyewitness to the explosion.

Defendant Virginia Chemicals ＊ ＊ ＊ sought to establish that it was Halloran's "usage and practice" to use an immersion coil to heat the water in which the Freon was placed. ＊ ＊ ＊

Of course, had an immersion heating coil been used at the time of the accident the unexplained and thus far unexplainable explosion would have been fully explained.

＊ ＊ ＊

To be sure, Halloran's practice prior to June 1, 1970 is not conclusive proof of the method he employed in working on the 1967 Chrysler. ＊ ＊ ＊ While courts of this State have in negligence cases traditionally excluded evidence of carefulness or carelessness as not probative of how one acted on a particular occasion, in other cases evidence of a consistent practice or method followed by a person has routinely been allowed ＊ ＊ ＊ . That a kind of habit, practice, or method was proffered in this case to establish negligence should not, without more, affect its admissibility.

Because one who has demonstrated a consistent response under given circumstances is more likely to repeat that response when the circumstances arise again, evidence of habit has, since the days of the common-law reports, generally been admissible to prove conformity on specified occasions ＊ ＊ ＊ . Hence, a lawyer, to prove due execution of a will, may testify that he always has wills executed according to statutory requirements. So too, to prove that notice is mailed on a specified day of the month, one is allowed to testify that he is in the habit of being home on that day of the month to transact such business.

When negligence is at issue, however, New York courts have long resisted allowing evidence of specific acts of carelessness or carefulness to create an inference that such conduct was repeated when like circumstances were again presented. Hence, evidence of a plaintiff's habit of jumping on streetcars may not be offered to prove he was negligent on the day of the accident. Nor could testimony that the deceased had usually looked both ways before crossing railroad tracks be introduced to establish his care on the particular occasion. Whether a carryover from the prohibition against using so-called "character" evidence in civil cases, or grounded on the assumption that even repeated instances of negligence or care do not sufficiently increase the probability of like conduct on a particular occasion, the statement that evidence of habit or regular usage is never admissible to establish negligence is too broad (see 1 Wigmore, Evidence [3d ed.], § 97, esp. p. 532).

At least, as in this kind of case, where the issue involves proof of a deliberate and repetitive practice, a party should be able, by introducing evidence of such habit or regular usage, to allow the inference of its persistence, and hence negligence on a particular occasion (see McCormick, Evidence [2d ed.], § 195, advocating an even more expansive approach; see, also, 1 Wigmore, Evidence [3d ed.], § 97). Far less likely to vary with the attendant circumstances, such repetitive conduct is more predictive than the frequency (or rarity) of jumping on streetcars or exercising stop-look-and-listen caution in crossing railroad tracks. On no view, under traditional analysis, can conduct involving not only oneself but particularly other persons or independently controlled instrumentalities produce a regular usage because of the likely variation of the circumstances in which such conduct will be indulged. Proof of a deliberate repetitive practice by one in complete control of the circumstances is quite another matter and it should therefore be admissible because it is so highly probative.

As previously noted, Halloran, in the course of his work as a mechanic, had serviced "hundreds" of automobile air conditioners and had used "thousands" of cans of Freon. From his testimony at trial it seems clear that in servicing these units he followed, as of course he would, a routine. If, indeed, the use of an immersion coil tended to be part of this routine whenever it was necessary to accelerate the flow of the refrigerant, as he indicated was often the case, the jury should not be precluded from considering such evidence as an aid to its determination.

Of course, to justify introduction of habit or regular usage, a party must be able to show on *voir dire,* to the satisfaction of the Trial Judge, that he expects to prove a sufficient number of instances of the conduct in question * * *. If defendant's witness was prepared to testify to seeing Halloran using an immersion coil on only one occasion, exclusion was proper. If, on the other hand, plaintiff was seen a sufficient number of times, and it is preferable that defendant be able to fix, at least generally, the times and places of such occurrences, a finding of habit or regular usage would be warranted and the evidence admissible for the jury's consideration.

* * *

* * * [T]he action remitted for a new trial on the issue of liability.

Jasen, Gabrielli, Jones, Wachtler, Fuchsberg and Cooke, JJ., concur.

* * *

RATHBUN v. HUMPHREY CO.

Court of Appeals of Ohio, 1953.
94 Ohio App. 429, 113 N.E.2d 877, 52 O.O. 145.

HURD, Presiding Judge.   This is an action of tort instituted by plaintiff in the Court of Common Pleas to recover for personal injuries received during a ride upon an amusement device. Plaintiff appeals from a judgment entered pursuant to a jury verdict for defendant.

Defendant, The Humphrey Company, owns and operates an amusement park in the city of Cleveland known as Euclid Beach Park. One of the attractions is a roller coaster called the "Thriller". It is composed of three separate cars, with four seats each joined together in a train. The train operates on rails supported by a trestle, built in the form of declivities, dips and curves. It is pulled by a chain from the loading platform to the top of the trestle. From there it descends by force of gravity. The ride covers a distance of about 2,800 feet in about two minutes.

Plaintiff, a young woman of about 32 years of age, entered the Thriller with her mother. They occupied the first seat of the second car, the mother to the right or outside, the daughter to the left or inside. The car ahead was filled to capacity with eight persons. The seats in back of plaintiff in the second car were wholly or partially filled. Plaintiff testified that as they were approaching the return curve, she turned slightly to her mother and told her to scream as they were approaching a series of dips. Plaintiff testified further that when she was thus turned slightly to her right, a branch of a tree suddenly whipped down from foliage overhanging the track area on the return or lower curve striking her forehead, nose and left eye, breaking her eyeglasses in such a manner that the left lens was shattered and the frame fell into her mother's lap. She claimed that she was seriously injured because pieces of the shattered lens lodged in her eye.

Six grounds of error were assigned, two of which were abandoned in this appeal. Combining the first two assignments of error, plaintiff asserts—(1) that the trial court erred prejudicially in permitting the manager of the Thriller to testify that during the summer of 1948 up to and including September 26, 1948, the date of the injury, no person had ever complained to him of having been struck by a branch or limb of a tree during a ride, and (2) in permitting defendant to introduce testimony of the number of persons who rode the roller coaster on the day of the injury.

The courts are divided on the question of the admissibility and competency of evidence showing non-occurrence or absence of other similar accidents in negligence cases generally. Some hold that such evidence is not admissible for the purpose of showing that the place of injury was free from danger. Others hold that such evidence is admissible for that purpose and that it tends to show reasonable care, thus negativing to a certain degree the charge of negligence. In any event, such testimony is admissible only if it has rational probative value bearing upon the issues made upon the pleadings. It is never conclusive, the persuasive effect or weight being for the jury alone under proper instructions. As a general rule, such testimony is admitted as applicable to static conditions where the danger is not obvious.

Considering now the issues made by the pleadings in the instant case, the plaintiff alleges and the defendant denies, (1) that the proximate cause of her injuries was the negligence of the defendant in failing to provide a route of travel which was reasonably safe for patrons to use; (2) in designing, operating and maintaining the Thriller in close proximity to abutting and overhanging trees; (3) in failing properly to care for said trees and to exercise vigilance to provide patrons with a ride free from danger, occasioned by the presence of such trees wholly under the control and management of the defendant; (4) in permitting said tree and the branches thereof to become a source of danger to patrons using said roller coaster; (5) in failing to warn plaintiff of the danger.

From these allegations it appears that plaintiff has created an issue as to the static condition of the amusement device in relation to external conditions surrounding its design, operation and maintenance in the particular location close to overhanging and abutting trees. Was this operation as there conducted safe for patrons, or, was it dangerous? How is this question to be determined? Is not experience a definite criterion, persuasive but not conclusive? We think so. True, it is as plaintiff argues that her claim is not based on any mechanical defect in the Thriller as such, nor is there any

claim of improper mechanical construction. This removes from consideration the doctrine of res ipsa loquitur, but it does not remove from consideration the claim that the design, operation and maintenance of the device as
located was dangerous for patrons under the static conditions there existing
and upon which the claim of negligence is predicated.

In Cleveland & Buffalo Transit Co. v. Roderick, 1918, 10 Ohio App.
119, evidence of non-occurrence of similar accidents was held admissible for
the purpose of showing defendant not guilty of negligence in not apprehend-
ing the accident where the danger was not obvious. In that case this court
reversed and remanded for prejudicial error in excluding such testimony.

* * *

In Murphy v. Steeple Chase Amusement Co., 1929, 250 N.Y. 479, 166
N.E. 173, 175, where plaintiff sued for injuries sustained while using an
amusement device known as the "Flopper", Cardozo, Ch.J., refers to
evidence offered by the President of the amusement company to the effect
that there had never been such an accident before and that, according to defendant's evidence, two hundred and fifty thousand visitors "were at the
Flopper in a year."

In Carlin v. Krout, 1923, 142 Md. 140, 120 A. 232, 29 A.L.R. 13, where
plaintiff sued for injuries received on an amusement device known as an
"Ocean Wave", it was held that the fact that no accident similar to plaintiff's had occurred to any of the thousands of persons who had used the device, during the two years which had elapsed since its installation, while not
conclusive of the absence of negligence, might properly be considered on the
question whether any part of the device was improperly designed or constructed.

The case of Wray v. Fairfield Amusement Co., 126 Conn. 221, 10 A.2d
600, is cited by plaintiff as being contra, but that case should be distinguished because there the evidence of the number of passengers who had
ridden the amusement device was excluded because the strap of one seat,
which plaintiff had occupied, was defective and evidence of the entire
number who had occupied other seats not defective would not be a reasonable test of experience, particularly in view of the fact that the plaintiff did
not claim that either the construction or operation of the roller coaster in
general was negligent.

We conclude, under the issues here made by the pleadings, together
with all the surrounding facts and circumstances appearing in the evidence,
that testimony tending to show the absence or non-occurrence of similar accidents during the summer season of 1948 (to which the testimony was limited) including the number of riders on the day of the accident without injury (in excess of 5,000) must be considered to have a rational probative value, bearing upon the claim of negligence made by plaintiff, in the design,
operation and maintenance of the amusement device in the place in
question. To hold that plaintiff could create such an issue so general and
comprehensive in its nature and implications and to deny the defendant the
right to meet it by the test of experience would not be in accord with sound
logic or judicial fairness.   * * *

Finding no error prejudicial to the rights of plaintiff, the judgment is
affirmed.

Kovachy and Skeel, JJ., concur.

MORRIS, STUDIES IN THE LAW OF TORTS

87–89 (1952).*
[Some footnotes omitted.]

* * * In the simple cases, safety-history evidence favorable to the defendant may be of greater weight than safety-history evidence favorable to the plaintiff. In Field v. Davis,[34] the plaintiff was hurt when his mules backed his wagon out of the defendant's grain elevator and over the side of a railing-protected inclined roadway. The defendant was allowed to prove that thousands of wagons had been driven into his elevator and no other accident had ever happened on the incline. The jury might have been able to visualize the incline and appreciate its safety without such evidence; nevertheless, the fact that the plaintiff was injured is itself some slight evidence of danger, and the defendant deserves the protection of safety-history evidence—which tends to check the jury from formulating unsound general theories as to the danger of inclined roadways.

The difference between evidence of safety history offered by a plaintiff and that offered by a defendant is illustrated perhaps more sharply in Charlton v. St. L. & S. F. R. R.[35] The plaintiff's deceased, a brakeman, was knocked off a ladder on the side of a moving boxcar by a standpipe maintained near the tracks. Another brakeman was allowed to testify that he brushed his arm on the same standpipe under similar circumstances. The problem of danger seems so simple that, after proof of the distance between cars and the standpipe, jurors could probably decide this case without the second brakeman's testimony as well as they could with it. While this testimony probably did no harm, a trial judge who excluded it would not have abused his discretion. But if the railroad had offered to prove that no brakeman other than the deceased had ever been brushed by the standpipe, in spite of constant exposure, the evidence should be received. The deceased's injury was proof that such an accident could happen. Unless the distance was so large that a trainman could be hit only by assuming an unlikely posture, jurors with the actual dimensions of the clearance before them are not likely to judge the clearance safe. But the situation may be safer than it seems to those without actual experience in railroading. Therefore, a defendant's proof of favorable safety history has greater probative value in this kind of case than a plaintiff's proof of unfavorable safety history. * * *

Hypothetical

A sues the X Golf Course for damages for personal injuries arising out of a slip-and-fall accident. A, a business invitee of X, was proceeding from the parking lot to the starting area and was walking across a new, level, cement veranda that has a smooth surface. A was wearing golf shoes with half-worn spikes and her feet slipped from under her, causing her serious injury. X calls B, the manager of the golf course, to testify that, during the year the cement veranda has been in existence, he had never been informed of any accidents on this area other than A's, and that between 3500 and 4000 persons per month had traversed the area wearing golf shoes. A objects to B's proposed testimony on the grounds of irrelevancy and that such negative evidence is precluded by law. What result?

*Copyright, 1952 by The Foundation Press, Inc.

34.　27 Kan. 400 (1882).

35.　200 Mo. 413, 98 S.W. 529 (1906).

PART C.   COMPROMISE

ESSER v. BROPHEY

Supreme Court of Minnesota, 1942.
212 Minn. 194, 3 N.W.2d 3.

PETERSON, Justice.   This is an action to recover for personal injuries and property damage sustained as the result of an automobile collision on the afternoon of November 19, 1939, on Wayzata Boulevard in Minneapolis. At and near the place of the accident the boulevard has a roadway 34 feet wide paved with brick. Although there were no lines marked on the pavement, it was wide enough for three lanes of traffic. Immediately prior to and at the time of the accident, the two northerly lanes were being used for westbound and the southerly one for eastbound traffic. The northernmost lane was used by "slow" and the middle lane by faster moving traffic.

Plaintiff was traveling easterly in the southernmost lane on her right side of the road at about 15 to 20 miles per hour. Defendant and one Hambly were traveling westerly in their automobiles, the former in the middle and the latter in the northernmost lane. Suddenly defendant's automobile turned into the southernmost lane about three or four car lengths ahead and in front of plaintiff, who was unable to avoid a collision. No claim was made at the trial that she was at fault.

Defendant attributed the collision solely to the negligence of Hambly. His claim was that Hambly, in violation of the law of the road, passed on his right and cut in short ahead of him in such a way that either the left rear bumper or fender of the Hambly car hooked into his right front fender or bumper and pulled his car into the path of plaintiff's oncoming car to cause the collision.

Hambly was called as a rebuttal witness by plaintiff and testified that he passed defendant on defendant's right; that after he had passed he gave defendant a signal that he was going to turn into the middle lane; that defendant collided with the rear of his car because he ignored the signal; and that the collision caused defendant's car to swerve over to the south side of the road. According to the witness's testimony, the accident was caused solely by defendant's negligence in running into his car after he had passed him and turned into the middle lane in front of him.

The testimony made it a fact issue whether the accident was caused by the sole negligence of defendant or Hambly or by the concurrent negligence of both.

On cross-examination of Hambly, defendant inquired whether or not he had paid defendant for the damage to his car. Plaintiff objected to the inquiry upon the ground that it was not material for the reason that the payment was made as a "compromise." The testimony, taken over plaintiff's objection, showed that defendant sued the witness in the conciliation court of Minneapolis for either $72 or $73 for the damage done to his car by the collision; that on the advice of counsel Hambly paid defendant $50 in settlement and obtained a release; and that the expense of defending the action was a factor inducing him to settle.

There was a verdict for defendant, and plaintiff appealed. Plaintiff urges that the court erred in permitting defendant to elicit the facts concerning Hambly's settlement with defendant and to argue to the jury that the settlement was an admission by the witness that his negligence was the cause of the collision.

The question for decision is whether a party to an action arising out of an automobile collision may show that he sued a witness for his adversary on a cause of action arising out of the same collision and that the witness settled the action by payment of a stipulated sum of money less than that sued for.

We have held in numerous cases that an unaccepted offer to compromise was inadmissible in a subsequent action against the party making it. [citations omitted] We said that "the law favors the settlement of disputed claims without litigation, and to encourage such settlements will not permit either party to use offers of settlement made by the other as evidence of an admission of liability." Bartels v. Schwake, 153 Minn. 251, 252, 190 N.W. 178, 179. In Stoakes v. Larson, 108 Minn. 234, 121 N.W. 1112, we expressly left open the question of whether or not the payment of like claims by persons sought to be charged, made to other parties, is proper evidence as an admission from conduct. In the Larson case the payment was made by a party not by a witness.

The exclusion of a compromise or an offer of compromise is put on one of three grounds, viz., privilege, contract, or relevancy. The theory of privilege is that the compromise negotiations are privileged communications like those between attorney and client, physician and patient, etc. The exclusion could not be sustained in the instant case on that ground because the communications were between the defendant and the witness. The privilege, if any, belonged to them as the parties to the compromise. Neither of them asserted the privilege. On the contrary, defendant disregarded and waived the alleged privilege by insisting on eliciting testimony concerning the settlement. Plaintiff is not entitled to assert the privilege. Privilege is personal to those to whom it belongs and is waived unless asserted by them. A party may not invoke the privilege of his witness, much less that of his adversary. This is but an application of the rule that a party may assert his own rights, but not those of others. The contract theory rests upon the basis of contract, express or implied, that the negotiations are "without prejudice." Assuming that parties may so stipulate, plaintiff is not entitled to claim the benefit of any contract between the witness and defendant relating to the privilege, since plaintiff was not a party to the contract and the contract was not made for her benefit.

Since the exclusion of the compromise cannot be justified on the grounds of either privilege or contract, determination of the question must depend on that of relevancy. By the test of relevancy, the admissibility of a compromise is made to depend on its tendency to prove an admission by conduct. "The true reason for excluding an offer of compromise is that it *does not* ordinarily proceed from and *imply a specific belief that the adversary's claim is well founded,* but rather a belief that the further prosecution of that claim, whether well founded or not, would in any event cause such annoyance as is preferably avoided by the payment of the sum offered.

In short, the offer implies merely a desire for peace, not a concession of wrong done." 4 Wigmore, Evidence, § 1061(c), p. 28. The weight of authority supports this view. [Citations omitted.] In Republic Fire Insurance Company v. Weides, 14 Wall. 375, 381, 20 L.Ed. 894, on error to the circuit court for the district of Minnesota, the court said: "A compromise proposed or accepted is not evidence of an admission of the amount of the debt."

Some texts cite Lord Mansfield's illustration that where a defendant is sued for 100 pounds and offers 20 pounds in compromise "without prejudice," the offer of compromise is irrelevant because it neither admits nor ascertains the debt and amounts to no more than saying that the defendant would pay the amount of the offer to be rid of the action. In Tennant v. Hamilton, 7 Cl. & F. 122, 133, 7 Reprint, 1012, the court said that "money paid upon a complaint made, paid merely to purchase peace, is no proof that the demand is well founded." In Wayman v. Hilliard, 7 Bing, 101, 131 Reprint, 39, Bosanquet, J., said that there is no acknowledgment of the adversary's claim in an offer to compromise.

Where, however, an admission of liability is made, it is admissible, although it is embraced in an offer of compromise. A common illustration is one where liability is admitted and the dispute relates to the amount due, as in Person v. Bowe, 79 Minn. 238, 82 N.W. 480. Where there is no compromise, but a payment of a claim asserted, the payment permits an inference of admission of liability because "it is the simple case of a claim made, and a yielding to it." Grimes v. Keene, 52 N.H. 330, 334.

Admissibility depends on whether an offer or payment was intended as an admission of liability or an effort to settle a dispute. "As his [the party making the offer of compromise] object could not be a matter of law, and he knows what it was, he may testify directly on that point." Colburn v. Groton, 66 N.H. 151, 157, 28 A. 95, 98, 22 L.R.A. 763. In this respect plaintiff was unduly restricted below on the redirect examination of the witness to show the facts concerning the settlement. Where, as here, there was no admission, but a compromise and settlement of a disputed claim, an inference of admission of liability is not permissible. The rulings below permitted defendant to show a compromise and settlement to get rid of a lawsuit, and that only. That fact was irrelevant because it implied no admission of liability on the part of the witness.

Defendant relies on Pym v. Pym, 118 Wis. 662, 671, 96 N.W. 429, 432, but that case involved admissions made in the course of a compromise and does not support his view. The court said: "But such settlement was not an admission on the part of the son that the facts alleged in his father's verified complaint were true. The extent of the son's admission was necessarily measured by what he said and did under the circumstances."

We have examined other cases cited by defendant and find that they are not in point. Some of them involve situations where a party was permitted to impeach a witness by showing that after a compromise and settlement between his adversary and the witness of a claim arising out of the same accident, the witness gave testimony favorable to such adversary inconsistent with the claim asserted. Such testimony is received not to establish an inference of liability, but to show bias of the witness in favor of the party calling him. The testimony relates entirely to the credibility of the witness. So far from sustaining defendant's contention that a settlement of a claim with the witness by the party calling him may be shown as an admission of liability, the case of St. Louis, S. F. & T. Ry. Co. v. Knowles, 44 Tex.Civ.App. 172, 99 S.W. 867, holds that such a settlement should be considered not as an admission of liability, but only as affecting the credibility of the witness, and that a cautionary instruction to that effect is proper. Subsequent to the decision in Keet v. Murrin, supra, it was held in Cochrane v. Fahey, 245 App.Div. 41, 280 N.Y.S. 622, that a compromise and settlement was not admissible to establish an admission of liability.

Of course it always is permissible to show the bias of a witness as affecting his credibility by such circumstances as family relationship, association, employment, and other facts showing a disposition to give testimony favorable to the party calling him, although such matters may not have independent relevancy.

We should, if we could, affirm on the ground that it was proper to prove the suit and settlement to show bias of the witness. A witness may be discredited by showing his hostility to the party against whom he testified. Where hostility is denied it may be proved by acts and declarations showing animosity, but not by showing that the witness had been sued by the party seeking to discredit him and that he had settled the lawsuit.

The compromise and settlement between the witness and defendant was not admissible to impeach the witness because it was not relevant to show either an admission of liability or the witness' hostility to defendant.

In the Herschmann case error in receiving testimony concerning the suit and settlement was held to be harmless. But we cannot so hold here. The testimony relating to the suit and settlement in the cited case was received simply to show bias arising from hostility. Here, it was received to show that the witness, not defendant, was solely responsible for the accident. The rule is well established that in cases like the instant one such evidence is inherently prejudicial notwithstanding an instruction (absent here) limiting its purpose and effect. Georgia Ry. & Elec. Co. v. Wallace & Co., 122 Ga. 547, 50 S.E. 478; Cochrane v. Fahey, 245 App.Div. 41, 280 N.Y.S. 622, supra. In the Wallace case, Mr. Justice Lamar, later of the Supreme Court of the United States, in stating the generally accepted judicial view concerning such evidence said (122 Ga. 551, 50 S.E. 480): "Nor was the error in the admission of the evidence of the witness cured by instructing them that the evidence as to the settlement could only be considered for the purposes of impeachment. The rule against allowing evidence of compromise is founded upon recognition of the fact that such testimony is inherently harmful, for the jury will draw conclusions therefrom in spite of anything said by the parties at the time of discussing the compromise, and in spite of anything which may be said by the judge in instructing them as to the weight to be given such evidence."

Argument based on the irrelevant testimony was objectionable, but requires no further comment here.

There must be a new trial because of prejudicial error.

Reversed and new trial granted.

See Federal Rules of Evidence 408, 409 at p. 911; California Evidence Code § § 1152, 1154 at p. 874.

KEETON, TRIAL TACTICS AND METHODS

52–54 (1954).*
[Most footnotes omitted.]

CASE 13.   *P* is suing for injuries sustained in a collision between his car and *D's* truck. *P's* car, after the impact with *D's* truck, veered into *W's* car. When *P's* lawyer interviews *W*, he learns that *D* paid *W* $75 for a release and that *W* tells a version of the facts favorable to *D*. *P's* lawyer anticipates that *D* will call *W* as a witness in the trial, and he wants to be prepared to get in evidence the payment of $75 by *D* to *W*, though the possibility of an objection on the ground that it was paid in compromise of a disputed claim is apparent.

In some exceptional instances, the asking of questions which are clearly improper and prejudicial is regarded as such misconduct of counsel as to warrant the granting of a mistrial or new trial. There is a widespread attitude that it is fair practice to offer objectionable evidence so long as there is no violation of these comparatively innocuous rules against misconduct of counsel. Some lawyers frankly state, and still more practice, the ethically indefensible proposition that such an improper question should be asked unless the question is of such prejudicial character that the refusal of the trial court to declare a mistrial would be reversible error. This practice is sometimes used for the very purpose of confronting adverse counsel with the difficult choice of waiving objection by failing to make it, or else making an objection which may lead the jury to conclude that he is attempting to withhold information from them. An advocate of this practice may seek to justify it on the basis that the exclusionary rule of evidence applying to his case is archaic, that the jury should have the benefit of the evidence, and that his adversary ought to have to pay the price if he wants to take advantage of some technical rule of evidence. Another argument often advanced is that since the right to exclude evidence may be waived by failure to object, it is not improper to make the offer and hope that objection will be waived. Both of these arguments, and the practice of deliberate use of improper questions, probably should be regarded as inconsistent with the provision of Canon 22[3] that "A lawyer should not offer evidence which he knows the Court should reject, in order to get the same before the jury by argument for its admissibility,   *   *   *   " and that kindred practices are condemned.

Protection against the deliberate use of clearly improper questions is inadequate under existing rules of law, unless the trial judge uses his discretionary powers to deal with the practice sternly. Even if ethical considerations are disregarded, however, some limitations exist as to advisability of asking objectionable questions, because of tactical considerations. The jury may recognize the unfairness of such tactics, after the court has sustained objection to the question, and may be influenced against the lawyer using such tactics and against his case. The jury's recognition of such unfairness might even occur without objection to the evidence, as in the case of a practice of continually leading the witness.

*Copyright, 1954 by Prentice-Hall, Inc.

3.   Canons of Professional Ethics of the American Bar Association. The second of the arguments stated above is the more troublesome. It might be urged that if the offering lawyer thinks his opponent may waive his ground of objection by failing to object either through design or by oversight, then the evidence offered is not "evidence which he knows the Court should reject," since the court should not reject it in the absence of an objection.

If admissibility is subject to reasonable doubt, on strictly ethical considerations the asking of the question is proper if the lawyer actually desires to insist on admission of the evidence, since it is the lawyer's right and duty to present the best case for his client that the facts and rules of law will support. Although it might be argued that he should first present such evidence to the court in the absence of the jury, for its admissibility to be determined, this attitude is rarely taken except in cases where the other attorney has presented an objection to the court in advance of the offer. On tactical considerations, offering evidence of doubtful admissibility should usually be avoided by the party (normally the plaintiff) who desires speedy termination of the case and has jury sympathy on his side, unless the evidence is actually important to persuasion of the jury, in the judgment of the lawyer. This is true for the reason that the admission of such evidence over objection may result in the granting of a new trial, if either the trial or appellate court later concludes that such admission was harmful error. The question might be asked with the purpose of not insisting upon admission of the evidence over objection, but it may be difficult to withdraw the question after it is asked. If the judge promptly overrules the objection when made, the lawyer who then tries to get the judge to withdraw the evidence by an instruction to the jury to disregard it will find it difficult to maintain even the appearance of good faith in making the offer.

If you conclude that the evidence of doubtful admissibility is likely to have a strong influence on the conclusion reached by the jury in the case, you may conclude that the chance of reversal is worth taking; the decision is based upon weighing the probable value of the evidence to you in its influence on the jury against the disadvantage of possible reversal of a favorable verdict and judgment. The evidence of payment of $75 to *W* by *D*, in Case 13, presents an illustration of this problem. If admissibility of this evidence is doubtful in the jurisdiction of trial, even on the alternative theory, the evidence probably should be offered unless plaintiff has a very strong case without it and a client whose circumstances make important prompt termination of the litigation (and avoidance of the possibility of new trial because of a decision that receipt of the evidence was harmful error).

ANDO v. WOODBERRY

Court of Appeals of New York, 1960.
8 N.Y.2d 165, 203 N.Y.Supp.2d 74, 168 N.E.2d 520.

FULD, Judge. This appeal calls upon us to decide a question of first impression in this court: May a defendant's prior plea of guilt to a traffic offense be introduced as evidence of his carelessness in a civil action for damages?

The relevant facts are simple and undisputed. Robert Ando, a police officer, driving a motorcycle, and Edward Nichols, driving an automobile owned by Essie Woodberry, were both proceeding north on Fifth Avenue, New York City, on the afternoon of December 28, 1955. Car and motorcycle collided when Mr. Nichols attempted to make a left turn at 110th Street, and Officer Ando was injured as a result of the collision. Mr. Nichols was given a summons which charged him with failing to make a proper turn and failing to signal before turning, and he subsequently appeared in the Manhattan Traffic Division of Magistrates' Court and pleaded guilty to both charges.

Upon the negligence trial, held in the Supreme Court, the only witnesses to the occurrence of the accident were the plaintiff and the defendant Nichols who drove the car. According to the plaintiff, Mr. Nichols, after first pulling over to the right, made a left turn without prior warning or signal and struck his motorcycle. Mr. Nichols not only denied that he had moved to the right, but asserted that he had given a signal upon making the turn. In order to strengthen his case, the plaintiff attempted to prove Mr. Nichols' plea of guilt in Traffic Court on the theory that it constituted an admission, but, upon the defendants' objection, the trial court excluded the proffered evidence. The jury returned a verdict in favor of the defendants and the Appellate Division, two Justices dissenting, affirmed the judgment subsequently rendered.

In deciding whether proof of a plea of guilty to a traffic violation should be received as evidence in chief in a subsequent civil action, it is well to recall the principle, basic to our law of evidence, that "All facts having rational probative value are admissible" unless there is sound reason to exclude them unless, that is "some specific rule forbids" (1 Wigmore, Evidence [3d ed., 1940], p. 293). It is this general principle which gives rationality, coherence and justification to our system of evidence and we may neglect it only at the risk of turning that system into a trackless morass of arbitrary and artificial Rules.

In view of the fact that Mr. Nichols' plea of guilty to the charges leveled against him—failing to signal and making an improper turn—is relevant to the issue of his negligence in turning off Fifth Avenue, we must simply decide whether there is any justification for excluding it. Two possible grounds of exclusion suggest themselves; the first, that such testimony is hearsay and, the second, that its introduction violates public policy.

Since a prior plea of guilt represents an admission, it is not obnoxious to the hearsay rule. Accordingly, the courts of this State, as well as of other jurisdictions, have generally sanctioned the receipt in evidence in a negligence action of a prior plea of guilty to a traffic violation. [Citations omitted.] Thus, when Mr. Nichols pleaded guilty to the traffic infractions charged against him, his plea of guilty amounted to a statement or admission by him that he did the act charged. As such, it should be treated like any other admission or confession, and subject to the same rules relating to its weight and effect.

The defendants insist, however, that there is a public policy which requires us to treat the admission implicit in pleading guilty to a traffic offense differently from others. It is the policy of this State, they urge, that a traffic infraction be distinguished from a crime and that it be recognized that a plea of guilt is entered in traffic court for numerous reasons unrelated to actual guilt. To support their contention, they point to subdivision 29 of section 2 of the Vehicle and Traffic Law, Consol.Laws, c. 40, Hart v. Mealey, 287 N.Y. 39, 38 N.E.2d 121 and Walther v. News Syndicate Co., 276 App.Div. 169, 93 N.Y.S.2d 537, supra.

The portion of the Vehicle and Traffic Law relied upon provides that "a traffic infraction is not a crime and the penalty or punishment imposed therefor * * * shall not affect or impair the credibility as a witness, or otherwise, of any person convicted thereof." (Vehicle and Traffic Law, §

2, subd. 29; see, also Civil Practice Act, § 355). Whatever else this provision may mean, it is clear that it is directed solely against the use of a conviction of a traffic infraction to "affect or impair * * * credibility as a witness" of the person convicted and not against the use of a plea as evidence in chief. The statute does no more than restate the rule of the common law that a prior conviction may be shown to attack the credibility of a witness only if it was a conviction of a *crime*.

Since a traffic infraction was declared not to be a crime, it was but natural for the Legislature to, in effect, codify the settled rule prohibiting the use of a conviction of such an offense to impeach the offender when called to testify as a witness. Had more than this been intended, had it been the legislative design to render evidence of a traffic infraction unavailable for *any* purpose in a subsequent civil action, it could easily have so provided. See, e.g., Minn.Stats.Ann. § 169.94, subd. 1; Colo.Rev.Stat., 13–4–140.[1] The Legislature of this State having written a clearly limited rule of exclusion, we may not apply it beyond its terms to exclude the use of a guilty plea as evidence in chief.

Nor may legislative policy be taken to justify its exclusion. Certain violations of the Vehicle and Traffic Law were denominated traffic infractions and distinguished from crimes in order to establish a new type of offense, one "with the stigma of criminality removed." Squadrito v. Griebsch, 1 N.Y.2d 471, 476, 154 N.Y.S.2d 37, 41, 136 N.E.2d 504, 507. The legislation simply represented a recognition of the fact that most traffic violations do not involve the degree of moral turpitude associated with crime.

In addition to their reliance on policy and precedent, the defendants also offer an argument based on what they label "experience". They contend that one charged with a traffic violation pleads guilty even though he believes himself innocent, in order to avoid the expenditure of time and money which would be involved if guilt were denied and the charge contested. Based on this assumption, they suggest that the plea of guilt must be looked upon as one *nolo contendere*. The contention has no merit. In the first place, the plea of *nolo contendere* has long been abolished in this State and may not be resurrected without legislative sanction. In the second place, while we are willing to assume that pleas to traffic charges are not infrequently prompted by considerations of expediency, we have no reliable means of judging how significant a portion of all guilty pleas to traffic charges are of this character. But, quite apart from this, there is no basis for the defendants' unverified generalization or "hunch" in cases where, as here, the alleged violation was attended with injury to the person or property of a third party and the plea carries with it serious consequences to the offender's future status as a motor vehicle operator (Vehicle and Traffic Law, § 71).[2]

1. The Minnesota statute declares that "No record of the conviction of any person for any violation of [the Highway Traffic Regulation Act] shall be admissible as evidence in any court in any civil action" (Minn.Stats.Ann. § 169.94, subd. 1).

2. Under the so-called "point system", in effect in New York, a plea of guilt, for instance, to the charge of failing to signal or of making an improper turn, is taken into account in determining whether the offender's license should be suspended or revoked. (See pamphlet issued by the Commissioner of Motor Vehicles, entitled, "What You Need to Know About New York State's Point System for Persistent Traffic Law Violators".)

What the defendant Nichols is actually arguing is that, when he pleaded guilty, he "really didn't mean what he said". This claim, however, goes to the weight of evidence and entitles the defendant not to exclusion of the plea, but to an "opportunity to explain" it. Chamberlain v. Iba, 181 N.Y. 486, 490, 74 N.E. 481, 482. After the defendant has given his explanation, his reasons for pleading guilty, it is for the jurors to evaluate his testimony and decide whether the plea is entitled to any weight. As this court wrote some years ago with respect to extra-judicial admissions, it is for the jury, noting "the conditions and circumstances under which [such admissions] were made", to determine their "effect * * * and their probative weight and value, which may range from the lowest, or none at all, to conclusiveness." Gangi v. Fradus, 227 N.Y. 452, 457, 125 N.E. 677, 679, supra. The traditional treatment accorded to admissions by our courts takes account of the very claim here made, namely, that the defendant's guilty plea was not an admission that he committed the acts charged against him.

To the claim that the jury will be unduly prejudiced by the introduction of a plea of guilt despite the opportunity to explain it away, we content ourselves with the statement that this underestimates the intelligence of jurors and overlooks their awareness of those very circumstances said to destroy the meaning and significance of the plea. If voluntarily and deliberately made, the plea was a statement of guilt, an admission by the defendant that he committed the acts charged, and it should be accorded no less force or effect than if made outside of court to a stranger.

The judgment of the Appellate Division should be reversed and a new trial granted, with costs to abide the event.

Van Voorhis, Judge (dissenting).

The law of evidence has its roots in experience, and in common experience men and women charged with minor traffic violations plead guilty to avoid inconvenience whether they are innocent or guilty. In the Federal courts it is possible for a defendant in a criminal action to plead *nolo contendere*, the accepted meaning of which is that the defendant chooses not to contest and takes the consequences of conviction but without admitting the truth of the charge against him. Such a plea could not be received in evidence as a voluntary admission against interest under the reasoning of the opinion by Judge Fuld in this case. The State procedure does not give opportunity to plead *nolo contendere* but that is exactly what persons accused of minor traffic violations generally mean to do and are understood to have done when they enter guilty pleas in such instances. They are subject to the punishment provided by law for the offenses to which they have pleaded guilty, but the criminal statutes do not impose the additional burden of having the conviction used in a civil action as a factual admission by the person charged that he or she did or omitted the act on which the traffic infraction depends. It is irrelevant that *nolo contendere* is not a form of plea that is used in the State courts, inasmuch as we are not confronted in this case with any of the consequences of conviction under the criminal law. We have before us merely the collateral effect of such a plea as bearing upon the civil rights of the party in an action for damages. It is contrary to ordinary experience to give that effect to this plea of guilty in the Magistrates' Court, as the Appellate Division has correctly held. When Mr. Nichols pleaded guilty in the Manhattan Traffic Division of Magistrates' Court, to failure to make a proper turn or to signal, he rendered himself liable to whatever penalties were involved but in my view it cannot be said with justice or a sense of reality that he conceded whatever facts he was accused of by the arresting officer. I think that it was not intended that the first steps in the enforcement or defense of damage claims in automobile negligence accident cases should be taken in traffic courts or police courts, nor does it aid their most effective functioning if that is so.

Desmond, C.J., and Dye, Froessel, Burke and Foster, JJ., concur with Fuld, J.

Van Voorhis, J., dissents in an opinion.

Judgment reversed, etc.

NOTE

See Federal Rules of Evidence 410 at p. 911; California Evidence Code § 1153 at p. 874.

In connection with Ando v. Woodberry, supra, and its problem of the admissibility in civil cases of prior pleas of guilty in criminal cases, two related problems should be considered: (1) the admissibility of judgments of conviction; and (2) the possible res judicata effect of judgments of conviction.

Judgments of conviction. See Hearsay Exceptions, supra, p. . Historically, judgments of conviction (other than for impeachment purposes) have been inadmissible as constituting hearsay and opinion. However, a growing number of courts are admitting in civil cases a judgment of conviction offered against the person convicted. California Evidence Code § 1300 provides that a final judgment of conviction for a felony is not inadmissible as hearsay when offered in a civil action to prove any fact essential to the judgment unless the judgment was based on a plea of *nolo contendere.*

Res judicata. Beyond the problem of admissibility is the doctrine in those jurisdictions where mutuality as a condition of res judicata has been abandoned, that the criminal judgment of conviction is conclusive in the civil case. But in California an exception has been legislated for violations of the Vehicle Code; judgments of conviction for such offenses are not res judicata in civil cases. West's Ann.Cal. Vehicle C. § 40834.

Hypotheticals

(1) A sues X and the Y Bus Company for damages for personal injuries suffered in a collision between an automobile driven by A and a bus owned by the Y Bus Company and driven by X, its employee. A makes an offer of proof that at the scene of the acccident X made the statement, "I know I blew the stop sign, but will you take $100 in settlement? I know the company will pay that much." Both X and the Y Bus Company make objections that X's statement is hearsay and also barred by the rule against admissions made during settlement negotiations. Should the objection be sustained?

(2) A sues the X Insurance Company for damages for intentional infliction of mental distress. A carried a disability-insurance policy with X, which provided for monthly payments of $150 to A as long as a disability continued. A is hurt and has a permanent disability. X pays A $150 per month until he has been paid $2,500. X then stops the payments, and seeks cancellation of the policy on the ground that A had made misrepresentations at the time of the policy application. A offers evidence that X was acting in bad faith in asserting that A had made any misrepresentations to secure the policy. A offers in evidence a letter from X to A, in which X offered to compromise A's claim that the policy was valid by permitting A to retain the $2,500 in payments, in return for X's cancellation of the policy and A's execution of a release of X. X makes an objection that its letter is inadmissible as an offer to compromise a claim. What result?

PART D.   SUBSEQUENT PRECAUTIONS

BARRY v. MANGLASS

Supreme Court, Appellate Division, Second Department, 1976.
55 A.D. 2d 1, 389 N.Y.S.2d 870.

SHAPIRO, Justice.

* * *

THE ACCIDENT.

On January 8, 1972, Gary A. Manglass was operating a 1969 Chevrolet Nova in Mount Ivy, Ramapo, New York. He was alone in the car. He made a left turn from Old Route 202 to go south on Route 45, a two-lane, north-south road, with a painted line down the center. The car was proceeding at a speed of 50 to 60 miles per hour either as it started into the turn or when it came into the southbound lane (the eyewitness testimony is not clear as to this). Suddenly the car appeared to be out of control and began weaving from one lane to the other. It struck a vehicle proceeding north which was operated by Beverly McElroy, injuring her and her passengers (her daughter Margo and Joanna and Jo-Ann Barry). Manglass was rendered unconscious and claimed that he had no recollection of the accident or of its immediate antecedents.

The Barrys and McElroys sued Gary A. Manglass and Janice E. Manglass, owner of the Nova, for negligence and they sued General Motors for alleged defects in the car which Gary Manglass was operating. The Manglasses sued General Motors but did not sue Beverly McElroy.

THE CONTENTION OF THE
PARTIES.

The basis of the claim against General Motors was an alleged defect in the left motor mount securing the engine block to the frame of Manglass' 1969 Nova. Experts testifying on behalf of the Barrys contended that the left motor mount separated into two parts prior to the collision and that that caused the engine to rise above its rotational axis and bind the accelerator linkage, resulting in an open-throttle posture.

General Motors, while admitting that, after the accident, the left motor mount was separated from the framework, contended that that condition was a result of the collision which, they claimed, was caused by Gary Manglass' loss of control of the car after making the turn at too great a speed. General Motors also contended that, because there was an absence of scarring on the surface of the motor mount, even if the separation had existed prior to the accident, it was not the cause of the malfunction of the accelerator linkage. Further, argued General Motors, motor mount failure would not have had an effect on the steering of the vehicle.

Experts on behalf of the Barrys testified that the motor mount failure preceded the accident and caused an unintended increase in the speed of the car as it was making the turn. However, there is more to these actions than the traditional battle of the experts. As part of the case against General Motors, there were submitted and accepted into evidence, over objection, portions of two recall letters issued to Chevrolet owners by General Motors, in March and November, 1972. The first was issued two months after the accident; however, the parties agree, awareness of the accident was not the cause of the issuance of the letters. The second letter was essentially a repeat of the first and was sent to those owners who had taken no action after receipt of the first. The relevant portions of the first letter are as follows:

"Dear Chevrolet Owner:

"This notification applies to 1969 Model Chevrolet passenger cars equipped with a V-8 engine except Chevelle and Corvette models

* * *

"[W]e are sending this letter to call to your attention a possible safety hazard which exists should separation of an engine mount occur on your vehicle. If you will take your vehicle to any Chevrolet dealer, restraints will be installed at 'no cost' to you, to eliminate this possible safety hazard. We urge that you do so.

"Your vehicle is equipped with two front engine mounts; one positioned on each side of the engine. An engine mount consists of a rubber cushion sandwiched between two metal plates. It supports and cushions the engine. Since the center portion of an engine mount is made of rubber, it is subject to fatigue from constant flexing during vehicle operation and from engine compartment heat. Replacement of fatigued engine mounts is a part of vehicle maintenance which is the responsibility of the owner.

"The possible safety hazard referred to exists when, as a result of fatigue or collision damage, the rubber portion of an engine mount has separated. When this condition exists, very rapid acceleration of the vehicle from a stop or from very low speeds can result in the engine rotating sufficiently to interfere with the accelerator linkage and to cause the throttle to be held open temporarily. This can occur suddenly and without warning when the vehicle is in either forward or reverse gear. A sharp left turn during forward acceleration can increase the possibility of engine rotation if the left engine mount has separated.

"If the throttle is unexpectedly held open, prompt reaction on the part of the driver will be required to avoid temporary loss of control of the vehicle. If that should occur, the driver should turn off the ignition and apply sufficient pressure on the brake pedal to bring the vehicle to a stop.

"Torque reaction forces, which can cause an engine with separated mounts to rotate sufficiently to affect vehicle operation can occur only during very rapid acceleration from a standing start or from very low speeds. It, therefore, is suggested that, except in emergency situations, you avoid such rapid acceleration from low speeds until after restraints have been installed in your vehicle by a Chevrolet dealer.

"Chevrolet has developed special restraints for installation in affected vehicles. In the event of engine mount separation, these restraints will limit engine rotation and thereby prevent interference with the normal operation of your vehicle. Installation of these restraints, therefore, will eliminate the possible safety hazard associated with engine mount separation which is described in this letter.

* * *

"If, in the future, it is necessary to replace engine mounts on your vehicle, it is important that you install only interlocking type engine
mounts. This type of mount limits engine rotation if separation occurs.

"Chevrolet Motor Division,

"General Motors Corporation"

General Motors alleges that it was reversible error for the court to admit those letters which were sent pursuant to the Motor Vehicle Safety Act
of 1966 and, more particularly, subdivision (a) of section 113 of the Act
(U.S. Code, tit. 15, § 1402, subd. [a]) which, at that time, provided:

"Every manufacturer of motor vehicles or tires shall furnish notification of any defect in any motor vehicle or motor vehicle equipment
produced by such manufacturer which he determines, in good faith,
relates to motor vehicle safety, to the purchaser (where known to the
manufacturer) of such motor vehicle or motor vehicle equipment,
within a reasonable time after such manufacturer has discovered such
defect."

General Motors analogizes the furnishing of such notification to
evidence of "subsequent repairs", which is classically inadmissible to prove
the existence of a defect. That rule came into being when most personal injury cases were based upon the negligence of the defendant. General Motors
contends that the admission into evidence of the letters, unfairly penalizes
manufacturers "who have come forward to announce the existence of a possible defect when it is found to exist." The analogy is inappropriate. Literally, of course, it does not apply because the letters were not an aftermath of
the accident. The rule precluding the admission of evidence of subsequent
repairs is that improvement of the condition of the injury-causing object indicates no more than a belief that it is *capable of causing such an injury,
but indicates nothing more*" (2 Wigmore on Evidence [3d ed.], § 283 [4]),
and that "[m]ere capacity of a place or thing to cause injury is not the fact
that constitutes a liability * * * it must be a capacity which could
have been known to an owner using reasonable diligence and foresight, and
a capacity to injure persons taking reasonable care in its use." Wigmore
then states:

"To be sure, it may be argued that, on the general theory of Relevancy
* * * it would suffice for admissibility if merely the inference was
a fairly possible one,—leaving it to the opponent to argue that it was
the less probable one. Theoretically, it would be perhaps difficult to
deny this. But in the present instance an argument of Policy has
always been invoked to strengthen the case for exclusion. That argument is that the admission of such acts, even though theoretically not
plainly improper, would be liable to over-emphasis by the jury, and
that it would discourage all owners, even those who had genuinely
been careful, from improving the place or thing that had caused the injury, because they would fear the evidential use of such acts to their
disadvantage; and thus not only would careful owners refrain from improvements, but even careless ones, who might have deserved to have
the evidence adduced against them, would by refraining from improvements subject innocent persons to the risk of the recurrence of
the injury.

"Whatever then might be the strength of the objection to such evidence from the point of view of Relevancy alone, the added considerations of Policy suffice to make clear the impropriety of resorting to it."

Even if the rule against admission of proof of subsequent repairs is not one which has outlived its usefulness and which should not now be discarded (see The Exclusionary Rule on Subsequent Repairs—A Rule in Need of Repair, 7 The Forum 1)[1], Wigmore's conclusion, and that of the other text writers in agreement with him, that regardless of the relevancy of the proffered proof it should be excluded because "the added considerations of Policy suffice to make clear the impropriety of resorting to it", should not be applied in products liability cases. The court, in Sutkowski v. Universal Marion Corp., (5 Ill.App.3d 313, 319, 281 N.E.2d 749, 753), stated that "policy considerations are involved which shift the emphasis from the defendant manufacturer's conduct to the character of the product" and that therefore the rule excluding evidence of postoccurrence repairs in negligence cases should not be applied to products liability cases. Thus, while it may be sound to exclude evidence of post-injury remedial safety measures in negligence cases because the repairs reflect hindsight rather than foresight and might militate against the making of such repairs, to extend the rule to cases of strict products liability would, without basis in reason, permit an arbitrary exclusionary rule to operate in the field of consumer protection. In such cases we are not dealing with *fault* or *negligence* or *culpability,* but, regardless of any of them, with a defect which existed in the product. The former deal with the defendant's conduct, the latter with the product.

In enunciating the same view, the Supreme Court of California, in Ault v. International Harvester Co., 13 Cal.3d 113, 120, 117 Cal.Rptr. 812, 815–816, 528 P.2d 1148, 1151–1152 said:

"When the context is transformed from a typical negligence setting to the modern products liability field, however, the 'public policy' assumptions justifying this evidentiary rule are no longer valid. The contemporary corporate mass producer of goods, the normal products liability defendant, manufactures tens of thousands of units of goods; it is manifestly unrealistic to suggest that such a producer will forego making improvements in its product, and risk innumerable additional lawsuits and the attendant adverse effect upon its public image, simply because evidence of adoption of such improvement may be admitted in an action founded on strict liability for recovery on an injury that preceded the improvement. In the products liability area, the exclusionary rule of section 1151 [a California procedural rule] does not affect the primary conduct of the mass producer of goods, but serves merely as a shield against potential liability. In short, the purpose of section 1151 is not applicable to a strict liability case and hence its exclusionary rule should not be gratuitously extended to that field.

---

1. The writer of the article in The Forum, Professor Victor E. Schwartz, properly states that "Throughout the rather long and tortuous history of the rule excluding repairs, no court or writer has produced any empirical data showing that the rule has resulted in a single repair or that its absence would discourage repair activity" (7 The Forum 1, 6).

"This view has been advanced by others. It has been pointed out that not only is the policy of encouraging repairs and improvements of doubtful validity in an action for strict liability since it is in the economic self interest of a manufacturer to improve and repair defective products, but that the application of the rule would be contrary to the public policy of encouraging the distributor of mass-produced goods to market safer products."

In analyzing the usual public policy argument which has been used by the courts to preclude the admission of proof of subsequent repairs in negligence cases, and in demonstrating its inapplicability in a products liability context, we find the following cogent and convincing statement in an article entitled Products Liability and Evidence of Subsequent Repairs (1972 Duke L.J. 837, 848–860):

"The assumption that the admission of evidence of subsequent repairs, discourages defendants from making required repairs may be erroneous. Manufacturers and distributors of mass-produced products may not be so callous to the safety of the consumer as the general exclusionary rule presumes. Furthermore, to the extent that admission of such evidence results in recovery by injured plaintiffs, it can be argued that evidence of subsequent repairs *encourages* future remedial action. A distributor of mass-produced goods may have thousands of goods on the market. If his products are defective, the distributor would probably face greater total liability by allowing such defective products to remain on the market or by continuing to put more defective products on the market than he would by being adjudged liable in one particular case where evidence of subsequent repairs was introduced. Also, concern on the part of the distributors for consumer protection is promoted by consumer organizations, federal agencies, and mass media exposure of product defects. To some extent, the economic self-interest of product distributors requires that they repair and improve defective products to avoid adverse publicity which might result from future litigation. Since a prior jury finding of product defectiveness is admissible in a subsequent suit when the product causing the second injury is substantially similar to the first, distributors of defective products are under pressure to repair or alter their products to insulate themselves from a finding of defectiveness which may be used against them in subsequent litigation.

"In conclusion, excluding evidence of subsequent repairs to encourage future remedial action may preclude recovery under theories of products liability which are themselves designed to ensure safety in marketed products. Relevant evidence should not be excluded from a products liability case by an obsolete evidentiary rule when modern legal theories, accompanied by economic and political pressures, will achieve the desired policy goals". [Emphasis in original.]

The latest case in an appellate court dealing with the admissibility of manufacturers' recall letters is Fields v. Volkswagen of Amer., Okl., 555 P.2d 48 (dec. July 27, 1976).

That was an action for damages for injuries suffered by the plaintiff (Fields) when his 1971 Volkswagen overturned while he was attempting to negotiate a left-hand curve. He contended that the steering wheel locked while he was driving, making it impossible for him to keep the car on the road. The car was equipped with an ignition lock system that prevented the steering wheel from being turned while the ignition was off. Plaintiff claimed that the locking mechanism was defective when the vehicle left the factory and that the failure of that system was the actual and proximate cause of the accident.

There, as here, the plaintiff, prior to offering the recall letter in evidence, established the claimed defect by expert testimony. There, as here, the recall letter was then admitted. On appeal the court sustained the ruling and said (p. 58):

> "The recall letter by itself does not make a prima facie case or shift the burden of proof. It does not prove that the defect existed at the time of the accident. This must be proved independently. But if a defect contributing to or causing the accident is the defect that is the subject of the recall letter, *then the letter would be some evidence that the 'defect existed at the time the product left the manufacturer'*". [Emphasis supplied.]

Furthermore, as the court said in *Comstock v. General Motors Corp.,* 358 Mich. 163, 176, 99 N.W.2d 627, 634:

> "The duty to warn of known danger inherent in a product, or in its contemplated use, has long been a part of the manufacturer's liability doctrine."

In the light of the foregoing, and since the plaintiff is required to prove that the defect existed not only at the time of the accident but also at the time when the product left the hands of the manufacturer, we believe that the relevancy of the recall letters outweighs any possible prejudice in their receipt; a jury is entitled to know that the existence of the defect in a particular model of vehicle was likely and that such likelihood was greater as to such model than it was as to other models.

* * *

True it is that some prejudice is inevitable in such a case, but it can, and should, be minimized by the court's *caveat,* at the time of its receipt in evidence, and when charging the jury, that such letters do not establish that the defect was present in the particular vehicle. Thus, to sustain a verdict for a plaintiff based upon an existing defect, such letters, standing alone, would be insufficient. Here, however, we have the testimony of plaintiff's experts (albeit contradicted by that of General Motors' expert witnesses), which was not unbelievable, and which justified the jury's conclusion that the defect existed prior to the accident and that it caused the accident. The statements contained in the letters could therefore properly be utilized by the jury as confirmation of that testimony.

There is an additional factor to be considered. We may take judicial notice that recall letters by automobile manufacturers have by now been sent out by the millions. The failure to mention the letters might well cause jurors to believe that no such letters were issued and that the claimed defect was a solitary one and did not in fact exist. In such case the prejudice to the injured plaintiff could not be minimized because it would relate to undisclosed matters.

As indicated, the admission of such exhibits must be handled with such circumspection that it is made clear to the jury that its consideration of them is not the end of the matter, but, rather, a circumstance to be considered along with the rest of the evidence in the case. Here there was no such circumspection. On the contrary, the trial court charged the jury that "[i]f you find from the fact that General Motors sent these letters *that it thereby admitted that the engine mounts in the Manglass vehicle were defective,* you may consider these letters as evidence * * * that *this vehicle* was defective." [Emphasis supplied.]

Obviously, the letters were not an admission that the *vehicle involved in this case was defective.* Further, the charge tended to eliminate the issue of proximate cause. Most importantly, it maximized, rather than minimized the implicit prejudice of the letters. As we have noted, the letters were admissible *despite* their prejudice, but the trial court should have balanced the scales and should not have unduly added to the one side which was already weighted. This basic error alone requires a new trial as to defendant General Motors.

* * *

Cohalan, Acting P.J., and Margett, Damiani and Titone, JJ., concur.

MAINE RULES OF EVIDENCE

June 1975.

Rule 407

SUBSEQUENT REMEDIAL MEASURES; NOTIFICATION OF DEFECT

(a) Subsequent remedial measures.   When, after an event, measures are taken which, if taken previously, would have made the event less likely to occur, evidence of the subsequent measures is admissible.

(b) Notification of defect.   A written notification by a manufacturer of any defect in a product produced by such manufacturer to purchasers thereof is admissible against the manufacturer on the issue of existence of the defect to the extent that it is relevant.

Compare with Federal Rules of Evidence 407 at p. 911; California Evidence Code § 1151 at p. 874.

DAGGETT v. ATCHISON, TOPEKA AND SANTE FE RY. CO.

Supreme Court of California, 1957.
48 Cal.2d 655, 313 P.2d 557.

CARTER, Justice.   Defendants, The Atchison, Topeka and Sante Fe Railway Company, G.H. Benton (motorman), and Irwin M. Pike (conductor) appeal from a judgment in favor of John S. Daggett for the loss of his two minor children in an action arising out of a collision between one of defendant's passenger trains and an automobile driven by Paula Smith Daggett, who died in the same accident, at a railway crossing in Solana Beach. Olga Smith and Paul R. Smith, the parents of Paula Smith Daggett (wife of John S. Daggett) were also plaintiffs in the action but as to them the jury found in favor of defendant railway company.

Neither the negligence of defendants, nor the contributory negligence of Paula Smith Daggett, are issues on this appeal. The only two assignments of error with respect to the evidence relate to the examination of defendant railway's employees called under section 2055 of the Code of Civil Procedure. The facts therefore will be set forth as briefly as possible but with particular emphasis on the disputed evidence.

The accident occured at approximately 11:18 a.m. on June 25, 1954. It was a clear day. Mrs. Daggett, who was 24 years of age and eight months pregnant, was driving in a westerly direction on Plaza Street, Solana Beach, accompanied by her two minor children, aged 3 years and 10 months, respectively. Defendant's train, which was traveling in a southerly direction at a speed of between 86 and 90 miles an hour crossed the intersection of Plaza Street on its railroad tracks at the same time as Mrs. Daggett's automobile which was estimated to be traveling at a speed of from 10 to 15 miles per hour. Mrs. Daggett and the two minor children were killed in the accident. On the north side of Plaza Street was a lumber company building about 75 feet from the crossing; on the same side of Plaza Street was a railroad siding on which stood a freight car about 100 feet from the crossing. Both the building and the freight car were on Mrs. Daggett's right (the direction from which the train approached the crossing) as she drove westerly on Plaza Street toward the railroad crossing. On the northeast corner (on Mrs. Daggett's right) of the intersection of the tracks and Plaza Street was an automatic wigwag signal located 12 feet 9 inches above the ground; on the southwest corner of the crossing was a standard crossarm. Running parallel to, and a very short distance from, defendant's railroad tracks is the Pacific Coast Highway which intersects Plaza Street after it crosses the tracks. At this intersection there is a traffic light for vehicular traffic.[1] Ringing circuits for the operation of the wigwag signal were set off by a southbound train at a point 3,023 feet north of Plaza Street where it intersects with the tracks. In view of the speed at which defendant's train was approaching the intersection, this would result in the operation of the automatic wigwag signal for approximately 22 seconds.

Glenn H. Benton, a defendant, and the motorman who was operating the train at the time of the accident, was the first witness called by plaintiffs under section 2055 of the Code of Civil Procedure.[2] Mr. Benton testified that the train which he was operating at the time of the accident was a four-unit Diesel with ten passenger cars; that it was capable of a speed of 100 miles an hour; that at the time of the accident he had the train in throttle "position 8" (the highest speed position) and that the train was going from 85 to 90 miles an hour; that the railroad speed limit for that crossing was 90 miles an hour and that this was considered a safe speed.[3] The witness also testified that on the day in question the train was 15 minutes late and

1. There was evidence in the record that this light, rather than the automatic wigwag signal predominated the view of vehicular traffic proceeding in a westerly direction on Plaza Street.

2. A party to the record of any civil action or proceeding * * * may be examined by the adverse party as if under cross-examination, subject to the rules applicable to the examination of other witnesses. The party calling such adverse witness shall not be bound by his testimony, and the testimony given by such witness may be rebutted by the party calling him for such examination by other evidence

* * *

3. The record shows that an average of 2,500 automobiles crossed the tracks daily at this intersection.

that he was trying to make up time. Mr. Benton testified that the area involved was part of the fourth district and that the speed limit for that district was 90 miles an hour. The witness testified that the speed "*is* 90 now on the first, second, and fourth districts." (Emphasis added.) Over objection by defense counsel the following occurred: "Q. [By plaintiffs' counsel]: Well, Mr. Benton, the restriction now is 50 miles an hour, isn't it?" Plaintiffs' counsel, in answer to the court's question concerning the district to which he was referring, replied: "He is referring to the fourth. He says the restriction in the fourth district now is 90 miles an hour. We are prepared to show that the restriction in this district at this crossing now, rather than being 90 miles an hour, is 50 miles an hour." In response to defense counsel's request to take "this matter" up out of the presence of the jury, the court ruled that "He has a right to say what he expects to prove or what he expects to get this witness to testify to. It is cross-examination, a legitimate statement." Over objection by defense counsel, the following took place: "Q. [Plaintiff's counsel]: Mr. Benton, you say that the speeds in these areas then and now are 90 miles an hour?" After objection and a holding that the question was a compound one, the witness answered a simplified question that the speed "now" at the "Plaza area" was 50 miles an hour.

The second witness called by plaintiffs was William Price, signal engineer for the defendant railway company. Mr. Price, who qualified as an expert witness, and who testified under section 2055 of the Code of Civil Procedure said that he was "absolutely sure" that the type of signal in use at the Plaza crossing at the time of the accident was "the safest type of signal." Counsel for plaintiffs, over objection, questioned the witness and brought out that since the accident the California Public Utilities Commission had requested defendant railway company to change the single wigwag signal to two "flashing light signals" located 8 feet above the ground level. Over objection, the court permitted the jury to view the scene of the accident at a time when a train crossed the intersection. At this time, of course, the speed limit had been reduced and the new signals installed. However, photographs of the crossing with the new signals installed had been theretofore admitted in evidence without objection by defense counsel.[4]

Defendants contend that the court committed prejudicial error in admitting evidence of changes made subsequent to the time of the accident. Plaintiffs argue that the evidence was not admitted for the purpose of showing changed conditions but to impeach the witnesses called by them under section 2055. It is also argued by defendants that evidence of changed conditions may not be used to impeach a witness called under section 2055, and that the error was magnified by plaintiffs' counsel during argument to the jury.

It is the general rule in this state that evidence of precautions taken and repairs made after the happening of the accident is not admissible to show a negligent condition at the time of the accident. The reason for the rule was well stated in Sappenfield v. Main St. & A. P. R. Co., 91 Cal. 48,

---

4. In Church v. Headrick & Brown, 101 Cal.App.2d 396, 413, 414, 225 P.2d 558, it was held that where evidence of changed conditions was admitted by the court without objection the admission of similar evidence from another witness, over objection, was not ground for a reversal. See, also, Dyas v. Southern Pac. Co., 140 Cal. 296, 306, 73 P. 972.

62, 27 P. 590, 593: "It would be unjust to hold that, because the employer seeks by all the aid he gets from the light of experience to make the implement free from danger, he is therefore to be charged with negligence in the use of all prior appliances, even though they were adopted with the best light then under his control. * * * He may have exercised all the care which the law requires, and yet in the light of a new experience, after an unexpected accident has occurred, he may adopt additional safeguards. To hold that the adoption of such new appliances which experience has demonstrated are more efficient than those previously in use, or which invention has developed from observing the defects in those originally adopted, shall be an admission that he was negligent prior thereto would prevent the very conduct in employers which they should be urged to follow."

This court has held, however, that "Although evidence of the character here in question may not be admissible to prove negligence at the time of the accident, it is proper to impeach the testimony of a witness. Inyo Chemical Co. v. City of Los Angeles, supra [5 Cal.2d 525, 55 P.2d 850]. * * * [W]here evidence is admissible for a limited purpose only, it is not the duty of a judge to instruct the jury as to such purpose unless requested to do so [citations omitted]. Having failed to request an instruction that the impeaching evidence was admitted only for that purpose and was not otherwise competent, defendants may not complain.

* * *

The judgment is affirmed.

Gibson, C.J., and Shenk and Traynor, JJ., concur.

Schauer, Justice (dissenting).

It is my view that it was prejudicial error to bring before the jury the fact that after the accident defendant railroad company reduced its speed limitation from 90 to 50 miles an hour at the intersection in Solana Beach where the railroad tracks crossed Plaza Street and where the accident occurred. The attempt to defend such an error as being merely the presentation of impeaching evidence appears to me to be without support in the record. To the contrary, the record affirmatively shows that at no time did the witness, Benton, testify that the limitation for the crossing remained at 90 miles an hour at the time of trial. His testimony was clearly to the effect that the general limitation for the entire fourth district—i. e., the area from Fullerton to San Diego—was 90 miles both at the time of the accident and at the time of trial, and he had further made clear that there were other limitations calling for lesser speeds at various smaller areas within the district. Moreover, any confusion as to speeds, times, and districts or areas appears from the record to have been invited and brought about by counsel for plaintiffs, who then seized upon such alleged confusion as an excuse to get before the jury otherwise inadmissible evidence of a change in the speed limitation after the accident. The following excerpts from the examination of Benton by counsel for plaintiffs, who had called him as a witness under section 2055 of the Code of Civil Procedure, will so demonstrate (all italics have been added):

"Q. [By counsel for plaintiff] What *was* [at the time of the accident] that crossing posted for as far as the railroad was concerned? A. 90 miles an hour. * * *

"Q.   Now, with reference to whether you were early or late, were you late on that run, on that day? A. We were. We were late.   *   *   *

"Q.   And where was the place to the Los Angeles side of Solana Beach where you had last attempted to pick up some time? A. The speed restriction down *at the district* is 90 miles per hour, *with the exception of where there is curve restrictions or restrictions otherwise.*   *   *   *

"Q.   Well, how fast *did* you usually go across that intersection in Solana Beach? A. Between 80—between 80 and 90 miles per hour.   *   *   *

"Q.   But across this intersection your speed varies [note present tense used by counsel for plaintiff] between 80 and 90 miles an hour; right? A. Yes, sir.   *   *   *

"Q.   Could you go as fast as 90 miles an hour around this curve that comes into Solana Beach or *is* [note the present tense] that restricted to less? A. That is 90 miles an hour.

"Q.   And do I understand that you could go 90 miles an hour all the way from Los Angeles to San Diego? A. *No,* sir, because *there is restrictions, curve restrictions and other forms of restrictions.*

"Q.   How about that curve from Cardiff into the place of the accident; *isn't* [note present tense] that curve restricted to 85? A. That's a 90 mile an hour curve.   *   *   *

"Q.   *   *   * Now, you have driven these diesels similar to the one you were driving on that day for some time, haven't you? A. Yes, sir.

"Q.   And in driving those diesels, have you gone over 90 miles an hour with them?   *   *   * A. I have. Those diesels are a hundred-mile-an-hour diesel, but *that* particular *district is 90 mile restriction* down there. *That's known as the fourth district.*   *   *   *

"Q.   What does fourth district mean; can you tell us? A. Well, that's the district from one station to the other.

"Q.   That has nothing to do with the type of speed, does it? A. No.

"Q.   Merely nomenclature of the area, merely geographically a description or appellation of the area, what it is called; is that right? A. What the company, what particular restriction they put on that particular district, why [the reason why] I don't know.

"Q.   *Is* [note present tense employed by counsel for plaintiff] that put on the whole district from Los Angeles all the way to San Diego? A. That just runs from Fullerton to San Diego, but from Los Angeles to Fullerton is a portion of the third district.

"Q.   And then you *have* [note present tense] to go slower in that area? A. That's right.

"Q.   What speed *do you go* [note present tense] in the area between Fullerton and Los Angeles?   *   *   * A. The speed *restriction on* all *districts* in the Santa Fe Los Angeles Division *is 90 miles* an hour.

"Q. How about between Fullerton and Los Angeles? A. That *is* 90 miles an hour, too.

"Q. So there *is* no more restriction there than there *is* down here? A. Not at this time. I don't recall whether—it was a hundred on all districts but the third and fourth districts it was less, but it *is* the same all over now, with the exception of the third district. That *is* 80.

"Q. You are not speaking of what it *is* now, are you? A. No. It *is* *90 now on the* first, second, and *fourth districts.*

"Q. Well, Mr. Benton, the *restriction now is 50 miles an hour,* *isn't it?*   *   *   *   "

From the above-quoted portion of the record it is apparent that counsel for plaintiffs, by swinging back and forth between past tense and present tense, and by discussing speed restrictions without specific indication of whether he referred to restrictions within entire railroad districts or to re-strictions at a smaller area within a district (such as at the Plaza Street crossing here involved), succeeded in confusing not only Benton, the wit-ness, but also the court itself. Counsel then seized upon the confusion which he himself had engendered, to not only bring before the jury the fact that the restriction at the Plaza Street crossing had been changed to 50 miles, but to emphasize that the change had taken place subsequent to the acci-dent. The admission of such improper evidence could not, and did not, tend to impeach the witness, who at no time had testified that the *Plaza Street* intersection speed had remained at 90 miles an hour up to the time of trial; on the contrary, the witness had clearly stated that the overall restriction in the fourth district (i.e., from Fullerton to San Diego) remained at 90 miles, but he had also several times referred to "curve restrictions and other forms of restrictions" within districts—references which were plainly understood by plaintiff's counsel, who himself likewise referred to such lesser restric-tions. Inasmuch as the issue of negligence on the part of defendants was close, it appears that the error of admitting such evidence of changed condi-tions was prejudicial.

Spence and McComb, JJ., concur.

Hypotheticals

(1) A sues X for damages for personal injuries arising out of A's slipping and falling on steps in a store owned and operated by X. A testifies that a strip of abrasive tape on the step on which she slipped was worn, and that the step was slip-pery. X calls B, the store manager, who testifies that the tape strips on the steps were not worn and that the steps were not slippery. In rebuttal, A offers to prove that a week after A's accident, X replaced the old strips of tape with new ones, and A of-fers in evidence photographs of the steps with the new strips of tape. X objects to A's offer of proof on the ground of the policy exclusion of evidence of subsequent re-medial conduct. What result?

(2) Assume the same facts as in Illustration (1), except that A adds to his offer of proof the fact that B, the store manager who testified for X, was the person who authorized installation of the new abrasive tape strips after A's accident. X makes the same objection that he makes in Illustration (1). How should the court rule?

(3) P, a savings company, sues D, a bank, for damages arising out of a long-period embezzlement of $500,000 by M, a manager of P's branch office. From

time to time, M placed the embezzled funds in a personal account with D and subsequently made withdrawals by checks to himself until all funds were withdrawn. P claims D was negligent in permitting M to make deposits and withdrawals from this account. D's defense is that P was negligent in its accounting and auditing procedures which allowed M to embezzle such a large amount without detection. After the embezzlement, P retained X, an accounting firm, to audit P and recommend accounting and auditing changes. P placed such recommended changes into effect after getting X's report. D makes a discovery motion to inspect and copy X's report. What result?

Chapter V

IMPEACHMENT AND CROSS EXAMINATION

PART A. THE RULE AGAINST IMPEACHING ONE'S OWN WITNESS AND OTHER FORENSIC PROBLEMS

KAPLAN AND WALTZ, THE TRIAL OF JACK RUBY

120–121 (1965).*

* * * Unlike the practice in most European countries, where the witness merely stands up and delivers a long narrative concerning what he knows about the case, in Anglo-American law the witnesses relate their stories through the question-and-answer method. Although some lawyers argue that by focusing the witnesses' attention on specific details, our method actually is simpler and faster, most lawyers would agree that it is in fact slower and more cumbersome. The reason it is used is that the rules of evidence in our jurisprudence are vastly more detailed, complicated and strict than those of most other countries. Relying on a jury untrained in the law, we make every possible effort to keep from the jurors the sort of information which they might rely on but which experience teaches is either unfair to the defendant or for some reason dangerously misleading. We therefore require the witness to give his answers in response to relatively pointed questions so that the opposing attorney, forewarned by the question that the jury may be about to hear inadmissible material, can object in time to prevent receipt of the damaging answer.

In Anglo-American law not only must the parties proceed by question and answer, but they must adhere to certain forms of questions. And the restrictions are far more severe on the side calling the witness to the stand. The examination of one's own witness—direct examination as distinguished from cross-examination—must be made without the use of leading questions, that is, questions which suggest their own answer. A typical leading question is, "Was the defendant's black automobile going about fifty miles an hour when you first saw it on the right, bearing down on you?" The witness may answer "Yes," but it is the attorney's version of the story that the jury hears. Leading questions, although technically prohibited, are generally used to save time on unimportant and background matters. "Is your name Joe Smith?" However, as soon as important matters are reached, most trial lawyers automatically switch from leading questions to avoid a barrage of objections which are properly sustained by the court.

A second major restriction encountered in direct examination is that the side calling the witness is, as lawyers say, "bound by his testimony." This means not that the lawyer must assume the truth of every fact testified to by his own witnesses but rather that he cannot argue with them or seek by further questioning to modify their testimony unless he can convince the judge that the witness is hostile or has taken him by surprise.

In cross-examination these restrictive rules do not apply. The cross-examiner can ask as many leading questions as he wishes and, if the

371

answers prove unsatisfactory, he can go at the matter again and again in as many different ways as he can devise to press the witness into delivering the desired answers.   *   *   *

MAGUIRE, EVIDENCE: COMMON SENSE AND COMMON LAW

41–43 (1947).*

Examination of Witnesses

In judicial and legislative provisions for the handling of witnesses the notion appears again and again that a litigant producing a witness vouches for, or in a sense commits his cause to, the probity of that witness and must consequently grin and bear it if the witness proves unfavorable. This may be a hazy heritage from the time when witnesses were not questioned as now, but rather, in the process termed compurgation, by the very weight of their oaths carried the day for the party in whose behalf they appeared. Or it may be a consequence of the fact that the presentation of evidence, particularly in jury trials began as a special privilege instead of as a right, with the result that a litigant would be denied leave to attack the credibility of a witness whom he had been granted the privilege of presenting. The notion does not stand up well under analytical criticism, because an honest man engaged in litigation cannot count upon having his choice of witnesses. Experts, to be sure, he may select within the limits of scientific controversy and scientific ethics, and in most commercial cases he may rest part of his reliance upon the testimony of associates likely to see matters his way. But in catch-as-catch-can litigation such as accident cases and criminal prosecutions the litigant who takes real witnesses as they come instead of trying to make artifical ones is often forced to put forward highly dubious human material.

One result of the vouching notion has been a doctrine that the party who places a witness on the stand and examines him directly or in chief may not impeach him if his testimony is disappointing or harmful. "Impeach" is a lawyers' word of art which may not be quite clear on first encounter. It really means something like "derogate from credibility". One impeaches a witness, for example, by seeking to show that he has a poor reputation for truth and veracity, or has been convicted of crime which reflects on veracity, or has out of court made statements inconsistent with his testimony, or is affected by some sort of bias with respect to the present litigation. Impeachment must be distinguished from contradicting one of your witnesses by counter-testimony of the others as to matters at issue on the merits. The latter process is always allowed. The anti-impeachment rule does not forbid contradiction.

The best argument concocted to sustain this "no impeachment of your own witness" doctrine is that if a witness finds himself exposed to battering by both sides, he may, to obtain the protective championship of one side, warp his testimony away from the truth to make it entirely favorable for that one side. The argument is not moving. To begin with, it stinks of the lamp, being manifestly some laborious scholar's rationalization of existing practice. Besides, if witnesses are such shrinking violets as this, the really thorough-going protective step would be to forbid impeachment by *anybody*. That is not usually done, although it may be brought about when *both* sides have called and examined the *same* witness to make out their respective cases. Finally and very practically, this argument is at loggerheads with the exception to the rule against impeaching one's own witnesses manifested in the case of the "necessary" witness. An example will suggest the scope of this exception. Very commonly in a will contest the proponent is required by law to call all the attesting witnesses of the alleged testamentary instrument, although he distrusts them and would like to pass them by. They thus become necessary or legally compelled witnesses, and because of the compulsion the proponent is allowed to impeach them if their testimony turns out adverse to the validity of the instrument they attested. But that opens such witnesses to hammering by both sides, and thus disregards the argument stated at the opening of this paragraph. And so, it is fair to remark, does the practice of having the trial judge call dubious witnesses to the stand, with permission for impeachment by all parties.

According to the best professional thought, sweeping prohibition of impeachment by a party of his own witnesses is nonsense—most regrettably not simple nonsense, but very complex nonsense; the underlying connotations extend far, as we shall see. It has been somewhat broken down here and there by decision and statute. Yet it has perverse vitality and will be with us in some jurisdictions for a long time to come.　　*　　*　　*

MATHEW, FORENSIC FABLES BY O

267–68 (1961).

THE BEGINNER WHO THOUGHT HE WOULD DO IT HIMSELF

A Beginner, in the Temporary Absence of his Leader, Found himself Opposed to a Big Pot in the Commercial Court. Though Greatly Alarmed, the Beginner Bore himself Bravely. To his Surprise and Delight the Beginner Managed to Cross-Examine the Big Pot's Principal Witness with Such Effect that he Needed a Good Deal of Rehabilitation. Rising to Re-Examine, the Big Pot Airily Observed to the Principal Witness: "I Suppose What You Meant by Your Last Answer was This," and Proceeded to Tell the Principal Witness Quite Clearly what he Meant. When the Beginner made a Dignified Protest the Judge Smilingly Suggested that the Big Pot might Shape his Question rather Differently. The Next Day the Beginner was in a County Court. The Plaintiff (for whom the Beginner Appeared) having Made an Awkward Admission to his Learned Friend on the Other Side, the Beginner Thought he would Employ the Excellent Formula of the Big Pot. He Did so. The Scene that Followed Beggars Description. The County Court Judge in a Voice of Thunder Ordered the Beginner to Sit Down. He then Rebuked the Beginner for his Gross Misconduct and Discussed the Question whether he would Commit him for Contempt, or Merely Report him to the General Council of the Bar. Finally he Expressed the Hope that the Incident would be a Lesson to the Beginner and Directed that the Case should be re-Heard on a Later Date before a Fresh Jury.

Moral.—*Wait till You're a Big Pot.*

See Federal Rules of Evidence 607, 611 at pp. 916–918; California Evidence Code § § 764, 767, 776, 785 at pp. 836, 837, 838, 841.

PART B.   CROSS EXAMINATION

1.   IN GENERAL*

SUSANNA AND THE ELDERS

(C. 130 B.C.).

from
THE BIBLE
designed to be read as living literature. The Old and the New
Testaments in The King James Version 1936
Simon and Schuster. New York

* * *

Then the two elders stood up in the midst of the people, and laid their hands upon her head. And she weeping looked up toward heaven: for her heart trusted in the Lord. And the elders said, "As we walked in the garden alone, this woman came in with two maids, and shut the garden doors, and sent the maids away. Then a young man, who there was hid, came unto her, and lay with her. Then we that stood in a corner of the garden, seeing this wickedness, ran unto them. And when we saw them together, the man we could not hold: for he was stronger than we, and opened the door, and leaped out. But having taken this woman, we asked who the young man was, but she would not tell us: these things so we testify."

Then the assembly believed them, as those that were the elders and judges of the people: so they condemned her to death.

Then Susanna cried out with a loud voice, and said, "O everlasting God, that knowest the secrets, and knowest all things before they be: thou knowest that they have borne false witness against me, and behold, I must die; whereas I never did such things as these men have maliciously invented against me."

The Lord heard her voice.

Therefore when she was led to be put to death, the Lord raised up the holy spirit of a young youth, whose name was Daniel: who cried with a loud voice, "I am clear from the blood of this woman."

Then all the people turned them toward him, and said, "What mean these words that thou hast spoken?"

So he standing in the midst of them said, "Are ye such fools, ye sons of Israel, that without examination or knowledge of the truth ye have condemned a daughter of Israel? Return again to the place of judgment: for they have borne false witness against her."

Wherefore all the people turned again in haste, and the elders said unto him, "Come, sit down among us, and show it us, seeing God hath given thee the honour of an elder."

Then said Daniel unto them, "Put these two aside one far from another, and I will examine them."

---

*Cross examination is also discussed in
Chapter I, Making the Record, supra.

So when they were put asunder one from another, he called one of them, and said unto him, "O thou that art waxed old in wickedness, now thy sins which thou has committed aforetime are come to light: for thus hast pronounced false judgment, and hast condemned the innocent, and hast let the guilty go free; albeit the Lord saith, 'The innocent and righteous shalt thou not slay.' Now then, if thou hast seen her, tell me under what tree sawest thou them companying together?"

Who answered, "Under the mastic tree."

And Daniel said, "Very well; thou hast lied against thine own head; for even now the angel of God hath received the sentence of God to cut thee in two."

So he put him aside, and commanded to bring the other, and said unto him, "O thou seed of Chanaan, and not of Juda, beauty hath deceived thee, and lust hath perverted thine heart. Thus have ye dealt with the daughters of Israel, and they for fear companied with you: but the daughter of Juda would not abide your wickedness. Now therefore tell me under what tree didst thou take them companying together?"

Who answered, "Under a holm tree."

Then said Daniel unto him, "Well; thou hast also lied against thine own head: for the angel of God waiteth with the sword to cut thee in two, that he may destroy you."

With that all the assembly cried out with a loud voice, and praised God, who saveth them that trust in him. And they arose against the two elders, for Daniel had convicted them of false witness by their own mouth: and according to the law of Moses they did unto them in such sort as they maliciously intended to do their neighbour: and they put them to death. Thus the innocent blood was saved the same day.

Therefore Chelcias and his wife praised God for their daughter Susanna, with Joacim her husband, and all the kindred, because there was no dishonesty found in her.

MATHEW, FORENSIC FABLES BY O

87–88 (1961).

MR. WHITEWIG AND THE RASH QUESTION

MR. WHITEWIG was Greatly Gratified when the Judge of Assize Invited him to Defend a Prisoner who was Charged with Having Stolen a Pair of Boots, a Mouse-Trap, and Fifteen Packets of Gold Flakes. It was his First Case and he Meant to Make a Good Show. Mr. Whitewig Studied the Depositions Carefully and Came to the Conclusion that a Skillful Cross-Examination of the Witnesses and a Tactful Speech would Secure the Acquittal of the Accused. When the Prisoner (an Ill-Looking Person) was Placed in the Dock, Mr. Whitewig Approached that Receptacle and Informed the Prisoner that he Might, if he Wished, Give Evidence on Oath. From the Prisoner's Reply (in which he Alluded to Grandmothers and Eggs) Mr. Whitewig Gathered that he did not Propose to Avail Himself of this Privilege. The Case Began. At First All Went Well. The Prosecutor Admitted to Mr. Whitewig that he Could not be Sure that the Man he had Seen Lurking in the Neighbourhood of his Emporium was the Prisoner; and the Prosecutor's Assistant Completely Failed to Identify the Boots, the

Mouse-Trap, or the Gold Flakes by Pointing to any Distinctive Peculiarities
which they Exhibited. By the Time the Police Inspector Entered the Wit-
ness-Box Mr. Whitewig Felt that the Case was Won. Mr. Whitewig Cun-
ningly Extracted from the Inspector the Fact that the Prisoner had Joined
Up in 1914, and that the Prisoner's Wife was Expecting an Addition to her
Family. He was about to Sit Down when a Final Question Occurred to him.
"Having Regard to this Man's Record," he Stearnly Asked, "How Came
You to Arrest him?" The Inspector Drew a Bundle of Blue Documents from
the Recesses of his Uniform, and, Moistening his Thumb, Read therefrom.
Mr. Whitewig Learned in Silent Horror that the Prisoner's Record Included
Nine Previous Convictions. When the Prisoner was Asked whether he had
Anything to say why Sentence should not be Passed Upon him, he Said
some Very Disagreeable Things about the Mug who had Defended him.

Moral.—*Leave Well Alone.*

KEETON, TRIAL TACTICS AND METHODS

87–90 (1954).*
[All footnotes omitted.]

Cross-examination is that phase of the trial which has potentialities of
being the most spectacular. It affords the opportunity for the most successful employment of an aptitude for quick thinking, sharp repartee, and
dramatics. To excel in these, one must have native ability. Nearly everyone
interested in trial work does have a degree of such ability, however, and it
can be developed by practice and experience, just as a talent for music or
acting may be so developed. But the talent for cross-examination, in this
sense, is the lesser part of the secret of effective cross-examination. Nearly
all effective cross-examination is planned, to one degree or another. For one
interested in entering trial practice without experience, adequate planning
can often produce effective cross-examination from the first. For one who is
experienced, greater success in cross-examination is possible as he prepares
more diligently and thoroughly for it. This chapter is devoted to consideration of methods customarily used in effective cross-examination, and ways
of planning for their use. In this broader sense of "talent," one can enter the
courtroom with considerable talent for cross-examination even in his
earliest cases.

The potential aims of cross-examination may be classified into four
groups: (1) discrediting the testimony of the witness being examined; (2) using testimony of this witness to discredit the unfavorable testimony of other
witnesses; (3) using the testimony of this witness to corroborate the favorable testimony of other witnesses; and (4) using the testimony of this witness to contribute independently to the favorable development of your own
case.

Accomplishing one of these aims may require an entirely different
method of dealing with the witness from that appropriate for another aim.
A method of cross-examination designed to serve one aim may defeat another. In such instances, adequate planning requires an appraisal of the relative advantages associated with each of these aims, as a factor in the
choice of methods.

*Copyright, 1954 by Prentice-Hall, Inc.

Your selection of methods of cross-examination of the witness will be influenced also by the type of witness before you—for example, whether the witness is an argumentative one, an expert, a woman, or one of a series of witnesses who appear to have a memorized story. The age, education, and mentality of the witness are other important factors. The most ignorant witness is often the hardest to cross-examine because you cannot get him set up to knock over. Also, you must exercise great care to avoid creating jury sympathy for him because you are exposing his ignorance or illiteracy. Your aim is to condemn his testimony as unreliable without condemning the witness for being ignorant. The infliction of personal ridicule upon an ignorant witness, or sarcastic treatment of the witness, may be regarded by jurors as your taking an unfair advantage of the differences in intelligence and education between yourself and the witness.

Some consideration should be given to your general attitude and demeanor toward the witness. Should you let your contempt for the reprobate be obvious for the jury to see, if you feel that way about him? Or should you be the paragon of courtesy? Usually an attitude of courtesy toward the witness should be adopted, for although the jurors expect a lawyer to be an advocate, they very quickly take up sympathy for the witness if they get the idea that the lawyer is badgering the witness unfairly. It is quite possible to be very polite and yet convey to the jury your distrust of the witness' testimony.

Most trial yarns concerning cross-examination are tales of the brilliant cross-examination which won the lawsuit. Others tell of the inept cross-examination which lost the lawsuit. While both types of yarns are usually influenced by a recognized license, like that of the poet and fisherman, they are founded on truths.

These are some of the risks which you incur in cross-examination:

(1) Confronting a witness with a prior written statement inconsistent with his present testimony may result in proof of other facts recorded in the statement and not previously proven, or it may result in incidental disclosure of the existence of liability insurance, where its existence would have been unknown to the jury otherwise.

(2) Confronting the witness with inconsistency between his testimony and that of your own witness may result in impeachment of the testimony of your own witness.

(3) The cross-examination intended to show want of good opportunity for observation of the facts related may serve only to demonstrate that the opportunity was good.

(4) An attempt to prove or even actual proof of bad character of the witness may provoke the sympathy of the jury for the witness and the case he supports.

(5) The cross-examination intended to reveal indirectly the bias of the witness by committing him to an untenable extreme may result in strengthening the direct examination.

(6) The cross-examination intended to bring out matters about which your adversary failed to inquire, in the belief that the answers will be favorable to your client, may result only in more evidence favorable to the adverse party who called the witness.

(7)   Calling on the witness to repeat and elaborate his testimony, as a foundation for proof of prior contradictions or inconsistencies, may emphasize and strengthen the witness' testimony if he has a plausible explanation for the apparent inconsistencies.

(8)   Cross-examination intended to show bias from animosity associated with termination of employment may provoke sympathy for the discharged employee.

(9)   Asking a "why" question in the belief that the witness can have no reasonable explanation may result in expression of prejudicial arguments which would have been clearly inadmissible in the absence of the invitation by the open question.

(10)   Insistence upon a clear answer from an evasive witness may lead to an unexpected and unfavorable disclosure.

(11)   Defendant's cross-examination of plaintiff's medical expert regarding fees may emphasize plaintiff's expenses and cause a higher damages finding.

(12)   Cross-examination of an expert concerning his qualifications may serve only to bolster less adequate proof of those qualifications during direct examination.

(13)   Methods of cross-examination intended to exact disclosures from an unwilling witness may be harmful because of a jury reaction that they are unfair methods.

2.   SCOPE OF CROSS EXAMINATION

CONLEY v. MERVIS

Supreme Court of Pennsylvania, 1936.
324 Pa. 577, 188 A. 350.

KEPHART, Chief Justice.   Appellees, plaintiffs in the court below, were injured by a truck bearing dealer's license plates owned by appellant, the defendant. Defendant denied ownership of the truck and that the driver was his servant. It appeared that dealer's license plates No. 3X547 for 1931 were on the truck at the time of the accident, and defendant was called by plaintiffs as on cross-examination and asked whether he had owned the license plates. Having admitted ownership, his counsel proposed to examine him further in connection therewith: whether they had been loaned to any one and whether the truck was driven by his servant in the scope of his employment. The court below refused to permit the examination, holding that these matters were part of defendant's case and could not be brought out under the guise of cross-examination. The defendant was forced to introduce this testimony as part of his own case. The issues having been submitted to the jury, it disagreed, and the refusal of defendant's request for judgment on the whole record caused this appeal.

It is conceded that the ownership of dealer's license plates appearing on a motor vehicle raises a rebuttable presumption that the truck belonged to the owner of the tags, and was driven by his agent or servant in the scope of employment; and this, without more, would require the submission of these questions to the jury, even though rebutted by the uncontradicted oral testimony of the dealer's witnesses. Defendant contends, however, that the court below should have permitted his cross-examination to embrace any matter touching upon or connected with the question of ownership of the tags, including all the inferences arising therefrom, and, if this had been allowed, the prima facie case arising from ownership would have been overcome by plaintiffs' own witness.

The scope of cross-examination in Pennsylvania is more restricted than that permitted in England, where it may embrace any matter material to the case, irrespective of whether it relates to a point testified to by the witness in his examination in chief. In this state it has been frequently stated that cross-examination must be strictly confined to matters touched upon in direct examination. This viewpoint originated in general statements which appear frequently in our cases discussing the permissible scope of cross-examination. "The cross-examination, as a general thing, is only regular when it is confined to the testimony given by the witness in chief." Helser v. McGrath, 52 Pa. 531, 532, 533. "It is certainly well settled in this state that cross-examination, must be confined to the matters which have been stated in the examination in chief." Jackson v. Litch, 62 Pa. 451, 455. Expressions of a similar nature will be found in numerous other cases. But this rigid rule has not been closely adhered to, and we have created well-defined exceptions. The conception that these general pronouncements are an accurate statement of the rule is erroneous. It disregards the limitations imposed on its operation and ignores the fundamental reasons for the imposition of any restrictions on the scope of cross-examination.

The underlying reason for confining the scope of cross-examination is to promote order and method in the presentation of a case. Each party must have an opportunity to present his side of the case without the introduction of matters unrelated to his case in chief and not touched upon in his evidence. The Pennsylvania rule makes the issues as clear as possible to the jury by reducing to a minimum the possibility of the intermingling of matters purely defensive in character with the facts of a plaintiff's case. The issues are clarified and confusion eliminated to the greatest possible extent by the separation of their respective contentions and the testimony produced in support thereof.   *   *   *

Nothing is better established than that cross-examination in many cases may reach beyond the facts elicited on direct examination and embrace new matter. As early as 1848 Chief Justice Gibson, the creator of the Pennsylvania rule, in Bank v. Fordyce, 9 Pa. 275, at page 277, 49 Am.Dec. 561, said: "A party is entitled [on cross-examination] to bring out every circumstance relating to a fact which an adverse witness is called to prove." Or, as the rule is sometimes stated, it is competent on cross-examination to develop all circumstances within the witness' knowledge which qualify or destroy his direct testimony, although strictly speaking, they constitute new matter and are part of the cross-examiner's own case. In Smith v. Traction Co., 202 Pa. 54, 57, 51 A. 345, 346, quoted with approval in the Felski Case, this court, after stating the broad principle that cross-examination should be confined to matters testified to in chief and cannot be used to bring out new matter in defense, said: "But it is equally true that, when the cross-examination is germane to what is inquired into in chief, or tends to elicit facts which, as in this case, the plaintiff ought to have brought out as part of the case, and which the court and jury should have known from him and his witnesses, the defendant should be allowed to develop what is withheld, intentionally or otherwise." Therefore it may be regarded as definitely settled that cross-examination may embrace any matter germane to the direct examination, qualifying or destroying it, or tending to develop facts which have been improperly suppressed or ignored by the plaintiff. It is equally established that, where a plaintiff offers himself as a witness, he may be cross-examined as to anything relevant, provided it is not purely a matter of defense, on the theory he should not withhold matters materially affecting his rights and facts may be elicited on cross-examination which are part of the res gestae, even though in a sense they constitute new matter. Finally, the decision as to the proper scope of cross-examination rests within the trial court's sound discretionary power, and its failure to properly limit it is not grounds for reversal in the absence of apparent injury as a result of the error.

The burden rested upon plaintiffs to prove that the truck driver was defendant's servant and that he was engaged in his master's business at the time of the accident. Defendant's testimony, on examination by plaintiffs, admitting ownership of the license plates, had much greater significance than the fact of ownership would seem to indicate and enabled them to meet this burden. The real purpose of a question may reach far beyond its apparent import. Under our decisions with respect to dealer's license plates, this admission had embodied in it not only the fact of ownership but inferences sufficient to take the case to the jury: namely, that the motor vehicle was owned by defendant; that the driver was his servant; and that the vehicle was being driven at the time on his business. It was not the fact of ownership which was harmful but the implications arising from it. Defendant proposed to cross-examine the witness as to the fact of ownership and the inferences that flowed from it, and, had he been permitted to do so plaintiffs' own testimony would have deprived them of the benefit of the presumption. It would have shown not only that he did not own the truck and that the driver had never been in his employ, but that the plates were taken from his place of business without his knowledge or consent or that of any one authorized to grant consent. This uncontradicted evidence would have rebutted the presumption in plaintiffs' case by their own witness. The trial court refused to permit this examination and compelled defendant to produce this evidence as part of his own case, thereby requiring submission of the issue to the jury.

The testimony given by defendant corresponded exactly with what his counsel had proposed to bring out on cross-examination. It revealed that the license plates were taken from his garage without his permission and given to one Samuels, an owner or operator of the Star Produce Company which owned the delivery truck, for use on the truck. Defendant had no interest in the produce company or the truck, and the driver of the truck had never been employed by him. The court below in refusing to permit this testimony on cross-examination proceeded upon the theory that it must be strictly and literally confined to the matter actually testified to in chief. It held that, as defendant's testimony had been limited to the question of ownership of the license plates on the truck at the time of the accident, his examination by his own counsel could not extend beyond this precise matter.

This strict limitation entirely ignored the purpose for which defendant's ownership of the license tags was introduced in evidence and its legal effect as proof of the existence of a master and servant relationship. This evidence was produced exclusively for the purpose of giving rise to a presumption of such relationship. The inferences flowing therefrom enabled plaintiffs to make out a prima facie case, and their probative value was the impelling and vital reason for securing from defendant an admission of ownership of the license plates. The fact of ownership, standing alone and stripped of these inferences, meant nothing to their case. The inferences are the damaging part of this testimony. Here is a patent case where cross-examination would be of little value if restricted to the actual facts elicited on direct examination. One of the purposes of cross-examination is to enable the jury to ascertain the truth of relevant facts deposed by a witness on direct examination and to properly guide them in drawing material inferences therefrom. If cross-examination is to be of any service, it must not be limited to the precise facts brought out on direct examination, but must extend to all inferences, deductions, or conclusions which may be drawn therefrom. In Haun v. McCabe, supra, where the defendant sought to create an erroneous impression by securing an answer from his witness which gave rise to an inference favoring him if additional facts were not brought to light to explain it away, this court, speaking through Mr. Justice Drew, said (308 Pa. 431, at page 438, 162 A. 906, 908): "Standing alone, the answer to the question asked by defendant's counsel would have left the jury with an erroneous and distorted view of plaintiff's testimony at the inquest. It was entirely proper to correct such a wrong impression on cross-examination by eliciting facts, germane to what was inquired into in chief, which qualified or destroyed the effect of the testimony on direct examination. [Authorities cited.]" In other words, the testimony in chief, for the purpose of determining the proper scope of cross-examination, consists not only of the bare facts brought out but in addition includes all inferences or deductions which may be made from them.

In the case at bar the court below should have permitted defendant's counsel to develop any facts pertaining to the inferences based upon ownership of the license plates or tending to qualify or destroy them. Plaintiffs cannot disclaim part of defendant's testimony simply on the ground it was unfavorable to them. Defendant was entitled to explain away the adverse effects of the facts elicited from him by plaintiffs' counsel, which necessarily include all possible relevant inferences, and his explanation bound them, if uncontradicted. Where a party calls a person adversely interested as if under cross-examination, he is bound by the testimony if uncontradicted. Readshaw v. Montgomery, supra, and authorities cited therein. Consequently defendant's explanation of his ownership and its inferences must be considered as part of plaintiffs' testimony and binding upon them.

Aside from the fact that the proposed examination of defendant by his counsel covered inferences flowing from his direct examination, there is another reason why it should have been permitted. As previously mentioned, the burden rested upon plaintiffs to establish affirmatively that the truck driver was defendant's servant and acting within his scope of employment. Having chosen to place defendant on the witness stand and examine him as to facts bearing on this question, plaintiffs were not at liberty to bring out only those matters favorable to them and ignore or otherwise suppress facts of an adverse and harmful character bearing a direct relation to it. To permit the concealment or suppression of facts which are germane or related to an issue touched upon in direct examination and are not purely matters of defense would be to bestow upon a plaintiff an unfair advantage and enable him to have the case submitted to the jury, in spite of the fact his own witnesses possessed knowledge of facts which would make it impossible for him to make out a prima facie case if these facts appeared on the record as part of his own case. This course would be simply juggling with judicial procedure. Any limitation on the scope of cross-examination opening the way for such an absurd situation would defeat one of the vital reasons for its existence. That the testimony on direct examination does not go sufficiently far to prove the ultimate fact in issue is immaterial. It is enough if it tends to establish it. Where testimony has been adduced relevant to a particular issue involved, cross-examination may embrace any circumstances pertaining thereto, though prejudicial to plaintiff's case and reaching beyond the direct testimony. The chief reason for limiting cross-examination is to promote order and clarity in the presentation of a case and prevent confusion, but there are circumstances where inculpatory evidence may appear in one's own case. To hold otherwise would be to give a party an opportunity to suppress and hide facts, intentionally or otherwise, which, though not affirmative defenses, would bar his right to recover. The Pennsylvania limitations on cross-examination were never designed to provide a cloak for the concealment of material facts pertaining to issues touched upon in direct examination.

The refusal to permit defendant's counsel to examine him regarding a master and servant relationship worked a serious injury, constituting an abuse of the trial court's discretionary power. Where a party has been improperly denied the right to cross-examine a witness, and the testimony (which should have been admitted as cross-examination) appears as part of his own case, on appeal it will be considered as though given on cross-examination. While it is true that, where plaintiff's case rests upon a presumption, he is entitled to have it submitted to the jury though rebutted by defendant's uncontradicted parol evidence (Coates v. Commercial Credit Co., supra), where the presumption is rebutted by plaintiff's own evidence, it disappears and a nonsuit will be granted (Readshaw v. Montgomery, supra; Felski v. Zeidman, supra). Plaintiffs failed to carry the burden of proof and judgment should have been entered for defendant on the whole record.   *   *   *

Reversed.

See Federal Rules of Evidence 611 at p. 918; California Evidence Codes §§ 772 & 773, at p. 838.

PART C.   CROSS EXAMINATION AND IMPEACHMENT

1.   CHARACTER OF THE WITNESS

See California Evidence Code § 780 at p.

A.   PRIOR BAD ACTS

PEOPLE v. SORGE

Court of Appeals of New York, 1950.
301 N.Y. 198, 93 N.E.2d 637.

FULD, Judge.   In this prosecution for the crime of abortion, the evidence given on behalf of the People was more than sufficient to justify the verdict of guilt—for the conflicting testimony of the victim and of the defendant but presented a question of veracity and credibility for the jury. Accordingly, an affirmance is compelled, unless prejudicial error was committed by the district attorney in conducting his cross-examination of defendant. He interrogated her about abortions which she had allegedly performed upon four other women and, after she had answered his questions in the negative, pressed her further as to whether she had not signed a statement admitting that she had aborted one of the women, as to whether that particular operation had not furnished the predicate for her plea of guilty to the crime of practicing medicine without a license, and as to whether she had not been present while a fifth abortion had been performed.

There can, of course, be no doubt as to the propriety of cross-examining a defendant concerning the commission of other specific criminal or immoral acts. A defendant, like any other witness, may be "interrogated upon cross-examination in regard to any vicious or criminal act of his life" that has a bearing on his credibility as a witness. It does not matter that the offenses or the acts inquired about are similar in nature and character to the crime for which the defendant is standing trial. See People v. Jones, supra, 297 N.Y. 459, 74 N.E.2d 173: murder prosecution, defendant interrogated as to another murder; People v. Brown, supra, 284 N.Y. 753, 31 N.E.2d 511: murder prosecution, defendant interrogated as to another murder; People v. Alex, 279 N.Y. 766, 18 N.E.2d 858: murder prosecution, defendant interrogated as to another murder; People v. Madison, 3 Cal.2d 668, 678, 46 P.2d 159: murder prosecution, defendant interrogated as to assault with gun; State v. Palko, 121 Conn. 669, 678–679, 188 A. 657: murder prosecution, defendant interrogated as to subsequent robbery. And if the questions have basis in fact and are asked by the district attorney in good faith, they are not rendered improper merely because of their number. Entitled to delve into past misdeeds, the prosecutor may not arbitrarily be shackled by the circumstance that the defendant has pursued a specialized field of crime and has committed many offenses.

Nor is it improper for a district attorney to continue his cross-examination about a specific crime after a defendant has denied committing it. As long as he acts in good faith, in the hope of inducing the witness to abandon his negative answers, the prosecutor may question further. In other words, a negative response will not fob off further interrogation of the witness himself, for, if it did, the witness would have it within his power to render futile most cross-examination. The rule is clear that while a witness' testimony regarding collateral matters may not be refuted by the calling of other witnesses or by the production of extrinsic evidence there is no prohibition against examining the witness himself further on the chance that he may change his testimony or his answer.

This principle covers not only the questions put to defendant which were based upon her prior statement, but also the questions grounded upon her prior conviction—following her guilty plea—of practicing medicine without a license. Since a witness may be examined properly with respect to criminal acts that have escaped prosecution, there is no reason why indictment followed by conviction should proscribe inquiry as to what those acts were. A knowledge of those acts casts light upon the degree of turpitude involved and assists the jury in evaluating the witness' credibility—all the more so in a case such as the present where conviction of a crime such as practicing medicine without a license gives no inkling whatsoever of the acts upon which the charge and conviction against defendant had been predicated. In point of fact, the matters sought to be elicited by the cross-examination were precisely those matters that could have been established by proof of the official record of defendant's conviction—a course which the People could unquestionably have pursued under section 2444 of the Penal Law, Consol.Laws, c. 40. See State v. Brames, supra, 154 Wash. 304, 310, 282 P. 48, involving a statute identical with section 2444.

While, for the reasons outlined above, we cannot single out any questions and say that they were improper as a matter of law, there still remains the problem of whether the cumulative effect of the sustained cross-examination constituted error, despite the propriety of the individual queries. Basic in this connection is the rule that "The manner and extent of the cross-examination lies largely within the discretion of the trial judge." [Citations omitted.]

Accordingly, although there may be room for a difference of opinion as to the scope and extent of cross-examination, the wide latitude and the broad discretion that must be vouchsafed to the trial judge, if he is to administer a trial effectively, precludes this court, in the absence of "plain abuse and injustice", La Beau v. People, 34 N.Y. 223, 230, from substituting its judgment for his and from making that difference of opinion, in the difficult and ineffable realm of discretion, a basis for reversal.

We may not here say that prejudice or "injustice" resulted from the district attorney's interrogation or that permitting the vigorous cross-examination constituted "plain abuse". The evidence against defendant was clear and, since the outcome of the case depended almost entirely upon whether the testimony of the victim or of the defendant was credited by the jury, there was good and ample reason to give both sides a relatively free hand on cross-examination in order to afford the jury full opportunity to weigh and evaluate the credibility of each witness.

The judgment should be affirmed.

Loughran, C.J., and Lewis, Conway, Desmond, Dye and Froessel, JJ., concur.

Judgment affirmed.

WELLMAN, THE ART OF CROSS-EXAMINATION
56–60 (1903, 1962).*

Henry E. Lazarus, a prominent merchant in this city, was indicted a few years ago by the Federal Grand Jury, charged with the offense of bribing a United States officer and violation of the Sabotage Act, but was honorably acquitted by a jury after a thirty minute deliberation. It was during the height of the war and Mr. Lazarus was a very large manufacturer of rubber coats and had manufactured hundreds of thousands for the Government under contract. The Government for its protection employed large numbers of inspectors, and in the heat and excitement of war times these inspectors occasionally tried to "make good." One of these efforts resulted in the indictment of Lazarus.

The chief witness against Lazarus was Charles L. Fuller, Supervising Inspector attached to the Depot Quartermaster's Office in New York City. Fuller testified that Lazarus gave money to him to influence him in regard to his general duties as an inspector, and to overlook the fact that Lazarus was manufacturing defective coats and thereby violating the Sabotage Act.

Martin W. Littleton acted as chief counsel for the defense and was fully appreciative of Mr. Lazarus's high character and of his conscientious discharge of his duties in the manufacture of material for the Government. He was also well informed as to the general character and history of Fuller. After Fuller testified in chief, he was first questioned closely as to the time when he became an employee of the Government, counsel knowing that he was *required to make and sign and swear to an application as to his prior experience.*

A messenger had been sent to the Government files to get the original of this application, signed by the witness, and came into court with the document in his hand just as counsel was putting the following question:

Q.   "Did you sign such an application?"

A.   "I did, sir."

Q.   "Did you swear to it?"

A.   "No, I did not swear to it."

Q.   "I show you your name signed on the bottom of this blank, and ask you if you signed that?"

A.   "Yes, sir."

Q.   "Do you see it is sworn to?"

A.   "I had forgotten it."

Q.   "You see there is a seal on it?"

A.   "I had forgotten that also."

Q.   "This application appears to be subscribed on the 24th of May, 1918, by Charles Lawrence Fuller."

A.   "It must be right if I have sworn to it on that date."

Q.   "Do you remember in May, 1918, that you signed and swore to this application?"

A.   "That is so, I must have sworn to it, sir."

Q.   "Do you remember it?"

A.   "Let me look at it and I can probably refresh my memory." (Paper handed to witness)

Q.   "Look at the signature. Does that help you?"

A.   "That is my signature."

Q.   "You said that. Do you remember in May, 1918, you signed and swore to this?"

A.   "Well, the date is there."

Q.   "Do you know that?"

A.   "Yes, sir, I must have sworn to it. I don't remember the date."

Q.   "Don't you remember you signed your name, Charles Lawrence Fuller, there?"

A.   "I did, sir."

Q.   "And you swore to this paper and signed it?"

A.   "That date is correct there, yes, sir."

Q.   "Don't you remember you swore to it the date you signed it?"

A.   "I swore to it."

Q.   "Was your name Fuller?"

A.   "Yes, sir."

Q.   "Has your name always been Fuller?"

A.   "No, sir."

Q.   "What was your name?"

The witness protested against any further inquiry along that line, but counsel was permitted to show that his name at one time was Finkler and that he changed his name, back and forth, from Finkler to Fuller.

Counsel then proceeded to bring the witness down to the actual oath he had taken in his application.

Q.   "Now, Mr. Fuller, in your application you made to the Government, on which I showed you your signature and affidavit, you attached your picture, did you not?"

A.   "Yes, sir."

Q.   "And you stated in your application you were born in Atlanta, Georgia, did you not?"

A.   "Yes, sir."

Q.   "You were asked, when you sought this position, these questions: 'When employed, the years and the months,' and you wrote in, 'February, 1897 to August, 1917, number of years 20; Where employed

—Brooklyn; Name of employer—Vulcan Proofing Company; Amount of salary,—$37.50 a week; also superintendent in the rubber and compound room.' "

Q. "You wrote that, didn't you?"

A. "Yes, sir."

Q. "And swore to that, didn't you?"

A. "Yes, sir."

Q. "Now, were you employed from February, 1897, to August, 1917, twenty years, with the Vulcan Proofing Company?"

A. "No, sir."

Q. "That was not true, was it?"

A. "No, sir."

Q. "And had you been assistant superintendent of the rubber and compound room?"

A. "No, sir."

Q. "That was false, wasn't it?"

A. "Yes, sir."

Q. " 'And through my experience as chief inspector of the rubber and slicker division,' that was false, wasn't it?"

A. "Yes, sir."

Q. "You knew it was false, didn't you?"

A. "Yes, sir."

Q. "And you knew you were swearing to a falsehood when you swore to it?"

A. "Yes, sir."

Q. "And you swore to it intentionally?"

A. "Yes, sir."

Q. "And you knew you were committing perjury when you swore to it?"

A. "I did not look at it in that light."

Q. "Didn't you know you were committing perjury by swearing and pretending you had been twenty years in this business?"

A. "Yes, sir."

Q. "And you are swearing now, aren't you?"

A. "Yes, sir."

Q. "In a matter in which a man's liberty is involved?"

A. "Yes, sir."

Q. "And you know that the jury is to be called upon to consider whether you are worthy of belief or not, don't you?"

A. "Yes, sir."

Q. "When you swore to this falsehood deliberately, and wrote it in your handwriting, you knew it was false, you swore to it intentionally, and you knew that you were committing perjury, didn't you?"

A.   "I did not look at it in that light."

Q.   "Well, now, when you know you are possibly swearing away the liberty of a citizen of this community, do you look at it in the same light?"

A.   "Yes, sir, I do."

Mr. Littleton then uncovered the fact that the witness, instead of having been twenty years superintendent of a rubber room with the Vulcan Proofing Company, as he had sworn in his own handwriting, was a stag entertainer in questionable houses, was a barker at a Coney Island show, was an advance agent of a cheap road show and had been published in the paper as having drawn checks that were worthless, the witness fully admitting all of the details of his twenty years of questionable transactions. The result was his utter collapse so far as his credibility was concerned, and the Government's case collapsed with him.

The point of the cross-examination and the design of the cross-examiner was to get the witness at the outset of his cross-examination in a position from which he could not possibly extricate himself, by confronting him with this document, written in his own handwriting in which he would be obliged to admit that he had sworn falsely. The witness having been thoroughly subjugated by this process would then, as he actually did, confess to twenty years of gadding about in questionable employment, under different names, and thus completely destroy himself as a reliable witness in the eyes of the jury.

HOUSE, GREAT TRIALS OF FAMOUS LAWYERS
180–81 (1962).

Max Steuer had the task of cross-examining Representative Foelker, a very popular member of Congress, who was the crucial witness against Steuer's client in a prosecution for bribery. When Steuer began his preparation for trial his * * * mental picture of Foelker's career was on the usual pattern of the crusader in politics. The first essential is that he be beholden to none. This most frequently results, in a young man, from a secure background of position and affluence, both generally inherited. Mr. Thain* gave an outline of Foelker's history. He was a German immigrant reaching this country in his early teens. After a short period in Troy, he settled in Brooklyn and attended public school. He left school early to go to work. He got a job in a law office, where he progressed from the minor tasks to a clerkship, eventually studying for the bar and being admitted. At the same time he interested himself in politics with the results already seen. So, in addition to being a knight errant he was also an Horatio Alger hero.

Now whatever Steuer may or may not have known about a Galahad career he was perfectly familiar with the life of the "Rags-to-Riches" type. He had lived it and when he got back to his office he compared his meager information with his intimate knowledge of the background. Two points loomed up. The first was that a man of that background gets rapid political preferment by being an asset first to a ward-heeler, then to a district leader. The most obvious service is the production of votes and the first vote to be

*[The Prosecutor].

produced is one's own. He decided to look into Foelker's voting record. It proved interesting. Foelker had followed the adage about voting early—by a year at least.

Secondly, in order to take the bar examination a candidate who is not a law-school graduate must pass a certain number of examinations set by the Board of Regents. The Regents examinations of those days were about the present equivalent of the graduation examinations for a junior high school. But they were all factual. An unprepared candidate could not pass them. There is obviously no way of knowing who won the battle of Lookout Mountain, the conjugations of the French irregular verbs or how to obtain the square root of X^2-Y^2 unless you have learned the answers. In the thumbnail sketch of Foelker, the necessary schooling was missing. He decided to find out how Foelker passed his Regents examinations.

Inquiry at the Board of Regents showed that the examination papers had been destroyed but the notation of the results, the correspondence and the like had been preserved. Foelker did remarkably well but the subject in which he must have been most proficient, German, did not appear in the list of his subjects. What writings there were from Foelker were not in a German script. And although Foelker had a residence and a business address at the time, the Regents Board were directed to correspond with him, care of Solinsky, at 54 Rutgers Street. Max Solinsky was traced and found. He proved to be a professional examination taker and was currently in Sing Sing prison for taking a civil-service examination under a false name.

That was all the ammunition there was, and it needed careful handling. In the first place there are the rules of evidence. When a witness takes the stand he puts his character in issue, and he can be cross-examined about anything in his life that will show he is not fit to be believed. But as to anything that he was not asked about on his direct examination, his answer is final and cannot be contradicted. For instance, if a lady takes the stand and testifies that the defendant stole her purse, you can call witnesses to show that she never had a purse, or that she was in Chicago at the time, or anything else to show that the purse was not stolen. But if you want to prove that she is no lady you must prove it out of her own mouth. You may have a dozen witnesses to show that she ran a gambling house, or tortured stray cats, or engaged in any number of activities that are not looked upon with approbation, but if she denies them (and you must ask her) that is the end of it.

Mr. Steuer had no illusions about Foelker's knowledge of this rule. If he was not already acquainted with it, he would be when he took the stand. Therefore he had to be so enmeshed by the time he was confronted with something important that a denial would be unavailing. But to get him in the toils would involve a series of questions about his schooling to which entirely credible answers would be that he did not remember. Who does remember at the age of 35 what he learned in school? Foelker had to have no excuse for not remembering. Mr. Steuer wrote Thain a letter telling him that he was going to question Foelker on these subjects, and asked him to refresh his recollection. If he ignored the request the jury would see that he had a good reason for doing it. On the other hand it would certainly warn Foelker that this incident was known and his care would make the questioning more difficult. It could not be helped.   *   *   *

STATE v. OSWALT

Supreme Court of Washington, 1963.
62 Wash.2d 118, 381 P.2d 617.

HAMILTON, Judge. Defendant appeals, upon a short record, from a conviction of robbery and first degree burglary. During trial, a defense of alibi was introduced. Error is assigned to the admission of certain rebuttal testimony, defendant contending such evidence constituted impeachment on a collateral matter.

The short record before us (testimony of two witnesses) indicates that on July 14, 1961, two armed men entered the King County residence of Frank L. Goodell. One man stood guard over a number of people at the home. The other man took Mr. Goodell to a Tradewell store and forced him to open the safe and turn over the money therein. Defendant was identified as one of the two men.

In presenting his defense of alibi, defendant called a Mr. August Ardiss of Portland, Oregon. On direct examination Mr. Ardiss testified in substance that: his wife and he operated a restaurant in Portland; he was acquainted with the defendant, as a fairly regular patron of the restaurant; defendant was in the restaurant at such times on July 14, 1961, as to render it impossible, as a practical matter, for defendant to be in Seattle at the time of the offense charged; and he remembered this occasion because defendant had accompanied a restaurant employee to work, assisted in a part of her work, and escorted her home.

On cross-examination by the state, the following exchange took place:

"Q. To the best of your knowledge would you say Oswalt had been in every day for the last couple of months or did he miss occasional periods of three or four days, or what was it? A. No, I think he was in there every day. I really think he was in there every day. Q. For the last couple months? A. Yes."

In rebuttal, a police detective was permitted to testify, over defense objections, as follows:

"Q. Did you see and talk to the defendant Mr. Oswalt on June 12, 1961? A. I did. Q. And in what city did you talk to him? A. In the City of Seattle. Q. And did you during that conversation ask him how long he had been in this city of Seattle at that time? * * * A. I did. Q. And how long did he state he had been in the City of Seattle? A. He stated he had arrived in Seattle a couple days before I talked to him. Q. Did he state where he had come from? A. Portland, Oregon."

During colloquy between the trial court and counsel relative to the admissibility of the detective's testimony, the trial court commented: "There is no claim by Oswalt he wasn't in Seattle, Gilman [a codefendant] claims that, but Oswalt doesn't."

It is to the rebuttal testimony of the police detective that defendant assigns error. The state, in response, contends such testimony to be admissible not only because it challenges the credibility of witness Ardiss, but also establishes defendant's presence in Seattle preparatory to the offense.

It is a well recognized and firmly established rule in this jurisdiction, and elsewhere, that a witness cannot be impeached upon matters collateral to the principal issues being tried. [Citations omitted.]

The purpose of the rule is basically two-fold: (1) avoidance of undue confusion of issues, and (2) prevention of unfair advantage over a witness unprepared to answer concerning matters unrelated or remote to the issues at hand.

We, in common with other jurisdictions, have stated the test of collateralness to be: Could the fact, as to which error is predicted, have been shown in evidence for any purpose independently of the contradiction?

We are handicapped by the limited record before us in evaluating the relationship of the contradictory evidence in question to the general issues presented in the trial.

So far as appears by this record, the sole issue raised by defendant's defense of alibi, through the direct testimony of witness Ardiss, was whether or not the defendant was or could have been in Seattle at the time of the offense on July 14, 1961. The defendant did not contend or seek to prove by this witness that he had not been in Seattle prior to such date. Thus, for purposes of impeaching this witness, whether the defendant was in Seattle on a given occasion one month prior to July 14th, was irrelevant and collateral. While a cross-examiner is, within the sound discretion of the trial court, permitted to inquire into collateral matters testing the credibility of a witness, he does so at the risk of being concluded by the answers given.

The state, however, contends that the quoted testimony of Ardiss, as elicited by its cross-examination, carries with it an inference that defendant could not have been in Seattle sufficiently in advance of July 14, 1961, to have participated in necessary planning of and preparation for the offense. Upon the inference so erected, the state asserts the questioned testimony becomes material and admissible independently of its contradictory nature. The state further supports this argument by testimony elicited from the police detective to the effect that defendant admitted, in the interview of June 12, 1961, that he had purchased some adhesive tape.

Admittedly, relevant and probative evidence of preparations by an accused for the commission of a crime is admissible. Based upon the limited record before us, however, the state's argument requires us to speculate that the defendant could not readily commute between Portland and Seattle, and that his presence in Seattle and acquisition of adhesive tape, upon an isolated occasion approximately a month before the offense in question, constituted significant evidence of planning and preparation for the offense in question, the particular mechanics of which are unrevealed by the record. This we decline to do, absent effort upon the part of the state to obtain a more complete record.

Upon the record before us, we must conclude it was error to admit the questioned testimony.

Having so concluded, we must next determine whether the error was prejudicial.

In State v. Britton, 27 Wash.2d 336, 341, 178 P.2d 341, we said:

"A harmless error is an error which is trivial, or formal, or merely academic, and was not prejudicial to the substantial rights of the party assigning it, and in no way affected the final outcome of the case.

* * *

* * *

"A prejudicial error is an error which affected the final result of the case and was prejudicial to a substantial right of the party assigning it. * * *"

In the instant case, the state's charge apparently rested upon an identification of the defendant by witnesses at the scene of the crime. The defense apparently rested upon alibi. The state seemingly considered the testimony of witness Ardiss sufficiently credible to require this attack. The defendant was convicted. It is difficult, therefore, to classify admission of the testimony in question trivial, formal, academic, or harmless, and to conclude that such did not affect the outcome of the case. The alternative is that it was prejudicial. We so hold.

The judgment is reversed and the cause remanded for new trial.

Ott, C.J., and Donworth, Hunter, and Finley, JJ., concur.

See Federal Rules of Evidence 608(b) at p. 916; California Evidence Code § 782 at p. 840.

Hypotheticals

(1) D is prosecuted for forcible rape of V, a 21-year-old female. D's defense is an alibi. At the preliminary hearing and at trial, V testifies on direct examination that D was the perpetrator and that she suffered great emotional distress and great physical pain because she had never had sexual intercourse with any man before. After V's direct examination, D files a motion to present an offer of proof with an affidavit by B that he, B, was V's former boyfriend and that he and V had engaged in several acts of sexual intercourse, setting forth specific dates and circumstances prior to the date of the charged offense. The trial judge conducts an in camera hearing at which V testifies that B was a former boyfriend but denies any intimacy with B. B testifies as set forth in his affidavit. The prosecutor makes impermissible-attempted-impeachment objection. How should the court rule?

(2) D is charged with rape of an unmarried female, V. V testifies and identifies D, by his voice, as the perpetrator. After the prosecution completes its case in chief, D calls V and elicits testimony that she had engaged in sexual relations within two days prior to the date of the alleged rape. D then asks V if she had taken a pregnancy test within two weeks prior to the date of the alleged rape. The prosecutor makes an improper impeachment objection. D then makes an oral offer of proof to the effect that his cross-examination question was relevant on the theory that V, on the date of the alleged rape, may have known that she was pregnant and had thus concocted the story of being raped to cover up for the fact of her pregnancy. What result?

(3) X is prosecuted for the murder of A. B is called by the prosecution and testifies that he saw the fight between A and X and that X struck the first blow. X calls C, who testifies that he was with B in a bar an hour before the fight. X proposes to have C testify that he saw B drink five shots of straight whiskey during that hour. The prosecutor objects that this is improper impeachment evidence. What result?

B. PSYCHIATRIC CONDITION

MOSLEY v. COMMONWEALTH

Court of Appeals of Kentucky, 1967.
420 S.W.2d 679.

WADDILL, Commissioner.

Appellant was convicted of the crime of rape and sentenced to ten years' servitude in the state penitentiary. The sole ground for reversal of the conviction is that the trial court erred in excluding the testimony of James Gay, a psychologist, concerning the mental condition of the prosecuting witness at the time of the alleged rape.

The record reflects that for several months prior to May 11, 1966, the date of the alleged offense, Geraldine Eden, the prosecuting witness, had been staying in the home of Elihu Asher where she was employed as a full-time baby-sitter. Geraldine, who is 27 years of age, testified that during the evening of May 11, 1966, the Ashers had left their residence to go bowling. Appellant, an acquaintance of Geraldine and a relative of Asher entered the Asher home for the purpose of staying overnight. Geraldine stated that after the Asher children went to bed, appellant tried to make love to her and when she resisted his amorous advances he forcibly tied her hands behind her back, pushed her down on a couch, removed her underclothing and raped her.

Appellant, age 54, testifed that upon his arrival at the Asher residence Geraldine informed him that she wanted to talk with him before he retired. He had waited only a short time when Geraldine came over and sat beside him on a couch where they immediately began making love and Geraldine voluntarily submitted to sexual intercourse with him as she had on several previous occasions. He stated that following the intercourse they went to the kitchen and Geraldine prepared a snack for them. When they were later questioned that night as to their conduct, appellant stated that much to his surprise Geraldine claimed he had raped her.

Appellant urges that the court erred in refusing to permit the jury to consider, for the purpose of impeaching Geraldine's credibility, the testimony of Doctor Gay concerning Geraldine's mental condition. Doctor Gay has obtained a Ph.D. degree in psychology and has been licensed by the state of Kentucky as clinical psychologist.   *   *   *

Doctor Gay, who is in charge of the treatment of Geraldine's mental disorder, testified, by way of avowal out of the presence of the jury, that Geraldine had entered a state hospital for mental treatment during October 1961. At that time she was complaining that her father and brothers had molested her sexually during her adolescence. She was discharged from the hospital in January 1962 and readmitted for treatment on a voluntary basis during 1964. She has been treated by Doctor Gay since September 1965.

While Doctor Gay believed that Geraldine was in a state of remission at the time of the alleged rape, it was his opinion that she is schizophrenic and is an immature individual. She could not tolerate frustration, was easily disturbed and had a guilt complex. Doctor Gay stated that schizophrenia is a complex phenomenon, that it is a disturbance of behavioral effect and thinking which has not been found to be caused or related to any physical or organic condition, but it has a psychiatric origin, i. e. an emotional basis. He further stated that one of the manifestations of schizophrenic reaction is fantasies and when asked whether Geraldine's fantasies extend to the area of sex, he answered, "In this particular case I think it does."

Since the Commonwealth relied upon the uncorroborated testimony of Geraldine to establish its case against appellant, the principal question at

394 IMPEACHMENT AND CROSS EXAMINATION Ch. 5

issue had reference to the credit to be given to the testimony of Geraldine. Therefore, Doctor Gay's testimony [, if admitted, might] have had an important impact on the jury as it tended to impeach Geraldine's credibility.

It is our opinion that the proferred testimony of Doctor Gay was relevant and competent and should have been received, not in extenuation of rape, but for its bearing upon the question of the weight to be accorded Geraldine's testimony. For this reason the court should admonish the jury that the expert testimony should be considered by it only for the purpose of affecting the credibility of this witness, if it does so.

Generally a witness may be impeached only as specified in our Rules of Civil Procedure (CR 43.07). However, the modern trend is to permit the jury to consider expert testimony in the field of mental disorders and relax the rule in sex offense cases. McCormick in his treatise on Evidence, Section 45 at page 99, observes:

"* * * Naturally, the use of psychiatric testimony as to mental disorders and defects suggests itself as a potential aid in determining the credibility of crucial witnesses in any kind of litigation. In one type of case, namely that of sex offenses, the indispensible value of this kind of testimony has been urged by Wigmore, and other commentators, and such testimony has been widely received by the courts. * * *."

* * *

In State v. Armstrong, 232 N.C. 727, 62 S.E.2d 50, the importance of permitting an accused to impeach a witness for the state was pointed out as follows:

"* * * It is always open to a defendant to challenge the credibility of the witnesses offered by the prosecution who testify against him. * * *.

"What could be more effective for the purpose than to impeach the mentality or the intellectual grasp of the witness? If his interest, bias, indelicate way of life, insobriety and general bad reputation in the community may be shown as bearing upon his unworthiness of belief, why not his imbecility, want of understanding, or moronic comprehension, which go more directly to the point? * * *."

A similar conclusion was reached by the United States District Court in United States v. Hiss, 88 F.Supp. 559, wherein it was observed:

"The existence of insanity or mental derangement is admissible for the purpose of discrediting a witness. Evidence of insanity is not merely for the judge on the preliminary question of competency, but does to the jury to affect credibility. * * *."

Also see Giles v. State of Maryland, 386 U.S. 66, 87 S.Ct. 793, 17 L.Ed.2d 737, which concerns itself with the prosecution's suppression of evidence relating to the credibility of the prosecution's witnesses.

We conclude that the jury was entitled to hear and consider the testimony of Doctor Gay and that its exclusion constituted prejudicial error in the case.

The judgment is reversed with directions to grant appellant a new trial.

Williams, C. J., and Edward P. Hill, Milliken, Steinfeld, Palmore and Osborne, JJ., concur.

1950 ANNUAL SURVEY OF AMERICAN LAW

804–808 (1950).*

EVIDENCE, BY JUDSON FALKNOR†

Witnesses: Impeachment by Psychiatric Testimony.—Although similar testimony had been rejected at the first trial of Alger Hiss,[1] Judge Goddard at the second trial held admissible psychiatric testimony designed to impeach the credibility of the Government witness Whittaker Chambers,[2] and in pursuance of this ruling a psychiatrist, Dr. Carl Binger, testified that Chambers was a "psychopath with a tendency toward making false accusations."[3] Dr. Binger testified that his opinion was based on "personal observation of Mr. Chambers at the first trial for five days and on one day at this trial" and that "he had read plays, poems, articles and book reviews written by Mr. Chambers and books he had translated from German." While it has been said that Dr. Binger's diagnosis was "based entirely on courtroom observation"[4] it appears from a trustworthy contemporary news-

---

†Judson F. Falknor has been Dean and Professor of Law at the University of Washington School of Law since 1936, is a Member of the Bar of the State of Washington, and during the school year 1949–1950 was Visiting Professor of Law at New York University School of Law.

1. N.Y. Times, July 1, 1949, p. 1, col. 2.

2. United States v. Hiss, 88 F.Supp. 559 (S.D.N.Y.1950).

3. N.Y. Times, Jan. 6, 1950, p. 1, col. 2. Amplifying this, the psychiatrist testified that Chambers suffered from a condition known as "a psychopathic personality, a disorder of character, the outstanding features of which are amoral and asocial behavior." This condition, said the witness, has "nothing to do with the conventional judgment of sanity"; it is rather a "personality deviation" that would not prevent Chambers from earning the $30,000 a year he got as senior editor of Time magazine up to Dec. 12, 1948. The symptoms of "a psychopathic personality" are variegated, including chronic, persistent and repetitious lying, stealing, and deception, abnormal sexuality, alcoholism, panhandling, vagabondage, inability to form regular habits and a tendency to make false accusations. Such a person, the doctor continued, is quite aware of what he is doing but does not always know why he is doing it. He is frequently impulsive and bizarre. The psychopathic holds some kind of middle ground between the psychotic and neurotic. He plays a role: he may be a hero one moment and a gangster the next, but he acts as though the fancied situation were true. He will claim friendships that do not exist and will make false accusations because he is under constant compulsion to make his fancies come true. He is "amazingly isolated and egocentric." Ibid.

The cross-examination of the psychiatrist (N.Y. Times, Jan. 11, 1950, p. 12, col. 4 and Jan. 12, 1950, p. 9, col. 1) appears to have been rather effective. For example: The witness on his direct examination had emphasized and apparently attached importance to Chambers' "untidiness." He agreed on cross-examination that that trait was manifested by such persons as Albert Einstein, Heywood Broun, Will Rogers, Owen D. Young, Bing Crosby and Thomas A. Edison. The expert had testified that Mr. Chambers habitually gazed at the ceiling while testifying and seemed to have no direct relation with his examiner. "We have made a count of the number of times you looked at the ceiling," the prosecutor told Dr. Binger. "During the first ten minutes you looked at the ceiling nineteen times. In the next fifteen minutes you looked up twenty times. For the next fifteen minutes ten times and for the last fifteen minutes ten times more. We counted a total of fifty-nine times that you looked at the ceiling in fifty minutes. Now I was wondering whether that was any symptom of a psychopathic personality?" Shifting in the witness chair, Dr. Binger smiled frostily and said: "Not alone." When the expert insisted that stealing was a psychopathic symptom the prosecutor asked: "Did you ever take a hotel towel or a Pullman towel?" "I can't swear whether I did or not," Dr. Binger replied, "I don't think so." "And if any member of this jury had stolen a towel, would that be evidence of psychopathic personality?" Mr. Murphy asked. "That would have no bearing on it," the psychiatrist said. It should be noted also that Dr. Binger conceded on cross-examination that he "could not form an opinion of a person merely by watching him from the witness stand."

4. 59 Yale L.J. 1324, 1339 (1950).

5. Note 3 supra.

paper account that Dr. Binger gave his opinion after listening to a 70-minute hypothetical question "that accentuated unpalatable aspects of Mr. Chamber's life."[5] These accounts leave obscure the tenor of the assumptions in the hypothetical question as well as the character and source of evidence in support thereof.

"Since the use of psychiatric testimony to impeach the credibility of a witness is a comparatively modern innovation," said Judge Goddard in his opinion, "there appear to be no Federal cases dealing with this precise question. However, the importance of insanity on the question of credibility of witnesses is often stressed.[6] There are some state cases in which such testimony has been held to be admissible or which indicate that if this question had been presented it would have been admissible."[7] Judge Goddard noted the contrary conclusion of the West Virginia court in State v. Driver,[8] but said, "This was in 1921—before the value of psychiatry had been recognized."[9]

Judge Goddard's instructions relative to the weight to be given the psychiatric testimony are set forth in the margin.[10]   *   *   *

6. Wigmore, Evidence §§ 931, 932 (3d ed. 1940).

7. The cases cited by the Court scarcely support this statement. The cases cited follow: People v. Cowles, 246 Mich. 429, 224 N.W. 387 (1929): In this rape case two physicians who had observed the prosecuting witness expressed the opinion that she was a "pathological falsifier, a nymphomaniac and a sexual pervert." But this testimony was received without objection. It is to be noted, however, that in holding improper the prosecutor's argument deprecating the medical testimony the Court said that "the term 'nymphomaniac' is a standard one in medical parlance * * * the opinion evidence that she was such is entitled to consideration"; State v. Wesler, 1 N.J. 58, 61 A.2d 746 (1948): This was also a rape case and the question on appeal was whether the verdict of guilty was against the weight of the evidence. In determining that it was not, the Court made reference to the testimony of two psychiatrists to the effect that the prosecuting witnesses were "psychopaths and immoral and that psychopaths are prone to be untruthful," but the admissibility of the evidence is not discussed. As far as the opinion discloses it was received without objection. In any case, the admissibility of the psychiatric testimony was not involved on the appeal; Ellarson v. Ellarson, 198 App.Div. 103, 190 N.Y. Supp. 6 (3d Dep't 1921): This case appears to go no further than to hold that extrinsic evidence of "insanity," in the traditional sense, is admissible for impeachment purposes. The holding is orthodox. Wigmore, Evidence § 932 (3d ed. 1940); Jeffers v. State, 145 Ga. 74, 88 S.E. 571 (1916): In this rape case a physician testified apparently as a State's witness, as to the result of a physical examination of the prosecutrix, a girl of thirteen, and also "rel-

ative to her mental condition he testified she was below the average and that he considered her a child." On appeal the convicted defendant questioned the admissibility of this evidence but it was held proper. The case does not seem apposite; Bouldin v. State, 87 Tex.Cr.R. 419, 222 S.W. 555 (1920): In a robbery prosecution defendant proposed to show that a state's witness was, if not insane, an idiot or feeble-minded and also that the mother of the witness was an idiot. On appeal the exclusion of this evidence was held erroneous. This is like the *Ellarson* case, supra.

8. 88 W.Va. 479, 107 S.E. 189 (1921). In this prosecution for rape the trial court excluded the opinions of a neurologist and a psychologist that the prosecuting witness was a moron and as such "untrustworthy of belief." This ruling was affirmed on appeal. The Court said that "we are not convinced that the time-honored and well-settled and defined rule of impeachment of the veracity of a witness [by evidence of bad reputation for truth and veracity] should be thus innovated upon. It is yet to be demonstrated that psychological and medical tests are practical, and will detect the lie on the witness stand."

9. Psychiatric Evaluation of the Mentally Abnormal Witness, 59 Yale L.J. 1324 (1950) contains a helpful summary of psychological and psychiatric theory touching the reliability of this sort of impeaching evidence. It is the conclusion of the writer that while the psychiatrist's opinion would be most helpful where he has had the benefit of a clinical examination, nevertheless his "diagnosis should be admitted whenever it is offered, whether based on clinical examination or courtroom observation alone. * * * Enough data may be presented in court to provide the basis for a psychological diagnosis which will be help-

Hypothetical

X is prosecuted for battery upon A, his girl friend. A testifies that she was trying to break off her relationship with X and that he got mad and beat her. On cross-examination, X asks A if it isn't true that she has been under the care of a pychiatrist for the last three years. The prosecutor makes an improper impeachment objection. X represents that he intends to prove that it was he who was trying to break off the relationship, because he found out that A had been under the care of a psychiatrist; that he never struck A at all; and that A's claim is a figment of her imagination.

ful to the jury. For example, by correlating all the factors of a witness' personality a psychiatrist may sometimes be able to detect a pathological liar in the courtroom as easily as in the clinic. These factors may include the witness' ability to adjust quickly to exposure of his lies, a case history denoting bizarre, insensitive or paranoidal tendencies and any convictions or indications of a bad reputation for veracity extrinsically revealed. Thus, whenever a qualified psychiatrist believes that he can make a competent courtroom diagnosis the Court should allow him to do so. Despite any shortcomings in a diagnosis of this sort, the psychiatrist is better qualified than a lay jury to assess personality disorders."

In a letter published in 123 N.Y.L.J., p. 414, col. 3, Feb. 2, 1950, A. S. Cutler criticizes the ruling as giving to the well-to-do litigant an unfair advantage. The poor litigant, because of the cost, will be unable to utilize this "new weapon in the armory of trial procedure." And in a letter published in 123 N.Y.L.J., p. 702, col. 2, Feb. 27, 1950, David L. Delman, besides agreeing with Cutler's point, calls attention to the frequent disagreement among experts "on scientific facts or pseudo-scientific facts" and says "especially is this true when we come to the nebulous field of psychology, psychiatry and psychoanalysis. * * * It is not generally known that this whole field of psychology is not a science at all because it is so inexact. * * * To have a psychologist or psychiatrist testify to the fact that a man is lying because the experts saw him look at the ceiling comes about as close to burlesquing justice as possible. * * * The jurors, by hearing testimony of the various witnesses and by using their own common sense are much more able to determine truth or falsehood than psychological experts." For a contrary view, see letter of Harry Silberschutz, 123 N.Y.L.J., p. 812, col. 2, March 7, 1950. He says: "The novelty of the offer of the testimony argued by counsel for the prosecution [in the Hiss case] is no insuperable obstacle. Progress in science has compelled changes in legal concepts and growth in medical knowledge is not legally of lesser significance. The psychopathic personality was not known in the days of Blackstone, so it is futile to dig deep into the past for cases on 'all fours'. * * * The constitutional infirmity of the psychopathic personality is not less a

factor in destruction of credibility than interest or bias or what is loosely denominated 'insanity'. * * * Psychiatrists are already well accepted as experts virtually everywhere in our courts, and deservedly so. That they sometimes differ among themselves in their findings is no more damaging than it is in the case of other experts."

10. "The defense has called Dr. Binger, a psychiatrist, and Dr. Murray, a psychologist, for the purpose of attacking Mr. Chambers' credibility. Dr. Binger, basing his opinion upon certain testimony which for the purpose of a hypothetical question he assumed to be true and on his observations of Mr. Chambers while Mr. Chambers was on the witness stand; and Dr. Murray, basing his opinion upon the same hypothetical situation which he assumed to be true, testified that in their opinion Mr. Chambers was a psychopathic personality and that this tended to reduce his credibility. As is the case with all expert testimony, these opinions are purely advisory. You may reject their opinions entirely if you find the hypothetical situation presented to them in the question to be incomplete or incorrect or if you believe their reasons to be unsound or not convincing. An expert does not pass on the truth of the testimony included in a hypothetical question. Similarly, he does not, and as a matter of law, he cannot pass on the truth of any part or parts of the testimony of the witness about whose mental condition he expresses his opinion. Assuming the facts in the hypothetical question to be true, the expert testifies that in his opinion the witness is suffering from a mental disorder which would tend to reduce his credibility in general. You yourselves have seen and heard Mr. Chambers for several days while he was on the witness stand and you have heard all the evidence. It is for you to say how much weight, if any, you will give to the testimony of the experts—and of Mr. Chambers. * * * Was Mr. Chambers telling the truth when he testified that he did see Mr. Hiss and that he did receive from him documents as charged? Those are the questions you must answer. Even though you may accept the experts' opinion as to Mr. Chambers' mental condition, you may still find that Mr. Chambers was telling the truth when he testified regarding those particular matters." N.Y. Times, Jan. 21, 1950, p. 2, col. 2.

C. PRIOR CONVICTIONS

UNITED STATES v. SMITH

United States Court of Appeals, District of Columbia Circuit, 1976.
551 F.2d 348.

McGOWAN, Circuit Judge.

On November 11, 1974, the Seventh Street branch of the National Bank of Washington was robbed by two armed men who wore hats completely covering their hair, but employed no other form of disguise. The bandits disarmed the bank's private security guard immediately upon entering the bank lobby. While one stood watch, the other proceeded through the bank managers' office into the tellers' cage area, where he filled a brown paper bag with bills of various denominations. The entire incident consumed less than five minutes. A subsequent audit revealed that the robbers fled with $13,214 in cash, as well as the bank guard's revolver.

Under an indictment filed in the District Court on February 12, 1975, appellant (was) * * * convicted by a jury of armed bank robbery and armed robbery * * *.

*   *   *

Appellant Gartrell seeks reversal of his conviction on the ground that the district judge erred in ruling that a prior conviction would be admissible for impeachment purposes if Gartrell chose to testify in his own defense. The trial in this case was held on July 17, 18, and 21, 1975. The new Federal Rules of Evidence became effective on July 1, 1975. The impeachment by prior conviction issue, therefore, was and is governed by Fed.R.Evid. 609(a).[16] Gartrell's claim in this regard presents difficulty, because the controlling relevance of Rule 609 was unrecognized at trial. In the colloquy of record about admissibility, the Rule was never mentioned by the prosecution, the defense, or the court. The district judge seems to have decided to permit use of Gartrell's prior conviction by reference to earlier law in this Circuit. See Luck v. United States, 121 U.S.App.D.C. 151, 348 F.2d 763 (1965); Gordon v. United States, 127 U.S.App.D.C. 343, 383 F.2d 936 (1967), cert. denied, 390 U.S. 1029, 88 S.Ct. 1421, 20 L.Ed.2d 287 (1968). This was error.

Despite substantial surface similarity, the inquiry to be conducted by the trial court under Rule 609(a) differs significantly from that mandated by *Luck* and its progeny. Adherence to the proper standard by the District Court might have produced a different ruling on the impeachment question. Had evidence of his prior conviction been excluded, appellant Gartrell in all likelihood would have taken the stand and the jury presumably would have heard him deny participation in the bank robbery. * * * [We]

---

16. Rule 609. Impeachment by Evidence of Conviction of Crime

(a) General rule. For the purpose of attacking the credibility of a witness, evidence that he has been convicted of a crime shall be admitted if elicited from him or established by public record during cross-examination but only if the crime (1) was punishable by death or imprisonment in excess of one year under the law under which he was convicted, and the court determines that the probative value of admitting this evidence outweighs its prejudicial effect to the defendant, or (2) involved dishonesty or false statement, regardless of the punishment.

cannot say, on the facts of this case, that failure to apply Rule 609 constituted harmless error. Therefore, we remand the case to the District Court for a determination of whether, within the meaning of Rule 609(a), the probative value of Gartrell's prior conviction outweighs its prejudicial effect. If it decides that the prior conviction was admissible, the conviction stands, subject to further review on appeal; if it decides that it should have been excluded, the conviction is reversed and a new trial ordered.

* * * Rule 609 has been designed to work at least three important changes in the approach of federal courts to the problems of impeachment by prior conviction:

(i) Evidence of *some* prior convictions (i.e., convictions for crimes involving dishonesty or false statement) is now *automatically* admissible for the purpose of attacking the credibility of a witness. With respect to these convictions, trial courts are no longer free to exercise the discretion they enjoyed under *Luck*.[20] Congress has substituted its judgment that evidence of such crimes is always sufficiently related to credibility to justify its admission, regardless of possible prejudice to the defendant. * * *

20. But see Fed.R.Evid. 403, which provides: Rule 403. Exclusion of Relevant Evidence on Grounds of Prejudice. Confusion, or Waste of Time

Although relevant, evidence may be excluded if its probative value is substantially outweighed by the danger of unfair prejudice, confusion of the issues, or misleading the jury, or by considerations of undue delay, waste of time, or needless presentation of cumulative evidence.

The potential interaction between Rule 403 and Rule 609(a) elicited comment at legislative hearings on the Proposed Federal Rules of Evidence. Although it offers no solutions, the following colloquy between Congressmen Dennis and Hungate and Judge Friendly is instructive:

Judge FRIENDLY. [D]o you really think if you were on a jury, you would not like to know if the witness had committed a murder. I think I would like to know.

Mr. DENNIS. I think I would like to know it, but I think it is very unfair to ask a man who is on trial for some irrelevant or unrelated offense, whether he committed murder or manslaughter 5 years ago. All it does is prejudice the case. It has nothing to do with his credibility in my judgment, especially murder. That is the primary example. Those are usually one time offenses.

Judge FRIENDLY. Perhaps in taking murder I chose an unfortunate case. But, of course, there is the overriding rule that the judge can always exclude testimony where probative value he thinks is outweighed by its prejudicial effect and perhaps in the case we are discussing he should do that.

Mr. HUNGATE. Would that be true with or without the rules?

Judge FRIENDLY. That is true today.

Mr. HUNGATE. Would it remain true if these rules became effective?

Judge FRIENDLY. I assume they have such a rule in here. I could easily check.

Mr. DENNIS. It seems to me if he has to follow this rule [i.e., Rule 609(a)] he does not have much discretion. Maybe he still could rule something out. I am not sure.

Mr. HUNGATE. I apologize for interrupting. Go ahead.

Mr. [sic] FRIENDLY. I want to check whether there was such a general rule. I thought there was.

* * *

Mr. HUNGATE. I believe section 403 is the rule to which you are referring. [Quotes the rule.]

Judge FRIENDLY. I think the Congressman's point is a good one. You have the problem: Does that apply when there is a specific rule on the subject? This just says relevant evidence may be excluded if it has this effect. But then somebody is going to argue, this other rule dealt very specifically with the question and rule 403 is out. I don't know what the answer would be.

Rules of Evidence, Hearings on S. 583, H.R. 4958, and H.R. 5463 Before the Special Subcomm. on Reform of Federal Criminal Laws of the House Comm. on the Judiciary, 93d Cong., 1st Sess., ser. 2 at 251–52 (1973). (In connection with Congressman Dennis's remark about the limited discretion available to a trial judge under Rule 609(a), at the time of the

(ii) The addition of the phrase "to the defendant" at the end of Rule 609(a)(1) reflects a deliberate choice to regulate impeachment by prior conviction *only* where the *defendant's* interests might be damaged by admission of evidence of past crimes, and *not* where the prosecution might suffer, or where a non-defendant witness complains of possible loss of reputation in the community.[21] This procedure may be

above exchange the version of the rule under consideration mandated that *all felony* convictions, as well as all convictions for crimes involving dishonesty or false statement, be automatically admissible for impeachment purposes.)

As Judge Friendly observed, the language of Rule 609(a)(2) is absolute in nature, suggesting that the subsection's command, authorizing use of prior convictions for crimes involving dishonesty or false statement, may not be abrogated by reference to Rule 403. Partial support for this proposition can be derived from the original Advisory Committee Note to Rule 403, a rule whose text remained unchanged throughout Congressional consideration. The Advisory Committee said that Rule 403 was "designed as a guide for the handling of situations for which no specific rules have been formulated." Since Gartrell's prior crime, attempted robbery, did not involve dishonesty or false statement as those terms are used in Rule 609(a)(2) we express no opinion on the issue of whether evidence admissible under Rule 609(a)(2) may nevertheless be excluded by a trial judge in the exercise of his discretion under Rule 403.

21. The Conference Committee Report states:

> The danger of prejudice to a witness other than the defendant * * * was considered and rejected by the Conference as an element to be weighed in determining admissibility. It was the judgment of the Conference that the danger of prejudice to a non-defendant witness is outweighed by the need for the trier of fact to have as much relevant evidence on the issue of credibility as possible. Such evidence should only be excluded where it presents a danger of improperly influencing the outcome of the trial by persuading the trier of fact to convict the defendant on the basis of his prior criminal record.

H.R.Conf.Rep.No. 93–1597, 93d Cong., 2d Sess. 9–10, *reprinted* in [1974] U.S. Code Cong. & Admin.News pp. 7098, 7103. In explaining the Conference Report and urging adoption of the new Federal Rules, Representative Hungate, the leading Conference Committee Manager, announced flatly that Rule 609(a) "means that in a criminal case the prior felony conviction

of a prosecution witness may always be used." 120 Cong.Rec.H. 12,254 (daily ed. Dec. 18, 1974). Similarly, Representative Dennis, another Conference Committee member, told the House that "now a defendant can cross examine a government witness about any of his previous felony convictions; he can always do it, because that will not prejudice him in anyway [sic] * * * . Only the Government is going to be limited. * * * " Id. at H. 12,257.

In his treatise on the Federal Rules of Evidence, Judge Weinstein recognizes the accuracy of the above descriptions of the effect of Rule 609(a). Prosecution witnesses may be impeached by their prior felony convictions, subject only to Rule 611(a)(3)'s instruction that the court exercise control over interrogation so as to "protect witnesses from harassment or undue embarrassment." See 3 Weinstein's Evidence ¶ 609[03], at 609–66 n. 11 and accompanying text (1975). However, in United States v. Jackson, 405 F.Supp. 938 (E.D.N.Y.1975), Judge Weinstein fashioned a significant modification of the rule that prior felony convictions may always be used to impeach prosecution witnesses.

Defendant in *Jackson* was charged with armed bank robbery. His record revealed a recent state felony conviction for assault. One or more government witnesses apparently also had prior assault convictions. Judge Weinstein excluded evidence of defendant's prior conviction, but conditioned the exclusion upon defense counsel's agreement to refrain from using prior assault convictions to impeach prosecution witnesses, absent the court's express advance approval of such tactics. Imposition of this condition was justified by a pretrial finding that if government witnesses *were* so impeached, then the probative value of *defendant's* assault conviction *would* outweigh the risk of prejudice under Rule 609(a). Judge Weinstein asserted that, under the general purpose formulation of Rule 102, district judges are obliged to "interpret the [Federal] Rules [of Evidence] creatively." 405 F.Supp. at 943. (Rule 102 directs that the rules "be construed to secure fairness in administration, * * * and promotion of growth and development of the law of evidence to the end that the truth may be ascertained and proceedings justly determined.")

contrasted with earlier possibilities under *Luck*. Although in practice *Luck* hearings were most frequently conducted to determine whether a criminal defendant who wished to testify could be impeached with evidence of his prior convictions, in theory the *Luck* discretionary standard was equally applicable to all witnesses and parties. In order to avoid undue prejudice to *any* individual, the trial court could exclude prior conviction evidence which it concluded had only limited probative value with respect to credibility.

(iii) Crucial for present purposes, the language of Rule 609(a)(1), as enacted, manifests an intent to shift the burden of persuasion with respect to admission of prior conviction evidence for impeachment. *Luck* held that such evidence could be excluded "where the trial judge believes the prejudicial effect of impeachment *far* outweighs the probative relevance of the prior conviction to the issue of credibility." 348 F.2d at 768 (emphasis added). *Gordon* reiterated this test, and emphasized that "[t]he burden of persuasion in this regard is on the accused * * * . The underlying assumption [of *Luck*] was that prior convictions would ordinarily be admissible unless this burden is met." 383 F.2d at 939. Presumably, the House Subcommittee version of Rule 609(a)(1) would have preserved the approach already developed by the case law in this Circuit. As amended by the Subcommittee, the rule provided that previous felony convictions could be used to impeach a witness *"unless* the court determines that the danger of unfair prejudice outweighs the probative value of the evidence of the conviction[s]." H.R.Rep.No. 93–650, 93d Cong., 1st Sess. 11, *reprinted in* [1974] U.S.Code Cong. & Admin.News, pp. 7075, 7084 (emphasis added). Rejecting this option, the version of Rule 609 which ultimately emerged from the Conference Committee and became law allows impeachment by prior felony conviction (for a crime not involving dishonesty or false statement) *"only* if * * * the court determines that the probative value of admitting this evidence outweighs its prejudicial effect to the defendant." Fed.R.Evid. 609(a)(1) (emphasis added). This modest variation in language is not purely semantic. The prosecution now must bear the burden of establishing that prior conviction evidence should be admitted. * * *

   * * * Rule 609 was one of the most hotly contested provisions in the Federal Rules of Evidence.[24] The current language of the Rule is unquestionably the product of careful deliberation and compromise. The

---

24. At least three alternatives were formally considered by the Advisory Committee before the Proposed Rules were transmitted to Congress. See 3 Weinstein's Evidence 609–46 to –49 (1975). Also during this preliminary period, several correspondents urged unsuccessfully that the Committee endorse the solution then embodied in Rule 21 of the Uniform Rules of Evidence. As approved in 1953 by the National Conference of Commissioners on Uniform State Laws, Rule 21 permitted introduction of prior conviction evidence only where the underlying crime involved dishonesty or false statement, and barred all

such impeachment of a criminal defendant who elected to testify in his own behalf, unless he had "first introduced evidence admissible solely for the purpose of supporting his credibility." The American Law Institute had taken the same approach a decade earlier in Rule 106 of its Model Code of Evidence (1942).

The final Supreme Court version of Rule 609 essentially represented a codification of existing law in the majority of American jurisdictions. A witness could be impeached by any prior conviction for a felony or a crime involving dishonesty or false state-

House of Representatives and the Senate Judiciary Committee agreed that *criminal defendants* should not be impeached by evidence of prior convictions unless the earlier offenses involved dishonesty or false statement. Adoption of this position by the full Senate was blocked only at the last moment, only by a bare majority, and only after Senator McClellan had succeeded in forcing a second vote on the matter.

Faced with the task of forging a consensus between views both strongly held and widely divergent, the Conference Committee was aware of the substantial sentiment in both chambers for limiting impeachment by prior conviction, especially in the criminal defendant-as-witness context. The House debate almost ten months earlier was particularly revealing. As reported by the Judiciary Committee, Rule 609 banned impeachment by prior conviction, regardless of the identity of the witness, except where the crime in question had involved dishonesty or false statement. Representative Hogan vigorously pressed for amendment of the proposal to authorize impeachment by any prior felony conviction. Resurrecting the suggestion previously advanced by a Special House Subcommittee, Representative Smith countered with a compromise amendment along the lines of *Luck*. Sitting as a Committee of the Whole, the House first replaced the Hogan amendment with the Smith amendment, and then rejected the latter in favor of the Judiciary Committee version by a vote of 48–10. * * * The small minority of members voting overwhelmingly favored the "dishonesty or false statement" approach. The Conference Committee sought a formula which would improve upon *Luck* in providing at least the appearance of more definite restrictions on the use of prior convictions for impeachment purposes. At the same time, the Conference could not avoid the fact that a narrow majority of the Senate wished to permit impeachment with any prior felony conviction. Rule 609, as currently effective, resolves these opposing tensions by retaining the trial court's discretion to allow impeachment with any prior felony, but shifting to the prosecution the burden of demonstrating that probative value on the issue of credibility outweighs prejudicial effect to the defendant.

The Government has contended, both in its brief and on oral argument, that Gartrell's earlier crime, attempted robbery, involved "dishonesty or false statement," as that phrase is used in the Federal Rules of Evidence. If this contention were accurate, the Government would be correct in its conclusion that Rule 609(a)(2) provides for the *automatic* admissibility of evidence of Gartrell's prior conviction. The District Court's decision could

ment. The Special House Subcommittee which initially examined the Proposed Rules rejected this, and offered a substitute based on *Luck*. Following the approach of the Uniform Rules and the Model Code, the full House Judiciary Committee elected to further restrict impeachment by prior conviction. Credibility was to be challenged only with convictions for crimes involving dishonesty or false statement. The House membership accepted this scheme, and sent the Judiciary Committee draft to the Senate. The corresponding Senate committee injected a new variable by advocating that Rule 609 be revised to differentiate between defendant and non-defendant witnesses. As to the former, the Senate Judiciary Committee concurred in the recommendation of its House counterpart. With respect to non-defendant witnesses, however, the Committee suggested a restrictive discretionary standard which allocated the burden of persuasion to the proponent of prior conviction evidence. On the Senate floor, Senator McClellan launched an attempt to scrap the new committee proposal in favor of a return to the original Supreme Court version of Rule 609. The McClellan amendment was first "defeated" by a tie vote, but was subsequently passed by a narrow margin on motion to reconsider.

be upheld, even though rendered without reference to the newly-applicable Rules. However, the Government has misconstrued the language in question, partially through a misplaced reliance on comments of this court in cases decided under *Luck*. Attempted robbery is not a crime involving "dishonesty or false statement" within the meaning of Rule 609(a)(2). If Gartrell's prior conviction is to be admitted at all, it must be admitted only after the court makes the determination prescribed in Rule 609(a)(1).

The Conference Committee Report fully supports this position:

> By the phrase "dishonesty and false statement" the Conference means crimes such as perjury or subornation of perjury, false statement, criminal fraud, embezzlement, or false pretense, or any other offense in the nature of crimen falsi, the commission of which involves some element of deceit, untruthfulness, or falsification bearing on the accused's propensity to testify truthfully.

H.R.Conf.Rep.No. 93–1597, 93d Cong., 2d Sess. 9, *reprinted in* [1974] U.S.Code Cong. & Admin.News, pp. 7098, 7103. Numerous remarks made in the course of floor debate, set forth in the Appendix to this opinion, substantiate the interpretation that robbery may not be classified legitimately as an "offense in the nature of crimen falsi." Congress clearly intended the phrase to denote a fairly narrow subset of criminal activity. Moreover, research into the derivation of the term "crimen falsi" indicates that Congress's restrictive construction comports with historical practice. While commentators have uncovered some divergence between civil and common law usage, the expression has never been thought to comprehend robbery or other crimes involving force.[26] Even in its broadest sense, the term "crimen

---

26.   Under Roman law, where the term originated, "crimen falsi" included "not only forgery, but every species of fraud and deceit." 1 S. Greenleaf, A Treatise on the Law of Evidence § 373, at 514 & n. 3 (16th ed. 1899). Apparently, no practical importance attached to the classification. Rather, it functioned purely as a label, referring to violations of the *Lex Cornelia de Falsis*. This statute, enacted in 81 B.C., was designed to curtail the then prevalent practice of "forging, altering, destroying, and substituting wills." 15 S.P. Scott, The Civil Law 47 n. 1 (1932). Severe sanctions (usually banishment, deportation, or death) were provided for transgressors. As was typical of the Roman criminal law, development and expansion of the *Lex Cornelia* was accomplished gradually through a combination of senate decrees, imperial constitutions, subsequent legislation, and judicial interpretation. *See* A. Berger, Encyclopedic Dictionary of Roman Law 418 (1953). This process was presumably still in progress at the time of Justinian (c. 530 A.D.), whose Institutes report that the *Lex Cornelia* "imposes a punishment on him who has written, sealed, read or substituted a forged testament or other document, or has made, engraved or impressed a false seal, knowingly and with evil intent." The Institutes of Justinian, 452 (J. Abdy and B. Walker trans. 1876). Ul-

timately, the scope of the *crimen falsi* was enlarged to include:

> false swearing, subornation of perjury, forgery, the execution or attestation of any written instrument, conspiracy to cause the death of innocent persons, counterfeiting, and the sale or suppression of testimony. This was the *crimen falsi* of Roman jurisprudence, which, while embracing nearly every species of deceit by whose agency anyone might be prejudiced, or deprived of his rights, was generally synonymous with the fabrication, or fraudulent alteration of documents to which, when not otherwise distinctly specified, it was presumed to refer.

15 S.P. Scott, supra at 47 n. 1. See also S. Hallifax, An Analysis of the Civil Law 170–71 (1836), listing as examples of the *crimen falsi* at Roman law (i) a supposititious birth [i.e. fraudulent substitution of one child for another]; (ii) false weights and measures; (iii) selling or mortgaging the same thing to two persons in two several contracts; and (iv) supporting the lawsuit of another by money, witnesses, or patronage.

At common law, the term had a more limited range, reflecting the purpose for which it had been borrowed from the civil systems.

falsi" has encompassed only those crimes characterized by an element of deceit or deliberate interference with a court's ascertainment of truth. As graphically observed by Senator McClellan, robbery is not such a crime:

> There is no deceit in armed robbery. You take a gun, walk out, and put it in a man's face and say, "Give me your money," or walk up to the counter of the cashier and say, "this is a holdup; give me your money." There is no deceit in that. They are not lying. They mean business. They will murder you if you do not do it.

120 Cong.Rec.S. 19913 (daily ed. Nov. 22, 1974).

* * *

* * * Two recent Third Circuit cases, decided the same day, have argued convincingly that petty larceny is not ordinarily a crime involving dishonesty or false statement under Rule 609(a)(1). *See* Government of Virgin Islands v. Toto, 529 F.2d 278, 282 (3rd Cir. 1976) (reviewing a March, 1975 trial, and therefore applying the circuit's traditional *crimen falsi* limitation on impeachment by misdemeanor conviction, but construing Rule 609(a)(2) in dictum);[28] and Government of Virgin Islands v. Testamark, 528

Along with conviction for treason or a felony, conviction of a crime subsumed under the heading *crimen falsi* disqualified an individual, at common law, from serving as a witness in a legal proceeding. Greenleaf explains:

> In regard to the two former, as all treasons, and almost all felonies, were punishable with death, it was very natural that crimes, deemed of so grave a character as to render the offender unworthy to live, should be considered as rendering him unworthy of belief in a court of justice.

1 S. Greenleaf, supra at 513–14. The *crimen falsi* category was added because a number of offenses, supposedly bearing directly on credibility, did not constitute felonies at common law. Among this group were perjury, subornation of perjury, suppression of testimony by bribery, conspiracy to procure the absence of a witness, and conspiracy to accuse another of a crime. Since, by hypothesis, persons convicted of such crimes had a special propensity to testify falsely, the common law sought to exclude them from the ranks of potential witnesses. The *crimen falsi* designation was employed to this end. The distinguishing characteristic of crimes listed under the *crimen falsi* rubric at common law was their close relationship to the judicial process. "[P]rivate cheats, such as the obtaining of goods by false pretenses, or the uttering of counterfeit coin or forged securities" were not included. Ex parte Wilson, 114 U.S. 417, 423, 5 S.Ct. 935, 938, 29 L.Ed. 89 (1885); 1 S. Greenleaf, supra at 514–15.

Pendock v. Mackinder, 125 Eng.Rep. 1375 (C.P. 1755), cited by the Supreme Court in *Wilson,* 114 U.S. at 422, is instructive for our purposes. *Pendock* involved a challenge to the validity of a will. The question presented was whether an individual convicted over twenty years earlier for petty larceny could legitimately serve as a witness to the signing of that will. The court decided that he could not, holding that petty larceny was sufficiently similar to the felony of grand larceny to justify imposition of testimonial incompetence upon persons convicted of the lesser offense. The court thus reached its result by analogizing a crime clearly not a true felony * * * to its more serious counterpart. The notion that an identical outcome could have been produced through the expedient of application of the *crimen falsi* label to petty larceny was not mentioned and apparently not considered. The term simply did not extend so far.

More recent sources have blurred the distinction between the civil and common law conceptions of the *crimen falsi.* However, this confusion should not obscure the fundamental point, which is that robbery and other crimes of violence were not included among the *crimen falsi* under *either* standard. Historically, some element of fraud or deceit has always been a prerequisite, even under the broadest reading of the ancient term.

28. Of course, if a statutory petty larceny offense is committed not by stealth, but by fraudulent or deceitful means, e. g., taking by false pretenses, it may qualify as a crime involving dishonesty or false statement. Where the formal title of an offense leaves room for doubt, automatic admissibility under Rule 609(a)(2) will normally not be permitted, unless the prosecution first demonstrates to the court, outside the jury's hearing, that a particular prior conviction rested on facts warranting the dishonesty or false statement description. Id. at 281 n. 3.

F.2d 742, 743 (3d Cir. 1976) (actually applying Rule 609(a)(2), and holding that the new enactment tracks the circuit's long-standing *crimen falsi* restriction). *Contra,* United States v. Carden, 529 F.2d 443, 446 (5th Cir. 1976) (holding, without the benefit of argument by the parties, that a petty larceny conviction was properly admitted for impeachment purposes, "since the crime at issue involved dishonesty"). The Seventh Circuit, in United States v. Mahone, 537 F.2d 922 (7th Cir. 1976) simply found it unnecessary to discuss whether evidence of a prior *robbery* conviction might be admitted under Rule 609's "dishonesty or false statement" provision, focusing its attention instead solely on the discretionary language of Rule 609(a)(1) * * *. In like manner, at least two District Courts have apparently regarded the "dishonesty" issue as too clear for comment.

The Government has invoked Gordon v. United States, 127 U.S.App.D.C. 343, 383 F.2d 936, *cert. denied,* 390 U.S. 1020, 88 S.Ct. 1421, 20 L.Ed.2d 287 (1967), and United States v. Simpson, 144 U.S.App.D.C. 259, 445 F.2d 735 (1970), in aid of the proposition that stealing, and in particular the crime of robbery, involves dishonesty or false statement under Rule 609(a)(2). *Gordon* and *Simpson* are not unique. Other cases decided by this court pursuant to the *Luck* standard might also have been cited. The simple answer to the Government's argument is that none of these cases involved Rule 609. *Luck* had held that, under the then applicable version of the D.C.Code * * * trial courts should exercise discretion in determining whether to permit impeachment by prior conviction. *Gordon* represented the effort of this tribunal to be helpful to the District Court in its exercise of that discretion. The nature of the prior crime was one factor identified in both the *Luck* and *Gordon* opinions as relevant to the impeachment issue. When Judge (now Chief Justice) BURGER, writing in *Gordon,* characterized stealing as "conduct which reflects adversely on a man's honesty and integrity," he was not holding that all prior convictions for theft and related crimes were automatically admissible for impeachment purposes. He said merely that such offenses had some bearing on an individual's credibility, a bearing which the trial court should consider in exercising its discretion. By contrast, the *Gordon* opinion noted, acts of violence "generally have little or no direct bearing on honesty and veracity." thus implying that virtually any showing of prejudicial effect should be sufficient to exclude evidence of such prior convictions.

The issue under Rule 609(a)(2) is entirely different from that confronted by this court in *Gordon, Simpson,* and other cases descendant from *Luck.* The new Rule provides that a prior conviction for a crime involving dishonesty or false statement is *automatically* admissible for impeachment purposes. With respect to such evidence, the trial court enjoys no discretion. * * * In its Conference Committee Report, Congress has spelled out the meaning of the phrase "dishonesty or false statement" as it is used in Rule 609(a)(2). * * * The Report plainly shows that the set of crimes involving dishonesty or false statement under the Rule is not coterminous with the set of crimes bearing on credibility in the *Luck-Gordon* analysis. * * *

As we indicated at the beginning of this part of our opinion, we cannot view as harmless error the trial court's failure to follow Rule 609 in deciding whether to permit impeachment of Gartrell by prior conviction evidence. * * *

* * *

* * * [T]he case is remanded to the District Court for the purpose of the inquiry described above * * *

It is so ordered.

APPENDIX

Consensus on the meaning of "dishonesty or false statement" appears to have transcended policy disagreements on the general impeachment by prior conviction issue. Senator McClellan's prepared statement, reprinted in the Congressional Record, concentrated predictably on the problem created when an accused takes the stand as a witness:

> Particularly relevant to a witness's credibility and worthiness of belief is the prior criminal record of such a witness.
>
> Those who favor the rule as reported in this bill [i.e., the Senate Judiciary Committee version; see note 24 supra] agree that prior convictions do have a bearing on credibility. But they want to limit that judgment only to crimes involving dishonesty or false statement. They make ineligible crimes of murder, rape, armed robbery and other serious felonies. They do not seem to believe that those who have committed these other serious felonies are just as likely to lie under oath as those who have committed crimes involving "dishonesty."
>
> I cannot accept that conclusion. Surely a person who has committed a serious crime—a felony—will just as readily lie under oath as someone who has committed a misdemeanor involving lying. Would a convicted rapist, cold-blooded murderer or armed robber really hesitate to lie under oath any more than a person who has previously lied? Would a convicted murderer or robber be more truthful than such a person?
>
> Of course not!

120 Cong.Rec.S. 19909 (daily ed. Nov. 22, 1974). * * *

The picture in the House was more unsettled. Congressman Hogan believed the drafters were ill-advised to use the phrase "dishonesty or false statement," because it was to imprecise.

> The courts would certainly have difficulty with the term "dishonesty" in the present proposal of rule 609(a). Although ordinarily one would think of car theft as involving dishonesty, it might be contended that the "joyriding" type of case did not involve dishonesty. Then, too, one might think that [sic] housebreaking as usually involving dishonesty, but there could be cases where the trespass was obviously not accompanied by any intention to steal or commit any other crime, so that argument could be made that some kinds of offenses normally thought to involve dishonesty did not involve dishonesty on the facts. The standard employed in the committee's rule is simply not a very satisfactory one.

* * *

What, really, is dishonesty or false statement in judicial or legal terms? Unless one practices in a jurisdiction which has statutorily defined crimen falsi, the common law definition of "any crime which may injuriously affect the administration of justice, by the introduction of falsehood and fraud" is applicable. This definition has been held to include forgery, perjury, subornation of perjury, suppression of testimony by bribery, conspiracy to procure the absence of a witness or to accuse of crime, obtaining money under false pretenses, stealing, moral turpitude, shoplifting, intoxication, petit larceny, jury tampering, embezzlement and filing a false estate tax return. In other jurisdictions, some of these same offenses have been found not to fit the crimen falsi definition.

120 Cong.Rec.H. 552 (daily ed. Feb. 6, 1974). Congressmen Dennis and Wiggins, not sharing the above reservations about the clarity of the drafters' expression, attempted to dispel their colleagues' doubts and to set the record straight.

> Mr. DENNIS. ✻ ✻ ✻ We [i.e., the House Judiciary Committee] have said that, for the purpose of attacking credibility of a witness, evidence that he has been convicted of a crime is admissible only if the crime involved dishonesty or false statement. In other words, if it in fact did bear on his credibility. Certainly, if he has been convicted of perjury or false pretense or fraud or something of that kind, it does reflect on his credibility, but if he stole an automobile when he was 18 years old or if he slugged somebody in a bar 10 years ago or something like that, then it has no connection to his credibility at all and it should not be inquired about on that basis.

Id. at 553.

> Mr. WIGGINS. ✻ ✻ ✻ The thrust of "dishonesty" as used in this bill [i.e., the House Judiciary Committee version, described above by Mr. Dennis] goes to his [i.e., a witness'] veracity and his ability to relate the truth. "Dishonesty" is tested, for example, by perjury convictions and convictions dealing with false statements, but not generally criminality. Evidence for a conviction of murder goes to criminality, not to dishonesty.

Id. at 555.

Unfortunately, these well-intentioned efforts by knowledgeable legislators did not completely eliminate uncertainty. The following exchange reflects the House's failure to achieve unanimity on the "dishonesty or false statement" matter.

> Mr. DANIELSON. ✻ ✻ ✻
>
> With respect, Mr. Chairman, to the distinction, if any, between the terms "dishonesty" and "false statement," I would like to point out that unless there has been a remarkable change in the meaning of words in recent years, "dishonesty" and "false statement" are not necessarily the same.
>
> I respectfully submit, there is no point in using both terms in section 609(a), unless they mean two different things, or at least that the term "dishonesty" is much broader than "false statement."
>
> Who can state that murder does not involve dishonesty? Who can, for instance, say stealing does not involve dishonesty, then what does it involve?

The terms "dishonest" and "false statement" are not synonymous as used in this code section, and to the extent that we are establishing legislative history here, I want today to make it clear that when I voted for this bill out of committee, and when I vote for it today, it was and is my intention that the term "dishonesty" is broader than "false statement," and any offense involving moral turpitude such as stealing, robbery, burglary, or what have you, in my opinion is an offense involving dishonesty.

I want to make the record eminently clear that I do not equate "dishonesty" precisely with "false statement."

Mr. HOGAN. Mr. Chairman, will the gentleman yield?

Mr. DANIELSON. Mr. Chairman, I yield to the gentleman from Maryland.

Mr. HOGAN. Mr. Chairman, if the gentleman believes what he said, which I am sure he does, he should support the Hogan amendment [impeachment by any prior felony and by misdemeanors involving dishonesty or false statement] rather than the committee version [impeachment only by crimes involving dishonest or false statement] or the substitute [*Luck* approach; * * *]. I agree with him precisely.

MR. DANIELSON. Mr. Chairman, I am glad we are in agreement. I just feel it is unnecessary to go that far, because I think the form the committee has brought out covers the field adequately. Unless we so stultify the meaning of "dishonesty" that it is limited to false statements, we have covered everything we need to do in this particular case.

Mr. DENNIS. Mr. Chairman, will the gentleman yield?

Mr. DANIELSON. Mr. Chairman, I yield to the gentleman from Indiana.

Mr. DENNIS. Mr. Chairman, I would agree with my friend that dishonesty is a bit broader than false statement, but I would not agree that it covers such things as crimes of violence. What we are getting at here is crimen falsi, in the technical language, perjury, false pretense, fraud, and perhaps some other things.

Mr. DANIELSON. Moral turpitude.

Mr. DENNIS. It goes to one's honesty and one's credibility, and it does not cover the waterfront on all crimes for which a person can be sent to jail in excess of a year such as my friend from Maryland (Mr. HOGAN) wants to do.

Mr. DANIELSON. Mr. Chairman, I am pleased to agree with the gentleman from Indiana that it involves that which shall be generally regarded as a dishonest act.

Mr. HOGAN. Mr. Chairman, will the gentleman yield?

Mr. DANIELSON. Mr. Chairman, I yield to the gentleman from Maryland.

Mr. HOGAN. Mr. Chairman, the courts have not borne out the gentleman's interpretation of what is dishonesty. The courts have sometimes rejected under this same guideline robbery, theft, and many other crimes that under the gentleman's definition would be considered "dishonesty."

Mr. DANIELSON. Mr. Chairman, I submit that, if the gentleman please, with the courts aided by this colloquy on the floors to what the Congress means when it says "dishonesty," they will be able to apply the rule correctly.

Id. at 555-56.   *   *   *

*   *   *

ABBY'S VIEW

DEAR ABBY: My husband and I went on a two-week trip last year and hired a woman to stay in our home and look after our children.

After we came home, I couldn't find my favorite pair of earrings. They were only costume jewelry, but I liked them and wore them with many outfits.

Last evening my husband and I went to a movie, and as we came out, there was this friend who stayed at our home last year, wearing my earrings! Up until that time I wanted to believe that I had just misplaced them. Needless to say, I was shocked. Shall I ask her to return my earrings? Or should I just wait and hope she reads your column and brings them back?

MRS. A

DEAR MRS. A: Ask, but don't expect her to return them. Any one who would steal would probably lie.

Hypotheticals

(1) X is prosecuted for the sale of heroin. He makes a pretrial motion to exclude the prosecutor's use of a 1945 Ohio felony conviction of burglary to impeach X as a witness, on the ground that he was denied right of counsel. At a pretrial hearing, X testifies that he was not represented by counsel in 1945 and was not advised that he had any right to counsel. The record of the Ohio judgment recites merely that X appeared and entered a plea of guilty. The prosecutor offers no evidence other than that record of X's conviction. X moves to preclude the use of the Ohio felony conviction to impeach him. What result?

(2) X is prosecuted for the offense of having sexual intercourse with A, his 13-year-old stepdaughter. A testifies, with minimal impeachment of her testimony. X testifies in denial of the charge. To impeach X, the prosecution proposes to establish, through cross-examination of X, that he has suffered prior felony convictions of rape, sale of heroin, and grand theft, all occurring within the 10-year-period prior to the offense charged. X requests the court to preclude such cross-examination. How should the court rule?

D.   BAD REPUTATION FOR TRUTH AND VERACITY
MATHES AND DEVITT, FEDERAL JURY PRACTICE

§ 9.10 (1965).*

§ 9.10 Impeachment—Evidence of Witness' Reputation for Truth and Veracity

When an attempt is made to impeach a witness by showing a bad general reputation for truth and veracity in the community where the witness now resides, or has recently resided, the jury should consider such evidence along with all evidence of good reputation as to those traits of character. Evidence that the witness' reputation for truth and veracity has not been discussed or, if discussed, those traits of the witness' character have not been questioned, may be sufficient to warrant an inference of good reputation as to those traits of character.

————

See Federal Rules of Evidence 608 at p. 916; California Evidence Code § 786 at p. 841.

Hypothetical

X is prosecuted for the sale of heroin to A, an informer for the police. A testifies that he made a purchase of heroin from X in a dimly lit bar, and that this was part of a "buy" program that covered a three-month period, with A's purchase from X coming in the second month. X's defense is an alibi. X calls B to testify that he has been a next-door neighbor to A for 10 years and has attended many social affairs which A also attended, and that A has a reputation in the community for having a bad memory. The prosecutor objects to the proposed testimony of B as improper impeachment evidence. What result?

2. PRIOR INCONSISTENT STATEMENTS

COLES v. HARSCH

Supreme Court of Oregon, 1929.
129 Or. 11, 276 P. 248.

In this action the plaintiff sought to recover a judgment for $50,000 upon charges that the defendant had maliciously alienated the affections of plaintiff's wife by improper attentions shown to her in the years 1923, 1924, and 1925. * * * The verdict and judgment were in favor of the plaintiff in the sum of $17,500. The defendant appealed.

ROSSMAN, J. (after stating the facts as above). The defendant presents for our disposal several assignments of error. We shall first consider the one which is based upon the endeavor of the plaintiff to impeach the testimony of one James A. Thompson, who was of the defendant's principal witnesses. In order to better understand the situation presented by this assignment of error, it seems desirable to state the following undisputed facts: While the parties were married to their former wives, the two couples belonged to the same social group; they frequently met at card parties, dances, and other social diversions, and frequently visited back and forth. The plaintiff contended that at some time in 1923 he noticed that the defendant was developing a propensity for wrestling with the plaintiff's wife, and engaging in other similar play with her. It was his contention that this propensity of the defendant did not abate with the passing of time, but that it grew more pronounced, and the plaintiff contended that it constituted one of the means which the defendant employed for winning the affections of the plaintiff's wife. This seems to be a rather unusual method of love making, yet if current reports are reliable, it is not the first instance where a cicisbeo has delved into the distant stone age and brought forth a somewhat rough and uncouth method of endearment, which well served his purpose, and brought about the desired result. Be this as it may, it will suffice to say that much time was consumed in the trial court in taking testimony concerning these wrestling and similar encounters and the extent to which other members of the parties participated in them; there was also testimony, not all in harmony, however, concerning the plaintiff's protests against the activities along these lines of his wife and the defendant and the latter's replies and rejoinders thereto.

As we have said, one of the defendant's principal witnesses was a Mr. James A. Thompson. The latter and his wife were members of this social group. His testimony, apparently important to the defendant, covered these wrestling encounters, the social diversions of the group, and the relationship between the defendant and Mrs. Coles, plaintiff's former wife. If his testimony was accepted as truthful by the jury, the defendant's conduct towards Mrs. Coles was the same as his conduct towards other women friends, and was proper and harmless. Apparently nothing developed upon cross-examination which obviously discredited this witness; but, upon rebuttal, the plaintiff was permitted over objection to testify that, "at the time I was in the garage where he works," Thompson told him that at a picnic held on the banks of the Pudding river the conduct of the defendant and Mrs. Coles towards each other was disgraceful. Before defendant's objection was ruled upon, plaintiff's counsel stated that the purpose of the contemplated answer was to "go to the credibility of Thompson." The objections of the defendant to the questions, which elicited the above answer, were specific and were reiterated; they were to the effect that, if the plaintiff sought this information to substantiate the charges of his complaint, the inquiry was in violation of the hearsay evidence rule: That if the plaintiff sought the answer for the purpose of impeaching Thompson, he had not laid the proper foundation by making a similar inquiry of Thompson accompanied with the details of time, place, and persons present. The merits of the first alternative of the objection are so self-evident, that we deem it necessary to set forth our consideration only of the second phase of the objection.

Section 864, Or. L., provides: "A witness may also be impeached by evidence that he has made, at other times, statements inconsistent with his present testimony; but before this can be done, the statements must be related to him, with the circumstances of times, places, and persons present; and he shall be asked whether he has made such statements, and if so, allowed to explain them. If the statements be in writing, they shall be shown to the witness before any question is put to him concerning them."

It is necessary, therefore, to examine the inquiries propounded to Thompson and determine whether a similar question was put to him which complied with this statutory rule. Pausing for a moment, it is worthwhile to observe that this requirement does not invoke an idle ceremony, but is intended to serve a useful purpose. Every witness, whose testimony is shown in conflict with a previous statement made by him, is not necessarily revealed thereby as a dishonest person; the impeachment, in many instances, may uncover only a faulty memory in the discredited witness. The requirement that the identifying circumstances of time, place, those present, and the statement that the witness then made shall be related to him, is founded upon the experience, which frequently presents itself in the courtroom, that a witness, who has stoutly denied having made an alleged statement, may finally blushingly and apologetically admit it, when the questioner throws into association with it identifying circumstances. It is a common observation that associated ideas, as they are related, one after another, not infrequently succeed in upturning a fact which previously had de-fied all efforts of recollection. And so this rule of evidence is intended to reveal not only the dishonest witness, but is also intended to afford all witnesses ample opportunity to recall a fact before they may be assailed as dishonest. The requirement also tends to reduce to the minimum a confusion of issues by eliminating unnecessary impeachments.

Approaching the statutory requirement thus broadly as one intended to serve a practical, useful end, let us see what the record presents. On direct examination Thompson was asked concerning a conversation he had had with the plaintiff at the Bybee Avenue Garage. The witness stated that the conversation occurred so long ago that his recollection had become somewhat vague, but he recalled that at that time the plaintiff said that his wife was going to get a divorce. No further questions were asked him on direct examination concerning that conversation. The time of this conversation was not fixed, nor were those present mentioned, and he was asked nothing concerning the Pudding river incident. On cross-examination he was asked whether he recalled "talking to Mr. Coles about that trip to the Pudding river." He replied in the negative. This was the only foundation laid for the impeaching question; we believe it was insufficient. It may be that Thompson was untruthful, but before the plaintiff could avail himself of such an argument he should have prepared the necessary premise by submitting to Thompson the alleged statement accompanied by the identifying circumstances. Since this was not done, error was committed when the impeaching witness was permitted to answer.   *   *   *

[Reversed.]

GOLDSTEIN, TRIAL TECHNIQUE

§ 601 (1935).*
[Most footnotes omitted.]

§ 601. Former contradictory oral statements[11]

In those instances where the lawyer is in possession of information as to verbal statements made by the witness which are directly contrary to his present testimony, the following procedure is suggested: First—get the witness to repeat upon cross-examination the statements that he has made on direct examination, then put a casual and general question as to whether or not he has ever made a statement to the contrary, at any time or place, then identify the person to whom the contradictory statement is purported to have been made, then direct his attention to the time, the place, and the exact language used or in substance, and again ask him whether or not he had made such contradictory statement. Upon his denial he might again be interrogated on the same question for psychological effect and upon a similar denial the witness should be excused.

After opponent's case is in and he rests, the lawyer should then produce the impeaching witness and prove the contradictory statement by him.

See Federal Rules of Evidence 613 at p. 919; California Evidence Code §§ 769, 770 at p. 837.

---

*Copyright 1935 by Callaghan & Co.   11.   The attention of the witness must be
                                            called to the statement.

BARMORE v. SAFETY CAS. CO.

Court of Civil Appeals of Texas, 1962.
363 S.W.2d 355.

McNEILL, Justice.   Appellant sought benefits under the Workmen's Compensation law for total and permanent incapacity resulting from an alleged injury of March 9, 1960. Since judgment was against him, the parties here will be referred to as they were in the trial court.

In answer to the first special issue submitted to it, the jury found that plaintiff had not sustained an injury on or about March 9, 1960. Seeking to set aside the judgment of the lower court and for remand, plaintiff urges a single point of error. This point asserts that, since the charge of "recent fabrication" had been leveled by defendant at plaintiff, the trial court erred in excluding the testimony of plaintiff's wife in rebuttal that he told her the morning after his claimed injury that he had been hurt on the job.

The question whether plaintiff had had an accident and sustained any injury on the occasion in question was vigorously contested. To put the question in proper perspective, we set forth a summary of pertinent events as they developed at the trial. Plaintiff was the first witness taking the stand and on direct examination, after having told about being employed by Socony-Mobil Oil Company as a tank-truck driver, stated that the night of March 9th, while driving along the highway some electric wires in the motor of the truck shorted and caught on fire. Upon discovering this he immediately pulled his truck off the highway and, just before he stopped its roll, he jumped out of the cab and claimed to have injured himself doing so. After waiting about an hour beside the road, another employee of the company, Sterling Hoke, coming from the opposite direction stopped his truck and plaintiff told him about the motor catching on fire. Plaintiff was then asked whether he told Sterling Hoke at that time that he had gotten hurt, in answer to which he said he did. He testified that Hoke flagged a car for him and the driver of that car brought plaintiff to the inspection station in Logansport, Louisiana. After he reached this inspection station plaintiff telephoned his boss, Zee P. Brooks, and reported the break down of the truck. After staying at the inspection station about four hours he caught a ride with his co-employee Hoke, who was then returning from a trip and going back to Center, where plaintiff lived.

On the following cross-examination, plaintiff stated, while he did not remember, he might have mentioned to Brooks that he had gotten hurt. He was then asked whether he had seen a doctor L.S. Oates after his claimed injury and whether he told him of his injury. Plaintiff said he did not remember doing so. He was then asked whether he had any explanation for this, and he stated, "No, sir, I don't." In reference to the way the accident happened, he was asked on this examination, "Of course, you had no skinned places on you? No, sir, not * * * "   Then he was asked, "You had no bruises to show anybody. You had no signs on you anywhere? A. No, sir." When asked whether he fell on his hands when he jumped from the truck, he said he could not answer that. Then: "Uh-huh. But you did not skin your hand and you had no skins any place on you? A. No, sir." A short time later in this cross-examination, defendant's counsel stated "As a matter of fact, don't you know you didn't have any accident there. You just had your truck short out and you stopped and first man come along, you didn't tell him you had any injury did you? A. I told him the truck was on fire." He was then asked if after he went to the inspection station "You didn't tell that man about being injured did you? A. I did." Then he was asked whether he told Brooks on the 'phone that he had gotten hurt, to which he stated he did not remember. Plaintiff was pressed for not having told Brooks about any injury, and in answer to this he said he had no reasonable opportunity to do so and that he knew that there was going to be some men laid off and he wanted to hold his job. As a matter of fact he was let out about two weeks after March 9th. Then defendant's counsel stated:

"Q.   Yeah. And he finally let you out and then you decided to file this claim and then you left him—you ever seen Dr. Dickerson up till then? A. No, sir.

"Q.   Till you decided to make a case and when you decided to make a case, you started hunting those kind of doctors didn't you? One that would swear there was something wrong with you? A. I didn't hunt Dr. Dickerson at all.

"Q.   Well, did you hunt the lawyers and the lawyers hunted the doctor for you? Who gave you this doctor's name? A. Well, I had heard of Dr. Dickerson.

"Q.   Well, did you see your lawyer here first? A. Yes, sir.

"Q.   And from him did you get Dr. Dickerson's name? A. Yes, sir.

"Q.   Uh-huh. And so at the time you got Dr. Dickerson you really wasn't trying to get treated, you was trying to file a lawsuit wasn't you? Trying to make out a case? A. We had talked about it."

After the above took place, plaintiff was then questioned as to who the man was who took him into the weighing station at Logansport. While he could not recall the man's name, he described him well and he was located and the man, C.R. Baker, later testified for the defendant to the effect that he did not remember plaintiff mentioning anything about an injury to him. In this connection plaintiff himself had previously testified that he did not remember telling Baker about his injury. Defendant also produced the weighing station witness who stated that while he recalled the incident when plaintiff stayed at the station March 9, 1960, to his knowledge plaintiff did not mention that he had gotten hurt. He heard his conversation with Mr. Brooks on the 'phone but did not remember that plaintiff mentioned his injury to Mr. Brooks. Defendant also placed Brooks on the stand, who testified that while plaintiff had several opportunities to tell him of the injury, he never mentioned it to him either on the telephone or in person. Defendant produced Dr. L.A. Oates, who also testified that insofar as he could recall plaintiff never mentioned an injury to him; that his record listed no such injury and if he had been told thereof, he would have made a note of it.

After defendant rested, plaintiff placed his wife on the stand in rebuttal. The following transpired, while plaintiff's counsel was examining her:

"Q.   Now then, after he had been in Louisiana, the time when his truck got on fire, when he came back, did he tell you anything about getting hurt? A. Yes he did.

"Q.   What did he tell you? A. Well, he—

"MR. LANE: Just a minute, I was listening here. We would object to what he told her some several hours or 6 or 8 hours after he came in. Wouldn't be res jeste.

"COURT: Sustain the objection as to what he told her.

"Q.   But did he tell you he got hurt? A. He did.

"MR. LANE: Well we—that's the same thing.

"MR. SEALE: Now your Honor, the whole case, every witness he's brought up here, he said 'Did he tell you he got hurt' 'Did he tell you he got hurt.' That's the big issue in the case. Now if he can ask his witnesses whether he told them, I think I ought to be able to.

"MR. LANE: That's different. He's the plaintiff. We're the defendants. We've got a right to ask that but he can't ask a self-serving declaration of that type. We've got them as admissions from him but he can't put this witness on unless it's res jeste.

"MR. SEALE: Silence of a witness can't be admission—

"MR. LANE: Certainly can be.

"MR. FITZPATRICK: If your Honor please Mr. Barmore testified he told these people things. We brought witnesses on to show that he had not. That's admissible under the hearsay rule.

"COURT: I'm going to exclude what he told her.

"MR. SEALE: Note our exception. And so that we won't disturb the proceedings, may it be understood I may complete by bill later in the absence of the jury.

"COURT: Very well."

The following stipulation was made at the close of the evidence:

"MR. SEALE: Can we stipulate her testimony would have been that he told her he got hurt?

"MR. FITZPATRICK: I guess so John.

"MR. SEALE: I assume—it seems obvious that's what she was going to do.

"MR. FITZPATRICK: Yes."

Plaintiff insists that as the issue of injury was hotly contested with the charge of "recent fabrication" having been thrown at him, plaintiff's wife should have been permitted to so testify in rebuttal, and that her testimony may thus have been sufficient to cause the jury to find that he had received an injury on the occasion in question. Defendant counters this upon several grounds: first, it denies that the charge of "recent fabrication" was made. In view of defendant's vigorous cross-examination of plaintiff, we hold that the charge was made. In fact, the charge was expressly made in this cross-examination twice. This is so in the above quoted statement: "As a matter of fact, don't you know you didn't have any accident there" and in the latter quotation, "Till you decided to make a case and when you decided to make a case, you started hunting those kind of doctors didn't you? One that would swear there was something wrong with you."

Undoubtedly the defendant has the right to produce testimony to meet evidence presented by plaintiff that he had sustained an accident, but the cross-examination went much further than this. In addition, although plaintiff did not say that he told Baker, who brought him into the inspection station, that he had gotten hurt, defendant produced him and he testified he had no memory that plaintiff mentioned that he had gotten hurt. Plaintiff stated he did not remember whether he told his boss that he had gotten hurt when he talked to him on the 'phone. Brooks, when placed on stand by defendant, testified plaintiff never mentioned receiving any injury. And though plaintiff had testified that he did not remember telling Dr. Oates he had gotten hurt, defendant produced Dr. Oates, who stated that plaintiff had not told him about his injury. Thus, the defendant, and not plaintiff, undoubtedly initiated the charge of "recent fabrication." In this respect the present case differs from Skillern & Sons, Inc. v. Rosen (Tex.Sup.Ct.) 359 S.W.2d 298.

When a witness is charged at the trial with recent fabrication, his former consistent declarations are admissible to corroborate his testimony, provided such declarations were made at a time when he had no motive to misrepresent the fact stated by him. It was held in Aetna Ins. Co. v. Eastman, 95 Tex. 34, 64 S.W. 863, and in Skillern & Sons, Inc. v. Rosen (Tex.Sup.Ct.) 359 S.W.2d 298, that prior consistent statements of the plaintiff were inadmissible for the reason that in each case plaintiff had the motive (whether influenced thereby or not) to falsify the fact. Or as alternatively stated in the Skillern case, after the time when its ultimate effect and operation could be foreseen. The prior consistent declarations in both Eastman and Rosen took place shortly after the event the plaintiffs claimed took place. Although the fire loss had not occurred in the former case and the consistent declaration was made the day after notice of taking out the second policy was given to the insurance company's agent, the court said (64 S.W. p. 864): "It is nevertheless true that at the time of the alleged statement it was to his interest to make it."

There is, however, a modification of the proposition above that prior consistent declarations to be admissible must be made before motive to misrepresent exists. This modification comes into play if defendant raises the charge of recent fabrication and produces witnesses who testify plaintiff was silent about his accident at a time when he could have been reasonably expected to speak of it and did not do so. It is then permissible for plaintiff to show by other witnesses that he did speak of the accident and injury at or near those particular times. This we think are the holdings in Houston & T. C. Ry. Co. v. Fox, 106 Tex. 317, 166 S.W. 693, and Texas Employers' Ins. Ass'n. v. Thames, Tex.Civ.App., 236 S.W.2d 203 (W.R.), as interpreted in Skillern v. Rosen, supra. In the latter circumstances the consistent declarations appear to be admissible even after plaintiff's claim is filed, provided there was not then, (at the time of making such declaration or claim), a motive to rebut the issue of recent fabrication. At the time, 6 or 8 hours after he had returned home, when plaintiff told his wife he had gotten hurt, there existed no charge of recent fabrication. In fact, defendant produced Dr. Oates to show that several days later, when plaintiff went to the doctor plaintiff did not mention getting hurt. This evidence was tendered upon the ground that it would have been the usual and customary thing for plaintiff to have then told his doctor, if he had gotten hurt. What Judge Hamilton said in the Skillern opinion, of the holding in the Texas Employers' Ins. Ass'n. v. Thames, supra, is presently pertinent (359 S.W.2d p. 304):

"* * * The notice of injury and claim in the Thames case was prepared before any motive could have existed to rebut the issue of recent fabrication raised by the failure of the plaintiff to tell the doctors of his general injury." * * *

[The court, however, holds the error "harmless", and the judgment is *affirmed.*]

UNITED STATES v. QUINTO

United States Court of Appeals, Second Circuit, 1978.
582 F.2d 224.

WATERMAN, Circuit Judge.

While it is superfluous to say that the intent of a tax evader is to try "to screw the government out of some cash if [he can]," what makes this contested tax evasion case remarkable is that, according to the government, Quinto, the alleged tax evader here, was gracious enough to acknowledge to two Internal Revenue Service agents when interviewed by them that that is precisely what he was hoping to accomplish by failing to report approximately $15,000 of income over a two-year period. Not surprisingly, though, Quinto's recollection of his interview with the IRS agents, as developed during his testimony in his own defense at his trial * * * on two charges of tax evasion and two charges of willfully subscribing false income tax returns is somewhat different.

* * *

Michael Quinto is a full-time employee of the Suffolk County (New York) Land Management Bureau, serving in the capacity of Senior Right of Way Agent. Since 1965, however, Quinto had also performed services on a part-time basis for the architectural and engineering firm of Wiedersum Associates. * * *

* * *

Inasmuch as the defense acknowledged that Quinto had failed to report the aggregate $15,700 received from Wiedersum during 1974 and 1975, the government's proof at trial was directed at establishing that at the time he had failed to report the income Quinto had had the willful intent that must exist for a defendant to be convicted of tax evasion and of willfully subscribing false income tax returns. To establish the willfulness of Quinto's failure to report income, the government relied upon the testimony of James Wallwork, a Special Agent in the Intelligence Division of the Internal Revenue Service. The crucial portion of the agent's testimony concerned an interview with Quinto conducted by Wallwork, Peter Fuhrman, another IRS Special Agent, and two Assistant United States Attorneys. * * * Quinto was * * * asked why he had not reported the money he had received from Wiedersum during 1974 and 1975, and according to Wallwork, Quinto, after some abortive attempts to extricate himself from his obvious predicament, blurted out: "Okay, I was trying to screw the government out of some cash if I could."

Defense counsel conducted a vigorous cross-examination of Wallwork which was designed to show that the meeting of August 20 had been more of an inquisition than an interview * * *

* * * [T]he prosecution on redirect examination elicited from Wallwork that the agents had prepared a memorandum following the August 20 "interview" with Quinto. The document, consisting of eight single-spaced, typed pages, purported to describe exactly what had happened at Quinto's session with the agents. It disclosed, * * * in what was protrayed as a verbatim quotation of Quinto's remarks, that Quinto had confessed that his purpose in failing to report the income was "to screw the government out of some cash if [he] could." Arguing that there had been "a general attack on the agent's credibility," the government attempted to introduce the memorandum as a prior consistent statement usable not only to corroborate Wallwork's in-court direct testimony but also usable under Fed.R.Evid. 801(d)(1)(B) as "substantive evidence" to prove that Quinto had made the fatal admission the IRS agents claim he made. The defense objected to the admission of the document, and, although the judge sustained the objection, he expressly left open the possibility that he might permit the document to be admitted later in the trial "if there [were] a challenge to its credibility, even the form of a contradiction."

Quinto testified in his own defense and his testimony covered two distinct areas. First of all, his recollection of what had transpired at his interview conducted by the IRS agents and the federal prosecutors differed materially from the version of that incident conveyed to the jury through Agent Wallwork's testimony and, importantly, the version which would eventually be conveyed to the jury through the later-admitted IRS memorandum of that interview as well. Quinto, claiming that he had been lured to the interview on the pretext that the discussions there would involve certain land condemnation procedures, stated that the interview had been conducted in inquisitorial fashion, his inquisitors "badgering" and "goading" him and calling him a "liar" at several points during the interview. Quinto stated that he had not been informed at the start of the interview that he was a target, and that he had no recollection of having been informed that he had the right to leave the room at any time, or that he could refuse to answer questions. As to the supposed admission that he was trying "to screw the government out of some cash," Quinto testified that Agent Wallwork had distorted what Quinto had actually said:

When they were goading me and goading me, I just said, "Do you think for one moment I would try to screw the Government out of a few dollars?" That's what I said, in just that tone, with a question mark on the end of it. (Tr. at 693.)

During Quinto's direct examination, defense counsel also attempted to establish that Quinto's failure to report income and to pay the taxes due on that income was attributable to his good faith belief that his undeclared business expenses for 1974 and 1975 exceeded his unreported income for those two years. During his cross-examination, Quinto denied that he had admitted at the interview that his purpose in not reporting the income had been to "screw the government out of some cash." Undaunted by this categorical denial, the prosecutor kept pressing the witness to concede that he had made the damaging statement and, to get Quinto to retract his denial, the prosecutor attempted to "refresh the witness's recollection" by showing him the IRS memorandum and directing his attention to the point in the memorandum where it was stated that Quinto had made the admission of guilt. At this point the prosecutor again offered the IRS memorandum into evidence, and again Judge Pratt refused to admit the document.

* * *

After the defense had rested, the judge, of his own accord, reopened the question of the admissibility of the IRS memorandum:

* * *

The Court: * * * I have been thinking about it further, and have wondered whether you were now taking the position that the implied attack upon Mr. Wallwork's credibility as to recent fabrication or improper motive or influence or something, had been sufficiently established to warrant its admission.

Mr. Marcus: That in fact, is the basis for the offer at that time. It would seem to me that at this point, we have had almost a day of Mr. Quinto, in essence, saying that Special Agent Wallwork lied in connection with saying "He was not given his rights," saying he was or was not told he was a target, etc.

The Court: I know what he said. Just when you made the offer, you didn't say anything that rang the bell that you were reasserting the argument, which you had previously made, and *which I expressly left open in the event the contradictions should occur.*

You did intend to reassert that—

Mr. Marcus: That is correct, your Honor.

The Court: I will reflect on the matter over lunch. I will give you my ruling after lunch.

* * *

After lunch, the judge did exactly that, ruling that "I have decided that I will admit [the memorandum] into evidence under 801(d)(1)(2) [sic], I believe it is." * * * Thereafter, the prosecutor distributed the memorandum, now an exhibit in the case, to the jurors and it was taken by them into the jury room when they retired to deliberate Quinto's fate.

Quinto's principal argument on appeal is that the district court committed reversible error by admitting the IRS memorandum into evidence as a prior consistent statement under Fed.R.Evid. 801(d)(1)(B). We agree, and we hold that the memorandum should have been excluded regardless of whether it was offered for the truth of the matters asserted therein or merely for the more limited purpose of rehabilitating the in-court testimony of Agent Wallwork of the Internal Revenue Service.

For nearly 200 years last past, the courts have enforced, except in certain very limited circumstances, a general prohibition against the use of prior consistent statements. While it is true that the use of such statements to prove the truth of the matters asserted has always been clearly barred by the hearsay rule, the courts have also generally prohibited the use of such evidence even when the proponent of the prior consistent statement was simply offering it for the more limited purpose of bolstering the witness's damaged credibility. * * * The rationale for excluding most, but not all, prior consistent statements being offered to establish the witness's credibility is one of relevancy. "The witness is not helped by [the prior consistent statement;] even if it is an improbable or untrustworthy story, it is not made more probable or more trustworthy by any number of repetitions of it." 4 Wigmore, Evidence § 1124, at 255 (Chadbourn rev. 1972). There have been situations, however, in which courts traditionally have felt that it is indeed relevant to the issue of whether the witness's in-court testimony should be believed that on prior occasions the witness has uttered statements which are consistent with his in-court testimony. "Prior consistent statements traditionally have been admissible to rebut charges of recent fabrication or improper influence or motive." Note to Rule 801, Notes of the Advisory Committee on the Proposed Rules of Evidence [hereinafter "Advisory Committee Notes"], 56 F.R.D. 183, 296 (1972); * * * But the prior consistent statements have been so admissible only when the statements were made prior to the time the supposed motive to falsify arose. Only then was the prior consistent statement "relevant" on the issue of credibility; that is, it tended to make the trustworthiness of the witness's in-court testimony more probable, after that testimony had been assailed, inasmuch as the consistency of the prior statement with the witness's testimony at trial made it "appear that the statement in the form now uttered was independent of the [alleged] discrediting influence." 4 Wigmore, Evidence § 1128, at 268 (Chadbourn rev. 1972).

To the extent that a prior consistent statement is used for rehabilitative purposes, the Federal Rules of Evidence have apparently not altered prior law. Fed.R.Evid. 402 laconically states that "[e]vidence which is not relevant is not admissible," and "relevant" evidence is defined in Fed.R.Evid. 401 as being "evidence having any tendency to make the existence of any fact that is of consequence to the determination of the action more probable or less probable than it would be without the evidence." Needless to say, irrelevant evidence is evidence which does not possess such a tendency. While credibility is always an issue of consequence and while "testimony which aids in the jury's determination of a [witness's] credibility and veracity [is always relevant]," Lewis v. Baker, 526 F.2d 470, 475 (2d Cir. 1975), it is well-recognized, as we have already explained, that only some well-defined classes of prior consistent statements can really so assist the jury. Therefore, it has been only those particular categories of prior consistent statements which have been able to withstand the objection that the prior consistent statement is irrelevant to the issue of the witness's credibility.

* * *

* * * [T]he standards for determining whether prior consistent statements can now be admitted as substantive evidence are precisely the same as the traditional standards and, * * * continue to be the standards used under the new rules of evidence for determining which varieties of prior consistent statements can be admitted for the more limited purpose of rehabilitation.

It is clear, therefore, that to avoid having the prior consistent statement found irrelevant under Fed.R.Evid. 402 or incapable of satisfying the requirements of Fed.R.Evid. 801(d)(1)(B), the proponent must demonstrate three things. First, he must show that the prior consistent statement is "consistent with [the witness's in-court] testimony." Fed.R.Evid. 801(d)(1)(B). Second, the party offering the prior consistent statement must establish that the statement is being "offered to rebut an express or implied charge against [the witness] of recent fabrication or improper influence or motive." Id. Finally, it is necessary that, as was the situation under the law of evidence prior to the adoption of the Federal Rules of Evidence, the proponent must demonstrate that the prior consistent statement was made prior to the time that the supposed motive to falsify arose.

Here, during oral argument before us, in response to pointed questioning from the bench the government has failed to satisfy this third requirement. The various improper motives the defense vigorously asserted the IRS agent might have had for lying on the witness stand—motives reducible essentially to a claim that, regardless of Quinto's actual guilt or innocence, throughout the entire investigation the government agents were ruthlessly seeking a conviction, presumably to enhance their own professional advancement and aggrandizement—would have been as operative at the time the IRS agents compiled the memorandum summarizing their interview with Quinto as those motives were at the time the IRS agents testified at trial. Indeed, Quinto's testimony attempted to show that the "interview" had been more in the nature of a trap and an inquisition and that, even at the time of the interview, the IRS agents and the prosecutors were, in common parlance, out "to get" him. Thus, the deeply rooted prejudice which Quinto claims was motivating the agents' actions existed both at the time the memorandum was compiled and at the time of Quinto's trial.

Moreover, while the admissibility of the memorandum was being debated at trial, at no time during his extended remarks on the subject did the prosecutor apparently point out to Judge Pratt exactly what improper motives might have existed at trial that did not also exist at the time of the compilation of the memorandum. Indeed, restricting his argument advocating the document's admission to the ground that there had been "a general attack on the agent's credibility," indeed a "broad based attack on motive, intent, integrity of not only this agent, but the Internal Revenue Service in the preparation and prosecution of this case," the prosecutor seemingly thought the memorandum admissible regardless of the time when the alleged motive to falsify might have arisen. Judge Pratt also mistakenly assumed that, regardless of the time when any motive to falsify might have arisen, the memorandum was admissible as soon as there had been a clear "challenge to [the agent's] credibility, even [in] the form of a contradiction," * * * or "contradictory testimony by someone else." Although the district judge refused to admit the document during the redirect examination of Agent Wallwork, he did permit it to be introduced after Wallwork's testimony had been "contradicted" by Quinto and several other witnesses. The judge's apparent reasons for allowing the document to be admitted are not, and historically have not been, a sufficient basis for admitting prior consistent statements for rehabilitative purposes.

> A former consistent statement helps in no respect to remove such discredit as may arise from a contradiction by other witnesses. When B is produced to swear to the contrary of what A has asserted on the stand, it cannot help us, in deciding between them, to know that A has asserted the same thing many times previously. If that were an argument, then the witness who had repeated his story to the greatest number of people would be the most credible.

4 Wigmore, Evidence § 1127, at 267 (Chadbourn rev. 1972).

We therefore conclude that the memorandum was irrelevant for the rehabilitative purpose of bolstering Agent Wallwork's challenged credibility and, to the extent that it was used or could be used as substantive evidence to prove the truth of the matters asserted in the memorandum, it did not satisfy the requirements of Fed.R.Evid. 801(d)(1)(B) and it therefore was not excluded from the definition of hearsay contained in Fed.R.Evid. 801(c). As a consequence, it was inadmissible * * * We therefore hold that the district court erred in admitting the IRS memorandum against Quinto.

* * *

Judgment order reversed and case remanded for a new trial on all counts of the indictment.

———

See Federal Rules of Evidence 801(d)(1) at p. 922; California Evidence Code § 791 at p. 842, § § 1235–36 at p. 880.

Hypotheticals

(1) X is indicted for child molestation. The victim is A, his 12-year-old stepdaughter. At X's trial the prosecution calls A, who testifies that she has no recollection of any molestation by X, or of having testified before the grand jury. The prosecution seeks to read into the record a transcript of A's testimony before the grand jury, describing X's acts of molestation. X objects. Is X correct?

(2) X is charged with the murder of A by use of a beer bottle in a barroom fight. X claims that he struck in self-defense when A came at him with a knife. There were no witnesses to the killing. B testifies for X that shortly before the final encounter he saw A and X fighting in the bar with their fists, and that A was getting the best of it; that X was retreating as if he were trying to stop fighting; and that he, B, stepped in between A and X, stopped the fighting and then left the bar. On cross-examination, B has no recollection of making any prior statement to C. The prosecution calls C to testify that a week after the killing B told him that X started the earlier fight with A and he (B) heard X say during that fight that he was going to get a gun and shoot A. X objects. What result?

(3) X is prosecuted for robbery of a gas station. Y, a codefendant, is tried first and convicted. At X's trial, the prosecutor calls Y who proves to be a recalcitrant witness and testifies that he and a friend had gone to the gas station together and that he, Y, had committed the robbery. Y gives an "I-don't-remember" answer to the prosecutor's question as to whether X was the friend with him at the gas station. In answer to the prosecutor's questions seeking a description of the friend, Y gives evasive and "I-don't-remember" answers. Y gives an "I-don't-remember" answer to the prosecutor's question as to whether Y had given a statement to B, a police officer, as to who was with him at the robbery. The prosecutor calls B and represents that B will testify that Y told him that X was his accomplice and told him the part each played in committing the robbery. X objects to B's proposed testimony, on the ground that Y's prior statements are not inconsistent with any of Y's testimony. How should the court rule?

(4) X is prosecuted for assault with a deadly weapon upon A. X calls B, who testifies that A was approaching X with a gun in his hand when struck by X with a billiard cue. On cross-examination, the prosecutor asks B, "Didn't you state after X's encounter with A that A had no weapon in his hand when he was struck by X with the billiard cue?" X makes a lack-of-foundation objection, in that no time, place, or persons present are given. Is X correct?

3. BIAS

PEOPLE v. TAYLOR

Supreme Court of Colorado, En Banc, 1976.
545 P.2d 703.

LEE, Justice.

* * *

* * * On the evening of February 15, 1974, Denver police Officers Malara and Leary approached defendant as he left the "Apex Social Club." Recognizing him as "the party wanted in our daily bulletin," they asked him for identification. Not satisfied with defendant's response, Officer Leary pulled a wallet out of defendant's pocket, opened it, and found a social security card revealing his true identity. Leary then returned the wallet, and was about to frisk defendant when the latter pushed Leary into Malara and fled. The officers testified that as he was running defendant turned and fired several shots, and the officers fired in return. Defendant made good his escape that night, but was apprehended the next day. He denied either having a firearm in his possession or firing any shots at the officers.

At trial, the defense attacked the credibility of Officer Leary by revealing his alleged racial bias toward the defendant. Both officers were white and defendant was black. The impeachment was sought to be accomplished by cross-examining Leary about several arrests of blacks he had made within a few months of defendant's arrest. The prosecution objected on the ground that such cross-examination would inject collateral issues into the proceedings and confuse the jury. The objection was overruled, and the defense attorney was permitted to inquire in considerable detail into these other arrests.

In each instance, the officer firmly disavowed the use of either racial slurs or of excess force. In rebuttal, the defense called several witnesses to testify as to what transpired at these other arrests, and to contradict Leary's version. The prosecutor renewed his objections but these were overruled on the ground that the proffered testimony went to the the officer's credibility. The testimony of the rebuttal witnesses again went into great detail concerning each incident, and was to the effect that Leary was sadistic and brutal in the manner in which he effected the arrests.

At the close of the evidence, the prosecution further renewed its objection and moved for a mistrial. The motion was denied.

I.

The trial court properly concluded that the alleged racial biases of Officer Leary might be inquired into for the purpose of impeaching his credibility. Cross-examination should be liberally extended to permit a thorough inquiry into the motives of witnesses. Within broad limits, any evidence tending to show bias or prejudice, or to throw light upon the inclinations of witnesses, may be permitted. The trial court must, however, exercise its sound discretion to preclude inquiries that have no probative force, or are irrelevant; or which would have little effect on the witness' credibility but would substantially impugn his moral character.

We hold that the cross-examination was proper insofar as the defense counsel inquired into the officer's asserted racial slurs. Such prejudice, if shown, might have greatly assisted the jury in its weighing of the conflicting testimony.

Once Leary denied that he was racially prejudiced, the defense counsel was entitled to present extrinsic evidence to contradict him. In other words, a party who on cross-examination inquires into bias is not bound by the denial of the witness, but may contradict him with the evidence of other witnesses. Indeed, this court has been more liberal than the majority of jurisdictions[1] in permitting the introduction of evidence as to the bias of a witness. In Kidd v. People, 97 Colo. 480, 51 P.2d 1020, we held that the court's failure to receive extrinsic evidence relating to the bias of a police officer-witness was reversible error, though the officer himself had not been cross-examined as to his possible bias. And in Angelopoulos v. Wise, 133 Colo. 133, 293 P.2d 294, we reaffirmed the proposition that to show bias by extrinsic evidence no foundation need be laid by cross-examination.

We hold that the trial court ruled correctly in admitting the rebuttal testimony about the racial slurs purportedly made by Officer Leary.

II.

We emphasize, however, the dangers of too readily admitting such extrinsic testimony relating to bias.

"∗ ∗ ∗ After all, impeachment is not a central matter, and the trial judge, though he may not deny a reasonable opportunity at either stage [i.e., cross-examination or rebuttal testimony] to prove the bias of the witness, has a discretion to control the extent to which the proof may go. He has the responsibility for seeing that the sideshow does not take over the circus. ∗ ∗ ∗" *McCormick*, supra.

Much of the controverted evidence admitted in this case dealt not so much with possible racial bias as with details of the arrests made on other occasions by Officer Leary. We believe that the trial judge erred in permitting inquiry into the details of those arrests, both on cross-examination and on rebuttal. Such questions were aimed not merely at impeaching the credibility of the officer, but at maligning his character and official conduct generally. To routinely allow this sort of questioning could greatly delay the trial and in effect make the officer the defendant in a series of mini-trials dealing with the manner in which he arrested countless other persons at other times. The potential for harm would become especially great if the defense could introduce witnesses to testify as to such other arrests; for, if the defense witnesses could give their view of the officer's conduct on these occasions, surely the officer himself should have the right to present witnesses to tell his side of the story. The sideshow could indeed "take over the circus."

∗ ∗ ∗

In this area, what may not be asked of the witness himself may not thereafter be proven by the testimony of defense witnesses. Defendant

1. For the majority rule, see Annot., 87 A.L.R. 2d 407, and Later Case Service. Most states require a "foundation" in the form of cross-examination of the witness as to his bias.

could, of course, have called witnesses to testify as to Officer Leary's reputation in the community for truth and veracity. But even then specific instances of alleged misconduct could not have been detailed.

The evidentiary rulings of the trial court permitting detailed examination into the collateral arrests are therefore disapproved, except that evidence relating directly to racial slurs in connection with collateral arrests was admissible.

WALTZ, CRIMINAL EVIDENCE

127–8.

* * *

Proof of bias and the like is always relevant to credibility and can be inquired into thoroughly. This can run the gamut from showing that the accused's solitary alibi witness is his devoted wife to demonstrating that the witness on the stand has been bribed by the side whose cause his testimony favors.

Thus it can be brought out that an accomplice who has turned "State's evidence" was granted immunity from prosecution or promised a reduced sentence as a *quid pro quo* for testimony advantageous to the prosecution. Less dramatic circumstances can be revealed. Perhaps the defendant's witnesses can all be shown to be his relatives or close friends. Or perhaps—and this will be more difficult for the criminal investigator to develop—the defendant's witnesses, such as alibi witnesses, are persons over whom the defendant has some sort of hold. He has threatened them, or gotten others to threaten them, with bodily harm unless they testify in his favor. Threats to the witness's loved ones can be shown, as can threats to destroy the witness's business or reputation. Promises of a monetary or other type of reward for favorable testimony can be brought out.

Sometimes defense counsel, lacking anything more solid, will bear down on the fact that the prosecution's key witness has been housed in a good hotel, wined and dined, and supported financially pending and during the trial.

Example:

BY THE PROSECUTING ATTORNEY: Let's get this straight, Miss Adams. You state, as I understand it, that the accused was with you during all of the night in question?

A.   That's correct.

Q.   It is a fact, is it not, that you have been living with the accused, although not married to him, for the past five years?

A.   That's true. But we're going to get married sometime. He's promised me.

Q.   That is your hope, is it?

A.   Yes.

Q.   You won't be able to get married if he goes to jail on this charge, will you?

A.   No. Maybe I could wait for him.

Q.   And the fact also is that the accused has been and is now your sole source of financial support, isn't that so?

A.   Yes.

Q.   And he could not continue to support you if he goes to prison, could he?

A.   I guess not. They don't earn much in there.

Q.   You have everything to gain if Charlie is acquitted and everything to lose if he is convicted, is that not correct?

A.   Yes, but I'm not lying.

Q.   Can you give the court and jury the name of any person who saw you and Charlie together on the night in question?

A.   No.

It is proper to ask expert witnesses, such as a psychiatrist who has supported an insanity defense, whether he is being paid a fee for his testimony, although a carefully coached expert will usually sidestep this sort of cross-examination fairly artfully.

———

See Federal Rules of Evidence 806 at p. 928; California Evidence Code § 1202 at p. 877.

Hypotheticals

(1)   A sues X, a police officer, and Y City, X's employer, for damages for false imprisonment growing out of X's arrest of A in a barroom brawl. B, a witness for A, testifies that A was a mere bystander and not a party to the brawl. On cross-examination, X asks B if he had not, on two occasions, slashed tires on marked police cars and been convicted of malicious mischief for so doing. A objects that this is improper cross-examination and improper attempted impeachment of B. What result?

(2)   A sues X, a police officer, and Y City, X's employer, for damages for false arrest and imprisonment growing out of X's arrest of A in a barroom brawl. B, a witness for A, testifies that A was a mere bystander and not a party to the brawl. On cross-examination, X seeks to question B to elicit that he had had three felony arrests by Y City police resulting in no convictions, and six arrests by Y City police resulting in misdemeanor convictions. A objects to this cross-examination as being irrelevant and improper impeachment by specific instances of conduct. X asserts he is offering the evidence to prove bias by B against Y City police and against X as a police officer. Should A's objections be sustained?

Chapter VI

CONFIDENTIALITY AND CONFIDENTIAL COMMUNICATION

PART A. THE ATTORNEY: PRIVILEGE, LOYALTY AND ETHICS

1. PRIVILEGE

JEREMY BENTHAM, 5 RATIONALE OF JUDICIAL EVIDENCE

pp. 302–304 (1827) (quoted in part in 8 Wigmore, Evidence,
§ 2291 pp. 549–550, McNaughton rev. 1961).

Lawyer and Client

English judges have taken care to exempt the professional members of the partnership from so unpleasant an obligation as that of rendering service to justice * * * When in consulting with a law adviser, attorney or advocate, a man has confessed his delinquency, or disclosed some fact which, if stated in court, might tend to operate in proof of it, such law adviser is not to be suffered to be examined as to any such point. The law adviser is neither to be compelled, nor so much as suffered, to betray the trust thus reposed in him. Not Suffered? Why not? Oh, because to betray a trust is treachery; and an act of treachery is an immoral act * * * But if such confidence, when reposed, is permitted to be violated, and if this be known, (which, if such be the law, it will be), the consequence will be, that no such confidence will be reposed. Not reposed?—Well: and if it be not, wherein will consist the mischief? The man by the supposition is guilty; if not, by the supposition there is nothing to betray: let the law adviser say every thing he has heard, every thing he can have heard from his client, the client cannot have any thing to fear from it * * * What then, will be the consequence? That a guilty person will not in general be able to derive quite so much assistance from his law adviser, in the way of concerting a false defence, as he may do at present. * * *

LOUISELL, CONFIDENTIALITY, CONFORMITY AND CONFUSION: PRIVILEGES IN FEDERAL COURT TODAY

31 Tul.L.Rev. 101, 109–115 (1956).*
[All footnotes omitted.]

* * *

THE NATURE OF THE PRIVILEGES

Although European legal thought seems to regard at least certain privileges as consistent with the goal of accurate fact-finding because they help

*Copyright, 1957 by the Tulane Law Review
Association.

avoid perjury, Anglo-American analysis commonly proceeds from the premise that recognition of the privileges constitutes a perpetual threat to the ascertainment of truth in litigation. Assuming for present purposes the validity of this premise (which should be further tested by comparative law inquiry), it is nevertheless submitted that there are things even more important to human liberty than accurate adjudication. One of them is the right to be left by the state unmolested in certain human relations. At least, there is no violence to history, logic or common sense in a legislative judgment to that effect. It is the historic judgment of the common law, as it apparently is of European law and is generally in western society, that whatever handicapping of the adjudicatory process is caused by recognition of the privileges, it is not too great a price to pay for secrecy in certain communicative relations—husband-wife, client-attorney, and penitent-clergyman.

Therefore, to conceive of the privileges merely as exclusionary rules, is to start out on the wrong road and, except by happy accident, to reach the wrong destination. They are, or rather by the chance of litigation may become, exclusionary rules; but this is incidental and secondary. Primarily they are a right to be let alone, a right to unfettered freedom, in certain narrowly prescribed relationships, from the state's coercive or supervisory powers and from the nuisance of its eavesdropping. Even when thrown into the lap of litigation, they are not the property of the adversaries as such; even in litigation, they may be exclusively the property of perfectly neutral persons who wish to preserve despite litigation, just as they preserved prior to litigation, their right to be left alone in their confidences.

" * * * The privilege is that the confidential matter be not revealed, not that it be not used against the holder of the privilege or any other. * * * "

It may be that Wigmore, despite his monumental contribution to the law of privileges, has conduced to the current confusion by his emphasis on strictly utilitarian bases for the privileges—bases which are sometimes highly conjectural and defy scientific validation. It will be remembered that he predicates four fundamental conditions necessary to establish a privilege as an exception to the general liability of all persons to testify fully on all facts in a judicial proceeding:

(1) The communications must originate in a *confidence* that they will not be disclosed;

(2) This element of *confidentiality must be essential* to the full and satisfactory maintenance of the relation between the parties;

(3) The *relation* must be one which in the opinion of the community ought to be sedulously *fostered;* and

(4) The *injury* that would inure to the relation by the disclosure of the communications must be *greater than the benefit* thereby gained for the correct disposal of litigation.

As is well known, he concludes that all of the requisites exist for the husband-wife, client-attorney, and penitent-priest communications, but that only the third requisite exists in the patient-physician relationship which he considers should not be privileged. The thesis of his main justification of the client-attorney privilege, for example, is that "In order to promote freedom of consultation of legal advisers by clients, the apprehension of compelled disclosure by the legal advisers must be removed; and hence the law must prohibit such disclosure except on the client's consent." A telling attack on this thesis is made by one of the most precise analysts in the history of common law evidence.* The theory that this privilege is necessary to ensure that the attorney gets all essential information, inevitably rests ultimately on sheer speculation. Wigmore comes much closer to the heart of the matter when, in responding to Bentham's onslaught on this privilege, Wigmore states:

> "The consideration of 'treachery,' so inviting an argument for Bentham's sarcasms, is after all not to be dismissed with a sneer. The *sense of treachery* in disclosing such confidences is impalpable and somewhat speculative; but it is there nevertheless. * * * If the counsellors were compellable to disclose, 'no man * * * of a noble or elevated mind would stoop to such an employment.' Certainly the position of the legal adviser would be a difficult and disagreeable one; for it must be repugnant to any honorable man to feel that the confidences which his relation naturally invites are liable at the opponent's behest to be laid open through his own testimony. He cannot but feel the disagreeable inconsistency of being at the same time solicitor and the revealer of the secrets of the cause. This double-minded attitude would create an unhealthy moral state in the practitioner. Its concrete impropriety could not be overbalanced by the recollection of its abstract desirability. If only for the sake of the peace of mind of the counsellor, it is better that the privilege should exist."

Why would compellability to reveal his clients' secrets "create an unhealthy moral state in the practitioner?" Because, it is submitted, he would know that he was perverting the function of counselling. * * *

If it will help clarify thinking about the nature of the privileges, let us by all means use terminology appropriate to describe protection for significant human freedoms. The privileges are guarantees for the benefit of their holders; they exist from the moment of their inception in the confidential communication; they normally survive all the vicissitudes of life save only waiver by the owner; they survive even his death. The law will protect them at all stages of their existence. If they are in the form of written documents, the law will protect them against theft, trespass, subpoena, or other infringement; if oral, from all types of seizure to which such are susceptible: coercion, physical or psychological, trickery or fraud. If the holder becomes involved in litigation, a new type of attack on his privilege may or may not be made, in the discretion of his adversary. But if the attack is made, if the infringing question is propounded, the law through the judge will continue its protection by now affirmatively enveloping the holder in a cloak of silence. Realization that all this protection is for the holder of the privilege as such, regardless of whether or not in litigation he becomes an adversary or neutral witness, perhaps most keenly focuses up that the exclusionary feature of the privileges, far from defining them, is only an incident of their vitality. It is also noteworthy that, whether or not evidence rules primarily ex-

*Morgan, Suggested Remedy for Obstructions to Expert Testimony by Rules of Evidence, 10 U.Chi.L.Rev. 285, 288–290 (1943).

clusionary in nature, such as the hearsay rule, are attributable to the jury trial, the composition of the tribunal has nothing to do with the privileges. It is equally important to prevent disclosure in a judge or jury trial, an administrative hearing, deposition or other discovery proceeding, or any other procedure whatsoever. Of course the privileges can be waived by the holder; but so can an automobile be sold, given away, abandoned or destroyed; so can realty be deliberately conveyed or let go for taxes.

I write primarily of the genuine privileges whose validity is proved at least to the extent that general acceptance by the common and apparently European law proves it. The courts should, it is true, accept in a democratic society the legislative judgment in providing privileged status for additional communications, although concededly the new privileges may be spurious, unwarranted and abusive of the social interest in accurate adjudication. But it is submitted that in the long run insistence upon precise analysis of the reason for privileged communications, and close inquiry into the true nature and psychological, social, historical and moral importance to human freedom of claims to privilege, will best separate the genuine from the spurious. Conversely, it is the hodge-podge treatment of all the privileges, throwing them into a single pot labelled "exclusionary rules," that conduces toward making all privilege a mere matter of professional jealousy and contention, with the resultant spawning of spurious privileges. It is in the area indicated in this paragraph that further careful inquiry into non-common law sources, particularly in respect of the ultimate historical roots of each privilege, should I believe prove exceptionally fruitful.

* * *

See Federal Rules of Evidence 501 at p. 914; California Evidence Code § § 911–913, 915–919 at pp. 851–852, 853.

MATTER OF FISCHEL

United States Court of Appeals, Ninth Circuit, 1977.
557 F.2d 209.

SNEED, Circuit Judge:

Appellant Elaine B. Fischel was a witness in the criminal trial of Harry Margolis, Ronald H. Adolphson, Quentin L. Breen and Banco Popular Antilliano, N.V. During the course of her testimony the district court ordered her to produce certain documents known as "system accountings." After consultation with counsel, appellant refused to furnish the majority[1] of these system accountings on the grounds that they were protected by the attorney-client and the work product privileges. * * * The district court adjudged her guilty of contempt for this refusal and appellant appeals therefrom. We affirm.

I.

Factual Background.

Appellant is an attorney who was associated in differing capacities with defendant Harry Margolis, also an attorney, from 1964 to 1971. During this

---

1. Appellant produced the system accountings pertaining to transactions involving two of her former clients, both of whom are now deceased. She now seeks to retrieve these system accountings as well. See part II(D), infra.

association, she performed tax planning services for her clients with the help of Margolis. These services included designing business transactions for her clients which it was hoped would reduce their taxes.

These business transactions were conducted with a group of business entities which Margolis used to effectuate his tax planning ideas. As a group these entities came to be designated as the "system." Appellant kept track of each of her client's dealings with each entity in the system. She recorded these transactions on a ledger to arrive at a composite picture of each client's business transactions with the system as a whole. These composite pictures are the system accountings which are the center of the controversy now before us.

To understand our decision, a brief description of a system accounting is required. It is a summary prepared by counsel of the business transactions with third party entities undertaken by a client to effectuate the tax planning program devised by Margolis and used by appellant. The information contained in this summary is derived from the entities themselves, records maintained by counsel, and documents of the client. It also includes the fees and costs of the tax planning service. It appears in balance sheet form, giving a very brief description of each transaction, and the amount of money involved. At the end of the year, a balance is computed reflecting whether the client is a debtor to or creditor of the system. A system accounting is not a summary of tax advice given by counsel, nor is it a summary of confidential communications from a client to his attorney.

The district court held the system accountings

are not protected by the attorney-client privilege in that they and each of them constitute a record or compilation of past transactions publicly conducted, that they and each of them constitute a communication and record of clerical information not conveyed or held in confidence as between attorney and client and that they and each of them do not represent communications made by a client to an attorney acting in a professional capacity as an attorney.

II.

Discussion.

A. *Attorney-Client Privilege.*

At the outset we note that federal, not state, law governs our decision. Fed.R.Evid. 501. Thus, it is to the federal common law we must turn for guidance in this case.

We begin with the formulation of the essential elements of the privilege found in 8 Wigmore Evidence § 2292 at 554. (McNaughton rev. 1961).

(1) Where legal advice of any kind is sought
(2) from a professional legal adviser in his capacity as such,
(3) the communications relating to that purpose,
(4) made in confidence
(5) by the client,
(6) are at his instance permanently protected
(7) from disclosure by himself or by the legal adviser,
(8) unless the protection be waived.

*   *   *

It is important to note that the privilege as defined in Wigmore is limited to "communications * * * made in confidence * * * by the client."[2] The privilege is so limited for a reason. The rationale for the rule is to encourage clients to confide fully in their attorneys without fear of future disclosure of such confidences. This in turn will enable attorneys to render more complete and competent legal advice. The purpose of the privilege is to protect and foster the client's freedom of expression. It is not to permit an attorney to conduct his client's business affairs in secret. 8 Wigmore, supra, § 2317; see generally Fisher v. United States, supra.

Of necessity the privilege is not limited to the actual communication by the client to the attorney. Ordinarily the compelled disclosure of an attorney's communications or advice to the client will effectively reveal the substance of the client's confidential communication to the attorney. To prevent this result, the privilege normally extends both to the substance of the client's communication as well as the attorney's advice in response thereto. It also extends to those papers prepared by an attorney or at an attorney's request for the purpose of advising a client, provided the papers are based on and would tend to reveal the client's confidential communications.

The privilege does not extend, however, beyond the substance of the client's confidential communications to the attorney. It will not conceal everything said and done in connection with an attorney's legal representation of a client in a matter. An attorney's involvement in, or recommendation of, a transaction does not place a cloak of secrecy around all the incidents of such a transaction.

For example, facts which an attorney receives from a third party about a client are not privileged. Extension of the privilege to this information would not serve to protect and foster the client's freedom of expression. A client has no expectation of confidentiality with respect to these facts. An attorney's subsequent use of this information in advising his client does not automatically make the information privileged. Thus, under the circumstances of this case, the facts of each transaction received from third parties are not privileged.

We must decide, however, whether summaries of a client's business transactions with third parties compiled by an attorney from unprivileged facts are entitled to the protection of the privilege. The claimant of the privilege, of course, must bear the burden of proving that he is entitled to this protection. These summaries, in addition to reflecting facts received from third parties, constitute a communication of sorts by the attorney to the client. To be within the privilege, appellant must show that these summaries directly or indirectly reveal communications of a confidential nature by the client to the attorney. Otherwise, disclosure of the summaries in no way infringes upon the confidentiality of the attorney-client relationship.

2. The Government contends that appellant was not acting in her capacity as a lawyer, but rather served as an investment counselor or business associate to her clients and consequently no attorney-client privilege is available. We do not pass on the merits of this contention.

On the record before us, we cannot say that the summaries will tend to reveal any such confidential communication.[3]

Perhaps an experienced tax planner could glean from the summaries sufficient information to enable him to understand the general tenor of the tax advice given by appellant. This does not, however, supply the required link between the summaries and the privileged communications which is required to extend the privilege.[4] To supply this link, the summaries, or any entry thereon, must be so interwoven with the privileged communications that disclosure of the former leads irresistibly to disclosure of the latter.

Appellant has not demonstrated that such a link exists in the system accountings which the district court ordered produced. Hence, we affirm the district court's holding with respect to the absence of the attorney-client privilege. After compliance with the order, appellant may wish to establish the necessary connection with respect to particular summaries or portions thereof. This she may attempt to do. The district court, after such an effort, should determine whether the connection exists. If it does not, appellant should surrender the information or * * * be adjudged in contempt.

B. *Work product immunity.*

Appellant argues that the work product immunity should extend to these summaries prepared by appellant as an attorney. We disagree. The limited work product immunity extends only to certain materials prepared by an attorney in anticipation of litigation. The summaries were not prepared in such a setting.

* * *

Affirmed.

Koelsch, Circuit Judge, concurring and dissenting:

* * *

* * * I wholly disagree with the majority's conclusion that on this record the attorney-client privilege does not operate to shield the summaries from production and disclosure.

The attorney-client privilege, as I understand it, is that of the client and is intended to protect from public disclosure confidential communications he makes to his attorney in connection with legal matters. Necessarily, the privilege is not narrowly applied, for it would be a poor thing indeed if an attorney could be compelled to disclose the advice given his client in response to such a communication, for the essence of the communication would necessarily inhere in the response and be fairly deducible from it.

---

3. The inclusion of fee information does not render the summaries confidential. United States v. Hodge and Zweig, 548 F.2d 1347 (9th Cir. 1977).

4. We note that the Supreme Court has taken a restrictive view of the reach of the attorney-client privilege.

> [S]ince the privilege has the effect of withholding relevant information from the fact-finder, it applies

only where necessary to achieve its purpose. Accordingly, it protects only those disclosures—necessary to obtain informed legal advice—which might not have been made absent the privilege.

Fisher v. United States, 425 U.S. 391, 403, 96 S.Ct. 1569, 1577, 48 L.Ed.2d 39 (1976); see 8 Wigmore, Evidence § 2291 (McNaughton rev. 1961).

Here we are not concerned with a recalcitrant attorney-witness but with documents prepared by the attorney. If the issue were as the majority postulates, simply "whether summaries of a client's business transactions with third persons compiled by an attorney from unprivileged facts are entitled to the protection of the privilege," I would certainly join in voting to affirm. But the record does not provide such an easy springboard. The summaries are constituted of a melange of facts. Appellant testified before the district court that the information from which the documents were compiled was derived from manifold sources: from communications by the client, from co-counsel, from public records, and in part from calculations made by counsel on the basis of such composite information and not reflected in any other document. The documents sought by the government are thus amalgams as far as the source of their content is concerned: in part derived from communications from the client intended to be confidential, in part from public, non-confidential sources.

Of course, as the majority points out, it is not enough that an experienced tax planner might be able to "glean from the summaries sufficient information to enable him to understand the general tenor of the tax advice given by appellant." If that were the extent of the deduction, then the privilege, being that of the client, would not be violated. But I suggest the "experienced tax planner" could most likely deduce much more. Advice in the abstract in tax matters is not the norm. It most generally is based upon specific information.

In my view, a document need not, as the majority declares, "irresistibly" disclose a confidential communication in order to be protected by the privilege; if it is such as to reasonably permit such a communication to be deduce, I would honor the privilege and protect the client.

I would reverse.

CITY AND COUNTY OF SAN FRANCISCO v. SUPERIOR COURT

Supreme Court of California, 1951.
37 Cal.2d 227, 231 P.2d 26, 25 A.L.R.2d 1418.

TRAYNOR, Justice.   James Hession brought an action for personal injuries against the City and County of San Francisco and the Western Pacific Railroad Company. He alleged that he suffered brain concussion, nerve root damage, and nervous shock. At the request of Hession's attorneys, Dr. Joseph Catton, a physician specializing in nervous and mental diseases, twice gave Hession a neurological and psychiatric examination. In his deposition Dr. Catton testified that there was no physician-patient relationship between him and Hession; that he did not advise or treat Hession; that the sole purpose of the examination was to aid Hession's attorneys in the preparation of a lawsuit for Hession; and that he was the agent of the attorneys. He refused to answer questions regarding Hession's condition on the grounds that the information sought was privileged under subdivisions 2 and 4 of Section 1881 of the Code of Civil Procedure and that the questions called for "the use of faculties of a physician, neurologist, and psychiatrist and for an opinion based thereon, which opinion is a portion of my property which I do not wish to be deprived of without due compensation and arrangement having been made in relation thereto." Hession's counsel also claimed that the information was privileged.

Petitioner, the City and County of San Francisco, seeks a writ of mandamus to compel respondent court to order Dr. Catton to answer the questions.

The Physician-Patient Privilege

[The court finds that the physician-patient privilege is inapplicable]

The Attorney-Client Privilege

Although Dr. Catton can invoke no privilege of his own and there was no physician-patient privilege in this case, we have concluded that Dr. Catton was an intermediate agent for communication between Hession and his attorneys and that Hession may therefore invoke the attorney-client privilege under section 1881, subdivision (2) of the Code of Civil Procedure. That subdivision reads: "An attorney, cannot, without the consent of his client, be examined as to any communication made by the client to him, or his advice given thereon in the course of professional employment; nor can an attorney's secretary, stenographer, or clerk be examined, without the consent of his employer, concerning any fact the knowledge of which has been acquired in such capacity." See also, Bus. & Prof.Code, § 6068(e). This privilege is strictly construed, since it suppresses relevant facts that may be necessary for a just decision. It cannot be invoked unless the client intended the communication to be confidential, and only communications made to an attorney in the course of professional employment are privileged.

The privilege is given on grounds of public policy in the belief that the benefits derived therefrom justify the risk that unjust decisions may sometimes result from the suppression of relevant evidence. Adequate legal representation in the ascertainment and enforcement of rights or the prosecution or defense of litigation compels a full disclosure of the facts by the client to his attorney. "Unless he makes known to the lawyer all the facts, the advice which follows will be useless, if not misleading; the lawsuit will be conducted along improper lines, the trial will be full of surprises, much useless litigation may result. Thirdly, unless the client knows that his lawyer cannot be compelled to reveal what is told him, the client will suppress what he thinks to be unfavorable facts." Morgan, Foreword, Am.Law.Inst. Code of Evidence, pp. 25–26. Given the privilege, a client may make such a disclosure without fear that his attorney may be forced to reveal the information confided to him. "[T]he absence of the privilege would convert the attorney habitually and inevitably into a mere informer for the benefit of the opponent." 8 Wigmore, supra, § 2380a, p. 813.

The privilege embraces not only oral or written statements but actions, signs, or other means of communicating information by a client to his attorney. "(A)lmost any act, done by the client in the sight of the attorney and during the consultation, may conceivably be done by the client as the subject of a communication, and the only question will be whether, in the circumstances of the case, it was intended to be done as such. The client, supposedly, may make a specimen of his handwriting for the attorney's information, or may exhibit an identifying scar, or may show a secret token. If any of these acts are done as part of a communication to the attorney, and if further the communication is intended to be confidential * * *, the privilege comes into play." 8 Wigmore, supra, § 2306, p. 590.

Petitioner contends that under the express terms of section 1881(2) it is only the attorney and the attorney's secretary, stenographer, or clerk who cannot be examined, and that since Dr. Catton was not engaged in any of these capacities he cannot withhold the information requested.

The statute specifically extends the client's privilege to preclude examination of the attorney's secretary, stenographer, or clerk regarding information of communications between attorney and client acquired in such capacities, to rule out the possibility of their coming within the general rule that the privilege does not preclude the examination of a third person who overhears or otherwise has knowledge of communications between a client and his attorney. It does not follow, however, that intermediate agents of communication between attorney and client fall within that general rule. Had Hession himself described his condition to his attorneys there could be no doubt that the communication would be privileged and that neither the attorney nor Hession could be compelled to reveal it, even though a client is not listed in section 1881(2) among those who cannot be examined. It is no less the client's communication to the attorney when it is given by the client to an agent for transmission to the attorney, and it is immaterial whether the agent is the agent of the attorney, the client, or both. "(T)he client's freedom of communication requires a liberty of employing other means than his own personal action. The privilege of confidence would be a vain one unless its exercise could be thus delegated. A communication, then by *any form of agency* employed or set in motion by the client is within the privilege.

"This of course includes communications through an *interpreter,* and also communications *through a messenger* or any other *agent of transmission,* as well as communications *originating with the client's agent* and made to the attorney. It follows, too, that the communications of the *attorney's agent* to the attorney are within the privilege, because the attorney's agent is also the client's sub-agent and is acting as such for the client." 8 Wigmore, supra, § 2317, pp. 616–617; * * * Thus, when communication by a client to his attorney regarding his physical or mental condition requires the assistance of a physician to interpret the client's condition to the attorney, the client may submit to an examination by the physician without fear that the latter will be compelled to reveal the information disclosed. In Arnold v. City of Maryville, 110 Mo.App. 254, 85 S.W. 107, 108, and McMillen v. Industrial Comm. of Ohio, Ohio App., 37 N.E.2d 632, on which petitioner relies, it was held, as we hold in the present case, that there was no physician-patient privilege. In neither case, however, was the attorney-client privilege invoked or considered.

It is contended that the purpose of the patient-litigant exception in subdivision 4 of section 1881 would be defeated if the attorney-client privilege in subdivision 2 can be invoked to prevent a physician from divulging the results of his examination of a person for the purpose of aiding his attorneys in the preparation of an action for personal injuries. The two subdivisions relate to two separate and distinct privileges. Since there was no physician-patient relationship, there was no physician-patient privilege to waive; the whole of subdivision 4 including the exception was therefore inapplicable. It does not follow that if there is no physician-patient privilege there can be no attorney-client privilege. The patient-litigant exception applies only to the physician-patient privilege in subdivision 4 and there is no corresponding client-litigant exception in subdivision 2. Had Dr. Catton treated Hession before being asked to serve as an intermediate agent between Hession and his attorneys, the patient-litigant exception would apply and Dr. Catton would then have been like any other witness with knowledge of facts pertinent to an issue to be tried. The exception could not be defeated by asking the physician to reveal his knowledge of the facts to the attorneys, for a litigant cannot silence a witness by having him reveal his knowledge to the litigant's attorney. Similarly, if Dr. Catton should now treat Hession, any information acquired in the course of that treatment would not be privileged, although the results of his previous examinations and his reports to Hession's attorneys would be.

The alternative writ of mandamus is discharged, and the petition for the peremptory writ is denied.

Gibson, C. J., and Shenk, Edmonds, Carter, Schauer and Spence, JJ., concur.

DIVERSIFIED INDUSTRIES, INC. v. MEREDITH

United States Court of Appeals, Eighth Circuit, 1978.
572 F.2d 596.

ON HEARING EN BANC

* * *

HEANEY, Circuit Judge.

This matter is before the Court en banc on a petition for a writ of mandamus. When the matter was first considered, a panel of this court * * * held that Diversified Industries, Inc., was not entitled to protect from discovery a memorandum dated June 19, 1975, and a report dated December, 1975, as well as certain corporate minutes and a letter dated January 30, 1976, from the President of Diversified by the Washington, D.C., These documents were prepared for Diversified by the Washington, D.C., law firm of Wilmer, Cutler & Pickering. It reasoned that the June 19 memorandum was not entitled to protection under the attorney-client privilege because the memorandum contained no confidential information and that the December report was not entitled to protection under the privilege because the law firm was not hired by Diversified to provide legal services or advice. * * *

* * *

A brief restatement of the facts will bring into focus the issues concerning the December, 1975, report, the corporate minutes and the January 30 letter.

* * *

In 1974 and 1975, during proxy fight litigation involving Diversified, facts surfaced indicating that Diversified may have established and maintained a "slush" fund to bribe purchasing agents of companies with whom Diversified dealt, presumably including Weatherhead [its customer].

On July 9, 1976, Weatherhead filed a complaint in the District Court alleging that Diversified conspired with Weatherhead employees to sell Weatherhead an inferior grade of copper and that in return for accepting the inferior copper, Weatherhead employees were paid bribes out of a "slush" fund. Weatherhead also alleged tortious interference with its employment contracts and violations of § 4 of the Clayton Act, 15 U.S.C. § 15.

As a result of the disclosures made during the 1974–1975 litigation, the Board of Directors of Diversified passed the following resolution:

RESOLVED, that, as this Board of Directors deems it to be in the best interests of this Corporation and its stockholders, the General Counsel of the Corporation be and he hereby is authorized, in behalf of this Board of Directors, to engage the services of Wilmer, Cutler & Pickering, Washington, D.C. to conduct an investigation and inquiry into the matters disclosed and discussed in this regard at this meeting for the purposes of eliciting facts, making certain findings, and providing to the Board of Directors of this Corporation a report possibly containing recommendations as to course of action, so that the Board of Directors of this Corporation may properly discharge its duties, and, further

RESOLVED, that Wilmer, Cutler & Pickering be and they hereby are authorized to procure assistance as may be reasonably required, in the above-designated inquiry, from accounting firms and others to conclude in a prompt and diligent manner the above commissioned inquiry and investigation, and, further

RESOLVED, that this Board of Directors hereby delegates to the Audit Committee of this Board the power and authority to review this matter in detail with Wilmer, Cutler & Pickering and, where necessary and appropriate, to provide to that firm any necessary interim authorizations or advice as may be necessary or desirable for the efficient handling and conclusion of the above mentioned inquiry and investigation, and, further

RESOLVED, that the officers and directors of this Corporation be and they hereby are directed to cooperate fully, and to ensure that all employees of this Corporation cooperate fully with Wilmer, Cutler & Pickering and such other persons as Wilmer, Cutler & Pickering may retain in the foregoing matters.

The law firm was subsequently directed to report to the Board of Directors rather than to the Audit Committee. The company President subsequently advised employees that he would take any steps necessary or appropriate to insure employee cooperation. During the course of the investigation, the law firm interviewed several employees of Diversified, including some who were not in a position to control or take a substantial part in a decision the corporation might make based on the law firm's advice. The December report summarized these interviews, analyzed the accounting data, evaluated the conduct of certain employees, drew conclusions as to the propriety of their conduct and made recommendations as to steps Diversified should take. Certain corporate minutes and parts of the January 30 letter restate critical portions of the report.

The attorney-client privilege applies to corporations. However, because a corporation can speak or hear only through its human agents, we must determine the circumstances in which employee communications can be classified as the corporate client's communications.

Two tests have developed in the federal courts. The first is the "control group" test formulated in City of Philadelphia v. Westinghouse Electric Corp., 210 F.Supp. 483 (E.D.Pa.), mandamus and prohibition denied sub nom., General Electric Co. v. Kirkpatrick, 312 F.2d 742 (3rd Cir. 1962), cert. denied, 372 U.S. 943, 83 S.Ct. 937, 9 L.Ed.2d 969 (1963). In this test, an employee's statement is not considered a corporate communication unless the employee "is in a position to control or even to take a substantial part in a decision about any action which the corporation may take upon the advice of the attorney, or if he is an authorized member of a body or group which has that authority [.]" Id. at 485. It is the most widely used test.

The second test is that formulated in Harper & Row Publishers, Inc. v. Decker, 423 F.2d 487 (7th Cir. 1970), *aff'd by an equally divided court,* 400 U.S. 348, 91 S.Ct. 479, 27 L.Ed.2d 433 (1971). In this test, "an employee of a corporation, though not a member of its control group, is sufficiently identified with the corporation * * * where the employee makes the communication at the direction of his superiors in the corporation and where the subject matter upon which the attorney's advice is sought by the corporation and dealt with in the communication is the performance by the employee of the duties of his employment." Id. at 491–492.

Although it predominates, the control group test has come under increasing criticism. * * * The principal criticism is that the control group test attempts to equate corporate clients with individual clients. An individual client both communicates to a lawyer and, based on the lawyer's advice, decides on an appropriate course of action. Similarly, before an employee's communiation will be deemed the corporate client's communication, the control group test demands that the employee communicate to the attorney and be in a position to control or play a substantial role in any decision based on the attorney's advice. In practice, this results in protecting only communications of top level executives which fails to take into account the realities of corporate life.

In a corporation, it may be necessary to glean information relevant to a legal problem from middle management and nonmanagement personnel as well as from top executives. The attorney dealing with a complex legal problem "is thus faced with a 'Hobson's choice'. If he interviews employees not having 'the very highest authority', their communications to him will not be privileged. If, on the other hand, he interviews *only* those with 'the very highest authority', he may find it extremely difficult, if not impossible, to determine what happened." * * * Thus, the control group test inhibits the free flow of information to a legal advisor and defeats the purpose of the attorney-client privilege. Moreover, the test may result in discouraging communications to lawyers made in a good faith effort to promote compliance with the complex laws governing corporate activity. * * * We conclude that the control group test is inadequate for determining the extent of a corporation's attorney-client privilege.

The *Harper & Row* test provides a more reasoned approach to the problem by focusing upon why an attorney was consulted, rather than with whom the attorney communicated. The test extends the privilege to communications made by any employee if a communication is made at the direction of the employee's superior and concerns the performance of his duties. In contrast to the control group test, it encourages the free flow of information to the corporation's counsel in those situations where it is most needed.

This test also has its critics. They argue, not unjustifiably, that the *Harper & Row* test can shield data from the discovery process. * * * The critics fear that many corporations will attempt to funnel most corporate communications through their attorneys in order to prevent subsequent disclosure. Judge Jack B. Weinstein, in his text on evidence, suggests several modifications that substantially limit whatever potential for abuse the *Harper & Row* test presents. 2 Weinstein's Evidence ¶ 503(b)[04] (1975).

We feel that the limitations suggested by Judge Weinstein have merit and that the attorney-client privilege is applicable to an employee's communication if (1) the communication was made for the purpose of securing legal advice; (2) the employee making the communication did so at the direction of his corporate superior; (3) the superior made the request so that the corporation could secure legal advice; (4) the subject matter of the communication is within the scope of the employee's corporate duties; and (5) the communication is not disseminated beyond those persons who, because of the corporate structure, need to know its contents. We note, moreover, that the corporation has the burden of showing that the communication in issue meets all of the above requirements.

This modified *Harper & Row* test will better protect the purpose underlying the attorney-client privilege. Under this test, the mere receipt of routine reports by the corporation's counsel will not make the communication privileged, either because the communication will have been made available to those who do not need to know or because the communication was not made for the purpose of securing legal advice. Moreover, application of the attorney-client privilege will do little to further encourage this type of communication since they will continue to be made for independent business reasons. By confining the subject matter of the communication to an employee's corporate duties, we remove from the scope of the privilege any communication in which the employee functions merely as a fortuitous witness. These are also communications that ordinarily would be made in any event.

We now apply these standards to the employee interviews to determine whether they are within the scope of the attorney-client privilege. We begin by deciding whether the communications were made for the purpose of securing legal advice for the corporation. We think it clear that they were.

Dean Wigmore has perceptively set forth the following generalized test:

It is not easy to frame a definite test for distinguishing *legal from non-legal advice*. * * * [T]he most that can be said by way of generalization is that a matter committed to a professional legal adviser *is prima facie so committed for the sake of the legal advice* which may be more or less desirable for some aspect of the matter, and is therefore within the privilege unless it clearly appears to be lacking in aspects requiring legal advice.

Obviously, much depends upon the circumstances of individual transactions.

8 Wigmore, Evidence § 2296 (McNaughton rev. 1961) [emphasis included].
*   *   *

Here, the matter was committed to Wilmer, Cutler & Pickering, a professional legal adviser. Thus, it was prima facie committed for the sake of legal advice and was, therefore, within the privilege absent a clear showing to the contrary. No such showing was made. Rather, the December report contained communications which were uniquely legal.

The charge to the professional legal adviser was a broad one. The law firm was given complete autonomy to conduct a professional investigation and inquiry. It was authorized to procure such assistance including accounting services as reasonably required. It was authorized to interview any employee of the corporation who might have knowledge of the facts—from the President to the nonmanagerial employees. Perhaps most importantly, it was given the authority to analyze the accounting data, to evaluate and draw conclusions as to the propriety of past actions and to make recommendations for possible future courses of action. Accountants could have been hired by Diversified to audit the books and records and lay investigators could have been employed to interview employees; but neither would have had the training, skills and background necessary to make the independent analysis and recommendations which the Board felt essential to the future welfare of the corporation. To be sure, there are possibilities of abuse, but the application of the attorney-client privilege to this matter and others like it will encourage corporations to seek out and correct wrongdoing in their own house and to do so with attorneys who are obligated by the Code of Professional Responsibility to conduct the inquiry in an independent and ethical manner.   *   *   *

It is clear that the remaining requirements of the test set forth by Judge Weinstein and adopted by us have been met. The resolution authorizing the law firm to conduct the investigation specifically instructed all corporate employees to cooperate fully with the law firm for purposes of the investigation. An examination of the report reveals that the interviews explored only areas within the bounds of the employees' corporate duties. Finally, the corporation scrupulously avoided disseminating this information to other than those immediately concerned with the results of the investigation.

We conclude that these employee interviews are confidential communications of the corporate client and entitled to the attorney-client privilege. Thus, the report and the relevant portions of the corporate minutes and January 30 letter are also privileged because disclosure would reveal directly or inferentially the contents of the interviews.

*   *   *

*   *   *   Each party shall bear its own costs.

NOTE

For the rules governing the attorney-client privilege, see California Evidence Code § § 950-962, at pp. 854-856; California Penal Code § 636.

LOUISELL, MODERN CALIFORNIA DISCOVERY*

From Chapter 10: Attorney-Client Confidential Communications
and "Work Product".

§ 10.02 GENERAL: THE NATURE OF THE PROBLEM

The principle of confidential communication between client and attorney as codified in C.C.P. § 1881–2, quoted supra, is basic in Anglo-American society as indeed it is throughout the Western World. Application of this principle occasions many difficult problems, theoretically and practically. Discovery, as such, does not seem to aggravate the problem but only to increase the occasions when inherent difficulties arise.

If a communication between client and attorney is confidential and hence truly privileged, it is privileged during discovery proceedings as well as at all other times. C.C.P. § 2016(b), quoted supra, clearly recognizes this fundamental fact by providing that all matters which are privileged against disclosure upon the trial under the law of this state are privileged against disclosure through any discovery procedure. Thus, in Grand Lake Drive In, Inc. v. Superior Court, 179 Cal.App.2d 122, 132, 3 Cal.Rptr. 621, 86 A.L.R.2d 129 (1960), it is stated: "No possible showing of good cause can dissipate or destroy [the attorney-client privilege] when it truly applies."

At the outset, the work product doctrine of Hickman v. Taylor, 329 U.S. 495, 67 S.Ct. 385, 91 L.Ed. 451 (1947)—in California the subject of recently enacted statutory provisions—should be clearly differentiated from the quite separate principle of confidentiality of attorney-client communications. This is not to deprecate the work product doctrine. To the contrary, reasonable privacy for the attorney in the conduct of litigation is an essential of the adversary system. This is true whether "work product" or some other phraseology is used to characterize the essential notion of privacy. But sharp distinction between the two principles—that of attorney-client confidences, on the one hand, and that of reasonable privacy for the attorney in his professional work, on the other—is essential to a clear analysis and to effectuation of the proper scope of each. When consideration of two distinct principles, each inherently difficult, is permitted to overlap, almost inevitably confusion is compounded.

§ 10.03 NATURE OF THE PROBLEM CONTINUED: GREYHOUND CORP. v. SUPERIOR COURT

Greyhound Corp. v. Superior Court, 56 Cal.2d 335, 15 Cal.Rptr. 90, 364 P.2d 266 (1961) well illustrates the separateness of the two principles, attorney-client confidential communications and the attorney's so-called "work product." In that case plaintiffs were injured in a collision between their vehicle and defendant's bus. Defendant's investigators took statements from witnesses, many of whom resided out of California and were subsequently unavailable to plaintiff. After filing suit, plaintiff moved under C.C.P. § 2031 to inspect and copy the statements. One of the defendant's grounds of opposition to the motion was that defendant should not be compelled to produce the statements of the independent witnesses for the reason that they came within the attorney-client confidential communications privilege. After reviewing the essentials of that privilege, the court explicitly overruled defendant's contention as follows, 56 Cal.2d at 397:

> These rules clearly demonstrate that the [defendant's] action of gathering and transmitting the witnesses' statements to its attorney did not create an attorney-client privilege unless such privilege existed, *ab initio*. That no privilege attached to those statements *ab initio* is demonstrated by the often-repeated proposition that the privilege created by subdivision 2 of section 1881 does not attach to matters communicated in the absence of a professional relationship or not intended to be confidential (citing cases). The witnesses, whose statements [defendant] has been ordered to disclose for inspection, did not intend their remarks to be confidential, and they were not in any sense parties to an attorney-client relationship. To attach privilege to the facts and matters which they voluntarily divulged to [defendant's] investigators would run contra to the rule expressed in Chronicle Pub. Co. v. Superior Court, supra, 54 Cal.2d 548, at p. 565: " ' * * * no new or common law privilege can be recognized in the absence of express statutory provision * * * ' The burden of establishing that the evidence is within the terms of the statute is upon the party asserting the privilege." Inasmuch as the witnesses' statements were not, of themselves, privileged, and since the inclusion of them in what may have been a confidential report did not extend any privilege to them, [defendant's] claim must fail.

The foregoing reasoning was reaffirmed in Suezaki v. Superior Court, 58 Cal.2d 166, 174, 23 Cal.Rptr. 368, 371, 373 P.2d 432 (1962), where the discovery of movies of plaintiff taken by the investigator for defendant's attorney, was held not precluded by the attorney-client privilege.

In *Greyhound* the defendant also invoked the work product doctrine. It argued that its attorney should not be required to disclose the statements of the independent witnesses for the reason that such were the product of its preparation for the defense of probable litigation. The court's consideration of this contention was separate from its consideration of the attorney-client confidential communication contention. This contention, too, was explicitly rejected by the court which said, 56 Cal.2d at 401:

> In its essence, the "work product rule" is a form of federally created privilege. The Legislature expressly refused to extend the concepts of privilege when adopting the discovery procedures. Since privilege is created by statute it should not be extended by judicial fiat. While the Hickman case, and any other case from a jurisdiction having a similar discovery statute, may be persuasive, and its reasoning accepted where applicable to California (citing cases) such should not be accepted as creating a privilege where none existed. We are therefore inclined to the view that the work product privilege does not exist in this state. This is not to say that discovery may not be denied, in proper cases, when disclosure of the attorney's efforts, opinions, conclusions or theories would be against public policy (citing case), or would be eminently unfair or unjust, or would impose an undue burden. * * *

Subsequently, the legislature enacted legislation which created a statutory work product privilege in California. But the separate consideration given by the court in *Greyhound* to the two distinct principles —attorney-client confidential communications on the one hand and "work product" on the other—should continue to be helpful to the bar in distinguishing carefully between them. While they often overlap, they proceed essentially from different bases and consequently when properly applied have different operative scopes. They are no more fungible than apples and oranges. * * *

CLARK v. STATE

Court of Criminal Appeals, Texas 1953.
159 Tex.Cr.R. 187, 261 S.W.2d 339.
Cert. denied 346 U.S. 855, 905, 74 S.Ct. 69(3), 217(2), 98 L.Ed. 360, 404.

MORRISON, Judge.   The offense is murder; the punishment, death.

The deceased secured a divorce from appellant on March 25, 1952. That night she was killed, as she lay at home in her bed, as the result of a gunshot wound. From the mattress on her bed, as well as from the bed of her daughter, were recovered bullets which were shown by a firearms expert to have been fired by a .38 special revolver having Colt characteristics. Appellant was shown to have purchased a Colt .38 Detective Special some ten months prior to the homicide.

* * *

Marjorie Bartz, a telephone operator in the City of San Angelo, testified that at 2:49 in the morning of March 26, 1952, while on duty, she received a call from the Golden Spur Hotel; that at first she thought the person placing the call was a Mr. Cox and so made out the slip; but that she then recognized appellant's voice, scratched out the word "Cox" and wrote "Clark." She stated that appellant told her he wanted to speak to his lawyer, Jimmy Martin in Dallas, and that she placed the call to him at telephone number Victor 1942 in that city and made a record thereof, which record was admitted in evidence. Miss Bartz testified that, contrary to company rules, she listened to the entire conversation that ensured, and that it went as follows:

The appellant: "Hello, Jimmy, I went to the extremes."

The voice in Dallas: "What did you do?"

The appellant: "I just went to the extremes."

The voice in Dallas: "You got to tell me what you did before I can help."

The appellant: "Well, I killed her."

The voice in Dallas: "Who did you kill; the driver?"

The appellant: "No, I killed her."

The voice in Dallas: "Did you get rid of the weapon?"

The appellant: "No, I still got the weapon."

The voice in Dallas: "Get rid of the weapon and sit tight and don't talk to anyone, and I will fly down in the morning."

It was stipulated that the Dallas telephone number of appellant's attorney was Victor 1942.

* * *

We now discuss the contentions raised by appellant's able counsel in their carefully prepared brief.

*   *   *

Proposition (1b) is predicated upon the contention that the court erred in admitting the testimony of the telephone operator, because the conversation related was a privileged communication between appellant and his attorney.

As a predicate to a discussion of this question, we note that the telephone operator heard this conversation through an act of eavesdropping.

In 20 Am.Jur., p. 361, we find the following:

"Evidence procured by eavesdropping, if otherwise relevant to the issue, is not to be excluded because of the manner in which it was obtained or procured   *   *   *   ."

This Court has recently, in Schwartz v. State, supra, affirmed by the Supreme Court of the United States on December 15, 1952, 73 S.Ct. 232, authorized the introduction of evidence secured by means of a mechanical interception of a telephone conversation.

We now discuss the question of the privileged nature of the conversation. Wigmore on Evidence (Third Edition), Section 2326, reads as follows:

"The law provides subjective freedom for the client by assuring him of exemption from its processes of disclosure against himself or the attorney or their agents of communication. This much, but not a whit more, is necessary for the maintenance of the privilege. Since the means of preserving secrecy of communication are entirely in the client's hands, and since the privilege is a derogation from the general testimonial duty and should be strictly construed, it would be improper to extend its prohibition to third persons who obtain knowledge of the communications."

The precise question here presented does not appear to have been passed upon in this or other jurisdictions.

In Hoy v. Morris, 13 Gray 519, 79 Mass. 519, a conversation between a client and his attorney was overheard by Aldrich, who was in the adjoining room. The Court therein said:

"Aldrich was not an attorney, not in any way connected with Mr. Todd; and certainly in no situation where he was either necessary or useful to the parties to enable them to understand each other. On the contrary, he was a mere bystander, and casually overheard conversation not addressed to him nor intended for his ear, but which the client and attorney meant to have respected as private and confidential. Mr. Todd could not lawfully have revealed it. But, in consequence of a want of proper precaution, the communications between him and his client were overheard by a mere stranger. As the latter stood in no relation of confidence to either of the parties, he was clearly not within the rule of exemption from giving testimony; and he might therefore, when summoned as a witness, be compelled to testify as to what he overheard, so far as it was pertinent to the subject matter of inquiry upon the trial   *   *   *   ."

In Walker v. State, 19 Tex.App. 176, we find the following:

"Mrs. Bridges was not incompetent or disqualified because she was present and heard the confessions made by defendant, even assuming that the relation of attorney and client subsisted in fact between him and Culberson."

The above holding is in conformity with our statute, Article 713, Code Cr.Proc.

"All other persons, except those enumerated in articles 708 and 714, whatever may be the relationship between the defendant and witness, are competent to testify, except that an attorney at law shall not disclose a communication made to him by his client during the existence of that relationship, nor disclose any other fact which came to the knowledge of such attorney by reason of such relationship."

Attention is also called to Russell v. State, 38 Tex.Cr.R. 590, 44 S.W. 159.

Appellant relies upon Gross v. State, 61 Tex.Cr.R. 176, 135 S.W. 373, 376, 33 L.R.A.,N.S., 477, wherein we held that a letter written by the accused to his wife remained privileged even though it had fallen into the hands of a third party. We think that such opinion is not authority herein, because therein we said:

"There is a broad distinction between the introduction of conversations overheard by third parties occurring between husband and wife and the introduction of letters written by one to the other, as shown by practically, if not all, the authorities. It is unnecessary to take up or discuss the question as to conversations going on between husband and wife which are overheard by other parties. That question is not in the case, and it is unnecessary to discuss it. We hold that the introduction of the contents of the letter through the witness Mrs. Maud Coleman was inadmissible. It was a privileged communication under the statute, and therefore interdicted. Article 774, Code of Criminal Procedure."

And, further on the opinion, we find the following:

"Not minimizing the same relation of client and attorney, but we do say that the relation between husband and wife is far more sacred, and to be the more strongly guarded, than that of relation between attorney and client."

We hold that the trial court properly admitted the evidence of the telephone operator.

* * *

Finding no reversible error, the judgment of the trial court is affirmed.

On Appellant's Motion for Rehearing

WOODLEY, Judge. We are favored with masterful briefs and arguments in support of appellant's motion for rehearing including amicus curiae brief by an eminent and able Texas lawyer addressed to the question of privileged communications between attorney and client.

* * *

As to the testimony of the telephone operator regarding the conversation between appellant and Mr. Martin, the conversation is set forth in full in our original opinion. Our holding as to the admissibility of the testimony of the operator is not to be considered as authority except in comparable fact situations.

For the purpose of this opinion we assume that the Dallas voice was that of Mr. Martin, appellant's attorney. If it was not appellant's attorney the conversation was not privileged.

It is in the interest of public justice that the client be able to make a full disclosure to his attorney of all facts that are material to his defense or that go to substantiate his claim. The purpose of the privilege is to encourage such disclosure of the facts. But the interests of public justice further require that no shield such as the protection afforded to communications between attorney and client shall be interposed to protect a person who takes counsel on how he can safely commit a crime.

We think this latter rule must extend to one who, having committed a crime, seeks or takes counsel as to how he shall escape arrest and punishment, such as advice regarding the destruction or disposition of the murder weapon or of the body following a murder.

One who knowing that an offense has been committed conceals the offender or aids him to evade arrest or trial becomes an accessory. The fact that the aider may be a member of the bar and the attorney for the offender will not prevent his becoming an accessory.

Art. 77, P.C. defining an accessory contains the exception "One who aids an offender in making or preparing his defense at law" is not an accessory.

The conversation as testified to by the telephone operator is not within the exception found in Art. 77, P.C. When the Dallas voice advised appellant to "get rid of the weapon" (which advice the evidence shows was followed) such aid cannot be said to constitute aid "in making or preparing his defense at law". It was aid to the perpetrator of the crime "in order that he may evade an arrest or trial."

Is such a conversation privileged as a communication between attorney and client?

If the adviser had been called to testify as to the conversation, would it not have been more appropriate for him to claim his privilege against self-incrimination rather than that the communication was privileged because it was between attorney and client?

Appellant, when he conversed with Mr. Martin, was not under arrest nor was he charged with a crime. He had just inflicted mortal wounds on his former wife and apparently had shot her daughter. Mr. Martin had acted as his attorney in the divorce suit which had been tried that day and had secured a satisfactory property settlement. Appellant called him and told him that he had gone to extremes and had killed "her", not "the driver". Mr. Martin appeared to understand these references and told appellant to get rid of "the weapon".

We are unwilling to subscribe to the theory that such counsel and advice should be privileged because of the attorney-client relationship which existed between the parties in the divorce suit. We think, on the other hand, that the conversation was admissible as not within the realm of legitimate professional counsel and employment.

The rule of public policy which calls for the privileged character of the communication between attorney and client, we think, demands that the rule be confined to the legitimate course of professional employment. It cannot consistent with the high purpose and policy supporting the rule be here applied.

The murder weapon was not found. The evidence indicates that appellant disposed of it as advised in the telephone conversation. Such advice or counsel was not such as merits protection because given by an attorney. It was not in the legitimate course of professional employment in making or preparing a defense at law.

Nothing is found in the record to indicate that appellant sought any advice from Mr. Martin other than that given in the conversation testified to by the telephone operator. We are not therefore dealing with a situation where the accused sought legitimate advice from his attorney in preparing his legal defense.

Some of the citations and quotations have been deleted from our original opinion.

We remain convinced that the appeal was properly disposed of on original submission.

Appellant's motion for rehearing is overruled.

CLIENT'S TIP-OFF LANDS
LAWYER IN A DILEMMA

The National Law Journal, March 26, 1979.

Lawyer Herschel Kozlov of Cherry Hill, N. J., was just trying to do the right thing.

He had learned from a client that a juror involved in convicting a police chief had held a secret grudge against the defendant. As was his duty, Mr. Kozlov told the trial judge.

But the trial judge wasn't satisfied. Nothing would suffice, he told Mr. Kozlov, but the name of his source.

Now, Mr. Kozlov had a conflicting duty: protecting the confidentiality of a client. Claiming the attorney-client privilege, he demurred. The judge rejected the claim and held Mr. Kozlov in contempt, fining him $50.

The New Jersey Supreme Court has rescued Mr. Kozlov, reversing the citation on Feb. 28. But his troubles may not be over.

Balancing Test

The high court said the lawyer passed a balancing test on when the attorney-client privilege must fall.

According to the court, the privilege yields under three circumstances: when there is a legitimate need for the evidence, when the evidence is material and relevant and when the information cannot be secured from a less intrusive source.

In this case, the "less intrusive source" would be juror Salvatore Yacovelli and his sister Luciana. No date has been set down yet for the court to interview them.

But if the Yacovellis are not forthcoming, the court warned, it may become necessary to call Mr. Kozlov on the carpet again.

Luciana Yacovelli had been convicted of shoplifting in 1974 after Sgt. Floard C. Catlett arrested her. Mr. Catlett went on to become chief in Lawnside, N.J., and was charged later with misconduct in office and bribery.

Mr. Yacovelli was on the jury that convicted Chief Catlett. Later the juror was heard bragging that he had gotten "even with the defendant for the arrest and prosecution of a member of his family," according to the State Supreme Court.

At this point a client came to Mr. Kozlov, who had no connection with the Catlett case, and told him about the juror's boasts. The high court called Mr. Kozlov "the classic innocent bystander."

Obeying DR 7-108(E), Mr. Kozlov "reveal(ed) promptly to the court improper conduct by * * * a juror."

But rather than question the implicated juror, Superior Court Judge Leon Wingate interrogated Mr. Kozlov, demanding his client's name. The lawyer kept the confidence.

[T]he high court freed the lawyer from his "dilemma of professional conscience."

"Privilege born of the common law, such as the attorney-client privilege here involved, is not an idle and anachronistic vestige of the ancient past," the court said.

"Vindicated"

"I feel vindicated," said Mr. Kozlov, 31, a lawyer since 1972. "I felt I had an obligation, and I had to discharge it. I don't regret it at all. The Supreme Court said we did the right thing."

However, as the court noted, if the interrogation of the Yacovellis is unsuccessful, "it may again become necessary to press attorney Kozlov and the case as to him may be reactivated."

"I'll cross that bridge when I come to it," Mr. Kozlov said.

Lawyer Charles Harp, who along with Joseph Kenney represented Mr. Kozlov, said the ruling saved his client but would be little help to other attorneys.

"It doesn't give attorneys much comfort in dealing with similar problems," Mr. Harp said. "They can tell their clients that there will be a weighing process involved, but there is no guarantee they can shield their clients."

UNITED STATES v. LIDDY

United States Court of Appeals, District of Columbia Circuit, 1974.
509 F.2d 428.
[Some footnotes and citations omitted.]

Before BAZELON, Chief Judge, and WRIGHT, McGOWAN, LEVENTHAL, ROBINSON, MacKINNON and WILKEY, Circuit Judges, sitting en banc.

LEVENTHAL, Circuit Judge:

Appellant Liddy seeks reversal of his conviction on charges relating to the burglary and wiretapping of the offices of the Democratic National Committee in the Watergate apartment-office building complex in the early morning hours of Saturday, June 17, 1972. Appellant was named in six counts of an eight count indictment returned against seven defendants[1] on September 15, 1972. On January 8, 1973, jury selection began before then Chief Judge John J. Sirica of the United States District Court for the District of Columbia. Shortly after the trial commenced, five defendants changed their pleas to guilty. On January 30, 1973, the remaining defendants, appellant Liddy and James W. McCord, Jr., were found guilty by the jury. Appellant was convicted of conspiracy in violation of 18 U.S.C. § 371 (count 1), burglary in violation of 22 D.C.Code § 1801(b) (counts 2 and 3), and unlawful endeavor to intercept oral and wire communications and interception of communications in violation of 18 U.S.C. § 2511(1)(a) (counts 4, 5, and 8). * * *

* * *

IV. INSTRUCTION REGARDING RETAINING OF COUNSEL

On direct examination, attorney Michael Douglas Caddy testified as follows: At approximately 3:40 a.m. Saturday morning, June 17, 1972, Howard Hunt arrived at his apartment and arranged with him to secure counsel for the five men arrested in the Democratic National Committee's offices an hour and a half earlier. At about 4:45 a.m. Hunt called Liddy and both Hunt and Caddy explained to Liddy the steps that had been taken to retain an attorney for those men. During this conversation, Liddy indicated that he desired to have Caddy represent him in this matter.

Appellant assigns as error the trial judge's instruction that the jury could draw no adverse inferences from the fact that Liddy retained counsel but could "consider the time and other surrounding circumstances at which Mr. Liddy retained Mr. Caddy with respect to the state of mind of Mr. Liddy only." Appellant claims that allowing the jury to draw inferences of guilty knowledge from his efforts to obtain counsel imposes a penalty on the exercise of his Sixth Amendment rights.[40] Liddy cites the Government's emphasis in closing argument on the unusual hour at which he retained counsel as evidence of the prejudicial nature of the alleged error.

Appellant bases his Sixth Amendment claim on Griffin v. California, 380 U.S. 609, 85 S.Ct. 1229, 14 L.Ed.2d 106 (1965). In that case the Court held that comment on the defendant's failure to testify was forbidden by the Fifth Amendment, because it was tantamount to a penalty for exercising a constitutional right. A number of courts, including this court, have extended the principle announced in *Griffin* to prohibit comment on the defendant's failure to make an exculpatory statement upon arrest.

---

1. The other defendants were James W. McCord, Jr., Everette Howard Hunt, Jr., Bernard L. Baker, Eugenio R. Martinez, Frank A. Sturgis and Virgilio R. Gonzalez.

40. Appellant's claim that the challenged testimony violated the attorney-client privilege is without merit. National Union Fire Ins. Co. v. Aetna Cas. & Sur. Co., 127 U.S.App.D.C. 364, 365 n. 4, 384 F.2d 316, 317 n. 4 (1967).

There is only scant law on the applicability of the penalty analysis employed in *Griffin* to the Sixth Amendment right to counsel. Some courts have found reversible error in circumstances in which the prosecutor has commented on the defendant's silence and request for counsel upon arrest. Those cases, though containing language referring generally to the right to counsel, appear to be bottomed on considerations involving the rights of an accused facing police interrogation—a context in which the right to counsel is intimately bound up with the privilege against self-incrimination. They are thus of marginal value in ascertaining the applicability of *Griffin* to the Sixth Amendment claim raised in the present case.

In the present case, the trial judge instructed the jury that no adverse inferences could be drawn from the fact that appellant Liddy exercised his constitutional right to counsel. The trial judge, however, drew a distinction between the fact of hiring counsel and the time and circumstances under which an attorney was retained by the defendant.

Although it is the latter action of the trial judge that is contested on this appeal, we may usefully begin our discussion by approval of his instruction prohibiting the drawing of an adverse inference from the mere fact of hiring an attorney, at least when the circumstances are such that admission of evidence of such a request provokes the possibility that it will be taken as self-incriminatory. This prohibition of adverse inference from the fact of hiring an attorney seems to us to be a fair corollary to the Supreme Court's opinion in *Griffin*. * * *

The trial judge erred, however, in limiting the application of the principle of *Griffin* with a ruling that apparently considered that it is generally proper to take into account the time and circumstances of retaining an attorney, and to draw whatever inferences as seem appropriate. Such a distinction generally raises problems that hobble the right to seek counsel. To the extent that an inference of criminality is operative, it invites probing of the very process of selection of counsel—who, why, when and where—and pressing the defendant to come forward with evidence concerning this process. The mischief of the approach is underlined by its semantic subtleties, which opens the door to maneuver and misunderstanding. It would be a rare case indeed where the prosecutor could not point out that the incriminating feature of the employment of counsel—in the absence of explanation—rests not in the employment as such but in the time and circumstances surrounding that event, and inferences therefrom that reflect adversely on the defendant.

The Third Circuit recently examined the application of *Griffin* to a Sixth Amendment contention in United States ex rel. Macon v. Yeager, 476 F.2d 613 (3rd Cir.), cert. denied, 414 U.S. 855, 94 S.Ct. 154, 38 L.Ed.2d 104 (1973). In that case the prosecutor in his summation to the jury commented upon the fact that the defendant called an attorney the morning after the alleged crime and argued that this action cast doubt on the defendant's claim that the shooting was an accident. Id. 476 F.2d at 614. Although the defendant neither objected to the comment nor requested an instruction, the court held that there was plain error that required a reversal of the conviction. The court read *Griffin* as an absolute prohibition against the imposition of any penalty for the exercise of a constitutional right in a criminal law context. Id. at 615–616.

We agree with the Third Circuit's analysis that the admission of a request for counsel raises Sixth Amendment problems under *Griffin.* We are not called upon in this case to determine whether the Third Circuit was correct in treating *Griffin* as a bar that is absolute—whether, for example, it would apply where the request for or retainer of counsel was part of the actions constituting the offense, sometimes called the res gestae, so that omission of the request or retainer would distort the underlying account of the witnesses or undercut the likelihood that it would be considered reasonable or natural.

In the present case, even if it be assumed that there was error in the admission of evidence, the prosecutor's summation, or the instruction, or all of these, the error would be "harmless beyond a reasonable doubt." * * * Here, the time at which Liddy retained counsel was but one of a number of factors that linked him to Hunt and the five defendants apprehended a couple of hours earlier. Moreover, the effect of the error was mitigated by the fact that evidence of part of Liddy's 5:00 a.m. conversation with Caddy was clearly admissible to show Liddy's involvement in his action of retaining counsel for those arrested during the break-in. His assertion of a right to Sixth Amendment protection against any use of his statements to obtain counsel for himself certainly does not prohibit inquiry into portions of his conversation with Caddy relating to his action in obtaining counsel for others. This evidence of Liddy's efforts on behalf of the five defendants only a few hours after their arrest was probative of his involvement in their venture.[45]

The evidence against the appellant, * * * was so overwhelming that even if there were constitutional error in the comment of the prosecutor and the instruction of the trial judge there is no reasonable possibility that it contributed to the conviction.

*   *   *

Affirmed.

Hypotheticals

(1)   D is charged with furnishing a restricted dangerous drug to V, a minor. V testifies and identifies D as the person who gave her pills. After the first day of trial, D disappears. X, D's attorney, testifies that D had expressed to him apprehension about whether V would show up to testify against him, and that upon seeing V enter the courtroom on the second day of trial, D departed. D is convicted by the jury. On appeal, D contends that it was error for the trial court to permit X to testify about D's communication to him as it violated D's lawyer-client privilege rights. Is D's contention correct?

(2)   D is charged with exploding a destruction device, causing great bodily injury to V. V testifies about a bomb in a package exploding as he opened the package. While testifying, V draws on the blackboard a diagram of the bomb. The prosecutor calls B, the court bailiff, who testifies, without objection, that while V was drawing the diagram, B was seated near the far end of the jury box and heard D tell his law-

---

45.   We are aware that this point, developed by Government's appellate counsel, differs from the trial prosecutor's use of the evidence—hammering away at the unusual hour. But it is properly taken into account in considering whether any error of the prosecutor at trial was harmless error.

yer: "It was not quite like that." D is convicted and makes a motion for a new trial on the ground that B's testimony was admitted in evidence in violation of D's lawyer-client privilege. How should the court rule?

(3)   X is prosecuted for perjury. X previously had been convicted of assault with a deadly weapon and sentenced to prison. X filed a habeas corpus petition, alleging that he had entered a plea of guilty to the assault charge because A, his lawyer, had assured him that the judge, with the prosecutor's concurrence, had agreed to a county jail sentence. In the habeas corpus proceeding, A denied giving X any such assurance. The perjury prosecution is based on X's allegations in the habeas corpus petition. At the perjury trial, the prosecutor calls A to testify to the communications between him and X when he represented X on the assault charge. X claims the lawyer-client privilege to prevent A's testimony. What result?

(4)   A was injured from a gas explosion occurring in a building under construction. A sues X, the contractor, and the Y Gas Co., which was installing gas equipment and machinery. Y Gas Co. files a cross-complaint against X. X takes the deposition of Z, an employee of Y Gas Co., who conducted an investigation of the explosion for Y. In answer to questions from X, Z testifies that he investigated the explosion upon the direction of his employer, Y Gas Co.; that he made a written report of the investigation; that one copy was sent to the accident-prevention department of the Y Gas Co. and the original was sent to the lawyer for Y Gas Co.; and that his job was to investigate all explosion-type accidents involving Y Gas Co.'s employees and equipment. Upon being asked what he discovered about the explosion and its cause, he answered that he had no present recollection and that he would have to look at his report. Y Gas Co.'s lawyer objects to Z's use of the report on the ground of the lawyer-client privilege. X seeks a court order to compel Z to answer the deposition questions through use of his report. How should the court rule?

(5)   A sues the X Gas Service Station for damages for personal injuries arising out of a freeway accident. A's car was stopped on the freeway, with part of it in a travel lane. A was standing in back of his car when he was struck by an oncoming car driven by Y. A settled with Y. A testifies that before getting on the freeway he got oil and gas from X and that X's employee failed to fasten the hood, which suddenly flew open on the freeway, causing him to stop. X calls P, a police officer, to testify that several weeks after the accident he (P) telephoned Z, A's attorney, and advised him that if P couldn't get a statement from A about how the accident happened, he would be forced to issue a traffic citation against A; that Z replied that A had been too ill to give a statement, but that Z knew the facts about the accident; that Z then said that A's engine had suddenly stopped and this was why A stopped; and that A first looked under the hood and then went to the back of his car to get some pliers when he was struck by Y's car. A objects to P's proposed testimony, on the ground that the lawyer-client privilege protects Z's disclosure to P of A's communication to Z. Is A's objection proper?

(6)   A sues the X Hospital, a corporation, for damages for injuries suffered in falling out of a hospital bed while he was a patient. A makes a pretrial discovery motion for inspection and copying of a report of the incident prepared by B, an employee of the X Hospital, in possession of X's lawyer. X opposes the motion by asserting the lawyer-client privilege. X files a declaration by C, the X Hospital administrator, that states that a few days after the accident to A, he directed B, who is head of nursing services, to prepare a report of the accident on a form provided by the Y Insurance Co., the hospital's liability-insurance carrier. The form read at the top, "Confidential—to be prepared for use of hospital attorneys in case of litigation." The declaration also states that B prepared the report and that it was sent to Y Insurance Co. without any copy being held by the hospital. Other declarations filed by X indicate that B was not a witness to A's fall, and that Y Insurance Co. sent B's report to the X Hospital's lawyer. Should A's motion be granted?

(7)   P sues D, a corporation, for damages arising out of a slip-and-fall accident at one of D's stores. At request of D's insurance carrier, D has M, the store manager, make a report of the accident. The report is transmitted to the carrier and then to defense counsel. P makes a discovery motion for inspection and copying of the report. D objects on the ground of the lawyer-client privilege. What result?

2.   ETHICS AND LOYALTY

HAZARD, ETHICS IN THE PRACTICE OF LAW
20–21, 127–135 (1978).*

[The American Bar Association Code of Professional Responsibility] deals with essentially three problems:

—Confidentiality: What matters learned by a lawyer should he treat as secret, and from whom, and under what conditions may the secrecy be lifted?

—Conflict of Interest: When and to what extent is a lawyer prohibited from acting because there is a conflict of interest between his clients or between himself and a client?

—Prohibited assistance: What kinds of things is a lawyer prohibited from doing for a client?

These are all tough problems, and not only for lawyers. What is perhaps not fully appreciated, by lawyers and laymen alike, is that similar problems arise in everyday life. If this fact were appreciated by lawyers, they might be able to perceive and to discuss the problems free of the introverted assumption that lawyers alone can appreciate their complex and stressful nature. If laymen recognized the similarity, they might regard the lawyers' ethical dilemmas with greater comprehension and perhaps even greater sympathy.

Many illustrations might be suggested from other walks of life, at work and at home, of problems involving confidentiality, conflict of interest, and prohibited assistance. A few will suffice to make the point. Thus, regarding confidentiality: What should a parent do who knows that his child has stolen something from a store? A pediatrician who discovers physical abuse of a child by its parents? A teacher who finds out that a student has been using drugs? An accountant who knows that his client is understating income for tax purposes? Regarding conflict of interest: Does a parent send a healthy child to college rather than send a sick one to the Mayo Clinic? A plant manager trim on safety systems to keep his company financially afloat? A doctor order hospitalization because medical insurance will not otherwise cover the patient? A supervisor commend a subordinate who may become a rival? Regarding prohibited assistance: Do you help a friend by lying to the police? Omit adverse information when asked to evaluate a former student or employee? Help sell stock that may be overvalued? Maintain the "character of a neighborhood" by not renting to a black?

If there is any peculiarity about these problems as they are confronted by lawyers, it is that a lawyer confronts them every day and is supposed to resolve them in a fashion that is compatible with a conception of his professional role. The Code of Professional Responsibility undertakes to tell him how he should do so.

* * *

No question of legal ethics is more difficult than the question whether an advocate can help suppress the truth in order to protect his client. In so far as litigation is concerned, the effect is to immobilize the law's enforcement. A lawyer can, within the limits of the law, obstruct its enforcement by advising his client to refuse to testify. At the borderland of the law, and without much risk to himself, he can go a considerable way in helping his client build a coverup. For example, he can advise the client about the consequences of preserving records or indicate to him the legal consequences of a certain line of testimony that the client might give. To the extent that such advice is given and acted upon, the effect is much the same as putting a client on the stand when it is known that his testimony will be false: The truth of the matter, which might have been discovered if the lawyer had not been involved, will less likely be discovered because he is involved. The problem is whether the benefits are worth that cost.

Paradoxically, the primary benefit of the system is often said to be the promotion of truth. For every instance in which truth is suppressed or distorted by the adversary system, it is thought there are more instances in which the system uncovers truth that otherwise would not have been uncovered. There is no practicable way to test this claim. It is worth considering, however, whether the situation would really be much better if we gave up the adversary system in favor of the interrogative system. But even if the claim were false we might want to keep the rule as it is. Under the present system, using ostensibly open competition for discovery of the truth, the law has troubles with suppression and distortion; what sort of troubles would it have if we depended on *ex officio* procedures for getting the evidence? If the truth suffers from our use of the adversary system, we ought to consider how it might suffer if we used some other system. In our political culture, the interrogative system of trial could well turn out to resemble Congressional hearings.

The real value of the adversary system thus may not be its contribution to truth but its contribution to the ideal of individual autonomy. This is the rationale underlying many rules that obscure the truth, such as the privilege against self-incrimination and the rule that private premises may not be searched without a warrant. The proposition, as applied to the adversary system, is that there is good in being able to say what one wants to say, even if it involves the commission of perjury. Stated baldly, the proposition is shocking. The norms of our society condemn lying, although it is perhaps worth noting that the biblical rule is the much narrower proposition that one should not bear false witness against a neighbor. At any rate, conventional morality does not openly recognize the value of being able to lie. Still, our commitment to truthfulness may actually go no futher than homily; when it comes to serious business such as negotiation and diplomacy, most people accept the utility, the inevitability, and perhaps even the desirability of dissimulation in various forms.

Why should dissimulation not be acceptable in court? There are many cultures in which it is assumed that parties to legal conflict lie on their own behalf; no pretense is made that they should be expected to do otherwise. The common law formerly exhibited the same attitude, for it did not allow testimony from a criminal defendant or any "party in interest" in civil litigation. The present ethical dilemma in the adversary system may therefore be ultimately traceable to the abolition of the common law rules of witness disqualification.

The reform of the common law rules occurred in the nineteenth century. It was based on the proposition that few injustices would result if interested persons were allowed to testify. It was believed that with cross-examination and the good sense of the jury, the truth will out most of the time. Perhaps it is time that this premise was reexamined, for it seems evident that if the stakes involved in a lawsuit are substantial, if the outcome depends on the truth, and if the parties are authorized to give evidence as to what the truth is, the parties will distort their submissions to the maximum extent possible. The artistry and self-conscious of the distortion will of course vary. In many cases it may be supposed that at least one party will tell the unvarnished truth, hoping if not trusting that it will be seen as such. But to require a party to choose between inprisonment or financial self-destruction on the one hand, and complete truthfulness on the other, is to impose a moral burden that may simply be too heavy. And, directly to the point of the present discussion, it imposes nearly as difficult a burden on the advocate who must advise the party in making the choice.

There is much ambivalence concerning the advocate's responsibility in this respect. The rules clearly say that, even in the defense of criminal cases, the advocate may not assist his client in committing perjury or in otherwise fabricating or suppressing evidence. In practice, lawyers often wind up violating these rules, some of them quite frequently. But they seek escapes from moral responsibility for having done so.

There are several escapes. It is said that no client is guilty until found so by a court; therefore, one cannot know what the truth is until then; therefore, one cannot conclude that a client's testimony will constitute perjury. This is pure casuistry. Of course there are doubtful situations, but there are also ones that are not doubtful. A thing is not made true or not by a court's pronouncing on it, and a lawyer can reach conclusions about an issue without having a judge tell him what to think.

Another escape is for the advocate to indicate to the client how inconvenient it would be if the evidence were such and so, and leave it to the client to do the dirty work—well illustrated in "the lecture" in *Anatomy of a Murder.* * Another is for the advocate to pretend that the rules governing his responsibility are different from what they are—to pretend that duty to client requires aiding him in whatever the client feels he must do to vindicate himself in court. The advocate is then absolved because he is merely an instrument.

As the situation stands, the advocate is supposed to be both the champion of his client and a gatekeeper having a duty to prevent his client from contaminating the courtroom. In principle, these responsibilities are compatible. The duty to the court simply limits the ways in which a lawyer can champion his client's cause. In practice, however, the duties have come to be in perhaps uncontrollable conflict.

* * *

*Traver, Anatomy of a Murder (1958).

If the adversary system is to be changed, it will not be a simple under-taking. The system as it exists expresses a number of strongly held beliefs and ideals. One is that justice should be free. It is this proposition that sup-ports the rule that the loser in litigation does not have to pay the winner's expenses. From this in turn follows the contingent fee system and the lack of inhibitions on running up an opposing party's costs, with the correspond-ing impairment of the advocate's gatekeeper function. Another belief is that entry into the legal profession should be relatively democratic. From this proposition it follows that admission is relatively easy, levels of training un-even, and professional esprit de corps weak. From this it follows that the images of professional lawyers are fuzzy and the potential for self-policing correspondingly low. Another is that litigation should secure not only jus-tice under law but natural and popular justice. From this it follows that liti-gation often has inherently political, redistributive, and sometimes sub-versive characteristics, which infuse not only the merits of the controversies but the way they are prosecuted or defended. The "Chicago Seven" trial is an illustration. Still another belief is the notion that militant advocacy is an especially genuine and efficacious expression of social conscience. Ex-emplars of this style are the relentless prosecutor, the fearless vindicator of the oppressed, the wily strategist for the establishment. It would be better if there were a larger constituency that understood, with Judge Learned Hand, that being in litigation, whatever its outcome, can justly be com-pared with sickness and death.

Perhaps the problem is this: We can have a system that does not charge user fees, lets everyone play, seeks both law and common justice, and is sub-ject to few inhibitions in style. We can also have a system in which a trial is a serious search for the truth or at least a ceremony whose essential virtue is solemnity. But we probably cannot have both. So long as the advocate in the American system is supposed to be at once a champion in forensic roughhouse and a guardian of the temple of justice, he can fulfill his respon-sibilities only if he combines extraordinary technical skill with an unusually disciplined sense of probity. That seems to be asking too much of any pro-fession.

LOWERY v. CARDWELL

United States Court of Appeals, Ninth Circuit, 1978.
575 F.2d 727.

MERRILL, Circuit Judge:

This habeas corpus appeal presents the problem of accommodating a criminal defendant's rights to fair trial and due process with the ethical duty of defense counsel to refrain from lending support to what he believes to be false testimony.

Appellant was charged by the State of Arizona with first degree murder. She pleaded not guilty and trial was had to the court without a jury. Testimony established that the victim's body had been found seated in his car, parked in front of a cafe. He had been shot twice at close range. The state's principal witness testified that he had seen appellant walk to the car with the deceased and stand on the far side of the car—the driv-er's side—while the deceased entered the car. Sounds similar to those of the popping of fire crackers had then been heard. *   *   *

The appellant took the stand and testified in part as follows:

"Q. * * * You heard Sarge's testimony that you walked outside with him?

A. No, I didn't.

Q. Did you walk out after him?

A. No.

Q. Did you at any time go to his car?

A. No.

Q. Did you shoot him?

A. Did I what?

Q. Shoot this man.

A. [Witness shakes head.]

Q. Do you understand my question?

A. Yes. You asked me did I shoot him.

Q. Yes.

A. No.

Q. You did not do so?

A. No."

Counsel then requested a recess which was granted. The trial transcript discloses that in chambers, without appellant being present, the following occurred:

"MR. LYDING: I'd like to put on the record that I move to withdraw.

THE COURT: State your reason.

MR. LYDING: I cannot state the reason.

THE COURT: Okay. The motion will be denied. Off the record.

[Whereupon, an off-the-record discussion was held.]"

Back in court counsel stated that he had no further questions of appellant. In closing argument to the court he made no reference to appellant's testimony to the effect that she had not accompanied the deceased to his car and had not shot him. Instead counsel argued that the state's case was subject to reasonable doubt and that if the court should find that appellant had pulled the trigger, still the case was not one of first degree murder.

The court found appellant guilty of second degree murder. The Supreme Court of Arizona affirmed. State v. Lowery, 111 Ariz. 26, 523 P.2d 54 (1974). After exhausting state remedies appellant sought habeas corpus in the District Court for the District of Arizona. * * *

* * *

[I]t was established that counsel had sought to withdraw because he believed appellant was lying; that for the same reason he had failed further to interrogate appellant or to argue her assertion that she had not shot the deceased; that nothing had occurred during the off-the-record period except an inquiry from the court as to how long trial would take. On the basis of this record the district court * * * dismissed appellant's petition for a writ of habeas corpus. * * *

* * * The due process question is whether the motion to withdraw, made when it was and under the circumstances then existing, served to deprive appellant of fair trial. We conclude that it did.

The problem presented is that which arises when defense counsel, in the course of a criminal trial, forms the belief that his client's defense is based on false testimony. We start with the basic proposition that if, under these circumstances, counsel informs the fact finder of his belief he has, by that action, disabled the fact finder from judging the merits of the defendant's defense. Further, he has by his action openly placed himself in opposition to his client upon her defense. The consequences of such action on the part of counsel, in our judgment, are such as to deprive the defendant of a fair trial. If in truth the defendant has committed perjury (a fact we do not know in this case) she does not by that falsehood forfeit her right to fair trial.

The question presented, then, is whether what here occurred amounted to such an unequivocal announcement to the fact finder as to deprive appellant of due process. In our judgment it must be said that it did. The judge, and not a jury, was the fact finder. From the testimony of appellant that we have quoted, from the fact that the examination of appellant ceased abruptly at that point with a request for a recess, from the making of the motion to withdraw and counsel's statement to the court that he could not state the reason for his motion, the only conclusion that could rationally be drawn by the judge was that in the belief of her counsel appellant had falsely denied shooting the deceased.

The result on these unusual facts is not inconsistent with the principles of professional responsibility under ethical standards as they are generally recognized today and does not expose counsel to a charge of subornation of perjury. The American Bar Association Code of Professional Responsibility states only that "In his representation of a client, a lawyer shall not * * * knowingly use perjured testimony or false evidence." Disciplinary Rule 7–102(A)(4). The ABA Defense Function Standards cast light on the rule and deal with the subject at greater length, although they do not deal specifically with trial before a judge without a jury or with the case where counsel is surprised by perjury in the course of examination of his client.[3]

---

3. Section 7.7 of the Standards states:

"Testimony by the defendant.

(a) If the defendant has admitted to his lawyer facts which establish guilt and the lawyer's independent investigation establishes that the admissions are true but the defendant insists on his right to trial, the lawyer must advise his client against taking the witness stand to testify falsely.

(b) If, before trial, the defendant insists that he will take the stand to testify falsely, the lawyer must withdraw from the case, if that is feasible, seeking leave of the court if necessary.

(c) If withdrawal from the case is not feasible or is not permitted by the court, or if the situation arises during the trial and the defendant insists upon testifying falsely in his own behalf, the lawyer may not lend his aid to the perjury. Before the defendant takes the stand in these circumstances, the lawyer should make a record of the fact that the defendant is taking the stand against the advice of counsel in some appropriate manner without revealing the fact to the court. The lawyer must confine his examination to identifying the witness as the defendant and permitting him to make his statement to the trier or the triers of the facts; the lawyer may not engage in direct examination of the defendant as a witness in the conventional manner and may not later argue the defendant's known false version of facts to the jury as worthy of belief and he may not recite or rely upon the false testimony in his closing argument."

The Standards, in brief, would appear to require that when, in the course of trial, counsel is surprised by his client's perjury he should not act to advance it. However, there is no requirement that he seek to withdraw, since, during trial, that course is likely not to be feasible. The Standards seem quite sensibly to assume that counsel will not be expected to act in such a fashion as to disclose his quandary to the fact finder.[4]

Thus it does not follow from our holding that a passive refusal to lend aid to what is believed to be perjury in accordance with the Defense Function Standards would violate due process. In our view, mere failure to pursue actively a certain course of defense, which counsel ethically is precluded from actively pursuing, cannot be said to constitute denial of fair trial. While a knowledgeable judge or juror, alert to the ethical problems faced by attorneys and the manner in which they traditionally are met, might infer perjury from inaction, counsel's belief would not appear in the clear and unequivocal manner presented by the facts here. There may be many reasons for failure actively to pursue a particular line of defense. And in the weighing of competing values in which we are engaged—the accommodation we specified at the outset of this opinion—the integrity of the judicial process must be allowed to play a respectable role; the concept of due process must allow room for it.

The distinction we draw is between a passive refusal to lend aid to perjury and such direct action as we find here—the addressing of the court in pursuit of court order granting leave to withdraw. By calling for a judicial decision upon counsel's motion in a case in which the judge served as fact finder, this conduct affirmatively and emphatically called the attention of the fact finder to the problem counsel was facing.[5]

---

4. An ABA panel, which included then Circuit Judge Warren E. Burger, in commenting on a hypothetical case submitted to it in 1966, anticipated the Standards on the question of the proper method of dealing with the client who insists on taking the stand to commit perjury. Judge Burger states:

"If in those circumstances the lawyer's immediate withdrawal from the case is either not feasible, or if the judge refuses to permit withdrawal, the lawyer's course is clear: He may not engage in direct examination of his client to facilitate known perjury. He should confine himself to asking the witness to identify himself and to make a statement, but he cannot participate in the fraud by conventional direct examination. Since this informal procedure is not uncommon with witnesses, there is no basis for saying that this tells the jury the witness is lying. A judge may infer that such is the case but lay jurors will not."

Burger, Standards of Conduct: A Judge's Viewpoint, 5 Am.Crim.Law Q. 11, 13 (1966).

5. The attorney may justifiably desire to establish a record for his own protection in the event that his professional conduct is later questioned. Especially in a case tried to the court, and even in a jury trial:

" * * * if the trial judge is informed of the situation, the defendant may be unduly prejudiced * * * and the lawyer may feel he is caught in a dilemma between protecting himself by making such a record and prejudicing his client's case by making it with the court. The dilemma can be avoided in most instances by making the record in some other appropriate manner, for example, by having the defendant subscribe to a file notation, witnessed, if possible, by another lawyer."

ABA Defense Function Standards § 7.7 Commentary at 277.

That this is an unhappy result cannot be denied. Trial counsel is to be commended for his attention to professional responsibility.[6] Nor can criticism be leveled at the trial judge for his confidence in his ability to remain unaffected by the motion to withdraw. We are acutely aware of the anomaly presented when mistrial must result from counsel's bona fide efforts to avoid professional irresponsibility. We find no escape, however, from the conclusion that fundamental requisites of fair trial have been irretrievably lost. Whether a just result nevertheless was reached would be a futile and irrelevant inquiry.

Reversed and remanded with instructions that the writ issue, unless, within fifteen days, the state shows good cause before the district court why the issuance should be delayed.

Hufstedler, Circuit Judge, specially concurring:

Although I do not disagree with the majority's due process analysis, I would rest the decision on the petitioner's Sixth Amendment right to effective assistance of counsel. The petitioner sustained her burden of proving that counsel failed to render reasonably effective assistance and that failure resulted in the denial of fundamental fairness.

*   *   *

STATE v. OLWELL

Supreme Court of Washington, 1964.
64 Wash.2d 828, 394 P.2d 681.

DONWORTH, Justice.   May an attorney refuse to produce, at a coroner's inquest, material evidence of a crime by asserting the attorney-client privilege or by claiming the privilege against self-incrimination on behalf of his client? These are the issues raised in this appeal.

September 18, 1962, a coroner's inquest was held for the purpose of investigating the circumstances surrounding the death of John W. Warren. Several days prior to the date of the inquest, appellant was served with a subpoena duces tecum, which said, in part:

" *   *   *   bring with you all knives in your possession and under your control relating to Henry LeRoy Gray, Gloria Pugh or John W. Warren."

Thereafter, at the coroner's inquest the following exchange took place between a deputy prosecutor and appellant:

" *   *   *

"Q.   Now, Mr. Olwell, did you comply with that? [Subpoena]

"A.   I do not have any knives in my possession that belong to Gloria Pugh, or to John W. Warren, and I did not comply with it as to the question of whether or not I have a knife belonging to Henry LeRoy Gray.

---

6.   Problems of ethics are not before us. Our sole concern relates to the requisites of due process and fair trial. Thus, we do not reach such questions as the extent to which counsel should satisfy himself that the testimony of his client is false, or the extent to which he should confer with his client before passively refusing to lend aid to her defense. Of course, we do not condone such misconduct as a deliberate and strategic causing of mistrial.

"Q. Now, I would ask you, do you have a knife in your possession or under your control relating to or belonging to Henry LeRoy Gray?

"A. I decline to answer that because of the confidential relationship of attorney and client; and to answer the question would be a violation of my oath as an attorney.

"   * * *

"Q. And for the record, Mr. Olwell, in the event you do have in your possession a knife or knives that would be called for under the subpoena duces tecum, I take it your answer would be that you received these at the time you were acting as the attorney for Mr.Gray, is that correct?

"A. That is correct."

Further, on examination by the coroner, the following occurred:

"Mr. Sowers: * * * As the Coroner of King County I order you to do so [answer] under the provisions of the law set forth in the legislature under R.C.W. 36.24.050.

"Mr. Olwell: I decline to surrender any of my client's possessions, if any, because of the confidential relationship of attorney and client because under the law I cannot give evidence which under the law cannot be compelled from my client himself."

The events preceding the issuance of the subpoena and the coroner's inquest (as shown by the record as supplemented by some undisputed statements in the parties' briefs) are substantially as follows: Henry LeRoy Gray and John W. Warren engaged in a fight on September 7, 1962, which resulted in Warren's being mortally injured by knife wounds. On or about September 8, 1962, Gray was taken into custody by the Seattle Police Department and placed in jail. During his incarceration, Gray admitted the stabbing of Warren and was willing to co-operate and to aid in the investigation of the homicide. According to a detective of the police department, Gray was not sure what became of the knife he had used in the fight with Warren.

September 10, 1962, David H. Olwell, appellant, was retained as attorney for Gray, who was still confined in jail. Mr. Olwell conferred with his client and then, between the time of that conference and the issuance of the subpoena duces tecum, he came into possession of certain evidence (a knife). It is not clear whether appellant came into possession of this knife through his own investigation while acting as attorney for Gray or whether possession of it was obtained as the result of some communication made by Gray to Olwell during the existence of their attorney and client relationship. This factor is important in determining whether the evidence could be considered as a privileged communication (which is discussed below.)

Therefore, at the time of the inquest, appellant was in possession of a knife that, at that time, was considered as a possible murder weapon.[1]

1. It is stated in respondent's brief that, on April 25, 1963, Henry LeRoy Gray was tried and convicted of murder and is now serving a life sentence for the crime. Furthermore, a knife other than the one involved in this proceeding was subsequently discovered to be the weapon used by Gray in the fight.

Thereafter, the coroner issued the subpoena duces tecum previously quoted.

Appellant appeared at the coroner's inquest and the exchange between appellant, the deputy prosecutor, and the coroner took place as described above. At that time, appellant refused to comply with the subpoena duces tecum and raised the issues presented in this appeal. Thereafter, appellant was cited to appear in the Superior Court of King County, where he was found to be in contempt because of his actions at the coroner's inquest on September 18, 1962. Appellant was given 10 days within which to purge himself of contempt, and, upon his failure to do so, an order was entered adjudging him to be in contempt and directing that he serve two days in the county jail. From that order finding him in contempt, Mr. Olwell appeals.

The attorney-client privilege is codified in RCW 5.60.060, which provides, in part:

> "The following persons shall not be examined as witnesses:
>
> "   *   *   *
>
> "(2)   An attorney or counselor shall not, without the consent of his client, be examined as to any communication made by the client to him, or his advice given thereon in the course of professional employment."

To be protected as a privileged communication, information or objects acquired by an attorney must have been communicated or delivered to him by the client, and not merely obtained by the attorney while acting in that capacity for the client. This means that the securing of the knife in this case must have been the direct result of information given to Mr. Olwell by his client at the time they conferred in order to come within the attorney-client privilege. Although there is no evidence relating thereto, we think it reasonable to infer from the record that appellant did, in fact, obtain the evidence as the result of information received from his client during their conference. Therefore, for the purposes of this opinion and the questions to be answered, we assume that the evidence in appellant's possession was obtained through a confidential communication from his client. If the knife were obtained from a third person with whom there was no attorney-client relationship, the communication would not be privileged, and the third person could be questioned concerning the transaction.[3]

Further, communications concerning an alleged crime or fraud, which are made by a client to the attorney after the crime or the fraudulent transaction has been completed, are within the attorney-client privilege, as long as the relationship of attorney and client has been established. Therefore, we find nothing significant in the fact that the communication was made after and concerned the events of a homicide.[4]

In the present case we do not have a situation that readily lends itself to the application of one of the general rules applicable to the attorney-client privilege. Here, we enter a balancing process which requires us to weigh that

---

3.   The state suggests that the knife was obtained from Gray's ex-wife, but it failed to offer any proof of this alleged fact to show that a privileged communication did not, in fact, exist.

4.   See State v. Cory, 62 Wash.2d 371, 382 P.2d 1019 (1963) on the question of the right of a client to confer privately with his attorney.

privilege (which is based on statute and common law), and, as discussed later herein, the privilege against self-incrimination (which is constitutional), against the public's interest in the criminal investigation process. Generally speaking, the public interest at times must yield to protect the individual. Also, we must not lose sight of the policy behind the attorney-client privilege, which is to afford the client freedom from fear of compulsory disclosure after consulting his legal adviser.

We must remember, also, that the attorney-client privilege is not absolute, for it can be waived by the client.

On the basis of the attorney-client privilege, the subpoena duces tecum issued by the coroner is defective on its face because it requires the attorney to give testimony concerning information received by him from his client in the course of their conferences. The subpoena names the client and requires his attorney to produce, in an open hearing, physical evidence allegedly received from the client. This is tantamount to requiring the attorney to testify against the client without the latter's consent. RCW 36.24.080 makes testifying in a coroner's inquest similar to testifying in a superior court, and, therefore, the attorney-client privilege should be equally applicable to witnesses at a coroner's inquest. We therefore, hold that appellant's refusal to testify at the inquest for the first reason stated by him was not contemptuous.

We do not, however, by so holding, mean to imply that evidence can be permanently withheld by the attorney under the claim of the attorney-client privilege. Here, we must consider the balancing process between the attorney-client privilege and the public interest in criminal investigation. We are in agreement that the attorney-client privilege is applicable to the knife held by appellant, but do not agree that the privilege warrants the attorney, as an officer of the court, from withholding it after being properly requested to produce the same. The attorney should not be a depository for criminal evidence (such as a knife, other weapons, stolen property, etc.), which in itself has little, if any, material value for the purposes of aiding counsel in the preparation of the defense of his client's case. Such evidence given the attorney during legal consultation for information purposes and used by the attorney in preparing the defense of his client's case, whether or not the case ever goes to trial, could clearly be withheld for a reasonable period of time. It follows that the attorney, after a reasonable period, should, as an officer of the court, on his own motion turn the same over to the prosecution.

We think the attorney-client privilege should and can be preserved even though the attorney surrenders the evidence he has in his possession. The prosecution, upon receipt of such evidence from an attorney, where charge against the attorney's client is contemplated (presently or in the future), should be well aware of the existence of the attorney-client privilege. Therefore, the state, when attempting to introduce such evidence at the trial, should take extreme precautions to make certain that the source of the evidence is not disclosed in the presence of the jury and prejudicial error is not committed.[5] By thus allowing the prosecution to recover such

5. See State v. Vindhurst, 63 Wash.Dec. 2d 611, 388 P.2d 552 (1964), where the defendant's former counsel was asked a question concerning the production of narcotics, a privileged communication. The question there was only whether or not the asking of the question alone was prejudicial error.

evidence, the public interest is served, and by refusing the prosecution an opportunity to disclose the source of the evidence, the client's privilege is preserved and a balance is reached between these conflicting interests. The burden of introducing such evidence at a trial would continue to be upon the prosecution. * * *

Because the subpoena duces tecum in this case is invalid, since it required the attorney to testify without the client's consent regarding matters arising out of the attorney-client relationship, the order of the trial court finding appellant to be in contempt and punishing him therefor is hereby reversed with directions to dismiss this proceeding.

Ott, C.J., Hamilton, J., and Langenbach, J., pro tem., concur.

Finley, J., concurs in the result.

IN RE RYDER

United States District Court, E.D. Virginia, 1967.
263 F.Supp. 360.

MEMORANDUM

PER CURIAM.   This proceeding was instituted to determine whether Richard R. Ryder should be removed from the roll of attorneys qualified to practice before this court. Ryder was admitted to this bar in 1953. He formerly served five years as an Assistant United States Attorney. He has an active trial practice, including both civil and criminal cases.

In proceedings of this kind the charges must be sustained by clear and convincing proof, the misconduct must be fraudulent, intentional, and the result of improper motives. We conclude that these strict requirements have been satisfied. Ryder took possession of stolen money and a sawed-off shotgun, knowing that the money had been stolen and that the gun had been used in an armed robbery. He intended to retain this property pending his client's trial unless the government discovered it. He intended by his possession to destroy the chain of evidence that linked the contraband to his client and to prevent its use to establish his client's guilt.

On August 24, 1966, a man armed with a sawed-off shotgun robbed the Varina Branch of the Bank of Virginia of $7,583. Included in the currency taken were $10 bills known as "bait money," the serial numbers of which had been recorded.

On August 26, 1966, Charles Richard Cook rented safety deposit box 14 at a branch of the Richmond National Bank. Later in the day Cook was interviewed at his home by agents of the Federal Bureau of Investigation, who obtained $348 from him. Cook telephoned Ryder, who had represented him in civil litigation. Ryder came to the house and advised the agents that he represented Cook. He said that if Cook were not to be placed under arrest, he intended to take him to his office for an interview. The agents left. Cook insisted to Ryder that he had not robbed the bank. He told Ryder that he had won the money, which the agents had taken from him, in a crap game. At this time Ryder believed Cook.

Later that afternoon Ryder telephoned one of the agents and asked whether any of the bills obtained from Cook had been identified as a part of the money taken in the bank robbery. The agent told him that some bills had been identified. Ryder made inquires about the number of bills taken and their denominations. The agent declined to give him specific information but indicated that several of the bills were recorded as bait money.

The next morning, Saturday, August 27, 1966, Ryder conferred with Cook again. He urged Cook to tell the truth, and Cook answered that a man, whose name he would not divulge, offered him $500 on the day of the robbery to put a package in a bank lockbox. Ryder did not believe this story. Ryder told Cook that if the government could trace the money in the box to him, it would be almost conclusive evidence of his guilt. He knew that Cook was under surveillance and he suspected that Cook might try to dispose of the money.

That afternoon Ryder telephoned a former officer of the Richmond Bar Association to discuss his course of action. He had known this attorney for many years and respected his judgment. The lawyer was at home and had no library available to him when Ryder telephoned. In their casual conversation Ryder told what he knew about the case, omitting names. He explained that he thought he would take the money from Cook's safety deposit box and place it in a box in his own name. This, he believed, would prevent Cook from attempting to dispose of the money. The lawyers thought that eventually F.B.I. agents would locate the money and that since it was in Ryder's possession, he could claim a privilege and thus effectively exclude it from evidence. This would prevent the government from linking Ryder's client with the bait money and would also destroy any presumption of guilt that might exist arising out of the client's exclusive possession of the evidence.

Ryder testified:

"I had sense enough to know, one, at that time that apparently the F.B.I. did have the serial numbers on the bills. I had sense enough to know, from many, many years of experience in this court and in working with the F.B.I. and, in fact, in directing the F.B.I. on some occasions, to know that eventually the bank—that the F.B.I. would find that money if I left that money in the bank. There was no doubt in my mind that eventually they would find it. The only thing I could think of to do was to get the money out of Mr. Cook's possession. * * *
[T]he idea was that I assumed that if anybody tried to go into a safety deposit box in my name, the bank officials would notify me and that I would get an opportunity to come in this court and argue a question of whether or not they could use that money as evidence."

The lawyers discussed and rejected alternatives, including having a third party get the money. At the conclusion of the conversation Ryder was advised, "Don't do it surreptitiously and be sure that you let your client know that it is going back to the rightful owners."

On Monday morning Ryder asked Cook to come by his office. He prepared a power of attorney, which Cook signed:

"KNOW YOU ALL MEN BY THESE PRESENTS, that I, CHARLES RICHARD COOK do hereby make, constitute and appoint, R. R. RYDER as my Attorney at Law and in fact and do authorize my said Attorney to enter a safety deposit box rented by me at the Richmond National Bank and Trust Company, 2604 Hull Street,

Richmond, Virginia, said box requiring Mosler Key Number 30 to open the same and I further authorize the said Attorney to remove the contents of the said box and so dispose of the said contents as he sees fit and I direct the officials of the said bank to cooperate with my said Attorney towards the accomplishment of this my stated purpose."

Ryder did not follow the advice he had received on Saturday. He did not let his client know the money was going back to the rightful owners. He testified about his omission:

"I prepared it myself and told Mr. Cook to sign it. In the power of attorney, I did not specifically say that Mr. Cook authorized me to deliver that money to the appropriate authorities at any time because for a number of reasons. One, in representing a man under these circumstances, you've got to keep the man's confidence, but I also put in that power of attorney that Mr. Cook authorized me to dispose of that money as I saw fit, and the reason for that being that I was going to turn the money over to the proper authorities at whatever time I deemed that it wouldn't hurt Mr. Cook."

Ryder took the power of attorney which Cook had signed to the Richmond National Bank. He rented box 13 in his name with his office address, presented the power of attorney, entered Cook's box, took both boxes into a booth, where he found a bag of money and a sawed-off shotgun in Cook's box. The box also contained miscellaneous items which are not pertinent to this proceeding. He transferred the contents of Cook's box to his own and returned the boxes to the vault. He left the bank, and neither he nor Cook returned.

Ryder testified that he had some slight hesitation about the propriety of what he was doing. Within a half-hour after he left the bank, he talked to a retired judge and distinguished professor of law. He told this person that he wanted to discuss something in confidence. Ryder then stated that he represented a man suspected of bank robbery. The judge recalled the main part of the conversation:

" * * * And that he had received from this client, under a power of attorney, a sum [of] money which he, Mr. Ryder, suspected was proceeds of the robbery, although he didn't know it, but he had a suspicion that it was; that he had placed this money in a safety deposit vault at a bank; that he had received it with the intention of returning it to the rightful owner after the case against his client had been finally disposed of one way or the other; that he considered that he had received it under the privilege of attorney and client and that he wanted responsible people in the community to know of that fact and that he was telling me in confidence of that as one of these people that he wanted to know of it.

"Q.   Did he say anything to you about a sawed-off shotgun? A. I don't recall. If Mr. Ryder says he did, I would not deny it, but I do not recall it, because the—my main attention in what he was saying was certainly drawn to the fact that the mony was involved, but I just cannot answer the question emphatically, but if Mr. Ryder says he told me, why, I certainly wouldn't deny it."

Ryder testified that he told about the shotgun. The judge also testified that Ryder certainly would not have been under the impression that he —the judge—thought that he was guilty of unethical conduct.

The same day Ryder also talked with other prominent persons in Richmond—a judge of a court of record and an attorney for the Commonwealth. Again, he stated that what he intended to say was confidential. He related the circumstances and was advised that a lawyer could not receive the property and if he had received it he could not retain possession of it.

On September 7, 1966 Cook was indicted for robbing the Varina Branch of the Bank of Virginia. A bench warrant was issued and the next day Ryder represented Cook at a bond hearing. Cook was identified as the robber by employees of the bank. He was released on bond. Cook was arraigned on a plea of not guilty on September 9, 1966.

On September 12, 1966 F.B.I. agents procured search warrants for Cook's and Ryder's safety deposit boxes in the Richmond National Bank. They found Cook's box empty. In Ryder's box they discovered $5,920 of the $7,583 taken in the bank robbery and the sawed-off shotgun used in the robbery.

On September 23, 1966 Ryder filed a motion to suppress the money obtained from Cook by the agents on August 26, 1966. The motion did not involve items taken from Ryder's safety deposit box. The motion came on to be heard October 6, 1966. Ryder called Cook as a witness for examination on matters limited to the motion to suppress. The court called to Ryder's attention papers pertaining to the search of the safety deposit boxes. Ryder moved for a continuance, stating that he intended to file a motion with respect to the seizure of the contents of the lockbox.

On October 14, 1966 the three judges of this court removed Ryder as an attorney for Cook; suspended him from practice before the court until further order; referred the matter to the United States Attorney, who was requested to file charges within five days; set the matter for hearing November 11, 1966; and granted Ryder leave to move for vacation or modification of its order pending hearing.

The United States Attorney charged Ryder with violations of Canons 15 and 32 of the Canons of Professional Ethics of the Virginia State Bar. Ryder did not move for vacation or modification of the order, and the case was heard as scheduled by the court en banc. After the transcript was prepared and the case briefed, the court heard the argument of counsel on December 27, 1966.

At the outset, we reject the suggestion that Ryder did not know the money which he transferred from Cook's box to his was stolen. We find that on August 29 when Ryder opened Cook's box and saw a bag of money and a sawed-off shotgun, he then knew Cook was involved in the bank robbery and that the money was stolen. The evidence clearly establishes this. Ryder knew that the man who had robbed the bank used a sawed-off shotgun. He disbelieved Cook's story about the source of the money in the lockbox. He knew that some of the bills in Cook's possession were bait money.

Judge Learned Hand observed in United States v. Werner, 160 F.2d 438, 441 (2d Cir. 1947):

"The defendants ask us to distinguish between 'knowing' that goods are stolen and merely being but upon an inquiry which would have led to discovery; but they have misconceived the distinction which the decisions have made. The receivers of stolen goods almost never 'know' that they have been stolen, in the sense that they could testify to it in a court room."

Judge Hand then went on to say (160 F.2d 442):

"But that the jury must find that the receiver did more than infer the theft from the circumstances has never been demanded, so far as we know; and to demand more would emasculate the statute * * * ."

In Melson v. United States, 207 F.2d 558, 559 (4th Cir. 1953), the court said:

"It is well settled that knowledge that goods have been stolen may be inferred from circumstances that would convince a man of ordinary intelligence that this is the fact."

We also find that Ryder was not motivated solely by certain expectation the government would discover the contents of his lockbox. He believed discovery was probable. In this event he intended to argue to the court that the contents of his box could not be revealed, and even if the contents were identified, his possession made the stolen money and the shotgun inadmissible against his client. He also recognized that discovery was not inevitable. His intention in this event, we find, was to assist Cook by keeping the stolen money and the shotgun concealed in his lockbox until after the trial. His conversations, and the secrecy he enjoined, immediately after he put the money and the gun in his box, show that he realized the government might not find the property.

We accept his statement that he intended eventually to return the money to its rightful owner, but we pause to say that no attorney should ever place himself in such a position. Matters involving the possible termination of an attorney-client relationship, or possible subsequent proceedings in the event of an acquittal, are too delicate to permit such a practice.

We reject the argument that Ryder's conduct was no more than the exercise of the attorney-client privilege. The fact that Cook had not been arrested or indicted at the time Ryder took possession of the gun and money is immaterial. Cook was Ryder's client and was entitled to the protection of the lawyer-client privilege. Continental Oil Co. v. United States, 330 F.2d 347 (9th Cir. 1964).

Regardless of Cook's status, however, Ryder's conduct was not encompassed by the attorney-client privilege. A frequently quoted definition of the privilege is found in United States v. United Shoe Mach. Corp., 89 F.Supp. 357, 358 (D.Mass.1950):

"The privilege applies only if (1) the asserted holder of the privilege is or sought to become a client; (2) the person to whom the communication was made (a) is a member of the bar of a court, or his subordinate and (b) in connection with this communication is acting as a lawyer; (3) the communication relates to a fact of which the attorney was informed (a) by his client (b) without the presence of strangers (c) for the purpose of securing primarily either (i) an opinion on law or (ii) legal services or (iii) assistance in some legal proceeding, and not (d) for the purpose of committing a crime or tort; and (4) the privilege has been (a) claimed and (b) not waived by the client."

The essentials of the privilege have been stated in 8 Wigmore, Evidence § 2292 (McNaughton Rev. 1961):

"(1) Where legal advice of any kind is sought (2) from a professional legal adviser in his capacity as such, (3) the communications relating to that purpose, (4) made in confidence (5) by the client, (6) are at his instance permanently protected (7) from disclosure by himself or by the legal adviser, (8) except the protection be waived."

It was Ryder, not his client, who took the initiative in transferring the incriminating possession of the stolen money and the shotgun from Cook. Ryder's conduct went far beyond the receipt and retention of a confidential communication from his client. Counsel for Ryder conceded, at the time of argument, that the acts of Ryder were not within the attorney-client privilege.

Ryder's reliance upon United States v. Judson, 322 F.2d 460 (9th Cir. 1963) and Schwimmer v. United States, 232 F.2d 855 (8th Cir. 1956), cert. denied 352 U.S. 833, 77 S.Ct. 48, 1 L.Ed.2d 52 (1956), is unfounded. In both of these cases subpoenas duces tecum were served upon lawyers requiring them to produce papers deposited with them by their clients. *Judson* turns upon the application of the Fifth Amendment. The court said at 322 F.2d 466:

"Clearly, if the taxpayer in this case * * * had been subpoenaed and directed to produce the documents in question, he could have properly refused. The government concedes this. But instead of closeting himself with his myriad tax data drawn up around him, the taxpayer retained counsel. Quite predictably, in the course of the ensuing attorney-client relationship the pertinent records were turned over to the attorney. The government would have us hold that the taxpayer walked into his attorney's office unquestionably shielded with the Amendment's protection, and walked out with something less.

* * *

"The thrust of the Fifth Amendment is that 'prosecutors are forced to search for independent evidence instead of relying upon proof extracted from individuals by force of law.' United States v. White, supra, 322 U.S. [694,] at 698 [64 S.Ct. 1248, 88 L.Ed. 1542]."

Schwimmer (232 F.2d 855) concerned papers which had been contained in a lawyer's files. The lawyer had discontinued his practice and had stored the papers with a manufacturing company. The court recognized that the lawyer had standing to quash a subpoena duces tecum. The case turned upon the Fourth Amendment. The court recognized that production of one's private books and papers by subpoena duces tecum for use against him in a criminal proceeding is prohibited by the Amendment. The fact that the papers were in the constructive possession of the attorney did not remove them from its protection. The court also recognized that the attorney had sufficient interest in the papers to be permitted to take a part in the proceedings to determine their admissibility. Not all papers in a lawyer's file are immune. The rule is summarized in McCormick, Evidence, § 93 at p. 188 (1954):

"[I]f a document would be subject to an order for production if it were in the hands of a client, it would be equally subject if it is in the hands of an attorney."

The basic difficulty with Ryder's reliance upon *Judson* and *Schwimmer* is that this proceeding is not concerned with the concealment of Cook's papers or other articles of an evidentiary nature. Neither Cook nor his attorney could be compelled to produce merely evidentiary articles nor could such articles be seized in a legal search. In Harris v. United States, 331 U.S. 145, 154, 67 S.Ct. 1098, 1103, 91 L.Ed. 1399 (1947), Mr. Chief Justice Vinson said:

"This Court has frequently recognized the distinction between merely evidentiary materials, on the one hand, which may not be seized either under the authority of a search warrant or during the course of a search incident to arrest, and on the other hand, those objects which may validly be seized including the instrumentalities and means by which a crime is committed, the fruits of crime such as stolen property, weapons by which escape of the person arrested might be effected, and property the possession of which is a crime."

Ryder, an experienced criminal attorney, recognized and acted upon the fact that the gun and money were subject to seizure while in the possession of Cook.

In Clark v. United States, 289 U.S. 1, 15, 53 S.Ct. 465, 469, 77 L.Ed. 993 (1933), Mr. Justice Cardozo expressed a dictum, which is apt to the aid Ryder gave Cook:

"We turn to the precedents in the search for an analogy, and the search is not in vain. There is a privilege protecting communications between attorney and client. The privilege takes flight if the relation is abused. A client who consults an attorney for advice that will serve him in the commission of a fraud will have no help from the law. He must let the truth be told."

Securities & Exchange Comm. v. Harrison, 80 F.Supp. 226, 230 (D.D.C.1948), aff'd, 87 U.S.App.D.C. 232, 184 F.2d 691 (1950), judgment order vacated as moot, 340 U.S. 908, 71 S.Ct. 290, 95 L.Ed. 656 (1951), describes the privilege and its limitations:

"That privilege has long been recognized as a very proper and necessary one to insure full and complete revelation by a person to an attorney to the end that the client may be properly advised, represented, and, in appropriate cases, defended by that attorney. To subject such revelations to exposure by the testimonial process would inevitably lead to concealments which would impair proper representation and thus interfere with proper administration of justice. While it relates to the rights of an individual, it is nonetheless recognized, as so many of our fundamental rights are, as essentially in the public interest. This privilege has, however, never been intended to be, and should not be, a cloak or shield for the perpetration of a crime or fraudulent wrong doing. One who consults an attorney to secure aid or assistance in the perpetration of a future crime or fraudulent wrong doing is not consulting that attorney for the legitimate purposes which are protected by the privilege. If, therefore, it be shown by evidence other than the disclosure of the communications between client and attorney that aid or assistance is being sought for the perpetration of crime or fraudulent wrongdoing, there is no immunity to the testimonial process respecting such communications."

In Clark v. State, 159 Tex.Cr.R. 187, 261 S.W.2d 339 (1953), cert. denied, reh. denied sub nom. Clark v. Texas, 346 U.S. 855, 905, 74 S.Ct. 69, 98 L.Ed. 369 (1953), a lawyer's advice to get rid of a gun used to commit a murder was admissible in evidence. The court observed the conversation was not within the realm of legitimate professional conduct and employment. In argument, it was generally conceded that Ryder could have been required to testify in the prosecution of Cook as to the transfer of the contents of the lockbox.

We conclude that Ryder violated Canons 15 and 32. His conduct is not sanctioned by Canons 5 or 37. In providing for the adoption and enforcement by the Supreme Court of Appeals of Virginia of rules and regulations prescribing a code of ethics to govern professional conduct of attorneys, the General Assembly of Virginia stated that "the Supreme Court of Appeals shall not adopt or promulgate rules or regulations prescribing a code of ethics * * * [for] attorneys * * * which shall be inconsistent with any statute * * * ." Va.Acts of Assembly 1940, ch. 314 at 508 (Mar. 28, 1940).

Pursuant to this legislation, the Supreme Court of Appeals of Virginia adopted the Canons of Professional Ethics, published in 205 Va. 1012. The Court followed the Canons of the American Bar Association. Pertinent to this case are Canons 5, 15, 32 and 37:

"5. *The Defense or Prosecution of Those Accused of Crime.* It is the right of the lawyer to undertake the defense of a person accused of crime, regardless of his personal opinion as to the guilt of the accused; otherwise innocent persons, victims only of suspicious circumstances, might be denied proper defense. Having undertaken such defense, the lawyer is bound by all fair and honorable means, to present every defense that the law of the land permits, to the end that no person may be deprived of life or liberty, but by due process of law.

"The primary duty of a lawyer engaged in public prosecution is not to convict, but to see that justice is done. The suppression of facts or the secreting of witnesses capable of establishing the innocence of the accused is highly reprehensible.

* * *

"15. *How Far a Lawyer May Go in Supporting a Client's Cause.* Nothing operates more certainly to create or to foster popular prejudice against lawyers as a class and to deprive the profession of that full measure of public esteem and confidence which belongs to the proper discharge of its duties than does the false claim, often set up the unscrupulous in defense of questionable transactions, that it is the duty of the lawyer to do whatever may enable him to succeed in winning his client's cause.

"It is improper for a lawyer to assert in argument his personal belief in his client's innocence or in the justice of his cause.

"The lawyer owes 'entire devotion to the interest of the client, warm zeal in the maintenance and defense of his rights and the exertion of his utmost learning and ability,' to the end that nothing be taken or be withheld from him, save by the rules of law, legally applied. No fear of judicial disfavor or public unpopularity should restrain him from the full discharge of his duty. In the judicial forum the client is entitled to the benefit of any and every remedy and defense that is authorized by the law of the land, and he may expect his lawyer to assert every such remedy or defense. But it is steadfastly to be borne in mind that the great trust of the lawyer is to be performed within and not without the bounds of the law. The office of attorney does not permit, much less does it demand of him for any client, violation of law or any manner of fraud or chicane. He must obey his own conscience and not that of his client.

* * *

"32. *The Lawyer's Duty In Its Last Analysis.* No client, corporate or individual, however powerful, nor any cause, civil or political, however important, is entitled to receive, nor should any lawyer render any service or advice involving disloyalty to the law whose ministers we are, or disrespect of the judicial office, which we are bound to uphold, or corruption of any person or persons exercising a public office or private trust, or deception or betrayal of the public. When rendering any such improper service or advice, the lawyer invites and merits stern and just condemnation. Correspondingly, he advances the honor of his profession and the best interests of his client when he renders service or gives advice tending to impress upon the client and his undertaking exact compliance with the strictest principles of moral law. He must also observe and advise his client to observe the statute law, though until a statute shall have been construed and interpreted by competent adjudication, he is free and is entitled to advise as to its validity and as to what he conscientiously believes to be its just meaning and extent. But above all a lawyer will find his highest honor in a deserved reputation for fidelity to private trust and to public duty, as an honest man and as a patriotic and loyal citizen.

* * *

"37. *Confidence of a Client.* It is the duty of a lawyer to preserve his client's confidences. This duty outlasts the lawyer's employment, and extends as well to his employees; and neither of them should accept employment which involves or may involve the disclosure or use of these confidences, either for the private advantage of the lawyer or his employees or to the disadvantage of the client, without his knowledge and consent, and even though there are other available sources of such information. A lawyer should not continue employment when he discovers that this obligation prevents the performance of his full duty to his former or to his new client.

"If a lawyer is accused by his client, he is not precluded from disclosing the truth in respect to the accusation. The announced intention of a client to commit a crime is not included within the confidences which he is bound to respect. He may properly make such disclosures as may be necessary to prevent the act or protect those against whom it is threatened."

The money in Cook's box belonged to the Bank of Virginia. The law did not authorize Cook to conceal this money or withhold it from the bank. His larceny was a continuing offense. Cook had no title or property interest in the money that he lawfully could pass to Ryder. The Act of Assembly authorizing the promulgation of the Canons of Ethics in Virginia forbids inconsistency with § 18.1–107 Code of Virginia, 1950, which provides:

"If any person buy or receive from another person, or aid in concealing, any stolen goods or other thing, knowing the same to have been stolen, he shall be deemed guilty of larceny thereof, and may be proceeded against, although the principal offender be not convicted."

No canon of ethics or law permitted Ryder to conceal from the Bank of Virginia its money to gain his client's acquittal.

Cook's possession of the sawed-off shotgun was illegal. 26 U.S.C. § 5851. Ryder could not lawfully receive the gun from Cook to assist Cook to avoid conviction of robbery. Cook had never mentioned the shotgun to Ryder. When Ryder discovered it in Cook's box, he took possession of it to hinder the government in the prosecution of its case, and he intended not to reveal it pending trial unless the government discovered it and a court compelled its production. No statute or canon of ethics authorized Ryder to take possession of the gun for this purpose.

Canon 15 states in part:

" * * * [T]he great trust of the lawyer is to be performed within and not without the bounds of law. The office of attorney does not permit, much less does it demand of him for any client, violation of law or any manner of fraud or chicane. He must obey his own conscience and not that of his client."

In helping Cook to conceal the shotgun and stolen money, Ryder acted without the bounds of law. He allowed the office of attorney to be used in violation of law. The scheme which he devised was a deceptive, legalistic subterfuge—rightfully denounced by the canon as chicane.

Ryder also violated Canon 32. He rendered Cook a service involving deception and disloyalty to the law. He intended that his actions should remove from Cook exclusive possession of stolen money, and thus destroy an evidentiary presumption. His service in taking possession of the shotgun and money, with the intention of retaining them until after the trial, unless discovered by the government merits the "stern and just condemnation" the canon prescribes.

Ryder's testimony that he intended to have the court rule on the admissibility of the evidence and the extent of the lawyer-client privilege does not afford justification for his action. He intended to do this only if the government discovered the shotgun and stolen money in his lockbox. If the government did not discover it, he had no intention of submitting any legal question about it to the court. If there were no discovery, he would continue to conceal the shotgun and money for Cook's benefit pending trial.

Ryder's action is not justified because he thought he was acting in the best interests of his client. To allow the individual lawyer's belief to determine the standards of professional conduct will in time reduce the ethics of the profession to the practices of the most unscrupulous. Moreover, Ryder knew that the law against concealing stolen property and the law forbidding receipt and possession of a sawed-off shotgun contain no exemptions for a lawyer who takes possession with the intent of protecting a criminal from the consequences of his crime.

Canon 15 warns against the reasoning urged in support of Ryder:

"Nothing operates more certainly to create or to foster popular prejudice against lawyers as a class and to deprive the profession of that full measure of esteem and confidence which belongs to the proper discharge of its duties than does the false claim, often set up by the unscrupulous in defense of questionable transactions, that it is the duty of the lawyer to do whatever may enable him to succeed in winning his client's cause."

We find it difficult to accept the argument that Ryder's action is excusable because if the government found Cook's box, Ryder's would easily be found, and if the government failed to find both Cook's and Ryder's boxes, no more harm would be done than if the agents failed to find only Cook's. Cook's concealment of the items in his box cannot be cited to excuse Ryder. Cook's conduct is not the measure of Ryder's ethics. The conduct of a lawyer should be above reproach. Concealment of the stolen money and the sawed-off shotgun to secure Cook's acquittal was wrong whether the property was in Cook's or Ryder's possession.

There is much to be said, however, for mitigation of the discipline to be imposed. Ryder intended to return the bank's money after his client was tried. He consulted reputable persons before and after he placed the property in his lockbox, although he did not precisely follow their advice. Were it not for these facts, we would deem proper his permanent exclusion from practice before this court. In view of the mitigating circumstances, he will be suspended from practice in this court for eighteen months effective October 14, 1966.   *   *   *

AN EXCHANGE OF LETTERS

The following correspondence is printed with the permission of the authors.

Charles Flynn
825 W. 8th
Anchorage, Alaska 99501

Dear Charles:

After conferring most recently on conference call with   *   *   *   , I have decided I would like to take them and you up on your offer to get an informal consensus from two members of the Ethics Committee. I understand you and   *   *   *   agree to send up your thoughts if I would submit the problem in the form of a hypothetical. So, here it is:

Defendant is arrested, charged with robbing a bank. The teller was held at gun point, bound with tape to a red bandana, while the safe was blown with plastic explosives.

Defendant tells me he is innocent—wasn't there. He can't get out of jail because of high bail. While defendant is in jail a friend comes to town and with defendant's consent occupies his trailer.

About a month after he is bound over by the grand jury and while he is still in jail, Defendant authorizes his friend to "clean out" the car in his driveway.

In the car, friend finds the following:

(1) a set of roller skates.

(2) a detailed floor plan of the bank robbed

(3) a list of "things to take with me", including roller skates, plastic explosives, and "tape and red bandana to tie teller"

(4) receipt for purchase of plastic explosives dated two days before robbery took place

Friend, without asking defendant's permission or disclosing to him his intentions, calls me, and turns over the above. I take possession of the writings.

All of the above were documents in handwriting of defendant. I approached defendant and asked him if he wrote them, he admitted it, however explained they were written "after I read of the bank robbery—I was fantasizing how I *would* have done it, if it were me". I, as his attorney cannot, in good faith, say I believe him.

QUESTIONS:

(1) Do I have an ethical obligation to turn over the material—or part of it, to the District Attorney or police? (If so, should I withdraw from the case?)

(2) If I keep the material, should I keep it in my personal possession or return it to the car where it was found?

Thanks for your work on this. I know you have a considerable time investment already Charles. If you and * * * could get your opinion off to me as soon as possible, I would appreciate it—especially if you determine I'll have to get off the case, and if he must get a new attorney he'll need all the time he can get.

Very truly yours,

STEPHEN R. CLINE
Ass't Public Defender

See also ABA Opinion 1057.

———

July 23, 1975

Stephen R. Cline
Assistant Public Defender
State of Alaska
Public Defender Agency
950 Cowles Street, Room 120
Fairbanks, Alaska 99701

Re: Ethics Committee
      Our File–1945

Dear Mr. Cline:

The Committee has considered the question posed in your letter of July 11, 1975, and has formulated an opinion as to your present ethically-required course of conduct.

I wish to stress, at the beginning, that this letter represents the opinion of the Ethics Committee solely, and has not been approved by the Board of Governors of the Alaska Bar Association, as is normally the case with our opinions. Likewise, our consideration and opinion is based solely upon the ethical requirements which may be imposed upon you as an attorney. You are also, of course, a citizen, and subject to the law in the same manner and to the same extent as other citizens. As you suggest in your letter, AS 11.30.315 may arguably impose upon you some duty with respect to the physical evidence in your possession. The Committee has taken the statute into consideration, but obviously can render no definitive opinion as to its applicability, or the applicability of other civil and criminal law of the State of Alaska. The course of conduct outlined in this letter is based upon ethical considerations, but if a different course of action is required by the statute, your observance of the statutory requirement would also be ethically proper. See DR4–101 (c) (2).

It is your duty under Canon 4 of the Code of Professional Responsibility to preserve the confidences and secrets of a client. As DR4–101 (c) points out, you may ethically reveal confidences or secrets of a client when required by law, but otherwise, such revelation of confidences or secrets is prohibited. As EC4–4 properly points out, this duty to safeguard the confidences and secrets of a client is broader than the attorney/client evidentiary privilege, and " * * * exists without regard to the nature or source of information or the fact that others share the knowledge." Thus, it seems clear to us that you are ethically obligated not to reveal the existence of the physical evidence which has come into your possession, unless required to do so by statute.

We have also considered informal opinion #1057 of the American Bar Association Committee on Ethics, and find the analysis therein persuasive. The American Bar Association has advised that when a client, or one acting on behalf of a client, presents evidence of the type you have described to us to the attorney, the attorney should decline to take possession of it and should advise the client with respect to his obligations regarding the evidence under relevant state law. If the client then declines to follow the course that he is legally obligated to follow, the attorney should either decline employment or withdraw from employment previously accepted. In our opinion, this is the correct balancing of the interests of society, the attorney's duty to preserve the confidences and secrets of a client.

Therefore, in the situation you have posed, it is our opinion that you are ethically required to contact the "friend" who tendered the evidence to you, return it to his possession, and advise him in the clearest possible terms as to his obligations and potential liabilities with respect to that physical evidence. This is done to re-create, as nearly as possible, the status quo ante.

If, after returning the physical evidence to the friend, you know, or it becomes obvious, that the physical evidence has been destroyed or concealed, we believe it is your ethical obligation, pursuant to DR7-102 and DR2-110, to withdraw from representation of the accused.

Finally, the Committee is concerned that the situation posed in your letter of July 11, 1975, or situations substantially similar and raising substantially the same issues, may arise with some frequency in the defense of those accused of crime. It is the Committee's view that attorneys should not be used, even temporarily, as a repository for the physical evidence of a crime. We therefore believe that it would be highly desirable, from an ethical standpoint, if yourself, Mr. Shortell, and the agency in general, were to formulate an office policy with respect to physical evidence such as that you have described in your letter, consistent with the Code of Professional Responsibility and the opinions of the various committees interpreting it.

Very truly yours,

ETHICS COMMITTEE OF THE
ALASKA BAR ASSOCIATION
By Charles P. Flynn, Chairman

NOTE

In Morrell v. State, 575 P.2d 1200 (Alaska, 1978), the Alaska Supreme Court found an affirmative duty requiring lawyers to turn over incriminating physical evidence in their possession, especially where the evidence comes from third parties. The case seems to be the culmination of the actual case involving public defender Stephen Cline discussed in the above exchange of letters. Mr. Cline, however, seems to have changed the facts in his letters * * * in case he later determined that the client's identity was to be kept secret.

FORMAL OPINION 341*

September 30, 1975.

This opinion is made in response to several inquiries regarding the effect of the February, 1974, amendment to Disciplinary Rule 7-102(B), which presently reads: "(B) A lawyer who receives information clearly establishing that (1) His client has, in the course of the representation, perpetrated a fraud upon a person or tribunal shall promptly call upon his client to rectify the same, and if his client refuses or is unable to do so, he shall reveal the fraud to the affected person or tribunal, *except when the in-*

*61 A.B.A.J. 1543 (Dec. 1975).

formation is protected as a privileged communication. "[Italicized language added by amendment February, 1974.][1]

The derivation of D.R. 7-102(B) (1) is informative. The prior American Bar Association Canons of Professional Ethics contained three mandatory revelation rules: Canon 1 (complaint against judge), Canon 29 (exposing dishonest conduct of lawyers and exposing perjury), and Canon 41 (informing injured person of fraud or deception by client). In the Code of Professional Responsibility, D.R. 1-103 contains a duty to reveal knowledge of misconduct by judge or lawyer.[2] But the preliminary draft of the Code of Professional Responsibility (January, 1969) did not contain a disciplinary rule requiring a lawyer to reveal misconduct of a client.

Perhaps the omission was due to the committee's consideration of the high fiduciary duty owed by lawyer to client and consideration of the firm support found in the law of evidence for the attorney-client privilege. The preliminary draft contained a disciplinary rule virtually identical to present D.R. 4-101(C), forbidding a lawyer, with certain exceptions, from knowingly revealing a confidence or secret of his client.[3] Some lawyers objected, however, to the preliminary draft because it did not carry into the Code of Professional Responsibility the substance of prior Canon 41. The result was the addition to the Code of Professional Responsibility, at that time, of D.R. 7-102(B).

When D.R. 7-102(B) was added to the Code of Professional Responsibility prior to its adoption in August, 1969, the full significance of D.R. 4-101(C) apparently was not appreciated, even though the preliminary draft contained a virtually identical provision stating that "[a] lawyer may reveal * * * [c]onfidences or secrets when permitted [under] Disciplinary Rules or required by law or court order."[4] That provision of D.R. 4-101(C), while quite proper in the preliminary draft, had the unacceptable result when combined with new D.R. 7-102(B)(1) of requiring a lawyer in certain instances to reveal privileged communications which he also was

---

1. Compare Rule 11, Code of Trial Conduct of the American College of Trial Lawyers (1971): "(d) Subject to whatever qualifications may exist from the confidential privilege that exists between a lawyer and his client, the lawyer should expose without fear before the proper tribunals perjury, subornation of perjury and any professional misconduct."

See Casenote, 50 Tex.L.Rev. 1265 (1972), for a view critical of D.R. 7-102(B) (1) prior to its amendment.

Some commentators are concerned that the 1974 amendment might encourage lawyers to refuse to reveal communications that are not within the attorney-client privilege; however, the rule exempts from disclosure only confidences and secrets. Other commentators seem concerned that even with the amendment there is too heavy a burden upon a lawyer to reveal a client's misconduct; see, e. g., Lipman *The SEC's Reluc-*

tant Police Force: A New Role for Lawyers, 49 N.Y.U.L. Rev. 437 (1974); Monroe Freedman, *Legal Ethics,* N.J.L.J., July 24, 1974; Freedman, *Letter to Editor,* 59 A.B. A.J. 114 (1973) (reporting the rejection of the original version of D.R. 7-102(B) (1) when the C.P.R. was adopted in the District of Columbia).

2. D.R. 7-108(G), revealing misconduct regarding juror, and D.R. 7-102(B) (2), revealing fraud on tribunal by one other than client, are other revelation rules contained in the Code of Professional Responsibility.

3. D.R. 5-101(A), (B), (C), and (E), Preliminary Draft, C.P.R., are identical, except for minor textual changes, with D.R. 4-101(A), (B), (C), and (D).

4. In the preliminary draft, "by" rather than "under" was used. The rule appeared as 4-101(C)(2) in the preliminary draft.

duty bound not to reveal according to the law of evidence. The amendment of February, 1974, was necessary in order to relieve lawyers of exposure to such diametrically opposed professional duties.

A similar impasse arising under the prior Canons of Professional Ethics was considered by this committee in Formal Opinion 287 (1953). Then Canon 37 required a lawyer to "preserve his client's confidences," although Canon 29 required a lawyer to reveal perjury to the prosecuting authorities and Canon 41 required a lawyer to inform against his client in certain circumstances in regard to "fraud or deception." The situation in Opinion 287 was that of a client who had committed perjury (which we assume constituted intrinsic fraud upon the tribunal) during the trial of his divorce action. Three months later the client sought advice from the same lawyer who had represented him in the divorce action. The advice was sought in regard to a dispute with his former wife over support money; in connection with this consultation the client told the lawyer that he had given false material testimony in the divorce action in which he had been represented by the same lawyer. Tracing the background of the evidentiary law concerning the attorney-client privilege, this committee held that the duty of the lawyer to preserve his client's confidences prevailed over the duty under Canon 41 to reveal fraud or deception, and over the duty under Canon 29 to bring knowledge of perjury to the attention of others. In Opinion 287 it was said that the lawyer, "despite Canons 29 and 41, should not disclose the facts to the court or to the authorities."[5]

One effect of the 1974 amendment to D.R. 7–102(B) (1) is to reinstate the essence of Opinion 287 which had prevailed from 1953 until 1969. It was as unthinkable then as now that a lawyer should be subject to disciplinary action for failing to reveal information which by law is not to be revealed without the consent of the client, and the lawyer is not now in that untenable position. The lawyer no longer can be confronted with the necessity of either breaching his client's privilege at law or breaching a disciplinary rule.[6]

While the derivation of D.R. 7–102(B) (1) indicates the necessity for the 1974 amendment, the scope of the 1974 amendment can be indicated only by considering the coverage of the basic requirement of D.R. 7–102(B) (1) and by examining the interrelation of D.R. 7–102(B) (1) and D.R. 4–101. The conflicting duties to reveal fraud and to preserve confidences have existed side-by-side for some time.

However, it is clear that there has long been an accommodation in favor of preserving confidences either through practice or interpretation. Through the bar's interpretation in practice of its responsibility to preserve confidences and secrets of clients, and through its interpretations like Formal Opinion 287, significant exceptions to any general duty to reveal fraud have been long accepted. Apparently, the exceptions were so broad or the policy underlying the duty to reveal so weak that the earlier drafts of the Code of Professional Responsibility omitted altogether the concept em-

---

5. See also New Jersey Ethics Opinion 163 (1969), 92 N.J.L.J. 825, citing A.B.A Opinion 287 with approval.

6. A lawyer who breaches his fiduciary duty to client by revealing confidences protected by the attorney-client privilege may be liable to client in tort. He also may be guilty of a crime in some jurisdictions. See Weinberg, Confidential and Other Communications 16 (1967).

bodied in Canon 41. Nonetheless, D.R. 7–102(B) is a part of the Code of Professional Responsibility and must be given some meaning. Some of the exceptions to a general duty to reveal have been built into the disciplinary rule itself (for example, that the information must "clearly establish" fraud; that it must be received "in the course of representation" and (since 1974) that it must not be information "protected as a privileged communication").

Formal Opinion 287, which dealt with a lawyer's duty to reveal a perjury committed earlier by his client, represents merely one of the exceptions to old Canon 41 (it also pertained to old Canon 29, dealing with revealing perjury to the affected tribunal). We do not think that Formal Opinion 287 was intended to be an *exclusive* exception to old Canon 41. Accordingly, limiting the 1974 amendment to matters of attorney-client privilege covered in Formal Opinion 287 will not necessarily bring D.R. 7–102 into line with past interpretations of a lawyer's duty when a client's confidences and secrets are involved.

The tradition (which is backed by substantial policy considerations) that permits a lawyer to assure a client that information (whether a confidence or a secret) given to him will not be revealed to third parties is so important that it should take precedence, in all the most serious cases, over the duty imposed by D.R. 7–102(B). The many annotations to D.R. 4–101 reflect this policy. Of course, there will be situations where a lawyer may reveal the secrets and confidences of his client. Some of these are recognized in D.R. 4–101(C).

The balancing of the lawyer's duty to preserve confidences and to reveal frauds is best made by interpreting the phrase "privileged communication" in the 1974 amendment to D.R. 7–102(B) as referring to those confidences and secrets that are required to be preserved by D.R. 4–101.

Such an interpretation does not wipe out D.R. 7–102(B), because D.R. 7–102(B) applies to information received from any source, and it is not limited to information gained in the professional relationship as is D.R. 4–101. Under the suggested interpretation, the duty imposed by D.R. 7–102(B) would remain in force if the information clearly establishing a fraud on a person or tribunal and committed by a client in the course of representation were obtained by the lawyer from a third party (but not in connection with his professional relationship with the client), because it would not be a confidence or secret of a client entitled to confidentiality. D.R. 4–102(C) sets out several circumstances under which revelation of a secret or confidence is permissible, and thus in cases where these exceptions, apply, D.R. 7–102(B) may make the optional disclosure of information under D.R. 4–101 a mandatory one. For example, when disclosure is required by a law, the "privileged communication" exception of D.R. 7–102(B) is not applicable and disclosure may be required.

An interpretation of the 1974 amendment which would limit its scope to the attorney-client privilege as it exists in each jurisdiction and under the Federal Rules of Evidence is undesirable because the lawyer's ethical duty would depend upon the rules of evidence in a particular jurisdiction. There may be significant problems in knowing which jurisdiction's evidentiary rule would be applied in a given case, and the scope of that privilege may vary widely among jurisdictions.[7] Furthermore, limiting the 1974 amendment to the scope of the attorney-client privilege raises problems as to the difference between waiver of privilege by a client and a consent to the lawyer's disclosure of a confidence.

It is not reasonable to put a lawyer at peril of discipline if, after determining that he has information that "clearly" establishes fraud (a difficult task in itself), he must also determine the relevant rule of attorney-client privilege in order to determine whether he must reveal the client's confidences and secrets. Also, we believe that it is inconsistent with the lawyer's confidential relationship with his client to impose at the same time a duty to evaluate the client's confidences to determine whether the level of evidence of "fraud" has been reached that would require disclosure of such confidences. The lawyer's problem is not lessened, in this respect, by interpreting fraud in D.R. 7-102(B), as we do, as being used in the sense of active fraud, with a requirement of *scienter* or intent to deceive.

The interpretation here adopted by the committee, which would preserve confidential information received in connection with the professional relationship, minimizes the problems. The committee believes that this interpretation does not go too far in relieving a lawyer of any responsibility to others because it does not alter the standing sanctions against the lawyer's involvement in a fraud nor alter the lawyer's duty under D.R. 7-102(B) when his information is obtained outside the confidential relationship.

7. Compare Rule 5-3 [503?—Ed.] of the Federal Rules of Evidence with the Texas rule discussed in Opinion 378 of the State Bar of Texas (1975).

PART B.   PATIENT-PHYSICIAN AND PSYCHOTHERAPIST-PATIENT PRIVILEGES

PRINK v. ROCKEFELLER CENTER INC.

Court of Appeals of New York, 1979.
48 N.Y.2d 309, 422 N.Y.S.2d 911, 398 N.E.2d 517.

MEYER, J.

The question presented by this appeal is whether evidentiary privileges prevent disclosure in a wrongful death action concerning the mental condition of the decedent whose unwitnessed death occurred under circumstances consistent with either negligence of the defendant or suicide.

* * *

Plaintiff is the administratrix of the estate of her husband, Robert Prink, who was an associate of a law firm whose offices were at 30 Rockefeller Plaza in New York City. On March 1, 1976, he was found dead on the sixth floor setback of the building. The window of the 36th floor office Mr. Prink had occupied was open. There were no eyewitnesses, but the deputy chief medical examiner noted on Mr. Prink's death certificate that Dr. Thomas Doyle, Mr. Prink's psychiatrist, had reported to him that Mr. Prink had been acutely tense and depressed.

Thereafter plaintiff commenced the present action against defendants, the owners and architects respectively of 30 Rockefeller Center, claiming that negligence in the design and installation of the window alcove desk at which decedent worked and in the maintenance of the window required that he kneel on the desk in order to open the window which was jammed, and that he lost his balance and fell when he attempted to do so. During the examination of plaintiff before trial she admitted that her husband had told her sometime before his death that he was seeing Dr. Doyle, a psychiatrist.
* * * She also admitted that after her husband's death she had spoken with Dr. Doyle, but refused to disclose the content of the conversation, claiming privilege.[1] On defendants' motion for an order compelling plaintiff to testify concerning the content of her conversations with * * * Dr. Doyle, Special Term ordered the questions answered. The Appellate Division affirmed, but certified to us the question "Was the order of the Supreme Court, as affirmed by this Court, properly made?" We answer the certified question in the affirmative and, therefore, affirm the Appellate Division's order.

The initial inquiry is whether privilege ever attached. * * * Mrs. Prink did not consult Dr. Doyle as a patient. Mr. Prink did, however, and Dr. Doyle's information concerning him was therefore, "acquired in attending a patient in a professional capacity" within the meaning of * * * (the New York Statute) and for purposes of the present inquiry at least may be presumed to have been "necessary to enable him to act in that capacity" as required by that provision.

---

1. While plaintiff's testimony concerning what Dr. Doyle told her is clearly hearsay, that would not protect her from the disclosure required by CPLR 3101 which requires revelation of inadmissible testimony that may lead to discovery of admissible evidence.

* * * [T]he physician-patient privilege is [not] terminated by death alone. * * * [The privilege applies] unless waived in some manner. To be borne in mind in deciding whether there has been a waiver is that * * * the physician-patient privilege belongs to the patient. * * * [I]t follows that Dr. Doyle's voluntary disclosures to the chief medical examiner and to Mrs. Prink after her husband's death, proper though they undoubtedly were as a matter of professional ethics cannot constitute a waiver making an otherwise privileged statement admissible. To hold that a recipient of confidential information by his sole fiat may destroy the privilege would be directly contrary to the salutary purpose for which the privilege was adopted.[2]

There is, however, another basis upon which we hold * * * the doctor-patient * * * privilege waived. The instant action is brought pursuant to EPTL 5-4.1, which authorizes an action for wrongful death only "for a wrongful act, neglect or default which *caused the decedent's death* against a person *who would have been liable to the decedent by reason of such wrongful conduct* if death had not ensued" (emphasis supplied). Thus to succeed in this action, which is wholly statutory in nature, plaintiff must establish that it could have been maintained by decedent had he survived * * * and that defendants' wrongful act caused his death. In final analysis, therefore, the issue is whether had Mr. Prink survived and brought the action he could successfully have resisted defendants' demand, in their effort to establish that his injuries resulted from attempted suicide rather than defendant's negligence, for disclosure of his conversations with Dr. Doyle * * * .

* * * [Because of] the unfairness of mulcting a defendant in damages without affording him an opportunity to prove his lack of culpability [cf. Chambers v. Mississippi, 410 U.S. 284, 93 S.Ct. 1038, 35 L.Ed.2d 297], Mr. Prink as plaintiff could (not) assert * * * the physician-patient privilege (Koump v. Smith, 25 N.Y.2d 287, 294; to foreclose inquiry concerning whether his injury was the result of an attempt at suicide.

In *Koump* plaintiff demanded authorization * * * to obtain defendant's hospital record in an effort to show that defendant was intoxicated at the time his car crossed a center divider striking plaintiff's car and injuring plaintiff. We upheld defendant's claim of privilege in that case because defendant had done no more than deny plaintiff's allegation that defendant was intoxicated and plaintiff's only evidence of intoxication was an attorney's affidavit reciting that the police report of the accident contained a hearsay statement that defendant appeared intoxicated. Nevertheless, we recognized (25 N.Y.2d, at p. 294 [303 N.Y.S.2d, at p. 864, 250 N.E. 2d, at p.

---

2. To be distinguished, of course, is the common-law rule permitting an eavesdropper to testify concerning an otherwise privileged communication * * * . Thus, had Mrs. Prink overheard Dr. Doyle's conversation with her husband as an eavesdropper rather than having learned its content from the doctor she could be required to disclose its content. The distinction, perhaps filagree in nature, is between the unauthorized act of the recipient of the confidence and the act of the eavesdropper who unauthorizedly intrudes himself upon the confidential conference. It results, apparently, from the confidant's negligence in the eavesdropper situation in not assuring absolute secrecy at the time of disclosure, and the contradiction in terms that would be involved in taxing the confidant with negligence in relying upon the trust which is the very root of his relationship to the person in whom he has confided.

861]): "that by bringing or defending personal injury action in which mental or physical condition is affirmatively put in issue, a party *waives* the privilege" (emphasis in original).

Whatever the ultimate determination of the triers of fact may be in the present case and notwithstanding the presumption against suicide which they will have to consider in reaching their determination, we conclude that it is a matter of common knowledge which we can judicially notice * * * that many apparently accidental deaths are in fact suicides and that a wrongful death complaint predicated upon an alleged accidental fall from a 36th story window is sufficiently equivocal in that respect to put in issue, by plaintiff's affirmative act in bringing the action, decedent's mental condition * * * . To hold otherwise is to ignore the realities of the factual situation and to come perilously close to a taking of defendants' property without due process of law (cf. Chambers v. Mississippi, 410 U.S. 284, [93 S.Ct. 1038, 35 L.Ed.2d 297] supra). An additional reason, not however essential to our conclusion, for holding the (privilege) waived by the bringing of the action is that determination of the pecuniary injury sustained by Mr. Prink's death necessarily involved his mental condition.

Bearing in mind the purpose for which the (privilege) in question (was) created, the affirmative stance of plaintiff who claims on behalf of decedent's distributees to have sustained pecuniary injury as a result of defendants' negligence, and the unfairness of permitting plaintiff to succeed by hiding behind the (privilege) asserted, we are satisfied on balance that the better policy is to hold the (privilege) waived. The basis for that conclusion * * * is set forth in Koump v. Smith (25 N.Y.2d 287 [303 N.Y.S.2d 858, 250 N.E.2d 857], supra; see, also, Wigmore, *op. cit.*, § 2380a). * * *

Accordingly the certified question should be answered in the affirmative and the order of the Appellate Division should be affirmed.

* * *

IN RE LIFSCHUTZ

Supreme Court of California, 1970.
2 C.3d 415, 85 Cal.Rptr. 829, 467 P.2d 557.
[Some footnotes and citations omitted.]

TOBRINER, Justice.

Dr. Joseph E. Lifschutz, a psychiatrist practicing in California, seeks a writ of habeas corpus to secure his release from the custody of the Sheriff of the County of San Mateo. Dr. Lifschutz was imprisoned after he was adjudged in contempt of court for refusing to obey an order of the San Mateo County Superior Court instructing him to answer questions and produce records relating to communications with a former patient. * * *

The instant proceeding arose out of a suit instituted by Joseph F. Housek against John Arabian on June 3, 1968, for damages resulting from an alleged assault. Housek's complaint alleged that the assault caused him "physical injuries, pain, suffering and severe mental and emotional distress." Defendant Arabian deposed the plaintiff and during the course of that deposition Housek stated that he had received psychiatric treatment from Dr. Lifschutz over a six-month period approximately 10 years earlier. Nothing in the record indicates that the plaintiff revealed the nature or contents of any conversation with or treatment by Dr. Lifschutz.

Arabian then subpoenaed for deposition Dr. Lipschutz and all of his medical records relating to the treatment of Housek. (Code Civ.Proc. §§ 2016, 2019, subd. (a).) Although Dr. Lifschutz appeared for the deposition, he refused to produce any of his medical records and refused to answer any questions relating to his treatment of patients; the psychiatrist declined even to disclose whether or not Housek had consulted him or had been his patient. Although notified, neither plaintiff Housek nor his attorney were present at this deposition and neither has appeared in any of the subsequent hearings related to this proceeding. Housek has neither expressly claimed a psychotherapist-patient privilege, statutory or constitutional, nor expressly waived such a privilege.

* * *

Dr. Lifschutz presents a novel challenge, attempting to raise far-reaching questions of constitutional law. From the affidavits and correspondence included in the record we note that a large segment of the psychiatric profession concurs in Dr. Lifschutz's strongly held belief that an absolute privilege of confidentiality is essential to the effective practice of psychotherapy.

We recognize the growing importance of the psychiatric profession in our modern, ultracomplex society. The swiftness of change—economic, cultural, and moral—produces accelerated tensions in our society, and the potential for relief of such emotional disturbances offered by psychotherapy undoubtedly establishes it as a profession essential to the preservation of societal health and well-being. Furthermore, a growing consensus throughout the country, reflected in a trend of legislative enactments,[3] acknowledges that an environment of confidentiality of treatment is vitally important to the successful operation of psychotherapy. California has embraced this view through the enactment of a broad, protective psychotherapist-patient privilege.

---

3.   Until 20 years ago, no statutes dealt specifically with the question of the privilege for psychotherapeutic communications; protection was available only under the terms of existing physician-patient privileges. Such privilege only applied to medical practitioners who fell within the terms of various state statutes; often psychiatrists were covered, but clinical psychologists, though using many of the same techniques of psychotherapy, were not. In the nineteen-fifties and sixties several states, responding to the demands of organized spokesmen of psychology, enacted new privilege statutes, often granting psychologist-patient communications much broader protection than was provided by existing physician-patient privileges. (See Ferster, "Statutory Summary of Physician-Patient Privileged Communication Laws" in Allen, Ferster & Ruben, Readings in Law & Psychiatry (1968) pp. 161–165). In 1960 California enacted such a statute, providing: "[T]he confidential relations and communications between psychologist and client shall be placed upon the same basis as those provided by law between attorney and client * * * ." (Bus. & Prof.Code, § 2904 (since repealed).)

Although commentators who analyzed the need for a privilege in this specific area unanimously supported the position that greater protection be extended to communications of psychotherapeutic treatment (see, e. g., Louisell, The Psychologist in Today's Legal World: Part II (1957) 41 Minn. L.Rev. 731; Slovenko, Psychiatry and a Second Look at the Medical Privilege (1960) 6 Wayne L.Rev. 175), they pointed out the anomaly of affording more protection to patients of psychologists than to patients of psychiatrists, as most of the existing statutory schemes did. To eliminate this irrational distinction, California enacted the current psychotherapist-patient privilege (Evid.Code, § 1014) in 1965.

* * *

Properly viewed, the broadest issue before our court is whether the Legislature, in attempting to accommodate the conceded need of confidentiality in the psychotherapeutic process with general societal needs of access to information for the ascertainment of truth in litigation, has unconstitutionally weighted its resolution in favor of disclosure by providing that a psychotherapist may be compelled to reveal relevant confidences of treatment when the patient tenders his mental or emotional condition in issue in litigation. For the reasons discussed below, we conclude that, under a properly limited interpretation, the litigant-patient exception to the psychotherapist-patient privilege, at issue in this case, does not unconstitutionally infringe the constitutional rights of privacy of either psychotherapists or psychotherapeutic patients. As we point out, however, because of the potential of invasion of patients' constitutional interests, trial courts should properly and carefully control compelled disclosures in this area in the light of accepted principles.

I. *The order requiring Dr. Lifschutz to answer appropriate questions concerning communications with a patient does not infringe the psychotherapist's constitutional rights.*

The primary contention of Dr. Lifschutz's attack on the judgment of contempt consists of the assertion of a constitutional right of a psychotherapist to absolute confidentiality in his communications with, and treatment of, patients. Although, as we understand it, the alleged right draws its substance primarily from the psychological needs and expectations of patients, Dr. Lifschutz claims that the Constitution grants him an absolute right to refuse to disclose such confidential communications, regardless of the wishes of a patient in a particular case. In separating the interest of the psychotherapist from that of the patient for the purposes of analyzing this contention, we conclude that the compelled disclosure of relevant information obtained in a confidential communication does not violate any constitutional privacy rights of the psychotherapist.

* * *

[The court in Griswold v. Connecticut, 381 U.S. 479 [85 S.Ct. 1678, 14 L.Ed.2d 510 (1965)] on which Dr. Lifschutz replies] * * * explained, however, that the constitutional privacy interests and rights underlying its decision were those of the "patients" of the birth control clinic, rather than of physicians. * * * It is the depth and intimacy of the *patients'* revelations that give rise to the concern over compelled disclosure; the psychotherapist, though undoubtedly deeply involved in the communicative treatment, does not exert a significant privacy interest separate from his patient.[6] We cannot accept petitioner's reliance on the *Griswold* decision as establishing broad constitutional privacy rights of psychotherapists.

In addition to his claim as to a "right of privacy," petitioner urges that the provisions of the Evidence Code requiring a psychotherapist to reveal

---

6. Indeed, in many instances a patient may desire to have a psychotherapist testify as to confidential communications. (See, e. g., Hampton v. Hampton (1965) 241 Or. 277, 405 P.2d 549.) The granting of petitioner's broad contention could foreclose access to psychotherapeutic sessions even when the patient has no desire to preserve his "privacy."

confidential matters under some circumstances unconstitutionally impair the practice of his profession. This position rests on two distinct legal contentions: first, that the impairment is so severe as to constitute an unconstitutional "taking" of a valuable property right, the doctor's right to practice psychotherapy; and second, that compelled disclosure of any psychotherapeutic communication renders the continued practice of psychotherapy impossible and thus unconstitutionally constricts the realm of available medical treatment. Although psychotherapists should, of course, be entitled to the constitutional protections requisite to the right to practice their profession we doubt that the disclosure involved here goes so far as to constitute the claimed unconstitutional deprivation of that right.

Insofar as petitioner's argument rests on the economic loss that psychotherapists may suffer as a result of the disclosure requirement, his position runs contra to the current trend of constitutional adjudication involving the regulation of economic interests. Legal requirements prescribing mandatory disclosure of confidential business records are of course regular occurrences and although all compelled disclosures may interfere to some extent with an individual's performance of his work, such requirements have been universally upheld so long as the compelled disclosure is reasonable in the light of a related and important governmental purpose.

* * *

The second basis of petitioner's contention raises a more serious problem. Petitioner claims that if the state is authorized to compel disclosure of some psychotherapeutic communications, psychotherapy can no longer be practiced successfully.[7] He asserts that the unique nature of psychotherapeutic treatment, involving a probing of the patient's subconscious thoughts and emotions, requires an environment of total confidentiality and absolute trust. Petitioner claims that unless a psychotherapist can truthfully assure his patient that all revelations will be held in strictest confidence and never disclosed, patients will be inhibited from participating fully in the psychotherapeutic process and proper treatment will be impossible. Petitioner concludes that the patient-litigant exception involved here conflicts with the preservation of an environment of absolute confidentiality and unconstitutionally constricts the field of medical practice.

Petitioner's argument, resting as it does on assertions of medical necessity, exemplifies the type of question to which the judiciary brings little expertise. Although petitioner has submitted affidavits of psychotherapists who concur in his assertion that total confidentiality is essential to the practice of their profession, we cannot blind ourselves to the fact that the practice of psychotherapy has grown, indeed flourished, in an environment of a

7. Petitioner's contention that the recognition of a privilege is necessary to the preservation of a given occupation or profession is by no means unique to psychotherapy. In the past, organized occupational groups of journalists, accountants, and social workers, among others, have sought the establishment of a legal privilege and have proclaimed, on principle, that required revelation of information received in confidence would mean the destruction of their calling. (See generally, 8 Wigmore, Evidence (McNaughton rev. 1961) § 2286, pp. 532–537.) In many instances such organized groups have been able to convince state legislatures of the wisdom of their position and as a result statutory privileges have been created; the broad psychotherapist-patient privilege enacted in California is such an example.

non-absolute privilege. No state in the country recognizes as broad a privilege as petitioner claims is constitutionally compelled.[8] * * *

* * *

The statutory provisions challenged here do not attempt to narrow the scope of psychotherapeutic treatment, by proscribing, for example, the discussion of certain subjects (cf. Poe v. Ullman (1961) 367 U.S. 497, 513–515, 81 S.Ct. 1752, 6 L.Ed.2d 989 (Douglas, J., dissenting) (state statute barring advice on the use of contraceptives)). Instead, the provisions are intended to serve the important state interest of facilitating the ascertainment of truth in legal proceedings. Although petitioner argues that, as a matter of social as well as medical policy, the benefits to be derived from a broadening of the existing privilege would outweigh the detriments resulting from a narrowing of evidence available in litigation, the balancing of those alternatives remains with the Legislature.

II. *The presence of a legislatively created absolute clergyman-penitent privilege does not render the absence of such an absolute psychotherapist-patient privilege a denial of equal protection.*

Section 1034 of the Evidence Code provides that: "a clergyman * * * has a privilege to refuse to disclose a penitential communication if he claims the privilege"; the code provides no exceptions to the clergyman-penitent privilege comparable to the numerous exceptions to the psychotherapist-patient privilege. (See Evid. Code, §§ 1016–1026.) Petitioner contends that the Legislature, in so distinguishing between clergymen and psychotherapists, has denied psychotherapists the equal protection of the laws in violation of the Fourteenth Amendment.

* * *

Petitioner maintains, however, that, given the purpose of the clergyman-penitent privilege, the distinction between clergymen and psychotherapists cannot stand. Dr. Lifschutz characterizes the "modern" purpose of the clergyman-penitent privilege as fostering a "sanctuary for the disclosure of emotional distress": as so characterized, relevant distinctions between clergymen and psychotherapists do diminish. Petitioner's portrayal of the clergyman-penitent privilege, however, while perhaps identifying one of the supporting threads of the statutory provision, does not reflect a complete analysis of the foundation of the privilege.

Realistically, the statutory privilege must be recognized as basically an explicit accommodation by the secular state to strongly held religious tenets of a large segment of its citizenry. As the Law Revision Commission Comment accompanying the adoption of California's current privilege explains: "At least one underlying reason seems to be that the law will not compel a clergyman to violate—nor punish him for refusing to violate—the tenets of his church which require him to maintain secrecy as to confidential statements made to him in the course of his religious duties." Wigmore, in his treatise, similarly relates the purpose of the privilege in a question and answer format: "Does the penitential relation deserve recognition and coun-

8. Indeed, only six states have any laws specifically granting to the psychiatric relationship any special protection, over and above that given to medical communications generally. (See Slawson, Patient-Litigant Exception: Hazard to Psychotherapy (1969), 21 Arch.Gen.Psychiat. 347, 348.)

tenance? In a state where toleration of religion exists by law, and where a substantial part of the community professes a religion practising a confessional system, this question must be answered in the affirmative." (8 Wigmore, Evidence, supra, § 2396 at p. 878;   *   *   *   .

Recognizing that the toleration of religious beliefs and practices forms the basis for this privilege, we cannot say that the Legislature acted irrationally in granting the privilege to clergymen and not to psychotherapists. Although in some circumstances clergymen and psychotherapists perform similar functions and serve similar needs, fundamental and significant differences remain. While many psychotherapists are no doubt strongly committed to the "tenets" of their profession,[9] as indeed Dr. Lifschutz has exhibited by his determined action in the instant proceeding, the source of this commitment can be reasonably distinguished from the distinctive religious conviction out of which the penitential privilege flows.

*   *   *

III.   *Under the facts of this case petitioner could assert no statutory authority to refuse to comply with requested disclosures.*

Although, as we have discussed above, Dr. Lifschutz on his own behalf can claim no constitutional privilege to avoid disclosure, he may in some circumstances assert the statutory privilege of his patient.[11] Evidence Code, section 1012 recognizes communications between patient and psychotherapist, diagnosis by the psychotherapist, and advice given during the therapy relationship as privileged communications. Section 1015 provides that: "[t]he psychotherapist who received or made a communication subject to the privilege under this article shall claim the privilege whenever he is present when the communication is sought to be disclosed and is authorized to claim the privilege under subdivision (c) of Section 1014." Section 1014, subdivision (c), indicates that the psychotherapist cannot claim the privilege of the patient "if there is no holder of the privilege in existence or if he is otherwise instructed by a person authorized to permit disclosure." The record in the present case shows no express instructions from plaintiff Housek directing Dr. Lifschutz to decline the privilege against disclosure. Thus, under Evidence Code, section 1015 Dr. Lifschutz could generally assert the privilege of his patient to prevent disclosure of privileged communications.

The psychotherapist, however, cannot assert his patient's privilege if that privilege has been waived or if the communication in question falls within the statutory exceptions to the privilege. Evidence Code, section 912,

---

9.   We note that this court has not been apprised of any present, established "tenet" of the medical profession that would be violated by petitioner's compliance with the order of the trial court. Section 9 of the "Principles of Medical Ethics" adopted by the American Medical Association, which petitioner submitted to the trial court, proclaims: "A physician may not reveal the confidences entrusted to him in the course of medical attendance, or the deficiencies he may observe in the character of patients, *unless he is required to do so by law* or unless it becomes necessary in order to protect the welfare of the individual or of the community." (Italics added.) Although there has been some criticism of this present principle (see, e. g., Sidel, Confidential Information and the Physician, supra, 264 New England J. of Med. 1133), we are not aware of any modification of the "official" principle of confidentiality.

11.   The statutory privilege established in section 1014 of the Evidence Code is a privilege of the patient, not of the psychotherapist. (Evid.Code, § 1013; cf. City and County of San Francisco v. Superior Court (1951) 37 Cal.2d 227, 233, 231 P.2d 26.

subdivision (a), provides that: " * * * the right of any person to claim a privilege provided by Section * * * 1014 (psychotherapist-patient privilege) * * * is waived with respect to a communication protected by such privilege if any holder of the privilege, without coercion, has disclosed a significant part of the communication or has consented to such disclosure made by anyone. Consent to disclosure is manifested by any statement or other conduct of the holder of the privilege indicating his consent to the disclosure, including his failure to claim the privilege in any proceeding in which he has the legal standing and opportunity to claim the privilege."

Since Housek, the holder of the privilege (see Evid.Code, § 1013), disclosed at a prior deposition that he had consulted Dr. Lifschutz for psychiatric treatment, he has waived whatever privilege he might have had to keep such information confidential.

The questions posed to Dr. Lifschutz, however, have inquired only into whether he treated Mr. Housek and whether he possessed records regarding this patient. Defendant has not yet asked Dr. Lifschutz about the nature of his treatment of the plaintiff, his diagnosis, or the content of any communication. Certainly, in admitting the existence of a psychotherapist-patient relationship, plaintiff has not disclosed "a significant part of the communication" (Evid.Code, § 912) between himself and Dr. Lifschutz so as to waive his right subsequently to claim the privilege as to other elements of the communication.

Defendant contended in the superior court, however, that *any* communication between the plaintiff and Dr. Lifschutz has lost its privileged status because the plaintiff has filed a personal injury action in which he claims recovery for "mental and emotional distress." Defendant relies on section 1016 of the Evidence Code, the patient-litigant exception to the psychotherapist-patient privilege, which provides that: "[t]here is no privilege under this article as to a communication relevant to an issue concerning the mental or emotional condition of the patient if such issue has been tendered by: (a) the patient * * * ." To avoid the necessity for further contempt proceedings or delaying appellate review in the instant case, we have considered whether defendant has accurately identified the proper reach of the patient-litigant exception.

* * * [T]he patient-litigant exception allows only a limited inquiry into the confidences of the psychotherapist-patient relationship, compelling disclosure of only those matters directly relevant to the nature of the specific "emotional or mental" condition which the patient has voluntarily disclosed and tendered in his pleadings or in answer to discovery inquiries. Furthermore, even when confidential information falls within this exception, trial courts, because of the intimate and potentially embarrassing nature of such communications, may utilize the protective measures at their disposal to avoid unwarranted intrusions into the confidences of the relationship.

In interpreting this exception we are necessarily mindful of the justifiable expectations of confidentiality that most individuals seeking psychotherapeutic treatment harbor. * * *

We believe that a patient's interest in keeping such confidential revelations from public purview, in retaining this substantial privacy, has deeper roots than the California statute and draws sustenance from our constitutional heritage. In Griswold v. Connecticut, supra, 381 U.S. 479, 484, 85 S.Ct. 1678, 1681, 14 L.Ed.2d 510, the United States Supreme Court declared that "Various guarantees [of the Bill of Rights] create zones of privacy," and we believe that the confidentiality of the psychotherapeutic session falls within one such zone. Although *Griswold* itself involved only the marital relationship, the open-ended quality of that decision's rationale evidences its far-reaching dimension.[12]   *   *   *

Even though a patient's interest in the confidentiality of the psychotherapist-patient relationship rests, in part, on constitutional underpinnings, all state "interference" with such confidentiality is not prohibited. In section 1016 we do not deal with a provision which seeks to proscribe the association of a psychotherapist and patient entirely, but instead we encounter a provision carefully tailored to serve the historically important state interest of facilitating the ascertainment of truth in connection with legal proceedings.[14] In the past this state interest has been viewed as substantial enough to compel the disclosure of a great variety of confidential material. Moreover, since the exception compels disclosure only in cases in which the patient's own action initiates the exposure, "intrusion" into a patient's privacy remains essentially under the patient's control. As such, we find no constitutional infirmity in it.

Although no previous cases have arisen under the patient-litigant exception to the psychotherapist-patient privilege, decisions applying an analogous exception to the physician-patient privilege[15] have identified two distinct grounds for the exception. First, the courts have noted that the patient, in raising the issue of a specific ailment or condition in litigation, in effect dispenses with the confidentiality of that ailment and may no longer justifiably seek protection from the humiliation of its exposure. Second, the exception represents a judgment that, in all fairness, a patient should not be permitted to establish a claim while simultaneously foreclosing inquiry

12.   The breadth of the principles of privacy and individual freedom recognized in *Griswold* is illustrated by the variety of the cases which have subsequently embraced that decision's conclusions. (See, e. g., Stanley v. Georgia (1969) 394 U.S. 557, 564, 89 S.Ct. 1243, 22 L.Ed.2d 542 (right to view all books and films in the privacy of one's home); Roberts v. Clement (E.D.Tenn. 1966) 252 F.Supp. 835, 848 (Darr, J., concurring) (right to practice nudism in private); Finot v. Pasadena City Board of Education (1967) 250 Cal.App.2d 189, 197–198, 58 Cal.Rptr. 520 (right of adult teacher to wear beard); cf. Jessin v. County of Shasta (1969) 274 A.C.A. 810, 821, 79 Cal.Rptr. 359 (right to obtain voluntary sterilization).)

14.   The justification for compelling disclosure of relevant psychotherapeutic communications when the patient himself has raised an issue of his mental condition has been recognized even by commentators who are strongly in favor of broadening the current psychotherapist-patient privilege. To "model" psychotherapist-patient privi-

lege acts, drafted by such proponents, have included a provision recognizing a patient-litigant exception. (See Model Psychotherapist-Patient Privilege (1968) 4 Harv.J.Legis. 307, 322; Fisher, The Psychotherapeutic Profession and the Law of Privileged Communication (1964) 10 Wayne L.Rev. 609, 644.)

15.   The present patient-litigant exception to the physician-patient privilege (Evid.Code, § 996) which parallels the exception to the psychotherapist-patient privilege precisely, superseded section 1881, subdivision 4, of the Code of Civil Procedure, the initial patient-litigant exception enacted in 1917 and the section under which most of the relevant case law arose. Section 1881, subdivision 4, limited the physician-patient privilege by providing: "[W]here any person brings an action to recover damages for personal injuries, such action shall be deemed to constitute a consent by the person bringing said action that any physician who has prescribed for or treated said person and *whose testimony is material in said action* shall testify." (Italics added.)

into relevant matters. As we explained in City and County of San Francisco v. Superior Court, supra, 37 Cal.2d 227, 232, 231 P.2d 26, 28 (the *Catton* case), "The whole purpose of the [physician-patient] privilege is to preclude the humiliation of the patient that might follow disclosure of his ailments. When the patient himself discloses those ailments by bringing an action in which they are in issue, there is no longer any reason for the privilege. The patient-litigant exception precludes one who has placed in issue his physical condition from invoking the privilege on the ground that disclosure of his condition would cause him humiliation. He cannot have his cake and eat it too."

Although defendant reads the above quoted language of the *Catton* case as implying that the patient-litigant exception contemplates an automatic, complete waiver of privilege whenever a patient institutes a claim for any physical or mental injury, we find nothing in either the rationale of the exception as explained in the *Catton* case, or in the cases applying the exception, to justify the breadth of this description. In previous physician-patient privilege cases the exception has been generally applied only to compel disclosure of medical treatment and communication concerning the very injury or impairment that was the subject matter of the litigation.[19] There is certainly nothing to suggest that in the context of the more liberal psychotherapist-patient privilege this exception should be given a broader reading.[20]

If the provision had as broad an effect as is suggested by petitioner, it might effectively deter many psychotherapeutic patients from instituting any general claim for mental suffering and damage out of fear of opening up all past communications to discovery. This result would clearly be an intolerable and overbroad intrusion into the patient's privacy, not sufficiently limited to the legitimate state interest embodied in the provision and would create opportunities for harassment and blackmail.

19. For example, in Ballard v. Pacific Greyhound Lines (1946) 28 Cal.2d 357, 360, 170 P.2d 465, the plaintiff, injured in a bus accident, had consulted a physician concerning the injuries she sustained therein. When the patient later sued the bus company for damages, the court permitted the defendant to examine the physician concerning the injuries of which plaintiff complained, finding the patient-litigant exception directly applicable. (Accord, San Francisco Unified Sch. Dist. v. Superior Court, supra, 55 Cal.2d 451, 454, 11 Cal.Rptr. 373, 374, 359 P.2d 925, 926 (exception applicable to doctor who had been consulted "to diagnose and treat [the plaintiff] for the injuries for which recovery is now sought").)

20. Our reliance on precedents rendered in the context of the physician-patient privilege is not intended to suggest that authorities involving the physician-patient privilege will always be helpful in resolving issues concerning the psycho-therapist-patient privilege. In the past the physician-patient privilege has been the subject of rather severe criticism (see, e. g., Chafee, Privileged Communications: Is Justice Served or Obstructed by Closing the Doctor's Mouth on the Witness Stand? (1943) 52 Yale L.J. 607; 8 Wigmore, Evidence, supra, § 2380a, at pp. 828–832), and in response the application of the privilege has been limited in a variety of circumstances (see, e. g., Evid.Code, §§ 998, 999, 1007). The psychotherapist-patient privilege, on the other hand, won legislative recognition in the face of legal antipathy toward privileges generally (see Louisell, The Psychologist in Today's Legal World: Part II, supra, 41 Minn.L.Rev. 731, 731-732); the Legislature acknowledged that the unique nature of psychotherapeutic treatment required and justified a greater degree of confidentiality than was legally afforded other medical treatment (see Legislative Committee Com. to Evid.Code, § 1014). Even commentators who concurred in the criticism of the general physician-patient privilege noted that the psychotherapeutic privilege rested on a much sounder basis and supported its adoption. (See, e. g., Louisell, supra, at pp. 740–746.) The differences that exist between these two medically oriented privileges caution against blind application of the precedents of the physician-patient privilege in future psychotherapist-patient privilege cases.

In light of these considerations, the "automatic" waiver of privilege contemplated by section 1016 must be construed not as a complete waiver of the privilege but only as a limited waiver concomitant with the purposes of the exception. Under section 1016 disclosure can be compelled only with respect to *those mental conditions* the patient-litigant has "disclose[d] * * * by bringing an action in which *they* are in issue" (City and County of San Francisco v. Superior Court, supra, 37 Cal.2d 227, 232, 231 P.2d 26); communications which are not directly relevant to those specific conditions do not fall within the terms of section 1016's exception and therefore remain privileged. Disclosure cannot be compelled with respect to other aspects of the patient-litigant's personality even though they may, in some sense, be "relevant" to the substantive issues of litigation.[21] The patient thus is not obligated to sacrifice all privacy to seek redress for a specific mental or emotional injury; the scope of the inquiry permitted depends upon the nature of the injuries which the patient-litigant himself has brought before the court.

* * *

Because only the patient, and not the party seeking disclosure, knows both the nature of the ailments for which recovery is sought and the general content of the psychotherapeutic communications, the burden rests upon the patient initially to submit some showing that a given confidential communication is not directly related to the issue he has tendered to the court. (Cf. Evid.Code, § 404 (person claiming privilege against incrimination bears burden of showing proffered evidence might tend to incriminate him).) A patient may have to delimit his claimed "mental or emotional distress" or explain, in general terms, the object of the psychotherapy[23] in order to illustrate that it is not reasonably probable that the psychotherapeutic communications sought are directly relevant to the mental condition that he has placed in issue. In determining whether communications sufficiently relate to the mental condition at issue to require disclosure, the court should heed the basic privacy interests involved in the privilege in general, the statutory psychotherapist-patient privilege "[is to] be liberally construed in favor of the patient."

* * *

* * * Moreover, as with any evidence, the court retains discretion to "exclude evidence if its probative value is substantially outweighted

---

21.   Thus in the instant case, for example, defendant would not be authorized to undertake an examination of psychotherapeutic communications to determine if the plaintiff has ever exhibited aggressive tendencies or had other personal attributes that might be related to the assault. The plaintiff has not disclosed such elements of his mental condition merely by instituting an action for damages resulting from an assault and thus the exception of section 1016 is not applicable.

23.   Although ordinarily a patient cannot be required to disclose privileged information in order to claim the privilege (Evid.Code, § 915, subd. (a)), because the privileged status of psychotherapeutic communications under the patient-litigant exception depends upon the *content* of the communication, a patient may have to reveal some information about a communication to enable the trial judge to pass on his claim of irrelevancy. Upon such revelation, the trial judge should take necessary precautions to protect the confidentiality of these communications; for example, he might routinely permit such disclosure to be made *ex parte* in his chambers. (Compare the procedure suggested in Evid.Code, § 915, subd. (b).) (See also Developments in the Law—Discovery (1964), 74 Harv.L.Rev. 940, 1017–1018.)

by the probability that its admission will * * * (b) create substantial danger of undue prejudice, * * * ." (Evid.Code, § 352.)[25] In this area, the careful exercise of this discretion is necessary to provide substantial protection for the patient's legitimate interests;[26] without this element of court supervision intensive examinations of psychotherapists and patients may often ultimately result in substantially more harm than benefit.

In sum, we conclude that no constitutional right enables the psychotherapist to assert an absolute privilege concerning all psychotherapeutic communications. We do not believe the patient-psychotherapists privilege should be frozen into the rigidity of absolutism. So extreme a conclusion neither harmonizes with the expressed legislative intent nor finds a clear source in constitutional law. Such an application would lock the patient into a vice which would prevent him from waiving the privilege without the psychotherapist's consent. The question whether such a ruling would have the medical merit claimed by petitioner must be addressed to the Legislature; we can find no basis for such a ruling in legal precedent or principle.

Furthermore, the existence of a broad statutory privilege in clergymen does not deny psychotherapists the equal protection of the laws. Finally, although we recognize the legitimacy and importance of the concern over governmentally sanctioned intrusions into a patient's psychotherapeutic history, the patient-litigant exception, as properly limited, does not necessarily entail an overbroad intrusion into the patient's privacy.

Inasmuch as plaintiff had already disclosed that he had consulted Dr. Lifschutz for psychotherapeutic treatment, petitioner could not properly have refused to answer at least that question concerning the communications; since neither plaintiff nor the psychotherapist has as yet made any claim that the subpoenaed records are not directly relevant to the specific "mental and emotional" injuries for which plaintiff is claiming relief, Dr. Lifschutz had no right to refuse to produce the records. Thus the trial court's order requiring the production of records and the answering of questions was valid; the trial court properly adjudged Dr. Lifschutz in contempt of court for intentionally violating that valid court order.

The order to show cause is discharged and the petition for writ of habeas corpus is denied.

Mosk, Acting C. J., McComb, Peters, Burke, and Sullivan, JJ., and *Molinari, J. pro tem., concur.

See California Evidence Code § § 1010–1017, 1024, 1027, 1028 at pp. 862–863, 864, 865.

25. Necessary information will often be accessible without delving deeply into specific intimate factual circumstances and such searching probes ought to be avoided whenever possible. The psychotherapist's general conclusions about specific emotional symptoms will often suffice to convey the needed information while preserving the patient's dignity and interest in privacy.

26. The draftsmen of two separate versions of "model" legislation in this field each suggested that only a "conditional" patient-litigant exception be adopted; under this suggestion, disclosure would be compelled only upon a finding of the court that it would be in "the best interests of justice." Similar protection can be afforded under the California statutory scheme through a sensitive exercise of the trial court's discretionary authority.

*Assigned by the Chairman of the Judicial Council.

Hypothetical

A sues Dr. X for damages for injuries in a medical malpractice action. A's injuries were received when Dr. X performed angiogram tests on A. During the deposition of Dr. X, taken by A, Dr. X, claiming the physician-patient privilege, refuses to answer questions as to the names and addresses of other patients upon whom he performed angiogram tests, both before and after those performed on A, including two patients who developed complications from such tests. A moves for an order to compel Dr. X to answer these questions. Should A's motion be granted?

PART C. THE MARITAL PRIVILEGES

TRAMMEL v. UNITED STATES

Supreme Court of the United States, 1980.
445 U.S. 40, 100 S.Ct. 906, 63 L.Ed 2d 186.

Mr. Chief Justice BURGER delivered the opinion of the Court.

We granted certiorari to consider whether an accused may invoke the privilege against adverse spousal testimony so as to exclude the voluntary testimony of his wife. This calls for a re-examination of Hawkins v. United States, 358 U.S. 74 [79 S.Ct. 136, 3L.Ed. 2d 125] (1958).

I

On March 10, 1976, petitioner Otis Trammel was indicted with two others, Edwin Lee Roberts and Joseph Freeman, for importing heroin into the United States from Thailand and the Philippine Islands and for conspiracy to import heroin in violation of 21 U.S.C. §§ 952 (a), 962 (a), and 963. The indictment also named six unindicted co-conspirators, including petitioner's wife Elizabeth Ann Trammel.

According to the indictment, petitioner and his wife, flew from the Philippines to California in August 1975, carrying with them a quantity of heroin. Freeman and Roberts assisted them in its distribution. Elizabeth Trammel then travelled to Thailand where she purchased another supply of the drug. On November 3, 1975, with four ounces of heroin on her person, she boarded a plane for the United States. During a routine customs search in Hawaii, she was searched, the heroin was discovered, and she was arrested. After discussions with Drug Enforcement Administration agents, she agreed to cooperate with the Government.

Prior to trial on this indictment, petitioner moved to sever his case from that of Roberts and Freeman. He advised the court that the Government intended to call his wife as an adverse witness and asserted his claim to a privilege to prevent her from testifying against him. At a hearing on the motion, Mrs. Trammel was called as a Government witness * * * .
She testified that she and petitioner were married in May 1975 and that they remained married.[1] She explained that her cooperation with the Government was based on assurances that she would be given lenient treatment.[2] She then described, in considerable detail, her role and that of her husband in the heroin distribution conspiracy.

After hearing this testimony, the District Court ruled that Mrs. Trammel could testify in support of the Government's case to any act she observed during the marriage and to any communication "made in the presence of a third person"; however, confidential communications between petitioner and his wife were held to be privileged and inadmissible. The motion to sever was denied.

---

1. In response to the question whether divorce was contemplated, Mrs. Trammel testified that her husband had said that "I would go my way and he would go his." (App., at 27).

2. The Government represents to the Court that Elizabeth Trammel has not been prosecuted for her role in the conspiracy.

At trial, Elizabeth Trammel testified within the limits of the court's pretrial ruling; her testimony, as the Government concedes, constituted virtually its entire case against petitioner. He was found guilty on both the substantive and conspiracy charges   *   *   *   .

In the Court of Appeals petitioner's only claim of error was that the admission of the adverse testimony of his wife, over his objection, contravened this Court's teaching in Hawkins v. United States, 358 U.S. 74 [79 S.Ct. 136, 3 L.Ed. 2d 125] (1958), and therefore constituted reversible error. The Court of Appeals rejected this contention. It concluded that *Hawkins* did not prohibit "the voluntary testimony of a spouse who appears as an unindicted co-conspirator under grant of immunity from the Government in return for her testimony." 583 F. 2d 1166, 1168 (CA10 1978).

II

The privilege claimed by petitioner has ancient roots. Writing in 1628, Lord Coke observed that "it hath been resolved by the Justices that a wife cannot be produced either against or for her husband." 1 Coke, A Commentarie upon Littleton 6b (1628). This spousal disqualification sprang from two canons of medieval jurisprudence; first, the rule that an accused was not permitted to testify in his own behalf because of his interest in the proceeding; second, the concept that husband and wife were one, and that since the woman had no recognized separate legal existence, the husband was that one. From those two now long-abandoned doctrines, it followed that what was inadmissible from the lips of the defendant-husband was also inadmissible from his wife.

Despite its medieval origins, this rule of spousal disqualification remained intact in most common-law jurisdictions well into the 19th century. It was applied by this Court in Stein v. Bowman, 13 Pet. 209, 220-223 [10 L. Ed. 129] (1839), in Graves v. United States, 150 U.S. 118 [14 S.Ct. 40, 37 L.Ed. 1021] (1893), and again in Jin Fuey Moy v. United States, 254 U.S. 189, 195 [41 S.Ct. 98, 101, 65 L.Ed. 214] (1920), where it was deemed so well established a proposition as to "hardly requir[e] mention." Indeed, it was not until 1933, in Funk v. United States, 290 U.S. 371 [54 S.Ct. 212, 78 L.Ed. 369], that this Court abolished the testimonial disqualification in the federal courts, so as to permit the spouse of a defendant to testify in the defendant's behalf. *Funk,* however, left undisturbed the rule that either spouse could prevent the other from giving adverse testimony. Id., at 373 [54 S.Ct., at 212]. The rule thus evolved into one of privilege rather than one of absolute disqualification.   *   *   *

The modern justification for this privilege against adverse spousal testimony is its perceived role in fostering the harmony and sanctity of the marriage relationship. Notwithstanding this benign purpose, the rule was sharply criticized. Professor Wigmore termed it "the merest anachronism in legal theory and an indefensible obstruction to truth in practice." 8 Wigmore, § 2228 at 221. The Committee on the Improvement of the Law of Evidence of the American Bar Association called for its abolition. 63 American Bar Association Reports, at 594–595 (1938). In its place, Wigmore and others suggested a privilege protecting only private marital communications, modeled on the privilege between priest and penitent, attorney and client and physician and patient.[5]

These criticisms influenced the American Law Institute, which, in its 1942 Model Code of Evidence, advocated a privilege for marital confidences, but expressly rejected a rule vesting in the defendant the right to exclude all adverse testimony of his spouse. See American Law Institute, Model Code of Evidence, Rule 215 (1942). In 1953 the Uniform Rules of Evidence, drafted by the National Conference of Commissioners on Uniform State Laws, followed a similar course; it limited the privilege to confidential communications and "abolishe[d] the rule, still existing in some states, and largely a sentimental relic, of not requiring one spouse to testify against the other in a criminal action." See Rule 23 (2) and comments. Several state legislatures enacted similarly patterned provisions into law.

In Hawkins v. United States, 358 U.S. 74 [79 S.Ct. 136, 3 L.Ed.2d 125] (1958), this Court considered the continued vitality of the privilege against adverse spousal testimony in the federal courts. There the District Court had permitted petitioner's wife, over his objection, to testify against him. With one questioning concurring opinion, the Court held the wife's testimony inadmissible; it took note of the critical comments that the common-law rule had engendered, id., at 76, and n. 4 [79 S.Ct., at 137], but chose not to abandon it. Also rejected was the Government's suggestion that the Court modify the privilege by vesting it in the witness spouse, with freedom to testify or not independent of the defendant's control. The Court viewed this proposed modification as antithetical to the widespread belief, evidenced in the rules then in effect in a majority of the States and in England, "that the law should not force or encourage testimony which might alienate husband and wife, or further inflame existing domestic differences." Id., at 79 [79 S.Ct., at 139].

Hawkins, then, left the federal privilege for adverse spousal testimony where it found it, continuing "a rule which bars the testimony of one spouse against the other unless both consent." Id., at 78 [79 S.Ct., at 138]. Accord, Wyatt v. United States, 362 U.S. 525, 528 [80 S.Ct. 901, 903, 4 L.Ed.2d 931] (1960).[7] However, in so doing, the Court made clear that its decision was not meant to "foreclose whatever changes in the rule may eventually be dictated by 'reason and experience.'" 358 U.S., at 79 [79 S.Ct., at 139].

5. This Court recognized just such a confidential marital communications privilege in Wolfle v. United States, 291 U.S. 7 [54 S.Ct. 279, 78 L.Ed. 617] (1934), and in Blau v. United States, 340 U.S. 332 [71 S.Ct. 301, 95 L.Ed. 306] (1951). In neither case, however, did the Court adopt the Wigmore view that the communications privilege be substituted *in place of* the privilege against adverse spousal testimony. The privilege as to confidential marital communications is not at issue in the instant case; accordingly, our holding today does not disturb *Wolfle* and *Blau.*

7. The decision in *Wyatt* recognized an exception to *Hawkins* for cases in which one spouse commits a crime against the other. 362 U.S., at 526 [80 S.Ct. at 902]. This exception placed on the ground of necessity, was a longstanding one at common law. See Lord Audley's Case, 123 Eng. Rep. 1140 (1931), 8 Wigmore § 2239. It has been expanded since then to include crimes against the spouse's property, see Herman v. United States, 220 F. 2d 219, 226 (C.A.4 1955), and in recent years crimes against children of either spouse, United States v. Allery, 526 F. 2d 1362 (C.A.8, 1975). Similar exceptions have been found to the confidential marital communications privilege. See 8 Wigmore, § 2338.

III

A

The Federal Rules of Evidence acknowledge the authority of the federal courts to continue the evolutionary development of testimonial privileges in federal criminal trials "governed by the principles of the common law as they may be interpreted   *   *   *   in the light of reason and experience." Fed. Rule Evid. 501. The general mandate of Rule 501 was substituted by the Congress for a set of privilege rules drafted by the Judicial Conference Advisory Committee on Rules of Evidence and approved by the Judicial Conference of the United States and by this Court. That proposal defined nine specific privileges, including a husband-wife privilege which would have codified the *Hawkins* rule and eliminated the privilege for confidential marital communications. See Fed. Rule of Evid., Proposed Rule 505. In rejecting the proposed rules and enacting Rule 501, Congress manifested an affirmative intention not to freeze the law of privilege. Its purpose rather was to "provide the courts with the flexibility to develop rules of privilege on a case-by-case basis," 120 Cong. Rec. 40891 (1974) (statement of Rep. Hungate), and to leave the door open to change.   *   *   *

Although Rule 501 confirms the authority of the federal courts to reconsider the continued validity of the *Hawkins* rule, the long history of the privilege suggests that it ought not to be casually cast aside. That the privilege is one affecting marriage, home, and family relationships—already subject to much erosion in our day—also counsels caution. At the same time we cannot escape the reality that the law on occasion adheres to doctrinal concepts long after the reasons which gave them birth have disappeared and after experience suggests the need for change. This was recognized in *Funk* where the Court "decline[d] to enforce   *   *   *   ancient rule[s] of the common law under conditions as they now exist." 290 U.S., at 382 [54 S.Ct., at 215]. For, as Mr. Justice Black admonished in another setting, "[w]hen precedent and precedent alone is all the argument that can be made to support a court-fashioned rule, it is time for the rule's creator to destroy it." Francis v. Southern Pacific Co., 333 U.S. 445, 471 [68 S.Ct. 611, 623, 92 L.Ed. 798] (1948) (Black, J., dissenting).

B

Since 1958, when *Hawkins* was decided, support for the privilege against adverse spousal testimony has been eroded further. Thirty-one jurisdictions, including Alaska and Hawaii, then allowed an accused a privilege to prevent adverse spousal testimony. 358 U.S., at 81, n. 3 [79 S.Ct., at 140], (Stewart, J., concurring). The number has now declined to 24.[9] In

---

9. Eight states provide that one spouse is incompetent to testify against the other in a criminal proceeding: *   *   *   .

Sixteen states provide a privilege against adverse spousal testimony and vest the privilege in both spouses or in the defendant-spouse alone;   *   *   *   .

Nine states entitle the witness-spouse alone to assert a privilege against adverse spousal testimony: *   *   *   .

The remaining 17 states have abolished the privilege in criminal cases: *   *   *   .

In 1901, Congress enacted a rule of evidence for the District of Columbia that made husband and wife "competent but not compellable to testify for or against each other," except as to confidential communications. This provision, which vests the privilege against adverse spousal testimony in the witness spouse, remains in effect. See 31 Stat. 1358, §§ 1068, 1069, recodified as D. C. Code § 14–306 (1973).

1974, the National Conference on Uniform States Laws revised its Uniform Rules of Evidence, but again rejected the *Hawkins* rule in favor of a limited privilege for confidential communications. See Uniform Rules of Evidence, Rule 504. That proposed rule has been enacted in Arkansas, North Dakota, and Oklahoma—each of which in 1958 permitted an accused to exclude adverse spousal testimony.[10] The trend in state law toward divesting the accused of the privilege to bar adverse spousal testimony has special relevance because of the law of marriage and domestic relations are concerns traditionally reserved to the states. Scholarly criticism of the *Hawkins* rule has also continued unabated.

C

Testimonial exclusionary rules and privileges contravene the fundamental principle that "the public * * * has a right to every man's evidence." United States v. Bryan, 339 U.S. 323, 331 [70 S.Ct. 724, 730, 94 L.Ed. 884] (1950). As such, they must be strictly construed and accepted "only to the very limited extent that permitting a refusal to testify or excluding relevant evidence has a public good transcending the normally predominant principle of utilizing all rational means for ascertaining truth." Elkins v. United States, 364 U.S. 206, 234 [80 S.Ct. 1437, 1454, 4 L.Ed.2d 1669] (1960) (Frankfurter, J., dissenting). Accord, United States v. Nixon, 418 U.S. 683, 709–710 [94 S.Ct. 3090, 3108–3109, 41 L.Ed.2d 1039] (1974). Here we must decide whether the privilege against adverse spousal testimony promotes sufficiently important interests to outweigh the need for probative evidence in the administration of criminal justice.

It is essential to remember that the *Hawkins* privilege is not needed to protect information privately disclosed between husband and wife in the confidence of the marital relationship—once described by this Court as "the best solace of human existence." Stein v. Bowman, 13 Pet., at 223. Those confidences are privileged under the independent rule protecting confidential marital communications. The *Hawkins* privilege is invoked, not to exclude private marital communications, but rather to exclude evidence of criminal acts and of communications made in the presence of third persons.

No other testimonial privilege sweeps so broadly. The privileges between priest and penitent, attorney and client, and physician and patient limit protection to private communications. These privileges are rooted in the imperative need for confidence and trust. The priest-penitent privilege recognizes the human need to disclose to a spiritual counselor, in total and absolute confidence, what are believed to be flawed acts or thoughts and to receive priestly consolation and guidance in return. The lawyer-client privi-

---

10. In 1965, California took the privilege from the defendant-spouse and vested it in the witness-spouse, accepting a study commission recommendation that the "latter [was] more likely than the former to determine whether or not to claim the privilege on the basis of the probable effect on the marital relationship." See Cal. Evid. Code §§ 970–973 * * * .

Support for the common-law rule has also diminished in England. In 1972 a study group there proposed giving the privilege to the witness-spouse, on the ground that "if [the wife] is willing to give evidence * * * the law would be showing excessive concern for the preservation of marital harmony if it were to say she must not do so." Criminal Law Revision Committee, Eleventh Report Evidence (General), at 93.

lege rests on the need for the advocate and counselor to know all that relates to the client's reasons for seeking representation if the professional mission is to be carried out. Similarly, the physician must know all that a patient can articulate in order to identify and to treat disease; barriers to full disclosure would impair diagnosis and treatment.

The *Hawkins* rule stands in marked contrast to these three privileges. Its protection is not limited to confidential communications; rather it permits an accused to exclude all adverse spousal testimony. As Jeremy Bentham observed more than a century and a half ago, such a privilege goes far beyond making "every man's house his castle," and permits a person to convert his house into "a den of thieves." 5 Rationale of Judicial Evidence 340 (1827). It "secures, to every man, one safe and unquestionable and ever ready accomplice for every imaginable crime." Id., at 338.

The ancient foundations for so sweeping a privilege have long since disappeared. Nowhere in the common-law world—indeed in any modern society—is a woman regarded as chattel or demeaned by denial of a separate legal identity and the dignity associated with recognition as a whole human being. Chip by chip, over the years those archaic notions have been cast aside so that "[n]o longer is the female destined solely for the home and the rearing of the family, and only the male for the marketplace and the world of ideas." Stanton v. Stanton, 421 U.S. 7, 14, 15 [95 S.Ct. 1373, 1377, 1378, 43 L.Ed.2d 688] (1975).

The contemporary justification for affording an accused such a privilege is also unpersuasive. When one spouse is willing to testify against the other in a criminal proceeding—whatever the motivation—their relationship is almost certainly in disrepair; there is probably little in the way of marital harmony for the privilege to preserve. In these circumstances, a rule of evidence that permits an accused to prevent adverse spousal testimony seems far more likely to frustrate justice than to foster family peace.[12] Indeed, there is reason to believe that vesting the privilege in the accused could actually undermine the marital relationship. For example, in a case such as this, the Government is unlikely to offer a wife immunity and lenient treatment if it knows that her husband can prevent her from giving adverse testimony. If the Government is dissuaded from making such an offer, the privilege can have the untoward effect of permitting one spouse to escape justice at the expense of the other. It hardly seems conducive to the preservation of the marital relation to place a wife in jeopardy solely by virtue of her husband's control over her testimony.

IV

Our consideration of the foundations for the privilege and its history satisfy us that "reason and experience" no longer justify so sweeping a rule as that found acceptable by the Court in *Hawkins*. Accordingly, we conclude that the existing rule should be modified so that the witness spouse alone has a privilege to refuse to testify adversely; the witness may be neither compelled to testify nor foreclosed from testifying. This mod-

---

12. It is argued that abolishing the privilege will permit the Government to come between husband and wife, pitting one against the other. That, too, misses the mark. Neither *Hawkins*, nor any other privilege, prevents the Government from enlisting one spouse to give information concerning the other or to aid in the other's apprehension. It is only the spouse's testimony in the courtroom that is prohibited.

ification—vesting the privilege in the witness spouse—furthers the important public interest in marital harmony without unduly burdening legitimate law enforcement needs.

Here, petitioner's spouse chose to testify against him. That she did so after a grant of immunity and assurances of lenient treatment does not render her testimony involuntary. Accordingly, the District Court and the Court of Appeals were correct in rejecting petitioner's claim of privilege, and the judgment of the Court of Appeals is affirmed.

Affirmed.

———

The concurring opinion of Mr. Justice Stewart is omitted.

———

See California Evidence Code § § 970–973, 980–982, 984–987, at pp. 857, 858.

Hypothetical

X is prosecuted for murder of A, a liquor-store clerk, during a holdup. The murder remained unsolved for several years. X's participation became known after B, X's wife at the time, secured an annulment. The prosecutor calls B to testify that she had her marriage to X annulled about six months ago because she married X before her divorce from Y became final, and that on the night of A's murder, X came home and told her he had pulled a robbery at the liquor store and killed the clerk. X objects to B's proposed testimony on the ground of the privilege for marital communications. What result?

PART D.   MISCELLANEOUS PRIVILEGES

STOKES, CHURCH & STATE IN THE UNITED STATES

555-6 (1964).*
[All footnotes omitted.]

The Seal of the Confessional

The question of the sacredness of confessions made to a priest has frequently been a matter of judicial consideration. In general, what is called the "seal of the confessional" has been recognized by the civil courts, though by the old common law confessions were not considered privileged. New York is said to have been the first of all English-speaking states from the time of the Reformation to protect by its courts and laws the secrecy and sanctity of auricular confession. The decision was made in June, 1813, by De Witt Clinton, then presiding in the mayor's court in New York City. It was judicially determined that auricular confession, being a recognized part of Church discipline, protects a priest from being compelled in a court of law to testify as to statements made to him in the confessional. Many states, following this decision, specifically protect a priest against the necessity of disclosing confessions made to him in confidence and in his professional capacity. In some states a characteristic provision is that found in an Arkansas statute:

No minister of the gospel or priest of any denomination shall be compelled to testify in relation to any confession made to him in his professional character, in the course of discipline by the rules or practice of such denomination.

In other states, such as Michigan and New York, the provision goes even farther and substitutes the word "allowed" for "compelled," which means that even if the clergyman were willing to testify concerning the confession made to him and none of the attorneys objected to the testimony, the court would still have to forbid him to do so.

There are states with no specific legislation, but attempts are extremely rare where any responsible court tries to compel a priest to disclose knowledge gained through the confessional. Perhaps the most interesting case that has come before the courts was in Richmond, Virginia, in 1855, when the vicar general, the Very Reverend John Teeling, D.D., was summoned to testify against a man who had fatally wounded his wife. The vicar general had taken her confession as she was dying and was ordered to reveal it. He replied, "Any statement made in her sacramental confession whether inculpatory or exculpatory of the prisoner, I am not at liberty to reveal." The presiding judge of the circuit court then gave a decision in which he said,

"I regard any infringement upon the tenets of any denomination as a violation of the fundamental law, which guarantees perfect freedom to all classes in the exercise of their religion. To encroach upon the confessional, which is well understood to be a fundamental tenet in the Catholic church, would be to ignore the Bill of Rights, so far as it is applicable to that Church. In view of these circumstances, as well as of other considerations connected with the subject, I feel no hesitation in ruling that a priest enjoys a privilege of exemption from revealing what is communicated to him in the confessional."

The records of the court were lost in the Civil War, and little information is available about either the defendant or the priest. Hence, it cannot be said what the ultimate outcome of the trial was or whether the defendant was convicted and executed. It should be noted that the priest refused to testify even if the testimony would have been "exculpatory of the prisoner." In these circumstances it can hardly be said that the moral issue was clearly in favor of upholding the execution of a man for a crime he never committed. Nevertheless, there is no exception made in the law in respect to exculpatory confessions, and in general the courts hold that the confidence which was recognized by the English common law as existing between lawyer and client should also exist between physician and patient and between priest as confessor and his parishioner or other penitent. This applies not only to the Roman Catholic Church with its regular confessional but to similar confidence between non-Catholic clergymen, when acting as such, and their parishioners.

See California Evidence Code § 1030–1034 at p. 865.

NOTE, FUNCTIONAL OVERLAP BETWEEN THE LAWYER AND OTHER PROFESSIONALS: ITS IMPLICATIONS FOR THE PRIVILEGED COMMUNICATIONS DOCTRINES

71 Yale L.J. 1226, 1247–49 (1962).*
[Footnotes omitted.]

THE ACCOUNTANT

At common law there was no testimonial privilege for communications between a man and his accountant, and courts continue to reject this claim of privilege unanimously. By enacting privileged communications statutes protecting confidences between accountants and their clients, fifteen American jurisdictions have changed the common law rule. Almost no case law exists which interprets these statutes. However, they may be narrowly construed if cases arise which invite their construction, since lawyers and jurists responding to our survey, leading commentators, legal organizations, and a number of federal courts disfavor this privilege. Almost certainly all the exceptions and limitations of the attorney-client privilege will be grafted onto these statutes. In a number of cases raising the question in States with such a privilege, federal courts have refused to apply the state accountant privilege statute, but have adhered to the common law rule. These cases involved either tax investigations or criminal prosecutions.

At first glance, it seems unfair that a conversation with a lawyer is protected while the same conversation if held with an accountant would not be. The possibility of an accountant-client privilege, however, is one which has not been enthusiastically embraced by all accountants. The American Institute of Certified Public Accountants officially opposes the privilege. The Executive Director of the National Society of Public Accountants explains this policy:

> Perhaps the reason for not pushing for privileged communication for our members practicing public accounting is the fact that much of their income is from tax work, and they maintain a good relationship with the Internal Revenue Service. There might be some question about cooperation and working relationships should there be privileged communication. Usually a client will tell the agent, "Go see my accountant." The agent would not be so amenable to this suggestion if the accountant were privileged.

Arguably, since the privilege is for the client's protection, not the professional's, the accountant's preference should defer to his client's. But no tension seems to exist between the views of the accountant and the client; a majority of the laymen surveyed who expressed an opinion disfavored the accountant privilege. Lawyers and judges, too, were heavily opposed, and accountants ambivalent at best. Thus, the practical political obstacles either to passage or successful administration of such a law are great.

Even discounting the public opinion against it, the accountant-client privilege is of dubious inherent desirability. It is likely that federal courts at least believe that an accountant-client privilege would greatly increase the government's difficulties in proving tax evasions. Tacit recognition of this privilege's obstructive effect is also found in the statutes of six of the fifteen States with this privilege. Those six suspend the privilege in criminal and bankruptcy cases. While personal counseling and advice about lawsuits may require guarantees of absolute confidentiality in order to be effectual, this is probably untrue of the tasks performed by the accountant —evidenced by the attitudes of their professional associations to the privilege. Although there is a functional overlap between accountants and attorneys, this is insufficient to justify a privilege for the former. The attorney-client privilege must cover all legitimate attorney tasks in order to shield those functions for which protection is essential. If the area of overlap could be separated, neither profession would be entitled to a privilege. In fact, courts have withdrawn the privilege from attorneys who were acting more like accountants than attorneys. Further, courts have curtailed accountant activity which resembled too closely the lawyer's work by declaring such tasks to have been unauthorized practice of law. In sum, therefore, the privilege should not be extended to the accountant.

See also California Evidence Code § § 1050 at p. 871, (privilege to protect secrecy of vote) 1060 at p. 871 (privilege to protect trade secret), 1070 at p. 871 (Newsman's refusal to disclose news source.)

PARENT-CHILD PRIVILEGE FOUND

The National Law Journal, November 19, 1979.*

A NEW YORK state court, in an apparently unprecedented ruling, has held that a parent cannot be forced to testify against his child, even if the child is an adult.

*Copyright 1979, National Law Journal.

Judge Gerard Delaney of the Westchester County Court, said that "the confidences extended between a parent and child are just as sacrosanct as between a doctor and a patient or a priest and a penitent. The privilege does not terminate simply because the child reaches majority. People v. Fitzgerald, 76-43.

Judge Jack B. Weinstein of the U.S. District Court in Brooklyn reportedly characterized the Nov. 1 ruling as "very unusual."

"It would never occur to most lawyers" to claim the privilege, he was quoted as saying. "It's not recognized in the federal courts at all or by any of the states."

Judge Delaney dismissed the case against Michael Fitzgerald of Briarcliff Manor, N.Y., who had been charged with criminally negligent homicide in a 1975 automobile accident in which an 18-year-old woman died. Mr. Fitzgerald was then 23 years old.

The dismissal came after Mr. Fitzgerald's father refused to testify against him. The elder Fitzgerald had previously testified before a grand jury about conversations he had with his son after the accident but before his son was arrested.

The younger Fitzgerald's attorney, John Keegan of White Plains, N.Y., said he relied on a state appellate division ruling, Matter of A&M, 61 A.D.2d 426. The appellate court supported the confidentiality between parent and child in principle, though it did not rule on the matter or address the issue of the child's majority, he said.

THE NEWS-PERSON'S PRIVILEGE

MATTER OF FARBER

Supreme Court of New Jersey, 1978.
78 N.J. 259, 394 A.2d 330.

MOUNTAIN, J.

In these consolidated appeals The New York Times Company and Myron Farber, a reporter employed by the newspaper, challenge judgments entered against them in two related matters—one a proceeding in aid of a litigant (civil contempt), the other for criminal contempt of court. The proceedings were instituted in an ongoing murder trial now in its seventh month, as a result of the appellants' failure to comply with two *subpoena duces tecum*, directing them to produce certain documents and materials compiled by one or both of these appellants in the course of Farber's investigative reporting of certain allegedly criminal activities. Farber's investigations and reporting are said to have contributed largely to the indictment and prosecution of Dr. Mario E. Jascalevich for murder. Appellants moved unsuccessfully before Judge William J. Arnold, the trial judge in State v. Jascalevich, to quash the two subpoenas; an order was entered directing that the subpoenaed material be produced for *in camera* inspection by the court. The appellant's applications for a stay of Judge Arnold's order were denied successively by the Appellate Division of the Superior Court, by this Court, and by two separate Justices of the Supreme Court of the United States.

Impelled by appellants' persistent refusal to produce the subpoenaed materials for *in camera* inspection, Judge Arnold issued an order returnable before Judge Theodore W. Trautwein, directing appellants to show cause why they should not be deemed in contempt of court. During the subsequent hearing, Judge Trautwein ordered counsel for Jascalevich to apply to Judge Arnold, pursuant to R 1:10–5, for an additional order to show cause, this to be in aid of litigants' rights. The order was issued, served and the hearing on the matter consolidated with the hearing on the criminal contempt charge.

Judge Trautwein determined that both appellants had wilfully contemned Judge Arnold's order directing that materials be produced for *in camera* inspection and found them guilty as charged. A fine of $100,000 was imposed on The New York Times and Farber was ordered to serve six months in the Bergen County jail and to pay a fine of $1,000. Additionally, in order to compel production of the materials subpoenaed on behalf of Jascalevich, a fine of $5,000 per day for every day that elapsed until compliance with Judge Arnold's order was imposed upon The Times; Farber was fined $1,000 and sentenced to confinement in the county jail until he complied with the order.

* * *

I

The First Amendment

Appellants claim a privilege to refrain from revealing information sought by the *subpoenas duces tecum* essentially for the reason that were they to divulge this material, confidential sources of such information would be made public. Were this to occur, they argue, newsgathering and the dissemination of news would be seriously impaired, because much information would never be forthcoming to the news media unless the persons who were the sources of such information could be entirely certain that their identities would remain secret. The final result, appellants claim, would be a substantial lessening in the supply of available news on a variety of important and sensitive issues, all to the detriment of the public interest. They contend further that this privilege to remain silent with respect to confidential information and the sources of such information emanates from the "free speech" and "free press" clauses of the First Amendment.[1]

In our view the Supreme Court of the United States has clearly rejected this claim and has squarely held that no such First Amendment right exists. In Branzburg v. Hayes, 408 U.S. 665, 92 S.Ct. 2646, 33 L.Ed.2d 626 (1972), three news media representatives argued that, for the same reason here advanced, they should not be required to appear and testify before grand juries, and that this privilege to refrain from divulging information, asserted to have been received from confidential sources, derived from the First Amendment. Justice White, noting that there was no common law privilege, stated the issue and gave the Court's answer in the first paragraph of his opinion:

---

1. The First Amendment of the United States Constitution reads as follows:

    Congress shall make no law respecting an establishment of religion, or prohibiting the free exercise thereof, or

abridging the freedom of speech, or of the press; or the right of the people peaceably to assemble, and to petition the Government for a redress of grievances.

The issue in these cases is whether requiring newsmen to appear and testify before state or federal grand juries abridges the freedom of speech and press guaranteed by the First Amendment. We hold that it does not. [Branzburg v. Hayes, supra, 408 U.S. at 667, 92 S.Ct. at 2649, 33 L.Ed.2d at 631 (1972)]

In that case one reporter, from Frankfort, Kentucky, had witnessed individuals making hashish from marijuana and had made a rather comprehensive survey of the drug scene in Frankfort. He had written an article in the Louisville Courier-Journal describing this illegal activity. Another, a newsman-photographer employed by a New Bedford, Massachusetts television station, had met with members of the Black Panther movement at the time that certain riots and disorders occurred in New Bedford. The material he assembled formed the basis for a televison program that followed. The third investigative reporter had met with members of the Black Panthers in northern California and had written an article about the nature and activities of the movement. In each instance there had been a commitment on the part of the media representative that he would not divulge the source of his article or story.

By a vote of 5 to 4 the Supreme Court held that newspaper reporters or other media representatives have no privilege deriving from the First Amendment to refrain from divulging confidential information and the sources of such information when properly subpoenaed to appear before a grand jury. The three media representatives were directed to appear and testify. The holding was later underscored and applied directly to this case by Justice White in a brief opinion filed in this cause upon the occasion of his denial of a stay sought by these appellants. He said:

There is no present authority in this Court either that newsmen are constitutionally privileged to withhold duly subpoenaed documents material to the prosecution or defense of a criminal case or that a defendant seeking the subpoena must show extraordinary circumstances before enforcement against newsmen will be had. [New York Times and Farber v. Jascalevich, 439 U.S. 1317, 99 S.Ct. 6, 10, 58 L.Ed.2d 25, 30-31 (1978)]

We pause to point out that despite the holding in *Branzburg,* those who gather and disseminate news are by no means without First Amendment protections. Some of these are referred to by Justice White in the *Branzburg* opinion. They include, among others, the right to publish what the press chooses to publish, to refrain from publishing what it chooses to withhold, to seek out news in any legal manner and to refrain from revealing its sources except upon legitimate demand. Demand is not legitimate when the desired information is patently irrelevant to the needs of the inquirer or his needs are not manifestly compelling. Nor will the First Amendment sanction harassment of the press. These do not exhaust, the list of such First Amendment protective rights.

The point to be made, however, is that among the many First Amendment protections that may be invoked by the press, there is not to be found the privilege of refusing to reveal relevant confidential information and its sources to a grand jury which is engaged in the fundamental governmental function of "[f]air and effective law enforcement aimed at providing security for the person and property of the individual * * * " [408 U.S. at

690, 92 S.Ct. at 2661, 33 L.Ed.2d at 644]. The reason this is so is that a majority of the members of the United States Supreme Court have so determined.

Faced with this conclusion, appellants appear to argue that Justice Powell's concurring opinion in *Branzburg* somehow fails to support this result. The argument is without merit. We do not read Justice Powell's opinion as in any way disagreeing with what is said by Justice White. But even if it did, it would not matter for present purposes. The important and conclusive point is that five members of the Court have all reached the conclusion that the First Amendment affords no privilege to a newsman to refuse to appear before a grand jury and testify as to relevant information he possesses, even though in so doing he may divulge confidential sources. The particular path that any Justice may have followed becomes unimportant when once it is seen that a majority have reached the same destination.

Thus we do no weighing or balancing of societal interests in reaching our determination that the First Amendment does not afford appellants the privilege they claim. The weighing and balancing has been done by a higher court.   *   *   *

II

The Shield Law[2]

In Branzburg v. Hayes, supra, the Court dealt with a newsman's claim of privilege based solely upon the First Amendment. As we have seen, this claim of privilege failed. In *Branzburg* no shield law was involved. Here we have a shield law, said to be as strongly worded as any in the country.

We read the legislative intent in adopting this statute in its present form as seeking to protect the confidential sources of the press as well as information so obtained by reporters and other news media representatives to the greatest extent permitted by the Constitution of the United States and that of the State of New Jersey. It is abundantly clear that appellants come fully within the literal language of the enactment. Extended discussion is quite unnecessary. Viewed solely as a matter of statutory construction, appellants are clearly entitled to the protections afforded by the act unless

---

2. The term "shield law" is commonly and widely applied to statutes granting newsmen and other media representatives the privilege of declining to reveal confidential sources of information. The New Jersey shield law reads as follows:

Subject to Rule 37, a person engaged on, engaged in, connected with, or employed by news media for the purpose of gathering, procuring, transmitting, compiling, editing or disseminating news for the general public or on whose behalf news is so gathered, procured, transmitted, compiled, edited or disseminated has a privilege to refuse to disclose, in any legal or quasi-legal proceeding or before any investigative body, including, but not limited to, any court, grand jury, petit jury, administrative agency, the Legislature or legislative committee, or elsewhere:

a. The source, author, means, agency or person from or through whom any information was procured, obtained, supplied, furnished, gathered, transmitted, compiled, edited, disseminated, or delivered; and

b. Any news or information obtained in the course of pursuing his professional activities whether or not it is disseminated.

The provisions of this rule insofar as it relates to radio or television stations shall not apply unless the radio or telvision station maintains and keeps open for inspection, for a period of at least 1 year from the date of an actual broadcast or telecast, an exact recording, transcription, kinescopic film or certified written transcript of the actual broadcast or telecast.

statutory exceptions including waiver are shown to apply. In view of the fundamental basis of our decision today, the question of waiver of privilege under the Shield Law need not be addressed by us.

III

The Sixth Amendment[3] and its New Jersey Counterpart[4]

Viewed on its face, considered solely as a reflection of legislative intent to bestow upon the press as broad a shield as possible to protect against forced revelation of confidential source materials, this legislation is entirely constitutional. Indeed, no one appears to have attacked its facial constitutionality.

It is, however, argued, and argued very strenuously, that if enforced under the facts of this case, the Shield Law violates the Sixth Amendment of the Federal Constitution as well as Article 1, ¶ 10 of the New Jersey Constitution. These provisions are set forth above. Essentially the argument is this: The Federal and State Constitutions each provide that in all criminal prosecutions the accused shall have the right "to have compulsory process for obtaining witnesses in his favor." Dr. Jascalevich seeks to obtain evidence to use in preparing and presenting his defense in the ongoing criminal trial in which he has been accused of multiple murders. He claims to come within the favor of these constitutional provisions—which he surely does. Finally, when faced with the Shield Law, he invokes the rather elementary but entirely sound proposition that where Constitution and statute collide, the latter must yield. Subject to what is said below, we find this argument unassailable.

The compulsory process clause of the Sixth Amendment has never been elaborately explicated by the Supreme Court. Not until 1967, when it decided Washington v. Texas, 388 U.S. 14, 87 S.Ct. 1920, 18 L.Ed.2d 1019 had the clause been directly construed. Westen, *Confrontation and Compulsory Process: A Unified Theory of Evidence for Criminal Cases,* 91 Harv.L.Rev. 567, 586 (1978). In *Washington* the petitioner sought the reversal of his conviction for murder. A Texas statute at the time provided that persons charged or convicted as co-participants in the same crime could not testify for one another. One Fuller, who had already been convicted of the murder, was prevented from testifying by virtue of the statute. The record indicated that had he testified his testimony would have been favorable to petitioner. The Court reversed the conviction on the ground that petitioner's Sixth

---

3. The Sixth Amendment of the United States Constitution reads as follows:

    In all criminal prosecutions, the accused shall enjoy the right to a speedy and public trial, by an impartial jury of the State and district wherein the crime shall have been committed, which district shall have been previously ascertained by law, and to be informed of the nature and cause of the accusation; to be confronted with the witnesses against him; to have compulsory process for obtaining witnesses in his favor; and to have the Assistance of Counsel for his defense.

4. Article 1, § 10 of the Constitution of the State of New Jersey reads as follows:

    In all criminal prosecutions the accused shall have the right to a speedy and public trial by an impartial jury; to be informed of the nature and cause of the accusation; to be confronted with the witnesses against him; to have compulsory process for obtaining witnesses in his favor; and to have the assistance of counsel in his defense.

Amendment right to compulsory process had been denied. At the same time it determined that the compulsory process clause in the Sixth Amendment was binding on state courts by virtue of the due process clause of the Fourteenth Amendment. It will be seen that *Washington* is like the present case in a significant respect. The Texas statute and the Sixth Amendment could not both stand. The latter of course prevailed. So must it be here.

Quite recently, in United States v. Nixon, 418 U.S. 683, 94 S.Ct. 3090, 41 L.Ed.2d 1039 (1974), the Court dealt with another compulsory process issue. There the Special Prosecutor, Leon Jaworski, subpoenaed various tape recordings and documents in the possession of President Nixon. The latter claimed an executive privilege and refused to deliver the tapes. The Supreme Court conceded that indeed there was an executive privilege and that although "[n]owhere in the Constitution * * * is there any explicit reference to a privilege of confidentiality, yet to the extent this interest relates to the effective discharge of a President's powers, it is constitutionally based." 418 U.S. at 711, 94 S.Ct. at 3109, 41 L.Ed.2d at 1065. Despite this conclusion that at least to some extent a president's executive privilege derives from the Constitution, the Court nonetheless concluded that the demands of our criminal justice system required that the privilege must yield.

We have elected to employ an adversary system of criminal justice in which the parties contest all issues before a court of law. The need to develop all relevant facts in the adversary system is both fundamental and comprehensive. The ends of criminal justice would be defeated if judgments were to be founded on a partial or speculative presentation of the facts. The very integrity of the judicial system and public confidence in the system depend on full disclosure of all the facts, within the framework of the rules of evidence. To ensure that justice is done, it is imperative to the function of courts that compulsory process be available for the production of evidence needed either by the prosecution or by the defense. [United States v. Nixon, supra, 418 U.S. at 709, 94 S.Ct. at 3108, 41 L.Ed.2d at 1064]

It is important to note that the Supreme Court in this case compelled the production of privileged material—the privilege acknowledged to rest in part upon the Constitution—even though there was no Sixth Amendment compulsion to do so. The Sixth Amendment affords rights to an accused but not to a prosecutor. The compulsion to require the production of the privileged material derived from the necessities of our system of administering criminal justice.

Article 1, ¶ 10 of the Constitution of the State of New Jersey contains, as we have seen, exactly the same language with respect to compulsory process as that found in the Sixth Amendment. There exists no authoritative explication of this constitutional provision. Indeed it has rarely been mentioned in our reported decisions. We interpret it as affording a defendant in a criminal prosecution the right to compel the attendance of witnesses and the production of documents and other material for which he may have, or may believe he has, a legitimate need in preparing or undertaking his defense. It also means that witnesses properly summoned will be required to testify and that material demanded by a properly phrased *subpoena duces tecum* will be forthcoming and available for appropriate examination and use.

Testimonial privileges, whether they derive from common law or from statute, which allow witnesses to withhold evidence seem to conflict with this provision. This conflict may arise in a variety of factual contexts with respect to different privileges. We confine our consideration here to the single privilege before us—that set forth in the Shield Law. We hold that Article 1,¶ 10 of our Constitution prevails over this statute, but in recognition of the strongly expressed legislative viewpoint favoring confidentiality, we prescribe the imposition of the safeguards set forth in Point IV below.

IV

Procedural Mechanism

Appellants insist that they are entitled to a full hearing on the issues of relevance, materiality and overbreadth of the subpoena. We agree. The trial court recognized its obligation to conduct such a hearing, but the appellants have aborted that hearing by refusing to submit the material subpoenaed for an *in camera* inspection by the court to assist it in determining the motion to quash. That inspection is no more than a procedural tool, a device to be used to ascertain the relevancy and materiality of that material. Such an *in camera* inspection is not in itself an invasion of the statutory privilege. Rather it is a preliminary step to determine whether, and if so to what extent, the statutory privilege must yield to the defendant's constitutional rights.

Appellants' position is that there must be a full showing and definitive judicial determination of relevance, materiality, absence of less intrusive access, and need, prior to any *in camera* inspection. The obvious objection to such a rule, however, is that it would, in many cases, effectively stultify the judicial criminal process. It might well do so here. The defendant properly recognizes Myron Farber as a unique repository of pertinent information. But he does not know the extent of this information nor is it possible for him to specify all of it with particularity, nor to tailor his subpoena to precise materials of which he is ignorant. Well aware of this, Judge Arnold refused to give ultimate rulings with respect to relevance and other preliminary matters until he had examined the material. We think he had no other course. It is not rational to ask a judge to ponder the relevance of the unknown.

The same objection applies with equal force to the contention that the subpoena is overbroad. Appellants do not assert that the subpoena is vague and uncertain, but that the data requested may not be relevant and material. To deal effectively with this assertion it is not only appropriate but absolutely necessary for the trial court to inspect *in camera* the subpoenaed items so that it can make its determinations on the basis of concrete materials rather than in a vaccum.   *   *   *

While we agree, then, that appellants should be afforded the hearing they are seeking, one procedural aspect of which calls for their compliance with the order for *in camera* inspection, we are also of the view that they, and those who in the future may be similarly situated, are entitled to a preliminary determination before being compelled to submit the subpoenaed materials to a trial judge for such inspection. Our decision in this regard is not, contrary to the suggestion in some of the briefs filed with us, mandated by the First Amendment; for in addition to ruling generally against the representatives of the press in *Branzburg,* the Court particularly and rather vigorously, rejected the claims there asserted that before going before the grand jury, each of the reporters, at the very least, was entitled to a preliminary hearing to establish a number of threshold issues. Branzburg v. Hayes, supra, 408 U.S. at 701–07, 92 S.Ct. at 2666–69, 33 L.Ed.2d at 651–55. Rather, our insistence upon such a threshold determination springs from our obligation to give as much effect as possible, within ever-present constitutional limitations, to the very positively expressed legislative intent to protect the confidentiality and secrecy of sources from which the media derive information. To this end such a determination would seem a necessity.

The threshold determination would normally follow the service of a subpoena by a defendant upon a newspaper, a reporter or other representative of the media. The latter foreseeably would respond with a motion to quash. If the status of the movant—newspaper or media representative —were not conceded, then there would follow the taking of proofs leading to a determination that the movant did or did not qualify for the statutory privilege. Assuming qualification, it would then become the obligation of the defense to satisfy the trial judge, by a fair preponderance of the evidence including all reasonable inferences, that there was a reasonable probability or likelihood that the information sought by the subpoena was material and relevant to his defense, that it could not be secured from any less intrusive source, and that the defendant had a legitimate need to see and otherwise use it.

* * *

Although in this case the trial judge did not articulate the findings prescribed above, it is perfectly clear that on the record before him a conclusion of materiality, relevancy, unavailability of another source, as well as need was quite inescapable. * * *

* * * Two and a half months before his June 30th decision, Judge Arnold observed:

The facts show that Farber has written articles for the *New York Times* about this matter, commencing in January 1976. According to an article printed in the *New York Times* (hereinafter the *Times*) on January 8, 1976, Farber showed Joseph Woodcock, the Bergen County Prosecutor at that time, a deposition not in the State's file and *provided additional information that convinced the prosecutor to reopen an investigation into some deaths that occurred at Riverdell Hospital.* [State v. Jascalevich; In the Matter of the Application of Myron Farber and the New York Times Company re: Sequestration, 158 N.J.Super. 488, 490, 386 A.2d 466, 467 (Law Div. 1978), (emphasis added).]

And

The court has examined the news stories in evidence and they demonstrate exceptional quality, a grasp of intricate scientific knowledge, and a style of a fine journalist. *They, also, demonstrate considerable knowledge of the case before the court and deep involvement by Farber,* showing his attributes as a first-rate investigative reporter. However, if a newspaper reporter assumes the duties of an investigator, he must also assume the responsibilities of an investigator and be treated equally under the law, unless he comes under some exception. [Id. at 493–94, 386 A.2d at 469 (emphasis added).]

In the same vein is a letter before the trial court dated January 14, 1977 from Assistant Prosecutor Moses to Judge Robert A. Matthews, sitting as a Presiding Judge in the Appellate Division, undertaking to explain "how the investigation, from which the [Jascalevich] indictment resulted, came to be reopened." In the course of that explanation it is revealed that sometime in the latter part of 1975 "a reporter for the *New York Times* began an investigation into the 1965–66 deaths and circumstances surrounding them. The results of the *New York Times* inquiry were made available to the Prosecutor. *It was thus determined that there were certain items which were not in the file of the Prosecutor.*" [Emphasis added.]

Further support for the determination that there is a reasonable probability that the subpoenaed materials meet the test formulated above appears in the following factual circumstances pointed to by this defendant and supported by documents and transcripts of testimony found in the appendix filed by the defendant:

1. A principal witness for the State is Dr. Michael Baden, a New York City Medical Examiner, who testified that Farber communicated with him prior to any official communication from the Prosecutor's office. The defendant would have one infer from this that Farber stimulated Baden's research into the causal connection among curare, the deaths, and Dr. Jascalevich, then turned the results of this joint effort over to the Prosecutor. (Trial testimony elicited from Dr. Baden after June 30th, the date of Judge Arnold's order, is said to furnish futher support for this inference.) While no sinister implications need flow from this, it arguably serves to buttress the defense assertion that the driving power behind this prosecution is Farber, and hence such materials, if any, that he may be secreting are reasonably likely to bear on the guilt or innocence of Dr. Jascalevich.

2. Dr. Stanley Harris was a surgeon at the hospital where the criminal activities are said to have occurred. His suspicions are said to have been aroused by the unexplained deaths of some of his patients. Dr. Harris admits having spoken to Farber five times before the New York Times articles appeared and before his reinterview by the Prosecutor's office in 1976. He is characterized by the criminal defendant as his "principal accuser," and therefore whatever otherwise unavailable information Farber extracted from him would, with reasonable probability, bear upon Dr. Jascalevich's guilt or innocence.

3. Lee Henderson was an attendant at Seton Hall Medical School at a time when, according to one statement allegedly made by Dr. Jascalevich, the latter was performing certain tests on dogs in the School laboratory. The tests supposedly involved the effects of curare (a drug said to have been administered by the criminal defendant in producing the deaths of the victims). Henderson may very well have information touching upon Dr. Jascalevich's activities, if any, in the laboratory. After considerable effort Farber succeeded in tracking down Henderson in South Carolina. When a Prosecutor's investigator was later able to communicate with Henderson (having presumably been led to him by information furnished by Farber), the witness initially refused to give a statement (later supplied) for fear that it would conflict with a written statement previously furnished to

Farber. The criminal defendant wishes to examine this earlier statement.

4.　Herman Fuhr was an operating room attendant who opened Dr. Jascalevich's locker at Riverdell Hospital, where curare was allegedly stored. Farber interviewed him. He will not speak to defense representatives.

5.　Dr. Charles Umberger was a toxicologist who worked on slides of one of the alleged victims. He gave notes to Farber who did not return them. Some of these notes are missing. Dr. Umberger died in 1977 before the defense could interview him.

6.　Barbara Kenderes was a lab technician at the hospital. She gave a statement to a Prosecutor's detective in 1966, which the State either has not furnished or cannot furnish to the defense. She testified before the grand jury in March, 1976. Several days later Mrs. Kenderes received a telephone call on her private, unlisted number from Myron Farber. During the course of the conversation he accused her of hiding something from him. She replied that, indeed, she was. Shortly thereafter, she received a call from Assistant Prosecutor Sybil Moses, who is handling the case. Mrs. Moses told Mrs. Kenderes that Myron Farber called her and said Mrs. Kenderes was hiding something. Mrs. Moses wanted to know what that was. Mrs. Kenderes replied that it was only the fact that she had appeared before the grand jury, which Mrs. Moses had cautioned her not to speak about. The only person to whom Mrs. Kenderes had given her private phone number in connection with this matter was Mrs. Moses. Again the inference defendant Jascalevich would have us draw is that early on there was complete cooperation and exchange of information between the Prosecutor's office and Farber, with the resultant likelihood that Farber is now, and for some time has been, in possession of material and relevant information not otherwise obtainable bearing on the guilt or innocence of Dr. Jascalevich.

We hasten to add that we need not, and do not, address (much less determine) the truth or falsity of these assertions. The point to be made is that these are the assertions of the criminal defendant supported by testimonial or documentary proof; and based thereon it is perfectly clear that there was more than enough before Judge Arnold to satisfy the tests formulated above. Of course all of this information detailed above has long been known to appellants. Accordingly we find that preliminary requirements for *in camera* inspection have been met.

* * *

The judgment of conviction of criminal contempt and that in aid of litigants' rights are affirmed. Stays heretofore entered are vacated effective as of 4:00 p.m., Tuesday, September 26, 1978.

For affirmance:　Chief Justice Hughes and Justices Mountain, Sullivan, Clifford and Schreiber—5.

For reversal:　Justices Pashman and Handler—2.

[Concurring and dissenting opinions omitted.]

Chapter VII

THE PRIVILEGE AGAINST COMPULSORY SELF-INCRIMINATION

CONSTITUTION OF THE UNITED STATES, AMENDMENT V

No person * * * shall be compelled in any criminal case to be a witness against himself * * * .

HISTORICAL BACKGROUND

The privilege against self-incrimination can only be understood against the background of English history which produced it. In very brief and simplified form, this is what happened:

Early in the reign of Henry VIII, about 450 years ago, England was a Roman Catholic state. Protestants were vigorously persecuted. Then, when Henry broke with the Roman Catholic Church and Parliament established the Church of England, the Protestants reversed the situation and began to persecute the Catholics, until Queen Mary once again persecuted the Protestants. This situation was reversed after the death of Mary, when Elizabeth took the throne. From the 1560's Elizabeth's Church began persecuting (in addition to the Catholics) dissident Protestants called Puritans. This continued under James I and Charles I and helped provoke the Revolution in which Puritans and their allies were victorious.

After the Puritan victory, the authorities continued to persecute Catholics, while also persecuting both the Anglican clergy, less reform-minded than themselves, and the "left wing" dissenters who broke away from the main body of Puritans. Then, after the accession to power of Oliver Cromwell, the center of the Puritan establishment moved left and began its own campaigns against the "ungodly," persecuting the Catholics, the High Anglicans and the right wing Puritans. By the time of the Restoration of the monarchy under Charles II, all England was sick of religious persecution and for the most part it ceased.

This history is quite remarkable. In the course of about 150 years, members of every major religious group in England had been both the initiators and the victims of persecution—and the roles had changed with bewildering rapidity.

Of course, these persecutions were only partly religious. They were also political. The divorce of religion from politics is, in historical terms, a relatively recent phenomenon. It is obvious that the break of Henry VIII with Rome (not to mention the later excommunication of Elizabeth) had political as well as religious significance.

In any event, a major method of these persecutions was the oath. During the persecution of the Puritans by the Church of England under Elizabeth and James, for example, Puritan ministers were called before the High Commission and asked questions under oath about their beliefs. Being men of God, they could not lie—and, if they admitted to their deviant and nonconformist views, they could be very seriously punished. As a result, increasingly, they claimed the right not to answer and the existence or non-existence of such a right gradually became a major issue in 17th century England. One of the most celebrated cases involving the right was that of John Lilburne:*

"In 1637, Lilburne, A Puritan dissenter, was brought before the Star Chamber. Having just returned from Holland, he was charged with sending "factitious and scandalous books" from there to England. Lilburne repeatedly contended that he was entitled to notice, indictment, and court trial under the known laws of England; that he had a right to have witnesses summoned in his behalf and be confronted by witnesses against him; and that he could not be compelled to testify against himself.

"For refusing to respond to the questions, Lilburne was fined, was tied to a cart and, his body bared, was whipped through the streets of London. At Westminster he was placed in a pillory—his body bent down, his neck in the hole, and his lacerated back bared to the midday sun; there he stood for two hours and exhorted all who would listen to resist the tyranny of the bishops. Refusing to be quiet, he was gagged so cruelly that his mouth bled. After all this, he was kept in solitary confinement in the Fleet Prison with irons on his hands and legs and without anything to eat for ten days. After Lilburne's release, his cruel treatment and bold resistance had two consequences. The first was the vote of the Long Parliament that his sentence was illegal and that he be paid reparations. The second was the abolition of both the Star Chamber and the Court of the High Commission by the same Parliament. * * * "

The development of the privilege was by no means complete at this point. As has been pointed out,

"[The] objections to compulsory self-incrimination were not, however, aimed at the practice in the regular criminal courts but, rather, at the practice as it was carried out by the Star Chamber and the High Commission. After the abolition of the Courts of the Star Chamber and of the High Commission, [q]uestioning of the accused at his trial continued unaltered for nearly two decades; the examination of the prisoner by the committing magistrate continued for as long as two centuries. Nevertheless, a gradual repugnance to compulsory self-incrimination developed. By the end of the reign of Charles II, the privilege was recognized in all courts when claimed by defendant or witness.**

See California Evidence Code § § 404 at p. 817, 930 at p. 854, 940 at p. 854.

*The Bill of Rights, A Source Book for Teach-   **Id. at 83.
ers, California State Department of Educa-
tion (1967, pp. 79–81).

MALLOY v. HOGAN

Supreme Court of the United States, 1964.
378 U.S. 1, 84 S.Ct. 1489, 12 L.Ed.2d 653.
[Most of the Court's footnotes are omitted.]

Mr. Justice BRENNAN delivered the opinion of the Court.

In this case we are asked to reconsider prior decisions holding that the privilege against self-incrimination is not safe-guarded against state action by the Fourteenth Amendment. Twining v. New Jersey, 211 U.S. 78, 29 S.Ct. 14, 53 L.Ed. 97; Adamson v. California, 332 U.S. 46, 67 S.Ct. 1672, 91 L.Ed. 1903.

The petitioner was arrested during a gambling raid in 1959 by Hartford, Connecticut, police. He pleaded guilty to the crime of pool selling, a misdemeanor, and was sentenced to one year in jail and fined $500. The sentence was ordered to be suspended after 90 days, at which time he was to be placed on probation for two years. About 16 months after his guilty plea, petitioner was ordered to testify before a referee appointed by the Superior Court of Hartford County to conduct an inquiry into alleged gambling and other criminal activities in the county. The petitioner was asked a number of questions related to events surrounding his arrest and conviction. He refused to answer any question "on the grounds it may tend to incriminate me." The Superior Court adjudged him in contempt, and committed him to prison until he was willing to answer the questions. Petitioner's application for a writ of habeas corpus was denied by the Superior Court, and the Connecticut Supreme Court of Errors affirmed. 150 Conn. 220, 187 A.2d 744. The latter court held that the Fifth Amendment's privilege against self-incrimination was not available to a witness in a state proceeding, that the Fourteenth Amendment extended no privilege to him, and that the petitioner had not properly invoked the privilege available under the Connecticut Constitution. We granted certiorari. 373 U.S. 948, 83 S.Ct. 1680, 10 L.Ed.2d 704. We reverse. We hold that the Fourteenth Amendment guaranteed the petitioner the protection of the Fifth Amendment's privilege against self-incrimination, and that under the applicable federal standard, the Connecticut Supreme Court of Errors erred in holding that the privilege was not properly invoked.

* * *

The marked shift to the federal standard in state cases began with Lisenba v. California, 314 U.S. 219, 62 S.Ct. 280, 86 L.Ed. 166, where the Court spoke of the accused's "free choice to admit, to deny, or to refuse to answer." Id., 314 U.S. at 241, 62 S.Ct. at 292. The shift reflects recognition that the American system of criminal prosecution is accusatorial, not inquisitorial, and that the Fifth Amendment privilege is its essential mainstay. Governments, state and federal, are thus constitutionally compelled to establish guilt by evidence independently and freely secured, and may not by coercion prove a charge against an accused out of his own mouth. Since the Fourteenth Amendment prohibits the States from inducing a person to confess through "sympathy falsely aroused." Spano v. New York, supra, 360 U.S., at 323, 79 S.Ct. at 1207, or other like inducement far short of "compulsion by torture," Haynes v. Washington, supra, it follows *a fortiori* that it also forbids the States to resort to imprisonment, as here, to compel him to answer questions that might incriminate him. The Fourteenth Amendment secures against state invasion the same privilege that the Fifth Amendment guarantees against federal infringement—the right of a person to remain silent unless he chooses to speak in the unfettered exercise of his own will, and to suffer no penalty, as held in Twining, for such silence. * * * In thus returning to the Boyd view that the privilege is one of the "principles of a free government." 116 U.S., at 632, 6 S.Ct., at 533,[7] Mapp necessarily repudiated the Twining concept of the privilege as a mere rule of evidence "best defended not as an unchangeable principle of universal justice, but as a law proved by experience to be expedient." 211 U.S., at 113, 29 S.Ct., at 25. * * *

We turn to the petitioner's claim that the State of Connecticut denied him the protection of his federal privilege. It must be considered irrelevant that the petitioner was a witness in a statutory inquiry and not a defendant in a criminal prosecution, for it has long been settled that the privilege protects witnesses in similar federal inquiries. Counselman v. Hitchcock, 142 U.S. 547, 12 S.Ct. 195, 35 L.Ed. 1110; McCarthy v. Arndstein, 266 U.S. 34, 45 S.Ct. 16, 69 L.Ed. 158; Hoffman v. United States, 341 U.S. 479, 71 S.Ct. 814, 95 L.Ed. 1118. We recently elaborated the content of the federal standard in Hoffman:

"The privilege afforded not only extends to answers that would in themselves support a conviction * * * but likewise embraces those which would furnish a link in the chain of evidence needed to prosecute. * * * [I]f the witness, upon interposing his claim, were required to prove the hazard * * * he would be compelled to surrender the very protection which the privilege is designed to guarantee. To sustain the privilege, it need only be evident from the implications of the question, in the setting in which it is asked, that a responsive answer to the question or an explanation of why it cannot be answered might be dangerous because injurious disclosure could result." 341 U.S., at 486–487, 71 S.Ct. at 818.

We also said that, in applying that test, the judge must be

" 'perfectly clear, from a careful consideration of all the circumstances in the case, that the witness is mistaken, and that the answer[s] cannot possibly have such tendency' to incriminate." 341 U.S., at 488, 71 S.Ct., at 819.

The State of Connecticut argues that the Connecticut courts properly applied the federal standards to the facts of this case. We disagree.

The investigation in the course of which petitioner was questioned began when the Superior Court in Hartford County appointed the Honorable Ernest A. Inglis, formerly Chief Justice of Connecticut, to conduct an inquiry into whether there was reasonable cause to believe that crimes, including gambling, were being committed in Hartford County. Petitioner

---

7. Boyd had said of the privilege, " * * * any compulsory discovery by extorting the party's oath * * * to convict him of crime * * * is contrary to the principles of a free government. It is abhorrent to the instincts of an Englishman; it is abhorrent to the instincts of an American. It may suit the purposes of despotic power, but it cannot abide the pure atmosphere of political liberty and personal freedom." 116 U.S., at 631–632, 6 S.Ct., at 533.

Dean Griswold has said: "I believe the Fifth Amendment is, and has been through this period of crisis, an expression of the moral striving of the community. It has been a reflection of our common conscience, a symbol of the America which stirs our hearts." The Fifth Amendment Today 73 (1955).

appeared on January 16 and 25, 1961, and in both instances he was asked substantially the same questions about the circumstances surrounding his arrest and conviction for pool selling in late 1959. The questions which petitioner refused to answer may be summarized as follows: (1) for whom did he work on September 11, 1959; (2) who selected and paid his counsel in connection with his arrest on that date and subsequent conviction; (3) who selected and paid his bondsman; (4) who paid his fine; (5) what was the name of the tenant of the apartment in which he was arrested; and (6) did he know John Bergoti. The Connecticut Supreme Court of Errors ruled that the answers to these questions could not tend to incriminate him because the defenses of double jeopardy and the running of the one-year statute of limitations on misdemeanors would defeat any prosecution growing out of his answers to the first five questions. As for the sixth question, the court held that petitioner's failure to explain how a revelation of his relationship with Bergoti would incriminate him vitiated his claim to the protection of the privilege afforded by state law.

The conclusions of the Court of Errors, tested by the federal standard, fail to take sufficient account of the setting in which the questions were asked. The interrogation was part of a wide-ranging inquiry into crime, including gambling, in Hartford. It was admitted on behalf of the State at oral argument—and indeed it is obvious from the questions themselves —that the State desired to elicit from the petitioner the identity of the person who ran the pool-selling operation in connection with which he had been arrested in 1959. It was apparent that petitioner might apprehend that if this person were still engaged in unlawful activity, disclosure of his name might furnish a link in a chain of evidence sufficient to connect the petitioner with a more recent crime for which he might still be prosecuted.

Analysis of the sixth question, concerning whether petitioner knew John Bergoti, yields a similar conclusion. In the context of the inquiry, it should have been apparent to the referee that Bergoti was suspected by the State to be involved in some way in the subject matter of the investigation. An affirmative answer to the question might well have either connected petitioner with a more recent crime, or at least have operated as a waiver of his privilege with reference to his relationship with a possible criminal. See Rogers v. United States, 340 U.S. 367, 71 S.Ct. 438, 95 L.Ed. 344. We conclude, therefore, that as to each of the questions, it was "evident from the implications of the question, in the setting in which it [was] asked, that a responsive answer to the question or an explanation of why it [could not] be answered might be dangerous because injurious disclosure could result," Hoffman v. United States, 341 U.S., at 486–487, 71 S.Ct. 818; see Singleton v. United States, 343 U.S. 944, 72 S.Ct. 1041.

Reversed.

(The dissenting opinions of Mr. Justice Harlan joined by Mr. Justice Clark and that of Mr. Justice White, joined by Mr. Justice Stewart, are omitted.)

WILLIAMS, THE PROOF OF GUILT
THE RIGHT NOT TO BE QUESTIONED*
[Most footnotes omitted.]

According to the rule, neither the judge nor the prosecution is entitled at any stage to question the accused unless he chooses to give evidence. "At the common law," says Blackstone, *"nemo tenebatur prodere seipsum:* and his fault was not to be wrung out of himself, but rather to be discovered by other means and other men." This rule may be called the accused's right not to be questioned; in America it is termed the privilege against self-incrimination. The latter expression is more apt as the name for another rule, the privilege of any witness to refuse to answer an incriminating question; this is different from the rule under discussion, which, applying only to persons accused of crime, prevents the question from being asked. The person charged with crime has not merely the liberty to refuse to answer a question incriminating himself; he is freed even from the embarrassment of being asked the question. The privilege against self-incrimination, as applied to witnesses generally, must be expressly claimed by the witness when the question is put to him in the box[2]; whereas the accused's freedom from being questioned prevents the prosecution from asking (much less compelling) him to enter the box, and from addressing questions to him in the dock.

* * * The first great opponent of the rule was Bentham, and his criticism of it is still the fullest and best in our literature. Bentham did not hesitate to adopt a strong attitude, calling the rule "one of the most pernicious and most irrational notions that ever found its way into the human mind." This attack took considerable courage, for then, as indeed to a lesser degree now, the rule was firmly entrenched in public favour as one of the most important safeguards of the English legal system.

Bentham recognized that the rule derived part of its attraction from the fact that it stood at the opposite pole from the tyranny practised on the Continent, and in England under the Star Chamber, which "presented the hateful spectacle of torture, and of judges eager to seize, and turn against the accused, every word which might escape him in the agony of pain." This reaction has lost none of its psychological force at the present day. It is a natural, if irrational, response to barbarity of this kind to refuse to permit any questioning of a defendant. However, as Bentham pointed out, the rule cannot, if dispassionately regarded, be supported by an argument referring to torture. No one supposes that in present-day England a permission to question an accused person, if accompanied, as it would be, by safeguards, would result in any ill treatment of him. The risk, if there is one, is just the opposite: that if dangerous criminals cannot be questioned before a magistrate or judge, the frustrated police may resort to illegal questioning and brutal "third degree" methods in order to obtain convictions. This has happened in the United States of America; and even if we have sufficient

---

*London, Stevens, 1955.

2.   The judge will not generally take the objection for the witness: Att.-Gen. v. Radloff (1854) 10 Ex. at 107, 156 E.R. 375, *per* Parke B.; but he ought to inform the witness of his rights. Cf. [1954] Crim.L.R. 916.

Whereas the witness' privilege causes little difficulty in England, it has caused innumerable problems in the United States, partly because of the multiplicity of jurisdictions which makes it impossible to be certain as a practical matter that the witness will not be charged.

confidence in our own police to discount the possibility of rubber-hose beatings here, we must recognise that the restraint on their part exists in spite of the defendant's freedom from examination in court and not because of it.

Bentham had no difficulty in disposing of the other argument for the rule, that it prevented the enforcement of bad laws, and above all restricted the operation of the too numerous laws carrying capital punishment. The simple answer was that the rule tended to prevent the enforcement of good law equally with bad, and thus acted as a debilitative upon the whole body of the penal law. As Stephen afterwards remarked, "people always protest with passionate eagerness against being deprived of technical defences against what they regard as bad laws, and such complaints often give a spurious value to technicalities when the cruelty of the laws against which they have offered protection has come to be commonly admitted."

The old laws of capital punishment were examples of such bad laws: and one of their evil effects was that they reduced the administration of justice to a gamble. Although almost all felonies were punishable with death, it was not in fact practicable to carry out executions on the scale that legal theory required, and public justice was regarded as satisfied if a comparatively small number of felons was executed each year. The rest might be allowed benefit of clergy, pardoned, or acquitted on technicalities or by the "pious perjury" of the jury. Historically regarded, the rule against questioning the defendant is one example of the indifference of society to the need for securing the conviction of the guilty. Bentham set his face against this system of haphazard punishment, arguing that "the more certain punishment is, the less severe it need be." Consequently he was against all rules making for the acquittal of offenders.

The third argument in favour of the law was again mere sentiment: that to try to get an accused person to give evidence against himself was not playing the game; it was hitting below the belt, or hitting a man when he was down. Bentham was scornful of the analogy between a criminal trial and a private combat. He pointed to the evil results of the rule: in so far as it hindered the conviction of the guilty it might operate to prevent the conviction of the apprentice in crime while he was yet open to redemption, besides neglecting the immediate interest of society that dangerous criminals should not be left free. "When the guilty is acquitted, society is punished." Moreover, the supposed rule of fair play was not logically applied, because no objection was seen to giving evidence against the accused of documents written by him, or even of conversations ascribed to him by other witnesses. "Thus," said Bentham, "what the technical procedure rejects is his own evidence in the purest and most authentic form; what it admits is the same testimony, provided that it be indirect, that it have passed through channels which may have altered it, and that it be reduced to the inferior and degraded state of hearsay." In fact, of course, the conventional notion of fairness could not be consistently applied in these other respects without destroying the law altogether. But, said Bentham, "if it is wished to protect the accused against punishment, it can be done at once, and with perfect efficacy, by not allowing any investigation."

With his clarity of mind Bentham perceived that the common use of the maxim *Nemo tenetur seipsum accusare* (or, *prodere*) was tendentious. Read as a proposition that no one was bound to start a prosecution against himself, the thing was so obvious that its mere statement was puerile. Read as an assertion that no one should be punished for refusing to make a confession of guilt, the maxim was again not in question. In this sense the maxim applies to all witnesses in all legal proceedings, not merely to the defendant to a criminal charge: no witness is punishable for refusing to answer a question which he claims may incriminate him. This rule has not been doubted for four centuries, because it is regarded as inhumane to place a person in a legal dilemma which must result in punishment one way or the other.[29] Those who seek to alter the accused's freedom from interrogation ask only that the prosecution should be permitted in court, to put questions to the accused person, whether (since 1898) he elects to give evidence or not. There would be no direct compulsion on the accused to answer the questions if he preferred to maintain a stolid silence; though of course this silence would almost certainly have a most serious effect upon his defence.

The crux of the matter is that immunity from being questioned is a rule which from its nature can protect the guilty only. It is not a rule that may operate to acquit some guilty for fear of convicting some innocent. To quote Bentham's words, "If all criminals of every class had assembled, and framed a system after their own wishes, is not this rule the very first which they would have established for their security? Innocence never takes advantage of it; innocence claims the right of speaking, as guilt invokes the privilege of silence."

NOONAN, INFERENCES FROM THE INVOCATION OF THE PRIVILEGE AGAINST SELF-INCRIMINATION

(41) Va.L.Rev. 311 (1955).*
[Most footnotes omitted.]

* * *

The most commonly accepted rationale today is Wigmore's—that unrestricted interrogation has a demoralizing effect on the prosecution. Wigmore illustrates this proposition by these specifications: such interrogation encourages incomplete investigations; and it induces a resort to bullying and even physical force. Neither of these specific examples of demoralization, however, has much persuasiveness. If investigation results in the conviction of a guilty person through his own admission, how can it be termed incomplete? Torture is already barred by the due process clause, and many observers have commented that the barrier to judicial interrogation interposed by the privilege achieves the contrary effect of encouraging the police to use the third degree to get the information they need. The famous red pepper story of Judge Stephen,[7] used to illustrate so many defenses of the privilege, is relevant only if it be supposed that abandonment of the privilege would entail abandonment of due proccess.

---

29. But Canada has resolved this problem in a different way, by providing that the witness who takes objection is compellable to answer but is protected from having his statement given in evidence against him in any subsequent criminal prosecution (Canada Evidence Act, 1952, s. 5, replacing earlier legislation).

7. An Indian officer observed to Judge Stephen, "It is far pleasanter to sit comfortably in the shade rubbing red pepper into a poor devil's eyes than to go about in the sun hunting up evidence." Stephen quotes the statement to illustrate the value of the privilege. 1 Stephen, History of the Criminal Law of England 442 n. 1 (1883).

Similarly, the argument cited by Wigmore that the privilege protects against the undignified and prejudicial examination of the accused by the court, a practice alleged to characterize the French courts, seems to be founded on a misconception; if the privilege did not exist, questioning would still be by counsel and no more a battle of wits between accused and court than any other examination of a witness. Another suggestion by Wigmore is that in an inquisitorial system blackmail is practiced on the timid by the unscrupulous. But he offers no empirical evidence of his own in support of this statement, and as far as can be seen, no study of French civic life, for example, would support him. His assertion can scarcely be given more weight than any speculation on general habits which seems to rest on no very common experience.

But Wigmore in the same section does go on to give more substantial support to his main proposition. "Under any system which permits John Doe to be forced to answer on the mere suspicion of an officer of the law, or on public rumor, or on secret betrayal," he writes, " * * * the petty judicial officer becomes a local tyrant and misuses his discretion for political or mercenary or malicious ends. * * * " The proposition has support in experience. Yet it must be examined in the light of a careful distinction between adversary and nonadversary proceedings.

Take his statement first in regard to criminal trials. Here there is some danger that an unjust prosecutor, by the use of circumstantial evidence obtained from the defendant or by collateral impeachment evidence of a prejudicial nature, could secure the conviction of an innocent man. In fact, the Amerian Bar Association's Committee on the Improvement of the Law of Evidence in 1937 recommended against the abolition of the privilege on this ground, that overzealous prosecutors might convict the innocent if it were abolished. Yet the most intensive study of the conviction of the innocent, Borchard's, actually recommends the abolition of the privilege.[13] In a criminal trial where both a grand jury and a petit jury stand in the way of the success of arbitrary prosecution, the Wigmore reason does not seem very substantial.

Wigmore's illustration carries more weight, however, in regard to inquisitorial proceedings. A Committee of the New York Constitutional Convention, in a thoughtful analysis of the advantages of the privilege noted the danger, if the privilige did not exist, of " * * * investigations that can be instituted for no other purpose than to appease groups, satisfy curiosity, or harass the unpopular." The history of the privilege is particularly pertinent here. It was originally asserted only against the inquisitorial proceedings of the High Commission and the Star Chamber, and the enthusiasm of the common lawyers for it apparently developed from dislike of these institutions. Hence, a rationale for the privilege which has little weight for a jury trial reacquires its historic validity when applied to an inquisition.

13. Borchard, Convicting the Innocent xvi–xvii (1932). Of course there might have been more convictions of the innocent without the privilege, a possibility Borchard's study cannot disprove. But what is significant is that one who has studied the conditions contributing to injustice to the innocent finds the privilege not a safeguard, but a nuisance.

Historically, the privilege was a shield for religious dissent. The privilege peculiarly protects the contents of a man's mind, his beliefs, at which the High Commission directed its questioning; and early respect for use of the privilege in heresy cases may have arisen partly from the secular community's unspoken reluctance to punish mere belief, partly from a sympathy for the witness' fear of entrapment by subtle theological questions. Yet protection of beliefs extended to acts of belief. The celebrated cases establishing the privilege, concerned overt acts of heresy, such as publishing heretical libels, or hearing Mass, or even treason. Given the closer relation of religious and political dissent in the seventeenth century, this protection was equally a defense for political heresy.

Later, in America, the colonial experience with the privilege was mainly in opposition to political inquiries by the prerogative courts of the governor and council of a colony. And two of the principal cases seem to have been free-speech cases, in which the right to silence was asserted against the inquisition of the governor.

Considering this historical background, we may conclude that one purpose of the constitutional provisions for the privilege was not merely to impede inquisitions, but to impede them especially in relation to crimes in which religious or political belief was a large element. It is here that the official tyranny of which Wigmore speaks is likely to be especially acute. Acceptance of the privilege on this ground would explain why the courts have found no invasion of the privilege in requiring corporations to incriminate themselves, in forcing business to keep incriminating records; or in holding motorists to have waived the privilege to the extent that anti-hit-and-run laws require. At the same time, this explanation of the privilege is largely valid only in relation to grand jury and legislative investigations, and for only a special type of these.

A second appealing basis for the privilege has been scouted by Bentham as the "old woman's reason," but still has much support. It is that a man should not be forced to do the unnatural act of bringing about his own conviction of crime. The most basic human urge is that of self-preservation; should the law command a man to stifle it? The argument has particular force when it is observed that even when the privilege as such did not exist before the ecclesiastical inquisitions, a moral privilege to deny a public accusation was recognized by some scholastic moralists, because it would be too harsh to make a man condemn himself. And as Dean Griswold has very recently expressed it,

> * * * We do not make even the most hardened criminal sign his own death warrant, or dig his own grave, or pull the lever that springs the trap on which he stands. We have through the course of history developed a considerable feeling of the dignity and intrinsic importance of the individual man.

The State in many ways may demand a curbing of the urge to self-preservation, as when it conscripts for war. But nowhere else is a man's voluntary act made so certain and deliberate a means of his own ruin. True, a man is evidence against himself when his body is used as evidence, as when he is compelled to submit to identification or fingerprinting, or even to blood tests. Yet there is a difference, at least in degree, between this and the use of the man's intelligence and memory. Finally, the exceptions to the privilege are consistent with this explanation. Corporations have no biological tendency to self-preservation; in the business records and automobile cases, a man is at least warned in advance that by running a business or a car he forfeits the right to protect his criminal secrets.

The strength of this natural tendency argument may vary with the temperament or philosophy of the reader. It is more a product of intuition than a fact capable of empirical demonstration. One can always answer to it, with Bentham, that the man who by his own acts has placed himself in an incriminating position has done so by voluntary choice, and the law does no more than attach consequences to his first choice. But as long as a number of authorities on the privilege find its justification here, this reason must be treated seriously as a major purpose of the privilege. It is applicable equally to adversary and nonadversary proceedings.

So far the purposes of the privilege have been but half-expressed. It is to protect against tyrannous inquisition and self-betrayal, but only if the inquisition and betrayal lead to punishment. The protection of the privilege is not, as it were, a privilege in the air; it is a protection against penal sanctions. Two types of cases seem to make this clear: (1) The cases denying that the privilege protects against disgrace; and, (2) The cases sustaining immunity statutes if they grant immunity to criminal prosecution and nothing more.

The first class of cases, ordering the witness to testify although his reputation will be destroyed, shows that the privilege is not intended to protect against the social consequences of compulsory testimony. Thus, disclosure of disgraceful conduct is not protected by the privilege, nor is disclosure of criminal behavior if the statute of limitations has run or the defendant has already been tried for the offense. The second class of cases shows that the legislature may investigate unrestrainedly if it counts the investigation serious enough to pay the price of immunity. Once immunity is granted, the testimony obtained may be used against the witness economically, as in the regulation of his business, and even professionally in disbarment proceedings.

These cases may be objected to on the ground that the main purposes of preventing self-destruction and restraining persecutive prosecutions are then defeated. The self-destruction of reputation can be forced, and a persecutive investigating group can achieve many of its ends, if testimony may ever be forced. The difference lies in degree. There is an attempt to balance a public interest in the truth against the interests served by protection; as happens wherever interests are balanced, no interests gets its full measure. Here the law protects the witness only from the most formidable types of State coercion; it is silent as to other sanctions.

LOUISELL, CRIMINAL DISCOVERY AND SELF-INCRIMINATION: ROGER TRAYNOR CONFRONTS THE DILEMMA

(53) Calif.L.Rev. 89, 93–96 (1965).*
[Footnotes omitted.]

[Written primarily as a commentary on the privilege against self-incrimination in the context of criminal discovery by the state, hereinafter considered p.   infra, this article necessarily confronted the opposing value judgments on the privilege itself. After mentioning a number of restrictions on the privilege such as immunity, hit-run and alibi statutes, the author continues:]

Why this ambivalence, this schizophrenia about the fifth amendment? If the principle against self-incrimination is so solid, valuable, and significant, why so many accepted encroachments? If the fifth amendment is such an old and good friend, why do we depart its company so readily? Is it primarily fear that so often severs our loyalty to this principle, as we stand relatively alone in liberty's narrow beam amidst an enshrouding and enlarging darkness? Or is it the perhaps ultimate predicament of the human conscience—to be plagued simultaneously in life's vital concerns by two competing, and maybe equally valid, principles?

There is, on the one hand, the supportive rationale for the rule against self-incrimination, the true justification—whatever it may be. I speak now not of its historic value; it has indeed been a good friend. I speak of present circumstances. We no longer have the rack and screw, at least not as officially acknowledged legitimate instruments. We have instead due process, elaborated notions against coerced confessions, careful articulation of and devotion to the requirement of proof beyond a reasonable doubt. Is not the real old friend—protection against brutality whether physical or psychological—now in the garb of fundamental fairness? Is it not an artifice to drape it also in the mantle of compelled abstention from the most rational inquiry available, questions to the suspect himself? To the innuendoes implicit in such queries as these, I long thought that the best answer lay in the realities of an accusatorial as opposed to inquisitorial system: that for our adversary system, the principle against self-incrimination is the logical fulfillment and best expression of the state's obligation to prove guilt to the highest degree known in practical human affairs. Indeed, Malloy v. Hogan now explicitly affirms this rationale: "[T]he American system of criminal prosecution is accusatorial, not inquisitorial, and * * * the Fifth Amendment privilege is its essential mainstay."

*   *   *

[Another justification of the privilege, that it is inherently cruel to make a man be the instrument of his own condemnation,] confronts the clear fact that the rule against self-incrimination is psychologically and morally unacceptable as a general governing principle in human relations. As Sidney Hook expresses it: "Let any sensible person ask himelf whether he would hire a secretary, nurse, or even a baby sitter for his children, if she refused to reply to a question bearing upon the proper execution of her duties with a response equivalent to the privilege against self-incrimination." From the lawyer's viewpoint, this case has been argued about as incisively as possible by Professor McNaughton—there is little to add.

There, to me, they are—the opposing desiderata, the starkly contrasting values: (1) That man, at least when he acts officially as government, must curb the instinct to cruelty, even if to do so he must maintain an artificial barrier against rational inquiry; (2) that man, intellectually feeble at best, should use all available instruments to find the truth provided they not be pernicious, and certainly should not eschew the most efficient one, namely, orderly and fair inquiry of the most knowledgeable person concerned.

Why must men as government be less logical than men as men? Why, when the state is the actor, do we tip the scales in favor of values other than accuracy in fact ascertainment? Is it only because of the awesome power of the state, with its corresponding capacity for tyranny and cruelty? Is it because of deep skepticism about the value of criminal law enforcement, even at its best, in relation to the human suffering it causes? Is it because so many of the criminal law's prohibitions, e.g., of gambling, are not rooted in anything like a substantially universal ethos, and involve no real victim to excite the passion for retribution? The individual cannot or at least will not afford to run the risk, which results from failure of proper inquiry and rational inference, of getting Sidney Hook's unsuitable secretary, nurse or baby sitter. American society, however, feels that it can, should, and will run that risk.   *   *   *

REINA v. UNITED STATES

Supreme Court of the United States, 1960.
364 U.S. 507, 81 S.Ct. 260, 5 L.Ed.2d 249.
[Most of the Court's footnotes are omitted.]

Mr. Justice BRENNAN delivered the opinion of the Court.

The Narcotic Control Act of 1956,[1] 18 U.S.C. § 1406, 18 U.S.C.A. § 1406, legislates immunity from prosecution for a witness compelled under the section by court order to testify before a federal grand jury investigating alleged violations of the federal narcotics laws. The questions presented are, primarily, whether the section grants immunity from state, as well as federal, prosecution, and, if state immunity, whether the section is constitutional.

The petitioner was serving a five-year sentence for a federal narcotics offense when, on December 5, 1958, he was subpoenaed before a federal grand jury sitting in the Southern District of New York. A number of questions were asked him concerning his crime, particularly as to the persons involved with him and their activities in the smuggling of narcotics into this country from Europe. The petitioner invoked the provision of the Fifth Amendment against being compelled to be a witness against himself and refused to answer any of the questions. The United States Attorney with the approval of the Attorney General obtained a court order pursuant to § 1406

---

1. Act of July 18, 1956, 70 Stat. 572 et seq.; 18 U.S.C. § 1401 et seq., 18 U.S.C.A. § 1401 et seq. The relevant portions of § 1406 are as follows:

    "§ 1406. Immunity of witnesses.

    "Whenever in the judgment of a United States attorney the testimony of any witness * * * in any case or proceeding before any grand jury or court of the United States involving any violation of [certain federal narcotics statutes] * * * is necessary to the public interest, he, upon the approval of the At-torney General, shall make application to the court that the witness shall be instructed to testify * * * . But no such witness shall be prosecuted or subjected to any penalty or forfeiture for or on account of any transaction, matter, or thing concerning which he is compelled, after having claimed his privilege against self-incrimination, to testify * * * nor shall testimony so compelled be used as evidence in any criminal proceeding * * * against him in any court. * * * "

directing him to answer. When he returned before the grand jury he again refused to testify. Proceedings against him in criminal contempt resulted in the judgment under review adjudging him guilty as charged. D.C., 170 F.Supp. 592. The Court of Appeals for the Second Circuit affirmed. 273 F.2d 234. Because of the importance of the questions of the construction and constitutionality of § 1406 raised by the case, we granted certiorari, 362 U.S. 939, 80 S.Ct. 805, 4 L.Ed.2d 769.

Petitioner's main argument in both courts below and here challenges § 1406 as granting him only federal immunity, and not state immunity, either because Congress meant the statute to be thus limited, or because the statute, if construed also to grant state immunity, would be unconstitutional. Both courts below passed the question whether the statute grants state immunity because, assuming only federal immunity is granted, they held that United States v. Murdock, 284 U.S. 141, 52 S.Ct. 63, 76 L.Ed. 210, settled that the Fifth Amendment does not protect a federal witness from answering questions which might incriminate him under state law. D.C., 170 F.Supp. at page 595; 2 Cir., 273 F.2d at page 235. Petitioner contends that Murdock should be re-examined and overruled. We have no occasion to consider this contention, since in our view § 1406 constitutionally grants immunity from both federal and state prosecutions.

We consider first whether the immunity provided by § 1406 covers state, as well as federal prosecutions. We have no doubt the section legislates immunity from both. The relevant words of the section have appeared in other immunity statutes [and] have been construed by this Court to cover both state and federal immunity. In Adams v. State of Maryland, 347 U.S. 179, 74 S.Ct. 442, 98 L.Ed. 608, a like provision in 18 U.S.C. § 3486, 18 U.S.C.A. § 3486, that the compelled testimony shall not "be used as evidence in *any* criminal proceeding against him in *any* court" was held to cover both federal and state courts. (Emphasis supplied.) The "Language could be no plainer," 347 U.S. at page 181, 74 S.Ct. at page 445. In Ullmann v. United States, 350 U.S. 422, 434–435, 76 S.Ct. 497, 504–505, 100 L.Ed. 511, 18 U.S.C. § 3486(c), 18 U.S.C.A. § 3486(c), added by the Immunity Act of 1954, of which § 1406 is virtually a carbon copy, was given the same construction. Moreover, the adoption of § 1406 followed close upon the Ullmann decision. That decision came down on March 26, 1956. Section 1406 was reported out of the House Ways and Means Committee only three months later on June 19, 1956, H.R.Rep.No.2388, 84th Cong., 2d Sess. It became law on July 18, 1956. 70 Stat. 574. We cannot believe that Congress would have used in § 1406 the very words construed in Ullmann to cover both state and federal prosecutions without giving the words the same meaning.   *   *   *

The petitioner urges that in any event he should not have been ordered to answer the grand jury's questions unless he first received a "general pardon or amnesty" covering the unserved portion of his sentence and his fine. This is a surprising contention, in light of the traditional purpose of immunity statutes to protect witnesses only as to the future. It suggests that the witness who has been convicted is entitled to ask more of the Government than the witness who has not but who may be compelled under § 1406 to reveal criminal conduct which, but for the immunity, would subject him to future federal or state prosecution. Yet the petitioner in his brief says that "the ordinary rule is that once a person is convicted of a crime, he no longer has the privilege against self-incrimination as he can no longer be incriminated by his testimony about said crime * * * ." There is indeed weighty authority for that proposition. United States v. Romero, 2 Cir., 249 F.2d 371; 8 Wigmore, Evidence (3d ed. 1940), § 2279; cf. Brown v. Walker, supra, 161 U.S. 597–600, 16 S.Ct. 647–648. Under it, immunity, at least from federal prosecution, need not have been offered the petitioner at all.

The petitioner does not argue that remission of his penalty was his due as a *quid pro quo* for further exposing himself to personal disgrace or opprobrium. That reason would not be tenable under Brown v. Walker, supra, in which the Court rejected the argument that the validity of an immunity statute should depend upon whether it shields "the witness from the personal disgrace or opprobrium attaching to the exposure of his crime." 161 U.S. at page 605, 16 S.Ct. at page 650. Nor does he support his contention with the argument that the prison sentence imposed for disobedience of the order directing him to testify is actually an additional punishment for his crime. His argument is the single one that the "said order was not a proper basis upon which to bottom a contempt proceeding in the face of a claim of privilege against self incrimination *as it did not grant this petitioner immunity coextensive with the constitutional privilege it sought to replace * * * .*" (Emphasis supplied.) The complete answer to this is that in safeguarding him against future federal and state prosecution "for or on account of any transaction, matter, or thing concerning which he is compelled" to testify, the statute grants him immunity fully coextensive with the constitutional privilege. Some language in Brown v. Walker, 161 U.S. at page 601, 16 S.Ct. at page 648, to which petitioner refers, compares immunity statutes to the traditional declarations of amnesty or pardon. But neither in that opinion nor elsewhere is it suggested that immunity statutes, to escape invalidity under the Fifth Amendment, need do more than protect a witness from future prosecutions. This § 1406 does.

The petitioner complains finally that his sentence is excessive. The District Court sentenced him to two years' imprisonment to commence at the expiration of the sentence he was then serving. However, the court also allowed the petitioner 60 days from the date of the judgment to purge himself of his contempt by appearing within that period before the grand jury and answering the questions. It was further provided that if he did so, "the sentence imposed herein shall be vacated." The District Court took this action because it found in effect that the petitioner asserted his legal position in good faith and was not contumaciously disrespectful of the court's order or obstinately flouting it. D.C., 170 F.Supp. at page 596. There is no occasion for us to consider the claim of excessiveness of the sentence, or the petitioner's companion claim that the conviction was invalid because the District Court did not advise him of the extent of the immunity conferred by § 1406. We construe the 60-day purge period as running from the effective date of this Court's mandate and the petitioner may avoid imprisonment by answering. Now that this Court has held that his fears of future state or federal prosecution are groundless, he knows that the only reason he gave for claiming his privilege has no substance. No question of an admixture of civil criminal contempt having been raised below or here, we do not reach the issues it might present.

Affirmed.

[The dissenting opinion of Mr. Justice Black, concurred in by Chief Justice Warren, is omitted.]

McCORMICK'S HANDBOOK ON THE LAW OF EVIDENCE

303–308 (2d ed.).*

REMOVING THE DANGER OF INCRIMINA-TION: IMMUNITY AND IMMUNITY STATUTES.

Since criminal liability for an act is a matter of legal mandate rather than an inherent characteristic of the act itself, it follows that the liability may also be removed by legal action. Removing liability removes the danger against which the privilege protects and makes the privilege unavailable. Thus if no conviction is possible * * * if the one from whom testimony is sought is effectively granted legal immunity from any danger arising from his testimony which is within the protection of the privilege.[91]

Although in some jurisdictions prosecuting attorneys have been found to have inherent power to confer immunity,[92] in most jurisdictions their ability to do so depends upon specific legislative authorization. Legislative activity in this area, however, has been piecemeal and the statutory provisions for conferring immunity are consequently varied and often confusing. Most jurisdictions have a number of different provisions each relating to a single crime or a limited category of crimes difficult to prove unless a participant "turns State's evidence"; these provisions often differ in phraseology and substance within a jurisdiction. Some states and the United States, however, have enacted general immunity statutes[95] and the Model State Witness Immunity Act[96] has been available as a guide for those jurisdictions that choose this course, although the act is now somewhat outmoded.

91. It has been argued that immunity statutes cannot confer adequate immunity because the witness may despite the immunity be subjected to prosecution and required to assert a plea in bar or obtain a favorable ruling on a motion to quash. Brown v. Walker, 161 U.S. 591, 621–22 [16 S.Ct. 644, 660, 40 L.Ed. 819] (1896) (Mr. Justice Shiras, dissenting). This view has found little support.

92. The Texas courts have found inherent power. Ex parte Copeland, 91 Tex.Cr.R. 549, 240 S.W. 314 (1922); Ex parte Muncy, 72 Tex.Cr.R. 541, 163 S.W. 29 (1914). Other courts have found less formal ways of avoiding the undesirable consequences which might flow from a promise of immunity without legislative authorization. Lowe v. State, 111 Md. 1, 73 A. 637 (1909) suggested that although an unauthorized promise of immunity from a prosecutor could not be pleaded in bar, the trial court should upon a showing of the promise continue the case to give the prosecutor an opportunity to file a *nolle prosequi* or to give the defendant an opportunity to apply for a pardon. The Illinois Supreme Court arrived at an interesting compromise. A defendant who testified pursuant to an unauthorized promise of immunity from the prosecutor was held entitled to a discharge in a subsequent prosecution brought in violation of the promise. People v. Bogolowski, 326 Ill. 253, 157 N.E. 181 (1927). But the court refused to give such a promise full logical effect, and a witness who refused to testify after receiving a prosecutor's promise of immunity could not be held in contempt. People v. Rockola, 339 Ill. 474, 171 N.E. 559 (1930). The actual reason underlying the decision probably was a reluctance in effect to confer a pardoning power upon prosecutors without judicial supervision.

95. West's Ann.Cal.Penal Code, §§ 1324, 1324 New York Penal Law of 1909 § 2447. (The New York statute was repealed in 1967 with the anticipation that the matter would be covered in the Code of Criminal Procedure. See McKinney's New York Criminal Procedure Law 50.10, 50.2d (1969).)

Title II of the Organized Crime Control Act of 1970 repealed more than fifty specific federal immunity statutes and substituted a general immunity statute, 84 Stat. 922 (codified as 18 U.S.C.A. §§ 6001, 6005). See

The constitutionally required scope of the immunity which must be conferred to render the privilege inoperative was not directly dealt with by the Supreme Court until 1964. In 1892 the Court had struck down a federal immunity statute on the ground that it did not protect the witness from "the use of his testimony to search out other testimony to be used in evidence against him."[98] The Court's dictum—"[W]e are clearly of the opinion that no statute which leaves the party or witness subject to prosecution after he answers the criminating questions put to him can have the effect of supplanting the privilege conferred by the Constitution of the United States"—[99] has been read as requiring that "transactional immunity" be conferred, that is, that the witness must be protected against prosecution based upon any transaction as to which he testified under compulsion. It was not sufficient, under this view, that the witness was protected against the use of the testimony or its fruits. He must be protected against prosecution. Although the Court's language referred to the federal privilege which was not held binding upon the states until much later, many state courts adopted the "transactional immunity" approach and much state as well as federal immunity legislation was drawn to confer this broad freedom from subsequent prosecution. The position has merit. That a witness is entitled to protection against indirect as well as direct use of his testimony has been generally accepted. Insofar as any lesser protection would require a defendant to prove that evidence offered by the prosecution was obtained by indirect use of his compelled testimony, it might well face him with an impossible task. Thus in practice a witness granted immunity only from the use of his testimony might well lack full protection by virtue of his inability to prove a causal relationship.

But in Murphy v. Waterfront Commission of New York Harbor,[2] the Court made clear that in some circumstances, at least, the federal constitutional privilege does not require the granting of transactional immunity. After concluding that a state could not compel a witness to give testimony if that testimony might give rise to a federal prosecution, the Court held only that the Federal Government "must be prohibited from making any * * * use [in a criminal prosecution] of [state] compelled testimony

---

McClellan, The Organized Crime Control Act (S. 30) or Its Critics: Which Threatens Civil Liberties? 46 Notre Dame Law. 55, 82–86 (1970).

96.   The text of the Model Act, omitting formal parts, is as follows:

"§ 1.   Compelling Evidence in Criminal Proceedings: Immunity. In any criminal proceeding before a court or grand jury, [or examining Magistrate] if a person refuses to answer a question or produce evidence of any other kind on the ground that he may be incriminated thereby, and if the prosecuting attorney, in writing [and with the approval of the Attorney General], requests the court to order that person to answer the question or produce the evidence the court after notice to the witness and hearing shall so order [, unless it finds that to do so would be clearly contrary to the public interest,] and that person shall comply

with the order. After complying, and if, but for this section, he would have been privileged to withhold the answer given or the evidence produced by him, that person shall not be prosecuted or subjected to penalty or forfeiture for or on account of any transaction, matter or thing concerning which, in accordance with the order, he gave answer or produced evidence. But he may nevertheless be prosecuted or subjected to penalty or forfeiture for any perjury, false swearing or contempt committed in answering, or failing to answer, or in producing, or failing to produce, evidence in accordance with the order."

98.   Counselman v. Hitchcock, 142 U.S. 547, 564 [12 S.Ct. 195, 198–99, 35 L.Ed. 1110] (1892).

99.   Id. at 586.

2.   378 U.S. 52 [84 S.Ct. 1594, 12 L.Ed.2d 678] (1964).

and its fruits."[3] As to the problem of proving the causal relationship between the testimony and offered proof, the Court held that a defendant need only establish that he has testified under a state grant of immunity to matters related to the federal prosecution. Federal prosecutors then have the burden of showing that offered evidence is not "tainted"; this can be done by establishing that they had an "independent, legitimate" source for the evidence.[4]

Murphy involved only the scope of immunity necessary when the jurisdiction seeking to prosecute is not the jurisdiction which compelled the testimony. Although the reasoning of *Murphy* could be applied when the prosecuting jurisdiction is also the compelling jurisdiction, three justices of the Supreme Court of the United States have indicated that they would distinguish such a case from *Murphy* and require that transactional immunity be granted when the prosecuting and compelling jurisdictions were the same.[5] The arguments in support of this position are essentially those in support of transactional immunity generally with several added factors. Where only one jurisdiction is involved, there is a greater likelihood that criminal prosecution will follow a grant of use immunity; this raises in more cases, then, the danger that one granted use immunity will not in fact be able successfully to establish a causal relationship between his testimony and offered evidence and consequently will not be able fully to assert his immunity. Moreover, where only a single jurisdiction is involved no need exists to permit use immunity as a means of preventing one jurisdiction from defeating another's interest in prosecuting a particular individual for a particular crime. Thus not only do the arguments in favor of transactional immunity apply more strongly in a one-jurisdiction situation, but one of the primary objections to transactional immunity in the multiple jurisdiction situation does not apply.

If, however, *Murphy* means that use immunity is sufficient in single jurisdiction as well as multiple jurisdiction situations, it has rendered much existing immunity legislation (including the Model State Witness Immunity Act) unnecessarily (although perhaps not undesirably) broad. This might be accommodated by judicial construction. The New York Court of Appeals apparently adopted the position that the state's immunity statute, although it used transactional immunity phraseology, was intended to confer only that immunity constitutionally required. Reading *Murphy* as requiring only use immunity in the single jurisdiction situation, the court read the statute as granting only use immunity,[10] although it subsequently reversed this position.[11]

Although procedures for bringing immunity into effect depend upon the specific statute involved, the better drafted statutes have in common

---

3. Id. at 79.

4. Id. at 79 n. 18.

5. Piccirillo v. New York, 400 U.S. 548 [91 S.Ct. 520, 27 L.Ed.2d 596] (1971) (Douglas, J., with Marshall, J., concurring, and Brennan, J., with Marshall, J. concurring, dissenting from dismissal of the writ of certiorari as improvidently granted).

10. Id. The same conclusion was reached by the California Supreme Court. Byers v. Justice Court, 71 Cal.2d 1039, 80 Cal.Rptr. 553, 458 P.2d 465 (1969), rev'd on other grounds, 402 U.S. 424, 39 U.S. Law Week 4579 (1971).

11. Gold v. Menna, 25 N.Y.2d 475, 307 N.Y.S.2d 33, 255 N.E.2d 235 (1969).

several important requirements that must be complied with in order to divest the witness of his privilege:[12]

(1) The witness must be faced with an attempt by the state to use its power of testimonial inquiry. Thus the witness's position must be such that if he wrongfully refused to answer he would be subject to legal sanctions.

(2) The witness must invoke the privilege.[13] If the witness is willing to testify without the grant of immunity, there would be little reason for the state to grant immunity and much reason not to do so. It is often required, therefore, that before immunity can be conferred the questions must be put to the witness and he must decline to answer them, relying on his privilege.

(3) The application for immunity must be made by the prosecution authorities. The decision to seek immunity in return for testimony involves a determination that the value of the testimony would ultimately be greater than the value of the right to prosecute the witness or to use any testimony that he might be persuaded to give without the immunity. This is essentially a matter within the province of prosecution authorities, and many statutes make explicit their option to decide whether to attempt to forfeit possible actions against the witness.

(4) The grant must be approved by the court, which under the Model Act and some statutes may decline to approve it if to do so would be clearly to the contrary of the public interest. This requirement serves the purpose of formalizing the "agreement" and making it a matter of formal court record. It also provides the witness with notice that immunity has been granted and that he may no longer rely on the privilege. In addition, however, many statutes appear to be based on the policy that there should be some check on the prosecutor's power to forfeit the state's right to proceed against individuals who may well be guilty of criminal offenses.

No such carefully defined procedure is defined in many of the statutes, especially the so-called "automatic" immunity statutes which by their terms provide only that in a given situation a witness shall not be excused from testifying and then direct that the witness is to be protected from prosecution or the use of his testimony.[14] Nevertheless, a witness may not be

12. See generally 8 Wigmore, Evidence § 2282. In the Model Act, note 11, supra, and some statutes the procedure is carefully defined. E. g., West's Ann.Cal.Penal Code, § 1324. In others, all or some of these requirements may be read in. Special difficulties are raised by the "automatic" immunity statutes; see note 14, infra.

13. See Annot., 145 A.L.R. 1416. But see United States v. Monia, 317 U.S. 424 [63 S.Ct. 409, 87 L.Ed. 376] (1943) (since statute would appear to layman to grant immunity to one who simply testifies on request, there is no need for witness specifically to claim privilege).

14. See Marcus v. United States, 310 F.2d 143 (3d Cir. 1962) ("The immunity con-

ferred by [47 U.S.C.A. § 409(1)] is the automatic statutory consequence of compulsory testimony."). The immunity conferred under these statutes has been held to extend only to matters which the testimony concerned "in a substantial way." Heike v. United States, 227 U.S. 131 [33 S.Ct. 226, 57 L.Ed. 450] (1913). The danger of the automatic immunity acts is that a government official may find after an investigation that by calling witnesses he has unintentionally conferred immunity upon them. United States v. Weber, 255 F.Supp. 40 (D.N.J.1965), aff'd sub nom. United States v. Fisher, 384 U.S. 212 [86 S.Ct. 1453, 16 L.Ed.2d 479] (1966); United States v. Niarchos, 125 F.Supp. 214 (D.D.C.1954) (immunity conferred without regard to

held in contempt for failure to testify under even these automatic statutes unless "it has been demonstrated to him that an immunity, as broad in scope as the privilege it replaces, is available and applicable to him."[15] It is reasonable that this demonstration must include a representation by the court that in fact the statutory requirements have been complied with and the immunity has been validly conferred.

It is generally held that the immunity conferred does not include immunity for crimes committed in the giving of the testimony. Thus one who is granted immunity is not immune from a prosecution for perjury based upon false testimony given under immunity.[16] An interesting situation arises if immunity is granted and the testimony given turns out not to be incriminating. If the statutory immunity is transactional, has the state forfeited its right to proceed against the witness? It is generally concluded, on the basis of scant authority, that the answer is negative, on the assumption that the legislature did not intend to confer immunity without obtaining an equivalent benefit, and if no benefit accrues because the testimony was such that the state was entitled to have it without the grant of immunity, the immunity is of no effect.

Some statutes by their terms apply only to witnesses called on behalf of the prosecution in a criminal trial,[18] and statutes whose wording might per-

prosecutor's intent to confer immunity when subject matter of inquiry was "substantially related" to offenses); State ex rel. Lurie v. Rosier, 226 So.2d 825 (Fla. App.1969). See generally Wexler, Automatic Witness Immunity Statutes and the Inadvertent Frustration of Criminal Prosecutions: A Call for Congressional Action, 55 Geo.L.J. 656 (1967), urging that the statutes be amended so that no immunity is conferred unless the witness specifically claims immunity and is nevertheless required to answer. The new general federal immunity provision (see n. 95, supra) provides for immunity only when "a witness refuses, on the basis of his privilege against self-incrimination, to testify or provide other information" and an order is communicated to him ordering him to testify or to provide such information. 18 U.S.C.A. § 6002.

15.   Stevens v. Marks, 383 U.S. 234, 246 [86 S.Ct. 788, 15 L.Ed.2d 724] (1966), relying on Raley v. Ohio, 360 U.S. 423 [79 S.Ct. 1257, 3 L.Ed.2d 1344] (1959). In *Raley* petitioners had been called to testify before a state commission. They had been expressly told that the privilege applied, and had declined to answer questions. Later, they were prosecuted under a statute making it a criminal offense to refuse to testify "when lawfully required" to do so; an automatic immunity statute, the state argued, made their reliance on the privilege improper. In view of commands that were not only vague and contradictory but "actively misleading," the Court held, the convictions could not be sustained. Cf. United States v. Monia, 317 U.S. 424 [63 S.Ct. 409, 87 L.Ed.

376] (1943) (in view of statutory language, a witness need not specifically assert the privilege when subpoenaed to testify in order to obtain immunity granted under statute). It follows that while a court may save a statute which compels self-incrimination by judicially creating a grant of immunity, Murphy v. Waterfront Commission of New York Harbor, 378 U.S. 52 [84 S.Ct. 1594, 12 L.Ed.2d 678] (1964) (right to have compelled testimony and fruits excluded in federal courts saves state immunity legislation); Byers v. Justice Court of Mendocino County, 71 Cal.2d 1039, 80 Cal.Rptr. 553, 458 P.2d 465 (1969), a witness cannot be punished for failure to comply with the compulsion unless he is made aware of the immunity and given a chance to answer. Murphy v. Waterfront Commission of New York Harbor, supra, at 79–80.

16.   Glickstein v. United States, 222 U.S. 139 [32 S.Ct. 71, 56 L.Ed. 128] (1911) (witness may be prosecuted for perjury committed while testifying pursuant to statute directing that "no testimony given [under immunity] * * * shall be offered in evidence against him in any criminal proceeding", and the witness' allegedly perjurious testimony may be admitted in evidence in the perjury prosecution); Washburn v. State, 167 Tex.Cr.R. 125, 318 S.W.2d 627 (1959), cert. denied 359 U.S. 965 [79 S.Ct. 876, 3 L.Ed.2d 834] (witness granted immunity was nevertheless subject to penalties for perjury and therefore competent).

18.   E. g., Idaho Code Ann. § 18–1308 (1948) (witnesses testifying in bribery prosecution "at the instance of the state").

mit another construction have been interpreted to authorize immunity only for prosecution witnesses.[19] In practice, since the prosecution often has a veto power over the application, immunity is granted under other statutes primarily for purposes of building up the prosecution's case. But what of the defendant whose case would be assisted if a key witness were granted immunity and required to testify in his behalf?[20] It is certainly arguable that without the right to have immunity granted a defendant lacks "compulsory process for obtaining witnesses in his favor" as guaranteed by the Sixth Amendment. Moreover, the imbalance created by the availability of this power to the prosecution but not to the defense may well constitute a deprivation of due process of law.[21]

UNITED STATES v. APFELBAUM

Supreme Court of the United States, 1980.
445 U.S. 115, 100 S.Ct. 948, 63 L.Ed.2d 250.

Mr. Justice REHNQUIST delivered the opinion of the Court.

Respondent Apfelbaum invoked his privilege against compulsory self-incrimination while being questioned before a grand jury in the Eastern District of Pennsylvania. The government then granted him immunity in accordance with 18 U.S.C. § 6002, and he answered the questions propounded to him. He was then charged with and convicted of making false statements in the course of those answers.[1] The Court of Appeals reversed the conviction, however, because the District Court had admitted into evidence relevant portions of respondent's grand jury testimony that had not been alleged in the indictment to constitute the *"corpus delicti"* or "core" of the false statement's offense. Because proper invocation of the Fifth Amendment privilege against compulsory self-incrimination allows a witness to remain silent, but not to swear falsely, we hold that neither the statute nor the Fifth Amendment requires that the admissibility of immunized testimony be governed by any different rules than other testimony at a trial for making false statements in violation of 18 U.S.C. § 1623 (a). We therefore reverse the judgment of the Court of Appeals.

19.   State v. Perry, 246 Iowa 861, 69 N.W.2d 412 (1955). Cf. Smith v. United States, 58 F.2d 735 (5th Cir. 1932) (witness for state in prosecution of federal agent which had been removed to federal court and was defended by United States Attorney could not be granted immunity under federal statute upon application of state prosecutor).

20.   Cf. State v. Shaw, 6 Ariz.App. 33, 429 P.2d 667 (1967), finding no error in the refusal on the part of the prosecution to grant immunity to a witness. The record established, however, that the anticipated testimony would not have established a defense.

21.   See J. Maguire, Evidence of Guilt § 2.081 (1959). Wigmore argues that an opposite result would permit an offender to secure immunity by contriving with a defendant to be called as a witness. 8 Wigmore, Evidence § 2282, p. 519. But a requirement that the court approve any grant of immunity would sufficiently minimize this danger.

1.   Title 18 U.S.C. § 1623(a) provides in pertinent part:

"Whoever under oath in any proceeding before * * * [a] grand jury of the United States knowingly makes any false material declaration * * * shall be fined not more than $10,000 or imprisoned not more than five years, or both."

I

The grand jury had been investigating alleged criminal activities in connection with an automobile dealership located in the Chestnut Hill section of Philadelphia. The investigation focused on a robbery of $175,000 in cash that occurred at the dealership on April 16, 1975, and on allegations that two officers of the dealership staged the robbery in order to repay loanshark debts. The grand jury also heard testimony that the officers were making extortionate extensions of credit through the Chestnut Hill Lincoln-Mercury dealership.

In 1976, respondent Apfelbaum, then an Administrative Assistant to the District Attorney in Philadelphia, was called to testify because it was thought likely that he was an aider or abettor or an accessory after the fact to the allegedly staged robbery. When the grand jury first sought to question him about his relationship with the two dealership officials suspected of the staged robbery, he claimed his Fifth Amendment privilege, against compulsory self-incrimination and refused to testify. The District Judge entered an order pursuant to 18 U.S.C. § 6002 granting him immunity and compelling him to testify.[3] Respondent ultimately complied with this order to testify.

During the course of his grand-jury testimony, respondent made two series of statements that served as the basis for his subsequent indictment and conviction for false swearing. The first series was made in response to questions concerning whether respondent had attempted to locate Harry Brown, one of the two dealership officials, while on a "fishing trip" in Ft. Lauderdale, Fla., during the month of December 1975. Respondent testified that he was "positive" he had not attempted to locate Brown, who was also apparently in the Ft. Lauderdale area at the time. In a second series of statements, respondent denied that he had told FBI agents that he had lent $10,000 to Brown. The grand jury later indicted respondent pursuant to 18 U.S.C. § 1623 for making these statements, charging that the two series of statements were false and that respondent knew they were false.

At trial the government introduced into evidence portions of respondent's grand-jury testimony in order to put the charged statements in context and to show that respondent knew they were false. Respondent objected to the use of all the immunized testimony except the portions charged in the indictment as false. The District Court overruled the objection and admitted the excerpts into evidence on the ground that they were

---

3. Title 18 U. S. C. § 6002 provides:

Whenever a witness refuses, on the basis of his privilege against self-incrimination, to testify or provide other information in a proceeding before or ancillary to—

"(1) a court or grand jury of the United States,

"(2) an agency of the United States, or

"(3) either House of Congress, a joint committee of the two Houses, or a committee or a subcommittee of either House,

"and the person presiding over the proceeding communicates to the witness an order issued under this part, the witness may not refuse to comply with the order on the basis of his privilege against self-incrimination; but no testimony or other information compelled under the order (or any information directly or indirectly derived from such testimony or other information) may be used against the witness in any criminal case, except a prosecution for perjury, giving a false statement, or otherwise failing to comply with the order."

relevant to prove that respondent had knowingly made the charged false statements. The jury found respondent guilty on both counts of the indictment.

The Court of Appeals for the Third Circuit reversed, holding that because the immunized testimony did not constitute "the *corpus delicti* or core of a defendant's false swearing indictment" it could not be introduced. 584 F. 2d 1264, 1265 (CA3 1978). We granted certiorari because of the importance of the issue and because of a difference in approach to it among the Courts of Appeals.[5]

* * *

II

Did Congress intend the Federal Immunity Statute, 18 U.S.C. § 6002, to limit the use of a witness's immunized grand jury testimony in a subsequent prosecution of the witness for false statements made at the grand jury proceeding? Respondent contends that while § 6002 permits the use of a witness's false statements in a prosecution for perjury or for making false declarations, it establishes an absolute prohibition against the use of truthful immunized testimony in such prosecutions. But this contention is wholly at odds with the explicit language of the statute, and finds no support even in its legislative history.

It is a well-established principle of statutory construction that absent clear evidence of a contrary legislative intention, a statute should be interpreted according to its plain language. Here 18 U.S.C. § 6002 provides that when a witness is compelled to testify over his claim of a Fifth Amendment privilege, "no testimony or other information compelled under the order (or any information directly or indirectly derived from such testimony or other information) may be used against the witness in any criminal case, *except a prosecution for perjury, giving a false statement, or otherwise failing to comply with the order.*" [Emphasis added.] The statute thus makes no distinction between truthful and untruthful statements made during the course of the immunized testimony. Rather it creates a blanket exemption from the bar against the use of immunized testimony in cases in which the witness is subsequently prosecuted for making false statements.

The legislative history of § 6002 shows that Congress intended the perjury and false declarations exception to be interpreted as broadly as constitutionally permissible. The present statute was enacted * * * not only to bring about uniformity in the operation of immunity grants within the federal system, but also to restrict the grant of immunity to that required by the United States Constitution. Thus, the statute derives from a 1969 report of the National Commission on the Reform of the Federal Criminal Laws, which proposed a general use immunity statute under which "the immunity conferred would be confined to the scope required by the Fifth Amendment." And as stated in both the Senate and House Reports on the proposed legislation:

5. The Seventh Circuit agrees with the Court of Appeals below that the government may introduce into evidence so much of the witness' testimony as is essential to establish the *corpus delicti* of the offense of perjury. The Second and Tenth Circuits have held that false immunized testimony is admissible, but truthful immunized testimony is not, in a subsequent prosecution for perjury. The Sixth and Eighth Circuits have held that immunized testimony may be used for any purpose in such a prosecution.

"This statutory immunity is intended to be as broad as, but no broader than, the privilege against self-incrimination * * * . It is designed to reflect the use-restriction immunity concept of Murphy v. Waterfront Commission, 378 U.S. 52, 84 S.Ct. 1594, 12 L.Ed.2d 678 (1964) rather [than] the transaction immunity concept of Counselman v. Hitchcock, 142 U.S. 547, 12 S.Ct. 195, 35 L.Ed. 1110 (1892)."[10]

In light of the language and legislative history of § 6002, the conclusion is inescapable that Congress intended to permit the use of both truthful and false statements made during the course of immunized testimony if such use was not prohibited by the Fifth Amendment.

III

The limitation placed on the use of relevant evidence by the Court of Appeals may be justified, then, only if required by the Fifth Amendment. Respondent contends that his conviction was properly reversed because under the Fifth Amendment his truthful immunized statements were inadmissible at his perjury trial, and the government never met its burden of showing that the immunized statements it introduced into evidence were not truthful. The Court of Appeals, as noted above, concluded that the Fifth Amendment prohibited the use of all immunized testimony except the *"corpus delicti"* or "core" of the false swearing indictment.

In reaching its conclusion, the Court of Appeals initially observed that a grant of immunity must be coextensive with the Fifth Amendment. Kastigar v. United States, supra, 406 U.S., at 440. It then reasoned that had respondent not been granted immunity, he would have been entitled under the Fifth Amendment to remain silent. And if he had remained silent, he would not have answered any questions, truthfully or falsely. There consequently would been no testimony whatsoever to use against him. A prosecution for perjury committed at the immunized proceeding, the Court of Appeals continued, must be permitted because "as a practical matter, if immunity constituted a license to lie, the purpose of immunity would be defeated." Such a prosecution is but a "narrow exception" carved out to preserve the integrity of the truth-seeking process. But the subsequent use of statements made at the immunized proceeding, other than those alleged in the indictment to be false, is impermissible because the introduction of such statements cannot be reconciled with the privilege against self-incrimination. 584 F.2d, at 1269-1271.

A

There is more than one flaw in this reasoning. Initially, it presumes that in order for a grant of immunity to be "coextensive with the Fifth Amendment privilege," the witness must be treated as if he had remained silent. This presumption focuses on the *effect* of the assertion of the Fifth

---

10. S. Rep. No. 91-617, 91st Cong., 1st Sess., 145 (1969); H. R. Rep. No. 91-1549, 91st Cong., 2d Sess., 42 (1970). Representative Poff, the bill's chief sponsor in the House, quoted Mr. Justice White's observation in Murphy v. Waterfront Commission, supra, 378 U.S., at 107 [84 S.Ct., at 1618,] that " 'Immunity must be as broad as, but not harmfully and wastefully broader than, the privilege against self-incrimination.' " 116 Cong. Rec. 35291 (1970). We express no opinion as to the possible intimation in the Reports that the Fifth Amendment would have prohibited an immunity statute any broader than § 6002.

Amendment privilege, rather than on the *protection* the privilege is designed to confer. In so doing, it calls into question the constitutionality of all immunity statutes, including "transactional" immunity statutes as well as "use" immunity statutes such as § 6002. Such grants of immunity would not provide a full and complete substitute for a witness's silence because, for example, they do not bar the use of the witness's statements in civil proceedings. Indeed, they fail to prevent the use of such statements for any purpose that might cause detriment to the witness other than that resulting from subsequent criminal prosecution.

The Court has never held, however, that the Fifth Amendment requires immunity statutes to preclude all uses of immunized testimony. Such a requirement would be inconsistent with the principle that the privilege does not extend to consequences of a noncriminal nature, such as threats of liability in civil suits, disgrace in the community, or the loss of employment.

And this Court has repeatedly recognized the validity of immunity statutes, Kastigar v. United States, supra, 406 U.S., at 449 [92 S.Ct., at 1658] (1972), acknowledged that Congress included immunity statutes in many of the regulatory measures adopted in the first half of this century, and that at the time of the enactment of 18 U.S.C. § 6002, the statute under which this prosecution was brought, there were in force over 50 federal immunity statutes as well as similar laws in every State of the Union. 406 U.S., at 448 [92 S.Ct., at 1658]. This Court in Ullmann v. United States, supra, 350 U.S. 422, [76 S.Ct. 497, 100 L.Ed. 511], stated that such statutes have "become part of our constitutional fabric." Id., at 438 [76 S.Ct., at 506]. And the validity of such statutes may be traced in our decisions at least as far back as Brown v. Walker, supra, 161 U.S. 591 [16 S.Ct. 644, 40 L.Ed. 819].

These cases also establish that a strict and literal reading of language in cases such as Counselman v. Hitchcock, supra, 142 U.S. 547 [12 S.Ct. 195, 35 L.Ed. 1110]—that an immunity statute "cannot abridge a constitutional privilege, and that it cannot replace or supply one, at least unless it is so broad as to have the same extent in scope and effect"—does not require the sort of "but for" analysis used by the Court of Appeals in order to enable it to survive attack as being violative of the privilege against compulsory self-incrimination. Indeed, in Brown v. Walker, supra, 161 U.S., at 600 [16 S.Ct., at 648], this Court stated that "[t]he danger of extending the principle announced in Counselman v. Hitchcock is that the privilege may be put forward for a sentimental reason, or for a purely fanciful protection of the witness against an imaginary danger, and for the real purpose of securing immunity to some third person, who is interested in concealing the facts to which he would testify." And in Kastigar v. United States, supra, 406 U.S. 454 [92 S.Ct. 1661], we concluded that "[t]he broad language in *Counselman* relied upon by petitioners was unnecessary to the Court's decision, and cannot be considered binding authority." Id., at 454–455 [92 S.Ct. at 1662]. *Kastigar* also expressly declined a request by the petitioner to reconsider and overrule Brown v. Walker, supra, and Ullmann v. United States, supra, and went on to expressly reaffirm the validity of those decisions.

The reasoning of the Court of Appeals is also internally inconsistent in that logically it would not permit a prosecution for perjury or false swearing committed during the course of the immunized testimony. If a witness must be treated as if he had remained silent, the mere requirement that he answer questions, thereby subjecting himself to the possibility of being subsequently prosecuted for perjury or false swearing, places him in a position that is substantially different from that he would have been in had he been permitted to remain silent.

All of the Courts of Appeals, however, have recognized that the statutory provision in 18 U.S.C. § 6002 allowing prosecutions for perjury in answering questions following a grant of immunity does not violate the Fifth Amendment privilege against compulsory self-incrimination. And we ourselves have repeatedly held that perjury prosecutions are permissible for false answers to questions following the grant of immunity. See, e.g., United States v. Wong, 431 U.S. 174 [97 S.Ct. 1823, 52 L.Ed. 2d 231] (1977); United States v. Mandujano, 425 U.S. 564 [96 S.Ct. 1768, 48 L.Ed. 2d 212] (1976) (plurality opinion); id., at 584–585 [96 S.Ct., at 1780–1781] (Brennan, J., concurring); id., at 609 (Stewart and Blackmun, JJ., concurring).

It is therefore analytically incorrect to equate the benefits of remaining silent as a result of invocation of the Fifth Amendment privilege with the protections conferred by the privilege—protections that may be invoked with respect to matters that pose substantial and real hazards of subjecting a witness to criminal liability at the time he asserts the privilege. For a grant of immunity to provide protection "coextensive" with that of the Fifth Amendment, it need not treat the witness as if he had remained silent. Such a conclusion, as noted above, is belied by the fact that immunity statutes and prosecutions for perjury committed during the course of immunized testimony are permissible at all.

B

The principle that the Fifth Amendment privilege against compulsory self-incrimination provides no protection for the commission of perjury has frequently been cited without any elaboration as to its underlying rationale. Its doctrinal foundation, as relied on in both *Wong and Mandujano,* is traceable to Glickstein v. United States, 222 U.S. 139, 142 [32 S.Ct. 71, 73, 56 L.Ed. 128] (1911). *Glickstein* stated that the Fifth Amendment "does not endow the person who testifies with a license to commit perjury," id., at 142 [32 S.Ct. at 73], and that statement has been so often repeated in our cases as to be firmly established constitutional law. But just as we have refused to read literally the broad *dicta* of *Counselman,* supra, we are likewise unwilling to decide this case solely upon an epigram contained in *Glickstein,* supra. Thus, even if, as the Court of Appeals said, a perjury prosecution is but a "narrow exception" to the principle that a witness should be treated as if he had remained silent, it does not follow that the Court of Appeals was correct in its view of the question before us now.

Perjury prosecutions based on immunized testimony, even if they be but a "narrow exception" to the principle that a witness should be treated as if he had remained silent after invoking the Fifth Amendment privilege, *are* permitted by our cases. And so long as they are, there is no principle or decision that limits the admissibility of evidence in a manner peculiar only to them. To so hold would not be an exercise in the balancing of competing constitutional rights, but in a comparison of apples and oranges.[11] For even if both truthful and untruthful testimony from the immunized proceeding are admissible in a subsequent perjury prosecution, the exception surely would still be properly regarded as "narrow," once it is recognized that the testimony remains inadmissible in all prosecutions for offenses committed prior to the grant of immunity that would have permitted the witness to invoke his Fifth Amendment privilege absent the grant.

While the application of the Fifth Amendment privilege to various types of claims has changed in some respects over the past three decades, the basic test reaffirmed in each case has been the same.

> "The central standard for the privilege's application has been whether the claimant is confronted by substantial and 'real,' and not merely trifling or imaginary, hazards of incrimination. Rogers v. United States, 340 U.S. 367, 374 [71 S.Ct. 438, 442, 95 L.Ed. 344]; Brown v. Walker, 161 U.S. 591, 600 [76 S.Ct. 644, 40 L.Ed. 819]." Marchetti v. United States, 390 U.S. 39, 53 [88 S.Ct. 697, 705, 519 L.Ed. 2d 889] (1968).

Marchetti, supra, which overruled earlier decisions of this Court in United States v. Kahriger, 345 U.S. 22 [73 S.Ct. 510, 97 L.Ed. 754] (1953), and Lewis v. United States, 348 U.S. 419 [75 S.Ct. 415, 99 L.Ed. 475] (1955), invalidated the federal wagering statutes at issue in *Kahriger* and *Lewis* on the ground that they contravened the petitioner's Fifth Amendment right against compulsory self-incrimination. The practical effect of the requirements of those statutes was to compel petitioner, a professional gambler engaged in ongoing gambling activities that he had commenced and was likely to continue, to choose between openly exposing himself as acting in violation of state and federal gambling laws and risking federal prosecution for tax avoidance.[12] The Court held that petitioner was entitled to assert his Fifth Amendment privilege in these circumstances. But it also observed that "prospective acts will doubtless ordinarily involve speculative and insubstantial risks of incrimination." 390 U.S., at 54 [88 S.Ct., at 705]. Thus, although *Marchetti* rejected "the rigid chronological distinction adopted in *Kahriger* and *Lewis,*" id., at 53 [88 S.Ct. at 705], that distinction does not aid respondent here.

---

11.   Thus, the Court of Appeals' position is basically a halfway house that does not withstand logical analysis. If the rule is that a witness who is granted immunity may be placed in no worse a position than if he had been permitted to remain silent, the principle that the Fifth Amendment does not protect false statements serves merely as a piece of a legal mosaic justified solely by *stare decisis,* rather than as part of a doctrinally consistent view of that Amendment.

12.   Thus, the Court observed:

"Petitioner was confronted by a comprehensive system of federal and state prohibitions against wagering activities, he was required, on pain of criminal prosecution, to provide information which he might reasonably suppose would be available to prosecuting authorities, and which would surely prove a significant 'link in a chain' of evidence tending to establish his guilt." 390 U.S., at 48 [88 S.Ct., at 703].

And "[e]very aspect of petitioner's wagering activities," the Court continued, "subjected him to possible state or federal prosecution," and the "[i]nformation obtained as a consequence of the federal wagering tax laws is readily available to assist efforts of state and federal authorities to enforce those penalties." 390 U.S., at 47 [88 S.Ct., at 702].

In United States v. Freed, 401 U.S. 601 [91 S.Ct. 1112, 28 L.Ed. 2d 356] (1971), this Court rejected the argument that a registration requirement of the National Firearms Act violated the Fifth Amendment because the information disclosed could be used in connection with offenses that the transferee of the firearm might commit in the future. In so doing, the Court stated:

> "Appellees' argument assumes the existence of a periphery of the Self-Incrimination Clause which protects a person against incrimination not only against past or present transgressions but which supplies insulation for a career of crime about to be launched. We cannot give the Self-Incrimination Clause such an expansive interpretation." Id., at 606–607 [91 S.Ct., at 1117].

And Mr. Justice Brennan in his concurring opinion added:

> "I agree with the Court that the Self-Incrimination Clause of the Fifth Amendment does not require that immunity be given as to the use of such information in connection with crimes that the transferee might possibly commit in the future with the registered firearm." Id., at 611 [91 S.Ct. at 1119].

In light of these decisions, we conclude that the Fifth Amendment does not prevent the use of respondent's immunized testimony at his trial for false swearing because, at the time he was granted immunity, the privilege would not have protected him against false testimony that he later might decide to give. Respondent's assertion of his Fifth Amendment privilege arose from his claim that the questions relating to his connection with the Chestnut Hill auto dealership would tend to incriminate him. The government consequently granted him "use" immunity under § 6002, which prevents the use and derivative use of his testimony with respect to any subsequent criminal case except prosecutions for perjury and false swearing offenses, in exchange for his compelled testimony.

The government has kept its part of the bargain; this is a perjury prosecution and not any other kind of criminal prosecution. The Court of Appeals agreed that such a prosecution might be maintained, but as noted above severely limited the admissibility of immunized testimony to prove the government's case. We believe that it could not be fairly said that respondent, at the time he asserted his privilege and was consequently granted immunity, was confronted with more than a "trifling or imaginary" hazard of compelled self-incrimination as a result of the possibility that he might commit perjury during the course of his immunized testimony. In United States v. Bryan, 339 U.S. 323 [70 S.Ct. 724, 94 L.Ed. 884] (1950), we held that an immunity statute that provided that "[n]o testimony given by a witness before * * * any committee of either House * * * shall be used as evidence in any criminal proceeding against him in any court, except in a prosecution for perjury committed in giving such testimony," did not bar the use at respondent's trial for willful default of the testimony given by her before a congressional committee. In so holding, we stated that "[t]here is, in our jurisprudence, no doctrine of 'anticipatory contempt.'" Id., at 341 [70 S.Ct., at 735].

We hold here that in our jurisprudence there likewise is no doctrine of "anticipatory perjury." In the criminal law, both a culpable *mens rea* and a criminal *actus reus* are generally required for an offense to occur.[13] Similarly, a future intention to commit perjury or to make false statements if granted immunity because of a claim of compulsory self-incrimination is not by itself sufficient to create a "substantial and 'real' " hazard that permits invocation of the Fifth Amendment. Therefore, neither the immunity statute nor the Fifth Amendment preclude the use of respondent's immunized testimony at a subsequent prosecution for making false statements, so long as that testimony conforms to otherwise applicable rules of evidence. The exception of a perjury prosecution from the use that may be made of immunized testimony may be a narrow one, but it is also a complete one. The Court of Appeals having held otherwise, its judgment is accordingly

   Reversed.

                            *   *   *

ROGERS v. UNITED STATES

Supreme Court of the United States, 1951.
340 U.S. 367, 71 S.Ct. 438, 95 L.Ed. 344.
[Some of the Court's footnotes are omitted.]

Mr. Chief Justice VINSON delivered the opinion of the Court.

This case arises out of an investigation by the regularly convened grand jury of the United States District Court for the District of Colorado. The books and records of the Communist Party of Denver were sought as necessary to that inquiry and were the subject of questioning by the grand jury. In September, 1948, petitioner, in response to a subpoena, appeared before the grand jury. She testified that she held the position of Treasurer of the Communist Party of Denver until January, 1948, and that, by virtue of her office, she had been in possession of membership lists and dues records of the Party. Petitioner denied having possession of the records and testified that she had turned them over to another. But she refused to identify the person to whom she had given the Party's books, stating to the court as her only reason: "I don't feel that I should subject a person or persons to the same thing that I'm going through."[1] The court thereupon committed peti-

---

13.   As recognized by one commentator, Shakespeare's lines here express sound legal doctrine:

   "His acts did not o'ertake his bad intent,
   And must be buried but as an intent
   That perish'd by the way: Thoughts are no subjects,
   Intents but merely thoughts." Measure for Measure, Act V, Scene 1.

1.   Transcript, p. 39 (September 21, 1948):

   "The Court: Now, what is the question?

   "Mr. Goldschein: Who has the books and records of the Communist Party of Denver now? Who did Mrs. Rogers give those books up to as she says she gave them up in January of this year?

   "The Court: Do you care to answer that question, madam?

   "Mrs. Rogers: I do not.

   "The Court: What?

   "Mrs. Rogers: I do not, and that's what I told them.

   "The Court: Why won't you answer?

   "Mrs. Rogers: I don't feel that I should subject a person or persons to the same thing that I'm going through.

   "The Court: It is the order or finding of the Court that you should answer those questions. Now, will you do that?

   "Mrs. Rogers: No."

tioner to the custody of the marshal until ten o'clock the next morning, expressly advising petitioner of her right to consult with counsel.[2]

The next day, counsel for petitioner informed the court that he had read the transcript of the prior day's proceedings and that, upon his advice, petitioner would answer the questions to purge herself of contempt.[3] However, upon reappearing before the grand jury, petitioner again refused to answer the question. The following day she was again brought into court. Called before the district judge immediately after he had heard oral argument concerning the privilege against self-incrimination in another case, petitioner repeated her refusal to answer the question, asserting this time the privilege against self-incrimination.[4] After ruling that her refusal was not privileged, the district judge imposed a sentence of four months for contempt, The Court of Appeals for the Tenth Circuit affirmed, 1950, 179 F.2d 559, and we granted certiorari, 1950, 339 U.S. 956, 70 S.Ct. 978.

If petitioner desired the protection of the privilege against self-incrimination, she was required to claim it. United States v. Monia, 1943, 317 U.S. 424, 427, 63 S.Ct. 409, 410, 87 L.Ed. 376. The privilege "is deemed waived unless invoked." United States v. Murdock, 1931, 284 U.S. 141, 148, 52 S.Ct. 63, 64, 76 L.Ed. 210. Furthermore, the decisions of this Court are explicit in holding that the privilege against self-incrimination "is

---

2. Transcript, p. 40 (September 21, 1948):

"The Court: You will be detained until tomorrow morning until ten o'clock. In the meantime, you may consult counsel and have a hearing tomorrow morning at ten o'clock on your reasons for refusal to answer questions.

"Mrs. Rogers: I can consult counsel between now and then? The Court: Yes, but you will be in the custody of the marshal all the time. Get your counsel and bring him over here if you want to, but you will have to be in the custody of the marshal and spend the night in jail, I'm afraid."

3. Transcript, pp. 43, 49 (September 22, 1948):

"Mr. Menin (After entering his appearance on behalf of petitioner): In regard to the witness Rogers, I've read the transcript of what has transpired in court here yesterday; and I believe that upon my advice she will answer questions which were propounded to her."

* * *

"Mr. Menin: As to the witness Jane Rogers, I think she will purge herself of her contempt by answering the questions.

"The Court: In the case of the witness Rogers, then, the order of the Court is that she return to the Grand Jury room and if she purges herself of contempt, then upon bringing the matter back to the Court, she will be discharged. In the meantime, she will remain in custody."

4. "No person * * * shall be compelled in any criminal case to be a witness against himself * * * ." U.S.Const. Amend. V. The proceedings leading to the claim of privilege by petitioner appear at Transcript, pp. 77–78 (September 23, 1948):

"The Court: Madam, do you still persist in not answering these questions? Mrs. Rogers: Well, on the basis of Mr. Menin's statements this morning—

"The Court: Will you please answer the question yes or no? Mrs. Rogers: Well, I think that's rather undemocratic. I'm a very honest person. Would you mind letting me consider—

"The Court: Make any statement you wish.

"Mrs. Rogers: Well, as I said before, I'm a very honest person and I'm not acquainted with the tricks of legal procedure, but I understand from the reading of these cases this morning that I am —and I do have a right to refuse to answer these questions, on the basis that they would tend to incriminate me, and you read it yourself, that I have a right to decide that.

"The Court: You have not the right to say.

"Mrs. Rogers: According to what you read, I do. I stand on that.

"The Court: All right. If you will make no changes, it is the judgment and sentence of the court you be confined to the custody of the Attorney General for four months. Call the next case."

solely for the benefit of the witness,"[6] and "is purely a personal privilege of the witness."[7] Petitioner expressly placed her original declination to answer on an untenable ground, since a refusal to answer cannot be justified by a desire to protect others from punishment, much less to protect another from interrogation by a grand jury. Petitioner's claim of the privilege against self-incrimination was pure afterthought. Although the claim was made at the time of her second refusal to answer in the presence of the court, it came only after she had voluntarily testified to her status as an officer of the Communist Party of Denver. To uphold a claim of privilege in this case would open the way to distortion of facts by permitting a witness to select any stopping place in the testimony.

The privilege against self-incrimination, even if claimed at the time the question as to the name of the person to whom petitioner turned over the Party records was asked, would not justify her refusal to answer. As a preliminary matter, we note that petitioner had no privilege with respect to the books of the Party, whether it be a corporation or an unincorporated association. Books and records kept "in a representative rather than in a personal capacity cannot be the subject of the personal privilege against self-incrimination, even though production of the papers might tend to incriminate (their keeper) personally." United States v. White, 1944, 322 U.S. 694, 699, 64 S.Ct. 1248, 1251, 88 L.Ed. 1542.[11] Since petitioner's claim of privilege cannot be asserted in relation to the books and records sought by the grand jury, the only claim for reversal of her conviction rests on the ground that mere disclosure of the name of the recipient of the books tends to incriminate.

In Blau v. United States, 1950, 340 U.S. 159, 71 S.Ct. 223, [95 L.Ed. 170] we held that questions as to connections with the Communist Party are subject to the privilege against self-incrimination as calling for disclosure of facts tending to criminate under the Smith Act, 18 U.S.C.A. § 2386.[12] But petitioner's conviction stands on an entirely different footing, for she had freely described her membership, activities and office in the Party. Since the privilege against self-incrimination presupposes a real danger of legal detriment arising from the disclosure, petitioner cannot invoke the privilege where response to the specific question in issue here would not further incriminate her. Disclosure of a fact waives the privilege as to details. As this Court stated in Brown v. Walker, 1896, 161 U.S. 591, 597, 16 S.Ct. 644, 647, 40 L.Ed. 819: "Thus, if the witness himself elects to waive his privilege, as

---

6.   United States v. Murdock, 1931, 284 U.S. 141, 148, 52 S.Ct. 63, 64, 76 L.Ed. 210.

7.   Hale v. Henkel, 1906, 201 U.S. 43, 69, 26 S.Ct. 370, 376, 50 L.Ed. 652; McAlister v. Henkel, 1906, 201 U.S. 90, 91, 26 S.Ct. 385, 50 L.Ed. 671.

11.   See also the cases cited in notes 7 and 8, supra. The privilege does not attach to the books of an organization, whether or not the books in question are "required records" of the type considered in Shapiro v. United States, 1948, 335 U.S. 1, 68 S.Ct. 1375, 92 L.Ed. 1787.

12.   Membership in the Communist Party was not, of itself, a crime at the time the questions in this case were asked. And Congress has since expressly provided, in the Internal Security Act of 1950, Act of Sept. 23, 1950, 64 Stat. 987, 992, § 4(f), 50 U.S.C.A. § 783(f), that "Neither the holding of office nor membership in any Communist organization by any person shall constitute per se a violation (of this Act) or of any other criminal statute." We, of course, express no opinion as to the implications of this legislation upon the issues presented by these cases.

he may doubtless do, since the privilege is for his protection and not for that of other parties, and discloses his criminal connections, he is not permitted to stop, but must go on and make a full disclosure."[13]

Following this rule, federal courts have uniformly held that, where criminating facts have been voluntarily revealed, the privilege cannot be invoked to avoid disclosure of the details. The decisions of this Court in Arndstein v. McCarthy, 1920, 254 U.S. 71, 41 S.Ct. 26, 65 L.Ed. 138, and McCarthy v. Arndstein, 1923, 262 U.S. 355, 43 S.Ct. 562, 67 L.Ed. 1023, further support the conviction in this case for, in sustaining the privilege on each appeal, the Court stressed the absence of any previous "admission of guilt *or incriminating facts*,"[15] and relied particularly upon Brown v. Walker, supra, and Foster v. People, 1869, 18 Mich. 266. The holding of the Michigan court is entirely apposite here: "(W)here a witness has voluntarily answered as to materially criminating facts, it is held with uniformity that he cannot then stop short and refuse further explanation, but must disclose fully what he has attempted to relate." 18 Mich. at page 276.[16]

Requiring full disclosure of details after a witness freely testifies as to a criminating fact does not rest upon a further "waiver" of the privilege against self-incrimination. Admittedly, petitioner had already "waived" her privilege of silence when she freely answered criminating questions relating to her connection with the Communist Party. But when petitioner was asked to furnish the name of the person to whom she turned over Party records, the court was required to determine, as it must whenever the privilege is claimed, whether the question presented a reasonable danger of further crimination in light of all the circumstances, including any previous disclosures. As to each question to which a claim of privilege is directed, the court must determine whether the answer to that particular question would subject the witness to a "real danger" of further crimination.[17] After petitioner's admission that she held the office of Treasurer of the Communist Party of Denver, disclosure of acquaintance with her successor presents no more than a "mere imaginary possibility" of increasing the danger of prosecution.

Petitioner's contention in the Court of Appeals and in this Court has been that, conceding her prior voluntary crimination as to one element of proof of a Smith Act violation, disclosure of the name of the recipient of the Party records would tend to incriminate as to the different crime of con-

---

13. Quoted with approval in Powers v. United States, 1912, 223 U.S. 303, 314, 32 S.Ct. 281, 283, 56 L.Ed. 448.

15. 262 U.S. at page 359, 43 S.Ct. at page 563, 67 L.Ed. 1023 (emphasis supplied). The Arndstein appeals, like the present case, arose out of an involuntary examination. The Court reserved, as we do here, the problems arising out of a possible abuse of the privilege against self-incrimination in adversary proceedings. Compare state court decisions collected in 147 A.L.R. 255 (1943).

16. VIII Wigmore, Evidence (1940) § 2276, quotes from Foster v. People, 1869, 18 Mich. 266, as authoritative and sum-

marizes the law as follows: "The case of the *ordinary witness* can hardly present any doubt. He may waive his privilege; this is conceded. He waives it by exercising his option of answering; this is conceded. Thus the only inquiry can be whether, by *answering as to fact X, he waived it for fact Y.* If the two are related facts, parts of a whole fact forming a single relevant topic, then his waiver as to a part is a waiver as to the remaining parts; because the privilege exists for the sake of the criminating fact as a whole." [Emphasis in original.]

17. Heike v. United States, 1913, 227 U.S. 131, 144, 33 S.Ct. 226, 228, 57 L.Ed. 450; Brown v. Walker, 1896, 161 U.S. 591, 600, 16 S.Ct. 644, 648, 40 L.Ed. 819.

spiracy to violate the Smith Act. Our opinion in Blau v. United States, supra, 340 U.S. at page 161, 71 S.Ct. at page 224, explicitly rejects petitioner's argument for reversal here in its holding that questions relating to activities in the Communist Party are criminating both as to "violation of (or conspiracy to violate) the Smith Act." Of course, at least two persons are required to constitute a conspiracy, but the identity of the other members of the conspiracy is not needed, inasmuch as one person can be convicted of conspiring with persons whose names are unknown.

Affirmed.

Mr. Justice Clark took no part in the consideration or decision of this case.

Mr. Justice Black, with whom Mr. Justice Frankfurter and Mr. Justice Douglas concur, dissenting.

* * *

Apparently, the Court's holding is that at some uncertain point in petitioner's testimony, regardless of her intention, admission of associations with the Communist Party automatically effected a "waiver" of her constitutional protection as to all related questions. To adopt such a rule for the privilege against self-incrimination, when other constitutional safeguards must be knowingly waived, relegates the Fifth Amendment's privilege to a second-rate position. Moreover, today's holding creates this dilemma for witnesses: On the one hand, they risk imprisonment for contempt by asserting the privilege prematurely; on the other, they might lose the privilege if they answer a single question. The Court's view makes the protection depend on timing so refined that lawyers, let alone laymen, will have difficulty in knowing when to claim it. In this very case, it never occurred to the trial judge that petitioner waived anything. And even if voluntary testimony can under some circumstances work a waiver, it did not do so here because what petitioner stated to the grand jury "standing alone did not amount to an admission of guilt or furnish clear proof of crime * * * ." Arndstein v. McCarthy, 254 U.S. 71, 72, 41 S.Ct. 26, 65 L.Ed. 138.

Furthermore, unlike the Court, I believe that the question which petitioner refused to answer did call for additional incriminating information. She was asked the names of the persons to whom she had turned over the Communist Party books and records. Her answer would not only have been relevant in any future prosecution of petitioner for violation of the Smith Act but also her conviction might depend on testimony of the witnesses she was thus asked to identify. For these reasons the question sought a disclosure which would have been incriminating to the highest degree. Certainly no one can say that the answer "[could not] possibly be used as a basis for, or in aid of, a criminal prosecution against the witness * * * ." Brown v. Walker, 161 U.S. 591, 597 [16 S.Ct. 644, 647, 40 L.Ed. 819] * * *

I would reverse the judgment of conviction.

[An appendix to the opinion of Mr. Justice Black giving the full transcript of the proceedngs under review is omitted.]

KENNEDY, THE ENEMY WITHIN

314–16 (1960).*

* * *

Some attorneys advise their clients to plead the Fifth Amendment on every question and not to be selective. There is some legal precedent indicating that such advice is well founded. Although I could never be sure until a particular question was asked whether the witness would claim the Fifth Amendment, I could often tell early in the questioning whether I was going to get many answers out of him. When a witness resorted to the Fifth Amendment on every request, I felt he should be interrogated only on matters I would have asked about if he were answering questions. In other words, I questioned him on a point only when the facts had already been established in the record or when I had some definite information to support the question. For instance, if we had a gangster or underworld figure from Chicago or New York who was taking the Fifth Amendment, I would not ask him whether he had been involved in a murder or armed robbery, or had been the gunman for Albert Anastasia, unless I had some specific information that he had been.

I am not claiming that when I questioned a witness I always had positive proof on the subject matter of interrogation. In many instances, where a gangster was concerned, the information came from police files and could not be positively verified. These people not only wouldn't talk to us, they wouldn't and haven't talked to anyone. However, if I had some information to support the question, I believed that I was justified in asking it.

But this is where abuses creep in.

For instance, a witness from the Midwest was pleading the Fifth Amendment on every question when suddenly Senator Curtis asked him what his relationship was with the Governor of Iowa. I knew this was an unfair question at the time, for we had no information that the man even knew the Governor of Iowa or had had any dealings with him. The witness, of course, did not have to plead the Fifth Amendment on that question, but since he was pleading it regularly, once more made no difference to him. In any case, he exercised his privilege and refused to answer on grounds of self-incrimination. And in Iowa, as I had expected, the story was "Gangster Takes Fifth Amendment on Ties with Governor." I immediately put out a statement that we had absolutely no information about any relationship between the Governor and the witness. But the damage had been done. It was low politics and a perversion of the use of the Congressional investigating committee.

Very early in the hearings in 1957, my brother pointed out the unfairness of this kind of procedure, but as late as one of our last hearings in 1959 it was still being practiced. For example, in September of that year a former UAW official who had taken some pay-offs from an employer invoked the Fifth Amendment in answer to all questions. In the course of his interrogation, he was asked by Senator Mundt if he had made kickbacks to Richard Gosser, vice president of the UAW. He took the Fifth Amendment. Robert Manual, an assistant counsel appointed by the Republicans, then asked if

*Harper & Brothers, New York; 1960.

Reuther had not instructed him to take the Fifth Amendment, with the implication that it was a cover-up for the UAW. My brother asked if there was any evidence whatever that the witness, Zvara, had kicked back to Richard Gosser. Senator Curtis and Robert Manual had to admit that there was not. My brother showed the unfairness of the questioning by asking Zvara if he had ever kicked back to Robert Manual. Again, on this, Zvara pleaded the Fifth Amendment. Manual also admitted that there was no evidence whatever that Walter Reuther had had any conversations with Zvara in connection with his appearancce before the Committee, let alone instructing him to plead the Fifth Amendment.

If my brother had not pointed these things out at the time, the record would have carried a completely unfair implication. As it was, one news story did report that Zvara pleaded the Fifth Amendment on kickbacks to Gosser. * * *

JOHNSON v. UNITED STATES

Supreme Court of the United States, 1943.
318 U.S. 189, 63 S.Ct. 549, 87 L.Ed. 704.

Mr. Justice DOUGLAS delivered the opinion of the Court.

Petitioner was convicted of wilfully attempting to defeat and evade his federal income taxes for the years 1936 and 1937. He was acquitted for 1935. Petitioner was a political leader in Atlantic City and Atlantic County, New Jersey. The prosecution's theory was that he had received large sums of money from those conducting the numbers game for protection against police interference and had not reported those sums in his income tax returns for 1935, 1936, and 1937. The defense was that his failure to return all the income he had received resulted from the mistaken but sincere belief that he was bound to return only the net balance remaining after deducting amounts expended for political purposes. The evidence was that one Weloff and one Towhey acting alternately delivered to petitioner on behalf of the numbers syndicate $1,200 a week from July 1935 to November 1937. About November 1, 1937, Weloff and Towhey were displaced by one Jack Southern to whom the syndicate delivered $1,200 a week. Neither the prosecution nor the defense would sponsor Southern's testimony. At the request of the prosecution the court called Southern as a witness. He testified that during November and December, 1937, he delivered the $1,200 a week to an inspector of police named Ferretti who was dead at the time of the trial. He denied that he ever made any weekly payments to petitioner. No evidence was adduced that petitioner received any sums from the syndicate during November or December, 1937. Petitioner took the stand and on direct examination admitted that he had received the weekly payments from Weloff and Towhey up to November, 1937. For 1937 these admitted payments totalled $50,400. Petitioner accounted for this sum by stating that he had reported $30,189.99 in his 1937 return as "Other commissions" and that he had paid out the balance, roughly $21,000, as political contributions for that year. On cross-examination he denied that he had received payments from Southern during November and December, 1937.[1] He was then asked "Did you receive any money from numbers in 1938?" Counsel for the defense objected

---

1. The indictment charged that the defendant had received $62,400 from the numbers game in 1937. It was the difference between that amount and $50,400 admittedly received which was in dispute.

to the question on the ground that it was not relevant to the issue and would tend to prove a different offense than the one charged in the indictment. The court overruled the objection. Petitioner then answered the question in the affirmative. He was then asked, "Who gave it to you?" Counsel for the defense objected. The court had the jury withdraw. The prosecutor asked that petitioner "also be excused from the court room during the argument, and that when he resumes the stand he should do so without having any opportunity to hear what the argument is about". The court said "that is a fair request" and ordered petitioner to retire, which he did. No objection was made to that action. Counsel for the prosecution argued that the questions asked in cross-examination were proper to establish a continuous practice of receiving the numbers income throughout 1937. Counsel for the defense insisted that the cross-examination should be limited to the subjects opened up by the examination in chief. The court expressed the view that the cross-examination was permissible since it bore directly upon credibility.* Counsel for the defense then pressed the point that even if it otherwise might be proper cross-examination, nevertheless it was "improper cross-examination for the reason that it is directed to a future prosecution." He asserted that he made the claim of privilege on behalf of the accused "in view of the avowed threat of the government to prosecute him for the very years concerning which he is now asked to testify." The court replied that it was for the accused, not his counsel, to make the claim and added, "You may advise him of his rights, of course, but it is for him to determine whether or not he wishes to take advantage of them". After further argument, the court stated:

"It seems to me that the testimony is perfectly relevant and material as cross examination directed to credibility.

"In view of the witness' testimony, unless it runs afoul of his right not to be required to incriminate himself, it seems to me that that is a right which he may waive or claim, and that that is a personal right that he may be advised by counsel when a question is asked, and that he will have to determine himself whether he is going to claim it or not."

Petitioner resumed the stand. The question "Who gave it to you?" was repeated. Counsel for petitioner then advised him of his constitutional privilege, which he thereupon claimed. The court ruled, "You may decline to answer."

The prosecutor in his address to the jury commented at some length on petitioner's assertion of his constitutional privilege:

"I asked him, 'Did you get the money in 1938?' and he said, 'Yes'. Well, of course, then a lot of little things happened. They didn't like that because naturally you say, 'Well, I don't understand that, Mr. Johnson.' I wish you could have asked him questions then. You say, 'Mr. Johnson, you say that suddenly November 1st, 1937 you stopped getting the $1200 from numbers; then in 1938 you started to get it again? How come?' You don't get it, you don't get it because it isn't the truth. That is what cross examination is for.

*[Compare FRE 608(b), second paragraph —Ed.]

"So then we went beyond that. We said, 'Who did you get it from?' He said, 'I claim my privilege against self-incrimination. I violated the income tax law in 1938; I don't want to tell you about that. I am having enough trouble with 1935, six and seven.' If he could have claimed his privilege on the stand here with respect to 1935, six and seven he would have done it. He would claim anything that is necessary to get him out of any predicament he is in. Well, now, ladies and gentlemen, if he got that numbers money in 1938 who did he get it from? He must have got it from Jack Southern. Maybe he got it from Inspector Ferretti, but he admits he got it. Well, then, if he got it he got it during the last two months of 1937. They didn't say anything about that to you because they were trapped. No need of them talking about it. It is for me to point that out to you.

"Now, ladies and gentlemen, can you believe that man told you the truth about anything on the witness stand when he admits that he got numbers money in 1938 but won't tell you who he got it from on the ground it would incriminate him? If you can believe that that man is innocent of this charge when he stands right up in front of you and says he cannot answer a question about 1938, that he just got through answering for 1937 on the ground it would incriminate him, well, then, I just don't get it."

An objection was made to these statements and overruled and an exception was noted. The next morning before the court charged the jury various other objections were submitted. During the colloquy the court stated that there "were a number of matters referred to last evening　*　*　*　I ruled on some of them, all of which rulings I indicted I would reconsider. Now, have you mentioned to me now all the points you desire to refer to?" Counsel for petitioner replied, "We withdraw whatever was said last night *　*　*　I think the only fair thing to do is to forget everything that happened last night and start this morning". The objection previously made to the prosecutor's comment on the accused's failure to testify was not renewed. Nor was any request made to the court to charge the jury to disregard petitioner's refusal to testify. Though the prosecutor's comment on the accused's failure to testify was again adverted to, it was in a different connection. Counsel for petitioner contended that the prosecutor's statement that the claim of privilege amounted to an admission of income tax violation in 1938 was "an entire misconception of　*　*　*　the claim of privilege" inasmuch as the basis of the claim "is that the testimony *　*　*　would have a tendency to incriminate him", and "not that it would prove him guilty". The court indicated that this objection was well taken and should be called to the attention of the jury. The court added, "He is not being charged with any 1938 tax." The prosecutor then said, "It is a question of his good faith and his credibility, and the answers he has already given on similar questions. That is the purpose for which the questions were permitted." The court thereupon stated, "I think I probably should indicate to the jury that that is the full extent of it." Counsel for petitioner remained silent, making no objection. No error was asserted in the motion for a new trial or in the assignments of error on the ground that the prosecutor's comment or the court's charge on the inference from the claim of privilege was improper.

The court in its charge stated that petitioner's refusal to answer the question on the ground that it would tend to incriminate him "may only be considered by you in testing his credibility as to the answers which he did give and his good faith in the matter" and that petitioner was not being tried for anything he did in 1938. To this charge no objection was made.

The Circuit Court of Appeals affirmed the judgment of conviction, one judge dissenting. 3 Cir., 129 F.2d 954. The court held that the exclusion of petitioner from the court room during the colloquy did not result in prejudice; that the cross-examination covering 1938 income was proper; and that the allowance of comment on the claim of privilege was justified. The case is here on a petition for a writ of certiorari.

The case of an accused who voluntarily takes the stand and the case of an accused who refrains from testifying (Bruno v. United States, 308 U.S. 287, 60 S.Ct. 198, 84 L.Ed. 257) are of course vastly different. Raffel v. United States, 271 U.S. 494, 46 S.Ct. 566, 70 L.Ed. 1054. His "voluntary offer of testimony upon any fact is a waiver as to all other relevant facts, because of the necessary connection between all." 8 Wigmore, Evidence (3d ed., 1940) § 2276(2). [Citations omitted.]

The cross-examination did not run afoul of the rule which prohibits inquiry into a collateral crime unconnected with the offense charged. Boyd v. United States, 142 U.S. 450, 12 S.Ct. 292, 35 L.Ed. 1077. Inquiry into petitioner's income for 1938 was relevant to the issue in the case. As contended by the prosecution, the receipt of money from the numbers syndicate prior to November, 1937 and after December, 1937 might well support a finding of the jury that in view of all the circumstances the payments were not in fact interrupted during the last two months of 1937. The amount and source of the 1938 income accordingly were relevant to show the continuous nature of the transactions in question. That line of inquiry therefore satisfied the test of relevancy and was a proper part of cross-examination. [Citations omitted.] Though the issue might have been more aptly phrased by the court in terms other than credibility, the meaning of the ruling in its context is plain. Thus we may assume that it would not have been error for the court to deny petitioner's claim of privilege. In such a case his failure to explain the source of his numbers income in 1938 could properly be the subject of comment and inference. As stated by this Court in Caminetti v. United States, 242 U.S. 470, 494, 37 S.Ct. 192, 198, 61 L.Ed. 442, L.R.A.1917F, 502, Ann.Cas.1917B, 1168, an accused who takes the stand "may not stop short in his testimony by omitting and failing to explain incriminating circumstances and events already in evidence, in which he participated and concerning which he is fully informed, without subjecting his silence to the inferences to be naturally drawn from it." But where the claim of privilege is asserted and unqualifiedly granted, the requirements of fair trial may preclude any comment. That certainly is true where the claim of privilege could not properly be denied. The rule which obtains when the accused fails to take the stand (Wilson v. United States, 149 U.S. 60, 13 S.Ct. 765, 37 L.Ed. 650) is then applicable. As stated by the Supreme Court of Pennsylvania, "If the privilege claimed by the witness be allowed, the matter is at an end. The claim of privilege and its allowance is properly no part of the evidence submitted to the jury, and no inferences whatever can be legitimately drawn by them from the legal assertion by the witness of his constitutional right. The allowance of the privilege would be a mockery of justice, if either party is to be affected injuriously by it." [Citations omitted.] We also think that the same result should obtain in any case where the court grants the claim of privilege and then submits the matter to the jury, if that action may be said to affect materially the accused's choice of claiming or waiving the privilege and results in prejudice. The fact that the privilege is mistakenly granted is immaterial.

The ruling of the court gave the petitioner the choice between testifying and refusing to testify as to his 1938 income. An accused having the assurance of the court that his claim of privilege would be granted might well be entrapped if his assertion of the privilege could then be used against him. His real choice might then be quite different from his apparent one. In this case it would lie between protection against an indictment for 1938 and the use of his claim of privilege as evidence that he did in fact receive the income during the last two months of 1937. Elementary fairness requires that an accused should not be misled on that score. If advised by the court that his claim of privilege though granted would be employed against him, he well might never claim it. If he receives assurance that it will be granted if claimed, or if it is claimed and granted outright, he has every right to expect that the ruling is made in good faith and that the rule against comment will be observed. Certainly the question whether petitioner had received income from the syndicate during November and December, 1937, was an extremely material issue in the case. As we have noted, petitioner admitted receiving $50,400 from the numbers syndicate during 1937. And all of this amount according to the testimony was received prior to November 1, 1937. Of this amount he reported only $30,189.99 in his 1937 income tax return. He testified, however, that he had paid out $21,000 in political contributions for that year. Thus he attempted to account for all the numbers income which he had received that year and defended on the ground that his failure to return the $21,000 was due to his mistaken but sincere belief that he was bound to return only the net balance remaining after deducting amounts expended for political purposes. The indictment, however, charged that he had received $62,400 from the numbers syndicate during 1937. And the prosecution claimed that the weekly payments of $1200 continued during November and December, 1937. If that were established, it would plainly destroy his defense and would be cogent evidence of his wilful attempt to evade the tax. All of the direct evidence in the record was to the effect that he had not received income from the numbers syndicate during November and December, 1937. There was no basis for concluding that he had unless that fact was to be inferred from the evidence that he had received the income until November, 1937 and that he received it again in 1938. Hence it would be highly valuable to the prosecution and equally damaging to the accused to have his failure to testify employed to bolster such an inference.

It is no answer to say that comment on a defendant's refusal to testify does not in any way place him in jeopardy of being charged with or convicted of the crime protected by his privilege. That may be admitted. The problem here is a different one. It is whether a procedure will be approved which deprives an accused on facts such as these of an intelligent choice between claiming or waiving his privilege. Knowledge that a failure to testify though permitted by the court would be submitted to the jury might seriously affect that choice. If the accused makes the choice without that knowledge, he may well be misled on one of the most important decisions in his defense. We would of course not be concerned with the matter if it turned only on the quality of legal advice which he received. But the responsibility for misuse of the grant of the claim of privilege is the court's. It is the court to whom an accused properly and necessarily looks for protection in such a matter. When it grants the claim of privilege but allows it to be used against the accused to his prejudice, we cannot disregard the matter. That procedure has such potentialities of oppressive use that we will not sanction its use in the federal courts over which we have supervisory powers.

We are mindful of the fact that there is eminent authority which may be said to represent the contrary view. State v. Ober, 52 N.H. 459, 13 Am.Rep. 88. That case stands for the general proposition that when the accused took the stand "without claiming his constitutional privilege, it was too late for him to halt at that point which suited his own convenience." Page 465 of 52 N.H. With that rule we agree. Whether the facts of that case and the stage of the proof when the privilege was claimed made the comment on the accused's failure to testify prejudicial, cannot be determined from the report of the case. The point with which we are here concerned was not adverted to in the opinion. Indeed the court stated (52 N.H. page 465) that the "whole argument of his counsel now proceeds upon the erroneous assumption that the ruling of the court [granting the claim of privilege] was right. That assumption being groundless, his argument fails." But as we have indicated, the problem in this case is quite different.

* * *

[The Court goes on to hold that petitioner waived the error by withdrawing his objection.]

Affirmed.

[Justices Murphy and Jackson did not participate in the consideration of this case. The concurring opinion of Mr. Justice Frankfurter is omitted.]

GRUNEWALD v. UNITED STATES

Supreme Court of the United States, 1957.
353 U.S. 391, 77 S.Ct. 963, 1 L.Ed.2d 931.
[Most of the Court's footnotes are omitted.]

Mr. Justice HARLAN delivered the opinion of the Court.

* * *

III.

What we have held as to the statute of limitations disposes of the conviction of the three petitioners under Count 1, but does not touch Halperin's conviction on Counts 5, 6, and 7 for violating 18 U.S.C. § 1503, 18 U.S.C.A. § 1503. As to those Counts, Halperin who took the stand in his own defense at the trial, contends (a) that the Government was improperly allowed to cross-examine him as to the assertion of his Fifth Amendment privilege before a grand jury investigating this conspiracy, before which he had been called as a witness,[26] and (b) that the evidence did not justify his conviction on these Counts. For the reasons given hereafter we think that the first contention is well taken, but that the second one is untenable.

26.　Grunewald and Bolich also make this contention on their own behalf.

In 1952 Halperin was subpoenaed before a Brooklyn grand jury which was investigating corruption in the Bureau of Internal Revenue. Testimony had already been received by the grand jury from the Patullo and Gotham taxpayers, which linked Halperin with the tax-finding ring. Halperin was asked a series of questions before the grand jury, including, among others, such questions as whether he knew Max Steinberg (an employee of the Bureau of Internal Revenue and a co-defendant in the charge under Count 1); whether he knew Grunewald; whether he had held and delivered escrow money paid to Grunewald by Gotham after the "no prosecution" ruling; and whether he had phoned Grunewald to arrange a meeting between one of his own associates and Bolich. Halperin declined to answer any of these questions, on the ground that the answers would tend to incriminate him and that the Fifth Amendment therefore entitled him not to answer. He repeatedly insisted before the grand jury that he was wholly innocent, and that he pleaded his Fifth Amendment privilege only on the advice of counsel that answers to these questions might furnish evidence which could be used against him, particularly when he was not represented by counsel and could not cross-examine witnesses before the grand jury.

When the Government cross-examined Halperin at the trial some of the questions which he had been asked before the grand jury were put to him. He answered each question in a way consistent with innocence. The Government was then allowed, over objection, to bring out in cross-examination that petitioner had pleaded his privilege before the grand jury as to these very questions. Later, in his charge to the jury, the trial judge informed them that petitioner's Fifth Amendment plea could be taken only as reflecting on his credibility, and that no inference as to guilt or innocence could be drawn therefrom as to Halperin or any co-defendant.[28]

In thus allowing this cross-examination, the District Court relied on Raffel v. United States, 271 U.S. 494, 46 S.Ct. 566, 70 L.Ed. 1054, where

28. The charge as to this point was as follows:

"During the cross examination of one of the defendants, the government questioned the defendant as to his previous statements before the Brooklyn Grand Jury in which he refused to answer certain questions on the ground that answers to them might tend to incriminate him. These questions related to matters similar to those to which the defendant testified at this trial when he took the stand. No witness is required to take the stand or required to give testimony that might tend to incriminate him; but when a defendant takes the stand in his own defense at a trial, it is proper to interrogate him as to previous statements which he may have made under oath concerning the same matter, including his assertion of his constitutional privilege to refuse to testify as to those matters before a grand jury. You may use this evidence of a defendant's prior assertions of the Fifth Amendment for the sole purpose of ascertaining the weight you choose to give to his present testimony with respect to the same matters upon which he previously invoked his privilege.

"The defendant had the right of asserting the Fifth Amendment when he appeared before the Grand Jury, and I charge you that you are not to draw any inference whatsoever as to the guilt or innocence of the defendant in this case by reason of the fact that he chose to assert his unquestioned right to invoke the Fifth Amendment, on that previous occasion. However, it was proper for the Government to question the defendant with respect to his previous invocation of the Fifth Amendment, but you may consider this evidence of his prior assertions of the Fifth Amendment only for the purpose of ascertaining the weight you choose to give to his present testimony with respect to the same matters upon which he previously asserted his constitutional privilege. It is not to be considered in a determination of the guilt or innocence of any co-defendant."

this Court held that a defendant's failure to take the stand at his first trial to deny testimony as to an incriminating admission could be used on cross-examination at the second trial, where he did take the stand, to impugn the credibility of his denial of the same admission. In upholding the District Court here, the Court of Appeals likewise relied on Raffel, and also on one of its own earlier decisions. Halperin attacks these rulings on these principal grounds: (a) Raffel is distinguishable from the present case; (b) if Raffel permitted this cross-examination, then the trial court erred in refusing to charge, as Halperin requested, that "an innocent man may honestly claim that his answers may tend to incriminate him"; (c) in any case Raffel has impliedly been overruled by Johnson v. United States, 318 U.S. 189, 63 S.Ct. 549, 87 L.Ed. 704; and (d) compelling Halperin to testify before the grand jury, when he had already been marked as a putative defendant, violated his constitutional rights, so that, by analogy to the rule of Weeks v. United States, 232 U.S. 383, 34 S.Ct. 341, 58 L.Ed. 652, his claim of privilege could in no event be used against him. We find that in the circumstances presented here Raffel is not controlling, and that this cross-examination was not permissible.

It is, of course, an elementary rule of evidence that prior statements may be used to impeach the credibility of a criminal defendant or an ordinary witness. But this can be done only if the judge is satisfied that the prior statements are in fact inconsistent. 3 Wigmore, Evidence, § 1040. And so the threshold question here is simply whether, in the circumstances of this case, the trial court erred in holding that Halperin's plea of the Fifth Amendment privilege before the grand jury involved such inconsistency with any of his trial testimony as to permit its use against him for impeachment purposes. We do not think that Raffel is properly to be read either as dispensing with the need for such preliminary scrutiny by the judge, or as establishing as a matter of law that such a prior claim of privilege with reference to a question later answered at the trial is always to be deemed to be a prior inconsistent statement, irrespective of the circumstances under which the claim of privilege was made. The issue decided in Raffel came to the Court as a certified question in quite an abstract form, and was really ·centered on the question whether a defendant who takes the stand on a second trial can continue to take advantage of the privilege asserted at the first trial. This Court held, in effect, that when a criminal defendant takes the stand, he waives his privilege completely and becomes subject to cross-examination impeaching his credibility just like any other witness: "His waiver is not partial; having once cast aside the cloak of immunity, he may not resume it at will, whenever cross-examination may be inconvenient or embarrassing." The Court in Raffel, did not focus on the question whether the cross-examination there involved was in fact probative in impeaching the defendant's credibility. In other words, we may assume that under Raffel, Halperin in this case was subject to cross-examination impeaching his credibility just like any other witness, and that his Fifth Amendment plea before the grand jury could not carry over any form of immunity when he voluntarily took the stand at the trial. This does not, however, solve the question whether in the particular circumstances of this case the cross-examination should have been excluded because its probative value on the issue of Halperin's credibility was so negligible as to be far outweighed by its possible impermissible impact on the jury. As we consider that in the circumstances of the present case, the trial court, in the exercise of a sound discretion, should have refused to permit this line of cross-examination, we are not faced with the necessity of deciding whether Raffel has been stripped of vitality by the later Johnson case, supra, or of otherwise re-examining Raffel.

We need not tarry long to reiterate our view that, as the two courts below held, no implication of guilt could be drawn from Halperin's invocation of his Fifth Amendment privilege before the grand jury. Recent re-examination of the history and meaning of the Fifth Amendment has emphasized anew that one of the basic functions of the privilege is to protect *innocent* men. Griswold, The Fifth Amendment Today, 9–30, 53–82. "Too many, even those who should be better advised, view this privilege as a shelter for wrongdoers. They too readily assume that those who invoke it are either guilty of crime or commit perjury in claiming the privilege." Ullmann v. United States, 350 U.S. 422, 426, 76 S.Ct. 497, 500, 100 L.Ed. 511. See also Slochower v. Board of Higher Eduction, 350 U.S. 551, at pages 557–558, 76 S.Ct. 637, at page 641, 100 L.Ed. 692, when, at the same Term, this Court said: "The privilege serves to protect the innocent who otherwise might be ensnared by ambiguous circumstances."

When we pass to the issue of credibility, we deem it evident that Halperin's claim of the Fifth Amendment privilege before the Brooklyn grand jury in response to questions which he answered at the trial was wholly consistent with innocence. Had he answered the questions put to him before the grand jury in the same way he subsequently answered them at trial, this nevertheless would have provided the Government with incriminating evidence from his own mouth. For example, had he stated to the grand jury that he knew Grunewald, the admission would have constituted a link between him and a criminal conspiracy, and this would be true even though he was entirely innocent and even though his friendship with Grunewald was above reproach. There was, therefore, as we see it, no inconsistency between Halperin's statement to the grand jury that answering the question whether he knew Grunewald would tend to furnish incriminating evidence against him, and his subsequent testimony at trial that his acquaintance with Grunewald   *   *   *   was free of criminal elements. And the same thing is also true, as we see it, as to his claim of privilege with respect to the other questions asked him before the grand jury and his answers to those same questions when they were put to him at the trial. These conclusions are fortified by a number of other considerations surrounding Halperin's claim of privilege:

First, Halperin repeatedly insisted before the grand jury that he was innocent and that he pleaded his Fifth Amendment privilege solely on the advice of counsel.

Second, the Fifth Amendment claim was made before a grand jury where Halperin was a compelled, and not a voluntary, witness; where he was not represented by counsel; where he could summon no witnesses; and where he had no opportunity to cross-examine witnesses testifying against him. These factors are crucial in weighing whether a plea of the privilege is inconsistent with later exculpatory testimony on the same questions, for the nature of the tribunal which subjects the witness to questioning bears heavily on what inferences can be drawn from a plea of the Fifth Amendment.

See Griswold, supra, at 62. Innocent men are more likely to plead the privilege in secret proceedings, where they testify without advice of counsel and without opportunity for cross-examination, than in open court proceedings, where cross-examination and judicially supervised procedure provide safeguards for the establishing of the whole, as against the possibility of merely partial, truth.

Finally, and most important, we cannot deem Halperin's plea of the Fifth Amendment to be inconsistent with his later testimony at the trial because of the nature of this particular grand-jury proceeding. For, when Halperin was questioned before the grand jury, he was quite evidently already considered a potential defendant. The taxpayers whose cases had been "fixed" by the conspiratorial ring had already testified before the grand jury, and they gave there largely the same evidence as they did later, at trial. The scheme was thus in essence already revealed when Halperin was called to testify. Under these circumstances it was evident that Halperin was faced with the possibility of an early indictment, and it was quite natural for him to fear that he was being asked questions for the very purpose of providing evidence against himself. It was thus quite consistent with innocence for him to refuse to provide evidence which could be used by the Government in building its incriminating chain. For many innocent men who know that they are about to be indicted will refuse to help create a case against themselves under circumstances where lack of counsel's assistance and lack of opportunity for cross-examination will prevent them from bringing out the exculpatory circumstances in the context of which superficially incriminating acts occurred.

We are not unmindful that the question whether a prior statement is sufficiently inconsistent to be allowed to go to the jury on the question of credibility is usually within the discretion of the trial judge. But where such evidentiary matter has grave constitutional overtones, as it does here, we feel justified in exercising this Court's supervisory control to pass on such a question. This is particularly so because in this case the dangers of impermissible use of this evidence far outweighed whatever advantage the Government might have derived from it if properly used. If the jury here followed the judge's instructions, namely, that the plea of the Fifth Amendment was relevant only to credibility, then the weight to be given this evidence was less than negligible, since, as we have outlined above, there was no true inconsistency involved; it could therefore hardly have affected the Government's case seriously to exclude the matter completely. On the other hand, the danger that the jury made impermissible use of the testimony by implicitly equating the plea of the Fifth Amendment with guilt is, in light of contemporary history, far from negligible. Weighing these factors, therefore, we feel that we should draw upon our supervisory power over the administration of federal criminal justice in order to rule on the matter. Cf. McNabb v. United States, 318 U.S. 332, 63 S.Ct. 608, 87 L.Ed. 819.

We hold that under the circumstances of this case it was prejudicial error for the trial judge to permit cross-examination of petitioner on his plea of the Fifth Amendment privilege before the grand jury, and that Halperin must therefore be given a new trial on Counts 5, 6, and 7.

Finally, we find no substance to Halperin's contention that he was in effect convicted for advising, as a lawyer, some of the witnesses before the grand jury that they had a right to plead their Fifth Amendment privilege. The evidence against Halperin under these Counts was quite sufficient to make out a case for submission to the jury.

For the reasons given we hold that the judgments below must be reversed, and the cases remanded to the District Court for further proceedings consistent with this opinion.

It is so ordered.

Reversed and remanded.

Mr. Justice Black, with whom The Chief Justice, Mr. Justice Douglas, and Mr. Justice Brennan join, concurring.

I concur in the reversal of these cases for the reasons given in the Court's opinion with one exception.

In No. 184, the petitioner, Halperin, appeared before a grand jury in response to a subpoena. There he declined to answer certain questions relying on the provision of the Fifth Amendment that "No person * * * shall be compelled in any criminal case to be a witness against himself."

Later, at his trial, Halperin took the stand to testify in his own behalf. On cross-examination the prosecuting attorney asked him the same questions that he had refused to answer before the grand jury. This time Halperin answered the questions; his answers tended to show that he was innocent of any wrong-doing. The Government was then permitted over objection to draw from him the fact that he had previously refused to answer these questions before the grand jury on the ground that his answers might tend to incriminate him.

At the conclusion of the trial the judge instructed the jury that Halperin's claim of his constitutional privilege not to be a witness against himself could be considered in determining what weight should be given to his testimony—in other words, whether Halperin was a truthful and trustworthy witness. I agree with the Court that use of this claim of constitutional privilege to reflect upon Halperin's credibility was error, but I do not, like the Court, rest my conclusion on the special circumstances of this case. I can think of no special circumstances that would justify use of a constitutional privilege to discredit or convict a person who asserts it. The value of constitutional privileges is largely destroyed if persons can be penalized for relying on them. It seems peculiarly incongruous and indefensible for courts which exist and act only under the Constitution to draw inferences of lack of honesty from invocation of a privilege deemed worthy of enshrinement in the Constitution. * * *

GRIFFIN v. CALIFORNIA

Supreme Court of the United States, 1965.
380 U.S. 609, 85 S.Ct. 1229, 14 L.Ed.2d 106.
[Most of the Court's footnotes are omitted.]

Mr. Justice DOUGLAS delivered the opinion of the Court.

Petitioner was convicted of murder in the first degree after a jury trial in a California court. He did not testify at the trial on the issue of guilt, though he did testify at the separate trial on the issue of penalty. The trial court instructed the jury on the issue of guilt, stating that a defendant has a constitutional right not to testify. But it told the jury:[2]

"As to any evidence or facts against him which the defendant can reasonably be expected to deny or explain because of facts within his knowledge, if he does not testify or if, though he does testify, he fails to deny or explain such evidence, the jury may take that failure into consideration as tending to indicate the truth of such evidence and as indicting that among the inferences that may be reasonably drawn therefrom those unfavorable to the defendant are the more probable."

It added, however, that no such inference could be drawn as to evidence respecting which he had no knowledge. It stated that failure of a defendant to deny or explain the evidence of which he had knowledge does not create a presumption of guilt nor by itself warrant an inference of guilt nor relieve the prosecution of any of its burden of proof.

Petitioner had been seen with the deceased the evening of her death, the evidence placing him with her in the alley where her body was found. The prosecutor made much of the failure of petitioner to testify:

"The defendant certainly knows whether Essie Mae had this beat up appearance at the time he left her apartment and went down the alley with her.

"What kind of a man is it that would want to have sex with a woman that beat up if she was beat up at the time he left?

"He would know that. He would know how she got down the alley. He would know how the blood got on the bottom of the concrete steps. He would know how long he was with her in that box. He would know how her wig got off. He would know whether he beat her or mistreated her. He would know whether he walked away from that place cool as a cucumber when he saw Mr. Villasenor because he was conscious of his own guilt and wanted to get away from that damaged or injured woman.

"These things he has not seen fit to take the stand and deny or explain.

"And in the whole world, if anybody would know, this defendant would know.

"Essie Mae is dead, she can't tell you her side of the story. The defendant won't."

The death penalty was imposed and the California Supreme Court affirmed. 60 Cal.2d 182, 32 Cal.Rptr. 24, 383 P.2d 432. The case is here on a writ of certiorari which we granted, 377 U.S. 989, 84 S.Ct. 1926, 12 L.Ed.2d 1043, to consider whether comment on the failure to testify violated the Self-Incrimination Clause of the Fifth Amendment which we made applicable to the States by the Fourteenth in Malloy v. Hogan, 378 U.S. 1, 84 S.Ct. 1489, 12 L.Ed.2d 653, decided after the Supreme Court of California had affirmed the present conviction.

---

2. Article I, § 13, of the California Constitution provides in part:

    " * * * in any criminal case, whether the defendant testifies or not, his failure to explain or to deny by his testimony any evidence or facts in the case against him may be commented upon by the court and by counsel, and may be considered by the court or the jury."

If this were a federal trial, reversible error would have been committed. Wilson v. United States, 149 U.S. 60, 13 S.Ct. 765, 37 L.Ed. 650, so holds. It is said, however, that the Wilson decision rested not on the Fifth Amendment, but on an Act of Congress, now 18 U.S.C. § 3481.[4] That indeed is the fact, as the opinion of the Court in the Wilson case states. But that is the beginning, not the end, of our inquiry. The question remains whether, statute or not, the comment rule, approved by California, violates the Fifth Amendment. We think it does. It is in substance a rule of evidence that allows the State the privilege of tendering to the jury for its consideration the failure of the accused to testify. No formal offer of proof is made as in other situations; but the prosecutor's comment and the court's acquiescence are the equivalent of an offer of evidence and its acceptance. The Court in the Wilson case stated:

" * * * the act was framed with a due regard also to those who might prefer to rely upon the presumption of innocence which the law gives to every one, and not wish to be witnesses. It is not every one who can safely venture on the witness stand, though entirely innocent of the charge against him. Excessive timidity, nervousness when facing others and attempting to explain transactions of a suspicious character, and offenses charged against him, will often confuse and embarrass him to such a degree as to increase rather than remove prejudices against him. It is not every one, however, honest, who would therefore willingly be placed on the witness stand. The statute, in tenderness to the weakness of those who from the causes mentioned might refuse to ask to be witnesses, particularly when they may have been in some degree compromised by their association with others, declares that the failure of a defendant in a criminal action to request to be a witness shall not create any presumption against him." 149 U.S., p. 66, 13 S.Ct., p. 766.

If the words "Fifth Amendment" are substituted for "act" and for "statute" the spirit of the Self-Incrimination Clause is reflected. For comment on the refusal to testify is a remnant of the "inquisitorial system of criminal justice," Murphy v. Waterfront Comm., 378 U.S. 52, 55, 84 S.Ct. 1594, 1596, 12 L.Ed.2d 678, which the Fifth Amendment outlaws.[5] It is a penalty imposed by courts for exercising a constitutional privilege. It cuts down on the privilege by making its assertion costly. It is said, however,

---

4. Section 3481 reads as follows:

"In trial of all persons charged with the commission of offenses against the United States and in all proceedings in courts martial and courts of inquiry in any State, District, Possession or Territory, the person charged shall, at his own request, be a competent witness. His failure to make such request shall not create any presumption against him." June 25, 1948, c. 645, 62 Stat. 833.

The legislative history shows that 18 U.S.C. § 3481 was designed, *inter alia*, to bar counsel for the prosecution from commenting on the defendant's refusal to testify. Mr. Frye of Maine, spokesman for the bill, said, "That is the law of Massachusetts, and we proposed to adopt it as a law of the United States." 7 Cong.Rec. 385. The reference was to

Mass.Stat.1866, c. 260, now Mass.Gen. Laws Ann., c. 233, § 20, cl. Third (1959), which is almost identical with 18 U.S.C. § 3481. See also Commonwealth v. Harlow, 110 Mass. 411; Commonwealth v. Scott, 123 Mass. 239; Opinion of the Justices, 300 Mass. 620, 15 N.E.2d 662.

5. Our decision today that the Fifth Amendment prohibits comment on the defendant's silence is no innovation, for on a previous occasion a majority of this Court indicated their acceptance of this proposition. In Adamson v. People of State of California, 332 U.S. 46, 67 S.Ct. 1672, the question was, as here, whether the Fifth Amendment proscribed California's comment practice. The four dissenters (Black, Douglas, Murphy and Rutledge, JJ.) would have answered this question in the af-

that the inference of guilt for failure to testify as to facts peculiarly within the accused's knowledge is in any event natural and irresistible, and that comment on the failure does not magnify that inference into a penalty for asserting a constitutional privilege. People v. Modesto, 62 Cal.2d 436, 452–453, 42 Cal.Rptr. 417, 426–427, 398 P.2d 753, 762–763. What the jury may infer, given no help from the court, is one thing. What it may infer when the court solemnizes the silence of the accused into evidence against him is quite another. That the inference of guilt is not always so natural or irresistible is brought out in the Modesto opinion itself:

> "Defendant contends that the reason a defendant refuses to testify is that his prior convictions will be introduced in evidence to impeach him ([Cal.] Code Civ. Proc. § 2051) and not that he is unable to deny the accusations. It is true that the defendant might fear that his prior convictions will prejudice the jury, and therefore another possible inference can be drawn from his refusal to take the stand." Id., p. 453, 42 Cal.Rptr., p. 427, 398 P.2d, p. 763.

We said in Malloy v. Hogan, supra, 378 U.S. p. 11, 84 S.Ct. p. 1495, that "the same standards must determine whether an accused's silence in either a federal or state proceeding is justified." We take that in its literal sense and hold that the Fifth Amendment, in its direct application to the Federal Government and in its bearing on the States by reason of the Fourteenth Amendment, forbids either comment by the prosecution on the accused's silence or instructions by the court that such silence is evidence of guilt.

Reversed.*

The Chief Justice took no part in the decision of this case.

[The concurring opinon of Mr. Justice Harlan is omitted.]

Mr. Justice Stewart, with whom Mr. Justice White joins, dissenting.

* * *

We must determine whether the petitioner has been "compelled * * * to be a witness against himself." Compulsion is the focus of the inquiry. * * *

* * * [T]he lurid realities which lay behind enactment of the Fifth Amendment [are] a far cry from the subject matter of the case before us. I think that the Court in this case stretches the concept of compulsion beyond all reasonable bounds, and that whatever compulsion may exist derives from the defendant's choice not to testify, not from any comment by court or counsel. * * *

* * *

firmative. A fifth member of the Court, Justice Frankfurter, stated in a separate opinion: "For historical reasons a limited immunity from the common duty to testify was written into the Federal Bill of Rights, and I am prepared to agree that, as part of that immunity, comment on the failure of an accused to take the witness stand is forbidden in federal prosecutions." Id., p. 61, 67 S.Ct., p. 1680. But, though he agreed with the dissenters on this point, he also agreed with Justices Vinson, Reed, Jackson, and Burton that the Fourteenth Amendment did not make the Self-Incrimination Clause of the Fifth Amendment applicable to the States; thus he joined the opinion of the Court which so held (the Court's opinion assumed that the Fifth Amendment barred comment, but it expressly disclaimed any intention to decide the point. Id., p. 50, 67 S.Ct., p. 1674).

*See also Fontaine v. California, 390 U.S. 593, 88 S.Ct. 1229 [20 L.Ed.2d 154] (1968) (comments on defendant's failure to testify not "harmless beyond a reasonable doubt.")

STATE v. DISTRICT COURT OF FOURTH JUDICIAL DISTRICT

Supreme Court of Wyoming, 1967.
426 P.2d 431.

Before GRAY, McINTYRE, and PARKER, JJ.

Mr. Justice McINTYRE delivered the opinion of the court.

This is an original proceeding in which Velma Moore Sheehan asks the supreme court to prohibit the district court of Johnson County, Fourth Judicial District, and district judge John P. Ilsley from proceeding further in connection with a civil action lodged against her in that court. The petitioner is one of three joint executors of the estate of Thomas C. Moore, deceased, her former husband. The other two joint executors are brothers of the deceased.

It is the claim of petitioner that she, while a resident of California and a nonresident of Wyoming, made application to the probate court of Johnson County for a widow's allowance; that she came to Wyoming as a witness to testify in behalf of her application; and that when she entered the courthouse of Johnson County for that purpose she was served with a summons requiring her to answer to a civil action brought by the two brothers of decedent. The brothers brought the action as co-executors of the estate of Thomas C. Moore, deceased, and as next friends of Jock Moore and Bret Moore, the minor children of deceased and petitioner. Such action was initiated July 26, 1966, in the district court of Johnson County as Civil No. 3927.

According to an amended complaint the plaintiffs, in their action against Mrs. Sheehan, are alleging in a first count that she unlawfully caused or procured her husband Moore's life to be taken by David R. M. Martin, who has been convicted of the murder of Thomas C. Moore. This count shows the cause of action therein asserted is based upon § 2–46, W.S.1957, and brought under the Uniform Declaratory Judgments Act, §§ 1–1049 to 1–1064, W.S.1957. A second count of the amended complaint alleges that Velma Moore Sheehan is liable in damages for the wrongful death of her husband Moore.

The prayer of the amended complaint is for a declaratory judgment that Velma Moore Sheehan is not entitled to inherit or take by devise or legacy any portion of the estate of Thomas C. Moore, nor retain any portion of the proceeds of any life insurance policy, nor take any other benefits arising upon the death of Thomas C. Moore. Also, judgment against the defendant is asked for the wrongful death of decedent.

[The court held there was jurisdiction of the person and subject matter, and therefore no basis for prohibition.]

* * *

Petitioner seems to be fearful that if a civil court tries the issues asserted in plaintiffs' complaint, she will suffer a lack of due process and denial of certain constitutional rights, in particular the right not to be compelled to testify against herself. She overlooks the fact, however, that constitutional guarantees and immunities are just as binding on civil courts as they are on criminal courts. She can therefore expect the civil court which tries the issues involved in civil case No. 3927 to be zealous in the protection of all her rights, and to see that she and plaintiffs also are afforded due process of law.

It is apparent from the papers before us that Mrs. Sheehan has already elected, in an attempted deposition, not to testify in this case for the reason that her testimony might tend to incriminate her. In view of this election, we think it would be improper for plaintiffs in the district court action to make any further attempt, in the presence of a jury, to call Mrs. Sheehan as a witness—unless she first opens the door herself and waives her immunity from testifying.

We also think it would be improper for plaintiffs or their attorneys to make any comment to a jury, which would directly or indirectly convey knowledge of the defendant's election, under her constitutional immunity, not to testify. Any violation of these rights on the part of defendant, by plaintiffs or their attorneys, might indeed cause a mistrial.

Of course, we are not unmindful that our rules of civil procedure give the right for a party in a civil action to call an adverse party for cross-examination. But constitutional provisions and guarantees necessarily supersede and override conflicting statutory provisions and rules, and in this instance the right of the defendant to be protected in the election she has already made supersedes the right of plaintiffs to call her as a witness.

* * *

[Prohibition denied.]

NOTE

[The following letter requesting a change in the California Evidence Code was written by Robert E. Hinerfeld, a Los Angeles attorney, to the California Law Revision Commission. Reprinted by permission.—Eds.]

In a recent civil action undertaken by this firm an interesting problem, apparently of first impression, was presented under the new California Evidence Code. The action was one for extrinsic fraud brought by a divorced wife against her former husband in which she claimed that in the settlement of their divorce case he had concealed from her the existence of certain community property in which she had an interest. On behalf of the plaintiff ex-wife, we served a set of 83 interrogatories on counsel for the husband. The husband's reply was to answer the first and second questions (his name and address) and to decline to answer the remaining 81 questions on the grounds that the answers to the questions might tend to incriminate him. The questions concerned his property holdings during and after the marriage.

We brought on a motion to compel answers to the interrogatories, contending that a bare refusal to answer them on the grounds of the privilege against compulsory self-incrimination was insufficient, especially without a detailed attempt by the questioned party to explain, question by question, how an answer to each question might tend to incriminate him. In response to our motion, the husband's counsel filed his declaration in support of the refusal to answer, stating in substance that his client was then under investigation by the Intelligence Division of the Internal Revenue Service for possible criminal violations of the Internal Revenue laws. We rejoined with the contention that the husband had waived his Fifth Amendment privilege by filing a verified answer to our complaint and alleging in the answer by various items of affirmative matter, including certain allegations responsive to the allegations in the complaint, to the effect that he had recovered a tax refund on account of tax years during the period of the marriage and had failed to divide that refund with the plaintiff.

The legal problem presented by the Evidence code arises under § 913 (a) which prohibits comment on, and adverse inference being drawn from, the exercise of any privilege covered by Division 8 of the Code, § 940, which incorporates into the Code the privilege against compulsory self-incrimination under the Constitution of the United States and the law of the State of California. We pointed out to the trial court that if it sustained the husband's claim of the privilege, § 913 (a) of the Evidence Code might have the effect of preventing any sanctions from being imposed against the defendant husband despite the sanction procedures authorized by Code of Civil Procedure § 2034.* The court indicated that it recognized the problem and that no ultimate solution was available in the face of the existing statutes. The court's resolution of the problem is reflected in the enclosed copy of a minute order** on the motion. The order amounts to a compromise of interests which is probably not a solution of the problem but may be the most that is permitted under the existing law.

The ruling is less than satisfactory to the plaintiff because it does not prohibit the defendant ex-husband from offering evidence other than his own testimony in support of his verified answer. In addition, the ruling does not in any way prohibit the husband, who is the manager of the community property owing fiduciary obligations to his wife, from freely concealing property in which the wife has an interest, thereby preventing her from obtaining any evidence which would tend to establish her property rights in a divorce action.

Indeed, if a subsequent motion, under Code of Civil Procedure § 2034 to strike the entirety of the defendant ex-husband's answer, were granted, the plaintiff ex-wife might be deprived of any opportunity to produce affirmative evidence in support of her complaint, which evidence may be exclusively within the knowledge of the defendant.

---

*This section authorizes sanctions for failure to make discovery.

**The court's opinion is as follows:

Later: Motion to compel further response is granted as to interrogatory # 3 and denied as to all others on the basis of defendant's claim of privilege against self incrimination. The court recognizes that in the event that defendant should elect to waive his privilege by testimony at the time of trial plaintiff should then be entitled to a continuance to pursue discovery. The court therefore, in the interest of control of its calendar, and of the ordinary process of this litigation, orders that defendant shall not be permitted to testify at the time of trial as to any matter concerning which the privilege of self incrimination has been claimed in resistance to this motion unless at least 60 days prior to pretrial hearing—or 90 days prior to trial if pretrial is waived—defendant shall have served and filed full and complete answers to the interrogatories which are the subject of this motion without further objection.

Motion for sanctions is denied.

Plaintiff may file and serve further interrogatories consistent with this order.

Compare Christenson v. Christenson, 281 Minn. 507, 162 N.W.2d 194 (1968) (plaintiff in a civil action must either waive the privilege against self-incrimination or become subject to dismissal of the action).

If the wife, or former wife, is barred by the Fifth Amendment privilege against compulsory self-incrimination from cross-examining the manager, or former manager, of the marital community, § 913 (a) of the Evidence Code may have the effect of substantially expropriating an innocent wife.

With the facts of this case in mind, it is our belief that the Law Revision Commission should consider the desirability of amending Evidence Code § 913 (a) to exclude from its scope in a civil action or proceeding the privilege against compulsory self-incrimination under Evidence Code § 940. Otherwise, in certain civil proceedings such as the instant one, the privilege against compulsory self-incrimination can be utilized by a malefactor as a sword rather than simply as a shield. Where information is peculiarly within the knowledge of one party to a civil action and pretrial discovery is effectively barred to the opposing party by reason of the Fifth Amendment, Evidence Code § 913 (a) in its present form can well have the unintended result of utterly destroying a plaintiff's cause of action.*

NOTE

The Supreme Court in Baxter v. Palmigiano, 425 U.S. 308, 96 S.Ct. 1551, 47 L.Ed.2d 810 (1976) declined to extend the *Griffin* rule to disciplinary proceedings in State prisons:

> Our conclusion is consistent with the prevailing rule that the Fifth Amendment does not forbid adverse inferences against parties to civil actions when they refuse to testify in response to probative evidence offered against them: the Amendment "does not preclude the inference where the privilege is claimed by a party to a *civil cause.*" 8 J. Wigmore, Evidence 439 (McNaughton rev. 1961). In criminal cases, where the stakes are higher and the State's sole interest is to convict, *Griffin* prohibits the judge and prosecutor from suggesting to the jury that it may treat the defendant's silence as substantive evidence of guilt. Disciplinary proceedings in state prisons, however, involve the correctional process and important state interests other than conviction for crime. We decline to extend the *Griffin* rule to this context. (425 U.S. at 318–319).

ALLEN v. SUPERIOR COURT

Supreme Court of California, 1976.
18 Cal. 3d 520, 134 Cal. Rptr. 774, 557 P.2d 65.

WRIGHT, Chief Justice.

Charles Allen seeks a writ of prohibition to restrain respondent court from enforcing an order compelling disclosure of the names of prospective defense witnesses in criminal proceedings pending against him. On the day set for commencement of petitioner's trial respondent court on its own motion ordered both the People and petitioner to disclose the names of their prospective witnesses. The court intended that those names would be read to potential jurors to ascertain whether any of them was acquainted with such prospective witnesses. The court advised counsel that those named would not be described to the jurors as defense or prosecution witnesses. The court also proposed to enjoin the People from contacting any individual named by the defense until the name of such person was otherwise disclosed during the course of the trial. Petitioner refused to reveal the names of his prospective witnesses and sought the instant relief.

Compare Christenson v. Christenson, 281 Minn. 507, 162 N.W.2d 194 (1968).

Petitioner contends that the disclosure sought by the foregoing order would violate his constitutional right against self-incrimination. * * * We have concluded that the court erred in ordering disclosure of prospective defense witnesses, and herewith issue our peremptory writ of prohibition.

* * *

In Prudhomme v. Superior Court (1970) 2 Cal.3d 320, 85 Cal. Rptr. 129, 466 P.2d 673 we concluded that the principal element in determining whether a compelled disclosure should be allowed is "whether disclosure thereof conceivably might lighten the prosecution's burden of proving its case in chief." (Id., at p. 326 [85 Cal. Rptr at p. 133, 466 P.2d at p. 677].) We observed that "in ruling upon a claim of privilege, the trial court must find that it clearly appears from a consideration of all the circumstances in the case that an answer to the challenged question cannot possibly have a tendency to incriminate the witness. [Citations.]" (Id., at p. 326 [85 Cal. Rptr. at p. 133, 466 P.2d at p. 677].)

The People and amicus curiae, arguing that *Prudhomme* is not in accord with subsequent United States Supreme Court decisions, urge that we reexamine our holding therein.

There are no decisions of the United States Supreme Court in direct conflict with *Prudhomme.* Nevertheless, we are mindful that the trend of the federal high court's decisions on questions of compelled defense disclosure to the prosecution is not wholly consistent with our interpretation of the privilege against self-incrimination. (See United States v. Nobles (1975) 422 U.S. 225, 95 S.Ct. 2160, 45 L.Ed.2d 141; Williams v. Florida (1970) 399 U.S. 78, 90 S.Ct. 1893, 26 L.Ed.2d 446.)[1]

Petitioner's claim of a violation of his privilege against self-incrimination is based on the Fifth and Fourteenth Amendments as well as state constitutional grounds. (Cal. Const., art. I, § 15.)[2] It is established that our Constitution is "a document of independent force" "whose construction is left to this court, informed but untrammeled by the United States Supreme Court's reading of parallel federal provisions. [Citations.]"

In [Reynolds v. Superior Court, 12 Cal. 3d 834, 117 Cal. Rptr. 437, 528 P.2d. 45 (1974).] we noted that "*Prudhomme* put this court on record as being considerably more solicitous of the privilege against self-incrimination than federal law currently requires." (Id., at p. 843 [117 Cal. Rptr. at 442, 528 P.2d at p. 50].) We maintain that solicitude and affirm the continued vitality of the stringent standards set forth in *Prudhomme* for the protection of the privilege against self-incrimination as embodied in article I, section 15.

The People and amici further contend that the state interest in securing a trial by an unbiased jury and avoiding the possibility of a disrupted trial is sufficient to permit the limited disclosure at time of trial of informa-

1. In *Nobles* the court held that the privilege is personal, and consequently upheld a trial court order compelling defendant to disclose portions of a defense investigator's report of statements taken from prosecution witnesses. In *Williams* the court upheld a Florida notice-of-alibi statute stressing that there would be no constitutional bar to the prosecutor's being granted a con- tinuance following the unanticipated presentation of alibi evidence.

2. Article I, section 15 provides in pertinent part: "['] * * * Persons may not * * * be compelled in a criminal cause to be a witness against themselves * * * ."

tion which defendent intends to disclose subsequently during the trial. This proposition suggests a balancing test in which the state's interest is weighed against and may offset the accused's interest in the risk of self-incrimination. The *Prudhomme* standard leaves no room for a balancing of interest. That standard plainly proscribes compelled defense disclosures which "*conceivably might lighten* the prosecution's burden of proving its case in chief." (Prudhomme v. Superior Court, supra, 2 Cal.3d 320, 326 [85 Cal. Rptr. 129, 133, 466 P.2d 673, 677]; italics added.) A disclosure order which fails to meet that standard is constitutionally impermissible.

Our conclusion in this regard should not be construed as demeaning the importance of the state interests. It should be noted, however, that these interests may be served by other measures not likely to infringe upon the privilege against self-incrimination. For example the names of the prospective witnesses might be read to the jurors prior to trial in the absence of counsel of both parties, or alternate jurors may be designated to substitute for any juror whose relationship with a witness is made known when such witness is called during trial. In any case where a relationship is indicated which suggests a possible conflict or bias voir dire would be feasible without the untimely disclosure to the prosecution of the names of prospective defense witnesses.

It is of no significance that while *Prudhomme* involved a trial court discovery order requiring disclosure to the prosecution of the names, addresses and expected testimony of defense witnesses, the instant order arose *sua sponte* and was not initiated by a motion for prosecutorial discovery. "[T]he privilege forbids *compelled* disclosures * * * " (id., at p. 326, [85 Cal. Rptr. at p. 133, 466 P.2d at p. 677] italics added) regardless of the form which the compulsion takes. Thus, the propriety of the court's order must be determined under the test articulated in *Prudhomme*.[3]

Applying that test to the order of the court below, we find that it does not clearly appear that the disclosure sought to be compelled cannot possibly have a tendency to incriminate petitioner. The trial judge did not make the careful inquiry which we mandated in *Prudhomme*. Moreover, the fact that the People would be enjoined from contacting defense witnesses until their names were otherwise revealed would not preclude investigation of other matters suggested by the names of the witnesses.[4] In *Prudhomme* we noted: "It requires no great effort or imagination to conceive of a variety of

3. It is also irrelevant that *Prudhomme* dealt with pretrial discovery, while the instant case involves disclosure at trial. In a companion case to *Prudhomme*, Bradshaw v. Superior Court (1970) 2 Cal.3d 332 [85 Cal.Rptr. 136, 466 P.2d 680] we rejected that portion of a discovery order which required defense disclosure of witnesses within 24 hours of expected use. We observed that "If the evidence might possibly incriminate petitioners, they cannot be compelled to disclose it at any time prior to its actual use at trial." (Id., at p. 333 [85 Cal.Rptr. at p. 137, 466 P.2d at p. 681] fn. 3.)

4. For example, if the defense witnesses identified are friends or relatives of an accused, the prosecution can anticipate an alibi defense; if police officers the defense of entrapment can be projected. The trial judge's qualification of the instant order in no way prevents the People from investigating the background of the designated witnesses or questioning their friends or acquaintances. Such investigation may reveal the details of the alibi or other defenses, or may yield other evidence useful to the prosecution including impeachment witnesses, inconsistent statements, and admissible evidence of specific instances of misconduct by the prospective witnesses.

situations wherein the disclosure of the expected testimony of defense witnesses *or even their names and addresses,* could easily provide an essential
link in a chain of evidence underlying the prosecution's case in chief."
(Prudhomme v. Superior Court, supra, 2 Cal.3d 320, 326; italics added.)
The possibility of self-incrimination is in no measure diminished by the
omission of addresses in the instant order since names lead directly and easily to addresses.

We conclude, therefore, that the disclosure order of respondent court
fails to satisfy the standards established in *Prudhomme* to secure the privilege against self-incrimination as set forth in article I, section 15 of the California Constitution.

Let a peremptory writ of prohibition issue restraining respondent court
from enforcing the disclosure order challenged herein.

Tobriner, J., and Mosk, J., concurred. [Concurring opinion of Sullivan,
J., omitted.]

* * *

RICHARDSON, Justice (dissenting).

I respectfully dissent, finding that my position in this case lies at a
point roughly midway between that of the majority and that of the dissent.
On the one hand, the majority reaffirm the strict standard imposed by
Prudhomme v. Superior Court (1970) 2 Cal.3d 320, 85 Cal.Rptr. 129, 466
P.2d 673, and, disregarding recent important federal Supreme Court hold-
ings, rest their decision exclusively upon the self-incrimination clause of the
California Constitution. On the other hand, the dissent would overrule
Prudhomme outright and embrace the conclusions of the United States Su-
preme Court in Williams v. Florida (1970) 399 U.S. 78 [90 S.Ct. 1893, 26
L.Ed.2d 446] and United States v. Nobles (1975) 422 U.S. 225 [95 S.Ct.
2160, 45 L.Ed.2d 141], decisions which interpret the self-incrimination
clause of the United States Constitution.

In my view, there are no easy answers to the thorny questions posed
herein. Only the most careful balancing of the respective interests of the defendant, the prosecution and the courts will enable us to chart a wise and
prudent course between the rigid strictures of *Prudhomme* and the expansive new principles announced in *Williams/Nobles.* I suggest the need
for a somewhat more extended analysis of this troublesome and complex issue. Although *Prudhomme* may indeed afford a satisfactory solution, we
should test that premise by a serious and thoughtful reconsideration of that
case in light of the subsequent and very significant holdings of the United
States Supreme Court.

* * * Relying upon what then appeared to be the federal trend, we
adopted in *Prudhomme* a cautious approach to the question of prosecutorial
discovery and determined that all such discovery should be denied if any
possible risk of self-incrimination existed.

Within a few weeks after *Prudhomme* was filed, the United States Supreme Court decided Williams v. Florida, supra, 399 U.S. 78, 90 S.Ct. 1893,
26 L.Ed.2d 446, which, by a vote of six to two, upheld Florida's "notice-of-alibi" statute. With respect to prosecutorial discovery in general, the
high court in *Williams* noted the state's "obvious and legitimate" interest
in protecting itself against an "eleventh-hour defense." "The adversary sys-

tem of trial," the court then observed, "is hardly an end in itself; it is not yet a poker game in which players enjoy an absolute right always to conceal their cards until played." (*Williams,* supra, at pp. 81-82, [90 S.Ct. at p. 1896, 26 L.Ed.2d at pp. 449-450] fn. omitted. Since a defendant has a free choice whether or not to rely upon an alibi defense, advance disclosure of facts concerning that defense cannot be considered "compelled" within the meaning of the Fifth Amendment. At most, the high court reasoned, the pretrial disclosure rule merely accelerates the *timing* of defendant's disclosure of information he has already chosen to divulge. (Id., at pp. 85-86 [90 S.Ct. 1893, 26 L.Ed.2d at pp. 452-453].)

Following *Williams,* the Supreme Court in United States v. Nobles, supra, 422 U.S. 225, [95 S.Ct. 2160, 45 L.Ed.2d 141] *unanimously* held that a defendant could be required to furnish the prosecution, after completion of the case in chief, with relevant portions of an investigator's report containing statements made by prosecution witnesses. The high court reasoned that the privilege against self-incrimination "is an 'intimate and personal one,' " which " 'adheres basically to the person, not to information that may incriminate him.' " (Id., at p. 233 [95 S.Ct. at p. 2167, 45 L.Ed.2d at pp. 150-151].) Since the report at issue contained only statements of third party witnesses, the privilege against self-incrimination was held to be inapplicable.

The "acceleration" rule enunciated in *Williams* and the "personal privilege" reasoning of *Nobles* clearly would permit prosecutorial discovery in certain instances where it is not available under the strict *Prudhomme* standard. Therefore, to the extent that our assessment of federal law determined the outcome in *Prudhomme,* the rationale of the case and indeed its validity have been manifestly and severely undercut. Its federal underpinnings sheared away, *Prudhomme* has now become a rule in search of a reason.

The majority, sensing this structural weakness, believe that the California Constitution supplies a new and sturdy foundation, as it contains (in art. I, § 15) a guarantee against compelled self-incrimination in language substantially identical to that of the Fifth Amendment self-incrimination clause. I adhere to, and reexpress without elaboration, the view that in the absence of strong countervailing circumstances or demonstrable policy reasons, " * * * we should defer to the leadership of the nation's highest court in its interpretation of nearly identical constitutional language, rather than attempt to create a separate echelon of state constitutional interpretations * * * ." (People v. Disbrow (1976) 16 Cal.3d 101, 119 [127 Cal.Rptr. 360, 372, 545 P.2d 272, 284], dis. opn. of Richardson, J.) * * * I do not think, in blindly repeating the *Prudhomme* rule which we ourselves posited in large part on what we then understood were "developments in the [federal] law," that we can or should so blithely ignore these very recent decisions of the United States Supreme Court, one of them the unanimous opinion of the highest court in the land.

I am equally disturbed, however, by the cursory treatment which the majority afford our own California law. At the time the *Prudhomme* rule was adopted, we thought we had no reasonable alternative under federal law. It is now clear that alternatives are available; but the majority inexplicably decline even to consider them. They choose simply to lift

Prudhomme from its crumbling federal foundations and resettle it on the sheltered ground of the California Constitution without considering the arguably nontestimonial nature of the material sought, and without discussion, analysis, policy exposition or indeed anything but an unamplified avowal of "solicitude * * * for the protection of the privilege against self-incrimination as embodied in article I, section 15." (Ante, p. 776 of 134 Cal.Rptr., p. 67 of 557 P.2d.) I respectfully suggest that the problem of prosecutorial discovery deserves a thoughtful and deliberative explication.

I do not necessarily advocate that *Prudhomme* be overruled and the federal approach adopted in its entirety. Indeed, we might be persuaded, after a careful consideration of the issues, that the wiser course in this instance is to adhere to a standard more restrictive than the relatively broad sweep of the federal cases. I am not as confident as the *Williams* majority, for instance, that the timing of defense disclosures is necessarily an inconsequential matter, nor am I convinced of the propriety of compelling a defendant, as in *Nobles,* to make pretrial disclosure of information that he does not intend to use at trial. I do, however, advocate a reexamination of a judicial rule which, as the majority interpret it, will effectively bar *all* prosecution discovery. (Today's decision implicitly disapproves even those few appellate cases in which some limited prosecutorial discovery has been permitted; see People v. Wiley (1976) 57 Cal.App.3d 149 [129 Cal.Rptr. 13]; People v. Ayers (1975) 51 Cal.App.3d 370 [124 Cal.Rptr. 283].) The possibility of a middle ground should at least be explored, and both the course and the result of that inquiry openly described.

The case before us presents a factual matrix very well adapted to such an analysis. The trial court's order required that petitioner produce, on the date set for trial, a list of defense witnesses. The names disclosed were then to be intermixed with those of prosecution witnesses and the entire list read to the jury to determine if any disqualifying connection existed between a juror and a witness, thereby avoiding the delay and disruption attendant upon a subsequent discovery of such disqualification. The trial judge offered to couple the initial order with a second one prohibiting the prosecution from contacting any defense witness before that witness was actually called to the stand.

First, it is clear from the record that petitioner advanced no claim that any *actual* and *substantial* possibility of incrimination existed; he challenged the order on the sole ground that it was in effect a form of prosecution discovery and as such was barred by *Prudhomme. Prudhomme* places upon the trial judge the burden of "determining that under the facts and circumstances in the case before him it clearly appears that disclosure *cannot possibly* tend to incriminate defendant." (Prudhomme v. Superior Court, supra, 2 Cal.3d at p. 327, [85 Cal.Rptr. at p. 134, 466 P.2d at 678] italics added.) The task imposed in such a situation upon the trial court is difficult enough at best. It should not have to speculate or hypothesize.

Even if it were necessary to indulge in conjecture, however, I have difficulty finding in the facts of this case any risk of self-incrimination. The effect of the orders was to require petitioner to disclose only facts he intented to make public within a day or two anyway. The prosecution was permitted to garner such new information as might be available about the defense witnesses only after completion of the state's case in chief. Advance disclosure of the names of prospective witnesses could at the most provide the prosecution with the barest indication of potential defenses. For example, a list of witnesses containing the names of petitioner's friends or relatives might suggest an alibi defense. It may, on the other hand, signal only routine character evidence. Names of police officers might suggest that petitioner planned to plead entrapment—an argument so predictable that any prudent prosecutor would have anticipated and prepared for it if the facts surrounding the arrest could possibly support such an interpretation.

It is conceivable, of course, that petitioner had located an eyewitness, as yet unknown to the prosecution, whose testimony was generally favorable to the defense but perhaps equivocal enough to supply the prosecution with a lead or suggest a fruitful line of inquiry. (Petitioner herein made no such assertion.) Even under such unlikely circumstances, compliance with the court order at issue here could hardly have created any substantial risk. At petitioner's request, the district attorney would have been barred by a parallel order from questioning or even contacting any defense witness who had not yet been called to the stand. Thus the prosecutor would have learned the substance of the alibi, the basis of the entrapment argument, the nature of the eyewitness' evidence, in precisely the same way and at the same time he would have if there had been no disclosure order—from the lips of defense witnesses when testifying on the stand. The prosecution, it is true, would gain a few additional days in which to investigate (as distinguished from questioning) potential defense witnesses, and to accumulate material bearing generally on credibility for impeachment purposes. I see nothing wrong with this. The alternative is either to grant a continuance to the prosecution with the resultant delay or to force the prosecution to proceed without the benefit of potential impeaching evidence. The conduct of a trial is a search for the truth. The state's ultimate burden of producing evidence sufficient for conviction is in no way lightened.

We need not repudiate the basic *Prudhomme* principle to uphold the disclosure order in this case, when even the freest speculation yields little to support any fear of self-incrimination. The majority, however, not only hold that the order in the present case is inconsistent with article I, section 15, but pronounce, by reflex, a rule of unlimited extremity: "The *Prudhomme* standard leaves no room for a balancing of interest." * * * Under this sweeping, all-encompassing pronouncement, evidently any free-floating hypothetical risk, no matter how remote, how tenuously related to the facts of the particular case, will bar all prosecutorial discovery. This approach is neither wise nor necessary.

* * *

It may fairly be said that we pioneered the development of liberal rules of discovery by the defendant. It is ironic that the majority now turn their backs upon the modern trend toward even a limited prosecutorial discovery without either full or fair discussion of the alternatives. Sometime ago former Chief Justice Traynor reminded us that since discovery serves " * * * to promote the orderly ascertainment of the truth * * * [t]hat procedure should not be a one-way street." (Jones v. Superior Court, supra, 58 Cal.2d at p. 60 [22 Cal.Rptr. at p. 881, 372 P.2d at p. 921].) The majority now reject this salutary observation, and erect artificial barriers preventing two-way passage on the street. They thereby assure that criminal discovery instead of constituting that "orderly ascertainment of the truth" remains, in effect, the poker game in which one player—the defendant—has "an absolute right always to conceal * * * [his] cards until played." (Williams v. Florida, supra, 399 U.S. at p. 82 [90 S.Ct. at 1896, 26 L.Ed. 2d at p. 450].)

I would deny the writ.

Clark, J., Dissenting.

Candor requires we correct the mistake of Prudhomme v. Superior Court * * *

I would deny the writ.

McComb, J., concurred.

TRAVER, ANATOMY OF A MURDER

Part One, Chapter 24, pp. 155–57 (1958).*

"That's one of the things I've been mulling over, Paul," Parnell said. "You know, of course, that under the statute we must serve timely notice on the prosecution of our intention to claim the defense of insanity and at least four days before the trial. When do you propose to serve that notice, boy? Time's a-flyin'."

"That problem's been bothering me most all night, Parn—ever since I read that damned letter. Up to now I've been putting off serving the notice for several reasons: till I saw we could actually get a psychiatrist; then with the vague idea of not tipping our hand to the other side any sooner than we had to; and also to possibly prevent or delay the People from sicking their own rebuttal psychiatrists on our man." I paused. "I'm glad you raised the subject because I've just about made up my mind that we should serve the notice now—today—and let the chips fall where they may. What do you think?"

"But won't that do just what you're trying to avoid?" Parnell said thoughfully. "Tip off our defense and give the other side a longer psychiatric crack at him, as it were? Mind, now, I'm not objectin', boy; I'm merely tryin' to test your thinkin'—our little game, you know. I'm listenin'."

So Parnell and I were away again, endlessly debating the pros and cons of our strategy for the fast approaching trial. I pointed out that if we delayed the serving of our notice this might in itself give the People their grounds for a continuance since Mitch could then argue that he needed additional time in which to obtain a decent rebuttal psychiatric examination. Parnell agreed and then raised the question of whether the People could ever get to examine our man.

"It's a little brainstorm I had during the night," he added.

"What do you mean?" I said. "Surely you're familiar with the procedure that permits a prosecutor in felony cases to file a petition with the Court suggesting insanity and asking for a psychiatric examination and sanity hearing? The moment we file our notice of insanity Mitch can petition

*St. Martin's Press, N.Y. Copyright, 1958 by Robert Traver.

the court—on the sole ground that we've thereby furnished him—that the defendant *may* have been insane (he needn't admit it), and hence get to paw over our man."

Parnell grinned evilly. "I'm aware of that procedure, boy," he said. "I have it fully in mind. If and when such a petition is filed we'll simply tell our man to clam up and tell the People's psychiatrist to go fly a kite. He simply won't play."

I figeted uneasily. "You mean, Parn, we'd tell Lieutenant Manion not to let the People's psychiatrist have at him?"

"Not only tell him not to let them examine him—but not even talk with them," he said. "I mean our man will tell 'em all to go plumb to hell."

"But how can you expect to get away with it, Parn? That procedure's on the law books, man, and has been for years. Won't I risk being jailed for contempt or something?"

"We'll chance it," Parnell replied. "There are a lot of rusty old things in the law and on the law books, boy, that couldn't stand up for five minutes if their constitutionality were seriously challenged. Nearly every new supreme court report that comes out has at least one shining example. The Legislature's forever getting some unconstitutional bug in its britches, and I think this old law is one of them. I've had my droopy eye on this statute for years and in my opinion it isn't worth the paper it's written on. Constitutionally, I mean."

"I'm beginning to see," I murmured. "I'm beginning to see * * * "

"Don't you see," Parnell went on, warming to his subject, "one of the basic provisions of both the State and Federal constitutions is that no man shall be compelled to testify against himself in any criminal case. That's of course the Fifth Amendment—the very one that's getting to be such a dirty word these days in certain sturdy flag-waving quarters. * * * "

"Let's not get on that now, Parn," I said, rolling up my eyes.

Parnell had awakened during the night with the whole argument laid out cold. "I must have put a nickel in me subconscious." If any statute or procedure purported to *force* a person charged with crime to submit to a hostile psychiatric examination, wasn't it thereby unconstitutional and bad?

"Hm," I mused, over the bold soundness of the old man's vision. "But supposing the good judge overrules all our fine constitutional arguments? Either we appeal—which is tantamount to a People's continuance—or the other side still gets its examination."

Parnell grinned and shook his head. "No, boy. No such thing. If the judge rules against us our man still tells 'em all to go to hell. And if he tells them that what're they going to do? The Judge, Mitch, the Doctor, anyone? If our man simply won't talk *who's* going to make him talk? They can't threaten to jail *him* for contempt, the poor bastard's already there. And you're in the clear, Polly. You co-operated. And what kind of a psychiatric examination would they have if he wouldn't play ball? The whole procedure of psychoanalysis, to be effective, presumes ardent co-operation from the subject; hence the overstuffed couch."

NOTE

Is an acccused whose defense is insanity denied his privilege against self-incrimination by compulsory examination by a court-appointed psychiatrist? In State v. Olson, 274 Minn. 225, 143 N.W.2d 69 (1966), the court held:

> We conclude that since there are no statutes in this state governing the procedure in cases where the accused pleads insanity as a defense and providing the necessary machinery and guidelines for the protection of the accused from self-incrimination, the courts have no legal basis, without the defendant's consent, for ordering an examination either to determine his mental condition at the time of the alleged criminal acts or to qualify an expert psychiatric witness by virtue of such examination to testify at trial.

Cf. People v. Combes, 56 Cal.2d 135, 149, 14 Cal.Rptr. 4, 363 P.2d 4 (1961) (West's Ann. Cal.Penal Code § 1007, providing for court appointment of alienists, does not require a defendant to be a witness against himself. Nothing in the section compels him to submit to an examination. If he does so the action is purely voluntary). But see State v. Marion County Criminal Court, 234 N.E.2d 636 (Ind.1968).

ARENS, THE DURHAM RULE IN ACTION
Judicial Psychiatry and Psychiatric Justice

1 Law and Society Review 41, 53 (1967)*

* * * Almost invariably an order for a mental examination entered by the District Court commits the criminal defendant to the diagnostic care and custody of St. Elizabeths Hospital. Even in the rare case in which the defendant has sufficient means to secure independent psychiatric examination, an order for his examination by the St. Elizabeths staff will usually be handed down by the court, and the defendant may be explicitly directed to cooperate with the St. Elizabeths physicians with the intimation that his lawyers may be cited for contempt if he does not.[28] * * *

KAMISAR, "EQUAL JUSTICE IN THE GATEHOUSES AND MANSIONS OF AMERICAN CRIMINAL PROCEDURE" IN CRIMINAL JUSTICE IN OUR TIME

25–32 (1965)*
(Ed. A.E. Dick Howard).
[Footnotes omitted.]

IS THE PRIVILEGE CHECKED AT THE "GATEHOUSE" DOOR?

Those who would not narrow the gap between the nobility of the principles we purport to cherish and the meanness of the station house proceedings we permit to continue may:

28. In United States v. John S. Sweeney, criminal case no. 466–60 (D.D.C. 1960) transcript of proceedings on December 16, 1960, the Government secured a court order directing a defendant, charged with murder, to cooperate with St. Elizabeths physicians on the ground that "it would be an intolerable situation if the Government should be deprived of the opportunity to ascertain the truth. * * * " In this context—since contempt proceedings against the defendant would be fatuous —Government counsel suggested that the defendant's lawyers would seem proper targets of criminal prosecution if they persisted in advising their client not to talk to Government physicians. See id. at 4–6.

1) Cite the language in the Fifth Amendment which forbids compelling any person "to be a witness against himself" "in any criminal case" and contend that in the police station the "criminal case" has not yet commenced. But it is hornbook law that the privilege extends to all judicial or official hearings where persons may be called upon to give testimony, even to civil proceedings.

2) Find some comfort in the assertion by the greatest master of the law of evidence, Wigmore, that the privilege against self-incrimination "covers only statements made in court under process as a witness." As other masters of the subject have pointed out, however, this is an "obviously inaccurate" statement; indeed it is in direct conflict with Wigmore's earlier declaration that the privilege applies "in investigations by a *grand jury*, in investigations by a *legislature* or a body having legislative functions, and in investigations by *administrative* officials."

3) Remind us (a) that the histories of the privilege and of the rule excluding "involuntary" confessions are "wide apart, differing by one hundred years in origin, and derived through separate lines of precedents"; "if the privilege, fully established by 1680, had sufficed for both classes of cases, there would have been no need for creating the distinct rule about confessions"; (b) that until recently, at any rate, the privilege has never been applicable to police interrogation and "all of the decisions admitting coerced statements of incriminating facts not amounting to a confession assume that the privilege is inapplicable, as does the constant recognition of the accepted police practice which, in the absence of statute, does not require that the accused be warned he need not answer."

Here, as elsewhere, to look to "history" is to see "through a screen of human values that gives importance to some antecedents and relegates others to obscurity"; is to be less impressed with historical facts "which do not fit into our theories * * * than [with] those that do."

For example, one who would apply the privilege to the police station may select, from the vast conglomerate of determinants which form its history, the fact that the maxim "no man shall be compelled to accuse himself" first meant (and until the seventeenth century probably only meant) that no man shall be compelled to make the *first charge* against himself, to submit to a "fishing" interrogation about his crimes, to furnish his own indictment from his own lips. Until the 1600's all parties concerned seemed to have operated on the premise that *after* pleading to the indictment, the accused could be compelled to incriminate himself.

Recent studies have disclosed that in Washington, D.C., in 1960, of 1,356 persons "arrested for investigation" and held for eight hours or more, only 1.2 per cent were ever formally charged, and that in Chicago in 1956, "50 per cent of the police prisoners produced in Felony Court [were] held without charge for 17 hours or longer" and "another 30 per cent could not be accounted for in terms of pre-booking detention because of police failure to complete the arrest slip." When we apply the privilege to "arrests for investigation" or "routine pickups," do we disguise a revolutionary idea in the garb of the past or do we restore the privilege to its primordial state?

Nor should it be forgotten that for many centuries there were simply no "police interrogators" to whom the privilege could be applied. Although what Dean Wigmore calls "the first part" of the history of the privilege, the opposition to the ex-officio oath of the ecclesiastical courts, began in the 1200's "criminal investigation by the police, with its concomitant of police interrogation, is a product of the late nineteenth century"; in eighteenth-century America as in eighteenth-century England "there were no police [in the modern sense] and, though some states seem to have had prosecutors, private prosecution was the rule rather than the exception." In fact as well as in theory, observes Professor Edmund M. Morgan, "there can be little question that the modern American police have taken over the functions performed originally by the English committing magistrates [and at least by some colonial magistrates]; they are in a real sense administrative officers and their questioning of the person under arrest is an investigative proceeding in which testimony is taken." If modern police are permitted to interrogate under the coercive influence of arrest and secret detention, then, insists Professor Albert R. Beisel, "they are doing the very same acts which historically the judiciary was doing in the seventeenth century but which the privilege against self-incrimination abolished."

I do not contend that "the implication[s] of a tangled and obscure history" dictate that the privilege apply to the police station, only that they permit it. I do not claim that this long and involved history displaces judgment, only that it liberates it. I do not say that the distinct origins of the confession and self-incrimination rules are irrelevant, only that it is more important (if we share Dean Charles T. McCormick's views) that "the kinship of the two rules is too apparent for denial" and that "such policy as modern writers are able to discover as a basis for the self-crimination privilege * * * pales to a flicker beside the flaming demands of justice and humanity for protection against extorted confessions."

Those who applaud the show in the mansion without hissing the show in the gatehouse may also:

4)   Find refuge in the notion that compulsion to testify means *legal* compulsion. Since he is threatened neither with perjury for testifying falsely nor contempt for refusing to testify at all, it cannot be said, runs the argument, that the man in the back room of the police station is being "compelled" to be a "witness against himself" within the meaning of the privilege. Since the police have no legal right to make him answer, "there is no legal obligation to which a privilege in the technical sense can apply."

Can we accept this analysis without forgetting as lawyers and judges what we know as men? Without permitting logic to triumph over life? So long as "what on their face are merely words of request take on color from the officer's uniform, badge, gun and demeanor"; so long as his interrogators neither advise him of his rights nor permit him to consult with a lawyer who will; can there be any doubt that many a "subject" will *assume* that the police have a legal right to an answer? That many an incriminating statement will be extracted under "color" of law? So long as the interrogator is instructed to "get the idea across * * * that [he] has 'all the time in the world' "; so long as "the power [legal or otherwise] to extract answers begets a forgetfulness of the just limitations of the power" and "the simple and peaceful process of questioning breeds a readiness to resort to bullying and to physical force"; can there be any doubt that many a subject will asume that there is an *extralegal* sanction for contumacy?

If these inferences are unfair, if very few "subjects" are misled to believe that there is either a legal obligation to talk or unlimited time and extralegal means available to make them do so—if, in short, they know they can "shut up"—why are the police so bent on preventing counsel from telling them what they already know? Why, at least, don't the officers themselves tell their "subjects" plainly and emphatically that they need not and cannot be made to answer? That they will be permitted to consult with counsel or be brought before a magistrate in short order? And why is the "subject" questioned in *secret?* Why does the modest proposal that a suspect be interrogated by or before an impartial functionary immediately after arrest "meet with scant favor in police circles, even from the most high-minded and highly respected elements in those circles?" * * *

MIRANDA v. ARIZONA

Supreme Court of the United States, 1966.
384 U.S. 436, 86 S.Ct. 1602, 1609–1618, 1655–1659, 16 L.Ed.2d 694.
[Most of the Court's footnotes are omitted.]

Mr. Chief Justice WARREN delivered the opinion of the Court.

The cases before us raise questions which go to the roots of our concepts of American criminal jurisprudence: the restraints society must observe consistent with the Federal Constitution in prosecuting individuals for crime. More specifically, we deal with the admissibility of statements obtained from an individual who is subjected to custodial police interrogation and the necessity for procedures which assure that the individual is accorded his privilege under the Fifth Amendment to the Constitution not to be compelled to incriminate himself.

* * *

Our holding will be spelled out with some specificity in the pages which follow but briefly stated it is this: the prosecution may not use statements, whether exculpatory or inculpatory, stemming from custodial interrogation of the defendant unless it demonstrates the use of procedural safeguards effective to secure the privilege against self-incrimination. By custodial interrogation, we mean questioning initiated by law enforcement officers after a person has been taken into custody or otherwise deprived of his freedom of action in any significant way.[4] As for the procedural safeguards to be employed, unless other fully effective means are devised to inform accused persons of their right of silence and to assure a continuous opportunity to exercise it, the following measures are required. Prior to any questioning, the person must be warned that he has a right to remain silent, that any statement he does make may be used as evidence against him, and that he has a right to the presence of an attorney, either retained or appointed. The defendant may waive effectuation of these rights, provided the waiver is made voluntarily, knowingly and intelligently. If, however, he indicates in any manner and at any stage of the process that he wishes to consult with an attorney before speaking there can be no questioning. Likewise, if the individ-

---

4. This what we meant in *Escobedo* when we spoke of an investigation which had focused on an accused.

ual is alone, and indicates in any manner that he does not wish to be interrogated, the police may not question him. There mere fact that he may have answered some questions or volunteered some statements on his own does not deprive him of the right to refrain from answering any further inquiries until he has consulted with an attorney and thereafter consents to be questioned.

I.

The constitutional issue we decide in each of these cases is the admissibility of statements obtained from a defendant questioned while in custody or otherwise deprived of his freedom of action in any significant way. In each, the defendant was questioned by police officers, detectives, or a prosecuting attorney in a room in which he was cut off from the outside world. In none of these cases was the defendant given a full and effective warning of his rights at the outset of the interrogation process. In all the cases, the questioning elicited oral admissions, and in three of them, signed statements as well which were admitted at their trials. They all thus share salient features—incommunicado interrogation of individuals in a police-dominated atmosphere, resulting in self-incriminating statements without full warnings of constitutional rights.

An understanding of the nature and setting of this in-custody interrogation is essential to our decisions today. The difficulty in depicting what transpires at such interrogations stems from the fact that in this country they have largely taken place incommunicado. From extensive factual studies undertaken in the early 1930's, including the famous Wickersham Report to Congress by a Presidential Commission, it is clear that police violence and the "third degree" flourished at that time. In a series of cases decided by this Court long after these studies, the police resorted to physical brutality—beatings, hanging, whipping—and to sustained and protracted questioning incommunicado in order to extort confessions. The Commission on Civil Rights in 1961 found much evidence to indicate that "some policemen still resort to physical force to obtain confessions," 1961 Comm'n on Civil Rights Rep., Justice, pt. 5, 17. The use of physical brutality and violence is not, unfortunately, relegated to the past or to any part of the country. Only recently in Kings County, New York, the police brutally beat, kicked and placed lighted cigarette butts on the back of a potential witness under interrogation for the purpose of securing a statement incriminating a third party. People v. Portelli, 15 N.Y.2d 235, 257 N.Y.S.2d 931, 205 N.E.2d 857 (1965).[7]

---

7.   In addition, see People v. Wakat, 415 Ill. 610, 114 N.E.2d 706 (1953); Wakat v. Harlib, 253 F.2d 59 (C.A. 7th Cir. 1958) (defendant suffering from broken bones, multiple bruises and injuries sufficiently serious to require eight months' medical treatment after being manhandled by five policemen); Kier v. State, 213 Md. 556, 132 A.2d 494 (1957) (police doctor told accused, who was strapped to a chair completely nude, that he proposed to take hair and skin scrapings from anything that looked like blood or sperm from various parts of his body); Bruner v. People, 113 Colo. 194, 156 P.2d 111 (1945) (defendant held in custody over two months, deprived of food for 15 hours, forced to submit to a lie detector test when he wanted to go to the toilet); People v. Matlock, 51 Cal.2d 682, 336 P.2d 505, 71 A.L.R.2d 605 (1959) (defendant questioned incessantly over an evening's time, made to lie on cold board and to answer questions whenever it appeared he was getting sleepy). Other cases are documented in American Civil Liberties Union, Illinois Division, Secret Detention by the Chicago Police (1959); Potts, The Preliminary Examination and "The Third Degree," 2 Baylor L.Rev. 131 (1950); Sterling, Police Interrogation and the Psychology of Confession, 14 J.Pub.L. 25 (1965).

The examples given above are undoubtedly the exception now, but they are sufficiently widespread to be the object of concern. Unless a proper limitation upon custodial interrogation is achieved—such as these decisions will advance—there can be no assurance that practices of this nature will be eradicated in the foreseeable future. The conclusion of the Wickersham Commission Report, made over 30 years ago, is still pertinent:

"To the contention that the third degree is necessary to get to the facts, the reporters aptly reply in the language of the present Lord Chancellor of England (Lord Sankey): 'It is not admissible to do a great right by doing a little wrong. * * * It is not sufficient to do justice by obtaining a proper result by irregular or improper means.' Not only does the use of the third degree involve a flagrant violation of law by the officers of the law, but it involves also the dangers of false confessions, and it tends to make police and prosecutors less zealous in the search for objective evidence. As the New York prosecutor quoted in the report said, 'It is a short cut and makes the police lazy and un-enterprising.' Or, as another official quoted remarked: 'If you use your fists, you are not so likely to use your wits.' We agree with the con-clusion expressed in the report, that 'The third degree brutalizes the police, hardens the prisoner against society, and lowers the esteem in which the administration of justice is held by the public.' " IV Na-tional Commission on Law Observance and Enforcement, Report on Lawlessness in Law Enforcement 5 (1931).

Again we stress that the modern practice of in-custody interrogation is psychologically rather than physically oriented. As we have stated before, "Since Chambers v. State of Florida, 309 U.S. 227, 60 S.Ct. 472, 84 L.Ed. 716, this Court has recognized that coercion can be mental as well as physi-cal, and that the blood of the accused is not the only hallmark of an un-constitutional inquisition." Blackburn v. State of Alabama, 361 U.S. 199, 206, 80 S.Ct. 274, 279, 4 L.Ed.2d 242 (1960). Interrogation still takes place in privacy. Privacy results in secrecy and this in turn results in a gap in our knowledge as to what in fact goes on in the interrogation rooms. A valuable source of information about present police practices, however, may be found in various police manuals and texts which document procedures em-ployed with success in the past, and which recommend various other effec-tive tactics. These texts are used by law enforcement agencies themselves as guides. It should be noted that these texts professedly present the most en-lightened and effective means presently used to obtain statements through custodial interrogation. By considering these texts and other data, it is pos-sible to describe procedures observed and noted around the country.

The officers are told by the manuals that the "principal psychological factor contributing to a successful interrogation is privacy—being alone with the person under interrogation." The efficacy of this tactic has been explained as follows:

"If at all practicable, the interrogation should take place in the investigator's office or at least in a room of his own choice. The subject should be deprived of every psychological advantage. In his own home he may be confident, indignant, or recalcitrant. He is more keenly aware of his rights and more reluctant to tell of his indiscretions or criminal behavior within the walls of his home. Moreover his family and other friends are nearby, their presence lending moral support. In his office, the investigator possesses all the advantages. The atmosphere suggests the invincibility of the forces of the law."

To highlight the isolation and unfamiliar surroundings, the manuals instruct the police to display an air of confidence in the suspect's guilt and from outward appearance to maintain only an interest in confirming certain details. The guilt of the subject is to be posited as a fact. The interrogator should direct his comments toward the reasons why the subject committed the act, rather than court failure by asking the subject whether he did it. Like other men, perhaps the subject has had a bad family life, had an unhappy childhood, had too much to drink, had an unrequited desire for women. The officers are instructed to minimize the moral seriousness of the offense, to cast blame on the victim or on society. These tactics are designed to put the subject in a psychological state where his story is but an elaboration of what the police purport to know already—that he is guilty. Explanations to the contrary are dismissed and discouraged.

The texts thus stress that the major qualities an interrogator should possess are patience and perseverance. One writer describes the efficacy of these characteristics in this manner:

"In the preceding paragraphs emphasis has been placed on kindness and stratagems. The investigator will, however, encounter many situations where the sheer weight of his personality will be the deciding factor. Where emotional appeals and tricks are employed to no avail, he must rely on an oppressive atmosphere of dogged persistence. He must interrogate steadily and without relent, leaving the subject no prospect of surcease. He must dominate his subject and overwhelm him with his inexorable will to obtain the truth. He should interrogate for a spell of several hours pausing only for the subject's necessities in acknowledgement of the need to avoid a charge of duress that can be technically substantiated. In a serious case, the interrogation may continue for days, with the required intervals for food and sleep, but with no respite from the atmosphere of domination. It is possible in this way to induce the subject to talk without resorting to duress or coercion. The method should be used only when the guilt of the subject appears highly probable."

The manuals suggest that the suspect be offered legal excuses for his actions in order to obtain an initial admission of guilt. Where there is a suspected revenge-killing, for example, the interrogator may say:

"Joe, you probably didn't go out looking for this fellow with the purpose of shooting him. My guess is, however, that you expected something from him and that's why you carried a gun—for your own protection. You knew him for what he was, no good. Then when you met him he probably started using foul, abusive language and he gave some indication that he was about to pull a gun on you, and that's when you had to act to save your own life. That's about it, isn't it, Joe?"

Having then obtained the admission of shooting, the interrogator is advised to refer to circumstantial evidence which negates the self-defense explanation. This should enable him to secure the entire story. One text notes that

"Even if he fails to do so, the inconsistency between the subject's original denial of the shooting and his present admission of at least doing the shooting will serve to deprive him of a self-defense 'out' at the time of trial."

When the techniques described above prove unavailing, the texts recommend they be alternated with a show of some hostility. One ploy often used has been termed the "friendly-unfriendly" or the "Mutt and Jeff" act:

" * * * In this technique, two agents are employed. Mutt, the relentless investigator, who knows the subject is guilty and is not going to waste any time. He's sent a dozen men away for this crime and he's going to send the subject away for the full term. Jeff, on the other hand, is obviously a kindhearted man. He has a family himself. He has a brother who was involved in a little scrape like this. He disapproves of Mutt and his tactics and will arrange to get him off the case if the subject will cooperate. He can't hold Mutt off for very long. The subject would be wise to make a quick decision. The technique is applied by having both investigators present while Mutt acts out his role. Jeff may stand by quietly and demur at some of Mutt's tactics. When Jeff makes his plea for cooperation, Mutt is not present in the room."[17]

The interrogators sometimes are instructed to induce a confession out of trickery. The technique here is quite effective in crimes which require identification or which run in series. In the identification situation, the interrogator may take a break in his questioning to place the subject among a group of men in a line-up. "The witness or complainant (previously coached, if necessary) studies the line-up and confidently points out the subject as the guilty party." Then the questioning resumes "as though there were now no doubt about the guilt of the subject." A variation on this technique is called the reverse line-up":

"The accused is placed in a line-up, but this time he is identified by several fictitious witnesses or victims who associated him with different offenses. It is expected that the subject will become desperate and confess to the offense under investigation in order to escape from the false accusations."

The manuals also contain instructions for police on how to handle the individual who refuses to discuss the matter entirely, or who asks for an attorney or relatives. The examiner is to concede him the right to remain silent. "This usually has a very undermining effect. First of all, he is disappointed in his expectation of an unfavorable reaction on the part of the interrogator. Secondly, a concession of this right to remain silent impresses the subject with the apparent fairness of his interrogator." After this psychological conditioning, however, the officer is told to point out the incriminating significance of the suspect's refusal to talk:

17.   O'Hara, supra, at 104, Inbau & Reid, supra, at 58–59. See Spano v. People of State of New York 360 U.S. 315, 79 S.Ct. 1202, 3 L.Ed.2d 1265 (1959) A variant on the technique of creating hostility is one of engendering fear. This is perhaps best described by the prosecuting attorney in Malinski v. People of State of New York, 324 U.S. 401, 407, 65 S.Ct. 781, 784, 89 L.Ed. 1029 (1945): "Why this talk about being undressed? Of course, they had a right to undress him to look for bullet scars, and keep the clothes off him. That was quite proper police procedure. That is some more psychology—let him sit around with a blanket on him, humiliate him there for a while; let him sit in the corner, let him think he is going to get a shellacking."

"Joe, you have a right to remain silent. That's your privilege and I'm the last person in the world who'll try to take it away from you. If that's the way you want to leave this, O.K. But let me ask you this. Suppose you were in my shoes and I were in yours and you called me in to ask me about this and I told you, 'I don't want to answer any of your questions.' You'd think I had something to hide, and you'd probably be right in thinking that. That's exactly what I'll have to think about you, and so will everybody else. So let's sit here and talk this whole thing over."

Few will persist in their initial refusal to talk, it is said, if this monologue is employed correctly.

In the event that the subject wishes to speak to a relative or an attorney, the following advice is tendered:

"[T]he interrogator should respond by suggesting that the subject first tell the truth to the interrogator himself rather than get anyone else involved in the matter. If the request is for an attorney, the interrogator may suggest that the subject save himself or his family the expense of any such professional service, particularly if he is innocent of the offense under investigation. The interrogator may also add, 'Joe, I'm only looking for the truth, and if you're telling the truth, that's it. You can handle this by yourself.'"   *   *   *

[The dissenting opinions of Justices Harlan, Clark, Stewart, and White are omitted.]

REPRINTED FROM HALL AND KAMISAR, MODERN CRIMINAL PROCEDURE

119–120 (1965).*

ANONYMOUS—AN HONEST CONFESSION MAY BE GOOD FOR THE SOUL, BUT NOT FOR THE F.B.I.

Scene: Office of F.B.I.

A few straight chairs, a desk, at which is seated an investigator for the F.B.I., reading the recent decision of McNabb v. the United States   *   *   *

Enter: A hill billy backwoodsman.

Hill Billy: Is this the F.B.I.?

Investigator: Yes. Is there anything I can do for you?

H.B.:   Yes, sir. I've killed a revenooer and I want to confess.

F.B.I.:   Wait a minute. I'll have to hunt you an upholstered and plush-covered chair. A man can't confess unless he is comfortable. It's been so held by the court.

H.B.:   But I'm only uncomfortable in mind. I don't keer to set.

*Copyright, 1965 by West Publishing Co.

F.B.I.:   You surely must not have read the ruling of Judge Frankfurter in which he held that you could not have a man uncomfortable who is about to confess a murder.

H.B.:   Shore nuff?

F.B.I.:   Where are your kin folks?

H.B.:   I ain't got none lessen you think my mother-in-law's kin.

F.B.I.:   You can't confess unless you brought your relatives along.

H.B.:   Well, me and her ain't a speakin' and she won't help me none.

F.B.I.:   Did you graduate from college?

H.B.:   Did I what?

F.B.I.:   How far did you get in school?

H.B.:   To the 4th grade.

F.B.I.:   I'm afraid you can't qualify. The Supreme Court has held that confessions by men who had not passed the 4th grade were no good. You've got to be educated to confess.

H.B.:   But that's agin the Preacher and the Good Book. They say confess yer sins, and they don't say nothin' about schoolin' and kin folks.

F.B.I.:   But it's the law, brother. Furthermore, I haven't seen your lawyer. Where's he?

H.B.:   Mister, you don't seem to understand. I want to tell the truth—not to git around it. I don't have to hire a lawyer before I can tell the truth, do I?

F.B.I.:   I'm sorry, but your notions are old fashioned. It used to be the law that a criminal could confess, provided he was advised and warned of his rights, and provided no force or violence was used, and provided no promise or reward was made to him, and provided he was not put in fear or duress. Lots of them used to confess when they found we had the proof on them, but that was horse and buggy law. Now a criminal must have his kin folks with him, must be comfortable, must have a lawyer, whether he asks for one or not, must have been educated past the 4th grade, and must have traveled at least further than Jasper. By the way, how far have you traveled away from home?

H.B.:   I ain't ever been out of the state in my life. I never run away. I jes' decided I'd stay and take my medicine.

F.B.I.:	Hell, that lets you out. You haven't got a single characteristic of a qualified confessor.
H.B.:	But mister, I killed a man—
F.B.I.:	Stop! I've been talking to you now nearly an hour, and that alone would disqualify you.
H.B.:	But the parson says that an honest confession is good for the soul.
F.B.I.:	I sympathize with you, brother, but there are only two courses left open to you: One is to bear your troubles in silence; the other is to go back to school, then travel abroad, marry you some kin folks, hire you a lawyer, and bring them down here with you. In the meantime, I'll try to get this office air-conditioned, and also have a nice overstuffed chair for you. Then I will hear your confession. But remember, you will have to make it short and snappy.
H.B.:	(Departing perplexedly) Well, I'll be damned.

HARRIS v. NEW YORK

Supreme Court of the United States, 1971.
401 U.S. 222, 91 S.Ct. 643, 28 L.Ed.2d 1.

Mr. Chief Justice BURGER delivered the opinion of the Court.

We granted the writ in this case to consider petitioner's claim that a statement made by him to police under circumstances rendering it inadmissible to establish the prosecution's case in chief under Miranda v. Arizona, 384 U.S. 436, 86 S.Ct. 1602, 16 L.Ed.2d 694 (1966), may not be used to impeach his credibility.

The State of New York charged petitioner in a two-count indictment with twice selling heroin to an undercover police officer. At a subsequent jury trial the officer was the State's chief witness, and he testified as to details of the two sales. A second officer verified collateral details of the sales, and a third offered testimony about the chemical analysis of the heroin.

Petitioner took the stand in his own defense. He admitted knowing the undercover police officer but denied a sale on January 4, 1966. He admitted making a sale of contents of a glassine bag to the officer on January 6 but claimed it was baking powder and part of a scheme to defraud the purchaser.

On cross-examination petitioner was asked seriatim whether he had made specified statements to the police immediately following his arrest on January 7—statements that partially contradicted petitioner's direct testimony at trial. In response to the cross-examination, petitioner testified that he could not remember virtually any of the questions or answers recited by the prosecutor. At the request of petitioner's counsel the written statement from which the prosecutor had read questions and answers in his impeaching process was placed in the record for possible use on appeal; the statement was not shown to the jury.

The trial judge instructed the jury that the statements attributed to petitioner by the prosecution could be considered only in passing on petitioner's credibility and not as evidence of guilt. In closing summations both counsel argued the substance of the impeaching statements. The jury then found petitioner guilty on the second count of the indictment.[1] The New York Court of Appeals affirmed in a *per curiam* opinion, 25 N.Y.2d 175, 303 N.Y.S.2d 71, 250 N.E.2d 349 (1969).

At trial the prosecution made no effort in its case in chief to use the statements allegedly made by petitioner, conceding that they were inadmissible under Miranda v. Arizona, 384 U.S. 436, 86 S.Ct. 1602, 16 L.Ed.2d 694 (1966). The transcript of the interrogation used in the impeachment, but not given to the jury, shows that no warning of a right to appointed counsel was given before questions were put to petitioner when he was taken into custody. Petitioner makes no claim that the statements made to the police were coerced or involuntary.

Some comments in the *Miranda* opinion can indeed be read as indicating a bar to use of an uncounseled statement for any purpose, but discussion of that issue was not at all necessary to the court's holding and cannot be regarded as controlling. *Miranda* barred the prosecution from making its case with statements of an accused made while in custody prior to having or effectively waiving counsel. It does not follow from *Miranda* that evidence inadmissible against an accused in the prosecution's case in chief is barred for all purposes, provided of course that the trustworthiness of the evidence satisfies legal standards.

In Walder v. United States, 347 U.S. 62, 74 S.Ct. 354, 98 L.Ed. 503 (1954), the Court permitted physical evidence, inadmissible in the case in chief, to be used for impeachment purposes.

"It is one thing to say that the Government cannot make an affirmative use of evidence unlawfully obtained. It is quite another to say that the defendant can turn the illegal method by which evidence in the Government's possession was obtained to his own advantage, and provide himself with a shield against contradiction of his untruths. Such an extension of the *Weeks* doctrine would be a perversion of the Fourth Amendment.

"[T]here is hardly justification for letting the defendant affirmatively resort to perjurious testimony in reliance on the Government's disability to challenge his credibility." 347 U.S., at 65, 74 S.Ct., at 356.

It is true that Walder was impeached as to collateral matters included in his direct examination, whereas petitioner here was impeached as to testimony bearing more directly on the crimes charged. We are not persuaded that there is a difference in principle that warrants a result different from that reached by the Court in *Walder*. Petitioner's testimony in his own behalf concerning the events of January 7 contrasted sharply with what he told the police shortly after his arrest. The impeachment process here undoubtedly provided valuable aid to the jury in assessing petitioner's credibility, and the benefits of this process should not be lost, in our view,

---

1.   No agreement was reached as to the first count. That count was later dropped by the State.

because of the speculative possibility that impermissible police conduct will be encouraged thereby. Assuming that the exclusionary rule has a deterrent effect on proscribed police conduct, sufficient deterrence flows when the evidence in question is made unavailable to the prosecution in its case in chief.

Every criminal defendant is privileged to testify in his own defense, or to refuse to do so. But that privilege cannot be construed to include the right to commit perjury. Having voluntarily taken the stand, petitioner was under an obligation to speak truthfully and accurately, and the prosecution here did no more than utilize the traditional truth-testing devices of the adversary process.[2] Had inconsistent statements been made by the accused to some third person, it could hardly be contended that the conflict could not be laid before the jury by way of cross-examination and impeachment.

The shield provided by *Miranda* cannot be perverted into a license to use perjury by way of a defense, free from the risk of confrontation with prior inconsistent utterances. We hold, therefore, that petitioner's credibility was appropriately impeached by use of his earlier conflicting statements.

Affirmed.

Mr. Justice BLACK dissents.

Mr. Justie BRENNAN, with whom Mr. Justice DOUGLAS and Mr. Justice MARSHALL join, dissenting.

It is conceded that the question-and-answer statement used to impeach petitioner's direct testimony was, under Miranda v. Arizona, 384 U.S. 436, 86 S.Ct. 1602, 16 L.Ed.2d 694 (1966), constitutionally inadmissible as part of the State's direct case against petitioner. I think that the Constitution also denied the State the use of the statement on cross-examination to impeach the credibility of petitioner's testimony given in his own defense. The decision in Walder v. United States, 347 U.S. 62, 74 S.Ct. 354, 98 L.Ed. 503 (1954), is not, as the Court today holds, dispositive to the contrary. Rather, that case supports my conclusion.

The State's case against Harris depended upon the jury's belief of the testimony of the undercover agent that petitioner "sold" the officer heroin on January 4 and again on January 6. Petitioner took the stand and flatly denied having sold anything to the officer on January 4. He countered the officer's testimony as to the January 6 sale with testimony that he had sold the officer two glassine bags containing what appeared to be heroin, but that actually the bags contained only baking powder intended to deceive the officer in order to obtain $12. The statement contradicted petitioner's direct testimony as to the events of both days. The statement's version of the events on January 4 was that the officer had used petitioner as a middleman to buy some heroin from a third person with money furnished by the officer. The version of the events on January 6 was that petitioner had again

---

2. If, for example, an accused confessed fully to a homicide and led the police to the body of the victim under circumstances making his confession inadmissible, the petitioner would have us allow that accused to take the stand and blandly deny every fact disclosed to the police or discovered as a "fruit" of his confession, free from confrontation with his prior statements and acts. The voluntariness of the confession would, on this thesis, be totally irrelevant. We reject such an extravagant extension of the Constitution. *Compare* Killough v. United States, 114 U.S.App.D.C. 305, 315 F.2d 241 (1962).

acted for the officer in buying two bags of heroin from a third person for which petitioner received $12 and a part of the heroin. Thus, it is clear that the statement was used to impeach petitioner's direct testimony not on collateral matters but on matters directly related to the crimes for which he was on trial.[1]

Walder v. United States was not a case where tainted evidence was used to impeach an accused's direct testimony on matters directly related to the case against him. In *Walder* the evidence was used to impeach the accused's testimony on matters *collateral* to the crime charged. Walder had been indicted in 1950 for purchasing and possessing heroin. When his motion to suppress use of the narcotics as illegally seized was granted, the Government dismissed the prosecution. Two years later Walder was indicted for another narcotics violation completely unrelated to the 1950 one. Testifying in his own defense, he said on direct examination that he had never in his life possessed narcotics. On cross-examination he denied that law enforcement officers had seized narcotics from his home two years earlier. The Government was then permitted to introduce the testimony of one of the officers involved in the 1950 seizure, that when he had raided Walder's home at that time he had seized narcotics there. The Court held that on facts where "the defendant went beyond a mere denial of complicity in the crimes of which he was charged and made the sweeping claim that he had never dealt in or possessed any narcotics," 347 U.S., at 65, the exclusionary rule of Weeks v. United States, 232 U.S. 383, 34 S.Ct. 341, 58 L.Ed. 652 (1914) would not extend to bar the Government from rebutting this testimony with evidence, although tainted, that petitioner had in fact possessed narcotics two years before. The Court was careful, however, to distinguish the situation of an accused whose testimony, as in the instant case, was a "denial of complicity in the crimes of which he was charged," that is, where illegally obtained evidence was used to impeach the accused's direct testimony on matters directly related to the case against him. As to that situation, the Court said:

> "Of course, the Constitution guarantees a defendant the fullest opportunity to meet the accusation against him. He must be free to deny all the elements of the case against him without thereby giving leave to the Government to introduce by way of rebuttal evidence illegally secured by it, and therefore not available for its case in chief." 347 U.S., at 65, 74 S.Ct., at 356.

From this recital of facts it is clear that the evidence used for impeachment in *Walder* was related to the earlier 1950 prosecution and had no direct bearing on "the elements of the case" being tried in 1952. The evidence tended solely to impeach the credibility of the defendant's direct testimony that he had never in his life possessed heroin. But that evidence was completely unrelated to the indictment on trial and did not in any way interfere with this freedom to deny all elements of that case against him. In contrast, here, the evidence used for impeachment, a statement concerning

---

1.   The trial transcript shows that petitioner testified that he remembered making a statement on January 7; that he remembered a few of the questions and answers; but that he did not "remember giving too many answers." When asked about his bad memory, petitioner, who had testified that he was a heroin addict, stated that "my joints was down and I needed drugs."

the details of the very sales alleged in the indictment, was directly related to the case against petitioner.

While *Walder* did not identify the constitutional specifics that guarantee "a defendant the fullest opportunity to meet the accusation against him * * * [and permit him to] be free to deny all the elements of the case against him," in my view Miranda v. Arizona, 384 U.S. 436, 86 S.Ct. 1602, 16 L.Ed.2d 694 (1966), identified the Fifth Amendment's privilege against self-incrimination as one of those specifics.[2] That privilege has been extended against the States. Malloy v. Hogan, 378 U.S. 1, 84 S.Ct. 1489, 12 L.Ed.2d 653 (1964). It is fulfilled only when an accused is guaranteed the right "to remain silent unless he chooses to speak in the *unfettered* exercise of his own will," id., at 8 (emphasis added). The choice of whether to testify in one's own defense must therefore be "unfettered," since that choice is an exercise of the constitutional privilege, Griffin v. California, 380 U.S. 609, 85 S.Ct. 1229, 14 L.Ed.2d 106 (1965). *Griffin* held that comment by the prosecution upon the accused's failure to take the stand or a court instruction that such silence is evidence of guilt is impermissible because it "fetters" that choice—"[i]t cuts down on the privilege by making its assertion costly." Id., at 614. For precisely the same reason the constitutional guarantee forbids the prosecution from using a tainted statement to impeach the accused who takes the stand: The prosecution's use of the tainted statement "cuts down on the privilege by making its assertion costly." Ibid. Thus, the accused is denied an "unfettered" choice when the decision whether to take the stand is burdened by the risk that an illegally obtained prior statement may be introduced to impeach his direct testimony denying

---

2.   Three of the five judges of the Appellate Division in this case agreed that the State's use of petitioner's illegally obtained statement was an error of constitutional dimension. People v. Harris, 31 A.D.2d 828, 298 N.Y.S.2d 245 (1969). However, one of the three held that the error did not play a meaningful role in the case and was therefore harmless under our decision in Chapman v. California, 386 U.S. 18, 87 S.Ct. 824, 17 L.Ed.2d 705 (1967). He therefore joined in affirming the conviction with the two judges who were of the view that there was no constitutional question involved. 31 A.D.2d, at 830, 298 N.Y.S.2d, at 249. I disagree that the error was harmless and subscribe to the reasoning of the dissenting judges, id., at 831–832, 298 N.Y.S.2d at 250:

Under the circumstances outlined above, I cannot agree that this error of constitutional dimension was 'harmless beyond a reasonable doubt' (Chapman v. California, 386 U.S. 18, 24, 87 S.Ct. 824, 17 L.Ed.2d 705). An error is not harmless if 'there is a reasonable possibility that the evidence complained of might have contributed to the conviction' (Fahy v. Connecticut, 375 U.S. 85, 86–87, 84 S.Ct. 229, 230, 11 L.Ed.2d 171). The burden of showing that a constitutional error is

harmless rests with the People who, in this case, have not even attempted to assume that demonstration (Chapman v. California, supra). Surely it cannot be said with any certainty that the improper use of defendant's statement did not tip the scales against him, especially when his conviction rests on the testimony of the same undercover agent whose testimony was apparently less than convincing on the January 4 charge (cf. Anderson v. Nelson, 390 U.S. 523, 525, 88 S.Ct. 1133, 20 L.Ed.2d 81). On the contrary, it is difficult to see how defendant could not have been damaged severely by use of the inconsistent statement in a case which, in the final analysis, pitted his word against the officer's. The judgment should be reversed and a new trial granted."

The Court of Appeals affirmed *per curiam* on the authority of its earlier opinion in People v. Kulis, 18 N.Y.2d 318, 274 N.Y.S.2d 873, 221 N.E.2d 541 (1966). Chief Judge Fuld and Judge Keating dissented in *Kulis* on the ground that *Miranda* precluded use of the statement for impeachment purposes, 18 N.Y.2d, at 323, 274 N.Y.S.2d at 875, 221 N.E.2d, at 542.

complicity in the crime charged against him.[3] We settled this proposition in *Miranda* where we said:

> "The privilege against self-incrimination protects the individual from being compelled to incriminate himself in *any* manner. * * * [S]tatements merely intended to be exculpatory by the defendant are often *used to impeach his testimony at trial. * * * These statements are incriminating in any meaningful sense of the word and may not be used without the full warnings and effective waiver required for any other statement.*" 384 U.S., at 476–477, 86 S.Ct., at 1629 (emphasis added).

This language completely disposes of any distinction between statements used on direct as opposed to cross-examination.[4] "An incriminating statement is as incriminating when used to impeach credibility as it is when used as direct proof of guilt and no constitutional distinction can legitimately be drawn." People v. Kulis, 18 N.Y.2d 318, 324, 274 N.Y.S.2d 873, 221 N.E.2d 541, 543 (1966) (dissenting opinion).

The objective of deterring improper police conduct is only part of the larger objective of safeguarding the integrity of our adversary system. The "essential mainstay" of that system, Miranda v. Arizona, 384 U.S., at 460, 86 S.Ct. 1602 is the privilege against self-incrimination, which for that reason has occupied a central place in our jurisprudence since before the Nation's birth. Moreover, "we may view the historical development of the privilege as one which groped for the proper scope of governmental power over the citizen. * * * All these policies point to one overriding thought: the constitutional foundation underlying the privilege is the respect a government * * * must accord to the dignity and integrity of its citizens." Ibid. These values are plainly jeopardized if an exception against admission of tainted statements is made for those used for impeachment purposes. Moreover, it is monstrous that courts should aid or abet the law-breaking police officer. It is abiding truth that "[n]othing can destroy a government more quickly than its failure to observe its own laws, or worse, its disregard of the charter of its own existence." Mapp v. Ohio, 367 U.S. 643, 659, 81 S.Ct. 1684, 1694, 6 L.Ed.2d 1081 (1961). Thus, even to the ex-

---

3. It is therefore unnecessary for me to consider petitioner's argument that *Miranda* has overruled the narrow exception of *Walder* admitting impeaching evidence on collateral matters.

4. Six federal courts of appeals and appellate courts of 14 States have reached the same result. United States v. Fox, 403 F.2d 97 (C.A.2, 1968); United States v. Pinto, 394 F.2d 470 (C.A.3, 1968); Breedlove v. Beto, 404 F.2d 1019 (C.A.5, 1968); Groshart v. United States, 392 F.2d 172 (C.A.9, 1968); Blair v. United States, 130 U.S.App.D.C. 322, 401 F.2d 387 (1968); Wheeler v. United States, 382 F.2d 998 (C.A.10, 1967); People v. Barry, 237 Cal.App.2d 154, 46 Cal.Rptr. 727 (1965), cert. denied, 386 U.S. 1024, 87 S.Ct. 1382, 18 L.Ed.2d 464 (1967); Velarde v. People, 171 Colo. 261, 466 P.2d 919 (1970); State v. Galasso, 217 So.2d 326 (Fla.1968); People v. Luna, 37 Ill.2d 299, 226 N.E.2d 586 (1967); Franklin v. State, 6 Md.App. 572, 252 A.2d 487 (1969); People v. Wilson, 20 Mich.App. 410, 174 N.W.2d 79 (1969); State v. Turnbow, 67 N.M. 241, 354 P.2d 533 (1960); State v. Catrett, 276 N.C. 86, 171 S.E.2d 398 (1970); State v. Brewton, 247 Or. 241, 422 P.2d 581, cert. denied, 387 U.S. 943, 87 S.Ct. 2074, 18 L.Ed.2d 1328 (1967); Commonwealth v. Padgett, 428 Pa. 229, 237 A.2d 209 (1968); Spann v. State, 448 S.W.2d 128 (Tex.Cr.App.1969); Cardwell v. Commonwealth, 209 Va. 412, 164 S.E.2d 699 (1968); Gaertner v. State, 35 Wis.2d 159, 150 N.W.2d 370 (1967); see also Kelly v. King, 196 So.2d 525 (Miss.1967). Only three state appellate courts have agreed with New York. State v. Kimbrough, 109 N.J.Super. 57, 262 A.2d 232 (1970); State v. Butler, 19 Ohio St. 2d 55, 249 N.E.2d 818 (1969); State v. Grant, 77 Wash.2d 47, 459 P.2d 639 (1969).

tent that *Miranda* was aimed at deterring police practices in disregard of the Constitution, I fear that today's holding will seriously undermine the achievement of that objective. The Court today tells the police that they may freely interrogate an accused incommunicado and without counsel and know that although any statement they obtain in violation of *Miranda* cannot be used on the State's direct case, it may be introduced if the defendant has the temerity to testify in his own defense. This goes far toward undoing much of the progress made in conforming police methods to the Constitution. I dissent.

FISHER v. UNITED STATES

Supreme Court of the United States, 1976.
425 U.S. 391, 96 S.Ct. 1569, 48 L.Ed.2d 39.

Mr. Justice WHITE delivered the opinion of the Court.

In these two cases we are called upon to decide whether a summons directing an attorney to produce documents delivered to him by his client in connection with the attorney-client relationship is enforceable over claims that the documents were constitutionally immune from summons in the hands of the client and retained that immunity in the hands of the attorney.

I

In each case, an Internal Revenue agent visited the taxpayer or taxpayers and interviewed them in connection with an investigation of possible civil or criminal liability under the federal income tax laws. Shortly after the interviews—one day later in No. 74–611 and a week or two later in No. 74–18—the taxpayers obtained from their respective accountants certain documents relating to the preparation by the accountants of their tax returns. Shortly after obtaining the documents—later the same day in No. 74–611 and few weeks later in No. 74–18—the taxpayers transferred the documents to their lawyers—respondent Kasmir and petitioner Fisher, respectively—each of whom was retained to assist the taxpayer in connection with the investigation. Upon learning of the whereabouts of the documents, the Internal Revenue Service served summonses on the attorneys directing them to produce documents listed therein. In No. 74-611, the documents were described as "the following records of Tannebaum Bindler & Lewis [the accounting firm].

"1. Accountant's workpapers pertaining to Dr. E. J. Mason's books and records of 1969, 1970 and 1971.[2]

"2. Retained copies of E. J. Mason's income tax returns for 1969, 1970 and 1971.

"3. Retained copies of reports and other correspondence between Tannebaum Bindler & Lewis and Dr. E. J. Mason during 1969, 1970 and 1971."

In No. 74–18, the documents demanded were analyses by the accountant of the taxpayers' income and expenses which had been copied by the accountant from the taxpayers' canceled checks and deposit receipts.[3] In No.

---

2. The "books and records" concerned the taxpayer's large medical practice.

3. The husband taxpayer's checks and deposit receipts related to his textile waste business. The wife's related to her women's wear shop.

74–611, a summons was also served on the accountant directing him to appear and testify concerning the documents to be produced by the lawyer. In each case, the lawyer declined to comply with the summons directing production of the documents, and enforcement actions were commenced by the Government under 26 U.S.C. §§ 7402(b) and 760(a). In No. 74–611, the attorney raised in defense of the enforcement action the taxpayer's * * * Fifth Amendment rights. In No. 74–18, the attorney claimed that enforcement would involve compulsory self-incrimination of the taxpayers in violation of their Fifth Amendment privilege * * * . In No. 74–18 the taxpayers intervened and made similar claims.

In each case the summons was ordered enforced by the District Court and its order was stayed pending appeal. In No. 74–18, * * * [T]he Court of Appeals for the Third Circuit after reargument en banc affirmed the enforcement order, * * *   In No. 74–611, a divided panel of the Court of Appeals for the Fifth Circuit reversed the enforcement order, 499 F.2d 444 (1974). The court reasoned that by virtue of the Fifth Amendment the documents would have been privileged from production pursuant to summons directed to the taxpayer had he retained possession and, in light of the confidential nature of the attorney-client relationship, the taxpayer retained, after the transfer to his attorney, "a legitimate expectation of privacy with regard to the materials he placed in his attorney's custody, that he retained constructive possession of the evidence, and thus * * * retained Fifth Amendment protection." Id., at 453. We granted certiorari to resolve the conflict created. 420 U.S. 906, 95 S.Ct. 824, 42 L.Ed.2d 835 (1975). * * *

II

All of the parties in these cases and the Court of Appeals for the Fifth Circuit have concurred in the proposition that if the Fifth Amendment would have excused a *taxpayer* from turning over the accountant's papers had he possessed them, the *attorney* to whom they are delivered for the purpose of obtaining legal advice should also be immune from subpoena. Although we agree with this proposition for the reasons set forth in Part III, infra, we are convinced that, under our decision in Couch v. United States, 409 U.S. 322, 93 S.Ct. 611, 34 L.Ed.2d 548 (1973), it is not the taxpayer's Fifth Amendment privilege that would excuse the *attorney* from production.

The relevant part of that Amendment provides:

"No person * * * shall be *compelled* in any criminal case to be a *witness against himself.*" (Emphasis added.)

The taxpayer's privilege under this Amendment is not violated by enforcement of the summonses involved in these cases because enforcement against a taxpayer's lawyer would not "compel" the taxpayer to do anything—and certainly would not compel him to be a "witness" against himself. The Court has held repeatedly that the Fifth Amendment is limited to prohibiting the use of "physical or moral compulsion" exerted on the person asserting the privilege. In Couch v. United States, supra, we recently ruled that the Fifth Amendment rights of a taxpayer were not violated by the enforcement of a documentary summons directed to her accountant and requiring production of the taxpayer's own records in the possession of the accountant. We did so on the ground that in such a case "the ingredient of personal compulsion against an accused is lacking." 409 U.S., at 329, 93 S.Ct., at 616, 34 L.Ed.2d, at 554.

Here, the taxpayers are compelled to do no more than was the taxpayer in *Couch*. The taxpayers' Fifth Amendment privilege is therefore not violated by enforcement of the summonses directed toward their attorneys. This is true whether or not the Amendment would have barred a subpoena directing the taxpayer to produce the documents while they were in his hands.

The fact that the attorneys are agents of the taxpayers does not change this result. *Couch* held as much, since the accountant there was also the taxpayer's agent, and in this respect reflected a longstanding view. In Hale v. Henkel, 201 U.S. 43, 69–70, 26 S.Ct. 370, 377, 50 L.Ed. 652, 663 (1906), the Court said that the privilege "was never intended to permit [a person] to plead the fact that some third person might be incriminated by his testimony, even though he were the agent of such person * * * . [T]he Amendment is limited to a person who shall be compelled in any criminal case to be a witness against *himself*." (Emphasis in original.) "It is extortion of information from the accused himself that offends our sense of justice." Couch v. United States, supra, 409 U.S., at 328, 93 S.Ct., at 616, 34 L.Ed.2d, at 554. Agent or no, the lawyer is not the taxpayer. The taxpayer is the "accused," and nothing is being extorted from him.

Nor is this one of those situations, which *Couch* suggested might exist, where constructive possession is so clear or relinquishment of possession so temporary and insignificant as to leave the personal compulsion upon the taxpayer substantially intact. 409 U.S., at 333, 93 S.Ct., at 618, 34 L.Ed.2d, at 556. In this respect we see no difference between the delivery to the attorneys in these cases and delivery to the accountant in the *Couch* case. As was true in *Couch*, the documents sought were obtainable without personal compulsion on the accused.

Respondents in No. 74–611 and petitioners in No. 74–18 argue, and the Court of Appeals for the Fifth Circuit apparently agreed, that if the summons was enforced, the taxpayers' Fifth Amendment privilege would be, but should not be, lost solely because they gave their documents to their lawyers in order to obtain legal advice. But this misconceives the nature of the constitutional privilege. The Amendment protects a person from being compelled to be a witness against himself. Here, the taxpayers retained any privilege they ever had not to be compelled to testify against themselves and not to be compelled themselves to produce private papers in their possession. *This* personal privilege was in no way decreased by the transfer. It is simply that by reason of the transfer of the documents to the attorneys, those papers may be subpoenaed without compulsion on the taxpayer. The protection of the Fifth Amendment is therefore not available. "A party is privileged from producing evidence but not from its production." Johnson v. United States, supra, 228 U.S., at 458, 33 S.Ct., at 572, 57 L.Ed., at 920.

The Court of Appeals for the Fifth Circuit suggested that because legally and ethically the attorney was required to respect the confidences of his client, the latter had a reasonable expectation of privacy for the records in the hands of the attorney and therefore did not forfeit his Fifth Amendment privilege with respect to the records by transferring them in order to obtain legal advice. It is true that the Court has often stated that one of the several purposes served by the constitutional privilege against compelled testimonial self-incrimination is that of protecting personal privacy. But the Court has never suggested that every invasion of privacy violates the privilege. Within the limits imposed by the language of the Fifth Amendment, which we necessarily observe, the privilege truly serves privacy interests; but the Court has never on any ground, personal privacy included, applied the Fifth Amendment to prevent the otherwise proper acquisition or use of evidence which, in the Court's view, did not involve compelled testimonial self-incrimination of some sort.[5]

The proposition that the Fifth Amendment protects private information obtained without compelling self-incriminating testimony is contrary to the clear statements of this Court that under appropriate safeguards private incriminating statements of an accused may be overheard and used in evidence, if they're not compelled at the time they were uttered, and that disclosure of private information may be compelled if immunity removes the risk of incrimination. If the Fifth Amendment protected generally against the obtaining of private information from a man's mouth or pen or house, its protections would presumably not be lifted by probable cause and a warrant or by immunity. The privacy invasion is not mitigated by immunity; and the Fifth Amendment's strictures, unlike the Fourth's, are not removed by showing reasonableness. The framers addressed the subject of personal privacy directly in the Fourth Amendment. They struck a balance so that when the State's reason to believe incriminating evidence will be found becomes sufficiently great, the invasion of privacy becomes justified and a warrant to search and seize will issue. They did not seek in still another Amendment—the Fifth—to achieve a general protection of privacy but to deal with the more specific issue of compelled self-incrimination.

We cannot cut the Fifth Amendment completely loose from the moorings of its language, and make it serve as a general protector of privacy—a word not mentioned in its text and a concept directly addressed in the Fourth Amendment. We adhere to the view that the Fifth Amendment protects against "compelled self-incrimination, not [the disclosure of] private information." United States v. Nobles, 422 U.S. 225, 233 n. 7, 95 S.Ct. 2160, 2167, 45 L.Ed.2d 141 (1975).

Insofar as private information not obtained through compelled self-incriminating testimony is legally protected, its protection stems from other sources[6]—the Fourth Amendment's protection against seizures

---

5. There is a line of cases in which the Court stated that the Fifth Amendment was offended by the use in evidence of documents or property seized in violation of the Fourth Amendment. But the Court purported to find elements of compulsion in such situations. "In either case he is the unwilling source of the evidence, and the Fifth Amendment forbids that he shall be compelled to be a witness against himself in a criminal case." Gouled v. United States, supra, 255 U.S., at 306, 41 S.Ct. at 264, 65 L.Ed., at 651. In any event the predicate for those cases, lacking here, was a violation of the Fourth Amendment.

6. In Couch v. United States, 409 U.S. 322, 93 S.Ct. 611, 34 L.Ed.2d 548 (1973), on which taxpayers rely for their claim that the Fifth Amendment protects their "legitimate expectation of privacy," the Court differentiated between the things protected by the Fourth and Fifth Amendments. "We hold today that no Fourth or Fifth Amendment claim can prevail where, as in this case, there exists no legitimate expectation of privacy and no semblance of governmental compulsion against the person of the accused." Id., 409 U.S., at 336, 93 S.Ct., at 620, 34 L.Ed.2d, at 558.

without warrant or probable cause and against subpoenas which suffer from "too much indefiniteness or breadth in the things required to be 'particularly described,' " Oklahoma Press Pub. Co. v. Walling, 327 U.S. 186, 208, 66 S.Ct. 494, 505, 90 L.Ed. 614, 629 (1946); In re Horowitz, 482 F.2d 72, 75–80 (CA2 1973) (Friendly, J.); the First Amendment, see NAACP v. Alabama, 357 U.S. 449, 462, 78 S.Ct. 1163, 1171, 2 L.Ed.2d 1488, 1499 (1958); or evidentiary privileges such as the attorney-client privilege.

* * *

[The Court next held that if the clients would have been privileged from production of the documents and the documents were transferred to their attorneys for the purpose of obtaining legal assistance, then the attorney-client privilege may be invoked to prevent compelled disclosure from the attorneys.]

Since each taxpayer transferred possession of the documents in question from himself to his attorney in order to obtain legal assistance in the tax investigations in question, the papers, if unobtainable by summons from the client, are unobtainable by summons directed to the attorney by reason of the attorney-client privilege. We accordingly proceed to the question whether the documents could have been obtained by summons addressed to the taxpayer while the documents were in his possession. The only bar to enforcement of such summons asserted by the parties or the courts below is the Fifth Amendment's privilege against self-incrimination.

* * *

IV

The proposition that the Fifth Amendment prevents compelled production of documents over objection that such production might incriminate stems from Boyd v. United States, 116 U.S. 616, 68 S.Ct. 524, 29 L.Ed. 746 (1886). *Boyd* involved a civil forfeiture proceeding brought by the Government against two partners for fraudulently attempting to import 35 cases of glass without paying the prescribed duty. The partnership had contracted with the Government to furnish the glass needed in the construction of a Government building. The glass specified was foreign glass, it being understood that if part or all of the glass was furnished from the partnership's existing duty-paid inventory, it could be replaced by duty-free imports. Pursuant to this arrangement, 29 cases of glass were imported by the partnership duty free. The partners then represented that they were entitled to duty-free entry of an additional 35 cases which were soon to arrive. The forfeiture action concerned these 35 cases. The Government's position was that the partnership had replaced all of the glass used in construction of the Government building when it imported the 29 cases. At trial, the Government obtained a court order directing the partners to produce an invoice the partnership had received from the shipper covering the previous 29-case shipment. The invoice was disclosed, offered in evidence, and used, over the Fifth Amendment objection of the partners, to establish that the partners were fraudulently claiming a greater exemption from duty than they were entitled to under the contract. This Court held that the invoice was inadmissible and reversed the judgment in favor of the Government. The Court ruled that the Fourth Amendment applied to court orders in the nature of subpoenas *duces tecum* in the same manner in which it applies to search warrants, id., at 622, 6 S.Ct., at 528, 29 L.Ed., at 748; and that the Government may not, consistent with the Fourth Amendment, seize a person's documents or other property as evidence unless it can claim a proprietary interest in the property superior to that of the person from whom the property is obtained. Id., at 623–624, 6 S.Ct., at 528–529, 29 L.Ed., at 748. The invoice in question was thus held to have been obtained in violation of the Fourth Amendment. The Court went on to hold that the accused in a criminal case or the defendant in a forfeiture action could not be forced to produce evidentiary items without violating the Fifth Amendment as well as the Fourth. More specifically, the Court declared, "a compulsory production of the private books and papers of the owner of goods sought to be forfeited * * * is compelling him to be a witness against himself, within the meaning of the Fifth Amendment to the Constitution." Id., at 634–635, 6 S.Ct., at 534, 29 L.Ed., at 752. Admitting the partnership invoice into evidence had violated both the Fifth and Fourth Amendments.

Among its several pronouncements, *Boyd* was understood to declare that the seizure, under warrant or otherwise, of any purely evidentiary materials violated the Fourth Amendment and that the Fifth Amendment rendered these seized materials inadmissible. * * * Private papers taken from the taxpayer, like other "mere evidence," could not be used against the accused over his Fourth and Fifth Amendment objections.

Several of Boyd's express or implicit declarations have not stood the test of time. Purely evidentiary (but "nontestimonial") materials, as well as contraband and fruits and instrumentalities of crime, may now be searched for and seized under proper circumstances, Warden v. Hayden, 387 U.S. 294, 87 S.Ct. 1642, 18 L.Ed.2d 782 (1967).[9] Also, any notion that "testimonial" evidence may never be seized and used in evidence is inconsistent with Katz v. United States, 389 U.S. 347, 88 S.Ct. 507, 19 L.Ed.2d 576 (1967); Osborn v. United States, 385 U.S. 323, 87 S.Ct. 429, 439, 17 L.Ed.2d 394 (1966); and Berger v. New York, 388 U.S. 41, 87 S.Ct. 1873, 18 L.Ed.2d 1040 (1967), approving the seizure under appropriate circumstances of conversations of a person suspected of crime.

It is also clear that the Fifth Amendment does not independently proscribe the compelled production of every sort of incriminating evidence but applies only when the accused is compelled to make a *testimonial* communication that is incriminating. We have, accordingly, declined to extend the protection of the privilege to the giving of blood samples, Schmerber v. California, 384 U.S. 757, 763–764, 86 S.Ct. 1826, 1831–1832, 16 L.Ed.2d 908, 915–916 (1966);[10] to the giving of handwriting exemplars, Gilbert v. California, 388 U.S. 263, 265–267, 87 S.Ct. 1951, 1952–1954, 18 L.Ed.2d 1178, 1181–1183 (1967); voice exemplars, United States v. Wade, 388 U.S. 218, 222–223, 87 S.Ct. 1926, 1929–1930, 18 L.Ed.2d 1149, 1154–1155 (1967); or the donning of a blouse worn by the perpetrator, Holt v. United States, 218 U.S. 245, 31 S.Ct. 2, 54 L.Ed. 1021 (1910). Furthermore, despite *Boyd,*

9. Citing to Schmerber v. California, 384 U.S. 757, 86 S.Ct. 1826, 16 L.Ed.2d 908 (1966), Warden v. Hayden, 387 U.S., at 302–303, 87 S.Ct., at 1648, 18 L.Ed.2d, at 789, reserved the question "whether there are items of evidential value whose very nature precludes them from being the object of a reasonable search and seizure."

10. The Court's holding was: "Since the blood test evidence, although an incriminating product of compulsion, was neither petitioner's testimony nor evidence relating to some communicative act or writing by petitioner, it was not inadmissible on privilege grounds." 384 U.S., at 765, 86 S.Ct., at 1833, 16 L.Ed.2d, at 916.

neither a partnership nor the individual partners are shielded from compelled production of partnership records on self-incrimination grounds. Bellis v. United States, 417 U.S. 85, 94 S.Ct. 2179, 40 L.Ed.2d 678 (1974). It would appear that under that case the precise claim sustained in *Boyd* would now be rejected for reasons not there considered.

The pronouncement in *Boyd* that a person may not be forced to produce his private papers has nonetheless often appeared as dictum in later opinions of this Court. To the extent, however, that the rule against compelling production of private papers rested on the proposition that seizures of or subpoenas for "mere evidence," including documents, violated the Fourth Amendment and therefore also transgressed the Fifth, Gouled v. United States, supra, the foundations for the rule have been washed away. In consequence, the prohibition against forcing the production of private papers has long been a rule searching for a rationale consistent with the proscriptions of the Fifth Amendment against compelling a person to give "testimony" that incriminates him. Accordingly, we turn to the question of what, if any, incriminating testimony within the Fifth Amendment's protection, is compelled by a documentary summons.

A subpoena served on a taxpayer requiring him to produce an accountant's workpapers in his possession without doubt involves substantial compulsion. But it does not compel oral testimony; nor would it ordinarily compel the taxpayer to restate, repeat, or affirm the truth of the contents of the documents sought. Therefore, the Fifth Amendment would not be violated by the fact alone that the papers on their face might incriminate the taxpayer, for the privilege protects a person only against being incriminated by his own compelled testimonial communications. The accountant's workpapers are not the taxpayer's. They were not prepared by the taxpayer, and they contain no testimonial declarations by him. Furthermore, as far as this record demonstrates, the preparation of all of the papers sought in these cases was wholly voluntary, and they cannot be said to contain compelled testimonial evidence, either of the taxpayers or anyone else.[11] The taxpayer cannot avoid compliance with the subpoena merely by asserting that the item of evidence which he is required to produce contains incriminating writing, whether his own or that of someone else.

The act of producing evidence in response to a subpoena nevertheless has communicative aspects of its own, wholly aside from the contents of the papers produced. Compliance with the subpoena tacitly concedes the existence of the papers demanded and their possession or control by the taxpayer. It also would indicate the taxpayer's belief that the papers are those described in the subpoena. The elements of compulsion are clearly present, but the more difficult issues are whether the tacit averments of the taxpayer are both "testimonial" and "incriminating" for purposes of applying the Fifth Amendment. These questions perhaps do not lend themselves to cate-

---

11. The fact that the documents may have been written by the person asserting the privilege is insufficient to trigger the privilege, and, unless the Government has compelled the subpoenaed person to write the document the fact that it was written by him is not controlling with respect to the Fifth Amendment issue. Conversations may be seized and introduced in evidence under proper safeguards, if not compelled. In the case of a documentary subpoena the only thing compelled is the act of producing the document and the compelled act is the same as the one performed when a chattel or document not authored by the producer is demanded. McCormick § 128, p. 261.

gorical answers; their resolution may instead depend on the facts and circumstances of particular cases or classes thereof. In light of the records now before us, we are confident that however incriminating the contents of the accountant's workpapers might be, the act of producing them—the only thing which the taxpayer is compelled to do—would not itself involve testimonial self-incrimination.

It is doubtful that implicity admitting the existence and possession of the papers rises to the level of testimony within the protection of the Fifth Amendment. The papers belong to the accountant, were prepared by him, and are the kind usually prepared by an accountant working on the tax returns of his client. Surely the Government is in no way relying on the "truth-telling" of the taxpayer to prove the existence of or his access to the documents. The existence and location of the papers are a foregone conclusion and the taxpayer adds little or nothing to the sum total of the Government's information by conceding that he in fact has the papers. Under these circumstances by enforcement of the summons "no constitutional rights are touched. The question is not of testimony but of surrender." In re Harris, 221 U.S. 274, 279, 31 S.Ct. 557, 558, 55 L.Ed. 732, 735 (1911).

When an accused is required to submit a handwriting exemplar he admits his ability to write and impliedly asserts that the exemplar is his writing. But in common experience, the first would be a near truism and the latter self-evident. In any event, although the exemplar may be incriminating to the accused and although he is compelled to furnish it, his Fifth Amendment privilege is not violated because nothing he has said or done is deemed to be sufficiently testimonial for purposes of the privilege. This Court has also time and again allowed subpoenas against the custodian of corporate documents or those belonging to other collective entities such as unions and partnerships and those of bankrupt businesses over claims that the documents will incriminate the custodian despite the fact that producing the documents tacitly admits their existence and their location in the hands of their possessor. The existence and possession or control of the subpoenaed documents being no more in issue here than in the above cases, the summons is equally enforceable.

Moreover, assuming that these aspects of producing the accountant's papers have some minimal testimonial significance, surely it is not illegal to seek accounting help in connection with one's tax returns or for the accountant to prepare workpapers and deliver them to the taxpayer. At this juncture, we are quite unprepared to hold that either the fact of existence of the papers or of their possession by the taxpayer poses any realistic threat of incrimination to the taxpayer.

As for the possibility that responding to the subpoena would authenticate[12] the workpapers, production would express nothing more

---

12. The "implicit authentication" rationale appears to be the prevailing justification for the Fifth Amendment's application to documentary subpoenas. Schmerber v. California, 384 U.S., at 763–764, 86 S.Ct., at 1832, 16 L.Ed.2d, at 915–916 ("the privilege reaches * * * the compulsion of responses which are also communications, for example, compliance with a subpoena to produce one's papers. Boyd v. United States, 116 U.S. 616, 6 S.Ct. 524, 29 L.Ed. 746"); Couch v. United States, 409 U.S., at 344, 346, 93 S.Ct., at 611, 625, 34 L.Ed.2d, at 548, 564 (Marshall, J., dissenting) (the person complying with the subpoena "implicitly testifies that the evidence he brings forth is in fact the evidence demanded"); United States v. Beattie, 522 F.2d 267, 270

than the taxpayer's belief that the papers are those described in the subpoena. The taxpayer would be no more competent to authenticate the accountant's workpapers or reports[13] by producing them than he would be to authenticate them if testifying orally. The taxpayer did not prepare the papers and could not vouch for their accuracy. The documents would not be admissible in evidence against the taxpayer without authenticating testimony. Without more, responding to the subpoena in the circumstances before us would not appear to represent a substantial threat of self-incrimination. Moreover, in Wilson v. United States, supra; Dreier v. United States, supra; United States v. White, supra; Bellis v. United States, supra; and In re Harris, supra, the custodian of corporate, union, or partnership books or those of a bankrupt business was ordered to respond to a subpoena for the business' books even though doing so involved a "representation that the documents produced are those demanded by the subpoena," Curcio v. United States, 354 U.S., at 125, 77 S.Ct., at 1150, 1 L.Ed.2d, at 1231.[14]

Whether the Fifth Amendment would shield the taxpayer from producing his own tax records in his possession is a question not involved here; for the papers demanded here are not his "private papers," see Boyd v. United States, supra, 116 U.S., at 634–635, 6 S.Ct., at 534, 29 L.Ed., at 752. We do hold that compliance with a summons directing the taxpayer to produce the accountant's documents involved in these cases would involve no incriminating testimony within the protection of the Fifth Amendment.

The judgment of the Court of Appeals for the Fifth Circuit in No. 74–611 is reversed. The judgment of the Court of Appeals for the Third Circuit in No. 74–18 is affirmed.

So ordered.

Affirmed in part; reversed in part.

Mr. Justice Stevens took no part in the consideration or disposition of these cases.

[Concurring opinions by Mr. Justice Brennan and Mr. Justice Marshall omitted.]

(CA2 1975) (Friendly, J.) ("[a] subpoena demanding that an accused produce his own records is * * * the equivalent of requiring him to take the stand and admit their genuineness"), cert. pending, Nos. 75–407, 75–700; 8 Wigmore § 2264, p. 380 (the testimonial component involved in compliance with an order for production of documents or chattels "is the witness' assurance, compelled as an incident of the process, that the articles produced are the ones demanded"); McCormick § 126, p. 268 ("[t]his rule [applying the Fifth Amendment privilege to documentary subpoenas] is defended on the theory that one who produces documents (or other matter) described in the subpoena duces tecum represents, by his production, that the documents produced are in fact the documents described in the subpoena"); People v. Defore, 242 N.Y. 13, 27, 150 N.E. 585, 590 (1926) (Cardozo, J.) ("A defendant is

'protected from producing his documents in response to a subpoena duces tecum, for his production of them in court would be his voucher of their genuineness.' There would then be 'testimonial compulsion' ").

13. In seeking the accountant's "retained copies" of correspondence with the taxpayer in No. 74–611, we assume that the summons sought only "copies" of original letters sent from the accountant to the taxpayer—the truth of the contents of which could be testified to only by the accountant.

14. In these cases compliance with the subpoena is required even though the books have been kept by the person subpoenaed and his producing them would itself be sufficient authentication to permit their introduction against him.

Hypotheticals

(1) X is prosecuted for assault with a deadly weapon upon A by shooting A. Prosecution offers evidence that X was the owner and driver of the automobile from which the shots came that struck A. X takes the witness stand and, on direct examination, testifies that he had let Y, his girl friend, have his car several hours before the shooting. On cross-examination, the prosecutor asks X if he had driven his car to Y's home when he let her have his car. X objects to the question and claims the self-incrimination privilege, contending that an answer may disclose the offense of driving with a suspended or revoked license. How should the court rule?

(2) Dr. X is prosecuted for rape of A. A testifies for the prosecution that she went to see Dr. X, thinking that she was pregnant, to have an abortion; that Dr. X told her she was pregnant and that he would fix things for her; that Dr. X had her come back to his office on three occasions; and that on each occasion he gave her injections which made her dizzy and unable to resist and that he had sexual intercourse with her on each occasion. The prosecutor calls B and C, and each testifies that she had an experience with Dr. X similar to that testified to by A. Dr. X takes the stand, testifies in his own defense and denies the rape charges by A. No questions are asked of Dr. X on direct examination, relative to the testimony of B and C. On cross-examination, the prosecutor asks Dr. X if he had ever given B a drug injection as she testified. Dr. X objects that the question violates his privilege against self-incrimination. Is Dr. X correct?

Chapter VIII

JUDICIAL NOTICE

A. ADJUDICATIVE FACTS

GOODMAN v. STALFORT, INC.

United States District Court, D. New Jersey, 1976.
411 F. Supp. 889.

BIUNNO, District Judge.

This suit, brought on diversity grounds, seeks damages for personal injuries sustained in the use of an inflammable fluid marketed for the specific purpose of igniting charcoal in an outdoor grill.

The defendant Inland Oil and Chemical Corp. (Inland) was the supplier who initially furnished the fluid to Stalfort, in bulk. The fluid was sold to one or the other of the Stalfort companies, which packaged the fluid in cans for defendant Great Atlantic & Pacific Tea Co., Inc. (A & P), which in turn marketed the product under its brand for retail sale. Plaintiff Goodman purchased the can of fluid from A & P.

In the late afternoon of a day in mid-June, 1970, Goodman, then 53 years old, set up a charcoal grill to cook steaks for expected guests. The grill was a rectangular one, a foot wide and two feet long, and perhaps 6 to 8 inches deep.

He set this up in his driveway on a picnic table in the sun near the rear of the house, and filled it "good and full" with charcoal briquettes he had bought at A & P that afternoon, along with the can of charcoal lighter fluid.

It was the first time he was using the grill; he had a round one before that he had used and lit charcoal fires in up to 5 times.

He then lifted the plastic cap of the can and began to sprinkle the fluid over the charcoal. The fluid did not come out fast enough to his satisfaction, so he took a garden tool—a long-handled, four-tined fork—and used it to enlarge the openings in a plastic sprinkler set below the cap. He could not say how many holes the sprinkler had, or whether he pressed the fork through the cap or enlarged one of the holes. In any event, after this operation, he had made a large hole and the fluid came out quite freely, in a stream.

He poured the fluid, going back and forth over the charcoal to soak it all, using about half the contents of the can. He was not sure whether it was a pint can or a quart can. He then put the can down some distance away, waited a while for the fluid to soak into the charcoal, and then lit it in several places with a match.

The flames came up immediately, and satisfied that the fire was started, he went into the house to help his wife prepare the steaks. He came out ten to fifteen minutes later to check the fire, and it seemed to him to be out. He saw no flames, and passing his hand back and forth over the grill, there seemed to be no warmth, there was no heat to amount to anything. He did not poke or turn the charcoal to look underneath. Some of the briquettes

603

on top were a grayish-white at the corners. In his prior experience with charcoal, he had observed that when the charcoal was fully burning, a whitish or grayish-white coating formed on the entire surface.

He then picked up the can again, and the moment he began pouring more fluid on the charcoal a flame shot up the stream of fluid and the can blew up in his hand.   *   *   *

*   *   *

Stalfort and Inland have moved for summary judgment against Goodman.   *   *   *   [Asserting that] he was guilty of contributory negligence as a matter of law.   *   *   *

*   *   *   There is no doubt that Goodman's testimony discloses contributory negligence; the issue here is whether it so clearly appears therefrom as to amount to contributory negligence as a matter of law. Was Goodman's conduct such as to "invite calamity" by proximately making himself "the instrumentality of his own injury"?

Taking the evidence which Goodman would be bound with at trial in its most favorable light, the court is satisfied that it clearly and convincingly shows proximate causative contributory negligence as a matter of law. There is no escape from this conclusion.

*   *   *

*   *   *   It is clear on the facts of this case, that the case could not go to a jury, and if it did a verdict for Goodman would be set aside. The factual account and analysis so far expressed is more than sufficient to support the determination. Beyond that, there are matters that would be judicially noticed in this context at a trial which strongly reinforce the conclusion reached.

Charcoal has been known to man for a long time, and is probably one of his earliest artifacts after the discovery of fire. Although also prepared from animal bone, sugar and coal (coke), its commonest form is prepared from wood. From a remote period, in areas where there is an abundance of wood, as in the forests of France, Austria and Sweden, it was customary to stack billets of wood into a conical pile, cover it with turf or moistened soil, and then burn the wood slowly in a restricted amount of air. This drives off more volatile materials, such as acetone, wood-tar, and the like, leaving a porous carbon, the major use of which is as a fuel that burns with considerable heat and with little or no smoke or odor. See, The Encyclopaedia Brittanica (11th Ed.), Vol. 5, "Carbon", p. 305, and "Charcoal", p. 856.

The antiquity of the occupation of making charcoal from wood is evidenced by the references in old fairy tales to "charcoal burners", who live in a "great forest". See, for example, "The Knapsack, the Hat and the Horn", in Kingston, "Fifty Famous Fairy Tales", (Whitman Publishing Co., Racine, Wis., 1917) at pp. 143–145.

Today, of course, the destructive distillation of wood is carried out more efficiently, with the wood being heated in closed retorts without access to air, and the many useful by-products driven off are captured and separated (e.g., creosote, acetone, acetic acid, wood alcohol, etc.) leaving the charcoal as the residue. See, Dull, "High School Chemistry" (Henry Holt & Co., New York, 1925), § 182.

Until recent decades, charcoal sold at retail for use in cooking on grills came in the form of irregular pieces of varying sizes that retained the shape of the pieces of wood from which it was made. In its modern form, it is first powdered and then shaped into square, rounded pillows called "briquettes" of uniform size.

Igniting charcoal has traditionally consisted of first making a layer of twisted paper, wood chips, "kindling" wood, and the like, placing the charcoal on top, and then lighting the paper with a spill, a long wooden match, or the like. The easily ignited paper lights the kindling, and the heat from that ignites the charcoal. When the charcoal is ignited, it forms a greyish-white coating of ash since the combustion occurs at the surface (where the carbon is in contact with air) and continues burning toward the interior.

Impatience or difficulty with the traditional method led to the marketing of charcoal lighter fluid. Many users had for years employed substances such as cigarette lighter fluid, kerosene and alcohol as liquid fuels to ignite the charcoal more easily. Modern commercial fluids marketed for the purpose are less dangerous than these makeshift methods, and are essentially odorless as well.

In any case, the building of a charcoal fire, as with a log fire, involves going from a cold fuel to a fuel sufficiently heated to sustain its own combustion. The rate at which the charcoal passes from the cold state to the fully heated state depends on obvious variables. Enough air must pass through the bed to sustain and expand combustion. Too much air will cool the bed; too little air will fail to sustain the fire. The quantity of fuel is another factor. If there is too little, much of the heat will be lost by convection and ignition will not spread. If there is too much, the mass of charcoal will require a longer time to heat up to combustion.

But at any stage of the process, from the lighting of the fire on, if there is any combustion occurring anywhere in the bed, it is a "lighted fire", and the addition of a flammable material, such as was done by Goodman, is certain to result in an instaneous flare-up of the volatile liquid coming in contact with burning charcoal.

These are all matters of such common knowledge that the court feels obliged to take judicial notice of them. Under the formulation of Fed.Ev. Rule 201, it is by no means clear whether these are "adjudicative facts", or what the Advisory Committee's Note confusingly calls "legislative facts." In either case, these facts are so well known and not open to challenge as to require that they be judicially noticed.

* * *

Applying the test for summary judgment as interpreted in this circuit, the court finds that there is no genuine issue as to any material fact, and that Goodman's conduct was the proximate cause of his own injury constituting contributory negligence as a matter of law.

STATE v. LAWRENCE

Supreme Court of Utah, 1951.
120 Utah 323, 234 P.2d 600.

CROCKETT, Justice.   This case comes to us on an appeal from a conviction of grand larceny, arising out of the theft of an automobile. Two questions are presented: First, where there is no evidence of value except a description of the property involved, is it prejudicial error for the court to instruct the jury that the value of the property is greater than $50 and that if defendant is guilty at all he is guilty of grand larceny. The necessity of answering the first question in the affirmative gives rise to the second: Where such error has been committed, can the cause be remanded for retrial without violating the constitutional guarantee of the accused not to be placed twice in jeopardy for the same offense. After a consideration of the problems involved touching upon those questions we answer both in the affirmative.

At the conclusion of the evidence, the defendant's counsel moved the court for a directed verdict on the ground that there had been no evidence of value of the stolen car. The State's attorney might properly and with little difficulty have moved to reopen and supply the missing evidence. He did not do so but instead argued that judicial notice could be taken of the value of the car. The court denied defendant's motion and included in its instructions to the jury the following:

"Grand Larceny so far as it might be material in this case is committed when the property taken is of a value exceeding $50.00.

"In this case you will take the value of this property as being in excess of $50.00 and therefore the defendant, if he is guilty at all, is guilty of grand larceny."

It is conceded by the State that there was no direct evidence of value and that the only testimony in the record upon which a finding of value could be based was that of the owner of the automobile describing it saying it was in excellent condition.

This is not a case where the defendant either expressly or impliedly admitted the value, nor by conduct or statements of himself or counsel, allowed it to be assumed that the matter was not disputed. His plea of not guilty cast upon the State the burden of proving every essential element of the offense by evidence sufficient to convince the jury beyond a reasonable doubt. In a charge of grand larceny, one of those essentials is that the value be greater than $50. A conviction for that offense cannot stand unless there is satisfactory evidence of the value of the property. State v. Harris, Mo., 267 S.W. 802; People v. Leach, 106 Cal.App. 442, 290 P. 131. Ordinarily, judicial notice will not be taken of the value of personal property, 31 C.J.S., Evidence, § 101, page 701, and as will later appear herein, this is unquestionably so in connection with the instruction given in this case.

We direct our attention to the argument of the prosecution that the court could take judicial notice of the value of the car and so instruct the jury: Judicial notice is the taking cognizance by the court of certain facts without the necessity of proof, 31 C.J.S., Evidence, § 6, page 509. One class of factual material which is the subject of judicial notice is that dealt with by statute. Section 104–46–1, U.C.A.1943, provides: "Courts take judicial

notice of the following facts:" and proceeds to list in eight separate categories, such things as English words, whatever is established by law, acts of
departments of government, seals of courts, states and the United States,
etc. It would be of no value to list them all here because the value of the car
in question could not be thought to come under any subdivision of that statute by any stretch of the imagination.

Section 104–54–4, U.C.A.1943, under the Code of Civil Procedure provides in part: " *   *   * Whenever the knowledge of the court is by law
made evidence of a fact, the court is to declare such knowledge to the jury,
who are bound to accept it."

The word "knowledge" in the foregoing section is apparently used advisedly, there being a distinction between "judicial knowledge" of public
records, laws, etc. which the court is deemed to know by virtue of his office
and "judicial notice" of things which are commonly known. The further discussion in this opinion will show that this statute has no application to the
instant case. We are not here concerned with what the result might be if the
evidence in question were such that the statute required that the jury be
bound to accept it.

Beyond the scope of the statute providing that certain matters will be
taken judicial notice of, there is another class of facts which are so well
known and accepted that they are judicially noticed without taking the
time, trouble and expense necessary to prove them. Under this doctrine the
court will consider, without proof of such generally known facts, its knowledge of what is known to all persons of ordinary intelligence. This court has
recognized that class of judicial notice in a great variety of matters, a few
examples of which are: Rugg v. Tolman, 39 Utah 295, 117 P. 54 (that assignment or garnishment of wages ordinarily imputes no wrong or misconduct to
the debtor); Union Savings & Inv. Co. v. District Court of Salt Lake County, 44 Utah 397, 140 P. 221 (the general purpose and methods of doing business of building and loan associations); Salt Lake City v. Board of Education of Salt Lake City, 52 Utah 540, 175 P. 654 (location of school buildings);
Utah State Fair Ass'n v. Green, 68 Utah 251, 249 P. 1016 (that betting follows horse racing); State Tax Commission v. City of Logan, 88 Utah 406, 54
P.2d 1197 (that most consumers of electrical energy are constant users). For
numerous cases on judicial notice of many different subjects of common
knowledge outside the classes covered by our statute see Pacific Digest,
Evidence ☞1 to 52, inc. The taking of judicial notice of this latter class of
commonly known evidentiary facts does not establish them so conclusively
as to prevent the presentation of contrary evidence or the making of a finding to the contrary. The subject is treated in Wigmore on Evidence, 3d Ed.,
Sections 2555 et sequi, and he states in Section 2567: "(a) That a matter is
judicially noticed means merely that it is taken as true without the offering
of proof by the party who should ordinarily have done so. This is because
the court assumes that the matter is so notorious that it will not be disputed. But the opponent is not prevented from disputing the matter by
evidence, if he believes it disputable."

In discussing this further, Wigmore refers to statutes which expressly
provide that the judicial notice is the final determination and binding on
the jury; and in Subsection b of the above section, continues: " *   *   *
Does it signify that the settlement of the matter rests with the judge and not

with the jury, that the jury are to accept the fact from the judge, and that so far as any futher investigation is concerned, it is for the judge alone? Such is the view sometimes found, in decisions as well as statutes [citing statutes including Utah]. *Yet it seems rather that the jury are not concluded; that* the process of notice is intended chiefly for expedition of proof; *and remains possible for the jury to negative it."* (Emphasis added.)

Accordingly, if we assume that the value of the car is of that class of facts which is so well known that judicial notice should be taken thereof, that would not necessarily be conclusive upon the jury. It would merely take the place of evidence. Upon that basis the court could have instructed the jury to this effect: If you believe from the evidence beyond a reasonable doubt that the defendant stole the automobile in question and that it was a 1947 Ford Sedan in good condition, then you may take into consideration your knowledge acquired in the every day affairs of life in determining what value you will place upon said automobile.

Suppose any number of thoroughly competent and credible witnesses had testified that the car was worth more than $50, and there had been no evidence to the contrary, no matter how clear and convincing the evidence might have been, in a criminal case it was not the prerogative of the court to tell the jury that they have to believe it and so find. See State v. Estrada, Utah, 1951, 227 P.2d 247, 248, wherein this court reiterated the time-honored rule that it is the sole and exclusive province of the jury to determine the facts in criminal cases, whether the evidence offered by the State is strong or weak; and expressly stated:

"If the trial judge may not find a verdict of guilty, so, likewise he may not find any of the facts which are necessary elements of the crime for which the accused is being tried. * * * The provision of our State Constitution which grants accused persons the right to a trial by jury extends to each and all of the facts which must be found to be present to constitute the crime charged, and *such right may not be invaded by the presiding judge indicating to the jury that any of such facts are established by the evidence."*
(Emphasis added.)

* * * It is to be admitted that upon the surface there doesn't appear to be much logic to the thought that a jury would not be bound to find that the car involved here (1947 Ford 2-Door Sedan) is worth more than $50. However, under our jury system, it is traditional that in criminal cases juries can, and sometimes do, make findings which are not based on logic, nor even common sense. No matter how positive the evidence of a man's guilt may be, the jury may find him not guilty and no court has any power to do anything about it. Notwithstanding the occasional incongruous result, this system of submitting all of the facts in criminal cases to the jury and letting them be the exclusive judges thereof has lasted for some little time now and with a fair degree of success. If the result in individual cases at times seems illogical, we can be consoled by the words of Mr. Justice Holmes, that in some areas of the law, "a page of history is worth a volume of logic." We, who live with it, have a fervent devotion to the jury system, in spite of its faults. We would not like to see it destroyed nor whittled away. If a court can take one important element of an offense from the jury and determine the facts for them because such fact seems plain enough to him,

then which element cannot be similarly taken away, and where would the process stop?

For the court to instruct the jury as it did in its Instruction No. 4 " * * * you will take the value of this property as being in excess of $50.00" was an invasion of their province as the exclusive triers of the fact and was prejudicial error * * * . No case has been cited which supports the action of the trial court. One case has been found, certain language of which seems to indicate that the court could take judicial notice of the value of the car, State v. Phillips, 106 Kan. 192, 186 P. 743, 744, the court said: "We must not assume to be more ignorant than everybody else, and everybody else knows that such a car is worth more than $20."

But that case did not involve an instruction as to the value the jury must place on the car as in the instant case. In the Phillips case, the judgment was attacked for failure to prove value but the court recited that the defendant himself testified that he and his accomplice had sold the car for $200 (ten times the amount necessary to make grand larceny in that State) and taken $100 each. The evidence of value was sufficient and the conviction was affirmed. * * *

Judgment of the lower court is reversed and the cause remanded for a new trial.

Wade, McDonough, and Henriod, JJ., concur.

Wolfe, Chief Justice (dissenting).

I dissent. It is a well known fact of common and general knowledge that a 1947 2-door Ford sedan in excellent condition was worth more than $50 when it was stolen in March, 1950. There is sufficient notoriety of the value of this model car for the trial court to properly take judicial notice thereof.

* * * Defendant argued that the jury should be directed to find a verdict of not guilty upon the ground that there was no evidence as to the value of this automobile. The court took judicial notice of the obvious fact that the car was worth more than $50 and so instructed the jury. The doctrine of judicial notice of generally well known facts has been invoked in many criminal cases. Wharton's Criminal Evidence, 10th Ed. Vol. 1, Chapter VI. The rule should be the same in civil cases as in criminal cases, American Law Institute, Model Code of Evidence, Rules 1, 2 and 801. The majority opinion incorrectly assumes that in this state our Constitution forbids the trial court in a criminal case to take judicial notice of any of the facts necessary to proof of the offense. * * *

The fact that this car was a 1947 model in excellent condition is itself very good evidence of the fact that it was worth substantially more than $50. This is a chattel with which we are all familiar and no reasonable mind could believe that it was worth less than $50. Thus, the testimony of the owner of the automobile as to its make, model and condition made out a prima facie case as to its value. Instead of presenting evidence to rebut what the value of the car was, defendant seeks a reversal of the conviction contending that the State failed in its burden of proof. But the proof is plainly there. * * *

In order to scrupulously refrain from permitting the trial court to invade the province of the jury, the majority opinion suggests that the court could have instructed the jury that "you may take into consideration your knowledge acquired in the every day affairs of life in determining what value you will place upon said automobile." The question thus arises: If the court takes judicial notice of a fact, or at least believes a fact is so obvious that proof thereof is unnecessary, in what manner must he see that a just verdict does not fail for want of that fact? How should his decision to take judicial notice of a fact be transmitted to the jury? Mr. Justice Crockett believes it to be prejudicial error if the trial court tells the jury forthright, what is obviously so—that the car is worth more than $50. He would rather have the jury instructed that they are to draw from their own everyday experience in determining what the car is worth.

There is no constitutional provision which prohibits the trial judge from taking judicial notice in a criminal case of a fact, sufficiently notorious. If the fact is so well known that judicial notice should be taken thereof, it then becomes the duty of the court to inform the jury that the matter should be taken to be established. Counsel not contending that the fact is controverted, the jury should be instructed as to what the fact is. The trial court in this case stated in effect that the evidence as to value of the property stolen warranted conviction of grand larceny, if defendant was guilty at all. The jury was fully instructed that before the defendant could be found guilty of grand larceny they must believe beyond a reasonable doubt that the defendant drove away the Ford automobile, with a felonious intent of stealing said property and of permanently depriving the owner thereof. The jury was left free to determine the ultimate fact of guilt or innocence. * * *

NOTE

14 Sw.L.J. 394 (1960).*

EVIDENCE—JUDICIAL NOTICE—RADAR

[Most footnotes omitted.]

Defendant was convicted of violating maximum speed laws. The basis of the conviction was a radar unit reading with respect to his speed. There was testimony that the radar unit had been set up and tested, but there was no evidence of the results of the test. *Held:* Where a conviction for speeding rests upon the reading of a radar unit, failure to prove the accuracy of that radar unit on location is reversible error. Wilson v. State, 163 Tex.Crim. 439, 328 S.W.2d 311 (1959).

The doctrine of judicial notice recognizes that certain facts may be so notorious or their existence so easily ascertained that proof of such will not be required. While there is strong authority to the contrary, the majority of jurisdictions support the view that when judicial notice of a fact is taken, evidence to the contrary is inadmissible, and the judge is required to instruct the jury that the fact is to be accepted as true. Judicial notice usually will be taken of scientific facts either notoriously true or capable of demonstration by authoritative sources. Courts have judicially noticed certain scientific facts e. g., the results of blood grouping tests in questions of paternity, X-ray photographs, fingerprints, speedometer readings, disc recordings, the arching propensity of electricity, the intoxicating character of various beverages, the liquid character of alcohol and ether at ordinary room temperatures, and certain passages in recognized books. Some courts, however, have refused to take judicial notice of such facts, holding them admissible to be considered by the fact finder in determining the particular issue if (1) the scientific apparatus producing the facts is accepted as dependable in the field of science involved; (2) the particular appartus used is in good condition for accurate work; and (3) the witness using the apparatus as the source of his testimony is qualified for its use by training and experience. Most courts are in agreement that certain scientific facts, e. g., the results of lie detector tests and sodium pentothal (truth serum) tests, not only will be denied judicial notice, but will not be admitted into evidence, reasoning that the reliability of such tests is not established with a sufficient degree of accuracy in the particular field of science.

The early cases on radar speedmeters refused to take judicial notice of their readings, but admitted them in evidence upon proof of (1) the accuracy of the general principles of radar by expert testimony, (2) the particular unit's accuracy at the time in question, and (3) the qualifications to operate the unit of the witness seeking to testify as to the reading of the unit regarding the defendant's speed. The courts began to modify their requirements with the New Jersey decision of State v. Dantonio,[20] where the court stated that there would be no need for expert testimony as to the accuracy of the scientific principles of radar if the particular unit in question were properly set up and tested by the police officers in charge. Subsequently, New York and Nebraska courts followed the same reasoning. However, for the first time in People v. Magri,[23] the courts completed the change in their requirements by giving express recognition to the applicability of the doctrine of judicial notice to radar readings. The present rule is that the results of radar will be judicially noticed if it is established that the particular unit in question was accurate and was properly operated at the time the defendant's speed was recorded.

The court's holding in the principal case is sound; for radar readings to be admitted in evidence or judicially noticed, the particular unit must be proven accurate. A conviction based on the readings of a unit, the accuracy of which has not been established, will require reversal. Although the principal case does not reach the issue of judicial notice, the court does indicate that the results of radar will be judicially noticed as true if there is proof of the accuracy of the unit in question and that the unit was operated by one qualified by training and experience. If this is true, Texas will be in accord with the majority of other jurisdictions which have considered the problem.

The prevailing authority, accepting the view that radar readings should be accorded judicial notice, will expedite trials by doing away with the necessity of proving the accuracy of the general principles of radar in every case. Moreover, the defendant will still be accorded sufficient protection since he may prevent judicial notice by showing that the particular instrument in question was inaccurate or that the operator of the unit was inexperienced. With over five hundred police departments in forty-three

---

20.   18 N.J. 570, 115 A.2d 35 (1955).   23.   3 N.Y.2d 562, 147 N.E.2d 728, 170 N.Y.S.2d 335 (1958).

states utilizing radar to aid in law enforcement and the increasing number of automobiles and super-highways across the nation, such a result is a desirable and progressive step forward in the law.

* * *

COMMENT, JUDICIAL NOTICE BY APPELLATE COURTS OF FACTS AND FOREIGN LAWS NOT BROUGHT TO THE ATTENTION OF THE TRIAL COURT

42 Mich.L.Rev. 509 (1943).*
[Footnotes omitted.]

The doctrine of judicial notice represents one of the oldest and most valuable constituents of our jurisprudence. From the days of the Yearbooks, courts have noticed matters of many diverse kinds which they have considered (a) sufficiently notorious and (b) commonly recognized. Thus courts have recognized that games such as ping-pong are not "toys," that short delays often occur in mail deliveries, * * * that tobacco is a farm product, that the front fender of an automobile is about the height of a man's knee [Grzybowski v. Connecticut Co., 116 Conn. 292, 164 A. 632 (1933)], * * * that a mule is a dangerous instrumentality. * * * Today, as in earlier times, the doctrine remains a kind of common-sense "taking-for-granted" of certain facts which experience has shown need not be proved. To put the matter another way, it declares that there are certain propositions in a party's case as to which he will not be required to offer evidence. * * *

SCHWARTZ, A SUGGESTION FOR THE DEMISE OF JUDICIAL NOTICE OF "JUDICIAL FACTS"

45 Tex.L.Rev. 1212 (1967).**

Judicial notice as presently conceived is a doctrine that allows a court to decide certain issues without reference to data submitted at an adversary hearing governed by the conventional rules of evidence. A court takes judicial notice of an issue for one of two reasons: (1) It is general in nature, relevant to a legal question such as statutory construction or constitutionality, and can better be explored by the judge free of the limitations imposed by the rules of evidence. (2) It is so indisputably settled that although normally in the province of the fact finder (usually a jury) it can be resolved by the judge without hearing evidence. This is commonly referred to as judicial notice of "judicial facts."

The latter aspect of judicial notice is formulated in rule 9(2) of the Uniform Rules of Evidence. The test for permitting judicial notice is whether the facts "are so generally known or of such common notoriety within the territorial jurisdiction * * * that they cannot reasonably be the subject of dispute. * * * [or] are capable of immediate and accurate determination by resort to easily accessible sources of indisputable accuracy."[1] This aspect of judicial notice performs essentially two functions. It serves to identify in advance issues that need not be formally tried, and it

---

1. Rule 9 also provides for judicial notice of various matters of local and foreign law. This portion of the rule, however, will not be considered here. This observation is also limited to civil cases.

provides a means for achieving a just result despite the failure of the parties to produce adequate proof.

The doctrine is, however, seriously deficient in accomplishing both of these objectives. It fails as a means of identifying issues that need be tried because of the extraneous limitation to facts that are of "common notoriety" or "capable of immediate and accurate determination." The only significant question should be whether the particular factual issue is genuinely in dispute. As a means of reaching a just result in the face of an inadequate record, judicial notice, of course, suffers from this same deficiency. More fundamental, however, is the failure to face squarely the questions of what should be the judge's responsibility in determining whether a factual record is inadequate and whether to take steps to cure it. Surely that responsibility should not be limited to supplying facts that are of "common notoriety" or "capable of immediate and accurate determination."

The following statute, together with presently available motions for summary judgment and directed verdict, would provide more inclusive and rational means for dealing with these problems:

(1)　If the trial court in a case in which both sides have rested and the case has not been decided shall determine that the evidence with respect to a material issue of fact is significantly less than may be available and that there is a substantial risk that decision based on the evidence of record measured by the applicable burdens of proof and persuasion may not comport with actual fact it may

(a)　in all cases where there is no jury and in jury cases where the additional evidence can be obtained without substantial delay stay all proceedings until the parties have an opportunity to obtain the additional evidence and then permit the evidence to be introduced and considered in the decision of the case, or

(b)　in jury cases where the additional evidence cannot be obtained without substantial delay discharge the jury and direct retrial of the case when the additional evidence is obtained.[2]

(2)　If the trial court after the case has been decided or an appellate court shall determine that the evidence with respect to a material issue of fact is significantly less than may be available and that there is a substantial risk that decision based on the evidence of record measured by the applicable burdens of proof and persuasion may not comport with actual fact it may

(a)　afford the parties the opportunity to demonstrate to the Court before whom the matter is pending their respective rights to summary judgment[3] with respect to the issue, or

2.　There are procedural devices that provide alternatives to directing complete retrial. Thus if the issue with respect to which the evidence is to be offered is severable the court can sever it and hear the remainder of the case. The jury verdict may then make the severed issue moot. A second possibility is that the party who will have to bear the expense of the extra proceedings (as provided in paragraph 3) may be agreeable to waiving jury trial. If the other party concurs, the case can simply be continued until the additional evidence is available. It is also possible that after the additional evidence is obtained summary judgment can be awarded and retrial thus avoided.

3.　A motion for summary judgment before the appellate court would be an unprecedented innovation. Since no oral testimony is required and the appellate court has gained familiarity with the case by hearing the appeal, there is no reason for a remand to the trial court.

(b)   remand the case for the taking of further evidence and reconsideration by the judge before whom the case was originally heard (who may be the judge issuing the order) or a retrial of the issue before a jury as may be appropriate.[4]

(3)   The party or parties against whom the issue would be resolved on the state of the record prior to the proceedings authorized by this Rule shall be responsible for all costs, including reasonable attorney's fees, incurred by the other parties in connection with proceedings authorized by this Rule.

There are two main conclusions underlying the proposed solution. First, a party who is aware that there is strong proof of his contention and would be entitled to have judicial notice taken should be able to demonstrate his right to summary judgment or a directed verdict. In addition to covering all cases within the scope of judicial notice as presently conceived, the summary judgment and directed verdict procedures serve to foreclose spurious issues that are beyond reach of judicial notice. The overlap between summary judgment or directed verdict on the one hand and judicial notice on the other creates the risk that a party may invoke judicial notice, overlook the other devices, and thus be denied relief to which he is entitled. Secondly, in those cases where all the evidence is in and the matter is pending before a trial or appellate court, judicial notice provides a poor way to cure a defective record—the real reason for its use. The question whether the record affords an inadequate basis for decision should be squarely faced and the court should have available the full range of practical alternatives for obtaining further factual guidance.

The principal reason for rejecting judicial notice in favor of summary judgment or directed verdict is that the judicial notice concept introduces the essentially extraneous concepts that the facts must be "so generally known or of such common notoriety that they cannot reasonably be the subject of dispute" or "capable of immediate and accurate determination by resort to easily accessible sources of indisputable accuracy." Whether the matter is commonly known or subject to immediate and accurate determination should be irrelevant if the truth of the particular fact in issue can be plainly demonstrated. This is precisely the approach of summary judgment and directed verdict, which foreclose the matter if the particular issue is not "genuine." These devices, moreover, should cover all cases where judicial notice can now be taken. If the matter is of "common notoriety," the affidavit or testimony of a knowledgeable person will be sufficient because presumably no denial will be possible. If the matter can be determined by reference to sources of "indisputable accuracy" the moving party will offer them; if indeed they are indisputable, they will not be disputed.

The use of judicial notice as a pretrial device is probably explicable in historical terms by the unavailability of summary judgment (and perhaps discovery devices such as requests for admissions that can also be used to eliminate spurious issues) as a means of limiting trials to matters genuinely in dispute. One other contemporary justification might be offered. Since the

4.   Of course, waiver of jury trial will avoid the necessity of repeating the evidence previously admitted on the issue.

exclusionary rules of evidence generally do not govern what a judge may consider in determining whether to take judicial notice, judicial notice may be viewed as a means of relaxing the hearsay limitations on the use of documentary evidence. This approach to the problem is unfortunate. If reliable documentation is being excluded by the hearsay rule, the rule ought to be changed. It is anomalous indeed for a scholarly work to be characterized as a "source of indisputable accuracy" for the purpose of allowing judicial notice and yet to be excluded as hearsay at trial.

In any event, with the advent of liberal discovery and summary judgment, the judicial notice doctrine is not significant where counsel realizes that his position may be so strong that he can avoid litigating the matter at trial. Its more significant use, however, is when it is discovered after all the evidence is in that a party has failed to offer adequate proof with respect to a contention that the court nevertheless feels is true. In this situation the limitations of the judicial notice doctrine can create more serious problems. The court can supply the missing proof only if the stated requirements are met. If they cannot be met, however, the case must be decided on the existing record no matter how strong the indications are that vital evidence has been omitted.

This is obviously a bad result. If there is still time to produce reliable proof before the case is submitted for decision, the court should advise counsel to obtain it. Or if the inadequacy is detected after an initial determination, the party should be permitted to demonstrate the fact by affidavit or other irrefutable proof. More fundamentally, the court should never decide a case on a record it regards as inadequate. Rather, it should invoke the alternative provided by the proposed Rule, which assures an informed resolution of the issue with the least possible expense and burden.

The proposal is completed by providing that the party who has failed to discharge his responsibility to prove the matter should bear the expense of the extra proceedings to cure the defective record. Indeed, if the party in turn succeeds in recovering these expenses from his own counsel, when his negligence has created the necessity for the additional proceedings, the consequences may be even more salutary.

In conclusion, judicial notice adds nothing as a means of selecting in advance issues that need not be the subject of proof at trial—with the exception of the doubtful contribution of indirect relaxation of the hearsay rule. As a means of achieving a just resolution when the trial record is inadequate it suffers most fundamentally from a failure squarely to face the problem. Moreover, it is far too limited and inflexible to afford appropriate relief in all cases where it is needed. The use of summary judgment and directed verdict to eliminate spurious issues, the relaxation of hearsay limitations on the consideration of reliable scholarly works, and the invocation of the proposed statute dealing directly with the problem of the inadequate trial record, together afford far better means for resolving the problems now handled under the judicial notice doctrine.

See Federal Rules of Evidence 201, at p. 908. California Evidence Code § § 450–460 at pp. 819–821. On judicial notice of foreign law see F.R.Civ.P.44.1 and F.R.Cr.P.26.1

MAGUIRE: EVIDENCE, COMMON SENSE AND COMMON LAW

168–171 (1947)*

* * *

To a large extent the subjects of judicial notice are, as already indicated, rudimentary commonplaces—propositions of generalized knowledge and specific fact so notorious as not to be either ignored or disputed. But judicial notice goes a great deal further than this. Judges of first instance and of appeal judicially notice the common law and public statutes, State or Federal, and of course all constitutional provisions, which are in force in their jurisdiction. The reason is obvious. This is their main judicial apparatus, and they are responsible for its proper recognition and application.

At common law judges usually have not been authorized to notice in this fashion private acts or resolves of local legislatures or Congress, or ordinances or regulations of subdivisions of their State governments. Likewise the decisions and statutes of other States or nations have not been subjects of notice at common law—but this limitation will be misunderstood unless it is remembered that so far as Federal courts act under their original jurisdiction conferred by the national constitution and laws, the law of every State is domestic to these tribunals. See, on this last matter, Hanley v. Donoghue, 166 U.S. 1, 6 S.Ct. 242 (1885), a case taken to the Supreme Court of the United States from a State court instead of an inferior Federal court.

Why the distinctions between foreign law and the law of the home State, between public and private legislation, and between the law of that State as a whole and the law of its municipal subdivisions? As to foreign law, two highly practical reasons at once suggest themselves: First, it might be very difficult for the judge of the District Court of Siwash to lay his hands on a reliable version of the decisions or statutes of Zanzibar; and, second, even if he could get the books, all their presuppositions might be so strange that he could not by solitary perusal assure himself of the true legal meaning. The second of these reasons will not apply to domestic private acts or county, city, and town law, but the first will. American municipalities have often fallen woefully short of presenting, in form upon which legal experts can rely, proper collations of their ordinances, regulations, and so on; nor have private acts and resolves always been reliably accessible.

The legal profession is coming to believe that under modern conditions important parts of the old rule about judicial notice of foreign law ought to be changed. A Uniform State Law carrying this view into effect has had numerous legislative adoptions. Other related legislation has gone through. Quite likely, before many years pass, we shall find the common practice in the United States to be that each State's courts notice the decisions and public statutes of sister States; that courts notice domestic ordinances, private acts, etc.; possibly even that within reasonable limits courts notice the law of foreign countries. Whether the law prescribing this practice is worded in mandatory or discretionary form will make little difference. No judge can possibly have at his instant command all these details or even the sources of information. Counsel will have to help the judiciary. No help, no notice. Unquestionably the desired assistance will be forthcoming. When a presiding judge asks the lawyers for an ordinary memorandum of law, he gets it; and so in this or any angle of judicial notice.

Broadly speaking, of course, such submission of information amounts to giving evidence. But the process is bound to be informal and direct, unhampered by any technical exclusionary rules. What seems to the judge reliable and convincing he will accept and use. Incidentally, when matters of law do have to be proved, instead of being noticed with or without informative assistance, it is the definite tendency of modern legislation to have the proof presented to the judge for his finding, instead of being put to the jury. Unquestionably the judge is a better trier of this kind of issue, and his employment in that capacity will tend to speed and simplify probative steps.

These extensions of the application of judicial notice to determinations about law are made practicable by the growing ease of access to trustworthy printed information. It is therefore consistent to find courts, often without special statutory authority, noticing a wide variety of other facts which, although not mere everyday commonplaces, are in the terms of the Law Institute Code "capable of immediate and accurate demonstration by resort to easily accessible sources of indisputable accuracy." Rule 802(c). For instance, the coincidence of days of the week and of the month in times past or to come, by inspecting calendars; the phases of the moon, by consulting standard almanacs; holders of public office, by examining records of appointment or election in the office of the Secretary of State or other appropriate functionary; relations between the United States and foreign nations, by communication with the Department of State; and so on through an indeterminable list. Some States have statutes scheduling considerable numbers of particular matters to be noticed; in other States the whole question is left for the judges to develop; hence the principle is applied with a good deal of variability.

The courts have not sharply and fully spelled out the procedure of judicial notice. There is speculation as to whether counsel must invariably request the taking of notice; how far the judge should consult counsel before he commits himself; whether a lawyer whose request for notice is improperly denied should submit evidence on the point which notice would have covered; whether and how far the jury may notice matters without instruction from the judge; what happens on appeal with respect to matters which escaped notice in the trial court although they ought to have been, or might have been there noticed; and a great many other details. * * *

B. JURY NOTICE

IX WIGMORE, EVIDENCE § 2570 (1940)*

[Some footnotes omitted.]

Judicial Notice by the Jury's Own Knowledge. In general, the jury may in modern times act only upon evidence properly laid before them in the course of the trial. But so far as the matter in question is one upon which men in general have a common fund of experience and knowledge, through data notoriously accepted by all, the analogy of judicial notice by the judge obtains here also, to some extent, and the jury are allowed to resort to this information in making up their minds.

This doctrine, of course, has several aspects. From the point of view of the jury's duty, it appears as an exception to the rule that they must act only upon what is presented to them at the trial. From the point of view of the Hearsay rule, it may also be thought of as a partial exception to that.[1] But additionally it must be considered from the present point of view. It authorizes the party to ask the *jury to refer to their general knowledge* upon matters *notorious and unquestioned,* and thus in effect and to that extent makes it unncessary for the party to have offered evidence on the matter:

1878, Hunter's Trial, N.J., 13 Amer.St.Tr. 57, 151; murder of Armstrong by Graham, at Hunter's instigation; a witness as to their doings placed Hunter on the Philadelphia ferry-boat on the evening of the murder. Mr. *George R. Robeson,* for the accused, arguing against this witness' credibility: "As to the testimony of Mrs. Auvache, think of the brilliancy of memory of a witness who could come into court five months after the 23d of January and positively identify Hunter as a man at whom she had taken a passing glance on the evening of that day. And her entry in the diary of her trip to Philadelphia on that day, only two other entries being made in the whole book! She insisted that the ladies' cabin on the boat she came over on was on the left-hand side of the boat, although the ladies' cabin is on the right side of the boat."

Mr. *Jenkins* [for the State]: *"Is there any proof in this case* as to what side the ladies cabin is located?"

Mr. *Robeson*: "Does the prosecutor dispute that fact?"

Mr. *Jenkins*: "I dispute that it is in testimony."

Mr. *Robeson*: "I don't care whether it is or not. I think Moore testified to the fact, but it does not matter; *the Court knows, the jury knows, the people know, and the prosecutor knows,* that the ladies' cabin on the boats of the Camden ferry is on the *right*-hand side. I gave Mrs. Auvache every opportunity to rectify her statement by asking her every form of question about it, but she stuck to her falsehood."

1908, Mr. *Arthur Train,* in the "Sunday Magazine," Nov. 7, 1908: "Most cases turn on an unconsidered point. A prosecutor once lost what seemed to him the clearest sort of a case. When it was all over, and the defendant had passed out of the courtroom rejoicing, he turned to the foreman and asked the reason for the verdict. 'Did you hear your chief witness say he was a carpenter?' inquired the foreman. 'Why, certainly,' answered the district attorney. 'Did you hear me ask him what he paid for that ready-made pine door he claimed to be working on when he saw the assault?' The prosecutor recalled the incident and nodded. 'Well, he said ten dollars—and I knew he was a liar.

---

1. Ante, § 1900 (jurors having personal knowledge must take the stand and state it publicly as witnesses subject to cross-examination). Distinguish, however, the propriety of *knowledge acquired at a view* (ante, § 1168).

A door like that don't cost but four-fifty!' It is, perhaps, too much to require a knowledge of carpentry on the part of a lawyer trying an assault case. Yet the juror was undoubtedly right in his deduction."

1884, Lyon, J., in Washburn v. R. Co., 59 Wis. 364, 370: "A jury is not bound to give and cannot give any weight to testimony which, although undisputed by witnesses, is contrary to what every person of ordinary intelligence knows to be true. To illustrate, should a witness testify that at Boston on a certain day the sun arose at midnight, or that the Mississippi river empties into Lake Michigan, or that white is black, the testimony would be rejected at once. * * * Beyond this the jury cannot properly go. To allow jurors to make up their verdict on their individual knowledge of disputed facts material to the case, not testified to by them in court, or upon their private opinions, would be most dangerous and unjust. It would deprive the losing party of the right of cross-examination and the benefit of all the tests of credibility which the law affords. Besides, the evidence of such knowledge or of the grounds of such opinions could not be preserved in a bill of exceptions or questioned on appeal."

1895, Hackney, J., Jenney Electric Co. v. Branham, 145 Ind. 314, 41 N.E. 448 (permitting the use of "your experience and relations among men" in judging of the credibility of witnesses): "It is argued that such a rule would permit the disposition of a cause upon the whims of jurors, rather than upon the law and the evidence as they were learned in the trial. Jurors should be, and, as a rule, are, selected because of their extensive experiences among men. The school of experience which men attend in their varied relations among men imparts a keenness of mental vision which enables them the more readily to see the motives and to judge of the selfish or unselfish interest of men. This education, be it much or little, is a part of the juror, and should not, if possible, be laid aside in passing upon the inducements which may surround a witness to speak falsely. It is this education which to a great extent enables a juror to discover in the faltering manner or the downcast eye whether the statement of the witness is made in modesty or in the guilt of falsehood. The value of experience is not to be given up when the man becomes a juror, and is required to apply the tests of credit to the heart and mind of the witness, but whatever qualification that experience gives should be employed to the end that the whole truth may be known and acted upon."

1921, Burnett, C.J., in Rostad v. Portland R.L. & P. Co., 101 Or. 569, 201 P. 184: "The *personal* knowledge of any juror concerning any probative fact involved in the case under consideration is not to be used in deciding the case. Such a juror should communicate his information to the Court, and if he is not excused from service and it is deemed proper to use his cognizance of such a fact in the trial, he must be sworn as a witness and examined, subject to cross-examination by the adverse party, the same as any other witness. But any juror must consider the testimony in the light of that *knowledge and experience which is common to all men.* For instance, it is a matter of common knowledge that a bullet piercing the brain of a human being will in all likelihood prove fatal. It is common knowledge, also, that a forest tree cut nearly in two at the butt will fall, if a high wind blows against it. If a witness should testify to the contrary to these ordinary phenomena, the common knowledge of the juror derived from his experience in such matters would naturally compel him to discredit that witness. Many illustrations might be given where men are normally and legitimately influenced in considering testimony by their general knowledge and experience. * * * It is utterly impracticable in the administration of courts of justice to secure a juror whose mind is totally blank as to questions involved in the ordinary transactions of life. Triers of fact cannot, in the nature of things, be divested of general knowledge of practical affairs. The Court cannot do otherwise than to direct them to use such experiences as are common to all men in the decision of questions of fact. It is part of the jury system which cannot be dispensed with."

But the scope of this doctrine is narrow; it is strictly limited to a few matters of elemental experience in human nature, commercial affairs, and everyday life. Thus, the natural instincts of human conduct, with reference to care or negligence at the time of danger, may be considered, the dangerousness of smoking a pipe in a barn near the straw, the conditions affecting the various kinds of values, the intoxicating nature of a certain liquor, and even (though this illustrates how local conditions may affect the application) that a game played with bone-counters was played for money. But such a matter of private and variable belief as the character of a particular witness cannot be so taken into consideration by the jury.

The range of such general knowledge is not precisely definable. But in these days when too much emphasis is placed, in the selection of jurors, on the blankness of their mental tablets, there can be no harm in the liberal application of the present principle.

As a natural part of its doctrine, of course, these matters may be referred to by counsel in their arguments.

HIGGINS v. LOS ANGELES GAS & ELECTRIC CO.

Supreme Court of California, 1911.
159 Cal. 651, 115 P. 313.

HENSHAW, J. This action was brought to recover damages from defendant for injuries caused to a building, the property of plaintiff. The damage was caused by an explosion of gas. This explosion occurred in a restaurant of a tenant of the plaintiff, Cressaty by name. The facts attending the explosion have recently been set forth by this court in its consideration of the case of Merrill v. Los Angeles Gas & Electric Company, 111 Pac. 534. It is sufficient to refer to that case; but it is to be borne in mind that that action was for personal injuries occasioned to a patron of Cressaty's restaurant, while the present action is to recover damages occasioned to plaintiff's building while in the possession of a tenant.

Trial was had before a jury. The defendant, as part of its evidence, showed that, the gas leak being in a dark and obscure place, its employés approached the leak with an electric flash light, and while the man holding the flash light was in close proximity to the leak the explosion occurred. The flash light used to inspect the leak was never recovered. It was probably destroyed by the explosion. But a similar flash light was introduced in evidence by the defendant, and the contention was made that it was impossible for this flash light as used to give out any spark which would cause the ignition and explosion of the gas. It was also in evidence that an oil stove in the restaurant was burning at the time of the explosion, and that this oil stove was some 44 feet from the place where the gas was escaping. It was contended by plaintiff that the explosion was probably occasioned by a spark from the electric flash light, and he introduced evidence to establish the fact that a flash light such as that before the jury could produce a spark. It was contended by defendant that the explosion was occasioned by the flame of the oil stove, and that Cressaty, plaintiff's tenant, was negligent in not having extinguished the light of the stove after demand by defendant's employés that he do so. To demonstrate that the flash light could give out, and might have given out, a spark sufficient to cause the explosion, plaintiff, in rebuttal of the evidence of defendant's experts to the contrary, put an expert witness on the stand who so testified. Asked to demonstrate before the jury how the spark could be produced and to produce it, he proceeded to unscrew the cap of the flash light and undertook to make a spark by the use of a pair of plyers. Under objection the court stopped this experiment, manifestly for the reason that, to be of value to the jury, a spark should be produced from the flash light under conditions of use like those attending the explosion. Argument was indulged in before the jury pro and con over the possibility of so producing a spark, and the flash light was passed from hand to hand and inspected by the jury. While deliberating over their verdict, the jury requested to have with them in the jury room the flash light. The court permitted them to do so. Special interrogatories were submitted to the jury, amongst them one in answer to which it declared that the explosion was caused by a spark from the flash light and not from the flame of the oil stove. The general verdict was for plaintiff. Defendant moved for a new trial.

The court denied the motion as to all grounds save one, and granted the new trial "on the sole ground that the court erred in sending into the jury in their consultation room the flash light." The terms of this order eliminate from consideration the question of the sufficiency or insufficiency of the evidence to support the verdict. There are left for consideration two matters: First, was it error calling for a new trial for the court to have permitted the jury to take with them to their room and to have with them during their deliberations the flash light introduced in evidence by respondent? Second, alleged errors of the court arising in the trial of the case.

The only express provision of the law bearing upon the right of juries to use exhibits or upon the right of the court to permit juries to use exhibits in their deliberations is found in section 612 of the Code of Civil Procedure, and this has to do solely with "papers" which have been introduced in evidence. One curious in such matters can learn from the common law why this section of the Code was adopted and why also it is confined to papers. The common-law rule was that jurors were allowed to take with them in their deliberations only such instruments as were under seal, and that they were not permitted to take with them any unsealed papers excepting by consent of the parties. The reason for this, according to Lord Hale and Lord Gilbert, was that jurors were supposed to be, and for the most part were, unlettered men. They could not read. A writing conveyed to them nothing. But in the case of sealed instruments, as these jurors were drawn from the vicinage, they were quite apt to be familiar with the armorial bearings of their neighborhood great from which the seals were derived. An instrument under seal, therefore, spoke for itself, and the jurors were permitted to take such instruments with them, not for the purpose of reading the instrument itself, but rather for the purpose of verifying their recollection of the seal and testing its genuineness. The curious inquirer will also find that it was not uncommon for one who had not risen to the dignity of possessing an armorial bearing to set the stamp of his teeth as his seal upon the instrument, and hence the old time phrase of "proving it to (by) his teeth." But, in the case of other exhibits not involving a knowledge of reading or writing, it seems to have been a matter of discretion with the court to allow the jury to take them into the jury room in aid of their deliberations. This rule, as to papers, however, was in force at a time when learning in letters was so rare and the premium upon such learning so high that a felon could save his neck by proving his ability to read a verse of scripture. It was to save the possibility of the question arising in this state as in 1812 it arose in the state of Pennsylvania (Alexander et al. v. Jameson et al., 5 Bin. 238) that the section of the Code was adopted. All distinction between sealed and unsealed instruments had been abolished, and, as the restrictive rule of the common law upon the power of the court had gone only to papers containing printing or writing, it was necessary only to modify that rule as was done by section 612. Therefore section 612 is not to be construed as a limitation of the power of the court in the matter of other exhibits, but as a modification and extension of the common-law rule touching exhibits containing writings.

It will be noted that depositions are excluded by the section. This is for the very obvious reason that depositions may, and usually do, contain matters not admissible in evidence which matters have been eliminated from the consideration of the jury. To permit the jury to take depositions with them would be to put them in possession of this excluded evidence.

In this lies the suggestion of the true rule guiding the court and governing the jury in the use of exhibits. The court may permit the jury to take with them and use in their deliberations any exhibit where the circumstances call for it, observing the proper precaution of instructing the jury in the nature of the use which they shall make of the exhibit. It is a fundamental rule that all evidence shall be taken in open court, and that each party to a controversy shall have knowledge of, and thus be enabled to meet and answer, any evidence brought against him. It is this fundmental rule which is to govern the use of such exhibits by the jury. They may use the exhibit according to its nature to aid them in weighing the evidence which has been given and in reaching a conclusion upon a controverted matter.

They may carry out experiments within the lines of offered evidence; but if their experiments shall invade new fields, and they shall be influenced in their verdict by discoveries from such experiments which will not fall fairly within the scope and purview of the evidence, then, manifestly, the jury has been itself taking evidence without the knowledge of either party, evidence which it is not possible for the party injured to meet, answer, or explain.

Typical instances of the improper and proper experimental use of exhibits by a jury are found, respectively, in Wilson v. United States, 116 F. 484, 53 C.C.A. 652, and Taylor v. Commonwealth, 90 Va. 109, 17 S.E. 812.

In the first of these cases the indictment charged the defendant with smuggling opium "prepared for smoking purposes." A sealed can had been introduced in evidence by the prosecution and asserted to contain a sample of the smuggled opium. No testimony was given tending to show that the can contained opium prepared for smoking purposes, and yet it was conceded that it was essential to a conviction (since the offense was so laid) to show not only that the can contained opium, and that it was smuggled opium, but also that it was opium "prepared for smoking purposes." In this condition of the evidence the court instructed the jury that it might take the can to the jury room, open it, and extract some of the contents; that they would not be permitted to make a chemical examination of the contents; but that they could in the jury room test the extracted samples and learn to their satisfaction whether or not it would burn, and use the information so obtained in determining whether the can contained "opium prepared for smoking purposes." The Circuit Court of Appeals, in holding this instruction to be erroneous, said: "Surely, if the attorney for the government, as was his duty, had offered evidence going to show that the can in question contained opium for smoking purposes, the defendants would have been legally and justly entitled to have proved, if they could, that it contained no such thing; in which latter event there must have been a verdict of not guilty, for there was nothing else offered tending to show that there was any opium prepared for smoking purposes in the case. Yet the jury was left to determine that essential fact for themselves, by experiment, and in the absence of the defendants, who were thus wholly deprived of the opportunity to contest the correctness of the jury's experiments, and of the possibility of giving any evidence upon one of the essential facts involved in the prosecution." Taylor v. Commonwealth was a case of murder. It was the assassination from ambush at midday of six or seven innocent and unsuspecting people. By the Supreme Court of Virginia it is described as "an inhuman and wholesale massacre of innocent and unsuspecting men, women and children traveling peaceably upon the public highway." In the ambuscade of the assassins were found certain cartridge shells which had been discharged from a 45-75 Winchester rifle. Defendant was charged with this murder. It was shown by the prosecution that he carried a rifle of this description and caliber. The defendant introduced his rifle in evidence and with it four empty shells which he proved were fired from his rifle. It was contended that the marks of the firing pin upon the cartridge shells found in the ambuscade were so different from the marks of the firing pin upon the shells introduced by the defendant in evidence as to establish to a certainty that the shells found in the ambuscade were not fired from defendant's rifle. During the trial the rifle admitted in evidence was inspected by the jury but was not taken to pieces. After retiring to deliberate the jury asked if the gun could be sent to them. This was done without objection from either side. After a verdict of guilty defendant moved in arrest of judgment, contending that the jury had improperly taken the gun to pieces and examined the plunger or firing pin. It was shown in support of the motion that the jury had actually done this thing, and that from their examination had concluded that the plunger or firing pin had been tampered with. The Supreme Court of Virginia very properly upheld the verdict, the conduct, and the experiment of the jury. The purpose of the introduction of the gun in evidence was to show that its firing pin did not strike the cartridge in a particular way. The gun was offered by the defendant to establish his contention in this regard. A more acute prosecuting attorney might have caused the examination to have been made in open court, and thus have demonstrated the trick and fraud; but his failure to do so afforded no ground for overthrowing the verdict of an intelligent and scrutinizing jury, which, making its own examination of the evidence admitted to prove or disprove the very fact, discovered that the plunger "had been recently tampered with and fixed for the occasion of the trial." These cases, we have said, are typical. In the one the jury was permitted to make an experiment without knowledge of the parties of the method or process which was employed. It was an experiment addressed to evidence necessary to the prosecution's case which should have been offered in court. To permit the jury to gather this evidence without the presence of the defendant and without the possibility of knowledge upon his part as to the method by which their conclusion was reached and without the possibility of contesting the correctness of their experiment was, as the court justly held, the equivalent of the taking by the jury of evidence out of court, and a deprivation of the constitutional right of the defendant to be present at the taking of all evidence in his case. Upon the other hand, in the Virginia case the jury was not experimenting along lines without the evidence. It merely subjected an exhibit to a more critical examination than had been made of it in court, and by such examination reached a conclusion upon a contested fact by a more careful scrutiny of an exhibit introduced for the very purpose of affording evidence of the fact.

In this state it was held, in People v. Conkling, 111 Cal. 616, 44 P. 314, that it was error demanding a new trial, when certain of the jurors, to satisfy themselves at what distance a rifle discharged would powder-mark cloth, procured a rifle out of the courtroom and experimented with it. Here was a clear case of the jury's obtaining evidence by unauthorized experiments made without the presence and knowledge of the defendant. But, on the other hand, in People v. Mahoney, 77 Cal. 530, 20 P. 73, clothing worn by the deceased at the time of the homicide was, upon the jury's request, sent to the jury room, and in the matter of the Thomas Estate, 155 Cal. 488, 101 P. 798, it was held that a memorandum book admitted in evidence was properly allowed in the jury room in aid of the jury's deliberations.

In most of the cases, because of the very nature of the exhibit and of all the possible uses to which it may be put in the jury room, there is no occasion for the court to admonish the jury or to caution and limit it as to the nature of the use or experiment which shall be made. But where, from its nature, it may be susceptible to improper use, as in the case of the can of opium, it is the duty of the court, by instruction to the jury, to limit and restrict that use.

Coming to the case at bar, it is certain that the trial judge conceived that he had fallen into error in allowing the jury to take with them and to experiment with an exhibit which they might subject to an improper use, without limiting the scope of their experiments by proper instruction. It will be remembered that the court checked one experiment in the courtroom during its progress, and it is probable that the judge thought that by delivering the exhibit to the jury he had prepared the way for them to perform the very experiment which he had forbidden.

Since a jury is not allowed to impeach its verdict by showing what improper methods it employed to reach it, the need of such cautionary instructions in a proper case becomes imperative, and we would by no means disturb the ruling of a trial court granting a new trial if it appeared that injury resulted from its failure to give such instructions.

But if, on the other hand, it could not have resulted in injury to the defendant even if the jury did perform an improper experiment and from it reached its conclusion that the explosion of gas was caused by a spark from the flash light, then clearly no new trial should be granted for an error which could not have resulted in injury. To this consideration we now come.

The special verdict that the explosion was caused by a spark from the flash light was not material to the case, and defendant's position would not have been bettered if the jury had found that the cause of the explosion was not the spark from the flash light, but the fire from Cressaty's stove. It is to be remembered that this is not Cressaty's action to recover, which might be defeated by proof of his own contributory negligence. It is the action of his landlord, and, unless it can be said that the landlord was responsible for the negligent act of the tenant so as to defeat the landlord's recovery, the statement just made is unanswerable.

[The order granting a new trial was reversed.]

C.   LEGISLATIVE FACTS

McCORMICK'S HANDBOOK OF THE LAW OF EVIDENCE

776–69 (2d ed. 1972).*

Social and Economic Data Used in Judicial Law-Making: "Legislative" Facts.

It is conventional wisdom today to observe that judges not only are charged to find what the law is, but must regularly make new law when deciding upon the constitutional validity of a statute, interpreting a statute, or extending or restricting a common law rule. The very nature of the judicial process necessitates that judges be guided, as legislators are, by considerations of expediency and public policy. They must, in the nature of things, act either upon knowledge already possessed or upon assumptions,[83] or upon investigation of the pertinent general facts, social,[84] economic,[85] political,[86] or scientific.[87]. An older tradition once prescribed that

---

83. See, e. g., Village of Euclid v. Ambler Realty Co., 272 U.S. 365, 47 S.Ct. 114, 71 L.Ed. 303 (1926) (proper exercise of police power to exclude apartment houses from residential districts because they tend to be mere parasites and come near to being nuisances); Potts v. Coe, 78 U.S.App.D.C. 297, 140 F.2d 470 (1944) (incentive to invent supplied by patent law will not work in organized research because it destroys teamwork).

84. Brown v. Board of Educ., 347 U.S. 483 [74 S.Ct. 686, 98 L.Ed. 873] (1954), supplemented 349 U.S. 294 [75 S.Ct. 753, 99 L.Ed. 1083], (racially segregated schools can never be equal notwithstanding their equality of teachers or equipment because the very act of segregation brands the segregated minority with a feeling of inferiority).

85. SEC v. Capital Gains Research Bureau, Inc., 300 F.2d 745 (2d Cir. 1961), rev'd 375 U.S. 180 [84 S.Ct. 275, 11 L.Ed.2d 237], (judicial notice taken that advice tendered by small advisory service could not influence stock market generally); same case, 375 U.S. 180 [84 S.Ct. 275, 11 L.Ed.2d 237] (1963) (judicial notice taken that the advice tendered could influence the market price).

86. Baker v. Carr, 369 U.S. 186 [82 S.Ct. 691, 7 L.Ed.2d 663] (1962) (contemporary notions of justice require that equal apportionment of voting districts be made a legal and perforce largely mathematical question rather than a purely political one).

87. Durham v. United States, 94 U.S. App. D.C. 228, 214 F.2d 862 (1954) (psychiatric learning pertinent to the scientific soundness of the right-and-wrong test of criminal insanity).

judges should rationalize their result solely in terms of analogy to old doctrines leaving the considerations of expediency unstated. Contemporary
practice indicates that judges in their opinions should render explicit their
policy-judgments and the factual grounds therefor. These latter have been
helpfully classed as "legislative facts," as contrasted with the "adjudicative
facts" which are historical facts pertaining to the incident which give rise to
lawsuits.

Constitutional cases argued in terms of due process typically involve reliance upon legislative facts for their proper resolution. Whether a statute
enacted pursuant to the police power is valid, after all, involves a twofold
analysis. First, it must be determined that the enactment is designed to
achieve an appropriate objective of the police power; that is, it must be designed to protect the public health, morals, safety, or general welfare. The
second question is whether, in light of the data on hand, a legislature still
beholden to reason could have adopted the means they did to achieve the
aim of their exercise of the police power.[90] In Burns Baking Co., v. Bryan,[91]
for example, the question was whether, concerned about consumers being
misled by confusing sizes of bread, the Nebraska legislature could decree
not only that the bakers bake bread according to distinctively different
weights but that they wrap their product in wax paper lest any post-oven
expansion of some loaves undo these distinctions. A majority of the court
held the enactment unconstitutional because, in their opinion, the wrapping
requirement was unreasonable. Mr. Justice Brandeis, correctly anticipating
the decline of substantive due process, dissented, pointing out that the only
question was whether the measure was a reasonable legislative response in
light of the facts available to the legislators themselves. Then, in a
marvellous illustration of the Brandeis-brief technique, he recited page after
page of data illustrating how widespread was the problem of shortweight
and how, in light of nationwide experience, the statute appeared to be a reasonable response to the environmental situation[93].

Given the bent to test due process according to the information available to the legislature, the truth-content of this data is not directly relevant.
The question is whether sufficient data exists which could influence a reasonable legislature to act, not whether ultimately this data is true.[94] This is
not the same case as when a court proceeds to interpret a constitutional
norm and, while they still rely upon data, the judges *qua* legislators them-

---

90. See the discussion running throughout
the several opinions in Griswold v. Connecticut, 381 U.S. 479 [85 S.Ct. 1678, 14
L.Ed.2d 510] (1965).

91. 264 U.S. 504 [44 S.Ct. 412, 68 L.Ed.
813] (1924).

93. The opponents of a statute can resort to
extra-record legislative facts to support
their argument that it is invalid. In Burns
Baking Co. v. Bryan, 264 U.S. 504 [44 S.Ct.
412, 68 L.Ed. 813] (1924), the statute regulating bread sizes was struck down because
it was "contrary to common experience and
unreasonable to assume there could be any
danger of * * * deception." See also
Defiance Milk Products Co. v. DuMond,
309 N.Y. 537, 132 N.E.2d 829 (1956) (stat-

ute requiring inordinately large size cans
for retail sale of evaporated skimmed milk
held invalid because judicial notice was
taken that it would be incredible to believe
consumers needed protection against deception practiced with regard to the nature
of this product).

94. In theory, at least, the Uniform Rules of
Evidence would not allow the judges to
take judicial notice of any of the data with
which the cases in this section are concerned since none of it is "indisputably"
true. See the text of these rules reproduced
in § 328, note 3, supra. Given the practice
of courts to notice less than indisputably
true facts within a legislative context, the
Uniform Rules might be interpreted to apply only to adjudicative facts. * * *

selves proceed to act as if the data were true. In Brown v. Board of Education,[95] for example, the Court faced the issue whether segregated schools, equal facility and teacher-wise, could any longer be tolerated under the equal protection clause. The question was not any longer whether a reasonable legislator could believe these schools could never be equal, but whether the *judges* believed that the very act of segregating branded certain children with a feeling of inferiority so deleterious that it would be impossible for them to obtain an equal education no matter how equal the facilities and teachers. Thus the intellectual legitimacy of this kind of decision turns upon the actual truth-content of the legislative facts taken into account by the judges who propound the decision. While not necessarily indisputably true, it would appear that these legislative facts must at least appear to be more likely than not true if the opinion is going to have the requisite intellectual legitimacy upon which the authority of judge-made rules is ultimately founded.[96]

When making new common law, judges must, like legislators, do the best they can assaying the data available to them and make the best decision they can of which course wisdom dictates they follow. Should they, for example, continue to invoke the common law rule of *caveat emptor* in the field of real property, or should they invoke a notion of implied warranty in the instance of the sale of new houses?[97] Should they require landlords of residential units to warrant their habitability and fitness for the use intended?[98] While sociological, economic, political and moral doctrine may abound about questions like this, none of this data is likely indisputable.[99]

Thus it is that, in practice, the legislative facts upon which judges rely when performing their lawmaking function are not indisputable. At the same time, cognizant of the fact that his decision as lawmaker can affect the public at large, in contradistinction to most rulings at trials which affect

95. 347 U.S. 483 [74 S.Ct. 686, 98 L.Ed. 873] (1954), supplemented 349 U.S. 294 [75 S.Ct. 753, 99 L.Ed. 1083].

96. See, e. g., the reaction to Durham v. United States, 94 U.S.App.D.C. 228, 214 F.2d 862 (1954), wherein on the basis of psychiatric data the court formulated a new test for criminal insanity. Some psychiatrists accepted the result: Roche, Criminality and Mental Illness—Two Faces of the Same Coin, 22 U.Chi.L.Rev. 320 (1955). The American Law Institute rejected it. Model Penal Code, Tentative Draft No. 4, 159–60 (1955). See also Brown v. Board of Education, 347 U.S. 483 [74 S.Ct. 686, 98 L.Ed. 873] (1954), supplemented 349 U.S. 294 [75 S.Ct. 753, 99 L.Ed. 1083] wherein for the psychological impact of segregation the court relied upon, inter alia, the work of Dr. Kenneth B. Clark. Dr. Clark felt compelled thereafter publicly to respond to critics of his work. Clark, The Desegregation Cases: Criticism of the Social Scientists Role, 5 Vill.L.Rev. 224, 236–40 (1960). But see Van den Haag, Social Science Testimony in the Desegregation Cases—A Reply to Professor Kenneth Clark, 6 Vill.L.Rev. 69 (1960).

97. Schipper v. Levitt & Sons, Inc., 44 N.J. 70, 207 A.2d 314 (1965) (mass developer of homes who assembled final product out of component parts treated as a manufacturer and implied warranty imposed).

98. Lemle v. Breeden, 51 Hawaii 426, 462 P.2d 470 (1969) (application of implied warranty recognizes changes in history of leasing transactions and takes into account contemporary housing realities).

99. See particularly Davis, A System of Judicial Notice Based on Fairness and Convenience, in Perspectives of Law, 69, 82 (Pound ed. 1964) ("judge-made law would stop growing if judges, in thinking about questions of law and policy, were forbidden to take into account the facts they believe, as distinguished from facts which are 'clearly * * * within the domain of the indisputable.' ") If the data available on appeal are conflicting, however, a court can remand the case to trial so these data can be more effectively explored by introducing them there in the form of evidence subject to cross-examination. See, e. g., Borden's Farm Products Co. v. Baldwin, 293 U.S. 194 [55 S.Ct. 187, 79 L.Ed.281](1934).

only the parties themselves, a judge is not likely to rely for his data only upon what opposing counsel tender him. Obviously enough, therefore, legislative facts tend to be the most elusive facts when it comes to propounding a codified system of judicial notice.[1]

332. The Parameters of Judicial Notice.

Agreement is not to be had whether the perimeters of the doctrine of judicial notice enclose only facts which are indisputably true or encompass also facts more than likely true. If, on the one hand, the function of the jury is to resolve disputed questions of fact, an argument can be made that judges should not purport to make decisions about facts unless they are indisputable facts. If this argument is accepted, it follows that once a fact has been judicially noticed, evidence contradicting the truth of the fact is inadmissible because by its very nature, a fact capable of being judicially noticed is an indisputable fact which the jury must be instructed to accept as true. If, on the other hand, the function of judicial notice is to expedite the trial of cases, an argument can be made that judges should dispense with the need for time-consuming formal evidence when the fact in question is likely true. If this argument is accepted, it follows that evidence contradicting the judicially noticed fact is admissible and that the jury are ultimately free to accept or reject the truth of the fact posited by judicial notice.

Hypotheticals

(1) A sues X to recover on a promissory note in which X is the maker and B is the payee. A is B's assignee. X's defense is that the note was given in payment of B's services as a real estate broker and that B did not possess a broker's license. On direct examination, A is asked whether B, his assignor, was a licensed real estate broker. X makes an objection that A lacks personal knowledge. The judge announces that he knows B personally, and is taking judicial notice of the fact that B is a licensed real estate broker. Is the judge correct?

(2) A sues X Construction Co. for damages for breach of a contract to build a brick chicken coop in Provo, Utah. X's defense is that it is illegal and impossible to build. At the trial, set for a two-day trial, X produces a volume labeled "Municipal Ordinances of Provo," and requests the court to take judicial notice of the fact that the building of brick chicken coops is prohibited by ordinance within the city of Provo. A objects on the ground that he has not been given advance notice of this judicial-notice request. What result?

1. Note that F.R.Ev. (R.D.1971) 201, reproduced at § 328, n. 3, supra, does not purport to regulate the notice of legislative facts.

Chapter IX
GOVERNMENTAL PRIVILEGES

UNITED STATES v. REYNOLDS

Supreme Court of the United States, 1953.
345 U.S. 1, 73 S.Ct. 528, 97 L.Ed. 727.
[Some of the Court's footnotes are omitted.]

Mr. Chief Justice VINSON delivered the opinion of the Court.

These suits under the Tort Claims Act[1] arise from the death of three civilians in the crash of a B–29 aircraft at Waycross, Georgia, on October 6, 1948. Because an important question of the Government's privilege to resist discovery[2] is involved, we granted certiorari. 343 U.S. 918, 72 S.Ct. 678, 96 L.Ed. 1332.

The aircraft had taken flight for the purpose of testing secret electronic equipment, with four civilian observers aboard. While aloft, fire broke out in one of the bomber's engines. Six of the nine crew members, and three of the four civilian observers were killed in the crash.

The widows of the three deceased civilian observers brought consolidated suits against the United States. In the pretrial stages the plaintiffs moved, under Rule 34 of the Federal Rules of Civil Procedure,[3] for production of the Air Force's official accident investigation report and the statements of the three surviving crew members, taken in connection with the official investigation. The Government moved to quash the motion, claiming that these matters were privileged against disclosure pursuant to Air Force regulations promulgated under R.S. § 161.[4] The District Judge sustained plaintiffs' motion, holding that good cause for production had been shown.[5] The claim of privilege under R.S. § 161 was rejected on the premise that the Tort Claims Act, in making the Government liable "in the same manner"

1. 28 U.S.C. §§ 1346, 2674, 28 U.S.C.A. §§ 1346, 2674.

2. Federal Rules of Civil Procedure, Rule 34, 28 U.S.C.A.

3. "Rule 34. *Discovery and Production of Documents and Things for Inspection, Copying, or Photographing.* Upon motion of any party showing good cause therefor and upon notice to all other parties, and subject to the provisions of Rule 30(b), the court in which an action is pending may (1) order any party to produce and permit the inspection and copying or photographing, by or on behalf of the moving party, of any designated documents, papers, books, accounts, letters, photographs, objects, or tangible things, not privileged, which constitute or contain evidence relating to any of the matters within the scope of the examination permitted by Rule 26(b) and which are in his possession, custody, or control; or (2) order any party to permit entry upon designated land or other property in his possession or control for the purpose of inspecting, measuring, surveying, or photographing the property or any designated object or operation thereon within the scope of the examination permitted by Rule 26(b). The order shall specify the time, place, and manner of making the inspection and taking the copies and photographs and may prescribe such terms and conditions as are just."

4. 5 U.S.C. § 22, 5 U.S.C.A. § 22:
   "The head of each department is authorized to prescribe regulations, not inconsistent with law, for the government of his department, the conduct of its officers and clerks, the distribution and performance of its business, and the custody, use, and preservation of the records, papers, and property appertaining to it."

   Air Force Regulation No. 62–7(5) (b) provides:
   "Reports of boards of officers, special accident reports, or extracts therefrom will not be furnished or made available to persons outside the authorized chain of command without the specific approval of the Secretary of the Air Force."

5. 10 F.R.D. 468.

629

as a private individual[6] had waived any privilege based upon executive control over governmental documents.

Shortly after this decision, the District Court received a letter from the Secretary of the Air Force, stating that "it has been determined that it would not be in the public interest to furnish this report. * * * " The court allowed a rehearing on its earlier order, and at the rehearing the Secretary of the Air Force filed a formal "Claim of Privilege." This document repeated the prior claim based generally on R.S. § 161, and then stated that the Government further objected to production of the documents "for the reason that the aircraft in question, together with the personnel on board, were engaged in a highly secret mission of the Air Force." An affidavit of the Judge Advocate General, United States Air Force, was also filed with the court, which asserted that the demanded material could not be furnished "without seriously hampering national security, flying safety and the development of highly technical and secret military equipment." The same affidavit offered to produce the three surviving crew members, without cost, for examination by the plaintiffs. The witnesses would be allowed to refresh their memories from any statement made by them to the Air Force, and authorized to testify as to all matters except those of a "classified nature."

The District Court ordered the Government to produce the documents in order that the court might determine whether they contained privileged matter. The Government declined, so the court entered an order, under Rule 37(b) (2) (i),[7] that the facts on the issue of negligence would be taken as established in plaintiffs' favor. After a hearing to determine damages, final judgment was entered for the plaintiffs. The Court of Appeals affirmed,[8] both as to the showing of good cause for production of the documents, and as to the ultimate disposition of the case as a consequence of the Government's refusal to produce the documents.

We have had broad propositions pressed upon us for decision. On behalf of the Government it has been urged that the executive department heads have power to withhold any documents in their custody from judicial view if they deem it to be in the public interest.[9] Respondents have asserted that the executive's power to withhold documents was waived by the Tort

---

6. 28 U.S.C. § 2674, 28 U.S.C.A. § 2674:

> "The United States shall be liable, respecting the provisions of this title relating to tort claims, in the same manner and to the same extent as a private individual under like circumstances, but shall not be liable for interest prior to judgment or for punitive damages."

7. "Rule 37. *Refusal to Make Discovery: Consequences*

* * *

> "(b) Failure to Comply With Order.

* * *

> "(2) *Other Consequences.* If any party or an officer or managing agent of a party refuses to obey * * * an order made under Rule 34 to produce any document * * * , the court may make such orders in regard to the refusal

as are just, and among others the following:

> "(i) An order that the matters regarding which the questions were asked, or the character or description of the thing or land, or the contents of the paper, or the physical or mental condition of the party, or any other designated facts shall be taken to be established for the purposes of the action in accordance with the claim of the party obtaining the order; * * *"

8. 192 F.2d 987.

9. While claim of executive power to suppress documents is based more immediately upon R.S. § 161 (see supra, note 4), the roots go much deeper. It is said that R.S. § 161 is only a legislative recognition of an inherent executive power which is protected in the constitutional system of separation of power.

Claims Act. Both positions have constitutional overtones which we find it unnecessary to pass upon, there being a narrower ground for decision.

The Tort Claims Act expressly makes the Federal Rules of Civil Procedure applicable to suits against the United States. The judgment in this case imposed liability upon the Government by operation of Rule 37, for refusal to produce documents under Rule 34. Since Rule 34 compels production only of matters "not privileged," the essential question is whether there was a valid claim of privilege under the Rule. We hold that there was, and that, therefore, the judgment below subjected the United States to liability on terms to which Congress did not consent by the Tort Claims Act.

We think it should be clear that the term "not privileged" as used in Rule 34, refers to "privileges" as that term is understood in the law of evidence. When the Secretary of the Air Force lodged his formal "Claim of Privilege," he attempted therein to invoke the privilege against revealing military secrets, a privilege which is well established in the law of evidence. The existence of the privilege is conceded by the court below, and, indeed, by the most outspoken critics of governmental claims to privilege.

Judicial experience with the privilege which protects military and state secrets has been limited in this country. English experience has been more extensive, but still relatively slight compared with other evidentiary privileges. Nevertheless, the principles which control the application of the privilege emerge quite clearly from the available precedents. The privilege belongs to the Government and must be asserted by it; it can neither be claimed nor waived by a private party. It is not to be lightly invoked. There must be a formal claim of privilege, lodged by the head of the department which has control over the matter, after actual personal consideration by that officer. The court itself must determine whether the circumstances are appropriate for the claim of privilege, and yet do so without forcing a disclosure of the very thing the privilege is designed to protect. The latter requirement is the only one which presents real difficulty. As to it, we find it helpful to draw upon judicial experience in dealing with an analogous privilege, the privilege against self-incrimination.

The privilege against self-incrimination presented the courts with a similar sort of problem. Too much judicial inquiry into the claim of privilege would force disclosure of the thing the privilege was meant to protect, while a complete abandonment of judicial control would lead to intolerable abuses. Indeed, in the earlier stages of judicial experience with the problem, both extremes were advocated, some saying that the bare assertion by the witness must be taken as conclusive, and others saying that the witness should be required to reveal the matter behind his claim of privilege to the judge for verification. Neither extreme prevailed, and a sound formula of compromise was developed. This formula received authoritative expression in this country as early as the Burr trial. There are differences in phraseology, but in substance it is agreed that the court must be satisfied from all the evidence and circumstances, and "from the implications of the question, in the setting in which it is asked, that a responsive answer to the question or an explanation of why it cannot be answered might be dangerous because injurious exposure could result." Hoffman v. United States, 1951, 341 U.S. 479, 486–487, 71 S.Ct. 814, 818, 95 L.Ed. 1118. If the court is so satisfied, the claim of the privilege will be accepted without requiring further disclosure.

Regardless of how it is articulated, some like formula of compromise must be applied here. Judicial control over the evidence in a case cannot be abdicated to the caprice of executive officers. Yet we will not go so far as to say that the court may automatically require a complete disclosure to the judge before the claim of privilege will be accepted in any case. It may be possible to satisfy the court, from all the circumstances of the case, that there is a reasonable danger that compulsion of the evidence will expose military matters which, in the interest of national security, should not be divulged. When this is the case, the occasion for the privilege is appropriate, and the court should not jeopardize the security which the privilege is meant to protect by insisting upon an examination of the evidence, even by the judge alone, in chambers.

In the instant case we cannot escape judicial notice that this is a time of vigorous preparation for national defense. Experience in the past war has made it common knowledge that air power is one of the most potent weapons in our scheme of defense, and that newly developing electronic devices have greatly enhanced the effective use of air power. It is equally apparent that these electronic devices must be kept secret if their full military advantage is to be exploited in the national interest. On the record before the trial court it appeared that this accident occurred to a military plane which had gone aloft to test secret electronic equipment. Certainly there was a reasonable danger that the accident investigation report would contain references to the secret electronic equipment which was the primary concern of the mission.

Of course, even with this information before him, the trial judge was in no position to decide that the report was privileged until there had been a formal claim of privilege. Thus it was entirely proper to rule initially that petitioner had shown probable cause for discovery of the documents. Thereafter, when the formal claim of privilege was filed by the Secretary of the Air Force, under circumstances indicating a reasonable possibility that military secrets were involved, there was certainly a sufficient showing of privilege to cut off further demand for the document on the showing of necessity for its compulsion that had then been made.

In each case, the showing of necessity which is made will determine how far the court should probe in satisfying itself that the occasion for invoking the privilege is appropriate. Where there is a strong showing of necessity, the claim of privilege should not be lightly accepted, but even the most compelling necessity cannot overcome the claim of privilege if the court is ultimately satisfied that military secrets are at stake.[26] *A fortiori*, where necessity is dubious, a formal claim of privilege, made under the circumstances of this case, will have to prevail. Here, necessity was greatly minimized by an available alternative, which might have given respondents the evidence to make out their case without forcing a showdown on the claim of privilege. By their failure to pursue that alternative, respondents have posed the privilege question for decision with the formal claim of privilege set against a dubious showing of necessity.

26. See Totten v. United States, 1875, 92 U.S. 105, 23 L.Ed. 605, where the very subject matter of the action, a contract to perform espionage, was a matter of state secret. The action was dismissed on the pleadings without ever reaching the question of evidence, since it was so obvious that the action should never prevail over the privilege.

There is nothing to suggest that the electronic equipment, in this case, had any casual connection with the accident. Therefore, it should be possible for respondents to adduce the essential facts as to causation without resort to material touching upon military secrets. Respondents were given a reasonable opportunity to do just that, when petitioner formally offered to make the surviving crew members available for examination. We think that offer should have been accepted.

Respondents have cited us to those cases in the criminal field, where it has been held that the Government can invoke its evidentiary privileges only at the price of letting the defendant go free. The rationale of the criminal cases is that, since the Government which prosecutes an accused also has the duty to see that justice is done, it is unconscionable to allow it to undertake prosecution and then invoke its governmental privileges to deprive the accused of anything which might be material to his defense. Such rationale has no application in a civil forum where the Government is not the moving party, but is a defendant only on terms to which it has consented.

The decision of the Court of Appeals is reversed and the case will be remanded to the District Court for further proceedings consistent with the views expressed in this opinion.

Reversed and remanded.

Mr. Justice Black, Mr. Justice Frankfurter, and Mr. Justice Jackson dissent, substantially for the reasons set forth in the opinion of Judge Marias below 192 F.2d 987.

EVIDENTIARY PRIVILEGE OF "STATE SECRETS" IN CONTRACT ACTION

55 Colum.L.Rev. 570–573 (1955).*
[Footnotes omitted.]

Defendant contracted to manufacture arming mechanisms for the United States Army. Plaintiff with whom he had subcontracted brought an action for breach of contract. Defendant moved to dismiss or, in the alternative, to stay all proceedings on the ground that prosecution and defense of the action would require disclosure of classified information in violation of the Espionage Act. *Held,* motions denied. Proceedings may continue along their ordinary course and the court if necessary will, at the appropriate time, take measures to ensure that national security is not endangered. Ticon Corp. v. Emerson Radio & Phonograph Corp., 206 Misc. 727, 134 N.Y.S.2d 716 (Sup.Ct.1954).

The courts have long recognized a privilege against disclosure of information affecting national security in essentially private litigation as well as when the government is a party. The basic policy underlying the decisions granting protection to state secrets is the paramount interest of the nation in safeguarding its military and diplomatic position, even to the subordination of individual interests.

Although the government has not raised the state secrets privilege while acting as plaintiff or prosecutor, it has asserted other privileges of nondisclosure resting upon different grounds. Ordinarily in these situations, however, the courts have not sustained the privilege where the defendant requested material documents in the government's possession. Apparently, the rationale of these decisions is that it is unconscionable to allow the government to initiate an action and then invoke a privilege that might deprive an accused of anything material to his defense. Although one case suggested that the government introduce secondary evidence in order to prevent disclosure, generally the courts have accommodated the conflicting interests of individuals and the government in favor of individuals. Thus, if the court finds that the information requested is material, the government is in the dilemma of either having to risk unsuccessful prosecution or being forced to disclose privileged information.

The government as defendant has not been estopped from raising the states secrets privilege by virtue of its consent to be sued. In United States v. Reynolds, the Supreme Court distinguished the role of government as prosecutor and reversed the trial court's finding of certain facts in favor of plaintiffs after the government had refused to produce documents in conformity with an order of the court. The Court noted the existence of international tension and emphasized that plaintiff had not demonstrated sufficient necessity to justify an order requiring initial disclosure to the judge of information involving ostensibly secret electronic data.

In private litigation the question of whether information comes within the states secrets privilege has been raised by motion or objection of a private party or by the court itself. The government's position in the matter, which may be stated by affidavit of the cognizant executive head —whether the government intervenes as a party or not—is apparently the crucial factor in determining whether the privilege is to be sustained. Thus, if the court has evidence that the government does not object to the introduction of documents, a refusal to disclose may subject the objector to comtempt proceedings.

Once a claim of privilege is properly made by the appropriate executive department head, the English view appears to be that whether there is a state secret involved is not justiciable. This view, granting the executive almost unlimited discretion, has been defended on the grounds that showing the information to the court may defeat the very secrecy required and that the court lacks the expertise that the executive possesses for a sound determination of the necessity for secrecy. *Reynolds,* while asserting the justiciable nature of the question, formulates a rule which considerably limits the court's discretion. If the government makes a showing that there is a reasonable danger that the evidence sought would expose military secrets, the privilege will be sustained without disclosure to the court. Although, theoretically, the showing required would be balanced against the opposing party's need, practically it appears that the government's burden of persuasion is relatively slight since the executive claim of secrecy is likely to be accepted on its face. Consequently, almost any assertion of privilege by the government will foreclose a private party's ability to litigate successfully.

The instant case in some measure reasserts judicial control over the privilege when a private party makes the claim, and the government apparently has not reviewed the question of secrecy in the light of the impending litigation. The decision does not require a disclosure of state secrets since production of classified documents or information was not requested by the opposing party or by the court. The court recognized that un-authorized disclosure by defendant would violate the espionage laws, but it apparently hoped to avoid the issue by taking a course of action which would stimulate the government to declassify the evidence, intervene in the action or arrange for a settlement between the parties. The court also rea-soned that a dismissal might unjustly deprive plaintiff of his rights by pre-cluding relief if declassification did not occur until after expiration of the statute of limitations and would encourage other litigants in the defen-dant's position to breach contracts and seek refuge under a privilege de-signed for the benefit of the state.

Although the prematureness of defendant's motions enabled the court to adjust the competing interests of nation and litigants, it is clear that the problem may be merely postponed. If plaintiff had utilized discovery mech-anisms the court would have been faced with the issue of compulsion of the requested information. Assuming the court determines that state secrets are not involved and orders production, a refusal risks possible contempt of court or loss of the suit whereas compliance may entail violation of the es-pionage laws and exposure of the nation's secrets. A dismissal by the court after a decision that state secrets are involved may cause an injustice to a deserving plaintiff. Present procedures seem inadequate to equitably adjust the interests of nation and individual both in ascertaining the presence of state secrets and in disposing of the controversy once it is decided they are involved.

Perhaps, in the sub-contract situation, a solution might be reached along the following lines: A federal statute, based upon the power of the na-tion to protect itself, could require that sub-contracts let under a govern-ment prime contract and classified as affecting the national security con-tain a clause requiring the parties to arbitrate all disputes arising under the contract, the dispute would, however, only proceed to arbitration if the ap-propriate executive department head certified that there was a continued need for secrecy. If the executive declassified the contract or took no action within a reasonable time, the information would be deemed unprivileged and the clause inapplicable; the disputants would be free to litigate in the courts. Otherwise, an arbitrator would be chosen by the parties from a list provided by the executive department concerned, or if no choice could be agreed upon one would be designated by the department. The parties would be represented by counsel of their choice, or if necessary, because of security considerations, by appointed counsel. The arbitrator would be empowered to enter a default award after prescribed notice to a recalcitrant party. An award would be confirmable in any federal district court. Although the arbi-trator's determination of the scope of the arbitration clause and the merits of the controversy would be final, an award would not be enforced if (1) the subject of the dispute had been declassified prior to arbitration proceedings, (2) reasonable notice was not given to a party against whom a default award was taken or, (3) the award was procured by means of fraud or corruption of the arbitrator.

At the minimum the proposal would ensure that individual interests receive a disposition on the merits while preserving the nation's interest in secrecy. Although parties would have to accept an arbitrator's disposition of the controversy with few of the safeguards of an independent judiciary, it is submitted that while the adjustment of individual and governmental interests requires something more than complete denial of relief to deserving litigants an effective security system precludes full judicial inquiry.

UNITED STATES v. NIXON

Supreme Court of the United States, 1974.
418 U.S. 683, 94 S.Ct. 3090, 41 L.Ed.2d 1039.
[Some footnotes and citations omitted.]

Mr. Chief Justice BURGER delivered the opinion of the Court.

* * *

On March 1, 1974, a grand jury of the United States District Court for the District of Columbia returned an indictment charging seven named individuals[3] with various offenses, including conspiracy to defraud the United States and to obstruct justice. Although he was not designated as such in the indictment, the grand jury named the President, among others, as an unindicted coconspirator. On April 18, 1974, upon motion of the Special Prosecutor, see n. 8, infra, a subpoena *duces tecum* was issued pursuant to Rule 17(c) to the President by the United States District Court and made returnable on May 2, 1974. This subpoena required the production, in advance of the September 9 trial date, of certain tapes, memoranda, papers, transcripts or other writings relating to certain precisely identified meetings between the President and others. The Special Prosecutor was able to fix the time, place, and persons present at these discussions because the White House daily logs and appointment records had been delivered to him. On April 30, the President publicly released edited transcripts of 43 conversations; portions of 20 conversations subject to subpoena in the present case were included. On May 1, 1974, the President's counsel, filed a "special appearance" and a motion to quash the subpoena under Rule 17(c). This motion was accompanied by a formal claim of privilege. At a subsequent hearing, futher motions to expunge the grand jury's action naming the President as an unindicted coconspirator and for protective orders against the disclosure of that information were filed or raised orally by counsel for the President.

On May 20, 1974, the District Court denied the motion to quash and the motions to expunge and for protective orders. 377 F.Supp. 1326. It further ordered "the President or any subordinate officer, official, or employee with custody or control of the documents or objects subpoenaed," id., at 1331 to deliver to the District Court, on or before May 31, 1974, the originals of all subpoenaed items, as well as an index and analysis of those items, together with tape copies of those portions of the subpoenaed recordings for which transcripts had been released to the public by the President on April 30. * * *

* * *

[The Court held that the order of the district judge was a final appealable order, despite the fact that no contempt adjudication had been

3. The seven defendants were John N. Mitchell, H. R. Haldeman, John D. Ehrlichman, Charles W. Colson, Robert C. Mardian, Kenneth W. Parkinson, and Gordon Strachan. Each had occupied either a position of responsibility on the White House staff or the Committee for the Re-election of the President. Colson entered a guilty plea on another charge and is no longer a defendant.

made; that the matter was within the Supreme Court's jurisdiction, despite the fact that the two contending parties, the President and the Special Prosecutor, were both within the executive branch; and that the subpoena in question met the requirements of specificity of Rule 17 of the Federal Rules of Criminal Procedure. Then, it moved on to the privilege issue.]

IV

THE CLAIM OF PRIVILEGE

A

* * * [W]e turn to the claim that the subpoena should be quashed because it demands "confidential conversations between a President and his close advisors that it would be inconsistent with the public interest to produce." The first contention is a broad claim that the separation of powers doctrine precludes judicial review of a President's claim of privilege. The second contention is that if he does not prevail on the claim of absolute privilege, the court should hold as a matter of constitutional law that the privilege prevails over the subpoena *duces tecum.*

In the performance of assigned constitutional duties each branch of the Government must initially interpret the Constitution, and the interpretation of its powers by any branch is due great respect from the others. The President's counsel, as we have noted, reads the Constitution as providing an absolute privilege of confidentiality for all Presidential communications. Many decisions of this Court, however, have unequivocally reaffirmed the holding of Marbury v. Madison, 1 Cranch. 137, 2 L.Ed. 60 (1803), that "[i]t is emphatically the province and duty of the judicial department to say what the law is." Id., at 177, 2 L.Ed. 60.

* * *

* * * Notwithstanding the deference each branch must accord the others, the "judicial Power of the United States" vested in the federal courts by Art. III, § 1, of the Constitution can no more be shared with the Executive Branch than the Chief Executive, for example, can share with the Judiciary the veto power, or the Congress share with the Judiciary the power to override a Presidential veto. Any other conclusion would be contrary to the basic concept of separation of powers and the checks and balances that flow from the scheme of a tripartite government. * * *

B

In support of his claim of absolute privilege, the President's counsel urges two grounds, one of which is common to all governments and one of which is peculiar to our system of separation of powers. The first ground is the valid need for protection of communications between high Government officials and those who advise and assist them in the performance of their manifold duties; the importance of this confidentiality is too plain to require further discussion. Human experience teaches that those who expect public dissemination of their remarks may well temper candor with a concern for appearances and for their own interests to the detriment of the decisionmaking process.[15] Whatever the nature of the privilege of confiden-

---

15. There is nothing novel about governmental confidentiality. The meetings of the Constitutional Convention in 1787 were conducted in complete privacy. 1 M. Farrand, The Records of the Federal Convention of 1787, pp. xi–xxv (1911). Moreover, all records of those meetings were sealed for more than 30 years after the Convention.

tiality of Presidential communications in the exercise of Art. II powers, the privilege can be said to derive from the supremacy of each branch within its own assigned area of constitutional duties. Certain powers and privileges flow from the nature of enumerated powers;[16] the protection of the confidentiality of Presidential communications has similar constitutional underpinnings.

The second ground asserted by the President's counsel in support of the claim of absolute privilege rests on the doctrine of separation of powers. Here it is argued that the independence of the Executive Branch within its own sphere, insulates a President from a judicial subpoena in an ongoing criminal prosecution, and thereby protects confidential Presidential communications.

However, neither the doctrine of separation of powers, nor the need for confidentiality of high-level communications, without more, can sustain an absolute, unqualified Presidential privilege of immunity from judicial process under all circumstances. The President's need for complete candor and objectivity from advisers calls for great deference from the courts. However, when the privilege depends solely on the broad, undifferentiated claim of public interest in the confidentiality of such conversations, a confrontation with other values arises. Absent a claim of need to protect military, diplomatic, or sensitive national security secrets, we find it difficult to accept the argument that even the very important interest in confidentiality of Presidential communications is significantly diminished by production of such material for *in camera* inspection with all the protection that a district court will be obliged to provide.

The impediment that an absolute, unqualified privilege would place in the way of the primary constitutional duty of the Judicial Branch to do justice in criminal prosecutions would plainly conflict with the function of the courts under Art. III. In designing the structure of our Government and dividing and allocating the sovereign power among three co-equal branches, the Framers of the Constitution sought to provide a comprehensive system, but the separate powers were not intended to operate with absolute independence.

> "While the Constitution diffuses power the better to secure liberty, it also contemplates that practice will integrate the dispersed powers into a workable government. It enjoins upon its branches separateness but interdependence, autonomy but reciprocity." Youngstown Sheet & Tube Co. v. Sawyer, 343 U.S., at 635, 72 S.Ct., at 870 (Jackson, J., concurring).

To read the Art. II powers of the President as providing an absolute privilege as against a subpoena essential to enforcement of criminal statutes on

See 3 Stat. 475, 15th Cong., 1st Sess., Res. 8 (1818). Most of the Framers acknowledge that without secrecy no constitution of the kind that was developed could have been written. C. Warren, The Making of the Constitution 134–139 (1937).

16. The Special Prosecutor argues that there is no provision in the Constitution for a Presidential privilege as to the President's communications corresponding to the privilege of Members of Congress under the Speech or Debate Clause. But the silence of the Constitution on this score is not dispositive. "The rule of constitutional interpretation announced in McCulloch v. Maryland, 4 Wheat. 316, 4 L.Ed. 579, that that which was reasonably appropriate and relevant to the exercise of a granted power was to be considered as accompanying the grant, has been so universally applied that it suffices merely to state it." Marshall v. Gordon, 243 U.S. 521, 537, 37 S.Ct. 448, 451, 61 L.Ed. 881 (1917).

no more than a generalized claim of the public interest in confidentiality of nonmilitary and nondiplomatic discussions would upset the constitutional balance of "a workable government" and gravely impair the role of the courts under Art. III.

C

Since we conclude that the legitimate needs of the judicial process may outweigh Presidential privilege, it is necessary to resolve those competing interests in a manner that preserves the essential functions of each branch. The right and indeed the duty to resolve that question does not free the Judiciary from according high respect to the representations made on behalf of the President.

The expectation of a President to the confidentiality of his conversations and correspondence, like the claim of confidentiality of judicial deliberations, for example, has all the values to which we accord deference for the privacy of all citizens and, added to those values, is the necessity for protection of the public interest in candid, objective, and even blunt or harsh opinions in Presidential decision-making. A President and those who assist him must be free to explore alternatives in the process of shaping policies and making decisions and to do so in a way many would be unwilling to express except privately. These are the considerations justifying a presumptive privilege for Presidential communications. The privilege is fundamental to the operation of Government and inextricably rooted in the separation of powers under the Constitution.[17] In Nixon v. Sirica, 159 U.S.App.D.C. 58, 487 F.2d 700 (1973), the Court of Appeals held that such Presidential communications are "presumptively privileged," id., at 75, 487 F.2d, at 717, and this position is accepted by both parties in the present litigation. We agree with Mr. Chief Justice Marshall's observation, therefore, that "[i]n no case of this kind would a court be required to proceed against the president as against an ordinary individual." United States v. Burr, 25 F.Cas., at 192.

But this presumptive privilege must be considered in light of our historic commitment to the rule of law. This is nowhere more profoundly manifest than in our view that "the twofold aim [of criminal justice] is that guilt shall not escape or innocence suffer." Berger v. United States, 295 U.S., at 88, 55 S.Ct., at 633. We have elected to employ an adversary system of criminal justice in which the parties contest all issues before a court of law. The need to develop all relevant facts in the adversary system is both fundmental and comprehensive. The ends of criminal justice would be defeated if judgments were to be founded on a partial or speculative presentation of the facts. The very integrity of the judicial system and public confidence in the system depend on full disclosure of all the facts, within the framework of the rules of evidence. To ensure that justice is done, it is imperative to the function of courts that compulsory process be available for the production of evidence needed either by the prosecution or by the defense.

17. "Freedom of communication vital to fulfillment of the aims of wholesome relationships is obtained only by removing the specter of compelled disclosure. * * * [G]overnment * * * needs open but protected channels for the kind of plain talk that is essential to the quality of its functioning." Carl Zeiss Stiftung v. V. E. B. Carl Zeiss, Jena, 40 F.R.D. 318, 325 (DC 1966). See Nixon v. Sirica, 159 U.S.App.D.C. 58, 71, 487 F.2d 700, 713 (1973); Kaiser Aluminum & Chemical Corp. v. United States, 141 Ct.Cl. 38, 157 F.Supp. 939 (1958) (Reed, J.); The Federalist, No. 64 (S. Mittell ed. 1938).

Only recently the Court restated the ancient proposition of law, albeit in the context of a grand jury inquiry rather than a trial,

"that 'the public ＊ ＊ ＊ has a right to every man's evidence,' except for those persons protected by a constitutional, common-law, or statutory privilege, United States v. Bryan, 339 U.S. [323, 331, 70 S.Ct. 724, 730 (1949)]; Blackmer v. United States, 284 U.S. 421, 438 [52 S.Ct. 252, 76 L.Ed. 375] (1932). ＊ ＊ ＊ " Branzburg v. Hayes. United States, 408 U.S. 665, 688 [92 S.Ct. 2646, 33 L.Ed.2d 626] (1972).

The privileges referred to by the Court are designed to protect weighty and legitimate competing interests. Thus, the Fifth Amendment to the Constitution provides that no man "shall be compelled in any criminal case to be a witness against himself." And, generally, an attorney or a priest may not be required to disclose what has been revealed in professional confidence. These and other interests are recognized in law by privileges against forced disclosure, established in the Constitution, by statute, or at common law. Whatever their origins, these exceptions to the demand for every man's evidence are not lightly created nor expansively construed, for they are in derogation of the search for truth.[18]

In this case the President challenges a subpoena served on him as a third party requiring the production of materials for use in a criminal prosecution; he does so on the claim that he has a privilege against disclosure of confidential communications. He does not place his claim of privilege on the ground they are military or diplomatic secrets. As to these areas of Art. II duties the courts have traditionally shown the utmost deference to Presidential responsibilities. In C. & S. Air Lines v. Waterman S.S. Corp., 333 U.S. 103, 111, 68 S.Ct. 431, 436, 92 L.Ed. 568 (1948), dealing with Presidential authority involving foreign policy considerations, the Court said:

"The President, both as Commander-in-Chief and as the Nation's organ for foreign affairs, has available intelligence services whose reports are not and ought not to be published to the world. It would be intolerable that courts, without the relevant information, should review and perhaps nullify actions of the Executive taken on information properly held secret."

In United States v. Reynolds, 345 U.S. 1, 73 S.Ct. 528, 97 L.Ed. 727 (1953), dealing with a claimant's demand for evidence in a Tort Claims Act case against the Government, the Court said:

"It may be possible to satisfy the court, from all the circumstances of the case, that there is a reasonable danger that compulsion of the evidence will expose military matters which, in the interest of national security, should not be divulged. When this is the case, the occasion for the privilege is appropriate, and the court should not jeopardize the security which the privilege is meant to protect by insisting upon

18. Because of the key role of the testimony of witnesses in the judicial process, courts have historically been cautious about privileges. Mr. Justice Frankfurter, dissenting in Elkins v. United States, 364 U.S. 206, 234, 80 S.Ct. 1437, 1454, 4 L.Ed.2d 1669 (1960), said of this: "Limitations are properly placed upon the operation of this general principle only to the very limited extent that permitting a refusal to testify or excluding relevant evidence has a public good transcending the normally predominant principle of utilizing all rational means for ascertaining truth."

an examination of the evidence, even by the judge alone, in chambers." Id., at 10.

No case of the Court, however, has extended this high degree of deference to a President's generalized interest in confidentiality. Nowhere in the Constitution, as we have noted earlier, is there any explicit reference to a privilege of confidentiality, yet to the extent this interest relates to the effective discharge of a President's powers, it is constitutionally based.

The right to the production of all evidence at a criminal trial similarly has constitutional dimensions. The Sixth Amendment explicitly confers upon every defendant in a criminal trial the right "to be confronted with the witnesses against him" and "to have compulsory process for obtaining witnesses in his favor. Moreover, the Fifth Amendment also guarantees that no person shall be deprived of liberty without due process of law. It is the manifest duty of the courts to vindicate those guarantees, and to accomplish that it is essential that all relevant and admissible evidence be produced.

In this case we must weigh the importance of the general privilege of confidentiality of Presidential communications in performance of the President's responsibilities against the inroads of such a privilege on the fair administration of criminal justice.[19] The interest in preserving confidentiality is weighty indeed and entitled to great respect. However, we cannot conclude that advisers will be moved to temper the candor of their remarks by the infrequent occasions of disclosure because of the possibility that such conversations will be called for in the context of a criminal prosecution.[20]

On the other hand, the allowance of the privilege to withhold evidence that is demonstrably relevant in a criminal trial would cut deeply into the guarantee of due process of law and gravely impair the basic function of the courts. A President's acknowledged need for confidentiality in the communications of his office is general in nature, whereas the constitutional need for production of relevant evidence in a criminal proceeding is specific and central to the fair adjudication of a particular criminal case in the administration of justice. Without access to specific facts a criminal prosecution may be totally frustrated. The President's broad interest in confidentiality of communications will not be vitiated by disclosure of a limited

19. We are not here concerned with the balance between the President's generalized interest in confidentiality and the need for relevant evidence in civil litigation, nor with that between the confidentiality interest and congressional demands for information, nor with the President's interest in preserving state secrets. We address only the conflict between the President's assertion of a generalized privilege of confidentiality and the constitutional need for relevant evidence in criminal trials.

20. Mr. Justice Cardozo made this point in an analogous context, speaking for a unanimous Court in Clark v. United States, 289 U.S. 1, 53 S.Ct. 465, 77 L.Ed. 993 (1933), he emphasized the importance of maintaining the secrecy of the deliberations of a petit jury in a criminal case. "Freedom of debate might be stifled and independence of thought checked if jurors were made to feel that their arguments and ballots were to be freely published to the world." Id., at 13, 53 S.Ct., at 469. Nonetheless, the Court also recognized that isolated inroads on confidentiality designed to serve the paramount need of the criminal law would not vitiate the interests served by secrecy:

A juror of integrity and reasonable firmness will not fear to speak his mind if the confidences of debate are barred to the ears of mere impertinence of malice. He will not expect to be shielded against the disclosure of his conduct in the event that there is evidence reflecting upon his honor. The chance that now and then there may be found some timid soul who will take counsel of his fears and give way to their repressive power is too remote and shadowy to shape the course of justice." Id., at 16, 53 S.Ct., at 470.

number of conversations preliminarily shown to have some bearing on the pending criminal cases.

We conclude that when the ground for asserting privilege as to subpoenaed materials sought for use in a criminal trial is based only on the generalized interest in confidentiality, it cannot prevail over the fundamental demands of due process of law in the fair administration of criminal justice. The generalized assertion of privilege must yield to the demonstrated, specific, need for evidence in a pending criminal trial.

D

We have earlier determined that the District Court did not err in authorizing the issuance of the subpoena. If a President concludes that compliance with a subpoena would be injurious to the public interest he may properly, as was done here, invoke a claim of privilege on the return of the subpoena. Upon receiving a claim of privilege from the Chief Executive, it became the further duty of the District Court to treat the subpoenaed material as presumptively privileged and to require the Special Prosecutor to demonstrate that the Presidential material was "essential to the justice of the [pending criminal] case." United States v. Burr, 25 Fed.Cas., at 192. Here the District Court treated the material as presumptively privileged, proceeded to find that the Special Prosecutor had made a sufficient showing to rebut the presumption, and ordered an *in camera* examination of the subpoenaed material. On the basis of our examination of the record we are unable to conclude that the District Court erred in ordering the inspection. Accordingly we affirm the order of the District Court that subpoenaed materials be transmitted to that court. We now turn to the important question of the District Court's responsibilities in conducting the *in camera* examination of Presidential materials or communications delivered under the compulsion of the subpoena *duces tecum*.

E

Enforcement of the subpoena *duces tecum* was stayed pending this Court's resolution of the issues raised by the petitions for certiorari. Those issues now having been disposed of, the matter of implementation will rest with the District Court. "[T]he guard, furnished to [the President] to protect him from being harassed by vexatious and unnecessary subpoenas, is to be looked for in the conduct of a [district] court after those subpoenas have issued; not in any circumstance, which is to precede their being issued." United States v. Burr, supra, at 34. Statements that meet the test of admissibility and relevance must be isolated; all other material must be excised. At this stage the District Court is not limited to representations of the Special Prosecutor as to the evidence sought by the subpoena; the material will be available to the District Court. It is elementary that *in camera* inspection of evidence is always a procedure calling for scrupulous protection against any release or publication of material not found by the court, at that stage, probably admissible in evidence and relevant to the issues of the trial for which it is sought. That being true of an ordinary situation, it is obvious that the District Court has a very heavy responsibility to see to it that Presidential conversations, which are either not relevant or not admissible, are accorded that high degree of respect due the President of the United States. Mr. Chief Justice Marshall, sitting as a trial judge in the *Burr* case, supra, was extraordinarily careful to point out that "[i]n no case of this kind would a court be required to proceed against the president as against an ordinary individual." at 192.

Marshall's statement cannot be read to mean in any sense that a President is above the law, but relates to the singularly unique role under Art. II of a President's communications and activities, related to the performance of duties under that Article. Moreover, a President's communications and activities encompass a vastly wider range of sensitive material than would be true of any "ordinary individual." It is therefore necessary[21] in the public interest to afford Presidential confidentiality the greatest protection consistent with the fair administration of justice. The need for confidentiality even as to idle conversations with associates in which casual reference might be made concerning political leaders within the country or foreign statesmen is too obvious to call for further treatment. We have no doubt that the District Judge will at all times accord to Presidential records that high degree of deference suggested in United States v. Burr, supra and will discharge his responsibility to see to it that until released to the Special Prosecutor no *in camera* material is revealed to anyone. This burden applies with even greater force to excised material; once the decision is made to excise, the material is restored to its privileged status and should be returned under seal to its lawful custodian.

* * *

Affirmed.

Mr. Justice Rehnquist took no part in the consideration or decision of these cases.

See California Evidence Code § 1040 at p. 868.

ROVIARO v. UNITED STATES

Supreme Court of the United States, 1957.
353 U.S. 53, 77 S.Ct. 623, 1 L.Ed.2d 639.
[Most of the Court's footnotes are omitted.]

Mr. Justice BURTON delivered the opinion of the Court.

This case concerns a conviction for violation of the Narcotic Drugs Import and Export Act, as amended. The principal issue is whether the United States District Court committed reversible error when it allowed the Government to refuse to disclose the identity of an undercover employee who had taken a material part in bringing about the possession of certain drugs by the accused, had been present with the accused at the occurrence of the alleged crime, and might be a material witness as to whether the accused knowingly, transported the drugs as charged. For the reasons hereafter stated, we hold that, under the circumstances here present, this was reversible error.

---

21. When the subpoenaed material is delivered to the District Judge *in camera,* questions may arise as to the excising of parts, and it lies within the discretion of that court to seek the aid of the Special Prosecutor and the President's counsel for *in camera* consideration of the validity of particular excisions, whether the basis of excision is relevancy or admissibility or under such cases as United States v. Reynolds, 345 U.S. 1, 73 S.Ct. 528, 97 L.Ed. 727 (1953), or C. & S. Air Lines v. Waterman S.S. Corp., 333 U.S. 103, 68 S.Ct. 431, 92 L.Ed. 568 (1948).

In 1955, in the Northern District of Illinois, petitioner, Albert Roviaro, was indicted on two counts by a federal grand jury. The first count charged that on August 12, 1954, at Chicago, Illinois, he sold heroin to one "John Doe" in violation of 26 U.S.C. § 2554(a), 26 U.S.C.A. § 2554(a). The second charged that on the same date and in the same city he "did then and there fraudulently and knowingly receive, conceal, buy and facilitate the transportation and concealment after importation of * * * heroin, knowing, the same to be imported into the United States contrary to law; in violation of Section 174, Title 21, United States Code."

Before trial, petitioner moved for a bill of particulars requesting, among other things, the name, address and occupation of "John Doe." The Government objected on the ground that John Doe was an informer and that his identity was privileged. The motion was denied.

Petitioner, who was represented by counsel, waived a jury and was tried by the District Court. During the trial John Doe's part in the charged transaction was described by government witnesses, and counsel for petitioner, in cross-examining them, sought repeatedly to learn Joe Doe's identity. The court declined to permit this cross-examination and John Doe was not produced, identified, or otherwise made available. Petitioner was found guilty on both counts and was sentenced to two years' imprisonment and a fine of $5 on each count, the sentences to run concurrently. The Court of Appeals sustained the conviction, holding that the concurrent sentence was supported by the conviction on Count 2 and that the trial court had not abused its discretion in denying petitioner's requests for disclosure of Doe's identity. * * *

At the trial, the Government relied on the testimony of two federal narcotics agents, Durham and Fields, and two Chicago police officers, Bryson and Sims, each of whom knew petitioner by sight. On the night of August 12, 1954, these four officers met at 75th Street and Prairie Avenue in Chicago with an informer described only as John Doe. Doe and his Cadillac car were searched and no narcotics were found. Bryson secreted himself in the trunk of Doe's Cadillac, taking with him a device with which to raise the trunk lid from the inside. Doe then drove the Cadillac to 70th Place and St. Lawrence Avenue, followed by Durham in one government car and Field and Sims in another. After an hour's wait at about 11 o'clock, petitioner arrived in a Pontiac, accompanied by an unidentified man. Petitioner immediately entered Doe's Cadillac, taking a front seat beside Doe. They then proceeded by a circuitous route to 74th Street near Champlain Avenue. Both government cars trailed the Cadillac but only the one driven by Durham managed to follow it to 74th Street. When the Cadillac came to a stop on 74th Street, Durham stepped out of his car onto the sidewalk and saw petitioner alight from the Cadillac about 100 feet away. Durham saw petitioner walk a few feet to a nearby tree, pick up a small package, return to the open right front door of the Cadillac, make a motion as if depositing the package in the car, and then wave to Doe and walk away. Durham went immediately to the Cadillac and recovered a package from the floor. He signaled to Bryson to come out of the trunk and then walked down the street in time to see petitioner re-enter the Pontiac, parked nearby, and ride away.

Meanwhile, Bryson, concealed in the trunk of the Cadillac, had heard a conversation between John Doe and petitioner after the latter had entered the car. He heard petitioner greet John Doe and direct him where to drive. At one point, petitioner admonished him to pull over to the curb, cut the motor, and turn out the lights so as to lose a "tail." He then told him to continue "further down." Petitioner asked about money Doe owed him. He advised Doe that he had brought him "three pieces this time." When Bryson heard Doe being ordered to stop the car, he raised the lid of the trunk slightly. After the car stopped, he saw petitioner walk to a tree, pick up a package, and return toward the car. He heard petitioner say, "Here it is," and "I'll call you in a couple of days." Shortly thereafter he heard Durham's signal to come out and emerged from the trunk to find Durham holding a small package found to contain three glassine envelopes containing a white powder.

A field test of the powder having indicated that it contained an opium derivative, the officers, at about 12:30 a.m., arrested petitioner at his home and took him, along with Doe, to Chicago police headquarters. There petitioner was confronted with Doe, who denied that he knew or had ever seen petitioner. Subsequent chemical analysis revealed that the powder contained heroin.

I.

Petitioner contends that the trial court erred in upholding the right of the Government to withhold the identity of John Doe. He argues that Doe was an active participant in the illegal activity charged and that, therefore, the Government could not withhold his identity, his whereabouts, and whether he was alive or dead at the time of trial.[5] The Government does not defend the nondisclosure of Doe's identity with respect to Count 1, which charged a sale of heroin to John Doe, but it attempts to sustain the judgment on the basis of the conviction on Count 2, charging illegal transportation of narcotics. It argues that the conviction on Count 2 may properly be upheld since the identity of the informer, in the circumstances of this case, has no real bearing on that charge and is therefore privileged.

What is usually referred to as the informer's privilege is in reality the Government's privilege to withhold from disclosure the identity of persons who furnish information of violations of law to officers charged with enforcement of that law. The purpose of the privilege is the furtherance and protection of the public interest in effective law enforcement. The privilege recognizes the obligation of citizens to communicate their knowledge of the com-

---

5. The following colloquy occurred between Chester E. Emanuelson, the government counsel, and Maurice J. Walsh, petitioner's counsel:

"Mr. Emanuelson: *   *   *

*   *   *

"The reason we do not want to reveal his [Doe's] name is that there are other matters that are pending. I have been told—I know of one myself—and the cases hold that we do not have to reveal the informer's name. Now, if there is some reason—

"Mr. Walsh: Well, is there any activity of the informer which will be curtailed by reason of the disclosure of his name?

Would you answer that?

"Mr. Emanuelson: Any activities?

"Mr. Walsh: Yes.

"Mr. Emanuelson: From this point forward, no.

"Mr. Walsh: Is there any occasion upon which he will be called to testify?

"Mr. Emanuelson: No."

In a later colloquy Mr. Emanuelson stated: "[A]s I understand it, the reason his [Doe's] name has not been disclosed is because he is acting as a Government employee in other cases and it would help other persons in other matters that are pending."

mission of crimes to law enforcement officials and, by preserving their anonymity, encourages them to perform that obligation.

The scope of the privilege is limited by its underlying purpose. Thus, where the disclosure of the contents of a communication will not tend to reveal the identity of an informer, the contents are not privileged. Likewise, once the identity of the informer has been disclosed to those who would have cause to resent the communication, the privilege is no longer applicable.[8]

A further limitation on the applicability of the privilege arises from the fundamental requirements of fairness. Where the disclosure of an informer's identity, or of the contents of his communication, is relevant and helpful to the defense of an accused, or is essential to a fair determination of a cause, the privilege must give way. In these situations the trial court may require disclosure and, if the Government withholds the information, dismiss the action. Most of the federal cases involving this limitation on the scope of the informer's privilege have arisen where the legality of a search without a warrant is in issue and the communications of an informer are claimed to establish probable cause. In these cases the Government has been required to disclose the identity of the informant unless there was sufficient evidence apart from his confidential communication.

Three recent cases in the Courts of Appeals have involved the identical problem raised here—the Government's right to withhold the identity of an informer who helped to set up the commission of the crime and who was present at its occurrence. Portomene v. United States, 5 Cir., 221 F.2d 582; United States v. Conforti, 7 Cir., 200 F.2d 365; Sorrentino v. United States, 9 Cir., 163 F.2d 627. In each case it was stated that the identity of such an informer must be disclosed whenever the informer's testimony may be relevant and helpful to the accused's defense.

We believe that no fixed rule with respect to disclosure is justifiable. The problem is one that calls for balancing the public interest in protecting the flow of information against the individual's right to prepare his defense. Whether a proper balance renders nondisclosure erroneous must depend on the particular circumstances of each case, taking into consideration the crime charged, the possible defenses, the possible significance of the informer's testimony, and other relevant factors.

II.

The materiality of John Doe's possible testimony must be determined by reference to the offense charged in Count 2 and the evidence relating to

8. The record contains several intimations that the identity of John Doe was known to petitioner and that John Doe died prior to the trial. In either situation, whatever privilege the Government might have had would have ceased to exist, since the purpose of the privilege is to maintain the Government's channels of communication by shielding the identity of an informer from those who would have cause to resent his conduct. The Government suggests that if petitioner knew John Doe's identity, the court's failure to require disclosure would not be prejudicial even if erroneous. See

Sorrentino v. United States, 9 Cir., 163 F.2d 627. However, any indications that petitioner, at the time of the trial, was aware of John Doe's identity are contradicted by the testimony of Officer Bryson that John Doe at police headquarters denied knowing, or ever having seen, petitioner. The trial court made no factual finding that petitioner knew Doe's identity. On this record we cannot assume that John Doe was known to petitioner, and, if alive, available to him as a witness. Nor can we conclude that John Doe died before the trial.

that count. The charge is in the language of the statute. It does not charge mere possession; it charges that petitioner did "fraudulently and knowingly receive, conceal, buy and facilitate the transportation and concealment after importation of * * * heroin, knowing the same to be imported into the United States contrary to law. * * * " While John Doe is not expressly mentioned, this charge, when viewed in connection with the evidence introduced at the trial, is so closely related to John Doe as to make his identity and testimony highly material.

It is true that the last sentence of subdivision (c) of § 2 authorizes a conviction when the Government has proved that the accused possessed narcotics, unless the accused explains or justifies such possession. But this statutory presumption does not reduce the offense to one of mere possession or shift the burden of proof; it merely places on the acccused, at a certain point, the burden of going forward with his defense. The fact that petitioner here was faced with the burden of explaining or justifying his alleged possession of the heroin emphasizes his vital need for access to any material witness. Otherwise, the burden of going forward might become unduly heavy.

The circumstances of this case demonstrate that John Doe's possible testimony was highly relevant and might have been helpful to the defense. So far as petitioner knew, he and John Doe were alone and unobserved during the crucial occurrence for which he was indicted. Unless petitioner waived his constitutional right not to take the stand in his own defense, John Doe was his one material witness. Petitioner's opportunity to cross-examine Police Officer Bryson and Federal Narcotics Agent Durham was hardly a substitute for an opportunity to examine the man who had been nearest to him and took part in the transaction. Doe had helped to set up the criminal occurrence and had played a prominent part in it. His testimony might have disclosed an entrapment. He might have thrown doubt upon petitioner's identity or on the identity of the package. He was the only witness who might have testified to petitioner's possible lack of knowledge of the contents of the package that he "transported" from the tree to John Doe's car. The desirability of calling John Doe as a witness, or at least interviewing him in preparation for trial, was a matter for the accused rather than the Government to decide.

Finally, the Government's use against petitioner of his conversation with John Doe while riding in Doe's car particularly emphasizes the unfairness of the nondisclosure in this case. The only person, other than petitioner himself, who could controvert, explain or amplify Bryson's report of this important conversation was John Doe. Contradiction or amplification might have borne upon petitioner's knowledge of the contents of the package or might have tended to show an entrapment.

This is a case where the Government's informer was the sole participant, other than the accused, in the transaction charged. The informer was the only witness in a position to amplify or contradict the testimony of government witnesses. Moreover, a government witness testified that Doe denied knowing petitioner or ever having seen him before. We conclude that, under these circumstances, the trial court committed prejudicial error in permitting the Government to withhold the identity of its undercover em-

ployee in the face of repeated demands by the accused for his disclosure.[15]
* * *

Reversed and remanded.

Mr. Justice Black and Mr. Justice Whittaker took no part in the consideration or decision of this case.

Mr. Justice Clark, dissenting.

It is with regret that I dissent from the opinion of the Court, not because I am alone, but for the reason that I have been unable to convince the majority of the unsoundness of its conclusion on the facts here and the destructive effect which that conclusion will have on the enforcement of the narcotic laws. The short of it is that the conviction of a self-confessed dope peddler is reversed because the Government refused to furnish the name of its informant whose identity the undisputed evidence indicated was well known to the peddler. Yet the Court reverses on the ground of "unfairness" because of the Government's failure to perform this fruitless gesture. In my view this does violence to the common understanding of what is fair and just. * * *

McCRAY v. ILLINOIS

Supreme Court of the United States, 1967.
386 U.S. 300, 87 S.Ct. 1056, 18 L.Ed.2d 62.
[Some of the Court's footnotes are omitted.]

Mr. Justice STEWART delivered the opinion of the Court.

The petitioner was arrested in Chicago, Illinois, on the morning of January 16, 1964, for possession of narcotics. The Chicago police officers who made the arrest found a package containing heroin on his person and he was indicted for its unlawful possession. Prior to trial he filed a motion to suppress the heroin as evidence against him, claiming that the police had acquired it in an unlawful search and seizure in violation of the Fourth and Fourteenth Amendments. See Mapp v. Ohio, 367 U.S. 643, 81 S.Ct. 1684 [6 L.Ed.2d 1081]. After a hearing, the court denied the motion, and the petitioner was subsequently convicted upon the evidence of the heroin the arresting officers had found in his possession. The judgment of conviction was affirmed by the Supreme Court of Illinois,[1] and we granted certiorari to consider the petitioner's claim that the hearing on his motion to suppress was constitutionally defective.[2]

The petitioner's arrest occurred near the intersection of 49th Street and Calumet Avenue at about seven in the morning. At the hearing on the motion to suppress, he testified that up until a half hour before he was arrested he had been at "a friend's house" about a block away, that after leaving the friend's house he had "walked with a lady from 48th to 48th and South

15. Thus far we have dealt largely with the trial court's refusal, at the trial, to require disclosure of the informer's identity. In view of the Government's exclusive reliance here upon Count 2, we have considered this question only with respect to that count. However, we think that the court erred also in denying, prior to the trial, petitioner's motion for a bill of particulars, insofar as it requested John Doe's identity and address. Since Count 1 was then before the court and expressly charged petitioner with a sale of heroin to John Doe, it was evident from the face of the indictment that Doe was a participant in and a material witness to that sale. Accordingly, when his name and address were thus requested, the Government should have been required to supply that information or suffer dismissal of that count.

1. 33 Ill.2d 66, 210 N.E.2d 161.

2. 384 U.S. 949, 86 S.Ct. 1575 [16 L.Ed.2d 546].

Park," and that, as he approached 49th Street and Calumet Avenue, "[t]he Officers stopped me going through the alley." "The officers," he said, "did not show me a search warrant for my person or an arrest warrant for my arrest." He said the officers then searched him and found the narcotics in question.[3] The petitioner did not identify the "friend" nor the "lady," and neither of them appeared as a witness.

The arresting officers then testified. Officer Jackson stated that he and two fellow officers had had a conversation with an informant on the morning of January 16 in their unmarked police car. The officer said that the informant had told them that the petitioner, with whom Jackson was acquainted, "was selling narcotics and had narcotics on his person and that he could be found in the vicinity of 47th and Calumet at this particular time." Jackson said that he and his fellow officers drove to that vicinity in the police car and that when they spotted the petitioner, the informant pointed him out and then departed on foot. Jackson stated that the officers observed the petitioner walking with a woman, then separating from her and meeting briefly with a man, then proceeding alone, and finally, after seeing the police car, "hurriedly walk[ing] between two buildings." "At this point," Jackson testified, "my partner and myself got out of the car and informed him we had information he had narcotics on his person, placed him in the police vehicle at this point." Jackson stated that the officers then searched the petitioner and found the heroin in a cigarette package.

Jackson testified that he had been acquainted with the informant for approximately a year, that during this period the informant had supplied him with information about narcotics activities "fifteen, sixteen times at least," that the information had proved to be accurate and had resulted in numerous arrests and convictions. On cross-examination, Jackson was even more specific as to the informant's previous reliability, giving the names of people who had been convicted of narcotics violations as the result of information the informant had supplied. When Jackson was asked for the informant's name and address, counsel for the State objected, and the objection was sustained by the court.[4]

---

3. The weather was "real cold," and the petitioner testified he "had on three coats." In order to conduct the search, the arresting officers, required the petitioner to remove some of his clothing, but even the petitioner's version of the circumstances of the search did not disclose any conduct remotely akin to that condemned by this Court in Rochin v. California, 342 U.S. 165, 72 S.Ct. 205 [96 L.Ed. 183].

4. "Q. What is the name of this informant that gave you this information?

"Mr. Engerman: Objection, Your Honor.

"The Court: State for the record the reasons for your objection.

"Mr. Engerman: Judge, based upon the testimony of the officer so far that they had used this informant for approximately a year, he has, worked with this individual, in the interest of the public, I see no reason why the officer should be forced to disclose the name of the informant, to cause harm or jeopardy to an individual who has cooperated with the police. The City of Chicago have a tremendous problem with narcotics. If the police are not able to withhold the name of the informant they will not be able to get informants. They are not willing to risk their lives if their names become known.

"In the interest of the City and the law enforcement of this community, I feel the officer should not be forced to reveal the name of the informant. And I also cite People vs. Durr.

"The Court: I will sustain that.

"Mr. Adam: Q. Where does this informant live?

"Mr. Engerman: Objection, your Honor, same basis.

"The Court: Sustained."

Officer Arnold gave substantially the same account of the circumstances of the petitioner's arrest and search, stating that the informant had told the officers that the petitioner "was selling narcotics and had narcotics on his person now in the vicinity of 47th and Calumet." The informant, Arnold testified, "said he had observed [the petitioner] selling narcotics to various people, meaning various addicts, in the area of 47th and Calumet." Arnold testified that he had known the informant "roughly two years," that the informant had given him information concerning narcotics "20 or 25 times," and that the information had resulted in convictions. Arnold too was asked on cross-examination for the informant's name and address, and objections to these questions were sustained by the court. * * * It is the petitioner's claim, however, that even though the officers' sworn testimony fully supported a finding of probable cause for the arrest and search, the state court nonetheless violated the Constitution when it sustained objections to the petitioner's questions as to the identity of the informant. We cannot agree.

In permitting the officers to withhold the informant's identity, the court was following well-settled Illinois law. When the issue is not guilt or innocence, but, as here, the question of probable cause for an arrest or search, the Illinois Supreme Court has held that police officers need not invariably be required to disclose an informant's identity if the trial judge is convinced, by evidence submitted in open court and subject to cross-examination, that the officers did rely in good faith upon credible information supplied by a reliable informant. This Illinois evidentiary rule is consistent with the law of many other States. * * *

The reasoning of the Supreme Court of New Jersey in judicially adopting the same basic evidentiary rule was instructively expressed by Chief Justice Weintraub in State v. Burnett, 42 N.J. 377, 201, A.2d 39:

"If a defendant may insist upon disclosure of the informant in order to test the truth of the officer's statement that there is an informant or as to what the informant related or as to the informant's reliability, we can be sure that every defendant will demand disclosure. He has nothing to lose and the prize may be the suppression of damaging evidence if the State cannot afford to reveal its source, as is so often the case. And since there is no way to test the good faith of a defendant who presses the demand, we must assume the routine demand would have to be routinely granted. The result would be that the State could use the informant's information only as a lead and could search only if it could gather adequate evidence of probable cause apart from the informant's data. Perhaps that approach would sharpen investigatorial techniques, but we doubt that there would be enough talent and time to cope with crime upon that basis. Rather we accept the premise that the informer is a vital part of society's defensive arsenal. The basic rule protecting his identity rests upon that belief.

* * *

"We must remember also that we are not dealing with the trial of the criminal charge itself. There the need for a truthful verdict outweighs society's need for the informer privilege. Here, however, the accused seeks to avoid the truth. The very purpose of a motion to suppress is to escape the inculpatory thrust of evidence in hand, not because its probative force is diluted in the least by the mode of seizure, but rather as a sanction to compel enforcement officers to respect the constitutional security of all of us under the Fourth Amendment. State v. Smith, 37 N.J. 481, 486, 181 A.2d 761 (1962). If the motion to suppress is denied, defendant will still be judged upon the untarnished truth.

* * *

"The Fourth Amendment is served if a judicial mind passes upon the existence of probable cause. Where the issue is submitted upon an application for a warrant, the magistrate is trusted to evaluate the credibility of the affiant in an *ex parte* proceeding. As we have said the magistrate is concerned, not with whether the informant lied, but with whether the affiant is truthful in his recitation of what he was told. If the magistrate doubts the credibility of the affiant, he may require that the informant be identified or even produced. It seems to us that the same approach is equally sufficient where the search was without a warrant, that is to say, that it should rest entirely with the judge who hears the motion to suppress to decide whether he needs such disclosure as to the informant in order to decide whether the officer is a believable witness." 42 N.J. at 385–388, 201 A. 2d, at 43–45.

What Illinois and her sister States have done is no more than recognize a well-established testimonial privilege, long familiar to the law of evidence. Professor Wigmore, not known as an enthusiastic advocate of testimonial privileges generally,[8] has described that privilege in these words:

"A genuine privilege, on * * * fundamental principle * * * , must be recognized for the *identity of persons supplying the government with information concerning the commission of crimes.* Communications of this kind ought to receive encouragement. They are discouraged if the informer's identity is disclosed. Whether an informer is motivated by good citizenship, promise of leniency or prospect of pecuniary reward, he will usually condition his cooperation on an assurance of anonymity—to protect himself and his family from harm, to preclude adverse social reactions and to avoid the risk of defamation or malicious prosecution actions against him. The government also has an interest in nondisclosure of the identity of its informers. Law enforcement officers often depend upon professional informers to furnish them with a flow of information about criminal activities. Revelation of the dual role played by such persons ends their usefulness to the government and discourages others from entering into a like relationship.

"That the government has this privilege is well established and its soundness cannot be questioned." (Footnotes omitted.) 8 Wigmore, Evidence § 2374 (McNaughton rev. 1961).

In the federal courts the rules of evidence in criminal trials are governed "by the principles of the common law as they may be interpreted by the courts of the United States in the light of reason and experience." This Court, therefore, has the ultimate task of defining the scope to be accorded

8. See 8 Wigmore, Evidence § 2192 (McNaughton rev. 1961).

to the various common law evidentiary privileges in the trial of federal criminal cases. This is a task which is quite different, of course, from the responsibility of constitutional adjudication. In the exercise of this supervisory jurisdiction the Court had occasion 10 years ago, in Roviaro v. United States, 353 U.S. 53, 77 S.Ct. 623 [1 L.Ed.2d 639], to give thorough consideration to one aspect of the informer's privilege, the privilege itself having long been recognized in the federal judicial system.

The *Roviaro* case involved the informer's privilege, not at a preliminary hearing to determine probable cause for an arrest or search, but at the trial itself where the issue was the fundamental one of innocence or guilt. * * *

What *Roviaro* thus makes clear is that this Court was unwilling to impose any absolute rule requiring disclosure of an informer's identity even in formulating evidentiary rules for federal criminal trials.

* * * Yet we are now asked to hold that the Constitution somehow compels Illinois to abolish the informer's privilege from its law of evidence, and to require disclosure of the informer's identity in every such preliminary hearing where it appears that the officers made the arrest or search in reliance upon facts supplied by an informer they had reason to trust. The argument is based upon the Due Process Clause of the Fourteenth Amendment, and upon the Sixth Amendment right of confrontation, applicable to the State through the Fourteenth Amendment. Pointer v. Texas, 380 U.S. 400, 85 S.Ct. 1065 [13 L.Ed.2d 923]. We find no support for the petitioner's position in either of those constitutional provisions.

The arresting officers in this case testified, in open court, fully and in precise detail as to what the informer told them and as to why they had reason to believe his information was trustworthy. Each officer was under oath. Each was subjected to searching cross-examination. The judge was obviously satisfied that each was telling the truth, and for that reason he exercised the discretion conferred upon him by the established law of Illinois to respect the informer's privilege.

Nothing in the Due Process Clause of the Fourteenth Amendment requires a state court judge in every such hearing to assume the arresting officers are committing perjury. "To take such a step would be quite beyond the pale of this Court's proper function in our federal system. It would be a wholly unjustifiable encroachment by this Court upon the constitutional power of States to promulgate their own rules of evidence * * * in their own state courts. * * * " Spencer v. Texas, 385 U.S. 554, 568–569, 87 S.Ct. 648, 656.

The petitioner does not explain precisely how he thinks his Sixth Amendment right to confrontation and cross-examination was violated by Illinois' recognition of the informer's privilege in this case. If the claim is that the State violated the Sixth Amendment by not producing the informer to testify against the petitioner, then we need no more than repeat the Court's answer to that claim a few weeks ago in Cooper v. California:

> "Petitioner also presents the contention here that he was unconstitutionally deprived of the right to confront a witness against him, because the State did not produce the informant to testify against him. This contention we consider absolutely devoid of merit." Ante, p. 58, at 62, n. 2, p. 788, at 791.

On the other hand, the claim may be that the petitioner was deprived of his Sixth Amendment right to cross-examine the arresting officers themselves, because their refusal to reveal the informer's identity was upheld. But it would follow from this argument that no witness on cross-examination could ever constitutionally assert a testimonial privilege, including the privilege against compulsory self-incrimination guaranteed by the Constitution itself. We have never given the Sixth Amendment such a construction, and we decline to do so now.

Affirmed.

[The opinion of Mr. Justice Douglas, with whom The Chief Justice, Mr. Justice Brennan and Mr. Justice Fortas concur, dissenting, is omitted.]

NON-DISCLOSURE OF COMPLAINANTS' NAMES IN SCHOOL DESEGREGATION CASES: TITLE IV OF THE CIVIL RIGHTS ACT OF 1964

Comment, 1967 Washington Univ. Law Quarterly 459.
[Some footnotes omitted.]

United States v. School Dist. No. 1, 40 F.R.D. 391 (D.S.C. 1966).

Title IV of the 1964 Civil Rights Act[1] permits the Attorney General to bring desegregation suits against local school boards "in the name of the United States" provided, among other requirements,[2] he believes the aggrieved persons cannot "initiate and maintain appropriate legal proceedings." Satisfied that the various requirements were met, the Attorney General commenced this action against the Lexington County School Board. The Board, stating it could not prepare its defense, posed numerous interrogatories, some of which the government refused to answer. The contested questions sought the name or names of the complainants and the nature of the complaint.[5] The government based its refusal to answer on subsection (b) of Title IV, which declares that a person is unable to initiate and maintain appropriate proceedings "∗ ∗ ∗ whenever he [the Attorney General] is satisfied that the institution of such litigation would jeopardize the personal safety, employment, or economic standing of such person or persons, their families, or their property." This provision, the government argued, was intended to protect the complainant by concealment, allowing suit to be brought in the name of the United States.

The court ordered the government to answer. Finding no reference to reprisals in desegregation cases to date, the court reasoned that there was

1. 42 U.S.C. § 2000c—6 (1964).

2. The Act also requires that the Attorney General: 1) receive a written complaint signed by parents stating that their children are being denied the equal protection of the laws, 2) believe the complaint is meritorious, 3) believe the action will "materially further the orderly achievement of desegregation of public education," 4) notify the school board of the complaint, 5) certify that he believes the school board has had a "reasonable time to adjust the conditions." 42 U.S.C. § 2000c—6(a) (1964).

5. A third question challenged the basis upon which the Attorney General determined the complainants' inability to initiate and maintain a suit. In sustaining the government's refusal to answer, the court followed precedent. See United States v. Junction City School Dist. No. 75, 253 F. Supp. 766 (W.D.Ark. 1966). It would have been difficult to draw a contrary conclusion because the House Judiciary Committee's Report states: "It is not intended that the determination on which the certification was based should be reviewable." 1964 (U.S.) Code Cong. & Ad. News 2355.

no basis for the concealment provision of the statute. Earlier cases involving non-disclosure were not directly in point. Moreover, the purpose and scope of pre-trial discovery demanded that this information be made available to the defendant school board.

   The court's decision raises three problems: congressional intent, troublesome language in earlier cases, and the scope of discovery. In his address to the Senate introducing the 1964 Civil Rights bill, the then Senator Hubert H. Humphrey stated:

> The bill requires the Attorney General to state in his complaint that in his judgment the persons who complained are unable to initiate or maintain appropriate legal proceedings. These statements by the Attorney General will not be subject to challenge either by the defendants or by the court. *Under no circumstances will the Attorney General be required to reveal the names of the particular complainants.*[8]

This unequivocal language is the sole statement about the non-disclosure provision. Congress accepted it without further debate. One federal court, after considering this provision, said:

> Section 407 of the Civil Rights Act of 1964 clearly expresses the legislative intent that the Attorney General be vested with exclusive and final determination of the sufficiency of the complaint. Thus, the Attorney General need not detail the facts behind the certificate nor disclose the names or identity of the person or persons complaining to him. The legislative history of the Act leaves no doubt that such was the contemplation of Congress.[9]

   But in *School Dist. No. 1,* the court questioned the need for concealment. Although it found no reprisals in desegregation cases, the court went on to say that even if there were reprisals, the "United States court is now available for the protection of the complainants."[10] What this precisely means remains obscure.   *   *   *

   Arguably, the "informer" in desegregation cases is substantially like the informer in an action brought under the Fair Labor Standards Act of 1938.[20] In these cases, after an employee complains to the Department of Labor about a violation of the Act, the Secretary is authorized to bring suit in his own name. After suits have commenced, employers, as part of the discovery process, have sought the names of the employees who complained. The Secretary has successfully raised the privilege to protect the informers' names.[22] In Wirtz v. Continental Finance & Loan Co., the court reasoned that employees are "particularly susceptible to the fear of retaliation," so that to obtain the information needed to insure compliance with the Act, the government must assure informers that their names would not be divulged. Summarizing the factors to be considered concerning informer's privilege, the court stated:

8. United States v. School Dist. No. 1, 40 F.R.D. 391, 393 (D.S.C.1966), citing 110 Cong.Rec. 6543 (1964) (emphasis added).

9. United States v. Junction City Sch. Dist. No. 75, 253 F.Supp. 766, 768 (W.D.Ark.1966).

10. United States v. Sch. Dist. No. 1, 40 F.R.D. 391, 394 (D.S.C.1966).

20. §§ 1–19, ch. 676, 52 Stat. 1060–69, as amended, 29 U.S.C. §§ 201–19 (1964).

22. Wirtz v. Continental Fin. & Loan Co., 326 F.2d 561 (5th Cir.1964); Wirtz v. B. A. C. Steel Prod., Inc., 312 F.2d 14 (4th Cir.1962); Mitchell v. Roma, 265 F.2d 633 (3d Cir.1959); Mitchell v. Neylon, 27 F.R.D. 438 (D.Neb.1960). Contra, Fleming v. Bernardi, 1 F.R.D. 624 (N.D. Ohio 1941).

This privilege may be invoked where a balancing of conflicting policy considerations shows that the public interest in protecting the flow of information outweighs the individual's rights to prepare his defense. If this type of weighing of conveniences is warranted in an action where the defendant may be subject to criminal penalties, it goes without saying that it is appropriate where only civil remedies are sought.

* * *

The government has decided to answer the interrogatories as ordered by the Court rather than suffer dismissal and appeal. There may be several reasons for this course of action: the government may not have feared reprisals in this locality, it may have decided that it must use the complainants at the trial, it may not have wished to delay this suit unless absolutely necessary. These are all matters of strategy whose importance is restricted to this particular case. They do not necessarily indicate any policy to be followed by the government in future cases.

See California Evidence Code § § 1041–1042 at pp. 868–869.

THE "JENCKS ACT", 18 U.S.C.A. § 3500

§ 3500. Demands for production of statements and reports of witnesses

(a)   In any criminal prosecution brought by the United States, no statement or report in the possession of the United States which was made by a Government witness or prospective Government witness (other than the defendant) shall be the subject of subpoena, discovery, or inspection until said witness has testified on direct examination in the trial of the case.

(b)   After a witness called by the United States has testified on direct examination, the court shall, on motion of the defendant, order the United States to produce any statement (as hereinafter defined) of the witness in the possession of the United States which relates to the subject matter as to which the witness has testified. If the entire contents of any such statement relate to the subject matter of the testimony of the witness, the court shall order it to be delivered directly to the defendant for his examination and use.

(c)   If the United States claims that any statement ordered to be produced under this section contains matter which does not relate to the subject matter of the testimony of the witness, the court shall order the United States to deliver such statement for the inspection of the court in camera. Upon such delivery the court shall excise the portions of such statement which do not relate to the subject matter of the testimony of the witness. With such material excised, the court shall then direct delivery of such statement to the defendant for his use. If, pursuant to such procedure, any portion of such statement is withheld from the defendant and the defendant objects to such withholding, and the trial is continued to an adjudication of the guilt of the defendant, the entire text of such statement shall be preserved by the United States and, in the event the defendant appeals, shall be made available to the appellate court for the purpose of determining the correctness of the ruling of the trial judge. Whenever any statement is delivered to a defendant pursuant to this section, the court in its discretion, upon application of said defendant, may recess proceedings in the trial for such time as it may determine to be reasonably required for the examination of such statement by said defendant and his preparation for its use in the trial.

Hypotheticals

(1) D is charged with committing battery against PO, a police officer. D makes a pretrial discovery motion to have the prosecution obtain from the Police Department its personnel or disciplinary record file on PO for inspection and copying by D. D asserts in his motion that his defense will be self-defense in response to the use of excessive force by PO. D's motion is supported by affidavits setting forth (a) that two named persons who had filed complaints against PO for use of excessive force are unavailable for interview by D and that these persons' prior statements to police investigators are necessary for D's effective cross-examination of PO at trial; (b) that two other named persons had previously reported misconduct on the part of PO and are available as witnesses but are unable to recall the details of the events and that the Police Department's files are necessary to refresh their recollection. The prosecutor claims the official information privilege as the person authorized by the Police Department to assert the privilege in opposition to D's motion. The trial judge makes an in camera inspection of the file in question and finds that the file does contain allegations by the four persons as set forth in D's affidavits. The trial judge then overrules the prosecutor's claim of privilege on the ground that the public-interest necessity for preserving the confidentiality of the information sought by D does not outweigh D's need for disclosure of the information to aid his defense in the interest of justice. Is this ruling of the trial judge correct?

(2) P sues D for damages for injuries received in an automobile accident on December 31, 1972. P alleges in his complaint that he lost a year's income of $20,000 for the year 1973, the year he was unable to work as a result of the accident. By a pretrial discovery motion, D seeks to inspect and copy P's copies of his federal and state income tax returns for the years 1971 and 1972, before the accident, and for 1973, the year after the accident. P resists D's motion on the ground of the official-information privilege. What result?

(3) A sues X for damages for injuries received in a collision between A's car and X's car. Shortly after the accident, A filed a claim for state disability-insurance benefits. The State Office for Disability Insurance Claims requests Dr. B to examine A for his ability or inability to work, and to make a confidential report to the state office. Dr. B examines A and sends his report to the state office. X takes Dr. B's deposition and has the state office served with a subpoena *duces tecum* to produce Dr. B's report at the deposition examination. A gives a written consent for the state office to disclose Dr. B's report to X. At the deposition examination, the state office claims an absolute privilege for nondisclosure. X seeks a court order to compel the state office to disclose Dr. B's report. How should the court rule?

(4) X is prosecuted for possession of heroin. At a pretrial hearing on X's motion to suppress, A, a police officer, testifies that he received a telephone call from a reliable informer who told him that X was selling heroin from his apartment and that he kept it in a telephone jack on the south wall of the bedroom; and that A then proceeded to X's apartment, without a warrant, found the heroin in the telephone jack and arrested X in the apartment. On cross-examination, A testifies that he did not learn from the informer whether he had ever been in X's apartment or in what way he obtained his information about the heroin location. X demands disclosure of the informer's identity, on the ground that there is the possibility that the informer could testify that another person put the heroin in the telephone jack, which would exonerate X of the heroin-possession charge. The prosecutor asserts the privilege for nondisclosure. Should the prosecutor's claim of privilege be sustained?

(5)   X is prosecuted for the sale of heroin. At the preliminary hearing, A, a police officer, testifies that he gave an informer a ten-dollar bill dusted with fluorescent powder, that he watched the informer go into an apartment and later come out with a bindle of heroin, that A then knocked on the apartment door, that X opened the door and was placed under arrest, and that X had traces of fluorescent powder on his hands. In cross-examination of A, X asks the name of the informer. A claims the identity-of-informer privilege. What result?

Chapter X

COMPETENCY OF WITNESSES

HILL v. SKINNER

Court of Appeals of Ohio, 1947.
81 Ohio App. 375, 79 N.E.2d 787.

DOYLE, Presiding Judge. This is an action under the Ohio statute, Section 5838, General Code, seeking to hold the owners and harborers of a dog called "Chang" with liability for damages arising out of an episode in which the dog, Chang, is alleged to have seized with his teeth and injured a youngster aged approximately four, the petitioner herein.

A jury, upon trial, awarded damages in the amount of $500. The judgment rendered thereon, in the Court of Common Pleas of Summit county, is part of the final order from which this appeal is taken, and consideration will be first given to the legality of this money judgment.

1. The appellants say "There was no evidence of a 'bite' anywhere in the record from any of the witnesses save the plaintiff himself. Without this * * * minor's testimony there was evidence of injury only with barbed wire, glass, a gashed steel barrel and other dogs being present as explanation."

It is a fact that there is no *direct* testimony of this dog's attack except that given by the child. If this evidence has probative worth, and is competent, it, coupled with the circumstances and other facts shown to exist, is sufficient to furnish the degree of proof necessary to sustain the judgment.

Section 11493, General Code, reads:

"All persons are competent witnesses except those of unsound mind, and children under ten years of age who appear incapable of receiving just impressions of the facts and transactions respecting which they are examined, or of relating them truly."

The Supreme Court of this state has recently ruled on that part of this statute pertaining to witnesses claimed to be of "unsound mind."

"2. The competency of an insane person to testify as a witness lies in the discretion of the trial judge and a reviewing court will not disturb the ruling thereon where there is no abuse of discretion." State v. Wildman, 145 Ohio St. 379, 61 N.E.2d 790, 791.

And in 2 Wigmore on Evidence (3 Ed.), Section 505, it is said:

"With reference to the general capacity to observe, recollect, and narrate, the same principles apply to Mental Immaturity that are applied to Mental Derangement."

The essential test of the competency of an infant witness is his comprehension of the obligation to tell the truth and his intellectual capacity of observation, recollection and communication. The nature of his conception of the obligation to tell the truth is of little importance if he shows that he will fulfill the obligation to speak truthfully as a duty which he owes a Diety or something held in reverence or regard, and if he has the intellectual capacity to communicate his observations and experiences.

The trial court, in chambers, examined the child at length, touching upon his qualifications to testify. Among other questions he was asked: "Do you know about telling the truth, what happens if you don't tell the truth?" and he answered, "They won't love me." Question: "Who won't love you?" Answer: "God won't love me." And in further answer to dozens of questions propounded by both the judge and counsel, the child demonstrated a capacity for memory of events, observation, recollection and communication.

Following this necessary and proper examination by the trial judge of the prospective witness, the court permitted him to testify. The child thereupon, upon direct examination, testified in part as follows:

"Q.　Cary do you remember when you went over to Skinner's? A. Sure.

"Q.　Tell the judge and jury what happened. A. The doggy bit me.

"Q.　What doggy bit you? A. Skinner's doggy.

"Q.　What were you doing with Skinner's dog? A. I was loving him.

"Q.　How? A. Like that. (indicating.)

"Q.　You mean around his neck? A. Yes."

On cross-examination appears the following:

"Q.　Where did Chang bite you, can you tell the ladies, take your fingers and show me where he bit you? A. He bit me when I was loving him.

"Q.　Where did he bite you, did he bite you on the leg? A. No, he bite me on the head and on my mouth here. (indicating.)"

As we view the testimony, the youthful narrator, except for a few nonresponsive answers, clearly described and explained the circumstances giving rise to this action. The evidence considered as a whole describes the wandering of the child out onto his neighbor's yard and the subsequent attack of the dog, under circumstances clearly related by the child. There is nothing in the record to show, except through pure guess and speculation, that the head injuries resulted from any other cause.

Paraphrasing a syllabus in State v. Wildman, supra, to fit this case, the rule may be pronounced to be that the competency of a child of mental immaturity to testify as a witness lies in the discretion of the trial judge, and a reviewing court will not disturb the ruling thereon when there is no abuse of discretion. In the instant case we find no such abuse. We further find that the evidence in the record is such as to warrant the jury in finding in favor of the petitioner.

Judgment modified to provide for the destruction of the dog, as required by the Ohio statute, and as modified, affirmed.

TRACY, HANDBOOK OF THE LAW OF EVIDENCE

120–133 (1952).*
[Footnotes omitted.]

COMPETENCY

In general. As we said in the Introduction, in the early days, the facts in a case were brought out only by the knowledge of the members of the jury; the calling of outside witnesses was a later development. It is not surprising that at first these outsiders were greeted with suspicion. Apparently the early courts looked on nearly every proffered witness as a possible prospective perjurer, and if there were any reason to suspect that certain characteristics or circumstances of a witness might incline him to lie, that person was considered incompetent to testify. Nearly all the old incompetencies have now been removed, but they will be discussed here briefly for their historical interest.

Religious belief. At common law, the religious belief of a prospective witness was most important, for unless he was found to believe in a Supreme Being who was a rewarder of truth and an avenger of falsehood, he was incapable of taking an oath and therefore of testifying. Ancient reports are full of cases dealing with this disability, but the common law rules on the subject have been made obsolete by the universal enactment of constitutional and statutory provisions. Such legislation has been along two lines: (1) abolishing any religious test as a prerequisite to taking an oath: (2) giving to those who have scruples against taking an oath the privilege to affirm.

In no American jurisdiction is religious belief now a test of the competency of a witness.

Infamy.   At early common law a part of the punishment for crime was that the person found guilty was thereby rendered infamous. He lost the rights of an ordinary citizen: the right to vote, the right to hold office, the right to serve on a jury, the right to testify in a court of law. The rule that he was incompetent to serve as a witness was based on the theory that such a person could not be expected to regard the obligation of an oath.

The reports and digests are full of cases construing this rule, but it has now been generally abolished. The reasons for its abolishment are obvious: (1) There is no logical connection between committing a crime (except probably the crime of perjury) and mendacity; there is no reason for believing that a person who has murdered will also lie. (2) Prosecutors in criminal cases discovered that by the enforcement of this rule they were being deprived of indispensable evidence in criminal cases, for the testimony of an accomplice who had himself pleaded guilty or who had stood trial and had been convicted could never be used. The rule is still applied by statute in a number of states to convictions for the crime of perjury, including subornation of perjury and, in a few southern states, to a specified list of infamous crimes. Most of these last-named jurisdictions, however, apply the rule in criminal trials only.

The attorney should examine the statutes of his state on this point. If there is no statute, there is no disability, for the common law rule on this subject no longer exists anywhere.

Interest. In the administration of justice at common law, it was considered essential to prevent a witness from testifying if he were interested in the outcome of the cause, as a party or otherwise. The reasons asserted to support this rule of disability were interestingly set out in a leading treatise on evidence published as late as 1824:

The law will not receive the evidence of any person, even under the sanction of an oath, who has an interest in giving the proposed evidence, and consequently whose interest conflicts with his duty. This rule of exclusion, considered in its principle, requires little explanation. It is founded on the known infirmities of human nature, which is too weak to be generally restrained by religious or moral obligations, when tempted and solicited in a contrary direction by temporal interests. There are, no doubt, many whom no interests could seduce from a sense of duty, and their exclusion by the operation of this rule may in particular cases shut out the truth. But the law must prescribe general rules; and experience proves that more mischief would result from the general reception of interested witnesses than is occasioned by their general exclusion.

Generations of experience in applying this rule of exclusion demonstrated to the satisfaction of jurists not only that the courts were wrong in assuming that pecuniary interest necessarily assures falsehood in testimony but that many apparently meritorious cases were rendered impossible of proof because the only persons who knew the facts could not testify, and that, consequently, more mischief resulted from the exclusion of the testimony of such witnesses than would have resulted from its reception. Therefore, by statutory enactment in practically every jurisdiction, such disability has been abolished, and interested persons may now testify fully, except in one class of cases—namely, where the survivor of a transaction with a deceased person undertakes to testify against the latter's estate. This exception exists by statute in all but a very few states, being popularly known as the "Dead Man's Act."

Testimony of interested survivor. * * * See pp. 667–668.

Mental capacity. A witness will ordinarily be presumed to have the mental capacity to testify. That capacity to testify may be challenged, however, in which event the mental capacity of the witness is to be determined by the trial judge as a preliminary question of fact. The three situations in which such challenge may be made are where the proffered witness is an infant, where he is alleged to be insane, or where he is alleged to be intoxicated.

Infancy. An infant of very tender years is, of course, incompetent to understand the nature of an oath or to narrate with understanding the facts of what he has seen. At what age does he become competent so to understand or narrate? Courts have struggled with that question, and certain judges have endeavored to lay down a rule determining the age at which a child should be admitted as a witness. There is so great a difference, however, in the mental growth of children that it is impossible to fix a proper age limit. Before a witness is permitted to testify, the court should be convinced on two points: that he understands the nature of an oath and the possible consequences of lying, and that he possesses the capacities of observation, recollection, and communication. In other words, he must be sufficiently mature to make an intelligent statement of what he saw take place.

The proper person to decide these two questions is the trial judge, after talking with the child and observing him. Sometimes, on the question of whether the child understands the nature of an oath, the judge may consult the child's minister or priest.

A word of caution on the use of child witnesses: The ordinary child is a great weaver of romances. He may often relate something he has read in a story as a personal experience. His story should be searched for its truth before he is called to the stand. If he is a witness for the opponent, he should be skillfully cross-examined.

Caution should also be used in preparing the child witness for his examination. An experienced attorney will not ordinarily call a witness to the stand unless he has first thoroughly gone over with him the story he is to tell to the court and jury and has prepared him for the cross-examination to which he may be subjected. But it is not safe to do this too thoroughly with a child witness, for if he is asked on cross-examination "Why did you say so-and-so?", he is likely to reply "Because Mr. Blank told me to."

A child witness is usually frightened at finding himself the center of attention in the court room, and it may be difficult to get him to talk at all or to talk loud enough to be heard. In such a case it is a common practice for the attorney to start out with some friendly, irrelevant questions to put the witness at his ease before bringing the examination around to the facts in the case. In this practice he will usually be indulged by the trial judge.

Mental derangement. In the early days, one whose mind was affected was regarded as not capable of giving testimony in a court of law. But as the knowledge of mental disease developed, it was seen how wrong such a rule may be. A person may be insane only on certain subjects or at certain times. For example, in a leading English case an attendant in an asylum for the insane was being prosecuted for manslaughter inflicted on an inmate. The prosecution called as one of its witnesses another inmate. There was no question but that this inmate was properly in the asylum. He stated on examination that he had 20,000 spirits speaking to him, who ascended from his stomach and head. Yet he appeared to understand the obligations of an oath and the consequences of perjury, and he gave a perfectly collected and rational account of the affair, which he reported himself to have witnessed. This testimony was admitted.

The rule is therefore now thoroughly established that an insane man can be a competent witness if he can pass these two tests: knowledge and appreciation of the obligation of an oath and the consequences of testifying falsely, and ability to tell an intelligent story of what he saw take place.

One question on which the courts have had some difficulty is whether, assuming that the witness can meet these two tests when called to the stand, he may still be held to be a competent witness if he was incapable of observing intelligently at the time of the event concerning which he is to testify. Ordinarily the courts will admit evidence of a derangement occurring before the time of testifying as affecting only the credibility of the witness, not his competency to testify.

Intoxication. The same rules that apply to mental derangement would seem to apply to a witness who is intoxicated when he appears on the stand or who was intoxicated at the time of the occurrence to which he testifies. The test to be applied to a witness who is intoxicated on the stand is whether he is capable of intelligent and truthful narration. That is a preliminary question of fact for the trial judge. If the witness is sober on the stand but was intoxicated at the time of the transaction to which he testifies, the fact of his intoxication at that time would be admissible as bearing on the credibility of his testimony, but not to bar him as a witness.

Marital relationship. Two questions are involved here: the competency of the husband or wife as a witness, and the privilege of husband or wife not to have the other spouse testify. Here only the question of competency will be discussed. The matter of privilege will be discussed later.

At common law a wife was not permitted to testify for or against her husband, or a husband for or against his wife, without the other's consent, except in such cases of necessity as assaults by one upon the other, actions for divorce, and the like. The disability was directed to the social end of preventing marital discord arising from one party's testifying against the other or being coerced to testify for him. It was most often applicable to the wife. As her social status improved and her independence of her husband increased, it was seen that often a greater harm was done to the cause of justice by depriving the courts of needed testimony than was warranted by the need of preserving family concord. So gradually legislation began to be enacted limiting the applicability of the rule. Practically every state now has some statute on the subject. Some of these statutes merely increase the number of common law exceptions; others abolish the common law rule altogether except as to confidential communications made by one spouse to the other during coverture. Inasmuch as Congress has never enacted any statute on the subject, the federal courts continued to apply the common law until 1933. In that year the Supreme Court handed down a decision that reviewed the history of the rule, recognized its abolishment or limitation by statute in nearly every common law jurisdiction and the fact that the reason for its original adoption no longer existed, and approved the admission of the testimony of the wife in the case before it.

The enactment of legislation on this subject has been so general that it can be said that, except in one or two jurisdictions, the incompetency of husband or wife as a witness in a case when a spouse is a party no longer exists. The marital relations problems that continue to confront the courts are those of privilege rather than of competency. [See supra pp. 497–503.—Ed.]

It should be noted, however, that it is the rule of many courts that on one subject married persons are still considered incompetent to testify: Neither husband nor wife will be permitted, as a witness, to bastardize the issue of the wife after marriage by testifying to the nonaccess of the husband. The rule is said to be one of public policy, in the interests of morality and decency.

Official connection with tribunal. Is a judge, a court clerk or bailiff, an attorney, or a juror a competent witness?

Judge

A judge is not incompetent to testify merely because he holds a judicial office, and this is so whether he is called upon to testify to actual facts or as a witness to character. The question may be asked whether he can take the stand as a witness in a case being tried before him. Fortunately this question rarely arises, since the judge will generally know in advance that he is to be called and will arrange to have another judge hear the case. If the possibility of his being called as a witness arises during the trial, the judge may either call in another judge to take over or order a retrial before another judge. On the strict question whether the judge is actually incompetent to testify if he is to continue to sit in the case, the modern rule is that a judge is not a competent witness in a case in which he is presiding unless there is a statute permitting it, but that if he does testify with the consent of all parties no reversible error occurs and he does not lose jurisdiction. A federal statute requires a judge to disqualify himself under such circumstances.

Court Officers

A court attaché, clerk, bailiff, stenographer may testify generally in the case being tried, and there is no question but that he is a competent witness.

Attorney

Whether an attorney may take the stand in a trial in which he is engaged as counsel has caused some controversy and a certain amount of loose thinking by the courts. There are two questions involved, one of evidence law, the other of professional ethics. It is a rule of legal ethics that, except on merely formal matters, he should not testify in a case in which he is engaged as counsel. It will not be unusual for him to testify to formal matters, such as the identification of a document or the calculation of interest on a mortgage, on which there will be no controversy. If, however, he is called upon to testify to matters of a controversial nature, he should immediately withdraw from the trial and have his case conducted by counsel already engaged in the trial or obtain a new trial counsel in his place. But there is nothing in the law of evidence that makes him incompetent to testify as a witness. If the attorney violates the canons of ethics by continuing in the trial after testifying, he is subject to bar discipline. Only a few courts have held that such action constitutes reversible error, and even these courts regard the conduct of the attorney as the error, not the admission of his testimony.

Jurors

A juror may be called as a witness in a trial in which he is engaged, returning to the box after he has finished his testimony. Although there are strong arguments against permitting this practice, the consequences of a refusal to let him testify—namely, that he would tell his story to his fellow jurors in their deliberations without being subject to cross-examination or impeachment—are such that the courts have chosen the lesser of two evils. If the testimony of the juror is on a vital point in the case, the court may consider it wise to declare a mistrial.

The situation of a juror's giving testimony on an ordinary issue in the case rarely arises, for usually his knowledge of the facts of the case will have been brought out on his voir dire examination, and he will have been challenged and excused for cause. The problem of the competency of a juror to testify will most often arise when, on the trial or after the verdict, he is called as a witness on a claim of misconduct on the part of the jury.

*   *   *

KLINE v. FORD MOTOR CO., INC.

United States Court of Appeals, Ninth Circuit, 1975.
523 F.2d 1067.

PER CURIAM.

Karen Kline ("Karen") and Jacqueline Selby ("Jacqueline") brought these consolidated personal injury actions against Ford Motor Company ("Ford") claiming that design deficiencies in the accelerator linkage system and the steering wheel lock mechanism in the Ford Pinto that Karen was driving and in which Jacqueline was riding caused Karen to lose control of the car resulting in the single-car crash that injured both of them. While the case was pending on appeal, Karen died from her injuries and her mother as administratrix of her estate has been substituted in her place as appellant. This diversity case was tried to a jury on the sole theory of strict liability in tort. At the close of plaintiffs' case in chief, the district court granted Ford's motion to dismiss pursuant to Rule 50(a) of the Federal Rules of Civil Procedure on the ground that plaintiffs had failed to prove any causal connection between the crash and the claimed design defects.   *   *   *   (An issue on appeal is) Did the district court err in refusing to permit Jacqueline to testify about the events immediately before the accident on the ground that she was incompetent to testify to those events because her memory of them had vanished before her recollection was restored under hypnosis?

*   *   *

The accident happened in the very early morning of October 31, 1970. Karen was driving the Pinto which had been purchased new about 30 days before the accident.   *   *   *   A truck driver, Paul Cave, saw the Pinto pass him going about 50 to 60 miles per hour. When the Pinto was approximately 150 feet in front of him in the number 2 lane, the car turned and went straight for the side of the embankment. The vehicle went over the embankment and crashed into a fence about 65 feet from the roadway.

*   *   *

Evidence was introduced, which if credited by the jury, would have supported findings that, at the time of the accident, the accelerator linkage system was capable of sticking in a depressed, open-throttle condition and that the steering wheel locking mechanism was capable of being activated and placed in a locked position independently of the position of the 4-speed manual transmission after the ignition had been turned off. The plaintiffs' problem was how to connect these deficiencies with the accident. The theory was that while Karen was driving along the freeway, the accelerator-carburetor control system failed to return from the depressed position and the vehicle continued to accelerate. Karen tried to turn off the engine and, in the process, her knee accidentally activated the steering column locking assembly, thereby locking the wheels.

Karen could not testify. She sustained severe head injuries and was in a coma from which she never revived before her death. Jacqueline suffered retrograde amnesia from her injuries. When her deposition was taken before the first trial, she could remember nothing about the accident or the events shortly before the accident. In the interim after her deposition and before trial, she had undergone hypnosis at the University of California at Los Angeles Medical Center under the supervision of a psychologist, Dr. Leonard

Ollinger. She testified that the session of hypnosis revived her memory and she testified to these events: The Pinto after entering the freeway was going upgrade requiring acceleration. Karen suddenly started screaming that the car would not slow down. Jacqueline noticed a sudden increase in speed as the car reached the crest of the hill and started on the downgrade near the Greenwood Avenue Overpass, just before the accident. Karen tried to turn off the key, and the car went off the side of the road.

The court granted a mistrial, set a date for a hearing to determine the admissibility of Jacqueline's testimony, and set a new trial date. At the hearing, the court received the testimony of Dr. Ollinger about the procedure and conduct of the hypnosis session, listened to tape recordings of the session, and heard argument. The court excluded Jacqueline's testimony to the events recalled after hypnosis, sustaining Ford's objections, on the ground she was not competent as a witness to testify to facts recalled under hypnosis. The ruling was erroneous.

Competence refers to the condition of the witness at the time he or she is called to testify. Jacqueline was fully capable of expressing herself and understanding her duty as a witness to tell the truth. (e. g., Cal.Evid.Code §§ 405, 701 and annexed Comment (West 1966). She was present and personally saw and heard the occurrences at the time of the accident. She was testifying about her present recollection of events that she had witnessed. That her present memory depends upon refreshment claimed to have been induced under hypnosis goes to the credibility of her testimony not to her competence as a witness. Although the device by which recollection was refreshed is unusual, in legal effect her situation is not different from that of a witness who claims that his recollection of an event that he could not earlier remember was revived when he thereafter read a particular document. (Wyller v. Fairchild Hiller Corp. (9th Cir. 1974) 503 F.2d 506; Cal.Evid. Code § 771 (West 1966); B. Witkin, *supra*, § 1167, at 1080—81.) Here, as in *Wyller*, "[w]e cannot accept [defendant's] argument that [plaintiff's] testimony was rendered inherently untrustworthy by [her] having undergone hypnosis. [Plaintiff] testified from [her] present recollection, refreshed by the treatments. [Her] credibility and the weight to be given such testimony were for the jury to determine." (503 F.2d at 509.)

* * *

The case must be reversed for error in excluding Jacqueline's testimony. With that testimony, the plaintiffs had enough evidence on liability to require submission to the jury. Accordingly, we need not decide whether the evidence was sufficient to go to the jury despite the exclusion of Jacqueline's testimony.

Reversed and remanded.

———

See Federal Rules of Evidence 601–606 at pp. 914–915. California Evidence Code § § 700–704 at pp. 830–831.

NEW YORK CIV. PRAC. ACT & RULES, § 4519

(Formerly N.Y.Civ.Prac.Act § 347).

§ 4519. Personal transaction or communication between witness and decedent or lunatic.

Upon the trial of an action or the hearing upon the merits of a special proceeding, a party or a person interested in the event, or a person from, through or under whom such a party or interested person derives his interest or title by assignment or otherwise, shall not be examined as a witness in his own behalf or interest, or in behalf of the party succeeding to his title or interest against the executor, administrator or survivor of a deceased person or the committee of a lunatic, or a person deriving his title or interest from, through or under a deceased person or lunatic, by assignment, or otherwise, concerning a personal transaction or communication between the witness and the deceased person or lunatic, except where the executor, administrator, survivor, committee or person so deriving title or interest is examined in his own behalf, or the testimony of the lunatic or deceased person is given in evidence, concerning the same transaction or communication. A person shall not be deemed interested for the purposes of this section by reason of being a stockholder or officer of any banking corporation which is a party to the action or proceeding, or interested in the event thereof. No party or person interested in the event, who is otherwise competent to testify, shall be disqualified from testifying by the possible imposition of costs against him or the award of costs to him. A party or person interested in the event or a person from, through or under whom such a party or interested person derives his interest or title by assignment or otherwise, shall not be qualified for the purposes of this section, to testify in his own behalf or interest, or in behalf of the party succeeding to his title or interest, to personal transactions or communications with the donee of a power of appointment in an action or proceeding for the probate of a will, which exercises or attempts to exercise a power of appointment granted by the will of a donor of such power, or in an action or proceeding involving the construction of the will of the donee after its admission to probate.

Nothing contained in this section, however, shall render a person incompetent to testify as to the facts of an accident or the results therefrom where the proceeding, hearing, defense or cause of action involves a claim of negligence or contributory negligence in an action wherein one or more parties is the representative of a deceased or incompetent person based upon, or by reason of, the operation or ownership of a motor vehicle being operated upon the highways of the state, or the operation or ownership of aircraft being operated in the air space over the state, or the operation or ownership of a vessel on any of the lakes, rivers, streams, canals or other waters of this state, but this provision shall not be construed as permitting testimony as to conversations with the deceased. As amended L.1963, c. 532, § 22.

See California Evidence Code § 1261 at p. 882.

Comment to Section 1261—Law Revision Commission

The dead man statute (subdivision 3 of Section 1880 of the Code of Civil Procedure) prohibits a party who sues on a claim against a decedent's estate from testifying to any fact occurring prior to the decedent's death. The theory apparently underlying the statute is that it would be unfair to permit the surviving claimant to testify to such facts when the decedent is precluded by his death from doing so. To balance the positions of the parties, the living may not speak because the dead cannot.

The dead man statute operates unsatisfactorily. It prohibits testimony concerning matters of which the decedent had no knowledge and, hence, to which he could not have testified even if he had survived. It operates unevenly since it does not prohibit testimony relating to claims under, as distinguished from claims against, the decedent's estate even though the effect of such a claim may be to frustrate the decedent's plan for the disposition of his property. See the Law Revision Commission's Comment to Code of Civil Procedure Section 1880 and 1 Cal.Law Revision Comm'n, Rep., Rec. & Studies, Recommendation and Study Relating to the Dead Man Statute at D–1 (1957). The dead man statute excludes otherwise relevant and competent evidence—even if it is the only available evidence—and frequently this forces the courts to decide cases with a minimum of information concerning the actual facts. See the Supreme Court's complaint in Light v. Stevens, 159 Cal. 288, 292, 113 P. 659, 660 (1911) ("Owing to the fact that the lips of one of the parties to the transaction are closed by death and those of the other party by the law, the evidence on this question is somewhat unsatisfactory."). Hence, the dead man statute is not continued in the Evidence Code.

Under the Evidence Code, the positions of the parties are balanced by throwing more light, not less, on the actual facts. Repeal of the dead man statute permits the claimant to testify without restriction. To balance this advantage, Section 1261 permits hearsay evidence of the decedent's statements to be admitted. Certain safeguards—i.e., personal knowledge, recent perception, and circumstantial evidence of trustworthiness—are included in the section to provide some protection for the party against whom the statements are offered, for he has no opportunity to test the hearsay by cross-examination.

Hypotheticals

(1)   D is charged with the sale of heroin to X. The prosecution's evidence is that X, a known heroin addict, was given $300 by the police to purchase heroin from D at D's barbershop. The prosecution calls X, and D objects to any testimony from X on the ground that X is incompetent to be a witness by virtue of drug use. The trial court conducts an in-chambers hearing on the question. D calls P, a psychiatrist, who testifies that the use of LSD may confuse one's perception, thereby impairing the capacity to perceive or remember one's observations. In this case, however, P states that he did not personally interview X, and that his opinion testimony is based upon his experience with LSD users who had a history of suffering blackouts. The prosecutor calls X, who testifies to excessive use of drugs, including LSD, but denies ever passing out, freaking out, or having loss of memory from use of LSD. The trial judge then overrules D's incompetency objection. Is this ruling correct?

(2)   A sues X for damages for personal injuries arising out of a two-car collision. A took X's deposition one month before trial. During his deposition, X testi-

fied that he had retrograde amnesia and could not remember the facts of the accident. At the trial, X takes the witness stand and his attorney asks him to relate how the accident happened. A objects that X is incompetent to testify in view of his deposition testimony. How should the court rule?

(3) Assume the same facts as in Hypothetical (2). A calls as a witness, C, who observed the accident after having escaped from a mental institution to which he had been committed as a manic-depressive psychotic. At the time of trial, C has been captured and is back in the institution. X objects to C as a witness, on the ground that C's commitment to a mental institution renders him incompetent to be a witness. How should the court rule?

(4) A sues X for damages for personal injuries arising out of a two-car, intersectional collision. A claims that X didn't stop at a stop sign. At a jury trial, A calls B to testify. X makes a lack-of-personal-knowledge objection. A represents that he will establish B's personal knowledge as B testifies. The trial judge permits B to testify conditionally, subject to X making a motion to strike. B then testifies that X "blew" the stop sign. On cross-examination, B finally admits that he reached the intersection just as the cars collided, and that he concluded that X blew the stop sign from observing the point of impact and from hearing other witnesses talk about what happened. X moves to strike B's testimony. What result?

Chapter XI
WRITINGS

PART A.   THE BEST EVIDENCE RULE

McCORMICK, EVIDENCE

409, 411–12 (1954).*
[All footnotes omitted.]

The specific tenor of [the best evidence rule] needs to be definitely stated and its limits clearly understood. The rule is this: in proving the terms of a writing, where such terms are material, the original writing must be produced, unless it is shown to be unavailable for some reason other than the serious fault of the proponent.

*   *   *

A rule which permitted the judge to insist that all evidence must pass his scrutiny as the "best" or most reliable means of proving the fact would be a sore incumbrance upon the parties, who in our system have the responsibility of proof. In fact,   *   *   *   no such general scrutiny is sanctioned, but only as to "writings" is a demand for the "best," the original, made. Accordingly, as to objects bearing no writing, the judge (unless in some exceptional cases when the exact features of the object have become as essential to the issue, as the precise words of a writing usually are) may not exclude oral testimony describing the object and demand that the object itself be produced.   *   *   *   If, however, the object, such as a policeman's badge, a revolver, an engagement ring, or a tombstone, bears a number or inscription the terms of which are relevant, we face the question, shall we treat it as a chattel or as a "writing"? Probably most modern cases would support the view advocated by Wigmore, that the judge shall have discretion, to follow the one analogy or the other in the light of such factors as the need for precise information as to the exact inscription, the ease or difficulty of production, and the simplicity or complexity of the inscription.

SIRICO v. COTTO

Civil Court of the City of New York, 1971.
67 Misc.2d 636, 324 N.Y.S.2d 483.
[Some citations omitted.]

Irving YOUNGER, Judge.

In the course of trying this personal injury action, there arose a problem in evidence the solution of which seemed to elude plaintiff's attorney. For whatever assistance it will be to him, and because others may find it useful, I am filing this memorandum.

To support her case on damages, plaintiff called as a witness Dr. Stanley Wolfson, a specialist in radiology. Dr. Wolfson testified that plaintiff had been sent to him by the treating physician and that, in due course, Dr. Wolfson had taken a number of X-ray photographs of plaintiff's spine. After studying them, he wrote a report setting forth his conclusions and sent it, together with the X-ray plates, directly to the treating physician. All that Dr. Wolfson had with him as he sat on the witness stand was a copy of his report. Having refreshed his recollection from it, he was asked to describe what he had found in the X-rays and to state his opinion with respect to plaintiff's physicial condition. At this point, defense counsel objected. In order to afford plaintiff an opportunity to make her record, the jury was excused, and Dr. Wolfson completed his testimony in its absence. He said that the X-rays showed a flattening of plaintiff's lumbar lordosis and a scoliosis of her midlumbar spine with convexity towards the left, from which he would conclude that plaintiff was suffering from the consequences of a lumbar-sacral sprain. As to the whereabouts of the X-ray plates, Dr. Wolfson knew only that he had sent them to the treating physician. That gentleman did not testify. Plaintiff's counsel did not have the plates in his possession, nor did he explain his failure to produce them. I sustained defendants' objection and, upon the jury's return to the courtroom, excused Dr. Wolfson.

The problem, then, is whether Dr. Wolfson, without the X-ray plates, might describe what he had seen in them and state the significance he ascribed to his observations. Two lines of analysis are available, each of which leads to the same conclusion—that Dr. Wolfson's testimony is inadmissible.

First, the best evidence rule. This oft-mentioned and much misunderstood rule merely requires a party who seeks to prove the contents of a document to offer in evidence the original copy of that document. If he does not, but rather offers secondary evidence (such as a photostat, a carbon, or a witness' *viva voce* description of the document), the adversary's objection must be sustained. But if the proponent explains his failure to offer the original copy of the document, he may then proceed to prove its contents by whatever secondary evidence is available to him. IV Wigmore, Evidence, Secs. 1192 et seq. (3d ed. 1940). A "document," within the meaning of the best evidence rule, is any physical embodiment of information or ideas—a letter, a contract, a receipt, a book of account, a blueprint, or an X-ray plate.

So much for basics. Here, plaintiff asked Dr. Wolfson to describe what he saw when he looked at the X-ray plates. This was secondary evidence of their contents. The best evidence rule, we see, requires plaintiff to offer the originals, which, in the instance of X-rays, would be the familiar negative plates one "reads" by affixing to a shadow box. Plaintiff's failure to offer these original plates would have been excused had counsel explained his failure (by proof competent for that purpose, needless to say.) This he did not do, and hence I sustained defendants' objection.

*   *   *

*   *   * [T]he consequence of my sustaining defendants' objection to Dr. Wolfson's testimony was a rather complicated excision from the jury's ken of part of another physician's opinion based upon Dr. Wolfson's. That, however, is a matter of interest only to counsel in this case, and so I leave it in the obscurity of the stenographer's minutes.

RECENT CASE NOTE

(64) Harv.L.Rev. 1369 (1951).*

EVIDENCE—DOCUMENTS—"BEST EVIDENCE" RULE AP-
PLIED TO PREVENT INTRODUCTION OF A RECORDING OF A DE-
STROYED RECORDING.—*A* and *B* were arrested and indicted for murder
and robbery. A tape recording of damaging admissions was obtained by
means of a microphone concealed in their cell. As was customary, the contents of the tape were recorded onto a disc, and the conversation was erased
from the tape, which was then placed back in stock for reuse. The disc recording was admitted in evidence by the trial court over objection by defendant *A*. On appeal, *held*, conviction affirmed. Admission of the recording
violated the "best evidence" rule, but there was enough other evidence to
sustain the conviction. People v. King, 225 P.2d 950, 954 (Cal.App.1950).

It is generally agreed that if the speakers are properly identified and
adequate safeguards are taken to ensure authenticity, a recording may be
introduced into evidence. E.g., United States v. Shanerman, 150 F.2d 941
(3d Cir. 1945). Hence, it would seem that the original tape recording could
properly have been admitted. However, in the instant case the disc recording raises the additional problem of the "best evidence" rule, which requires
that to prove the contents of a writing, the writing itself must be offered in
evidence unless adequate excuse is given for not presenting it. Although a
recording is not colloquially considered to be a writing, it is defined as such
in the Model Code of Evidence, Rule 1(17) (1942), and should be similarly
treated in relation to the best evidence rule since the policy of the rule—to
obtain the most truly probative evidence of a preserved communication—is
equally applicable to recordings. It may be argued that the disc recording in
the instant case is no more than a mechanical reproduction of the conversation on the tape and thus is a "duplicate original," which, under the best
evidence rule, may be introduced to prove the contents of a writing without
requiring an excuse for not producing the original. However, the only reproductions that have been categorized as duplicate originals are carbon and
printed copies. See International Harvester Co. v. Elfstrom, 101 Minn. 263,
112 N.W. 252 (1907). The courts have ordinarily labeled all other mechanically produced copies as secondary evidence lacking the necessary reliability to be treated as originals. E.g., People v. Wells, 380 Ill. 347, 44 N.E.2d 32
(1942) (photostat); see 4 Wigmore, Evidence § 1234 (3d ed. 1940). But since
most mechanical processes of reproduction are highly accurate and all are
susceptible in some degree to tampering, it would appear that the judicial
distinction, based upon relative reliability, is of doubtful validity. It would
seem that uniform treatment should be accorded all such devices, either
treating them as originals, or as secondary evidence, in which case the duplicate original doctrine would be restricted to copies possessing identical
legal significance, such as a duplicate will with the requisite testamentary
formalities.

The court indicates that it will not accept secondary evidence when the
original has been intentionally destroyed by the proponent even if such destruction was done in good faith. But see Cal.Code Civ.Proc.Ann. § 1855,
Code Commissioners' Note (Deering 1946). This is contrary to the generally

accepted view that the proponent may introduce secondary evidence upon a showing that the destruction was not fraudulent, e.g., McDonald v. United States, 89 F.2d 128 (8th Cir. 1937). Furthermore, where the destruction occurs pursuant to a usual course of business operations and without thought of evidentiary significance, as was alleged in the instant case [Brief for Respondent, p. 16], the burden on the proponent to justify his action should be materially lessened. Cf. Nelson v. Blake, 173 Atl. 625 (R.I.1934). It has been suggested that the entire problem of admissibility of copies should be left to the discretion of the trial court. 4 Wigmore, Evidence § 1231 (3d ed. 1940). Such discretion would allow courts to alleviate the rigidity of the best evidence rule and eliminate the necessity to classify so-called "super-reliable" copies as duplicate originals. Utilizing such an approach, mechanical reproductions would be treated as secondary evidence, and the proponent would have to account to the satisfaction of the trial court for failure to produce the original. If, however, trial courts are to remain bound by stringent rules governing the admissibility of secondary evidence, it would seem that mechanically reproduced copies should be admitted as duplicate originals, with the question of tampering left to the triers of fact.

HERZIG v. SWIFT & CO.

United States Court of Appeals, Second Circuit, 1945.
146 F.2d 444.
[All footnotes omitted.]

[Wrongful death action. Deceased had been a partner in a building construction firm. At trial, on the issue of damages, plaintiff offered testimony by one of the partners as to the amount of the partnership earnings and the deceased's share. This testimony was rejected on the ground that it was not the best evidence and that the firm's books should have been produced. Plaintiff appealed from a dismissal of her action.—Ed.]

FRANK, Circuit Judge. 1. Perhaps the most to be said for the "best evidence rule" is that it may serve on occasion as a good mnemonic device. It did not so serve the trial judge here, for it awoke in him an incorrect recollection when, in rejecting the oral testimony as to partnership earnings and in refusing to allow the plaintiff's counsel to argue for its admissibility, he said, "I am not going to hear an elementary argument on law school evidence."

"In its modern application, the best evidence rule amounts to little more than the requirement that the contents of a writing must be proved by the introduction of the writing itself, unless its absence can be satisfactorily accounted for." Here there was no attempt to prove the contents of a writing; the issue was the earnings of the partnership, which for convenience were recorded in books of account after the relevant facts occurred. Generally, this differentiation has been adopted by the courts. On the precise question of admitting oral testimony to prove matters that are contained in books of account, the courts have divided, some holding the oral testimony admissible, others excluding it. The federal courts have generally adopted the rationale limiting the "best evidence rule" to cases where the contents of the writing are to be proved. We hold, therefore, that the district judge erred in excluding the oral testimony as to the earnings of the partnership. A closer question arises as to whether proof of the decedent's share in the partnership must be proved by the partnership agreement; but we are not called upon to decide this question since the trial never reached the point where this question would be raised.   *   *   *

Reversed and remanded.

MEYERS v. UNITED STATES

United States Court of Appeals, District of Columbia, 1948.
84 U.S.App.D.C. 101, 171 F.2d 800, cert. denied 336 U.S. 912, 69 S.Ct. 602.
[All footnotes omitted.]

[This was a prosecution for subornation of perjury. At trial the prosecution sought to establish the content of one Lamarre's testimony for a committee of the United States Senate. Although a transcript of the stenographic record of Lamarre's testimony was available, the committee's counsel was permitted to recount orally the substance of Lamarre's testimony —Ed.]

Wilbur K. MILLER, Circuit Judge.   *   *   *   At the opening of the dissent it is said, "The testimony given by Lamarre before the Senate Committee was presented to the jury upon the trial in so unfair and prejudicial a fashion as to constitute reversible error."

The reference is to the fact that William P. Rogers, chief counsel to the senatorial committee, who had examined Lamarre before the subcommittee and consequently had heard all the testimony given by him before that body, was permitted to testify as to what Lamarre had sworn to the subcommittee. Later in the trial the government introduced in evidence a stenographic transcript of Lamarre's testimony at the senatorial hearing.

In his brief here the appellant characterizes this as a "bizarre procedure" but does not assign as error the reception of Rogers' testimony. The dissenting opinion, however, asserts it was reversible error to allow Rogers to testify at all as to what Lamarre had said to the subcommittee, on the theory that the transcript itself was the best evidence of Lamarre's testimony before the subcommittee.

That theory is, in our view, based upon a misconception of the best evidence rule. As applied generally in federal courts, the rule is limited to cases where the contents of a writing are to be proved. Here there was no attempt to prove the contents of a writing; the issue was what Lamarre had said, not what the transcript contained. The transcript made from shorthand notes of his testimony was, to be sure, evidence of what he had said, but it was not the only admissible evidence concerning it. Rogers' testimony was equally competent, and was admissible whether given before or after the transcript was received in evidence. Statements alleged to be perjurious may be proved by any person who heard them, as well as by a reporter who recorded them in shorthand.   *   *   *

As we have pointed out, there was no issue as to the contents of the transcript, and the government was not attempting to prove what it contained; the issue was what Lamarre actually had said. Rogers was not asked what the transcript contained but what Lamarre's testimony had been.

After remarking, "   *   *   *   there is a line of cases which holds that a stenographic transcript is not the best evidence of what was said. There is also a legal cliche that the best evidence rule applies only to documentary evidence", the dissenting opinion asserts that the rule is outmoded and that "the courts ought to establish a new and correct rule." We regard the principle set forth in the cases which we have cited as being, not a legal cliche, but an established and sound doctrine which we are not prepared to renounce.

* * *

Affirmed.

Prettyman, Circuit Judge (dissenting).

* * * From the theoretical viewpoint, I realize that there is a line of authority that (absent or incompetent the original witness) a bystander who hears testimony or other conversation may testify as to what was said, even though there be a stenographic report. And there is a line of cases which holds that a stenographic transcript is not the best evidence of what was said. There is also a legal cliche that the best evidence rule applies only to documentary evidence. The trial judge in this case was confronted with that authority, and a trial court is probably not the place to inaugurate a new line of authority. But I do not know why an appellate court should perpetuate a rule clearly outmoded by scientific development. I know that courts are reluctant to do so. I recognize the view that such matters should be left to Congress. But rules of evidence were originally judge-made and are an essential part of the judicial function. I know of no reason why the judicial branch of Government should abdicate to the legislative branch so important a part of its responsibility.

I am of opinion, and quite ready to hold, that the rules of evidence reflected by the cases to which I have just referred are outmoded and at variance with known fact, and that the courts ought to establish a new and correct rule. The rationale of the so-called "best evidence rule" requires that a party having available evidence which is relatively certain may not submit evidence which is far less certain. The law is concerned with the true fact, and with that alone; its procedures are directed to that objective, and to that alone. It should permit no procedure the sole use of which is to obscure and confuse that which is otherwise plain and certain.

We need not venture into full discussion of all the principles involved. As between two observers of an event, the law will not accept the evidence of one and exclude that of the other, because the law cannot say which is more accurate. But as between a document itself and a description of it, the law accepts the former and excludes the latter, because the former is certain and the latter is subject to many frailties. So as between the recollection of the parties to a contract evidenced by a writing and the writing itself, the law rejects the former and accepts the latter. To be sure, the writing may be attacked for forgery, alteration or some such circumstance. But absent such impeachment, the writing is immutable evidence from the date of the event, whereas human recollection is subject to many infirmities and human recitation is subject to the vices of prejudice and interest. Presented with that choice, the law accepts the certain and rejects the uncertain. The repeated statement in cases and elsewhere that the best evidence rule applies only to documents is a description of practice and not a pronouncement of principle. The principle is that as between human recollections the law makes no conclusive choice; it makes a conclusive choice only as between evidence which is certain and that which is uncertain.

It may be remarked at this point that the transcript in the case at bar is a document, not challenged for inaccuracy or alteration. It possesses every characteristic which the most literal devotee of established rules of evidence could ascribe to written evidence of a contract as justification for preference of such writing over the recollection of the parties.

In my view, the court iterates an error when it says that the best evidence rule is limited to cases where the contents of a writing are to be proved. The purpose of offering in evidence a "written contract" is not to prove the contents of the writing. The writing is not the contract; it is merely evidence of the contract. The contract itself is the agreement between the parties. Statutes such as the statute of frauds do not provide that a contract be in writing; they provide that the contract be evidenced by a writing, or that a written memorandum of it be made. The writing is offered as evidence of an agreement, not for the purpose of proving its own contents.

＊ ＊ ＊ From the theoretical point of view, the case poses this question: Given both (1) an accurate stenographic transcription of a witness' testimony during a two-day hearing and (2) the recollection of one of the complainants as to the substance of that testimony, is the latter admissible as evidence in a trial of the witness for perjury? I think not. To say that it is, is to apply a meaningless formula and ignore crystal-clear actualities. The transcript is, as a matter of simple, indisputable fact, the best evidence. The principle and not the rote of the law ought to be applied. ＊ ＊ ＊

PEOPLE v. ENSKAT

Appellate Department, Superior Court, Los Angeles County,California.
20 Cal.App.3d Supp. 1, 98 Cal.Rptr. 646 (1971).

ZACK, Judge. The complaint charges appellant with two counts of [exhibiting obscene motion pictures].

＊ ＊ ＊

The motion picture involved was not seized under a warrant, or otherwise offered or placed in evidence by the prosecution. The officers entered the theater and then took pictures of portions of the film. Such pictures, including pictures of the theater exterior, are People's 1 through 9, 11, and 12. The balance of the film, audio and visual, was the subject of testimony. A best evidence objection was overruled on the ground that the rule does not apply. Such ruling was error.

Evidence Code section 1500 states that " ＊ ＊ ＊ no evidence other than the writing itself is admissible to prove the content of a writing." There is no question but that the contents of the material must be considered in an obscenity case. ＊ ＊ ＊ Motion pictures are accorded the same constitutional protection as books and other forms of expression. ＊ ＊ ＊ As the content of a film is always an issue in an obscenity case, the best evidence rule will apply if a film is a writing under the Evidence Code.

Evidence Code section 250 defines a "writing" as including " ＊ ＊ ＊ photographing, and every other means of recording upon any tangible thing, any form of communication or representation, including letters, words, pictures, sounds, or symbols." A photographic transparency, e. g., a "slide," is a writing under this definition, because it is a picture recorded upon a tangible thing, the celluloid.[1] A motion picture film is a series

---

1. A photograph printed from a negative is still considered secondary evidence. (Hop- kins v. Hopkins (1958) 157 Cal.App.2d 313, 320 P.2d 918.)

of such pictures recorded upon a celluloid film strip. * * * Each picture in each frame is slightly different from the preceding one, so that when the film is moved through a projector, these individual pictures appear to merge into a continuous "moving" picture. This movement is only an optical illusion, for in actuality each separate picture is projected onto the screen for a split second, rapidly followed by the next one. That there *appears* to be a "motion picture" does not alter the fact that a series of single pictures on the filmstrip, each one a "writing," is casting an image on a screen.

Respondent argues, however, that it is not the film, but these light images on the screen, that constitute the offense of exhibiting an obscene motion picture. Respondent argues that as this moving image is unrecorded, it cannot be a writing, and therefore is not subject to the best evidence rule. This argument ignores the essential fact that the moving image is merely the consequence of passing a writing (the film) through a machine. Without the projector and the filmstrip, no moving image is cast at all. The content of the moving image, "evanescent" or not, is totally dependent upon the content of the filmstrip. Just as it is better for the trier of fact to read a document than have it described, it is better for the trier of fact to see a movie than have it described. The policy considerations upholding the rule for written documents apply with full force to movies as well. It is to be noted that the instant prosecution under Penal Code section 311.2 is for exhibiting *obscene matter.* The latter is defined in section 311, subdivisions (a) (2), (b) to include a "motion picture." It is the character of the contents of the motion picture exhibited which, strictly speaking is in issue, not the character of the images on the screen resulting from its exhibition.

Our ruling herein does not mean that obscenity cases may not, under any circumstances, be prosecuted by means of secondary evidence of the obscene material. It means that in this case, the prosecution, in presenting such secondary evidence, did not comply with the Evidence Code. An example of how the prosecution may proceed is contained in Evidence Code section 1503, subdivision (a): If (1) a defendant is in possession or control of the material at the time he is expressly or impliedly notified of the existence of a criminal action against him involving such alleged obscene material, and (2) if a request that he produce it is made at the trial (out of the presence of the jury), secondary evidence can be used.

But the prosecution has, as does the proponent of secondary evidence in any civil or criminal case, the burden of making a prima facie showing as to both (1) and (2). * * * Here, the proponent of the secondary evidence made no factual showing as to (1) nor did it do (2). Nor did the proponent attempt to make any other showing which might be construed as a foundation for use of secondary evidence other than the example we have mentioned. * * *

The judgment is reversed, and the cause remanded for a new trial.

Whyte, P.J., and Katz, J., concur.

See Federal Rules of Evidence 1001–08 at pp. 931–933, California Evidence Code § § 1500–10 at pp. 893–894, 1530 at p. 894, 1550 at p. 896.

Hypothetical

A, as administrator of B's estate, sues X to cancel a deed that B had delivered to X. A claims that the deed was given to X by reason of X's fraudulent representation that she would care for B during his declining years. X testifies that the deed was given in consideration of prior services performed by her. In rebuttal, A produces a cancelled check for $5000 from B to X. X then testifies that the $5000 check was a loan from B so that she could add a room to her house, that she had executed a promissory note for $5000 to B for this loan, and that the loan had been repaid and the note marked paid and returned to her. A moves to strike X's testimony on the ground that the paid note is the best evidence. What result?

PART B. AUTHENTICATION

McCORMICK, EVIDENCE

395–96 (1954).*
[Footnotes omitted.]

One who seeks to introduce evidence of a particular fact, or item of proof, must generally give evidence (or offer assurance that he will do so) of those circumstances which make this fact or item relevant to some issue in the case. In respect to writings one of the commonest and most obvious of these circumstances on which relevancy may depend is the *authorship* of the writing. By whom was it written, signed, or adopted? Certainly any intelligible system of procedure must require that if the legal significance of the writing depends upon its authorship by a particular person, some showing must be made that he was the author, if the writing is to be accepted for consideration. The question is, what showing? In the everyday affairs of business and social life, the practice is to look first to the writing itself and if it bears the purported signature of X, or recites that it was made by him, we assume if no question of authenticity is raised that the writing is what it purports to be, that is, the writing of X.

It is just here that the common law trial procedure departs sharply from men's customs in ordinary affairs, and adopts the opposite attitude, namely, that the purported signature or the recitation of authorship on the face of the writing will not be accepted as sufficient preliminary proof of authenticity to secure the admission of the writing in evidence. * * *

The term authentication is here used in the limited sense of proof of authorship. It is sometimes employed in a wider meaning, embracing all proof which may be required as a preliminary to the admission of a writing, chattel, photograph or the like. Thus in the case of business records not only is proof of authorship required for admission, but at common law various other facts such as that they were made in the course of the business must also be proved as part of the "foundation." Similarly the identity of a bullet offered in a murder case as the fatal bullet, or the correctness of a photograph would be part of the necessary foundation-proof for admission. * * *

MANCARI v. FRANK P. SMITH, INC.

United States Circuit Court of Appeals, District of Columbia Circuit, 1940.
114 F.2d 834.

STEPHENS, Associate Justice. This is an appeal from a judgment of the District Court of the United States for the District of Columbia entered upon a verdict directed for the appellee at the close of the appellant's case. Hereafter we refer to the appellant as plaintiff and to the appellee as defendant.

The plaintiff sued upon an alleged violation of his right of privacy. His complaint charged that the defendant Frank P. Smith, Inc., was engaged in business in the District of Columbia, and that for commercial and advertising purposes, and wrongfully and maliciously and without the plaintiff's knowledge or consent, it caused to be published in the District of Columbia a so-called advertising "tear sheet" in the form of the following purported newspaper article:

> "Salvatore Mancari is Missing—Wide Search being Made
>
> "Frank P. Smith, Inc., Offers Reward for Producing Valued
> Prospect
>
> "One of the most intensive manhunts in years was instituted to-day by Frank P. Smith, Inc., in an effort to solve a mysterious disappearance that has baffled the organization for months.
>
> "Today's bold step climaxes a long series of attempts to locate this missing man and discover some reason for his continued absence. The announcement of a worth-while reward in the nature of substantial savings on the kind of shoes he wears will do much, we believe, to bring about his return and solve the mystery.
>
> "Representatives of Frank P. Smith, Inc., were confident they could find their man, they honestly believe that once a man enjoys the style, fit, comfort and longer wear of 'Foot-Joy,' the shoe that's different, he will wear them again—in fact there is no fairer test of 'Foot-Joy's' economy than to compare the low cost of wear per day with that of many shoes in America.
>
> "Men who have worn 'Foot-Joy' know what a value they are at their regular price; they will be quick to take advantage of the present price before the increase. They know the quality is unchanged, they realize they are getting superior materials and workmanship that have built 'the shoe that's different,' they realize that 'Foot-Joy's' give them absolute comfort—that different feeling. When a man has once been fitted properly with 'Foot-Joy's' he will wear them on all occasions.
>
> "Wanted!
>
> "Reward Offered for Producing Salvatore Mancari
>
> "We want this man; he's too valuable to lose! When last seen he was wearing a pair of shoes and apparently well pleased. When found he probably will still be wearing them! If he will make his first visit to the Frank P. Smith, Inc., a substantial reward in foot comfort waits him. See details below.
>
> * * * "

The plaintiff charged that as a result of the publication of this material, he suffered mortification and humiliation—and for this he prayed damages.[1]

The defendant demurred to the plaintiff's complaint, but the demurrer was overruled. The defendant abided this ruling and entered three pleas. In the first of these it admitted that it was engaged in business in the District of Columbia, as alleged in the complaint; it denied each and every other allegation made in the complaint. In the second plea the defendant averred that: The defendant was a retailer of shoes, including "Foot-Joy" shoes manufactured by Field and Flint Company of Brockton, Massachusetts,

---

1. According to the record and briefs there was a second count in the plaintiff's complaint charging libel through publication of the "tear sheet." To this count a demurrer was sustained. The count, however, does not appear in the record and no point is made concerning it on this appeal.

and purchased outright by the defendant and held for sale on its own account and risk. Field and Flint Company, the manufacturer, had entered into an advertising contract with the Reuben H. Donnelley Corporation of New York, whereby the latter agreed to issue in behalf of the former advertising matter of the kind described in the plaintiff's complaint, with the names of prospective customers inserted by rubber stamp, this matter to be mailed by the Donnelley Corporation to prospective customers in Washington and elsewhere, these to be selected by the Donnelley Corporation itself. The defendant was not a party to this agreement, and had no knowledge until after the fact that such advertising matter had been sent to the plaintiff or to any other person. The defendant never authorized either Field and Flint Company or the Donnelley Corporation to act in the defendant's behalf in respect of this advertising. The third plea set up matter not material to the question involved in this appeal.

On the issues thus joined, the case went to trial before a jury. By Frances Mancari (the plaintiff's wife), and corroborating witnesses, the plaintiff proved that Mrs. Mancari had received through the mail, addressed to the plaintiff, the purported newspaper item, and that she had had it read to her—not herself readily reading English. Evidence was introduced on the subject of damages also. To prove that the defendant was responsible for the publication of the "tear sheet," the plaintiff introduced in evidence the "tear sheet" itself, pointing to the presence therein of the defendant's name. No other evidence was offered.

At the close of the plaintiff's case, the defendant moved for a directed verdict upon the ground that the evidence introduced failed to prove that the defendant was responsible for the publication of the article. The plaintiff urged that the presence of the defendant's name in the body of the advertisement was sufficient to raise a presumption of authorship and to take the case to the jury. The court granted the defendant's motion and directed a verdict. This appeal was then taken.

The ruling of the trial court that the evidence was insufficient to warrant submitting the case to the jury was correct. The mere presence in printed material of the name of a particular person constitutes no substantial evidence that that person caused such material to be written or published. Saenger Amusement Co. v. Murray, 1922, 128 Miss. 782, 91 So. 459; 4 Wigmore, Evidence (2d ed. 1923) § 2150. In the case cited Murray sued the Amusement Company for personal injuries charged to have been caused by the negligence of the Amusement Company as his employer. It was shown that at the time of his injury, in September 1919, Murray was employed as a janitor in the Lomo Theater, a moving picture house in Hattiesburg, Tennessee. To prove that this theater was operated by the Amusement Company and that he was accordingly its employee, Murray offered in evidence September issues of a newspaper, the Hattiesburg American, containing advertisements of moving picture attractions to appear in the Lomo Theater. That portion of the advertisements relied upon to show that the Amusement Company operated the Lomo Theater was in the following terms:

"Saenger Amusement Company presents today at Lomo Theater," etc. "Saenger's Lomo Theater." "Saenger's Lomo Theater, Progressive Amusements, Progressive People. Saenger Amusement Company presents Evelyn Nesbitt."

As in the instant case, no other evidence was offered that the defendant company had any connection with the publishing of the advertisements. Over the objection of the Amusement Company they were received in evidence. On an appeal by the company from a judgment rendered against it, the admission of the evidence was held erroneous as constituting no proof. The Supreme Court of Mississippi said:

"We are of the opinion that these advertisements proved nothing except the fact that they appeared in the newspaper in question. For aught that appears to the contrary, they may have been wholly unauthorized by appellant, or appellant may have furnished to the management of the Lomo Theater, by rental or otherwise, the picture reels which were being used therein, without having any control or interest whatever in the business, or appellant may have rented such reels to the management of said picture show, and as a part of the consideration for such rental authorized and paid for said advertisements. The advertisements utterly fail to establish the vital fact that appellee at the time of his injury was an employee of appellant by virtue of the alleged ownership or control by appellant of the said Lomo Theater. Therefore these newspaper advertisements, standing alone, should have been excluded by the trial court." [128 Miss. at 790, 91 So. at 461] Wigmore, cit. supra, states:

"Printed matter in general bears upon itself no marks of authorship other than contents. But there is ordinarily no necessity for resting upon such evidence, since the responsibility for printed matter, under the substantive law, usually arises from the act of causing publication, not merely of writing, and hence there is usually available as much evidence of the act of printing or of handing to a printer as there would be of any other act, such as chopping a tree or building a fence. There is therefore no judicial sanction for considering the contents alone as sufficient evidence."   *   *   *

Affirmed.

Rutledge, Associate Justice (dissenting).

Assuming that a cause of action was stated, as to which I express no opinion, I think the evidence was sufficient to put the defendant to proof of its denial of publication.

The rule that the contents of a document, purporting to be a particular person's, are not of themselves sufficient evidence of genuineness, is based on two principles: (1) that other, and better, evidence generally is available to prove authorship; (2) the danger that "too many would be found to take fraudulent advantage of this rule." 4 Wigmore, Evidence (2d ed. 1923) § 2148. But, as to the latter, there is also "danger of abuse in the opposite direction" (Id., § 2149) and, as to the former, there are situations in which other evidence is not available. In such a case, the first reason for the rule fails, and the contents become the best, in fact the only available, evidence of authorship. When this is true, evidence that the defendant did not publish the document generally would be within his peculiar knowledge and the situation, therefore, such as to require him to come forward with it. The rule is not invariable and in special circumstances the contents may be used as evidence of authorship or publication, particularly when they relate to other facts which, when admitted or proved, serve to identify the person named in the document as author. Cf. 4 Wigmore, Evidence (2d ed. 1923) §§ 2148–2150.

In the case of printed matter, the document itself generally contains no evidence of authorship other than its contents. Nothing in the record shows that the "tear sheet" contained a printer's label or any other means of identifying the printer, and through him the author. The article contained not only defendant's name, repeated in four places, but advertising solicitation for "Foot-Joy" shoes, together with specific mention of the plaintiff as prospective customer. It therefore identified defendant by name, by the general description of his business, by reference to the particular product in which he dealt, and it solicited business for the defendant and for that product. There was no indication of the manufacturer's identity or that the advertisement was issued by the manufacturer. The clear inference from the contents was that the defendant mailed the sheet. Nine out of ten persons, and possibly the tenth, on receiving such a document through the mails would assume that defendant had sent it. Furthermore, these facts were verified by statements in defendant's plea, which we may consider insofar as they are admissions, though we may not consider his denials. Defendant admits that it was engaged in retailing shoes in Washington and that "Foot-Joy" shoes were sold by it. To this extent its plea bars out the identification of defendant by the contents of the tear sheet, and made unnecessary production of proof by plaintiff to establish these facts. When the verdict was directed, therefore, the evidence, together with admissions in the pleadings, had established that defendant was a retail shoe dealer in Washington, selling "Foot-Joy" shoes, and that the tear sheet advertising this product and soliciting trade in it at defendant's store was sent through the mails and received at the intended address. Furthermore, there was nothing in the contents or in the advertising matter to indicate that another person was interested in the business, the product, the advertising, or having it distributed.

Under these circumstances, the natural and normal inference is that the sheet was mailed by the defendant. It is not customary or usual for strangers to advertise gratuitously another's business or product in a manner which involves, as this did, very considerable expense. According to common experience, that is done, generally by the owner or by another at his procurement. "National advertising" is an apparent exception, but the usual manner in which that is done is by indicating—and emphasizing—the name of the manufacturer, with or without the local dealer's name. Unless the mere mention of "Foot-Joy" shoes in the sheet, which did not mention or purport to be made on behalf of the manufacturer or anyone other than the defendant, can be taken as rebutting the clear inference created by the entire remaining contents and admitted facts, that inference would appear to be, if not the only, certainly a reasonable, one to make from them. If it was reasonable, the jury should have been allowed to make or refuse to make it, providing defendant did not succeed in rebutting it by his proof.

In Saenger Amusement Co. v. Murray, 1922, 128 Miss. 782, 91 So. 459, relied upon by the majority, several inferences were possible, equally consistent with that which the plaintiff insisted the jury should be permitted to draw. The decision held that the advertisement could not be admitted to prove that plaintiff was an employee of defendant, not that its contents did not prove authorship.

In my opinion, the judgment should be reversed and the cause remanded for further proceedings.

NOTE

In Keegan v. Green Giant Co., 150 Me. 283, 110 A.2d 599 (1954), plaintiff complained of injury produced by a piece of metal which had allegedly been included in a can of peas. To establish that the named defendant was the packer and distributor of the offending peas, plaintiff offered the metal can and the label surrounding it. The label read in part, "Green Giant Brand Great Big Tender Sweet Peas. Distributed by Green Giant Company." The Court held that exclusion of the exhibit was not error since the label had not been authenticated.

UNITED STATES v. GOICHMAN

United States Court of Appeals, Third Circuit, 1976.
547 F.2d 778.

[Defendant William A. Goichman was convicted of tax fraud and appeals.]

PER CURIAM:

* * *

The * * * alleged error is * * * a question of the admissibility of evidence. A document entitled "History of Children's Assets," exhibit G41(A), was admitted for the purpose of showing that various assets of Goichman's children were purchased by Goichman. The document was found in the clerk's office of the Court of Common Pleas in Montgomery County, Pennsylvania, by an IRS agent. There had been a proceeding in equity, William A. Goichman v. Beverly Goichman, in that court, in which Mr. Goichman claimed to have provided the funds for many of his wife's and children's assets, which he wanted retured to him. Several documents from that proceeding were introduced in the criminal case *sub judice*.

The "History of Children's Assets" is a two-page unsigned document, typewritten except for the title, which is in block printing by hand. Both pages contain the seal and signature of the clerk of the Court of Common Pleas, and a certification that they are "[f]rom original record docket." On the back of the second page is a mark in black felt-tip pen, about one-half inch in height, "D–15."

Appellant correctly contends that the certification on the document does not govern its admissibility. It is well-settled that "no certified copy whatever may be used where the original record itself is not admissible under the rules of evidence for the purpose in hand." 5 J.Wigmore, Evidence § 1677, p. 862 (Chadbourn rev. 1974).

Appellant contends the document is inadmissible because the only evidence to connect the document to Goichman was 1) references to "my wife" and "Gail, Jeff, and Daniel" (the first names of Goichman's three children) and 2) the "cryptic symbol, D–15" on the back. For the first point appellant relies on 7 J. Wigmore, Evidence § 2130, at 570 (3d ed. 1940), for the proposition that contents cannot be used until there has first been external evidence to connect the document to the defendant. For the second point, that "D–15" is merely a cryptic symbol, appellant argues that the government produced no evidence to show that the document was even used as an exhibit during the support proceeding.

Clearly this document could not be admitted without some proof of its authentication. As Wigmore puts it, "[t]he foundation on which rests the necessity of authentication is not any artificial principle of Evidence, but an *inherent logical necessity.*" Id. § 2129, at 564. And, generally, the contents themselves are not capable of providing this authentication unless they happen to reveal certain knowledge that could be true of only one individual, id. § 2148 at 606, which is not true here because Goichman's wife would be privy to the same knowledge alleged.

What appellant overlooks is that the showing of authenticity is not on a par with more technical evidentiary rules, such as hearsay exceptions, governing admissibility. Rather, there need be only a prima facie showing, to the court, of authenticity, not a full argument on admissibility. Once a prima facie case is made, the evidence goes to the jury and it is the jury who will ultimately determine the authenticity of the evidence, not the court. The only requirement is that there has been substantial evidence from which they could infer that the document was authentic.

Here there was sufficient evidence to let the jury consider the relevance and weight of the document. It was certified as being part of the docket record in the prior Montgomery County support proceeding; it referred to children having the same first names as did Goichman's; the contents are corroborated (as pertaining to Goichman) by Goichman's complaint in that Montgomery County proceeding, exhibit 639, which was correctly attributed to appellant, and by bank statements as well. In sum, the document was supported by a prima facie showing of authenticity.

* * *

* * * For the foregoing reasons, the judgment of the district court will be affirmed.

KORCH v. INDEMNITY INS. CO. OF NORTH AMERICA

Appellate Court of Illinois, 1946.
329 Ill.App. 96, 67 N.E.2d 298.

FRIEND, Presiding Justice. On June 22, 1944 Anton Korch, while driving his automobile, injured the plaintiff, Joseph Doody. Korch was covered by a casualty insurance policy issued by defendant, and the day following the accident he went to the office of the insurance company, reported the accident and gave a statement. Some time in August he received a letter from Doody's attorney, which he personally delivered to the claim department of the insurance company. In the meantime there had been investigations by the company and negotiations for settlement with Doody's attorney. On November 10, 1944 Doody filed suit against Korch. Summons was served on Korch by leaving a copy thereof with his daughter at their home on November 15, 1944, which she placed on his dresser without telling him about it. Korch did not see the summons until the evening of December 2, 1944, two days before the return day, which was December 4, 1944. He testified that during this time he was preoccupied and worried by his wife's serious illness and operation, and that on the day she came home from the hospital he started to open all his accumulated mail, found the summons and asked his daughter how and when it was received. He was considerably concerned because he thought that the trial was to be held on the following Monday, December 4, which was the return day, but he could not get in touch with the insurance company until Monday. Korch was a window cleaner by occupation, and on the following Monday he went to work at 7:30 in the morning, and about 9 o'clock when he thought the insurance company opened its office, he went to a near-by drug store and called up ANDover 3400, a number which he obtained from the telephone directory. He testified that the girl who answered the telephone said it was the Indemnity Insurance Company; that he told her his name was Anton Korch and that he wanted to talk to somebody about a summons which he had received requiring him to be in court on that day; that the girl said "Just a minute, I am going to connect you with the proper person"; that he waited a few minutes and then talked with some other person who inquired "You got a summons?" that he replied "Yes, my name is Anton Korch," gave the person to whom he was then speaking the number of his insurance policy and asked her "What should I do? I am late. I should be today in Court. Would you straighten those things out? I don't know how those things work. It is not my business"; that the girl to whom he was talking said "Yes, what is your name?", took it, and said that everything would be taken care of. He thereupon hung up the receiver "with satisfaction everything is settled," and returned to work.

It appears that nobody defended the suit; on January 11, 1945 an order of default was entered and on January 16, 1945 judgment was entered in favor of Doody and against Korch for $1500, with a finding of malice as the gist of the action. Subsequently, on March 29, 1945, Korch was requested to come to the office of the insurance company, where he was interrogated by its counsel and W.K. Faust, claims manager of the company. His statement at that time was substantially the same as his testimony in the garnishment proceeding as hereinbefore related.

The garnishment proceeding against the insurance company was instituted on February 21, 1945, and a hearing had therein before the court without a jury on May 10, 1945. The garnishee defendant contended that Korch had failed to comply with a clause of the policy providing that the insured forward summons to the company. Plaintiff, as well as counsel for Korch, claimed that the company had waived this provision of the policy. The court found for plaintiff and against the garnishee defendant for the amount of the original judgment, together with interest and costs, or a total of $1548.80. The defendant garnishee appeals from that judgment.

As the principal ground for reversal it is urged that Korch had breached a condition of the policy by failing to send the summons to the garnishee defendant, and that there was no waiver of such breach of policy conditions. It must be conceded, of course, that unless there was a waiver of the policy condition requiring Korch to deliver summons to the insurance company, Doody would not be entitled to prevail in this proceeding, and it being admitted that the summons was not delivered to the insurance company, the question presented is whether there was a waiver of that condition. We therefore revert to the testimony at the garnishment hearing touching upon the question of waiver. We have already set forth the pertinent portions of Korch's testimony with respect to the telephone conversation he had on the morning of December 4, 1944 reporting that summons had been served upon him, and asking for directions. W.K. Faust, manager of the claim department, and Edward A. Kirk, his assistant, both said that they did not talk to

Korch about any summons. Kirk testified that there were four inside men and seven women in the claim department. Faust stated that only he and Kirk handled matters in suit, and that two other men in the department handled matters of compensation. Thus, in addition to the four inside men in the office, there were seven or eight women, including the switchboard operator. None of these was produced at the hearing, and nothing was said by either Kirk or Faust as to who was authorized to receive any emergency calls in case neither of them was available.

The garnishee defendant contends that Korch's purported conversation with unidentified persons was not competent to establish waiver of paragraph E of the policy, which required that the insured should immediately forward to the company every summons, etc., received by him. The authorities are divided on this question. Some of the cases hold that recognition of the voice of the person on the other end of the circuit is indispensable to the admission of the conversation over the telephone, but there is ample authority to support the contention that such a rule is not applicable to a conversation with a business house in relation to the transaction of its affairs. Thus, in the leading case of Godair v. Ham Nat. Bank, 225 Ill. 572, 80 N.E. 407, 116 Am.St.Rep. 172, 8 Ann.Cas. 447, the bank sued Godair Commission Company to recover the amount of two drafts drawn by one Moreland through the bank upon the company. The bank paid Moreland but the drafts were not honored by the company. The question represented was whether Godair had authorized the bank to pay the drafts drawn by Moreland. Grant, a cashier of the bank, testified that on a previous occasion Moreland had asked the bank to cash certain drafts drawn by him upon the Godair Company; that before cashing the drafts he called up the office of the Godair Company by telephone and asked for Mr. Godair; that someone in the office answered that Godair was not in; that subsequently the commission company called back and said the party wanted by the bank was then in, and that he thereupon talked with someone connected with the Godair Company; that he inquired whether the drafts of Moreland would be paid, inasmuch as he wished to draw through the bank upon the Godair Company for a sufficient amount to pay for two or three carloads of cattle; that the party to whom he talked said the drafts would be paid; that he did not know Godair and did not recognize the voice and could not say with whom he talked. Grant's testimony was objected to as incompetent, but the court overruled the objection and admitted the conversation, relying on Wolfe v. Missouri Pacific Ry. Co., 97 Mo. 473, 11 S.W. 49, 51, 3 L.R.A. 539, 10 Am.St.Rep. 331. There it was sought to introduce conversations had by telephone with some unidentified person in plaintiffs' place of business. The court made the following observation: "The courts of justice do not ignore the great improvement in the means of intercommunication which the telephone has made. Its nature, operation, and ordinary uses are facts of general scientific knowledge, of which the courts will take judicial notice as part of public contemporary history. When a person places himself in connection with the telephone system through an instrument in his office, he thereby invites communication in relation to his business through that channel. Conversations so held are as admissible in evidence as personal interviews by a customer with an unknown clerk in charge of an ordinary shop would be in relation to the business there carried on. The fact that the voice at the telephone was not identified does not render the conversation inadmissible. The ruling here announced is intended to determine merely the admissibility of such conversations in such circumstances, but not the effect of such evidence after its admission. It may be entitled, in each instance, to much or little weight in the estimation of the triers of fact, according to their views of its credibility and of the other testimony in support, or in contradiction of it." Similarly, in Trapp v. Rockford Electric Co., 186 Ill.App. 379, wherein the Wolfe case was again cited with approval, a telephone conversation with an unknown person was held to be admissible, and the rule for which defendant contends was held inapplicable to a conversation with a business house over the telephone in relation to the business there carried on. * * * The rule enunciated in the Godair case has never been overruled or modified, and has generally been followed in this state. The essence of that rule is that any one who answers a telephone call at a place of business is presumed to speak for the company in respect to the general business carried on by such company; that a business concern, by installing a telephone to be used in the transaction of its affairs, impliedly invites the public to make use of that means of communication which is thereby made an agency for the transaction of its business, and persons dealing with it by telephone have the right to assume that the one answering the telephone of the company is clothed with authority to transact the business conducted.

Defendant cites and relies on Garden City Foundry Co. v. Indus. Comm'n, 307 Ill. 76, 138 N.E. 122, and Kimbark v. Illinois Car & Equipment Co., 103 Ill.App. 632, in support of its contention that a telephone conversation with an unknown person is inadmissible. We find, however, that in the Kimbark case the court itself drew the distinction between the admissibility of a conversation held with an unknown clerk at defendant's place of business, and the inadmissibility of a conversation tending to show that the speaker at the other end of the telephone was a Mr. Maris with whom plaintiff's agent thought he was speaking but whose voice he did not know. In the Garden City case the question arose as to whether there was sufficient notice of the accident, and the court held that there was not. In both cases the person calling the company asked for a particular individual whose voice he did not recognize. Moreover both cases were decided on the evidentiary weight of the conversations and not their admissibility. In the case at bar, however, Korch called the company and did not ask for any particular person. In other words, the crux of the differentiation, as plaintiff puts it, is that in the case at bar there was a person-to-company call, while in the cases cited by defendant there was a person-to-person call and the voice at the other end in the person-to-person call was unrecognized. It is also significant, as plaintiff points out in his brief, that in neither of the cases cited by defendant is any reference made to either the Godair or the Trapp case or to any of the decisions therein cited, thus indicating that the courts in those cases were dealing with an entirely different set of facts.

The authenticity of Korch's purported telephone call is questioned but not seriously disputed. The court who heard the witness evidently believed his testimony, and his prior conduct gives credence to his recitation as to what happened on the morning of December 4 and to his diligence and good faith in cooperating with the insurance company. The day after the accident occurred Korch went to the office of the defendant and made a report. As soon as he received a letter from Doody's lawyer he took it to the company's office. Later when the company's attorney requested him to appear and be interrogated, he appeared on the date requested, and although he was advised by the company's lawyer to obtain counsel of his own, he answered all questions freely without seeking legal advice. His telephone call on December 4 was in keeping with his prior willingness to cooperate with the company, and we think it deserves the credence which the court gave it.

* * *

For the reasons indicated we think the finding and judgment of the Circuit Court should be affirmed, and it is so ordered.

Finding and judgment affirmed.

Scanlan and Sullivan, JJ., concur.

NOTE

See Federal Rules of Evidence 901–903 at pp. 928–931; California Evidence Code § § 1400–1402 at p. 889, 1410–1421 at pp. 890–891. For additional discussion of procedures for authentication of writings, see Chapter I, Making the Record, supra.

Hypothetical

A sues X for damages for personal injuries suffered in a two-car collision. A testifies that X ran a red light. A produces a letter addressed to him and bearing a signature, "X," which states that X ran the red light. A testifies that he received this letter through the mail about a week after the accident. A offers the letter in evidence. X makes a lack-of-authentication objection. What result?

Chapter XII

THE BURDEN OF PROOF AND PRESUMPTIONS

JAMES, CIVIL PROCEDURE

248–266 (1965).*
[Most footnotes are omitted.]

§ 7.5. Burden of proof: The two meanings of the term. The term "burden of proof" is used in our law to refer to two separate and quite different concepts. The distinction was not clearly perceived until it was pointed out by James Bradley Thayer in 1898. The decisions before that time and many later ones are hopelessly confused in reasoning about the problem. The two distinct concepts may be referred to as (1) the risk of non-persuasion, or the burden of persuasion or simply persuasion burden; (2) the duty of producing evidence, the burden of going forward with the evidence, or simply the production burden or the burden of evidence.

§ 7.9. Burden of proof: Presumptions. The word "presumption" is used to mean many different things, but this they all have in common: they involve a relationship between a proven or admitted fact or group of facts, A, and another fact or conclusion of fact, B, which is sought to be proven.

At one end of the scale is the presumption of law, or conclusive or irrebuttable presumption. If A is shown, then B is to be presumed without question and the court will not even receive evidence or entertain argument to show the nonexistence of B. And the court will direct a jury that if they find A to be proven they *must* also find B. The conclusive presumption is not really a procedural device at all. Rather it is a process of concealing by fiction a change in the substantive law. When the law conclusively presumes the presence of B from A, this means that the substantive law no longer requires the existence of B in cases where A is present, although it hesitates as yet to say so forthrightly. We shall not here deal further with conclusive presumptions. Our concern is with those often called "rebuttable presumptions of fact."

The word "presumption" is occasionally used to refer to the logical inference of one fact from the existence of another. The process of judicial proof is constantly calling on circumstantial evidence and the inferences which may be drawn from it. If Smith mails at a postbox a letter to Jones, with proper address and postage on the envelope, the trier may infer that Jones received the letter. From long skid marks on a pavement great speed on the part of the vehicle that made them may be inferred. From the blowing of a horn in certain circumstances it may be inferred that a driver then saw a pedestrian. From handwriting similarities identity of authorship of two documents may be inferred. And so on, ad infinitum. As we shall see, courts set limits to the drawing of inferences and will permit juries to draw only those which the courts consider rational. But if a court determines that B is a rational inference from A, then the trier of fact is free to draw that inference as a matter of general lay reasoning and persuasion without the aid of any special procedural rules pertaining to litigation. Since there are such

---

*Copyright, 1965 by Fleming James, Jr.

special rules, since the word "presumption" is often used to refer to them, and since "inference" is the word generally used to refer to the process of drawing conclusions of fact on the basis of general lay reasoning and experience, it serves clarity and avoids confusion to observe this distinction between these two words.

Many careful courts and writers use the word "presumption" to refer only to a device for allocating the production burden. It operates thus: If *B* is presumed from *A*, then on a showing of *A*, *B must* be assumed by the trier in the absence of evidence of non-*B*. To put it another way, if *A* is shown, then the party who asserts non-*B* has the production burden on the issue of *B* vel non—that is, *B*'s existence or nonexistence. The word "presumption" will be used here only in this way.

In some situations, to be sure, *B* may be the only rational inference from *A* (absent further evidence), and we have seen that in all such cases the production burden shifts under rules of general application. But courts and legislatures have created presumptions in cases where either (1)   *B* would be a permissible inference from *A*, but not the *only* permissible one, or (2)   *B* would not even be a permissible inference from *A*. In such situations a presumption has an artificial procedural force and effect (at the point where proponent rests his case) over and above the logical probative effect of the evidence. In the first situation just described a presumption would call for a directed verdict on the issue of *B* vel non. If the opponent also rests, while, as we have seen, without the presumption the proponent on that issue would be entitled only to have it go to the jury. In the second situation the presumption has a double effect. It protects the proponent from an adverse directed verdict on the issue (or nonsuit or dismissal), which he would otherwise suffer for want of sufficient evidence. It also entitles the proponent to a directed verdict in his own favor on the issue, absent any countervailing evidence. Later in this section we shall inquire whether a presumption may have any further, continuing effect after evidence to rebut it has been introduced.

From the above it appears that a presumption may have important consequences. What, then, are the bases upon which courts or legislatures will create presumptions? For the most part they are the same kinds of reasons that influence the allocation of the production burden generally, and these may be summed up as reasons of convenience, fairness, and policy. What is *likely*, for instance, is often presumed. Most men are sane, as the law reckons sanity, and most properly sent letters reach their destination. In the absence of any evidence pointing to an opposite conclusion in the case at hand, it is both convenient and fair to assume that *this* testator, or *this* man accused of crime was sane when he made the will or did the act charged as criminal; or that *this* properly mailed letter reached the addressee. If nothing else, these assumptions will save a lot of time and trouble in making ponderous proof in every case of matters which will be controverted in only a small minority of cases.

Access to evidence is often the basis for creating a presumption. When goods are damaged in a bailee's possession, for instance, the bailee can more easily find out what happened to them than the bailor, so it is fair to presume the bailee's negligence as an initial matter and put him to the production of exculpatory evidence if he has any. The owner of an automobile has better means of knowing whether the driver was in his service when it struck the plaintiff than has the plaintiff. In such a case also there is an increasingly strong policy to make an automobile owner pay for the damage it causes even where there is no agency in the legal sense. Fairness and policy therefore combine to justify a presumption of agency from the mere fact of ownership. Here, it may be noted, is a presumption (usually created by statute) in a situation where most courts would not permit an inference.

If there is a presumption operating in proponent's favor when he rests his case, two questions then arise: (1) what must the opponent do to lift the production burden then resting upon him, and (2) if the opponent does lift this burden, what (if any) further effect does the presumption have?

Let us take up the first of these questions. It can be rephrased in terms of the simple symbols we have been using. If from A there is a presumption of B, and A is shown,[21] what must the opponent do to escape a compulsory finding of B? The answer is that the opponent must introduce evidence which will justify a finding of non-B. This requirement has, to use Maguire's terms, both an extensive and an intensive aspect. To satisfy the extensive aspect, the evidence must cover the whole of B. Thus a presumption of negligence on the part of the charterers of a vessel turned over to them in good condition and sinking while in their control is not met by a showing of care during *part* of the time it was in their control. Such evidence is not enough to lift the production burden. To satisfy the intensive aspect of the requirement, the evidence must satisfy the qualitative tests of sufficiency of the evidence to show non-B.

If, now, the opponent has lifted the production burden by rebutting evidence which satisfies the above standards, what happens to the presumption? The orthodox view, sired by Thayer, has it that the presumption is utterly destroyed and disappears, and this even though the trier disbelieves the countervailing evidence. If, for example, the addressee of a properly mailed letter testifies that he never received it, that testimony would, if believed, justify a finding of nonreceipt. It therefore satisfies the test of *sufficiency*—which is not concerned with *credibility*—whether it is believed or not. Under the orthodox view this testimony would, then, *end the presumption* even if everybody in the courtroom was convinced that the testimony was a lie. In the case put, the destruction of the presumption would not, however, compel a finding of nonreceipt because a properly addressed letter is so likely to reach its destination that a *rational inference* may be drawn that it did so. And while countervailing evidence banishes the artificial procedural effect given by a presumption to the facts proven, A (in this case the mailing of the letter, and so on), yet it does not destroy the rational probative effect of A. In our illustration, if the trier rejects the testimony of nonreceipt as false and believes the testimony as to proper mailing, it could and probably would find receipt as an inference from the mailing. On the suppositions here made, this result seems just and proper and the orthodox theory would not prevent it. But there are other situations wherein that view does present serious problems.

Suppose, first, that the mind of the trier in the case just described is in equipoise on all the evidence. If the proponent has the burden of persuading

---

21. Of course the evidence tending to show A may itself fall short of compelling such a finding. If so it will be a question for the trier to decide whether A exists.

the trier of *B*'s existence, he must lose. Does a presumption of *B*'s existence from proof of *A* have any effect on the persuasion burden? The orthodox doctrine says emphatically not—it declares that the effect of a presumption is entirely spent in shifting the production burden, and it denies that the persuasion burden ever shifts. But why should this necessarily be so? We have seen that the considerations which determine the allocation of the persuasion burden are of the same kind as those which lead to the creation of presumptions. If the developments of a trial bring forth a situation which justifies a presumption in the proponent's favor, might not the same considerations (though not necessarily) be sufficient to call for placing the persuasion burden also on the opponent? Why should a presumption always have the minimum effect prescribed for it by orthodoxy? The reasons that bring it forth will vary from mere administrative convenience, the necessity for getting the ball rolling, so to speak, to very strong policy. Should not the force of a presumption "be tough or tender according to the nature and force of those reasons"? Some courts say frankly that it should, and that a presumption may sometimes shift the persuasion burden; but on this particular point the weight of authority is probably that it may not. This problem is of importance, but only in cases where the trier's mind is in equipoise at the end of its deliberations, a situation which probably does not occur very often.

There is another situation where the orthodox theory gives more trouble. As we have seen, the fact(s), *A*, which give rise to a presumption of *B* in many instances are not sufficient to warrant an *inference* of *B*. A familiar example is the fairly common presumption of agency from the fact of ownership of an automobile. Suppose that Plaintiff, injured by Owner's automobile driven by Driver, has no available evidence on the issue of agency except the adverse testimony of Owner and Driver, and therefore rests on a presumption of agency, ownership being proven or admitted. Suppose further that Owner, sole defendant, puts on his own testimony and that of Driver, both of whom deny agency. If this testimony banishes the presumption, you may have the anomaly that the trier must find nonagency, even though it thoroughly disbelieves the denial as self-serving perjury. Such a result does indeed offend common sense and justice, and most courts reject it, although it is hard to reconcile its rejection with the orthodox view. Once a presumption comes into play the tendency is to send the matter to the jury unless the evidence to rebut the presumption leaves no reasonable room for the jury's function.

If the issue is sent to the jury, the question arises in this situation, as in the illustration involving the mailing of the letter, whether the persuasion burden is to be placed on plaintiff or defendant. And here again most courts will probably put it on plaintiff.[33]

33. See Jefferson Standard Life Ins. Co. v. Clemmer, 79 F.2d 724, 729–731 (4th Cir.1935); authorities cited note 32 supra; 9 Wigmore, Evidence § 2491 (3d ed. 1940).

The two alternative views set forth in the text are not the only possible ones, nor the only ones to attain some judicial support. Morgan, for example, lists the following: (1) The so-called orthodox view (see note 26 supra and accompanying text). (2) A presumption puts on the opponent the burden of persuading the jury "to believe so much of the evidence against the presumed fact as would justify a reasonable jury in finding against that fact." (3) It disappears when opponent puts in evidence upon which the trier's mind is in equipoise, if that evidence "is of the requisite quantity and quality to justify a reasonable jury in finding the nonexistence of the presumed fact." (4) It puts on opponent "the burden of persuading the

Another different problem has arisen in connection with presumptions. If a case goes to the jury, what if anything should be said to the jury about any presumptions which may have come into the case? The orthodox answer is unequivocal: nothing. If a presumption has been met with sufficient evidence, the presumption has vanished and the issue should go to the jury without mention of it. Of course, if the facts giving rise to the presumption also afford an inference, the jury may be told about the inference and if the word "presumption" is used so as to be clearly understood to mean only this permissible inference, choice of the wrong word may be harmless error.

Even where a court gives a presumption continuing effect after evidence has been introduced to rebut it, there is no need to mention the presumption to the jury and it is probably only confusing to do so. If the persuasion burden is shifted, that is the only burden the instructions need mention. If it is not, but the jury may find *B* if they disbelieve opponent's evidence of non-*B*, then a simple direction to that effect is all that is needed. The only justification for telling the jury about the presumption would be a desire to implement the policy behind the presumption by inviting the jury to weigh it, in some vague manner not easy to understand or articulate, as they would a part of the evidence. But if policy demands additional force to the presumption, better ways than this can be devised for giving it.

DYER v. MacDOUGALL

United States Court of Appeals, Second Circuit, 1952.
201 F.2d 265.

L. HAND, Circuit Judge. This case comes up on appeal by the plaintiff from a judgment summarily dismissing the third and fourth counts of a complaint for libel and slander. Two questions arise: (1) whether we have jurisdiction over the appeal; (2), whether the defendants showed that there was no "genuine issue" to try within the meaning of Rule 56(c) Fed.Rules Civ.Proc. 28 U.S.C. We may start with the amended complaint, which was filed on November 24, 1950. It was in four counts, of which the first alleged that the defendant, Albert E. MacDougall, had said of the plaintiff at a directors' meeting of the "Queensboro Corporation": "You are stabbing me in the back." The second count alleged that MacDougall had written a letter to one, Dorothy Russell Hope, the plaintiff's wife's sister, containing the words: "He"—the plaintiff—"has made false statements to my clients in Philadelphia," and "He has presented bills for work he has not done." The third count alleged that MacDougall had said to a lawyer, named Almirall, that a letter sent out by the plaintiff to the shareholders of the "Queensboro Corporation" was "a blackmailing letter." The fourth count alleged that MacDougall's wife, as MacDougall's agent, had said to Mrs. Hope that the

jury that the existence of the presumed fact is so doubtful that the jury cannot determine whether it exists." (5) It puts on opponent "the burden of persuading the jury that the presumed fact does not exist." (6) In addition to having one of the foregoing effects, the presumption is to be weighed by the jury together with the evidence in the case. (7) It may simply allow an inference of *B* from *A* when the or- dinary rules of proof would not allow it. (8) It may compel the finding of *B* unconditionally, if *A* is found (the conclusive presumption). Morgan, Instructing the Jury Upon Presumption and Burden of Proof, 47 Harv.L.Rev. 59, 60–62 (1933). A list of possibilities containing fewer refinements is found in O'Dea v. Amodco, 118 Conn. 58, 170 Atl. 486 (1934). See generally Morgan, supra, at 81–86.

plaintiff had "written and sent out a blackmailing letter." On December 26, 1950, the defendants, before answer, moved for judgment summarily dismissing the second, third and fourth counts, supporting their motion by affidavits of MacDougall, MacDougall's wife, and Almirall, and by a deposition of Mrs. Hope, which the plaintiff himself had already taken. Each of the defendants unequivocally denied the utterance of the slanders attributed to him or her; and Almirall and Mrs. Hope denied that he or she had heard the slanders uttered. On his part the plaintiff replied with several affidavits of his own, the contents of all of which would, however, be inadmissible as evidence at a trial upon the issue of utterance. On January 24, 1951, the defendants filed an unverified answer denying the defamatory utterances, and on the same day they brought on their motion for hearing before Judge Kennedy. He offered the plaintiff an opportunity to take depositions of Mr. and Mrs. MacDougall and of Almirall, and a second deposition of Mrs. Hope; and by consent the case was then adjourned to allow the plaintiff to take the depositions. However, towards the end of October 1951, he told the court that he did not wish to do so, and on December 28, 1951 (the defendants having meanwhile withdrawn their motion as to the second count), the judge decided the defendants' motion by summarily dismissing the third and fourth counts on the ground that upon the trial the plaintiff would have no evidence to offer in support of the slanders except the testimony of witnesses, all of whom would deny their utterance. On this opinion, D.C., 12 F.R.D. 357, he entered the judgment in suit on January 7, 1952, from which the plaintiff took no appeal within thirty days. However, on February 20, 1952, he wrote a letter to the judge, asking an extension under Rule 73(a) of thirty days within which to appeal; and this he followed on the 25th by a motion for a reargument, repeating his request for the extension. On March 4, 1952, the judge filed a second opinion, granting the reargument, but again deciding that counts three and four should be dismissed. D.C., 109 F.Supp. 444. However, he granted an extension of thirty days for the time to appeal, and, apparently *sua sponte,* "certified" "that I did give an express direction for the entry of judgment, and that there is no reason for delay." On March 4, 1952, the plaintiff filed a notice of appeal from the judgment.

* * *   The question is whether, in view of the defendants' affidavits and Mrs. Hope's deposition, there was any "genuine issue" under Rule 56(c) as to the utterance of the slanders. The defendants had the burden of proving that there was no such issue; on the other hand, at a trial the plaintiff would have the burden of proving the utterances; and therefore, if the defendants on the motion succeeded in proving that the plaintiff would not have enough evidence to go to the jury on the issue, the judgment was right. As the plaintiff has refused to avail himself of the privilege under Rule 56(f) of examining by deposition the witnesses whom the defendants proposed to call at the trial, we must assume that what they said in their affidavits they would have repeated in their depositions; and that what they would have said in their depositions, they would say at a trial, with one possible exception, the consideration of which we will postpone for the time being. With that reserve we will therefore first discuss the judgment on the assumption that the record before us contains all the testimony that would appear at a trial in support of the slanders. We have not forgotten that the plaintiff swears that his wife told him on March 8, 1950, that Mrs. Hope had said to her on March 7, 1950, that she, Mrs. Hope, could forgive the plaintiff "everything except that letter," meaning a letter, written by the plaintiff and addressed to the shareholders of the "Queensboro Corporation," which Mrs. MacDougall according to the complaint described as a "blackmailing letter." The plaintiff did not submit his wife's affidavit that Mrs. Hope had told her what he says his wife said to him she did; but we shall assume that such an affidavit is in the record. Mrs. Hope's putative declaration to Mrs. Dyer would of course be hearsay, but the plaintiff says that it would nevertheless be competent under the exception as to "spontaneous exclamations." We cannot agree. The time of Mrs. MacDougall's statement to Mrs. Hope is not fixed except that it is said to have been between December 13th and March 7th; and, strictly, we might dispose of the point because there is no reason to say that the interval was not two months. But let us suppose that Mrs. MacDougall had called up Mrs. Hope only the day before Mrs. Hope narrated the talk to her sister. The argument must be that the emotional stress set up in Mrs. Hope's mind by Mr. MacDougall's information endured for twenty-four hours and so far suspended her ordinary powers of deliberation as to make her declaration like the ejaculation of a person injured in an accident, or suddenly faced with a vital crisis. "The utterance must have been *before there has been time to contrive and fabricate,* i.e. while the nervous excitement may be supposed still to dominate and the reflective powers to be yet in abeyance." Wigmore § 1750(b). So we are to suppose that, when Mrs. Hope learned that her brother-in-law, whom incidentally she had recently "castigated," had sent out a letter that could be described as blackmailing MacDougall, it so far obsessed her deliberative faculties that, although she did not call up her sister that day, she remained unable to "contrive or fabricate" for twenty-four hours. Unless we are altogether to abandon the hearsay rule, it is difficult to imagine a situation more appropriate for its application. Finally, any declaration of Mrs. Hope would be incompetent as contradictory of her testimony, if the plaintiff should call her as his witness. It is true that Rule 43(b) makes competent inconsistent statements of a witness called by a party, if the witness is the adverse party himself, but Mrs. Hope is not a party. If the plaintiff called her and she repeated her deposition, he could not use his wife's contradictory version of the interview between her and Mrs. MacDougall.

Hence, if the cause went to trial, the plaintiff would have no witnesses by whom he could prove the slanders alleged in the third and fourth counts, except the two defendants, Almirall and Mrs. Hope; and they would all deny that the slanders had been uttered. On such a showing how could he escape a directed verdict? It is true that the carriage, behavior, bearing, manner and appearance of a witness—in short, his "demeanor"—is a part of the evidence. The words used are by no means all that we rely on in making up our minds about the truth of a question that arises in our ordinary affairs, and it is abundantly settled that a jury is as little confined to them as we are. They may, and indeed they should, take into consideration the whole nexus of sense impressions which they get from a witness. This we have again and again declared, and have rested our affirmance of findings of fact of a judge, or of a jury, on the hypothesis that this part of the evidence may have turned the scale. Moreover, such evidence may satisfy the tribunal, not only that the witness' testimony is not true, but that the truth is the opposite of his story; for the denial of one, who has a motive to deny, may be uttered with such hesitation, discomfort, arrogance or defiance, as to give assurance that he is fabricating, and that, if he is, there is no alternative but to assume the truth of what he denies.

Nevertheless, although it is therefore true that in strict theory a party having the affirmative might succeed in convincing a jury of the truth of his allegations in spite of the fact that all the witnesses denied them, we think it plain that a verdict would nevertheless have to be directed against him. This is owing to the fact that otherwise in such cases there could not be an effective appeal from the judge's disposition of a motion for a directed verdict. He, who has seen and heard the "demeanor" evidence, may have been right or wrong in thinking that it gave rational support to a verdict; yet, since that evidence has disappeared, it will be impossible for an appellate court to say which he was. Thus, he would become the final arbiter in all cases where the evidence of witnesses present in court might be determinative. We need not say that in setting aside a verdict the judge has not a broader discretion than in directing one, for we have before us only the equivalent of a direction. It may be argued that such a ruling may deprive a party of a possibly rational verdict, and indeed that is theoretically true, although the occasions must be to the last degree rare in which the chance so denied is more than fanciful. Nevertheless we do not hesitate to set against the chance so lost, the protection of a review of the judge's decision.

There remains the second point which we reserved for separate discussion: i.e. whether by an examination in open court the plaintiff might extract from the four witnesses admissions which he would not have got on the depositions that he refused. Although this is also at best a tenuous possibility, we need not say that there could never be situations in which it might justify denying summary judgment. It might appear for example that upon a deposition a witness had been recalcitrant, or crafty, or defiant, or evasive, so that the immediate presence of a judge in a court-room was likely to make him tell more. That would be another matter; and it might be enough. But the plaintiff is in no position to invoke such a possibility for he has refused to try out these witnesses upon deposition, where he might discover whether there was any basis for supposing that awe of a judge was necessary to make them more amenable. *A priori* we will not assume that that is true. The course of procedural reform has all indeed been towards bringing witnesses before the tribunal when it is possible; but that is not so much because more testimony can be got out of them as because only so can the "demeanor" evidence be brought before the tribunal.

Judgment affirmed.

Frank, Circuit Judge (concurring).

1.   The facts here are most peculiar, unlikely to recur often: The plaintiff in his complaint asserts that defendant slandered plaintiff in the plaintiff's absence but in the presence of only two other persons. If there were a trial, plaintiff could not himself testify, for he knows of his own knowlege none of the facts necessary to support his case. To prove his case, he would have to call the defendant who, in his oral testimony, would deny that he had uttered the alleged slanderous statement. For plaintiff is aware that the only two other possible witnesses he could summon would corroborate defendant; and, if he called them, he could not impeach them.

Judge Hand's opinion states that, if defendant and the other witnesses testified, the trial court, evaluating their credibility in the light of their demeanor as witnesses, could rationally find not only that defendant's denial was false but that the opposite was true, i.e., that defendant had made the slanderous statement. Yet Judge Hand holds that a trial judge in a jury trial of such a case would be obliged not to let the jury reach a verdict for plaintiff on that rational basis. As I understand Judge Hand, he says that the result of holding otherwise would be that the trial judge's disposition of a motion for a directed verdict (or a verdict n. o. v.) could not be effectively reviewed on appeal. On that ground alone—i. e., the supposed obstacle, in a jury trial of such a case, to review of a directed verdict— Judge Hand's opinion affirms the summary judgment for defendant here.

Since, then, the sole reason given in Judge Hand's opinion for affirmance is something peculiar to a jury trial, I take it that, were there a jury waiver here, so that if there were a trial, it would be a judge trial, Judge Hand would hold erroneous the summary judgment here. This is a curious distinction. It would make the propriety of a summary judgment in such a case turn exclusively on whether or not the parties, if entitled to any trial, are entitled to one by jury.[1] In such a case as this, it would prevent a jury from relying on demeanor but permit a judge in a judge trial to do so (although, if he did, his decision, in so far as he relied on demeanor, would not ordinarily be reviewable).

I agree with Judge Hand that (at least in some cases)[2] a trial judge should be allowed to find that a plaintiff has discharged his burden of proof when the judge disbelieves oral testimony all of which is adverse to plaintiff, solely because of the trial court's reaction to the witnesses' demeanor and there is no evidence for plaintiff except that "demeanor evidence."[3] But I think it most unfortunate to hold that this rule applies in judge trials and not in jury trials. Such a distinction should be avoided if possible.

But I read Judge Hand's opinion as saying it is unavoidable for the following reason: If, in a jury trial, the jury, solely on the basis of its evaluation of credibility as affected by the jury's reaction to a witness' demeanor, were allowed to bring in a plaintiff's verdict, then necessarily (says Judge Hand) the judge in that same trial could also properly take into account demeanor in passing on the defendant's motion for a directed verdict; but, were that true, the judge's action on the motion could never be reviewed, as demeanor cannot appear in the printed record on appeal.[4]

1. That is, whether or not they both have failed to demand a jury, or whether or not plaintiff seeks relief (e. g., specific performance) precluding a jury trial.

2. This parenthetical qualification I shall explain later.

3. We have already held that, solely on the basis of a trial judge's disbelief in the oral testimony of a plaintiff's witness—a disbelief resulting entirely from the witness' demeanor—the judge may decide for the defendant. Broadcast Music, Inc. v. Havana Madrid Restaurant Corp., 2 Cir., 175 F.2d 77. There, however, the disbelief in this testimony—uncontradicted by anything other than the witnesses' demeanor

—meant that plaintiff had not discharged his burden of proof. In the instant case, the question is whether plaintiff can discharge his burden of proof where the judge disbelieves the testimony of witnesses all of whom testified against him.

4. This reasoning, spelled out more in detail, is as follows:

   (a) If a jury, solely on the basis of its evaluation of credibility as affected by its reaction to a witness' demeanor in a case like this, could properly bring in a verdict for the plaintiff, then (says Judge Hand) necessarily a trial judge could also properly take into account credibility in the light of demeanor, and solely because

I cannot accept that distinction for the following reasons: Judge Hand argues from the alleged unreviewability of a directed verdict in a case like this, if demeanor were a factor. But this argument cuts too far. For, if Judge Hand is correct, the same difficulty will attend the review of any directed verdict in any case where any important evidence consists of oral testimony. In any such case, one could say, as Judge Hand says here: If the jury (should the case go to the jury) could rely on "demeanor evidence," then necessarily the trial judge could do likewise, on a motion for a directed verdict; and, if he could, no directed verdict would be reviewable when important testimony is oral. But this is exactly not the rule in the federal courts: The well-settled rule is that, in passing on a motion for a directed verdict, the trial judge always must utterly disregard his own views of witnesses' credibility, and therefore of their demeanor; that he believes or disbelieves some of the testimony is irrelevant. When asked to direct a verdict for the defendant, the judge must assume that if he lets the case go to the the jury, the jurymen will believe all evidence—including "demeanor evidence" —favorable to the plaintiff. In other words, the judge must not deprive plaintiff of any advantage that plaintiff might derive from having the jury pass upon the oral testimony. Indeed, the important difference between a trial judge's power on a motion for a new trial and on a motion for a directed verdict is precisely that on a new-trial motion he may base his action on his belief or disbelief in some of the witnesses, while on a directed-verdict motion he may not.

Lurton, J., in a much quoted opinion,[5] expressed the difference thus: "We do not think * * * that it is a proper test of whether the court should direct a verdict, that the court, on weighing the evidence, would, upon motion, grant a new trial. * * * In passing upon such motions [for new trial] he is necessarily required to weigh the evidence * * * . But, in passing upon a motion to direct a verdict, his functions are altogether different. In the latter case we think he cannot properly undertake to weigh the evidence. His duty is to take that view of the evidence most favorable to the party against whom it is moved to direct a verdict, and from that evidence, and the inferences reasonably and justifiably to be drawn therefrom, determine whether or not, under the law, a verdict might be found for the party having the onus."

Taft, J., held similarly in Felton v. Spiro, 6 Cir., 78 F. 576, 582–583. The cases in accord are legion. They are excellently discussed by Judge Parker in Aetna Cas. & Sur. Co. v. Yeatts, 4 Cir., 122 F.2d 350, 352–355 and

of resulting evaluation of the witnesses' reliability, could grant or deny the defendant's motion for a directed verdict.

(b) But (says Judge Hand) if the trial judge could thus consider demeanor, then in no case where there was oral testimony could the grant or denial of a directed verdict motion ever be reviewed and reversed, because the printed record before the upper court necessarily omits demeanor.

(c) Since, however, such directed-verdict orders can and should be reviewable this follows according to Judge Hand:

(1) The jury in a case like this may not properly return a plaintiff's verdict on the sole basis of "demeanor evidence."

(2) Therefore in such a case, on defendant's motion for a directed verdict, the trial judge must disregard the possibility that, were the case allowed to go to the jury, it might decide for plaintiff on the sole basis of "demeanor evidence."

5.   Mt. Adams & E. P. Inclined Ry. Co. v. Lowery, 6 Cir., 74 F. 463, 477.

by Judge Sibley in Marsh v. Illinois Central R. Co., 5 Cir., 175 F.2d 498, 499–500.

In Brady v. Southern Ry. Co., 320 U.S. 476, 479–480, 64 S.Ct. 232, 234, 88 L.Ed. 239, the Court said: "When the evidence is such that *without weighing the credibility of the witnesses* there can be but one reasonable conclusion as to the verdict, the court should determine the proceeding by non-suit, directed verdict or otherwise in accordance with the applicable practice without submission to the jury, or by judgment notwithstanding the verdict." (Emphasis added.) As Moore puts it, a motion for new trial may invoke "the exercise of the trial court's discretion, such as that the verdict is inadequate or excessive, or that the verdict is against the weight of the evidence. In reference to this latter matter this function of the motion for a new trial must be sharply distinguished from the motion for a directed verdict."[6] A "verdict may be set aside as contrary to the preponderance of the evidence, although a directed verdict is not justified."[7]

On a motion for new trial, the judge acts "as the thirteenth juror",[8] i. e., he evaluates the credibility of the orally-testifying witnesses and therefore their demeanor. But on a motion for a directed verdict he does not. The rule that a trial judge may legitimately consider demeanor in ordering new trials means that his new-trial orders are seldom reviewable; on the other hand, the rule that he may not legitimately consider demeanor in considering directed verdict motions means that his orders on such motions are readily reviewable.

Frequently this sort of case arises: The defendant urges his motion for a directed verdict on the ground that, although there is oral testimony, the record contains no testimony (or other evidence) from which any rational inference can be drawn for the existence of a fact indispensable to plaintiff's case. If the trial judge, then, directs a defendant's verdict,[9] the upper court, on appeal, in testing the propriety of his direction, adopts the postulate that the trial judge assumed that the jury, were it allowed to render a verdict, would regard the oral testimony—and therefore the witnesses' demeanor—in a manner most favorable to plaintiff. The upper court makes the same assumption; as a consequence, the trial judge's attitude towards that demeanor is not a factor on such an appeal, and so constitutes no obstacle to review.

If I am correct, there is no foundation for Judge Hand's distinction; and, as I gather that he would have held it error to enter summary judgment for defendant here, if there had been no jury demand, he should, I think, hold that the judgment here must be reversed, despite the request for trial by jury.

2.   One can imagine a case in which a man would suffer a grave injustice, if it were the invariable rule that a plaintiff can never win a case when (1) he can offer only the oral testimony of the defendant, the one available witness, which is flatly and unswervingly against the plaintiff but

---

6.   Moore, Federal Practice (2d ed. 1951) § 50.02(1), p. 2317.

7.   Moore, loc. cit., § 50.03, p. 2318. See also § 50.11, pp. 2338–2339, and Wigmore, Evidence (3d ed.) § 2494, pp. 298–299.

8.   McBride v. Neal, 7 Cir., 214 F. 966, 968;

Binder v. Commercial Travellers Mut.; Acc. Ass'n, 2 Cir., 165 F.2d 896, 902; cf. General American Life Ins. Co. v. Central Nat'l Bank, 6 Cir., 136 F.2d 821, 823; Moore, loc. cit., § 50.13, p. 2347.

9.   Or if he denies defendant's motion for such a verdict.

(2) the jury (in a jury trial) or the judge (in a judge trial) is thoroughly convinced by that witness' demeanor that he is an unmitigated liar. On that account, I would oppose such a rule.

But this is not such a case. As already noted, the facts here are most unusual: The plaintiff asserts that in his absence he was slandered by defendant in the presence of but two other persons. As this fact is denied by all three, only plaintiff's own suit serves to publicize the alleged slander. In these peculiar circumstances, the plaintiff should not have the chance at a trial to discharge his burden of proof by nothing except the trial court's disbelief in the oral testimony of witnesses all of whom will deny that the alleged slanderous statement was made. Wherefore I concur.

MAGUIRE, EVIDENCE: COMMON SENSE AND COMMON LAW

177–79, 182–84 (1947).*

* * * Now let us illustrate with a fascinating little case from which can be spun our whole discussion of these topics. Plaintiff sued defendant to quiet plaintiff's title to Blackacre. It seems to be assumed throughout that he had the burden of persuasion that he was the owner at the time he brought suit. Plaintiff alleged that he had acquired title on a specified date, and had ever since retained possession and title, but that defendant without right made some claim to Blackacre. Defendant admitted that plaintiff became owner of Blackacre on the date specified but denied that plaintiff was the present owner and also denied that defendant's claim was without right.

If on the issues shaped by these pleadings defendant had offered at trial evidence of acquisition of title to Blackacre by a sale for taxes, and plaintiff had given evidence tending to prove the sale invalid, apparently plaintiff would have had the burden of persuasion on the consequent issue. But that was not the way the parties tried the case. Plaintiff stood on the admission of the answer as to his acquisition of title and rested, urging that the status of ownership thus established was presumed to continue. Defendant, offering no evidence, moved for a non-suit. The motion was granted, and plaintiff appealed. Held error; reversed and remanded with a plain intimation that if defendant persisted in giving no evidence, judgment should be entered for plaintiff. Gatrell v. Salt Lake County, 105 Utah 409, 149 P.2d 827, 153 A.L.R. 1100 (1944); the court had trouble with the case; there are a brief main opinion, a slightly longer concurring opinion, and a still longer dissent.

The holding here is that although plaintiff had the ultimate burden of persuasion on the issue of continued ownership, the case had been left in a posture which cast upon defendant the burden of producing evidence on that issue. Evidently the cardinal point of the whole business is defendant's partial admission of plaintiff's allegations. The majority argue that this admission is in the nature of evidence conclusively establishing plaintiff's acquisition of title to Blackacre. Once getting title, plaintiff is presumed to retain title. Defendant has done nothing to displace or rebut this presumption. Therefore defendant could not win.

By reasoning thus the majority allow plaintiff to pick and choose among defendant's allegations, accepting the favorable and rejecting the unfavorable. The dissenter argues that plaintiff might not do this; he must take the bitter with the sweet; the whole matter is to be decided on the pleading level and, for purposes of pleading, defendant's denial of continued ownership nullifies the effect of his admission of plaintiff's acquisition of title. The majority seems to deny that the problem is one of pleading, treating it rather as a problem of evidence. They assume in that aspect the propriety of plaintiff's taking what he likes, and only what he likes, from defendant's various utterances about the issue of ownership.

This controversy within the court is aside from our immediate interest. Let us grant the soundness of the majority's method of attack on the case and examine its elements. First, burden of persuasion—why was it upon plaintiff and what does the term signify when translated into mental operations of the trier of fact? As to placement of burden of persuasion, all sorts of explanatory formulae can be found in the books. It is with the party seeking to sustain an affirmative; it is determined by the form of the pleadings; it is to be borne by the party having peculiar knowledge of the facts; it is imposed on the party whose contentions depart further from normal likelihood. This plurality of so-called decisive factors proves forthwith that no single simple formula for allocating burden of persuasion will be found. All four factors mentioned might be found in the same case, some pointing to one litigant, some to the other. Here, as in many large legal problems, we must work out our answers issue by issue, taking into consideration all elements of fairness and expediency. Of course this does not mean that the answers have to be worked out case by case. As already remarked, precedents will build up for recurrent issues, and these precedents will be serviceable analogies. It merely means that there is no wondrous touchstone to solve all problems without pain of thought.

Think back now to our *Gatrell* case about title to Blackacre. The decision rendered necessarily connoted that the finding *must* be for plaintiff unless defendant came forward with evidence to prove that plaintiff had somehow lost title between the date when he acquired it and the date when he began his suit. But, as a purely original proposition, there might be difference of opinion as to whether proof of getting title say in 1931 without more made it impossible reasonably to find that the grantee had lost title by say 1940. A lot could happen to shift ownership of Blackacre in nine years. Here, though, the courts step in with a judicial control. They say there is a presumption of continuance of the status of ownership, and that this presumption has an effect comparable to overwhelming proof in taking the issue out of debatability.

Here we had better slow down, make some comparisons, and take stock of difficulties. There is trouble with terminology. This word presumption has suffered badly from rough and careless handling. It has been used as a synonym for inference and sometimes as the operative part of weasel-worded formulae for saying that from the judicial or legislative point of view certain things are taken as so and attempts to contradict them will be futile. In the former usage the word has often been expanded into the term "presumption of fact" and in the latter into "presumption of law" or "conclusive presumption". As our text has shown, we are rejecting both these usages and employing presumption to denote the concept, illustrated specifically dozens of times in common and statute law, that when a designated basic fact or aggregate of facts exists, existence of another fact or aggregate of facts, called the presumed fact or facts, must be assumed in absence of adequate rebuttal. In the *Gatrell* case the basic fact was plaintiff's acquisition of title to Blackacre and the presumed fact the continuance of his ownership down to and through the date when he began his suit. This careful, particularized use of the word presumption, by the way, is getting more and more consistent acceptance in the courts; nobody has ever succeeded in making consistent the legislative use of this or any other important word.

Our text has steadily conceded that the state of decisive one-sidedness may not always be permanent. Temporarily overwhelming proof on an issue of fact may be met and controlled by counter-proof. Likewise the text has indicated that presumptions may be rebutted—that is, the presumed facts thrown open for deliberative findings instead of being coercively assumed. But a mighty battle has raged, and is still raging, over this matter of rebutting presumptions. Without being foolhardy enough to offer an infallible solution to terminate the battle for good and all, we should at least see what all the shooting is about.

It may be said that a presumption has both extensity and intensity. Rebuttal, we should expect, ought to be correspondingly wide and forceful. Suppose our presumption is that if a ship, hired under charter party, is turned over to the hirer in seaworthy condition and thereafter sinks, the sinking is due to the fault of the hirer. In case the rebuttal evidence offered by the hirer, when sued for damages because of the loss of the ship, tends to show due care on his part for *only a portion of the time* he controlled the ship, the evidence is not extensive enough to rebut the presumption. * * *

LEGILLE v. DANN

United States Court of Appeals, District of Columbia Circuit, 1976.
544 F.2d 1.

SPOTTSWOOD W. ROBINSON, III, Circuit Judge:

* * *

I

* * * On March 1, 1973, appellees' attorney mailed from East Hartford, Connecticut, to the Patent Office in Washington, D.C., a package containing four patent applications. Each of the applications had previously been filed in the Grand Duchy of Luxembourg, three on March 6, 1972, and the fourth on the following August 11. The package was marked "Airmail," bore sufficient airmail postage and was properly addressed. Delivery of air mail from East Hartford to Washington at that time was normally two days.

The applications were date-stamped "March 8, 1973," by the Patent Office. Each of the four applications was assigned that filing date on the ground that the stamped date was the date of receipt by the Patent Office. If the action of the Patent Office is to stand, three of appellees' applications, on which Luxembourg patents had been granted, fail in this country.

Appellees petitioned the Commissioner of Patents to reassign the filing date. The petition was denied. Appellees then sued in the District Court for a judgment directing the Commissioner to accord the applications a filing date not later than March 6, 1973. Both sides moved for summary judgment on the basis of the pleadings and affidavits respectively submitted. Not surprisingly, none of the affidavits reflected any direct evidence of the date on which the applications were actually delivered to the Patent Office.[12]

The District Court correctly identified the central issue: "whether there exists a genuine issue of fact as to when these applications were received by the Patent Office." By the court's appraisal, appellees' suit was "predicated upon the legal presumption that postal employees discharge their duties in a proper manner and that properly addressed, stamped and deposited mail is presumed to reach the addressee in due course and without unusual delay, unless evidence to the contrary is proven." The court believed, however, that the Commissioner's position rested "primarily upon a presumption of procedural regularity based upon the normal manner, custom, practice and habit established for the handling of incoming mail at the Patent Office and upon the absence of evidence showing that the subject applications were not handled routinely in accordance with those established procedures." On this analysis, the court "concluded that the presumption relied upon by the [Commissioner] is insufficient to overcome the strong presumption that mails, properly addressed, having fully prepaid postage, and deposited in the proper receptacles, will be received by the addressee in the ordinary course of the mails." "This latter presumption," the court held, "can only be rebutted by proof of specific facts and not by invoking another presumption"; "the negative evidence in this case detailing the manner, custom, practice and habit of handling incoming mail by the Patent Office fails to overcome or rebut the strong presumption that the applications were timely delivered in the regular course of the mails to the Patent Office." In sum,

> [appellees] rely upon the strong presumption of the regularity of the mails to show that, in the normal course of postal business, these applications would be delivered within two days from March 1, 1973. [The Commissioner] does not show nor offer to show by way of any positive evidence that the presumption is inapplicable in this case. On the contrary, he relies on negative evidence as to custom, habit and usual procedure to create a conflicting presumption that the agency's business and procedure were followed in this case. Under the circumstances of this case, this Court holds, as a matter of law, that this presumption is insufficient to rebut or overcome the presumption of the regularity of the mails.

II

Proof that mail matter is properly addressed, stamped and deposited in an appropriate receptacle has long been accepted as evidence of delivery to the addressee. On proof of the foundation facts, innumerable cases recognize a presumption to that effect. Some presume more specifically that the delivery occurred in due course of the mails. The cases concede, however, that the presumption is rebuttable. We think the District Court erred in adhering to the presumption in the face of the evidentiary showing which the Commissioner was prepared to make.

Rebuttable presumptions[24] are rules of law attaching to proven evidentiary facts certain procedural consequences as to the opponent's duty to come forward with other evidence. In the instant case, the presumption would normally mean no more than that proof of proper airmailing of appellees' applications required a finding, in the absence of countervailing evidence, that they arrived at the Patent Office within the usual delivery time. There is abundant authority undergirding the proposition that, as a presumption, it did not remain viable in the face of antithetical evidence. As Dean Wigmore has explained, "the peculiar effect of a presumption 'of law' (that is, the real presumption) is merely to invoke a rule of law compelling the [trier of fact] to reach a conclusion in the absence of evidence to the contrary from the opponent. If the opponent does offer evidence to the contrary (sufficient to satisfy the judge's requirement of some evidence), the presumption disappears as a rule of law, and the case is in the [factfinder's] hands free from any rule." As more poetically the explanation has been put, "[p]resumptions * * * may be looked on as the bats of the law, flitting in the twilight, but disappearing in the sunshine of actual facts."

We are aware of the fact that this view of presumptions—the so-called "bursting bubble" theory—has not won universal acclaim. Nonetheless, it is the prevailing view, to which jurists preponderantly have subscribed; it is the view of the Supreme Court, and of this court as well. It is also the approach taken by the Model Code of Evidence and, very importantly, by the newly-adopted Federal Rules of Evidence.[37] These considerations hardly leave us free to assume a contrary position. Beyond that, we perceive no legal or practical justification for preferring either of the two involved presumptions over the other. In light of the Commissioner's showing on the motions for summary judgment, then, we conclude that the District Court should have declined a summary disposition in favor of a trial.

24. We distinguish the presumption "of law"—the procedural rule dictating a factual conclusion in the absence of contrary evidence—from the presumption "of fact," which in reality is not a presumption at all, see 9 J. Wigmore, Evidence § 2491 at 288–289 (3d ed. 1940), and from the "conclusive" presumption, which is actually a substantive rule of law. See 9 J. Wigmore, Evidence § 2492 (3d ed. 1940); C. McCormick, Evidence § 342 at 804 (2d ed. 1972). We also differentiate presumptions from inferences, a dissimilarity which "is subtle, but not unreal. A presumption, sometimes called a presumption of law, is an inference which the law directs the [trier of fact] to draw if it finds a given set of facts; an inference is a conclusion which the [trier of fact] is *permitted*, but not compelled, to draw from the facts."

37. "In all civil actions and proceedings not otherwise provided for by Act of Congress or by these rules, a presumption imposes on the party against whom it is directed the burden of going forward with evidence to rebut or meet the presumption, but does not shift to such party the burden of proof in the sense of the risk of nonpersuasion, which remains throughout the trial upon the party on whom it was originally cast." Fed. R. Evid. 301. The history of this provision portrays a fluctuating evolution. As originally proposed by the Supreme Court, the presumptions governed were given the effect of placing on the opposing party the burden of establishing the nonexistence of the presumed fact, and "[t]he so-called 'bursting bubble' theory, under which a presumption vanishes upon the introduction of evidence which would support a finding of the nonexistence of the presumed fact, even though not believed, [was] rejected as according presumptions too 'slight and evanescent' an effect." Advisory Committee's Note to original Rule 301. The House Committee on the Judiciary agreed, but substituted a shift in the burden of going forward in place of a shift of the burden of proof, and conferred evidentiary value on the presumption. H.R. Rep. No. 93–650, 93d Cong., 1st Sess. 7 (1973), U.S. Code Cong. & Admin. News 1974, p. 7075. The Senate Committee on the Judiciary felt, however, that "the House amendment is ill-advised. * * * 'Presumptions are not evidence, but ways of dealing with evidence.' [footnote omitted]. This treatment requires juries to perform the task of considering 'as evidence' facts upon which

III

Conservatively estimated, the Patent Office receives through the mails an average of at least 100,000 items per month. The procedures utilized for the handling of that volume of mail were meticulously described in an affidavit by an official of the Patent Office, whose principal duties included superintendence of incoming mail. Ordinary mail—other than special delivery, registered and certified—arrives at the Patent Office in bags, which are date-marked if the items contained were placed by the postal service in the Patent Office pouch earlier than the date of delivery of the bags. A number of readers open the wrappers, compare the contents against any included listing—such as a letter of transmittal or a return postcard—and note any discrepancy, and apply to at least the principal included paper a stamp recording thereon the receipt date and the reader's identification number. Another employee then applies to the separate papers the official mail-room stamp, which likewise records the date; the two stamps are used in order to minimize the chance of error. The date recorded in each instance is the date on which the Patent Office actually receives the particular bag of mail, or a previous date when the bag is so marked. From every indication, the affidavit avers, appellees' applications were not delivered to the Patent Office until March 8, 1973.

We cannot agree with the District Court that an evidentiary presentation of this caliber would do no more than raise "a presumption of procedural regularity" in the Patent Office. Certainly it would accomplish that much; it would cast upon appellees the burden of producing contradictory evidence, but its effect would not be exhausted at that point. The facts giving rise to the presumption would also have evidentiary force, and as evidence would command the respect normally accorded proof of any fact. In other words, the evidence reflected by the affidavit, beyond creation of a presumption of regularity in date-stamping incoming mail, would have probative value on the issue of date of receipt of appellees' applications; and even if the presumption were dispelled, that evidence would be entitled to consideration, along with appellees' own evidence, when a resolution of the issue is undertaken. And, clearly, a fact-finder convinced of the integrity of the Patent Office's mail-handling procedures would inexorably be led to the conclusion that appellees' applications simply did not arrive until the date which was stamped on them.

In the final analysis, the District Court's misstep was the treatment of the parties' opposing affidavits as a contest postulating a question of law as to the relative strength of the two presumptions rather than as a prelude to conflicting evidence necessitating a trial. Viewed as the mere procedural devices we hold that they are, presumptions are incapable of waging war among themselves. Even more importantly, the court's disposition of the case on a legal ruling disregarded the divergent inferences which the evidentiary tenders warranted, and consequently the inappropriateness of a reso-

they have no direct evidence and which may confuse them in performance of their duties." S. Rep. No. 93-1277, 93d Cong., 2d Sess. 9–10 (1974), first quoting Hearings on H.R. 2463 Before the Senate Committee on Judiciary, 93d Cong., 2d Sess. 96 (1974) U.S. Code Cong. & Admin. News 1974, pp.

7051, 7056. The Senate Committee accordingly modified Rule 301 to its present form, and the Conference Committee adopted the Senate version. H.R. Rep. No. 93-1597, 93d Cong., 2d Sess. 5–6 (1974) U.S.Code Cong. & Admin. News 1974, p. 7098.

* * *

lution of the opposing claims by summary judgment. As only recently we said, "[t]he court's function is not to resolve any factual issue, but to ascertain whether any exists, and all doubts in that regard must be resolved against summary judgment." Here the District Court was presented with an issue of material fact as to the date on which appellees' applications were received by the Patent Office, and summary judgment was not in order.

The judgment appealed from is accordingly reversed, and the case is remanded to the District Court for further proceedings. The cross-motions for summary judgment will be denied, and the case will be set down for trial on the merits in regular course.

So ordered.

* * *

NOTE

See Federal Rules of Evidence 301–302 at pp. 908–909, California Evidence Code § § 110 at p. 810, 115 at p. 810, 500–502 at p. 822, 520–522 at pp. 822–823, 550 at p. 823, 600–607 at pp. 823–824, 620–624 at pp. 824–825, 630–645 at pp. 825–827, 660, 662–668 at p. 828.

DEGNAN, SYLLABUS ON CALIFORNIA EVIDENCE CODE

(11th Annual Summer Program for California Lawyers,
U. of Calif. at Berkeley, 1965) pp. 18–25.

B. Presumptions

The Code of Civil Procedure § 1957 divides all "indirect" (i.e., circumstantial) evidence into two forms or kinds, inferences and presumptions. In §§ 1958 and 1959 these two forms are defined. Without repeating the unnecessary division of § 1957, Evidence Code § 600 restates in more modern expression the substance of the existing definitions. An inference is a deduction which reasonable men could draw from another fact or facts which have been proved or established; a presumption is an assumption of fact that the law *requires* to be made when another fact or facts have been proved or established.

Evidence Code § 601 divides presumptions further into conclusive and rebuttable presumptions; so does C.C.P. § 1961. Retention of the term "conclusive presumption" is unfortunate because the kinds of things described in §§ 621–624 are not presumptions at all but rules of law. None of the things which will subsequently be said about management of presumptions generally have any reference to conclusive presumptions.

There have been two perennially difficult problems about presumptions in civil cases in California. First to be treated is the difficult concept of the presumption as evidence. The second is what impact the presumption has on the burdens of producing evidence and of persuasion. These two will be discussed separately.

1. Presumptions as Evidence

All theories about presumption agree on one thing. If the basic facts which support the presumption are established, and there is no contradiction, the jury *must* find the presumed fact to be true. This is the result of C.C.P. § 1961, and it is much more explicitly stated in Evidence Code §§ 604 and 606. The difficulty under the C.C.P. was the meaning of the word "controverted" in § 1961. Did contradictory evidence so "controvert" the presumption that it disappeared entirely, never to be mentioned by judge or jury? Or was a controverted presumption merely no longer binding, but still retaining some probative force? In part because of some language (§ § 1957, 1963) which refers to presumptions as "evidence," the Supreme Court in Smellie v. Southern Pac. Co., 212 Cal. 540, 299 P. 529 (1931), held that presumptions are evidence, and that they continue in the case even after controverting evidence has been introduced. The jury should be so instructed. Although abundantly criticized, this holding has endured and is the prime basis for the instructions framed under BAJI series 135. The case also held that while a presumption could be totally dispelled by testimony, that could be accomplished only by the testimony the holder of the presumption offered on his own behalf, and not by that extracted from him under C.C.P. § 2055.

To meet this uniquely California view, Evidence Code § 600 (a), after defining presumptions, expressly declares: "A presumption is not evidence." No longer should juries be instructed that it is evidence, and that it is to be weighed by them along with all other evidence on the particular issue. And there should no longer be a problem about whether the presumption is "dispelled" (i.e., totally eliminated) from the case in the sense of the *Smellie* opinion, for it was only as to the existence of the presumption as evidence that this question had any content.

2.   The Two Kinds of Presumptions

Evidence Code § 601, after dividing presumptions into conclusive and rebuttable, further classifies the latter as those affecting only the burden of producing evidence and those also affecting the burden of proof. Each of these classes, and the consequences of the classification, is elaborated in § § 603–606.

The basic theoretical dispute in other states and in the scholarly literature (somewhat concealed in California because of the doctrine that a presumption is evidence) has been about the effect of contrary or controverting evidence. One view, identified with Professors Thayer and Wigmore, has been that presumptions are created to resolve issues when no evidence has been produced on the point; when evidence is produced, the presumption is exhausted and plays no further role in the case. The burden of persuading the jury about the existence of the fact in question remains where it was at the outset. To the extent that the underlying facts of the presumption have some probative, circumstantial force (e.g., that a properly addressed and mailed letter was received) the jury may consider those facts, balancing them against the testimony of the other party that he did not receive it. But those basic facts, once contradicted, are not reinforced by the presumption.

The other major view, identified largely with Professors Morgan and McCormick and essentially adopted by the Uniform Rules of Evidence, is that a presumption that has a logical basis (again the letter doctrine) should not be robbed of its force merely by a denial or by the production of some evidence that, if believed, would support a finding. This view would continue the presumption in force, in the form of an instruction to the jury that if they believe that the basic facts exist they should find that the letter was received, unless the contrary evidence persuaded them (usually by a preponderance) that it was not achieved. Thus it may be that a party who started with the burden of proof on a given issue will have shifted that burden to the opponent by establishing the basic facts of a presumption.

No state has consistently followed either of these two theories. A court that solemnly declares that the burden of proof never shifts will, when encountering certain kinds of presumptions, declare that the presumption may be overcome only by persuasive evidence, and that the jury should find the presumed fact unless persuaded by the contrary evidence. Thus in California a child born of a married woman, or within ten months of the end of the marriage, is presumed to be the child of the husband, and that presumption can be overcome only by clear and convincing evidence. Kusior v. Silver, 54 Cal.2d 603, 354 P.2d 657, 7 Cal.Rptr. 129 (1960).

The Law Revision Commission resolved the seeming contradiction between theories by determining that some presumptions are created merely to expedite the proof of law suits, or to shift to a person who has superior access to proof the obligation to come forward with an explanation of an event. § 603. These it classified as presumptions affecting only the burden of producing evidence. Under this section, the stages are:

a) Evidence supporting the basic facts is produced by the party initially bearing the burden of proof. If no contrary evidence is produced the judge must direct the jury to find (or find himself) that the presumed fact exists if it or he believes the basic facts.

b) If evidence sufficient to support a contrary finding is produced, the case goes to the jury without mention of the presumption; they resolve it as they would any case of conflicting inferences and testimony.

Some other presumptions founded more in policy considerations than in mere expedition are given greater force under §§ 605–606. The presumption of legitimacy found in § 661 is illustrative. The stages here are:

a) Evidence supporting the basic facts is produced by the party initially bearing the burden of proof. If no contrary evidence is produced, the consequences are the same as above—a peremptory finding.

b) If contrary evidence sufficient to support a finding is produced, the jury will be instructed that the husband bears the burden of persuading them that he is not the father.

Admittedly the classification of presumptions as one form or the other will not be a simple task. The code helps by classifying some of the standard and commonly encountered presumptions. As to others (either those found in other codes or in the case law), the judges must do as they have done before.

C. Prima Facie Evidence

Code of Civil Procedure § 1833 defines prima facie evidence as "that which suffices for the proof of a particular fact, until contradicted and overcome by other evidence." The phrase is troublesome because it has been and is used with several different meanings. To the original code commissioners, it meant evidence that "in the absence of all controlling evidence or discrediting circumstances, becomes conclusive of the fact; that is, it should operate upon the minds of the jury as decisive to found their verdict as to the fact." As such, it is hard to distinguish from a presumption. The term is often used also as the equivalent of a reasonable inference —evidence which, if believed, is sufficient to support but not to compel, a finding. And the code commissioners themselves often used it when the only probable purpose was to create a hearsay exception. E. g., C.C.P. §§ 1936, 1946. To avoid the confusion, the commission has eliminated from the Evidence Code both the definition and the usage of "prima facie." But the problem remains, for other codes contain many sections making one thing, usually a writing or recording prima facie evidence of some fact or facts. E. g., Health & S.C. § 10577 (death certificate). Sometimes the courts have treated these as presumptions affecting the burden of proof. Miller & Lux, Inc. v. Secara, 193 Cal. 755, 227 P. 171 (1924). At other times they appear to be regarded as merely shifting the burden of producing evidence. Pacific Freight Lines v. Industrial Acc. Comm'n, 26 Cal.2d 234, 157 P.2d 634 (1945).

Although the Commission eliminated the term from the Evidence Code, it could not eliminate the many instances in which the term is used in other codes. Section 602 therefore provides:

"A statute providing that a fact or group of facts is prima facie evidence of another fact establishes a rebuttable presumption."

Whether it is a presumption shifting the burden of producing evidence only, or one shifting the burden of proof as well, the courts must in each instance decide by ascertaining the legislative purpose. And in most instances, of course, the special statute will serve the additional purpose of creating a hearsay exception. Evidence Code § 1205 expressly disclaims any intention to repeal hearsay exceptions found in other codes.

KUSIOR v. SILVER

Supreme Court of California, 1960.
54 Cal.2d 603, 7 Cal.Rptr.129, 354 P.2d 657.

DOOLING, Justice. Plaintiff appeals from a judgment for defendant in an action to establish the paternity and to provide for the support of her child. Plaintiff's child was born July 29, 1954, nine days after the entry of a final decree of divorce dissolving her marriage to Thaddeus Kusior.

It appears from the settled statement that plaintiff and her husband separated in February 1953, and that an interlocutory decree of divorce was secured in July 1953. The child was probably conceived in October or November 1953.

Both plaintiff and her husband testified that sexual relations between them ceased at the time of separation. However, Mr. Kusior exercised his right to visit their eight-year-old daughter at regular intervals. On these occasions, he would perform maintenance work on the property, and he took plaintiff and their daughter out to dinner on at least one occasion. Several times he remained in plaintiff's home until the early hours of the morning. Plaintiff testified: "I had to have someone to talk to. Yes, we sat and talked until 3 or 4 in the morning." Mr. Kusior continued these visits even after their daughter was sent east on a visit in May 1954, but plaintiff had long since been pregnant at that time.

Two neighbors testified that Mr. Kusior was seen by them, sometimes in the evenings, during the period of possible conception. They were unable to say whether he stayed all night but did state that plaintiff and her husband did "not live together" after the separation.

Mrs. Nelson lived in the house as a roomer until some time in October. She testified that plaintiff did not live together with any man during that period, although she did see one man, not Mr. Kusior, both in the evening and the following morning. There were, however, as many as ten men who visited plaintiff; they would sit with her in the den and sometimes bring groceries. Mrs. Nelson also saw one man leave amidst a commotion at four o'clock one morning.

Plaintiff testified that she first had intercourse with defendant early in June 1953, and subsequently about four more times until she underwent an operation in September of that year. She testified that she had intercourse with defendant several times thereafter. He slept in the den the first time he came to her house, about the middle of October 1953, shortly after Mrs. Nelson moved out of the house. Mrs. Nelson testified that she never saw defendant until her appearance in court.

Plaintiff also testified that she went out with other men during the period of possible conception, and also frequented a certain cocktail bar. She stated, however, that defendant was the only man with whom she had intercourse.

Blood tests were taken of the parties pursuant to section 1980.3 of the Code of Civil Procedure. These tests established that plaintiff's husband could not have been the father of the child but that defendant was within the class of persons who could have been.

The sufficiency of the evidence to support a judgment for defendant is not disputed, but plaintiff contends that certain instructions involving the effect of the blood tests and the presumptions of legitimacy were in error, and could have caused the jury to dispose of the proceedings by improperly determining that Mr. Kusior must be considered to be the child's father.

The trial court gave instructions based on the following sections of our code, which set forth conclusive and rebuttable presumptions of legitimacy. Code of Civil Procedure, § 1962, subdivision 5, provides: "Notwithstanding any other provision of law, the issue of a wife cohabiting with her husband, who is not impotent, is indisputably presumed to be legitimate." Section 1963, subdivision 31, sets forth as a disputable presumption: "That a child born in lawful wedlock, there being no divorce from bed and board, is legitimate." Civil Code, § 193, provides: "All children born in wedlock are presumed to be legitimate." Section 194 makes that presumption applicable to all children born within ten months of the "dissolution of the marriage." Section 195 provides that the only persons who can dispute that presumption are the state in an action for support under section 270 of the Penal Code, or the "husband or wife, or the descendant of one or both of them."

The instructions given to the jury based on these sections were to the effect that a conclusive presumption, which none of the other evidence in the case can contradict, would apply if there was a failure to show that there was not "a reasonable possibility of access." The jury was also instructed that if they found that the conclusive presumption did not apply, then only the rebuttable presumption applies, and any evidence, including the blood tests, might be considered to rebut it. The relevant instructions are set forth below.[1]

[The court discusses the authorities on the meaning of co-habitation].

* * * We conclude that "cohabiting" in section 1962, subdivision 5, should be construed to mean "living together as husband and wife," and any language giving or suggesting a broader meaning in any of the cases in the District Courts of Appeal * * * is to that extent disapproved.

---

1. "Now, you will observe there are two conditions which must exist and which you must find to exist before this conclusive presumption applies: 'The issue of a wife cohabiting with her husband, who is not impotent.'

"There is no question that Mrs. Kusior was married to Mr. Kusior, so she is a wife, but you must find that she cohabited with him during the period of conception involved in this case.

"You must also find that Mr. Kusior is not impotent. From the uncontradicted evidence in this case, you may accept as a fact that Mr. Kusior is not impotent; that is to say, he could father a child.

"So, then, the only question remaining for you to determine from the preliminary facts, is whether Mr. and Mrs. Kusior cohabited at any time and for any time during the period that conception must have taken place according to the laws of nature in this case.

"Hence, to invoke the conclusive presumption just read you, you need only find that Mr. and Mrs. Kusior cohabited, that is, at any time and for any time, lived together as husband and wife during the period when conception normally would have occurred in this case, or if you find from the evidence that Mr. Kusior, the husband, had access to his wife, Mrs. Kusior, during that period of conception involved here.

"There is evidence that the Kusiors had separated and had no sexual relations since or during the separation, but separation alone is not the test.

"To prevent this strong conclusive presumption from arising, where the child is conceived during marriage, which is the case here, the evidence must be clear and convincing that there in fact was no access; not simply that the parties were separated. If there was reasonable possibility of access, the conclusive presumption arises, and no evidence can be considered by you to contradict it.

"In that situation, the child is conclusively presumed to be legitimate and your verdict would have to be for the defendant, Dr. Silver.

"But, on the other hand, should you find that there was in fact no cohabitation by Mr. and Mrs. Kusior during the period in which conception normally would have occurred in this case, the conclusive presumption would not apply, but only the rebuttable presumption which was the one to the effect that a child born of a married woman within ten months after the dissolution of her marriage is presumed legitimate." (Court's Instruction "A.")

"You should bear in mind that if you find the fact of cohabitation existing between Mr. and Mrs. Kusior during the period of conception in this case the conclusive presumption applies and you may not consider any of the evidence in the case for the purpose of contradicting that presumption.

"But, if you find that it does not apply, and only the rebuttable presumption applies, then you may consider all the evidence in accordance with these instructions." (Court's Instruction "B.")

"There is another presumption which applies, depending as to whether you find certain preliminary facts to exist. That presumption says: 'The issue of a wife cohabiting with her husband, who is not impotent, is indisputably presumed to be legitimate.' That presumption cannot be contradicted, if it applies." (Court's Instruction "C.")

"The law throws certain protections around a family and the children of the family, for obvious reasons.

"There is a presumption established by law which says that all children of a woman who has been married, born within ten months of dissolution of the marriage, are presumed to be legitimate children of that marriage.

"This presumption, which is rebuttable, applies in this instance.

"The child was born of a woman who had been married, born nine days after the dissolution of the marriage.

"As I say, the presumption is rebuttable and you may apply, either in support of or contradiction of this presumption, any of the evidence that has been

We conclude that the trial court committed error in instructing that the conclusive presumption applies if the husband had "access" or "reasonable possibility of access" to his wife during the period of conception.

Appellant also contends that the instructions with regard to the conclusive presumption should not have been given at all in view of the fact that the blood tests showed that her husband could not have been the father. She argues that the conclusive presumption is subject to well-recognized exceptions, and that blood tests should be added to the exceptions. She relies principally on the explanation for the exceptions set forth in In re McNamara's Estate, supra, 181 Cal. 82, 96, 183 P. 552, 558, 7 A.L.R. 313: "The reason why the conclusive presumption is not applied in such instances is that the element of indeterminability which is the reason for the presumption in the ordinary case is absent. * * * The actual fact, in other words, is capable of definite determination, and for this reason the conclusive presumption which is a substitute for such determination is not properly applicable."

Appellant cites the scientific reliability of blood-grouping tests which was accorded recognition by the adoption of the Uniform Act on Blood Tests to Determine Paternity (Code Civ.Proc., §§ 1980.1–1980.7) and argues that the "actual fact" is here capable of definite determination, and thus under the reasoning in Estate of McNamara, supra, the "conclusive presumption is not applicable." However, the actions of the Legislature have clearly established the effect of the blood-grouping tests in relation to the application of the conclusive presumption to be otherwise.

The judicial decisions prior to the adoption of the Uniform Act in 1953 have a direct bearing on the present problem. In Arais v. Kalensnikoff, 10 Cal.2d 428, 74 P.2d 1043, 115 A.L.R. 163, the defendant was adjudged the father despite blood tests to the contrary. We affirmed, stating at page 432 of 10 Cal.2d, at page 1046 of 74 P.2d: "Whatever claims the medical profession may make for the test, in California 'no evidence is by law made conclusive or unanswerable unless so declared by this code.' Section 1978, Code Civ.Proc." In Berry v. Chaplin, supra, the same reasoning was applied and the same result was reached. Neither case involved a mother who was married at the time of conception or birth. However, in Hill v. Johnson, supra, 102 Cal.App.2d 94, 226 P.2d 655, a wife who was living in the same house with her husband at all times, including the time of conception, birth, and even the time of trial, brought suit against a third party for support. Blood tests disclosed that the husband could not have been the father, and he testified that he was sick at the relevant time and hence did not have intercourse with his wife. "From this plaintiff argues that Mr. Hill could not

received in this case, including the two blood tests." (Court's Instruction "F.")

Pertaining to the results of the blood tests, the court instructed the jury as follows: "The doctor's report of the results of the blood tests made of the parties to this action, and of the minor child Dorothy, does not establish that the defendant is the father of the minor child Dorothy. It merely establishes that the defendant is one of that group of men whose blood is such that, physiologically, any one of them could

father a child, having blood such as Dorothy, so that therefore it is physiologically possible for the defendant to be Dorothy's father. This report is to be considered by you, together with all of the other evidence presented in this case, in resolving the issue of whether the defendant is the father of the minor child Dorothy. The other report, you will recall, gave its interpretation of the findings that Thaddeus Kusior was excluded from the class of those who could be the father of the child." (Court's Instruction "E.")

have been the father of the child and that defendant could have been. Evidence of the result of a blood test is to be considered with all other evidence in the case and is not conclusive. [Citation.] It was error to admit the evidence since it is contrary to the conclusive presumption of legitimacy." 102 Cal.App.2d 96, 226 P.2d 656. The Hill case was decided in 1951, and the Legislature in 1953 enacted our version of the Uniform Act on Blood Tests to Determine Paternity, providing: "In a civil action, in which paternity is a relevant fact, the court * * * may * * * order the mother, child and alleged father to submit to blood tests." Code Civ.Proc. § 1980.3. "If the court finds that the conclusions of all the experts * * * are that the alleged father is not the father of the child, the question of paternity shall be resolved accordingly." Code Civ.Proc. § 1980.6. However, the Legislature significantly refrained from adopting section 5 of the Uniform Act, which provides: "The presumption of legitimacy of a child born during wedlock is overcome if the court finds that the conclusions of all the experts, as disclosed by the evidence based upon the tests, show that the husband is not the father of the child." Our law emerged without this section or any reference to the subject matter contained therein.

Statutes are to be interpreted by assuming that the Legislature was aware of the existing judicial decisions. Moreover, failure to make changes in a given statute in a particular respect when the subject is before the Legislature, and changes are made in other respects, is indicative of an intention to leave the law unchanged in that respect. That rule can be applied by analogy where a section is omitted in the face of our decisional law. Thus, it is clear that the Uniform Act negatives the possibility of another Arais v. Kalensnikoff, supra, or Berry v. Chaplin, supra, neither of which involved a married mother. But it is apparent that the failure of the Legislature to enact that part of the act which would specifically have enabled the result of a blood test to overcome the conclusive presumption declared in section 1962, subdivision 5, must be deemed an intention not to change the rule stated in Hill v. Johnson, supra.

Moreover, section 1962, subdivision 5, was amended in 1955 by the addition of the emphasized words: *"Notwithstanding any other provision of law,* the issue of a wife cohabiting with her husband, who is not impotent, is indisputably presumed to be legitimate." This addition was part of an act which gave the state power to dispute the rebuttable presumption by adding the state to the parties enumerated in Civil Code, § 195, and also by adding a provision to Penal Code, § 270, to the effect that the state could prove nonaccess "or any other fact establishing nonpaternity of a husband." Since the people have been equated with all others who may rebut presumptions, it is apparent that they and all others were not meant to be able to use this section, or any other provision of law, as against section 1962, subdivision 5. It is further apparent that blood tests are one of the ways in which paternity could be disputed other than nonintercourse, and that the overall legislative intent manifestly precludes any other construction of the statutes.

Appellant contends that such a construction is not consistent with constitutional principles in that there is no reasonable relationship between the presumption and the fact sought to be presumed in a case in which there is scientific evidence to the contrary. However, appellant does not suggest that the Legislature has no interest in or power to determine, as a matter of overriding social policy, that given a certain relationship between the husband and wife, the husband is to be held responsible for the child. There are significant reasons why the integrity of the family when husband and wife are living together as such should not be impugned. A conclusive presumption is in actuality a substantive rule of law and cannot be said to be unconstitutional unless it transcends such a power of the Legislature. * * *

Appellant's final contention is that the trial court was in error in instructing the jury that the blood tests were not conclusive as against the rebuttable presumption but were only evidence to be weighed with all the other evidence. A similar argument was rejected in McKee v. McKee, 156 Cal.App.2d 764, 320 P.2d 510, 512, a case in which the conclusive presumption was inapplicable, but the judgment was affirmed on the basis of the rebuttable presumption despite a blood test which negatived paternity. "It has not been determined whether paternity is a relevant fact in a case like the instant one where the child's mother is married at the time of conception and the husband denies paternity or whether the statute is limited to filiation proceedings where the child's mother is unwed. As the version of the statute adopted by our Legislature specifically excluded that portion of the act which provided that 'The presumption of legitimacy * * * is overcome' * * * defendant's argument would appear to be without merit." 156 Cal.App.2d 766–767, 320 P.2d 512. However, disputable presumptions are evidentiary devices which can be overcome by clear and convincing evidence. Although a rebuttable presumption is treated by our court as evidence which may outweigh positive evidence against it, there has been a legislative determination here that blood test evidence is conclusive. Code Civ.Proc. § 1980.6. Unless there can be found a manifested intent that this section specifically dealing with the effect of blood tests does not define the effect of such blood tests in every case in which they are admissible into evidence, then it seems clear that since they have always been admissible for whatever their worth as evidence capable of overcoming a rebuttable presumption (McKee v. McKee, supra, even assumes that they are), they ought, in view of the overall recognition by the statute of their accuracy, to be conclusive against a merely rebuttable presumption. Statutes are to be interpreted to give a reasonable result consistent with legislative purpose, and it cannot be said that such a result is not the most reasonable, nor can it be said that legislative purpose demands a contrary result. The fact that section 5 of the Uniform Act was omitted can be explained by assuming that the Legislature did not intend to affect the conclusive presumption, but that the statute as enacted was to have whatever effect on the rebuttal presumption a reasonable interpretation thereof would give it. If we did not have the dual system of presumption, then we might be forced to give a greater weight to the omission, but in the face of the dual system, we need not do so.

We conclude that the result of blood tests taken under the Uniform Act (Code Civ.Proc. § 1980.1 et seq.) may not be used to controvert the conclusive presumption of paternity created by subdivision 5 of section 1962 of the Code of Civil Procedure, but that under the language of section 1980.6, if "the conclusions of all the experts * * * are that the alleged father is not the father of the child, the question of paternity shall be resolved accordingly,"[5] where the tests so taken establish that the mother's husband could not be the father of the child the rebuttable presumptions of paternity are conclusively rebutted. The dictum in McKee v. McKee, supra, 156 Cal.App.2d 764, 320 P.2d 510, inconsistent with this conclusion, is disapproved.

The jury after deliberating returned to court and asked to be reinstructed on the effect of the presumptions of legitimacy. After being so instructed, they returned shortly with their verdict. Under the circumstances the prejudice from the error in defining "cohabiting" seems clear.

The judgment is reversed.

Gibson, C.J., and Traynor, Schauer, McComb, Peters, and White, JJ., concur.

COUNTY COURT OF ULSTER COUNTY v. ALLEN

Supreme Court of the United States, 1979.
442 U.S. 140, 99 S.Ct. 2213, 60 L.Ed.2d 777.

Mr. Justice STEVENS delivered the opinion of the Court.

A New York statute provides that, with certain exceptions, the presence of a firearm in an automobile is presumptive evidence of its illegal possession by all persons then occupying the vehicle.[1] The United States Court of Appeals for the Second Circuit held that * * *

Four persons, three adult males (respondents) and a 16-year-old girl (Jane Doe, who is not a respondent here), were jointly tried on charges that they possessed two loaded handguns, a loaded machinegun, and over a pound of heroin found in a Chevrolet in which they were riding when it was

---

5.   There appears to have been only one test made in this case of the blood of the husband. Since section 1980.6 speaks of "the conclusions of all the experts," it would seem that more than one expert must make the tests and agree upon the results to require that "the question of paternity shall be resolved accordingly." State by Dolloff v. Sargent, 100 N.H. 29, 118 A.2d 596, 597. While referring to this fact in his answer to the petition for hearing before this court, respondent concedes that this does not affect the legal questions posed. "Though not affecting the legal points involved in this appeal, it is perhaps of passing interest that * * * there was but one test. * * * " (Answer to Petition for Hearing, p. 11.) Since more than one expert may readily be appointed to examine the blood of the husband, the mother, and the child on a new trial, we have deemed it proper to consider the points raised as to the construction which should be given to the Uniform Act in relation to the presumption of legitimacy.

1.   New York Penal Law § 265.15(3):

"The presence in an automobile, other than a stolen one or a public omnibus, of any firearm, defaced firearm, firearm silencer, bomb, bombshell, gravity knife, switchblade knife, dagger, dirk, stiletto, billy, blackjack, metal knuckles, sandbag, sandclub or slungshot is presumptive evidence of its possession by all persons occupying such automobile at the time such weapon, instrument or appliance is found, except under the following circumstances:

"(a)   if such weapon, instrument or appliance is found upon the person of one of the occupants therein;

"(b)   if such weapon, instrument or appliance is found in an automobile which is being operated for hire by a duly licensed driver in the due, lawful and proper pursuit of his trade, then such presumption shall not apply to the driver; or

"(c)   if the weapon so found is a pistol or revolver and one of the occupants, not present under duress, has in his possession a valid license to have and carry concealed the same." In addition to the three exceptions delineated in §§ 265.15(3)(a)–(c) above as well as the stolen-vehicle and public-omnibus exception in § 265.15(3) itself, § 265.20 contains various exceptions that apply when weapons are present in an automobile pursuant to certain military, law enforcement, recreational, and commercial endeavors.

stopped for speeding on the New York Thruway shortly after noon on March 28, 1973. The two large-caliber handguns, which together with their ammunition weighed approximately six pounds, were seen through the window of the car by the investigating police officer. They were positioned crosswise in an open handbag on either the front floor or the front seat of the car on the passenger side where Jane Doe was sitting. Jane Doe admitted that the handbag was hers. The machinegun and the heroin were discovered in the trunk after the police pried it open. The car had been borrowed from the driver's brother earlier that day; the key to the trunk could not be found in the car or on the person of any of its occupants, although there was testimony that two of the occupants had placed something in the trunk before embarking in the borrowed car. The jury convicted all four of possession of the handguns and acquitted them of possession of the contents of the trunk.

Counsel for all four defendants objected to the introduction into evidence of the two handguns, the machinegun, and the drugs, arguing that the State had not adequately demonstrated a connection between their clients and the contraband. The trial court overruled the objection, relying on the presumption of possession created by the New York statute. Tr., at 474–483. Because that presumption does not apply if a weapon is found "upon the person" of one of the occupants of the car,   *   *   *   the three male defendants also moved to dismiss the charges relating to the handguns on the ground that the guns were found on the person of Jane Doe. Respondents made this motion both at the close of the prosecution's case and at the close of all evidence. The trial judge twice denied it, concluding that the applicability of the "on the person" exception was a question of fact for the jury. Tr., at 544–557, 589–590.

At the close of the trial, the judge instructed the jurors that they were entitled to infer possession from the defendants' presence in the car. He did not make any reference to the "upon the person" exception in his explanation of the statutory presumption, nor did any of the defendants object to this omission or request alternative or additional instructions on the subject.

Defendants filed a post-trial motion in which they challenged the constitutionality of the New York statute as applied in this case. The challenge was made in support of their argument that the evidence, apart from the presumption, was insufficient to sustain the convictions. The motion was denied, Tr., at 775–776, and the convictions were affirmed by the Appellate Division without opinion. 49 App.Div.2d 639, 370 N.Y.S.2d 243 (1975).

The New York Court of Appeals also affirmed.   *   *   *

Respondents filed a petition for a writ of habeas corpus in the United States District Court for the Southern District of New York contending that they were denied due process of law by the application of the statutory presumption of possession. The District Court issued the writ, holding that   *   *   *   the mere presence of two guns in a woman's handbag in a car could not reasonably give rise to the inference that they were in the possession of three other persons in the car.   *   *   *

The Court of Appeals for the Second Circuit   *   *   *   concluded that the statute is unconstitutional on its face because the "presumption obviously sweeps within its compass (1) many occupants who may not know they are riding with a gun (which may be out of their sight), and (2) many who may be aware of the presence of the gun but not permitted access to it. * * *

* * *

In this case the Court of Appeals undertook the task of deciding the constitutionality of the New York statute "on its face." Its conclusion that the statutory presumption was arbitrary rested entirely on its view of the fairness of applying the presumption in hypothetical situations—situations, indeed, in which it is improbable that a jury would return a conviction, or that a prosecution would ever be instituted. We must accordingly inquire whether these respondents had standing to advance the arguments that the Court of Appeals considered decisive. An analysis of our prior cases indicates that the answer to this inquiry depends on the type of presumption that is involved in the case.

Inferences and presumptions are a staple of our adversarial system of factfinding. It is often necessary for the trier of fact to determine the existence of an element of the crime—that is, an "ultimate" or "elemental" fact—from the existence of one or more "evidentiary" or "basic" facts. The value of these evidentiary devices, and their validity under the Due Process Clause, vary from case to case, however, depending on the strength of the connection between the particular basic and elemental facts involved and on the degree to which the device curtails the factfinder's freedom to assess the evidence independently. Nonetheless, in criminal cases, the ultimate test of any device's constitutional validity in a given case remains constant: the device must not undermine the factfinder's responsibility at trial, based on evidence adduced by the State, to find the ultimate facts beyond a reasonable doubt.

The most common evidentiary device is the entirely permissive inference or presumption, which allows—but does not require—the trier of fact to infer the elemental fact from proof by the prosecutor of the basic one and that places no burden of any kind on the defendant. In that situation the basic fact may constitute prima facie evidence of the elemental fact. When reviewing this type of device, the Court has required the party challenging it to demonstrate its invalidity as applied to him. Because this permissive presumption leaves the trier of fact free to credit or reject the inference and does not shift the burden of proof, it affects the application of the "beyond a reasonable doubt" standard only if, under the facts of the case, there is no rational way the trier could make the connection permitted by the inference. For only in that situation is there any risk that an explanation of the permissible inference to a jury, or its use by a jury, has caused the presumptively rational factfinder to make an erroneous factual determination.

A mandatory presumption is a far more troublesome evidentiary device. For it may affect not only the strength of the "no reasonable doubt" burden but also the placement of that burden; it tells the trier that he or they *must* find the elemental fact upon proof of the basic fact, at least unless the defendant has come forward with some evidence to rebut the presumed connection between the two facts.[16] * * * In this situation, the

16. This class of more or less mandatory presumptions can be subdivided into two parts: presumptions that merely shift the burden of production to the defendant, fol-

lowing the satisfaction of which the ultimate burden of persuasion returns to the prosecution; and presumptions that entirely shift the burden of proof to the defen-

Court has generally examined the presumption on its face to determine the extent to which the basic and elemental facts coincide. * * * To the extent that the trier of fact is forced to abide by the presumption, and may not reject it based on an independent evaluation of the particular facts presented by the State, the analysis of the presumption's constitutional validity is logically divorced from those facts and based on the presumption's accuracy in the run of cases.[17] It is for this reason that the Court has held it irrelevant in analyzing a mandatory presumption, but not in analyzing a purely permissive one, that there is ample evidence in the record other than the presumption to support a conviction.

dant. The mandatory presumptions examined by our cases have almost uniformly fit into the former subclass, in that they never totally removed the ultimate burden of proof beyond a reasonable doubt from the prosecution. * * *

To the extent that a presumption imposes an extremely low burden of production—e. g., being satisfied by "any" evidence—it may well be that its impact is no greater than that of a permissive inference and it may be proper to analyze it as such.

In deciding what type of inference or presumption is involved in a case, the jury instructions will generally be controlling, although their interpretation may require recourse to the statute involved and the cases decided under it. Turner v. United States, supra, provides a useful illustration of the different types of presumptions. It analyzes the constitutionality of two different presumption statutes (one mandatory and one permissive) as they apply to the basic fact of possession of both heroin and cocaine, and the presumed facts of importation and distribution of narcotic drugs. The jury was charged essentially in the terms of the two statutes.

The importance of focusing attention on the precise presentation of the presumption to the jury and the scope of that presumption is illustrated by a comparison of United States v. Gainey, 380 U.S. 63, 85 S.Ct. 754, 13 L.Ed.2d 658, with United States v. Romano, 382 U.S. 136, 86 S.Ct. 279, 15 L.Ed.2d 210. Both cases involved statutory presumptions based on proof that the defendant was present at the site of an illegal still. In Gainey the Court sustained a conviction "for carrying on" the business of the distillery in violation of 26 U.S.C. § 5601(a)(4), whereas in Romano, the Court set aside a conviction for being in "possession, custody, and * * * control" of such a distillery in violation of § 5601(a)(1). The difference in outcome was attributable to two important differences between the cases. Because the statute involved in Gainey was a sweeping prohibition of almost any activity associated with the still, whereas the Romano statute involved only one narrow aspect of the total undertaking, there was a much higher probability that mere presence could support an inference of guilt in the former case than in the latter.

Of perhaps greater importance, however, was the difference between the trial judge's instructions to the jury in the two cases. In Gainey the judge had explained that the presumption was permissive; it did not require the jury to convict the defendant even if it was convinced that he was present at the site. On the contrary, the instructions made it clear that presence was only "a circumstance to be considered along with all the other circumstances in the case." As we emphasized, the "jury was thus specifically told that the statutory [presumption] was not conclusive." 380 U.S., at 69–70, 85 S.Ct., at 758–759. In Romano the trial judge told the jury that the defendant's presence at the still "shall be deemed sufficient evidence to authorize conviction." 382 U.S., at 182, 86 S.Ct., at 281. Although there was other evidence of guilt, that instruction authorized conviction even if the jury disbelieved all of the testimony, except the proof of presence at the site. This Court's holding that the statutory presumption could not support the Romano conviction was thus dependent, in part, on the specific instructions given by the trial judge. Under those instructions it was necessary to decide whether, regardless of the specific circumstances of the particular case, the statutory presumption adequately supported the guilty verdict.

17.   In addition to the discussion of Romano in n. 16, supra, this point is illustrated by Leary v. United States, supra. In that case, Dr. Timothy Leary, a professor at Harvard University was stopped by customs inspectors in Laredo, Texas as he was returning from the Mexican side of the international border. Marihuana seeds and a silver snuff box filled with semirefined marihuana and three partially smoked marihuana cigarettes were discovered in his car. He was convicted of having knowingly transported marihuana which he knew had been illegally imported into this country in violation of 21 U.S.C. § 176a. That statute includes a mandatory presumption: "possession shall be deemed sufficient evidence to authorize conviction [for importation] unless the defendant explains his possession to the satisfaction of the jury." Leary admitted possession of the

Without determining whether the presumption in this case was mandatory, the Court of Appeals analyzed it on its face as if it were. In fact, it was not, * * *.

The trial judge's instructions make it clear that the presumption was merely a part of the prosecution's case,[19] that it gave rise to a permissive inference available only in certain circumstances, rather than a mandatory conclusion of possession, and that it could be ignored by the jury even if there was no affirmative proof offered by defendants in rebuttal. The judge explained that possession could be actual or constructive, but that constructive possession could not exist without the intent and ability to exercise control or dominion over the weapons. He also carefully instructed the jury that there is a mandatory presumption of innocence in favor of the defendants that controls unless it, as the exclusive trier of fact, is satisfied beyond a reasonable doubt that the defendants possessed the handguns in the manner described by the judge. In short, the instructions plainly directed the jury to consider all the circumstances tending to support or contradict the inference that all four occupants of the car had possession of the two loaded handguns and to decide the matter for itself without regard to how much evidence the defendants introduced.

Our cases considering the validity of permissive statutory presumptions such as the one involved here have rested on an evaluation of the presumption as applied to the record before the Court. None suggests that a court should pass on the constitutionality of this kind of statute "on its face." It was error for the Court of Appeals to make such a determination in this case.

marihuana and claimed that he had carried it from New York to Mexico and then back.

Justice Harlan for the Court noted that under one theory of the case, the jury could have found direct proof of all of the necessary elements of the offense without recourse to, the presumption. But he deemed that insufficient reason to affirm the conviction because under another theory the jury might have found knowledge of importation on the basis of either direct evidence or the presumption, and there was accordingly no certainty that the jury had not relied on the presumption. 395 U.S., at 31–32, 89 S.Ct., at 1545–1546. The Court therefore found it necessary to test the presumption against the Due Process Clause. Its analysis was facial. Despite the fact that the defendant was well educated and had recently traveled to a country that is a major exporter of marihuana to this country, the Court found the presumption of knowledge of importation from possession irrational. It did so not because Dr. Leary was unlikely to know the source of the marihuana but instead because "a majority of possessors" were unlikely to have such knowledge. Id., at 53, 89 S.Ct., at 1557. Because the jury had been instructed to rely on the presumption even if it did not believe the Government's direct evidence of knowledge of importation (unless, of course, the defendant met his burden of

"satisfying" the jury to the contrary), the Court reversed the conviction.

19. "It is your duty to consider all the testimony in this case, to weigh it carefully and assess the credit to be given to a witness by his apparent intention to speak the truth and by the accuracy of his memory to reconcile, if possible, conflicting statements as to material facts and in such ways to try and get at the truth and to reach a verdict upon the evidence." Tr., at 739–740.

* * *

"To establish the unlawful possession of the weapons, again the People relied upon the presumption and, in addition thereto, the testimony of Anderson and Lemmons who testified in their case in chief." Tr., at 744.

* * *

"Accordingly, you would be warranted in returning a verdict of guilt against the defendants or defendant if you find the defendants or defendant was in possession of a machine gun and the other weapons and that the fact of possession was proven to you by the People beyond a reasonable doubt, and an element of such proof is the reasonable presumption of illegal possession of a machine gun or the presumption of illegal possession of firearms, as I have just before explained to you." Tr., at 746.

III

As applied to the facts of this case, the presumption of possession is entirely rational. Notwithstanding the Court of Appeals' analysis, respondents were not "hitch-hikers or other casual passengers," and the guns were neither "a few inches in length" nor "out of [respondents'] sight." * * * The argument against possession by any of the respondents was predicated solely on the fact that the guns were in Jane Doe's pocketbook. But several circumstances * * * made it highly improbable that she was the sole custodian of those weapons.

Even if it was reasonable to conclude that she had placed the guns in her purse before the car was stopped by police, the facts strongly suggest that Jane Doe was not the only person able to exercise dominion over them. The two guns were too large to be concealed in her handbag.[24] The bag was consequently open, and part of one of the guns was in plain view, within easy access of the driver of the car and even, perhaps, of the other two respondents who were riding in the rear seat.

Moreover, it is highly improbable that the loaded guns belonged to Jane Doe or that she was solely responsible for their being in her purse. As a 16-year-old girl in the company of three adult men she was the least likely of the four to be carrying one, let alone two, heavy handguns. It is far more probable that she relied on the pocketknife found in her brassiere for any necessary self-protection. Under these circumstances, it was not unreasonable for her counsel to argue and for the jury to infer that when the car was halted for speeding, the other passengers in the car anticipated the risk of a search and attempted to conceal their weapons in a pocketbook in the front seat. The inference is surely more likely than the notion that these weapons were the sole property of the 16-year-old girl.

Under these circumstances, the jury would have been entirely reasonable in rejecting the suggestion— * * * that the handguns were in the sole possession of Jane Doe. Assuming that the jury did reject it, the case is tantamount to one in which the guns were lying on the floor or the seat of the car in the plain view of the three other occupants of the automobile. In such a case it is surely rational to infer that each of the respondents was fully aware of the presence of the guns and had both the ability and the intent to exercise dominion and control over the weapons. The application of the statutory presumption in this case therefore comports with the standard laid down in Tot v. United States, 319 U.S. 463, 467, 63 S.Ct. 1241, 1244, 87 L.Ed.2d 1519, and restated in Leary v. United States, supra, 395 U.S., at 36, 89 S.Ct., at 1548. For there is a "rational connection" between the basic facts that the prosecution proved and the ultimate fact presumed, and the latter is "more likely than not to flow from" the former.

Respondents argue, however, that the validity of the New York presumption must be judged by a "reasonable doubt" test rather than the "more likely than not" standard employed in Leary.[28] Under the more stringent test, it is argued that a statutory presumption must be rejected

---

24. Jane Doe's counsel referred to the .45 caliber automatic pistol as a "cannon." Tr., at 306.

28. "The upshot of *Tot, Gainey,* and *Romano* is, we think, that a criminal statutory presumption must be regarded as 'irrational' or 'arbitrary,' and hence unconstitutional, unless it can at least be said with substantial assurance that the presumed fact is more likely than not to flow from the proved fact on which it is made to depend."

unless the evidence necessary to invoke the inference is sufficient for a rational jury to find the inferred fact beyond a reasonable doubt. Respondents' argument again overlooks the distinction between a permissive presumption on which the prosecution is entitled to rely as one not-necessarily-sufficient part of its proof and a mandatory presumption which the jury must accept even if it is the sole evidence of an element of the offense.

In the latter situation, since the prosecution bears the burden of establishing guilt, it may not rest its case entirely on a presumption unless the fact proved is sufficient to support the inference of guilt beyond a reasonable doubt. But in the former situation, the prosecution may rely on all of the evidence in the record to meet the reasonable doubt standard. There is no more reason to require a permissive statutory presumption to meet a reasonable doubt standard before it may be permitted to play any part in a trial than there is to require that degree of probative force for other relevant evidence before it may be admitted. As long as it is clear that the presumption is not the sole and sufficient basis for a finding of guilt, it need only satisfy the test described in *Leary*.

The permissive presumption, as used in this case, satisfied the *Leary* test. And, as already noted, the New York Court of Appeals has concluded that the record as a whole was sufficient to establish guilt beyond a reasonable doubt.

The judgment is reversed.

———

See Federal Rules of Evidence 301–302 at pp. 908–909; California Evidence Code § 646 at p. 827.

Hypotheticals

(1) A sues X Insurance Company for $8000 damages for breach of a liability insurance policy. A had rear-ended B's car, injuring B. B sued A and got a judgment for $8000. X refused to defend A in B's lawsuit on the ground that the policy had been canceled before the accident occurred. At A's trial against X, it is admitted that A paid a year's premium on the policy when it was issued six months before the accident. X's defense is that the policy had been canceled two months before the accident under a policy provision for ten days' notice to the insured and a return of the unused premium. X calls C, a clerk for X, who identifies a copy of a letter from X to A canceling the policy 15 days from the date of the letter, which was two months prior to the A-B accident. C also testifies that she personally mailed the original to A, properly addressed and stamped, and that she enclosed X's check to A for the unused premium. A calls Y who testifies that she and C lived together and that on the date C claims to have mailed the letter to A, C was home sick in bed and didn't go to work that day, the day before, or the day after. X requests the court to instruct the jury that if the jury finds that X's letter to A was correctly addressed and properly mailed, the jury must find that A received the letter in the ordinary course of mail. Should the court grant X's requested instruction?

(2) Assume the same facts as in Illustration (1). In addition to presenting Y's testimony, A testifies that she has lived continuously at the same address to which the canceling notice was allegedly mailed, but has never received any letter from X Insurance Company; that she had no other insurance on her car than the policy issued by X Insurance Company; and that she had driven continuously for five years preceding the accident and has always carried liability insurance coverage. X requests the court to instruct the jury that a letter correctly addressed and properly mailed is presumed to have been received in the ordinary course of mail. What result?

Chapter XIII

OPINION, EXPERTISE AND EXPERTS; SCIENTIFIC AND DEMONSTRATIVE EVIDENCE

PART A.   OPINION, EXPERTISE AND EXPERTS

MAGUIRE, EVIDENCE: COMMON SENSE AND COMMON LAW

23–27 (1947).*

OPINION

Another kind of evidence toward which courts manifest hostility is described as opinion. Indications are not lacking that wiser members of bench and bar have come to consider this hostility rather overdone in the past. But, even when shrunk to diminished proportions by the best of common sense, the opinion rule is important enough to merit description as our second working tool.

In a way, all human assertions are opinions. It may have seemed pedantic to write, a few pages back, the phrase "manifestations of people's belief about * * * matters of fact" instead of merely saying "statements", but the wording was advisedly chosen. Our whole conscious life is a process of forming working beliefs or opinions from the evidence of our senses, few of them exactly accurate, most of them near enough correct for practical use, some of them seriously erroneous. Every assertion involves the expression of one or more of these opinions. A rule of evidence which called for the exclusion of opinion in this broad sense would therefore make trials quite impossible.

There certainly *is*, though, an exclusionary opinion rule. We can get a fair idea of its general scope by splitting opinions two different ways—first, into the categories of impulsive and deliberate opinions; second, into the categories of commonplace and expert opinions. When Professor Gray said in his teaching notes: "A witness may give his opinion when it is of a kind which a normal man forms justly and correctly but on reasoning which is unconscious or difficult of analysis," he was using both these kinds of classification at once. The complement of his statement, phrased in broad terms without any attempt at meticulous exactitude, would be: "A non-expert witness may not give an opinion as to matters calling for expertness, nor may any witness give a deliberate opinion as to commonplace matters which can be analyzed or broken down into rudimental factors." While we shall have to say something more about expert testimony to round out the topic, this latter complementary statement contains the meat of the exclusionary opinion doctrine.

One great trouble with this doctrine is obviously difficulty in determining when its prohibition does, and when it does not, apply. But before taking up practical application and consequences, let us try to phrase the underlying concepts. It is, of course, plain good sense to refuse to let a non-expert purport to give evidence about matters he does not understand. He is more likely to mislead than to afford sound guidance. The trier of fact is equally capable of forming his own conclusions. By expanding this last statement we shall get a phrasing of the practice under which courts have tended to exclude testimony consciously cast in terms of opinion and referring to commonplace matters, whenever they believe this testimony can be broken down into its rudiments—that is, normally, into statements of perception from which the relevant opinion or conclusion is to be derived. It is fundamental to our method of litigating factual issues that the trier of fact, whether judge or juror, shall so far as his capacities and the nature of the issues permit draw for himself all the conclusions which build themselves into his determination. Witnesses are to state their perceptions of fact, the triers to appraise credibility, make findings of fundamental fact, and draw the inferences necessary to decision.

It scarcely needs illustration to show that restriction of layman's opinion testimony to the limits indicated by Gray can be the cause of endless difficulty. Indeed, this possibility has been painfully realized in practice. Great play has been made of distinction between "opinion" and "shorthand rendition of fact". Much dispute has arisen as to what matters are, and what are not, "difficult of analysis". In tort cases where plaintiffs have been hurt by falling down stairs, off platforms, into areas, along theatre aisles, and so forth, there is constant bickering as to whether witnesses may characterize the place or structure or condition as dangerous, or must confine themselves to attempted recital of its physical characteristics. So foreign to ordinary human communication has the latter method of expression proved in many of these trials as almost to tongue-tie the witnesses.

Some judges refuse to worry much about this difficulty of thought and statement. They have an easy practical solution based on the belief that a little superfluous opinion evidence in matters of this kind is not likely to do any great harm. What really counts is full presentation to the jury or judge of the evidence about rudimental facts, with free rein to draw the correct conclusions. If perchance some needless and maybe unserviceable expressions of opinion are mixed in by the fact witnesses, nothing worse than slight loss of time has been suffered; even in these terms, the lost minutes will probably be fewer than those resulting from frequent wrangles over admissibility. Rule 401 of the Model Code of Evidence is deliberately very liberal in this respect.

The emphasis just thrown upon the rudimental facts suggests an interesting parallel between opinion evidence and hearsay. Often and often a bare opinion, without exposition of its premises, and a bare hearsay assertion, without exposition of the declarant's power, opportunity, and inclination to perceive, remember, and narrate truly, are equally and for the same reason worthless as items of proof. The old Bible metaphor of the house built upon sand cannot safely be put out of mind until sound, solid rock foundation is shown. Indeed, the present author has asserted, and not altogether jocosely, that the hearsay rule is nothing more than a specialized manifestation of the opinion rule. Hearsay About Hearsay, 8 Univ.Chi.L.Rev. 621 (1941). The reasoning ventured is that hearsay is customarily offered without any adequate effort to demonstrate its value by evidence as to the reliability of the declarant; that an attempt to supply this defect by testimony of non-expert witnesses concerning his reliability would fail because on such an issue such witnesses are not deemed capable of giving effective evidence; but that an attempt to supply the defect by the testimony of a witness who could qualify as an expert on human credibility in general, and had adequate personal knowledge of the very declarant, might raise a meritorious contention.

COMMONWEALTH v. HOLDEN

Supreme Court of Pennsylvania, 1957.
390 Pa. 221, 134 A.2d 868.

[Prosecution for first degree murder. The court affirmed the judgment of conviction, holding the evidence sufficient. The court gave no attention to the point discussed in the following dissenting opinion—Ed.]

MUSMANNO, Justice (dissenting).   The Majority Opinion fails to discuss a very important matter raised by the defendant Charles Holden in his appeal to this Court for a new trial.

On December 31, 1955, between 5:15 and 6:40 a.m., Cora Smith was killed in her home as the result of being struck over the head. The defendant, Charles Holden, was accused, tried, and convicted of her murder. He maintained in his defense that he was innocent since he was not in the victim's home at the time of the brutal attack.

At the time of Holden's arrest, he was taken by the police to the home of a Ralph Jones who had been with Holden for several hours prior to the killing. In Holden's presence, Jones was questioned by the police. The matter of this questioning became a subject for inquiry at the later trial. The assistant district attorney representing the Commonwealth asked Jones if, at the time he was being quizzed by the police in Holden's presence, Holden did anything that was unusual. Jones replied:

"Well, during the period of time that the detectives were questioning me in his presence, I believe one of them noticed him to sort of wink or something."

The assistant district attorney then asked Jones what Holden meant, and Jones replied:

"I didn't rightfully know whether it was a wink or something that was in his eye."

The prosecuting attorney's question was a flagrant violation of the rules of evidence and should not have been permitted. What Jones may have thought that Holden meant by the wink, if it was a wink, was entirely speculative. The prosecuting attorney might just as well have asked: "What was Holden thinking of at the time?" In fact, the question imported that very type of query because obviously the eye, no matter how eloquent it is supposed to be in the minds of poets, novelists, and dreamers, is still not capable, by a blink, to telegraph complicated messages, unless, of course, the blinker and the blinkee have previously agreed upon a code.

When Jones replied that he did not know whether Holden had actually winked or had been troubled by a foreign substance in his eye, the Commonwealth's attorney asked him about a statement he had made to the police some time following the winking incident. On January 11th, a few days after the blinking affiar, Captain Flynn of the City Detective Bureau asked Jones: "What did you take this wink to be?" and Jones replied:

"I think he was trying to get me to make an alibi for him to cover up some of his actions and I don't know nothing about any of his actions."

Commonwealth's counsel sought to introduce this statement at the trial and defense counsel properly objected, explaining:

"We object to that. Whatever it was, it wasn't made in the presence of the defendant, Charles Holden."

The objection was overruled and the jury was thus informed that the defendant endeavored to have Jones frame an alibi for him. On what evidence was this information based? On a wink.

And what did the wink say? I repeat:

"I think he was trying to get me to make an alibi for him to cover up some of his actions and I don't know nothing about any of his actions."

It will be noted that the stupendous and compendious wink not only solicited the fabrication of a spurious alibi but specified that it was "to cover up some of his actions." One movement of the eyelid conveyed a message of 21 words. Not even the most abbreviated Morse code could say so much with such little expenditure of muscular and mechanical power.

Although the statement of the interpretation of the wink is preposterous on its face, I can see how it could be made to seem very informative and convincing to the jury, since it was given to the jury with the Court's approval. If Holden had actually spoken to Jones the words which Jones related in his interpretation of the wink, no more effective admission of guilty knowledge could be imagined. Jones and Holden had been together prior to the killing. Holden tells Jones to make up an alibi so that Jones can extend their companionship of the evening to an hour including and beyond the time of the killing. And then Jones not only refuses to do what Holden asks him to do, but relates the criminal attempt on the part of Holden to suborn perjury.

But the fact of the matter is that Holden did not ask Jones to fabricate an alibi. He did not ask him to "cover up some of his actions." All that Holden did was to wink. No one knows whether he was trying to convey a message, whether he was attempting to shut out a strong ray of light, or whether a bit of dust troubled him at the moment. The Court, however, allowed the jury to believe that the wink was a semaphoric signal to Jones to commit perjury.

Was ever more ridiculous evidence presented in a murder trial? What is to happen to our rules of evidence in criminal trials if they can be breached so glaringly, without reproof or criticism by this Court? Holden was convicted and sentenced to life imprisonment. He might have been sentenced to death. On a wink.

And the Majority does not consider the matter of sufficient importance even to mention it.

If a witness is to be allowed to state what he believes a wink said, why should he not be allowed to interpret a cough? Or a sneeze? Or a grunt? Or a hiccough? Why should he indeed not be empowered to testify as to what is passing through an accused's brain? Why not permit mind readers to read a defendant's mind, and thus eliminate the jury system completely because who knows better than the defendant himself whether or not he committed the crime of which he stands accused?

The refusal of this Court to grant a new trial, with so momentous a violation of the defendant's rights, duly noted and excepted to on the record, would suggest that here the law has not only winked but closed both eyes.

WALTZ, CRIMINAL EVIDENCE

298–319 (1975).*

OPINION, EXPERTISE, AND EXPERTS

A.

The Opinon Rule

Opinion Testimony by a Layman. The law of evidence includes a well-known general rule against testimony by laymen in the form of an *opinion* or *conclusion*. (In lawyer series on television one is forever hearing counsel say, "Object, Your Honor, calls for a conclusion!") Generally speaking, it is true that a layman, called to the stand to give testimony, must restrict himself to describing material facts about which he has firsthand knowledge. He cannot ordinarily unburden himself of opinions and conclusions which he has drawn from his firsthand observations. This is true for one of two reasons: either the lay witness is technically unqualified, for lack of some essential skill, training, or experience, to draw such a conclusion; or the jurors themselves are fully capable of drawing the right conclusion from the recited facts—and if they are, the witness's opinion testimony would invade the rightful province of the jury.

Not all jurisdictions enforce the opinion rule with equal force. Judges will be quick to exclude opinions on ultimate issues—for example, "In my opinion the defendant is guilty of this crime"—but may be slower to react to conclusory statements that do not go to the very heart of the case.

Furthermore, there are numerous realistic exceptions to the rule against opinion testimony. Most of them involve lay "shorthand" testimony where it is next to impossible to express the matter in any other way.

Examples:

    a. *Matters of taste and smell*—"It smelled like gunpowder."

    b. *Another's emotions*—"He seemed nervous."

    c. *Vehicular speed*—"He was going very, very fast."

    d. *Voice identification*—"I've known Clyde Bushmat for fifteen years and I'd recognize his voice anywhere. It was Bushmat's voice on the telephone."

    e. *A witness's own intent, where relevant*—"I was planning on crossing the street."

    f. *Genuineness of another's handwriting*—"That's my husband's signature."

    g. *Another's irrational conduct*—"He was acting like a crazy man."

h.   *Intoxication*—"The man was drunk."

Reasoning Behind the Rule Against Lay Opinion Testimony.   A fundamental aspect of the reasoning underlying the opinion rule is that factual conclusions that are within the grasp or comprehension of the average layman should be left to the jury, which supposedly is made up of just such average laymen. If a juror can just as well arrive at his own conclusions by adding together the factual components provided by the witnesses, there is no need for the witnesses to inject their own conclusions.

Example a.:

In State v. Thorp, 72 N.C. 186 (1875), the defendant was charged with drowning her son Robert. The prosecution offered a witness who had known Robert. He testified that he was too far away from the defendant and the child she was holding to be certain that the child was Robert. He did testify, however, that it was "his best impression" that the child was Robert. The defendant's conviction was overturned on appeal because the witness had given prohibited opinion testimony.

Example b.:

In Commonwealth v. Holden, 134 A.2d 868 (1957), the accused was convicted of murder. While he was in custody he gave the police an alibi to the effect that he had been with one Ralph Jones at the crucial time. Jones, questioned by the police, denied this. During the questioning of Jones, the accused, who was present, had winked at him. At trial Jones testified about the wink and stated that he interpreted it as a signal to him to supply the defendant with an alibi. Although the accused's conviction was affirmed without consideration of the opinion rule problem in any detail, one justice of the Pennsylvania Supreme Court noted that Jones's testimony reflected an opinion.

Example c.:

In United States v. Schneiderman, 106 F.Supp. 892 (S.D.Cal.1952), the defendants were charged with Smith Act violations. The Government offered the testimony of former members of the Communist party that the defendants, by their actions, appeared to be members of the party. The trial court held that this was permissible since there was no other way the witnesses could convey to the jury what they had observed. (This was a questionable ruling, made during the era of Senator Joseph R. McCarthy.)

The Federal Approach.   Rule 701 of the Federal Rules of Evidence takes a practical approach: "If the witness is not testifying as an expert, his testimony in the form of opinions or inferences is limited to those opinions or inferences which are (a) rationally based on the perception of the witness and (b) helpful to a clear understanding of his testimony or the determination of a fact in issue."

B.

Experts and Expertise

An Exception to the Opinion Rule.   Opinion testimony by expert witnesses comes in through an important exception to the general rule against opinion testimony.

The Definition of "Expert." There are those who have the mistaken notion that the title of "expert" can properly be bestowed only on a few members of professional groups who have a cluster of postgraduate degrees after their names. Some people think that only a scientist of one sort or another and perhaps a few engineers can rightly be called experts. But the term "expert," at least in the law and in common sense, is far broader in meaning than this. Anyone who has ever tried to repair his own automobile or television set knows that some people are experts at these kinds of work and some are not. The proficient garage mechanic is an expert in his field even though a Ph.D. may be the last thing he ever hoped to acquire; the trained and experienced television repairman is just as surely an expert as the most renowned neurosurgeon. The same sort of thing can be said of the brick mason, the sheet metal worker, the plumber, the carpenter, and the electrician, just to name a few more genuine experts.

Getting closer to the immediate point, the label "expert" applies to the firearms identification technician and those who are proficient at fingerprint or handwriting comparison. And it applies to the policeman who knows how to use, interpret, and explain special equipment, such as radar vehicular speed measuring devices and equipment for measuring blood-alcohol ratios. Thus a basic law dictionary, Black's, sweepingly defines experts as "men of science educated in the art, or persons possessing special or peculiar knowledge *acquired from practical experience*" (italics added).

The Four Basic Conditions of Expert Testimony. An expert witness, such as a pathologist or ballistics technician, can testify to an opinion, inference, or conclusion if four basic conditions are met:

(1) The opinions, inferences, or conclusions depend on special knowledge, skill, or training not within the ordinary experience of lay jurors;

(2) The witness must be shown to be qualified as a true expert in the particular field of expertise;

(3) The witness must testify to a reasonable degree of certainty (probability) regarding his opinion, inference, or conclusion; and

(4) Although this fourth condition is currently in the process of modification, at least in times past it has generally been true that an expert witness must first describe the data (facts) on which his opinion, inference, or conclusion is based or, in the alternative, he must testify in response to a hypothetical question that sets forth the underlying data.

Rationale Behind the Expert Witness Exception to the Rule Against Opinion Testimony. The reasoning behind letting expert witnesses give testimony in the form of opinions or conclusions is that experts have special training, knowledge, and skill in drawing conclusions from certain sorts of data that lay jurors do not have. Expert witnesses and their opinions are permissible only in areas in which lay jurors cannot draw conclusions unassisted.

* * *

Qualifying the Witness as an Expert. From what has been said thus far it follows that the exception for expert testimony is available only when the witness is shown to be a true expert in the field that is involved. Before a witness can testify to an expert opinion, examining counsel must lay the necessary foundation by bringing out the witness's training, experience, and special skills. Trial lawyers call this process "qualifying the witness."

At the conclusion of the direct questions aimed at qualifying the witness as an expert, and before examining counsel gets into the meat of the witness's testimony, opposing counsel is entitled to interrupt and engage in cross-examination as to the witness's expertise. This examination will be limited strictly to probing the witness's credentials as an expert.

Example a.:

BY THE PROSECUTING ATTORNEY: Give your full name if you would, please.

A.　Fred Stitz.

Q.　Where do you live, Mr. Stitz?

A.　In Chicago, Illinois. 373 West Pavon Street.

Q.　What is your occupation or profession?

A.　I'm an examiner of questioned documents.

Q.　What does your work consist of?

A.　I examine disputed documents and make reports as to their genuineness. I examine typewriting and matters of disputed interlineations, erasures, and deal with matters of papers, pens, and inks.

Q.　How long have you had this profession?

A.　I have been doing this work since 1940.

Q.　Do you devote all of your time to this work?

A.　Yes, I do.

Q.　Have you ever testified before in a court regarding questioned documents?

A.　I have testified in forty-two of the states and in Canada.

Q.　Have you had any special study to prepare yourself to be an examiner of questioned documents?

A.　Oh, yes. I have read all of the texts on the subject of questioned documents and on the related subjects that I mentioned. I have studied microscopy, inks and their manufacture, paper and paper manufacturing, and photography. I have all the necessary equipment. I have an office and a laboratory for my work and I exchange ideas constantly with other experts in this field.

Q.　Where is your office and lab?

A.　662 North Pennell Street, Chicago.

Q.　You are able, I take it, to compare handwriting of known origin with handwriting of unknown origin and form a conclusion or opinion as to whether they were written by the same person?

A.　That's right.

Q.　Then I will show you what has been marked Prosecution Exhibit Number 3 for Identification.

BY DEFENSE COUNSEL:　Just a moment, if you please. May I ask this witness a few questions, Your Honor?

THE COURT:　With respect to his qualifications?

BY DEFENSE COUNSEL:　Yes.

THE COURT:　You may proceed.

BY DEFENSE COUNSEL:　Mr. Stitz, have you attended any special schools that teach one how to become a handwriting expert?

A.　No, I don't think there are any.

Q.　So you have no special degrees or certificates that reflect special study in a college or university?

A.　No, I do not.

Q.　Your supposed expertise is simply based on your own experience in examining documents, is that it?

A.　That's right, and my reading and so on.

BY DEFENSE COUNSEL:　Well, we have no strong objection to this witness testifying, Your Honor.

THE COURT:　If that is supposed to be some kind of objection, counsel, it is overruled.

Example b.:

Q.　What is your name, sir?

A.　John V. DeMarco.

Q.　Where do you live?

A.　At the Belmont Hotel here in the city.

Q.　What is your occupation or profession, sir?

A.　I am a physician and toxicologist.

Q.　Of what medical school are you a graduate, Doctor?

A.　The Northwestern University Medical School in Chicago.

Q.　When did you graduate?

A.　In 1930.

Q.　What was your undergraduate school?

A.　The University of Michigan.

Q.　What was your major field of study at Michigan?

A.　Chemistry.

Q.　After your graduation from medical school, what did you do?

A.　I was with the Health Department in Chicago for three years and then in 1933 I became the toxicologist for the Coroner's Office in Chicago.

Q.　Do you hold that position today?

A.　Yes, I have held it continuously since 1933, with time off for military service during World War II.

Q.　What have your duties been as a toxicologist?

A.　My duties involve the examination of organs for the presence of poisons and research concerning poisons. I have conducted many post mortems.

Q.   About how many since 1933?

A.   Probably around ten thousand. And I examined the organs of many people on whom I did not do a post mortem.

Q.   Do you hold any teaching positions at the present time?

A.   Yes, I am Professor of Toxicology at Rush Medical College in Chicago.

Q.   How long have you had this professorship, Doctor DeMarco?

A.   Since 1947.

Q.   Have you ever written anything on the subject of toxicology?

A.   Yes, I've written a number of articles on poisons and their detection. I have written chapters that were included in texts on toxicology, and I have delivered papers at professional seminars.

Q.   Would you describe toxicology for us, Doctor?

A.   It is the science that deals with toxic substances, poisons, their origin, and their detection by chemical or other means.

Q.   When you speak of a poison, what precisely do you mean?

THE COURT: Just a moment, counsel. Are you now going to get into this witness's substantive testimony?

BY EXAMINING COUNSEL: That was my intention, Your Honor.

THE COURT: Let me inquire of opposing counsel whether he desires at this point to examine further into the witness's qualifications.

BY OPPOSING COUNSEL: We reserve the right to cross-examine Doctor DeMarco on the substance of his testimony, Your Honor, but we do not dispute his qualifications as an expert in the field of toxicology.

THE COURT: Very well. You may proceed, counsel.

BY EXAMINING COUNSEL: What is it that you mean when you talk of a poison, Doctor?

A.   A poison is a substance which, when taken into the system, is capable of seriously affecting health adversely or of causing death, and that's its principal action.

Stipulating to the Witness's Expertise.   Sometimes counsel, realizing that the opposing side's witness has impressive credentials that will probably awe the jurors, will try to prevent the jury from hearing them described. Counsel does this by offering to stipulate (agree) that the witness is qualified to testify as an expert, thereby magnanimously saving opposing counsel from having to elicit the witness's full catalogue of credentials through the questioning process. This gambit is not usually successful. Opposing counsel is not obligated to accept an offered stipulation unless it gives him everything that he would be entitled to prove with evidence. And counsel is entitled to prove his expert witness's qualifications in some detail; a mere stipulation that he is qualified to testify does not give the side offering him anything to which it is entitled. Experienced counsel will know that it is important to show the details of his expert's training and experience in any case in which there is to be a battle of experts. This is so because the jurors must decide what weight to attach to the testimony of each side's experts. They can rationally apportion evidentiary weight only if they are in a position to compare the witnesses' relative qualifications.

Example:

Q. Doctor, will you give the jury your full name?

A. Jeffrey Eddy.

Q. Where do you reside?

A. 820 West Addison Street, Chicago, Illinois.

Q. What is your profession?

A. Physician and surgeon.

Q. Are you duly licensed to practice as a physician and surgeon in Illinois?

A. Yes, I am.

Q. What specialty, if any, have you made in your medical practice?

A. I specialize in neurosurgery.

Q. We'll come back to that, Doctor Eddy. How long have you practiced medicine?

A. Thirteen years this coming April.

Q. Of what medical school are you a graduate?

A. Northwestern University Medical School in Chicago.

Q. Have you done any postgraduate work?

BY OPPOSING COUNSEL: Pardon me just a moment. We would be willing to stipulate that Doctor Eddy is a qualified neurosurgeon and can testify here.

BY EXAMINING COUNSEL: We would rather make our proof on this, Your Honor. The jurors are entitled to hear his training and his experience in medicine and neurosurgery. They have to decide what weight to give his testimony, possibly in comparison with the testimony of an expert called by the other side, and they can't very well make that decision without hearing his qualifications.

THE COURT: It might speed things up a little if you accepted the stipulation, counsel, but I can't force you to do so. You may proceed to establish the witness's qualifications. Just don't get into the most minute details.

BY EXAMINING COUNSEL: Very well, Your Honor. We'll limit ourselves to the most important things. Doctor Eddy, have you had some postgraduate training?

BY OPPOSING COUNSEL: In view of our offer to stipulate, we object to counsel's going into this, Your Honor.

THE COURT: Overruled.

Sources of the Expert Witness's Data. Three sources of information are open to the expert witness in the formation of his opinions.

(1) The expert witness can express an opinion or conclusion based on facts personally observed by him, as occurs in the case of a medical ex-

aminer who renders a conclusion concerning cause of death on the basis of data clinically observed. (Such an expert can take into account facts communicated to him by another expert. For example, the medical examiner can base his opinion in part on the report of a X-ray technician. If the data upon which the expert bases his opinion or inference are of a type reasonable relied on by experts in the field when forming opinions or inferences on the subject in question, the data need not themselves be independently admissible in evidence.)

(2)   An expert witness who has been present in the courtroom can base an opinion on the evidence adduced if that evidence is not in conflict. (An expert will not be permitted to weigh conflicting evidence since, unbeknownst to anyone, he might accord it a weight different from that given it by the jurors.)

(3)   An expert witness can base an opinion on data conveyed to him by means of a hypothetical question that is drawn from the evidence introduced during the trial.

Efforts to Eliminate the Hypothetical Question. Obviously, the hypothetical question is often awkward and hypertechnical. It is fraught with possibilities of reversible error. Hypothetical questions can be extremely time-consuming and they are frequently confusing to jurors. More often than not they are used by counsel to make an extra summation in the middle of the case. Although counsel may think there is some advantage in getting this opportunity to summarize the evidence far in advance of closing arguments, it is more likely that he is putting the jurors to sleep. Still, there are lawyers who believe that the hypothetical question represents the best method yet devised for extracting helpful opinions from an expert witness who is not directly familiar with the facts of the case.

Efforts are occasionally made to do away with the necessity for using hypothetical questions. For example, Rule 705 of the Proposed Federal Rules of Evidence would provide that an expert can testify in terms of opinion "without prior disclosure of the underlying facts or data." The major change intended to be accomplished by this language is the elimination of the necessity for the hypothetical question in eliciting expert testimony. Under Rule 705 examining counsel does not have to disclose underlying facts to his expert witness by means of a hypothetical question posed to him in open court as a preliminary to his opinion. The necessary data can be conveyed to the expert prior to his direct examination and it need not be disclosed during that examination. Of course, opposing counsel can cross-examine the expert about the data on which his opinion testimony is based.

* * *

Court-Appointed Experts. Ever since 1946 there has been a comprehensive procedure for court-appointed experts in Rule 28 of the Federal Rules of Criminal Procedure and many states have similar procedures. Under Rule 28 a trial judge can order the accused or the Government, or both, to show cause why expert witnesses should not be appointed and can request the parties to submit the names of possible witnesses. The judge can either appoint experts agreed upon by the parties or he can appoint experts of his own selection. A court-appointed expert is informed of his duties by the judge, either in writing or at a conference at which the parties have an opportunity to take part. A court-appointed expert will inform the parties of his findings and can thereafter be called to the stand by the trial judge or any party to give testimony. Court-appointed experts are subject to full cross-examination by all parties.

Experts appointed by the trial court are most commonly encountered in cases in which it is suggested either that the accused was legally insane at the time of the offense charged or that the accused is presently incompetent to stand trial because of his inability to comprehend the proceedings and cooperate with his defense counsel. In such situations the trial court may appoint one or more psychiatrists to examine the accused and report.

The use of court-appointed experts occasionally avoids the frustrating phenomenon known as the battle of experts. Both sides in criminal and civil cases alike will shop for experts who are receptive to the position being taken by the side retaining them. Furthermore, some experts are in fact venal; one often hears remarks about "the best expert witness money can buy." And many reputable experts are unwilling to involve themselves in litigation. So, although the suggestion is occasionally made that court-appointed experts take on an aura of infallibility which they may not deserve, the trend is increasingly to provide for their use. The very availability of this appointment procedure reduces the need for resorting to it. This is because the mere possibility that the trial judge *might* appoint an objective, disinterested expert in a given case exerts a sobering influence on a party's expert and on the lawyer who is making use of his services.

Impeachment of Expert Witnesses. Aside from attacking his qualifications and disinterestedness or the thoroughness and competence of his investigation, there are two commonly encountered methods of attacking or impeaching an expert witness's opinion. They involve (1) contradictory material in authoritative publications in the field and (2) alteration of the facts of a hypothetical question put to the witness during his direct examination.

1. An expert witness can be confronted, on cross-examination, with contradictory material from authoritative published works in the pertinent field of expertise. In most jurisdictions it is not essential that the witness have relied on the particular treatise or other items of literature in forming the conclusions given in his direct examination, although this was once a common requirement and can still be found in § 721(b) of the California Evidence Code.

Example:

BY THE PROSECUTING ATTORNEY: Dr. Faust, you insisted in your direct testimony earlier this afternoon that a person who is a manic depressive may have a propensity for committing murder or assault to murder, didn't you?

A. Well, "insist" is a pretty strong word but that's what I said.

Q. And you believe your statement to be correct? You think it is medically and psychiatrically sound?

A. Certainly I do.

Q. Dr. Faust, at any given time a manic depressive can be in either the manic or exhilarated phase or the depressive, the subdued or depressed phase of the psychosis, can he not?

A.   That's true.

Q.   Would your statement about a propensity to commit violent acts be as true of a person in the depressive state as it would be of a person who was in a manic state?

A.   I think so, yes.

Q.   Do other psychiatrists agree with your position in this respect?

A.   I don't know specifically but I would presume so. My position is the correct one.

Q.   I see. Do you know Dr. Carl S. Milcher's work entitled *The Murderer's Mind?*

A.   I know of it. Everyone does.

Q.   Is Dr. Milcher a recognized authority on the psychotic condition of persons who have committed murder?

A.   I would say so. He is a distinguished psychiatrist.

Q.   And has done a great deal of work in this area?

A.   Yes.

Q.   Did you in any way rely on Dr. Milcher's work in forming your opinions regarding the accused in this case? [This question, although not required in a number of jurisdictions, is usually asked anyway.]

A.   I may have unconsciously. His work is a part of the fund of knowledge that I carry around in my head.

Q.   Dr. Faust, I hand you a copy of Dr. Milcher's book, *The Murderer's Mind,* published in 1973, which I have opened to page 492. On that page Dr. Milcher is discussing the manic depressive state, is he not? Take your time and look at it, Dr. Faust, and then you can answer.

A.   Yes, he describes the state here.

Q.   He mentions there that a person in the manic phase may have a propensity for murder or assault to murder, doesn't he?

A.   Yes, he does.

Q.   And Dr. Milcher is a widely recognized expert, is he not?

A.   I said so.

Q.   Yes, you did. Now look at the last full sentence on page 492 of Dr. Milcher's book. I want you to read that sentence to the court and jury. You can read it over to yourself first, if you want to, but then read it to the members of the jury, loud and clear.

A.   [Reading.] "The depressive aspect of the illness manifests itself more commonly in suicide."

BY THE PROSECUTING ATTORNEY: Thank you, sir. That will be all.

2. Examining counsel will frequently omit certain facts from a hypothetical question put to his expert witness on direct examination. It is entirely permissible for opposing counsel to inquire whether consideration of the omitted facts would have an impact on the witness's opinion.

Example:

BY THE PROSECUTING ATTORNEY: Doctor Faust, if you were requested to assume these additional facts, which were not mentioned by defense counsel in his hypothetical question to you, namely [the omitted facts are recounted], would your opinion remain the same?

A.   No, it wouldn't.

Q.   What would your opinion be if we include those facts, Doctor?

A.   [The witness gives his revised opinion.]

Sometimes facts included in a hypothetical question are later disproved by the evidence. In this situation the expert witness will be asked on cross-examination whether his conclusion would remain the same if those facts were eliminated from the hypothetical question.

Example:

BY THE PROSECUTING ATTORNEY: Doctor Faust, would your response to the hypothetical question have been different if in putting the question to you defense counsel had left out of consideration the statement that the blood found under the left shoulder was clotted?

A.   My answer would have been different, yes.

* * *

WALTZ & INBAU, MEDICAL JURISPRUDENCE

54–56 (1971).*
[Footnotes omitted.]

THE REQUIREMENT OF EXPERT TESTIMONY

The plaintiff in a medical malpractice action is ordinarily required to produce, in support of his claim, the testimony of qualified medical experts. This is true, as we have earlier said, because the technical aspects of his claim will ordinarily be far beyond the competence of the lay jurors whose duty it is to assess the defendant doctor's conduct. The plaintiff, himself a layman in most instances, is not free simply to enter the courtroom, announce under oath that the defendant surgeon amputated his leg instead of saving it, and then request the jury to find the surgeon negligent.

The jurors, possessing no special expertise in the relevant field, are incapable of judging whether the facts described by the plaintiff, even assuming an accurate narration by him, add up to negligent conduct. And the plaintiff himself is incompetent to supply guidance; he, too, lacks the training and experience that would qualify him to characterize the defendant's conduct. Unless the facts in our hypothetical amputation case spoke for themselves and unmistakably pointed to malpractice (the defendant, although operating in a fully equipped hospital, unaccountably removed plaintiff's leg with a dull ax), the judge would direct a verdict in defendant's favor immediately after the plaintiff's presentation of evidence. The judge would say that there had been a failure of proof on the issue of negligence, as to which the plaintiff had the burden of proof. Since the mere filing of a lawsuit, unsupported at trial by any probative evidence, does not entitle one to the payment of damages, the plaintiff here must lose. The plaintiff could hope to prevail only if he came to court backed by one or more qualified expert witnesses.

There is nothing unique about the requirement of expert testimony in medical malpractice cases. All sorts of lawsuits involve technical issues that exceed the competence of lay witnesses and lay jurors. A successful criminal prosecution may depend on the testimony of a firearms identification expert, a fingerprint expert, a handwriting expert, a pathologist, and a couple of psychiatrists. Many types of civil suits other than malpractice cases may call forth an array of essential experts: mechanical or aeronautical engineers and metallurgists in a case involving an airplane that allegedly crashed as a consequence of metal fatigue in the wing structure; pathologists in a product liability case against a food processor (was the corn borer that slipped into defendant's canned corn truly toxic?); handwriting experts in a will contest; accountants, entomologists, civil engineers —the catalog of potentially vital expert witnesses in civil cases goes on and on. It is so lengthy a list because lawsuits so often involve esoteric issues which a jury, unaided, could not possibly resolve on any basis other than guesswork. To the extent that it can, the Anglo-American system of justice prohibits verdicts having baseless speculation as their only support. The requirement of expert testimony on technical issues is one designed to avoid guesswork verdicts.

In short, lay jurors have a reasonable basis in their own life experience for deciding that it is negligent—that it poses an unreasonable risk of harm to others—to drive an automobile down the wrong side of the highway at ninety miles an hour; on the other hand, their life experience gives them no basis for assessing, for example, a delicate and difficult surgical procedure.

In our hypothetical malpractice case involving the defendant's amputation of plaintiff's leg, then, the plaintiff would be required to produce qualified medical experts who were prepared (1) to explain the accepted medical procedures and considerations applicable to plaintiff's condition and (2) to express an opinion, based on the proved facts, that the defendant surgeon had unjustifiably failed to follow those procedures or had followed them incompetently. In a less obvious case the plaintiff's experts would have to provide an answer to a third question—that is, whether the defendant's improper conduct probably was the cause of the plaintiff's injury. Indeed, in a less clear case than one involving an amputation it might even be essential that medical experts establish that the plaintiff had in fact suffered injury.

To recapitulate in sequence, in a typical medical malpractice lawsuit the plaintiff must put qualified medical experts on the witness stand to testify (1) that plaintiff suffered an injury that produced the disability and other ill effects claimed by him; (2) that the cause of this injury, or at least a significant contributing cause of it, was the professional services rendered by the defendant doctor; (3) that the standard methods, procedures, and treatments in cases such as plaintiff's were such-and-so; and (4) that defendant's professional conduct toward plaintiff fell below or otherwise unjustifiably departed from the described standard. In steps 1 and 2 the plaintiff's experts are used to establish damage and the causal connection with that damage of defendant's conduct. These two steps are common to every type of personal injury action, whether it be an automobile collision case or a medical malpractice case. Steps 3 and 4 are peculiar to professional negligence cases for they impart content and meaning to the generalized standard of care uniquely applicable to such cases.

KAPLAN & WALTZ, THE TRIAL OF JACK RUBY

194–201 (1965).*

* * *

Belli now inquired whether Dr. Schafer had an opinion whether Ruby "does or does not have organic brain damage." The witness replied that he did have an opinion. "I came to the conclusion," said Schafer, "that he did have organic brain damage, and that the most likely specific nature of it was psychomotor epilepsy."

The psychologist, in conformity with his usual practice, had taken no case history from Ruby when he visited him in late December. Dr. Schafer preferred to foreclose any risk that such subjective data might lead him to form preconceptions that would impede "clear perception of the test results themselves." He pointed out that history-taking was part of the psychiatrist's function. At this juncture Henry Wade injected a remark that was at odds with a bizarre position that the prosecution was to adopt minutes later. Commented Wade, "This is the psychologist and he's asking what the psychiatrist does."

Belli changed the subject, asking how many tests the witness had administered to the defendant. Schafer had given ten different psychological tests to Ruby, starting with an intelligence test and the Rorschach ink-blot test. Discussing the intelligence test—the Wechsler Adult Intelligence Scale, better known as the IQ test—Schafer revealed that a brain-damaged person might possess "an adequate or even somewhat more than adequate IQ" but that it would be unusual to find in such a person an extremely high intelligence level. Ruby had an IQ of 109, a score which, the witness continued, "exceeds 73 percent of American men of his age." Belli then asked Schafer to describe the various other tests he had employed. The witness was about to explain the significance of the ink-blot test when Bill Alexander interrupted with an objection.

MR. ALEXANDER: May it please the Court, at this time we want to object to all this. He has not asked the witness if he has an opinion as to soundness or unsoundness of the defendant's mind. If he does not have an opinion, then this is needless. If he does have an opinion, then we should know what that opinion is and what the basis is that he has based it on.

Melvin Belli, failing to grasp the import of the objection, responded that a number of experts would be called by the defense. "And we can only have one at a time." Now Jim Bowie joined in the prosecution refrain.

MR. BOWIE: The question before the Court, your Honor, is the sanity or insanity and the degree, under the charge of the Court as of November 24, 1963. If he has no opinion about that, then we haven't laid a proper predicate for this testimony.

Belli was becoming irritated at the prosecution's repeated interruptions of his examination. "Judge, may I conduct this my own way?" he snapped. "We're going to come to that and, I assure the Court, very thoroughly we'll come to that, even to the *M'Naughten* rule." Judge Joe B. Brown leaned forward and asked, humorlessly, "Counsel, how far off is it?"

Belli replied that it would take him about an hour to lay the groundwork with the witness then on the stand and Judge Brown said, "The Court has no objection to going into what he found." The skirmish seemingly won, Belli returned to Dr. Schafer, who testified that Ruby's ink-blot test findings "were * * * a very important part of the final conclusions I came to." They disclosed, he said, "signs of confusion, fluidity of thinking, tendencies toward incoherence and misuse of words, breakdown of sentence structure—a kind of impairment which is referred to as concreteness of thinking, which has been commonly described as part of the organic brain damage syndrome." The Rorschach, Dr. Schafer continued, had also picked up indications of emotionality, instability, impulsiveness, irrational thinking and a "readiness toward reactions of anger of an explosive nature."

After a brief recess, Ruby's defense counsel asked the witness to describe the various known types of epilepsy. Before Dr. Schafer could answer, however, the prosecution returned to its earlier theme.

MR. ALEXANDER: Your Honor, counsel has not asked the question as to whether or not this man has an opinion as to whether the defendant knew the difference between right and wrong, and understood the nature and consequences of his acts. For all we know, he may not have an opinion, or he may have an opinion that he is sane.

Again Henry Wade's first assistant, Jim Bowie, seconded the objection. "And we think," he said, "we should first find out if he has an opinion, and then these things might be admissible as the basis of his opinion."

Belli was furious at this repetition of an objection which he thought he had previously put permanently to rest. He could not be certain whether the prosecution was simply seeking to throw him off his stride or whether Alexander and Bowie actually thought that a psychologist had to be asked for an ultimate opinion on the insanity issue. Belli patiently, and patronizingly, responded to this latest interruption.

MR. BELLI: Judge, I tried to make an opening statement here and I could have laid this out very specifically so that each one of these four gentlemen would have had a blueprint of what we were trying to do and if there was anything wrong with it they could have gotten any doctor in the United States to combat it. Now, I've got to put on an X-ray technician, a nurse to test the urine and the protein of spinal fluid and then give this all to the internist or the diagnostician and ask him, "What do you make of all this melange of these various different tests?" Now, today you've got to have a psychologist go through all these tests.   * * *

Bill Alexander was unperturbed. In a bored voice he remarked, "Now, your Honor, I don't believe we need a lecture on what the law is in Texas. We objected to it because he hasn't asked the proper question, and we ask the Court—" The court interrupted the assistant prosecutor and suddenly Melvin Belli discovered that, whatever might be the prosecution's secret evaluation of its objection, Judge Joe B. Brown was impressed.

THE COURT: The Court's going to sustain the objection to it, Mr. Belli. You may ask the witness what his opinion is, and then go into it.

Ruby's attorney was baffled. "Well," he said, "I've asked him his opinion already, Judge, and he stated it to us."

"Ask him the legal question," directed Judge Brown.

"I thought I already had," replied Belli.

But no; when Judge Brown spoke of "the legal question" he meant not just any legally proper question but *the* legal question at issue in the case, the right-wrong *M'Naughten* inquiry. "Let's get down to the meat of the question, Mr. Belli; the legal test of insanity. Let's get on to that."

Melvin Belli insisted that he could only call upon his current witness for testimony concerning the psychological tests Ruby had undergone. Jim Bowie popped up to reiterate the prosecution's objection, asserting that "all of this is irrelevant and immaterial" unless psychologist Schafer were prepared to answer the *M'Naughten* question.

"The Court's going to sustain you in that, Counsel," said Judge Brown.

"Sustain him in what?" asked the perplexed defense attorney.

"Whether or not the man, according to the *M'Naughten* rule, knew right from wrong and if he has an opinion as to his ability to determine the nature and consequences of his act," Judge Brown replied in a tone of voice which is ordinarily reserved for children and the not-quite-bright.

Incomprehensible as it seemed to him, Belli now realized that the defense's medical case was in serious jeopardy even before it had been fairly launched. He gritted his teeth—spellbound spectators could almost hear him counting slowly to ten—and attempted to explain to the judge that a psychologist, in the context of a sanity determination, was in a real sense only a technician whose testing methods produced some but not all of the raw data relied upon diagnostically by the psychiatrists. He could no more ask a psychologist to express an opinion concerning insanity than he could demand that a laboratory technician diagnose a cancer. As the red-faced chief defense attorney put it:

> Judge, this man hasn't even taken a case history from him. You can't ask the nurse who has taken a temperature, or a bowel specimen, whether she thinks a man has smallpox. That comes from someone else. Now, the only way that I can ask Towler or these other doctors what they appreciate as to a man's mental condition at a particular time is to tell them what the psychologist found. I think that if he answered a question like that, that he'd be infringing the medical domain. He is a Ph.D. and a psychologist is in a particular field. Now, I'll go as far as I can with this man but I'm certainly not going to extend him or ask him questions beyond his own field. I say that respectfully, your Honor.

But Judge Brown was unmoved:

> The Court has sustained the State's objection. I do not want to make any comment about it. You may have an exception, sir, to the sustaining of the objection.

Belli tried to plunge forward in defiance of the court's ruling. "I don't want an exception," he shouted. "I want what this man has done laboriously over a hundred hours, your Honor." He asked the court reporter to locate in her notes and reread his last question to the witness—who had listened to the arguments of counsel and the comments of the judge with an increasingly puzzled expression on his face. But again the prosecution objected and now Belli made an offer of proof. The offer of proof is a technique for preserving for appellate review the propriety of a ruling excluding testimony. Counsel reads into the record a description of the testimony his witness would have given had he not been foreclosed by the trial judge's sustaining of an objection to it. Only when the substance of excluded matter is thus preserved can a reviewing court determine whether the witness's testimony should have been allowed. Belli's offer of proof revealed that the defense was still relying on a theory that the accused had been in an epileptic seizure at the time of his shooting of Oswald. "I make an offer of proof," he said "to show that psychomotor epilepsy does give these blackout states."

Judge Brown, quite correctly, interjected, "That's not what you asked." The judge apparently felt that Dr. Schafer was permitted to speak in the abstract about the consequences of various mental aberrations but could not relate his diagnosis of Ruby unless he held an opinion on whether Ruby was within the *M'Naughten* rule. Nor was the judge moved by Melvin Belli's argument that: "If he were dishonest and I were dishonest, we'd pop right out and say that this is the *M'Naughten*-rule case, but I want your Honor to hear what this man has to say."

Now Judge Brown suddenly became aware that the entire argument over whether the jury should be permitted to hear Dr. Schafer's testimony was taking place in the presence of the jury. He halted all discussion while the jury was led from the courtroom. Then he announced, "I'm going to hold him to testimony concerning the law of insanity in Texas."

Belli tried a slightly different tack. He informed the judge that Dr. Schafer's testimony would be connected, at a later time, with the testimony of Drs. Towler and Guttmacher, who "have told me that this man did not know the difference between right and wrong, the nature and consequences of his act, or what he was doing at the time he shot Mr. Oswald." Again Belli attempted to make it clear that, with Dr. Schafer, he was simply building a foundation for later medical and psychiatric witnesses' testimony:

> Now, he has to build a predicate. He's not going to go all the way. I'm not permitted to ask him, under Texas law, his opinion with reference to *M'Naughten*'s rule, because he's not the doctor. I can ask him these questions; what disease did this man have, and that's because of his study of this disease of epilepsy. I can then ask him what is his opinion of the most likely cause of his condition at the time that he shot someone in a moment of great stress, and he can answer that. But I cannot press him beyond that into the field of psychiatry, because if I did, your Honor, the Supreme Court would wonder why they are allowing a psychologist to testify in psychiatry.

Belli's reference to the Supreme Court appeared to have some effect on the prosecution and the judge. Both were trying the case with an eye on the High Court and every mention of it was a veiled threat by the defense. True, in the case Belli put, the Supreme Court would probably never worry in the least about a trial court having permitted a defense psychologist to testify on a matter of psychiatry, since that was a matter of state law and in any event would seem to favor the defense. Belli, of course, was engaged in battling on an entirely different question: Did the defense have a right to place before the jury testimony of a psychologist who did not have an opinion on the ultimate question of the *M'Naughten* rule where that testimony was used by other expert witnesses in reaching their conclusion as to the *M'Naughten* test? The answer, under Texas law as well as under that of about every other state, was clearly Yes.

Belli argued long and eloquently on the point, finally putting it flatly, "I'm not going to ask him that ultimate question about *M'Naughten's* test, because that's not in the domain of the psychologist." At the prosecution table Bill Alexander was the first to see the light. He realized that Belli was quite correct in arguing that Schafer's testimony was admissible on the question of Ruby's sanity even if Schafer himself was not qualified to hold an opinion on that issue. With a deft maneuver Alexander then completely changed the thrust of the prosecution objection, arguing merely that Schafer should first tell the jury that he had no opinion on the legal question of insanity and then (when presumably the jury would be much less interested) go into his tests.

MR. ALEXANDER: May it please the Court, we're not trying to cut them off from any testimony, but we're entitled to have that legal question asked before we get any farther. Whatever his answer is, then the jury can decide—he can tell them what the basis of his answer is. Undoubtedly there are only three ways he can answer the question. The question should be asked and the jury will have a basis for saying whether the basis he gives for his opinion is valid or not. And we think that counsel cannot proceed further until he does ask that legal question, asks the proper question.

Judge Brown, however, missed, the change in the prosecution tactics. He directed Belli to take Dr. Schafer off the stand and put on someone else. "I'm going to exclude his testimony. I sustain the objection to it, Mr. Belli." By now, Melvin Belli was distraught.

MR. BELLI: Your Honor is going to tell this jury in 1964 not to take the testimony of this great man from Yale University, in Dallas?

THE COURT: Yes.

Then light struck elsewhere at the prosecution table and the prosecution shifted its ground again. The original objection was on the ground that the jury should hear no testimony from a witness who could not venture an opinion on the *M'Naughten* right-wrong test. Then the complaint was merely that the testimony could come only after the witness has first admitted that he had no opinion on the question. Now Jim Bowie argued that the evidence of Dr. Schafer's testing was not admissible unless it would be connected to the *M'Naughten* rule by the testimony of this *or another* witness. This was not only the correct rule but precisely what Belli had been arguing all along. By then, however, his attitude had changed. He was convinced that Judge Brown's ruling constituted a bungle of the most prejudicial sort and that the prosecutors now realized this. They would have to rescue the judge somehow and Belli was in no hurry to assist in this task.

MR. BOWIE: But we have no assurance that the doctors who are coming in here to testify to insanity, if they ever used this opinion, or if they ever used any tests whatsoever. They might have seen this good doctor's report, and rejected it entirely, and then we would have nothing on which this testimony could be relevant; neither an opinion or use. Now if they want to assure us that—

MR. BELLI: I'm not assuring anyone of anything at this stage of the game, your Honor. We play it according to Texas law, and we tell nobody nothing. That's what your Honor is ordering us to do.

In fact, of course, Mr. Belli had already given the assurance asked for by the prosecution.

The prosecution was now in full retreat and Belli knew it. Said he, "I believe my brother is very concerned with the error that he has again led your Honor into in striking this testimony."

MR. BOWIE: If they want to assure us—this is premature, but if some doctor has used his test, has used his results in forming an opinion, and it is the basis of some opinion that might later come into this case, that may be somewhat legal—we would have no objections to it. But at this time to put a witness on to testify to all these matters without connecting it up in any way with the insanity issue before the jury, it's irrelevant and immaterial.

We have no objection to going into it if they will assure us that some doctor, sometime, some place, and I hope in this courtroom, will say that he used it as the basis of his opinion. Now, that's our objection to it.

Now Judge Brown saw the point.

THE COURT: Mr. Belli, are you going to connect it up?

MR. BELLI: Certainly. Yes, I have already said I certainly shall, your Honor. This is the basis of all of it.

And the prosecution collapsed. Henry Wade spoke: "Judge, let's let him go on. I think we could have finished by now. So, let's go on and let him testify."

Judge Brown agreed, "All right."

Melvin Belli had the last word: "I think that they see the magnitude of the error."*

PEOPLE v. CLAY

District Court of Appeal, First District, Division 1, California, 1964.
227 Cal.App.2d 87, 38 Cal.Rptr. 431.

SULLIVAN, Justice.

Defendants Ernest L. Clay and Arthur Junior Davis were charged in the first count of an information with burglary (Pen.Code § 459) and in a second count with grand theft (Pen.Code §§ 484–487). A jury found defendants guilty on both counts, finding the degree of burglary under the first count as second degree. (Pen.Code §§ 460, 1157.) * * * [Clay alone appealed.]

On November 19, 1962, * * * defendant and Davis entered Butler's Market in Cloverdale. Although defendant testified that he walked

*The conviction of Jack Ruby was reversed in Rubenstein v. State, 407 S.W.2d 793 (1966); however, Ruby died before a new trial could be had.

into the store by himself and that to his knowledge Davis was never in the store, Charles Thurow, one of the owners, testified that while he was taking an order on the telephone he saw both men who were Negroes come in the door together. Thurow stated that to his knowledge there were no other colored persons in his store on the day in question and that the store had no regular Negro customers. Later, as he looked down an aisle from his position at the telephone, Thurow saw Davis standing near the frozen food compartment.

At about this time, Earl Giacolini, the other owner of the store who was stocking shelves, saw defendant at the check-out stand and went up to the front of the store to wait on him. Defendant had a ten-cent bag of potato chips for his purchase and handed Giacolini a one-dollar bill. The latter rang up the sale on the cash register located to his right behind the counter, placed the bill in the till and returned the change to the customer. Defendant then requested a package of snuff which was located in a rack behind Giacolini, about three or four feet from the cash register, and about twelve to fifteen inches from the floor. Giacolini reached for the snuff, causing him to turn partially and to lose vision of both the register and the defendant. As Giacolini brought up a red can of snuff the defendant told him, "No, I prefer the other," so he (Giacolini) reached for the other, after which the defendant asked for some cigarette papers located next to the snuff. Giacolini took twenty cents in payment for the two items and returned the balance of the change to defendant. During this transaction, which occurred in a "matter of seconds," the defendant was standing approximately three to four feet distant from the cash register, and Giacolini did not notice any change in his position.

* * *

During the course of the above events, one Milton Holt, a Cloverdale merchant, entered Butler's Market by the rear entrance. * * * When he reached a point about five or six feet from Giacolini, Holt saw Davis' "hand, his arm through the opening, his hand balled in a fist coming out of the till." * * * Holt then saw Davis walk to the rear of the store with his right hand held out but "still balled up in a fist." He could not see whether there was anything in the hand. Davis went out the rear exit.

Holt immediately told Thurow what he had seen * * * Giacolini and Thurow found that $380 was missing from the cash register.

Thurow reported the incident to the Cloverdale Chief of Police and went with the latter in a police car along the highway in pursuit of the two men. Eventually they overtook them a short distance south of Cloverdale. Thurow stated that some money was missing from his store and Davis replied that he had never been in the store. Defendant and Davis voluntarily returned with the chief in the police car leaving their own car, a Cadillac, on the side of the road. Both men were searched at the police station. No money at all was found on Davis; defendant had only a dollar and some change. Searches of the Cadillac uncovered no money.

* * *

Over defendant's objection, Inspector Robert Reed of the Oakland Police Department testified as an expert on the crime of "till tapping" and, as we discuss in more detail infra, expressed an opinion that a hypothetical set of facts similar to those in the instant case revealed the "usual procedure of till tappers."

Both defendant and Davis took the stand on their own behalf. Both denied taking the money. Defendant asserted that he entered the store alone and never saw Davis there at any time. Davis insisted that he had never been in the store. According to defendant, they were returning from Eureka, Davis had parked the Cadillac on the side street and defendant had entered the store alone to buy something to eat. He explained that he told the police he did not know Davis because "at first I was unaware what was happening and I didn't want to be involved in nothing, so that's why I told him that." The stolen money was never found.

Defendant contends that the court committed error in admitting in evidence over defendant's objection the expert testimony of Inspector Reed "as to the crime of 'till-tapping' in general" and the opinion testimony of the inspector "as to the guilt" of defendant. The witness was qualified as an expert in the investigation of "till tapping" because of his 26 years service in the Oakland Police Department, incuding 8 years on the burglary and grand theft detail.[2] Immediately after the voir dire examination the prosecutor directed to the witness a hypothetical question predicated on an assumed set of facts similar to those appearing from the prosecution's evidence[3] and concluding thusly: "Now, assuming the facts that I have given to you, Inspector, would you as a—from your experience in the field have any opinion as to what, if any, crime had been committed from those facts?" The witness replied: "That is the usual procedure." Defendant thereupon made certain objections to the questions which appear in the reporter's transcript after the above answer but were nevertheless entertained by the court. The witness was thereupon asked to assume as suggested by the court an additional fact as part of the hypothesis that the two men in question "were seen entering into a four-walled building known as a grocery store." The following then took place: "THE COURT: The objections then are overruled, and the question concerning your opinion as to that set of

2. In testifying to his qualifications, the inspector stated *inter alia* that for three or four years while on the above details he "handled all the till taps and store boosts in the City of Oakland," that he conducted training programs for retail stores on till tapping and store boosting and that he made a study of till tapping operations by talking to persons actually participating therein.

3. The hypothesis of the question was as follows: " * * * Inspector, assuming the following facts: One, that in a grocery store at a check-out counter a customer comes up and presents a dollar bill for a ten cent purchase. The purchase is then rung up on a cash register, the door of which opens at the time the sale is rung up, that the clerk then counts out the cash to the customer, at which time the customer requests another article, said article being placed such that the clerk must turn away from the cash register and reach down for that article; that as the clerk turns back up with

this article, the customer states 'Not that one, but the other kind,' causing the clerk to turn back, replace the article, pick up another article, and again start to turn around to face the customer. At which time the customer then states, 'I want another article,' in the same approximate location as the first, causing the clerk to again turn and pick up another article before he finally turns to face the customer and take the money from him for these two further articles. Further assuming that at the time that the clerk is bent over picking up these articles, that another man is seen with his hand leaving the open cash drawer of the cash register, his hand being in the shape of a fist. Further assuming that after this time a sum of money is found to be missing from the cash register. And further assuming that after the transaction at the check-out stand, the two men, the customer and the one who is seen with the hand coming out of the till are seen together on the street getting into the same automobile. * * * "

facts and what, if any, crime it involved may be answered. THE WITNESS: That is the usual procedure of till tappers."

Thereafter in response to a number of prosecution questions, the witness explained his definition of till tapping and what, from his experience, was the "consistent procedure" of till tapping. Among other things, he stated that he could recall of no particular case in his experience where the money was *actually seen being taken* although there were instances where the store clerk would immediately notice that the money was gone and, an alarm having been sounded, the persons involved would be apprehended on the street together. At this point the following testimony was given: "Q. Now, the till tapping then is a crime, that is committed in the stores during the daylight hours, is that correct? A. Any time the store is open."

All of Inspector Reed's testimony was admitted over objection. At its conclusion defendant moved to strike the testimony on the grounds of the previously raised objection. The motion was denied. The People then rested.

Although defendant objected in the court below that Inspector Reed did not qualify as an expert, he has not raised any issue before us either in his brief or at oral argument as to the witness' testimonial qualifications. "It is for the trial court to determine, in the exercise of a sound discretion, the competency and qualification of an expert witness to give his opinion in evidence [citation], and its ruling will not be disturbed upon appeal unless a manifest abuse of that discretion is shown." We find no abuse here. The issue before us is not as to the competency of the witness but whether the matter on which the witness made certain statements—namely the nature and *modus operandi* of till tapping—was a proper subject of expert testimony. No California case answering this precise question has been called to our attention or disclosed by our independent research.

As the court said in People v. Cole (1956) 47 Cal.2d 99, 103, 301 P.2d 854, 856, 56 A.L.R.2d 1435: "[T]he decisive consideration in determining the admissibility of expert opinion evidence is whether the subject of inquiry is one of such common knowledge that men of ordinary education could reach a conclusion as intelligently as the witness or whether, on the other hand, the matter is sufficiently beyond common experience that the opinion of an expert would assist the trier of fact. [Citations.]" Wigmore, cited in Cole in support of the above excerpt, proffers the test thusly: "But the only true criterion is: On *this subject* can a jury from *this person* receive appreciable help? In other words, the test is a relative one, depending on the particular subject and the particular witness with reference to that subject and is not fixed or limited to any class of persons acting professionally." (7 Wigmore on Evidence, § 1923, p. 21.)

Examining the facts of the instant case in the light of these principles, we think that the subject matter of the inspector's expert testimony was "sufficiently beyond common experience that the opinion of an expert would assist the trier of fact." (People v. Cole, supra.) The evidence shows that at the crucial moment when Holt saw Davis' hand coming out of the till, defendant was to all appearances not participating in such act but was on the contrary merely a customer engaged in the seemingly innocent act of making additional purchases at the check stand. While defendant, in so doing, directed Giacolini's attention to articles behind the counter and thus caused the latter to turn away from the cash register, defendant's conduct in itself manifested no evil purpose. It is true that from the evidence that defendant and Davis were seen entering the store together and that they were later seen together hurrying to their car, the jury might have inferred that the two men while at the check stand were in fact confederates working together. On the other hand the jury might have concluded that defendant was no more than an innocent bystander at the time when Davis made his own personal decision to take advantage of the open drawer of the register.

It was the testimony of the inspector on the *modus operandi* of till tapping which threw a spotlight on the episode as a whole and thus enabled the jury to see the possibility of a relationship between the acts of the two men. This gave meaning to the evidence and permitted the jury to appreciate that defendant's activities while in themselves seemingly harmless, when considered with those of Davis, might well have been part of a cleverly planned and precisely executed scheme known as "till tapping." Thus the inspector's testimony clearly assisted the jury in determining whether or not defendant's conduct was felonious under all the circumstances.

Somewhat analogous to the case at bench, as we think the Attorney General correctly points out, are those cases where expert testimony has been received in respect to gambling activities. Thus is People v. Newman (1944) 24 Cal.2d 168, 174–176, 148 P.2d 4, 152 A.L.R. 365, it was held permissible for a police officer who was qualified as an expert in such matters to testify as to the meaning of signs, symbols, letters and figures appearing on betting markers, scratch sheets and other memoranda used in the business of bookmaking and to explain the *modus operandi* of recording bets in such business.[4] The court in Newman relied upon People v. Hinkle (1923) 64 Cal.App. 375, 378, 221 P. 693; People v. Hatfield (1926) 77 Cal.App.212, 218, 246 P. 95; and People v. Derrick (1927) 85 Cal.App. 406, 408, 259 P. 481. In Hinkle, arresting officers qualified by experience to give expert testimony as to race-track gambling and bookmaking were permitted to give expert testimony that two papers taken from the defendant were respectively a register of bets and a bookmaker's chart and to state their opinion as to the meaning of certain cryptic letters and figures appearing on the documents. The court there said: "[T]hey [the officers] had made a study of race track gambling and its *modus operandi.* * * * They had acquired some special knowledge of a subject which is not within the common experience of mankind generally. They possessed a knowledge which ordinarily does not come within the ken of the average member of a mixed jury of men and women—the juror who has moved in only the routine walks of an exemplary life and has not permitted his feet to wander into the forbidden byways frequented by the gamester." (64 Cal.App. at p. 378, 221 P. at p. 694.) In Hatfield, supra, the court regarded Hinkle as controlling in upholding the expert testimony of police officers establishing that certain slips and papers were such as were used by gamblers for recording bets on horse races. Derrick, supra, is to the same effect.

We are persuaded that a valid and helpful analogy exists between the foregoing cases and the instant one. Certainly if police officers qualified by

---

4. In Newman, supra, the court held that the action of the trial court in striking out the testimony of the officer was erroneous.

experience in the investigation of bookmakers, can properly give expert testimony concerning the *modus operandi* of gambling activities as reflected in betting markers and other memoranda used in the course of such activities, it would appear that such officers qualified by experience in the investigation of till tappers, can give similar testimony concerning the *modus operandi* of till tapping as reflected in the conduct exhibited by those participating in the latter activities. In each instance the witness possesses a "special knowledge of a subject which is not within the common experience of mankind generally." (People v. Hinkle, supra.) In each instance the jury can receive appreciable help from the witness on the subject.

Closer to the point at hand and in our view of persuasive authority is the case of Commonwealth v. Townsend, 1942, 149 Pa.Super. 337, 27 A.2d 462, cited by the People. There the court upheld the admission in evidence of the expert testimony of a police officer in charge of a police bureau dealing with pickpockets, con men, shoplifting and all larcencies by trick, describing the *modus operandi* of a larceny trick known as "flim-flam" or "drop-pigeon." The court observed that the testimony "was properly received. The ingenuity of crooks and swindlers is being constantly exercised in the invention of new forms of bunco games or confidence games, by which to trick credulous and gullible victims out of their money, and it is entirely proper that one who is familiar with the details of such tricks should describe them to the jury, who probably are not acquainted with the methods of operating them used by light-fingered gentry and who, otherwise, might not fully understand that the occurrence was a recognized form of bunco or confidence game. Similar testimony has been admitted in prosecutions dealing with methods of gambling and lotteries, such as craps, policy writing, numbers game, etc., and other forms of illegal activities." (27 A.2d pp. 463–464.)

Defendant argues that the expert testimony here introduced was improper on the authority of People v. Rose (1890) 85 Cal. 378, 382, 24 P. 817. In that case Rose was convicted of fraudulently winning money by means of a game of bunco. A detective called by the prosecution as an expert, described the game of bunco generally but not the game actually played by defendants. In connection with this testimony the trial court stated that the question whether the game played by the defendants was a bunco game or not was one of fact for the jury. Affirming an order granting a new trial, the court stated that "[t]he testimony admitted was clearly incompetent, under the decision of this court in People v. Carroll, 80 Cal. 153, 22 Pac.Rep. 129". In Carroll the defendant was charged with conducting a banking game in violation of section 330 of the Penal Code. An expert witness called by the prosecution was allowed to testify as to what constituted a banking game. The court stated that whether the game played was a banking game or not was one of law for the court[5] rather than one of fact for the jury. Carroll was followed by People v. Gosset (1892) 93 Cal. 641, 29 P. 246, where the defendant was convicted of playing the game of faro. In that case the court, relying on Carroll, held that a witness could not be called for the sole purpose of defining or describing faro since it was for the court to instruct the jury as to what constituted the game charged to have been played.

5. In Carroll the judgment and order denying new trial were reversed for the insufficiency of the information, the court holding that no offense was charged under section 330 or any other section.

The principle found in the above cases is that an expert may not attempt to define a statutory term when its definition is a matter of law on which the court should instruct. It is the court and not the witness which must declare what the law is, it not being within the province of a witness, for example, to testify as to what constitutes larceny or burglary. (Cf. Wigmore, op. cit., § 1952.)[6] The instant case is distinguishable from the above cases. Here the expert witness did not testify as to what constituted the crime charged but merely described the *modus operandi* of a certain class of criminals. His expert testimony was not directed to a question of law but towards assisting the jury in determining a factual issue, namely that of defendant's *intent* at the time he diverted Giacolini's attention.

Since the witness was testimonially qualified and since, as we have explained, the matter about which he testified was a proper subject of expert testimony, it was permissible to elicit his special knowledge through the use of a hypothetical question however unsatisfactory such a method of examination may be. Defendant complains that by the particular hypothetical question employed in the instant case (see footnote 3, ante), the inspector "was thus permitted to state his opinion that the defendants were guilty of the crimes charged."

It is a settled and long established rule, solidly supported by authority in California as well as in other jurisdictions, that a witness cannot express an opinion concerning the guilt or innocence of the defendant. Nevertheless "in this state we have followed the modern tendency and have refused to hold that expert opinion is inadmissible merely because it coincides with an ultimate issue of fact". (People v. Cole, supra, 47 Cal.2d 99, 105, 301 P.2d 854, 857, 56 A.L.R.2d 1435 and authorities there collected) and "[i]t is now well settled that there is in this state no absolute rule that an expert cannot testify to an ultimate issue of fact." (People v. Brown (1958) 49 Cal.2d 577, 587, 320 P.2d 5, 11.)

The result of the hypothetical question in the case at bench was to place before the jury the witness' opinion that the conduct of defendant and Davis under the facts of the case was consistent with the procedure of a till tapping operation. This was a permissible opinion although directed to an ultimate issue in the case. While we think that the hypothetical question could have been improved by eliminating any use of the word "crime" it is notable that the witness' response was expressed only in terms of the "usual procedure of till tappers." Defendant does not contend here that the hypothesis of the question was not supported by the evidence. In net effect, the question and answer told the jury that the pertinent facts and circumstances were consistent with the *modus operandi* of till tappers. The inspector's opinion was not binding on the jury who were free to determine its weight or to disregard it entirely if they found it unreasonable. (People v. Cole, supra, 47 Cal.2d 99, 105, 301 P.2d 854, 857.) As Cole points out,

6. Wigmore states: "The exclusion of testimonial opinion here [i. e., in respect to law] rests on a ground slightly different from that of all the other instances. The general principle * * * is exemplified, to be sure, that the tribunal does not need the witness' judgment and hence will insist on dispensing with it. But here it is not that the *jury* can of themselves determine equal-ly well; it is that the *judge* (or the jury as instructed by the judge) can determine equally well. The principle is the same; but the peculiarity is that a different member of the tribunal is relied upon as equipped with the data. It is not the common knowledge of the jury which renders the witness' opinion unnecessary, but the special legal knowledge of the judge." (Pp. 81–82.)

"[w]here expert opinion evidence is offered, much must be left to the discretion of the trial court." We are satisfied that the trial court did not abuse its discretion in admitting and refusing to strike the inspector's testimony.

* * *

The judgment and sentence are affirmed.

BRAY, P.J., and MOLINARI, J., concur.

INGRAM v. McCUISTON

Supreme Court of North Carolina, 1964.
261 N.C. 392, 134 S.E.2d 705.

Plaintiff instituted this action to recover for personal injuries which she alleges she sustained on March 16, 1961 when the automobile of the defendant collided with the rear of her vehicle on South Tryon Street in the City of Charlotte. In broad outline the facts are these:

About 5:00 p.m. plaintiff, operating a Volkswagen, made a left turn from Woodlawn Road onto Tryon Street, a two-lane roadway at that point. At the same time, the defendant Linda Lee McCuiston was approaching this intersection from the north on Tryon Street in a Dodge automobile owned by her mother, the other defendant. The distance of the Dodge from the intersection at the time of plaintiff's entrance is a matter of dispute between the parties. After plaintiff had proceeded south on Tryon Street in front of the defendant for about two hundred and sixty feet, she stopped three to four feet behind the last car in a long line of traffic which was waiting on a red traffic signal at the Yorkmont Road intersection approximately five hundred and twenty feet ahead. The defendant's Dodge then collided with the rear of plaintiff's Volkswagen causing it to strike the car immediately in front. Again the evidence is conflicting. Plaintiff contends she came to a gradual stop; defendant contends she stopped suddenly. In the two impacts plaintiff sustained an injury to her neck and back which, in the opinion of Dr. Robert E. Miller, the orthopedic specialist who treated her, resulted in a five percent permanent disability to her neck and thoracic spine. Plaintiff was "a nervous type individual," and at the time of the collision she was three months pregnant. She contends that her nervous condition was so aggravated by the collision that in May 1962 she required psychiatric treatment. Plaintiff's psychiatrist, Dr. Thomas A. Wright, Jr., discharged her in August 1962 as much improved. In his opinion the emotional condition he observed in plaintiff at the time she was referred to him could have been produced by the automobile accident.

The pleadings and evidence raised issues of negligence, contributory negligence, and damages. The jury answered each in favor of the plaintiff and awarded her substantial damages. From judgment entered on the verdict the defendants appealed.

SHARP, Justice. To establish the cause of plaintiff's injuries her counsel propounded to Dr. Miller a hypothetical question which covers six pages in the record. The defendants' objections to this question, and to another which incorporated it by reference, were overruled. The defendants assign these rulings as error and contend that they were prejudicial because: (1) The question was based on assumed facts of which there was no evidence; (2) it was based in part on the opinion of another expert as to the plaintiff's condition; (3) it included assumed facts totally unnecessary to enable the doctor to form a satisfactory medical opinion; and (4) it was argumentative and unduly colored the evidence in plaintiff's favor.

We have concluded that in order to discuss appellants' contentions intelligibly we are forced to reproduce the hypothetical question here. Therefore, it follows:

(1) Q. "Now, Dr. Miller, for the purpose of this hypothetical question, assuming that the jury finds the facts to be, from the evidence, and by its greater weight, that on March 16, 1961, and prior thereto, plaintiff Betty Pat Ingram was in excellent physical, emotional and psychological health, and suffering from no disability whatsoever, being an extremely active person from birth, having been brought up on a farm and actually worked in the fields, having held down a full-time job and being gainfully employed as of March 16, 1961; and that on March 16, 1961, at approximately 4:50 P.M., plaintiff Betty Pat Ingram was operating her husband's car, a 1960 Volkswagen, two-door sedan automobile, proceeding in a westerly direction on Woodlawn Road just inside the city limits of Charlotte, Mecklenburg County, North Carolina, and approaching the intersection of Woodlawn Road and South Tryon Street.

(2) "That the plaintiff *safely* brought her car to a complete stop on Woodlawn Road, in *lawful* obedience to a stop sign erected on said Woodlawn Road, directing traffic to stop completely before entering South Tryon Street, turning either left or right; and

(3) "That the plaintiff, after first having observed that no traffic was approaching on South Tryon Street close enough or in such a manner as to interfere with her safely entering South Tryon Street, and thus after first observing that her actions would not affect the movement of any other vehicle, and having given a *proper signal* of her intention to turn to her left, did then *lawfully* make a left turn, entering South Tryon Street and thereafter proceeding south along South Tryon St., in the right-hand or westerly lane.

(4) "Assuming, further, that the jury should find from the evidence and by its greater weight, that minor defendant Linda Lee McCuiston was operating her mother's 1950 Dodge and traveling in a southerly direction on South Tryon Street, here in Charlotte, also, approaching the intersection of South Tryon Street and Woodlawn Road, at approximately 4:57 P.M.; and

(5) "Further, that at the time mentioned herein, traffic was *extremely heavy* and practically bumper to bumper from the intersection of South Tryon Street and Woodlawn Road all the way down to the intersection of South Tryon Street or York Road and Yorkmont Road, and at which intersection there was located a red traffic light; and

(6) "That, as plaintiff Betty Pat Ingram started her left turn and started proceeding into South Tryon Street, *she saw, and anyone who was properly observant could and should have seen,* that the

traffic south of Betty Pat Ingram's vehicle was just barely moving and obviously preparing to make a stop, in obedience to the traffic control device aforementioned; and

(7) "That, after the plaintiff had driven a very few feet south on South Tryon Street, she saw all of the cars, numbering between 15 and 20, south of her from a certain bridge on South Tryon Street all the way to the traffic signal aforementioned come to a complete stop, at which time the plaintiff also began slowing down and preparing to stop behind the long line of traffic;

(8) "Assuming, further, that the jury should find from the evidence and by its greater weight that when the plaintiff started slowing down and preparing to stop, as aforementioned, the minor defendant, Linda Lee McCuiston, was directly behind the plaintiff's vehicle, some two or three or more car-lengths north, traveling exactly the same direction in the same traffic lane; and

(9) "That the plaintiff had no difficulty in stopping her car and did stop her car three or four feet behind another vehicle operated by a Mr. Guy V. Soule, at a point near the center of the bridge on South Tryon Street, at which time the plaintiff was sitting with the brake pedal on her car completely and fully depressed; and

(10) "That a very short time after the plaintiff stopped her vehicle, *in obedience to the traffic control device and because of the traffic stopped ahead of her,* she observed the minor defendant approaching at a rapid rate of speed, but did not have time to brace herself properly before her car was struck, *and actually had no place to go in her car anyhow;* and that the minor defendant struck the rear of the 1960 Volkswagen with the front of her larger 1950 Dodge, with such force as to drive the plaintiff's automobile forward *and ram the same* into the rear of the vehicle in front of her, despite the locked brakes on the car; and

(11) "Assuming that the jury further finds from the evidence and by its greater weight that at the moment of the first impact, *when the defendant rammed the front of her car into the rear of the car the plaintiff was driving, the* car was suddenly thrown forward, with the result that the body of the plaintiff was thrown back, snapping and whipping her neck and upper portion of her body; and that at the time of the second impact when the front of the plaintiff's car was driven by the force of the defendant's car into the rear of the vehicle operated by Mr. Guy V. Soule, that that impact caused the plaintiff's body to be *sharply* thrown forward, again snapping her neck in the manner of a whip and, likewise, throwing her suddenly and *with great force* forward, at which time her abdomen sustained, a *severe impact* with the steering wheel of the car the plaintiff was driving; and

(12) "Further, assuming the jury should find from the evidence and by its greater weight that the accident and the two impacts aforementioned subjected the plaintiff to a *severe jolt and strain,* the force of the two said impacts producing immediately excruciating pain *and agony,* in the plaintiff's neck, back, shoulder and arms; and

(13) "That at the time of the collision on March 16, 1961, the plaintiff had been pregnant for approximately three and a half months; and

(14) "Assuming, further, that the jury should find from the evidence and by its greater weight, that whereas plaintiff had not suffered any substantial emotional difficulty or disability prior to the accident, that the collision and the separate impact, coupled with the pregnant condition of the plaintiff, proximately caused the plaintiff from the date of the accident through the entire remainder of her pregnancy, up until the child was born on September 2, 1961, or for a period of more than five months, *constant mental anguish and shock,* caused by the *reasonable fear* that her serious personal injuries and the blow to her abdomen might cause her to sustain a miscarriage; and

(15) "Assuming, further, that the jury should find from the evidence and by its greater weight that the impact and the collision aforementioned subjected the plaintiff to *an extremely severe nervous and mental shock,* which permanently, to some extent, injured her nervous and mental systems, causing extensive and *permanent dislocation, psychoneurosis, nervous shock, nervousness, and traumatic neurosis or anxiety neurosis,* with the result that whereas plaintiff had never suffered such prior to the date of the accident, from the date of the accident and even for a considerable period of time after the birth of the plaintiff's baby, on September 2, 1961, the plaintiff suffered extremely from nightmares, worry and constant fear, and became in such a condition, as the result of the impact and the collision aforementioned, that she cried easily, became depressed and subject to suicidal tendencies; and

(16) "That her emotional condition became such that her orthopedic specialist, Dr. Robert E. Miller, referred her to a duly accredited psychiatrist, Dr. Thomas H. Wright, Jr., which psychiatrist diagnosed her condition as being an extremely depressive reaction, with nervous tension and depression greatly intensified since the date of the accident on March 16, 1961; and

(17) "That at the time the psychiatrist first examined the plaintiff in June of 1962, he found the plaintiff to have lost interest in life, being unable to concentrate and at times even not wishing to live; and

(18) "Assuming, further, that the jury finds from the evidence and by its greater weight that the plaintiff is still suffering emotional damage as the proximate result of the collision and the pain and suffering she endured, as above set out; and

(19) "Assuming, further, that from the time of the accident on March 16, 1961, despite extreme pain suffered in the neck, shoulder, back and other portions of the body, it was unsafe and impossible, safely, to take X-rays of the plaintiff, due to her pregnant condition, which in turn increased her anxiety and mental anguish; and

(20) "Assuming, further, that the jury should find from the evidence and by its greater weight that the plaintiff suffered from an extremely severe sprain of the cervical spine, thoracic spine, and the lumbar spine, and further, that the plaintiff presently is permanently partially disabled to the extent of 5% disability of said cervical spine, thoracic spine and lumbar spine; and

(21) "That the plaintiff, as a proximate result of the accident and the injuries sustained in the accident, has incurred medical expenses to date in the sum of approximately $600.00, including the cost of drugs and prescriptions, the charges to the Miller Clinic, the charges of the psychiatrist, the charges of the Presbyterian [Hospital] and the charges of the x-ray specialist, the charges for a special corrective girdle and for a cervical collar prescribed by the Miller Clinic; and

(22) "That the plaintiff would be likely to incur additional future medical expenses, directly attributable to her condition caused by the injuries; then

(23) "Assuming that the jury finds the above facts to be true, from the evidence and by its greater weight, then do you have an opinion satisfactory to yourself, as to whether or not the accident in which the plaintiff was involved on March 16, 1961, when the plaintiff was stopped in her husband's automobile on South Tryon Street, sitting with her foot on the brake, when the defendant *crashed* into the rear of the plaintiff's vehicle, *with tremendous force* and at a rapid rate of speed, driving the vehicle forward, and actually knocking the front of the plaintiff's vehicle into the rear of another vehicle, with the two separate impacts first knocking the plaintiff's body to the rear and then throwing the plaintiff's body to the front, *striking her abdomen, with a severe blow,* she being then and there three and a half months' pregnant, could or might have produced the severe nervous and mental shock, which injured her nervous and mental system, and further, could or might have produced the extensive and permanent psychoneurosis, nervous shock, nervous and traumatic neurosis, and further, could or might have caused the plaintiff to suffer from the nightmares, worry and constant fear, the depression and being subject to crying easily, and without reason and being subject to suicidal tendencies, and further, could or might have produced the 5% permanent partial disability to the cervical spine, the thoracic spine and the lumbar spine." (Italics ours).

The doctor answered that in his opinion the collision could or might have produced the conditions described.

The next question was:

"Q. Dr. Miller, assuming that the jury finds the facts to be from the evidence and by its greater weight, as set out in the hypothetical question that was just put to you, do you have an opinion satisfactory to yourself as to whether or not the plaintiff has sustained any permanent injury, mentally or emotionally, or whether she presently is still partially disabled from the standpoint of her mental health?

"A.   Well, you have got an expert sitting back there in the Court. He can answer that question better than I can.   *   *   *   Yes, I have an opinion. The question is, of course, in two parts. One is whether she has permanent partial disability from the emotional status and I think she does. The other is as to the permanent anxiety, and there is some permanency."

Under our system the jury finds the facts and draws the inferences therefrom. The use of the hypothetical question is required if it is to have the benefit of expert opinions upon factual situations of which the experts have no personal knowledge. However, under the adversary method of trial, the hypothetical question has been so abused that criticism of it is now widespread and noted by every authority on evidence. E. g., Stansbury, N. C. Evidence, s. 137 (2d ed. 1963); McCormick on Evidence, s. 16; Ladd, Expert Testimony, 5 Vand.L.Rev. 414, 427. Wigmore has urged that the hypothetical question be abolished: "Its abuses have become so obstructive and nauseous that no remedy short of extirpation will suffice. It is a logical necessity, but a practical incubus; and logic must here be sacrificed. After all, Law (in Mr. Justice Holmes' phrase) is much more than Logic. It is a strange irony that the hypothetical question, which is one of the few truly scientific features of the rules of Evidence, should have become that feature which does most to disgust men of science with the law of Evidence." II Wigmore, Evidence, s. 686 (3d ed. 1940). The comment contained in 2 Jones, Evidence, s. 422 (5th ed. 1958) might well have been directed at the hypothetical question involved in this appeal.

"The most meritorious of the criticisms are that the questions are often slanted for partisan advantage and are often so long and involved as to confuse rather than assist the jury, and, like some appellate court opinions, contain detailed recitals of factual surplusage not essential to support the conclusion reached."

To be competent, a hypothetical question may include only facts which are already in evidence or those which the jury might logically infer therefrom. Jackson v. Stancil, 253 N.C. 291, 116 S.E.2d 817; Stansbury, N.C. Evidence, s. 137 (2d ed. 1963) and cases therein cited. After a careful examination of the record, we find no evidence to support the following facts which were assumed in the hypothetical question involved on this appeal: (Figures in parentheses refer to correspondingly numbered paragraphs of the question.)

1.   That the plaintiff "was in excellent physical, emotional, and psychological health," (1). All the evidence indicates that plaintiff had "always had some nervousness." Indeed, she told Dr. Miller that she was "an extremely apprehensive type individual."

2.   That as a result of the collision plaintiff "became depressed and subject to suicidal tendencies," (15). There was ample evidence that plaintiff was abnormally depressed after the accident and during her entire pregnancy. However, there is no evidence either that she developed suicidal tendencies or that she lost the desire to live, as paragraph (17) of the question assumes the psychiatrist "found." Depression and suicidal tendencies are not necessarily synonymous.

3.   "That the plaintiff presently is permanently partially disabled to the extent of 5% disability of said cervical spine, thoracic spine and lumbar

spine," (20), (23). The evidence of such disability related only to the neck and thoracic spine. The doctor testified to no such disability in the lumbar spine.

Defendants' objection that the hypothetical question asked Dr. Miller, an orthopedic surgeon, was based in part upon the opinion of Dr. Wright, a psychiatrist, must also be sustained. Paragraphs (16) and (17) of the question reveal its reference to Dr. Wright's diagnosis of the plaintiff's condition "as being an extremely depressive reaction, with nervous tension and depression greatly intensified since the date of the accident on March 16, 1961." The question does not assume that plaintiff was actually suffering from an extreme depressive reaction; it merely states that Dr. Wright made this diagnosis. The inclusion of such a statement violates the rule in this jurisdiction that the opinion of an expert witness may not be predicated in whole or in part upon the opinions, inferences, or conclusions of other witnesses, whether they be expert or lay, unless their testimony is put to him hypothetically as an assumed fact. State v. David, 222 N.C. 242, 22 S.E.2d 633. When the hypothetical question is properly asked the jury can determine whether the assumed facts have been proven and weigh the opinion of the expert accordingly. An excellent statement of this rule appears in Quimby v. Greenhawk, 166 Md. 335, 340, 171 A. 59, 61:

> "Although a medical expert may base his opinion upon the facts testified to by another expert, the witness may not have submitted to him, as a part of the facts to be considered in the formation of his inference and conclusion, the opinion of such other expert on all or some of the facts to be considered by the witness from whom the answer is sought. To do so would destroy the premises of fact upon which an expert, by reason of his own peculiar technical skill and knowledge, is permitted to give in evidence his own inference and opinion."

The purpose of the first hypothetical question asked Dr. Miller was to elicit his opinion whether the collision on March 16, 1961 could have produced the five percent permanent disability which he found in plaintiff's neck and thoracic spine. The references therein to plaintiff's mental health had no bearing on the query whether the collision might have caused the injury to her neck and thoracic spine.

The purpose of the second question, which incorporated the first, was to find out whether, in his opinion, the plaintiff had sustained any permanent mental or emotional injury. As Dr. Miller himself told counsel, that question might have been more properly addressed to Dr. Wright, the psychiatrist. Furthermore, when paragraph (15) of the question stated that the collision on March 16, 1961 did proximately cause some "permanent dislocation, psychoneurosis, nervous shock, nervousness, and traumatic neurosis or anxiety neurosis," it assumed the very fact which plaintiff's counsel sought to establish by the doctor's opinion.

The references in the question to plaintiff's childhood on the farm, the route and manner of driving which brought her to Tryon Street immediately before the collision, her consultations with Dr. Wright and his diagnosis of her condition, the fact that her lumbar spine could not be X-rayed because of her pregnancy, and the cost of medical bills in the past and in the future were totally irrelevant to the question of causation. An examination of paragraphs (2), (3), (4), (5), (6), (16), (17), (18), (19), (21), and (22) discloses the validity of defendants' objection to the question on grounds that it contained an assumption of irrelevant facts. Each of the other paragraphs in question contain one or more references to facts which, more succinctly phrased, might be included in a properly stated question.

The italicized words in paragraphs (3), (6), (11), (12), (14), and (23) are examples of the repetitious, slanted, and argumentative words and phrases of which the defendants properly complain. It was no part of the legitimate purpose of the hypothetical question under consideration to establish defendants' negligence; nor are six pages required to state a proper hypothetical question based on the relevant evidence in this case. A shorter question should be no more difficult to frame and it will be easier for the court to rule upon and the jury to understand.

Defendants' assignments of error based on their objections to the hypothetical questions must be sustained. Since the case goes back for a new trial, it is not necessary to consider the other assignments involving questions which may not arise thereon.

New trial.

DIAMOND & LOUISELL, THE PSYCHIATRIST AS AN EXPERT WITNESS: SOME RUMINATIONS AND SPECULATIONS

63 Mich.L.Rev. 1335 (1965).*

Consider the difference between the expert testimony of an orthopedic surgeon in a personal injury suit and the testimony of a psychiatrist in a murder trial in which some elements of the *mens rea* are at issue. In both instances an expert opinion is received in evidence, providing the trier of fact with technical, specialized information which must, or should, be available in order to permit a rational decision-making process. Well-established rules govern the nature of expert evidence and its mode of presentation.[1] In legal theory, the orthopedic surgeon and the psychiatrist are both experts —physicians—who perform comparable functions in the court proceedings. Presumably, they are governed by the same rules of evidence, they are subject to the same restrictions, and their testimony bears an essential, though perhaps fragmentary, relationship to the chief issues at trial.

In actual practice, however, there can be a vast difference between the functions which these two experts play in the legal process.

In a typical, relatively uncomplicated accident suit involving an injury to the body, the questions to be decided are capable of reasonably precise definition and resolution: What was the negligent act or omission by the defendant? What was the causal relationship between that act or omission of the defendant and the injury and disability of the plaintiff? Was the plaintiff free of contributory negligence? What is the nature of the injury? What is the extent and permanency of the consequent disability? Obviously, even in simple litigation there are also less well-defined questions that are incapable of easy resolution. How much pain and suffering has the plaintiff

1. McCormick, Evidence §§ 13–18 (1954); 3 Wigmore, Evidence §§ 555–71, 387–88, 1923, 1925 (3d ed. 1940); Louisell, The Psychologist in Today's Legal World, 39 Minn.L.Rev. 235 (1955).

undergone in the past and how much may he anticipate in the future? What is the monetary value of an hour, a day, or a month of pain? But these are subordinate to, and distinguishable from, the central questions which are at the heart of the litigation.

In such a situation the expert witness should have little or no difficulty defining his own functional role in the trial. He is to supply particular, specialized information to the court—information derived both from his direct observation of the plaintiff and from his fund of general professional knowledge about the structure and mechanics of the human body and the nature of the injuries which the body suffers from external forces. If the witness is a man of high integrity, experienced, and professional competency, he will find it easy to communicate to the court which of his answers are based upon firm, objective facts and which veer off into more speculative hypotheses. He need not become defensive about his technical knowledge and his expertise, and he should be able to avoid becoming involved in those issues at trial which clearly have no relationship to his area of competency.

Particularly, the form in which such an expert's evidence is presented in the courtroom should not normally concern him seriously. He can testify almost as capably if his evidence is given in reply to a series of questions as if it is given as a continuous narrative. Cross-examination should hold no terrors for him. It should be of no grave consequence to him whether the questions are proposed as real or as hypothetical, provided they be put intelligibly. In short, this expert witness should be capable of easily adapting himself and his testimony to whatever rules, restrictions, and modes of presentation the law, in its own wisdom, deems best. Most especially, he should experience no need to involve himself emotionally or intellectually in the outcome of the trial.

It is possible to look upon the rules of evidence simply as logical, necessary devices to ensure that all of this takes place: that the expert witness be truly an expert and that he be exposed if he is not; that his evidence be objective and relevant and that it be presented in such a fashion that its weight and significance may be judged. The ordinary rules of evidence can, in most instances, ensure that the expert is not drawn into issues that do not concern him or that could be better determined by other kinds of witnesses giving other kinds of evidence.

Thus, in a well-run personal injury trial, the orthopedic surgeon of competence and integrity can be close to the ideal of the uninvolved, objective, impartial expert. If this ideal is not too frequently achieved, it is not necessarily because the rules of trial procedure are at fault. It is more likely the result of human failings and the exigencies of the expert's professional practice. Often, surgeons habitually will be either a defendant's or a plaintiff's witness. Some degree of bias is inevitable and its nature depends upon the orientation of the surgeon's medico-legal practice. Permanent emotional bias may also exist within the expert's own personality. He may be strongly identified with authority and conservative ideas of individual responsibility and determined, at least unconsciously, that the plaintiff receive a minimum of compensation. Or he may over-identify with the patient's position as the underdog and engage in a crusade from the witness stand on the patient's behalf. But these defects should be demonstrable by the questioning of a skillful attorney. No basic change in procedure or departure from the time-honored adversary system is necessary to cope with these problems. The fact that orthopedic surgeons for reasons of temperament and training frequently dislike the adversary system, as physicians often do, is not of great materiality to the law, except as it limits available competent expertise.

* * *

IV. THE NEED FOR PROCEDURAL CHANGES

If the psychiatrist is to be useful to the law, not as an oracle, fortune-teller, or pseudo-exact scientist, but rather as a man possessed of a certain modicum of wisdom about human beings and their behavior, it might be desirable for the law to modify some of its procedures in order to facilitate this. Some of the traditional ways of doing business in a courtroom might not be the most appropriate or useful for communicating what the psychiatrist has to say to the trier of fact. Nor are the traditional ways necessarily the best to reveal whether in truth the psychiatrist is a wise man who comprehends the goals of the law.

We wish to limit the remainder of our discussion in this paper to a few of the possible modifications of procedure which might improve psychiatric testimony and which would be more compatible with the psychiatrist's true role in the decision-making process of the trial. No claim is made that these are radical innovations.

A. *The Fallacy of Impartiality*

One of the authors has had considerable experience as a psychiatric expert for the defense in criminal trials. Taking advantage of judicial leniency he had experimented with different modes of participation in the criminal process. Out of this experience has come the conviction that the psychiatrist achieves a more significant, and at the same time, more honest and ethical relationship to the trial process if many of the customary pretenses of the expert witness are discarded.

The law too much assumes that psychiatric experts, especially court-appointed ones but to a degree also those called by parties, are impartial; that they furnish *neutral expertise* rather than *professional viewpoint*. The reality of this is open to question.[10] In former years, the psychiatrist who relied solely upon the obvious and objectively visible evidence of mental disease and who spent only a brief time with the defendant could, perhaps, retain a kind of impartiality. But now, when most of the better trained psychiatrists are keenly interested in the deeper and more obscure workings of the pathological mind and may develop a close and intimate emotional relationship with the defendant-patient through many hours of probing clinical examination, it becomes difficult to continue the pretext of detachment and impartiality.

Of even greater importance is the present trend toward a closer and more prolonged working relationship between the psychiatrist and the attorney. It is not unusual for an attorney (either prosecution or defense) to consult a psychiatrist very early in a criminal case. The attorney may depend heavily upon the advice and experience of the psychiatrist in planning

10. Diamond, The Fallacy of the Impartial Expert, 3 Archives of Criminal Psychodynamics 221 (1959), reprinted (in part) in Louisell & Hazard, Pleading and Procedure 1291 (1962) [2nd ed. 1256 (1968), 3d ed. 1289 (1973)].

the basic strategy of the entire legal proceeding, from the preliminary investigations to the concluding argument to the jury. Not infrequently the mental state of the defendant is the sole issue in dispute during the trial, and the problems of the mental state—the *mens rea*—may be most complicated and difficult of demonstration and resolution. Hence, the attorney may wisely utilize the collaboration of the psychiatrist at every step of the way.

Should the law then permit the illusion that the psychiatrist remains impartial and outside the adversary system? We think not. The remedy must lie in the full disclosure to the jury of the psychiatrist's role and function in the particular case. And it should not be necessary to drag this information from the reluctant witness through sharp and vigorous cross-examination. Rather, the psychiatrist should be prepared to describe his complete relationship to the defense (or to the prosecution) in his primary testimony as a legitimate part of the clinical information upon which his opinion is based. In this way, not only the opinion of the expert but also his role and participation become matters for the jury to weigh.

B.   *The Form of the Testimony*

Traditionally, the expert witness presents his testimony, as does the ordinary witness, in the form of direct answers to specific questions proposed by the attorney. This interrogatory form of communication probably developed out of the necessity of presenting evidence in tiny fragments, each fragment an entity in itself which could then be evaluated, determined if competent, relevant, and material, and then affirmed or contradicted by further interrogation. This may be the best method for the presentation of so-called objective facts, although this has been incisively questioned by able observers. In any event, it is gravely doubtful that it is the best means of communicating the psychological essence of the human mind.

Only a few decades ago psychiatrists were trained to imitate the systematic precision of the physician and surgeon. The mental examination, as set forth in the medical records of that time, followed very closely the form used by other physicians. It was divided into a great many different elements, each with a suitable rubric such as chief complaint, present illness, family history, past history, developmental history, educational and employment record, orientation to time, place, and person, recent and recall memory, contact with reality, insight, affect, and many more specific items, ending with a diagnosis, prognosis, and prescription for treatment. The psychodynamic psychiatrist of today no longer describes his patients this way, and he avoids thinking in such a fragmented manner. The human mind, normal or pathological, is best and most meaningfully described as a continuous story that begins with the individual's birth, or even before, with his family, social, and cultural heritage, and ends with the present moment which, in a criminal trial, means the defendant sitting in the presence of the jury, under its scrutiny, and awaiting its decision.

It is no small task for the psychiatrist to describe and interpret all of this from the witness stand. Particularly, it is difficult, but nevertheless essential, that he convincingly communicate to the jury the relevancy of the total life history of the defendant to that critical moment of the alleged criminal act upon which the jury must pass judgment.

To do this successfully and meaningfully, the psychiatrist must use the narrative form. He has a story to tell, a story of another man's whole life, thoughts, feelings, hopes, fears, fantasies, loves, hates, delusions, and dreams. Unavoidably, the clinical history, like all good stories, will contain exaggerations for the sake of emphasis, discrepancies and inconsistencies, loose ends, and unresolved contradictions. But these can be dealt with in cross-examination. For it is in clarifying, criticizing, verifying, and validating that the technique of question and answer works best.

So we propose that the psychiatrist be permitted and encouraged to tell his story as a narrative, all in one piece, taking as long as reasonably necessary, to relate to the jury who he, the witness, is, how he came to be involved with the defendant, what functions he has played in the development of the case, his interaction with the defendant, how he elicited the information he received, how he reconstructed the events of the defendant's life, and what he has inferred about the secret and invisible processes of the defendant's mind.

Then, upon the completion of this story, it becomes appropriate for the criticism and clarification to begin. For this, the traditional techniques of cross-examination seem well suited. It is in cross-examination that our method of utilizing expertise seems to excel in relation to typical European methods.[11]

C. *Full Disclosure and the Hypothetical Question*

It is recognized that a few situations exist in law (as, for example, an issue of testamentary capacity) where no approach other than the hypothetical question is normally possible. But if one accepts the principle that the validity of the psychiatrist's observations and inferences is dependent upon the totality of his approach, upon his taking everything, including his own personal and subjective interaction with his patient, into account, then the hypothetical question generally becomes a dubious technique.

No hypothetical question can ever be formulated which would contain sufficient facts to justify a really valid psychiatric inference. This is because the modern, psychodynamically oriented psychiatrist simply does not assemble diagnostic facts *A, B,* and *C* about his patient and thus arrive at conclusion *D.* The psychiatrist may be very much interested in observed phenomena, such as mannerisms, delusional and hallucinated behavior, and the like, but he can not derive a valid conclusion from such phenomena until he puts them together with his own subjective relationship to the examinee within the context of the latter's total background. There are few, if any, pathognomonic signs of mental disease.

The problem of the hypothetical question usually arises in a criminal trial under two circumstances. First, it arises when the psychiatrist has not actually examined the defendant. Such hypothetical testimony is of doubtful worth and often of dubious ethical quality. Secondly, it arises when it is used as a device to restrict the information admitted to the jury. A defendant may not wish to testify on his own behalf, being unwilling to admit the facts of the deed. The strategy of the trial may demand that all

11.   See Schlesinger, Cases on Comparative
Law 224, 250 (1959).

sorts of information about the crime and the criminal be withheld from the jury's knowledge, including evidence of previous offenses. The hypothetical question can be used for this purpose, restricting the psychiatrist to only certain facts and aspects of the case. This is the defendant's constitutional right. But it is not necessarily the psychiatrist's ethical duty to cooperate with such strategy. He should not and, if he is conscientious, he will not, wholly shrug off the responsibility for the consequences of his testimony.

There are two basic and radically different strategies available to the defense in a criminal trial involving a psychiatric defense. The defense can, in effect, say, "We admit nothing—prove your case." Or the defense can say, "We admit all the objective facts, we want you to hear the total account of this man's life, mind, and deed, and after you have heard everything you, the jury, will be better able to reach a just decision."

It seems to us that the psychiatrist may well have conscientious scruples as to the legitimacy of a role in the typical "admit nothing" defense. Of what possible use can such a role typically have other than to obscure the issues and befuddle the jury with professional jargon and abstract theories? Good psychiatric testimony generally is compatible only with full disclosure. It is, in fact, a type of full disclosure which goes far beyond that customary in the courtroom. The jury is asked to listen to and consider evidence of a type rarely disclosed in normal human relations. The defendant relinquishes all right of privacy, both as to his past and as to the inner depths of his mind, even as to matters of which he, himself, may be unaware.

We doubt that compromise can be possible here. To be willing to disclose in depth only those aspects about the self of the defendant that are strategically useful can quickly place the psychiatrist in the position of a dupe, in the position of one whose knowledge and skills are being used for purposes foreign to the values of his own discipline. Here, the remedy lies with the ethical and professional responsibility of the psychiatrist rather than with a change of the legal rules. The psychiatrist may insist that he will not participate in legal work unless he is permitted to disclose all. And he may wish to keep a careful watch over the uses to which his testimony is put.

It is true that the law can exercise its prerogative of saying to the psychiatrist, "This is none of your business. We want the answers to certain technical questions, and what we do with your answers is no concern of yours." But the price of such legal arrogance is the limitation of courtroom psychiatric expertise to the incompetent, the indifferent, and the pseudo-scientific purveyor of jargon. The leaders and the thinkers of the psychiatric profession simply will not participate on such terms.

*   *   *

E.   *The Problem of Hearsay*

*   *   *

[See Cal.Ev.C. § 801 at p. 843; FRE 703, at p.920.]

See Federal Rules of Evidence 602, at p. 915, 706 at p. 921; California Evidence Code § § 702, at p. 830, 720–723 at p. 832, 730–733 at pp. 833–834, 800–805 at pp. 843–844.

WALTZ, THE NEW FEDERAL RULES OF EVIDENCE: AN ANALYSIS

112–113 (2d ed. 1975).*

Rule 705 is important and, rightly or wrongly, somewhat controversial. It provides that an expert can testify in terms of opinion "without prior disclosure of the underlying facts or data."

*   *   *

Rule 705 does not do away with the hypothetical question absolutely; it simply does away with any absolute requirement that a hypothetical be used by counsel. The use of the hypothetical question sometimes has its advantages and it remains to be seen whether trial lawyers will accept with any frequency this Rule's invitation to forego its use.

In any event, Rule 705 probably forecloses successful assignments of error based on a claim that opposing counsel's hypothetical question was incomplete, i. e., did not include all of the "underlying facts or data." In effect, the new rule places on the cross-examiner the burden of eliciting any missing data. Thus Rule 705 should serve to make examining counsel less nervous about the use of hypotheticals; no longer will it be essential to include each and every scrap of arguably pertinent data on pain of a successful objection or reversal.

KAUFMAN v. EDELSTEIN

United States Court of Appeals, Second Circuit, 1976.
539 F.2d 811.

FRIENDLY, Circuit Judge:

We have here appeals from and petitions for mandamus to vacate two orders of Chief Judge Edelstein in the Government's civil antitrust action in the District Court for the Southern District of New York against International Business Machines Corporation (IBM). These orders denied motions to quash subpoenas directing Felix Kaufman, a partner in the international accounting firm of Coopers & Lybrand, and Frederic G. Withington, a senior staff member of the well-known management consulting firm of Arthur D. Little, Inc., to appear and testify on behalf of the Government. The issue is entirely between the United States on the one hand and Dr. Kaufman and Mr. Withington on the other; IBM has taken no position either in the District Court or here.

As the cases now stand, the sole issue sought to be raised on the merits is whether Dr. Kaufman and Mr. Withington are entitled to be excused from responding to the subpoenas because the Government is seeking to interrogate them on the basis of their expert knowledge of the computer industry. In affidavits opposing the motions to quash the subpoenas, the Government stated its desire as being to develop testimony "concerning the nature and structure of the general purpose electronic digital computer systems market, and of the electronic data processing industry in general"—a subject on which petitioners are highly qualified.[1] So far as concerned opin-

---

1.   Dr. Kaufman has had fifteen years experience, first as Regional Director for the Northeast Region and then as National Director of Consulting Services for Coopers & Lybrand. Mr. Withington affirms that he is "a management consultant to a wide variety of manufacturers, sellers and users of electronic computers" served by Arthur D.

ion testimony, the Government made clear that it would not require appellants to state their present opinions but rather "prior opinions expressed during the period from 1960 through 1972." In its brief here the Government has somewhat amplified the range of the proposed testimony; it intends also to ask the witnesses "to explain the nature of their duties as computer systems consultants, and especially to recount the advice which they gave to various users and potential users of computer systems." It states, however, that the witnesses "will not be asked at trial for their expert evaluation of the government's evidence" and that "their testimony will be confined to events which occurred between 1960–1972." It is not seeking to have either witness or his firm conduct any examinations or undertake any special studies in preparation for trial.

The Government also states in brief that it "will pay both witnesses as experts for their services" in amounts to be negotiated between them and Government counsel. According to the Government's affidavits, although contested in part by petitioners, both witnesses had initially agreed to testify but later declined at the direction of their firms. * * * The issue on the merits is posed most bluntly in the concluding paragraph of Mr. Withington's affidavit—"the government is seeking the very core of my expertise which I do not wish to provide and which I consider to be a proprietary asset available solely to my employer or to those for whom I wish to work."

Chief Judge Edelstein, in opinions, denied the motions to quash. His rulings were based largely on statements in this court's opinion in Carter-Wallace, Inc. v. Otte, 474 F.2d 529, 536 (2 Cir. 1972), cert. denied, 412 U.S. 929, 93 S.Ct. 2753, 37 L.Ed.2d 156 (1973), which are discussed below. He added "that an even stronger basis may be said to exist in the case at bar for recognizing the court's power to compel expert testimony than existed in *Carter-Wallace,*" since "[t]his is not an attempt by a litigant in a private controversy to support its case through the assistance of an unwilling expert" but "an attempt by the United States to summon a member of the public to testify in a major government antitrust case, a case which, by definition, greatly affects the commonweal," citing Pennsylvania Co. for Insurances On Lives and Granting Annuities v. City of Philadelphia, 262 Pa. 439, 441, 105 A. 630 (1918). Dr. Kaufman and Mr. Withington have appealed and also have petitioned for writs of mandamus to require Chief Judge Edelstein to grant their motions. * * *

* * *

 * * * The only reference to the need of consent by an expert is in [Federal] Rule 706(a), dealing with court appointed experts. This provides in part that "An expert witness shall not be appointed by the court unless he consents to act"—language taken verbatim from the former F.R.Cr.P. 28. The situation of the court appointed expert who is expected to delve deeply into the problem and arrive at an informed and unbiased opinion

Little. He also is "primarily responsible for preparing analyses and forecasts of the computer industry based on Arthur D. Little estimates of the performance of the participants" which are distributed periodically to paying subscribers, and is the author of three books and numerous articles concerning the industry. The books are entitled "The Organization of the Data Processing Function," "The Real Computer —Its Influences, Uses and Effects," and "The Use of Computers in Business Organizations."

differs utterly from that of an expert called by a party to state what facts he may know and what opinion he may have formed without being asked to make any further investigation. If any inference is to be drawn from the Federal Rules of Evidence, it is thus against the claim of privilege by an expert, not for it.

* * *

We think it plain * * * that, quite apart from the inference to be drawn from the provision with respect to court-appointed experts, Rule 706(a), "the principles of the common law as they may be interpreted by the courts of the United States in the light of reason and experience," Federal Rule 501 of Evidence, do not recognize any general privilege for experts.

In a notable case the Supreme Court has recently quoted its statement in Branzburg v. Hayes, 408 U.S. 665, 688, 92 S.Ct. 2646, 2660, 33 L.Ed.2d 626, 643 (1972), "that 'the public * * * has a right to every man's evidence,' except for those persons protected by a constitutional, common-law, or statutory privilege," United States v. Nixon, 418 U.S. 683, 709, 94 S.Ct. 3090, 3108, 41 L.Ed.2d 1039, 1064 (1974).[11] Admittedly there is no constitutional or statutory privilege against the compulsion of expert testimony, and we perceive no sufficient basis in principle or precedent for holding that the common law recognizes any general privilege to withhold his expert knowledge.

The truth of the proposition that the high degree of a person's knowledge of a subject excuses him from giving testimony about it is not self-evident, to say the least. As Wigmore says, 8 Evidence § 2192 at 72 (McNaughton rev. 1961), the giving of such testimony

> may be a sacrifice of time and labor, and thus of ease, of profits, of livelihood. This contribution is not to be regarded as a gratuity, or a courtesy, or an ill-required favor. It is a duty not to be grudged or evaded. Whoever is impelled to evade or to resent it should retire from the society of organized and civilized communities, and become a hermit. He who will live by society must let society live by him, when it requires to.

He adds that *"all privileges of exemption from this duty* [of giving testimony] *are exceptional,* and are therefore to be discountenanced. There must be good reason, plainly shown, for their existence." Id. at 73 (emphasis in original). The opinion which, on its facts, most directly supports the view espoused by petitioners, People ex rel. Kraushaar Bros. & Co. v. Thorpe, 296 N.Y. 223, 72 N.E.2d 165 (1947), itself conceded that, as compared with three other states recognizing a privilege for experts,[12] there were

---

11. The inner quote contains the words of Lord Hardwicke. See 8 Wigmore, Evidence § 2192 at 70 (McNaughton rev. 1961).

12. One of the three, Pennsylvania, would not allow the privilege in a situation where the state or, as here, the United States is seeking the testimony. See Pennsylvania Co. for Insurance on Loans and Granting Annuities v. City of Philadelphia, 262 Pa. 439, 441, 105 A. 630 (1918), cited in Chief Judge Edelstein's opinion.

In Cheatham Electric S.D. Co. v Transit De-velopment Co., 261 F. 792, 796 (2 Cir. 1919), appeal dismissed for want of jurisdiction, 252 U.S. 567, 40 S.Ct. 343, 64 L.Ed. 719 (1920), holding that expert witness fees were not taxable as costs, Judge Hough argued that this was an *a fortiori* case as compared with the non-taxability of attorneys' fees since "An expert sells his opinions, as counsel sells his services, and he cannot by law be compelled to testify at all, while an attorney may be compelled to serve." No authority was cited for this dictum.

eleven which compelled experts to testify to opinions which they "are able to give without study of the facts or other preparation."[13] * * * The reasoning in *Kraushaar Bros.* for regarding the majority rule as "quite unsatisfactory"[14] ignores several important points. One is the enormous range of "expert" knowledge in modern life; if there is a privilege against the compulsion of "expert" testimony, this must extend not only to such learned professions as "medicine, law [and] science" but to the builder, the tug boat captain, the carpenter, the real estate broker, the stock broker, and a legion of other callings. Furthermore it assumes that the only purpose in calling an expert is to ask him to express an opinion about facts of which he has no personal knowledge. In such a case we see no reason why an expert cannot decline to testify "without reflection upon his professional ability" if, as may often happen, he believes that a hypothetical question does not give all the facts required for a full and fair answer. Often the inquiry may be about the development of techniques, the stage they had reached, opinions already formulated or expressed, even—as the Government claims to be the situation here—relevant knowledge about a party to the case or its products. To clothe all such expert testimony with privilege solely on the basis that the expert "owns" his knowledge free of any testimonial easement[15] would be to seal off too much evidence important to the just determination of disputes.

What gives some pause about compelling expert testimony is not that the expert is called upon to make available to the community relevant knowledge that he has acquired through time and labor, but that since his knowledge, in contrast to that of the ordinary witness, is relevant to many cases, he may be summoned too often, both because of his eminence and because published views may eliminate the usual practical deterrent against calling an expert with whom counsel has not conferred in advance. A court would indeed have cause for concern if, for example, a world-renowned surgeon were forced to spend a considerable share of his time in the courtroom rather than the operating room;[16] the interest in the saving of lives would outweigh a party's interest in obtaining testimony from an expert having no previous connection with the case. But to say, as we do, that there is no privilege to withhold testimony simply because it represents the result of study or experience does not entail a holding that courts may never extend protection when good cause is shown. It will be time for a federal court to consider what should be done about cases like the one we have

---

13. Petitioners' suggestion that in this case we should look to state law, and follow *Kraushaar Bros.* on that basis, flies in the face of Fed.Rule of Evidence 501.

14. This was that:

In the realms of medicine, law, science, and many other callings where highly specialized knowledge is essential, only the most eminent are competent to answer ex tempore and defend impromptu opinions upon cross-examination, but none, without reflection upon his professional ability, may confess ignorance.

15. In view of the United States' offer to pay fair compensation to petitioners, we need not here express an opinion whether they could be compelled to testify for the ordinary witness fees. See the discussion in 8 Wigmore, Evidence § 2203(2)(c) (McNaughton rev. 1961), and the authorities there cited.

16. For a case that might have implicated this problem, see Karp v. Cooley, 493 F.2d 408, 424–25 (5 Cir.), cert. denied, 419 U.S. 845, 95 S.Ct. 79, 42 L.Ed.2d 73 (1974) (attempt to elicit testimony of Dr. Michael DeBakey in a malpractice action against another eminent heart surgeon with whom he was known to disagree).

framed when and if they should arise in situations governed by the first sentence of Rule 501. We can find no justification for a federal rule that would wholly exempt experts from placing before a tribunal factual knowledge relating to the case in hand, opinions already formulated, or, even, in the rare case where a party may seek this and the witness feels able to answer, a freshly formed opinion, simply because they have become expert in a particular calling.

We likewise see no basis for recognizing a narrower principle that an expert is privileged against being called against his will in the absence of a preliminary showing of the unavailability of a voluntary expert equally qualified. The task of determining whether the country contains a voluntary expert who is really as qualified and useful as the witness sought to be compelled would be an almost impossible one. Indeed, the facts of this case vividly illustrate the unworkability of such a "necessity" principle. A substantial part of the testimony which the Government here seeks from petitioners is testimony no one else can give. While it would seem that there must be other experts who could describe "the nature and structure of the general purpose electronic digital computer systems market, and of the electronic data processing industry in general," no one not connected with Coopers & Lybrand or Arthur D. Little can testify what advice these two important consultants gave to the large purchasers of computers who were their clients.[18] To be sure, there probably are other accounting and management consulting firms with clienteles as large as petitioners'. But if, and it would be a bit naive to assume otherwise, the Government has some reason to think the petitioners will give testimony on this subject considered favorable to its position, we see no reason why it must go down the list of great accounting and consulting firms until it finds one—if it should—that presents the combination of willingness to furnish a qualified expert and the helpfulness of his testimony which the Government evidently thinks it has found in Dr. Kaufman and Mr. Withington.

* * *

NOTE

U.S. CONST. AMENDMENT 13, SECTION 1

"Neither slavery nor involuntary servitude, except as a punishment for crime whereof the party shall have been duly convicted, shall exist within the United States, or any place subject to their jurisdiction."

Hypotheticals

(1) X is prosecuted for possession of marijuana. X makes a motion to suppress the marijuana found in his possession on the ground of unreasonable search and seizure. At the hearing, A, a police officer, testifies that he saw a water pipe through an open window of X's home and then went into the home without a search warrant and made the arrest and seizure. On direct examination A testifies that he was a high school graduate, that he had received police-academy training, that he had taken several academic courses at a college, that he had read numerous textbooks on narcotics, that he had worked with various officers

---

18. We do not and on this meagre record could not pass on the relevancy of such evidence; it suffices for this opinion that we cannot now say it necessarily would be irrelevant at least if connected with evidence of what the clients did. Petitioners have made no such argument.

on narcotic cases, that he had testified in narcotic violation cases, that he had seen narcotics used and demonstrated, that he had been working on the narcotics squad for two years; and that the pipe he saw in X's window was similar to a pipe he had seen in connection with other marijuana cases. The prosecutor then asked A for his opinion as to what use was made of the water pipe he observed in X's home. X requests permission to question A on voir dire on the ground that the witness lacks the qualification of an expert witness to testify to an opinion on the use of the water pipe. How should the court rule?

(2)   H sues D, a builder, for damages for wrongful death and property loss. H's wife, W, was drowned and H's home was destroyed in a flood. H and W had bought the home, built by D at the foot of a canyon. H's claim of liability of D is that D should have guarded against the danger of flooding by constructing a wall or building the house on a higher foundation. H calls ME, a mechanical engineer, and qualifies ME as an expert by eliciting that he had been trained in hydraulics and hydrology; that he was familiar with the characteristics of flooding in hillside areas; that he had observed construction of several hundred residential developments in hillside areas such as that involved in H's case. On voir dire examination of ME by D, ME testifies that he has had no close involvement in the construction of homes and is unfamiliar with building practices of home builders. H then asks ME to state his opinion as to whether a reasonably prudent builder in the area, taking into account the topography of the area and the location of the house, would have utilized a retaining wall as a portion of the design for the structure. D makes a lack-of-qualification objection to H's question. The trial judge sustains D's objection. Is this correct?

(3)   P was injured by using a power rotary lawn mower manufactured by D Mfg. Company. P sues D for damages, claiming that the lawn mower was defectively designed. P calls E, an expert on lawn mowers, to testify that the lawn mower was defectively designed. E states that his opinion is based on (1) articles published in Reader's Digest, Today's Health and consumer-bulletin magazines discussing the great number of injuries occurring from the use of rotary power lawn mowers, and (2) statistical surveys on the same subject in a book entitled, "Accidental Injuries Associated with Rotary Lawn Mowers," published by a department of the federal government. D moves to strike E's testimony on the ground that it is based on improper hearsay matter. The trial judge denies D's motion. Is this a proper ruling?

PART B.   SCIENTIFIC AND DEMONSTRATIVE EVIDENCE

STATE v. VALDEZ

Supreme Court of Arizona, 1962.
91 Ariz. 274, 371 P.2d 894.
[Some footnotes omitted.]

UDALL, Vice Chief Justice.   Defendant was tried for and convicted of possession of narcotics. Pursuant to a written stipulation entered into by defendant, his counsel and the county attorney before trial defendant submitted to a polygraph (lie-detector) examination. The stipulation also provided that the results of such examination would be admissible at the trial. Accordingly, the polygraph operator was permitted, over objection by defendant to testify to the results of the examination (unfavorable to defendant) at defendant's jury trial. After the jury returned a verdict of guilty and before sentence was entered, the trial court, pursuant to Rule 346 of the Arizona Rules of Criminal Procedure, 17 A.R.S., certified the following question to this court:

"In a criminal case, if prior to trial the defense attorney, on behalf of his client and with his client's consent, and the deputy county attorney agree in a written stipulation that the results of a polygraph test, to be taken by the defendant, will be admissible as evidence at the trial, on behalf of either the State of Arizona or the accused, may the trial court admit the results of the test over the objection of defense counsel?"

Because *any* case involving admissibility of lie-detector evidence would be one of first impression in Arizona and also because of the particular disposition herein of the question certified the following observations and review of the authorities are set forth for the guidance of the Bar.

The polygraph or lie-detector is a pneumatically operated device which simultaneously records changes in a subject's blood pressure, pulse, respiration rate and depth, psychogalvanic skin reflex (skin resistance to electrical current) and, in some cases, muscular activity. "The basis for the use of the so-called lie-detector * * * is the hypothesis that conscious deception can be deduced from certain involuntary physiological responses in the same manner as physicians diagnose various diseases. The thesis is that lying engenders emotional disturbances which are transmuted into tangible bodily manifestations."[3] The machine itself reflects and records only the subject's physiological responses to the questions propounded by the operator. He then interprets the poly*graph* (meaning, literally, "many pictures") and determines whether the subject is lying.

I   *Admissibility in General*

The first reported American case involving admissibility of lie-detector evidence was Frye v. United States, 54 App.D.C. 46, 293 F. 1013, 34 A.L.R. 145 (1923). Frye, convicted of murder in the second degree, appealed alleg-

---

3.   Kleinfeld, The Detection Of Deception
—A Résumé, 8 Fed.B.J. 153, 157 (1947).

ing as his sole assignment of error the trial court's refusal to allow an expert to testify as to the results of a systolic blood pressure test to which Frye had submitted. In affirming the conviction and in upholding the trial court's refusal of the proffered testimony the Circuit Court observed:

"Just when a scientific principle or discovery crosses the line between the experimental and demonstrable stages is difficult to define. Somewhere in this twilight zone the evidential force of the principle must be recognized, and while courts will go a long way in admitting expert testimony deduced from a well-recognized scientific principle or discovery, the thing from which the deduction is made must be sufficiently established to have gained general acceptance in the particular field in which it belongs.

"We think the systolic blood pressure deception test has not yet gained such standing and scientific recognition among physiological and psychological authorities as would justify the courts in admitting expert testimony deduced from the discovery, development, and experiments thus far made."[4]

Ten years later the Supreme Court of Wisconsin reached the same result in State v. Bohner, 210 Wis. 651, 246 N.W. 314, 86 A.L.R. 611 (1933). Bohner's conviction for robbery was affirmed and it was held that the trial judge had correctly excluded defendant's offer of lie-detector results. The Wisconsin court added the following:

"We are not satisfied that this instrument, during the ten years that have elapsed since the decision in the Frye Case, has progressed from the experimental to the demonstrable stage." 210 Wis. at 658, 246 N.W. at 317.

And the judicial attitude toward lie-detector evidence expressed in Bohner has not changed markedly in the numerous cases decided since 1933. Thus, in 1961 a New Jersey appellate court was correct in pointing out:

"* * * that there is not a single reported decision where an appellate court has permitted the introduction of the results of a polygraph or lie-detector test as evidence in the absence of a sanctioning agreement of stipulation between the parties."

State v. Arnwine, 67 N.J.Super. 483, 495, 171 A.2d 124, 131 (1961).[5] Consistent with this approach appellate courts have reversed convictions in cases where lie-detector results unfavorable to defendants were placed before the juries inferentially. E. g., State v. Arnwine, supra; People v. Wochnick, 98

---

4. 293 F. at 1014. Interestingly, after Frye was convicted and sentenced to life imprisonment the real murderer confessed to the crime. See Wicker, The Polygraphic Truth Test And The Law Of Evidence, 22 Tenn.L.Rev. 711, 715 (1953).

5. In People v. Kenny, 167 Misc. 51, 3 N.Y.S.2d 348 (1938) the Queens County Court, over objection by the prosecution, permitted an expert to testify as to the results of a pathometer (psychogalvanometer) test administered to the defendant. The Kenny case remains the only reported decision wherein lie-detector evidence was admitted absent a stipulation to effect. And the force of even that decision has been eroded if not obliterated by the decision of the New York Court of Appeals in the same year in People v. Forte, 279 N.Y. 204, 18 N.E.2d 31, 119 A.L.R. 1198 (1938). In Forte the highest New York court affirmed a murder conviction and the trial judge's exclusion of proffered lie-detector test results without mentioning the Kenny holding. It has been argued that the two cases are distinguishable, see Note, 29 Cornell L.Q. 535 (1944), but, absent a stipulation, Forte is probably controlling on the admissibility issue in New York today. See People v. Ford, 304 N.Y. 679, 682, 107 N.E.2d 595, 597 (1952).

Cal.App.2d 124, 219 P.2d 70 (1950). Further, it is uniformly held that a defendant is not permitted to introduce evidence of his willingness to take a lie-detector test. E. g., Commonwealth v. Saunders, 386 Pa. 149, 156–157, 125 A.2d 442, 445–46 (1956). Nor can a defendant's refusal to submit to polygraphic interrogation be shown by the state directly, State v. Kolander, 236 Minn. 209, 52 N.W.2d 458 (1952), or indirectly, People v. Carter, 48 Cal.2d 737, 752, 312 P.2d 665, 674 (1957).[6]

But judicial reluctance to recognize generally the worth of lie-detector evidence in the court room has not been due to mere inertia. For, in affirming a first degree rape conviction, the Oklahoma Criminal Court of Appeals quoted from two leading authorities the following " ' * * * factors which occasion the chief difficulties in the diagnosis of deception by the lie-detector technique * * * .' "

" '(1)   Emotional tension—,"nervousness"—experienced by a subject who is innocent and telling the truth regarding the offense in question, but who is nevertheless affected by

" '(a)   fear induced by the mere fact that suspicion or accusation has been directed against him, and particularly so in instances where the subject has been extensively interrogated or perhaps physically abused by investigators prior to the time of the interview and testing by the lie-detector examiner; and

" '(b)   a guilt complex involving another offense of which he is guilty.

" '(2)   Physiological abnormalities, such as

" '(a)   excessively high or excessively low blood pressure;

" '(b)   diseases of the heart;

" '(c)   respiratory disorders, etc.

" '(3)   Mental abnormalities, such as

" '(a)   feeblemindedness, as in idiots, imbeciles, and morons;

" '(b)   psychoses or insanities, as in manic depressives, paranoids, schizophrenics, paretics, etc.;

" '(c)   psychoneuroses, and psychopathia, as among so-called "peculiar" or "emotionally unstable" persons—those who are neither psychotic nor normal, and who form the borderline between these two groups.

" '(4)   Unresponsiveness in a lying or guilty subject, because of

" '(a)   lack of fear of detection;

" '(b)   apparent ability to consciously control responses by means of certain mental sets or attitudes;

" '(c)   a condition of "sub-shock" or "adrenal exhaustion" at the time of the test;

---

6.   In Carter the California Supreme Court ruled that the trial court erred in not striking all of the testimony of a witness who stated that he had been willing to take a lie-detector test but that " ' * * * some other people wouldn't take [such a test] * * * '." The reviewing court held that " * * * the implication survived that defendant had refused to take a lie detector test and that his refusal furnished some evidence of guilty knowledge." 48 Cal.2d at 752, 312 P.2d at 674.

" '(d) rationalization of the crime in advance of the test to such an extent that lying about the offense arouses little or no emotional disturbance;

" '(e) extensive interrogation prior to the test.

" '(5) Unobserved muscular movements which produce ambiguities or misleading indications in the blood pressure tracing.' "

Henderson v. State, 94 Okl.Crim. 45, 51–52, 230 P.2d 495, 501–02, 23 A.L.R.2d 1292, cert. denied, 342 U.S. 898, 72 S.Ct. 234, 96 L.Ed. 673 (1951). And in addition to the above enumerated scientific shortcomings of the polygraph technique the following objections to the unrestricted use of its results in the court room have been registered:

(1) The supposed tendency of judges and juries to treat lie-detector evidence as conclusive on the issue of defendants' guilt. See Highleyman, The Deceptive Certainty Of The "Lie Detector", 10 Hastings L.Rev. 47 (1958); Kleinfeld, The Detection of Deception—A Résumé, 8 Fed.B.J. 153 (1947).

(2) Lack of standardization of test procedure, (Burack, A Critical Analysis Of The Theory, Method, And Limitations Of The "Lie Detector", 46 J.Crim.L., C. & P.S., 414 (1955); Koffler, The Lie Detector—A Critical Appraisal Of The Technique As A Potential Undermining Factor In The Judicial Process, 3 N.Y.L.F. 123 (1957)), examiner qualifications and instrumentation.

(3) Difficulty for jury evaluation of examiners' opinions.

Finally, it appears " * * * that at the present time the technique is not an 'accepted' one among the scientists whose approval is a prerequisite to judicial recognition." Inbau and Reid, Lie Detection and Criminal Interrogation, (3rd ed. 1953) at 130. See also Cureton, A Consensus As To The Validity Of Polygraph Procedures, 22 Tenn.L.Rev. 728, 739–41 (1953). Of course absolute infallibility is not the standard for admissibility of scientific evidence. But at this time it seems wise to demand greater standardization of the instrument, technique and examiner qualifications and the endorsement by a larger segment of the psychology and physiology branches of science before permitting general use of lie-detector evidence in court. Accordingly, in the absence of a stipulation lie-detector evidence should not be received in an Arizona court for the present.

II *Admissibility Upon Stipulation*

The first reported decision involving stipulated admissibility of lie-detector results was LeFevre v. State, 242 Wis. 416, 8 N.W.2d 288 (1943). Before the trial defendant submitted to a lie-detector (Keeler polygraph) test the results of which were favorable to him. At trial, however, on objection by the district attorney to defendant's proffer of the test results, the trial judge excluded them. This ruling was upheld on appeal although the conviction was reversed on the grounds of insufficient evidence. Without mentioning the stipulation the Wisconsin Supreme Court simply cited the Bohner case, supra, and said "They were properly excluded." Oddly enought the court then referred to testimony of the district attorney to the effect that the test results indicated defendant was not lying, and remarked that:

"We have the word of the district attorney that those tests were favorable to the defendant. While the findings of these experts were properly excluded from the jury, the district attorney's testimony came in without objection and we regard it as very significant." 242 Wis. at 427, 8 N.W.2d at 293.

Further, a note critical of LeFevre in 1943 Wis.L.Rev. at 430 points out that the district attorney objected to the introduction of the reports *by themselves* and only on the ground that the examiners, not present in court, should have been called to testify to the results of the examination.

Five years later, however, a California District Court of Appeal held that the test results and the examiner's testimony relating thereto were properly admitted pursuant to a written stipulation. Determination of the value and weight of such evidence was left to the jury. People v. Houser, 85 Cal.App.2d 686, 193 P.2d 937 (1948). It does not appear from the decision whether an objection was made thereto at trial. In affirming Houser's conviction for a lewd and lascivious act the court remarked that:

"It would be difficult to hold that defendant should now be permitted on this appeal to take advantage of any claim that such operator was not an expert and that as to the results of the test such evidence was inadmissible, merely because it happened to indicate that he was not telling the truth. * * * ." 85 Cal.App.2d at 695, 193 P.2d at 942.

The next case in this area was Stone v. Earp, 331 Mich. 606, 50 N.W.2d 172 (1951). In Stone, a civil case, plaintiff sought a declaration that he was the legal and equitable owner of a truck and trailer. During the course of the trial the court required the parties to take lie-detector examinations. They consented and the examiner testified that in his opinion the plaintiff was not telling the truth. A decree for defendant was affirmed by the Michigan Supreme Court. The reviewing court, however, pointed out that the trial court committed error (though not prejudicial error, because, aside from the test results, there was a preponderance of evidence in defendant's favor) in receiving the lie-detector results in evidence. And in this connection the court remarked that " * * * whether by voluntary agreement, court direction, or coercion, the results of such tests do not attain the stature of competent evidence." 331 Mich. at 611, 50 N.W.2d at 174.

In 1960 the Iowa Supreme Court held that there was sufficient evidence to affirm a woman's second-degree murder conviction and then disposed of her contention that lie-detector evidence was improperly admitted notwithstanding a stipulation by announcing that:

"We hold the lie-detector evidence was admissible by reason of her agreement."

State v. McNamara, 252 Iowa 19, 104 N.W.2d 568, 574 (1960). Significantly, "at the trial defendant [McNamara] strenuously objected to any evidence regarding the tests on the ground that they were unreliable and prejudicial." 252 Iowa at 28, 104 N.W.2d at 573.

An opposite result was reached by the Supreme Court of New Mexico in the recent case of State v. Trimble, 68 N.M. 406, 362 P.2d 788 (1961). Without extended discussion of the authorities, indeed with no mention at all of the Houser or McNamara decisions, the court reversed defendant's conviction for incest on the ground that "The signing of a waiver did not alter the rule with regard to the admissibility of　＊　＊　＊　[lie-detector] evidence." 68 N.M. at 408, 362 P.2d at 789.　＊　＊　＊

Generally speaking, even those experts who warn against admissibility in the absence of a stipulation favor admission of lie-detector evidence upon a proper stipulation. And although polygraphic interrogation has not attained that degree of scientific acceptance in the fields to which it belongs to be admissible at the instance of either the state or defendant (supra, section I of this opinion), it has been considerably improved since Frye v. United States, supra, was decided in 1923. A conservative estimate of the accuracy of such tests is as follows:

(1)　In 75-80 per cent of the cases the examination correctly indicates the guilt or innocence of the accused;

(2)　in 15-20 per cent of the cases the results are too indefinite to warrant a conclusion by the examiner one way or the other; and

(3)　5 per cent or less is the margin of proven error.[10]

With improvement in and standardization of instrumentation, technique and examiner qualifications the margin of proven error is certain to shrink. "Modern court procedure must embrace recognized modern conditions of mechanics, psychology, sociology, medicine, or other sciences, philosophy, and history. The failure to do so will only serve to question the ability of courts to efficiently administer justice." Chappell, J., concurring in Bocche v. State, 151 Neb. 368, 383, 37 N.W.2d 593, 596, 600 (1949). Although much remains to be done to perfect the lie-detector as a means of determining credibility we think it has been developed to a state in which its results are probative enough to warrant admissibility upon stipulation. Cf., People v. Zavaleta, 182 Cal.App.2d 422, 6 Cal.Rptr. 166, 171 (1960).

Accordingly, and subject to the qualifications announced herein, we hold that polygraphs and expert testimony relating thereto are admissible upon stipulation in Arizona criminal cases. And in such cases the lie-detector evidence is admissible to corroborate other evidence of a defendant's participation in the crime charged. If he takes the stand such evidence is admissible to corroborate or impeach his own testimony.

The "qualifications" are as follows:

(1)　That the county attorney, defendant and his counsel all sign a written stipulation providing for defendant's submission to the test and for the subsequent admission at trial of the graphs and the examiner's opinion thereon on behalf of either defendant or the state.

(2)　That notwithstanding the stipulation the admissibility of the test results is subject to the discretion of the trial judge, i. e. if the trial judge is not convinced that the examiner is qualified or that the test was conducted under proper conditions he may refuse to accept such evidence.

(3)　That if the graphs and examiner's opinion are offered in evidence the opposing party shall have the right to cross-examine the examiner respecting:

10.　These statistics are taken from Dean Wicker's discussion of Inbau's experiments regarding accuracy of the polygraph. See 22 Tenn.L.Rev. at 713.

    a.   the examiner's qualifications and training;

    b.   the conditions under which the test was administered;

    c.   the limitations of and possibilities for error in the technique of polygraphic interrogation; and

    d.   at the discretion of the trial judge, any other matter deemed pertinent to the inquiry.

(4)   That if such evidence is admitted the trial judge should instruct the jury that the examiner's testimony does not tend to prove or disprove any element of the crime with which a defendant is charged but at most tends only to indicate that at the time of the examination defendant was not telling the truth. Further, the jury members should be instructed that it is for them to determine what corroborative weight and effect such testimony should be given.

The case as certified is remanded for action consistent with this opinion.

Bernstein, C.J., and Struckmeyer, Jennings and Lockwood, JJ., concur.

STATE v. WILLIAMS

Supreme Judicial Court of Maine, 1978.
388 A.2d 500.

WERNICK, Justice.

On May 26, 1976, defendant Thomas Williams was indicted in the Superior Court (Kennebec County) for the offense of terrorizing, in violation of 17–A M.R.S.A. § 210. A jury found defendant guilty as charged, and he has appealed from the judgment of conviction entered on the verdict.

* * *

On May 20, 1976, an unidentified person made a telephone call to a dispatcher at the Augusta Police Department and stated that a bomb was going to go off at the Augusta State Airport. While the call was in process, the Augusta police recorded it on magnetic tape. Thereafter, Officer Richard Gary Judkins of the Augusta Police Department listened to the tape recording and recognized the voice of the person telephoning as the voice of defendant. Later that day, at the request of the police, defendant came to the Augusta police station and read aloud a rough transcript of the threatening telephone call previously received and recorded at the police station. With defendant's agreement, a tape recording was made of defendant's reading. The police thereafter submitted both the tape recording of the threatening telephone call and of defendant's reading to Dr. Oscar Tosi of Michigan State University and Lieutenant Lonnie Smrkovski of the Michigan Department of State Police, each to make a voice identification analysis through the use of a speech spectrograph.

At trial, Dr. Tosi gave preliminary testimony as to the nature, reliability and scientific acceptance of the "scientific" voice identification process known as speech spectrography or "voiceprint" analysis. Dr. Louis J. Gertsman, of City College in New York, and Faulsto Poza, a consultant to the Stanford Research Institute, testified, preliminarily, in opposition to allowing in evidence testimony as to voice identification achieved by the use of speech spectrography.

At the conclusion of the extensive preliminary testimony the presiding Justice ruled, over defendant's objection, that adequate foundation had been shown to satisfy him that (1) voiceprint identification has such scientific acceptance and reliability as warrants its admissibility in evidence, (2) the experts whose opinions were here being sought as evidence were qualified to assist the jury in its determinations.

Thereafter, Dr. Tosi and Lt. Smrkovski testified that through use of a speech spectrograph each of them had independently analyzed the voices recorded on the two tapes and had independently made a "positive identification" that the unknown voice from the telephone call and the known voice of the defendant belonged to the same person. Officer Judkins then testified that he had recognized defendant's voice when he had listened to the recording of the bomb threat.

Defendant's position on appeal is that it was error to admit the speech spectrograph evidence because the scientific community has not generally accepted the speech spectrograph as a scientifically reliable method of voice identification. Defendant further contends that in any event speech spectrograph voice identification evidence is unreliable in forensic situations.

1.

The threshold question we confront is to determine what standard, under the law of evidence, governs *admissibility* in relation to the type of evidence here involved.

The preliminary evidence of record shows that the process of voice identification used by Dr. Tosi and Lt. Smrkovski consists of an aural comparison of two recorded voices and a visual comparison of graphic representations or "spectrograms" of the recorded voices. The spectrograms used in the visual comparison process are plotted by a machine known as a spectrograph. The spectrograph separates the sounds of a voice into elements of time, frequency and intensity and plots these variables on electronically sensitive paper.[1] Since the spectrograms of the voice of a person often vary over time and under a variety of conditions and circumstances, the accuracy of the spectrogram voice identification process is largely dependent on the ability, experience and judgmental consistency of the examiner. There is no dispute that for most of the 20th century the sound spectrograph has been widely resorted to for the analysis and classification of human speech sounds, but it had not been used to identify individual human voices until the early 1960's when Lawrence Kersta, a scientist with the Bell Telephone Laboratories, undertook such projects. Thereafter, Dr. Tosi conducted a number of significant experiments in individual voice identification with the use of the speech spectrograph. The publication in 1971 and 1972 of the results of these experiments and expert testimony given in cases by Dr. Tosi and his associates have induced many courts to allow as evidence individual voice identifications made by use of speech spectrographs.

Defendant argues that speech spectrograph voice identification rests on new developments in the application of scientific principles and therefore

---

1. The horizontal axis of the spectrogram represents the time lapse of each sound, the verticle axis indicates frequency and the thickness of the lines discloses the intensity of the voice.

its admissibility as evidence should be governed by a special standard, as set forth in Frye v. United States, 54 App.D.C. 46, 47, 293 F. 1013, 1014 (1923):

> "Just when a scientific principle or discovery crosses the line between the experimental and demonstrable stages is difficult to define. Somewhere in this twilight zone the evidential force of the principle must be recognized. And while courts will go a long way in admitting expert testimony deduced from a well-recognized scientific principle or discovery, the thing from which the deduction is made must be sufficiently established to have gained general acceptance in the particular field in which it belongs."

Prior to the adoption of the Maine Rules of Evidence in 1976, the law of Maine was unclear about the evidentiary rules governing the admissibility of evidence involving the new ascertainment, or application, of scientific principles. In State v. Knight, 43 Me. 11, 133, 134 (1857), the Court upheld the admissibility of scientific testimony as to the properties and appearance of human blood and animal blood. *Knight* gave the following rationale:

> "The history of the development of scientific principles by actual experiments, within a few of the last years, show[s] us that many things which were once regarded generally as incredible, are now admitted universally to be established facts. And as long as the existence of facts, which are the result of experiments, made by those versed in the department of science to which they pertain, are received as evidence, it would be legally erroneous for the court to determine that the absurdity of such facts was so great as to require their exclusion." (43 Me., at 133, 134)

It is questionable from this language whether *Knight* was suggesting a special standard, such as is stated in *Frye,* supra, to govern the admissibility of expert testimony resting on newly ascertained, or applied, scientific principles. More recently, this Court may have given stronger indication of following the *Frye* rule in regard to evidence of the results of lie detector or polygraph tests. Holding polygraph evidence generally inadmissible, this Court in State v. Casale, 150 Me. 310, 320, 110 A.2d 588 (1954) resorted to language contained in the Nebraska opinion in Boeche v. State, 151 Neb. 368, 37 N.W.2d 593, 597 (1949), as follows:

> " 'It is apparent from the foregoing authorities that the scientific principle involved in the use of such polygraph has not yet gone beyond the experimental and reached the demonstrable stage, and that it has not yet received general scientific acceptance.' "

The reference to a special standard of admissibility in *Casale,* however, was occasioned by the peculiarly special nature of lie detector tests as evidence.[2] Lie detector evidence directly and pervasively impinges upon that function which is so uniquely the prerogative of the jury as fact-finder: to decide the credibility of witnesses. The admissibility of lie detector evidence therefore poses the serious danger that a mechanical device, rather than the judgment of the jury, will decide credibility. For this reason, it remains questionable whether this Court by its language in *Casale* was

---

2.   The *Frye* case also involved the exclusion of polygraph evidence.

purporting to establish a specially restrictive standard regarding the admissibility of *any* type of expert testimony which may rest on new, or new applications of, scientific principles.

The Maine Rules of Evidence adopted in 1976 do not purport to establish a special standard to govern the admissibility of testimony involving newly ascertained, or applied, scientific principles. Under the Rules of Evidence all "relevant" evidence[3] is admissible

> "except as limited by constitutional requirements or as otherwise provided by statute or by   *   *   *   rules applicable in the courts of this state." Rule 402, M.R.Evid.

In Rule 702, specific reference is made to the admissibility of scientific testimony:

> "If scientific, technical, or other specialized knowledge will assist the trier of fact to understand the evidence or to determine a fact in issue, a witness qualified as an expert by knowledge, skill, experience, training, or education, may testify thereto in the form of an opinion or otherwise."

As also potentially affecting a case of this nature, Rule 403 provides a general limitation on the admissibility of relevant evidence:

> "Although relevant, evidence may be excluded if its probative value is substantially outweighed by the danger of unfair prejudice, confusion of the issues, or misleading the jury, or by considerations of undue delay, waste of time, or needless presentation of cumulative evidence."

Defendant's argument relies on the fact that the Rules of Evidence do not deal *specifically* with the admissibility problem as it may arise by virtue of newness in the development, or application, of scientific principles. Defendant asks us to fill this gap by establishing an additional precondition of admissibility as applicable *specially* to the situation in which proffered expert testimony will rest on a new ascertainment, or new application, of scientific principles—this further condition to be that there must be "general acceptance" of such newly discovered scientific principle, or new application of scientific principle, in the relevant scientific field.

We refuse to take the course for which defendant argues. We believe it would be at odds with the fundamental philosophy of our Rules of Evidence, as revealed more particularly in Rules 402 and 702, generally favoring the *admissibility* of expert testimony whenever it is relevant and can be of assistance to the trier of fact.[4] As stated in McCormick on Evidence § 203 at 491 (2d ed. 1972):

> " 'General scientific acceptance' is a proper condition for taking *judicial notice* of scientific *facts,* but not a criterion for the *admissibility* of scientific *evidence.* Any relevant conclusions which are supported by a

---

3. "Relevant" evidence is defined in Rule 401 to mean "evidence having any tendency to make the existence of any fact that is of consequence to the determination of the action more probable or less probable than it would be without the evidence."

4. We reach this conclusion, too, because of the difficulties experienced by courts in applying the *Frye* rule. As explained in Mc-

Cormick on Evidence § 203 at 490 (2d ed. 1972): "The difficulty of determining how to distinguish scientific evidence from other expert testimony, of deciding what is the particular field of science to which the evidence belongs, and of settling what is general acceptance, has led to an application of the   *   *   *   [Frye] test which is highly selective, although not enlightening as to its details."

qualified expert witness should be received unless there are other reasons for exclusion. Particularly, probative value may be overborne by the familiar dangers of prejudicing or misleading the jury, and undue consumption of time." (emphasis supplied)

In accordance with the provisions and basic spirit, of our Rules of Evidence in regard to the admissibility of expert testimony, we conclude that there is no justifiable distinction in principle arising because such expert testimony may happen to involve newly ascertained or newly applied scientific principles. The controlling criteria regarding the admissibility of expert testimony, so long as the proffered expert is qualified and probative value is not substantially outweighed by the factors mentioned in Rule 403, are whether in the sound judgment of the presiding Justice the testimony to be given is relevant and will assist the trier of fact to understand the evidence or to determine a fact in issue.

In particular cases where the expert testimony proffered rests on newly ascertained, or applied, scientific principles, a stronger showing may become necessary before the presiding Justice is satisfied that the preconditions of admissibility, in terms of relevance and helpfulness to the fact-finder, have been met. Thus, in the particular circumstances of a given case the presiding Justice may see fit to place greater emphasis on the consideration whether or not the scientific matters involved in the proffered testimony have been generally accepted or conform to a generally accepted explanatory theory. The Justice may believe this appropriate either (1) to avoid prejudice which might arise because the assertion that the principle, or technique, has a "scientific" basis may import an objectivity which could unduly influence the jury as a lay fact-finder or (2) to assist the presiding Justice in his responsibility to determine relevance, within the definition of Rule 401 M.R.Evid., i. e., whether the proffered testimony is likely to make the existence of any fact or consequence more probable or less probable than it would be without the evidence.

This, however, is not the same as saying, as does the *Frye* rule, that the presiding Justice is *bound* by an additional, *independently controlling* standard which exists over and above relevance (Rule 401 M.R.Evid.) and the capability of the expert testimony to assist the trier of fact (Rule 702 M.R.Evid.). On the approach we adopt the presiding Justice will be allowed a latitude, which the *Frye* rule denies, to hold admissible in a particular case proffered evidence involving newly ascertained, or applied, scientific principles which have not yet achieved general acceptance in whatever might be thought to be the applicable scientific community, if a showing has been made which satisfies the Justice that the proffered evidence is sufficiently reliable to be held relevant.

2.

With the criteria of admissibility thus decided, we address whether the presiding Justice committed error, here, by admitting the spectrograph testimony in evidence.

Dr. Tosi's testimony related to the nature of the human voice and the spectrograph process, the results of his experiments and the reliability of the spectrograph voice identification process. Simultaneously, however, Dr. Tosi was careful to explain that the spectrograph voice identification process is not infallible. According to Dr. Tosi, the reliability of the spectrograph voice identification method is highly dependent on the experience, ability and judgment of the person who makes the spectrograph comparisons.

Testimony was also given by acoustical scientists who oppose the use of spectrograph as evidence. In their view, (1) the examiners of spectrographic data cannot maintain firm and stable criteria of decision; (2) they may tend to relax their threshold standards for making a "positive identification", in particular where only a single sample voice exemplar is presented for comparison with the known voice; and (3) the spectrograph experiments generally have not accounted for many variables such as telephone recordings, disguised voices, noncontemporaneous recordings, background noise and voices of persons under psychological stress.

Yet, none of the acoustical scientists who testified questioned as facts that recordings of different human voices vary more in time, frequency and intensity than recordings of the same voice and that the spectrograph can accurately plot these variables. The opposition experts focused only on the difficulties of comparison and the exercise of judgment and the failure of the spectrograph experiments to account for many real world variables.

In view of the evidence of reliability presented by Dr. Tosi, we conclude that it was not error for the presiding Justice to admit the expert voice identification testimony in this case. The Justice was justified in finding that the spectrograph principle was sufficiently reliable to qualify as "relevant" within the definition of Rule 401 M.R.Evid., and that the qualified expert testimony based on it could be of assistance to the jury as fact-finder.

The issue raised by defendant regarding the application of the spectrograph process to forensic situations concerns the weight, not the admissibility, of the evidence[5] and was exclusively for the jury's determination.

The entry is:

Appeal denied.

Judgment affirmed.

* * *

NORFOLK & W. RY. CO. v. HENDERSON

Supreme Court of Appeals of Virginia, 1922.
132 Va. 297, 111 S.E. 277.

KELLY, P. This action was brought to recover damages for the death of the plaintiff's intestate, Marian Henderson, a child 26 months old, who was run over and killed by one of the defendant's trains. There was a verdict and judgment for the plaintiff, and the defendant assigns error.

The accident occurred about 9 o'clock a.m. on a clear day within the corporate limits of the town of Brookneal in Campbell county. For many years the railway tracks at that point had, with the knowledge of the railway company and its employees, been used as a walkway by men, women,

5. A number of courts in other jurisdictions have admitted spectrograph evidence either on the basis of the general acceptability test of *Frye* or on the basis of some type of reliability standard. Some courts, relying primarily on the *Frye* rule, have excluded spectrograph evidence because of the substantial opposition to it of many acoustical scientists.

and children. Marian Henderson had wandered away from the home of her parents, about 100 yards from the railroad, and was sitting down on or beside the rail. She wore a light-colored dress with a stocking net cap over her head, and was stooping or bending over, with her hands down, as if trying to pick something up from the track. For a distance of nearly 1,200 feet in the direction from which the train was approaching the track was perfectly straight. In the engine at the time were the engineer, fireman, and two brakemen, and they all testify that they saw the child as soon as the engine reached the straight track, but thought the object was a piece of paper, or as one of the brakemen said, either a piece of paper or a big white chicken. According to their testimony, they kept their eyes on this object, but did not discover its identity until they were within about 350 feet of the point at which the child was struck. It was then too late to stop the train, but the engineer blew his whistle, applied his brakes in emergency, and did all he could towards saving the child's life.

The speed of the train was about 25 miles an hour, and with prompt action could have been stopped within a distance of about 600 feet. It is thus apparent that there was ample opportunity to stop after the object was first seen and before it was struck, but no chance of doing so after the engineer and others in the engine first discovered the character of the object.

Of course, it is not contended, nor is it to be imagined, that the defendant's employees intentionally ran over the child. Furthermore, it is clear that, if the jury were bound to accept the testimony of these employees as conclusive, the verdict was wrong, and the judgment ought to be reversed. If, as claimed by them, they saw the object as soon as they could see it, and at that time had no reason from its appearance to believe it was a human being, and, in the exercise of the diligence required of them at a place regularly used by men, women, and children, had no reason to believe sooner than they did that it probably was a child, and, after making the discovery, used every reasonable means to avoid the injury, the defendant was not liable. All of these conditions of nonliability were established, if the evidence given by the only persons who could see the situation from the engine was conclusively binding upon the jury. Was it conclusive? The answer to this inquiry must precede the determination of the final and decisive question in the case, which is whether they discovered or ought to have discovered that the object was probably a child in peril before it was too late to take effective measures for its safety.   *   *   *

3. The leading assignment of error, presented to us with marked earnestness and ability, is that the court permitted certain witnesses to testify as to several tests or experiments which they made for the purpose of determining the distance up the track from which they could recognize a child as such when it was sitting on the rail at the point of the accident. There were two or more of these experiments made by sundry persons, some when the day was perfectly clear, and others in dark and cloudy weather. A child about the size of the one who was killed, and similarly dressed, was placed at the same place and in substantially the same position, and the witnesses in question then went up the track to see how far away they could recognize the object as a child. The result of the testimony was that, when the day was clear, they could recognize the child at a distance of something like 1,100 feet away, and that on a dark or cloudy day they could identify it

at a distance of 900 feet. These witnesses, of course, knew from the outset what the object was, but they were very positive in their testimony that under weather conditions as above indicated they could clearly and unquestionably recognize the child as such at the respective distances stated.

The contention of the defendant is that these tests were inadmissible because the conditions under which they were made were not substantially the same as those by which the engineer was surrounded.

One of the differences pointed out is that the engineer was on an engine, the motion and vibration of which would interfere with clear vision, while the witnesses who were making the tests were on the ground. This particular difference in the situation of the parties, however, is shown by the evidence to have been unsubstantial. The witness, Harvey, an old engineer, testified that he had participated in one of the tests, and that, in his opinion, a man in the engine moving as this one was would have been in a more favorable position for making the discovery than a man on the track. Nobody testified to the contrary. Moreover, and perhaps even more to the point, the engineer in charge of the engine, after saying that he did not think these tests were fair, upon being asked to specify the reason why he did not think they were fair, said:

"Knowing a thing is there and having your mind to help you out makes a great deal of difference."

This was a pointed, sensible, and comprehensive answer; and it is this difference, very appropriately called in the petition for the writ of error "the difference in the mental attitude of the parties," which the defendant chiefly relies upon, and, in view of the testimony, must solely rely upon, is a reason why the evidence should not have been admitted.

We may say, therefore, that the real question as to the admissibility of these tests is whether the fact that the witnesses making them knew from the outset that a child had been placed on the track constituted such a difference between their situation and that of the engineer and others with him in the engine as to render the tests incompetent as evidence. The position of the defendant in this respect does not seem to us to be well taken. We do not mean to say that this difference is of no consequence, but we think that its effect upon the value of the tests as proof was a question to be determined by the jury. * * *

After all, the question is one of relevancy, as to which, in debatable instances, the discretion of the trial judge is entitled to much consideration. 1 Jones on Evidence, § 164; 1 Wigmore on Evidence, § 444; Riverside Cotton Mills v. Waugh, 117 Va. 386, 393, 84 S.E. 658. Where the conditions are substantially similar in essential particulars, the evidence is admissible, and its weight is to be determined by the jury. As said in 22 Corpus Juris, p. 759:

"The weight to be attached to evidence of experiments is for the jury, and varies according to the circumstances of similarity existing between the experiments made and the actual occurrence, the facts of which are under investigation." * * *

The judgment is accordingly affirmed.

STATE v. BAKER

Supreme Court of Washington, 1960.
56 Wash.2d 846, 355 P.2d 806.

DONWORTH, Judge. Appellant was charged by information with the crime of negligent homicide under RCW 46.56.040. The charging portion of the information reads as follows:

"That the said Charles E. Baker in the County of Pierce, in the State of Washington, on or about the 13th day of September, Nineteen Hundred and Fifty-eight did then and there being unlawfully and feloniously operate a motor vehicle in a reckless manner with disregard for the safety of others, and while under the influence of or affected by the use of intoxicating liquor, and while so operating said vehicle and being in physical control thereof, did, as a result of such negligent operation strike and injure Ernest E. Eichhorn, a human being, from which said injuries the said Ernest E. Eichhorn, did on the 16th day of September, 1958, die, contrary to the form of the statute in such cases made and provided, and against the peace and dignity of the State of Washington."

The facts giving rise to the above charge may be briefly summarized as follows:

On Saturday evening, September 13, 1958 the opening night of the western Washington fair in Puyallup, Washington, Ernest E. Eichhorn, an officer of the Washington state patrol, was directing traffic at the intersection of Seventh avenue southeast and Meridian avenue, which is located approximately one block north of the fair grounds. The intersection was lighted by a single mercury vapor light, and Officer Eichhorn was wearing a light blue state patrol jacket with white threading in the material, which would reflect light.

Appellant was driving his automobile south along Meridian avenue on his way to the fair grounds to pick up his wife who was employed at the fair. As he approached the intersection, Officer Eichhorn had just stopped the east-west traffic, and the north-south traffic had commenced to move. There is a conflict in the evidence as to the precise manner in which the accident occurred. However, as appellant passed through the intersection, his car struck Officer Eichhorn, whose body was flung through the air. It came to rest in front of a Ford automobile which was traveling north on Meridian avenue and stopped with its front wheel touching Officer Eichhorn's body. Although it had been raining shortly prior to the accident, the evidence was conflicting as to whether or not it was raining at the time of the accident. The accident occurred a few minutes before eleven o'clock p.m.

Appellant admitted that he had consumed one stubby and four eight-ounce glasses of beer between six o'clock p.m. and the time of the accident. He denied that he was then under the influence of, or affected by, intoxicating liquor.

Shortly after the accident, appellant was taken in a patrol car by Officer Alfred F. Stewart of the state patrol to the police station of the neighboring city of Sumner, Washington. Officer Richard E. Mefferd of the Sumner police department put appellant through various physical observation tests for intoxication, and also administered a breathalyzer test, which appellant took of his own volition.

Neither Officer Stewart nor Officer Mefferd was able to form an opinion as to appellant's sobriety from their physical observations of him. However, the result of the breathalyzer test indicated that appellant had .185 per cent alcohol by weight in his blood (185 milligrams in 100 cc. of blood).

Appellant entered a plea of not guilty. The case was tried to the court sitting with a jury. At the close of the state's case, appellant moved to dismiss the case on the ground that the state had failed to produce sufficient legally admissible evidence to support a conviction. The motion was denied. Appellant renewed his motion at the close of all the evidence and it was again denied. The case was then submitted to the jury, which returned a verdict of guilty. Appellant's motion in arrest of judgment or, in the alternative, for a new trial was denied, and judgment and sentence was entered upon the verdict. This appeal followed.

The case, in so far as it relates to the breathalyzer test, is one of first impression in this state. Since the few cases that have been cited to us from other jurisdictions pertaining to breath-testing devices do not cover the precise issues that have been raised here, we make no reference to them.

There are twenty-one assignments of error, nine of which relate to the admissibility in evidence of the breathalyzer test result. We shall first consider these nine assignments. In order to understand the problems presented thereby, it is necessary to describe in some detail the nature of the breathalyzer and its method of operation as shown by the state's evidence.

The breathalyzer is a machine designed to measure the amount of alcohol in the alveolar breath and is based upon the principle that the ratio between the amount of alcohol in the blood and the amount in the alveolar breath from the lungs is a constant 2100 to 1. In other words, the machine analyzes a sample of breath to determine the alcoholic content of the blood. At the time of the trial of this case, there were twenty-three such machines in operation in the state of Washington.

To operate the machine, the subject blows into the machine through a mouthpiece until he has emptied his lungs in one breath. The machine is so designed that it traps only the last 52½ cubic centimeters of air that has been blown into it. This air is then forced, by weight of a piston, through a test ampoule containing a solution of sulphuric acid and potassium dichromate. This test solution has a yellow hue to it. As the breath sample bubbles through the test solution, the sulphuric acid extracts the alcohol, if any, therefrom, and the potassium dichromate then changes the alcohol to acetic acid, thereby causing the solution to lose some of its original yellow color. The greater the alcoholic content of the breath sample, the greater will be the loss in color of the test solution. By causing a light to pass through the test ampoule and through a standard ampoule containing the same chemical solution as the test ampoule (but through which no breath sample has passed), the amount of the change in color can be measured by photoelectric cells which are connected to a galvanometer. By balancing the galvanometer, a reading can be obtained from a gauge which has been calibrated in terms of percentage of alcohol in the blood.

It should be made clear at the outset that appellant does not contend that results of breathalyzer tests, in general, are not admissible in evidence.

He does contend that four basic requirements must be shown by the state before the results of such tests may be admitted in evidence, to wit: (1) That the machine was properly checked and in proper working order at the time of conducting the test; (2) that the chemicals employed were of the correct kind and compounded in the proper proportions; (3) that the subject had nothing in his mouth at the time of the test and that he had taken no food or drink within fifteen minutes prior to taking the test; (4) that the test be given by a qualified operator and in the proper manner.

The expert testimony introduced by the state in this case pertaining to the breathalyzer and its operation shows that unless the above four requirements are satisfied, the result of the test is wholly unreliable. We therefore hold that before the result of a breathalyzer test can be admitted into evidence, the state must produce *prima facie* evidence that each of the four requirements listed above have been complied with.

Appellant takes the position that the first three requirements were not met in the instant case. As to the first requirement, it is contended that the machine was not properly checked, in that Lt. DeWitt Whitman of the Washington state patrol did not use a test thermometer to check the temperature of the breath chamber of the machine during his periodic maintenance checks. Along this same line, it is further intended that Lt. Whitman failed to properly test the machine because he did not use a *test* thermometer to check the temperature of the test ampoule.

Neither contention has any merit. The breath chamber is heated to a temperature between forty-five to fifty degrees centigrade to prevent condensation. If condensation is present in the breath chamber, there is a danger that the piston which compresses the air through the test ampoule will stick and not operate properly. The test ampoule is heated to about sixty-five degrees centigrade so that it can rapidly oxidize the alcohol in the breath sample.

Lt. Whitman testified that he was in charge of the chemical testing program for the state patrol, and that he had studied and worked in that field since 1944. He said that the breathalyzer came into existence in 1955, and that he has been familiar with its operation since that time. He performed maintenance checks on the machine involved herein on July 1, 1958, and on November 14, 1958, and that on both occasions he checked the chamber and ampoule heat with the thermometer which is located in the machine itself, and that the temperatures were accurately recorded in each instance.

Appellant argues that the temperature checks should have been made with a thermometer other than the one used in the machine itself, as the machine thermometer could be faulty.

Lt. Whitman testified that the machine thermometer was checked against a calibrated thermometer at the time the machine was first obtained. In the absence of any indication that the machine thermometer was defective, we think the initial check was sufficient to establish its probable accuracy.

The evidence also discloses that both the ampoule and the chamber heat may vary somewhat without affecting the results of the test. The chamber heat (45-50 degrees centigrade) is marked on the thermometer by a green area, and the ampoule heat (65 degrees centigrade) is designated by a red mark. Lt. Whitman testified that if the temperature of either were substantially higher or lower, the only *possible* result would be a lower reading on the alcoholic content gauge. Thus, appellant could not be prejudiced even if the machine thermometer were inaccurate as any error in temperature would only result in his favor.

Lt. Whitman was cross-examined on the *voir dire* and, in the absence of the jury, appellant's counsel argued his objection to the witness' testifying as to whether in his opinion the machine had been properly checked and, also, argued a motion to strike all evidence as to the breathalyzer. The trial court gave careful consideration to these motions and, after stating his reasons, denied them.

It is next contended that the state failed to satisfy the second basic requirement for the admissibility of the breathalyzer test in that the test ampoule used in the test given appellant was never checked to insure that the chemicals therein were of the correct kind and compounded in the proper proportions.

The ampoules are sealed glass containers which are made and compounded by the same company which makes the breathalyzer machine. The ampoule cannot be tested as to chemical content without being broken, and once it is broken it can no longer be used. Thus, it was impossible to check the particular test ampoule that was used in the test on appellant. However, the state's evidence shows that the ampoules are shipped from the manufacturer in batches and each batch has a control number, which is stamped on each and every ampoule in that particular batch. Every time a new batch is received, Lt. Whitman spot checks at least six ampoules from that particular batch. During the course of his work, Lt. Whitman has tested hundreds of ampoules and has never found one which did not contain what it was certified to contain.

The fact that the *sealed* ampoules are delivered by the manufacturer of the breathalyzer machine for exclusive use in such machine plus the additional fact of regular spot checking of the ampoules is, in our opinion, sufficient *prima facie* proof that the chemicals in any one ampoule are of the proper kind and mixed to the proper proportion.

Appellant argues further that Lt. Whitman was not qualified to conduct spot checks to determine the chemical contents of the ampoules as he was not a chemist.

Lt. Whitman described the method of spot checking as follows:

"I run, first, a check using known alcohol samples. By using an equilibrating device, I can then check this ampoule against a known alcohol solution and find out if the answer arrived at is the proper answer. If you arrive at the proper answer, then there has to be the proper solution in this ampoule. I then use, by another method, by titration, I titrate against the potassium dichromate in this solution with a solution which will reduce the potassium dichromate."

It is not contended that the methods of testing employed by Lt. Whitman are improper. Appellant did not produce a chemist or other qualified expert witness at the trial to challenge the methods of testing used by Lt. Whitman. The qualifications which Lt. Whitman possessed, according to his testimony, are that he is in charge of the chemical testing program of the state patrol; that he took a course in chemical testing at Northwestern University Traffic Institute; that since 1944 he has received extensive training in the field of chemical testing from leading pathologists and toxicologists; and that he has done considerable independent study of his own.

Although Lt. Whitman is not a chemist, he has had sufficient experience in the field of chemical testing of the type involved in this case to warrant the trial court's allowing him to testify concerning his spot checking of the ampoules.

Appellant contends the state failed to meet the third basic requirement in two respects, to wit, (1) Officer Mefferd failed to examine appellant's mouth for the presence of any foreign matter prior to giving him the test; and (2) the police did not have appellant under observation for fifteen minutes prior to giving him the test.

From our examination of the record, we think that this contention is well taken. The testimony of both Lt. Whitman and Dr. Charles P. Larson, the state's two experts on the operation of the breathalyzer machine, makes it clear that unless a subject's mouth is free of all alcohol the test result will be unreliable. Their testimony further establishes that the subject must be kept under observation for at least fifteen minutes to insure that he has not taken anything alcoholic to drink during that period and to allow any alcohol present in the mouth to be absorbed by the skin.

Officer Mefferd candidly admitted that he did not examine appellant's mouth before giving him the test. There is evidence tending to show that appellant may have had an absorbent poultice and a packing impregnated with a medicine (toothache drops) containing alcohol in a cavity in his tooth at the time he took the test. Furthermore, there is evidence tending to show that appellant may have taken some cough medicine containing forty-five to forty-six per cent alcohol by volume within fifteen minutes of the test.

Appellant testified that he took a drink of cough medicine just before being brought to the Sumner police station. Officer Steward testified that the trip to Sumner took six to ten minutes. Officer Mefferd testified that appellant was in his presence at the police station for eight to ten minutes. Thus, under the state's own evidence, appellant may have been given the test after having been under observation for only fourteen minutes. Although this is only one minute less than the required fifteen-minute minimum, the state is bound by its own evidence to the effect that the minimum period of delay must be *fifteen* minutes.

This rule is recognized by Robert L. Donigan, general counsel for the Traffic Institute of Northwestern University, in his work entitled "Chemical Tests and the Law," at page 173, where the author states:

"A breath test will only give an accurate measure of the concentration of alcohol in the circulating blood, if there has been a lapse of *at least* 15 minutes between the taking of the last drink and the taking of the breath for analysis. During this 15-minute interval, any alcoholic liquor remaining in the mouth and throat or under dental plate will have been washed down by saliva. Thereafter, the alcohol concentration of the *breathed* air (alveolar breath) will reflect the alcohol concentration of the blood circulating through the lungs." (First italics ours.)

Both Lt. Whitman and Dr. Larson testified at some length as to the reliability and accuracy of breath-testing machines in general. In addition, Dr. Larson, a physician specializing in forensic pathology and a leading authority on the subject of breath tests, described in great detail what various percentages of alcohol by weight in the blood meant in terms of intoxication. His testimony, if believed by the jury, could leave no doubt that a reading of .185 on the breathalyzer would indicate that the subject was very intoxicated.

We have no way of knowing whether the verdict of guilty stemmed from the jury's finding that, at the time of the accident, appellant was driving in a reckless manner, or that he was then under the influence of, or affected by, intoxicating liquor, or that both of these facts were proven beyond a reasonable doubt. Since the state failed to satisfy the third requirement for the admissibility of the breathalyzer test, the admission of such test was error. In view of the evidence in this case concerning the reliability of breathalyzer tests and the significance of a .185 reading, we are further of the opinion that the error was prejudicial. Appellant is therefore entitled to a new trial.

*   *   *

Because of the trial court's error in admitting in evidence the result of the breathalyzer test, the judgment and sentence are reversed and the case is remanded with directions to grant appellant a new trial.

Weaver, C.J., and Finley, Ott, Rosellini, Foster and Hunter, JJ., concur.

Mallery and Hill, JJ., dissent.

PEOPLE v. BURNS

District Court of Appeal of California, 1952.
109 Cal.App. 524, 241 P.2d 308.

BRAY, Justice. Defendant appeals   *   *   *   from a conviction by a jury of murder in the second degree and an order denying a new trial. *   *   *

Facts.

It is the theory of the prosecution that deceased died from being beaten about the head by defendant. The defendant contends that her death was due to injuries from falls.   *   *   *

Over defendant's objection three photographs of deceased were admitted in evidence. They were pictures of the face, neck, and torso, taken after the autopsy. They were particularly horrible because the head was completely shaved. The head shows large incisions which had been made for the autopsy and were thereafter sewn together. In two pictures the lips were practically turned inside out and held with instruments to show the cuts. Both arms showed marks or punctures made by the surgeon, one being particularly ugly. Bruises and abrasions appear on the face, neck and arms. Most of them are quite faint. No one disputed that the deceased received them. Defendant contended that they came from the falls and striking the objects on the beach. The prosecution claimed that they came from defendant's fists and hands. How looking at the pictures would help the jury understand what caused them or how they could cause death, it is difficult to understand. The completely bald head, the surgical cuts and sutures, the ugly punctures, the inverted lips with the instruments attached, make the body so grotesque and horrible that it is doubtful if the average juror could be persuaded to look at the pictures while the witness pointed out the bruises and abrasions. In view of the fact that no question was raised as to these bruises and abrasions, and the fact that a view of them was of no particular value to the jury, it is obvious that the only purpose of exhibiting them was to inflame the jury's emotions against defendant. In Pennsylvania these photographs would be inadmissible for that reason. In California it has been held that photographs of this kind are admissible even though they show marks of the incisions for the autopsy, and even though they might inflame the minds of the jurors against the defendant. However, in every case in which they were admitted, with the possible exception of the Burkhart case, supra, where the "evidence points positively and unmistakably to the defendant as the perpetrator of the homicide", 211 Cal. at page 730, 297 P. at page 13, there was some necessity for exhibiting the wound or wounds to the jury. In People v. Elmore, 167 Cal. 205, 212, 138 P. 989, the court pointed out that photographs should not be offered or admitted for any purpose other than to help the jury. The admission of photographs of this type is within the sound discretion of the trial court. Surely, there is a line between admitting a photograph which is of some help to the jury in solving the facts of the case and one which is of no value other than to inflame the minds of the jurors. That line was crossed in this case. The error was not waived by the fact that after the court had admitted the photographs and the district attorney asked the doctor to point out on them the injuries shown thereon, defendant objected on the ground that the photographs speak for themselves. There was an abuse of discretion here.

* * *

The judgment and order denying a new trial are reversed.

SHAFFER: JUDGES, REPULSIVE EVIDENCE AND THE ABILITY TO RESPOND

43 Notre Dame Lawyer 503, 505–509 (1968).†
[Some footnotes omitted]

Repulsive Evidence as a Question of Accuracy

A.   Reaction to Repulsive Evidence

The first hypothesis is that prejudice is less important than accuracy, a conclusion that rests on my impression that these trial judges were ambivalent on the "law" of repulsive evidence. On the one hand, in abstract discussion they expressed themselves in terms taken pretty much from the appellate literature—that admissibility of real and demonstrative evidence is a matter of balancing prejudicial effect against probative value; as Judge Spencer Gard* put it in the 1963 conference, the question is one of impact.[8]

---

†Copyright 1968 by the University of Notre Dame.

*Of the Kansas bench.

8.   Judge Gard said that, in his opinion, the color photography issue is not necessarily a question of accuracy at all; it may be a question of impact. Concededly, honest color photography is more accurate than black and white photography. But the readers of newspapers and custodians of family picture albums who sit on juries are accustomed to seeing their photographs in black and white.

It is interesting to compare this with the fact that the 1967 judges expressed virtually no objection to color, and assented to Judge

However, their responses to particular pieces of evidence and the distinctions they made among demonstrative devices focus more on accuracy than on impact and seem to involve relatively little conscious balancing.

Judge Coleman** brought with him a set of color slides that had been taken in the police morgue in Detroit. He projected these slides for the Indiana judges with little or no advance explanation. The judges' reactions to three cases illustrate my hypothesis on accuracy.

In one case (three slides), a young man had been beaten to death by blows on his head with a pistol. The first slide showed his head and shoulders, on a morgue table, and illustrated clearly the location and nature of his wounds. The second and third slides had a less revolting perspective and an additional element: someone was holding a pistol by the dead man's head to demonstrate how the wounds were made.

The second case was very similar; death had been caused by a beating on the head with a lead pipe. The wounds were on the back of the skull, which had been shaved to make them visible. The first slide showed the wounds. The second slide was taken further back and was somewhat less revolting; it also showed a piece of pipe which was held next to the wounds it supposedly made.

The third case showed no body at all. The victim had been killed by a knife wound that pierced his heart. The slides (three of them) were of an excised portion of the aorta. One showed only a small, pale piece of tissue on a morgue table; the second showed the same tissue with a serrated knife next to it; and the third was an enlarged version of the second.

Judge Coleman posed the same question for all three sets of slides—a case (civil or criminal) in which death and the cause of death were at issue. In terms solely of their rulings, a majority of the judges in each of the groups would have (1) admitted slides from the first and second cases which showed the wounds alone, (2) excluded slides from those two cases which included the pistol or the lead pipe, and (3) admitted all of the slides from the third case.

In the first and second (pistol and lead pipe) cases, the pictures that did not show the pistol and pipe were more revolting than the pictures that did—this was because they were taken closer to the bodies and because the presence of the metal object tended to divert attention from the bodies. None of the judges, however, objected to the repulsive exhibits before them, although many of them expressly objected to the attempt at demonstration that was involved in the pictures comparing the wounds with the pistol or

Coleman's observation that amateur use of color photography by judges was one reason for its general acceptance as evidence. "Color pictures are true to life"; "If that is a true likeness of what they [witnesses] saw, then they [litigants] have a right to have it introduced."

Another interesting comparison, and one that supports a generalization in terms of accuracy, is the relatively greater judicial suspicion of movies as evidence. Most judges have allowed them, but they have taken the precaution of routinely previewing them before they are shown to the jury.

Some of the judges said their orders on editing often resulted in such broad removal of material from the movie that counsel decided not to use it. Other judges suspected misuse: "More splicing takes place after the judge has seen the movie than before" (this comment, by the way, from an appellate judge). Another judge said he explained the films to the jury himself while they ran. The judges seemed generally to feel that movies required a more exhaustive foundation than still photographs.

**Of the Michigan bench.

pipe. Some of their comments: "Let that come in by testimony * * * this is too theoretical." "The jury's guess is as accurate as the fellow's who posed the photograph. * * * It's unrealistic to pose the pipe." "This enters into the realm of speculation * * * don't know as how I could go along with that." The last judge emphasized that he thought the comparison similar to testimony by a morgue police officer on how the death occurred, which would be excluded because the officer was not present when the wounds were inflicted. One judge thought this visual comparison was in effect hearsay testimony; another thought that, in a criminal case, the comparison would violate the defendant's right to confront and cross-examine his accusers. "You're introducing a separate element, a foreign object," one judge said, although he admitted that he would allow a comparison of the pipe and the picture of the wounded skull by a witness whose competence to testify on the issue was shown. This alternative, another judge at the same session said, would remove the hearsay objection.[9] It did not alter these conclusions to point out, as Judge Coleman did in one session, that the officer who "posed" the weapon was present and testifying when the slide was shown.[10]

In the third case, the knife-aorta pictures were not repulsive, but they clearly involved a certain amount of posing. The two most representative comments on these pictures were probably that of a judge who expressed spontaneous admiration for the close detective work the "posed" slides demonstrated and that of a judge who said that the fundamental purpose of trials is to discover truth—"you have to use common sense." All of the judges would have admitted the picture of aortic tissue without the knife; a very clear majority of them would have admitted the aorta and knife; a bare majority of them would have admitted the enlarged picture of the aorta and knife. The general and strong objection against posed pictures that was demonstrated in the skull-wound cases was eroded when the demonstration involved was clearly accurate, as it was in the posed knife-aorta pictures.

Can the difference be explained in terms of gruesomeness? The aorta slides were not really gruesome at all. The lead-pipe slides were very gruesome and the pistol-whipping slides relatively gruesome. But I did not detect the balancing between probative value and gruesomeness that is found in the appellate literature.[11] I detected instead clear dispositions (1) to let the jury see the results of what happened (the skull pictures), (2) to

9. Judge Coleman also suggested a hypothetical sand box, used to demonstrate comparisons of footprints. A bare majority of the judges would have allowed the box; some of the objections: "A little far-fetched"; "You're quite a ways from home base on that"; "Might lose a lot in the translation there."

10. The fact that these slides were in color raised a small amount of interesting discussion. At one session, Judge Coleman asked, before he showed any of these slides, whether the judges objected to color photography when black-and-white pictures of the same matter were available. No one said he had general objections to color —although some indicated that they had changed attitudes on that point in the last decade. See note 8, supra. Furthermore, no one indicated a change of mind after he saw the slides. Some, in fact, said they preferred color pictures. "Blood is red, isn't it?" Judge Coleman said to them. However, each of the groups demonstrated revulsion ("Holy cow!") at graphic color slides.

11. See 4 Wigmore, Evidence §§ 1157–58 (3d ed. 1940). "Gruesome" is probably the usual word to describe this sort of evidence, but I prefer "repulsive" (which Fowler says is better for my purposes than "repellant"), because "repulsive" covers the observer's reaction more than it covers a supposed inherent quality in the exhibit.

protect them from conjecture as to *how* it happened—at least from conjecture outside the courtroom (the pistol and lead-pipe pictures), but (3) to expose them to conjecture which tended to demonstrate clearly its own probative sanction (the aorta and knife pictures). The generalization in terms of accuracy, rather than impact, is certainly suggested in this bit of data.

This is not to say, though, that revulsion is unimportant. The pistol-whipping and lead-pipe demonstrations were not only less accurate, they were also more repulsive, although those with demonstrative elements were less repulsive than those without demonstrative elements. I think it is fair to say that the test of accuracy is applied somewhat more closely where revulsion is involved. In other words, it is possible that a demand for accuracy almost instinctively burst forth when bloody pictures were presented, a demand that was not so intense where the evidence was not so repulsive. That generalization is subject to two further verifications in my data.

The aorta slides are an inadequate test because they were relatively less repulsive than the skull slides, as well as relatively more accurate. The best test would be a picture that was as gruesome as the skull slides yet as accurate as the aorta slides. Judge Coleman had a possible case for that test —two slides showing the head and shoulders of a young woman who had been fatally shot through the head. One of these slides showed the corpse only; the other showed the corpse with a probe inserted into and out of the fatal wound, demonstrating the path the bullet took. One group would have allowed the second of these slides on the expressed theory that otherwise the party having the burden of proof could not have demonstrated the path of the bullet. (Testimony, though, was available on that point.) Another group, however, would have allowed it only after a testimonial foundation from the person who inserted the probe; otherwise "how can you tell it's not pinned?" The third group agreed that the question was one of the illustrative value of the probe. In the fourth group, one judge said he had allowed a similar picture. This bit of first-hand experience tended to dampen discussion; one other participant, though, said he thought that the picture without the probe proved nothing that testimony could not prove as well. The probe picture, therefore, may demonstrate that a repulsive picture with an accurate demonstration in it is admissible, even though an equally repulsive picture with a less accurate demonstration is not. It should at least indicate that the test is one of accuracy, not of revulsion.

Another way to test the hypothesis would be to see if accuracy is less closely guarded where the evidence is not repulsive. Judge Coleman had several exhibits and orally presented several abstract problems, which were relatively bland and involved varying degrees of accuracy:

    1.   A building collapses and the builder is sued for defective construction. There are offered in evidence (A) samples of the brick and mortar from the defective building and (B) samples from a "good" building not otherwise at issue. Most judges would have overruled objections to the defective material, but sustained objections to the "good" material. The articulated reason for the difference was that the second exhibit involved an out-of-court demonstration of the way bricks are properly laid. Some of the judges, however, said they would allow a demonstration to the same effect in the courtroom.

2.   In a slip-and-fall accident case, plaintiff's counsel offers exhibits of properly roughened tile to illustrate why the defendant's smooth tile fell below the standard of care. Most judges would not have admitted the tile, absent evidence of a custom in the business community. Judge Coleman mentioned that, in a recent case in his court, he had not permitted evidence on reflectorized tape on railroad cars, nor a showing of Interstate Commerce Commission regulations requiring its use.

3.   In a narcotics prosecution, the government offers a spoon and syringe used in taking heroin. Most judges would have permitted the spoon and syringe the defendant used, but not any sort of model.

4.   In a will contest involving mental capacity a snapshot of the testator taken at about the time of the will execution is offered by the proponent. Most judges would have required a showing of the relevance of physical condition; their discussion suggested that a physical image of the testator might otherwise influence the jurors improperly. (That it might not be *accurate* on the issue of mental capacity?) In one session, this question evoked a relatively vigorous debate:

Judge *A*: "That could be very misleading to a jury." (Murmurs all around.)

Judge *B* (to Judge *A*):   "What right do you have to substitute your judgment for that of the jury?"

Judge *C*:   "There's no probative value in that." (Murmurs all around.) Judge Coleman then asked whether the judges would allow sound movies of an entire will execution, and the judges replied, with renewed unanimity, that they would.[12]

5.   Judge Coleman presented an interesting contrast between Indiana's little-used rules on jury views and the use of composite pictures and models. The picture involved was used in a rape-murder prosecution. It showed a hundred yards of verdant, residential river bank. The victim had been knocked down at the far right edge of the scene, raped at about the center and murdered at the far left. The picture was a clear, exactly done composite of twelve enlarged exposures. No one at any of the sessions disapproved of it. What is the difference between this picture and the "posed" comparisons of skulls and murder weapons? Which has the greater possibility of error? Which is repulsive? (It is interesting to note that some of the judges who approved of this picture would not have allowed the slides showing the probe through the gunshot wound or the knife-aorta slides.)

The model, which Judge Coleman described orally, showed a curved section of highway on which a collision occurred. It presented an aerial view, which was inadequate to illustrate the perspective presented to the driver of an automobile on the highway. The model maker had corrected this inadequacy by providing a sort of periscope, into which jurors could look, which simulated the scene as it was presented to the driver. The judges expressed nothing but admiration for this reconstruction and ap-

12.   Time, Dec. 22, 1967, at 49, describes the use of this device by Mr. Thomas Cassidy of the Peoria, Illinois, Bar—apparently more as insurance against contest being brought, though, than as potential evidence of capacity.

proved of the Michigan trial judge who had admitted it into evidence. One judge recalled that he had allowed a similar model showing automotive acceleration; another had allowed a model of a tree which had been struck by an automobile. Judge Coleman remarked to these judges that most questions of accuracy go to weight, not admissibility. Compare the reconstructions involved in the autopsy pictures of the pistol and lead pipe in terms of their accuracy and repulsiveness. The judges who admitted composite photographs and models but disapproved of photographic comparison of weapons and bodies seemed to be referring to degrees of demonstrated accuracy rather than to degrees of revulsion. A judgment on accuracy, rather than a balancing between gruesomeness and probative value, seems to me the best explanation of the "law" as it was developed in these sessions.

HOUTS, PHOTOGRAPHIC MISREPRESENTATION

Matthew Bender & Co.; San Franciso; 1964, pp. 5–46 to 5–49.

[8]—Lens Performance: Position of Automobiles

* * *

Figures 54 & 55 are taken from the same camera position behind the convertible automobile. A short focal length lens is used in *Figure 54.* This makes it appear that there is a substantial distance between the two vehicles and that perhaps the driver of the convertible would have had ample time to stop when the other car pulled out in front of him. *Figure 55* was taken with a long focal length lens which "pulls" the two vehicles together, making it appear that the driver of the convertible would not have had time to stop. * * *

WALTZ, CRIMINAL EVIDENCE

416–424 (1975).*

DEMONSTRATIVE EVIDENCE

A.

Historical Background

It is pointed out in [an earlier chapter] that demonstrative evidence is to be distinguished from real evidence in that demonstrative evidence consists of tangible materials that are used for illustrative or explanatory purposes only and do not purport to be "the real thing"—the murder weapon, the burglary tools actually used by the accused, the heroin seized by the narcotics agents when they arrested the defendant. It was also mentioned in [an earlier chapter] that there are two basic types of demonstrative evidence: (1) *selected* demonstrative evidence, such as handwriting exemplars, and (2) *prepared* or *reproduced* demonstrative evidence, such as a sketch or diagram * * * . In this chapter we go into somewhat greater depth in describing types of demonstrative evidence and the range of possible objections to its use.

Figure 54

Figure 55

There has been a resurgence of interest in the imaginative use of demonstrative evidence, after a lengthy period during which trial lawyers were reluctant to rely on it for fear of causing an adverse reaction by jurors who might draw the implication that an essentially weak case was being overproved by means of unsubstantial gimmickry. Unquestionably, the use of demonstrative evidence has had its ups and downs, as the following commentary—made almost a hundred years ago—attests:

> In the early and rude ages there was a strong leaning toward the adoption of demonstrative and practical tests upon disputed questions. Doubting Thomases demanded the satisfaction of their senses. * * * As society grew civilized and refined, it seemed disposed to despise these demonstrative methods, and inclined more to the preference of a narration, at second-hand, by eye and ear witnesses. But in this busy century there seems to have been a relapse toward the earlier experimental spirit, and a disposition to make assurance doubly sure by any practical method addressed to the senses. (Browne, Practical Tests in Evidence, 4 Green Bag 510 (1892).)

Of course, there is nothing inherently wrong with evidence which is addressed to some sense other than that of hearing. One character in the musical My Fair Lady may have unwittingly summed up the attitude of many jury members when she said, "Words, words, words—I'm sick of words. Is that all you lawyers can do? *Show me!*" (Italics added.)

For a number of years now, trial lawyers have paid increasing attention to demonstrative evidence as a means of *showing* the elements of a case to the fact-finder.

Perhaps the earliest reported use of demonstrative evidence was in the *Case of James Watson, the elder, Surgeon, on an Indictment charging him with High Treason,* 32 Howard State Trials 1 (1817). There was offered into evidence in that case a sketch of a flag that allegedly had been used to whip up a "treasonous assemblage" in England. Defense counsel objected, arguing that the flag "was a matter of verbal description not of description by drawing." The trial judge sneered and overruled the objection: "Can there be any objection to the production of a drawing, or a model, as illustrative of evidence? Surely there is nothing in the objection."

Another leading case, this time arising in America but not many years after the Watson trial, is Commonwealth v. Webster, 5 Cush. 295 (Sup.Jud.Ct.Mass.1850). Professor Webster had been charged with murdering Doctor Parkman and burning his body in a furnace. A mold of Doctor Parkman's jaw, made several years previously when he had been fitted for dentures, taken together with some teeth that had survived the furnace fire, was credited with securing Webster's conviction.

Today the propriety, in fact the wisdom, of using demonstrative evidence to help jurors follow the trial evidence goes pretty much without question in many cases, both criminal and civil. Objections to demonstrative evidence are frequently voiced, however.

B.

Bases for Objection to Demonstrative Evidence

Misguided Objections. Some objections to demonstrative evidence are misguided and will be swiftly overruled. Occasionally a lawyer will become confused about the proper application of the best evidence rule, discussed [earlier], and contend that the "original," and not "a mere example," must be produced in court. Thus one hears about the Texas judge who prohibited the use of a skeletal model because it did not consist of the very bones of the complaining witness (who was not dead). This judge had forgotten, if he ever knew, that the best evidence rule applies only to written documents.

Then, too, one sometimes encounters a misguided hearsay objection to demonstrative evidence. Defense counsel leaps up to object to the prosecution's offer of a witness's freehand sketch of a crime scene, asking, "How can we cross-examine a sketch, Your Honor?" What this objection misses, of course, is the fact that the sketch is being offered as a part of the testimony of a witness on the stand who is fully subject to confrontation and cross-examination.

Objections Grounded on Lack of Verity or Accuracy. As was suggested in [an earlier chapter], dealing with the perfecting of the trial record, a proper foundation or predicate must be laid before an item of demonstrative evidence can successfully be offered. The witness who is in a position to "sponsor" (authenticate) the exhibit must identify it and verify the verity, the accuracy of whatever it portrays. This does not mean that the sponsoring witness must be the person who took the photograph or prepared the drawing, chart, or map.

Example:

BY THE PROSECUTING ATTORNEY: Officer Ham, you have testified that you were present, in your investigative capacity, at the scene of the murders, isn't that correct?

A.   That's right, I was in the room for maybe three hours.

Q.   And you have testified to its general layout and appearance, have you not?

A.   I have.

Q.   To your knowledge, were photographs of the room taken while you were there?

A.   Yes, our photographer took a number of shots of the place.

Q.   Officer Ham, I now hand you what previously has been marked Prosecution Exhibit 12 for Identification, being a photographic print, and ask you whether or not it is a fair and accurate representation of the room at 421 Melrose Street on the day in question?

A.   Yes, sir, it is. That's exactly the way it looked.

BY THE PROSECUTING ATTORNEY: Your Honor, we offer prosecution's 12 into evidence.

BY DEFENSE COUNSEL: We have no objection.

THE COURT: The exhibit will be received.

There can be no stronger an objection to demonstrative evidence than that it is not a fair representation of what it supposedly depicts. If, for example, a photograph or map significantly distorts relevant aspects of the scene depicted, it will be subject to successful objection, or at least to an instruction that the jury is to disregard the distorted parts.

Occasionally photographs can be obtained only after autopsy procedures have in a sense distorted the picture of a deceased: the head has been shaved; large incisions have been made; sutures may be visible. Still, the tendency is to admit such photographs if they add to the case anything of real probative value. Thus in Young v. State, 299 P. 682 (S.Ct.Ariz.1931), the court, commenting on the receipt in evidence of post-autopsy photographs, said, "[T]he fact that the ghastly appearance of the wounds, even though such appearance was heightened by the shaving of the head and the use of mercurochrome * * * did not make [the photographs] inadmissible."

So long as the color has not been artificially and misleadingly heightened, there is a trend toward preferring natural color to black-and-white photographs. Some years ago Professor Conrad, an authority on photographic evidence, wrote, "[W]e have used black and white photographs for so long that we accept them as the real thing. Actually, black and white photography is considered an abstract medium and does not represent reality as such. * * * The inherent realism of color photography has been urged [as preferable to black and white]. * * * " (Conrad, Evidential Aspects of Color Photography, 4 Jour. of Forensic Science 176, 178 (1959).)

The fact that a photograph or other item of demonstrative evidence has been retouched or marked will not, in and of itself, result in inadmissibility. For example, in State v. Weston, 64 P.2d 536 (S.Ct.Or.1937), plaster casts of a body containing gunshot wounds had been prepared prior to autopsy. Many small blue dots had been placed on the casts by a witness who compared the casts with the body in order to distinguish the bullet wounds from air bubbles in the plaster casts. When the casts were offered in evidence to exemplify the location of the bullet wounds, defense counsel objected that "after the blue dots which indicate the wounds had been placed upon the cast it was no longer * * * a true representation of deceased's forearm and hand." The Oregon Supreme Court laid down the applicable principles:

> The jury was amply informed that the sole purpose of the blue dots was to indicate the presence of the wounds. Since the jurors could rightfully look at the indications of the wounds, we cannot understand how the help which these small dots gave them in locating the wounds would have prejudiced any interest properly claimed by the defendant. * * *
>
> [W]e deduce the rule that maps, photographs et cetera, containing markings, are not inadmissible if they are otherwise relevant and if the individual who made the mark or wrote the legend was familiar with the facts and so testifies, or if some other witness, familiar with the facts, adopts the mark or legend as his own. (See also Busch, Photographic Evidence, 4 DePaul Law Rev. 195 (1955).)

Models are sometimes rejected by trial courts because they may be misleading or confusing due to difference in scale.

Example a.:

San Mateo County v. Christian, 71 P.2d 88 (Cal.App. 1937) ("While models may frequently be of great assistance to a court and jury, it is common knowledge that, even when constructed to scale, they may frequently, because of the great disparity in size between the model and the original, also be very misleading. * * * ").

Example b.:

Martindale v. City of Mountain View, 25 Cal.Rptr. 148 (Cal.App.1962) (in assault and battery case, testimony was that victim had been beaten with 2′ stick; offer in evidence of axe handle 3′ long rejected).

Courts are suspicious of filmed reenactments and posed photographs, lest they be misleading. A leading case, Richardson v. Missouri-K. T. R. Co. of Texas, 205 S.W.2d 819 (Tex.Civ.App.1947), arose on the civil side. To establish that the plaintiff himself had been negligent, the defendant introduced a color film showing plaintiff's shop foreman demonstrating how plaintiff's hand "*could* be caught and run through the blades" of a shaping machine (italics added). The foreman testified that "he did not know how the fingers of [plaintiff] were caught in the machine and therefore his experiments did not undertake to show how [plaintiff] was operating it at the time."

The Texas court brushed aside the plaintiff's objections to this filmed reenactment. "In the final analysis," the court said, "the increased danger of fraud peculiar to posed photographs must be weighed against their communicative value. Only the additional danger of fraud or suggestion separates this question from that of the admissibility of ordinary photographs."

In line with the Richardson decision, posed and photographed reenactments of a crime are sometimes admitted in evidence after a careful foundation, which manifests the accuracy of the reenactment, has been laid by the prosecuting attorney.

Gruesome Films and Photographs. Another prime basis of objections to demonstrative evidence is that the motion picture, or still photograph is gruesome and inflammatory; in other words, that its potential for prejudice to the accused's right to a fair trial outweighs whatever probative worth it may have. An objection of this sort is directed to the trial judge's discretion.

A photograph or motion picture is not inadmissible simply because it is gruesome. That has been understood ever since the opinion in Franklin v. State, 69 Ga. 36 (S.Ct. Ga.1882), involving some gruesome photographs:

The throat of the deceased was cut; the character of the wound was important * * * ; the man was killed and buried * * * ; we cannot conceive of a more impartial and truthful witness than the sun, as its light stamps and seals the similitude of the wound on the photograph put before the jury; it would be more accurate than the memory of witnesses, and as the object of all evidence is to show the truth, why should not this dumb [in the sense of mute] witness show it?

Ever since *Franklin* it has been the rule that photographs and films are not rendered inadmissible simply because they depict in a graphic way the details of a shocking or revolting crime. They will be deemed inadmissible only if they are irrelevant to the issues in the case or where their probative worth is outweighed by their potential for unfair prejudice.

Example a:

Johnson v. Commonwealth, 445 S.W.2d 704 (S.Ct. Ky.1970) (hideous photographs showing mangled body in morgue, *held,* admissible to support autopsy surgeon's explanatory testimony).

Example b:

Henninger v. State, 251 So.2d 862 (S.Ct. Fla.1971) (three gruesome photographs showing knife wounds in back, partially severed head, and pantyhose wrapped around neck, *held,* admissible to establish identity of accused, cause of death, and to rebut claim of self-defense).

Appellate courts will conclude that it was an abuse of judicial discretion to receive gruesome photographs only when they were unnecessary, cumulative to the narrative testimony of witnesses, or where, although of minimal evidentiary value, they have been overemphasized to the jury. Thus it may be error to admit gruesome photographs when the testimony of an available pathologist would do just as well (see, e.g., State v. Bischert, 308 P.2d 969 (S.Ct. Mont.1957)). In an early California case, Thrall v. Smiley, 9 Cal.Rep. 529 (S.Ct. Cal.1858), the court rejected drawings of the defendant's damaged teeth, noting that the sketches were not "necessary to illustrate the fact asserted [since] the extent of the injury could be as well understood from the statement of the dentist who repaired them." And projecting color slides of the deceased's wounds for a full half day during a four and one-half day trial has led to reversal. (Commonwealth v. Johnson, 167 A.2d 511 (S.Ct. Pa.1961).) Some additional examples are given below:

Example a:

Commonwealth v. Dankel, 301 A.2d 365 (S.Ct. Pa. 1973) (where only factual dispute was whether accused aided in burglary during which a homicide occurred, introduction by prosecution of four gruesome photographs of victim, showing face eroded by ammonia burns, was reversible error).

Example b:

Terry v. State, 491 S.W.2d 161 (Tex.Crim.App.1973) (where bruises and other injures sustained by infant homicide victim had already been shown with pre-autopsy photographs, it was prejudicial error to receive four post-autopsy photographs depicting massive mutilation to child caused by autopsy procedures).

Example c:

Beagles v. State, 273 So.2d 796 (Fla.App.1973) (where defense in first degree murder case admitted victim's death, the cause of death, and her identity, the admission of numerous gruesome color photographs of the victim was error: "Photographs should be received in evidence with great caution and photographs which show nothing more than a gory or gruesome portrayal should not be admitted.").

Trial judges will protect an accused against the use of demonstrative evidence the primary purpose of which is to whip jurors into a vindictive mood. But demonstrative evidence has a firmly settled place in criminal litigation. If it is used sparingly, with scrupulous accuracy, and only when it holds out genuine promise of making the case more readily understandable by judge and jurors, courts can be expected to be liberal in their rulings on the admissibility question.

EXPANDED USE OF EXPERT WITNESSES
POSE NEW PROBLEMS FOR COUNSEL

The National Law Journal, Dec. 31, 1979.

Recent years have seen a quantum jump in the use of economic and other expert witnesses in complex commercial litigation in the federal courts. Forbes magazine recently commented upon this dramatic growth, and perhaps inferentially conjectured on the reason, observing "if prostitution is the oldest profession, economics may well be the newest."[1]

An example of the Dickensian proportions of this phenomenon is the trial in United States v. IBM Corp., 69 Civ. 200, before Chief Judge David Edelstein of the U.S. District Court for Southern District of New York. It began in May 1975 and its end is not yet in sight. The government, which ended its direct case in April 1978, utilized the testimony of four different expert witnesses. IBM is expected to use at least that many, if neither the pending settlement negotiations nor the proceedings to disqualify Chief Judge Edelstein interfere with the progress of the case.

Three of the government's expert witnesses were economists and the fourth was a computer industry consultant. These witnesses testified for a total period well over three months and comprised about 25 percent of the government's case. The government's principal economist testified for 78 days.

While the IBM case is not typical, other cases before judges, juries and administrative law judges present analogous problems of preparation and cross-examination.

The extensive growth in the use of expert witnesses is due in some considerable part to the liberal treatment afforded expert testimony under the Federal Rules of Evidence and particularly Rule 702.[2] The definition of an expert is broadly defined to include any witness qualified by special "knowledge, skill, experience, training or education," clearly going beyond traditional or restricted definitions of the term. The distinction between "expert" and "skilled" witnesses has been blurred or eliminated.

Unlike some state rules which permit an expert to testify only when such testimony is "necessary" to aid the trier of fact, Rule 702 broadens the ability to utilize such testimony by merely requiring that the testimony of the expert be "helpful" or "assist" the trier of fact in arriving at the truth. Once these rather modest qualifications are met, the expert may well be free to answer hypothetical questions and give a wide range of opinions so long as these statements are within his or her purported area of competence. Rule 704[6] also removes another arguable limitation by specifically providing that an expert may give opinions on so-called "ultimate issues."

1. Cheerful Days In The Dismal Science, Forbes, Jan. 8, 1979, p. 35.

2. Federal Rule of Evidence 702:

    If scientific, technical, or other specialized knowledge will assist the trier of fact to understand the evidence or to determine a fact in issue, a witness qualified as an expert by knowledge, skill, experience, training, or education, may testify thereto in the form of an opinion or otherwise.

6. Federal Rule of Evidence 704:

    Testimony in the form of an opinion or inference otherwise admissible is not objectionable because it embraces an ultimate issue to be decided by the trier of fact. Nielson v. Armstrong Rubber Co., 570 F.2d 272 (8th Cir. 1978); United States v. Morgan, 554 F.2d 31 (2d Cir. 1977).

The Federal Rules also present a change from past practice with respect to the predicate or foundation for expert testimony. Under Rule 703 expert testimony need not necessarily be based on personal knowledge of the expert or evidence in the record. So long as there is suitable "indicia of trustworthiness" or "reasonable basis of reliability," an expert is permitted wide latitude as to the materials on which he may base his testimony.[7]

Not surprisingly many practitioners have made wide and effective use of this broad latitude by resorting broadly to phrased "expert opinions" on ultimate issues, often based on little support in a record, to provide essential elements of a case for which little direct proof was available. Conjectural theories of liability or damages may thus assume the dignity of proof when asserted by an expert. Able advocates have, however, been able to respond to these tactics by effective use of discovery and cross-examination to the point where it may well be that the dangers of extensive use of experts can outweigh the advantages.   *   *   *

*   *   * The discovery devices available to the party confronted with an opponent's expert witness include principally: (1) F.R. Civ. P. Rule 26(b)(4), which generally provides for further discovery of experts as ordered by the court upon motion, and has been widely employed to authorize depositions of experts; (2) Rule 705 of the Federal Rules of Evidence which broadly defines, the scope of cross-examination of an expert; and (3) Rule 612 of the Federal Rules of Evidence, which has, in some instances, provided for broad discovery of materials used by an expert to "refresh his memory."

Depositions and production of documents will generally not be granted until such interrogatories have been served. United States v. IBM Corp., 72 F.R.D. 78 (S.D.N.Y. 1976).[8] Rule 26(b)(4)(A) does not provide for the production of documents indicating that they can be obtained only upon court order, a matter within the broad discretion of the trial judge.

While the full scope of these discovery devices remains to be developed, it is already clear that Rule 612 will be a valuable tool for counsel who are confronted with an expert. More ominously, Rule 612 represents a frequently unexpected and extreme risk to the party employing the expert. The most important caveat is the danger of an inadvertent waiver of otherwise available privilege or immunity from discovery which is assumed to attach to preliminary factual or legal position papers or summaries.

For example, in preparing a case an attorney will generally find it valuable to work in close association with an expert. Counsel will seek to design a case with an eye toward economic or other theoretical concepts. Legal and economic thesis should be co-ordinated and each can be used to test the other. Because the attorney's work product and the experts analysis can easily become "so interrelated as to become a composite work of both," the attorney, working in such close proximity with the expert who is being prepared to testify runs the risk of losing the protection that present discovery rules generally afford "work product."

---

7.   Fraier v. Continental Oil Co., 568 F.2d 378 (5th Cir. 1978); Merit Motors Inc. v. Chrysler Corp., 569 F.2d 666 (D.C. Cir. 1977).

8.   See also In Re IBM Peripheral EDP Devices Antitrust Litigation, 77 F.R.D. 39 (N.D. Cal. 1977).

A recent series of cases have highlighted the questions as to the scope of Rule 612[10] and its role in the disclosure of materials related to expert testimony.

A critical aspect of the controversy concerns whether Rule 612 allows for the broad discovery of records and documents that were used by an expert in preparation of testimony at a disposition or trial, or is limited to the discovery of materials actually referred to while testifying.

The literal terms of the rule provide for mandatory disclosure on request of documents actually used to refresh a witness' recollection while testifying. Disclosure of materials consulted before testifying can become available upon application to the court. The scope of the term "before testifying" has been the basis for much of the expansion and uncertainty attendant to the rule. Read broadly it gives the court discretion to require disclosure of all sources of information that the expert used in forming his evaluation. These sources often include documents prepared by, or for, an attorney, that otherwise would probably be immune from disclosure. It then threatens to be the basis of an embarrassing, and substantively damaging, finding of waiver.

Bailey v. Meister Brau, Inc., 57 F.R.D. 11 (N.D. Ill. 1972) was an early case dealing with this question. The defendants sought to gain access to documents used by plaintiff's expert at his deposition, which were claimed to be protected by attorney-client privilege. The court held that (a) "counsel is entitled to inspect any writing used by a witness to refresh his recollection," and (b) that any claim of privilege was waived by the manner of use of the otherwise privileged documents. The court concluded that to deny discovery would provide an unfair advantage to the attorney who used the documents to prepare a witness by handicapping the opponent who sought to cross examine the same witness.

Some later cases have limited *Bailey* and the reach of Rule 612 to materials or documents used to refresh recollection *while* testifying. However, a recent line of cases has rather explicitly sought to alert the bar that that Rule 612 can be construed to allow broad access to information and materials seen or used by experts, not necessarily with a direct nexus to testimony, notwithstanding the fact that it might otherwise be exempt from discovery.

In Berkey Photo, Inc. v. Eastman Kodak Co., 74 F.R.D. 613 (S.D.N.Y. 1977), plaintiff sought, at a deposition ordered by a magistrate under Rule 26, production of all documents used by the defendant's expert, including attorney notebooks which were claimed to be protected as work product. The notebooks had been prepared by counsel for his own use and were made available to aid the expert in his efforts to become familiar with the case. Defense counsel claimed they revealed intimate details of his strategy and efforts.

After an in camera review of the notebooks, and deciding that prior law did not give a clear enough warning of the dangers of waivers of the privilege, District Judge Marvin E. Frankel did not require production of the

10.　Rule provides in part: " * * * if a witness uses a writing to refresh his memory for the purpose of testifying, either (1) while testifying, or (2) before testifying, if the court in its discretion determines it is necessary in the interest of justice, an ad- verse party is entitled to have the writing produced at the hearing, to inspect it, to cross-examine the witness thereon, and to introduce in evidence those portions which relate to the testimony of the witness * * * ."

notebooks. Judge Frankel did indicate that Rule 612 is broad enough and designed to permit "access to those writings which may fairly be said to have an impact upon the testimony of the witness" and counsel working with an expert will henceforth have "powerful reason" to limit what the expert may review. He ruled that in subsequent cases a demand for documents reviewed by an expert should be honored so long as it seeks to "promote the search of credibility and memory" and that attorneys should expect this result when sharing their efforts with the testifying expert.

In Wheeling-Pittsburgh Steel Corp. v. Underwriters Laboratories, 81 F.R.D. 385 (N.D. Ill. 1978) the court addressed these same issues and permitted the inspection of an attorney's file labeled "communications with clients" which was taken for review by plaintiff's metallurgical engineer several months earlier and returned the day before his testimony was to be given.

While the court cited *Bailey* and attempted to limit the scope of Rule 612, the decision was clearly premised upon the notion that any "writings which may fairly be said to have an impact upon" the testimony of the witness are discoverable. The fact that the documents were used to refresh the witness' recollection prior to his testimony rather than during his testimony was deemed to be of no moment. In addressing the question of privilege, the court held that such use of once privileged material constituted a waiver.

A device which has been employed to avoid some of these pitfalls in complex commercial litigation involves the use of so-called non-testimonial expert witnesses. Under Rule 26 (b) (4)(B) of the Federal Rules of Civil Procedure, discovery of facts known or opinions held by an expert who is not expected to be called as a witness is limited to showings of "exceptional circumstances.[16]" This test seeks to minimize unfair advantage and to prevent unwarranted free rides on discovery when similar information is sufficiently obtainable.

Therefore, absent "exceptional circumstances," an attorney may generally retain a non-testimonial expert to help him gain an adequate understanding of the complexities of a particular area without running the same risk of disclosure as is involved in the use of testimonial experts. Bryan v. John Beam Division of FMC Corp., 566 F. 2d 541 (5th Cir. 1978) indicates that when an expert testifies as to subject matter also addressed by a non-testimonial expert, a court may impose considerable limitations on the extent to which the particulars of the non-testimonial expert's research or preparation may be uncovered.

In *Bryan*, the court held that reports of non-testifying experts, examined and relied on by a testifying expert but inconsistent with his own * * * testimony, were not admissible even as impeachment evidence "unless the testifying expert based his opinion on the opinion in the examined report or testified directly from the report."[18] This result obtained, even though the testifying expert relied on data set forth in the reports. The law and practice in this area await further development.

In sum, * * * practitioners are urged to think long and hard about whether you really want a long and important case to turn on whether a single expert witness can stand up on cross-examination.

---

16.   See FRCP 26 (b) (4) (B) at Note 8.   18.   Bryan, supra, 566 F. 2d at 546.

*

APPENDIX A

THE
EVIDENCE CODE
OF THE
STATE OF CALIFORNIA

AN ACT to establish an Evidence Code, thereby consolidating and revising the law relating to evidence; amending various sections of the Business and Professions Code, Civil Code, Code of Civil Procedure, Corporations Code, Government Code, Health and Safety Code, Penal Code, and Public Utilities Code to make them consistent therewith; adding Sections 164.5, 3544, 3545, 3546, 3547, and 3548 to the Civil Code; adding Sections 631.7 and 1908.5 to the Code of Civil Procedure; and repealing legislation inconsistent therewith.

Stats.1965, c. 299.

Approved and filed May 18, 1965.

Effective January 1, 1967.

As amended through the 1979 portion of the 1979–1980 Regular Session.

The people of the State of California do enact as follows:

Division 1
PRELIMINARY PROVISIONS AND CONSTRUCTION

§ 1. Short title

This code shall be known as the Evidence Code.
(Stats.1965, c. 299, § 2.)

§ 2. Common law rule construing code abrogated

The rule of the common law, that statutes in derogation thereof are to be strictly construed, has no application to this code. This code establishes the law of this state respecting the subject to which it relates, and its provisions are to be liberally construed with a view to effecting its objects and promoting justice.
(Stats.1965, c. 299, § 2.)

§ 3. Constitutionality

If any provision or clause of this code or application thereof to any person or circumstances is held invalid, such invalidity shall not affect other provisions or applications of the code which can be given effect without the invalid provision or application, and to this end the provisions of this code are declared to be severable.
(Stats.1965, c. 299, § 2.)

§ 4. Construction of code

Unless the provision or context otherwise requires, these preliminary provisions and rules of construction shall govern the construction of this code.
(Stats.1965, c. 299, § 2.)

§ 5. Effect of headings

Division, chapter, article, and section headings do not in any manner affect the scope, meaning, or intent of the provisions of this code.
(Stats.1965, c. 299, § 2.)

§ 6. References to statutes

Whenever any reference is made to any portion of this code or of any other statute, such reference shall apply to all amendments and additions heretofore or hereafter made.
(Stats.1965, c. 299, § 2.)

§ 7. "Division," "chapter," "article," "section," "subdivision," and "paragraph"

Unless otherwise expressly stated:

(a) "Division" means a division of this code.

(b) "Chapter" means a chapter of the division in which that term occurs.

(c) "Article" means an article of the chapter in which that term occurs.

(d) "Section" means a section of this code.

(e) "Subdivision" means a subdivision of the section in which that term occurs.

(f) "Paragraph" means a paragraph of the subdivision in which that term occurs.
(Stats.1965, c. 299, § 2.)

§ 8. Construction of tenses

The present tense includes the past and future tenses; and the future, the present.
(Stats.1965, c. 299, § 2.)

§ 9. Construction of genders

The masculine gender includes the feminine and neuter.
(Stats.1965, c. 299, § 2.)

§ 10. Construction of singular and plural

The singular number includes the plural; and the plural, the singular.
(Stats.1965, c. 299, § 2.)

§ 11. "Shall" and "may"

"Shall" is mandatory and "may" is permissive.
(Stats.1965, c. 299, § 2.)

§ 12. Code becomes operative January 1, 1967; effect on pending proceedings

(a) This code shall become operative on January 1, 1967, and shall govern proceedings in actions brought on or after that date and, except as provided in subdivision (b), further proceedings in actions pending on that date.

(b) Subject to subdivision (c), a trial commenced before January 1, 1967, shall not be governed by this code. For the purpose of this subdivision:

(1) A trial is commenced when the first witness is sworn or the first exhibit is admitted into evidence and is terminated when the issue upon which such evidence is received is submitted to the trier of fact. A new trial, or a separate trial of a different issue, commenced on or after January 1, 1967, shall be governed by this code.

(2) If an appeal is taken from a ruling made at a trial commenced before January 1, 1967, the appellate court shall apply the law applicable at the time of the commencement of the trial.

(c) The provisions of Division 8 (commencing with Section 900) relating to privileges shall govern any claim of privilege made after December 31, 1966.
(Stats.1965, c. 299, § 2.)

Division 2
WORDS AND PHRASES DEFINED

§ 100. Application of definitions

Unless the provision or context otherwise requires, these definitions govern the construction of this code.

(Stats.1965, c. 299, § 2.)

§ 105. "Action"

"Action" includes a civil action and a criminal action.

(Stats.1965, c. 299, § 2.)

§ 110. "Burden of producing evidence"

"Burden of producing evidence" means the obligation of a party to introduce evidence sufficient to avoid a ruling against him on the issue.

(Stats.1965, c. 299, § 2.)

§ 115. "Burden of proof"

"Burden of proof" means the obligation of a party to establish by evidence a requisite degree of belief concerning a fact in the mind of the trier of fact or the court. The burden of proof may require a party to raise a reasonable doubt concerning the existence or nonexistence of a fact or that he establish the existence or nonexistence of a fact by a preponderance of the evidence, by clear and convincing proof, or by proof beyond a reasonable doubt.

Except as otherwise provided by law, the burden of proof requires proof by a preponderance of the evidence.

(Stats.1965, c. 299, § 2.)

§ 120. "Civil action"

"Civil action" includes civil proceedings.
(Stats.1965, c. 299, § 2.)

§ 125. "Conduct"

"Conduct" includes all active and passive behavior, both verbal and nonverbal.
(Stats.1965, c. 299, § 2.)

§ 130. "Criminal action"

"Criminal action" includes criminal proceedings.
(Stats.1965, c. 299, § 2.)

§ 135. "Declarant"

"Declarant" is a person who makes a statement.
(Stats.1965, c. 299, § 2.)

§ 140. "Evidence"

"Evidence" means testimony, writings, material objects, or other things presented to the senses that are offered to prove the existence or nonexistence of a fact.
(Stats.1965, c. 299, § 2.)

§ 145. "The hearing"

"The hearing" means the hearing at which a question under this code arises, and not some earlier or later hearing.
(Stats.1965, c. 299, § 2.)

§ 150. "Hearsay evidence"

"Hearsay evidence" is defined in Section 1200.
(Stats.1965, c. 299, § 2.)

§ 160. "Law"

"Law" includes constitutional, statutory, and decisional law.
(Stats.1965, c. 299, § 2.)

§ 165. "Oath"

"Oath" includes affirmation or declaration under penalty of perjury.
(Stats.1965, c. 299, § 2.)

§ 170. "Perceive"

"Perceive" means to acquire knowledge through one's senses.
(Stats.1965, c. 299, § 2.)

§ 175. "Person"

"Person" includes a natural person, firm, association, organization, partnership, business trust, corporation, or public entity.
(Stats.1965, c. 299, § 2.)

§ 180. "Personal property"

"Personal property" includes money, goods, chattels, things in action, and evidences of debt.
(Stats.1965, c. 299, § 2.)

§ 185. "Property"

"Property" includes both real and personal property.
(Stats.1965, c. 299, § 2.)

§ 190. "Proof"

"Proof" is the establishment by evidence of a requisite degree of belief concerning a fact in the mind of the trier of fact or the court.
(Stats.1965, c. 299, § 2.)

§ 195. "Public employee"

"Public employee" means an officer, agent, or employee of a public entity.
(Stats.1965, c. 299, § 2.)

§ 200. "Public entity"

"Public entity" includes a nation, state, county, city and county, city, district, public authority, public agency, or any other political subdivision or public corporation, whether foreign or domestic.
(Stats.1965, c. 299, § 2.)

§ 205. "Real property"

"Real property" includes lands, tenements, and hereditaments.
(Stats.1965, c. 299, § 2.)

§ 210. "Relevant evidence"

"Relevant evidence" means evidence, including evidence relevant to the credibility of a witness or hearsay declarant, having any tendency in reason to prove or disprove any disputed fact that is of consequence to the determination of the action.
(Stats.1965, c. 299, § 2.)

§ 220. "State"

"State" means the State of California, unless applied to the different parts of the United States. In the latter case, it includes any state, district, commonwealth, territory, or insular possession of the United States.
(Stats.1965, c. 299, § 2.)

§ 225. "Statement"

"Statement" means (a) oral or written verbal expression or (b) nonverbal conduct of a person intended by him as a substitute for oral or written verbal expression.
(Stats.1965, c. 299, § 2.)

§ 230. "Statute"

"Statute" includes a treaty and a constitutional provision.
(Stats.1965, c. 299, § 2.)

§ 235. "Trier of fact"

"Trier of fact" includes (a) the jury and (b) the court when the court is trying an issue of fact other than one relating to the admissibility of evidence.
(Stats.1965, c. 299, § 2.)

§ 240. "Unavailable as a witness"

(a) Except as otherwise provided in subdivision (b), "unavailable as a witness" means that the declarant is:

(1) Exempted or precluded on the ground of privilege from testifying concerning the matter to which his statement is relevant;

(2) Disqualified from testifying to the matter;

(3) Dead or unable to attend or to testify at the hearing because of then existing physical or mental illness or infirmity;

(4) Absent from the hearing and the court is unable to compel his attendance by its process; or

(5) Absent from the hearing and the proponent of his statement has exercised reasonable diligence but has been unable to procure his attendance by the court's process.

(b) A declarant is not unavailable as a witness if the exemption, preclusion, disqualification, death, inability, or absence of the declarant was brought about by the procurement or wrongdoing of the proponent of his statement for the purpose of preventing the declarant from attending or testifying.
(Stats.1965, c. 299, § 2.)

§ 250. "Writing"

"Writing" means handwriting, typewriting, printing, photostating, photographing, and every other means of recording upon any tangible thing any form of communication or representation, including letters, words, pictures, sounds, or symbols, or combinations thereof.
(Stats.1965, c. 299, § 2.)

§ 255. "Original"

"Original" means the writing itself or any counterpart intended to have the same effect by a person executing or issuing it. An "original" of a photograph includes the negative or any print therefrom. If data are stored in a computer or similar device, any printout or other output readable by sight, shown to reflect the data accurately, is an "original."
(Added by Stats.1977, c. 708, § 1.)

§ 260. "Duplicate"

A "duplicate" is a counterpart produced by the same impression as the original, or from the same matrix, or by means of photography, including enlargements and miniatures, or by mechanical or electronic rerecording, or by chemical reproduction, or by other equivalent technique which accurately reproduces the original.
(Added by Stats.1977, c. 708, § 2.)

Division 3
GENERAL PROVISIONS

CHAPTER 1. APPLICABILITY OF CODE

Sec.
300. Applicability of code.

§ 300. Applicability of code

Except as otherwise provided by statute, this code applies in every action before the Supreme Court or a court of appeal, superior court, municipal court, or justice court, including proceedings in such actions conducted by a referee, court commissioner, or similar officer, but does not apply in grand jury proceedings.
(Stats.1965, c. 299, § 300. Amended by Stats.1967, c. 17, § 35.)

CHAPTER 2. PROVINCE OF COURT AND JURY

Sec.
310. Questions of law for court.
311. Procedure when foreign or sister-state law cannot be determined.
312. Jury as trier of fact.

§ 310. Questions of law for court

(a) All questions of law (including but not limited to questions concerning the construction of statutes and other writings, the admissibility of evidence, and other rules of evidence) are to be decided by the court. Determination of issues of fact preliminary to the admission of evidence are to be decided by the court as provided in Article 2 (commencing with Section 400) of Chapter 4.

(b) Determination of the law of an organization of nations or of the law of a foreign nation or a public entity in a foreign nation is a question of law to be determined in the manner provided in Division 4 (commencing with Section 450).
(Stats.1965, c. 299, § 2.)

§ 311. Procedure when foreign or sister-state law cannot be determined

If the law of an organization of nations, a foreign nation or a state other than this state, or a public entity in a foreign nation or a state other than this state, is applicable and such law cannot be determined, the court may, as the ends of justice require, either:

(a) Apply the law of this state if the court can do so consistently with the Constitution of the United States and the Constitution of this state; or

(b) Dismiss the action without prejudice or, in the case of a reviewing court, remand the case to the trial court with directions to dismiss the action without prejudice.
(Stats.1965, c. 299, § 2.)

§ 312. Jury as trier of fact

Except as otherwise provided by law, where the trial is by jury:

(a) All questions of fact are to be decided by the jury.

(b) Subject to the control of the court, the jury is to determine the effect and value of the evidence addressed to it, including the credibility of witnesses and hearsay declarants.
(Stats.1965, c. 299, § 2.)

CHAPTER 3. ORDER OF PROOF

Sec.
320. Power of court to regulate order of proof.

§ 320. Power of court to regulate order of proof

Except as otherwise provided by law, the court in its discretion shall regulate the order of proof.

(Stats.1965, c. 299, § 2.)

CHAPTER 4. ADMITTING AND EXCLUDING EVIDENCE

ARTICLE 1. GENERAL PROVISIONS

Sec.
350. Only relevant evidence admissible.
351. Admissibility of relevant evidence.
352. Discretion of court to exclude evidence.
352.1. Criminal sex acts; victim's address and telephone number.
353. Effect of erroneous admission of evidence.
354. Effect of erroneous exclusion of evidence.
355. Limited admissibility.
356. Entire act, declaration, conversation, or writing may be brought out to elucidate part offered.

§ 350. Only relevant evidence admissible

No evidence is admissible except relevant evidence.

(Stats.1965, c. 299, § 2.)

§ 351. Admissibility of relevant evidence

Except as otherwise provided by statute, all relevant evidence is admissible.

(Stats.1965, c. 299, § 2.)

§ 352. Discretion of court to exclude evidence

The court in its discretion may exclude evidence if its probative value is substantially outweighed by the probability that its admission will (a) necessitate undue consumption of time or (b) create substantial danger of undue prejudice, of confusing the issues, or of misleading the jury.

(Stats.1965, c. 299, § 2.)

§ 352.1. Criminal sex acts; victim's address and telephone number

In any criminal proceeding under Section 261, Section 264.1, subdivision (d) of Section 286, or subdivision (d) of Section 288a of the Penal Code, or in any criminal proceeding under subdivision (c) of Section 286 or subdivision (c) of Section 288a of the Penal Code in which the defendant is alleged to have compelled the participation of the victim by force, violence, duress, menace, or threat of great bodily harm, the district attorney may, upon written motion with notice to the defendant or the defendant's attorney, if he or she is represented by an attorney, within a reasonable time prior to any hearing, move to exclude from evidence the current address and telephone number of any victim at such hearing.

The court may order that evidence of the victim's current address and telephone number be excluded from any hearings conducted pursuant to such criminal proceeding if the court finds that the probative value of such evidence is outweighed by the creation of substantial danger to the victim.

Nothing in this section shall abridge or limit the defendant's right to discover or investigate such information.

(Added by Stats.1977, c. 34, § 1.)

§ 353. Effect of erroneous admission of evidence

A verdict or finding shall not be set aside, nor shall the judgment or decision based thereon be reversed, by reason of the erroneous admission of evidence unless:

(a) There appears of record an objection to or a motion to exclude or to strike the evidence that was timely made and so stated as to make clear the specific ground of the objection or motion; and

(b) The court which passes upon the effect of the error or errors is of the opinion that the admitted evidence should have been excluded on the ground stated and that the error or errors complained of resulted in a miscarriage of justice.
(Stats.1965, c. 299, § 2.)

§ 354. Effect of erroneous exclusion of evidence

A verdict or finding shall not be set aside, nor shall the judgment or decision based thereon be reversed, by reason of the erroneous exclusion of evidence unless the court which passes upon the effect of the error or errors is of the opinion that the error or errors complained of resulted in a miscarriage of justice and it appears of record that:

(a) The substance, purpose, and relevance of the excluded evidence was made known to the court by the questions asked, an offer of proof, or by any other means;

(b) The rulings of the court made compliance with subdivision (a) futile; or

(c) The evidence was sought by questions asked during cross-examination or recross-examination.
(Stats.1965, c. 299, § 2.)

§ 355. Limited admissibility

When evidence is admissible as to one party or for one purpose and is inadmissible as to another party or for another purpose, the court upon request shall restrict the evidence to its proper scope and instruct the jury accordingly.
(Stats.1965, c. 299, § 2.)

§ 356. Entire act, declaration, conversation, or writing may be brought out to elucidate part offered

Where part of an act, declaration, conversation, or writing is given in evidence by one party, the whole on the same subject may be inquired into by an adverse party; when a letter is read, the answer may be given; and when a detached act, declaration, conversation, or writing is given in evidence, any other act, declaration, conversation, or writing which is necessary to make it understood may also be given in evidence.
(Stats.1965, c. 299, § 2.)

ARTICLE 2. PRELIMINARY DETERMINATIONS ON ADMISSIBILITY OF EVIDENCE

§ 400. "Preliminary fact"

As used in this article, "preliminary fact" means a fact upon the existence or nonexistence of which depends the admissibility or inadmissibility of evidence. The phrase "the admissibility or inadmissibility of evidence" includes the qualification or disqualification of a person to be a witness and the existence or nonexistence of a privilege.
(Stats.1965, c. 299, § 2.)

§ 401. "Proffered evidence"

As used in this article, "proffered evidence" means evidence, the admissibility or inadmissibility of which is dependent upon the existence or nonexistence of a preliminary fact.

(Stats.1965, c. 299, § 2.)

§ 402. Procedure for determining foundational and other preliminary facts

(a) When the existence of a preliminary fact is disputed, its existence or nonexistence shall be determined as provided in this article.

(b) The court may hear and determine the question of the admissibility of evidence out of the presence or hearing of the jury; but in a criminal action, the court shall hear and determine the question of the admissibility of a confession or admission of the defendant out of the presence and hearing of the jury if any party so requests.

(c) A ruling on the admissibility of evidence implies whatever finding of fact is prerequisite thereto; a separate or formal finding is unnecessary unless required by statute.

(Stats.1965, c. 299, § 2.)

§ 403. Determination of foundational and other preliminary facts where relevancy, personal knowledge, or authenticity is disputed

(a) The proponent of the proffered evidence has the burden of producing evidence as to the existence of the preliminary fact, and the proffered evidence is inadmissible unless the court finds that there is evidence sufficient to sustain a finding of the existence of the preliminary fact, when:

(1) The relevance of the proffered evidence depends on the existence of the preliminary fact;

(2) The preliminary fact is the personal knowledge of a witness concerning the subject matter of his testimony;

(3) The preliminary fact is the authenticity of a writing; or

(4) The proffered evidence is of a statement or other conduct of a particular person and the preliminary fact is whether that person made the statement or so conducted himself.

(b) Subject to Section 702, the court may admit conditionally the proffered evidence under this section, subject to evidence of the preliminary fact being supplied later in the course of the trial.

(c) If the court admits the proffered evidence under this section, the court:

(1) May, and on request shall, instruct the jury to determine whether the preliminary fact exists and to disregard the proffered evidence unless the jury finds that the preliminary fact does exist.

(2) Shall instruct the jury to disregard the proffered evidence if the court subsequently determines that a jury could not reasonably find that the preliminary fact exists.

(Stats.1965, c. 299, § 2.)

§ 404. Determination of whether proffered evidence is incriminatory

Whenever the proffered evidence is claimed to be privileged under Section 940, the person claiming the privilege has the burden of showing that the proffered evidence might tend to incriminate him; and the proffered evidence is inadmissible unless it clearly appears to the court that the proffered evidence cannot possibly have a tendency to incriminate the person claiming the privilege.

(Stats.1965, c. 299, § 2.)

§ 405. Determination of foundational and other preliminary facts in other cases

With respect to preliminary fact determinations not governed by Section 403 or 404:

(a) When the existence of a preliminary fact is disputed, the court shall indicate which party has the burden of producing evidence and the burden of proof on the issue as implied by the rule of law under which the question arises. The court shall determine the existence or nonexistence of the preliminary fact and shall admit or exclude the proffered evidence as required by the rule of law under which the question arises.

(b) If a preliminary fact is also a fact in issue in the action:

(1) The jury shall not be informed of the court's determination as to the existence or nonexistence of the preliminary fact:

(2) If the proffered evidence is admitted, the jury shall not be instructed to disregard the evidence if its determination of the fact differs from the court's determination of the preliminary fact.
(Stats.1965, c. 299, § 2.)

§ 406. Evidence affecting weight or credibility

This article does not limit the right of a party to introduce before the trier of fact evidence relevant to weight or credibility.
(Stats.1965, c. 299, § 2.)

CHAPTER 5. WEIGHT OF EVIDENCE GENERALLY

Sec.
410. "Direct evidence."
411. Direct evidence of one witness sufficient.
412. Party having power to produce better evidence.
413. Party's failure to explain or deny evidence.

§ 410. "Direct evidence"

As used in this chapter, "direct evidence" means evidence that directly proves a fact, without an inference or presumption, and which in itself, if true, conclusively establishes that fact.
(Stats.1965, c. 299, § 2.)

§ 411. Direct evidence of one witness sufficient

Except where additional evidence is required by statute, the direct evidence of one witness who is entitled to full credit is sufficient for proof of any fact.
(Stats.1965, c. 299, § 2.)

§ 412. Party having power to produce better evidence

If weaker and less satisfactory evidence is offered when it was within the power of the party to produce stronger and more satisfactory evidence, the evidence offered should be viewed with distrust.
(Stats.1965, c. 299, § 2.)

§ 413. Party's failure to explain or deny evidence

In determining what inferences to draw from the evidence or facts in the case against a party, the trier of fact may consider, among other things, the party's failure to explain or to deny by his testimony such evidence or facts in the case against him, or his willful suppression of evidence relating thereto, if such be the case.
(Stats.1965, c. 299, § 2.)

Division 4
JUDICIAL NOTICE

Sec.
450. Judicial notice may be taken only as authorized by law.
451. Matters which must be judicially noticed.
452. Matters which may be judicially noticed.
453. Compulsory judicial notice upon request.
454. Information that may be used in taking judicial notice.
455. Opportunity to present information to court.
456. Noting for record denial of request to take judicial notice.
457. Instructing jury on matter judicially noticed.
458. Judicial notice by trial court in subsequent proceedings.
459. Judicial notice by reviewing court.
460. Appointment of expert by court.

§ 450. Judicial notice may be taken only as authorized by law

Judicial notice may not be taken of any matter unless authorized or required by law. (Stats.1965, c. 299, § 2.)

§ 451. Matters which must be judicially noticed

Judicial notice shall be taken of:

(a) The decisional, constitutional, and public statutory law of this state and of the United States and the provisions of any charter described in Section 3, 4, or 5 of Article XI of the California Constitution.

(b) Any matter made a subject of judicial notice by Section 11383, 11384, or 18576 of the Government Code or by Section 1507 of Title 44 of the United States Code.[1]

(c) Rules of professional conduct for members of the bar adopted pursuant to Section 6076 of the Business and Professions Code and rules of practice and procedure for the courts of this state adopted by the Judicial Council.

(d) Rules of pleading, practice, and procedure prescribed by the United States Supreme Court, such as the Rules of the United States Supreme Court, the Federal Rules of Civil Procedure, the Federal Rules of Criminal Procedure, the Admiralty Rules, the Rules of the Court of Claims, the Rules of the Customs Court, and the General Orders and Forms in Bankruptcy.

(e) The true signification of all English words and phrases and of all legal expressions.

(f) Facts and propositions of generalized knowledge that are so universally known that they cannot reasonably be the subject of dispute.
(Stats.1965, c. 299, § 2. Amended by Stats.1971, c. 438, § 88; Stats.1972, c. 764, § 1.)
[1] 44 U.S.C.A. § 1507.

§ 452. Matters which may be judicially noticed

Judicial notice may be taken of the following matters to the extent that they are not embraced within Section 451:

(a) The decisional, constitutional, and statutory law of any state of the United States and the resolutions and private acts of the Congress of the United States and of the Legislature of this state.

(b) Regulations and legislative enactments issued by or under the authority of the United States or any public entity in the United States.

(c) Official acts of the legislative, executive, and judicial departments of the United States and of any state of the United States.

(d) Records of (1) any court of this state or (2) any court of record of the United States or of any state of the United States.

(e) Rules of court of (1) any court of this state or (2) any court of record of the United States or of any state of the United States.

(f) The law of an organization of nations and of foreign nations and public entities in foreign nations.

(g) Facts and propositions that are of such common knowledge within the territorial jurisdiction of the court that they cannot reasonably be the subject of dispute.

(h) Facts and propositions that are not reasonably subject to dispute and are capable of immediate and accurate determination by resort to sources of reasonably indisputable accuracy.
(Stats.1965, c. 299, § 2.)

§ 453. Compulsory judicial notice upon request

The trial court shall take judicial notice of any matter specified in Section 452 if a party requests it and:

(a) Gives each adverse party sufficient notice of the request, through the pleadings or otherwise, to enable such adverse party to prepare to meet the request; and

(b) Furnishes the court with sufficient information to enable it to take judicial notice of the matter.
(Stats.1965, c. 299, § 2.)

§ 454. Information that may be used in taking judicial notice

(a) In determining the propriety of taking judicial notice of a matter, or the tenor thereof:

(1) Any source of pertinent information, including the advice of persons learned in the subject matter, may be consulted or used, whether or not furnished by a party.

(2) Exclusionary rules of evidence do not apply except for Section 352 and the rules of privilege.

(b) Where the subject of judicial notice is the law of an organization of nations, a foreign nation, or a public entity in a foreign nation and the court resorts to the advice of persons learned in the subject matter, such advice, if not received in open court, shall be in writing.
(Stats.1965, c. 299, § 2.)

§ 455. Opportunity to present information to court

With respect to any matter specified in Section 452 or in subdivision (f) of Section 451 that is of substantial consequence to the determination of the action:

(a) If the trial court has been requested to take or has taken or proposes to take judicial notice of such matter, the court shall afford each party reasonable opportunity, before the jury is instructed or before the cause is submitted for decision by the court, to present to the court information relevant to (1) the propriety of taking judicial notice of the matter and (2) the tenor of the matter to be noticed.

(b) If the trial court resorts to any source of information not received in open court, including the advice of persons learned in the subject matter, such information and its source shall be made a part of the record in the action and the court shall afford each party reasonable opportunity to meet such information before judicial notice of the matter may be taken.
(Stats.1965, c. 299, § 2.)

§ 456. Noting for record denial of request to take judicial notice

If the trial court denies a request to take judicial notice of any matter, the court shall at the earliest practicable time so advise the parties and indicate for the record that it has denied the request.

(Stats.1965, c. 299, § 2.)

§ 457. Instructing jury on matter judicially noticed

If a matter judicially noticed is a matter which would otherwise have been for determination by the jury, the trial court may, and upon request shall, instruct the jury to accept as a fact the matter so noticed.

(Stats.1965, c. 299, § 2.)

§ 458. Judicial notice by trial court in subsequent proceedings

The failure or refusal of the trial court to take judicial notice of a matter, or to instruct the jury with respect to the matter, does not preclude the trial court in subsequent proceedings in the action from taking judicial notice of the matter in accordance with the procedure specified in this division.

(Stats.1965, c. 299, § 2.)

§ 459. Judicial notice by reviewing court

(a) The reviewing court shall take judicial notice of (1) each matter properly noticed by the trial court and (2) each matter that the trial court was required to notice under Section 451 or 453. The reviewing court may take judicial notice of any matter specified in Section 452. The reviewing court may take judicial notice of a matter in a tenor different from that noticed by the trial court.

(b) In determining the propriety of taking judicial notice of a matter, or the tenor thereof, the reviewing court has the same power as the trial court under Section 454.

(c) When taking judicial notice under this section of a matter specified in Section 452 or in subdivision (f) of Section 451 that is of substantial consequence to the determination of the action, the reviewing court shall comply with the provisions of subdivision (a) of Section 455 if the matter was not theretofore judicially noticed in the action.

(d) In determining the propriety of taking judicial notice of a matter specified in Section 452 or in subdivision (f) of Section 451 that is of substantial consequence to the determination of the action, or the tenor thereof, if the reviewing court resorts to any source of information not received in open court or not included in the record of the action, including the advice of persons learned in the subject matter, the reviewing court shall afford each party reasonable opportunity to meet such information before judicial notice of the matter may be taken.

(Stats.1965, c. 299, § 2.)

§ 460. Appointment of expert by court

Where the advice of persons learned in the subject matter is required in order to enable the court to take judicial notice of a matter, the court on its own motion or on motion of any party may appoint one or more such persons to provide such advice. If the court determines to appoint such a person, he shall be appointed and compensated in the manner provided in Article 2 (commencing with Section 730) of Chapter 3 of Division 6.

(Stats.1965, c. 299, § 2.)

Division 5

BURDEN OF PROOF; BURDEN OF PRODUCING EVIDENCE; PRESUMPTIONS AND INFERENCES

CHAPTER 1. BURDEN OF PROOF

ARTICLE 1.   GENERAL

§ 500. Party who has the burden of proof

Except as otherwise provided by law, a party has the burden of proof as to each fact the existence or nonexistence of which is essential to the claim for relief or defense that he is asserting.

(Stats.1965, c. 299, § 2.)

§ 501. Burden of proof in criminal action generally

Insofar as any statute, except Section 522, assigns the burden of proof in a criminal action, such statute is subject to Penal Code Section 1096.

(Stats.1965, c. 299, § 2.)

§ 502. Instructions on burden of proof

The court on all proper occasions shall instruct the jury as to which party bears the burden of proof on each issue and as to whether that burden requires that a party raise a reasonable doubt concerning the existence or nonexistence of a fact or that he establish the existence or nonexistence of a fact by a preponderance of the evidence, by clear and convincing proof, or by proof beyond a reasonable doubt.

(Stats.1965, c. 299, § 2.)

ARTICLE 2.   BURDEN OF PROOF ON SPECIFIC ISSUES

§ 520. Claim that person guilty of crime or wrongdoing

The party claiming that a person is guilty of crime or wrongdoing has the burden of proof on that issue.

(Stats.1965, c. 299, § 520.)

§ 521. Claim that person did not exercise care

The party claiming that a person did not exercise a requisite degree of care has the burden of proof on that issue.

(Stats.1965, c. 299, § 2.)

§ 522. Claim that person is or was insane

The party claiming that any person, including himself, is or was insane has the burden of proof on that issue.
(Stats.1965, c. 299, § 2.)

CHAPTER 2. BURDEN OF PRODUCING EVIDENCE

Sec.
550. Party who has the burden of producing evidence.

§ 550. Party who has the burden of producing evidence

(a) The burden of producing evidence as to a particular fact is on the party against whom a finding on that fact would be required in the absence of further evidence.

(b) The burden of producing evidence as to a particular fact is initially on the party with the burden of proof as to that fact.
(Stats.1965, c. 299, § 2.)

CHAPTER 3. PRESUMPTIONS AND INFERENCES

ARTICLE 1. GENERAL

Sec.
600. Presumption and inference defined.
601. Classification of presumptions.
602. Statute making one fact prima facie evidence of another fact.
603. Presumption affecting the burden of producing evidence defined.
604. Effect of presumption affecting burden of producing evidence.
605. Presumption affecting the burden of proof defined.
606. Effect of presumption affecting burden of proof.
607. Effect of certain presumptions in a criminal action.

§ 600. Presumption and inference defined

(a) A presumption is an assumption of fact that the law requires to be made from another fact or group of facts found or otherwise established in the action. A presumption is not evidence.

(b) An inference is a deduction of fact that may logically and reasonably be drawn from another fact or group of facts found or otherwise established in the action.
(Stats.1965, c. 299, § 2.)

§ 601. Classification of presumptions

A presumption is either conclusive or rebuttable. Every rebuttable presumption is either (a) a presumption affecting the burden of producing evidence or (b) a presumption affecting the burden of proof.
(Stats.1965, c. 299, § 2.)

§ 602. Statute making one fact prima facie evidence of another fact

A statute providing that a fact or group of facts is prima facie evidence of another fact establishes a rebuttable presumption.
(Stats.1965, c. 299, § 2.)

§ 603. Presumption affecting the burden of producing evidence defined

A presumption affecting the burden of producing evidence is a presumption established to implement no public policy other than to facilitate the determination of the particular action in which the presumption is applied.
(Stats.1965, c. 299, § 2.)

§ 604. Effect of presumption affecting burden of producing evidence

The effect of a presumption affecting the burden of producing evidence is to require the trier of fact to assume the existence of the presumed fact unless and until evidence is introduced which would support a finding of its nonexistence, in which case the trier of fact shall determine the existence or nonexistence of the presumed fact from the evidence and without regard to the presumption. Nothing in this section shall be construed to prevent the drawing of any inference that may be appropriate.
(Stats.1965, c. 299, § 2.)

§ 605. Presumption affecting the burden of proof defined

A presumption affecting the burden of proof is a presumption established to implement some public policy other than to facilitate the determination of the particular action in which the presumption is applied, such as the policy in favor of establishment of a parent and child relationship, the validity of marriage, the stability of titles to property, or the security of those who entrust themselves or their property to the administration of others.
(Stats.1965, c. 299, § 2. Amended by Stats.1975, c. 1244, § 12.)

§ 606. Effect of presumption affecting burden of proof

The effect of a presumption affecting the burden of proof is to impose upon the party against whom it operates the burden of proof as to the nonexistence of the presumed fact.
(Stats.1965, c. 299, § 2.)

§ 607. Effect of certain presumptions in a criminal action

When a presumption affecting the burden of proof operates in a criminal action to establish presumptively any fact that is essential to the defendant's guilt, the presumption operates only if the facts that give rise to the presumption have been found or otherwise established beyond a reasonable doubt, and, in such case, the defendant need only raise a reasonable doubt as to the existence of the presumed fact.
(Stats.1965, c. 299, § 2.)

ARTICLE 2. CONCLUSIVE PRESUMPTIONS

§ 620. Conclusive presumptions

The presumptions established by this article, and all other presumptions declared by law to be conclusive, are conclusive presumptions.
(Stats.1965, c. 299, § 2.)

§ 621. Child of marriage; notice of motion for blood tests

(a) Except as provided in subdivision (b), the issue of a wife cohabiting with her husband, who is not impotent or sterile, is conclusively presumed to be a child of the marriage.

(b) Notwithstanding the provisions of subdivision (a), if the court finds that the conclusions of all the experts, as disclosed by the evidence based upon blood tests performed pursuant to Chapter 2 (commencing with Section 890) of Division 7 are that the husband is not the father of the child, the question of paternity of the husband shall be resolved accordingly.

The notice of motion for blood tests under this subdivision shall only be raised by the husband and shall be raised not later than two years from the date of birth of the child.

The notice of motion for the blood tests pursuant to this subdivision must be supported by a declaration under oath submitted by the moving party stating the factual basis for placing the issue of paternity before the court. This requirement shall not apply to any case pending before the court on the effective date of the amendment to this section adopted at the 1979–80 Regular Session of the Legislature.

The provisions of this subdivision shall not apply to any case which has reached final judgment of paternity on the effective date of the amendment to this section adopted at the 1979–80 Regular Session of the Legislature.
(Stats.1965, c. 299, § 2.   Amended by Stats.1975, c. 1244, § 13;   Stats.1980, c. 1310, § 1.)

§ 622. Facts recited in written instrument

The facts recited in a written instrument are conclusively presumed to be true as between the parties thereto, or their successors in interest; but this rule does not apply to the recital of a consideration.
(Stats.1965, c. 299, § 2.)

§ 623. Estoppel by own statement or conduct

Whenever a party has, by his own statement or conduct, intentionally and deliberately led another to believe a particular thing true and to act upon such belief, he is not, in any litigation arising out of such statement or conduct, permitted to contradict it.
(Stats.1965, c. 299, § 2.)

§ 624. Estoppel of tenant to deny title of landlord

A tenant is not permitted to deny the title of his landlord at the time of the commencement of the relation.
(Stats.1965, c. 299, § 2.)

ARTICLE 3. PRESUMPTIONS AFFECTING THE BURDEN OF PRODUCING EVIDENCE

§ 630. Presumptions affecting the burden of producing evidence

The presumptions established by this article, and all other rebuttable presumptions established by law that fall within the criteria of Section 603, are presumptions affecting the burden of producing evidence.
(Stats.1965, c. 299, § 2.)

§ 631. Money delivered by one to another

Money delivered by one to another is presumed to have been due to the latter.
(Stats.1965, c. 299, § 2.)

§ 632. Thing delivered by one to another

A thing delivered by one to another is presumed to have belonged to the latter.
(Stats.1965, c. 299, § 2.)

§ 633. Obligation delivered up to the debtor

An obligation delivered up to the debtor is presumed to have been paid.
(Stats.1965, c. 299, § 2.)

§ 634. Person in possession of order on himself

A person in possession of an order on himself for the payment of money, or delivery of a thing, is presumed to have paid the money or delivered the thing accordingly.
(Stats.1965, c. 299, § 2.)

§ 635. Obligation possessed by creditor

An obligation possessed by the creditor is presumed not to have been paid.
(Stats.1965, c. 299, § 2.)

§ 636. Payment of earlier rent or installments

The payment of earlier rent or installments is presumed from a receipt for later rent or installments.
(Stats.1965, c. 299, § 2.)

§ 637. Ownership of things possessed

The things which a person possesses are presumed to be owned by him.
(Stats.1965, c. 299, § 2.)

§ 638. Ownership of property by person who exercises acts of ownership

A person who exercises acts of ownership over property is presumed to be the owner of it.
(Stats.1965, c. 299, § 2.)

§ 639. Judgment correctly determines rights of parties

A judgment, when not conclusive, is presumed to correctly determine or set forth the rights of the parties, but there is no presumption that the facts essential to the judgment have been correctly determined.
(Stats.1965, c. 299, § 2.)

§ 640. Writing truly dated

A writing is presumed to have been truly dated.
(Stats.1965, c. 299, § 2.)

§ 641. Letter received in ordinary course of mail

A letter correctly addressed and properly mailed is presumed to have been received in the ordinary course of mail.
(Stats.1965, c. 299, § 2.)

§ 642. Conveyance by person having duty to convey real property

A trustee or other person, whose duty it was to convey real property to a particular person, is presumed to have actually conveyed to him when such presumption is necessary to perfect title of such person or his successor in interest.
(Stats.1965, c. 299, § 2.)

§ 643. Authenticity of ancient document

A deed or will or other writing purporting to create, terminate, or affect an interest in real or personal property is presumed to be authentic if it:

(a) Is at least 30 years old;

(b) Is in such condition as to create no suspicion concerning its authenticity;

(c) Was kept, or if found was found, in a place where such writing, if authentic, would be likely to be kept or found; and

(d) Has been generally acted upon as authentic by persons having an interest in the matter.
(Stats.1965, c. 299, § 2.)

§ 644. Book purporting to be published by public authority

A book, purporting to be printed or published by public authority, is presumed to have been so printed or published.
(Stats.1965, c. 299, § 2.)

§ 645. Book purporting to contain reports of cases

A book, purporting to contain reports of cases adjudged in the tribunals of the state or nation where the book is published, is presumed to contain correct reports of such cases.
(Stats.1965, c. 299, § 2.)

§ 646. Res ipsa loquitur; instruction

(a) As used in this section, "defendant" includes any party against whom the res ipsa loquitur presumption operates.

(b) The judicial doctrine of res ipsa loquitur is a presumption affecting the burden of producing evidence.

(c) If the evidence, or facts otherwise established, would support a res ipsa loquitur presumption and the defendant has introduced evidence which would support a finding that he was not negligent or that any negligence on his part was not a proximate cause of the occurrence, the court may, and upon request shall, instruct the jury to the effect that:

(1) If the facts which would give rise to a res ipsa loquitur presumption are found or otherwise established, the jury may draw the inference from such facts that a proximate cause of the occurrence was some negligent conduct on the part of the defendant; and

(2) The jury shall not find that a proximate cause of the occurrence was some negligent conduct on the part of the defendant unless the jury believes, after weighing all the evidence in the case and drawing such inferences therefrom as the jury believes are warranted, that it is more probable than not that the occurrence was caused by some negligent conduct on the part of the defendant.
(Added by Stats.1970, c. 69, § 1.)

§ 647. Return of process served by registered process server

The return of a process server registered pursuant to Chapter 16 (commencing with Section 22350) of Division 8 of the Business and Professions Code upon process or notice establishes a presumption, affecting the burden of producing evidence, of the facts stated in the return.
(Added by Stats.1978, c. 528, § 1.)

ARTICLE 4. PRESUMPTIONS AFFECTING THE BURDEN OF PROOF

§ 660. Presumptions affecting the burden of proof

The presumptions established by this article, and all other rebuttable presumptions established by law that fall within the criteria of Section 605, are presumptions affecting the burden of proof.
(Stats.1965, c. 299, § 2.)

§ 661. Repealed by Stats.1975, c. 1244, § 14

See, now, Civ.C. § 7004.

§ 662. Owner of legal title to property is owner of beneficial title

The owner of the legal title to property is presumed to be the owner of the full beneficial title. This presumption may be rebutted only by clear and convincing proof.
(Stats.1965, c. 299, § 2.)

§ 663. Ceremonial marriage

A ceremonial marriage is presumed to be valid.
(Stats.1965, c. 299, § 2.)

§ 664. Official duty regularly performed

It is presumed that official duty has been regularly performed. This presumption does not apply on an issue as to the lawfulness of an arrest if it is found or otherwise established that the arrest was made without a warrant.
(Stats.1965, c. 299, § 2.)

§ 665. Ordinary consequences of voluntary act

A person is presumed to intend the ordinary consequences of his voluntary act. This presumption is inapplicable in a criminal action to establish the specific intent of the defendant where specific intent is an element of the crime charged.
(Stats.1965, c. 299, § 2.)

§ 666. Judicial action lawful exercise of jurisdiction

Any court of this state or the United States, or any court of general jurisdiction in any other state or nation, or any judge of such a court, acting as such, is presumed to have acted in the lawful exercise of its jurisdiction. This presumption applies only when the act of the court or judge is under collateral attack.
(Stats.1965, c. 299, § 2.)

§ 667. Death of person not heard from in seven years

A person not heard from in seven years is presumed to be dead.
(Stats.1965, c. 299, § 2.)

§ 668. Unlawful intent

An unlawful intent is presumed from the doing of an unlawful act. This presumption is inapplicable in a criminal action to establish the specific intent of the defendant where specific intent is an element of the crime charged.
(Stats.1965, c. 299, § 2.)

§ 669. Failure to exercise due care

(a) The failure of a person to exercise due care is presumed if:

(1) He violated a statute, ordinance, or regulation of a public entity;

(2) The violation proximately caused death or injury to person or property;

(3) The death or injury resulted from an occurrence of the nature which the statute, ordinance, or regulation was designed to prevent; and

(4) The person suffering the death or the injury to his person or property was one of the class of persons for whose protection the statute, ordinance, or regulation was adopted.

(b) This presumption may be rebutted by proof that:

(1) The person violating the statute, ordinance, or regulation did what might reasonably be expected of a person of ordinary prudence, acting under similar circumstances, who desired to comply with the law; or

(2) The person violating the statute, ordinance, or regulation was a child and exercised the degree of care ordinarily exercised by persons of his maturity, intelligence, and capacity under similar circumstances, but the presumption may not be rebutted by such proof if the violation occurred in the course of an activity normally engaged in only by adults and requiring adult qualifications.
(Added by Stats.1967, c. 650, § 1.)

§ 669.5. Ordinances limiting building permits or development of buildable lots for residential purposes; impact on supply of residential units; actions challenging validity

(a) Any ordinance enacted by the governing body of a city, county, or city and county which directly limits, by number, (1) the building permits that may be issued for residential construction or (2) the buildable lots which may be developed for residential purposes, is presumed to have an impact on the supply of residential units available in an area which includes territory outside the jurisdiction of such city, county, or city and county.

(b) With respect to any action which challenges the validity of such an ordinance, the city, county, or city and county enacting such ordinance shall bear the burden of proof that such ordinance is necessary for the protection of the public health, safety, or welfare of the population of such city, county, or city and county.

(c) This section does not apply to ordinances which (1) impose a moratorium, to protect the public health and safety, on residential construction for a specified period of time, if, under the terms of the ordinance, the moratorium will cease when the public health or safety is no longer jeopardized by such construction, or (2) create agricultural preserves under Chapter 7 (commencing with Section 51200) of Part 1 of Division 1 of Title 5 of the Government Code, or (3) restrict the number of buildable parcels by limiting the minimum size of buildable parcels within a zone or by designating lands within a zone for nonresidential uses.

(d) This section shall not apply to a voter approved ordinance adopted by referendum or initiative prior to the effective date of this section which (1) requires the city, county, or city and county to establish a population growth limit which represents its fair share of each year's statewide population growth, or (2) which sets a growth rate of no more than the average population growth rate experienced by the state as a whole.
(Added by Stats.1980, c. 1144, § 2.)

Division 6
WITNESSES

CHAPTER 1. COMPETENCY

§ 700. General rule as to competency

Except as otherwise provided by statute, every person is qualified to be a witness and no person is disqualified to testify to any matter.
(Stats.1965, c. 299, § 2.)

§ 701. Disqualification of witness

A person is disqualified to be a witness if he is:

(a) Incapable of expressing himself concerning the matter so as to be understood, either directly or through interpretation by one who can understand him; or

(b) Incapable of understanding the duty of a witness to tell the truth.
(Stats.1965, c. 299, § 2.)

§ 702. Personal knowledge of witness

(a) Subject to Section 801, the testimony of a witness concerning a particular matter is inadmissible unless he has personal knowledge of the matter. Against the objection of a party, such personal knowledge must be shown before the witness may testify concerning the matter.

(b) A witness' personal knowledge of a matter may be shown by any otherwise admissible evidence, including his own testimony.
(Stats.1965, c. 299, § 2.)

§ 703. Judge as witness

(a) Before the judge presiding at the trial of an action may be called to testify in that trial as a witness, he shall, in proceedings held out of the presence and hearing of the jury, inform the parties of the information he has concerning any fact or matter about which he will be called to testify.

(b) Against the objection of a party, the judge presiding at the trial of an action may not testify in that trial as a witness. Upon such objection, the judge shall declare a mistrial and order the action assigned for trial before another judge.

(c) The calling of the judge presiding at a trial to testify in that trial as a witness shall be deemed a consent to the granting of a motion for mistrial, and an objection to such calling of a judge shall be deemed a motion for mistrial.

(d) In the absence of objection by a party, the judge presiding at the trial of an action may testify in that trial as a witness.
(Stats.1965, c. 299, § 2.)

§ 703.5. Judge as witness; subsequent civil proceeding; exceptions

No person presiding at any judicial or quasi-judicial proceeding shall be competent to testify, in any subsequent civil proceeding, as to any statement or conduct occurring at the prior proceeding, except as to a statement or conduct that could (a) give rise to civil or criminal contempt, (b) constitute a crime, (c) be the subject of investigation by the State Bar or Commission on Judicial Performance, or (d) give rise to disqualification proceedings under subdivision (5) of Section 170 of the Code of Civil Procedure.
(Added by Stats.1979, c. 205, § 1. Amended by Stats.1980, c. 290, § 1.)

§ 704. Juror as witness

(a) Before a juror sworn and impaneled in the trial of an action may be called to testify before the jury in that trial as a witness, he shall, in proceedings conducted by the court out of the presence and hearing of the remaining jurors, inform the parties of the information he has concerning any fact or matter about which he will be called to testify.

(b) Against the objection of a party, a juror sworn and impaneled in the trial of an action may not testify before the jury in that trial as a witness. Upon such objection, the court shall declare a mistrial and order the action assigned for trial before another jury.

(c) The calling of a juror to testify before the jury as a witness shall be deemed a consent to the granting of a motion for mistrial, and an objection to such calling of a juror shall be deemed a motion for mistrial.

(d) In the absence of objection by a party, a juror sworn and impaneled in the trial of an action may be compelled to testify in that trial as a witness.
(Stats.1965, c. 299, § 2.)

CHAPTER 2. OATH AND CONFRONTATION

Sec.
710. Oath required.
711. Confrontation.
712. Blood samples; technique in taking; affidavits in criminal actions; service; objections.

§ 710. Oath required

Every witness before testifying shall take an oath or make an affirmation or declaration in the form provided by law.
(Stats.1965, c. 299, § 2.)

§ 711. Confrontation

At the trial of an action, a witness can be heard only in the presence and subject to the examination of all the parties to the action, if they choose to attend and examine.
(Stats.1965, c. 299, § 2.)

§ 712. Blood samples; technique in taking; affidavits in criminal actions; service; objections

Notwithstanding Sections 711 and 1200, at the trial of a criminal action, evidence of the technique used in taking blood samples may be given by a registered nurse, licensed vocational nurse, or licensed clinical laboratory technologist or clinical laboratory bioanalyst, by means of an affidavit. The affidavit shall be admissible, provided the party offering the affidavit as evidence has served all other parties to the action, or their counsel, with a copy of the affidavit no less than 10 days prior to trial. Nothing in this section shall preclude any party or his counsel from objecting to the introduction of the affidavit at any time, and requiring the attendance of the affiant, or compelling attendance by subpoena.
(Added by Stats.1978, c. 93, § 1.)

CHAPTER 3. EXPERT WITNESSES

ARTICLE 1. EXPERT WITNESSES GENERALLY

§ 720. Qualification as an expert witness

(a) A person is qualified to testify as an expert if he has special knowledge, skill, experience, training, or education sufficient to qualify him as an expert on the subject to which his testimony relates. Against the objection of a party, such special knowledge, skill, experience, training, or education must be shown before the witness may testify as an expert.

(b) A witness' special knowledge, skill, experience, training, or education may be shown by any otherwise admissible evidence, including his own testimony.
(Stats.1965, c. 299, § 2.)

§ 721. Cross-examination of expert witness

(a) Subject to subdivision (b), a witness testifying as an expert may be cross-examined to the same extent as any other witness and, in addition, may be fully cross-examined as to (1) his qualifications, (2) the subject to which his expert testimony relates, and (3) the matter upon which his opinion is based and the reasons for his opinion.

(b) If a witness testifying as an expert testifies in the form of an opinion, he may not be cross-examined in regard to the content or tenor of any scientific, technical, or professional text, treatise, journal, or similar publication unless:

(1) The witness referred to, considered, or relied upon such publication in arriving at or forming his opinion; or

(2) Such publication has been admitted in evidence.
(Stats.1965, c. 299, § 2.)

§ 722. Credibility of expert witness

(a) The fact of the appointment of an expert witness by the court may be revealed to the trier of fact.

(b) The compensation and expenses paid or to be paid to an expert witness by the party calling him is a proper subject of inquiry by any adverse party as relevant to the credibility of the witness and the weight of his testimony.
(Stats.1965, c. 299, § 2.)

§ 723. Limit on number of expert witnesses

The court may, at any time before or during the trial of an action, limit the number of expert witnesses to be called by any party.
(Stats.1965, c. 299, § 2.)

ARTICLE 2. APPOINTMENT OF EXPERT WITNESS BY COURT

§ 730. Appointment of expert by court; duration of section

Text of section operative until Jan. 1, 1983

(a) When it appears to the court, at any time before or during the trial of an action, that expert evidence is or may be required by the court or by any party to the action, the court on its own motion or on motion of any party may appoint one or more experts to investigate, to render a report as may be ordered by the court, and to testify as an expert at the trial of the action relative to the fact or matter as to which such expert evidence is or may be required. The court may fix the compensation for such services, if any, rendered by any person appointed under this section, in addition to any service as a witness, at such amount as seems reasonable to the court.

(b) The court shall not advise the jury that such expert witness has been appointed by the court, but this shall not preclude the court from calling and examining such expert witness.

This section shall remain in effect only until January 1, 1983, and, as of such date, is repealed.
(Stats.1965, c. 299, § 2. Amended by Stats.1979, c. 746, § 2.)

For text of section operative Jan. 1, 1983, see § 730, post.

§ 730. Appointment of expert by court

Text of section operative Jan. 1, 1983

When it appears to the court, at any time before or during the trial of an action, that expert evidence is or may be required by the court or by any party to the action, the court on its own motion or on motion of any party may appoint one or more experts to investigate, to render a report as may be ordered by the court, and to testify as an expert at the trial of the action relative to the fact or matter as to which such expert evidence is or may be required. The court may fix the compensation for such services, if any, rendered by any person appointed under this section, in addition to any service as a witness, at such amount as seems reasonable to the court.
(Stats.1965, c. 299, § 2. Amended by Stats.1979, c. 746, § 2; Stats.1979, c. 746, § 3.)

For text of section operative until Jan. 1, 1983, see § 730, ante.

§ 731. Payment of court-appointed expert; duration of section

Text of section operative until Jan. 1, 1983

(a) In all criminal actions and juvenile court proceedings, the compensation fixed under Section 730 shall be a charge against the county in which such action or proceeding is pending and shall be paid out of the treasury of such county on order of the court.

(b) The compensation fixed under Section 730 for experts in all civil actions in a county shall, in the first instance and in the discretion of the court, either be paid by the parties, as apportioned by the court, or be a charge against and paid out of the treasury of such county on order of the court. If the court orders that the compensation shall be a charge against and paid out of the treasury of the county, the county shall be entitled to reimbursement for such compensation as provided in Section 1031.5 of the Code of Civil Procedure.

This section shall remain in effect only until January 1, 1983, and, as of such date, is repealed.
(Stats.1965, c. 299, § 2. Amended by Stats.1979, c. 746, § 4.)

For text of section operative Jan. 1, 1983, see § 731, post.

§ 731. Payment of court-appointed expert

Text of section operative Jan. 1, 1983

(a) In all criminal actions and juvenile court proceedings, the compensation fixed under Section 730 shall be a charge against the county in which such action or proceeding is pending and shall be paid out of the treasury of such county on order of the court.

(b) In any county in which the board of supervisors so provides, the compensation fixed under Section 730 for medical experts in civil actions in such county shall be a charge against and paid out of the treasury of such county on order of the court.

(c) Except as otherwise provided in this section, in all civil actions, the compensation fixed under Section 730 shall, in the first instance, be apportioned and charged to the several parties in such proportion as the court may determine and may thereafter be taxed and allowed in like manner as other costs.

(Stats.1965, c. 299, § 2. Amended by Stats.1979, c. 746, § 4; Stats.1979, c. 746, § 5.)

For text of section operative until Jan. 1, 1983, see § 731, ante.

§ 732. Calling and examining court-appointed expert

Any expert appointed by the court under Section 730 may be called and examined by the court or by any party to the action. When such witness is called and examined by the court, the parties have the same right as is expressed in Section 775 to cross-examine the witness and to object to the questions asked and the evidence adduced.

(Stats.1965, c. 299, § 2.)

§ 733. Right to produce other expert evidence

Nothing contained in this article shall be deemed or construed to prevent any party to any action from producing other expert evidence on the same fact or matter mentioned in Section 730; but, where other expert witnesses are called by a party to the action, their fees shall be paid by the party calling them and only ordinary witness fees shall be taxed as costs in the action.

(Stats.1965, c. 299, § 2.)

CHAPTER 4. INTERPRETERS AND TRANSLATORS

§ 750. Rules relating to witnesses apply to interpreters and translators

A person who serves as an interpreter or translator in any action is subject to all the rules of law relating to witnesses.

(Stats.1965, c. 299, § 2.)

§ 751. Oath required of interpreters and translators

(a) An interpreter shall take an oath that he will make a true interpretation to the witness in a language that the witness understands and that he will make a true interpretation of the witness' answers to questions to counsel, court, or jury, in the English language, with his best skill and judgment.

(b) A translator shall take an oath that he will make a true translation in the English language of any writing he is to decipher or translate.

(Stats.1965, c. 299, § 2.)

§ 752. Interpreters for witnesses

(a) When a witness is incapable of hearing or understanding the English language or is incapable of expressing himself in the English language so as to be understood directly by counsel, court, and jury, an interpreter whom he can understand and who can understand him shall be sworn to interpret for him.

(b) The interpreter may be appointed and compensated as provided in Article 2 (commencing with Section 730) of Chapter 3.
(Stats.1965, c. 299, § 2.)

§ 753. Translators of writings

(a) When the written characters in a writing offered in evidence are incapable of being deciphered or understood directly, a translator who can decipher the characters or understand the language shall be sworn to decipher or translate the writing.

(b) The translator may be appointed and compensated as provided in Article 2 (commencing with Section 730) of Chapter 3.
(Stats.1965, c. 299, § 2.)

§ 754. Deaf persons; interpreters; criminal actions; juvenile cases or proceedings; mental competency proceedings; administrative hearings

(a) As used in this section, "deaf person" means a person with a hearing loss so great as to prevent his understanding language spoken in a normal tone.

(b) In any criminal action, including any juvenile case or proceeding, or any proceeding to determine the mental competency of a person, or any administrative hearing, where a party or witness is a deaf person and such deaf person is required to be present, the proceedings shall be interpreted in a language that the deaf person understands by a qualified interpreter appointed by the court, tribunal, or hearing officer, or as agreed upon by the parties.

(c) For the purposes of this section, "qualified interpreter" shall mean only a person who meets both of the following criteria:

(1) Has been issued a certificate of competency by the National Registry of Interpreters for the Deaf, or by a state group affiliated with the National Registry of Interpreters for the Deaf, or by any other group determined by the Judicial Council to possess a level of competence in training, testing, and certification of interpreters for the deaf equivalent to that of the National Registry of Interpreters for the Deaf, which certificate has been determined by the issuing agency to be appropriate for the purpose of interpreting the proceedings specified in subdivision (b); and

(2) Has been included on a list of recommended court interpreters which shall be established by the superior court in each county.

(d) In the event that the only available interpreter is not considered to possess adequate interpreting skills for the particular situation, or the interpreter is not familiar with use of slang, the deaf person may be permitted by the court, tribunal, or hearing officer to nominate another person to act as intermediary between himself and the appointed qualified interpreter during the proceedings.

(e) Persons appointed to serve as interpreters under this section shall be paid, in addition to actual travel costs, the prevailing rate paid to persons employed by the court to provide other interpreter services unless such service is considered to be a part of the person's regular duties as an employee of the state, county, or other political subdivision of the state. Payment of the interpreter's fee shall be a charge against the county, or other political subdivision of the state, in which such action is pending. Payment of the interpreter's fee in administrative proceedings shall be a charge against the appointing board, agency, commission or licensing authority.

(f) No statement, written or oral, made by a person who is deaf in reply to a question of a peace officer, or any other person having prosecutorial function in any criminal or quasi-criminal proceeding, may be used against that deaf person unless either the statement was made or elicited through a qualified interpreter and was made knowingly, voluntarily, and intelligently, or the court makes a special finding that any statement made by a deaf person was made knowingly, voluntarily, and intelligently.

(g) In any action or proceeding in which a deaf person is a participant, the court or administrative authority shall not commence proceedings until the appointed interpreter is in full view of and spatially situated to assure proper communication with the deaf person or persons involved as participants.

(Stats.1965, c. 299 § 2. Amended by Stats.1977, c. 1182, § 1.)

CHAPTER 5. METHOD AND SCOPE OF EXAMINATION

ARTICLE 1. DEFINITIONS

§ 760. "Direct examination"

"Direct examination" is the first examination of a witness upon a matter that is not within the scope of a previous examination of the witness.
(Stats.1965, c. 299, § 2.)

§ 761. "Cross-examination"

"Cross-examination" is the examination of a witness by a party other than the direct examiner upon a matter that is within the scope of the direct examination of the witness.
(Stats.1965, c. 299, § 2.)

§ 762. "Redirect examination"

"Redirect examination" is an examination of a witness by the direct examiner subsequent to the cross-examination of the witness.
(Stats.1965, c. 299, § 2.)

§ 763. "Recross-examination"

"Recross-examination" is an examination of a witness by a cross-examiner subsequent to a redirect examination of the witness.
(Stats.1965, c. 299, § 2.)

§ 764. "Leading question"

A "leading question" is a question that suggests to the witness the answer that the examining party desires.
(Stats.1965, c. 299, § 2.)

ARTICLE 2. EXAMINATION OF WITNESSES

§ 765. Court to control mode of interrogation

The court shall exercise reasonable control over the mode of interrogation of a witness so as (a) to make such interrogation as rapid, as distinct, and as effective for the ascertainment of the truth, as may be, and (b) to protect the witness from undue harassment or embarrassment.
(Stats.1965, c. 299, § 2.)

§ 766. Responsive answers

A witness must give responsive answers to questions, and answers that are not responsive shall be stricken on motion of any party.
(Stats.1965, c. 299, § 2.)

§ 767. Leading questions

Except under special circumstances where the interests of justice otherwise require:

(a) A leading question may not be asked of a witness on direct or redirect examination.

(b) A leading question may be asked of a witness on cross-examination or recross-examination.
(Stats.1965, c. 299, § 2.)

§ 768. Writings

(a) In examining a witness concerning a writing, it is not necessary to show, read, or disclose to him any part of the writing.

(b) If a writing is shown to a witness, all parties to the action must be given an opportunity to inspect it before any question concerning it may be asked of the witness.
(Stats.1965, c. 299, § 2.)

§ 769. Inconsistent statement or conduct

In examining a witness concerning a statement or other conduct by him that is inconsistent with any part of his testimony at the hearing, it is not necessary to disclose to him any information concerning the statement or other conduct.
(Stats.1965, c. 299, § 2.)

§ 770. Evidence of inconsistent statement of witness

Unless the interests of justice otherwise require, extrinsic evidence of a statement made by a witness that is inconsistent with any part of his testimony at the hearing shall be excluded unless:

(a) The witness was so examined while testifying as to give him an opportunity to explain or to deny the statement; or

(b) The witness has not been excused from giving further testimony in the action.
(Stats.1965, c. 299, § 2.)

§ 771. Production of writing used to refresh memory

(a) Subject to subdivision (c), if a witness, either while testifying or prior thereto, uses a writing to refresh his memory with respect to any matter about which he testifies, such writing must be produced at the hearing at the request of an adverse party and, unless the writing is so produced, the testimony of the witness concerning such matter shall be stricken.

(b) If the writing is produced at the hearing, the adverse party may, if he chooses, inspect the writing, cross-examine the witness concerning it, and introduce in evidence such portion of it as may be pertinent to the testimony of the witness.

(c) Production of the writing is excused, and the testimony of the witness shall not be stricken, if the writing:

(1) Is not in the possession or control of the witness or the party who produced his testimony concerning the matter; and

(2) Was not reasonably procurable by such party through the use of the court's process or other available means.
(Stats.1965, c. 299, § 2.)

§ 772. Order of examination

(a) The examination of a witness shall proceed in the following phases: direct examination, cross-examination, redirect examination, recross-examination, and continuing thereafter by redirect and recross-examination.

(b) Unless for good cause the court otherwise directs, each phase of the examination of a witness must be concluded before the succeeding phase begins.

(c) Subject to subdivision (d), a party may, in the discretion of the court, interrupt his cross-examination, redirect examination, or recross-examination of a witness, in order to examine the witness upon a matter not within the scope of a previous examination of the witness.

(d) If the witness is the defendant in a criminal action, the witness may not, without his consent, be examined under direct examination by another party.
(Stats.1965, c. 299, § 2.)

§ 773. Cross-examination

(a) A witness examined by one party may be cross-examined upon any matter within the scope of the direct examination by each other party to the action in such order as the court directs.

(b) The cross-examination of a witness by any party whose interest is not adverse to the party calling him is subject to the same rules that are applicable to the direct examination.
(Stats.1965, c. 299, § 2.)

§ 774. Re-examination

A witness once examined cannot be reexamined as to the same matter without leave of the court, but he may be reexamined as to any new matter upon which he has been examined by another party to the action. Leave may be granted or withheld in the court's discretion.
(Stats.1965, c. 299, § 2.)

§ 775. Court may call witnesses

The court, on its own motion or on the motion of any party, may call witnesses and interrogate them the same as if they had been produced by a party to the action, and the parties may object to the questions asked and the evidence adduced the same as if such witnesses were called and examined by an adverse party. Such witnesses may be cross-examined by all parties to the action in such order as the court directs.
(Stats.1965, c. 299, § 2.)

§ 776. Examination of adverse party or witness

(a) A party to the record of any civil action, or a person identified with such a party, may be called and examined as if under cross-examination by any adverse party at any time during the presentation of evidence by the party calling the witness.

(b) A witness examined by a party under this section may be cross-examined by all other parties to the action in such order as the court directs; but, subject to subdivision (e), the witness may be examined only as if under redirect examination by:

(1) In the case of a witness who is a party, his own counsel and counsel for a party who is not adverse to the witness.

(2) In the case of a witness who is not a party, counsel for the party with whom the witness is identified and counsel for a party who is not adverse to the party with whom the witness is identified.

(c) For the purpose of this section, parties represented by the same counsel are deemed to be a single party.

(d) For the purpose of this section, a person is identified with a party if he is:

(1) A person for whose immediate benefit the action is prosecuted or defended by the party.

(2) A director, officer, superintendent, member, agent, employee, or managing agent of the party or of a person specified in paragraph (1), or any public employee of a public entity when such public entity is the party.

(3) A person who was in any of the relationships specified in paragraph (2) at the time of the act or omission giving rise to the cause of action.

(4) A person who was in any of the relationships specified in paragraph (2) at the time he obtained knowledge of the matter concerning which he is sought to be examined under this section.

(e) Paragraph (2) of subdivision (b) does not require counsel for the party with whom the witness is identified and counsel for a party who is not adverse to the party with whom the witness is identified to examine the witness as if under redirect examination if the party who called the witness for examination under this section:

(1) Is also a person identified with the same party with whom the witness is identified.

(2) Is the personal representative, heir, successor, or assignee of a person identified with the same party with whom the witness is identified.
(Stats. 1965, c. 299, § 2. Amended by Stats.1967, c. 650, § 2.)

§ 777. Exclusion of witness

(a) Subject to subdivisions (b) and (c), the court may exclude from the courtroom any witness not at the time under examination so that such witness cannot hear the testimony of other witnesses.

(b) A party to the action cannot be excluded under this section.

(c) If a person other than a natural person is a party to the action, an officer or employee designated by its attorney is entitled to be present.
(Stats.1965, c. 299, § 2.)

§ 778. Recall of witness

After a witness has been excused from giving further testimony in the action, he cannot be recalled without leave of the court. Leave may be granted or withheld in the court's discretion.
(Stats.1965, c. 299, § 2.)

CHAPTER 6. CREDIBILITY OF WITNESSES

ARTICLE I. GENERALLY

Sec.
780. General rule as to credibility.
782. Rape; evidence of sexual conduct of complaining witness; procedure for admissibility.

§ 780. General rule as to credibility

Except as otherwise provided by statute, the court or jury may consider in determining the credibility of a witness any matter that has any tendency in reason to prove or disprove the truthfulness of his testimony at the hearing, including but not limited to any of the following:

(a) His demeanor while testifying and the manner in which he testifies.

(b) The character of his testimony.

(c) The extent of his capacity to perceive, to recollect, or to communicate any matter about which he testifies.

(d) The extent of his opportunity to perceive any matter about which he testifies.

(e) His character for honesty or veracity or their opposites.

(f) The existence or nonexistence of a bias, interest, or other motive.

(g) A statement previously made by him that is consistent with his testimony at the hearing.

(h) A statement made by him that is inconsistent with any part of his testimony at the hearing.

(i) The existence or nonexistence of any fact testified to by him.

(j) His attitude toward the action in which he testifies or toward the giving of testimony.

(k) His admission of untruthfulness.
(Stats.1965, c. 299, § 2.)

§ 782. Rape; evidence of sexual conduct of complaining witness; procedure for admissibility

(a) In any prosecution under Section 261, or 264.1 of the Penal Code, or for assault with intent to commit, attempt to commit, or conspiracy to commit any crime defined in any such section, if evidence of sexual conduct of the complaining witness is offered to attack the credibility of the complaining witness under Section 780, the following procedure shall be followed:

(1) A written motion shall be made by the defendant to the court and prosecutor stating that the defense has an offer of proof of the relevancy of evidence of the sexual conduct of the complaining witness proposed to be presented and its relevancy in attacking the credibility of the complaining witness.

(2) The written motion shall be accompanied by an affidavit in which the offer of proof shall be stated.

(3) If the court finds that the offer of proof is sufficient, the court shall order a hearing out of the presence of the jury, if any, and at such hearing allow the questioning of the complaining witness regarding the offer of proof made by the defendant.

(4) At the conclusion of the hearing, if the court finds that evidence proposed to be offered by the defendant regarding the sexual conduct of the complaining witness is relevant pursuant to Section 780, and is not inadmissible pursuant to Section 352 of this

code, the court may make an order stating what evidence may be introduced by the defendant, and the nature of the questions to be permitted. The defendant may then offer evidence pursuant to the order of the court.

(b) As used in this section, "complaining witness" means the alleged victim of the crime charged, the prosecution of which is subject to this section.
(Added by Stats.1974, c. 569, § 1.)

ARTICLE 2. ATTACKING OR SUPPORTING CREDIBILITY

Sec.

§ 785. Parties may attack or support credibility

The credibility of a witness may be attacked or supported by any party, including the party calling him.
(Stats.1965, c. 299, § 2.)

§ 786. Character evidence generally

Evidence of traits of his character other than honesty or veracity, or their opposites, is inadmissible to attack or support the credibility of a witness.
(Stats.1965, c. 299, § 2.)

§ 787. Specific instances of conduct

Subject to Section 788, evidence of specific instances of his conduct relevant only as tending to prove a trait of his character is inadmissible to attack or support the credibility of a witness.
(Stats.1965, c. 299, § 2.)

§ 788. Prior felony conviction

For the purpose of attacking the credibility of a witness, it may be shown by the examination of the witness or by the record of the judgment that he has been convicted of a felony unless:

(a) A pardon based on his innocence has been granted to the witness by the jurisdiction in which he was convicted.

(b) A certificate of rehabilitation and pardon has been granted to the witness under the provisions of Chapter 3.5 (commencing with Section 4852.01) of Title 6 of Part 3 of the Penal Code.

(c) The accusatory pleading against the witness has been dismissed under the provisions of Penal Code Section 1203.4, but this exception does not apply to any criminal trial where the witness is being prosecuted for a subsequent offense.

(d) The conviction was under the laws of another jurisdiction and the witness has been relieved of the penalties and disabilities arising from the conviction pursuant to a procedure substantially equivalent to that referred to in subdivision (b) or (c).
(Stats.1965, c. 299, § 2.)

§ 789. Religious belief

Evidence of his religious belief or lack thereof is inadmissible to attack or support the credibility of a witness.
(Stats.1965, c. 299, § 2.)

§ 790. Good character of witness

Evidence of the good character of a witness is inadmissible to support his credibility unless evidence of his bad character has been admitted for the purpose of attacking his credibility.

(Stats.1965, c. 299, § 2.)

§ 791. Prior consistent statement of witness

Evidence of a statement previously made by a witness that is consistent with his testimony at the hearing is inadmissible to support his credibility unless it is offered after:

(a) Evidence of a statement made by him that is inconsistent with any part of his testimony at the hearing has been admitted for the purpose of attacking his credibility, and the statement was made before the alleged inconsistent statement; or

(b) An express or implied charge has been made that his testimony at the hearing is recently fabricated or is influenced by bias or other improper motive, and the statement was made before the bias, motive for fabrication, or other improper motive is alleged to have arisen.

(Stats.1965, c. 299, § 2.)

Division 7

OPINION TESTIMONY AND SCIENTIFIC EVIDENCE

CHAPTER 1. EXPERT AND OTHER OPINION TESTIMONY

ARTICLE 1. EXPERT AND OTHER OPINION TESTIMONY GENERALLY

§ 800. Opinion testimony by lay witness

If a witness is not testifying as an expert, his testimony in the form of an opinion is limited to such an opinion as is permitted by law, including but not limited to an opinion that is:

(a) Rationally based on the perception of the witness; and

(b) Helpful to a clear understanding of his testimony.

(Stats.1965, c. 299, § 2.)

§ 801. Opinion testimony by expert witness

If a witness is testifying as an expert, his testimony in the form of an opinion is limited to such an opinion as is:

(a) Related to a subject that is sufficiently beyond common experience that the opinion of an expert would assist the trier of fact; and

(b) Based on matter (including his special knowledge, skill, experience, training, and education) perceived by or personally known to the witness or made known to him at or before the hearing, whether or not admissible, that is of a type that reasonably may be relied upon by an expert in forming an opinion upon the subject to which his testimony relates, unless an expert is precluded by law from using such matter as a basis for his opinion.

(Stats.1965, c. 299, § 2.)

§ 802. Statement of basis of opinion

A witness testifying in the form of an opinion may state on direct examination the reasons for his opinion and the matter (including, in the case of an expert, his special knowledge, skill, experience, training, and education) upon which it is based, unless he is precluded by law from using such reasons or matter as a basis for his opinion. The court in its discretion may require that a witness before testifying in the form of an opinion be first examined concerning the matter upon which his opinion is based.

(Stats.1965, c. 299, § 2.)

§ 803. Opinion based on improper matter

The court may, and upon objection shall, exclude testimony in the form of an opinion that is based in whole or in significant part on matter that is not a proper basis for such an opinion. In such case, the witness may, if there remains a proper basis for his opinion, then state his opinion after excluding from consideration the matter determined to be improper. (Stats.1965, c. 299, § 2.)

§ 804. Opinion based on opinion or statement of another

(a) If a witness testifying as an expert testifies that his opinion is based in whole or in part upon the opinion or statement of another person, such other person may be called and examined by any adverse party as if under cross-examination concerning the opinion or statement.

(b) This section is not applicable if the person upon whose opinion or statement the expert witness has relied is (1) a party, (2) a person identified with a party within the meaning of subdivision (d) of Section 776, or (3) a witness who has testified in the action concerning the subject matter of the opinion or statement upon which the expert witness has relied.

(c) Nothing in this section makes admissible an expert opinion that is inadmissible because it is based in whole or in part on the opinion or statement of another person.

(d) An expert opinion otherwise admissible is not made inadmissible by this section because it is based on the opinion or statement of a person who is unavailable for examination pursuant to this section. (Stats.1965, c. 299, § 2.)

§ 805. Opinion on ultimate issue

Testimony in the form of an opinion that is otherwise admissible is not objectionable because it embraces the ultimate issue to be decided by the trier of fact. (Stats.1965, c. 299, § 2.)

ARTICLE 2. EVIDENCE OF MARKET VALUE OF PROPERTY

Article 2 Value, Damages, and Benefits in Eminent Domain and Inverse Condemnation Cases, was added by Stats.1965, c. 1151, § 4.

The heading of Article 2 was amended by Stats.1978, c. 294, § 2, to read as it now appears.

Article heading preceding § 870 et seq., added by Stats.1965, c. 299, as Article 2, was amended to be Article 3 by Stats.1965, c. 1151, § 3.

§ 810. Application of article

(a) Except where another rule is provided by statute, this article provides special rules of evidence applicable to any action in which the value of property is to be ascertained.

(b) This article does not govern ad valorem property tax assessment or equalization proceedings.
(Stats.1965, c. 1151, § 4, operative January 1, 1967. Amended by Stats.1978, c. 294, § 3; Stats.1980, c. 381, § 1.)

§ 811. Value of property

As used in this article, "value of property" means market value of any of the following:

(a) Real property or any interest therein.

(b) Real property or any interest therein and tangible personal property valued as a unit.
(Added by Stats.1965, c. 1151, § 4, operative January 1, 1967. Amended by Stats.1975, c. 1240, § 15, operative July 1, 1976; Stats.1978, c. 294, § 4; Stats.1980, c. 381, § 2.)

§ 812. Market value; interpretation of meaning

This article is not intended to alter or change the existing substantive law, whether statutory or decisional, interpreting the meaning of "market value," whether denominated "fair market value" or otherwise.
(Added by Stats.1965, c. 1151, § 4, operative January 1, 1967. Amended by Stats.1975, c. 1240, § 16, operative July 1, 1976; Stats.1978, c. 294, § 5.)

§ 813. Value of property; authorized opinions; view of property; admissible evidence

(a) The value of property may be shown only by the opinions of any of the following:

(1) Witnesses qualified to express such opinions.

(2) The owner or the spouse of the owner of the property or property interest being valued.

(3) An officer, regular employee, or partner designated by a corporation, partnership, or unincorporated association that is the owner of the property or property interest being valued, if the designee is knowledgeable as to the value of the property or property interest.

(b) Nothing in this section prohibits a view of the property being valued or the admission of any other admissible evidence (including but not limited to evidence as to the nature and condition of the property and, in an eminent domain proceeding, the character of the improvement proposed to be constructed by the plaintiff) for the limited purpose of enabling the court, jury, or referee to understand and weigh the testimony given under subdivision (a); and such evidence, except evidence of the character of the improvement proposed to be constructed by the plaintiff in an eminent domain proceeding, is subject to impeachment and rebuttal.

(c) For the purposes of subdivision (a), "owner of the property or property interest being valued" includes, but is not limited to, the following persons:

(1) A person entitled to possession of the property.

(2) Either party in an action or proceeding to determine the ownership of the property between the parties if the court determines that it would not be in the interest of efficient administration of justice to determine the issue of ownership prior to the admission of the opinion of the party.
(Added by Stats.1965, c. 1151, § 4, operative January 1, 1967. Amended by Stats.1978, c. 294, § 6; Stats.1980, c. 381, § 3.)

§ 814. Matter upon which opinion must be based

The opinion of a witness as to the value of property is limited to such an opinion as is based on matter perceived by or personally known to the witness or made known to the witness at or before the hearing, whether or not admissible, that is of a type that reasonably may be relied upon by an expert in forming an opinion as to the value of property, including but not limited to the matters listed in Sections 815 to 821, inclusive, unless a witness is precluded by law from using such matter as a basis for an opinion.
(Added by Stats.1965, c. 1151, § 4, operative January 1, 1967. Amended by Stats.1975, c. 1240, § 17; Stats.1980, c. 381, § 4.)

§ 814.5. Repealed by Stats.1971, c. 1574, § 1.4, operative July 1, 1972
See, now, Civil Code § 7004.

§ 815. Sales of subject property
When relevant to the determination of the value of property, a witness may take into account as a basis for an opinion the price and other terms and circumstances of any sale or contract to sell and purchase which included the property or property interest being valued or any part thereof if the sale or contract was freely made in good faith within a reasonable time before or after the date of valuation, except that in an eminent domain proceeding where the sale or contract to sell and purchase includes only the property or property interest being taken or a part thereof, such sale or contract to sell and purchase may not be taken into account if it occurs after the filing of the lis pendens.
(Added by Stats.1965, c. 1151, § 4, operative January 1, 1967. Amended by Stats.1978, c. 294, § 7.)

§ 816. Comparable sales
When relevant to the determination of the value of property, a witness may take into account as a basis for his opinion the price and other terms and circumstances of any sale or contract to sell and purchase comparable property if the sale or contract was freely made in good faith within a reasonable time before or after the date of valuation. In order to be considered comparable, the sale or contract must have been made sufficiently near in time to the date of valuation, and the property sold must be located sufficiently near the property being valued, and must be sufficiently alike in respect to character, size, situation, usability, and improvements, to make it clear that the property sold and the property being valued are comparable in value and that the price realized for the property sold may fairly be considered as shedding light on the value of the property being valued.
(Added by Stats.1965, c. 1151, § 4, operative January 1, 1967.)

§ 817. Leases of subject property
(a) Subject to subdivision (b), when relevant to the determination of the value of property, a witness may take into account as a basis for an opinion the rent reserved and other terms and circumstances of any lease which included the property or property interest being valued or any part thereof which was in effect within a reasonable time before or after the date of valuation, except that in an eminent domain proceeding where the lease includes only the property or property interest being taken or a part thereof, such lease may not be taken into account in the determination of the value of property if it is entered into after the filing of the lis pendens.

(b) A witness may take into account a lease providing for a rental fixed by a percentage or other measurable portion of gross sales or gross income from a business conducted on the leased property only for the purpose of arriving at an opinion as to the reasonable net rental value attributable to the property or property interest being valued as provided in Section 819 or determining the value of a leasehold interest.
(Added by Stats.1965, c. 1151, § 4, operative January 1, 1967. Amended by Stats.1978, c. 294, § 8.)

§ 818. Comparable leases
For the purpose of determining the capitalized value of the reasonable net rental value attributable to the property or property interest being valued as provided in Section 819 or determining the value of a leasehold interest, a witness may take into account as a basis for his opinion the rent reserved and other terms and circumstances of any lease of comparable property if the lease was freely made in good faith within a reasonable time before or after the date of valuation.
(Added by Stats.1965, c. 1151, § 4, operative January 1, 1967.)

§ 819. Capitalization of income
When relevant to the determination of the value of property, a witness may take into account as a basis for his opinion the capitalized value of the reasonable net rental value

attributable to the land and existing improvements thereon (as distinguished from the capitalized value of the income or profits attributable to the business conducted thereon). (Added by Stats.1965, c. 1151, § 4, operative January 1, 1967.)

§ 820. Reproduction cost

When relevant to the determination of the value of property, a witness may take into account as a basis for his opinion the value of the property or property interest being valued as indicated by the value of the land together with the cost of replacing or reproducing the existing improvements thereon, if the improvements enhance the value of the property or property interest for its highest and best use, less whatever depreciation or obsolescence the improvements have suffered. (Added by Stats.1965, c. 1151, § 4, operative January 1, 1967.)

§ 821. Conditions in general vicinity of subject property

When relevant to the determination of the value of property, a witness may take into account as a basis for his opinion the nature of the improvements on properties in the general vicinity of the property or property interest being valued and the character of the existing uses being made of such properties. (Added by Stats.1965, c. 1151, § 4, operative January 1, 1967.)

§ 822. Matter upon which opinion may not be based

(a) In an eminent domain or inverse condemnation proceeding, notwithstanding the provisions of Sections 814 to 821, the following matter is inadmissible as evidence and shall not be taken into account as a basis for an opinion as to the value of property:

(1) The price or other terms and circumstances of an acquisition of property or a property interest if the acquisition was for a public use for which the property could have been taken by eminent domain.

(2) The price at which an offer or option to purchase or lease the property or property interest being valued or any other property was made, or the price at which such property or interest was optioned, offered, or listed for sale or lease, except that an option, offer, or listing may be introduced by a party as an admission of another party to the proceeding; but nothing in this subdivision permits an admission to be used as direct evidence upon any matter that may be shown only by opinion evidence under Section 813.

(3) The value of any property or property interest as assessed for taxation purposes or the amount of taxes which may be due on the property, but nothing in this subdivision prohibits the consideration of actual or estimated taxes for the purpose of determining the reasonable net rental value attributable to the property or property interest being valued.

(4) An opinion as to the value of any property or property interest other than that being valued.

(5) The influence upon the value of the property or property interest being valued of any noncompensable items of value, damage, or injury.

(6) The capitalized value of the income or rental from any property or property interest other than that being valued.

(b) In an action other than an eminent domain or inverse condemnation proceeding, the matters listed in subdivision (a) are not admissible as evidence, and may not be taken into account as a basis for an opinion as to the value of property, except to the extent permitted under the rules of law otherwise applicable. (Added by Stats.1965, c. 1151, § 4, operative January 1, 1967. Amended by Stats.1978, c. 294, § 9; Stats.1980, c. 381, § 5.)

§ 823. No relevant market for property

Notwithstanding any other provision of this article, the value of property for which there is no relevant market may be determined by any method of valuation that is just and equitable. (Added by Stats.1980, c. 381, § 6.)

ARTICLE 3. OPINION TESTIMONY ON PARTICULAR SUBJECTS

Article heading, added by Stats.1965, c. 299, as Article 2, was changed to Article 3 by Stats.1965, c. 1151, § 3.

§ 870. Opinion as to sanity

A witness may state his opinion as to the sanity of a person when:

(a) The witness is an intimate acquaintance of the person whose sanity is in question;

(b) The witness was a subscribing witness to a writing, the validity of which is in dispute, signed by the person whose sanity is in question and the opinion relates to the sanity of such person at the time the writing was signed; or

(c) The witness is qualified under Section 800 or 801 to testify in the form of an opinion. (Stats.1965, c. 299, § 2.)

CHAPTER 2. BLOOD TESTS TO DETERMINE PATERNITY

UNIFORM ACT ON BLOOD TESTS TO DETERMINE PATERNITY
Table Of Jurisdictions Wherein Act Has Been Adopted

Jurisdiction	Statutory Citation
California	West's Ann.Evidence Code §§ 890 to 897.
Illinois	S.H.A. ch. 40, §§ 1401 to 1407.
Louisiana	LSA–R.S. 9.396 to 9.398.
New Hampshire	RSA 522:1 to 522:10.
Oklahoma	10 Okl.St.Ann. §§ 501 to 508.
Oregon	ORS 109.250 to 109.262.
Panama Canal Zone	8 C.Z.C. §§ 491 to 497.
Pennsylvania	42 Pa.C.S.A. §§ 6131 to 6137.
Utah	U.C.A.1953, 78–25–18 to 78–25–23.

§ 890. Short title

This chapter may be cited as the Uniform Act on Blood Tests to Determine Paternity. (Stats.1965, c. 299, § 2.)

§ 891. Interpretation

This act shall be so interpreted and construed as to effectuate its general purpose to make uniform the law of those states which enact it. (Stats.1965, c. 299, § 2.)

§ 892. Order for blood tests in civil actions involving paternity

In a civil action in which paternity is a relevant fact, the court may upon its own initiative or upon suggestion made by or on behalf of any person whose blood is involved, and shall upon motion of any party to the action made at a time so as not to delay the proceedings unduly, order the mother, child, and alleged father to submit to blood tests. If any party refuses to submit to such tests, the court may resolve the question of paternity

against such party or enforce its order if the rights of others and the interests of justice so require.
(Stats.1965, c. 299, § 2.)

§ 893. Tests made by experts

The tests shall be made by experts qualified as examiners of blood types who shall be appointed by the court. The experts shall be called by the court as witnesses to testify to their findings and shall be subject to cross-examination by the parties. Any party or person at whose suggestion the tests have been ordered may demand that other experts, qualified as examiners of blood types, perform independent tests under order of the court, the results of which may be offered in evidence. The number and qualifications of such experts shall be determined by the court.
(Stats.1965, c. 299, § 2.)

§ 894. Compensation of experts

The compensation of each expert witness appointed by the court shall be fixed at a reasonable amount. It shall be paid as the court shall order. The court may order that it be paid by the parties in such proportions and at such times as it shall prescribe, or that the proportion of any party be paid by the county, and that, after payment by the parties or the county or both, all or part or none of it be taxed as costs in the action.
(Stats.1965, c. 299, § 2.)

§ 895. Determination of paternity

If the court finds that the conclusions of all the experts, as disclosed by the evidence based upon the tests, are that the alleged father is not the father of the child, the question of paternity shall be resolved accordingly. If the experts disagree in their findings or conclusions, the question shall be submitted upon all the evidence.
(Stats.1965, c. 299, § 2.)

§ 896. Limitation on application in criminal matters

This chapter applies to criminal actions subject to the following limitations and provisions:

(a) An order for the tests shall be made only upon application of a party or on the court's initiative.

(b) The compensation of the experts shall be paid by the county under order of court.

(c) The court may direct a verdict of acquittal upon the conclusions of all the experts under the provisions of Section 895; otherwise, the case shall be submitted for determination upon all the evidence.
(Stats.1965, c. 299, § 2.)

§ 897. Right to produce other expert evidence

Nothing contained in this chapter shall be deemed or construed to prevent any party to any action from producing other expert evidence on the matter covered by this chapter; but, where other expert witnesses are called by a party to the action, their fees shall be paid by the party calling them and only ordinary witness fees shall be taxed as costs in the action.
(Stats.1965, c. 299, § 2.)

Division 8
PRIVILEGES

CHAPTER 1. DEFINITIONS

Sec.
900. Application of definitions.
901. "Proceeding."
902. "Civil proceeding."
903. "Criminal proceeding."
904. Blank.
905. "Presiding officer."

§ 900. Application of definitions

Unless the provision or context otherwise requires, the definitions in this chapter govern the construction of this division. They do not govern the construction of any other division.

(Stats.1965, c. 299, § 2.)

§ 901. "Proceeding"

"Proceeding" means any action, hearing, investigation, inquest, or inquiry (whether conducted by a court, administrative agency, hearing officer, arbitrator, legislative body, or any other person authorized by law) in which, pursuant to law, testimony can be compelled to be given.

(Stats.1965, c. 299, § 2.)

§ 902. "Civil proceeding"

"Civil proceeding" means any proceeding except a criminal proceeding.

(Stats.1965, c. 299, § 2.)

§ 903. "Criminal proceeding"

"Criminal proceeding" means:

(a) A criminal action; and

(b) A proceeding pursuant to Article 3 (commencing with Section 3060) of Chapter 7 of Division 4 of Title 1 of the Government Code to determine whether a public officer should be removed from office for willful or corrupt misconduct in office.

(Stats.1965, c. 299, § 2.)

§ 904. Blank

§ 905. "Presiding officer"

"Presiding officer" means the person authorized to rule on a claim of privilege in the proceeding in which the claim is made.

(Stats.1965, c. 299, § 2.)

CHAPTER 2. APPLICABILITY OF DIVISION

§ 910. Applicability of division

Except as otherwise provided by statute, the provisions of this division apply in all proceedings. The provisions of any statute making rules of evidence inapplicable in particular proceedings, or limiting the applicability of rules of evidence in particular proceedings, do not make this division inapplicable to such proceedings.
(Stats.1965, c. 299, § 2.)

CHAPTER 3. GENERAL PROVISIONS RELATING TO PRIVILEGES

§ 911. General rule as to privileges

Except as otherwise provided by statute:

(a) No person has a privilege to refuse to be a witness.

(b) No person has a privilege to refuse to disclose any matter or to refuse to produce any writing, object, or other thing.

(c) No person has a privilege that another shall not be a witness or shall not disclose any matter or shall not produce any writing, object, or other thing.
(Stats.1965, c. 299, § 2.)

§ 912. Waiver of privilege

(a) Except as otherwise provided in this section, the right of any person to claim a privilege provided by Section 954 (lawyer-client privilege), 980 (privilege for confidential marital communications), 994 (physician-patient privilege), 1014 (psychotherapist-patient privilege), 1033 (privilege of penitent), 1034 (privilege of clergyman), or 1035.8 (sexual assault victim-counselor privilege) is waived with respect to a communication protected by such privilege if any holder of the privilege, without coercion, has disclosed a significant part of the communication or has consented to such disclosure made by anyone. Consent to disclosure is manifested by any statement or other conduct of the holder of the privilege indicating consent to the disclosure, including failure to claim the privilege in any proceeding in which the holder has the legal standing and opportunity to claim the privilege.

(b) Where two or more persons are joint holders of a privilege provided by Section 954 (lawyer-client privilege), 994 (physician-patient privilege), 1014 (psychotherapist-patient privilege), or 1035.8 (sexual assault victim-counselor privilege), a waiver of the right of a particular joint holder of the privilege to claim the privilege does not affect the right of another joint holder to claim the privilege. In the case of the privilege provided by Section 980 (privilege for confidential marital communications), a waiver of the right of one spouse to claim the privilege does not affect the right of the other spouse to claim the privilege.

(c) A disclosure that is itself privileged is not a waiver of any privilege.

(d) A disclosure in confidence of a communication that is protected by a privilege provided by Section 954 (lawyer-client privilege), 994 (physician-patient privilege), 1014 (psychotherapist-patient privilege), or 1035.8 (sexual assault victim-counselor privilege), when such disclosure is reasonably necessary for the accomplishment of the purpose for which the lawyer, physician, psychotherapist, or sexual assault counselor was consulted, is not a waiver of the privilege.
(Stats.1965, c. 299, § 2; Stats.1980, c. 917, § 1.)

§ 913. Comment on, and inferences from, exercise of privilege

(a) If in the instant proceeding or on a prior occasion a privilege is or was exercised not to testify with respect to any matter, or to refuse to disclose or to prevent another from disclosing any matter, neither the presiding officer nor counsel may comment thereon, no presumption shall arise because of the exercise of the privilege, and the trier of fact may not draw any inference therefrom as to the credibility of the witness or as to any matter at issue in the proceeding.

(b) The court, at the request of a party who may be adversely affected because an unfavorable inference may be drawn by the jury because a privilege has been exercised, shall instruct the jury that no presumption arises because of the exercise of the privilege and that the jury may not draw any inference therefrom as to the credibility of the witness or as to any matter at issue in the proceeding.
(Stats.1965, c. 299, § 2.)

§ 914. Determination of claim of privilege; limitation on punishment for contempt

(a) The presiding officer shall determine a claim of privilege in any proceeding in the same manner as a court determines such a claim under Article 2 (commencing with Section 400) of Chapter 4 of Division 3.

(b) No person may be held in contempt for failure to disclose information claimed to be privileged unless he has failed to comply with an order of a court that he disclose such information. This subdivision does not apply to any governmental agency that has constitutional contempt power, nor does it apply to hearings and investigations of the Industrial Accident Commission, nor does it impliedly repeal Chapter 4 (commencing with Section 9400) of Part 1 of Division 2 of Title 2 of the Government Code. If no other statutory procedure is applicable, the procedure prescribed by Section 1991 of the Code of Civil Procedure shall be followed in seeking an order of a court that the person disclose the information claimed to be privileged.
(Stats.1965, c. 299, § 2.)

§ 915. Disclosure of privileged information in ruling on claim of privilege

(a) Subject to subdivision (b), the presiding officer may not require disclosure of information claimed to be privileged under this division in order to rule on the claim of privilege; provided, however, that in any hearing conducted pursuant to subdivision (c) of Section 1524 of the Penal Code in which a claim of privilege is made and the court determines that there is no other feasible means to rule on the validity of such claim other than to require disclosure, the court shall proceed in accordance with subdivision (b).

(b) When a court is ruling on a claim of privilege under Article 9 (commencing with Section 1040) of Chapter 4 (official information and identity of informer) or under Section 1060 (trade secret) and is unable to do so without requiring disclosure of the information claimed to be privileged, the court may require the person from whom disclosure is sought or the person authorized to claim the privilege, or both, to disclose the information in chambers out of the presence and hearing of all persons except the person authorized to claim the privilege and such other persons as the person authorized to claim the privilege is willing to have present. If the judge determines that the information is privileged, neither he nor any other person may ever disclose, without the consent of a person authorized to permit disclosure, what was disclosed in the course of the proceedings in chambers. (Stats.1965, c. 299, § 2. Amended by Stats.1979, c. 1034, § 1.)

§ 916. Exclusion of privileged information where persons authorized to claim privilege are not present

(a) The presiding officer, on his own motion or on the motion of any party, shall exclude information that is subject to a claim of privilege under this division if:

(1) The person from whom the information is sought is not a person authorized to claim the privilege; and

(2) There is no party to the proceeding who is a person authorized to claim the privilege.

(b) The presiding officer may not exclude information under this section if:

(1) He is otherwise instructed by a person authorized to permit disclosure; or

(2) The proponent of the evidence establishes that there is no person authorized to claim the privilege in existence.
(Stats.1965, c. 299, § 2.)

§ 917. Presumption that certain communications are confidential

Whenever a privilege is claimed on the ground that the matter sought to be disclosed is a communication made in confidence in the course of the lawyer-client, physician-patient, psychotherapist-patient, clergy-man-penitent, or husband-wife relationship, the communication is presumed to have been made in confidence and the opponent of the claim of privilege has the burden of proof to establish that the communication was not confidential.
(Stats.1965, c. 299, § 2.)

§ 918. Effect of error in overruling claim of privilege

A party may predicate error on a ruling disallowing a claim of privilege only if he is the holder of the privilege, except that a party may predicate error on a ruling disallowing a claim of privilege by his spouse under Section 970 or 971.
(Stats.1965, c. 299, § 2.)

§ 919. Admissibility where disclosure erroneously compelled; claim of privilege coercion

(a) Evidence of a statement or other disclosure of privileged information is inadmissible against a holder of the privilege if:

(1) A person authorized to claim the privilege claimed it but nevertheless disclosure erroneously was required to be made; or

(2) The presiding officer did not exclude the privileged information as required by Section 916.

(b) If a person authorized to claim the privilege claimed it, whether in the same or a prior proceeding, but nevertheless disclosure erroneously was required by the presiding officer to be made, neither the failure to refuse to disclose nor the failure to seek review of the order of the presiding officer requiring disclosure indicates consent to the disclosure or constitutes a waiver and, under these circumstances, the disclosure is one made under coercion.

(Stats.1965, c. 299, § 2. Amended by Stats.1974, c. 227, § 1.)

§ 920. No implied repeal

Nothing in this division shall be construed to repeal by implication any other statute relating to privileges.
(Stats.1965, c. 299, § 2.)

CHAPTER 4. PARTICULAR PRIVILEGES

ARTICLE 1. PRIVILEGE OF DEFENDANT IN CRIMINAL CASE

Sec.
930. Privilege not to be called as a witness and not to testify.

§ 930. Privilege not to be called as a witness and not to testify

To the extent that such privilege exists under the Constitution of the United States or the State of California, a defendant in a criminal case has a privilege not to be called as a witness and not to testify.

(Stats.1965, c. 299, § 2.)

ARTICLE 2. PRIVILEGE AGAINST SELF–INCRIMINATION

Sec.
940. Privilege against self-incrimination.

§ 940. Privilege against self-incrimination

To the extent that such privilege exists under the Constitution of the United States or the State of California, a person has a privilege to refuse to disclose any matter that may tend to incriminate him.

(Stats.1965, c. 299, § 2.)

ARTICLE 3. LAWYER–CLIENT PRIVILEGE

Sec.
950. "Lawyer."
951. "Client."
952. "Confidential communication between client and lawyer."
953. "Holder of the privilege."
954. Lawyer-client privilege.
955. When lawyer required to claim privilege.
956. Exception: Crime or fraud.
957. Exception: Parties claiming through deceased client.
958. Exception: Breach of duty arising out of lawyer-client relationship.
959. Exception: Lawyer as attesting witness.
960. Exception: Intention of deceased client concerning writing affecting property interest.
961. Exception: Validity of writing affecting property interest.
962. Exception: Joint clients.

§ 950. "Lawyer"

As used in this article, "lawyer" means a person authorized, or reasonably believed by the client to be authorized, to practice law in any state or nation.

(Stats.1965, c. 299, § 2.)

854

§ 951. "Client"

As used in this article, "client" means a person who, directly or through an authorized representative, consults a lawyer for the purpose of retaining the lawyer or securing legal service or advice from him in his professional capacity, and includes an incompetent (a) who himself so consults the lawyer or (b) whose guardian or conservator so consults the lawyer in behalf of the incompetent.
(Stats.1965, c. 299, § 2.)

§ 952. "Confidential communication between client and lawyer"

As used in this article, "confidential communication between client and lawyer" means information transmitted between a client and his lawyer in the course of that relationship and in confidence by a means which, so far as the client is aware, discloses the information to no third persons other than those who are present to further the interest of the client in the consultation or those to whom disclosure is reasonably necessary for the transmission of the information or the accomplishment of the purpose for which the lawyer is consulted, and includes a legal opinion formed and the advice given by the lawyer in the course of that relationship.
(Stats.1965, c. 299, § 2. Amended by Stats.1967, c. 650, § 3.)

§ 953. "Holder of the privilege"

As used in this article, "holder of the privilege" means:

(a) The client when he has no guardian or conservator.

(b) A guardian or conservator of the client when the client has a guardian or conservator.

(c) The personal representative of the client if the client is dead.

(d) A successor, assign, trustee in dissolution, or any similar representative of a firm, association, organization, partnership, business trust, corporation, or public entity that is no longer in existence.
(Stats.1965, c. 299, § 2.)

§ 954. Lawyer-client privilege

Subject to Section 912 and except as otherwise provided in this article, the client, whether or not a party, has a privilege to refuse to disclose, and to prevent another from disclosing, a confidential communication between client and lawyer if the privilege is claimed by:

(a) The holder of the privilege;

(b) A person who is authorized to claim the privilege by the holder of the privilege; or

(c) The person who was the lawyer at the time of the confidential communication, but such person may not claim the privilege if there is no holder of the privilege in existence or if he is otherwise instructed by a person authorized to permit disclosure.

The relationship of attorney and client shall exist between a law corporation as defined in Article 10 (commencing with Section 6160) of Chapter 4 of Division 3 of the Business and Professions Code and the persons to whom it renders professional services, as well as between such persons and members of the State Bar employed by such corporation to render services to such persons. The word "persons" as used in this subdivision includes partnerships, corporations, associations and other groups and entities.
(Stats.1965, c. 299, § 2. Amended by Stats.1968, c. 1375, § 2.)

§ 955. When lawyer required to claim privilege

The lawyer who received or made a communication subject to the privilege under this article shall claim the privilege whenever he is present when the communication is sought to be disclosed and is authorized to claim the privilege under subdivision (c) of Section 954.
(Stats.1965, c. 299, § 2.)

§ 956. Exception: Crime or fraud

There is no privilege under this article if the services of the lawyer were sought or obtained to enable or aid anyone to commit or plan to commit a crime or a fraud. (Stats.1965, c. 299, § 2.)

§ 957. Exception: Parties claiming through deceased client

There is no privilege under this article as to a communication relevant to an issue between parties all of whom claim through a deceased client, regardless of whether the claims are by testate or intestate succession or by inter vivos transaction. (Stats.1965, c. 299, § 2.)

§ 958. Exception: Breach of duty arising out of lawyer-client relationship

There is no privilege under this article as to a communication relevant to an issue of breach, by the lawyer or by the client, of a duty arising out of the lawyer-client relationship. (Stats.1965, c. 299, § 2.)

§ 959. Exception: Lawyer as attesting witness

There is no privilege under this article as to a communication relevant to an issue concerning the intention or competence of a client executing an attested document of which the lawyer is an attesting witness, or concerning the execution or attestation of such a document. (Stats.1965, c. 299, § 2.)

§ 960. Exception: Intention of deceased client concerning writing affecting property interest

There is no privilege under this article as to a communication relevant to an issue concerning the intention of a client, now deceased, with respect to a deed of conveyance, will, or other writing, executed by the client, purporting to affect an interest in property. (Stats.1965, c. 299, § 2.)

§ 961. Exception: Validity of writing affecting property interest

There is no privilege under this article as to a communication relevant to an issue concerning the validity of a deed of conveyance, will, or other writing, executed by a client, now deceased, purporting to affect an interest in property. (Stats.1965, c. 299, § 2.)

§ 962. Exception: Joint clients

Where two or more clients have retained or consulted a lawyer upon a matter of common interest, none of them, nor the successor in interest of any of them, may claim a privilege under this article as to a communication made in the course of that relationship when such communication is offered in a civil proceeding between one of such clients (or his successor in interest) and another of such clients (or his successor in interest). (Stats.1965, c. 299, § 2.)

ARTICLE 4. PRIVILEGE NOT TO TESTIFY AGAINST SPOUSE

§ 970. Privilege not to testify against spouse

Except as otherwise provided by statute, a married person has a privilege not to testify against his spouse in any proceeding.
(Stats.1965, c. 299, § 2.)

§ 971. Privilege not to be called as a witness against spouse

Except as otherwise provided by statute, a married person whose spouse is a party to a proceeding has a privilege not to be called as a witness by an adverse party to that proceeding without the prior express consent of the spouse having the privilege under this section unless the party calling the spouse does so in good faith without knowledge of the marital relationship.
(Stats.1965, c. 299, § 2.)

§ 972. When privilege not applicable

A married person does not have a privilege under this article in:

(a) A proceeding brought by or on behalf of one spouse against the other spouse.

(b) A proceeding to commit or otherwise place his spouse or his spouse's property, or both, under the control of another because of the spouse's alleged mental or physical condition.

(c) A proceeding brought by or on behalf of a spouse to establish his competence.

(d) A proceeding under the Juvenile Court Law, Chapter 2 (commencing with Section 500) of Part 1 of Division 2 of the Welfare and Institutions Code.

(e) A criminal proceeding in which one spouse is charged with:

(1) A crime against the person or property of the other spouse or of a child of either, whether committed before or during marriage.

(2) A crime against the person or property of a third person committed in the course of committing a crime against the person or property of the other spouse, whether committed before or during marriage.

(3) Bigamy.

(4) A crime defined by Section 270 or 270a of the Penal Code.
(Stats.1965, c. 299, § 2. Amended by Stats.1975, c. 71, § 2.)

§ 973. Waiver of privilege

(a) Unless erroneously compelled to do so, a married person who testifies in a proceeding to which his spouse is a party, or who testifies against his spouse in any proceeding, does not have a privilege under this article in the proceeding in which such testimony is given.

(b) There is no privilege under this article in a civil proceeding brought or defended by a married person for the immediate benefit of his spouse or of himself and his spouse.
(Stats.1965, c. 299, § 2.)

ARTICLE 5. PRIVILEGE FOR CONFIDENTIAL MARITAL COMMUNICATIONS

§ 980. Privilege for confidential marital communications

Subject to Section 912 and except as otherwise provided in this article, a spouse (or his guardian or conservator when he has a guardian or conservator), whether or not a party,

has a privilege during the marital relationship and afterwards to refuse to disclose, and to prevent another from disclosing, a communication if he claims the privilege and the communication was made in confidence between him and the other spouse while they were husband and wife.
(Stats.1965, c. 299, § 2.)

§ 981. Exception: Crime or fraud

There is no privilege under this article if the communication was made, in whole or in part, to enable or aid anyone to commit or plan to commit a crime or a fraud.
(Stats.1965, c. 299, § 2.)

§ 982. Exception: Commitment or similar proceeding

There is no privilege under this article in a proceeding to commit either spouse or otherwise place him or his property, or both, under the control of another because of his alleged mental or physical condition.
(Stats.1965, c. 299, § 2.)

§ 983. Exception: Proceeding to establish competence

There is no privilege under this article in a proceeding brought by or on behalf of either spouse to establish his competence.
(Stats.1965, c. 299, § 2.)

§ 984. Exception: Proceeding between spouses

There is no privilege under this article in:

(a) A proceeding brought by or on behalf of one spouse against the other spouse.

(b) A proceeding between a surviving spouse and a person who claims through the deceased spouse, regardless of whether such claim is by testate or intestate succession or by inter vivos transaction.
(Stats.1965, c. 299, § 2.)

§ 985. Exception: Certain criminal proceedings

There is no privilege under this article in a criminal proceeding in which one spouse is charged with:

(a) A crime committed at any time against the person or property of the other spouse or of a child of either.

(b) A crime committed at any time against the person or property of a third person committed in the course of committing a crime against the person or property of the other spouse.

(c) Bigamy.

(d) A crime defined by Section 270 or 270a of the Penal Code.
(Stats.1965, c. 299, § 2. Amended by Stats.1975, c. 71, § 3.)

§ 986. Exception: Juvenile court proceedings

There is no privilege under this article in a proceeding under the Juvenile Court Law, Chapter 2 (commencing with Section 500) of Part 1 of Division 2 of the Welfare and Institutions Code.
(Stats.1965, c. 299, § 2.)

§ 987. Exception: Communication offered by spouse who is criminal defendant

There is no privilege under this article in a criminal proceeding in which the communication is offered in evidence by a defendant who is one of the spouses between whom the communication was made.
(Stats.1965, c. 299, § 2.)

ARTICLE 6. PHYSICIAN–PATIENT PRIVILEGE

§ 990. "Physician"

As used in this article, "physician" means a person authorized, or reasonably believed by the patient to be authorized, to practice medicine in any state or nation.
(Stats.1965, c. 299, § 2.)

§ 991. "Patient"

As used in this article, "patient" means a person who consults a physician or submits to an examination by a physician for the purpose of securing a diagnosis or preventive, palliative, or curative treatment of his physical or mental or emotional condition.
(Stats.1965, c. 299, § 2.)

§ 992. "Confidential communication between patient and physician"

As used in this article, "confidential communication between patient and physician" means information, including information obtained by an examination of the patient, transmitted between a patient and his physician in the course of that relationship and in confidence by a means which, so far as the patient is aware, discloses the information to no third persons other than those who are present to further the interest of the patient in the consultation or those to whom disclosure is reasonably necessary for the transmission of the information or the accomplishment of the purpose for which the physician is consulted, and includes a diagnosis made and the advice given by the physician in the course of that relationship.
(Stats.1965, c. 299, § 2. Amended by Stats.1967, c. 650, § 4.)

§ 993. "Holder of the privilege"

As used in this article, "holder of the privilege" means:

(a) The patient when he has no guardian or conservator.

(b) A guardian or conservator of the patient when the patient has a guardian or conservator.

(c) The personal representative of the patient if the patient is dead.
(Stats.1965, c. 299, § 2.)

§ 994. Physician-patient privilege

Subject to Section 912 and except as otherwise provided in this article, the patient, whether or not a party, has a privilege to refuse to disclose, and to prevent another from disclosing, a confidential communication between patient and physician if the privilege is claimed by:

(a) The holder of the privilege;

(b) A person who is authorized to claim the privilege by the holder of the privilege; or

(c) The person who was the physician at the time of the confidential communication, but such person may not claim the privilege if there is no holder of the privilege in existence or if he is otherwise instructed by a person authorized to permit disclosure.

The relationship of a physician and patient shall exist between a medical or podiatry corporation as defined in the Medical Practice Act and the patient to whom it renders professional services, as well as between such patients and licensed physicians and surgeons employed by such corporation to render services to such patients. The word "persons" as used in this subdivision includes partnerships, corporations, associations, and other groups and entities.
(Stats.1965, c. 299, § 2.   Amended by Stats.1968, c. 1375, § 3;   Stats.1980, c. 1313, § 12.)

§ 995. When physician required to claim privilege

The physician who received or made a communication subject to the privilege under this article shall claim the privilege whenever he is present when the communication is sought to be disclosed and is authorized to claim the privilege under subdivision (c) of Section 994.
(Stats.1965, c. 299, § 2.)

§ 996. Exception: Patient-litigant exception

There is no privilege under this article as to a communication relevant to an issue concerning the condition of the patient if such issue has been tendered by:

(a) The patient;

(b) Any party claiming through or under the patient;

(c) Any party claiming as a beneficiary of the patient through a contract to which the patient is or was a party; or

(d) The plaintiff in an action brought under Section 376 or 377 of the Code of Civil Procedure for damages for the injury or death of the patient.
(Stats.1965, c. 299, § 2.)

§ 997. Exception: Crime or tort

There is no privilege under this article if the services of the physician were sought or obtained to enable or aid anyone to commit or plan to commit a crime or a tort or to escape detection or apprehension after the commission of a crime or a tort.
(Stats.1965, c. 299, § 2.)

§ 998. Exception: Criminal proceeding

There is no privilege under this article in a criminal proceeding.
(Stats.1965, c. 299, § 2.)

§ 999. Exception: communication relating to patient condition in proceeding to recover damages; good cause

There is no privilege under this article as to a communication relevant to an issue concerning the condition of the patient in a proceeding to recover damages on account of the conduct of the patient if good cause for disclosure of the communication is shown.
(Stats.1965, c. 299, § 2.   Amended by Stats.1975, c. 318, § 1.)

§ 1000. Exception: Parties claiming through deceased patient

There is no privilege under this article as to a communication relevant to an issue between parties all of whom claim through a deceased patient, regardless of whether the claims are by testate or intestate succession or by inter vivos transaction.
(Stats.1965, c. 299, § 2.)

§ 1001. Exception: Breach of duty arising out of physician-patient relationship

There is no privilege under this article as to a communication relevant to an issue of breach, by the physician or by the patient, of a duty arising out of the physician-patient relationship.

(Stats.1965, c. 299, § 2.)

§ 1002. Exception: Intention of deceased patient concerning writing affecting property interest

There is no privilege under this article as to a communication relevant to an issue concerning the intention of a patient, now deceased, with respect to a deed of conveyance, will, or other writing, executed by the patient, purporting to affect an interest in property.

(Stats.1965, c. 299, § 2.)

§ 1003. Exception: Validity of writing affecting property interest

There is no privilege under this article as to a communication relevant to an issue concerning the validity of a deed of conveyance, will, or other writing, executed by a patient, now deceased, purporting to affect an interest in property.

(Stats.1965, c. 299, § 2.)

§ 1004. Exception: Commitment or similar proceeding

There is no privilege under this article in a proceeding to commit the patient or otherwise place him or his property, or both, under the control of another because of his alleged mental or physical condition.

(Stats.1965, c. 299, § 2.)

§ 1005. Exception: Proceeding to establish competence

There is no privilege under this article in a proceeding brought by or on behalf of the patient to establish his competence.

(Stats.1965, c. 299, § 2.)

§ 1006. Exception: Required report

There is no privilege under this article as to information that the physician or the patient is required to report to a public employee, or as to information required to be recorded in a public office, if such report or record is open to public inspection.

(Stats.1965, c. 299, § 2.)

§ 1007. Exception: Proceeding to terminate right, license or privilege

There is no privilege under this article in a proceeding brought by a public entity to determine whether a right, authority, license, or privilege (including the right or privilege to be employed by the public entity or to hold a public office) should be revoked, suspended, terminated, limited, or conditioned.

(Stats.1965, c. 299, § 2.)

ARTICLE 7. PSYCHOTHERAPIST–PATIENT PRIVILEGE

§ 1010. "Psychotherapist"

As used in this article, "psychotherapist" means:

(a) A person authorized, or reasonably believed by the patient to be authorized, to practice medicine in any state or nation who devotes, or is reasonably believed by the patient to devote, a substantial portion of his time to the practice of psychiatry;

(b) A person licensed as a psychologist under Chapter 6.6 (commencing with Section 2900) of Division 2 of the Business and Professions Code;

(c) A person licensed as a clinical social worker under Article 4 (commencing with Section 9040) of Chapter 17 of Division 3 of the Business and Professions Code, when he is engaged in applied psychotherapy of a nonmedical nature.

(d) A person who is serving as a school psychologist and holds a credential authorizing such service issued by the state.

(e) A person licensed as a marriage, family and child counselor under Chapter 4 (commencing with Section 17800) of Part 3, Division 5 of the Business and Professions Code.
(Stats.1965, c. 299, § 2. Amended by Stats.1967, c. 1677, § 3; Stats.1970, c. 1396, § 1.5; Stats.1970, c. 1397, § 1.5; Stats.1972, c. 888, § 1; Stats.1974, c. 546, § 16.)

§ 1011. "Patient"

As used in this article, "patient" means a person who consults a psychotherapist or submits to an examination by a psychotherapist for the purpose of securing a diagnosis or preventive, palliative, or curative treatment of his mental or emotional condition or who submits to an examination of his mental or emotional condition for the purpose of scientific research on mental or emotional problems.
(Stats.1965, c. 299, § 2.)

§ 1012. "Confidential communication between patient and psychotherapist"

As used in this article, "confidential communication between patient and psychotherapist" means information, including information obtained by an examination of the patient, transmitted between a patient and his psychotherapist in the course of that relationship and in confidence by a means which, so far as the patient is aware, discloses the information to no third persons other than those who are present to further the interest of the patient in the consultation, or those to whom disclosure is reasonably necessary for the transmission of the information or the accomplishment of the purpose for which the psychotherapist is consulted, and includes a diagnosis made and the advice given by the psychotherapist in the course of that relationship.
(Stats.1965, c. 299, § 2. Amended by Stats.1967, c. 650, § 5; Stats.1970, c. 1396, § 2; Stats.1970, c. 1397, § 2.)

§ 1013. "Holder of the privilege"

As used in this article, "holder of the privilege" means:

(a) The patient when he has no guardian or conservator.

(b) A guardian or conservator of the patient when the patient has a guardian or conservator.

(c) The personal representative of the patient if the patient is dead.
(Stats.1965, c. 299, § 2.)

§ 1014. Psychotherapist-patient privilege; application to individuals and entities

Subject to Section 912 and except as otherwise provided in this article, the patient, whether or not a party, has a privilege to refuse to disclose, and to prevent another from disclosing, a confidential communication between patient and psychotherapist if the privilege is claimed by:

(a) The holder of the privilege;

(b) A person who is authorized to claim the privilege by the holder of the privilege; or

(c) The person who was the psychotherapist at the time of the confidential communication, but such person may not claim the privilege if there is no holder of the privilege in existence or if he is otherwise instructed by a person authorized to permit disclosure.

The relationship of a psychotherapist and patient shall exist between a psychological corporation as defined in Article 9 (commencing with Section 2995) of Chapter 6.6 of Division 2 of the Business and Professions Code or a licensed clinical social workers corporation as defined in Article 5 (commencing with Section 9070) of Chapter 17 of Division 3 of the Business and Professions Code, and the patient to whom it renders professional services, as well as between such patients and psychotherapists employed by such corporations to render services to such patients. The word "persons" as used in this subdivision includes partnerships, corporations, associations and other groups and entities.
(Stats.1965, c. 299, § 2. Amended by Stats.1969, c. 1436, § 1; Stats.1972, c. 1286, § 6.)

§ 1014.5. Minor under mental health treatment or counseling

Notwithstanding any other provision of law, with respect to situations in which a minor has requested and been given mental health treatment or counseling pursuant to Section 25.9 of the Civil Code, the professional person rendering such mental health treatment or counseling has the psychotherapist-patient privilege.
(Added by Stats.1979, c. 832, § 2.)

§ 1015. When psychotherapist required to claim privilege

The psychotherapist who received or made a communication subject to the privilege under this article shall claim the privilege whenever he is present when the communication is sought to be disclosed and is authorized to claim the privilege under subdivision (c) of Section 1014.
(Stats.1965, c. 299, § 2.)

§ 1016. Exception: Patient-litigant exception

There is no privilege under this article as to a communication relevant to an issue concerning the mental or emotional condition of the patient if such issue has been tendered by:

(a) The patient;

(b) Any party claiming through or under the patient;

(c) Any party claiming as a beneficiary of the patient through a contract to which the patient is or was a party; or

(d) The plaintiff in an action brought under Section 376 or 377 of the Code of Civil Procedure for damages for the injury or death of the patient.
(Stats.1965, c. 299, § 2.)

§ 1017. Exception: Court-appointed psychotherapist

There is no privilege under this article if the psychotherapist is appointed by order of a court to examine the patient, but this exception does not apply where the psychotherapist is appointed by order of the court upon the request of the lawyer for the defendant in a

criminal proceeding in order to provide the lawyer with information needed so that he may advise the defendant whether to enter or withdraw a plea based on insanity or to present a defense based on his mental or emotional condition.
(Stats.1965, c. 299, § 2. Amended by Stats.1967, c. 650, § 6.)

§ 1018. Exception: Crime or tort

There is no privilege under this article if the services of the psychotherapist were sought or obtained to enable or aid anyone to commit or plan to commit a crime or a tort or to escape detection or apprehension after the commission of a crime or a tort.
(Stats.1965, c. 299, § 2.)

§ 1019. Exception: Parties claiming through deceased patient

There is no privilege under this article as to a communication relevant to an issue between parties all of whom claim through a deceased patient, regardless of whether the claims are by testate or intestate succession or by inter vivos transaction.
(Stats.1965, c. 299, § 2.)

§ 1020. Exception: Breach of duty arising out of psychotherapist-patient relationship

There is no privilege under this article as to a communication relevant to an issue of breach, by the psychotherapist or by the patient, of a duty arising out of the psychotherapist-patient relationship.
(Stats.1965, c. 299, § 2.)

§ 1021. Exception: Intention of deceased patient concerning writing affecting property interest

There is no privilege under this article as to a communication relevant to an issue concerning the intention of a patient, now deceased, with respect to a deed of conveyance, will, or other writing, executed by the patient, purporting to affect an interest in property.
(Stats.1965, c. 299, § 2.)

§ 1022. Exception: Validity of writing affecting property interest

There is no privilege under this article as to a communication relevant to an issue concerning the validity of a deed of conveyance, will, or other writing, executed by a patient, now deceased, purporting to affect an interest in property.
(Stats.1965, c. 299, § 2.)

§ 1023. Exception: Proceeding to determine sanity of criminal defendant

There is no privilege under this article in a proceeding under Chapter 6 (commencing with Section 1367) of Title 10 of Part 2 of the Penal Code initiated at the request of the defendant in a criminal action to determine his sanity.
(Stats.1965, c. 299, § 2.)

§ 1024. Exception: Patient dangerous to himself or others

There is no privilege under this article if the psychotherapist has reasonable cause to believe that the patient is in such mental or emotional condition as to be dangerous to himself or to the person or property of another and that disclosure of the communication is necessary to prevent the threatened danger.
(Stats.1965, c. 299, § 2.)

§ 1025. Exception: Proceeding to establish competence

There is no privilege under this article in a proceeding brought by or on behalf of the patient to establish his competence.
(Stats.1965, c. 299, § 2.)

§ 1026. Exception: Required report

There is no privilege under this article as to information that the psychotherapist or the patient is required to report to a public employee or as to information required to be recorded in a public office, if such report or record is open to public inspection. (Stats.1965, c. 299, § 2.)

§ 1027. Exception: Child under 16 victim of crime

There is no privilege under this article if all of the following circumstances exist:

(a) The patient is a child under the age of 16.

(b) The psychotherapist has reasonable cause to believe that the patient has been the victim of a crime and that disclosure of the communication is in the best interest of the child.

(Added by Stats.1970, c. 1396, § 3; Stats.1970, c. 1397, § 3.)

§ 1028. Exception: Unqualified psychotherapist

Unless the psychotherapist is a person described in subdivision (a) or (b) of Section 1010, there is no privilege under this article in a criminal proceeding. (Added by Stats.1970, c. 1396, § 4; Stats.1970, c. 1397, § 4.)

ARTICLE 8. CLERGYMAN–PENITENT PRIVILEGES

§ 1030. "Clergyman"

As used in this article, "clergyman" means a priest, minister, religious practitioner, or similar functionary of a church or of a religious denomination or religious organization. (Stats.1965, c. 299, § 2.)

§ 1031. "Penitent"

As used in this article, "penitent" means a person who has made a penitential communication to a clergyman. (Stats.1965, c. 299, § 2.)

§ 1032. "Penitential communication"

As used in this article, "penitential communication" means a communication made in confidence, in the presence of no third person so far as the penitent is aware, to a clergyman who, in the course of the discipline or practice of his church, denomination, or organization, is authorized or accustomed to hear such communications and, under the discipline or tenets of his church, denomination, or organization, has a duty to keep such communications secret. (Stats.1965, c. 299, § 2.)

§ 1033. Privilege of penitent

Subject to Section 912, a penitent, whether or not a party, has a privilege to refuse to disclose, and to prevent another from disclosing, a penitential communication if he claims the privilege. (Stats.1965, c. 299, § 2.)

§ 1034. Privilege of clergyman

Subject to Section 912, a clergyman, whether or not a party, has a privilege to refuse to disclose a penitential communication if he claims the privilege. (Stats.1965, c. 299, § 2.)

ARTICLE 8.5. SEXUAL ASSAULT VICTIM–COUNSELOR PRIVILEGE

Article 8.5 was added by Stats.1980, c. 917, § 2.

§ 1035. Victim

As used in this article, "victim" means a person who consults a sexual assault victim counselor for the purpose of securing advice or assistance concerning a mental, physical, or emotional condition caused by a sexual assault.

(Added by Stats.1980, c. 917, § 2.)

§ 1035.2. Sexual assault victim counselor

As used in this article, "sexual assault victim counselor" means a person who is engaged in any office, hospital, institution, or center commonly known as a rape crisis center, whose primary purpose is the rendering of advice or assistance to victims of sexual assault and who is registered as a sexual assault victim counselor with the Division of Allied Health Professions of the Board of Medical Quality Assurance. To register, a sexual assault counselor shall meet one of the following requirements:

(a) Be a psychotherapist as defined in Section 1010; or have a master's degree in counseling or a related field; or have two years of supervised counseling experience, at least one of which is in rape crisis counseling; or

(b) Have 40 hours of training as described below and be supervised by an individual who qualifies as a counselor under subdivision (a). The training, to be supervised by a person qualified under subdivision (a), shall include, but not be limited to, the following areas: law, medicine, societal attitudes, crisis intervention and counseling techniques, role playing, referral services, and sexuality.

(Added by Stats.1980, c. 917, § 2.)

§ 1035.4. Confidential communication between the sexual assault counselor and the victim

As used in this article, "confidential communication between the sexual assault counselor and the victim" means information transmitted between the victim and the sexual assault counselor in the course of their relationship and in confidence by a means which, so far as the victim is aware, discloses the information to no third persons other than those who are present to further the interests of the victim in the consultation or those to whom disclosures are reasonably necessary for the transmission of the information or an accomplishment of the purposes for which the sexual assault counselor is consulted. The term includes all information regarding the victim's prior or subsequent sexual conduct, and opinions regarding the victim's sexual conduct or reputation in sexual matters. The term does not include advice given by the sexual assault counselor on potential testimony in court.

Information received by the sexual assault counselor which constitutes relevant evidence of the facts and circumstances involving an alleged sexual assault about which the victim is complaining and which is the subject of a criminal proceeding is not a confidential communication.

In the event of a dispute regarding what is or is not a confidential communication, the following procedure shall be followed:

(1) A written motion shall be made by the defendant to the court and prosecutor stating that the defense has an offer of proof of the relevancy of evidence containing prior

inconsistent statements for the purposes of impeachment or evidence that any element of the offense charged is not present.

(2) The written motion shall be accompanied by an affidavit in which the offer of proof shall be stated.

(3) If the court finds that the offer of proof is sufficient, the court shall order a hearing out of the presence of the jury, if any, and at such hearing allow the questioning of the sexual assault counselor regarding the offer of proof made by the defendant.

(4) At the conclusion of the hearing, if the court finds that evidence proposed to be offered by the defendant regarding the sexual conduct of the complaining witness is relevant pursuant to Section 780, and is admissible pursuant to Section 352, the court may make an order stating what evidence may be introduced by the defendant, and the nature of the questions to be permitted. The defendant may then offer evidence pursuant to the order of the court.

(Added by Stats.1980, c. 917, § 2.)

§ 1035.6. Holder of the privilege

As used in this article, "holder of the privilege" means:

(a) The victim when such person has no guardian or conservator.

(b) A guardian or conservator of the victim when the victim has a guardian or conservator.

(c) The personal representative of the victim if the victim is dead.

(Added by Stats.1980, c. 917, § 2.)

§ 1035.8. Refusal and prevention of disclosure by victim

A victim of a sexual assault, whether or not a party, has a privilege to refuse to disclose, and to prevent another from disclosing, a confidential communication between the victim and a sexual assault victim counselor if the privilege is claimed by:

(a) The holder of the privilege;

(b) A person who is authorized to claim the privilege by the holder of the privilege; or

(c) The person who was the sexual assault victim counselor at the time of the confidential communication, but such person may not claim the privilege if there is no holder of the privilege in existence or if he is otherwise instructed by a person authorized to permit disclosure.

(Added by Stats.1980, c. 917, § 2.)

§ 1036. Claim of privilege by sexual assault victim counselor

The sexual assault victim counselor who received or made a communication subject to the privilege under this article shall claim the privilege whenever he is present when the communication is sought to be disclosed and is authorized to claim the privilege under subdivision (c) of Section 1035.8.

(Added by Stats.1980, c. 917, § 2.)

§ 1036.2. Sexual assault

As used in this article, "sexual assault" includes:

(a) Rape, as defined in Section 261 of the Penal Code;

(b) Unlawful sexual intercourse, as defined in Section 261.5 of the Penal Code;

(c) Rape in concert with force and violence, as defined in Section 264.1 of the Penal Code;

(d) Sodomy, as defined in Section 286 of the Penal Code, except a violation of subdivision (e) of that section;

(e) A violation of Section 288 of the Penal Code;

(f) Oral copulation, as defined in Section 288a of the Penal Code, except a violation of subdivision (e) of that section;

(g) Annoying or molesting a child under 18, as defined in Section 647a of the Penal Code; or

(h) Any attempt to commit any of the above acts.

(Added by Stats.1980, c. 917, § 2.)

ARTICLE 9. OFFICIAL INFORMATION AND IDENTITY OF INFORMER

§ 1040. Privilege for official information

(a) As used in this section, "official information" means information acquired in confidence by a public employee in the course of his duty and not open, or officially disclosed, to the public prior to the time the claim of privilege is made.

(b) A public entity has a privilege to refuse to disclose official information, and to prevent another from disclosing such information, if the privilege is claimed by a person authorized by the public entity to do so and:

(1) Disclosure is forbidden by an act of the Congress of the United States or a statute of this state; or

(2) Disclosure of the information is against the public interest because there is a necessity for preserving the confidentiality of the information that outweighs the necessity for disclosure in the interest of justice; but no privilege may be claimed under this paragraph if any person authorized to do so has consented that the information be disclosed in the proceeding. In determining whether disclosure of the information is against the public interest, the interest of the public entity as a party in the outcome of the proceeding may not be considered.

(Stats.1965, c. 299, § 2.)

§ 1041. Privilege for identity of informer

(a) Except as provided in this section, a public entity has a privilege to refuse to disclose the identity of a person who has furnished information as provided in subdivision (b) purporting to disclose a violation of a law of the United States or of this state or of a public entity in this state, and to prevent another from disclosing such identity, if the privilege is claimed by a person authorized by the public entity to do so and:

(1) Disclosure is forbidden by an act of the Congress of the United States or a statute of this state; or

(2) Disclosure of the identity of the informer is against the public interest because there is a necessity for preserving the confidentiality of his identity that outweighs the necessity for disclosure in the interest of justice; but no privilege may be claimed under this paragraph if any person authorized to do so has consented that the identity of the informer be disclosed in the proceeding. In determining whether disclosure of the identity of the informer is against the public interest, the interest of the public entity as a party in the outcome of the proceeding may not be considered.

(b) This section applies only if the information is furnished in confidence by the informer to:

(1) A law enforcement officer;

(2) A representative of an administrative agency charged with the administration or enforcement of the law alleged to be violated; or

(3) Any person for the purpose of transmittal to a person listed in paragraph (1) or (2).

(c) There is no privilege under this section to prevent the informer from disclosing his identity.
(Stats.1965, c. 299, § 2.)

§ 1042. Adverse order or finding in certain cases

(a) Except where disclosure is forbidden by an act of the Congress of the United States, if a claim of privilege under this article by the state or a public entity in this state is sustained in a criminal proceeding, the presiding officer shall make such order or finding of fact adverse to the public entity bringing the proceeding as is required by law upon any issue in the proceeding to which the privileged information is material.

(b) Notwithstanding subdivision (a), where a search is made pursuant to a warrant valid on its face, the public entity bringing a criminal proceeding is not required to reveal to the defendant official information or the identity of an informer in order to establish the legality of the search or the admissibility of any evidence obtained as a result of it.

(c) Notwithstanding subdivision (a), in any preliminary hearing, criminal trial, or other criminal proceeding, any otherwise admissible evidence of information communicated to a peace officer by a confidential informant, who is not a material witness to the guilt or innocence of the accused of the offense charged, is admissible on the issue of reasonable cause to make an arrest or search without requiring that the name or identity of the informant be disclosed if the judge or magistrate is satisfied, based upon evidence produced in open court, out of the presence of the jury, that such information was received from a reliable informant and in his discretion does not require such disclosure.

(d) When, in any such criminal proceeding, a party demands disclosure of the identity of the informant on the ground the informant is a material witness on the issue of guilt, the court shall conduct a hearing at which all parties may present evidence on the issue of disclosure. Such hearing shall be conducted outside the presence of the jury, if any. During the hearing, if the privilege provided for in Section 1041 is claimed by a person authorized to do so or if a person who is authorized to claim such privilege refuses to answer any question on the ground that the answer would tend to disclose the identity of the informant, the prosecuting attorney may request that the court hold an in camera hearing. If such a request is made, the court shall hold such a hearing outside the presence of the defendant and his counsel. At the in camera hearing, the prosecution may offer evidence which would tend to disclose or which discloses the identity of the informant to aid the court in its determination whether there is a reasonable possibility that nondisclosure might deprive the defendant of a fair trial. A reporter shall be present at the in camera hearing. Any transcription of the proceedings at the in camera hearing, as well as any physical evidence presented at the hearing, shall be ordered sealed by the court, and only a court may have access to its contents. The court shall not order disclosure, nor strike the testimony of the witness who invokes the privilege, nor dismiss the criminal proceeding, if the party offering the witness refuses to disclose the identity of the informant, unless, based upon the evidence presented at the hearing held in the presence of the defendant and his counsel and the evidence presented at the in camera hearing, the court concludes that there is a reasonable possibility that nondisclosure might deprive the defendant of a fair trial.
(Stats.1965, c. 299, § 2. Amended by Stats.1965, c. 937, § 2; Stats.1969, c. 1412, § 1.)

§ 1043. Peace officer personnel records; discovery or disclosure; procedure

(a) In any case in which discovery or disclosure is sought of peace officer personnel records or records maintained pursuant to Section 832.5 of the Penal Code or information from such records, the party seeking such discovery or disclosure shall file a written motion with the appropriate court or administrative body upon 10 days' written notice to the governmental agency which has custody and control of such records. Upon receipt of such notice the governmental agency served shall immediately notify the individual whose records are sought.

(b) Such motion shall include:

(1) Identification of the proceeding in which discovery or disclosure is sought, the party seeking discovery or disclosure, the peace officer whose records are sought, the governmental agency which has custody and control of such records, and the time and place at which the motion for discovery or disclosure shall be heard;

(2) A description of the type of records or information sought; and

(3) Affidavits showing good cause for the discovery or disclosure sought, setting forth the materiality thereof to the subject matter involved in the pending litigation and stating upon reasonable belief that such governmental agency identified has such records or information from such records.

(c) No hearing upon a motion for discovery or disclosure shall be held without full compliance with the notice provisions of this section except upon a showing by the moving party of good cause for noncompliance, or upon a waiver of such hearing by the governmental agency identified as having such records.

(Added by Stats.1978, c. 630, § 1.)

§ 1044. Medical or psychological history records; right of access

Nothing in this article shall be construed to affect the right of access to records of medical or psychological history where such access would otherwise be available under Section 996 or 1016.

(Added by Stats.1978, c. 630, § 2.)

§ 1045. Peace officers; access to records of complaints or discipline imposed; relevancy; protective orders

(a) Nothing in this article shall be construed to affect the right of access to records of complaints, or investigations of complaints, or discipline imposed as a result of such investigations, concerning an event or transaction in which the peace officer participated, or which he perceived, and pertaining to the manner in which he performed his duties, provided that such information is relevant to the subject matter involved in the pending litigation.

(b) In determining relevance the court shall examine the information in chambers in conformity with Section 915, and shall exclude from disclosure:

(1) Information consisting of complaints concerning conduct occurring more than five years before the event or transaction which is the subject of the litigation in aid of which discovery or disclosure is sought.

(2) In any criminal proceeding the conclusions of any officer investigating a complaint filed pursuant to Section 832.5 of the Penal Code.

(3) Facts sought to be disclosed which are so remote as to make disclosure of little or no practical benefit.

(c) In determining relevance where the issue in litigation concerns the policies or pattern of conduct of the employing agency, the court shall consider whether the information sought may be obtained from other records maintained by the employing agency in the regular course of agency business which would not necessitate the disclosure of individual personnel records.

(d) Upon motion seasonably made by the governmental agency which has custody or control of the records to be examined or by the officer whose records are sought, and upon good cause showing the necessity thereof, the court may make any order which justice requires to protect the officer or agency from unnecessary annoyance, embarrassment or oppression.

(Added by Stats.1978, c. 630, § 3.)

ARTICLE 10. POLITICAL VOTE

Sec.
1050. Privilege to protest secrecy of vote.

§ 1050. Privilege to protect secrecy of vote

If he claims the privilege, a person has a privilege to refuse to disclose the tenor of his vote at a public election where the voting is by secret ballot unless he voted illegally or he previously made an unprivileged disclosure of the tenor of his vote.
(Stats.1965, c. 299, § 2.)

ARTICLE 11. TRADE SECRET

Sec.
1060. Privilege to protect trade secret.

§ 1060. Privilege to protect trade secret

If he or his agent or employee claims the privilege, the owner of a trade secret has a privilege to refuse to disclose the secret, and to prevent another from disclosing it, if the allowance of the privilege will not tend to conceal fraud or otherwise work injustice.
(Stats.1965, c. 299, § 2.)

CHAPTER 5. IMMUNITY OF NEWSMAN FROM CITATION FOR CONTEMPT

Sec.
1070. Newsmen's refusal to disclose news source.

§ 1070. Newsmen's refusal to disclose news source

(a) A publisher, editor, reporter, or other person connected with or employed upon a newspaper, magazine, or other periodical publication, or by a press association or wire service, or any person who has been so connected or employed, cannot be adjudged in contempt by a judicial, legislative, administrative body, or any other body having the power to issue subpoenas, for refusing to disclose, in any proceeding as defined in Section 901, the source of any information procured while so connected or employed for publication in a newspaper, magazine or other periodical publication, or for refusing to disclose any unpublished information obtained or prepared in gathering, receiving or processing of information for communication to the public.

(b) Nor can a radio or television news reporter or other person connected with or employed by a radio or television station, or any person who has been so connected or employed, be so adjudged in contempt for refusing to disclose the source of any information procured while so connected or employed for news or news commentary purposes on radio or television, or for refusing to disclose any unpublished information obtained or prepared in gathering, receiving or processing of information for communication to the public.

(c) As used in this section, "unpublished information" includes information not disseminated to the public by the person from whom disclosure is sought, whether or not related information has been disseminated and includes, but is not limited to, all notes, outtakes, photographs, tapes or other data of whatever sort not itself disseminated to the public through a medium of communication, whether or not published information based upon or related to such material has been disseminated.
(Stats.1965, c. 299, § 2. Amended by Stats.1971, c. 1717, § 1; Stats.1972, c. 1431, § 1; Stats.1974, c. 1323, § 1; Stats.1974, c. 1456, § 2.)

Division 9
EVIDENCE AFFECTED OR EXCLUDED BY EXTRINSIC POLICIES

CHAPTER 1. EVIDENCE OF CHARACTER, HABIT, OR CUSTOM

§ 1100. Manner of proof of character

Except as otherwise provided by statute, any otherwise admissible evidence (including evidence in the form of an opinion, evidence of reputation, and evidence of specific instances of such person's conduct) is admissible to prove a person's character or a trait of his character.
(Stats.1965, c. 299, § 2.)

§ 1101. Evidence of character to prove conduct

(a) Except as provided in this section and in Sections 1102 and 1103, evidence of a person's character or a trait of his character (whether in the form of an opinion, evidence of reputation, or evidence of specific instances of his conduct) is inadmissible when offered to prove his conduct on a specified occasion.

(b) Nothing in this section prohibits the admission of evidence that a person committed a crime, civil wrong, or other act when relevant to prove some fact (such as motive, opportunity, intent, preparation, plan, knowledge, identity, or absence of mistake or accident) other than his disposition to commit such acts.

(c) Nothing in this section affects the admissibility of evidence offered to support or attack the credibility of a witness.
(Stats.1965, c. 299, § 2.)

§ 1102. Opinion and reputation evidence of character of criminal defendant to prove conduct

In a criminal action, evidence of the defendant's character or a trait of his character in the form of an opinion or evidence of his reputation is not made inadmissible by Section 1101 if such evidence is:

(a) Offered by the defendant to prove his conduct in conformity with such character or trait of character.

(b) Offered by the prosecution to rebut evidence adduced by the defendant under subdivision (a).
(Stats.1965, c. 299, § 2.)

§ 1103. Evidence of character of victim of crime to prove conduct; evidence of complaining witness' sexual conduct in rape prosecution

(1) In a criminal action, evidence of the character or a trait of character (in the form of an opinion, evidence of reputation, or evidence of specific instances of conduct) of the

victim of the crime for which the defendant is being prosecuted is not made inadmissible by Section 1101 if such evidence is:

(a) Offered by the defendant to prove conduct of the victim in conformity with such character or trait of character.

(b) Offered by the prosecution to rebut evidence adduced by the defendant under subdivision (a).

(2) (a) Notwithstanding any other provision of this code to the contrary, and except as provided in this subdivision, in any prosecution under Section 261, or 264.1 of the Penal Code, or for assault with intent to commit, attempt to commit, or conspiracy to commit a crime defined in any such section, opinion evidence, reputation evidence, and evidence of specific instances of the complaining witness' sexual conduct, or any of such evidence, is not admissible by the defendant in order to prove consent by the complaining witness.

(b) Paragraph (a) of this subdivision shall not be applicable to evidence of the complaining witness' sexual conduct with the defendant.

(c) If the prosecutor introduces evidence, including testimony of a witness, or the complaining witness as a witness gives testimony, and such evidence or testimony relates to the complaining witness' sexual conduct, the defendant may cross-examine the witness who gives such testimony and offer relevant evidence limited specifically to the rebuttal of such evidence introduced by the prosecutor or given by the complaining witness.

(d) Nothing in this subdivision shall be construed to make inadmissible any evidence offered to attack the credibility of the complaining witness as provided in Section 782.

(e) As used in this section, "complaining witness" means the alleged victim of the crime charged, the prosecution of which is subject to this subdivision.
(Stats.1965, c. 299, § 2. Amended by Stats.1974, c. 569, § 2.)

§ 1104. Character trait for care or skill

Except as provided in Sections 1102 and 1103, evidence of a trait of a person's character with respect to care or skill is inadmissible to prove the quality of his conduct on a specified occasion.
(Stats.1965, c. 299, § 2.)

§ 1105. Habit or custom to prove specific behavior

Any otherwise admissible evidence of habit or custom is admissible to prove conduct on a specified occasion in conformity with the habit or custom.
(Stats.1965, c. 299, § 2.)

CHAPTER 2. OTHER EVIDENCE AFFECTED OR EXCLUDED BY EXTRINSIC POLICIES

§ 1150. Evidence to test a verdict

(a) Upon an inquiry as to the validity of a verdict, any otherwise admissible evidence may be received as to statements made, or conduct, conditions, or events occurring, either within or without the jury room, of such a character as is likely to have influenced the verdict improperly.   No evidence is admissible to show the effect of such statement, conduct, condition, or event upon a juror either in influencing him to assent to or dissent from the verdict or concerning the mental processes by which it was determined.

(b) Nothing in this code affects the law relating to the competence of a juror to give evidence to impeach or support a verdict.
(Stats.1965, c. 299, § 2.)

§ 1151. Subsequent remedial conduct

When, after the occurrence of an event, remedial or precautionary measures are taken, which, if taken previously, would have tended to make the event less likely to occur, evidence of such subsequent measures is inadmissible to prove negligence or culpable conduct in connection with the event.
(Stats.1965, c. 299, § 2.)

§ 1152. Offer to compromise and the like

(a) Evidence that a person has, in compromise or from humanitarian motives, furnished or offered or promised to furnish money or any other thing, act, or service to another who has sustained or will sustain or claims that he has sustained or will sustain loss or damage, as well as any conduct or statements made in negotiation thereof, is inadmissible to prove his liability for the loss or damage or any part of it.

(b) This section does not affect the admissibility of evidence of:

(1) Partial satisfaction of an asserted claim or demand without questioning its validity when such evidence is offered to prove the validity of the claim; or

(2) A debtor's payment or promise to pay all or a part of his preexisting debt when such evidence is offered to prove the creation of a new duty on his part or a revival of his preexisting duty.
(Stats.1965, c. 299, § 2.   Amended by Stats.1967, c. 650, § 7.)

§ 1153. Offer to plead guilty or withdraw plea of guilty by criminal defendant

Evidence of a plea of guilty, later withdrawn, or of an offer to plead guilty to the crime charged or to any other crime, made by the defendant in a criminal action is inadmissible in any action or in any proceeding of any nature, including proceedings before agencies, commissions, boards, and tribunals.
(Stats.1965, c. 299, § 2.)

§ 1154. Offer to discount a claim

Evidence that a person has accepted or offered or promised to accept a sum of money or any other thing, act, or service in satisfaction of a claim, as well as any conduct or statements made in negotiation thereof, is inadmissible to prove the invalidity of the claim or any part of it.
(Stats.1965, c. 299, § 2.)

§ 1155. Liability insurance

Evidence that a person was, at the time a harm was suffered by another, insured wholly or partially against loss arising from liability for that harm is inadmissible to prove negligence or other wrongdoing.
(Stats.1965, c. 299, § 2.)

§ 1156. Records of medical study of in-hospital staff committee

(a) In-hospital medical or medical-dental staff committees of a licensed hospital may engage in research and medical or dental study for the purpose of reducing morbidity or mortality, and may make findings and recommendations relating to such purpose.   Except as provided in subdivision (b), the written records of interviews, reports, statements, or memoranda of such in-hospital medical or medical-dental staff committees relating to such medical or dental studies are subject to Sections 2016 to 2036, inclusive, of the Code of Civil Procedure (relating to discovery proceedings) but, subject to subdivisions (c) and (d), shall not be admitted as evidence in any action or before any administrative body, agency, or person.

(b) The disclosure, with or without the consent of the patient, of information concerning him to such in-hospital medical or medical-dental staff committee does not make unprivileged any information that would otherwise be privileged under Section 994 or 1014; but, notwithstanding Sections 994 and 1014, such information is subject to discovery under subdivision (a) except that the identity of any patient may not be discovered under subdivision (a) unless the patient consents to such disclosure.

(c) This section does not affect the admissibility in evidence of the original medical or dental records of any patient.

(d) This section does not exclude evidence which is relevant evidence in a criminal action. (Stats.1965, c. 299, § 2. Amended by Stats.1975, c. 674, p. 1468, § 1.)

§ 1157. Proceedings and records of hospital medical or medical-dental staff review committees; local medical, dental, dental hygienist or chiropractic society review committees

Neither the proceedings nor the records of organized committees of medical or medical-dental staffs in hospitals having the responsibility of evaluation and improvement of the quality of care rendered in the hospital or medical or dental review or dental hygienist review or chiropractive review committees of local medical, dental, dental hygienist, or chiropractic societies shall be subject to discovery. Except as hereinafter provided, no person in attendance at a meeting of any such committee shall be required to testify as to what transpired thereat. The prohibition relating to discovery or testimony shall not apply to the statements made by any person in attendance at such a meeting who is a party to an action or proceeding the subject matter of which was reviewed at such meeting, or to any person requesting hospital staff privileges, or in any action against an insurance carrier alleging bad faith by the carrier in refusing to accept a settlement offer within the policy limits.

The prohibitions contained in this section shall not apply to medical, dental, dental hygienist, or chiropractic society committees that exceed 10 percent of the membership of the society, nor to any such committee if any person serves upon the committee when his own conduct or practice is being reviewed. (Added by Stats.1968, c. 1122, § 1. Amended by Stats.1975, c. 674, § 2; Stats.1978, c. 7, § 1; Stats.1978, c. 503, § 2.)

§ 1157.5. Organized committee of nonprofit medical care foundation or professional standards review organization; proceedings and records

Except in actions involving a claim of a provider of health care services for payment for such services, the prohibition relating to discovery or testimony provided by Section 1157 shall be applicable to the proceedings or records of an organized committee of any nonprofit medical care foundation or professional standards review organization which is organized in a manner which makes available professional competence to review health care services with respect to medical necessity, quality of care, or economic justification of charges or level of care. (Added by Stats.1973, c. 848, § 1. Amended by Stats.1980, c. 524, § 1.)

§ 1158. Presentation of authorization for inspection and copying of patient's records; failure to comply; costs

Whenever, prior to the filing of any action or the appearance of a defendant in an action, an attorney at law presents a written authorization therefor signed by an adult patient, by the guardian or conservator of his person or estate, or, in the case of a minor, by a parent or guardian of such minor, or by the personal representative or an heir of a deceased patient, or a copy thereof, a physician and surgeon, dentist, registered nurse, dispensing optician, registered physical therapist, podiatrist, licensed psychologist, osteopath, chiropractor, clinical laboratory bioanalyst, clinical laboratory technologist, or pharmacist or pharmacy, duly licensed as such under the laws of the state, or a licensed hospital, shall make all of the patient's records under his or its custody or control available for inspection and copying by such attorney at law or his representative, promptly upon the presentation of the written authorization.

Failure to make such records available, during business hours, within five days after the presentation of the written authorization, may subject the person or entity having custody or control of the records to liability for all reasonable expenses, including attorney's fees, incurred in any proceeding to enforce the provisions of this section.

All reasonable costs incurred by any person or entity enumerated above in making patient records available pursuant to this section may be charged against the person whose written authorization required the availability of such records. "Reasonable cost" as used in this paragraph means actual copying costs, not to exceed ten cents ($0.10) per page, plus any additional reasonable clerical costs incurred in locating and making the records available. Such additional clerical costs shall be based on a computation of the time spent locating and making the records available multiplied by the employee's hourly wage. (Added by Stats.1968, c. 1122, § 2. Amended by Stats.1970, c. 556, § 1; Stats.1974, c. 250, § 1; Stats.1974, c. 667, § 1; Stats.1975, c. 563, § 1; Stats.1978, c. 493, § 1; Stats.1980, c. 697, § 1.)

Division 10
HEARSAY EVIDENCE

CHAPTER 1. GENERAL PROVISIONS

Sec.
1200. The hearsay rule.
1201. Multiple hearsay.
1202. Credibility of hearsay declarant.
1203. Cross-examination of hearsay declarant.
1204. Hearsay statement offered against criminal defendant.
1205. No implied repeal.

§ 1200. The hearsay rule

(a) "Hearsay evidence" is evidence of a statement that was made other than by a witness while testifying at the hearing and that is offered to prove the truth of the matter stated.

(b) Except as provided by law, hearsay evidence is inadmissible.

(c) This section shall be known and may be cited as the hearsay rule.
(Stats.1965, c. 229, § 1200.)

§ 1201. Multiple hearsay

A statement within the scope of an exception to the hearsay rule is not inadmissible on the ground that the evidence of such statement is hearsay evidence if such hearsay evidence consists of one or more statements each of which meets the requirements of an exception to the hearsay rule.
(Stats.1965, c. 299, § 2. Amended by Stats.1967, c. 650, § 8.)

§ 1202. Credibility of hearsay declarant

Evidence of a statement or other conduct by a declarant that is inconsistent with a statement by such declarant received in evidence as hearsay evidence is not inadmissible for the purpose of attacking the credibility of the declarant though he is not given and has not had an opportunity to explain or to deny such inconsistent statement or other conduct. Any other evidence offered to attack or support the credibility of the declarant is admissible if it would have been admissible had the declarant been a witness at the hearing. For the purposes of this section, the deponent of a deposition taken in the action in which it is offered shall be deemed to be a hearsay declarant.
(Stats.1965, c. 299, § 2.)

§ 1203. Cross-examination of hearsay declarant

(a) The declarant of a statement that is admitted as hearsay evidence may be called and examined by any adverse party as if under cross-examination concerning the statement.

(b) This section is not applicable if the declarant is (1) a party, (2) a person identified with a party within the meaning of subdivision (d) of Section 776, or (3) a witness who has testified in the action concerning the subject matter of the statement.

(c) This section is not applicable if the statement is one described in Article 1 (commencing with Section 1220), Article 3 (commencing with Section 1235), or Article 10 (commencing with Section 1300) of Chapter 2 of this division.

(d) A statement that is otherwise admissible as hearsay evidence is not made inadmissible by this section because the declarant who made the statement is unavailable for examination pursuant to this section.
(Stats.1965, c. 299, § 2.)

§ 1204. Hearsay statement offered against criminal defendant

A statement that is otherwise admissible as hearsay evidence is inadmissible against the defendant in a criminal action if the statement was made, either by the defendant or by another, under such circumstances that it is inadmissible against the defendant under the Constitution of the United States or the State of California.
(Stats.1965, c. 299, § 2.)

§ 1205. No implied repeal

Nothing in this division shall be construed to repeal by implication any other statute relating to hearsay evidence.
(Stats.1965, c. 299, § 2.)

CHAPTER 2. EXCEPTIONS TO THE HEARSAY RULE

ARTICLE 1. CONFESSIONS AND ADMISSIONS

§ 1220. Admission of party

Evidence of a statement is not made inadmissible by the hearsay rule when offered against the declarant in an action to which he is a party in either his individual or representative capacity, regardless of whether the statement was made in his individual or representative capacity.
(Stats.1965, c. 299, § 2.)

§ 1221. Adoptive admission

Evidence of a statement offered against a party is not made inadmissible by the hearsay rule if the statement is one of which the party, with knowledge of the content thereof, has by words or other conduct manifested his adoption or his belief in its truth.
(Stats.1965, c. 299, § 2.)

§ 1222. Authorized admission

Evidence of a statement offered against a party is not made inadmissible by the hearsay rule if:

(a) The statement was made by a person authorized by the party to make a statement or statements for him concerning the subject matter of the statement; and

(b) The evidence is offered either after admission of evidence sufficient to sustain a finding of such authority or, in the court's discretion as to the order of proof, subject to the admission of such evidence.
(Stats.1965, c. 299, § 2.)

§ 1223. Admission of co-conspirator

Evidence of a statement offered against a party is not made inadmissible by the hearsay rule if:

(a) The statement was made by the declarant while participating in a conspiracy to commit a crime or civil wrong and in furtherance of the objective of that conspiracy;

(b) The statement was made prior to or during the time that the party was participating in that conspiracy; and

(c) The evidence is offered either after admission of evidence sufficient to sustain a finding of the facts specified in subdivisions (a) and (b) or, in the court's discretion as to the order of proof, subject to the admission of such evidence.
(Stats.1965, c. 299, § 2.)

§ 1224. Statement of declarant whose liability or breach of duty is in issue

When the liability, obligation, or duty of a party to a civil action is based in whole or in part upon the liability, obligation, or duty of the declarant, or when the claim or right asserted by a party to a civil action is barred or diminished by a breach of duty by the declarant, evidence of a statement made by the declarant is as admissible against the party as it would be if offered against the declarant in an action involving that liability, obligation, duty, or breach of duty.
(Stats.1965, c. 299, § 2.)

§ 1225. Statement of declarant whose right or title is in issue

When a right, title, or interest in any property or claim asserted by a party to a civil action requires a determination that a right, title, or interest exists or existed in the declarant, evidence of a statement made by the declarant during the time the party now claims the declarant was the holder of the right, title, or interest is as admissible against the party as it would be if offered against the declarant in an action involving that right, title, or interest.
(Stats.1965, c. 299, § 2.)

§ 1226. Statement of minor child in parent's action for child's injury

Evidence of a statement by a minor child is not made inadmissible by the hearsay rule if offered against the plaintiff in an action brought under Section 376 of the Code of Civil Procedure for injury to such minor child.
(Stats.1965, c. 299, § 2.)

§ 1227. Statement of declarant in action for his wrongful death

Evidence of a statement by the deceased is not made inadmissible by the hearsay rule if offered against the plaintiff in an action for wrongful death brought under Section 377 of the Code of Civil Procedure.
(Stats.1965, c. 299, § 2.)

ARTICLE 2. DECLARATIONS AGAINST INTEREST

Sec.
1230. Declarations against interest.

§ 1230. Declarations against interest

Evidence of a statement by a declarant having sufficient knowledge of the subject is not made inadmissible by the hearsay rule if the declarant is unavailable as a witness and the statement, when made, was so far contrary to the declarant's pecuniary or proprietary interest, or so far subjected him to the risk of civil or criminal liability, or so far tended to render invalid a claim by him against another, or created such a risk of making him an object of hatred, ridicule, or social disgrace in the community, that a reasonable man in his position would not have made the statement unless he believed it to be true.
(Stats.1965, c. 299, § 2.)

ARTICLE 3. PRIOR STATEMENTS OF WITNESSES

Sec.
1235. Inconsistent statement.
1236. Prior consistent statement.
1237. Past recollection recorded.
1238. Prior identification.

§ 1235. Inconsistent statement

Evidence of a statement made by a witness is not made inadmissible by the hearsay rule if the statement is inconsistent with his testimony at the hearing and is offered in compliance with Section 770.
(Stats.1965, c. 299, § 2.)

§ 1236. Prior consistent statement

Evidence of a statement previously made by a witness is not made inadmissible by the hearsay rule if the statement is consistent with his testimony at the hearing and is offered in compliance with Section 791.
(Stats.1965, c. 299, § 2.)

§ 1237. Past recollection recorded

(a) Evidence of a statement previously made by a witness is not made inadmissible by the hearsay rule if the statement would have been admissible if made by him while testifying, the statement concerns a matter as to which the witness has insufficient present recollection to enable him to testify fully and accurately, and the statement is contained in a writing which:

(1) Was made at a time when the fact recorded in the writing actually occurred or was fresh in the witness' memory;

(2) Was made (i) by the witness himself or under his direction or (ii) by some other person for the purpose of recording the witness' statement at the time it was made;

(3) Is offered after the witness testifies that the statement he made was a true statement of such fact; and

(4) Is offered after the writing is authenticated as an accurate record of the statement.

(b) The writing may be read into evidence, but the writing itself may not be received in evidence unless offered by an adverse party.
(Stats.1965, c. 299, § 2.)

§ 1238. Prior identification

Evidence of a statement previously made by a witness is not made inadmissible by the hearsay rule if the statement would have been admissible if made by him while testifying and:

(a) The statement is an identification of a party or another as a person who participated in a crime or other occurrence;

(b) The statement was made at a time when the crime or other occurrence was fresh in the witness' memory; and

(c) The evidence of the statement is offered after the witness testifies that he made the identification and that it was a true reflection of his opinion at that time.
(Stats.1965, c. 299, § 2.)

ARTICLE 4. SPONTANEOUS, CONTEMPORANEOUS, AND DYING DECLARATIONS

Sec.
1240. Spontaneous statement.
1241. Contemporaneous statement.
1242. Dying declaration.

§ 1240. Spontaneous statement

Evidence of a statement is not made inadmissible by the hearsay rule if the statement:

(a) Purports to narrate, describe, or explain an act, condition, or event perceived by the declarant; and

(b) Was made spontaneously while the declarant was under the stress of excitement caused by such perception.
(Stats.1965, c. 299, § 2.)

§ 1241. Contemporaneous statement

Evidence of a statement is not made inadmissible by the hearsay rule if the statement:

(a) Is offered to explain, qualify, or make understandable conduct of the declarant; and

(b) Was made while the declarant was engaged in such conduct.
(Stats.1965, c. 299, § 2.)

§ 1242. Dying declaration

Evidence of a statement made by a dying person respecting the cause and circumstances of his death is not made inadmissible by the hearsay rule if the statement was made upon his personal knowledge and under a sense of immediately impending death.
(Stats.1965, c. 299, § 2.)

ARTICLE 5. STATEMENTS OF MENTAL OR PHYSICAL STATE

Sec.
1250. Statement of declarant's then existing mental or physical state.
1251. Statement of declarant's previously existing mental or physical state.
1252. Limitation on admissibility of statement of mental or physical state.

§ 1250. Statement of declarant's then existing mental or physical state

(a) Subject to Section 1252, evidence of a statement of the declarant's then existing state of mind, emotion, or physical sensation (including a statement of intent, plan, motive, design, mental feeling, pain, or bodily health) is not made inadmissible by the hearsay rule when:

(1) The evidence is offered to prove the declarant's state of mind, emotion, or physical sensation at that time or at any other time when it is itself an issue in the action; or

(2) The evidence is offered to prove or explain acts or conduct of the declarant.

(b) This section does not make admissible evidence of a statement of memory or belief to prove the fact remembered or believed.
(Stats.1965, c. 299, § 2.)

§ 1251. Statement of declarant's previously existing mental or physical state

Subject to Section 1252, evidence of a statement of the declarant's state of mind, emotion, or physical sensation (including a statement of intent, plan, motive, design, mental feeling, pain, or bodily health) at a time prior to the statement is not made inadmissible by the hearsay rule if:

(a) The declarant is unavailable as a witness; and

(b) The evidence is offered to prove such prior state of mind, emotion, or physical sensation when it is itself an issue in the action and the evidence is not offered to prove any fact other than such state of mind, emotion, or physical sensation.
(Stats.1965, c. 299, § 2.)

§ 1252. Limitation on admissibility of statement of mental or physical state

Evidence of a statement is inadmissible under this article if the statement was made under circumstances such as to indicate its lack of trustworthiness.
(Stats.1965, c. 299, § 2.)

ARTICLE 6.   STATEMENTS RELATING TO WILLS AND TO CLAIMS AGAINST ESTATES

Sec.

§ 1260. Statement concerning declarant's will

(a) Evidence of a statement made by a declarant who is unavailable as a witness that he has or has not made a will, or has or has not revoked his will, or that identifies his will, is not made inadmissible by the hearsay rule.

(b) Evidence of a statement is inadmissible under this section if the statement was made under circumstances such as to indicate its lack of trustworthiness.
(Stats.1965, c. 299, § 2.)

§ 1261. Statement of decedent offered in action against his estate

(a) Evidence of a statement is not made inadmissible by the hearsay rule when offered in an action upon a claim or demand against the estate of the declarant if the statement was made upon the personal knowledge of the declarant at a time when the matter had been recently perceived by him and while his recollection was clear.

(b) Evidence of a statement is inadmissible under this section if the statement was made under circumstances such as to indicate its lack of trustworthiness.
(Stats.1965, c. 299, § 2.)

ARTICLE 7.   BUSINESS RECORDS

Sec.

§ 1270. "A business"

As used in this article, "a business" includes every kind of business, governmental activity, profession, occupation, calling, or operation of institutions, whether carried on for profit or not.
(Stats.1965, c. 299, § 2.)

§ 1271. Business record

Evidence of a writing made as a record of an act, condition, or event is not made inadmissible by the hearsay rule when offered to prove the act, condition, or event if:

(a) The writing was made in the regular course of a business;

(b) The writing was made at or near the time of the act, condition, or event;

(c) The custodian or other qualified witness testifies to its identity and the mode of its preparation; and

(d) The sources of information and method and time of preparation were such as to indicate its trustworthiness.

(Stats.1965, c. 299, § 2.)

§ 1272. Absence of entry in business records

Evidence of the absence from the records of a business of a record of an asserted act, condition, or event is not made inadmissible by the hearsay rule when offered to prove the nonoccurrence of the act or event, or the nonexistence of the condition, if:

(a) It was the regular course of that business to make records of all such acts, conditions, or events at or near the time of the act, condition, or event and to preserve them; and

(b) The sources of information and method and time of preparation of the records of that business were such that the absence of a record of an act, condition, or event is a trustworthy indication that the act or event did not occur or the condition did not exist.

(Stats.1965, c. 299, § 2.)

ARTICLE 8. OFFICIAL RECORDS AND OTHER OFFICIAL WRITINGS

§ 1280. Record by public employee

Evidence of a writing made as a record of an act, condition, or event is not made inadmissible by the hearsay rule when offered to prove the act, condition, or event if:

(a) The writing was made by and within the scope of duty of a public employee;

(b) The writing was made at or near the time of the act, condition, or event; and

(c) The sources of information and method and time of preparation were such as to indicate its trustworthiness.

(Stats.1965, c. 299, § 2.)

§ 1281. Record of vital statistic

Evidence of a writing made as a record of a birth, fetal death, death, or marriage is not made inadmissible by the hearsay rule if the maker was required by law to file the writing in a designated public office and the writing was made and filed as required by law.

(Stats.1965, c. 299, § 2.)

§ 1282. Finding of presumed death by authorized federal employee

A written finding of presumed death made by an employee of the United States authorized to make such finding pursuant to the Federal Missing Persons Act (56 Stats. 143, 1092, and P.L. 408, Ch. 371, 2d Sess. 78th Cong.; 50 U.S.C. App. 1001–1016), as enacted or as heretofore or hereafter amended, shall be received in any court, office, or other place in this state as evidence of the death of the person therein found to be dead and of the date, circumstances, and place of his disappearance.

(Stats.1965, c. 299, § 2.)

§ 1283. Record by federal employee that person is missing, captured, or the like

An official written report or record that a person is missing, missing in action, interned in a foreign country, captured by a hostile force, beleaguered by a hostile force, besieged by a hostile force, or detained in a foreign country against his will, or is dead or is alive, made by an employee of the United States authorized by any law of the United States to make such report or record shall be received in any court, office, or other place in this state as evidence that such person is missing, missing in action, interned in a foreign country, captured by a hostile force, beleaguered by a hostile force, besieged by a hostile force, or detained in a foreign country against his will, or is dead or is alive.
(Stats.1965, c. 299, § 2.)

§ 1284. Statement of absence of public record

Evidence of a writing made by the public employee who is the official custodian of the records in a public office, reciting diligent search and failure to find a record, is not made inadmissible by the hearsay rule when offered to prove the absence of a record in that office.
(Stats.1965, c. 299, § 2.)

ARTICLE 9.   FORMER TESTIMONY

Sec.
1290. "Former testimony."
1291. Former testimony offered against party to former proceeding.
1292. Former testimony offered against person not a party to former proceeding.

§ 1290. "Former testimony"

As used in this article, "former testimony" means testimony given under oath in:

(a) Another action or in a former hearing or trial of the same action;

(b) A proceeding to determine a controversy conducted by or under the supervision of an agency that has the power to determine such a controversy and is an agency of the United States or a public entity in the United States;

(c) A deposition taken in compliance with law in another action; or

(d) An arbitration proceeding if the evidence of such former testimony is a verbatim transcript thereof.
(Stats.1965, c. 299, § 2.)

§ 1291. Former testimony offered against party to former proceeding

(a) Evidence of former testimony is not made inadmissible by the hearsay rule if the declarant is unavailable as a witness and:

(1) The former testimony is offered against a person who offered it in evidence in his own behalf on the former occasion or against the successor in interest of such person; or

(2) The party against whom the former testimony is offered was a party to the action or proceeding in which the testimony was given and had the right and opportunity to cross-examine the declarant with an interest and motive similar to that which he has at the hearing.

(b) The admissibility of former testimony under this section is subject to the same limitations and objections as though the declarant were testifying at the hearing, except that former testimony offered under this section is not subject to:

(1) Objections to the form of the question which were not made at the time the former testimony was given.

(2) Objections based on competency or privilege which did not exist at the time the former testimony was given.
(Stats.1965, c. 299, § 2.)

§ 1292. Former testimony offered against person not a party to former proceeding

(a) Evidence of former testimony is not made inadmissible by the hearsay rule if:

(1) The declarant is unavailable as a witness;

(2) The former testimony is offered in a civil action; and

(3) The issue is such that the party to the action or proceeding in which the former testimony was given had the right and opportunity to cross-examine the declarant with an interest and motive similar to that which the party against whom the testimony is offered has at the hearing.

(b) The admissibility of former testimony under this section is subject to the same limitations and objections as though the declarant were testifying at the hearing, except that former testimony offered under this section is not subject to objections based on competency or privilege which did not exist at the time the former testimony was given. (Stats.1965, c. 299, § 2.)

ARTICLE 10. JUDGMENTS

§ 1300. Judgment of conviction of crime punishable as felony

Evidence of a final judgment adjudging a person guilty of a crime punishable as a felony is not made inadmissible by the hearsay rule when offered in a civil action to prove any fact essential to the judgment unless the judgment was based on a plea of nolo contendere. (Stats.1965, c. 299, § 2.)

§ 1301. Judgment against person entitled to indemnity

Evidence of a final judgment is not made inadmissible by the hearsay rule when offered by the judgment debtor to prove any fact which was essential to the judgment in an action in which he seeks to:

(a) Recover partial or total indemnity or exoneration for money paid or liability incurred because of the judgment;

(b) Enforce a warranty to protect the judgment debtor against the liability determined by the judgment; or

(c) Recover damages for breach of warranty substantially the same as the warranty determined by the judgment to have been breached. (Stats.1965, c. 299, § 2.)

§ 1302. Judgment determining liability of third person

When the liability, obligation, or duty of a third person is in issue in a civil action, evidence of a final judgment against that person is not made inadmissible by the hearsay rule when offered to prove such liability, obligation, or duty. (Stats.1965, c. 299, § 2.)

ARTICLE 11. FAMILY HISTORY

§ 1310. Statement concerning declarant's own family history

(a) Subject to subdivision (b), evidence of a statement by a declarant who is unavailable as a witness concerning his own birth, marriage, divorce, a parent and child relationship, relationship by blood or marriage, race, ancestry, or other similar fact of his family history is not made inadmissible by the hearsay rule, even though the declarant had no means of acquiring personal knowledge of the matter declared.

(b) Evidence of a statement is inadmissible under this section if the statement was made under circumstances such as to indicate its lack of trustworthiness.
(Stats.1965, c. 299, § 2. Amended by Stats.1975, c. 1244, § 15.)

§ 1311. Statement concerning family history of another

(a) Subject to subdivision (b), evidence of a statement concerning the birth, marriage, divorce, death, parent and child relationship, race, ancestry, relationship by blood or marriage, or other similar fact of the family history of a person other than the declarant is not made inadmissible by the hearsay rule if the declarant is unavailable as a witness and:

(1) The declarant was related to the other by blood or marriage; or

(2) The declarant was otherwise so intimately associated with the other's family as to be likely to have had accurate information concerning the matter declared and made the statement (i) upon information received from the other or from a person related by blood or marriage to the other or (ii) upon repute in the other's family.

(b) Evidence of a statement is inadmissible under this section if the statement was made under circumstances such as to indicate its lack of trustworthiness.
(Stats.1965, c. 299, § 2. Amended by Stats.1975, c. 1244, § 16.)

§ 1312. Entries in family records and the like

Evidence of entries in family Bibles or other family books or charts, engravings on rings, family portraits, engravings on urns, crypts, or tombstones, and the like, is not made inadmissible by the hearsay rule when offered to prove the birth, marriage, divorce, death, parent and child relationship, race, ancestry, relationship by blood or marriage, or other similar fact of the family history of a member of the family by blood or marriage.
(Stats.1965, c. 299, § 2. Amended by Stats.1975, c. 1244, § 17.)

§ 1313. Reputation in family concerning family history

Evidence of reputation among members of a family is not made inadmissible by the hearsay rule if the reputation concerns the birth, marriage, divorce, death, parent and child relationship, race, ancestry, relationship by blood or marriage, or other similar fact of the family history of a member of the family by blood or marriage.
(Stats.1965, c. 299, § 2. Amended by Stats.1975, c. 1244, § 18.)

§ 1314. Reputation in community concerning family history

Evidence of reputation in a community concerning the date or fact of birth, marriage, divorce, or death of a person resident in the community at the time of the reputation is not made inadmissible by the hearsay rule.
(Stats.1965, c. 299, § 2.)

§ 1315. Church records concerning family history

Evidence of a statement concerning a person's birth, marriage, divorce, death, parent and child relationship, race, ancestry, relationship by blood or marriage, or other similar fact of family history which is contained in a writing made as a record of a church, religious denomination, or religious society is not made inadmissible by the hearsay rule if:

(a) The statement is contained in a writing made as a record of an act, condition, or event that would be admissible as evidence of such act, condition, or event under Section 1271; and

(b) The statement is of a kind customarily recorded in connection with the act, condition, or event recorded in the writing.
(Stats.1965, c. 299, § 2. Amended by Stats.1975, c. 1244, § 19.)

§ 1316. Marriage, baptismal and similar certificates

Evidence of a statement concerning a person's birth, marriage, divorce, death, parent and child relationship, race, ancestry, relationship by blood or marriage, or other similar fact of family history is not made inadmissible by the hearsay rule if the statement is contained in a certificate that the maker thereof performed a marriage or other ceremony or administered a sacrament and:

(a) The maker was a clergyman, civil officer, or other person authorized to perform the acts reported in the certificate by law or by the rules, regulations, or requirements of a church, religious denomination, or religious society; and

(b) The certificate was issued by the maker at the time and place of the ceremony or sacrament or within a reasonable time thereafter.
(Stats.1965, c. 299, § 2. Amended by Stats.1975, c. 1244, § 20.)

ARTICLE 12. REPUTATION AND STATEMENTS CONCERNING COMMUNITY HISTORY, PROPERTY INTERESTS, AND CHARACTER

§ 1320. Reputation concerning community history

Evidence of reputation in a community is not made inadmissible by the hearsay rule if the reputation concerns an event of general history of the community or of the state or nation of which the community is a part and the event was of importance to the community.
(Stats.1965, c. 299, § 2.)

§ 1321. Reputation concerning public interest in property

Evidence of reputation in a community is not made inadmissible by the hearsay rule if the reputation concerns the interest of the public in property in the community and the reputation arose before controversy.
(Stats.1965, c. 299, § 2.)

§ 1322. Reputation concerning boundary or custom affecting land

Evidence of reputation in a community is not made inadmissible by the hearsay rule if the reputation concerns boundaries of, or customs affecting, land in the community and the reputation arose before controversy.
(Stats.1965, c. 299, § 2.)

§ 1323. Statement concerning boundary

Evidence of a statement concerning the boundary of land is not made inadmissible by the hearsay rule if the declarant is unavailable as a witness and had sufficient knowledge of the subject, but evidence of a statement is not admissible under this section if the statement was made under circumstances such as to indicate its lack of trustworthiness.
(Stats.1965, c. 299, § 2.)

§ 1324. Reputation concerning character

Evidence of a person's general reputation with reference to his character or a trait of his character at a relevant time in the community in which he then resided or in a group with which he then habitually associated is not made inadmissible by the hearsay rule. (Stats.1965, c. 299, § 2.)

ARTICLE 13. DISPOSITIVE INSTRUMENTS AND ANCIENT WRITINGS

§ 1330. Recitals in writings affecting property

Evidence of a statement contained in a deed of conveyance or a will or other writing purporting to affect an interest in real or personal property is not made inadmissible by the hearsay rule if:

(a) The matter stated was relevant to the purpose of the writing;

(b) The matter stated would be relevant to an issue as to an interest in the property; and

(c) The dealings with the property since the statement was made have not been inconsistent with the truth of the statement. (Stats.1965, c. 299, § 2.)

§ 1331. Recitals in ancient writings

Evidence of a statement is not made inadmissible by the hearsay rule if the statement is contained in a writing more than 30 years old and the statement has been since generally acted upon as true by persons having an interest in the matter. (Stats.1965, c. 299, § 2.)

ARTICLE 14. COMMERCIAL, SCIENTIFIC, AND SIMILAR PUBLICATIONS

§ 1340. Commercial lists and the like

Evidence of a statement, other than an opinion, contained in a tabulation, list, directory, register, or other published compilation is not made inadmissible by the hearsay rule if the compilation is generally used and relied upon as accurate in the course of a business as defined in Section 1270. (Stats.1965, c. 299, § 2.)

§ 1341. Publications concerning facts of general notoriety and interest

Historical works, books of science or art, and published maps or charts, made by persons indifferent between the parties, are not made inadmissible by the hearsay rule when offered to prove facts of general notoriety and interest. (Stats.1965, c. 299, § 2.)

Division 11
WRITINGS

CHAPTER 1. AUTHENTICATION AND PROOF OF WRITINGS

ARTICLE 1. REQUIREMENT OF AUTHENTICATION

§ 1400. Authentication defined
Authentication of a writing means (a) the introduction of evidence sufficient to sustain a finding that it is the writing that the proponent of the evidence claims it is or (b) the establishment of such facts by any other means provided by law.
(Stats.1965, c. 299, § 2.)

§ 1401. Authentication required
(a) Authentication of a writing is required before it may be received in evidence.

(b) Authentication of a writing is required before secondary evidence of its content may be received in evidence.
(Stats.1965, c. 299, § 2.)

§ 1402. Authentication of altered writing
The party producing a writing as genuine which has been altered, or appears to have been altered, after its execution, in a part material to the question in dispute, must account for the alteration or appearance thereof. He may show that the alteration was made by another, without his concurrence, or was made with the consent of the parties affected by it, or otherwise properly or innocently made, or that the alteration did not change the meaning or language of the instrument. If he does that, he may give the writing in evidence, but not otherwise.
(Stats.1965, c. 299, § 2.)

ARTICLE 2. MEANS OF AUTHENTICATING AND PROVING WRITINGS

§ 1410. Article not exclusive

Nothing in this article shall be construed to limit the means by which a writing may be authenticated or proved.

(Stats.1965, c. 299, § 2.)

§ 1411. Subscribing witness' testimony unnecessary

Except as provided by statute, the testimony of a subscribing witness is not required to authenticate a writing.

(Stats.1965, c. 299, § 2.)

§ 1412. Use of other evidence when subscribing witness' testimony required

If the testimony of a subscribing witness is required by statute to authenticate a writing and the subscribing witness denies or does not recollect the execution of the writing, the writing may be authenticated by other evidence.

(Stats.1965, c. 299, § 2.)

§ 1413. Witness to the execution of a writing

A writing may be authenticated by anyone who saw the writing made or executed, including a subscribing witness.

(Stats.1965, c. 299, § 2.)

§ 1414. Authentication by admission

A writing may be authenticated by evidence that:

(a) The party against whom it is offered has at any time admitted its authenticity; or

(b) The writing has been acted upon as authentic by the party against whom it is offered.

(Stats.1965, c. 299, § 2.)

§ 1415. Authentication by handwriting evidence

A writing may be authenticated by evidence of the genuineness of the handwriting of the maker.

(Stats.1965, c. 299, § 2.)

§ 1416. Proof of handwriting by person familiar therewith

A witness who is not otherwise qualified to testify as an expert may state his opinion whether a writing is in the handwriting of a supposed writer if the court finds that he has personal knowledge of the handwriting of the supposed writer. Such personal knowledge may be acquired from:

(a) Having seen the supposed writer write;

(b) Having seen a writing purporting to be in the handwriting of the supposed writer and upon which the supposed writer has acted or been charged;

(c) Having received letters in the due course of mail purporting to be from the supposed writer in response to letters duly addressed and mailed by him to the supposed writer; or

(d) Any other means of obtaining personal knowledge of the handwriting of the supposed writer.

(Stats.1965, c. 299, § 2.)

OFFICIAL FORMS
Proof of holographic instrument, see form set out following Probate Code § 331.

§ 1417. Comparison of handwriting by trier of fact

The genuineness of handwriting, or the lack thereof, may be proved by a comparison made by the trier of fact with handwriting (a) which the court finds was admitted or

treated as genuine by the party against whom the evidence is offered or (b) otherwise proved to be genuine to the satisfaction of the court.
(Stats.1965, c. 299, § 2.)

§ 1418. Comparison of writing by expert witness

The genuineness of writing, or the lack thereof, may be proved by a comparison made by an expert witness with writing (a) which the court finds was admitted or treated as genuine by the party against whom the evidence is offered or (b) otherwise proved to be genuine to the satisfaction of the court.
(Stats.1965, c. 299, § 2.)

§ 1419. Exemplars when writing is 30 years old

Where a writing whose genuineness is sought to be proved is more than 30 years old, the comparison under Section 1417 or 1418 may be made with writing purporting to be genuine, and generally respected and acted upon as such, by persons having an interest in knowing whether it is genuine.
(Stats.1965, c. 299, § 2.)

§ 1420. Authentication by evidence of reply

A writing may be authenticated by evidence that the writing was received in response to a communication sent to the person who is claimed by the proponent of the evidence to be the author of the writing.
(Stats.1965, c. 299, § 2.)

§ 1421. Authentication by content

A writing may be authenticated by evidence that the writing refers to or states matters that are unlikely to be known to anyone other than the person who is claimed by the proponent of the evidence to be the author of the writing.
(Stats.1965, c. 299, § 2.)

ARTICLE 3. PRESUMPTIONS AFFECTING ACKNOWLEDGED WRITINGS AND OFFICIAL WRITINGS

§ 1450. Classification of presumptions in article

The presumptions established by this article are presumptions affecting the burden of producing evidence.
(Stats.1965, c. 299, § 2.)

§ 1451. Acknowledged writings

A certificate of the acknowledgment of a writing other than a will, or a certificate of the proof of such a writing, is prima facie evidence of the facts recited in the certificate and the genuineness of the signature of each person by whom the writing purports to have been signed if the certificate meets the requirements of Article 3 (commencing with Section 1180) of Chapter 4, Title 4, Part 4, Division 2 of the Civil Code.
(Stats.1965, c. 299, § 2.)

§ 1452. Official seals

A seal is presumed to be genuine and its use authorized if it purports to be the seal of:

(a) The United States or a department, agency, or public employee of the United States.

(b) A public entity in the United States or a department, agency, or public employee of such public entity.

(c) A nation recognized by the executive power of the United States or a department, agency, or officer of such nation.

(d) A public entity in a nation recognized by the executive power of the United States or a department, agency, or officer of such public entity.

(e) A court of admiralty or maritime jurisdiction.

(f) A notary public within any state of the United States.
(Stats.1965, c. 299, § 2.)

§ 1453. Domestic official signatures

A signature is presumed to be genuine and authorized if it purports to be the signature, affixed in his official capacity, of:

(a) A public employee of the United States.

(b) A public employee of any public entity in the United States.

(c) A notary public within any state of the United States.
(Stats.1965, c. 299, § 2.)

§ 1454. Foreign official signatures

A signature is presumed to be genuine and authorized if it purports to be the signature, affixed in his official capacity, of an officer, or deputy of an officer, of a nation or public entity in a nation recognized by the executive power of the United States and the writing to which the signature is affixed is accompanied by a final statement certifying the genuineness of the signature and the official position of (a) the person who executed the writing or (b) any foreign official who has certified either the genuineness of the signature and official position of the person executing the writing or the genuineness of the signature and official position of another foreign official who has executed a similar certificate in a chain of such certificates beginning with a certificate of the genuineness of the signature and official position of the person executing the writing. The final statement may be made only by a secretary of an embassy or legation, consul general, consul, vice consul, consular agent, or other officer in the foreign service of the United States stationed in the nation, authenticated by the seal of his office.
(Stats.1965, c. 299, § 2.)

CHAPTER 2. SECONDARY EVIDENCE OF WRITINGS

ARTICLE 1. BEST EVIDENCE RULE

§ 1500. The best evidence rule

Except as otherwise provided by statute, no evidence other than the original of a writing is admissible to prove the content of a writing. This section shall be known and may be cited as the best evidence rule.
(Stats.1965, c. 299, § 2. Amended by Stats.1977, c. 708, § 3.)

§ 1501. Copy of lost or destroyed writing

A copy of a writing is not made inadmissible by the best evidence rule if the writing is lost or has been destroyed without fraudulent intent on the part of the proponent of the evidence.
(Stats.1965, c. 299, § 2.)

§ 1502. Copy of unavailable writing

A copy of a writing is not made inadmissible by the best evidence rule if the writing was not reasonably procurable by the proponent by use of the court's process or by other available means.
(Stats.1965, c. 299, § 2.)

§ 1503. Copy of writing under control of opponent

(a) A copy of a writing is not made inadmissible by the best evidence rule if, at a time when the writing was under the control of the opponent, the opponent was expressly or impliedly notified, by the pleadings or otherwise, that the writing would be needed at the hearing, and on request at the hearing the opponent has failed to produce the writing. In a criminal action, the request at the hearing to produce the writing may not be made in the presence of the jury.

(b) Though a writing requested by one party is produced by another, and is thereupon inspected by the party calling for it, the party calling for the writing is not obliged to introduce it as evidence in the action.
(Stats.1965, c. 299, § 2.)

§ 1504. Copy of collateral writing

A copy of a writing is not made inadmissible by the best evidence rule if the writing is not closely related to the controlling issues and it would be inexpedient to require its production.
(Stats.1965, c. 299, § 2.)

§ 1505. Other secondary evidence of writings described in Sections 1501 to 1504

If the proponent does not have in his possession or under his control a copy of a writing described in Section 1501, 1502, 1503, or 1504, other secondary evidence of the content of the writing is not made inadmissible by the best evidence rule. This section does not apply to a writing that is also described in Section 1506 or 1507.
(Stats.1965, c. 299, § 2.)

§ 1506. Copy of public writing

A copy of a writing is not made inadmissible by the best evidence rule if the writing is a record or other writing that is in the custody of a public entity.
(Stats.1965, c. 299, § 2.)

§ 1507. Copy of recorded writing

A copy of a writing is not made inadmissible by the best evidence rule if the writing has been recorded in the public records and the record or an attested or a certified copy thereof is made evidence of the writing by statute.
(Stats.1965, c. 299, § 2.)

§ 1508. Other secondary evidence of writings described in Sections 1506 and 1507

If the proponent does not have in his possession a copy of a writing described in Section 1506 or 1507 and could not in the exercise of reasonable diligence have obtained a copy, other secondary evidence of the content of the writing is not made inadmissible by the best evidence rule.
(Stats.1965, c. 299, § 2.)

§ 1509. Voluminous writings

Secondary evidence, whether written or oral, of the content of a writing is not made inadmissible by the best evidence rule if the writing consists of numerous accounts or other writings that cannot be examined in court without great loss of time, and the evidence sought from them is only the general result of the whole; but the court in its discretion may require that such accounts or other writings be produced for inspection by the adverse party.
(Stats.1965, c. 299, § 2.)

§ 1510. Copy of writing produced at the hearing

A copy of a writing is not made inadmissible by the best evidence rule if the writing has been produced at the hearing and made available for inspection by the adverse party.
(Stats.1965, c. 299, § 2.)

§ 1511. Duplicate of a writing; admissibility; conditions

A duplicate of a writing is not made inadmissible by the best evidence rule if:

(a) No later than 30 days before the hearing the proponent has served written notice upon each other party to the proceeding that a duplicate will be offered in evidence at the hearing in lieu of the original, and has (1) attached a duplicate to the notice, or (2) when it would be inconvenient or impractical to serve a duplicate on each other party, has described the writing in the notice and has made the original or a duplicate available to each other party to the proceeding for inspection or copying in the county in which the hearing will be held; and

(b) Within 10 days after service of the notice provided in subdivision (a), no party to the proceeding has served upon the proponent an objection to the duplicate and a demand that the original be produced at the hearing.
(Added by Stats.1977, c. 708, § 4.)

ARTICLE 2. OFFICIAL WRITINGS AND RECORDED WRITINGS

§ 1530. Copy of writing in official custody

(a) A purported copy of a writing in the custody of a public entity, or of an entry in such a writing, is prima facie evidence of the existence and content of such writing or entry if:

(1) The copy purports to be published by the authority of the nation or state, or public entity therein in which the writing is kept;

(2) The office in which the writing is kept is within the United States or within the Panama Canal Zone, the Trust Territory of the Pacific Islands, or the Ryukyu Islands, and

the copy is attested or certified as a correct copy of the writing or entry by a public employee, or a deputy of a public employee, having the legal custody of the writing; or

(3) The office in which the writing is kept is not within the United States or any other place described in paragraph (2) and the copy is attested as a correct copy of the writing or entry by a person having authority to make attestation. The attestation must be accompanied by a final statement certifying the genuineness of the signature and the official position of (i) the person who attested the copy as a correct copy or (ii) any foreign official who has certified either the genuineness of the signature and official position of the person attesting the copy or the genuineness of the signature and official position of another foreign official who has executed a similar certificate in a chain of such certificates beginning with a certificate of the genuineness of the signature and official position of the person attesting the copy. Except as provided in the next sentence, the final statement may be made only by a secretary of an embassy or legation, consul general, consul, vice consul, or consular agent of the United States, or a diplomatic or consular official of the foreign country assigned or accredited to the United States. Prior to January 1, 1971, the final statement may also be made by a secretary of an embassy or legation, consul general, consul, vice consul, consular agent, or other officer in the foreign service of the United States stationed in the nation in which the writing is kept, authenticated by the seal of his office. If reasonable opportunity has been given to all parties to investigate the authenticity and accuracy of the documents, the court may, for good cause shown, (i) admit an attested copy without the final statement or (ii) permit the writing or entry in foreign custody to be evidenced by an attested summary with or without a final statement.

(b) The presumptions established by this section are presumptions affecting the burden of producing evidence.
(Stats.1965, c. 299, § 2. Amended by Stats.1970, c. 41, § 1, urgency, eff. April 3, 1970.)

§ 1531. Certification of copy for evidence

For the purpose of evidence, whenever a copy of a writing is attested or certified, the attestation or certificate must state in substance that the copy is a correct copy of the original, or of a specified part thereof, as the case may be.
(Stats.1965, c. 299, § 2.)

OFFICIAL FORMS

Abstract of judgment, certification, see form set out following Code of Civil Procedure § 674.

Letters of administration, letters testamentary, letters of administration with will annexed, letters of special administration, certification, see form set out following Probate Code § 501.

Letters of guardianship/conservatorship, certification, see form set out following Probate Code § 1481.

§ 1532. Official record of recorded writing

(a) The official record of a writing is prima facie evidence of the existence and content of the original recorded writing if:

(1) The record is in fact a record of an office of a public entity; and

(2) A statute authorized such a writing to be recorded in that office.

(b) The presumption established by this section is a presumption affecting the burden of producing evidence.
(Stats.1965, c. 299, § 2.)

ARTICLE 3. PHOTOGRAPHIC COPIES OF WRITINGS

UNIFORM PHOTOGRAPHIC COPIES OF BUSINESS AND
PUBLIC RECORDS AS EVIDENCE ACT

Table Of Jurisdictions Wherein Act Has Been Adopted

Jurisdiction	Statutory Citation
Alabama	Code of Ala.1975, § 12–21–44.
Arkansas	Ark.Stats. § 28–932.
California	West's Ann.Evidence Code §§ 1550, 1551.
Colorado	C.R.S. '73, 13–26–101 to 13–26–104.
Connecticut	C.G.S.A. § 52–180.
Delaware	10 Del.C. § 4310.
Georgia	Code, § 38–710.
Hawaii	HRS § 622–4.
Idaho	I.C. §§ 9–417 to 9–419.
Iowa	I.C.A. § 622.30.
Kansas	K.S.A. 60–469.
Kentucky	KRS 422.105.
Maine	16 M.R.S.A. § 456.
Maryland	Code, Courts and Judicial Proceedings, § 10–102.
Massachusetts	M.G.L.A. c. 233 § 79E.
Michigan	M.C.L.A. § 600.2147.
Minnesota	M.S.A. § 600.135.
Montana	R.C.M.1947, §§ 93–801–5, 93–801–6.
Nebraska	R.R.S.1943, §§ 25–12,112 to 25–12,114.
New Hampshire	RSA 520:1 to 520:3.
New Jersey	N.J.S.A. 2A:82–38 to 2A:82–40.
New York	McKinney's CPLR 4539.
North Carolina	G.S. §§ 8–45.1 to 8–45.4.
North Dakota	NDCC 31–08–01.1.
Oklahoma	12 Okl.St.Ann. §§ 521 to 523.
Pennsylvania	42 Pa.C.S.A. § 6109.
Rhode Island	Gen.Laws 1956, § 9–19–14.
South Carolina	Code 1976, § 19–5–610.
South Dakota	SDCL 19–7–12.
Tennessee	T.C.A. § 24–711.
Utah	U.C.A.1953, 78–25–16.
Vermont	12 V.S.A. § 1701.
Virgin Islands	5 V.I.C. § 956.
Virginia	Code 1950, § 8.01–391.
Washington	RCWA 5.46.010 to 5.46.920.
West Virginia	Code, 57–1–7b.
Wisconsin	W.S.A. 889.29.

§ 1550. Photographic copies made as business records

A photostatic, microfilm, microcard, miniature photographic or other photographic copy or reproduction, or an enlargement thereof, of a writing is as admissible as the writing itself if such copy or reproduction was made and preserved as a part of the records of a business (as defined by Section 1270) in the regular course of such business. The introduction of such copy, reproduction, or enlargement does not preclude admission of the original writing if it is still in existence.
(Stats.1965, c. 299, § 2.)

§ 1551. Photographic copies where original destroyed or lost

A print, whether enlarged or not, from a photographic film (including a photographic plate, microphotographic film, photostatic negative, or similar reproduction) of an original writing destroyed or lost after such film was taken or a reproduction from an electronic recording of video images on magnetic surfaces is admissible as the original writing itself if, at the time of the taking of such film or electronic recording, the person under whose direction and control it was taken attached thereto, or to the sealed container in which it was placed and has been kept, or incorporated in the film or electronic recording, a certification complying with the provisions of Section 1531 and stating the date on which, and the fact that, it was so taken under his direction and control.
(Stats.1965, c. 299, § 2. Amended by Stats.1969, c. 646, § 1.)

ARTICLE 4. PRODUCTION OF BUSINESS RECORDS

§ 1560. Compliance with subpoena duces tecum for business records

(a) As used in this article:

(1) "Business" includes every kind of business described in Section 1270.

(2) "Record" includes every kind of record maintained by such a business.

(b) Except as provided in Section 1564, when a subpoena duces tecum is served upon the custodian of records or other qualified witness of a business in an action in which the business is neither a party nor the place where any cause of action is alleged to have arisen, and such subpoena requires the production of all or any part of the records of the business, it is sufficient compliance therewith if the custodian or other qualified witness, within five days after the receipt of such subpoena, delivers by mail or otherwise a true, legible, and durable copy of all the records described in such subpoena to the clerk of court or to the judge if there be no clerk or to such other person as described in subdivision (a) of Section 2018 of the Code of Civil Procedure, together with the affidavit described in Section 1561.

(c) The copy of the records shall be separately enclosed in an inner envelope or wrapper, sealed, with the title and number of the action, name of witness, and date of subpoena clearly inscribed thereon; the sealed envelope or wrapper shall then be enclosed in an outer envelope or wrapper, sealed, directed as follows:

(1) If the subpoena directs attendance in court, to the clerk of such court, or to the judge thereof if there be no clerk.

(2) If the subpoena directs attendance at a deposition, to the officer before whom the deposition is to be taken, at the place designated in the subpoena for the taking of the deposition or at his place of business.

(3) In other cases, to the officer, body, or tribunal conducting the hearing, at a like address.

(d) Unless the parties to the proceeding otherwise agree, or unless the sealed envelope or wrapper is returned to a witness who is to appear personally, the copy of the records shall remain sealed and shall be opened only at the time of trial, deposition, or other hearing, upon the direction of the judge, officer, body, or tribunal conducting the proceeding, in the presence of all parties who have appeared in person or by counsel at such trial, deposition, or hearing. Records which are not introduced in evidence or required as part of the record shall be returned to the person or entity from whom received.
(Stats.1965, c. 299, § 2. Amended by Stats.1969, c. 199, § 2.)

§ 1561. Affidavit accompanying records

(a) The records shall be accompanied by the affidavit of the custodian or other qualified witness, stating in substance each of the following:

(1) The affiant is the duly authorized custodian of the records or other qualified witness and has authority to certify the records.

(2) The copy is a true copy of all the records described in the subpoena.

(3) The records were prepared by the personnel of the business in the ordinary course of business at or near the time of the act, condition, or event.

(b) If the business has none of the records described, or only part thereof, the custodian or other qualified witness shall so state in the affidavit, and deliver the affidavit and such records as are available in the manner provided in Section 1560.
(Stats.1965, c. 299, § 2.   Amended by Stats.1969, c. 199, § 3.)

§ 1562. Admissibility of affidavit and copy of records

The copy of the records is admissible in evidence to the same extent as though the original thereof were offered and the custodian had been present and testified to the matters stated in the affidavit. The affidavit is admissible as evidence of the matters stated therein pursuant to Section 1561 and the matters so stated are presumed true. When more than one person has knowledge of the facts, more than one affidavit may be made. The presumption established by this section is a presumption affecting the burden of producing evidence.
(Stats.1965, c. 299, § 2.)

§ 1563. One witness and mileage fee

(a) This article shall not be interpreted to require tender or payment of more than one witness fee and one mileage fee or other charge unless there is an agreement to the contrary.

(b) Where the business records described in a subpoena issued pursuant to Section 1560 are patient records of a public or licensed hospital or of a physician and surgeon, osteopath, or dentist licensed to practice in this state, or a group of such practitioners, and the personal attendance of the custodian of such records or other qualified witness is not required, the sole fee for complying with such subpoena is twelve dollars ($12).

(c) When the personal attendance of the custodian of a record or other qualified witness is required pursuant to Section 1564, he shall be entitled to 20 cents ($0.20) a mile for mileage actually traveled, one way only, and to twelve dollars ($12) for each day of actual attendance.
(Stats.1965, c. 299, § 2.   Amended by Stats.1972, c. 396, § 1.)

§ 1564. Personal attendance of custodian and production of original records

The personal attendance of the custodian or other qualified witness and the production of the original records is required if the subpoena duces tecum contains a clause which reads:

"The personal attendance of the custodian or other qualified witness and the production of the original records is required by this subpoena. The procedure authorized pursuant to subdivision (b) of Section 1560, the Sections 1561 and 1562, of the Evidence Code will not be deemed sufficient compliance with this subpoena."
(Stats.1965, c. 299, § 2.)

§ 1565. Service of more than one subpoena duces tecum

If more than one subpoena duces tecum is served upon the custodian of records or other qualified witness and the personal attendance of the custodian or other qualified witness is required pursuant to Section 1564, the witness shall be deemed to be the witness of the party serving the first such subpoena duces tecum.
(Stats.1965, c. 299, § 2.   Amended by Stats.1969, c. 199, § 4.)

§ 1566. Applicability of article

This article applies in any proceeding in which testimony can be compelled.
(Stats.1965, c. 299, § 2.)

CHAPTER 3. OFFICIAL WRITINGS AFFECTING PROPERTY

Sec.
1603. Deed by officer in pursuance of court process.
1604. Certificate of purchase or of location of lands.
1605. Authenticated Spanish title records.

§ 1600. Record of document affecting property interest

(a) The record of an instrument or other document purporting to establish or affect an interest in property is prima facie evidence of the existence and content of the original recorded document and its execution and delivery by each person by whom it purports to have been executed if:

(1) The record is in fact a record of an office of a public entity; and

(2) A statute authorized such a document to be recorded in that office.

(b) The presumption established by this section is a presumption affecting the burden of proof.

(Stats.1965, c. 299, § 2. Amended by Stats.1967, c. 650, § 9.)

§ 1601. Proof of content of lost official record affecting property

(a) Subject to subdivisions (b) and (c), when in any action it is desired to prove the contents of the official record of any writing lost or destroyed by conflagration or other public calamity, after proof of such loss or destruction, the following may, without further proof, be admitted in evidence to prove the contents of such record:

(1) Any abstract of title made and issued and certified as correct prior to such loss or destruction, and purporting to have been prepared and made in the ordinary course of business by any person engaged in the business of preparing and making abstracts of title prior to such loss or destruction; or

(2) Any abstract of title, or of any instrument affecting title, made, issued, and certified as correct by any person engaged in the business of insuring titles or issuing abstracts of title to real estate, whether the same was made, issued, or certified before or after such loss or destruction and whether the same was made from the original records or from abstract and notes, or either, taken from such records in the preparation and upkeeping of its plant in the ordinary course of its business.

(b) No proof of the loss of the original writing is required other than the fact that the original is not known to the party desiring to prove its contents to be in existence.

(c) Any party desiring to use evidence admissible under this section shall give reasonable notice in writing to all other parties to the action who have appeared therein, of his intention to use such evidence at the trial of the action, and shall give all such other parties a reasonable opportunity to inspect the evidence, and also the abstracts, memoranda, or notes from which it was compiled, and to take copies thereof.

(Stats.1965, c. 299, § 2.)

§ 1602. Repealed by Stats.1967, c. 650, § 10

§ 1603. Deed by officer in pursuance of court process

A deed of conveyance of real property, purporting to have been executed by a proper officer in pursuance of legal process of any of the courts of record of this state, acknowledged and recorded in the office of the recorder of the county wherein the real property therein described is situated, or the record of such deed, or a certified copy of such record, is prima facie evidence that the property or interest therein described was thereby conveyed to the grantee named in such deed. The presumption established by this section is a presumption affecting the burden of proof.

(Stats.1965, c. 299, § 2. Amended by Stats.1967, c. 650, § 11.)

§ 1604. Certificate of purchase or of location of lands

A certificate of purchase, or of location, of any lands in this state, issued or made in pursuance of any law of the United States or of this state, is prima facie evidence that the

holder or assignee of such certificate is the owner of the land described therein; but this evidence may be overcome by proof that, at the time of the location, or time of filing a preemption claim on which the certificate may have been issued, the land was in the adverse possession of the adverse party, or those under whom he claims, or that the adverse party is holding the land for mining purposes.
(Stats.1965, c. 299, § 2.)

§ 1605. Authenticated Spanish title records

Duplicate copies and authenticated translations of original Spanish title papers relating to land claims in this state, derived from the Spanish or Mexican governments, prepared under the supervision of the Keeper of Archives, authenticated by the Surveyor-General or his successor and by the Keeper of Archives, and filed with a county recorder, in accordance with Chapter 281 of the Statutes of 1865–66, are admissible as evidence with like force and effect as the originals and without proving the execution of such originals.
(Stats.1965, c. 299, § 2.   Amended by Stats.1967, c. 650, § 12.)

APPENDIX B

RULES OF EVIDENCE
FOR
UNITED STATES COURTS
AND
MAGISTRATES

Effective July 1, 1975
Amended to October 1, 1980

Table of Rules

Article IV. Relevancy and Its Limits.
Rule

Article V. Privileges.
Rule

Article VI. Witnesses.
Rule

Article VIII. Hearsay.—Continued

Rule

803. Hearsay Exceptions: Availability of Declarant Immaterial.—
Continued

    (8) Public records and reports

    (9) Records of vital statistics

    (10) Absence of public record or entry

    (11) Records of religious organizations

    (12) Marriage, baptismal, and similar certificates

    (13) Family records

    (14) Records of documents affecting an interest in property

    (15) Statements in documents affecting an interest in property

    (16) Statements in ancient documents

    (17) Market reports, commercial publications

    (18) Learned treatises

    (19) Reputation concerning personal or family history

    (20) Reputation concerning boundaries or general history

    (21) Reputation as to character

    (22) Judgment of previous conviction

    (23) Judgment as to personal, family, or general history, or boundaries

    (24) Other exceptions

804. Hearsay Exceptions: Declarant Unavailable.

    (a) Definition of unavailability

    (b) Hearsay exceptions.

        (1) Former testimony

        (2) Statement under belief of impending death

        (3) Statement against interest

        (4) Statement of personal or family history

        (5) Other exceptions

805. Hearsay Within Hearsay.

806. Attacking and Supporting Credibility of Declarant.

Article IX. Authentication and Identification.

Rule

901. Requirement of Authentication or Identification.

    (a) General provision

    (b) Illustrations

        (1) Testimony of witness with knowledge

        (2) Nonexpert opinion on handwriting

        (3) Comparison by trier or expert witness

        (4) Distinctive characteristics and the like

        (5) Voice identification

        (6) Telephone conversations

        (7) Public records or reports

        (8) Ancient documents or data compilations

        (9) Process or system

        (10) Methods provided by statute or rule

ARTICLE I.　GENERAL PROVISIONS

Rule 101.

SCOPE

These rules govern proceedings in the courts of the United States and before United States magistrates, to the extent and with the exceptions stated in Rule 1101.

Rule 102.

PURPOSE AND CONSTRUCTION

These rules shall be construed to secure fairness in administration, elimination of unjustifiable expense and delay, and promotion of growth and development of the law of evidence to the end that the truth may be ascertained and proceedings justly determined.

Rule 103.

RULINGS ON EVIDENCE

(a) Effect of erroneous ruling.　Error may not be predicated upon a ruling which admits or excludes evidence unless a substantial right of the party is affected, and

(1) *Objection.*　In case the ruling is one admitting evidence a timely objection or motion to strike appears of record, stating the specific ground of objection, if the specific ground was not apparent from the context; or

(2) *Offer of proof.*　In case the ruling is one excluding evidence, the substance of the evidence was made known to the judge by offer or was apparent from the context within which questions were asked.

(b) Record of offer and ruling.　The court may add any other or further statement which shows the character of the evidence, the form in which it was offered, the objection made, and the ruling thereon.　It may direct the making of an offer in question and answer form.

(c) Hearing of jury.　In jury cases, proceedings shall be conducted, to the extent practicable, so as to prevent inadmissible evidence from being suggested to the jury by any means, such as making statements or offers of proof or asking questions in the hearing of the jury.

(d) Plain error.　Nothing in this rule precludes taking notice of plain errors affecting substantial rights although they were not brought to the attention of the court.

Rule 104.

PRELIMINARY QUESTIONS

(a) Questions of admissibility generally. Preliminary questions concerning the qualification of a person to be a witness, the existence of a privilege, or the admissibility of evidence shall be determined by the court, subject to the provisions of subdivision (b). In making its determination it is not bound by the rules of evidence except those with respect to privileges.

(b) Relevancy conditioned on fact. When the relevancy of evidence depends upon the fulfillment of a condition of fact, the judge shall admit it upon, or subject to, the introduction of evidence sufficient to support a finding of the fulfillment of the condition.

(c) Hearing of jury. Hearings on the admissibility of confessions shall in all cases be conducted out of the hearing of the jury. Hearings on other preliminary matters shall be so conducted when the interests of justice require or, when an accused is a witness, if he so requests.

(d) Testimony by accused. The accused does not, by testifying upon a preliminary matter, subject himself to cross-examination as to other issues in the case.

(e) Weight and credibility. This rule does not limit the right of a party to introduce before the jury evidence relevant to weight or credibility.

Rule 105.

LIMITED ADMISSIBILITY

When evidence which is admissible as to one party or for one purpose but not admissible as to another party or for another purpose is admitted, the court, upon request, shall restrict the evidence to its proper scope and instruct the jury accordingly.

Rule 106.

REMAINDER OF OR RELATED WRITINGS OR RECORDED STATEMENTS

When a writing or recorded statement or part thereof is introduced by a party, an adverse party may require him at that time to introduce any other part or any other writing or recorded statement which ought in fairness to be considered contemporaneously with it.

ARTICLE II. JUDICIAL NOTICE

Rule 201.

JUDICIAL NOTICE OF ADJUDICATIVE FACTS

(a) Scope of rule. This rule governs only judicial notice of adjudicative facts.

(b) Kinds of facts. A judicially noticed fact must be one not subject to reasonable dispute in that it is either (1) generally known within the territorial jurisdiction of the trial court or (2) capable of accurate and ready determination by resort to sources whose accuracy cannot reasonably be questioned.

(c) When discretionary. A court may take judicial notice, whether requested or not.

(d) When mandatory. A court shall take judicial notice if requested by a party and supplied with the necessary information.

(e) Opportunity to be heard. A party is entitled upon timely request to an opportunity to be heard as to the propriety of taking judicial notice and the tenor of the matter noticed. In the absence of prior notification, the request may be made after judicial notice has been taken.

(f) Time of taking notice. Judicial notice may be taken at any stage of the proceeding.

(g) Instructing jury. In a civil action or proceeding, the court shall instruct the jury to accept as conclusive any fact judicially noticed. In a criminal case, the court shall instruct the jury that it may, but is not required to, accept as conclusive any fact judicially noticed.

ARTICLE III. PRESUMPTIONS IN CIVIL ACTIONS AND PROCEEDINGS

Rule 301.

PRESUMPTIONS IN GENERAL IN CIVIL ACTIONS AND PROCEEDINGS

In all civil actions and proceedings not otherwise provided for by Act of Congress or by these rules, a presumption imposes on the party against whom it is directed the burden of going forward with evidence to rebut or meet the presumption, but does not shift to such party the burden of proof in the sense of the risk of nonpersuasion, which remains throughout the trial upon the party on whom it was originally cast.

Rule 302.

APPLICABILITY OF STATE LAW IN CIVIL ACTIONS AND PROCEEDINGS

In civil actions and proceedings, the effect of a presumption respecting a fact which is an element of a claim or defense as to which state law supplies the rule of decision is determined in accordance with state law.

ARTICLE IV. RELEVANCY AND ITS LIMITS

Rule 401.

DEFINITION OF "RELEVANT EVIDENCE"

"Relevant evidence" means evidence having any tendency to make the existence of any fact that is of consequence to the determination of the action more probable or less probable than it would be without the evidence.

Rule 402.

RELEVANT EVIDENCE GENERALLY ADMISSIBLE; IRRELEVANT EVIDENCE INADMISSIBLE

All relevant evidence is admissible, except as otherwise provided by the Constitution of the United States, by Act of Congress, by these rules, or by other rules prescribed by the Supreme Court pursuant to statutory authority. Evidence which is not relevant is not admissible.

Rule 403.

EXCLUSION OF RELEVANT EVIDENCE ON GROUNDS OF PREJUDICE, CONFUSION, OR WASTE OF TIME

Although relevant, evidence may be excluded if its probative value is substantially outweighed by the danger of unfair prejudice, confusion of the issues, or misleading the jury, or by considerations of undue delay, waste of time, or needless presentation of cumulative evidence.

Rule 404.

CHARACTER EVIDENCE NOT ADMISSIBLE TO PROVE CONDUCT; EXCEPTIONS; OTHER CRIMES

(a) **Character evidence generally.** Evidence of a person's character or a trait of his character is not admissible for the purpose of proving that he acted in conformity therewith on a particular occasion, except:

(1) *Character of accused.* Evidence of a pertinent trait of his character offered by an accused, or by the prosecution to rebut the same;

(2) *Character of victim.* Evidence of a pertinent trait of character of the victim of the crime offered by an accused, or by the prosecution to rebut the same, or evidence of a character trait of peacefulness of the victim offered by the prosecution in a homicide case to rebut evidence that the victim was the first aggressor;

(3) *Character of witness.* Evidence of the character of a witness, as provided in Rules 607, 608, and 609.

(b) **Other crimes, wrongs, or acts.** Evidence of other crimes, wrongs, or acts is not admissible to prove the character of a person in order to show that he acted in conformity therewith. It may, however, be admissible for other purposes, such as proof of motive, opportunity, intent, preparation, plan, knowledge, identity, or absence of mistake or accident.

Rule 405.

METHODS OF PROVING CHARACTER

(a) **Reputation or opinion.** In all cases in which evidence of character or a trait of character of a person is admissible, proof may be made by testimony as to reputation or by testimony in the form of an opinion. On cross-examination, inquiry is allowable into relevant specific instances of conduct.

(b) **Specific instances of conduct.** In cases in which character or a trait of character of a person is an essential element of a charge, claim, or defense, proof may also be made of specific instances of his conduct.

Rule 406.

HABIT; ROUTINE PRACTICE

Evidence of the habit of a person or of the routine practice of an organization, whether corroborated or not and regardless of the presence of eyewitnesses, is relevant to prove that the conduct of the person or organization on a particular occasion was in conformity with the habit or routine practice.

Rule 407.

SUBSEQUENT REMEDIAL MEASURES

When, after an event, measures are taken which, if taken previously, would have made the event less likely to occur, evidence of the subsequent measures is not admissible to prove negligence or culpable conduct in connection with the event. This rule does not require the exclusion of evidence of subsequent measures when offered for another purpose, such as proving ownership, control, or feasibility of precautionary measures, if controverted, or impeachment.

Rule 408.

COMPROMISE AND OFFERS TO COMPROMISE

Evidence of (1) furnishing or offering or promising to furnish, or (2) accepting or offering or promising to accept, a valuable consideration in compromising or attempting to compromise a claim which was disputed as to either validity or amount, is not admissible to prove liability for or invalidity of the claim or its amount. Evidence of conduct or statements made in compromise negotiations is likewise not admissible. This rule does not require the exclusion of any evidence otherwise discoverable merely because it is presented in the course of compromise negotiations. This rule also does not require exclusion when the evidence is offered for another purpose, such as proving bias or prejudice of a witness, negativing a contention of undue delay, or proving an effort to obstruct a criminal investigation or prosecution.

Rule 409.

PAYMENT OF MEDICAL AND SIMILAR EXPENSES

Evidence of furnishing or offering or promising to pay medical, hospital, or similar expenses occasioned by an injury is not admissible to prove liability for the injury.

Rule 410.

INADMISSIBILITY OF PLEAS, OFFERS OF PLEAS, AND RELATED STATEMENTS

Except as otherwise provided in this rule, evidence of a plea of guilty, later withdrawn, or a plea of nolo contendere, or of an offer to plead guilty or nolo contendere to the crime charged or any other crime, or of statements made in connection with, and relevant to, any of the foregoing pleas or offers, is not admissible in any civil or criminal proceeding against the person who made the plea or offer. However, evidence of a statement made in connection with, and relevant to, a plea of guilty, later withdrawn, a plea of nolo contendere, or an offer to plead guilty or nolo contendere to the crime charged or any other crime, is admissible in a criminal proceeding for perjury or false statement if the statement was made by the defendant under oath, on the record, and in the presence of counsel.

Rule 410.*
INADMISSIBILITY OF PLEAS, PLEA DISCUSSIONS, AND RELATED STATEMENTS

Except as otherwise provided in this rule, evidence of the following is not, in any civil or criminal proceeding, admissible against the defendant who made the plea or was a participant in the plea discussions:

(1) a plea of guilty which was later withdrawn;

(2) a plea of nolo contendere;

(3) any statement made in the course of any proceedings under Rule 11 of the Federal Rules of Criminal Procedure or comparable state procedure regarding either of the foregoing pleas; or

(4) any statement made in the course of plea discussions with an attorney for the prosecuting authority which do not result in a plea of guilty or which result in a plea of guilty later withdrawn.

However, such a statement is admissible (i) in any proceeding wherein another statement made in the course of the same plea or plea discussions has been introduced and the statement ought in fairness be considered contemporaneously with it, or (ii) in a criminal proceeding for perjury or false statement if the statement was made by the defendant under oath, on the record and in the presence of counsel.

Rule 411.

LIABILITY INSURANCE

Evidence that a person was or was not insured against liability is not admissible upon the issue whether he acted negligently or otherwise wrongfully. This rule does not require the exclusion of evidence of insurance against liability when offered for another purpose, such as proof of agency, ownership, or control, or bias or prejudice of a witness.

* Rule 410 was amended by the Supreme Court April 30, 1979 to take effect November 10, 1979. Congress however delayed the effective date until December 1, 1980, or until and then only to the extent approved by an Act of Congress, whichever is earlier. Pub.L. 96-42, 93 Stat. 326.

Rule 412.

CAL - 1102

RAPE CASES: RELEVANCE OF VICTIM'S PAST BEHAVIOR

(a) Notwithstanding any other provision of law, in a criminal case in which a person is accused of rape or of assault with intent to commit rape, reputation or opinion evidence of the past sexual behavior of an alleged victim of such rape or assault is not admissible.

(b) Notwithstanding any other provision of law, in a criminal case in which a person is accused of rape or of assault with intent to commit rape, evidence of a victim's past sexual behavior other than reputation or opinion evidence is also not admissible, unless such evidence other than reputation or opinion evidence is—

(1) admitted in accordance with subdivisions (c)(1) and (c)(2) and is constitutionally required to be admitted; or

(2) admitted in accordance with subdivision (c) and is evidence of—

(A) past sexual behavior with persons other than the accused, offered by the accused upon the issue of whether the accused was or was not, with respect to the alleged victim, the source of semen or injury; or

(B) past sexual behavior with the accused and is offered by the accused upon the issue of whether the alleged victim consented to the sexual behavior with respect to which rape or assault is alleged.

(c)(1) If the person accused of committing rape or assault with intent to commit rape intends to offer under subdivision (b) evidence of specific instances of the alleged victim's past sexual behavior, the accused shall make a written motion to offer such evidence not later than fifteen days before the date on which the trial in which such evidence is to be offered is scheduled to begin, except that the court may allow the motion to be made at a later date, including during trial, if the court determines either that the evidence is newly discovered and could not have been obtained earlier through the exercise of due diligence or that the issue to which such evidence relates has newly arisen in the case. Any motion made under this paragraph shall be served on all other parties and on the alleged victim.

(2) The motion described in paragraph (1) shall be accompanied by a written offer of proof. If the court determines that the offer of proof contains evidence described in subdivision (b), the court shall order a hearing in chambers to determine if such evidence is admissible. At such hearing the parties may call witnesses, including the alleged victim, and offer relevant evidence. Notwithstanding subdivision (b) of rule 104, if the relevancy of

the evidence which the accused seeks to offer in the trial depends upon the fulfillment of a condition of fact, the court, at the hearing in chambers or at a subsequent hearing in chambers scheduled for such purpose, shall accept evidence on the issue of whether such condition of fact is fulfilled and shall determine such issue.

(3) If the court determines on the basis of the hearing described in paragraph (2) that the evidence which the accused seeks to offer is relevant and that the probative value of such evidence outweighs the danger of unfair prejudice, such evidence shall be admissible in the trial to the extent an order made by the court specifies evidence which may be offered and areas with respect to which the alleged victim may be examined or cross-examined.

(d) For purposes of this rule, the term 'past sexual behavior' means sexual behavior other than the sexual behavior with respect to which rape or assault with intent to commit rape is alleged.

ARTICLE V.   PRIVILEGES

Rule 501.

GENERAL RULE

cAL

951-959

Except as otherwise required by the Constitution of the United States or provided by Act of Congress or in rules prescribed by the Supreme Court pursuant to statutory authority, the privilege of a witness, person, government, State, or political subdivision thereof shall be governed by the principles of the common law as they may be interpreted by the courts of the United States in the light of reason and experience.   However, in civil actions and proceedings, with respect to an element of a claim or defense as to which State law supplies the rule of decision, the privilege of a witness, person, government, State, or political subdivision thereof shall be determined in accordance with State law.

ARTICLE VI.   WITNESSES

Rule 601.

GENERAL RULE OF COMPETENCY

cAL.

700

Every person is competent to be a witness except as otherwise provided in these rules.   However, in civil actions and proceedings, with respect to an element of a claim or defense as to which State law supplies the rule of decision, the competency of a witness shall be determined in accordance with State law.

Rule 602.

LACK OF PERSONAL KNOWLEDGE

CA l
702

A witness may not testify to a matter unless evidence is introduced sufficient to support a finding that he has personal knowledge of the matter. Evidence to prove personal knowledge may, but need not, consist of the testimony of the witness himself. This rule is subject to the provisions of Rule 703, relating to opinion testimony by expert witnesses.

Rule 603.

OATH OR AFFIRMATION

cA L.
710

Before testifying, every witness shall be required to declare that he will testify truthfully, by oath or affirmation administered in a form calculated to awaken his conscience and impress his mind with his duty to do so.

Rule 604.

INTERPRETERS

An interpreter is subject to the provisions of these rules relating to qualification as an expert and the administration of an oath or affirmation that he will make a true translation.

Rule 605.

COMPETENCY OF JUDGE AS WITNESS

The judge presiding at the trial may not testify in that trial as a witness. No objection need be made in order to preserve the point.

Rule 606.

COMPETENCY OF JUROR AS WITNESS

(a) **At the trial.** A member of the jury may not testify as a witness before that jury in the trial of the case in which he is sitting as a juror. If he is called so to testify, the opposing party shall be afforded an opportunity to object out of the presence of the jury.

(b) **Inquiry into validity of verdict or indictment.** Upon an inquiry into the validity of a verdict or indictment, a juror may not testify as to any matter or statement occurring during the course of the jury's deliberations or to the effect of anything upon his or any other juror's mind or emotions as influencing him to assent to or dissent from the verdict or indictment or concerning his mental processes in connection therewith, except that a juror may testify on the question whether extraneous prejudicial information was improperly brought to the jury's attention or whether any outside influence was improperly brought to bear upon any juror. Nor may his affidavit or evidence of any statement by him concerning a matter about which he would be precluded from testifying be received for these purposes.

Rule 607.

WHO MAY IMPEACH

CAL. 785

The credibility of a witness may be attacked by any party, including the party calling him.

Rule 608.

EVIDENCE OF CHARACTER AND CONDUCT OF WITNESS

CAL. 790

(a) Opinion and reputation evidence of character. The credibility of a witness may be attacked or supported by evidence in the form of opinion or reputation, but subject to these limitations: (1) the evidence may refer only to character for truthfulness or untruthfulness, and (2) evidence of truthful character is admissible only after the character of the witness for truthfulness has been attacked by opinion or reputation evidence or otherwise.

(b) Specific instances of conduct. Specific instances of the conduct of a witness, for the purpose of attacking or supporting his credibility, other than conviction of crime as provided in Rule 609, may not be proved by extrinsic evidence. They may, however, in the discretion of the court, if probative of truthfulness or untruthfulness, be inquired into on cross-examination of the witness (1) concerning his character for truthfulness or untruthfulness, or (2) concerning the character for truthfulness or untruthfulness of another witness as to which character the witness being cross-examined has testified.

The giving of testimony, whether by an accused or by any other witness, does not operate as a waiver of his privilege against self-incrimination when examined with respect to matters which relate only to credibility.

Rule 609.

IMPEACHMENT BY EVIDENCE OF CONVICTION OF CRIME

CAL. 788

(a) General rule. For the purpose of attacking the credibility of a witness, evidence that he has been convicted of a crime shall be admitted if elicited from him or established by public record during cross-examination but only if the crime (1) was punishable by death or imprisonment in excess of one year under the law under which he was convicted, and the court determines that the probative value of admitting this evidence outweighs its prejudicial effect to the defendant, or (2) involved dishonesty or false statement, regardless of the punishment.

(b) Time limit. Evidence of a conviction under this rule is not admissible if a period of more than ten years has elapsed since the date of the conviction or of the release of the witness from the confinement imposed for that conviction, whichever is the later date, unless the court determines, in the interests of justice, that the probative value of the conviction supported by specific facts and circumstances substantially outweighs its prejudicial effect. However, evidence of a conviction more than 10 years old as calculated herein, is not admissible unless the proponent gives to the adverse party sufficient advance written notice of intent to use such evidence to provide the adverse party with a fair opportunity to contest the use of such evidence.

(c) Effect of pardon, annulment, or certificate of rehabilitation. Evidence of a conviction is not admissible under this rule if (1) the conviction has been the subject of a pardon, annulment, certificate of rehabilitation, or other equivalent procedure based on a finding of the rehabilitation of the person convicted, and that person has not been convicted of a subsequent crime which was punishable by death or imprisonment in excess of one year, or (2) the conviction has been the subject of a pardon, annulment, or other equivalent procedure based on a finding of innocence.

(d) Juvenile adjudications. Evidence of juvenile adjudications is generally not admissible under this rule. The court may, however, in a criminal case allow evidence of a juvenile adjudication of a witness other than the accused if conviction of the offense would be admissible to attack the credibility of an adult and the court is satisfied that admission in evidence is necessary for a fair determination of the issue of guilt or innocence.

(e) Pendency of appeal. The pendency of an appeal therefrom does not render evidence of a conviction inadmissible. Evidence of the pendency of an appeal is admissible.

Rule 610.

RELIGIOUS BELIEFS OR OPINIONS

Evidence of the beliefs or opinions of a witness on matters of religion is not admissible for the purpose of showing that by reason of their nature his credibility is impaired or enhanced.

Rule 611.

MODE AND ORDER OF INTERROGATION AND PRESENTATION

(a) **Control by court.** The court shall exercise reasonable control over the mode and order of interrogating witnesses and presenting evidence so as to (1) make the interrogation and presentation effective for the ascertainment of the truth, (2) avoid needless consumption of time, and (3) protect witnesses from harassment or undue embarrassment.

(b) **Scope of cross-examination.** Cross-examination should be limited to the subject matter of the direct examination and matters affecting the credibility of the witness. The court may, in the exercise of discretion, permit inquiry into additional matters as if on direct examination.

(c) **Leading questions.** Leading questions should not be used on the direct examination of a witness except as may be necessary to develop his testimony. Ordinarily leading questions should be permitted on cross-examination. When a party calls a hostile witness, an adverse party, or a witness identified with an adverse party, interrogation may be by leading questions.

Rule 612.

WRITING USED TO REFRESH MEMORY

Except as otherwise provided in criminal proceedings by section 3500 of title 18, United States Code, if a witness uses a writing to refresh his memory for the purpose of testifying, either—

(1) while testifying, or

(2) before testifying, if the court in its discretion determines it is necessary in the interests of justice,

an adverse party is entitled to have the writing produced at the hearing, to inspect it, to cross-examine the witness thereon, and to introduce in evidence those portions which relate to the testimony of the witness. If it is claimed that the writing contains matters not related to the subject matter of the testimony the court shall examine the writing in camera, excise any portions not so related, and order delivery of the remainder to the party entitled thereto. Any portion withheld over objections shall be preserved and made available to the appellate court in the event of an appeal. If a writing is not produced or delivered pursuant to order under this rule, the court shall make any order justice requires, except that in criminal cases when the prosecution elects not to comply, the order shall be one striking the testimony or, if the court in its discretion determines that the interests of justice so require, declaring a mistrial.

Rule 613.

PRIOR STATEMENTS OF WITNESSES   *IMPEACHMENT*

CAL.
1235

(a) Examining witness concerning prior statement. In examining a witness concerning a prior statement made by him, whether written or not, the statement need not be shown nor its contents disclosed to him at that time, but on request the same shall be shown or disclosed to opposing counsel.

(b) Extrinsic evidence of prior inconsistent statement of witness. Extrinsic evidence of a prior inconsistent statement by a witness is not admissible unless the witness is afforded an opportunity to explain or deny the same and the opposite party is afforded an opportunity to interrogate him thereon, or the interests of justice otherwise require. This provision does not apply to admissions of a party-opponent as defined in Rule 801 (d) (2).

Rule 614.

CALLING AND INTERROGATION OF WITNESSES BY COURT

(a) Calling by court. The court may, on its own motion or at the suggestion of a party, call witnesses, and all parties are entitled to cross-examine witnesses thus called.

(b) Interrogation by court. The court may interrogate witnesses, whether called by itself or by a party.

(c) Objections. Objections to the calling of witnesses by the court or to interrogation by it may be made at the time or at the next available opportunity when the jury is not present.

Rule 615.

EXCLUSION OF WITNESSES

At the request of a party the court shall order witnesses excluded so that they cannot hear the testimony of other witnesses, and it may make the order of its own motion. This rule does not authorize exclusion of (1) a party who is a natural person, or (2) an officer or employee of a party which is not a natural person designated as its representative by its attorney, or (3) a person whose presence is shown by a party to be essential to the presentation of his cause.

ARTICLE VII.   OPINIONS AND EXPERT TESTIMONY

Rule 701.

OPINION TESTIMONY BY LAY WITNESSES

CAL. 800

If the witness is not testifying as an expert, his testimony in the form of opinions or inferences is limited to those opinions or inferences which are (a) rationally based on the perception of the witness and (b) helpful to a clear understanding of his testimony or the determination of a fact in issue.

Rule 702.

TESTIMONY BY EXPERTS

CAL. 801

If scientific, technical, or other specialized knowledge will assist the trier of fact to understand the evidence or to determine a fact in issue, a witness qualified as an expert by knowledge, skill, experience, training, or education, may testify thereto in the form of an opinion or otherwise.

Rule 703.

BASES OF OPINION TESTIMONY BY EXPERTS

The facts or data in the particular case upon which an expert bases an opinion or inference may be those perceived by or made known to him at or before the hearing. If of a type reasonably relied upon by experts in the particular field in forming opinions or inferences upon the subject, the facts or data need not be admissible in evidence.

Rule 704.

OPINION ON ULTIMATE ISSUE

Testimony in the form of an opinion or inference otherwise admissible is not objectionable because it embraces an ultimate issue to be decided by the trier of fact.

Rule 705.

DISCLOSURE OF FACTS OR DATA UNDERLYING EXPERT OPINION

The expert may testify in terms of opinion or inference and give his reasons therefor without prior disclosure of the underlying facts or data, unless the judge requires otherwise. The expert may in any event be required to disclose the underlying facts or data on cross-examination.

Rule 706.

COURT APPOINTED EXPERTS

(a) Appointment. The court may on its own motion or on the motion of any party enter an order to show cause why expert witnesses should not be appointed, and may request the parties to submit nominations. The court may appoint any expert witnesses agreed upon by the parties, and may appoint witnesses of his own selection. An expert witness shall not be appointed by the court unless he consents to act. A witness so appointed shall be informed of his duties by the court in writing, a copy of which shall be filed with the clerk, or at a conference in which the parties shall have opportunity to participate. A witness so appointed shall advise the parties of his findings, if any; his deposition may be taken by any party; and he may be called to testify by the court or any party. He shall be subject to cross-examination by each party, including a party calling him as a witness.

(b) Compensation. Expert witnesses so appointed are entitled to reasonable compensation in whatever sum the court may allow. The compensation thus fixed is payable from funds which may be provided by law in criminal cases and civil actions and proceedings involving just compensation under the Fifth Amendment. In other civil actions and proceedings the compensation shall be paid by the parties in such proportion and at such time as the court directs, and thereafter charged in like manner as other costs.

(c) Disclosure of appointment. In the exercise of its discretion, the court may authorize disclosure to the jury of the fact that the court appointed the expert witness.

(d) Parties' experts of own selection. Nothing in this rule limits the parties in calling expert witnesses of their own selection.

ARTICLE VIII. HEARSAY

Rule 801.   *CAL. 1200 (a)*
2 25

DEFINITIONS

The following definitions apply under this Article:

(a) Statement. A "statement" is (1) an oral or written assertion or (2) nonverbal conduct of a person, if it is intended by him as an assertion.

(b) Declarant. A "declarant" is a person who makes a statement.

(c) Hearsay. "Hearsay" is a statement, other than one made by the declarant while testifying at the trial or hearing, offered in evidence to prove the truth of the matter asserted.

(d) Statements which are not hearsay. A statement is not hearsay if—

ADMISSIONS
CAL.1220

(1) *Prior statement by witness.* The declarant testifies at the trial or hearing and is subject to cross-examination concerning the statement, and the statement is (A) inconsistent with his testimony, and was given under oath subject to the penalty of perjury at a trial, hearing, or other proceeding, or in a deposition, or (B) consistent with his testimony and is offered to rebut an express or implied charge against him of recent fabrication or improper influence or motive, or (C) one of identification of a person made after perceiving him; or   *CAL. 1238 (c)*

(2) *Admission by party-opponent.* The statement is offered against a party and is (A) his own statement, in either his individual or a representative capacity or (B) a statement of which he has manifested his adoption or belief in its truth, or
CAL. 1222
AGENT
(C) a statement by a person authorized by him to make a statement concerning the subject, or (D) a statement by his agent or servant concerning a matter within the scope of his agency or employment, made during the existence of the relationship, or (E) a statement by a co-conspirator of a party during the course and in furtherance of the conspiracy.

Rule 802.

HEARSAY RULE

Hearsay is not admissible except as provided by these rules or by other rules prescribed by the Supreme Court pursuant to statutory authority or by Act of Congress.

Rule 803.

HEARSAY EXCEPTIONS: AVAILABILITY OF DECLARANT IMMATERIAL

The following are not excluded by the hearsay rule, even though the declarant is available as a witness:

(1) Present sense impression. A statement describing or explaining an event or condition made while the declarant was perceiving the event or condition, or immediately thereafter.

CAL. 1240
(2) Excited utterance. A statement relating to a startling event or condition made while the declarant was under the stress of excitement caused by the event or condition.

CAL. 1250
, 251
1252

(3) Then existing mental, emotional, or physical condition. A statement of the declarant's then existing state of mind, emotion, sensation, or physical condition (such as intent, plan, motive, design, mental feeling, pain, and bodily health), but not including a statement of memory or belief to prove the fact remembered or believed unless it relates to the execution, revocation, identification, or terms of declarant's will.

CAL
125'

(4) Statements for purposes of medical diagnosis or treatment. Statements made for purposes of medical diagnosis or treatment and describing medical history, or past or present symptoms, pain, or sensations, or the inception or general character of the cause or external source thereof insofar as reasonably pertinent to diagnosis or treatment.

CAL.
1237

(5) Recorded recollection. A memorandum or record concerning a matter about which a witness once had knowledge but now has insufficient recollection to enable him to testify fully and accurately, shown to have been made or adopted by the witness when the matter was fresh in his memory and to reflect that knowledge correctly. If admitted, the memorandum or record may be read into evidence but may not itself be received as an exhibit unless offered by an adverse party.

CAL.
1270
1271

(6) Records of regularly conducted activity. A memorandum, report, record, or data compilation, in any form, of acts, events, conditions, opinions, or diagnoses, made at or near the time by, or from information transmitted by, a person with knowledge, if kept in the course of a regularly conducted business activity, and if it was the regular practice of that business activity to make the memorandum, report, record, or data compilation, all as shown by the testimony of the custodian or other qualified witness, unless the source of information or the method or circumstances of preparation indicate lack of trustworthiness. The term "business" as used in this paragraph includes business, institution, association, profession, occupation, and calling of every kind, whether or not conducted for profit.

(7) Absence of entry in records kept in accordance with the provisions of paragraph (6). Evidence that a matter is not included in the memoranda reports, records, or data compilations, in any form, kept in accordance with the provisions of paragraph (6), to prove the nonoccurrence or nonexistence of the matter, if the matter was of a kind of which a memorandum, report, record, or data compilation was regularly made and preserved, unless the sources of information or other circumstances indicate lack of trustworthiness.

(8) Public records and reports. Records, reports, statements, or data compilations, in any form, of public offices or agencies, setting forth (A) the activities of the office or agency, or (B) matters observed pursuant to duty imposed by law as to which matters there was a duty to report, excluding, however, in criminal cases matters observed by police officers and other law enforcement personnel, or (C) in civil actions and proceedings and against the Government in criminal cases, factual findings resulting from an investigation made pursuant to authority granted by law, unless the sources of information or other circumstances indicate lack of trustworthiness.

CAL.
1281

(9) Records of vital statistics. Records or data compilations, in any form, of births, fetal deaths, deaths, or marriages, if the report thereof was made to a public office pursuant to requirements of law.

(10) Absence of public record or entry. To prove the absence of a record, report, statement, or data compilation, in any form, or the nonoccurrence or nonexistence of a matter of which a record, report, statement, or data compilation, in any form, was regularly made and preserved by a public office or agency, evidence in the form of a certification in accordance with Rule 902, or testimony, that diligent search failed to disclose the record, report, statement, or data compilation, or entry.

CAL.1315

(11) Records of religious organizations. Statements of births, marriages, divorces, deaths, legitimacy, ancestry, relationship by blood or marriage, or other similar facts of personal or family history, contained in a regularly kept record of a religious organization.

CAL. 1316

(12) Marriage, baptismal, and similar certificates. Statements of fact contained in a certificate that the maker performed a marriage or other ceremony or administered a sacrament, made by a clergyman, public official, or other person authorized by the rules or practices of a religious organization or by law to perform the act certified, and purporting to have been issued at the time of the act or within a reasonable time thereafter.

CAL.1312

(13) Family records. Statements of fact concerning personal or family history contained in family Bibles, genealogies, charts, engravings on rings, inscription on family portraits, engravings on urns, crypts, or tombstones, or the like.

(14) Records of documents affecting an interest in property. The record of a document purporting to establish or affect an interest in property, as proof of the content of the original recorded document and its execution and delivery by each person by whom it purports to have been executed, if the record is a record of a public office and an applicable statute authorized the recording of documents of that kind in that office.

(15) Statements in documents affecting an interest in property. A statement contained in a document purporting to establish or affect an interest in property if the matter stated was relevant to the purpose of the document, unless dealings with the property since the document was made have been inconsistent with the truth of the statement or the purport of the document.

CAL. 1331
(→
901(5)(8)

(16) Statements in ancient documents. Statements in a document in existence 20 years or more whose authenticity is established.

(17) Market reports, commercial publications. Market quotations, tabulations, lists, directories, or other published compilations, generally used and relied upon by the public or by persons in particular occupations.

(18) Learned treatises. To the extent called to the attention of an expert witness upon cross-examination or relied upon by him in direct examination, statements contained in published treatises, periodicals, or pamphlets on a subject of history, medicine, or other science or art, established as a reliable authority by the testimony or admission of the witness or by other expert testimony or by judicial notice. If admitted, the statements may be read into evidence but may not be received as exhibits.

(19) Reputation concerning personal or family history. Reputation among members of his family by blood, adoption, or marriage, or among his associates, or in the community, concerning a person's birth, adoption, marriage, divorce, death, legitimacy, relationship by blood, adoption, or marriage, ancestry, or other similar fact of his personal or family history.

CAL. 1313

(20) Reputation concerning boundaries or general history. Reputation in a community, arising before the controversy, as to boundaries of or customs affecting lands in the community, and reputation as to events of general history important to the community or state or nation in which located.

CAL. 1322

(21) Reputation as to character. Reputation of a person's character among his associates or in the community.

(22) Judgment of previous conviction. Evidence of a final judgment, entered after a trial or upon a plea of guilty (but not upon a plea of *nolo contendere*), adjudging a person guilty of a crime punishable by death or imprisonment in excess of one year, to prove any fact essential to sustain the judgment, but not including, when offered by the government in a criminal prosecution for purposes other than impeachment, judgments against persons other than the accused. The pendency of an appeal may be shown but does not affect admissibility.

CAL. 1300

(23) Judgment as to personal, family or general history, or boundaries. Judgments as proof of matters of personal, family, or general history, or boundaries, essential to the judgment, if the same would be provable by evidence of reputation.

(24) Other exceptions. A statement not specifically covered by any of the foregoing exceptions but having equivalent circumstantial guarantees of trustworthiness, if the court determines that (A) the statement is offered as evidence of a material fact; (B) the statement is more probative on the point for which it is offered than any other evidence which the proponent can procure through reasonable efforts; and (C) the general purposes of these rules and the interests of justice will best be served by admission of the statement into evidence. However, a statement may not be admitted under this exception unless the proponent of it makes known to the adverse party sufficiently in advance of the trial or hearing to provide the adverse party with a fair opportunity to prepare to meet it, his intention to offer the statement and the particulars of it, including the name and address of the declarant.

Rule 804.

HEARSAY EXCEPTIONS: DECLARANT UNAVAILABLE

CAL. 1290

(a) Definition of unavailability. "Unavailability as a witness" includes situations in which the declarant:

(1) Is exempted by ruling of the court on the ground of privilege from testifying concerning the subject matter of his statement; or

(2) Persists in refusing to testify concerning the subject matter of his statement despite an order of the court to do so; or

CAL. 1242

(3) Testifies to a lack of memory of the subject matter of his statement; or

(4) Is unable to be present or to testify at the hearing because of death or then existing physical or mental illness or infirmity; or

(5) Is absent from the hearing and the proponent of his statement has been unable to procure his attendance (or in the case of a hearsay exception under subdivision (b)(2), (3), or (4), his attendance or testimony) by process or other reasonable means.

A declarant is not unavailable as a witness if his exemption, refusal, claim of lack of memory, inability, or absence is due to the procurement or wrongdoing of the proponent of his statement for the purpose of preventing the witness from attending or testifying.

(b) Hearsay exceptions. The following are not excluded by the hearsay rule if the declarant is unavailable as a witness:

(1) *Former testimony.* Testimony given as a witness at another hearing of the same or a different proceeding, or in a deposition taken in compliance with law in the course of the same or another proceeding, if the party against whom the testimony is now offered, or, in a civil action or proceeding, a predecessor in interest, had an opportunity and similar motive to develop the testimony by direct, cross, or redirect examination.

(2) *Statement under belief of impending death.* In a prosecution for homicide or in a civil action or proceeding, a statement made by a declarant while believing that his death was imminent, concerning the cause or circumstances of what he believed to be his impending death.

(3) *Statement against interest.* A statement which was at the time of its making so far contrary to the declarant's pecuniary or proprietary interest, or so far tended to subject him to civil or criminal liability, or to render invalid a claim by him against another, that a reasonable man in his position would not have made the statement unless he believed it to be true. A statement tending to expose the declarant to criminal liability and offered to exculpate the accused is not admissible unless corroborating circumstances clearly indicate the trustworthiness of the statement.

(4) *Statement of personal or family history.* (A) A statement concerning the declarant's own birth, adoption, marriage, divorce, legitimacy, relationship by blood, adoption, or marriage, ancestry, or other similar fact of personal or family history, even though declarant had no means of acquiring personal knowledge of the matter stated; or (B) a statement concerning the foregoing matters, and death also, of another person, if the declarant was related to the other by blood, adoption, or marriage or was so intimately associated with the other's family as to be likely to have accurate information concerning the matter declared.

(5) *Other exceptions.* A statement not specifically covered by any of the foregoing exceptions but having equivalent circumstantial guarantees of trustworthiness, if the court determines that (A) the statement is offered as evidence of a material fact; (B) the statement is more probative on the point for which it is offered than any other evidence which the proponent can procure through reasonable efforts; and (C) the general purposes of these rules and the interests of justice will best be served by admission of the statement into evidence. However, a statement may not be admitted under this exception unless the proponent of it makes known to the adverse party sufficiently in advance of

the trial or hearing to provide the adverse party with a fair opportunity to prepare to meet it, his intention to offer the statement and the particulars of it, including the name and address of the declarant.

Rule 805.

HEARSAY WITHIN HEARSAY

Hearsay included within hearsay is not excluded under the hearsay rule if each part of the combined statements conforms with an exception to the hearsay rule provided in these rules.

Rule 806.

ATTACKING AND SUPPORTING CREDIBILITY OF DECLARANT

When a hearsay statement, or a statement defined in Rule 801 (d) (2), (C), (D), or (E), has been admitted in evidence, the credibility of the declarant may be attacked, and if attacked may be supported, by any evidence which would be admissible for those purposes if declarant had testified as a witness. Evidence of a statement or conduct by the declarant at any time, inconsistent with his hearsay statement, is not subject to any requirement that he may have been afforded an opportunity to deny or explain. If the party against whom a hearsay statement has been admitted calls the declarant as a witness, the party is entitled to examine him on the statement as if under cross-examination.

ARTICLE IX.   AUTHENTICATION AND IDENTIFICATION

Rule 901.

REQUIREMENT OF AUTHENTICATION OR IDENTIFICATION

CA L.
1414

(a) **General provision.** The requirement of authentication or identification as a condition precedent to admissibility is satisfied by evidence sufficient to support a finding that the matter in question is what its proponent claims.

(b) **Illustrations.** By way of illustration only, and not by way of limitation, the following are examples of authentication or identification conforming with the requirements of this rule:

(1) Testimony of witness with knowledge. Testimony that a matter is what it is claimed to be.

(2) Nonexpert opinion on handwriting. Nonexpert opinion as to the genuineness of handwriting, based upon familiarity not acquired for purposes of the litigation.

(3) Comparison by trier or expert witness. Comparison by the trier of fact or by expert witnesses with specimens which have been authenticated.

(4) Distinctive characteristics and the like. Appearance, contents, substance, internal patterns, or other distinctive characteristics, taken in conjunction with circumstances.

(5) Voice identification. Identification of a voice, whether heard firsthand or through mechanical or electronic transmission ˅ recording, by opinion based upon hearing the voice at any time under circumstances connecting it with the alleged speaker.

(6) Telephone conversations. Telephone conversations, by evidence that a call was made to the number assigned at the time by the telephone company to a particular person or business, if (A) in the case of a person, circumstances, including self-identification, show the person answering to be the one called, or (B) in the case of a business, the call was made to a place of business and the conversation related to business reasonably transacted over the telephone.

(7) Public records or reports. Evidence that a writing authorized by law to be recorded or filed and in fact recorded or filed in a public office, or a purported public record, report, statement, or data compilation, in any form, is from the public office where items of this nature are kept.

(8) Ancient documents or data compilations. Evidence that a document or data compilation, in any form, (A) is in such condition as to create no suspicion concerning its authenticity, (B) was in a place where it, if authentic, would likely be, and (C) has been in existence 20 years or more at the time it is offered.

(9) Process or system. Evidence describing a process or system used to produce a result and showing that the process or system produces an accurate result.

(10) Methods provided by statute or rule. Any method of authentication or identification provided by Act of Congress or by other rules prescribed by the Supreme Court pursuant to statutory authority.

Rule 902.

SELF-AUTHENTICATION

Extrinsic evidence of authenticity as a condition precedent to admissibility is not required with respect to the following:

(1) Domestic public documents under seal. A document bearing a seal purporting to be that of the United States, or of any state, district, commonwealth, territory, or insular possession thereof, or the Panama Canal Zone, or the Trust Territory of the Pacific Islands, or of a political subdivision, department, officer, or agency thereof, and a signature purporting to be an attestation or execution.

(2) Domestic public documents not under seal. A document purporting to bear the signature in his official capacity of an officer or employee of any entity included in paragraph (1) hereof, having no seal, if a public officer having a seal and having official duties in the district or political subdivision of the officer or employee certifies under seal that the signer has the official capacity and that the signature is genuine.

(3) Foreign public documents. A document purporting to be executed or attested in his official capacity by a person authorized by the laws of a foreign country to make the execution or attestation, and accompanied by a final certification as to the genuineness of the signature and official position (A) of the executing or attesting person, or (B) of any foreign official whose certificate of genuineness of signature and official position relates to the execution or attestation or is in a chain of certificates of genuineness of signature and official position relating to the execution or attestation. A final certification may be made by a secretary of embassy or legation, consul general, consul, vice consul, or consular agent of the United States, or a diplomatic or consular official of the foreign country assigned or accredited to the United States. If reasonable opportunity has been given to all parties to investigate the authenticity and accuracy of official documents, the court may, for good cause shown, order that they be treated as presumptively authentic without final certification or permit them to be evidenced by an attested summary with or without final certification.

(4) Certified copies of public records. A copy of an official record or report or entry therein, or of a document authorized by law to be recorded or filed and actually recorded or filed in a public office, including data compilations in any form, certified as correct by the custodian or other person authorized to make the certification, by certificate complying with paragraph (1), (2), or (3) of this Rule or complying with any Act of Congress or rule prescribed by the Supreme Court pursuant to statutory authority.

(5) Official publications. Books, pamphlets, or other publications purporting to be issued by public authority.

(6) Newspapers and periodicals. Printed materials purporting to be newspapers or periodicals.

(7) Trade inscriptions and the like. Inscriptions, signs, tags, or labels purporting to have been affixed in the course of business and indicating ownership, control, or origin.

(8) Acknowledged documents. Documents accompanied by a certificate of acknowledgment executed in the manner provided by law by a notary public or other officer authorized by law to take acknowledgments.

(9) Commercial paper and related documents. Commercial paper, signatures thereon, and documents relating thereto to the extent provided by general commercial law.

(10) Presumptions under Acts of Congress. Any signature, document, or other matter declared by Act of Congress to be presumptively or prima facie genuine or authentic.

Rule 903.

SUBSCRIBING WITNESS' TESTIMONY UNNECESSARY

The testimony of a subscribing witness is not necessary to authenticate a writing unless required by the laws of the jurisdiction whose laws govern the validity of the writing.

ARTICLE X.   CONTENTS OF WRITINGS, RECORDINGS, AND PHOTOGRAPHS

Rule 1001.

DEFINITIONS

For purposes of this article the following definitions are applicable.

(1) Writings and recordings. "Writings" and "recordings" consist of letters, words, or numbers, or their equivalent, set down by handwriting, typewriting, printing, photostating, photographing, magnetic impulse, mechanical or electronic recording, or other form of data compilation.

(2) Photographs. "Photographs" include still photographs, X-ray films, and motion pictures.

(3) Original. An "original" of a writing or recording is the writing or recording itself or any counterpart intended to have the same effect by a person executing or issuing it. An "original" of a photograph includes the negative or any print therefrom. If data are stored in a computer or similar device, any printout or other output readable by sight, shown to reflect the data accurately, is an "original."

(4) Duplicate. A "duplicate" is a counterpart produced by the same impression as the original, or from the same matrix, or by means of photography, including enlargements and miniatures, or by mechanical or electronic re-recording, or by chemical reproduction, or by other equivalent techniques which accurately reproduces the original.

931

Rule 1002.

REQUIREMENT OF ORIGINAL

To prove the content of a writing, recording, or photograph, the original writing, recording, or photograph is required, except as otherwise provided in these rules or by Act of Congress.

Rule 1003.

ADMISSIBILITY OF DUPLICATES

A duplicate is admissible to the same extent as an original unless (1) a genuine question is raised as to the authenticity of the original or (2) in the circumstances it would be unfair to admit the duplicate in lieu of the original.

Rule 1004.

ADMISSIBILITY OF OTHER EVIDENCE OF CONTENTS

The original is not required, and other evidence of the contents of a writing, recording, or photograph is admissible if——

(1) Originals lost or destroyed. All originals are lost or have been destroyed, unless the proponent lost or destroyed them in bad faith; or

(2) Original not obtainable. No original can be obtained by any available judicial process or procedure; or

(3) Original in possession of opponent. At a time when an original was under the control of the party against whom offered, he was put on notice, by the pleadings or otherwise, that the contents would be a subject of proof at the hearing, and he does not produce the original at the hearing; or

(4) Collateral matters. The writing, recording, or photograph is not closely related to a controlling issue.

Rule 1005.

PUBLIC RECORDS

The contents of an official record, or of a document authorized to be recorded or filed and actually recorded or filed, including data compilations in any form, if otherwise admissible, may be proved by copy, certified as correct in accordance with Rule 902 or testified to be correct by a witness who has compared it with the original. If a copy which complies with the foregoing cannot be obtained by the exercise of reasonable diligence, then other evidence of the contents may be given.

Rule 1006.

SUMMARIES

The contents of voluminous writings, recordings, or photographs which cannot conveniently be examined in court may be presented in the form of a chart, summary, or calculation. The originals, or duplicates, shall be made available for examination or copying, or both, by other parties at reasonable time and place. The court may order that they be produced in court.

Rule 1007.

TESTIMONY OR WRITTEN ADMISSION OF PARTY

Contents of writings, recordings, or photographs may be proved by the testimony or deposition of the party against whom offered or by his written admission, without accounting for the nonproduction of the original.

Rule 1008.

FUNCTIONS OF COURT AND JURY

When the admissibility of other evidence of contents of writings, recordings, or photographs under these rules depends upon the fulfillment of a condition of fact, the question whether the condition has been fulfilled is ordinarily for the court to determine in accordance with the provisions of Rule 104. However, when an issue is raised (a) whether the asserted writing ever existed, or (b) whether another writing, recording, or photograph produced at the trial is the original, or (c) whether other evidence of contents correctly reflects the contents, the issue is for the trier of fact to determine as in the case of other issues of fact.

ARTICLE XI. MISCELLANEOUS RULES

Rule 1101.

APPLICABILITY OF RULES

(a) **Courts and magistrates.** These rules apply to the United States district courts, the District Court of Guam, the District Court of the Virgin Islands, the District Court for the District of the Canal Zone, the United States courts of appeals, the Court of Claims, and to United States magistrates, in the actions, cases, and proceedings and to the extent hereinafter set forth. The terms "judge" and "court" in these rules include United States magistrates, referees in bankruptcy, and commissioners of the Court of Claims.

(b) **Proceedings generally.** These rules apply generally to civil actions and proceedings, including admiralty and maritime cases, to criminal cases and proceedings, to contempt proceedings except those in which the court may act summarily, and to proceedings and cases under the Bankruptcy Act.

(c) Rule of privilege. The rule with respect to privileges applies at all stages of all actions, cases, and proceedings.

(d) Rules inapplicable. The rules (other than with respect to privileges) do not apply in the following situations:

(1) *Preliminary questions of fact.* The determination of questions of fact preliminary to admissibility of evidence when the issue is to be determined by the court under rule 104.

(2) *Grand jury.* Proceedings before grand juries.

(3) *Miscellaneous proceedings.* Proceedings for extradition or rendition; preliminary examinations in criminal cases; sentencing, or granting or revoking probation; issuance of warrants for arrest, criminal summonses, and search warrants; and proceedings with respect to release on bail or otherwise.

(e) Rules applicable in part. In the following proceedings these rules apply to the extent that matters of evidence are not provided for in the statutes which govern procedure therein or in other rules prescribed by the Supreme Court pursuant to statutory authority; the trial of minor and petty offenses by United States magistrates; review of agency actions when the facts are subject to trial de novo under section 706(2)(F) of title 5, United States Code; review of orders of the Secretary of Agriculture under section 2 of the Act entitled "An Act to authorize association of producers of agricultural products" approved February 18, 1922 (7 U.S.C. 292), and under sections 6 and 7(c) of the Perishable Agricultural Commodities Act, 1930 (7 U.S.C. 499f, 499g(c)); naturalization and revocation of naturalization under sections 310–318 of the Immigration and Nationality Act (8 U.S.C. 1421–1429); prize proceedings in admiralty under sections 7651–7681 of title 10, United States Code; review of orders of the Secretary of the Interior under section 2 of the Act entitled "An Act authorizing associations of producers of aquatic products" approved June 25, 1931 (15 U.S.C. 522); review of orders of petroleum control boards under section 5 of the Act entitled "An Act to regulate interstate and foreign commerce in petroleum and its products by prohibiting the shipment in such commerce of petroleum and its products produced in violation of State law, and for other purposes", approved February 22, 1935 (15 U.S.C. 715d); actions for fines, penalties, or forfeitures under part V of title IV of the Tariff Act of 1930 (19 U.S.C. 1581–1624), or under the Anti-Smuggling Act (19 U.S.C. 1701–1711); criminal libel for condemnation, exclusion of imports, or other proceedings under the Federal Food, Drug, and Cosmetic Act (21 U.S.C. 301–392); disputes between seamen under sections 4079, 4080, and 4081 of the Revised Statutes (22 U.S.C. 256–258; habeas corpus under sections 2241–2254 of title 28, United States Code; motions to vacate, set aside or correct sentence under section 2255 of title 28, United States Code; actions for penalties for refusal to transport destitute seamen under section 4578 of the Revised Statutes (46 U.S.C. 679); actions against the United States under the Act entitled "An Act authorizing suits against the United States in admiralty for damage caused by and salvage service rendered to public vessels belonging to the United States, and for other purposes", approved March 3, 1925 (46 U.S.C. 781–790), as implemented by section 7730 of title 10, United States Code.

Rule 1102.

AMENDMENTS

Amendments to the Federal Rules of Evidence may be made as provided in section 2076 of title 28 of the United States Code.

Rule 1103.

TITLE

These rules may be known and cited as the Federal Rules of Evidence.

*

INDEX

TREATISES
See Hearsay, Exceptions

VERBAL ACT
See Hearsay

VERDICTS
See Record, Making The

VOICEPRINT ANALYSIS
See Scientific Evidence

VOUCHER RULE
See Hearsay

WITNESSES
See also Opinion Testimony
Competency, 658–669
Dead man's statute, 667–668
Hypnosis, restoration of memory
through, 665–666
Infamy, 660
Infancy, 658–659, 661–662
Interest, 661
Intoxication, 662–663
Marital relationship, 663
See also Privileges, Marital
Mental,
Capacity, 661
Derangement, 662
Religious belief, 660
Tribunal, official connection with,
Attorney, 664
Court officers, 664
Judge, 663–664
Jurors, 664
Cross examination, 15–16, 374–382
Aims, 376
"Bound" by witness' testimony, not,
371–372
Risks, 377–378
Scope of, 378–382
Direct examination, 10–15
"Bound" by testimony of one's own
witness, 371
Compound and otherwise confusing
questions, 13
Experts, 13–15
Leading questions, 11–13, 371
Questions assuming unproved facts, 13

WITNESSES—Cont'd
Expert,
See also Opinion Testimony
Direct examination of, 13–15
Impeachment, 383–426
See also Circumstantial Evidence,
Subsequent precautions
Bad acts, prior, 383–392
Bad reputation for truth and veracity,
409–410
Bias, 423–426
Character of witness, 383–410
Collateral matters, 390–392
Convictions, prior, 398–409
Federal Rules of Evidence,
Dishonesty or false statement,
399–409
Cross-examination, 15–16
Expert witness, 735–737
See also Opinion Testimony, Expert
witness
Own witness, 371–373
Prior inconsistent statements, 410–422
Foundation, laying proper, 411–412
Psychiatric condition, 393–397
Rehabilitation,
Prior consistent statement, 413–422
Federal Rules of Evidence,
419–422
Interpreter, use of, 15
Leading questions, 11–13
Prior consistent statements, 417–422
See also Impeachment, Rehabilita-
tion, this topic
Federal Rules of Evidence, 419–422
Questions,
Assuming unproved facts, 13
Compound and otherwise confusing, 13
Leading, 11–13
Impeachment purposes, 16

WORK PRODUCT DOCTRINE
See Privileges

WRITINGS
See Authentication ; Best Evidence Rule ;
Record, Making The

†

943